✧ God in All Worlds ✧

✢ God in All Worlds ✢

An Anthology of
Contemporary Spiritual Writing

Edited and with Introductions by

Lucinda Vardey

PANTHEON BOOKS
New York

Library of Congress Cataloging-in-Publication Data
God in all worlds : an anthology of contemporary spiritual writing / edited and
with introductions by Lucinda Vardey.
p. cm.
Includes bibliographical references and index.
ISBN 0-679-44214-6
1. Religion. 2. Spirituality. 3. Religions. I. Vardey, Lucinda.
BL48.G59 1995
291.4—DC20
95-14680

BOOK DESIGN BY LAURA HOUGH

Manufactured in the United States of America

First American Edition
2 4 6 8 9 7 5 3 1

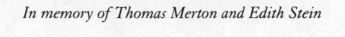
In memory of Thomas Merton and Edith Stein

✢ Contents ✦

Introduction xv

✢ Part I: The Quest ✦

✦ Part II: Revelation ✦

4: The Spiritual Experience 77

5: Strengthening the Self 134

6: Archetypes, Myth, and Ritual 197

7: Awakening the Great Mother 219

✦ PART III: TRIALS ✦

8: The Struggle with Evil 297

9: The Hidden Face of God 333

10: Liberation 367

❖ PART IV: SURRENDER ❖

11: The Way 387

12: Being for God 395

13: Doing for God 419

14: The Guides 435

15: The Gifts 471

Contents

⤞ PART V: DEATH AND THE ETERNAL LIFE ⤝

16: Death 545

17: The Gate of Life 575

18: Rebirth 610

❖ Part VI: Awe ❖

Contents

✦ Introduction ✦

"That which does the seeing, cannot be seen; that which does the hearing, cannot be heard; and that which does the thinking, cannot be thought."

—THE VEDAS

In the Vedas, the five-thousand-year-old yogic scriptures, it is recorded that we are constituted of two bodies—the corporal and the spiritual—and that it is the spiritual that defines us, sustains us, and provides meaning and purpose to our existence. German theologian Hans Küng has written that the spirit is "perceptible and yet not perceptible, invisible and yet powerful, real like the energy-charged air, the wind, the storm, as important for life as the air we breathe."

Religion has provided a tenet for spiritual expression and many have turned to it for guidance. The organized religions offer not only a sense of community bound by common beliefs, the collective study of scripture, the performance of ritual and the use of disciplines and practices, commandments and sacraments but also ways of taking care of our souls. Yet spirituality can embrace a wide range of thoughts and experiences—from the mystical to the metaphysical, including psychic episodes and miraculous occurrences in the supernatural realms—and so following an orthodox and traditional religion can sometimes prove limiting.

To live in spiritual truth requires a deep commitment to the divine in ourselves and others and can lead to transcended states of awareness, of consciousness that unites the mind, the heart, and the soul. Spirituality is about being open to the different realities of existence, about being guided by our intuition, which is nothing less than the truth within us. But we also live in a time when the moral order in the world is seesawing between liberal beliefs and rigid fundamentalism, and science and technology are advancing so rapidly that we lose sight of the need to reflect. This in turn can contribute to the sense of struggle, of being without direction, as we search for ways of finding meaning and peace in our lives.

In this confusion, I believe that it is possible to give form to a personal spirituality and I have compiled this anthology as a guide. Here are writings from the past fifty years—1945 to the present day—writings that touch upon the conservatism of the 1950s, the nonconformity and experimental rebelliousness of the 1960s, the commune life and feminist movements of the 1970s, through the heady materialism of the 1980s, to the soul-seeking, spiritually hungry "New Age" of the 1990s. During this period we have seen teachers and gurus from the East set up centres and ashrams in the West, thus bringing awareness of the Eastern religions and philosophy to the Western seeker. We have witnessed changes in traditional Christian churches—from the Roman Catholic Vatican II Council of reform to the ordination of women in the Protestant churches. The consciousness studies—from early drug experimentation, to the understanding of the workings of the human psyche—preceded the emergence of feminist spirituality, ecoconsciousness, energy healing, and goddess worship. We have seen how scientific knowledge has advanced spiritual awareness, giving rise to the ideas of cosmology and creation. The spiritual writing herein addresses these many evolutions and more.

Writings of spiritual guidance in the ancient traditions of Buddhism, Hinduism, Christianity, Judaism, Sufism, and Islam are available for anyone who seeks truth and wisdom, yet reading the texts of our contemporaries, many of whom come from traditional religious backgrounds, is, I believe, not only exciting and challenging but necessary. The writers gathered here express the spiritual concerns of this time and of the future. They consist of academics, scientists, ecumenical theologians, Eastern philosophers, priests, rabbis, monks and mystics, feminists, novelists, essayists, teachers, and New Age philosophers. Here too are the writings of ordinary people who have experienced the extraordinary. They all document experiences in spiritual awakening, manifestations, visions, enlightening episodes—and even the traumas and struggles on the way. In doing so, they offer a deeper understanding of the spirituality of ourselves, uplift our souls, and assist us on our own path to the higher way of life.

I have organized this material to follow the spiritual journey of the soul in this life. I began my journey as a Catholic, born and educated in England. I was similar to other members of my generation—the so-called Baby Boomers. I experienced the drugged and music-filled sixties in London. When I moved to North America in the early 1970s, I rapidly climbed the career ladder to a top executive position, then founded and ran my own international company of literary agents. My crisis came in the late 1980s when, after working long hours without a break for over twenty years, I realized how empty I felt outside my office. When I was younger, I was quite happy to make my work central to my life, but in middle age I became frustrated with the imbalance of a daily life driven by deadlines. I began to thirst for some peace, some joy, and some time for myself. Then I became depressed and ill and had to undergo surgery. During the time of my physical recuperation, I started on the course of transition and transformation of myself. Although I had always attended Mass on Sundays and called myself a liberal Catholic—I had even written a book about how to remain a Catholic and live in the modern world—I knew that I had to find a way to help myself recover.

My illness was a transforming gift as it brought me back to prayer, and through prayer I found my lost soul. I visited a Hindu ashram and began chanting and practising yoga. I felt at home in such a loving, holy place and became intrigued with the Eastern religions. I went on to study Buddhism and Taoism. While I wanted to remain a Christian, as this was culturally and intellectually the religion I knew and therefore the basis of my faith, I found that I could not go forward on my journey without the Eastern yogic disciplines and Buddhist meditation, so Christ became my "guru." I began to recognize Him in Buddhism and Hinduism as well as in Christian doctrine, and I was soon teaching yoga and experimenting with East/West devotion. I began to experience deep insights in my meditation which precipitated three years of contemplation, study, and prayer, through which I forged a closer relationship with God and vowed to put God central in my life and work. A lot had to change—mostly within myself—and as I experienced this very necessary process of change, my soul began to heal. And I began to experience the joy and the peace for which I had searched.

Spiritual experiences are unique to every individual, yet there is a familiar form of awakening and journeying that does not change. It is prevalent in the mystical writings of the past as it is in the writings collected here. In this life, the search for the spiritual begins with the longing of the soul for nourishment. This longing prompts the search for meaning and goes on to the quest itself. And this in turn usually leads to an excitement about what is revealed. And then to the trials of change. Through these trials we become strong enough to be humbled and wise enough to surrender. As our life is a preparation for our death, which is itself the ultimate surrender, endings and beginnings become more fully understood and guide us to the expansive feelings of awe and the great possibilities of renewal.

As I have formed this anthology like a spiritual journey, I have placed the selections themselves under the applicable signposts along the way. I picked the most lucid writing and the finest wisdom I could find to define the particular issue or experience. During my research, I found that there was a well-defined group of writers who were the most profound, honest, and proficient in the area of philosophy and religion, or spirituality or science, so a number appear quite frequently throughout this book. There are too the Eastern spiritual beliefs and religions—Hindu yoga, Zen Buddhism, Taoism and Sufism—which are always difficult to write about because of their experiential qualities, yet I have attempted to find the most clarified and eloquent of pieces. The contemporary writings of Islam are very scarce and therefore not extensive in this book. It was also my decision to not include the psychic and the occult areas because they are full of uncertainty and doubt, far too erratic and lacking in a sound theological base. The essayist and novelist Aldous Huxley wrote in a letter to the American priest Thomas Merton that "psychic powers without humility and without the guiding insights of spirituality will lead astray even more fatally than material powers, similarly unguided, are doing at present."

The language of patriarchy is ever present in a number of the pieces in this anthology. The use of "man" to describe men, women, and children, and "He" for describing God are a common occurrence, particularly in the selections written prior to the 1980s, when linguistic xenophobia was the accepted norm. Today, it is still customary to refer to "God" as masculine, and in the beginning of this book, I attempt to show the limitations that exist when searching for words to describe truth. Even using the word "God" limits our perception of the creator, conjuring up all kinds of images and emotions. For the Buddhists and Taoists God as the creator does not exist at all, yet if the word "truth" or "the Tao" replaced the word "God," it would be recognizable, familiar, and acceptable. So in writings on spirituality, monotheistic and patriarchal language is frequently used, yet I hope too that a new, fresh way of interpreting our spiritual existence and experiences will also be revealed in parts.

I trust that as you absorb the diversity and richness of the writings in this collection, this book will serve as a teacher and a guide, be helpful as a meditation, bring solace and comfort, inspiration and consolation, insight and knowledge, and perceptible hope. It is not my intention for this anthology to be authoritative on the subject of contemporary spirituality but rather that it contribute to the understanding of the revelation of the spirit in our time. As the famous Swiss psychologist Carl Jung has written, the living spirit is eternally renewed and "pursues its goal in manifold and inconceivable ways throughout the history of mankind. Measured against it, the names and forms which men have given it means very little; they are only the changing leaves and blossoms on the stem of the eternal tree."

❧ I ❧

The Quest

To seek is the start of any quest. The mythic quests of old are commonly recorded in fairy tales and tell of the conquering hero or heroine who overcomes the mightiest of obstacles in search of the experience to find the treasure or the reward, the thing most needed, most wanted, and most loved. Spiritual quests are similar to these mythical quests, except that the reward of the spiritual quest is the deeper understanding of the Self and a discovery of a new and different way of being. There are times in our lives when we long for change, when we have an insatiable need to pierce the safer boundaries of our existence to find what is beyond. We seek a sense of unity with each other, a sense of loving and being loved, of finding the peace that comes when a balanced life is lived. This is the treasure found at the end of any spiritual quest: that with the right ingredients of wisdom discovered on the way, we can joyfully live in the perfection of being wholly ourselves.

I believe we begin our search for meaning with doubt, pain, and a lot of questions. Why is the world the way it is? Does God exist, and if so, where is He/She? What is eternal Truth? What do I really believe? How much can I embrace? What are these alternative realities?

In the forthcoming chapters I have gathered writings that address the issue of divine existence, the mystery of creation, and questions of faith and truth. The writers represent the breadth of religious and spiritual backgrounds: Christian, Jewish, Islamic, Hindu, and Buddhist. Here are the works of ecumenical German theologican Hans Küng, whose *Does God Exist?* is perhaps one of the most broadly informed arguments for the existence of God ever published, and selections by the Canadian biblical scholar Northrop Frye and Mother Teresa of Calcutta. The late American priest Thomas Merton, who spent most of his adult life as a member of a Trappist monastic community in Kentucky and whose contribution to the understanding of the mystical relationship and of Zen and Christianity is unsurpassed, is quoted extensively throughout this anthology. Here too are Judaic philosopher Martin Buber, well known for his work on the Jewish faith in the modern world, and Czech dissident and later president Vaclav Havel, who wrote much of his philosophy in letters to his wife, Olga, while in prison for his anti-Communist writing. Indian teacher Jiddu Krishnamurti;

Englishman Paul Brunton, who spearheaded much Eastern aesthetic teachings to the West; and Christian/Buddhist Alan Watts all have a true talent in explaining much of the unexplained of the East to the Western mind.

All together these writers offer ways of linking personal quest to the divine and insight on the importance and the experience of faith, and through that faith the pursuit of truth, which writer Frithjof Schuon describes as "the fire beyond the tomb."

I

The Fire Beyond the Tomb
Contemplating God, Faith, and Truth

In most traditional religions, with the exception of Buddhism and Taoism, the quest is understood as a longing of the soul for its creator, God. However, the idea of "God" as male deity who rules, judges, loves and understands, guides and leads, as many traditions have taught, restricts the possibility for some people to find what they are seeking. It is hard for these individuals to refer to "God" in their attempt to describe the broadest form of spiritual existence. Some who have had faith or believe in certain principles know that there is a mystery in the reality of God. That when the search for the divine begins, the first step is towards a deeper way of relating, of understanding the dimensions of the mysterious, of seeking evidence of truth, and trusting in the "presence that exists" (R. D. Laing).

→←

The concept of God need not necessarily be theistic. When I was fifteen years old or so I came up with a definition of God to which, in my old age, I come back more and more. I would call it an operational definition. It reads as follows: God is the partner of your most intimate soliloquies.
Viktor E. Frankl, *"The Unheard Cry for Meaning"*

What I am concerned with at present is not the question whether God is dead or obsolete, but with the question of what resources of language may be dead or obsolete. The metaphorical and metonymic phases of language have been in large measure outgrown because of the obvious limitations that they imposed on the human mind. But it seems clear that the descriptive phase also has limitations, in a world where its distinction of subject and object so often does not work. There is no question of giving up descriptive language, only of relating it to a broader spectrum of verbal expression. The word "God" is a noun, and so falls into the category of things and objects. For metonymic writing this is not an insuperable problem: what is beyond all things and objects can still be a noun, or at any rate have a name. For most writers of the second phase, God represents an immutable being, set over against the dissolving flow of the world of becoming in which we are; and practically the only grammatical device for conveying this sense of the immutable is the abstract noun. For third-phase writing, founded as it is on a sense-apprehended distinction between objects that are there and objects that are not, "God" can go only into the illusory class. But perhaps this kind of noun-thinking is, at least here, a fallacy of the type that Whitehead calls a fallacy of misplaced concreteness.

In Exodus 3:14, though God also gives himself a name, he defines himself (according to the AV) as "I am that I am," which scholars say is more accurately rendered "I will be what I will be." That is, we might come closer to what is meant in the Bible by the word "God" if we understood it as a verb, and not a verb of simple asserted existence but a verb implying a process accomplishing itself. This would involve trying to think our way back to a conception of language in which words were words of power, conveying primarily the sense of forces and energies rather than analogues of physical bodies. To some extent this would be a reversion to the metaphorical language of primitive communities, as our earlier references to a cycle of language and the "primitive" word "mana" suggested. But it would also be oddly contemporary with post-Einsteinian physics, where atoms and electrons are no longer thought of as things but rather as traces of processes. God may have lost his function as the subject or object of a predicate, but may not be so much dead as entombed in a dead language.

Northrop Frye, *The Great Code*

Even the word "god" is being defined by many theologians today in such a way as to exclude the conception of a person with a form, a voice, a beard, etc. If God gets to be defined as "Being itself," or as "the integrating principle in the universe," or as "the whole of everything," or as "the meaningfulness of the cosmos," or in some other non-personal way, then what will atheists be fighting against? They may very well agree with "integrating principles" or "the principle of harmony."

Abraham H. Maslow, *Religions, Values, and Peak-Experiences*

God is not neuter, not an "it," but a God of men, who provokes the decision for belief or unbelief. He is spirit in creative freedom, the primordial identity of justice and love, one who faces me as founding and embracing all interhuman personality. If, with the religious philosophers of the East, we want to call the absolutely last and absolutely first reality the "void" or "Absolute Nothingness," then we must also call it "being itself," which manifests itself with an infinite claim and with infinite understanding. It will be better to call the most real reality not personal or nonpersonal but—if we attach importance to the terminology—transpersonal or suprapersonal.

Hans Küng, *Does God Exist?*

Can you think about God? Can you be convinced about the existence of God because you have read all the evidence? The atheist also has his evidence; he has probably studied as much as you, and he says there is no God. You believe that there is God, and he believes that there is not; both of you have beliefs, both of you spend your time thinking about God. But before you think about something that you do not know, you must find out what thinking is, must you not? How can you think about something that you do not know? You may have read the Bible, the Bhagavad Gita, or other books in which various erudite scholars have skilfully described what God is, asserting this and contradicting that, but as long as you do not know the process of your own thinking, what you think about God may be stupid and petty, and generally it is. You may collect a lot of evidence for the existence of God and write very clever articles about it, but surely the first question is, how do you know what you think is true? Can thinking ever bring about the experience of that which is unknowable? Which doesn't mean that you must emotionally, sentimentally *accept* some rubbish about God.

So is it not important to find out whether your mind is conditioned, rather than to seek that which is unconditioned? Surely if your mind is conditioned, which it is, however much it may inquire into the reality of God, it can only gather knowledge or information according to its conditioning. So your thinking about God is an utter waste of time, it is a speculation that has no value. It is like my sitting in this grove and wishing to be on the top of that mountain [in the background]. If I really want to find out what is on the top of the mountain and beyond, I must go to it. It is no good my sitting here speculating, building temples, churches, and getting excited about them. What I have to do is to stand up, walk, struggle, push, get there, and find out; but as most of us are unwilling to do that, we are satisfied to sit here and speculate about something that we do not know. And I say such speculation is a hindrance, it is a deterioration of the mind, it has no value at all; it only brings more confusion, more sorrow to man.

God is something that cannot be talked about, that cannot be described, that cannot be put into words, because it must ever remain the unknown. The moment the recognizing process takes place, you are back in the field of memory. Do you understand? Say, for instance, you have a momentary experience of something extraordinary. At that precise moment there is no thinker who says, "I must remember it." There is only the state of experiencing. But when that moment goes by, the process of recognition comes into being. Please follow this. The mind says, "I have had a marvellous experience and I wish I could have more of it," so the struggle for the more begins. The acquisitive instinct, the possessive pursuit of the more, comes into being for various reasons: because it gives you pleasure, prestige, knowledge, you become an authority, and all the rest of that nonsense.

The mind pursues that which it has experienced, but that which it has experienced is already over, dead, gone. To discover that which is, the mind must die to that which it has experienced. This is not something that can be cultivated day after day, that can be gathered, accumulated, held, and then talked and written about. All that we can do is to see that the mind is conditioned and through self-knowledge to understand the process of our own thinking. I must know myself, not as I would ideologically like to be, but as I actually am, however ugly or beautiful, however jealous, envious, acquisitive. But it is very difficult just to see what one is without wishing to change it, and that very desire to change it is another form of conditioning; and so we go on, moving from conditioning to conditioning, never experiencing something beyond that which is limited.

J. Krishnamurti, *On God*

The history of religion has shown that God can be called "father" in a great variety of religions. In Israel's vicinity, the Greeks had learned from Homer's epics that Zeus, son of Chronos, was the father of the family of gods; in stoic philosophy, the Deity was regarded in cosmological terms as father of the reason-permeated cosmos and of human beings endowed with reason, related to him and cared for by him.

But the very fact that God can be called "father" in the pagan religions should make us cautious about using this title. And this particularly in an age of women's emancipation, which has, again, made us sharply aware of the problems involved. There is no doubt that the conception of God as Father very often had to serve as a religious justification of a sociological paternalism at the expense of women and especially as a means of permanently suppressing the feminine element in the Church. For this father ideology is, again, the basis of an exclusively male Son Christology, which in turn is misused—as in one of the more recent Roman Catholic documents—with the aid of abstruse biblical arguments for continuing to refuse ordination to women.

In general, the gods in the history of religion appear as sexually differentiated, although at the very beginning there might have been bisexual or sexually neutral beings and, later, bisexual features continued to be displayed. But is it not striking that in the matriarchal cultures, in place of the Father God there is the "Great Mother," out of whose fertile womb all things and beings emerged and into which they return? This throws a light on the historical relativity of a masculine deity. From a historical standpoint, it is quite possible—even though now, as formerly, disputed among historians—that matriarchy is older than patriarchy. In that case, the cult of the mother deity—which exercised some influence, for instance, in Asia Minor on the cult of Mary—would also have preceded chronologically that of the Father God.

In the Old Testament also, the designation of "father" for God is not determined solely by the uniqueness of Yahweh. It appears also to be sociologically conditioned, bearing the imprint of a male-oriented society. But, however the historical questions may be decided, *God is certainly not simply male*. Even in the Old Testament, with the prophets, God displays also feminine, maternal features. And it is this very thing that must be seen more clearly from the modern standpoint, for the sake of the urgently needed revaluation of women in the churches; for Christianity—and even more, the other world religions—is a man's religion that, however, in practice is largely sustained by women. Consequently one thing must never be forgotten:

> *The designation of "father" for God is misunderstood if it is taken as the opposite of "mother" instead of symbolically (analogically). "Father" is a patriarchal symbol—but also with matriarchal traits—for a transhuman, transsexual, absolutely last/absolutely first reality.*

God, then, is not masculine and must not be seen through the screen of the masculine-paternal, as an all-too-masculine theology did. The feminine-maternal element must also be recognized in him.

Hans Küng, Does God Exist?

QUESTIONER: There are many concepts of God in the world today. What is your thought concerning God?

KRISHNAMURTI: First of all, we must find out what we mean by a concept. What do we mean by the process of thinking? Because, after all, when we formulate a concept, let us say of God, our formula or concept must be the result of our conditioning, must it not? If we believe in God, surely our belief is the result of our environment. There are those who are trained from childhood to deny God and those who are trained to believe in God, as most of you have been. So we formulate a concept of God according to our training, according to our background, according to our idiosyncrasies, likes and dislikes, hopes and fears. Obviously then, as long as we do not understand the process of our own thinking, mere concepts of God have no value at all, have they? Because thought can project anything it likes. It can create and deny God. Each person can invent or destroy God according to his inclinations, pleasures, and pains. Therefore, as long as thought is active, formulating, inventing, that which is beyond time can never be discovered. God, or reality, is to be discovered only when thought comes to an end.

Now, when you ask, "What is your thought concerning God?" you have already formulated your own thought, have you not? Thought can create God and experience that which it has created. But surely that is not true experience. It is only its own projection that thought experiences, and therefore it is not real. But if you and I can see the truth of this, then perhaps we shall experience something much greater than a mere projection of thought.

At the present time, when there is greater and greater insecurity outwardly, there is obviously a yearning for inward security. Since we cannot find security outside, we seek it in an idea, in thought, and so we create that which we call God, and that concept becomes our security. Now a mind that seeks security surely cannot find the real, the true. To understand that which is beyond time, the fabrications of thought must come to an end. Thought cannot exist without words, symbols, images. And only when the mind is quiet, free of its own creations, is there a possibility of finding out what is real. So merely to ask if there is or is not God is an immature response to the problem, is it not? To formulate opinions about God is really childish.

To experience, to realize that which is beyond time, we must obviously understand the process of time. The mind is the result of time, it is based on the memories of yesterday. And is it possible to be free from the multiplication of yesterdays that is the process of time? Surely this is a very serious problem; it is not a matter of belief or disbelief? Believing and disbelieving is a process of ignorance, whereas understanding the time-binding quality of thought brings freedom in which alone there can be discovery. But most of us want to believe because it is much more convenient; it gives us a sense of security, a sense of belonging to the group. Surely this very belief separates us; you believe in one thing and I believe in another. So belief acts as a barrier; it is a process of disintegration.

What is important, then, is not the cultivation of belief or disbelief, but to understand the process of the mind. It is the mind, it is thought that creates time. Thought is time, and whatever thought projects must be of time; therefore, thought cannot possibly go beyond itself. To discover what is beyond time, thought must come to an end, and that is a most difficult thing because the ending of thought does not come about through discipline, through control, through denial or suppression. Thought ends only when we understand the whole process of thinking, and to understand thinking there must be self-knowledge. Thought is the self, thought is the word that identifies itself as the "me" and, at whatever level the self is placed, high or low, it is still within the field of thought.

To find God, that which is beyond time, we must understand the process of thought—that is, the process of oneself. The self is very complex; it is not at any one level, but is made up of many thoughts, many entities, each in contradiction with the others. There must be a constant awareness of them all, an awareness in which there is no choice, no condemnation or comparison; that is, there must be the capacity to see things as they are without distorting or translating them. The moment we judge or translate what is seen, we distort it according to our background. To discover reality or God, there can be no belief because acceptance or denial is a barrier to discovery. We all want to be secure both outwardly and inwardly, and the mind must understand that the search for security is an illusion. It is only the mind that is insecure, completely free from any form of possession that can discover—and this is an arduous task. It does not mean retiring into the woods, or to a monastery, or isolating oneself in some peculiar belief; on the contrary, nothing can exist in isolation. To be is to be related; it is only in the midst of relationship that we can spontaneously discover ourselves as we are. It is this very discovery of ourselves as we are, without any sense of condemnation or justification, that brings about a fundamental transformation in what we are. And that is the beginning of wisdom.

J. Krishnamurti, *On God*

We do not create "God," we choose him.

C. G. Jung, *Psychology and Religion: West and East*

Faith rises and falls like the tides of an invisible sea.... You realize, I think, that it is more valuable, more mysterious, altogether more immense than anything you can learn or decide upon in college.

From a letter to Alfred Corn, May 30, 1962,
in Flannery O'Connor, *The Habit of Being*

"Where there is mystery, there must be faith. Faith, you cannot change no matter how you look at it. Either you have it, or you don't. For us, it is very simple because our feet are on the ground. We have more of the living reality. There was a time when the Church had to show majesty and greatness. But today, people have found that it does not pay. They have found the emptiness of all that pomp so they are coming down more to the ground, and in coming down there is the danger that they are not finding their proper place.

"God has created all things. All the butterflies, the animals—the whole of nature He has created for us. To them He has not given the will power to choose. They have only an instinct. Animals can be very lovable and love very beautifully, but that is out of instinct. But the human being can choose. That is the one thing that God does not take from us. The will power, the power to will. I want to go to heaven and I will, with the grace of God. If I choose to commit sin and go to hell, that is my choice. God cannot force me to do otherwise. That's why when we become religious we give up that will power. That is why the sacrifice is so great: the vow of obedience is very difficult. Because in making that vow you surrender the only thing that is your own—your will power. Otherwise my health, my body, my eyes, my everything are all His and He can take them. I can fall, I can break, but my will power doesn't go like this. I must choose to give it and that is beautiful."

> Mother Teresa, in Desmond Doig's
> *Mother Teresa: Her People and Her Work*

Indeed, every true word ever uttered, every thought sincerely and lucidly entertained, every harmonious note sung or sounded, laughter flashing like lightning between the head and the heart, human love in all its diversity binding together husbands and wives, parents and children, grandparents and grandchildren, and making of all mankind one family and our earth their home; the earth itself with its colours and shapes and smells, and its setting in a universe growing ever vaster and its basic components becoming ever more microscopic—seen with the eyes of Faith, it all adds up to a oneness, an image of everlasting reality.

> From "A Spiritual Journey," in Malcolm Muggeridge, *Conversion*

The fairest thing we can experience is the mysterious. It is the fundamental emotion which stands at the cradle of true art and true science. He who knows it not and can no longer wonder, no longer feel amazement, is as good as dead, a snuffed-out candle. It was the experience of mystery—even if mixed with fear—that engendered religion. A knowledge of the existence of something we cannot penetrate, of the manifestations of the profoundest reason and the most radiant beauty, which are only accessible to our reason in their most elementary forms—it is this knowledge and this emotion that constitute the truly religious attitude; in this sense, and in this alone, I am a deeply religious man. I cannot conceive of a God who rewards and punishes his creatures, or has a will of the type of which we are conscious in ourselves. An individual who should survive his physical death is also beyond my comprehension, nor do I wish it otherwise; such notions are for the fears or absurd egoism of feeble souls. Enough for me the mystery of the eternity of life, and the inkling of the marvellous structure of reality, together with the single-hearted endeavour to comprehend a portion, be it never so tiny, of the reason that manifests itself in nature.

Albert Einstein, *The World As I See It*

With reference to the beginning of the universe, then, what point can there be today in speaking not only—scientifically—about a big bang, models of the universe, theories of the cosmos, but also with a perfect right—theologically—about a *God who created heaven and earth*: a God whom people, particularly Christians and Jews, have acknowledged over and over again in the light of the Old Testament? Certainly my age is nothing in comparison with the age of mankind; but the age of mankind is nothing by comparison with the thirteen billion years of this cosmos. And this earth of ours is a speck of dust in comparison with the totality of the Milky Way, which includes some hundred billion individual stars, one of them being the sun. And, again, this Milky Way of ours is a speck of dust by comparison with galactic clusters, some of which contain ten thousand galaxies, so that the number of observable galaxies may well amount to a hundred million. The more, then, I reflect on the amazing conclusions of astrophysics and, again, like human beings from time immemorial, look up into the clear night sky, am I not to wonder what it all means, where it all comes from? To answer, "Out of nothing," is no explanation. Reasons cannot be satisfied with that. The only serious alternative—which, like so many other things, pure reason admittedly cannot prove, since it transcends its horizon of experience—is that *the whole stems from that first creative cause of causes, which we call God and indeed the Creator God*. And even if I cannot prove him, I can with good reason affirm him: in that reasonable, tested and *enlightened trust* in which I have already affirmed his existence. For if the God who exists is truly God, then he is not only God for me here and now, but God at the beginning, God from all eternity.

Could this be merely an illusion, could it be suspected of being a projection, as Feuerbach and Freud suggested? Do I make this existing Creator

God for myself because I am afraid to be alone in the universe, because I feel the horror of a vacuum, because I fear to draw the harsh conclusion that man is abandoned to nothingness? Does not believing in God mean remaining always a child and never growing up—as Freud expressed it? As we saw, there can be no knowledge without some projection. Obviously, projection is involved in my knowledge of the Creator God. Even someone who affirms a nothingness likewise links a projection with nothingness. And yet I have every reason to assume that my projection is not merely a projection, but that a reality corresponds to it, that the reality of the Creator God meets my image of it, confirming, correcting, infinitely surpassing it. What, then, does it mean to believe in the Creator God?

Believing in the Creator of the world does not mean believing in any sort of myths; neither does it mean imagining God as Creator in the form depicted—for instance—by Michelangelo as artist when he painted him in a completely human way on the ceiling of the Sistine Chapel. At this point, all representations come to an end. Nor does believing in God as Creator of the world mean deciding for one or another of the varying models of the universe produced by leading scholars. This is impossible simply because we are here concerned with what is presupposed to all models and to the universe as a whole. Believing in the Creator of the world means affirming in enlightened trust that the world and man do not remain inexplicable in their ultimate source, that the world and man are not pointlessly hurled from nothing into nothing, but that in their totality they are meaningful and valuable, not chaos but cosmos; that they find their security first and last in God their primal ground, originator, creator. Nothing forces me into this faith. *I can decide for it absolutely freely.* Once I have decided, then this faith changes my position in the world, my attitude to the world; *it establishes my fundamental trust and gives concrete shape to my trust in God.*

Since I believe in God as Creator, I can also affirm the world and man as God's creation: respect men as my fellow men (and not as inferior beings); respect and care for nonhuman nature—especially animals—as my environment (and not as my natural enemies, not as material for arbitrary exploitation). It is not although but because I am God's creature, because my fellow men and my environment are also God's creatures, that I and my fellow men acquire and that my environment also—despite all differences—acquires a dignity that has to be respected. The "subdue the earth" of the creation story can never be a license for uninhibited exploitation and destruction of nature and the environment: a principle that does not apply only at a time when we are increasingly aware of the "limits of growth." Believing in the Creator God of the world thus means accepting with greater seriousness, greater realism, and greater hope my responsibility for my fellow men and for the environment and the tasks assigned to me. Is it not appropriate to make such a decision of faith in the Creator God for myself? *Credo in Deum omnipotentem, creatorem caeli et terrae.*

Hans Küng, *Does God Exist?*

Faith in God is not an irrational, blind, daring leap, but a trust that is responsible in the eyes of reason and grounded in reality itself.

Hans Küng, *Theology for the Third Millennium*

There is no doubt, it seems to me, that there have been profound changes in the experience of man in the last thousand years. In some ways this is more evident than changes in the patterns of his behavior. There is everything to suggest that man experienced God. Faith was never a matter of believing He existed, but of trusting in the Presence that was experienced and known to exist as a self-validating datum. It seems likely that far more people in our time neither experience the Presence of God, nor the Presence of His absence, but the absence of His Presence.

R. D. Laing, in Stanislav and Christina Grof, *Spiritual Emergency*

How is this God—who so obviously cannot be proved—actually to be found? Must we from the outset refrain from a rational approach to him, throw ourselves blindly—so to speak—into his arms and then perhaps in this very way fall into nothingness? Believe? Has belief, then, nothing to do with thinking? Is belief without thought not unconsidered, unjustifiable belief? Or is belief in God to be something only for devout fanatics and not for thinking people?

Hans Küng, *Does God Exist?*

Very many people today think in such terms as these: "either God exists, or He does not; if He exists and is what people say He is, then He will recognize that we are good and do not deserve punishment." This means that they are prepared to believe in His existence provided He conforms to their own imaginings and recognizes the value they attribute to themselves. This is to forget, on the one hand, that we cannot know the standards by which the Absolute judges us, and on the other that the "fire" beyond the tomb is definitively nothing but our own intellect actualized in opposition to our own falseness; in other words, it is the immanent truth breaking forth into the full light of day.

Frithjof Schuon, *Understanding Islam*

It is impossible to ask anyone to believe in truths revealed by God unless he first understand that there is a God and that He can reveal Truth.

Thomas Merton, *The Ascent to Truth*

Thirst was made for water; inquiry for truth.

C. S. Lewis, *The Great Divorce*

A monk once went to Gensha, and wanted to learn where the entrance to the path of truth was. Gensha asked him, "Do you hear the murmuring of the brook?" "Yes, I hear it," answered the monk. "There is the entrance," the Master instructed him.

C. G. Jung, *Psychology and Religion: West and East*

There is, there can be only a single universal and external truth. Because the Real exists always and can never vanish, the True exists always and can never vanish. No prophet ever reveals it for the first time, no seer discovers it. All only rediscover it. It never changes or evolves; only its form of presentation does that. But before it can manifest in our world, it must find human minds sufficiently prepared to be able to receive it and sufficiently developed to be able to comprehend and teach it.

Paul Brunton, *The Spiritual Crisis of Man*

There is no path to truth, historically or religiously. It is not to be experienced or found through dialectics; it is not to be seen in shifting opinions and beliefs. You will come upon it when the mind is free of all the things it has put together. That majestic peak is also the miracle of life.

J. Krishnamurti, *Krishnamurti's Journal*

You know, passion is necessary to understand truth—I am using the word *passion* in its full significance—because to feel strongly, to feel deeply, with all your being, is essential; otherwise that strange thing called reality will never come to you. But your religions, your saints say that you must not have desire, you must control, suppress, overcome, destroy, which means that you come to truth burnt out, worn out, empty, dead. You must have passion to meet this strange thing called life, and you cannot have passion, intense feeling, if you are mesmerized by society, by custom, if you are entangled in beliefs, dogmas, rituals. So to understand that light, that truth, that immeasurable reality, we must first understand what we call religion and be free of it—not verbally, not intellectually, not through explanations, but actually be free; because freedom—not your intellectual freedom but the actual state of freedom—gives vitality. When you have walked through all this rubbish, when you have put aside all these confusing, traditional imitative things, then the mind is free, then the mind is alert, then the mind is passionate. And it is only such a mind that can proceed.

J. Krishnamurti, *On God*

Truth is that which does not contaminate you, but empowers you.

Gary Zukav, *The Seat of the Soul*

Truth, in things, is their reality. In our minds, it is the conformity of our knowledge with the things known. In our words, it is the conformity of our words to what we think. In our conduct, it is the conformity of our acts to what we are supposed to be.

Thomas Merton, *No Man Is an Island*

Individuals can be alienated from themselves only because there is *something* in them to alienate. The terrain of this violation is their authentic existence. Living the truth is thus woven directly into the texture of living a lie. It is the repressed alternative, the authentic aim to which living a lie is an inauthentic response. Only against this background does living a lie make any sense: it exists *because* of that background. In its excusatory, chimerical rootedness in the human order, it is a response to nothing other than the human predisposition to truth. Under the orderly surface of the life of lies, therefore, there slumbers the hidden sphere of life in its real aims, of its hidden openness to truth.

The singular, explosive, incalculable political power of living within the truth resides in the fact that living openly within the truth has an ally, invisible to be sure, but omnipresent: this hidden sphere. It is from this sphere that life lived openly in the truth grows; it is to this sphere that it speaks, and in it that it finds understanding. This is where the potential for communication exists. But this place is hidden and therefore, from the perspective of power, very dangerous. The complex ferment that takes place within it goes on in semi-darkness, and by the time it finally surfaces into the light of day as an assortment of shocking surprises to the system, it is usually too late to cover them up in the usual fashion. Thus they create a situation in which the regime is confounded, invariably causing panic and driving it to react in inappropriate ways.

It seems that the primary breeding ground for what might, in the widest possible sense of the word, be understood as an opposition in the post-totalitarian system is living within the truth. The confrontation between these opposition forces and the powers that be, of course, will obviously take a form essentially different from that typical of an open society or a classical dictatorship. Initially, this confrontation does not take place on the level of real, institutionalized, quantifiable power which relies on the various instruments of power, but on a different level altogether: the level of human consciousness and conscience, the existential level. The effective range of this special power cannot be measured in terms of disciples, voters, or soldiers, because it lies spread out in the fifth column of social consciousness, in the hidden aims of life, in human beings' repressed longing for dignity and fundamental rights, for the realization of their real social and political interests. Its power, therefore, does not reside in the strength of definable political or social groups, but chiefly in the strength of a potential, which is hidden throughout the whole of society, including the official power structures of that society. Therefore this power does not rely on soldiers of its own, but on the soldiers of the enemy as it were—that is to say, on everyone who is living within the lie and who may be struck at any moment (in theory, at least) by the force of truth (or who, out of an instinctive desire to protect their position, may at last adapt to that force). It is a bacteriological weapon, so to speak, utilized when conditions are ripe by a single civilian to disarm an entire division. This power does not participate in any direct struggle for power; rather it makes its influence felt in the obscure arena of being itself. The hidden movements it gives rise to there, however, can issue forth (when, where, under what circumstances, and to what extent are difficult to predict) in something visible: a real political act or event, a social movement, a sudden explosion of civil unrest, a sharp conflict inside an apparently monolithic power structure, or simply an irrepressible transformation in the social and intellectual climate. And since all genuine problems and matters of critical importance are hidden beneath a thick crust of lies, it is never quite clear when the proverbial last straw will fall, or what that straw will be. This, too, is why the regime prosecutes, almost as a reflex action preventively, even the most modest attempts to live within the truth.

Why was Solzhenitsyn driven out of his own country? Certainly not because he represented a unit of real power, that is, not because any of the regime's representatives felt he might unseat them and take their place in government. Solzhenitsyn's expulsion was something else: a desperate attempt to plug up the dreadful wellspring of truth, a truth which might cause incalculable transformations in social consciousness, which in turn might one day produce political debacles unpredictable in their consequences. And so the post-totalitarian system behaved in a characteristic way: it defended the integrity of the world of appearances in order to defend itself. For the crust presented by the life of lies is made of strange stuff. As long as it seals off hermetically the entire society, it appears to be made of stone. But the moment someone breaks through in one place, when one person cries out, "The emperor is naked!"—when a single person breaks the rules of the game, thus exposing it as a game—everything suddenly appears in another light and the whole crust seems then to be made of a tissue on the point of tearing and disintegrating uncontrollably.

Vaclav Havel, Living in Truth

→ 2 ←

Looking for Meaning and the Way

A significant aspect of the quest for meaning is the search within ourselves for answers. To find them, we must trust that the divine speaks to us through our intuition. And to do this we must recognize our own divinity, get to know our souls and learn how to nourish them. In *A Different Drum*, renowned American psychiatrist, psychotherapist, and author M. Scott Peck writes that to reach this place of recognition we must move through four stages of spiritual development: (1) chaotic, antisocial; (2) formal, institutional; (3) sceptic, individual; (4) mystic, communal. Stanislav and Christina Grof, leaders in understanding and counselling psychological and emotional shifts in behaviour during what they term "spiritual emergence" and "spiritual emergencies," explain how the intensity of these experiences transform a person's perceptions of life and accelerates spiritual awareness. For some, shifting behaviour or attitudinal patterns in order to reach a place of trust can cause much stress and distress. This is only natural as we relinquish the old worn ways of controlling our lives to seeing what may happen as we open ourselves to a new and relatively unknown spiritual way of being.

This section charts the emotional journey to awareness, from the growing need of the soul for acknowledgement, healing, and nourishment, to the sometimes painful transition from the old familiar ways of life, to the growing trust in the new.

→←

The Reckoning

Later some of these heroic worshippers
May live out one thrift in a world of options,
The crown of thorns, the bridal wreath of love,
Desires in all their motions.
"As below, darling, so above."
In one thought focus and resume
The thousand contradictions,
And still with a sigh these warring fictions.

Timeless as water into language flowing,
Molten as snow on new burns,
The limbo of half-knowing
Where the gagged conscience twists and turns,
Will plant the flag of their unknowing.

It is not peace we seek but meaning.

To convince at last that all is possible,
That the feeble human finite must belong
Within the starry circumference of wonder,
And waking alone at night so suddenly
Realise how careful one must be with hate—
For you become what you hate too much,
As when you love too much you fraction
By insolence the fine delight...

It is not meaning that we need but sight.

Lawrence Durrell, *Collected Poems*

The Great Way

Zen story:
    A monk said to Joshu: "What is the way?"
    Joshu replied: "Outside the fence."
    The monk insisted: "I mean the Great Way? What is the Great Way?"
    Joshu replied: "The Great Way is that which leads to the Capital."

The Great Way is right in the middle of the story, and I should remember it when I get excited about war and peace. I sometimes think I have an urgent duty to make all kinds of protest and clarification—but, above all, the important thing is to be on the Great Way and stay on it, whether one speaks or not. It is not necessary to run all over the countryside shouting "peace, peace!" But it is essential to stay on the Great Way which leads to the Capital, for only on the Great Way is there peace. If no one follows the way, there will be no peace in the world, no matter how much men may preach it.

It is easy to know that "there is a way somewhere," and even perhaps to know that others are not on it (by analogy with one's own lostness, wandering far from the way). But this knowledge is useless unless it helps one find the way.

Thomas Merton, *Conjectures of a Guilty Bystander*

We search for meaning, we search for belonging, and that means that we are all exploring God-territory. But that territory is so vast that you can go on forever and ever exploring one part of it and never meet other groups that explore other parts. There are certain crossroads where you choose to go in a certain direction. After that, you are not likely to reach the territory others are exploring who took a different turn.

One of those crossroads is the discovery that belonging is mutual. If we belong to God, God belongs to us; we are in a relationship. This is mysticism of course, but any one of us can experience it daily. God is related to us in a personal way. That's the experiential basis for the notion that God must have all the perfection that makes me a person and none of the limitations.

David Steindl-Rast, in Fritjof Capra, David Steindl-Rast
with Thomas Matus, *Belonging to the Universe*

Life must be played by ear—which is only to say that we must trust, not symbolic rules and linear principles, but our brains or natures. Yet this must bring one back to the faith that nature makes no mistake. In such a universe a decision which results in one's own death is not a mistake: it is simply a way of dying at the right moment.

But nothing can be right in a universe where nothing can be wrong, and every perception is an awareness of contrast, of a right/wrong, is/isn't, bright/dark, hard/soft situation. If this is the very nature of awareness, any and every circumstance, however fortunate, will have to be experienced as a good/bad or plus/minus in order to be experienced at all. By such reflections I think myself into silence and, by writing, help others similarly spellbound by thoughts and words to come to silence—which is the realization that a linear code cannot justly represent a nonlinear world. But this intellectual silence is not failure, defeat, or suicide. It is a return to that naked awareness, that vision unclouded by commentary, which we enjoyed as babies in the days when we saw no difference between knower and known, deed and happening. This time, however, we are babies reborn—babies who remember all the rules and tricks of human games and can therefore communicate with other people as if we were normal adults. We can also feel, as a just-born baby cannot, compassion for their confusions.

Now, from the standpoint of the wise-baby, the confusions of the normal adult world cannot be straightened out without becoming even more confused. There is no solution except to regain the baby's vision and so realize that the confusions are not really serious, but only the games whereby adults pass the time and pretend to be important. Seen thus, the world becomes immeasurably rich in color and detail because we no longer ignore aspects of life which adults pass over and screen out in their haste after serious matters. As in music, the point of life is its pattern at every stage of its development, and in a world where there is neither self nor other, the only identity is just This—which is all, which is energy, which is God by no name.

Alan Watts, *In My Own Way*

There is something that can be found in one place. It is a great treasure, which may be called the fulfillment of existence. The place where this treasure can be found is the place on which one stands.

Most of us achieve only at rare moments a clear realization of the fact that they have never tasted the fulfillment of existence, that their life does not participate in true, fulfilled existence, that, as it were, it passes true existence by. We nevertheless feel the deficiency at every moment, and in some measure strive to find—somewhere—what we are seeking. Somewhere, in some province of the world or of the mind, except where we stand, where we have been set—but it is there and nowhere else that the treasure can be found. The environment which I feel to be the natural one, the situation which has been assigned to me as my fate, the things that happen to me day after day, the things that claim me day after day—these contain my essential task and such fulfillment of existence as is open to me. It is said of a certain Talmudic master that the paths of Heaven were as bright to him as the streets of his native town. Hasidism inverts the order: It is a greater thing if the streets of a man's native town are as bright to him as the paths of Heaven. For it is here, where we stand, that we should try to make shine the light of the hidden divine life.

Martin Buber, *The Way of Man*

The fact that our being necessarily demands to be expressed in action should not lead us to believe that as soon as we stop acting we cease to exist. We do not live merely in order to "do something"—no matter what. Activity is just one of the normal expressions of life, and the life it expresses is all the more perfect when it sustains itself with an ordered economy of action. This order demands a wise alternation of activity and rest. We do not live more fully merely by doing more, seeing more, tasting more, and experiencing more than we ever have before. On the contrary, some of us need to discover that we will not begin to live more fully until we have the courage to do and see and taste and experience much less than usual.

A tourist may go through a museum with a Baedeker, looking conscientiously at everything important, and come out less alive than when he went in. He has looked at everything and seen nothing. He has done a great deal and it has only made him tired. If he had stopped for a moment to look at one picture he really liked and forgotten about all the others, he might console himself with the thought that he had not completely wasted his time. He would have discovered something not only outside himself but in himself. He would have become aware of a new level of being in himself and his life would have been increased by a new capacity for being and for doing.

Our being is not to be enriched merely by activity or experience as such. Everything depends on the *quality* of our acts and our experiences. A multitude of badly performed actions and of experiences only half-lived exhausts and depletes our being. By doing things badly we make ourselves less real. This growing unreality cannot help but make us unhappy and fill us with a sense of guilt. But the purity of our conscience has a natural proportion with the depth of our being and the quality of our acts: and when our activity is habitually disordered, our malformed conscience can think of nothing better to tell us than to multiply the *quantity* of our acts, without perfecting their quality. And so we go from bad to worse, exhaust ourselves, empty our whole life of all content, and fall into despair.

There are times, then, when in order to keep ourselves in existence at all we simply have to sit back for a while and do nothing. And for a man who has let himself be drawn completely out of himself by his activity, nothing is more difficult than to sit still and rest, doing nothing at all. The very act of resting is the hardest and most courageous act he can perform: and often it is quite beyond his power.

We must first recover the possession of our own being before we can act wisely or taste any experience in its human reality. As long as we are not in our own possession, all our activity is futile. If we let all our wine run out of the barrel and down the street, how will our thirst be quenched?

Thomas Merton, *No Man Is an Island*

What matters is being spontaneously open to the *reality* of God.
Thomas Merton, *The Springs of Contemplation*

You know always in your heart that you need God more than everything;
but do you not know that God needs you—in the fullness of His eternity
needs you? How would man be, how would you be, if God did not need
him, did not need you? You need God, in order to be—and God needs you,
for the very meaning of your life. In instruction and in poems men are at
pains to say more, and they say too much—what turgid and presumptuous
talk that is about the "God who becomes"; but we know unshakably in our
hearts that there is a becoming of the God that is. The world is not divine
sport, it is divine destiny. There is divine meaning in the life of the world, of
man, of human persons, of you and of me.
Martin Buber, *I and Thou*

The experiential process of interacting with the divine is what counts, the
walking along the road, not the milestones.
David Steindl-Rast, in Fritjof Capra, David Steindl-Rast,
with Thomas Matus, *Belonging to the Universe*

The basis of spiritual ascent is that God is pure Spirit and that man resembles
Him fundamentally through the intelligence; man goes towards God by
means of that which is, in him, most conformable to God—the intellect—
which is at the same time both penetration and contemplation and has as its
"supernaturally natural" content the Absolute which illumines and delivers.
The character of a way depends on a particular preliminary definition of man:
if man is defined as passion, as the general perspective of Christianity would
have it—though there is here no principal restriction—then the way is suffering; if as desire, then the way is renunciation; if as will, then the way is effort;
if as intelligence, then the way is discernment, concentration, contemplation.
Frithjof Schuon, *Understanding Islam*

Many Famous Feet Have Trod

Many famous feet have trod
Sublunary paths, and famous hands have weighed
The strength they have against the strength they need;

And famous lips interrogated God
Concerning franchise in eternity;
And in many differing times and places
Truth was attained (a moment's harmony);
Yet endless mornings break on endless faces:

Gold surf of the sun, each day
Exhausted through the world, gathers and whips
Irrevocably from eclipse;
The trodden way becomes the untrodden way,
We are born each morning, shelled upon
A sheet of light that paves
The palaces of sight, and brings again
The river shining through the field of graves.

Such renewal argues down
Our unsuccessful legacies of thought,
Annals of men who fought
Untiringly to change their hearts to stone,
Or to a wafer's poverty,
Or to a flower, but never tried to learn
The difficult triple sanity
Or being wafer, stone, and flower in turn.

Turn out your pockets on the tablecloth:
Consider what we know. A silver piece:
That's life; and, dealing in dichotomies,
This old discoloured copper coin is death.
Turn it about: it is impenetrable.
Reverse and obverse, neither bear
A sign or word remotely legible:
But spin the silver to a sphere,

Look in, and testify. Our mortal state
In turn is twisted in a double warp:
The light is waking and the dark is sleep
And twice a day before their gate
We kneel between them. There is more
Knowledge of sleep than death, and yet
Who knows the nature of our casting there,
Trawled inaccessible pool, or set

A line to haul its logic into speech?
Easier to balance on the hand
The waking that our senses can command,
For jewels are pebbles on a beach
Before this weaving, scattering, winged-and-footed
Privilege, this first, untold
And unrecurring luck that is never completed
Even in distance out of our hands' hold,

That makes, this waking traffic, this one last,
One paramount division. I declare
Two lineages electrify the air,
That will like pennons from a mast
Fly over sleep and life and death
Till sun is powerless to decoy
A single seed above the earth:
Lineage of sorrow: lineage of joy;

No longer think them aspects of the same;
Beyond each figured shield I trace
A different ancestry, a different face,
And sorrow must be held to blame
Because I follow it to my own heart
To find it feeding there on all that's bad:
It is sanctionable and right
Always to be ashamed of being sad.

Ashamed that sorrow's beckoned in
By each foiled weakness in the almanac
Engendered by the instinct-to-turn-back
—Which, if there are sins, should be called a sin—
Instinct that so worships my own face
It would halt time herewith
And put my wishes in its place:
And for this reason has great fear of death.

Because tides wound it;
The scuttling sand; the noose
Of what I have and shall lose,
Or have not and cannot get;
Partings in time or space

Wound it; it weeps sorely;
Holds sorrow before its face,
And all to pretend it is not part of me,

The blind part. I know what it will not know:
All stopping-up of cracks
Against dissolution builds a house of wax,
While years in wingspans go
Across and over our heads. Watch them:
They are flying east. They are flying to the ebb
Of dark. They are making sorrow seem
A spider busy on a forgotten web.

They are calling every fibre of the world
Into rejoicing, a mile-long silken cloth
Of wings moving lightwards out of death:
Lineage of joy into mortality hurled,
Endowing every actual bone
With motionless excitement. If quick feet
Must tread sublunary paths, attest this one:
Perpetual study to defeat

Each slovenly grief; the patience to expose
Untrue desire; assurance that, in sum,
Nothing's to reach, but something's to become,
That must be pitched upon the luminous,
Denying rest. Joy has no cause:
Though cut to pieces with a knife,
Cannot keep silence. What else should magnetize
Our drudging, hypocritical, ecstatic life?

15 October 1946

Philip Larkin, *Collected Poems*

God approaches our minds by receding from them.

We can never fully know Him if we think of Him as an object of capture, to be fenced in by the enclosure of our own ideas.

We know Him better after our minds have let Him go.

The Lord travels in all directions at once.

The Lord arrives from all directions at once.

Wherever we are, we find that He has just departed.

Wherever we go, we discover that He has just arrived before us.

Our rest can be neither in the beginning of this pursuit, nor in the pursuit itself, nor in its apparent end. For the true end, which is Heaven, is an end without end. It is a totally new dimension, in which we come to rest in the secret that He must arrive at the moment of His departure; His arrival is at every moment and His departure is not fixed in time.

Thomas Merton, *No Man Is an Island*

A Door Opens

A door opens in the center of our being and we seem to fall through it into immense depths which, although they are infinite, are all accessible to us; all eternity seems to have become ours in this one placid and breathless contact.

God touches us with a touch that is emptiness, and empties us. He moves us with a simplicity that simplifies us. All variety, all complexity, all paradox, all multiplicity cease. Our mind swims in the air of an understanding, a reality that is dark and serene and includes in itself everything. Nothing more is desired. Nothing more is wanting. Our only sorrow, if sorrow be possible at all, is the awareness that we ourselves still live outside of God.

For already a supernatural instinct teaches us that the function of this abyss of freedom, which has been opened out within our own midst, is to draw us utterly out of our own selfhood and into its own immensity of liberty and joy.

Thomas Merton, *New Seeds of Contemplation*

June 19, 1982

Dear Olga,

Again, I call to mind that distant moment in Heřmanice when on a hot, cloudless summer day, I sat on a pile of rusty iron and gazed into the crown of an enormous tree that stretched, with dignified repose, up and over all the fences, wires, bars and watchtowers that separated me from it. As I watched the imperceptible trembling of its leaves against an endless sky, I was overcome by a sensation that is difficult to describe: all at once, I seemed to rise above all the coordinates of my momentary existence in the world into a kind of state outside time in which all the beautiful things I had ever seen and experienced existed in a total "co-present"; I felt a sense of reconciliation, indeed of an almost gentle consent to the inevitable course of things as revealed to me now, and this combined with a carefree determination to face what had to be faced. A profound amazement at the sovereignty of Being became a dizzying sensation of tumbling endlessly into the abyss of its mystery; an unbounded joy at being alive, at having been given the chance to live through all I have lived through, and at the fact that everything has a deep and obvious meaning—this joy formed a strange alliance in me with a vague horror at the inapprehensibility and unattainability of everything I was so close to in that moment, standing at the very "edge of the finite"; I was flooded with a sense of ultimate happiness and harmony with the world and myself, with that moment, with all the moments I could call up, and with everything invisible that lies behind it and which has meaning. I would even say that I was somehow "struck by love," though I don't know precisely for whom or what. Once, in one of my letters, I reflected upon this experience; now I think—at least in the perspective of these essays—that I understand it better.

Evidently there exists an experience in which the longing of separated Being for remerging with the integrity of Being is satisfied, as it were, in the most mature and complete manner. That experience is typically and most profoundly human: it is the experience of meaning, and of meaningfulness. The need for meaning and the search for it—regardless of their form, their strength or their depth, or how definite or indefinite they may be, though they be nothing more than a vague sensation of the absence of "something" without which life is worthless—accompany the human "I" from its beginning right through to its end. They are inseparable and its most important dimension (because it embraces all the rest), its maturest and most complete expression, and the instrument of its self-constitution. Perhaps it could be said that the "I" is, in fact, this search for meaning—the meaning of things, events, its own life, itself. Certainly this dimension of its longing for "Being in Being," or rather this aspect of its thrownness into its source in Being, is somehow the "last" to come to light: it is something more than just the spontaneous intention of the "pre-I," in which there are still echoes of the "prenatal" state of nonseparation; it is even something more than the vigorous effort of the mind to grasp Being by perceiving and throwing light on it; these intentions are, of course, present in the "I," but they do not explain it entirely: it transcends them—by virtue, for example, of how it contains them within itself, mutually increases their strength and consummates them: paradoxically, the "I" seeks fullness of participation, but an alert participation, one that already knows of itself; it seeks a totality of merging, but a totality—so to speak—that is fully aware of its own unrealizability.

The experience of meaning is thus, essentially, the maturest or "highest" form of the "I"'s quasi-identification with the integrity of Being. It is the experience of genuine "contact," but contact as something both autonomous and integral—paradoxical as that may be. Perhaps it might be described as the experience of "counterpoint" between the "voice of Being" in the "I" (in its source) and the "voice of Being" in the "non-I" (in the world), wherein the meaning of this counterpoint does not just lie in a harmony that amplifies the original quality, but in the new quality it brings, a quality that knows neither of the two intersecting voices. It is in this counterpoint that it first seems possible (if only for a fleeting moment) to hear a suggestion or an echo of the as yet unfamiliar theme from the symphony of Being. The semipresence of Being in the "I" and its hidden presence in the "non-I" encounter each other here for an instant as "insight," a joyous sensation of participation and the vertigo that comes with it. The reflection of Being in the "I" renders us open to the mystery of Being in the "non-I"; Being concealed in the world, or the Being of the world, opens itself up to us. It is a meeting of two opennesses— but opennesses that are directed exclusively toward each other: it is not just that we seem to be here because of Being, but that Being seems to be here because of us. The greatest attainable closeness, fullness and completeness of Being would therefore seem to call forth the greatest degree of fullness and completeness of the "I."

Perhaps it will now be clear why I link the experience of meaning with what I called the third paradox of our thrownnesses: the nearest we can come to the fullness of Being also gives us the clearest indication of how unattainable it is; the most mature identification is most powerfully revealed as quasi-identification. Joy has an undertone of horror, tranquillity of anxiety, good fortune a touch of the fatally tragic. This experience reveals to us that in complete and unlimited identification, total insight, utter happiness, lies the end of the "I," death. It is by no means accidental that at the very heights of meaningfulness, happiness, joy and love, the specter of death inevitably appears with particular clarity. The experience of meaning also differs from less mature expressions of our longing for Being in that it contains within it—while at the same time, oddly enough, losing nothing of that sense of supreme happiness—the most forceful awareness of futility. But is it not precisely this that brings it closest to the contradictory essence itself of human life and the human mission?

Being spellbound within me and Being spellbound within the world can join hands anytime, anywhere and in any way: when I look into the crown of a tree or into someone's eyes, when I succeed in writing you a good letter, when I am moved by an opera on television, when a passage from Levinas sets my thoughts swirling, when our visits work out, when I understand the meaning of my compassion for the weatherwoman, when I help someone or when someone helps me, when something important happens, or when nothing in particular happens at all. But whenever and however it happens, such moments tend to be rare and fleeting. Given the contradictory nature of separated Being, it can't be any other way and it is right that it should be so: after all, the uniqueness and the unpredictability of such moments combine to create their meaning: it is the meaning of "islands of meaning" in the ocean of our struggling, the meaning of lanterns whose light is cast into the darkness of our life's journey, illuminating all the many meanings of its direction.

I kiss you,
Vašek

Vaclav Havel, *Letters to Olga*

Suppose you're God. Suppose you have all time, eternity, and all power at your disposal. What would you do? I believe you would say to yourself after a while, "Man, get lost." It's like asking another question which amounts to supposing you were given the power to dream any dream you wanted to dream every night. Naturally, you could dream any span of time—you could dream seventy-five years of time in one night, a hundred years of time in one night, a thousand years of time in one night—and it could be anything you wanted—because you make up your mind before you go to sleep. "Tonight I'm going to dream of so-and-so." Naturally, you would start out by fulfilling all your wishes. You would have all the pleasures you could imagine, the most marvelous meals, the most entrancing love affairs, the most romantic journeys; you could listen to music such as no mortal has heard, and see landscapes beyond your wildest dreams.

And for several nights, oh, maybe for a whole month of nights, you would go on that way, having a wonderful time. But then, after a while, you would begin to think, "Well, I've seen quite a bit, let's spice it up, let's have a little adventure." And you would dream of yourself being threatened by all sorts of dangers. You would rescue princesses from dragons, you would perhaps engage in notable battles, you would be a hero. And then as time went on, you would dare yourself to do more and more outrageous things, and at some point in the game you would say, "Tonight I am going to dream in such a way that I don't know that I'm dreaming," and by so doing you would take the experience of the drama for complete reality. What a shock when you woke up! You could really scare yourself!

And then on successive nights you might dare yourself to experience even more extraordinary things just for the contrast when you woke up. You could, for example, dream yourself in situations of extreme poverty, disease, agony. You could, as it were, live the essence of suffering to its most intense point, and then, suddenly, wake up and find it was after all nothing but a dream and everything's perfectly OK.

Well, how do you know that's not what you're doing already. You, reading, sitting there with all your problems, with all your whole complicated life situations, it may just be the very dream you decided to get into. If you don't like it, what fun it'll be when you wake up!

This is the essence of drama. In drama, all the people who see it know it's only a play. The proscenium arch, the cinema screen tells us, "Well, this is an illusion, it is not for real." In other words, they are going to act their parts so convincingly that they're going to have us sitting on the edge of our seats in anxiety, they're going to make us laugh, they're going to make us cry, they're going to make us feel horror. And all the time, in the back of our minds we have what Germans call *hintergedanken*, which is a thought way, way, way in the back of our minds, that we're hardly aware of but really know all the time. In the theater, we have a *hintergedanken* that it's only a play. But the mastery of the actors is going to almost convince us that it's real.

And, so, imagine a situation in which you have the best of all possible actors, namely God, and the best of all possible audiences ready to be taken in and convinced that it's real, namely God, and that you are all many, many masks which the basic consciousness, the basic mind of the universe, is assuming. To use a verse from G. K. Chesterton:

> But now a great thing in the street
> Seems any human nod
> Where shift in strange democracy
> The million masks of God.

It is like the mask of Vishnu, the preserver of the universe, a multiple mask which illustrates the fact that the one who looks out of my eyes and out of everyone's eyes is the same center. So, when I look at another human being, and I look straight into their eyes, I don't like doing that, there's something embarrassing about looking into someone's eyes too closely. Don't look at me that closely because I might give myself away! You might find out who I really am! And what do you suppose that would be? Do you suppose that another person who looks deeply into your eyes will read all the things you're ashamed of, all your faults, all the things you are guilty of? Or is there some deeper secret than that?

The eyes are our most sensitive organ, and when you look and look and look into another person's eyes you are looking at the most beautiful jewels in the universe. And if you look down beyond that surface beauty, it's the most beautiful jewel in the universe, because that's the universe looking at you. We are the eyes of the cosmos. So that in a way, when you look deeply into somebody's eyes, you're looking deep into yourself, and the other person is looking deeply into the same self, which many-eyed, as the mask of Vishnu is many-faced, is looking out everywhere, one energy playing myriads of different parts. Why?

It's perfectly obvious, because if you were God, and you knew everything and were in control of everything, you would be bored to death. It would be like making love to a plastic woman. Everything would be completely predictable, completely known, completely clear, no mystery, no surprise whatever.

Look at it another way. The object of our technology is to control the world, to have a superelectronic pushbutton universe, where we can get anything we want, fulfill any desires simply by pushing a button. You're Aladdin with the lamp, you rub it, the jinni comes and says, "Salaam, I'm your humble servant, what do you wish? Anything you want."

And after a while, just as in those dreams I described, you would decide one day to forget that you were dreaming, you would say to the jinni of the lamp, "I would like a surprise." Or God, in the Court of Heaven, might turn to his vizier and say, "Oh, Commander of the Faithful, we are bored." And the vizier of the Court would reply, "Oh King, live forever, surely out of the infinitude of your wisdom you can discover some way of not being bored." And the King would reply, "Oh vizier, give us a surprise." That's the whole basis of the story of the Arabian Nights. Here was a very powerful sultan who was bored. And therefore he challenged Scheherazade to tell him a new story every night so that the telling of the tales, getting involved in adventures, would never, never end.

Isn't that the reason why we go to the theater, why we go to the movies, because we want to get out of ourselves? We want a surprise; and a surprise means that you have to *other* yourself. That is to say, there has to enter into your experience some element that is not under your control.

So if our technology were to succeed completely, and everything were to be under our control, we should eventually say, "We need a new button." With all these control buttons, we always have to have a button labeled SURPRISE, and just so it doesn't become too dangerous, we'll put a time limit on it—surprise for 15 minutes, for an hour, for a day, for a month, a year, a lifetime. Then, in the end, when the surprise circuit is finished, we'll be back in control and we'll all know where we are. And we'll heave a sigh of relief, but, after a while, we'll press the button labeled SURPRISE once more.

You will notice a curious rhythm to what I have been explaining, and this rhythm corresponds to the Hindu idea of the course of time and the way evolution works, an idea drastically different from ours. First of all, Hindus think of time as circular, as going round—look at your watch, it goes round. But Westerners tend to think of time in a straight line, a one-way street, and we got that idea from Hebrew religion, and from St. Augustine.

There is a time of creation, then a course of history which leads up to final, eschatological catastrophe, the end of the world, and after that, the judgment, in which all things will be put to right, all questions answered, and justice dealt out to everyone according to his merits. And that'll be that! Thereafter the universe will be, in a way, static; there will be the eternally saved and the eternally damned.

Now, many people may not believe that today, but that has been a dominating belief throughout the course of Western history, and it has had a tremendously powerful influence on our culture. But the Hindus think half of the world as going round and round for always, in a rhythm. They calculate the rounds in periods that in Sanskrit are called *kalpas*, and each *kalpa* lasts for 4,320,000 years. And so a *kalpa* is the period or *manvantara* during which the world as we know it is manifested. And it is followed by a period, also a *kalpa* long, 4,320,000 years, which is called *pralaya*, and this means when the world is not manifested anymore.

And these are the days and nights of Brahma, the godhead. During the *manvantara*, when the world is manifested, Brahma is asleep, dreaming that he is all of us and everything that's going on, and during the *pralaya*, which is his day, he's awake, and knows himself, or itself (because it's beyond sex), for who and what he/she/it is. And then, once again, presses the button— surprise! As in the course of our dreaming, we would very naturally dream the most pleasant and rapturous dreams first and then get more adventurous, and experience and explore the more venturesome dimensions of experience, in the same way, the Hindus think of a *kalpa* of the manifested universe *manvantara* as divided into four periods. These four periods are of different lengths. The first is the longest, and the last is the shortest. They are named in accordance with the throws in the Hindu game of dice. There are four throws and the throw of four is always the best throw, like the six in our game, the throw of one, the worst throw.

Now, therefore, the first throw is called *krita* and the epoch, the long, long period for which this throw lasts, is called a *yuga*. So we will translate *yuga* as an "epoch," and we will translate *kalpa* as an "eon." Now the word *krita* means "done," as when we say, "well done," and that is a period of the world's existence that we call the Golden Age when everything is perfect, done to perfection. When it comes to an end, we get *treta-yuga* that means "the throw of three," and in this period of manifestation there's an element of the uncertain, an element of insecurity, an element of adventure in things. It's like a three-legged stool is not as secure as a four-legged one—you're a little more liable to be thrown off balance.

That lasts for a very long time, too, but then we get next what is called *dvapara-yuga*. In this period, the good and the bad, the pleasurable and the painful, are equally balanced. But, finally, there comes *kali-yuga*. *Kali* means "the worst throw," and this lasts for the shortest time. This is the period of manifestation in which the unpleasurable, painful, diabolical principle finally takes over—but it has the shortest innings.

And at the end of the *kali-yuga*, the great destroyer of the worlds, God manifested as the destructive principle Shiva does a dance called the *tandava*, and he appears, blue-bodied with ten arms, with lightning and fire appearing from every pore in his skin, and does a dance in which the universe is finally destroyed. The moment of cosmic death is the waking up of Brahma, the creator, for as Shiva turns round and walks off the stage, seen from behind, he is Brahma, the creator, the beginning of it all again. And Vishnu is the preserver, that is to say, the going on of it all, the whole state of the god-head being manifested as many, many faces. So, you see, this is a philosophy of the role of evil in life which is rational and merciful.

If we think God is playing with the world, has created it for his pleasure, and has created all these other beings and they go through the most horrible torments—terminal cancer, children being burned with napalm, concentration camps, the Inquisition, the horrors that human beings go through—how is that possibly justifiable? We try by saying, "Well, some God must have created it; if a God didn't create it, there's nobody in charge and there's no rationality to the whole thing. It's just a tale told by an idiot, full of sound and fury signifying nothing. It's a ridiculous system and the only out is suicide."

But suppose it's the kind of thing I've described to you, supposing it isn't that God is pleasing himself with all these victims, showing off his justice by either rewarding them or punishing them—supposing it's quite different from that. Suppose that God is the one playing all the parts, that God is the child being burned to death with napalm. There is no victim except the victor. All the different roles which are being experienced, all the different feelings which are being felt, are being felt by the one who originally desires, decides, wills to go into that very situation.

Curiously enough, there is something parallel to this in Christianity. There's a passage in St. Paul's Epistle to the Philippians in which he says a very curious thing: "Let this mind be in you which was also in Christ Jesus, who being in the form of God, did not think identity with God a thing to be clung to, but humbled himself and made himself of no reputation, and was found in fashion as a man and became obedient to death, even the death of the cross." Here you have exactly the same idea, the idea of God becoming human, suffering all that human beings can suffer, even death. And St. Paul is saying, "Let this mind be in you," that is to say, let the same kind of consciousness be in you that was in Jesus Christ. Jesus Christ knew he was God.

Wake up and find out eventually who you really are. In our culture, of course, they'll say you're crazy or you're blasphemous, and they'll either put you in jail or in the nut house (which is the same thing). But if you wake up in India and tell your friends and relations, "My goodness, I've just discovered that I'm God," they'll laugh and say, "Oh, congratulations, at last you found out."

Alan Watts, "The Drama of It All," in *The Essential Alan Watts*

When you live everyday with "what is" and observe "what is," not only out there but inwardly, then you will create a society that will be without conflict.

J. Krishnamurti, *On Nature and the Environment*

If one purpose of human life upon this earth is to unfold spiritually and if a section of humanity is driven by the pressures of crisis and the sufferings of war to seek such unfoldment, why should not the World Mind permit these drastic happenings? The same Nature which gives us mild balmy summers also gives us arctic cold winters. The same universal laws which bring the sunlight of noon also bring the midnight of darkness. The same Power which is bringing infant humanity through its first fumbling steps towards self-realization, is also permitting it to fall and bruise itself because only so will humanity ever learn to walk. Who can deny that at least one section of humanity needs the whip of suffering to act as a lesson in its moral education or as punishment for its blind sins or as stimulant to awaken it from stagnation into evolutionary movement? Those who will take the trouble to look deep beneath appearances for realities may even see in these very same world happenings the vindication of the World Mind's care for humanity and a demonstration of Its presence in the world.

To seek any way of escape from devastating happenings which seem to creep closer and closer, without including the way of trying sincerely to fulfil the spiritual purpose of his life on earth, is to live in a fool's paradise. The indifference of man to the silent pleading of Truth and his displacement from the spiritual centre of his being, cannot last for ever. It took the dangerous stresses of an unexampled war to offer the second chance of a great initiation to the world. That could and should have been a purifying process for those who had become too attached to earthly things and who did not trouble to bother about why they were here at all. Since pain and suffering are never welcome and seldom understood, the voice of woe rose in a long lament and echoed over the whole planet. All were being given another chance for self-regeneration, yet few knew it in their surface consciousness! Not only may intense suffering help to arouse a lethargic nation or an inert individual to neglected duties but if not too prolonged, it may also tend to awaken latent will-power.

It would be absurd to declare that all affliction serves destiny's ends. After we have made all allowance for those calamities which are born out of our own errors and sins; and also for those with which the Overself forces our individual or collective development; and after we have further allowed for those which are the natural consequences of the interdependence of mankind, affecting us through the frailty any imperfections of other people, it must nevertheless be admitted that there remains a proportion which are not of our own making at all. Whence do they come then? Although the suffering of human beings is often indicative that they have strayed from the right path, a part of it is always coincidental with human existence itself. The affliction to which they are exposed may not necessarily be the consequence of personal karma. It may be the consequence of being human. Whoever understands this statement, understands already a quarter of the Buddha's teaching. When he pointed out on how precarious a balance all human happiness rests, he pointed out a salutary fact. The truth of his teaching about the essentially sorrowful character of life is usually disguised by the pleasures and relaxations of life. It becomes apparent to the generality of people only when it is thrust prominently into their consciousness by horrors and tragedies such as those of war. Our generation has had the tragic character of existence thrown into sharp relief. It has glimpsed dimly by its own painful experience what philosophy always knew clearly by its tranquil reflection. Among many other things the war and crisis have been bold and unforgettable demonstrations of the fact that suffering is inseparably allied to life in this world. It is in fact forever with us, albeit on an unimpressive and unimposing scale. It is so familiar that we tend to remain untouched by its normal existence. Only the extremely thoughtful who love truth or seek peace take note of its ever-presence and seek also for some deeper solution of its meaning or durable escape from its burden. Where is the joy which is not sooner or later mingled with sorrow? A happiness which is not mixed at some point or at some time with misery, can nowhere be found on earth.

Paul Brunton, *The Spiritual Crisis of Man*

Out of the Pain

The pain, which until now had had sole dominion and been its own universe, slowly rotating on its own enigmatic axis, at last started to change color from whitish green to red.

He became aware of a stubborn voice drilling and drilling inside of him, a nagging voice which went through Greek verb forms, a teacher in his old boarding school with its dark vaults, who must have died a long time ago. And now he went through the aorist forms of one Greek verb after the other; he never wanted to stop, and the terrible thing was that it was completely unnecessary.

He already knew all the Greek verbs in both the imperfect and the aorist tense.

In this world, the gray-green world where he was, there ought not to be any Greek verbs, and slowly he was reminded that once there must have been another world, one where such conditions existed.

The world of pain was full, complete, a universe where nothing could be subtracted or added. This was the most perfect of all worlds, for it contained a single characteristic, and this characteristic was spread evenly through space.

In this other world, the one which must have existed once, like the monotonous droning of an old high school teacher, like the faint movements of ivy outside the windows just before afternoon rain, like the smell of chalk and ink, like the traces of generations of penknives in desk tops of sturdy ash, like the smell of vomit from his own pillow (evidently this time it hadn't helped to put a basin next to the couch when his migraine attack started) which he found undescribably disgusting, and which at the same time reminded him that in that other world, something like himself must exist—in *this* other world, there was a sense of loss. It was less perfect.

It was toward the end of the fourth day of one of his really major migraine attacks, the ones that surpassed all understanding, and while the afternoon outside the drawn brown curtains slowly changed to evening, he gradually became aware that he must be in a room in a pension—one of the cheaper pensions—on the shore of Lago Maggiore where the cheap hotels were, east of Lugano, and the wallpaper, which was very dark, had a rhomboid pattern.

The rhombs were drawn with lines that must once have been a kind of golden color but which had now turned green.

Between him and the oilcloth-covered desk, the kerosene lamp, the travel inkbottle with its safety cork, the green notebooks that he had busied himself with last week, there was now a sea. Portugal or the Cyclades could not be any harder to reach than his desk.

There wasn't much else in the room. The bed he was lying on, which you could convert into a couch in the daytime, with a pillowcase now smeared with his own greenish vomit.

The washstand with the basin he had moved temporarily close to the bed, two bulging leather trunks, worn, once elegant perhaps, with traces of careless handling by innumerable coachmen and porters, the always well-brushed but ever more frayed overcoat on its hook by the door.

The lake was not having one of its great sunsets. As soon as dusk had fallen, quick gusts of wind—the kind that makes it so dangerous for sailors—swept across the northern part of the lake; from the vicinity of Brissago, the sound of thunder.

The raindrops beat against the window like the children's hands.

Every time he tried to open his eyes, he could see a little more clearly. And—something that was a still better sign—his double vision had almost completely disappeared. It seemed that this was the end of one of his really big, totally devastating migraine attacks. However, he could not discount the possibility that it was simply a pause, a lull in the storm, morbidly still water in the eye of the tropical storm, where, in principle, he might be able to stay for twenty-four hours, hardly longer.

This sort of thing had happened before: he had started hoping too soon.

Right in the eye of the storm, in these lulls between the pain that seared his head with white heat and this terrible nausea, which continued day in and day out, long after his stomach was emptied of its thin contents, here in the middle of the lull there was knowledge to be had, strange, almost *yellowish* knowledge (in this condition even the most abstract phenomena had colors).

It might be about words, about how *the words* turned into narrow, as it were Newtonian rings in all the colors of the rainbow, gliding swiftly across the not completely pure surface into very deep and dark water. When the words collided with each other, they could either repel each other or attract each other, forming long molecular chains.

Until the chain became too heavy, or too pretentious, and then it would break again.

It might be about *history*, about events, about monarchs, about war, about crowds of people moving restlessly through the narrow, stepped alleys of Oriental cities, about speakers in town squares, where sharp sunlight made the shadows fall hard and pitiless.

And all this, the noise in the squares, the throngs of people, the pitiless light across bent backs, assumed the shape of a rising and falling surge, the surge of sound in a large seashell.

Or the sound of the movements on the surface when, deep down in moving water, you still sense the movements of the surface, its ringing, rising, and falling sounds, like the fragments of distant music.

And this history existed. Or did not exist. Just as you liked.

He no longer remembered how many weeks there had been since he last saw blue sky.

He needed a clear sky, a great, completely spotless—no, he meant cloudless—sky in order to think clearly.

Under gray skies, the shadows threatened him.

Oh, if only he were in Sils, if it had been lovely late summer in the Upper Engadin instead of heavy November in the lowlands!

But Sils was long since covered by deep snow; all the passes were closed, and the lodges were closed. Across the green meadows up by Ley, across the paths to Val Fex, there was now only this heavy whirl of darkness and snow-storms.

And the child-hands of the rain continued to beat against the window-pane, knocking restlessly as if they really wanted to get in.

If only there had been someone!

But the single person from whom he might count on something that even remotely resembled human interest was the blond proprietress of the pension, already past her prime, who pattered uneasily along the hallways, up and downstairs at late hours like a restless spirit, and who, on at least one occasion, had looked in on him to "see if he was sick."

God how he detested her!

There was—in her witchlike, stooping gait, in her slovenly stockings, sagging around her ankles, in her sharp, determined nose, in her shrill voice—something which, in some awful way, reminded him of his sister.

One of those connoisseurs of souls, one of those who venture forth at dusk to stalk their prey. A word to the wise is sufficient.

At this moment, he realized that he was on his way back into the ordi-nary world; he was again capable of hatred, and that was enough to tell him that once again he had survived, that he had grown stronger again.

These moments when he returned he liked to imagine as a hunter's return from a long hunt in a deep, impenetrable forest. If only he knew what kind of prey he carried with him from there.

It had been the same thing for almost his entire life. It wasn't true that it had started in Basel—it was only the pain that had started in Basel. He'd felt it much earlier than that, as early as Pforta—like some strange state between dream and waking, which could sneak up on him in the middle of a class, a buzzing in the deepest layer of his consciousness as if a wasp were shut up in there.

Perhaps it had started after the winter when one of his stubborn boy-hood colds had turned into an ear infection and, quite obviously, penetrated the fine membranes of his brain. No one had actually taken it seriously.

Or else it might have been part of him from birth: his mother, too, had a frail, precarious constitution.

No matter: it had broken out in Basel. It had turned into fate, destiny. Perhaps it was in Basel that he had decided on it—or it had decided on him.

The dusk outside, which had never been proper day, was changing into night. For the first time in a long while he started feeling something resembling ordinary, normal sleepiness. That was always a good sign.

He started thinking about how many years it might be since he had left his professorship in Basel, the blessed professorship, along with his students, his friends, his colleagues, the friendly, ancient city with its green-shimmering roofs, its little friendly bars with windows of leaded glass and heavy oak tables, Basel with its friendly smells of beer, sausage, and ash-wood fires, Basel where so much water flows under the bridges.

Paradise, but hell at the same time. Of course, it was the pain that drove him away from there, but just as much the awareness that it wasn't his life. He calculated it must be twelve years already—twelve years of loneliness, of illness, of days and nights such that only the bravest person would dare to imagine them repeated.

Hours, and again hours, of uninterrupted nearsighted writing, his whole head bent over the table, his thick glasses only an inch above the paper; happy, ecstatic writing, while the ticking of the clocks receded and became unimportant, while mealtimes passed and were forgotten; writing like a silent, ongoing feast, where the music that slumbered at the heart of things became audible and was transformed into a note endurable to human sense.

For this mysterious music you had to be prepared to sacrifice a lot.

And so: Ariadne, faceless, or faceless in memory, deep inside the labyrinth, in memory surrounded by a music inaudible in the ordinary world. Ariadne, surrounded by nothing but her music; Ariadne, who was at once his key and his jailer.

How far in the past those secret days in Treibchen, those short trips across the big lake, how fragile those memories! And just the same, they held him captive.

Like reflections in a lake, this world multiplied continuously.

And yet he could never be sure whether this world of repetitions was the real world or he was moving among mirrors a sorcerer had arranged in his prison to ensure his calmness or docility.

Around him, outside the windows, the world darkened; the squalls over the lake took on renewed force. Around him, Europe was industrializing itself—

a Europe which, with each passing year, became more unlike itself, more and more a parody, an evil repetition created by inferior gods. From the desolate autumnal fields streamed the poor of the earth, the former bond slaves of Pomerania and Mecklenburg, to fill the factories. The English cities grew like evil mushrooms under their clouds of smoke.

Old bonds and old curses were being replaced by others, heavier, unfamiliar.

Soon the smoke of the locomotives would rise toward the ceilings of the railroad stations' cast-iron cathedrals: oh, he knew them already. How often hadn't he seen them at night out of a dirty, steamed-up window, wrapped in his lap robe, cold as always, squeezed into a corner of the compartment, taking cover from night and loneliness.

Truly, wasn't he a Minotaur, alone in the night, alone at his own birth, forever locked into the labyrinth of this century?

From that thought there was only a very short step to the leave-taking from his friends, from the disdained, misunderstood friends, Paul Ree and Lou.

He wanted, and he didn't want, to imagine that leave-taking one last time. He had thought about it all too many times, and always with the same horrible feeling of *having made himself less than he was*.

Oh, he remembered everything as if it had happened just a few minutes ago: the leave-taking, the conversations, his sister's awful intervention, his own childish surprise *that someone was capable of abandoning him*.

And although he had thought these thoughts so many times, it was only at this moment he realized that *everything would have been perfect without him*.

The lives of his friends, the lives of his parents, this new world with its rootless proletarian masses journeying from one kind of slavery to another, from the rainy earth to the dark factories, these new smithies capable of forging the bonds of the future. And everything taking place during hopeful singing of Sankey's evangelical hymns in new houses of prayer with other rhythms than the pietistic rhythms of his childhood: the Crucified One, on his way to conquer India with cotton cloth and rob Asia of its budding industries in favor of a Christian world market, everything, from beginning to end, from the first lesson in morphology in the dark halls of Pforta, *everything would have been perfect without him*.

And—it suddenly struck him—his task was exactly that. *He was a truth*. He was the point of an incidental but very clever joke.

This leave-taking—so far back in time—whose hands still beat on the window, from Ree, from Lou, was, in spite of the continuing fever of the wound, the most beautiful thing he had experienced. So light and cheerful, and at the same time so serious and deep that he could still recall its breathing, it was a vehement reminder that life is easy, that it consists of purest lust, and that it only exists for those who are able to dance and to laugh.

Lars Gustafsson, "Out of the Pain," in *Stories of Happy People*

To know God in His essence is evidently something which transcends the powers of every created or creatable nature, for it is to possess God intuitively, in a vision in which there is no mediation of any idea, but in which the divine essence itself replaces every idea born in our mind, so that it immediately forms and determines our intellect. This is to know God divinely, as He Himself knows Himself and as He knows us, in His own uncreated light.

Nothing is more human that for man to desire naturally things impossible to his nature. It is, indeed, the property of a nature which is not closed up in matter like the nature of physical things, but which is intellectual or infinitized by the spirit. It is the property of a metaphysical nature. Such desires reach for the infinite, because the intellect thirsts for being and being is infinite.

Jacques Maritain, *Approaches to God*

Sometimes the process of spiritual awakening is so subtle and gradual that it is almost imperceptible. After a period of months or years, a person looks back and notices that there has been a profound shift in his or her understanding of the world, values, ethical standards, and life strategies. This change might start by reading a book that contains a message so clear and convincing that it is impossible to ignore. One is left with a longing to know and experience more; then, coincidentally, the author comes to town to give a lecture. This leads to associations with other people who share this excitement, to the discovery of other books, and to attending additional lectures and workshops. The spiritual journey has begun!

At other times, spiritual awareness enters one's life in the form of a deeper and changed perception of certain situations of everyday life. A person might walk into the cathedral in Chartres with a tour group and, completely unexpectedly, feel overwhelmed by the choir and the organ music, by the play of light in the stained-glass windows, and by the grandeur of the Gothic arches. The memory of this rapture and the sense of being connected with something greater than oneself remains. Similar transformations of perception have occurred in people during a raft trip through the majestic beauty of the Grand Canyon or in some other stunning natural setting. For many, the entry into the transcendental domain has been opened by art.

None of these individuals will ever again think of themselves as completely separate. They all have had vivid and convincing experiences that transported them beyond the restrictions of their physical bodies and limited self-concept to a connection with something outside of themselves.

When spiritual emergence is very rapid and dramatic, however, this natural process can become a crisis, and spiritual emergence becomes spiritual emergency. People who are in such a crisis are bombarded with inner experiences that abruptly challenge their old beliefs and ways of existing, and their relationship with reality shifts very rapidly. Suddenly they feel uncomfortable in the formerly familiar world and may find it difficult to meet the demands of everyday life. They can have great problems distinguishing their inner visionary world from the external world of daily reality. Physically, they may experience forceful energies streaming through their bodies and causing uncontrollable tremors.

Fearful and resistant, they might spend much time and effort trying to control what feels like an overwhelming inner event. And they may feel impelled to talk about their experiences and insights to anyone who is within range, sounding out of touch with reality, disjointed, or messianic. However, when offered understanding and guidance, they are usually cooperative and grateful to have someone with whom they can share their journey. The basic criteria for assessing when spiritual emergence has become a crisis are summarized in table 1.

Table 1. Differences Between Spiritual Emergence and Spiritual Emergency

EMERGENCE	EMERGENCY
Inner experiences are fluid, mild, easy to integrate.	Inner experiences are dynamic, jarring, difficult to integrate.
New spiritual insights are welcome, desirable, expansive.	New spiritual insights may be philosophically challenging and threatening.
Gradual infusion of ideas and insights into life.	Overwhelming influx of experiences and insights.
Experiences of energy that are contained and are easily manageable.	Experiences of jolting tremors, shaking, energy disruptive to daily life.

EMERGENCE	EMERGENCY
Easy differentiation between internal and external experiences and transition from one to other.	Sometimes difficult to distinguish between internal and external experiences, or simultaneous occurrence of both.
Ease in incorporating nonordinary states of consciousness into daily life.	Inner experiences interrupt and disturb daily life.
Slow, gradual change in awareness of self and world.	Abrupt, rapid shift in perception of self and world.
Excitement about inner experiences as they arise, willingness and ability to cooperate with them.	Ambivalence toward inner experiences, but willingness and ability to cooperate with them using guidance.
Accepting attitude toward change.	Resistance to change.
Ease in giving up control.	Need to be in control.
Trust in process.	Dislike, mistrust, of process.
Difficult experiences treated as opportunities for change.	Difficult experiences are overwhelming, often unwelcome.
Positive experiences accepted as gifts.	Positive experiences are difficult to accept, seem undeserved, can be painful.
Infrequent need to discuss experiences.	Frequent urgent need to discuss experiences.
Discriminating when communicating about process (when, how, with whom).	Indiscriminate communication about process (when, how, with whom).

Stanislav and Christina Grof,
The Stormy Search for the Self

Throughout history, people in intense spiritual crises were acknowledged by many cultures as blessed; they were thought to be in direct communication with the sacred realms and divine beings. Their societies supported them through these crucial episodes, offering sanctuary and suspending the usual demands. Respected members of their communities had been through their own emergencies, could recognize and understand a similar process in others, and, as a result, were able to honor the expression of the creative, mystical impulse. The often colorful and dramatic experiences were nourished with the trust that these individuals would eventually return to the community with greater wisdom and an enhanced capacity to conduct themselves in the world, to their own benefit as well as that of society.

With the advent of modern science and the industrial age, this tolerant and even nurturing attitude changed drastically. The notion of acceptable reality was narrowed to include only those aspects of existence that are material, tangible, and measurable. Spirituality in any form was exiled from the modern scientific worldview. Western cultures adopted a restricted and rigid interpretation of what is "normal" in human experience and behavior and rarely accepted those who sought to go beyond these limits.

Psychiatry found biological explanations for certain mental disorders in the form of infections, tumors, chemical imbalances, and other afflictions of the brain or body. It also discovered powerful ways of controlling symptoms of various conditions for which the causes remained unknown, including the manifestations of spiritual crises. As a result of these successes, psychiatry became firmly established as a medical discipline, and the term *mental disease* was extended to include many states that, strictly speaking, were natural conditions that could not be linked to biological causes. The process of spiritual emergence in general, along with its more dramatic manifestations, came to be viewed as an illness, and those who demonstrated signs of what had been previously thought of as inner transformation and growth were in most cases now considered to be sick.

Consequently, many people who have emotional or psychosomatic symptoms are automatically classified as having a medical problem, and their difficulties are seen as diseases of unknown origin, although clinical and laboratory tests do not offer any supportive evidence for such an approach. Most nonordinary states of consciousness are considered pathological and are treated with traditional psychiatric methods such as suppressive medication and hospitalization. As a result of this bias, many people who are involved in the natural healing process of spiritual emergence are automatically put in the same category as those with true mental illness—especially if their experiences are causing a crisis in their lives or are creating difficulties for their families.

This interpretation is further fueled by the fact that much of our culture does not recognize the significance and value of the mystical domains within human beings. The spiritual elements inherent in personal transformation seem alien and threatening to those who are unfamiliar with them.

In the last couple of decades, however, this situation has been changing rapidly. Spirituality has been reintroduced into the mainstream culture through renewed interest in sacred systems such as those found in Eastern religions, Western mystical literature, and Native American traditions. Numerous people are experimenting with meditation and other forms of spiritual practice; others are involved in self-exploration using various new therapies. Through these methods, they are discovering new dimensions and possibilities within themselves. At the same time, revolutionary developments in many disciplines are rapidly closing the gap between science and spirituality, and modern physicists and researchers in other fields are moving toward a worldview similar to that described by the mystics.

Along with the renewed interest in mysticism, we are seeing another phenomenon: growing numbers of people are having spiritual and paranormal experiences and are willing to talk more openly about them. A survey by the Gallup Organization showed that 43 percent of the people polled admitted to having had unusual spiritual experiences, and 95 percent said that they believed in God or a universal spirit. From our own observations, it appears that coinciding with this expanded interest is a growing incidence of difficulties related to the transformation process.

We became deeply aware of this apparent increase in spiritual emergencies as we traveled around the world in the past decade, presenting workshops and lectures in which we talked about our personal experiences and our alternative understanding of some states that have automatically been labeled as psychotic. We were amazed to find many people who resonated with various elements of our stories. Some had been through transformative experiences and felt more fulfilled as a result. Many others had had similar experiences but told us tragic stories of families and professionals who misunderstood them, of hospital commitments, unnecessary tranquilizers, and stigmatizing psychiatric labels. Often, a process that had originally begun as healing and transformative had been interrupted and even complicated by psychiatric intervention.

We have also met creative, compassionate, and innovative mental-health professionals—psychiatrists, psychologists, and others—who are looking for or are already providing alternatives for their patients. Many have expressed their frustration at not being able to pursue their ideas and approaches within their hospitals or clinics, largely due to their organizations' rigid adherence to the medical model, traditional administrative policy, and bureaucratic restrictions. They have told us of their professional loneliness and their desire to connect with like-minded people in their field.

As more and more people face spiritual emergencies, a growing number are becoming dissatisfied with the application of traditional psychiatric treatment during such events. Just as in recent years potential parents have actively pressured medical professionals to return to a sense of the time-honored reverence for birth and its dynamics, people involved in a transformational crisis are beginning to demand that professionals recognize their difficulties for what they are: challenging stages in a potentially life-changing process.

Stanislav and Christina Grof,
The Stormy Search for the Self

→ 3 ←

Finding the Soul and the
Flowering of the Spirit

"The real essence of personality is the divine soul."
— PAUL BRUNTON

The soul has been defined in most religious texts as the link with our spiritual destiny, the receptacle of grace and the centre of our being, that which was there before and exists after we die. It is how our own divinity feels at a deep emotional level. And it is the essential tool for uniting the outer self—personality formed by family, society, and career—with the true self—the character that was there in its innocence as a child, before expectations, limitations, and restrictions were imposed upon it.

Rediscovering the soul, the true inner self, is what the quest is about. The thirst of the human soul is to live in joy. It is the "one thing necessary" (Merton) for happiness and fulfilment, it is the instigator of the feeling of joy and bliss. To be able to feel this genuine joy—and the bliss, peace, and happiness that accompanies it—we must first find our souls again, as adults, and learn what it is we need to know from them now.

In this section, English writer and teacher Paul Brunton refers to the soul as the Overself, "the higher individuality, the permanent self eternal and undying." French Jesuit priest, writer, and scientist Pierre Teilhard de Chardin believes "My self is given to me far more than it is formed by me." Canadian Jungian analyst, writer, and lecturer Marion Woodman introduces the intrinsic partnership of the body with the soul. And Gary Zukav, one of the most influential pioneers of the New Age movement, explains the law of karma and its relationship with the soul.

→←

The Inner Fields

There is a brighter ether than this blue
   Pretence of an enveloping heavenly vault,
   Royaler investiture than this massed assault*
Of emerald rapture pearled with tears of dew.
Immortal spaces of caerulean hue
   Are in our reach and fields without this fault
   Of drab brown earth and streams that never halt
In their deep murmur which white flowers strew

Floating like stars upon a strip of sky.
   This world behind is made of truer stuff
   Than the manufactured tissue of earth's grace.
There we can walk and see the gods go by
   And sip from Hebe's cup nectar enough
   To make for us heavenly limbs and deathless face.

               Sri Aurobindo, *Collected Poems*

What does the word "soul" mean? . . . No one can give a definition of the soul. But we know what it feels like. The soul is the sense of something higher than ourselves, something that stirs in us thoughts, hopes, and aspirations which go out to the world of goodness, truth, and beauty. The soul is a burning desire to breathe in this world of light and never to lose it—to remain children of light.

               Albert Schweitzer, *Reverence for Life*

I, who am thinking, have always existed, but not in myself or within the limits of my own personality—and not by an impersonal existence or life either (for without personality there is no thought, and there must have been thought there, since it is now in me); therefore I have always existed by a suprapersonal existence or life. Where then? It must have been in a Being of transcendent personality, in whom all that there is of perfection in my thought and in all thought existed in a supereminent manner, and who was, in His own infinite Self, before I was, and is, now while I am, more I than I myself, who is eternal, and from whom I, the self which is thinking now, proceeded one day into temporal existence. I had (but without being able to

*A deeper greenness than this laughing assault

say "I") an eternal existence in God before receiving a temporal existence in my own nature and my own personality.

Jacques Maritain, *Approaches to God*

What science will ever be able to reveal to man the origin, nature and character of that conscious power to will and to love which constitutes his life? It is certainly not our effort, nor the effort of anyone around us, which set that current in motion. And it is certainly not our solicitude, nor that of any friend, which prevents its ebb or controls its turbulence. We can, of course, trace back through generations some of the antecedents of the torrent which bears us along; and we can, by means of certain moral and physical disciplines and stimulations, regularise or enlarge the aperture through which the torrent is released into us. But neither that geography nor those artifices help us in theory or in practice to harness the sources of life. My self is given to me far more than it is formed by me. Man, Scripture says, cannot add a cubit to his stature. Still less can he add a unit to the potential of his love, or accelerate by another unit the fundamental rhythm which regulates the ripening of his mind and heart. In the last resort the profound life, the fontal life, the new-born life, escape our grasp entirely.

Stirred by my discovery, I then wanted to return to the light of day and forget the disturbing enigma in the comfortable surroundings of familiar things—to begin living again at the surface without imprudently plumbing the depths of the abyss. But then, beneath this very spectacle of the turmoil of life, there re-appeared, before my newly opened eyes, the unknown that I wanted to escape. This time it was not hiding at the bottom of an abyss; it was concealed beneath the innumerable strands which form the web of chance, the very stuff of which the universe and my own small individuality are woven. Yet it was the same mystery without a doubt: I recognised it. Our mind is perplexed when we try to plumb the depth of the world beneath us. But it reels still more when we try to number the favourable chances which must conjoin at every moment if the least of living things is to survive and to succeed. After the consciousness of being something other and something greater than myself—a second thing made me dizzy: namely, the supreme improbability, the tremendous unlikelihood of finding myself existing in the midst of a world that has survived and succeeded.

Pierre Teilhard de Chardin, *The Divine Milieu*

Every moment and every event of every man's life on earth plants something in his soul.

Thomas Merton, *Seeds of Contemplation*

Where are the roots of our being? In the first place they plunge back and down into the unfathomable past. How great is the mystery of the first cells which were one day animated by the breath of our souls! How impossible to decipher the synthesis of successive influences in which we are for ever incorporated! In each one of us, through matter, the whole history of the world is in part reflected. And however autonomous our soul, it is heir to an existence worked upon from all sides—before it came into being—by the totality of the energies of the earth: it meets and rejoins life at a determined level. Then, hardly has it entered actively into the universe at that particular point than it feels, in its turn, besieged and penetrated by the flow of cosmic influences which have to be ordered and assimilated. Let us look around us: the waves come from all sides and from the farthest horizon. Through every cleft the sensible world inundates us with its riches—food for the body, nourishment for the eyes, harmony of sounds and fulness of the heart, unknown phenomena and new truths, all these treasures, all these urges, all these calls, coming from the four quarters of the world, pass through our consciousness at every moment. What is their role within us? What will their effect be, even if we receive them passively or indistinctly, like bad work-men? They will merge into the most intimate life of our soul, and either develop it or poison it. We only have to look at ourselves for one moment to realise this, and feel either delight or anxiety. If even the most humble and most material of our nourishment is capable of deeply influencing our most spiritual faculties, what can be said of the infinitely more penetrating ener-gies conveyed to us by the music of tones, of notes, of words, of ideas? We have not, in us, a body to be nourished independently of our soul. Everything that the body has admitted and has begun to transform must be sublimated by the soul in its turn. The soul does this, no doubt, in its own way and with its own dignity. But it cannot escape from this universal contact nor from that unremitting labour. And that is how the characteristic power of under-standing and loving, which will form its immaterial individuality, is gradu-ally perfected in it for its own good and at its own risk. We hardly know in what proportions and under what guise our natural faculties will pass over into the final act of the divine vision. But it can hardly be doubted that, with God's help, it is here below that we give ourselves the eyes and the heart which a final transfiguration will transmute into organs of a capacity for adoration and beatification special to each one of us.

The masters of the spiritual life continue to repeat that God wants only souls. To give those words their true value, we must not forget that the human soul, however independently created our philosophy imagines it to be, is inseparable, in its birth and in its growth, from the universe into which it is born. In each soul, God loves and partly saves the whole world which that soul sums up in an incommunicable and particular way. Now this summing-up, this synthesis is not given to us ready-made and complete with the first awakening of consciousness. It is we who, through our own activity, must industriously assemble the widely scattered elements. The labour of seaweed as it concentrates in its tissues the substances dispersed, in infinitesimal quantities, throughout the vast layers of the ocean; the industry of bees as they make honey from the juices scattered in so many flowers—these are but pale images of the continuous process of elaboration which all the forces of the universe undergo in us in order to become spirit.

Pierre Teilhard de Chardin, *The Divine Milieu*

A soul is an immaterial thing. It is a principle of activity, it is an "act," a "form," an energizing principle. It is the life of the body, and it must also have a life of its own. But the life of the soul does not inhere in any physical, material subject.

Thomas Merton, *The Seven Storey Mountain*

Being that has soul is living being. Soul is the living thing in man, that which lives of itself and causes life. Therefore God breathed into Adam a living breath, that he might live. With her cunning play of illusions the soul lures into life the inertness of matter that does not want to live. She makes us believe incredible things, that life may be lived. She is full of snares and traps, in order that man should fall, should reach the earth, entangle himself there, and stay caught, so that life should be lived; as Eve in the garden of Eden could not rest content until she had convinced Adam of the goodness of the forbidden apple. Were it not for the leaping and twinkling of the soul, man would rot away in his greatest passion, idleness. A certain kind of reasonableness is its advocate, and a certain kind of morality adds its blessing. But to have soul is the whole venture of life, for soul is a life-giving daemon who plays his elfin game above and below human existence, for which reason—in the realm of dogma—he is threatened and propitiated with superhuman punishments and blessings that go far beyond the possible deserts of human beings. Heaven and hell are the fates meted out to the soul and not to civilized man, who in his nakedness and timidity would have no idea of what to do with himself in a heavenly Jerusalem.

C. G. Jung, *The Archetypes and the Collective Unconscious*

So powerful is the energy of the soul that it could not advance into a physical form without, literally, exploding that form. In the creation of a personality, the soul calibrates parts of itself, reduces parts of itself, to take on the human experience. Your higher self is that aspect of your soul that is in you, but it is not the fullness of your soul. It is a smaller soul self. Therefore, "higher self" is another term for "soul," yet the soul is more than the higher self.

Picture a cup, a gallon and a water tank. The water tank is the soul. An aspect of the soul becomes a gallon. That gallon is still soul, but not the fullness of the soul. It is that part of the soul that is on mission, so to speak. The personality is the cup. The cup contacts the gallon, the higher self soul, but not the full-bodied water tank.

Gary Zukav, *The Seat of the Soul*

Your soul is not a passive or a theoretical entity that occupies a space in the vicinity of your chest cavity. It is a positive, purposeful force at the core of your being. It is that part of you that understands the impersonal nature of the energy dynamics in which you are involved, that loves without restriction and accepts without judgment.

If you desire to know your soul, the first step is to recognize that you have a soul. The next step is to allow yourself to consider, "If I have a soul, what *is* my soul? What does my soul want? What is the relationship between my soul and me? How does my soul affect my life?"

When the energy of the soul is recognized, acknowledged, and valued, it begins to infuse the life of the personality. When the personality comes fully to serve the energy of its soul, that is authentic empowerment. This is the goal of the evolutionary process in which we are involved and the reason for our being. Every experience that you have and will have upon the Earth encourages the alignment of your personality with your soul. Every circumstance and situation gives you the opportunity to choose this path, to allow your soul to shine through you, to bring into the physical world through you its unending and unfathomable reverence for and love of Life.

Gary Zukav, *The Seat of the Soul*

With Mahatma Gandhi at Wardha

"Mahatmaji, you are an exceptional man. You must not expect the world to act as you do." A critic once made this observation.

"It is curious how we delude ourselves, fancying that the body can be improved, but that it is impossible to evoke the hidden powers of the soul," Gandhi replied. "I am engaged in trying to show that if I have any of those powers, I am as frail a mortal as any of us and that I never had anything extraordinary about me nor have I now. I am a simple individual liable to err like any other fellow mortal. I own, however, that I have enough humility to confess my errors and to retrace my steps. I own that I have an immovable faith in God and His goodness, and an unconsumable passion for truth and love. But is that not what every person has latent in him?" He added: "If we may make new discoveries and inventions in the phenomenal world, must we declare our bankruptcy in the spiritual domain? Is it impossible to multiply the exceptions so as to make them the rule? Must man always be brute first and man after, if at all?"

Paramahansa Yogananda, *Autobiography of a Yogi*

Body awareness has become an important focus in my analytic practice because of my experience with both women and men who, despite earnest commitment to their dreams and to their own growth, are still unable to trust the process. Their souls are dislocated in bodies so wounded that the ego's willingness in itself is simply not enough.

Failure in travailing life's junctures is not necessarily the failure of the ego to adopt a new attitude toward the Self by sacrificing the old. Many of my analysands have what I believe to be appropriate ego attitudes; their bodies, however, have at some point been traumatized. While their egos can be approached through confrontation, challenge or humor, their bodies cannot respond. The more quickly the ego moves ahead, the more terrorized the body becomes. The task then is to find some means of going back to the point of wounding to reconnect with the abandoned child. The body, like the child, tells the truth, and tells it through movement or lack of movement.

A trained observer can discern whether the soul has taken up residence in the body, or whether the body image is so intolerable that the flesh is barely inhabited. The body can be so retarded that it cannot even imagine itself as an adult. If, as James Hillman says, "the image by which the flesh lives is the ultimate ruling necessity," then some means must be found to create an adequate image—physically as well as psychically. Body awareness, as I understand it, has nothing to do with the technology of the body. It is not fitness or longevity that is at stake, although these may be by-products. What is at stake is the integration of body, soul and spirit.

So long as we are in this world, the psyche is enacted through the medium of the body. William Blake described the body as "that portion of Soul discerned by the five Senses." The soul is, of course, much more than the bodily "portion" of itself. It is not limited to manifesting in the physical body; it manifests also in that infinite body which constitutes the "body" of the imagination, a body that includes the entire visionary world of the arts— music, sculpture, painting, poetry, dance, architecture. Each of these visionary or imaginary worlds may be thought of as larger human bodies, or a single giant human body. That it may act in another world, of which the arts are an expression, is one of the oldest speculations about the immortality of the soul, and art as an expression of it.

The soul, then, manifests in a multiplicity of forms. While it is on earth, it must have a body image as its home, as its primary medium of expression. The soul will not naturally reject its body image any more than the mother's breast will naturally reject her baby. The body mirrors the soul. Where rejection occurs, something has gone seriously wrong. But no matter what went wrong, the soul will do everything in its power to correct it. How then do we explain the blockage of the body as the soul's medium of expression? Seen from this point of view, anorexia nervosa and bulimia, for example, are the result of an abnormal release of psychic energy in an effort to overcome body blockage. Obesity is a manifestation of a soul that has more energy than the body can deal with.

Blocked bodies, metaphorically (sometimes literally), have hardened arteries, arteries blocked by too much cholesterol that makes it hard for the heart to pump blood through the system. They place mounting obstacles in the way of psychic energy. The result is that the energy has to find other modes of action, other modes of expression. Some of these are very creative and make for brilliant careers in the professions and the arts. But always, people whose psychic energy has had to carve out other channels of expression because their bodies were blocked, are haunted by their refusal, conscious or unconscious, to permit their souls to take up residence in their bodies. The result is that, without quite understanding what they are feeling or why they are feeling it, they are possessed by homeless souls who wander like ghosts in a bleak twilight zone where they cannot find shelter or rest. They are haunted by their own wandering souls that hover somewhere near the earth, crying in vain to be let in. Refusing them entrance into their own bodies, such people become the enemies of their souls. They unconsciously realize that they have sentenced their souls to perpetual exile.

Marion Woodman, *The Pregnant Virgin*

Fear is perhaps the greatest enemy of candor. How many men fear to follow their consciences because they would rather conform to the opinion of other men than to the truth they know in their souls? How can I be sincere if I am constantly changing my mind to conform with the shadow of what I think others expect of me? Others have no right to demand that I be anything other than what I ought to be in the sight of God.

Thomas Merton, *No Man Is an Island*

The soul is. It has no beginning and no end but flows toward wholeness. The personality emerges as a natural force from the soul. It is an energy tool that the soul adapts to function within the physical world. Each personality is unique because the configuration of energy of the soul that formed it is unique. It is the persona of the soul, so to speak, that interacts with physical matter. It is a product that is formed from the vibrational aspect of your name, the vibrational aspect of your relationship to planets at the time of your incarnation, and vibrational aspects of your energy environment, as well as from the splintered aspects of your soul that need to interact in physical matter in order to be brought into wholeness.

The personality does not operate independently from the soul. To the extent that a person is in touch with spiritual depths, the personality is soothed because the energy of consciousness is focused on its energy core and not on its artificial facade, which is the personality.

The personality sometimes appears as a force running rampant in the world with no attachment to the energy of its soul. This situation can be the origin of what we call an evil human being, and it can be the origin of a schizophrenic human being. It is the result of the personality being unable to find its reference point, or connection, to its mothership, which is its soul. The conflicts of a human's life are directly proportional to the distance at which an energy of personality exists separately from the soul, and, therefore, as we shall see, in an irresponsible position of creation. When a personality is in full balance, you cannot see where it ends and the soul begins. That is a whole human being.

What is involved in the healing of a soul?

Most of us are accustomed to the idea that we are responsible for some of our actions, but not all of them. We consider ourselves responsible, for example, for the good deed that brings our neighbor and us together, or for responding to it positively, but we do not consider ourselves responsible for the argument between us and our neighbor, or for responding to it negatively. We consider ourselves responsible for having a safe trip if we take the time to check the condition of the car before starting, but if we speed around a car that, in our opinion, has been traveling too slowly, and almost cause an accident by doing that, we consider the other driver to be responsible. If we feed and clothe ourselves through our successful business, we credit ourselves. If we feed and clothe ourselves by burglarizing apartments, we blame our difficult childhood.

For many of us, being held responsible is equal to getting caught. A friend who returns each year to his native Italy told me, with a twinkle in his eye, of a dinner out with his family. When the bill came, my friend's father, who is fastidious, examined each scribbled item. After some study, he deciphered the last entry and recognized it to be a short expression that translates, roughly, "If it goes, it goes." He called the waiter and asked, "What is this item?" The waiter shrugged, "It didn't go." Many of us feel that if a clerk gives us too much change, and we take it, our life has been affected only to the extent that we have come into an unexpected gain. In fact, each of our acts affects us in far-reaching ways.

Every action, thought, and feeling is motivated by an intention, and that intention is a cause that exists as one with an effect. If we participate in the cause, it is not possible for us not to participate in the effect. In this most profound way, we are held responsible for our every action, thought, and feeling, which is to say, for our every intention. We, ourselves, shall partake of the fruit of our every intention. It is, therefore, wise for us to become aware of the many intentions that inform our experience, to sort out which intentions produce which effects, and to choose our intentions according to the effects that we desire to produce.

This is the way that we learned about physical reality as children, and that we refine our knowledge of it as adults. We learn the effect of crying when we are hungry, and we repeat the cause that brings us the effect that we desire. We learn the effect of putting a finger in a light socket, and we do not repeat the cause that produces that effect.

We also learn about intentions and their effects through our experiences in physical reality, but learning that intentions produce specific effects, and what those effects are, proceeds slowly when our learning must be done solely through the density of physical matter. Anger, for example, causes distance and hostile interactions. If we must learn this solely through physical experience, we may have to experience ten, or fifty, or one hundred and fifty circumstances of distance from another and hostile interaction before we come to understand that it is the orientation of anger on our part, the intention of hostility and distance, and not this particular action or that, which produces the effect that we do not want. This is predominantly the way that a five-sensory human learns.

The relationship of cause and effect within the domain of physical objects and phenomena reflects a dynamic that is not limited to physical reality. This is the dynamic of karma. Everything in the physical world, including each of us, is a small part of dynamics that are more extensive than a five-sensory human can perceive. The love, fear, compassion, and anger that you experience, for example, are only a small part of the love, fear, compassion, and anger of a larger energy system that you do not see.

Within physical reality, the dynamic of karma is reflected by the third law of motion: "For every action there is an equal and opposite reaction." In other words, the great law of karma that governs the balancing of energy within our evolutionary system is reflected within the domain of physical objects and phenomena by the last of three principles, three laws of motion, that govern the balancing of energy within physical reality.

The law of karma is an impersonal energy dynamic. When its effects are personalized, that is, experienced from the point of view of the personality, they are experienced as a reversal in the direction, a coming back to the intender, of the energy of his or her intention. This is how the personality experiences the impersonal dynamic that is described by the third law as an "equal and opposite reaction." The person who intends hatred for others experiences the intention of hatred from others. The person who intends love for others experiences the intention of love from others, and so forth. The Golden Rule is a behavioral guide that is based upon the dynamic of karma. A personalized statement of karma would be, "You receive from the world what you give to the world."

Karma is not a moral dynamic. Morality is a human creation. The Universe does not judge. The law of karma governs the balancing of energy within our system of morality and within those of our neighbors. It serves humanity as an impersonal and Universal teacher of responsibility.

Every cause that has not yet produced its effect is an event that has not yet come to completion. It is an imbalance of energy that is in the process of becoming balanced. That balancing of energy does not always occur within the span of a single lifetime. The karma of your soul is created and balanced by the activities of its many personalities, including you. Often a personality experiences effects that were created by other of its soul's personalities, and, conversely, creates energy imbalances that are not able to right themselves within its own lifetime. Therefore, without knowledge of its soul, reincarnation, and karma, it is not always possible for a personality to understand the significance or the meaning of the events of its life, or to understand the effects of its responses to them.

For example, a personality that takes advantage of others creates an imbalance of energy that must be righted by the experience of being taken advantage of by others. If that cannot be accomplished within the lifetime of this personality, another of its soul's personalities will experience being taken advantage of by other people. If that personality does not understand that the experience of being taken advantage of by others is the effect of a previous cause, and that this experience is bringing to completion an impersonal process, it will react from a personal point of view rather than from the point of view of its soul. It may become angry, for example, or vengeful or depressed. It may lash out, or grow cynical or withdraw into sorrow. Each of these responses creates karma, another imbalance of energy which, in turn, must be balanced. In this way, one karmic debt has been paid, so to speak, but another, or others, has been created.

If a child dies early in its life, we do not know what agreement was made between that child's soul and the souls of its parents, or what healing was served by that experience. Although we are sympathetic to the anguish of the parents, we cannot judge this event. If we, or the parents of this child, do not understand the impersonal nature of the dynamic that is in motion, we may react with anger towards the Universe, or towards each other, or with guilt if we feel that our actions were inadequate. All of these rejections create karma, and more lessons for the soul to learn—more karmic debts for the soul to pay—appear.

In order to become whole, the soul must balance its energy. It must experience the effects that it has caused. The energy imbalances in the soul are the incomplete parts of the soul that form the personality. Personalities in interaction are souls that are seeking to heal. Whether an interaction between souls is healing or not depends upon whether the personality involved can see beyond itself and that of the other personality to the interaction of their souls. This perception automatically draws forth compassion. Every experience, and every interaction, provides you with an opportunity to look from the point of view of your soul or from the point of view of your personality.

What does this mean in practical terms? How does a personality begin to look beyond itself and to see its soul in interaction with the souls of others?

Since we cannot know what is being healed through each interaction—what karmic debts are coming to conclusion—we cannot judge what we see. For example, when we see a person sleeping in the gutter in the winter, we do not know what is being completed for that soul. We do not know whether that soul has engaged in cruelty in another lifetime, and now has chosen to experience the same dynamic from an entirely different point of view, as, for example, the target of charity. It is appropriate that we respond to his or her circumstance with compassion, but it is not appropriate that we perceive it as unfair, because it is not.

There are personalities that are selfish and hostile and negative, but even in these cases we cannot fully know the reasons why. These are hidden from view. That does not mean that we cannot recognize negativity when we see it, but we cannot judge it. That is not our place. If we intervene in an argument, or break up a fight, it is not appropriate that we judge the participants. Of one thing we can be certain: a person that is engaging in violence is hurting deeply, because a healthy and balanced soul is incapable of harming another.

When we judge, we create negative karma. Judgment is a function of the personality. When we say of another soul, "She is worthy," or, "He is not worthy," we create negative karma. When we say of an action, "This is right," or, "That is wrong," we create negative karma. This does not mean that we should not act appropriately to the circumstances in which we find ourselves.

If our car is hit by another car, for example, and the driver of the other car is drunk, it is appropriate that the other driver be held responsible, through the courts, for the repair of our car. It is appropriate that he or she be prohibited from driving while intoxicated. It is not appropriate that we allow our actions to be motivated by feelings of indignation, righteousness, or victimization. These feelings are the result of judgments that we make about ourselves and the other person, assessments through which we see ourselves as superior to another being.

If we act upon these feelings, not only do we increase the karmic obligations of our soul, but we also are not able to enter into these feelings and learn from them. Feelings, as we shall see, are the means through which we can discern the parts of itself that the soul seeks to heal, and through which we come to see the action of the soul in physical matter. The road to your soul is through your heart.

If we are to engage the viewpoint of the soul, we must cease from judging, even those events that appear to be unfathomable, such as the cruelty of an inquisition or a holocaust, the death of an infant, the prolonged agony of a death by cancer, or a life confined to a bed. We do not know what is being healed in these sufferings, or the details of the energetic circumstance that is coming into balance. It is appropriate that we allow ourselves to feel the compassion that such circumstances call forth in us and to act upon it, but if we allow ourselves to judge these events and those who participate in them, we create negative karma that must be balanced, and we, ourselves, will be among those souls that choose to participate in circumstances that are necessary to that balancing.

If we do not judge, how can there be justice?

Gandhi was beaten several times during his life. Although on two occasions he nearly died, he refused to prosecute his attackers because he saw that they were doing "what they thought was right." This position of non-judgmental acceptance was central in Gandhi's life. The Christ did not judge even those who spit in His face, and who subjected Him without mercy to His pain and humiliation. He asked forgiveness, not vengeance, for those who tortured Him. Did neither the Christ nor Gandhi know the meaning of justice? They knew non-judgmental justice.

What is non-judgmental justice?

Non-judgmental justice is a perception that allows you to see everything in life, but does not engage your negative emotions. Non-judgmental justice relieves you of the self-appointed job of judge and jury because you know that everything is being seen—nothing escapes the law of karma—and this brings forth understanding and compassion. Non-judgmental justice is the freedom of seeing what you see and experiencing what you experience without responding negatively. It allows you to experience directly the unobstructed flow of the intelligence, radiance, and love of the Universe of which our physical reality is a part. Non-judgmental justice flows naturally from understanding the soul and how it evolves.

This, then, is the framework of our evolutionary process: the continual incarnation and reincarnation of the energy of the soul into physical reality for the purposes of healing and balancing its energy in accordance with the law of karma. Within this framework we evolve, as individuals and as a species, through the cycle of being unempowered to becoming empowered, yet the experiences that we encounter in this process need not be the kind that we have encountered to now.

Gary Zukav, The Seat of the Soul

There is a general agreement, East and West, that life in a body provides uniquely good opportunities for achieving salvation or deliverance. Catholic and Mahayana Buddhist doctrine is alike in insisting that the soul in its disembodied state after death cannot acquire merit, but merely suffers in purgatory the consequences of its past acts. But whereas Catholic orthodoxy declares that there is no possibility of progress in the next world, and that the degree of the soul's beatitude is determined solely by what it has done and thought in its earthly life, the eschatologists of the Orient affirm that there are certain posthumous conditions in which meritorious souls are capable of advancing from a heaven of happy personal survival to genuine immortality in union with the timeless, eternal Godhead. And, of course, there is also the possibility (indeed, for most individuals, the necessity) of returning to some form of embodied life, in which the advance towards complete beatification, or deliverance through enlightenment, can be continued. Meanwhile, the fact that one has been born in a human body is one of the things for which, says Shankara, one should daily give thanks to God.

Aldous Huxley, The Perennial Philosophy

Souls are like wax waiting for a seal. By themselves they have no special identity. The wax that has melted in God's will can easily receive the stamp of its identity, the truth of what it was meant to be.

Thomas Merton, New Seeds of Contemplation

A baby, after an exhibition on the pot, with much anger and howling, stretches out her arms with a little cry, as when her pram is passing under

[63]

trees, to reveal an immense wonder and love for life,—a Soul. I have read that the cuckoo enters the world with two advantages over other birds; a special muscle on its back for throwing them from the nest; and a cry which is irresistible to the foster-parents. This sudden cry of recognition and pleasure is what keeps us all on the go from grab-all to crave. *Volupté!* The eternal cuckoo call.

Cyril Connolly, The Unquiet Grave

Out of the union of soul and spirit a child is conceived—the Jewel in the Lotus, the new consciousness dedicated to the possibility of Being. The child is the new energy that steps out of the past and turns its face to the future with hope, but lives in the *now*.

Organized religion once recognized the mystery of the union of the soul with God and the fear involved. Church rituals were set up, not to do away with the mystery, but to allow people to experience it. Western science finds a mystery intolerable and sets out to explain it away, or even to prove it evil. Logos thinking tries to solve the mystery, rather than enter into it. Ritual and contemplation are not an attempt to explain the mystery, but rather an attempt to orient individuals toward the mystery so that it may be approached without fear. When the Holy Spirit speaks it can be terrifying because it evokes profound fear of the unknown, fear of life, fear of stepping into our own destiny. If, however, men and women can find their own virgin within, they can learn to *Be*, both alone and with each other. The mystery lives in the possibility of Being. Love chooses us.

Marion Woodman, The Pregnant Virgin

Oh thou soul, endowed with the dignity of choice, which will you take, the race toward life or drift toward death? Will you labor to scale the pinnacle of Selfhood, alone leading to union and bliss, or by way of descent, through dimming consciousness and the unraveling of Self, re-enter the Unformed and await a new Creation?

Here—oh look quickly before it hides behind one of its thousand masks —here it lies, coiled at the centre of every fear known to humankind—the Original Fear: loss of being. Ages-old, primeval fear, fear of the fall from *I am* to *I am not*, formless recall from before the long breath of Creation, from the very deeps of the Mind of God, where dissolution and reabsorption are purged of their agony and the terror passes into the Great Memory.

To be obliterated, extinguished, waters closing over where once was I, individual, unique among others. And is it with the spiritual death as with the small human dying, that the whole life repeats before the eye in its moment of closing?

Think of it! The I, perceived all at once, its infinitude finally encapsuled, too late revealed. I! formed from a thousand forms, made from billions of years, millions of births and deaths, composed more of minutes and seconds than of years, for I cannot exult in a year but can feel an instant expand me to the limits of joy, a limit always widening toward the limitless. I, born and cherished of families uncounted, perhaps exalted by multitudes, revered in the trappings of royalty, no doubt burned at stakes and hanged from ancient trees...and no scrap of it without purpose and gain. I of so many talents! My fingers hold memories of stringed instruments, sculptors' clay, soft hair of my thousands of children. I have spoken with the tongues of all countries, lived, bled and died in the skin of all races, inhabited cities now buried deep under the earth, their life still vibrant within the Collective Mind.

And always, in all times and all places, I have loved. I have followed, hand over hand, the invisible thread that runs through the centre of all and which, if it were to be snapped, would cause the whole of Creation to spill into the Void.

I am fed by the Universe and feed it also, for all that I gain by my labors is given into the whole; and all others' advances advance me, enmeshed in the web of the great purposeful Life.

But if I move out of position, disturbing the exquisite balance which holds me in perfect relation to all? There will be an immense shift in the whole as aid rushes to me. But I am the mover and chooser, and respect will be shown for my will. I may refuse the aid: I am allowed. I may fall. I may vacate my place: none will refuse me. Perhaps I spin, free-falling and laughing at the serious God, planning to stop myself when I please.

And long ages after, deep in my fall, when I am helpless and will-less, even though all Life be held out to stay me, I still must make the saving grasp—and find I cannot.

Now to the mourning of God is added the necessity of mending the fabric of the once-perfect Work. Such a small tear—might not it be patched? ... or the space pulled together by a mere closing-in of the nearest souls in the hierarchy of rejoining?

No: the great mathematical scheme of Departure and Return does not permit a simple adjustment. Where the smallest part is affected, the largest is equally affected. In torment and groaning labor the entire created universe reassembles itself, from the far firmaments to the tiny unopened eye of the embryo fieldmouse. Oh, had I known my immense significance!

Patricia Joudry and Maurie D. Pressman, *Twin Souls*

One of the deepest needs of the human soul is for a center, a focus which confers meaning on the shapelessness of temporal existence. Perhaps the most basic, after the awareness of family, is man's apprehension of his immediate locale. For the surrounding landscape represents something markedly other—indeed the eternal presence of Otherness—and as such it carries the vibration of divinity. In man's identification with his region he realizes what he is by intuiting everything he is not. Close at hand and yet aloofly apart, it stands as the mandala of his unconscious associations, one of the ineradicable patterns of psychic life. As such, the recourse to landscape in the need for coherence has from time immemorial elevated man to his most profound religious intuitions. Mountains, valleys, rivers, islands. Always he has looked to the configuration of the world about him for the Face of God.

William Everson, *Birth of a Poet*

The real essence of personality is the divine soul. Because this soul continually exists in a state of unbroken happiness. Because even if we find all that we want physically and intellectually, we would still remain discontented, still go on with the search for happiness, for the single reason that we had not yet found the soul itself. Because we unconsciously and indirectly know this and therefore always hope on and hold on clinging to life despite all the sufferings and struggles that it brings us. Because whenever we observe how innumerable are the creatures, whether human or animal, who cling desperately to life even under the most horrible conditions, we observe also evidence of a subconscious recognition that the earthly incarnation possesses a value, purpose, and meaning beyond its immediate ones.

How little, at this immature stage of seeking amid externals, do men know that the treasures of bliss, satisfaction, and possession are really all in themselves! The feeling of being incomplete, unfinished, and imperfect harasses them; much of their unrest arises from it. But although they may experiment with various means of assuaging it, although they may seek satisfaction on different paths, they cannot overcome it except by taking to the final quest. Although they think they are seeking happiness through the physical body, they are in fact seeking it through the spiritual mind. This is so and must be so because of the constitution of their own nature. This is why no sooner is one desire satisfied than another arises to replace it. Thus, every thirst of the inebriate for further drink is really a thirst, at a physical and lower level of development, for the Overself's bliss. All men are engaged in this search for the second self but most men are engaged quite unconsciously. They are seeking its stable satisfaction in different transient ways. How few comprehend that their need of the divine self is a permanent one!

Most want to enjoy life in their way, which often is entirely dependent on external things or on other persons, not in the philosophic way, which, whilst including these things or persons, is yet inwardly independent of them. All troubling desires fall away and unchanging emotional rest is attained only when the goal is attained.

The serene happiness of the soul can never be broken by the anguish and misery of its shadow the person. No grief or passion, no fear or pain can get into it. That part of his being which always remains in heaven, is the Overself. That part which descends to suffer and struggle on earth, is the personality. The two are indissolubly linked, although ignorance sees only the person. This separation in consciousness from the Overself is the fundamental, if hidden, cause of man's perennial search for happiness, now in one thing or through one person and then in or through another. But a happiness unhindered by some accompanying or subsequent sorrow, he never finds. How could he, if it does not exist in anything or anyone outside? His longing will never be satisfied until it is diverted to, and satisfied by, the transcendental Overself. All through his successive appearances in different bodies, he is seeking the wholeness, the benign happiness, and the blessed fulfilment of union with his higher nature. When he discovers and finally accepts that earthly things are transient and contradictory, that the pleasurable are tied to the painful, and thereupon makes this search a conscious one, he is said to have entered on the Quest.

All forms of life in this world, being finite and limited, involve suffering. But life in the heavenly world, which is not a distant place but an inner state, which is findable even before death, is gloriously free and therefore without suffering. The six things mentioned on the opening page of this chapter,* always desired but never found on earth, are so elusive precisely because they belong to heaven. But heaven is a state of mind. It is indeed mind in its own purest being. Therefore, man may yet attain them here and now so long as he searches for them in the region of thought and feeling and does not limit himself to the region of flesh and blood. "The cause of happiness or misery is no other than one's self;' it is an idea of the mind," teaches Krishna, the divine messenger, in another ancient Indian text, the *Srimad Bhagavata*.

Paul Brunton, The Spiritual Crisis of Man

---

* "A happiness unmixed with sorrow,
   a life unbroken by death,
   a health unsaddened by sickness,
   a freedom unhindered by restraints,
   a knowledge untormented by questions and
   a harmony with all other people."

Happiness consists in finding out precisely what the "one thing necessary" may be, in our lives, and in gladly relinquishing all the rest. For then, by a divine paradox, we find that everything else is given us together with the one thing we needed.

Thomas Merton, *No Man Is an Island*

But this joy must not be the goal toward which you strive. It will be vouch-safed to you if you strive to "give joy to God." Your personal joy will rise up when you want nothing but the joy of God—nothing but joy in itself.

Martin Buber, *The Early Masters*

We are warmed by fire, not by the smoke of the fire. We are carried over the sea by a ship, not by the wake of a ship. So too, what we are is to be sought in the invisible depths of our own being, not in our outward reflection in our own acts. We must find our real selves not in the froth stirred up by the impact of our being upon the beings around us, but in our own soul, which is the principle of all our acts.

But my soul is hidden and invisible. I cannot see it directly, for it is hidden even from myself. Nor can I see my own eyes. They are too close to me for me to see them. They are not meant to see themselves. I know I have eyes when I see other things with them.

I can see my eyes in a mirror. My soul can also reflect itself in the mirror of its own activity. But what is seen in the mirror is only the reflection of who I am, not my true being. The mirror of words and actions only partly manifests my being.

The words and acts that proceed from myself and are accomplished outside myself are dead things compared with the hidden life from which they spring. These acts are transient and superficial. They are quickly gone, even though their effects may persist for a little while. But the soul itself remains. Much depends on how the soul sees itself in the mirror of its own activity.

My soul does not find itself unless it acts. Therefore it must act. Stagnation and inactivity bring spiritual death. But my soul must not project itself entirely into the outward effects of its activity. I do not need to *see* myself, I merely need to *be* myself. I must think and act like a living being, but I must not plunge my whole self into what I think and do, or seek always to find myself in the work I have done. The soul that projects itself entirely into activity, and seeks itself outside itself in the work of its own will is like a madman who sleeps on the sidewalk in front of his house instead of living inside where it is quiet and warm. The soul that throws itself outdoors in order to find itself in the effects of its own work is like a fire that has no desire to burn but seeks only to go up in smoke.

Thomas Merton, *No Man Is an Island*

It struck me at that moment that I was beginning to understand an inner truth that I had been trying to articulate with difficulty for so many months. As a boy at St. Wilfred's I had once listened during Easter week to a Franciscan retreat leader, talking of the strict vocation to the contemplative life in the silence and austerity of a Carthusian monastery. Afterwards I had walked in these same gardens thinking how heroic, how unattainable an ideal that was. How I longed for the courage to love God that much! And now, thirty years or so later, I was only just beginning to understand that the desert wilderness of spirituality is not to be found exclusively in those convents and houses of prayer where men and women dedicate themselves, externally, to the service of God. The desert may lie at the very heart of a person's life, in the depths of one's being.

Many people who have turned away from religion—even with a sense of hatred, rejecting all its idiosyncratic externals—to embrace scepticism, agnosticism, even militant atheism, are perhaps as much in the desert, in the "dark night of the soul," as any contemplative. What we are fleeing, perhaps, is not God at all, but the false or the inadequate representations of him which hinder any possibility of ever making progress in coming to recognize him or reach out for him. What we are rejecting, even hating, is not God, but the "trash and tinsel" that passes for him.

And thus it is that "Hatred of God may bring the soul to God."

John Cornwell, *Powers of Darkness, Powers of Light*

There are still many difficulties that cannot be touched on here. The problem for the "civilization" is the adoption of a religious attitude that can be assimilated as *objectively* as the headlines of last Sunday's newspapers. But the problem for the individual always will be the opposite of this, the conscious striving *not* to limit the amount of experience seen and touched; the intolerable struggle to expose the sensitive areas of being to what may possibly hurt them; the attempt to see as a whole, although the instinct of self-preservation fights against the pain of the internal widening, and all the impulses of spiritual laziness build into waves of sleep with every new effort. The individual begins that long effort as an Outsider; he may finish it as a saint.

Colin Wilson, *The Outsider*

You are the content of your consciousness; in knowing yourself you will know the universe. This knowing is beyond the word for the word is not the thing. The freedom from the known, every minute, is the essence of intelligence. It's this intelligence that is in operation in the universe if you leave it alone. You are destroying this sacredness of order through the ignorance of yourself. This ignorance is not banished by the studies others have made about you or themselves. You yourself have to study the content of your own consciousness.

J. Krishnamurti, *Krishnamurti's Journal*

Your moonlight shines in my wide open soul when everything is silent.

Thomas Merton, *The Sign of Jonas*

The enlightened person remains what he is, and is never more than his own limited ego before the One who dwells within him, whose form has no knowable boundaries, who encompasses him on all sides, fathomless as the abysms of the earth and vast as the sky.

C. G. Jung, *Answer to Job*

Once we have grasped this concept of an "inner world," we can see that we *always* inhabit it, even when we feel most trapped in external reality. And when I intensely enjoy any experience, it is because I am simultaneously in two worlds at once: the reality around me and the reality inside me. When a man deeply enjoys a book, it is as if he has taken the book into a cave inside himself, where he can be free from interruption. When he is absorbed in playing golf, he has taken the golf course inside him. When he is absorbed in making love, he has taken the girl inside him. The deeper he can retreat into that inner world, the more he can enjoy his experience of the outer world. Conversely, when he feels trapped in the outer world by boredom or tension, all his experience becomes unsatisfying and superficial. In order to begin to understand the mechanism of 3-D consciousness, we need to recognize the independent reality of that inner world, and to grasp the error of the view that we are creatures of the physical world around us.

We should also note that Shelley's capacity for "absorption" meant that he could "enter into" a book and abandon himself to its reality. When a man is in a state of boredom or tension, he cannot "enter" the book, and so cannot experience its reality. What do I *do* if I read some description by Dickens or Balzac and feel so absorbed that I actually seem to be there? I somehow add my own experience to the description, so it "becomes real." This is what Proust did spontaneously as he tasted the cake dipped in tea. This is what Arnold Toynbee did spontaneously as he sat in the citadel of Mistra and became aware of the reality of its destruction. In short, we are speaking of the capacity I have labelled "Faculty X."

As soon as we experience the flash of "three-dimensional consciousness," we recognize that this *is* "normal" consciousness—or at least, a step in the right direction. Ordinary consciousness is a mistake. It is an error that has been created by our "intermediate" stage of evolution. Left-brain awareness—the ability to examine the world through a magnifying glass—is essential, but its "close-upness" has deprived us of meaning. We are stranded in an oversized world of magnified objects, and we can see the trees but not the wood. And at this point, the emotional body intervenes, with its negativity and self-pity and mistrust, and turns the wood into a forest of nightmare. This is the state that Sartre calls "nausea," and that I have called "depression." It can be overcome only by recognizing that it *is* a mistake. And the "absurd good news" is the recognition that this insight, in itself, can transform subjective into objective consciousness. The bogies created by the mind can be destroyed by the mind.

Colin Wilson, The Essential Colin Wilson

Elijah

You wanted to descend like a storm wind
And to be mighty in deed like the tempest,
You wanted to blow being to being
And bless human souls while scourging them,
To admonish weary hearts in the hot whirlpool
And to stir the rigid to agitated light,
—You sought me on your stormy paths
And did not find me.

You wanted to soar upward like a fire
And wipe out all that did not stand your test,
Sun-powerful, you wanted to scorch worlds
And to refine worlds in sacrificial flame,

With sudden force to kindle a young nothingness
To new becoming of blessed poem,
—You sought me in your flaming abysses
And did not find me.

Then my messenger came to you
And placed your ear next to the still life of my earth,
Then you felt how seed after seed began to stir,
And all the movements of growing things encircled you,
Blood hammered against blood, and the silence overcame you,
The eternally complete, soft and motherly
—Then you had to incline upon yourself,
Then you found me.

Martin Buber, *A Believing Humanism,*
My Testament 1902–1965

❖ II ❖

Revelation

At some point in the seeker's journey, there comes revelation of the higher realms, a recognition either through what has been a gradually growing awareness, or flashes of sudden knowledge, or through "meaningful coincidences" (Jung), commonly known as synchronistic experiences—thinking the same thoughts as others at the same time, receiving an object, information, or confirmation very close thereafter. Revelation can also happen in dramatic visions, dreams; ecstatic, ritualistic, and mystical events. Without a doubt, these revelations change, often transform, people's lives; priorities shift and an alternative way of life is pursued. A person is reborn to a whole other level of reality, a vast kingdom where the energies of matter and what Hungarian-British writer Arthur Koestler terms "the perennial duellists"—emotion and reason—"are for once in complete harmony."

In the first part of the section, "The Spiritual Experience," I have gathered pieces that describe its manifold forms. All the senses can be involved in a revelation. Some see miracles like statues, moving or dazzling plays of light and colour. Others smell the scents of nature, incense, or some other subtle sweetness, and still others hear a voice or voices or music. Visions, scents, and sounds are usually accompanied by expansive feelings of love, compassion, and relief, joy and gratitude. For in this experience, a person receives a gift, an all-knowing connection to something very true, something very ancient or someone very close. The revelatory experience is a momentous event and marks the beginning of the highest relationship; the divine reward in the form of what Paramahansa Yogananda termed "the joyful presence of God." And in this presence one finds evidence that the Self is unique, great, and loved. The late Bede Griffiths, a former Benedictine monk (and one of the few Christian clergy to found a community in India incorporating the customs of a Hindu ashram), described this in his autobiography, *The Golden String*, where he writes, "I suddenly saw that all the time it was not I who had been seeking God, but God who had been seeking me."

Revelation of the Self can also come through practising various disciplines like yoga and meditation. In "Strengthening the Self," I have collected the words of such masters as Muktananda, Paul Brunton, Krishnamurti, Thich Nhat Hanh, and Gopi Krishna to describe these disciplines that raise consciousness of the partnership of the divine and the Self. This growing awareness can also provide ways of living the spiritual in the everyday and can sometimes lead to peak mystical experiences (ecstatic visions or feelings). Because revelatory experiences are intangible in many ways, and associated with the paranormal and the strange, many people who undergo them are either frightened by them or unaware of what they are and how valuable they can be. We are usually given signs and messages in symbols, ideas, and situations in codes that need to be deciphered, thought about, analyzed. As the Self is unique and its journey and destiny original and unlike any other, it is only by interpreting the signs and messages given that we can fully incorporate the revelation and give it significance in our lives.

The divine and the Self—therefore, the divine self—can be comprehended and honoured by exploring the mythic element in human life. The various archetypes that the subconscious offers us prove to be essential tools of guidance, especially during these chaotic and changing times. Traditional worship in churches, synagogues, and temples is only one way of making space and time sacred. Partaking in rituals, even making rituals to honour happenings and stages in our lives, imbues them with a sacredness and allows us the opportunity of honouring the spirit's guiding hand.

I conclude this section with "Awakening the Great Mother," and "The Emerging Woman" in particular, which to me represents the quintessential archetype of the last fifty years. Because so much has happened spiritually to women and therefore to the feminine energy in both men and women as a result of the women's liberation movement, I have included some new and exciting material here about feminist spirituality, as well as the feminine archetypes that are becoming more relevant—even essential—in our spiritual lives.

The Spiritual Experience

"The courage of confidence is in no way based on anything finite besides oneself, not even on the Church. It is based on God and solely on God, who is experienced in a unique and personal encounter."

—PAUL TILLICH

David Steindl-Rast, a member of the Camaldolese Benedictine community in Big Sur, California, and a leader in bridging the Eastern and Western spiritual traditions, once said in a conversation with Austrian physicist Fritjof Capra, author of the *Tao of Physics*, "By spiritual we mean, of course, fully alive, since spirit means life breath. The spirit is the life breath of God within us. If you are fully alive, alert, and responsive to the challenge of every moment then you are living a spiritual life."

In this chapter there are many examples of experiences beyond our everyday. They range from the peaceful sense of being all with everything, one with all, to the more dramatic, super-conscious revelations. For any type of experience, the overall revelation which accompanies it is that of excitement—of recognizing that there is a different way of existing in this world than we had known before. The American physicist David Bohm, who was a student of Einstein's and has achieved more than most scientists in linking the connections between physics and the realms of higher consciousness, wrote in the book *Changing Consciousness* that "whatever we know of the world, there is always more." The British journalist Malcolm Muggeridge converted to Catholicism late in his life and became a modern-day prophet. As controversial as he was clever, he used the media (appearing on television and writing books and newspaper columns and articles) to deliver his rhetoric on the sad state of secularity in the world. In this chapter, he records a very special time in his youth when he was saved from despair by "a kind of spiritual adolescence; whereby, thenceforth, all his values and pursuits and hopes were going to undergo a total transformation—from the carnal towards the spiritual; from the immediate, the now, towards the everlasting, the eternal." Here Muggeridge chose, like the Indian teacher Jiddu Krishnamurti, to write of himself in the third person.

As I mentioned earlier, the revelations of eternal reality are often accompanied by changing visual energies. French Jesuit Pierre Teilhard de Chardin watched a picture of Christ transform into the vision of the whole Universe vibrating. His revelation is similar to American anthropologist Carlos Castaneda's experience of seeing "the lines of the world" while a pupil of an Yaqui Indian shaman. Both speak of a particular kind of light—de Chardin's is "luminous," "iridescent." Castaneda's is "from the sun."

In the East, the practice of yoga can awaken kundalini—the spiritual energy and life force that moves like a snake from the base of the spine through the seven chakras (energy centres) in the body to the top of the head. The Indian writer and businessman Pandit Gopi Krishna, who practised yoga alone regularly at home for many years, recounts his own kundalini awakening in his autobiography. It is by far the most comprehensive and accessible written account we have of a meditative and gradual spiritual transformation culminating in a peak experience through physical and mental manifestation. This experience changed his life completely—he received wisdom and knowledge and the power to write—and his story gives us a captivating insight into the rebirth that spiritual practice can obtain.

>⊀

Each of us has at least once in his life experienced the momentous reality of God.

Abraham Joshua Heschel, *I Asked for Wonder*

The person who believes in God, then, sees in the fact that right must prevail an experience of what is above humanity, an experience of transcendence, in other words, he experiences the absolute and saving presence of God in that confusion of meaning and non-sense that we call "human existence."

Edward Schillebeeckx, *God Is New Each Moment*

For the sake of general coherence, I think that we do have to make the assumption that whatever we know or think about is part of a more fundamental and broader actual reality that is not generated by thought. We have been saying that thought doesn't cover everything; it is limited. Therefore, whatever we know of the world, there is always more. We find things that we didn't know about, and we find things that contradict what we already know. This is a sign of reality that is beyond our knowledge, our will, our intention, and our desire, as well as being beyond what we have created. The feeling that has arisen from the consideration of all this is that we exist in a vast, illimitable reality out of which we emerged, probably, as suggested by scientific evidence, through a process of evolution. But, of course, religious people say it came from God. Whichever assumption we make, we are here in this reality; we are participating in it.

David Bohm and Mark Edwards, *Changing Consciousness*

Illusion all—
Yet where for us the real
Unless what seems?
These cloud-capped towers
More durable than brass
Our dreams.

Say I must recognize
I but imagined love
Where no love was,
Say all is a dream
In whose brief span
Childhood, womanhood, the grave
Where my love lies:
That dream is all I am.

Cast not before swine—
The rational animal
Oysters' soft aphrodisiac flesh prefers:
Who values then a pearl
At so great price
As to sell all
To purchase one?

Kathleen Raine, from *On a Deserted Shore*

"We had been set to learn a passage from one of Paul's Epistles by heart. I had already got this, and I sat turning the dreary-looking pages of the school edition of the Bible, covered in shiny black. One hand was thrust into my inside pocket, clasping the tiny silver watch as a talisman. The other stopped at the page opening on the Fourth Gospel. I saw the phrase, 'In the beginning was the Word, and the Word was with God, and the Word was God.'

"I felt the hair on my head tingling, and a curtain of red blood appeared to fall before my eyes. I leaned forward, clasping myself close, while the world rocked around me. And as this earthquake subsided, I saw a new skyline defined. It was a landscape in which objects and words were fused. All was one, with the word as the verbal reality brought to material life by Mind, by man. It was therefore the very obvious, tangible presence of the Creator.

"Sitting in Surrey Lane School...I received a philosophy which I have never lost, a working faith in the oneness of all life. My fears of evil, the old Satanic dreads due to the division between the flesh and the spirit, vanished in that *moment* [my italics] of revelation. Everything was now contained, for me, in the power of the Word.

"... on this sharp and concise symbolism I was to build a concept of universal singleness that gave me authority over the horrors, the divisions, the guilt complexes, that beset us all as we go through life, in a world supposedly split into two, the flesh and the spirit, where civil war rages eternally, in sombre Miltonic gloom and hopelessness."

Richard Church, from "Over the Bridge,"
in Marghanita Laski, *Ecstasy*

I was in my room. It was night. The light was on. Suddenly it seemed to me that Father, who had now been dead more than a year, was there with me. The sense of his presence was as vivid and as real and as startling as if he had touched my arm or spoken to me. The whole thing passed in a flash, but in that flash, instantly, I was overwhelmed with a sudden and profound insight into the misery and corruption of my own soul, and I was pierced deeply with a light that made me realize something of the condition I was in, and I was filled with horror at what I saw, and my whole being rose up in revolt against what was within me, and my soul desired escape and liberation and freedom from all this with an intensity and an urgency unlike anything I had ever known before. And now I think for the first time in my whole life I really began to pray—praying not with my lips and with my intellect and my imagination, but praying out of the very roots of my life and of my being, and praying to the God I had never known, to reach down towards me out of His darkness and to help me to get free of the thousand terrible things that held my will in their slavery.

There were a lot of tears connected with this, and they did me good, and all the while, although I had lost that first vivid, agonizing sense of the presence of my father in the room, I had him in my mind, and I was talking to him as well as to God, as though he were a sort of intermediary. I do not mean this in any way that might be interpreted that I thought he was among the saints. I did not really know what that might mean then, and now that I do know I would hesitate to say that I thought he was in Heaven. Judging by my memory of the experience I should say it was "as if" he had been sent to me out of Purgatory. For after all, there is no reason why the souls in Purgatory should not help those on earth by their prayers and influence, just like those in Heaven: although usually they need our help more than we need theirs. But in this case, assuming my guess has some truth in it, things were the other way 'round.

However, this is not a thing on which I would place any great stress. And I do not offer any definite explanation of it. How do I know it was not merely my own imagination, or something that could be traced to a purely natural, psychological cause—I mean the part about my father? It is impossible to say. I do not offer any explanation. And I have always had a great antipathy for everything that smells of necromancy—table-turning and communications with the dead, and I would never deliberately try to enter in to any such thing. But whether it was imagination or nerves or whatever else it may have been, I can say truly that I did feel, most vividly, as if my father were present there, and the consequences that I have described followed from this, as though he had communicated to me without words an interior light from God, about the condition of my own soul—although I wasn't even sure I had a soul.

The one thing that seems to me morally certain is that this was really a grace, and a great grace. If I had only followed it through, my life might have been very different and much less miserable for the years that were to come.

Before now I had never prayed in the churches I had visited. But I remember the morning that followed this experience. I remember how I climbed the deserted Aventine, in the spring sun, with my soul broken up with contrition, but broken and clean, painful but sanitary like a lanced abscess, like a bone broken and re-set. And it was true contrition, too, for I don't think I was capable of mere attrition, since I did not believe in hell. I went to the Dominicans' Church, Santa Sabina. And it was a very definite experience, something that amounted to a capitulation, a surrender, a conversion, not without struggle, even now, to walk deliberately into the church with no other purpose than to kneel down and pray to God. Ordinarily, I never knelt in these churches, and never paid any formal or official attention to Whose house it was. But now I took holy water at the door and went straight up to the altar rail and knelt down and said, slowly, with all the belief I had in me, the Our Father.

It seems almost unbelievable to me that I did no more than this, for the memory remains in me as that of such an experience that it would seem to have implied at least a half hour of impassioned prayer and tears. The thing to remember is that I had not prayed at all for some years.

Another thing which Catholics do not realize about converts is the tremendous, agonizing embarrassment and self-consciousness which they feel about praying publicly in a Catholic church. The effort it takes to overcome all the strange imaginary fears that everyone is looking at you, and that they all think you are crazy or ridiculous, is something that costs a tremendous effort. And that day in Santa Sabina, although the church was almost entirely empty, I walked across the stone floor mortally afraid that a poor devout old Italian woman was following me with suspicious eyes. As I knelt to pray, I wondered if she would run out and accuse me at once to the priests, with scandalous horror, for coming and praying in their church—as if Catholics were perfectly content to have a lot of heretic tourists walking about their churches with complete indifference and irreverence, and would get angry if one of them so far acknowledged God's presence there as to go on his knees for a few seconds and say a prayer!

However, I prayed, then I looked about the church, and went into a room where there was a picture by Sassoferrato, and stuck my face out a door into a tiny, simple cloister, where the sun shone down on an orange tree. After that I walked out into the open feeling as if I had been reborn, and crossed the street, and strolled through the suburban fields to another deserted church where I did not pray, being scared by some carpenters and scaffolding. I sat outside, in the sun, on a wall and tasted the joy of my own inner peace, and turned over in my mind how my life was now going to change, and how I would become better.

Thomas Merton, *The Seven Storey Mountain*

To the convert, his conversion appears as a single and indivisible act, a spiritual rebirth in which emotion and reason, the perennial duellists, are for once in complete harmony.

Arthur Koestler, *Arrow in the Blue*

I returned home with the intention of preparing myself for taking orders in the Church of England and I was advised to go and stay at the Oxford Mission in Bethnal Green to get some practical experience of work in the slums. This decision cost me more than any previous decision of my life. I had still deeply ingrained in me my prejudice against any form of ecclesiasticism and especially of the clerical life, but I realised that it was the test of my faith, if I really believed in the Church, to submit myself to its discipline, and the idea of work in the East End of London appealed to me. To my mother this was the cause of the greatest joy. She had always had a special affection for me, which I had returned at first quite spontaneously, taking pleasure in helping her in the house and confiding all my ambitions to her. Now that I had begun to think as a Christian, this bond was strengthened not only by my own feelings of the duty and love which were due to her, but also by our common feeling for religion. I used always to go to Communion with her and the thought of my taking orders was her highest ambition for me.

No doubt, this had a considerable effect on my decision to settle in the Church of England, but I was not allowed to rest long in this state of mind. I read some of Archbishop Laud's writings, in particular his controversy with Fisher, the Jesuit, and on the whole I think I considered that he had the best of the argument. I also learned more of the sacramental doctrine of the Church and of the idea of the Real Presence, though I never found anything more satisfactory than I had learned from Hooker. I also studied Bishop Butler's *Analogy of Religion*, which made a deep impression on me, and I was much taken with the mystical works of William Law. This was, I think, the first time that I encountered any mystical doctrine, and it had a powerful effect on me. Law was a disciple of the German mystic Jacob Boehme, and brought into the Church of England a current of mystical teaching which, though not precisely orthodox, was of great power and beauty, and saved the Church in the eighteenth century from succumbing to the universal spirit of rationalism. Though Bishop Butler's sane rationalism appealed to me, Law answered to a deeper need of my soul, of which I was now becoming conscious.

I had continued at home to keep up the practice of saying Morning and Evening Prayer every day and I tried to live as strict and regular a life as possible. But I found that the difficulty of adjusting myself to the normal round of life was immense. I had a strong inclination now to fasting. I found that when I fasted my brain became clear and my prayer gained in fervour and intensity, but the moment I relaxed everything began to fall away from me. My mother did not interfere, but many of my friends tried to dissuade me from it, and it became a constant burden to me. I felt that if I abandoned it, I was giving up all my hard-won faith, while if I continued I felt myself becoming more and more isolated from other people. I found in William Law and the High Church tradition for which he stood a justification for my practice and this encouraged me to continue, but it caused an almost intolerable conflict. My reason counselled me often to give way, especially as I began to grow incredibly thin and weak, but at the same time I felt a constant renewal of spiritual power and a deep longing for prayer which increased from day to day.

Often I would take long bicycle rides of sixty or eighty miles, as I still refused to go anywhere by train, and in the course of these rides I went through astounding experiences. I would usually stop for some bread and cheese and beer at midday, but otherwise I tried to do without food. Towards the end of the day, however, I often found myself getting tired out and would be tempted to stop and take some tea. This would often raise an appalling conflict in my mind between reason and common sense on the one hand, the spirit of prayer and faith on the other hand: but I found that if I resisted the temptation it often brought with it a renewal of strength, both physical and spiritual, which seemed almost miraculous. Thus I was strengthened in my determination to continue.

If the conflict at home in the country was considerable, when I came to London and settled at Bethnal Green, it became intolerable. I now felt the full weight of that world which I had rejected pressing upon me. The life of prayer and austerity which I had been leading had increased my sensibility to an extreme degree, and I felt the presence of the surrounding world as a violent oppression. It was not simply a matter of sensibility. The life around Bethnal Green among the poor and in the open market attracted me; I felt that here was the human world which I loved; and the vegetables displayed in the stalls in the market made me feel the contact with the earth and the country. But my mind had grown so deeply antagonistic to the whole civilisation for which London stood that it filled me with horror. I felt it as a giant force opposed to all that I loved, ceaselessly beating against the doors of my mind, breaking down my resistance and driving out the spirit of prayer. I had read with deep conviction when I was at home the words of St. John: "Love not the world, nor the things that are in the world. If any man love the world, the love of the Father is not in him. For all that is in the world, the lust of the flesh, the lust of the eyes and the pride of life, is not of the Father, but of the world. And the world passeth away with the lust thereof, but he that doeth the will of God abideth for ever." These words had sunk into my soul, and now I felt this "world" around me, the world of time and flux and change and sensation, and I knew that it was at war with the world of that eternal order in which I believed.

I went to St. Paul's Cathedral and Westminster Abbey, the British Museum and the National Gallery, to try to recover my sense of these eternal values, but nothing could give me any peace. I attended services also at Anglo-Catholic churches, and there I felt some sense of continuity with the past, but it was like a small island in a flood: the deep unrest in my soul remained. At last this sense of unrest came to a head. I had bought a book of

Bishop Ken, one of the "non-juring" bishops of the seventeenth century who stood for the pure tradition of the Church of England, and in it I read some words about the need for repentance. Up to this time my religion had been to some extent external. I had engaged my mind and imagination, my feelings and my will, but it had never really touched my heart. Behind all my fervour and enthusiasm there had been an intense egoism. I acknowledged no real authority over myself. My religion was based on my own reason and my own will, and though I had come theoretically to accept the authority of the Church, it had no real effect on me.

Now for the first time I felt an overwhelming need to repent. I did not clearly understand what repentance was, nor was I aware of any particular sin of which I had to repent. It was simply that the unrest in my soul had turned from discontent with the world to a feeling of discontent with myself. There was nothing conscious or deliberate about it; it came to me as a command, and I kept saying to myself, scarcely knowing the meaning of what I said: "I must repent, I must repent." I went up in this state of mind to a small chapel at the top of the house one evening, and there, as I prayed, a resolution formed itself in my mind that I would not go to bed that night but would spend the whole night in prayer. Again the resolution seemed not to come from my own volition; it was an instinct with the force of a command.

I went, therefore, to my room and began to pray kneeling on the floor beside the bed, and immediately a furious conflict started in my mind. Reason and common sense told me that it was absurd to behave in this way. Beneath my unconventional behaviour, in many ways I was still deeply conventional, and I dreaded what people might think of me. Although I affected to despise the world, I was in fact still governed by its standards, and the idea of staying up all night in prayer appeared to me utterly absurd. I was also frightened of the isolation into which I felt that I was being driven. I had no real contact with anyone in London, and the people with whom I was staying, though good and kind, would have had no understanding of the conflict in my mind. I felt myself to be utterly alone in this vast city and I could find no human justification for what I was doing.

However, these were comparatively external considerations; what really terrified me was the conflict with my own reason. Until this time my reason and instinct had always gone hand in hand. My first experience of the beauty and mystery of nature had been confirmed by my reading of the poets and then of the philosophers. My discovery of Christianity had also gone on rational lines; at each stage I had seemed to find the book which I needed to satisfy both my reason and my instinct for beauty and holiness. Even my prayer had been perfectly rational and had been satisfied by the ordered beauty of the Book of Common Prayer, but now something irrational seemed to be coming into my life. There had been the desire for fasting which, though I might justify it by reason to some extent, came upon me as an irrational impulse; and now this call to repentance had come, as an apparently irrational urge, and my reason rose up against it. Which was I to obey, this obscure instinct, this apparently irrational urge, or my reason and common sense? The conflict was the most intense that I had ever endured, and it was part of the terms of the conflict, that it could not be answered by reason, because it was precisely the place of reason in my life which was in question.

The conflict went deeper than I could possibly understand. I had lived up till now by my own will. I had worked out my own philosophy and religion for myself and without knowing it I had made a God of my own reason. I had made myself the judge of everything in heaven and earth, and I acknowledged no power or authority over me. Even if theoretically I now acknowledged the authority of God and the Church, in practice I was still the ruler and the judge. I was the centre of my own existence, and my isolation from the rest of the world was due to the fact that I had deliberately shut myself up within the barriers of my own will and reason. Now I was being summoned to surrender this independence. Something had arisen in the depths of my own nature which my reason was powerless to control. I was being called to surrender the very citadel of my self. I was completely in the dark. I did not really know what repentance was or what I was required to repent of. It was this darkness which really made me afraid. Is not this the one thing of which we are all afraid? The darkness which is outside the sphere of our consciousness, the abyss where all known landmarks fail? This was what I was really facing and it was this which filled me with such unspeakable horror. I do not wish to exaggerate the nature of this ordeal, but it was indeed the turning point of my life. The struggle went on for many hours, but I realised at length that it was my reason which I had to renounce. My reason was the serpent which was threatening to devour my life. It was not merely the reason of convention and common sense, but the very autonomy of my reason which I was required to sacrifice. I had to surrender myself into the hands of a power which was above my reason, which would not allow me to argue, but commanded me to obey. Yet this power presented itself as nothing but darkness, as an utter blank.

In this state of mind I had but one resource. I had never been in the habit of meditating on the passion of Christ, but the scene in the Garden of Gethsemane had impressed itself on my imagination. I had always felt that in those hours Christ had faced the utter darkness of death and dereliction, the full tide of the power of evil sweeping over the world. Now I felt that this hour had come upon me, and I could only place myself beside him in the Garden of Gethsemane and wait for the night to pass. Once I had made up my mind not to listen to reason, the conflict ceased. It was only a matter of enduring to the end. So I set myself to remain kneeling on the floor, fighting against sleep and keeping my mind fixed on the figure of Christ. Somehow I managed to endure until it was morning. When I rose, I felt worn out and hopeless; I did not know what was to become of me. I did not feel that I could stay where I was and nothing else offered itself to me.

But as I was leaving my room, I suddenly heard a voice say: "You must go to a retreat." When I say that I heard a voice, I do not mean that I heard any sound. It was simply that this was signified to me interiorly, but in such a way that it did not appear to come from myself. I believe that I had heard the word "retreat" used once, but I am certain that I did not know what it meant. I associated it, I think, with some kind of clerical conference which I had heard of taking place in the country. The message came to me as a direct inspiration, though I did not know what it signified. I went, therefore, to an Anglo-Catholic church nearby and asked the priest if there was such a thing as a retreat to which I could go. He thought for a minute and then said: "Yes, there is one beginning this morning at Westminster House." The retreat was for a group of ordinands, but he thought that it would be possible for me to attend it. I went round to Westminster House, which I found to be a house of the Cowley Fathers.

It is difficult to describe what happened when I reached there. The retreat conferences were given by an old priest called Father Tovey. They were very simple in character and dealt with the fundamental doctrines of Original Sin and Redemption, of the Incarnation and the Holy Trinity. This was the first time that I had ever heard these doctrines expounded in a way which had any meaning to me. He based himself on St. Thomas, which I recognised with pleasure, but he gave them a living personal application which touched my heart. I had studied philosophy and theology, and I knew the elements of church history and church doctrine, but the simple truth of the faith had never before been set before me. Now it penetrated my soul in such a way that I was appalled to think that I had never understood it before. I had rejected the Church and gone my own way, working out my religion for myself, and here all the time the truth had been among the people I had despised. My whole life seemed to have been one gigantic mistake. I had turned my back on the truth, and sought it blindly in the opposite direction, and now I had been forced back to the point from which I started.

The repentance for which I had blindly asked the night before now came over me like a flood. I went to confession for the first time in my life and tears poured from my eyes, tears of a kind which I had never known before. My whole being seemed to be renewed. When I went into the church and heard the chanting of the Psalms, it seemed that the words were being spoken in the depths of my own soul and were the utterances of my own prayer. They were chanting the 119th Psalm; it must have been in plain-chant, though I did not know it, and no doubt this must have stirred my soul, for there is no music on earth like it; but it was the words which engraved themselves on my mind:

> Blessed are those that are undefiled in the way: and walk in the law of the Lord.
>
> Blessed are they that keep his testimonies and seek him with their whole heart....
>
> With my whole heart have I sought thee: O let me not go wrong out of thy commandments....
>
> Open thou my eyes that I may see the wondrous things of thy law.

I had come through the darkness into a world of light. That eternal truth and beauty which the sights and sounds of London threatened to banish from my sight was here the universal law. I heard its voice sounding in my ears. The very stones of the house seemed to be the living stones of a temple in which this song ascended. It was as though I had been given a new power of vision. Everything seemed to lose its hardness and rigidity and to become alive. When I looked at the crucifix on the wall, the figure on it seemed to be a living person; I felt that I was in the house of God. When I went outside I found that the world about me no longer oppressed me as it had done. The hard casing of exterior reality seemed to have been broken through, and everything disclosed its inner being. The buses in the street seemed to have lost their solidity and to be glowing with light. I hardly felt the ground as I trod, and I think that I must have been in some danger of being run over. I was like a bird which has broken the shell of its egg and finds itself in a new world; like a child who has forced its way out of the womb and sees the light of day for the first time.

When I returned to the house I went to my room and took up the New Testament. There I read the words of St. John: "Not that we loved God, but that He loved us," and suddenly the meaning of what had happened dawned on my mind. Through all these years I had thought that I had been seeking God. The presence which had appeared to me beneath the forms of nature that day at school; the beauty which I had found in the poets; the truth which philosophy had opened to me; and finally the revelation of Christianity; all these had seemed to be steps on my way of ascent towards God. Now I suddenly saw that all the time it was not I who had been seeking God, but God who had been seeking me. I had made myself the centre of my own existence and had my back turned to God. All the beauty and truth which I had discovered had come to me as a reflection of his beauty, but I had kept my eyes fixed on the reflection and was always looking at myself. But God had brought me to the point at which I was compelled to turn away from the reflection, both of myself and of the world which could only mirror my own image. During that night the mirror had been broken, and I had felt abandoned because I could no longer gaze upon the image of my own reason and the finite world which it knew. God had brought me to my knees and made me acknowledge my own nothingness, and out of that knowledge I had been reborn. I was no longer the centre of my life and therefore I could see God in everything.

That night before I went to bed I opened a book by St. John of the Cross and read in it the words: "I will lead thee by a way thou knowest not to the secret chamber of love." The words struck home to me as though they had been spoken to me. Though I had never been without affection for my family and had had many friends, yet I had never till this moment really known the meaning of love. My strongest feelings had gone into my love for nature and for poetry. Yet always I had had the feeling that in love the secret of life was to be found. And now I felt that love take possession of my soul. It was as though a wave of love flowed over me, a love as real and personal as any human love could be, and yet infinitely transcending all human limitations. It invaded my being and seemed to fill not only my soul but also my body. My body seemed to dissolve, as things about me had done, and felt light and buoyant. When I lay down I felt as though I might float on the bed, and I experienced such rapture that I could imagine no ecstasy of love beyond it.

During the retreat Father Tovey had compared the action of grace to a small child standing over an open trapdoor into a cellar where his father is standing. The cellar is in darkness and the child can see nothing. But he knows that his father is there, and his father tells him to jump. That is what had happened to me; I had jumped into the darkness, and I had been caught in the arms of love.

Bede Griffiths, The Golden String

To be unable to *understand* the mysteries of faith is by no means to be unable to *believe* them. And yet, as I have said, faith is in no way the blind acceptance of a truth which we have no hope of understanding. Although we can never comprehend the full meaning of these mysteries, yet faith is the key to a relative understanding of them. It is after the initial act of belief that the believer begins to see. Only then can the intellectual difficulties presented by these mysteries be dealt with in a way that is in some sense satisfactory.

Thomas Merton, The Ascent to Truth

He drove to the furthest point along the coast road, some six miles from Lourenço Marques, and there got out of the car and undressed. The lights were still on in Peter's Café and Costa da Sol. As the tide was far out, he had to wade on and on before there was enough water to swim in. So this was the end of his life, his last little while on earth. He kept on trying to think of the French word for "drown." Everything seemed to him unreal—had there been a single moment in his life when he had truly lived? Everything false—love, hate, despair, all equally false. Even his dying seemed false. Was it him, wading on to the open sea? Was it really happening? The bottom he trod on was muddy now, the water creeping up and cold, the air damp. At last there was enough water to swim in. He started swimming, the dark water churning white as his arms beat through it. Soon he was out of his depth, and still swam on. Now he felt easy, now it was settled. Looking back he could scarcely see the shore; only the lights of Peter's Café and Costa da Sol, far, far, away. He began to tremble, all his body trembled; he went under the water, trembling, came up again and reposed himself as though on a bed. He could sleep on this watery mattress, sleep. Then, suddenly, without thinking or deciding, he started swimming back to shore. He was very tired, and kept feeling as if he was in his depth again, and wasn't; he shouted foolishly for help, and kept his eyes fixed on the lights of Peter's Café and Costa da Sol.

They were lights of the world; they were the lights of his home, his habitat, where he belonged. He must reach them. There followed an over-whelming joy such as he had never experienced before; an ecstasy. *In some mysterious way it became clear to him that there was no darkness, only the possibility of losing sight of a light which shone eternally*; that our clumsy appetites are no more than the blind reaching of a newly born child after the teat through which to suck the milk of life; that our sufferings, our affliction, are part of a drama—an essential, even an ecstatic, part—endlessly revolving round the two great propositions of good and evil, of light and darkness. A brief interlude, an incarnation, reaching back into the beginning of time, and forward into an ultimate fulfilment in the universal spirit of love which informs, animates, illuminates all creation, from the tiniest particle of insentient matter to the radiance of God's very throne.

Now he felt the bottom, and began to wade laboriously back to the shore, reaching it by the estuary of a river, a long way away from where he had first gone into the sea. All round him was deep black mud, through which, shaking with cold, he floundered until, by luck more than any sense of direction, he saw his car where he had left it. Even at the time he realized, and realizes now ever more clearly, that this floundering was a sort of parable. Plodding and floundering on through deep mud, but never again without hope; thenceforth always knowing, deep in his heart, remembering even when he forgot, that it was not by chance or for nothing that the lights of Peter's Café and Costa da Sol had called him back. That he, too, had something he must try to say and be, until the time came for God to put him to sleep, as he had tried, in his own fatuous and sinful wilfulness, to put himself to sleep in the sea off Lourenço Marques. When, finally, he reached his car and clothes, the morning was just breaking; the black African sky just beginning to be tinged with grey. He breathed in the dawn air, greedily; after all, he was still alive.

Though he scarcely realized it at the time, and subsequently only very slowly and dimly, this episode represented for him one of those deep changes which take place in our lives.... A kind of spiritual adolescence, whereby, thenceforth, all his values and pursuits and hopes were going to undergo a total transformation—from the carnal towards the spiritual; from the immediate, the now, towards the everlasting, the eternal. In a tiny dark dungeon of the ego, chained and manacled, he had glimpsed a glimmer of light coming in through the barred window high above him. It was the light of Peter's Café and Costa da Sol calling him back to earth, his mortal home; it was the grey light of morning heralding another day as he floundered and struggled through the black mud; it was the light of the world. The bars of the window, as he looked more closely, took on the form of a Cross.

Malcolm Muggeridge, *Chronicles of Wasted Time*

"One night when the land was still fresh from the rain, I was wandering near our camp enjoying the moonlight when an immense exaltation took possession of me. It was as though the White Goddess of the moon had thrown some bewitching power into her rays. It seemed to me that our arid satellite was itself a living presence bounding in the sky—I do not myself understand this use of the word 'bounding,' but it comes insistently, and I cannot but use it to express some deeply felt vitality. Indeed, the whole night was dancing about me.

"It appeared that the moonlight had ceased to be a physical thing and now represented a state of illumination in my own mind. As here in the night landscape the steady white light threw every olive leaf and pebble into sharp relief, so it seemed that my thoughts and feelings had been given an extraordinary clarity and truth.

"So powerfully was I moved by this sense of possession that I climbed up on to a high outcrop of rock against the mouth of the wadi and knelt down there. The moonlight swam round, and in, my head as I knelt looking across the plain to the shining silver bar of the Mediterranean.

"From far behind me, still muffled in the folds of the mountain, I heard the bronze sound of camel-bells. To my sharpened but converging senses they seemed like a row of brown flowers blooming in the moonlight. In truth the sound of bells came from nothing more remarkable than a caravan, perhaps twenty camels with packs and riders, coming down the wadi on its way northward to Haifa. But even now I cannot recognise that caravan in such everyday terms; my memory of it is dreamlike, yet embodies one of the most intense sensuous and emotional experiences of my life. For those minutes, and I have no notion how many they were, I had the heightened sensibility of one passionately in love and with it the power to transmute all that the senses perceived into symbols of burning significance. This surely is one of the best rewards of humanity. To be filled with comprehension of the beauty and marvellous complexity of the physical world, and for this happy excitement of the senses to lead directly into an awareness of spiritual significance. The fact that such experience comes most surely with love, with possession by the creative eros, suggests that it belongs near the root of our mystery. Certainly it grants man a state of mind in which I believe he must come more and more to live: a mood of intensely conscious individuality which serves only to strengthen an intense consciousness of unity with all being. His mind is one infinitesimal node in the mind present throughout all being, just as his body shares in the unity of matter.

"The bells came nearer and another sound mingled with theirs; a low, monotonous chanting. I looked behind me for a moment and saw the dark procession swaying out from behind the last bend in the wadi, then I turned back so that the column should pass me and enter my world of vision from behind. I found myself comprehending every physical fact of their passage as though it were a part of my own existence. I knew how the big soft feet of the camels pressed down upon and embraced the rough stones of the path; I knew the warm depth of their fur and the friction upon it of leather harness and the legs of the riders; I knew the blood flowing through the bodies of men and beasts and thought of it as echoing the life of the anemones which now showed black among the rocks around me. The sound of bells and the chanting seemed rich and glowing as the stuff of the caravan itself.

"So the swaying line came from behind, went past, and moved away across the plain. It was a procession of life moving through the icy moonlight. It was coming from the mountain and going towards the sea. That was all I knew, but as the moon leapt and bounded in the sky I took full possession of a love and confidence that have not yet forsaken me."

Jacquetta Hawkes, from "Man on Earth,"

in Marghanita Laski, *Ecstasy*

We have the two fundamental elements: the ecstatic and the rational element united. There is ecstasy but the highest creation of the ecstasy is love in the sense of *agape*. There is ecstasy but the other creation of ecstasy is *gnosis*, the knowledge of God. It is knowledge, and it is not disorder and chaos.

Paul Tillich, *The Future of Religion*

The Picture

... At that time, he began, my mind was concerned with a problem that was half philosophic and half aesthetic. Suppose, I used to think, that Christ should deign to appear here, in the flesh, before my very eyes—what would he look like? Most important of all, in what way would he fit himself into Matter and so be sensibly apprehended? How would he impinge on the objects around him? And I felt that there was something vaguely distressing, something that grated on me, in the idea that the Body of the Lord could be jostled in the world-scene by the multitude of inferior bodies without the latter's noticing or recognizing by some perceptible change the Intensity that brushed against them.

Meanwhile, my eyes had unconsciously come to rest on a picture that represented Christ with his Heart offered to men. This picture was hanging in front of me, on the wall of a church into which I had gone to pray. And, continuing my line of thought, I could not see how it could be possible for an artist to represent the sacred Humanity of Jesus without giving him this over-exact physical definition, which seemed to cut him off from all other men: without giving him a face whose expression was too individual—a beautiful face, no doubt, but beautiful in a particular way which excluded all other types of beauty.

I was worrying and wondering about all this; and I was still looking at the picture when the vision began.

(Indeed, I cannot be certain exactly when it began, because it had already reached a certain pitch of intensity when I became aware of it....)

All I know is that as I let my eyes roam over the outlines of the picture, I suddenly realized that they *were melting*. They were melting, but in a very special way that I find it difficult to describe. When I tried to distinguish the drawing of the Person of Christ, the lines seemed to be sharply defined. And then, if I relaxed my visual concentration, the whole of Christ's outline, the folds of his robe, the bloom of his skin, merged (though without disappearing) into all the rest.

You might have said that the edge which divided Christ from the surrounding World was changing into a layer of vibration in which all distinct delimitation was lost.

As I remember it, the change must first have been noticeable in a particular spot on the edge of the picture; it started there, and then ran all round the outline of the figure—it was in that order, at any rate, that I became aware of it. And then, after that, the metamorphosis spread rapidly and included every detail.

First I noticed that the vibrant atmosphere which formed a halo around Christ was not confined to a narrow strip encircling him, but radiated into Infinity. From time to time what seemed to be trails of phosphorescence streamed across it, in which could be seen a continuous pulsing surge which reached out to the furthest spheres of Matter—forming a sort of crimson ganglion, or nervous network, running across every substance.

The whole Universe was vibrating. And yet, when I tried to look at the details one by one, I found them still as sharply drawn, their individual character still intact.

All this movement seemed to emanate from Christ—from his Heart in particular. And it was while I was trying to find my way back to the source of this effluence and determine its rhythm that my attention returned to the portrait itself, and then I saw the vision rapidly mount to its climax.

...I see that I have forgotten to tell you how Christ was dressed. His "raiment was white as the light," as we read in the account of the Transfiguration. But what struck me most was that it was not woven on any loom—unless the hand of the Angels is the hand of Matter. It was from no crudely spun thread that warp and weft were made; but Matter, a florescence of Matter, had spontaneously woven itself, working with the most intimate essence of its substance, to produce a magically textured lawn. And I thought I could see the interlocked fibres running on and on, harmoniously combining to form a natural design which was built into them from their first beginning.

And yet, you must understand, I could not give my full attention to this garment, so marvellously woven by the endless co-operation of all the energies of Matter and its whole order. It was the transfigured Face of the Master that drew me and held me.

At night time, you have often seen some stars that change the quality of their light: at one moment they are blood-red beads, and then they take on the shimmer of purple velvet. Similarly, you have seen the colours of the rainbow float in a transparent bubble.

It was thus that the light and the colours of all the beauties we know shone, with an inexpressible iridescence, over the face of Jesus, itself unmoved. I cannot say whether it was an expression of my own wishes or whether it was the choice of Him who determined and knew my tastes; but one thing I know, that these countless modifications, instinct with majesty, sweetness, and irresistible appeal, followed one another in succession, were transformed, melted into one another in a harmony that was utterly satisfying to me.

And all this time, beneath this surface movement—both supporting it and concentrating it in a higher unity—floated the incommunicable Beauty of Christ.... Again, I guessed at rather than apprehended that Beauty; for every time I tried to see through the screen of lesser beauties that hid it from me, other particular and fragmentary beauties came to the surface and drew a veil between me and *True Beauty*, even as they allowed me to glimpse it and stimulated my longing.

The whole Face gave out this radiance regulated by this same law. But the centre of radiation and iridescence was hidden in the eyes of the transfigured portrait.

The Reflection—or was it the Creative Form, the Idea?—of all that can charm, of all that has life, overlaid, in a rainbow, the rich depths of those eyes...And as I tried to read the secret of the luminous simplicity of their fire, it dissolved into a fathomless complexity in which were united all that the expressive eye has ever held to bring warmth to the heart of man and enthral it. For example, those eyes, which at first were so sweet and tender that I thought it was my mother that I saw, became in the next moment as full of passion and as dominating as those of a sovereign lady—so imperiously pure, at the same time, that it would have been physically impossible for sensibility to be misguided. And then again they were filled with a great and virile majesty, akin to that which can be seen in the eyes of a man who has great courage or great strength—and yet incomparably more lofty and more delightful in its mastery.

This scintillation of beauties was so total, so all-embracing, and at the same time so swift, that it reached down into the very powerhouse of my being, flooding through it in one surge, so that my whole self vibrated to the very core of me, with a full note of explosive bliss that was completely and utterly unique.

Now, while I eagerly concentrated my attention on the very pupils of Christ's eyes, in which I saw an infinite depth of Life, enchanting and glowing, from those same depths I saw a sort of cloud forming, which overlaid and drowned the shifting play of expression that I have been trying to describe. Gradually a look of extraordinary intensity spread over the fluctuating shades of emphasis I could read in the divine glance, first seeping into them and then absorbing them into itself.

I was completely at a loss.

I found it impossible to decipher this final expression, which dominated and summed up all that had gone before. I could not say whether it evidenced an unspeakable agony or, on the contrary, an excess of triumphant joy. All I know is that, since that occasion, I believe I have seen a hint of it once, and that was in the eyes of a dying soldier.

My own eyes were instantly dimmed by tears. But when I was able to look again at the picture of Christ in the church, it had resumed its over-defined outline and the blank immobility of its features.

Pierre Teilhard de Chardin, *The Heart of Matter*

I drove south and then east, following the roads I had always taken when driving with don Juan. I parked my car around the place where the dirt road ended and then I hiked on a familiar trail until I reached a high plateau. I had no idea what to do there. I began to meander, looking for a resting place. Suddenly I became aware of a small area to my left. It seemed that the chemical composition of the soil was different on that spot, yet when I focused my eyes on it there was nothing visible that would account for the difference. I stood a few feet away and tried to "feel" as don Juan had always recommended I should do.

I stayed motionless for perhaps an hour. My thoughts began to diminish by degrees until I was no longer talking to myself. I then had a sensation of annoyance. The feeling seemed to be confined to my stomach and was more acute when I faced the spot in question. I was repulsed by it and felt compelled to move away from it. I began scanning the area with crossed eyes and after a short walk I came upon a large flat rock. I stopped in front of it. There was nothing in particular about the rock that attracted me. I did not detect any specific color or any shine on it, and yet I liked it. My body felt good. I experienced a sensation of physical comfort and sat down for a while.

I meandered in the high plateau and the surrounding mountains all day without knowing what to do or what to expect. I came back to the flat rock at dusk. I knew that if I spent the night there I would be safe.

The next day I ventured farther east into the high mountains. By late afternoon I came to another even higher plateau. I thought I had been there before. I looked around to orient myself but I could not recognize any of the surrounding peaks. After carefully selecting a suitable place I sat down to rest at the edge of a barren rocky area. I felt very warm and peaceful there. I tried to pour out some food from my gourd, but it was empty. I drank some water. It was warm and stale. I thought that I had nothing else to do but to return to don Juan's house and began to wonder whether or not I should start on my way back right away. I lay down on my stomach and rested my head on my arm. I felt uneasy and changed positions various times until I found myself facing the west. The sun was already low. My eyes were tired. I looked down at the ground and caught sight of a large black beetle. It came out from behind a small rock, pushing a ball of dung twice its size. I followed its movements for a long time. The insect seemed unconcerned with my presence and kept on pushing its load over rocks, roots, depressions, and pro-tuberances on the ground. For all I knew, the beetle was not aware that I was there. The thought occurred to me that I could not possibly be sure that the insect was not aware of me; that thought triggered a series of rational evalu-ations about the nature of the insect's world as opposed to mine. The beetle and I were in the same world and obviously the world was not the same for both of us. I became immersed in watching it and marveled at the gigantic strength it needed to carry its load over rocks and down crevices.

I observed the insect for a long time and then I became aware of the silence around me. Only the wind hissed between the branches and leaves of the chaparral. I looked up, turned to my left in a quick and involuntary fash-ion, and caught a glimpse of a faint shadow or a flicker on a rock a few feet away. At first I paid no attention to it but then I realized that that flicker had been to my left. I turned again suddenly and was able to clearly perceive a shadow on the rock. I had the weird sensation that the shadow instantly slid down to the ground and the soil absorbed it as a blotter dries an ink blotch. A chill ran down my back. The thought crossed my mind that death was watching me and the beetle.

I looked for the insect again but I could not find it. I thought that it must have arrived at its destination and then had dropped its load into a hole in the ground. I put my face against a smooth rock.

The beetle emerged from a deep hole and stopped a few inches away from my face. It seemed to look at me and for a moment I felt that it became aware of my presence, perhaps as I was aware of the presence of my death. I experienced a shiver. The beetle and I were not that different after all. Death, like a shadow, was stalking both of us from behind the boulder. I had an extraordinary moment of elation. The beetle and I were on a par. Neither of us was better than the other. Our death made us equal.

My elation and joy were so overwhelming that I began to weep. Don Juan was right. He had always been right. I was living in a most mysterious world and, like everyone else, I was a most mysterious thing, and yet I was no more important than a beetle. I wiped my eyes and as I rubbed them with the back of my hand I saw a man, or something which had the shape of a man. It was to my right about fifty yards away. I sat up straight and strained to see. The sun was almost on the horizon and its yellowish glow prevented me from getting a clear view. I heard a peculiar roar at that moment. It was like the sound of a distant jet plane. As I focused my attention on it, the roar increased to a prolonged sharp metallic whizzing and then it softened until it was a mesmerizing, melodious sound. The melody was like the vibration of an electrical current. The image that came to my mind was that two electrified spheres were coming together, or two square blocks of electrified metal were rubbing against each other and then coming to rest with a thump when they were perfectly leveled with each other. I again strained to see if I could distinguish the person that seemed to be hiding from me, but I could only detect a dark shape against the bushes. I shielded my eyes by placing my hands above them. The brilliancy of the sunlight changed at that moment and then I realized that what I was seeing was only an optical illusion, a play of shadows and foliage.

I moved my eyes away and I saw a coyote calmly trotting across the field. The coyote was around the spot where I thought I had seen the man. It moved about fifty yards in a southerly direction and then it stopped, turned, and began walking toward me. I yelled a couple of times to scare it away, but it kept on coming. I had a moment of apprehension. I thought that it might be rabid and I even considered gathering some rocks to defend myself in case of an attack. When the animal was ten to fifteen feet away I noticed that it was not agitated in any way; on the contrary, it seemed calm and unafraid. It slowed down its gait, coming to a halt barely four or five feet from me. We looked at each other, and then the coyote came even closer. Its brown eyes were friendly and clear. I sat down on the rocks and the coyote stood almost touching me. I was dumbfounded. I had never seen a wild coyote that close, and the only thing that occurred to me at that moment was to talk to it. I began as one would talk to a friendly dog. And then I thought that the coyote "talked" back to me. I had the absolute certainty that it had said something. I felt confused but I did not have time to ponder upon my feelings, because the coyote "talked" again. It was not that the animal was voicing words the way I am accustomed to hearing words being voiced by human beings, it was rather a "feeling" that it was talking. But it was not like a feeling that one has when a pet seems to communicate with its master either. The coyote actually said something; it relayed a thought and that communication came out in something quite similar to a sentence. I had said, "How are you, little coyote?" and I thought I had heard the animal respond, "I'm all right, and you?" Then the coyote repeated the sentence and I jumped to my feet. The animal did not make a single movement. It was not even startled by my sudden jump. Its eyes were still friendly and clear. It lay down on its stomach and tilted its head and asked, "Why are you afraid?" I sat down facing it and I carried on the weirdest conversation I had ever had. Finally it asked me what I was doing there and I said I had come there to "stop the world." The coyote said, "Que bueno!" and then I realized that it was a bilingual coyote. The nouns and verbs of its sentences were in English, but the conjunctions and exclamations were in Spanish. The thought crossed my mind that I was in the presence of a Chicano coyote. I began to laugh at the absurdity of it all and I laughed so hard that I became almost hysterical. Then the full weight of the impossibility of what was happening struck me and my mind wobbled. The coyote stood up and our eyes met. I stared fixedly into them. I felt they were pulling me and suddenly the animal became iridescent; it began to glow. It was as if my mind were replaying the memory of another event that had taken place ten years before, when under the influence of peyote I witnessed the metamorphosis of an ordinary dog into an unforgettable iridescent being. It was as though the coyote had triggered the recollection, and the memory of that previous event was summoned and became superimposed on the coyote's shape; the coyote was a fluid, liquid, luminous being. Its luminosity was dazzling. I wanted to cover my eyes with my hands to protect them, but I could not move. The luminous being touched me in some undefined part of myself and my body experienced such an exquisite indescribable warmth and well-being that it was as if the touch had made me explode. I became transfixed. I could not feel my feet, or my legs, or any part of my body, yet something was sustaining me erect.

I have no idea how long I stayed in that position. In the meantime, the luminous coyote and the hilltop where I stood melted away. I had no thoughts or feelings. Everything had been turned off and I was floating freely.

Suddenly I felt that my body had been struck and then it became enveloped by something that kindled me. I became aware then that the sun was shining on me. I could vaguely distinguish a distant range of mountains towards the west. The sun was almost over the horizon. I was looking directly into it and then I saw the "lines of the world." I actually perceived the most extraordinary profusion of fluorescent white lines which criss-crossed everything around me. For a moment I thought that I was perhaps experiencing sunlight as it was being refracted by my eyelashes. I blinked and looked again. The lines were constant and were superimposed on or were coming through everything in the surroundings. I turned around and examined an extraordinarily new world. The lines were visible and steady even if I looked away from the sun.

I stayed on the hilltop in a state of ecstasy for what appeared to be an endless time, yet the whole event may have lasted only a few minutes, perhaps only as long as the sun shone before it reached the horizon, but to me it seemed an endless time. I felt something warm and soothing oozing out of the world and out of my own body. I knew I had discovered a secret. It was so simple. I experienced an unknown flood of feelings. Never in my life had I had such a divine euphoria, such peace, such an encompassing grasp, and yet I could not put the discovered secret into words, or even into thoughts, but my body knew it.

Then I either fell asleep or I fainted. When I again became aware of myself I was lying on the rocks. I stood up. The world was as I had always seen it. It was getting dark and I automatically started on my way back to my car.

Carlos Castaneda, Journey to Ixtlan

Again, in the essence of the mind there is transcendence, the effort to step beyond all horizons. From this, of course, it also follows that the mind violates its own horizon as well; we reflect on our ability to reflect; we know that we know; we know that we know that we know; we know that we have been separated, we know of our thrownnesses, we know of the unattainability of what we strive toward, and we know that we cannot help but strive toward it; we know what we don't know and what we cannot know—so that the more radically we step beyond our limitations, the better we know them, and the better we know them, the more obviously we step beyond them.

Vaclav Havel, Letters to Olga

The Tower

I was in Bollingen just as the first tower was being finished. This was the winter of 1923–24. As far as I can recall, there was no snow on the ground; perhaps it was early spring. I had been alone perhaps for a week, perhaps longer. An indescribable stillness prevailed.

One evening—I can still remember it precisely—I was sitting by the fireplace and had put a big kettle on the fire to make hot water for washing up. The water began to boil and the kettle to sing. It sounded like many voices, or stringed instruments, or even like a whole orchestra. It was just like polyphonic music, which in reality I cannot abide, though in this case it seemed to me peculiarly interesting. It was as though there were one orchestra inside the Tower and another one outside. Now one dominated, now the other, as though they were responding to each other.

I sat and listened, fascinated. For far more than an hour I listened to the concert, to this natural melody. It was soft music, containing, as well, all the discords of nature. And that was right, for nature is not only harmonious; she is also dreadfully contradictory and chaotic. The music was that way too: an outpouring of sounds, having the quality of water and of wind—so strange that it is simply impossible to describe it.

On another such still night when I was alone in Bollingen (it was in the late winter or early spring of 1924) I awoke to the sound of soft footsteps going around the Tower. Distant music sounded, coming closer and closer, and then I heard voices laughing and talking. I thought, "Who can be prowling around? What is this all about? There is only the little footpath along the lake, and scarcely anybody ever walks on it!" While I was thinking these things I became wide awake, and went to the window. I opened the shutters—all was still. There was no one in sight, nothing to be heard—no wind—nothing—nothing at all.

"This is really strange," I thought. I was certain that the footsteps, the laughter and talk, had been real. But apparently I had only been dreaming. I returned to bed and mulled over the way we can deceive ourselves after all, and what might have been the cause of such a strange dream. In the midst of this, I fell asleep again—and at once the same dream began: once more I heard footsteps, talk, laughter, music. At the same time I had a visual image of several hundred dark-clad figures, possibly peasant boys in their Sunday clothes, who had come down from the mountains and were pouring in around the Tower, on both sides, with a great deal of loud trampling, laughing, singing, and playing of accordions. Irritably, I thought, "This is really the limit! I thought it was a dream and now it turns out to be reality!" At this point, I woke up. Once again I jumped up, opened the window and shutters, and found everything just the same as before: a deathly still moonlit night. Then I thought: "Why, this is simply a case of haunting!"

Naturally I asked myself what it meant when a dream was so insistent on its reality and at the same time on my being awake. Usually we experience that only when we see a ghost. Being awake means perceiving reality. The dream therefore represented a situation equivalent to reality, in which it created a kind of wakened state. In this sort of dream, as opposed to ordinary dreams, the unconscious seems bent on conveying a powerful impression of reality to the dreamer, an impression which is emphasized by repetition. The sources of such realities are known to be physical sensations on the one hand, and archetypal figures on the other.

That night everything was so completely real, or at least seemed to be so, that I could scarcely sort out the two realities. Nor could I make anything of the dream itself. What was the meaning of these music-making peasant boys passing by in a long procession? It seemed to me they had come out of curiosity, in order to look at the Tower.

Never again did I experience or dream anything similar, and I cannot recall ever having heard of a parallel to it. It was only much later that I found an explanation. This was when I came across the seventeenth-century Lucerne chronicle by Rennward Cysat. He tells the following story: On a high pasture of Mount Pilatus, which is particularly notorious for spooks—it is said that Wotan to this day practices his magic arts there—Cysat, while climbing the mountain, was disturbed one night by a procession of men who poured past his hut on both sides, playing music and singing—precisely what I had experienced at the Tower.

The next morning Cysat asked the herdsman with whom he had spent that night what could have been the meaning of it. The man had a ready explanation: those must be the departed folk—*sälig Lüt*, in Swiss dialect; the phrase also means blessed folk—namely, Wotan's army of departed souls. These, he said, were in the habit of walking abroad and showing themselves.

It may be suggested that this is a phenomenon of solitude, the outward emptiness and silence being compensated by the image of a crowd of people. This would put it in the same class with the hallucinations of hermits, which are likewise compensatory. But do we know what realities such stories may be founded on? It is also possible that I had been so sensitized by the solitude that I was able to perceive the procession of "departed folk" who passed by.

The explanation of this experience as a psychic compensation never entirely satisfied me, and to say that it was a hallucination seemed to me to beg the question. I felt obliged to consider the possibility of its reality, especially in view of the seventeenth-century account which had come my way.

It would seem most likely to have been a synchronistic phenomenon. Such phenomena demonstrate that premonitions or visions very often have some correspondence in external reality. There actually existed, as I discovered, a real parallel to my experience. In the Middle Ages just such gatherings of young men took place. These were the *Reisläufer* (mercenaries) who usually assembled in spring, marched from Central Switzerland to Locarno, met at the Casa di Ferro in Minusio and then marched on together to Milan. In Italy they served as soldiers, fighting for foreign princes. My vision, therefore, might have been one of these gatherings which took place regularly each spring when the young men, with singing and jollity, bade farewell to their native land.

C. G. Jung, Memories, Dreams, Reflections

For many who have experienced it, this vision of a changeless reality has been so powerful and so self-evidently true that they have concluded that the changing world of everyday experience is somehow less real. The impermanence of things in this world is an appearance or reflection or illusion. Underlying everything is the true reality which neither comes into being nor passes away.

Rupert Sheldrake, Presence of the Past

In London I met my companion of the *Île de France*, who was surrendering herself to the surprises of a European summer. She had rented a Morris Minor and was a jaunty chauffeur for a merry ride to Canterbury. We had not been together for more than fifteen minutes before I began to relate my story of the previous two days. Perhaps it was the shock of those events to my nervous system or the lack of sleep, but I told the story in two or three different versions. Her woman's eye for the absurd and her general good spirits cast a warm spell around me and I began to sort out the deceptive complexity of that brief visit to Scotland.

While she drove, I fell into a reverie. Pleasant and seemingly random thoughts softened by the green English countryside, then vivid scenes from my past forming and reforming, sorting themselves out, leading me back to childhood like hypnotic regression. I was in warm, unaccountable spirits, anticipation spreading in my cells as if I knew this reverie would bring some marvelous secret. Both of us felt that sense of zero gravity that comes when you are traveling without an immediate or particular goal. In Canterbury we got into the old cathedral sometime after midnight because the wizened caretaker liked the gleam emanating from this loosening of my brain.

The next day we drove to Dover and crossed the channel to Calais. I still remember the smell of a store there, a smell that was familiar at once for it was the one I grew up with in my grandparents' laundry and kitchen— salamis and parsleys and spices and consommés, a combination of ingredients I could never forget. The store in Calais brought memories of vacations in San Francisco when I was a child, with my fun-loving, pleasure-loving Grand'mère and Grand'père and all their children and cousins (many of them gourmet cooks); a peasant world, a breath of air from the Pyrenees, full of the very same smells I found in this store in Calais. These smells from the past gave body to my reverie as we drove toward Rheims, absorbing me all that day until we arrived at the great cathedral and I saw the banner and figure of Saint Jeanne d'Arc.

The memories began in earliest infancy, feelings with no graspable image or event to hold them: feelings of cradling and rocking and my mother's pleasure, a time of membranes' sensuous stretching, with textures of reassuring blankets and diapers like warm water-beds, adventures of water and air, a trip well begun; then an image of a kindergarten class, watching all the others on the merry-go-round but too uneasy to get on myself, the shy one standing near the teacher while most of the kids screamed and laughed and fell on the whirling frame; and a third-grade teacher with a wall of bugs and spiders in bottles filled with formaldehyde, my peering through protective glass at those mysterious many-legged creepy-crawlies, knowing at once what they felt like and curious thereafter about other beings, teeming worlds of them appearing in books I could find on my parents' shelves and in fortunate classrooms; then books about stars and planets and finally the mystery underlying. I became an early philosopher—late into puberty, early into God—wandering into bookstores and feeling my way to the right shelf, the opening in the mystery: somewhere in that store was a word, it never failed, I would tell my friends that I could dowse for books, for the Word—the trip began into those reachings of the mind when I was still five feet four. And then the memory of that shattering day in a class I came to by mistake, the class of Frederic Spiegelberg, known to many of the students in those nonphilosophical nonapocalyptic days of 1950 as the best teacher on the Stanford campus, remembered him rolling the Sanskrit words, intoning the *Brahman* and the Vedic Hymns and knowing that I could never be the same again, that all the dowsing for books in my teen-age years was coming into focus—at Stanford, the fun-loving school, Spiegelberg rolling out the Vedic Hymns, bringing a few of us home to the beginning of things; and then our little group of dropouts in 1951, led by Walter Page, older than we with his streak of white hair running Mohawk-style down the middle of his head; Walt Page and his closet full of books— a forerunner of Shivas Irons. The memory of all my teachers and conversions rolled through me that sunny summer day in 1956.

We drove into Rheims and circled round the great cathedral, viewing it first from our car before we found our room. I had read a long shelf of history books before this trip, for I had decided to recapitulate the march of Western history on my way to India: I wanted to get my bearings, perhaps, on my way out to sea. The cathedral of Rheims and the armor of Jeanne d'Arc were special places on that journey back. I had read Shaw's play and preface and two or three books about her, for her life was one of those intersections I needed to comprehend if I was going to find the link between this world and the ones I was about to explore. She was a *pitha*, as the Indians say, a place where something breaks into our workaday world and bothers us forevermore with the hints it gives.

We found the small hotel we had heard about and asked for a room. Then I caused a scene by asking for *two* rooms. My companion, first of several good women confounded by sudden turnings of the erratic compass needle of asceticism and sensuality in my soul, was angry and hurt, and the innkeeper—well, I had never encountered one so jealous of his rooms; he thought I had asked for another because I didn't like the one we saw first, so came like a gallant Frenchman to my companion's defense. After much argument he said that this was the very last room in his inn, that, moreover, there was not another left in the entire town. So I said we would go on to Paris that night. In spite of all the trouble I was making, I had to make the renunciation, there was no resisting it; I had to prepare for whatever was emerging in these days of reverie and catharsis.

Jeanne d'Arc. I remembered seeing sailors from a French warship with her name on their caps while I was stationed in Puerto Rico, remembered my uncle's joke about being captain of the ship since he had been aboard it once in San Francisco; he had joked about it during every party at the Frenchmen's gatherings when I was a child, never tired of getting us to salute, my brother and I and all our cousins, whenever he announced he was "Captain Pierre" of the French fleet, captain of the *Jeanne d'Arc*.* As we walked toward the Gothic spires looming now above the town I remembered these and other associations to her name, an arc joining this world to the others, the charts on Shivas's wall with lines joining vertical columns, one entitled DANGEROUS CONNECTIONS, another GOD IS WAKING UP, and his notion that God gives us a million clues but because we are so dense he must shove some of them right in our face.

Then we came to the cathedral façade. There was construction under way inside and you could see at once that much of it was newly built. The ravages of bombardment during the war were still being repaired, we were told, that was why this rear part of the towering nave looked so clean, so free of soot and all the centuries' calefactions, almost as if it had shed a skin. It was not at all as I had anticipated it, not dark and libidinous and full of mystery; it reminded me in fact of a gigantic bower, full of springtime leaves and sunbeams streaming through the unstained glass. On all sides there bustled children from some French school, whispering and giggling as they scampered after their brisk and upright teachers: their chirping voices echoed off the tall, empty windows and airy vaults, receding into waves of formless sound and the beginnings of music. The cathedral of Rheims was for all the world like an airy bower, its power and mystery was in the sound it gave back.

---

* I have only to turn my head as I write to see the *Jeanne d'Arc* moored at a pier on the San Francisco waterfront.

I wrote this epilogue in Big Sur (in the spring of 1971) and returned to find a ship glowing in the water beneath me like an illuminated cathedral. At first I did not know its name. Then an announcement came over a local radio station that the *Jeanne d'Arc* was receiving visitors at pier 39—the pier beneath my window! I focused my binoculars on it, and there were the words spelled on its bow; there was no mistaking them. As a friend remarked, my ship had come in.

The sound. I was struck by the amazing swirl of it through the towering vaults: giggling children, hollow footsteps, the occasional shout of a workman rising above a quiet roar like distant surf.

The sound and then the tiny figure at the end of the nave. For there she was as I had hoped, the figure of the Maid in the original armor, carrying a banner of white that seemed four times her size.

I circled away from my friend and walked alone toward the statue, poised at last on insight's very edge. Memories recalled and impulses cleansed, mind empty now, a pious bore to my friend but ready nevertheless for the omens, I came like a sleepwalker to the point of intersections embodied in the relics of Saint Joan.

Then the omens began.

As I walked up the side aisle on the right, a weathered old lady dressed in black rose from her prayers near the aisle and watched me intently. As I passed her she grabbed my arm. Her face had a simian look, with flaring nostrils and flat high cheeks, and her eyes showed white as if they were rolled back permanently from so much prayer. "Entendez vous les voix sous les voûtes?" she asked with an urgent voice—did I hear the voices in the vaults? She rolled back her eyes and looked toward the cathedral roof, then repeated the question. I started to pull away but felt drawn to her strangely importuning look, for a moment I was going two ways at once.

She asked the question again with growing agitation—did I hear the voices? What was she driving at? She was mad, I thought, an eccentric old peasant woman centering her delusions in her prayers. But I followed her gestures and looked up into the cathedral vault. As I did, the echoes of the place engulfed me.

Distant ocean waves, elusive whispers were forming in the sibilant echoes. Yes, I could hear them, I could hear the voices. I sat down next to her and listened. The memories and catharsis of the last few days had prepared me perhaps for this unlikely event. I looked into the Gothic arches, up into the overturned keel of the nave. What were they saying? What were the old lady's voices saying? If I let some door in my brain swing open, there would be a voice and a word, I had learned how to do that during long hours of meditation. There was a resistance though, for the voice invariably left me with nausea—something was threatened by such interventions and reacted with an automatic visceral no. But now I was in a mood to let it come, the last few days had given me a taste for abandon, yes, whatever had begun at Burningbush was carrying me to this cathedral bench. I closed my eyes, let the swirl of sound congeal round that elusive door in my head, and sure enough the arches spoke. A tiny voice coming as if through distant echo chambers said, "Come home"—"Come home," it said again and then like distant choirs came the beginnings of music, emblazoning those words on my brain forever. Come home, come home, I was breaking through to another realm: come home, it said, follow the music home at last.

I will never know what happened next, for when I opened my eyes the old lady was gone and in her stead there sat my companion of recent days. I stretched my arms and reached out to touch her. Her hair in the sunlight was like a halo and her eyes and mouth curled upward with fond amusement. We looked at each other for a moment and I could see that she understood something of what I had seen. She leaned toward me and kissed my cheek and whispered that she would meet me outside when I was ready, then rose with a little wave and slipped away.

Perhaps an hour or two had passed, judging from the change of light. It seemed to be late afternoon and there was a hush in the cathedral now. The armor on Saint Joan's statue caught a ray of sunshine and flashed it back down the lengthening nave—perhaps the Maid was sending me signals. I felt a faint impulse to rise and explore the place, but the afterglow of trance held me in its blissful field: in the heavy stillness there was the subtlest suggestion of the fairy dust Shivas had mentioned filtering through the membranes of the inner body, as if my ordinary frame were being transformed by the explosion of light and sound triggered by the strange old lady. I sat for several minutes savoring the quiet and the process of change going on inside me and thought again of Shivas. This was the kind of thing he was into— what a pleasure and what a privilege! The thought occurred that he had passed the secret of it on to me. For it was said in most of the ancient books that *darshan*, as the Indians called it, the passing of the light, could only come directly from teacher to student, that it was rarely mediated in any other way. I said a little prayer of thanks to my Scottish golfing teacher.

The beams of light shaped by the tapering walls of glass were softening now and casting longer shadows among the branches and spreading trees on the walls of the church. I looked around the enormous space, at Saint Joan, at the people filing out the great rear doors, at the figures kneeling in prayer, then up to the Gothic columns, and the catwalks high above. High in the shadows of the nave, some 90 or 100 feet above me, a tiny figure was looking down, perhaps a workman looking for his helper. As I watched him I realized he wasn't moving, that he was looking in my direction. I could not discern his features but could see he was dressed in black with a frizzy beard, that he seemed to have a smile on his face, a mad, gay little smile.

I looked around the nave, then up at the ceiling again: the bearded face was staring down at me still, with the same little smile.

The relentless scrutiny of the distant figure was obscene. I stood up and started down the aisle toward the cathedral sanctuary to get another angle from which to see him. His head turned to follow my movement. There was no doubt about it, he was watching me intently. An old lady was sweeping at the edge of the choir; I pointed toward the figure in the rafters and asked her who it was. She shrugged her shoulders and said she did not speak English. "Qui est-ce?" I asked insistently, pointing again at the peering face. "Mais de qui parlez vous? Je ne vois rien," she said in a rasping voice as she looked toward the distant ceiling, "I don't understand."

I jabbed my finger at the smiling face. "There, right there, don't you see it?"

"I don't understand," she answered with a shrug and turned back to her sweeping.

For a moment the lights grew dim. I looked for someone to help me, but there was no one else in this part of the cathedral. Then I noticed a figure walking toward me up the center aisle, a tall man with a dark beard and priestly suit of black, a rabbi perhaps. He seemed to be looking at the figure of Saint Joan, for as he approached his head turned slowly to keep the statue in sight. As he passed I cleared my throat and touched his arm.

"Excuse me, sir, but would you do me a favor?" As I asked the question I glanced up to check on the figure above. It was in exactly the same position, peering down at me with a clearly discernible smile.

"Yes?" the stranger paused and looked at me with a kind and curious expression. He seemed strangely familiar.

"Forgive me for this," I asked, "but I think someone is watching me from the roof. Would you please see if you can see him?"

The stranger in black smiled through his bushy beard with a wide, slightly bucktoothed smile and said in what seemed to be a British accent, "I don't think one can get into those arches."

"But look, would you please look?" I asked again, an edge of pleading in my voice now.

"Well, then, show me where he is," he said and turned to follow my pointing finger. "I don't think there is anyone there," he said after he had scanned the long sweep of arches in the cathedral vault.

"But look, look there," I insisted, holding my arm so he could look down the line of my finger. I could see the face as clearly as ever.

"I'm sorry, I'm very sorry," he turned to face me. "I simply cannot see him. Perhaps you've mistaken a gargoyle for a living face." He smiled another bucktoothed smile and put an arm around my shoulder. "Young man," he said, "let me show you the banner of Saint Joan. That is far more interesting than a face in the roof."

I glanced again at the staring figure. But I followed the stranger, for his presence reassured me.

He led me to the base of the little statue. I could see when we got there that the Maid must have been less than five feet tall. We stood looking up at her in silence for several moments, then the kindly man in black said in his British accent, "That banner, have you ever seen it before?" I said that I had read about it and had seen it on a postcard. It was surprisingly long and I wondered how the little woman could have carried it; she must have been as strong as an ox. The stranger moved closer and reached over to touch it. Then he stroked it gently and brushed some dust from a fleur-de-lis. "She designed it herself, you know," he said. "Can you imagine the inspiration it must have been?" I was touched by his fond regard for the ancient object. My upset was going away. "Do you think it has some power still?" he murmured, almost as if he were asking himself the question. "I would love to pick it up." He touched the dusty banner now with both his hands, and for a moment I thought he might take it from the statue. I had an image of him holding it above his head and marching around the cathedral. He must have sensed what I was thinking for he turned to me and winked and said, "You be the Dauphin and I'll be the Maid." I was at ease by now and gave a little laugh. Then he smiled through his bushy beard.

The bells were tolling in the cathedral of Rheims and acolytes were lighting candles. It was time for Mass.

"Would you like to join me for the service here?" my new friend asked with an engaging smile. "Then I will tell you some secrets about Jeanne d'Arc." I was about to say yes, but at that very moment I saw him looking skeptically over my shoulder—I remember his look so well. Then I felt a hand on my neck and knew it was Dulce, my good companion come after these many hours to get me. There she was with her golden hair and twinkling eyes, patient to the end with all my dallyings.

"I'm sorry," I said to the stranger, "but we have to drive to Paris tonight. There's not a room left in Rheims."

He seemed to be disappointed. "Well," he said, with a gesture toward the cathedral roof, "at least we got rid of the ghost." I looked up and indeed the figure was gone. "I do that sometimes, see faces like that," my embarrassment must have been plain. "Thanks for your time."

I reached out to shake his hand and he gave me a bone-crunching grip. Then he smiled his bucktoothed smile for the last time and I saw that his gaze was ever so slightly crossed.

"Whenever you feel oppressed," he said, "remember Saint Joan and her angels and remember that she made herself a banner." He raised a large hand in farewell and waved it in front of his face as if he were opening and closing some invisible curtain. We waved good-bye, then arm in arm we walked outside into the light of the setting sun.

Michael Murphy, Golf in the Kingdom

(The scene is a jazz-club)

"We're there, thought Ray, we've done it. They're roaring, shouting, threshing, but they can't beat us. They can't drown us. He leant the mike into the guts of the open upright, and let Louie come in with the heavy, sharp chords off-rhythm, till they didn't know, any of them, who was playing, who was listening, but they were all playing and all listening, and Larry came in high up in triplets, catching them by the throat and holding them with sweet bitterness, his notes silver and hard, cleanly coming and high again, Ray taking his note and Larry cutting out, so that the change-over was impeccable. The crowd was gone, its noise the sea's noise or a waterfall, coming to it round the side of a hill, rising and retreating, and he was alone on the hill, blasting and challenging the sky with his lasciviously toned sax till the sky opened and there was nothing beyond, and the challenge turned to praise, ecstatic, believing, strong. The notes kept coming and the inspiration flowed in Ray like blood, essential. The passion rushed out of him, and then Larry and Louie and Hank were up there with him, all on the hilltop, all praising, and there was nothing beyond nothing, and again nothing. There was rushing wind in his ears, waves on sand, thunder, and the voice of the world in peace. The hillside darkened and split, a negro stumbled up the slope, tears on his face. His pink palms rattled on tight drum skins, giving an edge to the deeper tenor. He swayed like a snake. The bass crashed to the ground and Dix's voice called to the soul wildly, extemporising mad parabolas of sound. Larry hit G in altissimo and held it, a screaming fury, and then shaking on it till the hillside crumbled and the sky came together and they were back in the room with the lights and the crowd and the heat.

"There was stillness in the small room.... There was no cheering, no applause, just a gentle murmur as [the crowd's] breath escaped. They stared at Ray as though hypnotised, and a little afraid of what they had seen and heard. They had seen Ray crouched over his alto, blind to everything but the music, blowing something that was either profanity or a prayer....

"[Ray] lurched to the centre of the dais, still dazed and still on the hill alone, only now instead of nothing, there was poison, evil, staring hatred. He stared back at the evil and the hatred with equal hatred.

" 'Is that what you wanted? Is that what you were yelling for? Well, you got it. You got what you wanted. Do you know what you got? You got everything, heart, soul, guts and bones. There's nothing else left. Do you understand? You bled me, sucked me dry. You asked for everything and you got it.

Do you know what you got? You got the world's passion, the force of the hill I was on, where I saw nothing and everything and it was beautiful....' "

Frederick Woods, from "Sessions from Departure,"

in Marghanita Laski, *Ecstasy*

The reality of the holy can only be grasped from the standpoint of the mystery. Then one sees that the holy is not a segregated, isolated sphere of Being, but signifies the realm open to all spheres, in which they can alone find fulfilment. The face of the holy is not turned away from but towards the profane; it does not want to hover over the profane but to take it up into itself. "The mysteries always teach us to combine the holy with the profane." The strict division between them has its place not in the character and attitude of the holy but in those of the profane; it is the profane which makes a fundamental and unsurmountable division between itself and the holy, and on the other side the inadequate "usual" holiness consists only in being separate from the profane, whereas the perfectly holy thinks and wills nothing but unity. The contradictions between the spheres of the holy and the profane exist only in the subjectivity of man who has not yet attained to spiritual unity and is unable, with his limited powers of understanding, to mediate between the two. In reality the main purpose of life is to raise everything that is profane to the level of the holy.

Martin Buber, *On Zion*

I have likened the peak-experience in a metaphor to a visit to a personally defined heaven from which the person then returns to earth. This is like giving a naturalistic meaning to the concept of heaven. Of course, it is quite different from the conception of heaven as a place somewhere into which one physically steps after life on this earth is over. The conception of heaven that emerges from the peak-experiences is one which exists all the time all around us, always available to step into for a little while at least.

Abraham H. Maslow, *Religions, Values and Peak-Experiences*

The Seeds of Utopia

Ecstatic experience will be described in some or most of the following terms:

> *feelings of a new life, another world, satisfaction, joy, salvation, glory;*
> *of new and/or mystical knowledge; of loss of words, images, sense; of*
> *unity, eternity, heaven; of up-feelings; of contact; of loss of worldliness,*

*desire, sorrow, sin; of enlargement and improvement; of loss of self; of
inside-feelings; of loss of feelings of difference, time, place, of light
and/or fire feelings; of peace and calm; of liquidity; of ineffability; of
release; of pain.*

To believe one has had some or most of these feelings is belief war-
ranted by ecstatic experience. If we were to postulate the most probable
unwarranted beliefs that would be held as a result of ecstatic experience, we
could reasonably surmise that they would include belief in the existence of a
joyful and satisfactory condition in which, purified, one could enter a glorious new world or life; in which one gained ineffable knowledge aided by losing the impediment of normal perceptions; in which all was timelessly one;
in which worldliness, desire, sorrow, sin were unknown; to which one was
raised or elevated; in which one made contact with Someone or Something
or everyone or everything; by which one was enlarged or improved; to which
all differences, all divisions or time, all localized places were irrelevant; by
which one was illumined and warmed; was at peace; felt a beneficial flow;
endured delicious pain.

Marghanita Laski, Ecstasy

One morning during the Christmas of 1937 I sat cross-legged in a small
room in a little house on the outskirts of the town of Jammu, the winter capital of the Jammu and Kashmir State in northern India. I was meditating
with my face towards the window on the east through which the first grey
streaks of the slowly brightening dawn fell into the room. Long practice had
accustomed me to sit in the same posture for hours at a time without the least
discomfort, and I sat breathing slowly and rhythmically, my attention drawn
towards the crown of my head, contemplating an imaginary lotus in full
bloom, radiating light.

I sat steadily, unmoving and erect, my thoughts uninterruptedly centred on the shining lotus, intent on keeping my attention from wandering
and bringing it back again and again whenever it moved in any other direction. The intensity of concentration interrupted my breathing; gradually it
slowed down to such an extent that at times it was barely perceptible. My
whole being was so engrossed in the contemplation of the lotus that for several minutes at a time I lost touch with my body and surroundings. During
such intervals I used to feel as if I were poised in mid-air, without any feeling of a body around me. The only object of which I was aware was a lotus
of brilliant colour, emitting rays of light. This experience has happened to

many people who practise meditation in any form regularly for a sufficient length of time, but what followed on that fateful morning in my case, changing the whole course of my life and outlook, has happened to few.

During one such spell of intense concentration I suddenly felt a strange sensation below the base of the spine, at the place touching the seat, while I sat cross-legged on a folded blanket spread on the floor. The sensation was so extraordinary and so pleasing that my attention was forcibly drawn towards it. The moment my attention was thus unexpectedly withdrawn from the point on which it was focused, the sensation ceased. Thinking it to be a trick played by my imagination to relax the tension, I dismissed the matter from my mind and brought my attention back to the point from which it had wandered. Again I fixed it on the lotus, and as the image grew clear and distinct at the top of my head, again the sensation occurred. This time I tried to maintain the fixity of my attention and succeeded for a few seconds, but the sensation extending upward grew so intense and was so extraordinary, as compared to anything I had experienced before, that in spite of myself my mind went towards it, and at that very moment it again disappeared. I was now convinced that something unusual had happened for which my daily practice of concentration was probably responsible.

I had read glowing accounts, written by learned men, of great benefits resulting from concentration, and of the miraculous powers acquired by yogis through such exercises. My heart began to beat wildly, and I found it difficult to bring my attention to the required degree of fixity. After a while I grew composed and was soon as deep in meditation as before. When completely immersed I again experienced the sensation, but this time, instead of allowing my mind to leave the point where I had fixed it, I maintained a rigidity of attention throughout. The sensation again extended upward, growing in intensity, and I felt myself wavering; but with a great effort I kept my attention centred round the lotus. Suddenly, with a roar like that of a waterfall, I felt a stream of liquid light entering my brain through the spinal cord.

Entirely unprepared for such a development, I was completely taken by surprise; but regaining self-control instantaneously, I remained sitting in the same posture, keeping my mind on the point of concentration. The illumination grew brighter and brighter, the roaring louder, I experienced a rocking sensation and then felt myself slipping out of my body, entirely enveloped in a halo of light. It is impossible to describe the experience accurately. I felt the point of consciousness that was myself growing wider, surrounded by waves of light. It grew wider and wider, spreading outward while the body, normally the immediate object of its perception, appeared to have receded into the distance until I became entirely unconscious of it. I was now all consciousness, without any outline, without any idea of a corporeal appendage, without any feeling or sensation coming from the senses, immersed in a sea of light simultaneously conscious and aware of every point, spread out, as it were, in all directions without any barrier or material obstruction. I was no longer myself, or to be more accurate, no longer as I knew myself to be, a small point of awareness confined in a body, but instead was a vast circle of consciousness in which the body was but a point, bathed in light and in a state of exaltation and happiness impossible to describe.

After some time, the duration of which I could not judge, the circle began to narrow down; I felt myself contracting, becoming smaller and smaller, until I again became dimly conscious of the outline of my body, then more clearly; and as I slipped back to my old condition, I became suddenly aware of the noises in the street, felt again my arms and legs and head, and once more became my narrow self in touch with body and surroundings. When I opened my eyes and looked about, I felt a little dazed and bewildered, as if coming back from a strange land completely foreign to me. The sun had risen and was shining full on my face, warm and soothing. I tried to lift my hands, which always rested in my lap, one upon the other, during meditation. My arms felt limp and lifeless. With an effort I raised them up and stretched them to enable the blood to flow freely. Then I tried to free my legs from the posture in which I was sitting and to place them in a more comfortable position but could not. They were heavy and stiff. With the help of my hands I freed them and stretched them out, then put my back against the wall, reclining in a position of ease and comfort.

What had happened to me? Was I the victim of a hallucination? Or had I by some strange vagary of fate succeeded in experiencing the Transcendental? Had I really succeeded where millions of others had failed? Was there, after all, really some truth in the oft-repeated claim of the sages and ascetics of India, made for thousands of years and verified and repeated generation after generation, that it was possible to apprehend reality in this life if one followed certain rules of conduct and practised meditation in a certain way? My thoughts were in a daze. I could hardly believe that I had a vision of divinity. There had been an expansion of my own self, my own consciousness, and the transformation had been brought about by the vital current that had started from below the spine and found access to my brain through the backbone. I recalled that I had read long ago in books on Yoga of a certain vital mechanism called Kundalini, connected with the lower end of the spine, which becomes active by means of certain exercises, and when once roused carries the limited human consciousness to transcendental heights, endowing the individual with incredible psychic and mental powers. Had I been lucky enough to find the key to this wonderful mechanism, which was wrapped up in the legendary mist of ages, about which people talked and whispered without having once seen it in action in themselves or in others? I tried once again to repeat the experience, but was so weak and flabbergasted that I could not collect my thoughts sufficiently enough to induce a state of concentration. My mind was in a ferment. I looked at the sun. Could it be that in my condition of extreme concentration I had mistaken it for the effulgent halo that had surrounded me in the superconscious state? I closed my eyes again, allowing the rays of the sun to play upon my face. No, the glow that I could perceive across my closed eyelids was quite different. It was external and had not that splendor. The light I had experienced was internal, an integral part of enlarged consciousness, a part of my self.

I stood up. My legs felt weak and tottered under me. It seemed as if my vitality had been drained out. My arms were no better. I massaged my thighs and legs gently, and, feeling a little better, slowly walked downstairs. Saying nothing to my wife, I took my meal in silence and left for work. My appetite was not as keen as usual, my mouth appeared dry, and I could not put my thoughts into my work in the office. I was in a state of exhaustion and lassitude, disinclined to talk. After a while, feeling suffocated and ill at ease, I left for a short walk in the street with the idea of finding diversion for my thoughts. My mind reverted again and again to the experience of the morning, trying to recreate in imagination the marvellous phenomenon I had witnessed, but without success. My body, especially the legs, still felt weak, and I could not walk for long. I took no interest in the people whom I met, and walked with a sense of detachment and indifference to my surroundings quite foreign to me. I returned to my desk sooner than I had intended, and passed the remaining hours toying with my pen and papers, unable to compose my thoughts sufficiently to work.

When I returned home in the afternoon I felt no better. I could not bring myself to sit down and read, my usual habit in the evening. I ate supper in silence, without appetite or relish, and retired to bed. Usually I was asleep within minutes of putting my head to the pillow, but this night I felt strangely restless and disturbed. I could not reconcile the exaltation of the morning with the depression that sat heavily on me while I tossed from side to side on the bed. I had an unaccountable feeling of fear and uncertainty. At last in the midst of misgivings I fell asleep. I slept fitfully, dreaming strange dreams, and woke up after short intervals in sharp contrast to my usual deep, uninterrupted sleep. After about 3 a.m. sleep refused to come. I sat up in bed for some time. Sleep had not refreshed me. I still felt fatigued and my thoughts lacked clarity. The usual time for my meditation was approaching. I decided to begin earlier so that I would not have the sun on my hands and face, and without disturbing my wife, went upstairs to my study. I spread the blanket and, sitting cross-legged as usual, began to meditate.

I could not concentrate with the same intensity as on the previous day, though I tried my best. My thoughts wandered, and instead of being in a state of happy expectancy I felt strangely nervous and uneasy. At last, after repeated efforts, I held my attention at the usual point for some time, waiting for results. Nothing happened and I began to feel doubts about the validity of my previous experience. I tried again, this time with better success. Pulling myself together, I steadied my wandering thoughts, and fixing my attention on the crown, tried to visualize a lotus in full bloom as was my custom. As soon as I arrived at the usual pitch of mental fixity, I again felt the current moving upward. I did not allow my attention to waver, and again with a rush and a roaring noise in my ears the stream of effulgent light entered my brain, filling me with power and vitality, and I felt myself expanding in all directions, spreading beyond the boundaries of flesh, entirely absorbed in the contemplation of a brilliant conscious glow, one with it and yet not entirely merged in it. The condition lasted for a shorter duration than it had done yesterday. The feeling of exaltation was not so strong. When I came back to normal, I felt my heart thumping wildly and there was a bitter taste in my mouth. It seemed as if a scorching blast of hot air had passed through my body. The feeling of exhaustion and weariness was more pronounced than it had been yesterday.

I rested for some time to recover my strength and poise. It was still dark. I had now no doubts that the experience was real and that the sun had nothing to do with the internal lustre that I saw. But, why did I feel uneasy and depressed? Instead of feeling exceedingly happy at my luck and blessing my stars, why had despondency overtaken me? I felt as if I were in imminent danger of something beyond my understanding and power, something intangible and mysterious, which I could neither grasp nor analyse. A heavy cloud of depression and gloom seemed to hang round me, rising from my own internal depths without relation to external circumstances, I did not feel I was the same man I had been but a few days before, and a condition of horror, on account of the inexplicable change, began to settle on me, from which, try as I might, I could not make myself free by any effort of my will. Little did I realize that from that day onwards I was never to be my old normal self again, that I had unwittingly and without preparation or even adequate knowledge of it roused to activity the most wonderful and stern power in man, that I had stepped unknowingly upon the key to the most guarded secret of the ancients, and that thenceforth for a long time I had to live suspended by a thread, swinging between life on the one hand and death on the other, between sanity and insanity, between light and darkness, between heaven and earth.

><

The sudden awakening of Kundalini in one whose nervous system has reached the ripe stage of development as a result of favourable heredity, correct mode of living, and proper mental application, is often liable to create a most bewildering effect on the mind. The reason for it, though extremely simple, may not be easily acceptable to the present-day intellect, which treats the human mind as a finally sealed product, dependent, according to some, exclusively on the activity of the brain cells, beginning and ending with the body; according to others, on the responsiveness of the bone-shielded grey and white matter to the extremely subtle all-pervading cosmic mind or Universal spirit; and according to still others, on the existence of an immortal individual soul in the body. Without entering into a discussion of the correctness of these hypotheses advanced to account for the existence of mind, it is sufficient for our purpose to say that according to the authorities on Yoga, the activity of the brain and the nervous system, irrespective of whether it proceeds from an eternal self-existing spiritual source or from an embodied soul, depends on the existence in the body of a subtle life element known as *prana*, which pervades each cell of every tissue and fluid in the organism, much in the same way that electricity pervades each atom of a battery.

This vital element has a biological counterpart as thought has a biological complement in the brain, in the shape of an extremely fine biochemical essence of a highly delicate and volatile nature, extracted by the nerves from the surrounding organic mass. After extraction, this vital essence resides in the brain and the nervous system, and is capable of generating a subtle radiation impossible to isolate by laboratory analysis. It circulates in the organism as motor impulse and sensation, conducting all the organic functions of the body, permeated and worked by the super-intelligent cosmic life energy, or *prana*, by which it is continuously affected, just as the sensitive chemical layer on a photographic plate is affected by light. The term *prana*, as used by authorities on Yoga, signifies both the cosmic life energy and its subtle biological conductor in the body, the two being inseparable. At the very moment the body dies, the rare organic essence immediately undergoes chemical changes, ceasing to serve as a channel for the former in the previous capacity. Normally, the work of extraction of *prana* to feed the brain is done by a limited group of nerves, operating in a circumscribed area of the organism, with the result that the consciousness of an individual displays no variation in its nature or extent during the span of his life, exhibiting a constancy which is in sharp contrast to the continuously changing appearance of his body. With the awakening of Kundalini, the arrangement suffers a radical alteration affecting the entire nervous system, as a result of which other and more extensive groups of nerves are stirred to activity, leading to the transmission of an enormously enhanced supply of a more concentrated form of *pranic* radiation into the brain drawn from a vastly increased area of the body. The far-reaching effects of this immensely augmented flow of a new form of vital current into the cephalic cavity through the spinal cord before the system becomes fully accustomed to it may be visualized by considering the effects of a sudden increase in the flow of blood to the brain such as faintness, complete insensibility, excitement, irritability, or, in extreme cases, delirium, paralysis, death.

The awakening may be gradual or sudden, varying in intensity and effect according to the development, constitution, and temperament of different individuals; but in most cases it results in a greater instability of the emotional nature and a greater liability to aberrant mental conditions in the subject, mainly owing to tainted heredity, faulty modes of conduct, or immoderation in any shape or form. Leaving out the extreme cases, which end in madness, this generalization applies to all the categories of men in whom Kundalini is congenitally more or less active, comprising mystics, mediums, men of genius, and those of an exceptionally high intellectual or artistic development only a shade removed from genius. In the case of those in whom the awakening occurs all at once as the result of Yoga or other spiritual practices, the sudden impact of powerful vital currents on the brain and other organs is often attended with grave risk and strange mental conditions, varying from moment to moment, exhibiting in the beginning the abnormal peculiarities of a medium, mystic, genius, and madman all rolled into one.

I had absolutely no knowledge of the technicalities of the science or the mode of operation of the great energy or of the spheres of its activity, as vast and as varied as humanity itself. I did not know that I had dug down to the very roots of my being and that my whole life was at stake. Like the vast majority of men interested in Yoga I had no idea that a system designed to develop the latent possibilities and nobler qualities in man could be fraught with such danger at times as to destroy the sanity or crush life out of one by the sheer weight of entirely foreign and uncontrollable conditions of the mind.

On the third day of the awakening I did not feel myself in a mood for meditation and passed the time in bed, not a little uneasy about the abnormal state of my mind and the exhausted condition of my body. The next day when I sat for meditation, after a practically sleepless night, I found to my consternation that I completely lacked the power to concentrate my attention on any point for even a brief interval and that a thin stream of the radiant essence, which had impinged on my brain with such vivifying and elevating effect on the first two occasions, was now pouring into it automatically with a sinister light that instead of uplifting had a most depressing influence on me.

The days that followed had all the appearance of a prolonged nightmare. It seemed as if I had abruptly precipitated myself from the steady rock of normality into a madly racing whirlpool of abnormal existence. The keen desire to sit and meditate, which had always been present during the preceding days, disappeared suddenly and was replaced by a feeling of horror of the supernatural. I wanted to fly from even the thought of it. At the same time I felt a sudden distaste for work and conversation, with the inevitable result that being left with nothing to keep myself engaged, time hung heavily on me, adding to the already distraught condition of my mind. The nights were even more terrible. I could not bear to have a light in my room after I had retired to bed. The moment my head touched the pillow a large tongue of flame sped across the spine into the interior of my head. It appeared as if the stream of living light continuously rushing through the spinal cord into the cranium gathered greater speed and volume during the hours of darkness. Whenever I closed my eyes I found myself looking into a weird circle of light, in which luminous currents swirled and eddied, moving rapidly from side to side. The spectacle was fascinating but awful, invested with a supernatural awe which sometimes chilled the very marrow in my bones.

Only a few days before it had been my habit, when in bed at night, to invite sleep by pursuing a pleasant chain of thoughts which often led me, without revealing the exact moment when it happened, from the waking state into the fantastic realm of dreams. Now everything was altered. I tossed restlessly from side to side without being able for hours to bring my agitated mind to the degree of composure needed to bring sleep. After extinguishing the lights, instead of seeing myself in darkness wafted gradually to a delicious state of rest preparatory to sleep, I found myself staring fearfully into a vast internal glow, disquieting and threatening at times, always in rapid motion as if the particles of an ethereal luminous stuff crossed and recrossed each other, resembling the ceaseless movement of wildly leaping lustrous clouds of spray rising from a waterfall which, lighted by the sun, rushes down foaming into a seething pool.

Sometimes it seemed as if a jet of molten copper, mounting up through the spine, dashed against my crown and fell in a scintillating shower of vast dimensions all around me. I gazed at it fascinated, with fear gripping my heart. Occasionally it resembled a fireworks display of great magnitude. As far as I could look inwardly with my mental eye, I saw only a brilliant shower or a glowing pool of light. I seemed to shrink in size when compared to the gigantic halo that surrounded me, stretching out on every side in undulating waves of copper colour distinctly perceptible in the surrounding darkness, as if the optic centre in the brain was now in direct contact with an extremely subtle, luminous substance in perpetual motion, flooding the brain and nervous system, without the intervention of the intermediary channels of the retina and the optic nerve.

I seemed to have touched accidentally the lever of an unknown mechanism, hidden in the extremely intricate and yet unexplored nervous structure in the body, releasing a hitherto held up torrent which, impinging upon the auditory and optic regions, created the sensation of roaring sounds and weirdly moving lights, introducing an entirely new and unexpected feature in the normal working of the mind that gave to all my thoughts and actions the semblance of unreality and abnormality. For a few days I thought I was suffering from hallucinations, hoping that my condition would become normal again after some time. But instead of disappearing or even diminishing as the days went by, the abnormality became more and more pronounced, assuming gradually the state of an obsession, which grew in intensity as the luminous appearances became wilder and more fantastic and the noises louder and more uncanny. The dreadful thought began to take hold of my mind that I was irretrievably heading towards a disaster from which I was powerless to save myself.

To one uninitiated in the esoteric science of Kundalini, as I was at that time, all that transpired afterwards presented such an abnormal and unnatural appearance that I became extremely nervous about the outcome. I passed every minute of the time in a state of acute anxiety and tension, at a loss to know what had happened to me and why my system was functioning in such an entirely abnormal manner. I felt exhausted and spent. The day after the experience I suffered loss of appetite, and food tasted like ash in my mouth. My tongue was coated white, and there was a redness in the eyes never noticed before. My face wore a haggard and anxious expression, and there were acute disturbances in the digestive and excretory organs. I lost my regularity and found myself at the mercy of a newly released force about which I knew nothing, creating a tumultuous and agitated condition of the mind as the sweep of a tempest creates an agitation in the placid waters of a lake.

There was no remission in the current rising from the seat of Kundalini. I could feel it leaping across the nerves in my back and even across those lining the front part of my body from the loins upward. But most alarming was the way in which my mind acted and behaved after the incident. I felt as if I were looking at the world from a higher elevation than that from which I saw it before. It is very difficult to express my mental condition accurately. All I can say is that it seemed as if my cognitive faculty had undergone a transformation and that I had, as it were, mentally expanded. What was more startling and terrifying was the fact that the point of consciousness in me was not as invariable nor its condition as stable as it had been before. It expanded and contracted, regulated in a mysterious way by the radiant current that was flowing up from the lowest plexus. This widening and narrowing were accompanied by a host of terrors for me. At times I felt slightly elated with a transient morbid sense of well-being and achievement, forgetting for the time being the abnormal state I was in, but soon after was made acutely conscious of my critical condition and again oppressed by a tormenting cloud of fear. The few brief intervals of mental elation were followed by fits of depression much more prolonged and so acute that I had to muster all my strength and will-power to keep myself from succumbing completely to their influence. I sometimes gagged my mouth to keep from crying and fled from the solitude of my room to the crowded street to prevent myself from doing some desperate act.

For weeks I had no respite. Each morning heralded for me a new kind of terror, a fresh complication in the already disordered system, a deeper fit of melancholy or more irritable condition of the mind which I had to restrain to prevent it from completely overwhelming me by keeping myself alert, usually after a completely sleepless night; and after withstanding patiently the tortures of the day, I had to prepare myself for the even worse torment of the night. A man cheerfully overcomes insurmountable difficulties and bravely faces overwhelming odds when he is confident of his mental and physical condition. I completely lost confidence in my own mind and body and lived like a haunted, terror-stricken stranger in my own flesh, constantly reminded of my precarious state. My consciousness was in such a state of unceasing flux that I was never certain how it would behave within the next few minutes. It rose and fell like a wave, raising me one moment out of the clutches of fear to dash me again the next into the depths of despair. It seemed as if the stream of vitality rising into my brain through the backbone connected mysteriously with the region near the base of the spine was playing strange tricks with my imagination. Also I was unable to stop it or to resist its effect on my thoughts. Was I losing my mind? Were these the first indications of mental disorder? This thought constantly drove me to desperation. It was not so much the extremely weird nature of my mental condition as the fear of incipient madness or some grave disorder of the nervous system which filled me with growing dismay.

I lost all feeling of love for my wife and children. I had loved them fondly from the depths of my being. The fountain of love in me seemed to have dried up completely. It appeared as if a scorching blast had raced through every pore in my body, wiping out every trace of affection. I looked at my children again and again, trying to evoke the deep feeling with which I had regarded them previously, but in vain. My love for them seemed to be dead beyond recall. They appeared to me no better than strangers. To reawaken the emotion of love in my heart I fondled and caressed them, talked to them in endearing terms, but never succeeded in experiencing that spontaneity and warmth which are characteristic of true attachment. I knew they were my flesh and blood and was conscious of the duty I owed to them. My critical judgment was unimpaired, but love was dead. The recollection of my departed mother, whom I always remembered with deep affection, brought with it no wave of the deep emotion which I had invariably felt at the thought of her. I viewed this unnatural disappearance of a deep-rooted feeling with despondency, finding myself a different man altogether and my unhappiness increased at seeing myself robbed of that which gives life its greatest charm.

I studied my mental condition constantly with fear at my heart. When I compared my new conscious personality with what it had been before, I could definitely see a radical change. There had been an unmistakable extension. The vital energy which lighted the flame of being was pouring visibly inside my brain; this had not been the case before. The light, too, was impure and variable. The flame was not burning with a pure, imperceptible and steady lustre as in normal consciousness. It grew brighter and fainter by turns. No doubt the illumination spread over a wider circle, but it was not as clear and transparent as before. It seemed as if I were looking at the world through a haze. When I glanced at the sky I failed to notice the lovely azure I used to see before. My eyesight had always been good and even now there was nothing obviously wrong with it. I could easily read the smallest type and clearly distinguish objects at a distance. Obviously my vision was unimpaired, but there was something wrong with the cognitive faculty. The recording instrument was still in good order, but something was amiss with the observer.

In the normal man, the flow of the stream of consciousness is so nicely regulated that he can notice no variation in it from boyhood to death. He knows himself as a conscious entity, a nondimensional point of awareness located more particularly in the head with a faint extension covering the trunk and limbs. When he closes his eyes to study it attentively, he ends by observing a conscious presence, himself in fact, round the region of the head. As I could easily discern even in that condition of mental disquietude, this field of consciousness in me had vastly increased. It was akin to that which I had experienced in the vision, but divested of every trace of happiness which had characterized my first experience. On the contrary, it was gloomy and fear-ridden, depressed instead of cheerful, murky instead of clearly transparent. It seemed as if prolonged concentration had opened a yet partially developed centre in the brain which depended for its fuel on the stream of energy constantly rushing upward from the reproductive region. The enlarged conscious field was the creation of this hitherto closed chamber, which was now functioning imperfectly, first because it had been forced open prematurely, and secondly because I was utterly ignorant of the way to adjust myself to the new development.

For weeks I wrestled with the mental gloom caused by my abnormal condition, growing more despondent each day. My face became extremely pale and my body thin and weak. I felt a distaste for food and found fear clutching my heart the moment I swallowed anything. Often I left the plate untouched. Very soon my whole intake of food amounted to a cup or two of milk and a few oranges. Beyond that I could eat nothing. I knew I could not survive for long on such an insufficient diet, but I could not help it. I was burning inside but had no means to assuage the fire. While my intake of food was drastically reduced, the daily expenditure of energy increased tremendously. My restlessness had assumed such a state that I could not sit quietly for even half an hour. When I did so, my attention was drawn irresistibly towards the strange behaviour of my mind. Immediately the ever-present sense of fear was intensified, and my heart thumped violently. I had to divert my attention somehow to free myself from the horror of my condition.

In order to prevent my mind from dwelling again and again on itself, I took recourse to walking. On rising in the morning, as long as I possessed the strength to do so, I left immediately for a slow walk to counteract the effect of an oppressive sleepless night, when, forced to lie quiet in the darkness, I had no alternative but to be an awed spectator of the weird and fearsome display visible inside. On the way, I met scores of my acquaintances taking their morning constitutional, laughing and talking as they went. I could not share their enjoyment, and passed them in silence with merely a nod or gesture of salutation. I had no interest in any person or in any subject in the world. My own abnormality blotted out everything else from my mind. During the day I walked in my room or in the compound, diverting my attention from object to object without allowing it to rest on one particular thing for any length of time. I counted my steps or looked at the ceiling or at the wall, at the floor or at the surrounding objects one by one, at each for but a fleeting instant, thus with all the will-power at my command preventing my brain from attaining a state of fixity at any time. I was fighting desperately against my own unruly mind.

But how long could my resistance last? How long could I save myself from madness creeping upon me? My starving body was becoming weaker and weaker; my legs tottered under me while I walked, and yet walk I had to if I was to rid myself of the clutching terror which gripped my heart as soon as I allowed my mind to brood upon itself. My memory became weaker and I faltered in my talk, while the anxious expression on my face deepened. At the blackest moments, my eyebrows drew together into an anxious frown, the thickly wrinkled forehead and a wild look in my gleaming eyes giving my countenance a maniacal expression. Several times during the day I glanced at myself in the looking-glass or felt my pulse, and to my horror found myself deteriorating more and more. I do not know what sustained my will so that even in a state of extreme terror I could maintain control over my actions and gestures. No one could even suspect what was happening to me inside. I knew that but a thin line now separated me from lunacy, and yet I gave no indication of my condition to anyone. I suffered unbearable torture in silence, weeping internally at the sad turn of events, blaming myself bitterly again and again for having delved into the supernatural without first acquiring a fuller knowledge of the subject and providing against the dangers and risks of the path.

Even at the times of greatest dejection, and even when almost at the breaking point, something inside prevented me from consulting a physician. There was no psychiatrist at Jammu in those days, and even if there had been one, I am sure I should not have gone to see him. It was well that I did not do so. The little knowledge of diseases that I possessed was enough to tell me that my abnormality was unique, that it was neither purely psychic nor purely physical, but the outcome of an alteration in the nervous activity of my body, which no therapist on earth could correctly diagnose or cure. On the other hand, a single mistake in treatment in that highly dangerous condition, when the whole system was in a state of complete disorder and not amenable to control, might have proved fatal. Mistakes were inevitable in view of the entirely obscure and unidentifiable nature of the disease.

A skilled physician bases his observations on the symptoms present in an ailment, relying for the success of his treatment on the uniformity of pathological conditions in the normal human body. Physiological processes follow a certain specific rhythm which the body tries to maintain under all ordinary circumstances. In my case, since the basic element responsible for the rhythm and the uniformity was at the moment itself in a state of turmoil, the anarchy prevailing not only in the system but also in the sphere of thought, nay in the innermost recesses of my being, can be better imagined than described. I did not know then what I came to grasp later on—that an automatic mechanism, forced by the practice of meditation, had suddenly started to function with the object of reshaping my mind to make it fit for the expression of a more heightened and extended consciousness, by means of biological processes as natural and as governed by inviolable laws as the evolution of species or the development and birth of a child. But to my great misfortune I did not know this at the time. To the best of my knowledge, this mighty secret of nature is not known on earth today, although there is ample evidence to show that certain methods to deal with the condition, when brought about suddenly by the practice of Hatha Yoga, were fully known to the ancient adepts.

I studied my condition thoroughly from day to day to assure myself that what I experienced was real and not imaginary. Just as a man finding himself in an unbelievable situation pinches himself to make certain that he is not dreaming but awake, I invariably studied my bodily symptoms to find corroboration for my mental condition. It would be a fallacy to assume that I was the victim of a hallucination. Subsequent events and my present condition absolutely rule out that possibility. No, the crisis I was passing through was not a creation of my own imagination. It had a real physiological basis and was interwoven with the whole organic structure of my body. The entire machinery from the brain to the smallest organ was deeply involved, and there was no escape for me from the storm of nervous forces which blew through my system day and night, released unexpectedly by my own effort.

><

During recent times there have hardly been any instances of individuals in whom the serpent fire burnt ceaselessly from the day of awakening of Kundalini to the last, bringing about mental transformations known to and hinted at by the ancient sages of India. But that there have been many cases of a sporadic type in which the shakti* was active intermittently admits of no doubt. The mystics and saints of all countries, who from an early age are prone to transcendental visions and pass occasionally into ecstatic trances, thereafter reverting to their normal consciousness, belong to the latter category. The psychics and mediums and all those possessing the power of clairvoyance, mind reading, prediction, and similar supernormal faculties owe their surprising gifts to the action of an awakened Kundalini, operating in a limited way in the head without reaching the highest centre, when it only overshadows the whole consciousness. The same is true of the men of genius in whom the energy feeds certain specific regions of the brain, stimulating them to extraordinary phases of intellectual, literary, or artistic activity.

* Spiritual power manifesting itself as female energy in relation to its partner Shiva, the masculine "possessor of power."

In all the cases mentioned above, either the flow of the more potent vital current is so regulated and circumscribed that it does not create any disturbance in the system or, as in the case of mystics in whom the impact of the current on the brain is very powerful at times, the condition begins at birth so that the nervous system usually becomes accustomed to it from infancy, when one is not aware of the variations in consciousness nor able to place a meaning on the abnormal happenings in the body and feel the sense of fear. But even so, the latter have often to face many a crisis and to endure unusual suffering and torment before they acquire a stable and peaceful condition of the mind and are in a position to study and express comprehensively the experience which marks them as a class apart from the normal run of mortals. The individuals belonging to these categories, excepting mystics, do not perceive the luminosity and the movement of nervous currents, except in exceptional cases, as the flow of the vital energy is too restricted to create weird effects. Moreover, having been an integral part of the organism from birth, it becomes an inherent trait of their personalities.

The popular books on Yoga that I had read years before contained no hint of such an abnormal development and nerve-shattering experience. The learned authors confined themselves to the description of various postures and methods, all borrowed from the ancient writings on the subject. Few of them claimed to have had the experience but were eager to teach to others what they had never learned themselves. In some of the books there was a passing reference to Kundalini Yoga. A couple of pages or a small chapter was all that the authors thought sufficient for describing this most difficult and least known form of Yoga. It was stated that Kundalini represents the cosmic vital energy lying dormant in the human body which is coiled round the base of the spine, a little below the sexual organ, like a serpent, fast asleep and closing with her mouth the aperture of the *Sushumna*, the hairlike duct rising through the spinal cord to the conscious centre at the top of the head. When roused, Kundalini, they said, rises through the *Sushumna* like a streak of lightning carrying with her the vital energy of the body, which for the time being becomes cold and lifeless, with complete or partial cessation of vital functions, to join her divine spouse Shiva in the last or seventh centre in the brain. In the course of this process, the embodied self, freed from the bondage of flesh, passes into a condition of ecstasy known as *Samadhi*, realizing itself as deathless, full of bliss, and one with the all-pervading supreme consciousness. In only one or two writings were there vague hints of dangers to be met on the path. The nature of the danger and the methods to prevent or overcome it were not explained by the authors.

From the vague ideas I had gathered from these works or picked up in the course of discussions or talks about Yoga, it was only natural for me to infer that the abnormal condition I had brought upon myself was the direct outcome of my meditation. The experience I was having corresponded in every respect with the descriptions given of the ecstatic state by those who had attained this condition themselves; there was therefore no reason for me to doubt the validity or the possibility of my vision. There could be no mistake about the sounds I had heard and the effulgence I had perceived. Above all, there certainly could be no mistake about the transformation of my own consciousness, the nearest and the most intimate part of me, that I had experienced more than once, and the memory of which was so strong that it could never be effaced or mistaken for any other condition. It could not be a mere figment of my fancy because during the vision I still possessed the capacity to make a comparison between the extended state of consciousness and the normal one, and when it began to fade, I could perceive the contraction that was taking place. It was undoubtedly a real experience, and has been described with all the power of expression at their command by mystics and saints all over the world. But in my case there was one particular and unmistakable deviation from the usual type of vision: the most extraordinary sensation at the base of the spine followed by the flow of a radiant current through the spinal column into the head. This part of the strange experience tallied with the phenomena associated with the awakening of Kundalini, and hence I could not be mistaken in supposing that I had unknowingly aroused the coiled serpent, and that the serious disturbance in my nervous system as well as the extraordinary but most awful state I was in, was in some way occasioned by it.

I made no mention of my condition to anyone save my brother-in-law, who came to Jammu during those days on a short business visit. He was many years older than I and loved me like a son. I talked to him unreservedly, aware of his deep affection for me. He had himself practised meditation for many years under the guidance of a preceptor who claimed knowledge of Kundalini Yoga. Frank and noble by nature, he often narrated to me his own experiences in the simple manner of a child, seeking corroboration from me for the results he had achieved by his labours. Without the least pretension to knowledge, he gave me every bit of information he possessed, and thus in a way was instrumental in saving my life. My wife knew nothing of the life and death struggle in which I was engaged, but alarmed by my strange behaviour, lack of appetite, bodily disturbances, constant walks, and above all by the never-lifting cloud of anxiety and gloom on my face, she advised me again and again to consult a physician and constantly watched over me day and night, frantic with anxiety.

My brother-in-law could not grasp the significance of what I related to him, but said that his *guru* had once remarked that if by mistake Kundalini were aroused through any other *nadi* (nerve) except *Sushumna*, there was every danger of serious psychic and physical disturbances, ending in permanent disability, insanity, or death. This was particularly the case, the teacher had said, if the awakening occurred through *pingala* on the right side of the spine when the unfortunate man is literally burned to death due to excessive internal heat, which cannot be controlled by any external means. I was horrified by this statement and in desperation went to consult a learned ascetic from Kashmir who had come to spend the winter at Jammu. He heard me with patience and said that the experience I had undergone could not at all be due to the awakening of the serpent power, as that was always blissful and could not be associated with any agency liable to cause disease or disturbance. He made another gruesome suggestion, heard from his teacher or picked up from some ancient work, to the effect that my malady was probably due to the venom of malignant spirits that beset the path of Yogis, and prescribed a decoction, which I never took.

On the suggestion of someone I glanced through a couple of books on Kundalini Yoga, translations in English of ancient Sanskrit texts. I could not read even a page attentively, the attempt involving fixity of attention which I was incapable of maintaining for any length of time. The least effort instantly aggravated my condition by increasing the flow of the newborn energy into the brain, which added to my terror and misery. I just glanced through the books, reading a line here and a paragraph there. The description of the symptoms that followed the awakening corroborated my own experience and firmly strengthened my conviction that I had roused the vital force dormant in me; but whether the agony of mind and body that I was passing through was an inevitable result of the awakening or whether I had drawn up the energy through a wrong nerve, I could not be sure. There was, however, one very briefly stated injunction—call it accident or divine guidance—I picked up from the huge mass of material in that very cursory glance. It was to the effect that during the course of the practice the student is not permitted to keep his stomach empty, but should take a light meal every three hours. This brief advice, flashing across my brain at a most critical moment when I hovered between life and death and had lost every hope of survival, saved my life and sanity and continues to do so to this day.

At the time I paid no attention to this significant hint which, based on the experience of countless men, many of whom had probably lost their lives in the attempt to arouse the serpent, had come down through the ages as guidance for the initiates. Even if I had tried my hardest to do so, I could not have acted upon the advice at that time, as food was so abhorrent to me that my stomach revolted at the mere thought of it. I was burning in every part of my body while my mind, like a floating balloon, bobbed up and down and swayed sideways erratically, unable to keep itself steady even for a moment.

Whenever my mind turned upon itself I always found myself staring with growing panic into the unearthly radiance that filled my head, swirling and eddying like a fearsome whirlpool; even found its reflection in the pitch darkness of my room during the slowly dragging hours of the night. Not infrequently it assumed horrible shapes and postures, as if satanic faces were grinning and inhuman forms gesticulating at me in the blackness. This happened night after night for months, weakening my will and sapping my resistance until I felt unable to endure the fearful ordeal any longer, certain that at any moment I might succumb to the relentlessly pursuing horror and, bidding farewell to my life and sanity, rush out of the room a raving maniac. But I persisted, determined to hold on as long as I had a vestige of will-power, resolved at the first sign of breaking to surrender my life rather than lose myself in the ghastly wilderness of insanity.

When it was day I longed for the night and during the night I fervently prayed for the day. As the time wore on, my hope dwindled and desperation seized me. There was no relaxation in the tension or any abatement in the ceaselessly haunting fear or any relief from the fiery stream that darted through my nerves and poured into my agonized brain. On the other hand, as my vitality ebbed as a result of fasts, and my resistance weakened, the malady was aggravated to such a pitch that every moment I expected the end.

It was in such a frame of mind that the holy festival of Shivratri or the night of Shiva, came to pass towards the end of February. As usual every year my wife had prepared painstakingly some dainty dishes on the day and gently insisted that I, too, should partake of the food. Not to disappoint her and cast a cloud of gloom on her already anxiety-filled mind, I acquiesced and forcibly swallowed a few morsels, then gave up and washed my hands. Immediately I felt a sinking sensation at the pit of my stomach, a fiery stream of energy shot into my head, and I felt myself lifted up and up, expanding awfully with unbearable terror clutching at me from every side. I felt a reeling sensation while my hands and feet grew cold as ice, as if all the heat had escaped from them to feed the fiery vapour in the head which had risen through the cord like the ruddy blast from a furnace and now, acting like a poison on the brain, struck me numb. I was overpowered by faintness and giddiness.

I staggered to my feet and dragged myself heavily towards my bed in the adjacent room. With trembling hands I lifted up the cover and slipped in, trying to stretch myself into a position of ease. But I was in a terrible condition, burning internally from head to toes, outwardly cold as ice, and shivering as if stricken with ague. I felt my pulse; it was racing madly and my heart was thumping wildly below my ribs, its pounding distinctly audible to me. But what horrified me was the intensity of the fiery currents that now darted through my body, penetrating into every part and every organ. My brain worked desperately, unable to give coherence to my frenzied thoughts. To call in a doctor for consultation in such an unheard of disease would be a mere waste of effort. His first thought on hearing of my symptoms would be to turn to a lunatic asylum. It would be futile on my part to seek help from any other quarter for such an affliction. What could I do then to save myself from this torture? Could it be that in my previous semi-starved condition, subsisting only on a few oranges and a little milk, the fiery current could not attain such awful intensity as it had done now with the entry of solid food in my stomach? How could I save myself? Where could I go to escape from the furnace raging in my interior?

The heat grew every moment, causing such unbearable pain that I writhed and twisted from side to side while streams of cold perspiration poured down my face and limbs. But still the heat increased and soon it seemed as if innumerable red-hot pins were coursing through my body, scorching and blistering the organs and tissues like flying sparks. Suffering the most excruciating torture, I clenched my hands and bit my lips to stop myself from leaping out of bed and crying at the top of my voice. The throbbing of my heart grew more and more terrific, acquiring such a spasmodic violence that I thought it must either stop beating or burst. Flesh and blood could not stand such strain without giving way any moment. It was easy to see that the body was valiantly trying to fight the virulent poison speeding across the nerves and pouring into the brain. But the fight was so unequal and the fury let loose in my system so lethal that there could be not the least doubt about the outcome. There were dreadful disturbances in all the organs, each so alarming and painful that I wonder how I managed to retain my self-possession under the onslaught. The whole delicate organism was burning, withering away completely under the fiery blast racing through its interior.

I knew I was dying and that my heart could not stand the tremendous strain for long. My throat was scorched and every part of my body flaming and burning, but I could do nothing to alleviate the dreadful suffering. If a well or river had been near I would have jumped into its cold depths, preferring death to what I was undergoing. But there was no well and the river was half a mile away. With a great effort I got up, trembling, with the idea of pouring a few buckets of cold water over my head to abate the dreadful heat. But at that moment my eyes fell on my small daughter, Ragina, lying in the next bed awake, watching my feverish movements with wide-open anxious eyes. With the remnant of sense still left in me I could understand that the least unusual movement on my part at that time would make her cry and that if I started to pour water over my body at such an unearthly hour, both she and her mother, who was busy in the kitchen, would almost die with fright. The thought restrained me and I decided to bear the internal agony until the end, which could not be far off.

What had happened to me all of a sudden? What devilish power of the underworld held me in its relentless grasp? Was I doomed to die in this dreadful way, leaving a corpse with blackened face and limbs to make people wonder what unheard-of horror had overtaken me as a punishment for crimes committed in a previous birth? I racked my distracted brain for a way of escape, only to meet blank despair on every side. The effort exhausted me and I felt myself sinking, dully conscious of the scalding sea of pain in which I was drowning. I tried desperately to rouse myself, only to sink back again, deadened by a torment beyond my power to endure. After a while with a sudden, inexplicable revival of strength, marking the onset of delirium, I came back to life with a shred of sanity left, Almighty alone knows how, just sufficient to prevent me from giving way completely to acts of madness and self-violence.

Pulling the cover over my face, I stretched myself to my full length on the bed, burning in every fibre, lashed as it were by a fiery rain of red-hot needles piercing my skin. At this moment a fearful idea struck me. Could it be that I had aroused Kundalini through *pingala* or the solar nerve which regulates the flow of heat in the body and is located on the right side of *Sushumna*? If so, I was doomed, I thought desperately and as if by divine dispensation the idea flashed across my brain to make a last-minute attempt to rouse *Ida*, or the lunar nerve on the left side, to activity, thus neutralizing the dreadful burning effect of the devouring fire within. With my mind reeling and senses deadened with pain, but with all the will-power left at my command, I brought my attention to bear on the left side of the seat of Kundalini, and tried to force an imaginary cold current upward through the middle of the spinal cord. In that extraordinarily extended, agonized, and exhausted state of consciousness, I distinctly felt the location of the nerve and strained hard mentally to divert its flow into the central channel. Then, as if waiting for the destined moment, a miracle happened.

There was a sound like a nerve thread snapping and instantaneously a silvery streak passed zigzag through the spinal cord, exactly like the sinuous movement of a white serpent in rapid flight, pouring an effulgent, cascading shower of brilliant vital energy into my brain, filling my head with a blissful lustre in place of the flame that had been tormenting me for the last three hours. Completely taken by surprise at this sudden transformation of the fiery current, darting across the entire network of my nerves only a moment before, and overjoyed at the cessation of pain, I remained absolutely quiet and motionless for some time, tasting the bliss of relief with a mind flooded with emotion, unable to believe I was really free of the horror. Tortured and exhausted almost to the point of collapse by the agony I had suffered during the terrible interval, I immediately fell asleep, bathed in light and for the first time after weeks of anguish felt the sweet embrace of restful sleep.

As if rudely shaken out of my slumber I awoke after about an hour. The stream of lustre was still pouring in my head, my brain was clear, my heart and pulse had stopped racing, the burning sensations and the fear had almost vanished; but my throat was still dry, my mouth parched, and I found myself in a state of extreme exhaustion, as if every ounce of energy had been drained out of me. Exactly at that moment another idea occurred to me; as if suggested by an invisible intelligence, and with irresistible power came the direction that I should eat something immediately. I motioned to my wife, who as usual was lying awake in her bed anxiously watching my every movement, to fetch me a cup of milk and a little bread. Taken aback by this unusual and untimely request, she hesitated a moment, and then complied without a word. I ate the bread, swallowing it with difficulty with the help of the milk and immediately fell asleep again.

I woke up again after about two hours, considerably refreshed by the sleep. My head was still filled with the glowing radiance and, to my surprise, in this heightened and lustrous state of consciousness I could distinctly perceive a tongue of the golden flame searching my stomach for food and moving round along the nerves lining it. I took a few bites of bread and another cup of milk, and as soon as I had done so I found the halo in the head contracting and a larger tongue of flame licking my stomach, as if a part of the streaming energy pouring into my brain was being diverted to the gastric region to expedite the process of digestion. I lay awake, dumb with wonder, watching this living radiance moving from place to place through the whole digestive tract, caressing the intestines and the liver, while another stream poured into the kidneys and the heart. I pinched myself to make sure whether I was dreaming or asleep, absolutely dumbfounded by what I was witnessing in my own body, entirely powerless to regulate or to guide the current. Unlike the horror I had experienced before, I felt no discomfort now; all that I could feel was a gentle and soothing warmth moving through my body as the current travelled from point to point. I watched this wonderful play silently, my whole being filled with boundless gratitude to the Unseen for this timely deliverance from a dreadful fate; and a new assurance began to shape itself in my mind that the serpent fire was in reality now at work in my exhausted and agonized body; and that I was safe.

Gopi Krishna, *Kundalini: The Evolutionary Energy in Man*

Truth comes full circle
As departing light
From infinite space
Returns to the heart
Still what it was,
Embracing all.

              Kathleen Raine, from *On a Deserted Shore*

→ 5 ←

Strengthening the Self

Carl Jung said, "We count for something only because of the essential we embody, and if we do not embody that, life is wasted."

In the process of revelation, after the initial experience of a broader reality, of the existence of the spiritual realms, comes the strengthening of the Self. The Self is our higher being, composed of the divinity that stirs within us—our individual and unique soul and the purpose of its role in our lives and the lives of others. It manifests itself subtly in our bodies, which is often called the causal body of our being, and in our minds as the consciousness of our being. All these aspects of the Self need acknowledgement and care through wilful spiritual practices that fortify and sustain it as it prepares to break free from the previous self-imposed blockages to transcend into the greater consciousness at work in the world. This "multisignificational journey between Being and the world" as Vaclav Havel describes it in his letter to his wife, Olga, is a submission to spiritual destiny.

The recognition of the individuality and uniqueness of the Self is only the beginning. The incorporation of the Self into the broader community is the next step. Thomas Merton's and Bede Griffiths' personal revelations led them to monasteries and the monastic life, where they became part of a spiritual community. Ram Dass, respected leader, counsellor, and writer on spiritual wisdom, writes in his classic *Be Here Now* of "living faith in what is possible"—of going forward united with the whole. Ram Dass' story of his revelation of his future purpose is as amusing and poignant and as down-to-earth as Ram Dass is himself. In his earlier life as a Harvard professor of psychology, Richard Alpert and his colleague Timothy Leary caused quite a controversy in the mid-sixties for using psychedelic experiences—initiated by the mushroom *Psilocybe mexicana* and LSD—as means to mind expansion.

In this chapter, I have introduced two subsections to explore the ways of strengthening the Self, one being the spiritual disciplines for the body, the mind, and the soul—the separation from community to pursue individual conscious awareness; the other being Consciousness Transcendence, where the mind, body, and soul join as partners in receptivity to the greater whole, the collective consciousness which operates simultaneously in the higher realms around us.

><

The root-word *buddh* means to wake up, to know, to understand; and he or she who wakes up and understands is called a Buddha. It is as simple as that. The capacity to wake up, to understand, and to love is called Buddha nature. When Buddhists say "I take refuge in the Buddha," they are expressing trust in their own capacity of understanding, of becoming awake. The Chinese and the Vietnamese say, "I go back and rely on the Buddha in me." Adding "in me" makes it very clear that you yourself are the Buddha.

Thich Nhat Hanh, *Being Peace*

God is everywhere, in everything. Most of all He is right within yourself. You do not exist for the world—the world exists for you.

Meher Baba, *Life at Its Best*

The foolish being who lives making even the slightest distinction between the supreme Self and his own Self will always be subject to fear.

Swami Muktananda, *Play of Consciousness*

Dear Olga,

Birth from the maternal womb—as the moment one sets out on one's journey through life—presents a telling image of the initial condition of humanity: a state of separation. Of release. Of breaking away. The human race becomes distinct from the animal kingdom; a living cell comes into being in a dead ocean; a planet that will one day be occupied by man becomes self-sustaining: in these events can be read the history, or the prehistory, of a constant, and constantly recurring, state of separation. The idea that the human spirit and reason are constituted by a severing of something from the hidden spirit and reason of Being is one that is constantly occurring to us in one form or another, and at the very least, it suggests that "separation" is a fundamental experience that man has of himself and his existence in the world. With the advent of humanity, however, something intrinsically new has appeared, something that ultimately is not referrable to anything else, something that is, but is no longer spontaneously in "Being as such"; something that is, but somehow "otherwise," that stands against everything, even against itself. The miracle of the subject is born. The secret of the "I." The awareness of self. The awareness of the world. The mystery of freedom and responsibility. Man as a being that has fallen out of Being and therefore continually reaches toward it, as the only entity by which and to which Being has revealed itself as a question, as a secret and as meaning.

It seems to me that the notion of separation as humanity's starting point helps us establish our bearings when we explore the stage on which human existence is constituted and its drama unfolded.

Separation creates a deeply contradictory situation: man is not what he has set out into, or rather, he is not his experience of what he has set out into. To him, this terrain—the world—is an alien land. Every step of the way, he comes up against his own "otherness" in the world and his otherness vis-à-vis himself. This terrain is essentially unintelligible to man. He feels unsettled and threatened by it. We experience the world as something not our own, something from which meaning must first be wrested and which, on the contrary, is constantly taking meaning away from us. No longer protected and hidden by spontaneous, unseparated participation in Being, we are exposed to what Being, for us, has become by virtue of our separation— the world of existing entities. Exposed and vulnerable to it. On the other hand, we are no longer what we have become separated from, either: we lose the certitude of Being, of our former rootedness in its integrity, totality, and universality, of our involvement in its general "identity." In other words, we are no longer identical with Being. We do not experience it simply, from "inside," but only as our own alienation from it. The certitude of our being in Being has irredeemably become a thing of the past, clouds have darkened the sky and we are flung into the uncertainty of the world. A recollection of this past, its birthmark and the ineradicable seal of our origins in it go with us every step we take. But even that, to a considerable extent, is alienated from us (if only because we reflect upon it) and as such, it is in fact a part of what we have been thrown into or what we have fallen into and what drives us—in the alienness of the world—into situations we do not fully understand, which we suffer, but cannot avoid.

This inner echo of a home or a paradise forever lost to us—as a constitutive part of our "I"—defines the extent of what we are destined to lack and what we therefore cannot help but reach toward: for does not the hunger for meaning, for an answer to the question of what—in the process of becoming ourselves—we have become, derive from the recollection of a separated being for its state of primordial being in Being? From the other side, the alien world into which we are thrown beckons to us and tempts us. On the one hand we are constantly exposed to the temptation to stop asking questions and adapt ourselves to the world as it presents itself to us, to sink into it, to forget ourselves in it, to lie our way out of our selves and our "otherness" and thus to simplify our existence-in-the-world. At the same time we are persuaded over and over again that we can only reach toward meaning within the dimensions of this world, as it lies before us, by being open to the opening out of meaning within the world.

Thus is man alienated from Being, but precisely because of this he is seared by longing for its intensity (which he understands as meaningfulness), by a desire to merge with it and thus to transcend himself totally. As such, however, he is also alienated from the world in which he finds himself, a world that captivates and imprisons him. He is an alien in the world because he is still somehow bound up in Being, and he is alienated from Being because he has been thrown into the world. His drama unfolds in the rupture between his orientation "upward" and "backward" and a constant falling "downward" and into "now." He is surrounded by the horizon of the world, from which there is no escape, and at the same time, consumed by a longing to break through this horizon and step beyond it.

The absurdity of being at the intersection of this dual state of "thrownness," or rather this dual expulsion, can understandably give a person a reason (or an excuse) for giving up. He may also, however, accept it as a unique challenge enjoined upon his freedom, a challenge to set out—by virtue of all his thrownnesses—on a multisignificational journey between Being and the world (and thus, at the same time, to establish the outlines of his identity); to undertake it, aware that his goal lies beyond his field of vision, but also that precisely and only that fact can reveal the journey, make it possible and ultimately give it meaning; to fulfill uniquely the enigmatic mission of humanity in the history of Being by submitting to his destiny in an authentic, thoughtful way, a way that is faithful to everything originally good and therefore effective, and to make this entirely lucid acceptance of his entirely obscure task a source of sage delight to him.

I kiss you,
Vašek

Vaclav Havel, *Letters to Olga*

Love is our true destiny. We do not find the meaning of life by ourselves alone—we find it with another. We do not discover the secret of our lives merely by study and calculation in our own isolated meditations. The meaning of our life is a secret that has to be revealed to us in love, *by the one we love*. And if this love is unreal, the secret will not be found, the meaning will never reveal itself, the message will never be decoded. At best, we will receive a scrambled and partial message, one that will deceive and confuse us. We will never be fully real until we let ourselves fall in love—either with another human person or with God.

Thomas Merton, *Love and Living*

Only in the mirror of relationship do you see the face of what is.

J. Krishnamurti, *Krishnamurti's Journal*

Bhagwan Dass

I was in the Blue Tibetan with my friend and these other people, and in walked this very extraordinary guy, at least extraordinary with regard to his height. He was 6'7" and he had long blond hair and a long blond beard. He was a Westerner, an American, and was wearing holy clothes—a dhoti (a cloth Indian men wear instead of pants) and so on, and when he entered, he came directly over to our table and sat down.

Now, up until then, I had found this interesting thing that I don't think I could have labeled until that moment. Once, when I had met Gesha Wangyal at Freehold, N.J., I knew I was meeting a being who "knew," but I couldn't get to it because I wasn't ready, somehow. We were very close— we loved each other extraordinarily, but I hadn't been able to really absorb whatever I needed to absorb. Now here was this young fellow and again, I had the feeling I had met somebody who "Knew."

I don't know how to describe this to you, except that I was deep in my despair: I had gone through game, after game, after game, first being a professor at Harvard, then being a psychedelic spokesman, and still people were constantly looking into my eyes, like "Do you know?" Just that subtle little look, and I was constantly looking into their eyes—"Do you know?" And there we were, "Do you?" "Do you?" "Maybe he…" "Do you…?" And there was always that feeling that everybody was very close and we all knew we knew, but nobody quite knew. I don't know how to describe it, other than that.

And I met this guy and there was no doubt in my mind. It was just like meeting a rock. It was just solid, all the way through. Everywhere I pressed, there he was!

We were staying in a hotel owned by the King or the Prince, or something, because we were going first class, so we spirited this fellow up to our suite in the Sewalti Hotel and for five days we had a continuing seminar. We had this extraordinarily beautiful Indian sculptor Harish Johari, who was our guide and friend. Harish, this fellow, Bhagwan Dass and David and I sat there and for five days high on Peach Melbas and Hashish and Mescaline, we had a seminar with Alexandra David Neehl's books and Sir John Woodroffe's Serpent Power, and so on. At the end of five days, I was still absolutely staggered by this guy. He had started to teach me some mantras and working with beads. When it came time to leave, to go to Japan, I had the choice of going on to Japan on my first-class route, or going off with this guy, back into India on a temple pilgrimage. He had no money and I had no money and it was going to change my style of life considerably. I thought, "Well, look, I came to India to find something and I still think this guy knows—I'm going to follow him."

But there was also the counter thought, "How absurd—who's writing this bizarre script. Here I am—I've come half-way around the world and I'm going to follow, through India, a 23-year-old guy from Laguna Beach, California."

I said to Harish and to David, "Do you think I'm making a mistake?" And Harish said, "No, he is a very high guy." And so I started to follow him—literally follow him.

Now, I'm suddenly barefoot. He has said, "You're not going to wear shoes, are you?" That sort of thing. And I've got a shoulder bag and my dhoti and blisters on my feet and dysentery, the likes of which you can't imagine, and all he says is, "Well, fast for a few days."

He's very compassionate, but no pity.

And we're sleeping on the ground, or on these wooden tables that you get when you stop at monasteries, and my hip bones ache. I go through an extraordinary physical breakdown, become very childlike and he takes care of me. And we start to travel through temples—to Baneshwar and Konarak and so on.

I see that he's very powerful, so extraordinarily powerful—he's got an ectara, a one-stringed instrument, and I've got a little Tibetan drum, and we go around to the villages and people rush out and they touch our feet because we're holy men, which is embarrassing to me because I'm not a holy man—I'm obviously who I am—a sort of overage hippie, Western explorer, and I feel very embarrassed when they do that and they give us food. And he plays and sings and the Hindu people love him and revere him. And he's giving away all my money....

But I'm clinging tight to my passport and my return ticket to America, and a traveler's check that I'll need to get me to Delhi. Those things I'm going to hold on to. And my bottle of LSD, in case I should find something interesting.

And during these travels he's starting to train me in a most interesting way. We'd be sitting somewhere and I'd say,

"Did I ever tell you about the time that Tim and I..."

And he'd say, "Don't think about the past. Just be here now."

Silence.

And I'd say, "How long do you think we're going to be on this trip?"

And he'd say, "Don't think about the future. Just be here now."

I'd say, "You know, I really feel crummy, my hips are hurting..."

"Emotions are like waves. Watch them disappear in the distance on the vast calm ocean."

He had just sort of wiped out my whole game. That was it—that was my whole trip—emotions, and past experiences, and future plans. I was, after all, a great story teller.

So we were silent. There was nothing to say.

He'd say, "You eat this," or, "Now you sleep here." And all the rest of the time we sang holy songs. That was all there was to do.

Or he would teach me Asanas—Hatha Yoga postures.

But there was no conversation. I didn't know anything about his life. He didn't know anything about my life. He wasn't the least bit interested in all of the extraordinary dramas that I had collected.... He was the first person I couldn't seduce into being interested in all this. He just didn't care.

And yet, I never felt so profound an intimacy with another being. It was as if he were inside of my heart. And what started to blow my mind was that everywhere we went, he was at home.

If we went to a Thereavaden Buddhist monastery, he would be welcomed and suddenly he would be called Dharma Sara, a Southern Buddhist name, and some piece of clothing he wore, I suddenly saw, was also worn by all the other monks and I realized that he was an initiate in that scene and they'd welcomed him and he'd be in the inner temple and he knew all the chants and he was doing them.

We'd come across some Shavites, followers of Shiva, or some of the Swamis, and I suddenly realized that he was one of them. On his forehead would be the appropriate tilik, or mark, and he would be doing their chanting.

We'd meet Kargyupa lamas from Tibet and they would all welcome him as a brother, and he knew all their stuff. He had been in India for five years, and he was so high that everybody just welcomed him, feeling "he's obviously one of us."

I couldn't figure out what his scene was. All I personally felt was this tremendous pull toward Buddhism because Hinduism always seemed a little gauche—the paintings were a little too gross—the colors were bizarre and the whole thing was too melodramatic and too much emotion. I was pulling toward that clean, crystal-clear simplicity of the Southern Buddhists or the Zen Buddhists.

After about three months, I had a visa problem and we went to Delhi, and I was still quite unsure of my new role as a holy man and so when I got to Delhi, I took $4.00 out of my little traveler's check and bought a pair of pants and a shirt and a tie and took my horn-rimmed glasses out of my shoulder bag and stuck them back on and I became again Dr. Alpert, to go to the visa office. Dr. Alpert, who had a grant from the Folk Art Museum of New Mexico for collecting musical instruments and I did my whole thing.

I kept my beads in my pocket. Because I didn't feel valid in this other role. And then the minute I got my visa fixed, he had to have his annual visa worked over, and he had to go to a town nearby, which we went to, and we were welcomed at this big estate and given a holy man's house, and food brought to us, and he said, "You sit here. I'm going to see about my visa."

He told me just what to do. I was just like a baby. "Eat this." "Sit here." "Do this." And I just gave up. He knew. Do you know? I'll follow you.

He spoke Hindi fluently. My Hindi was very faltering. So he could handle it all.

We had spent a few weeks in a Chinese Buddhist monastery in Sarnath, which was extraordinarily powerful and beautiful, and something was happening to me but I couldn't grasp the total nature of it at all.

There was a strange thing about him. At night he didn't seem to sleep like I did. That is, any time I'd wake up at night, I'd look over and he would be sitting in the lotus position. And sometimes I'd make believe I was asleep and then open sort of a half-eye to see if he wasn't cheating—maybe he was sleeping Now—but he was always in the lotus posture.

Sometimes I'd see him lie down, but I would say that 80 percent of the time when I would be sleeping heavily, he would be sitting in some state or other, which he'd never describe to me. But he was not in personal contact— I mean, there was no wave or moving around, or nothing seemed to happen to him..

The night at that estate, I went out—I had to go to the bathroom and I went out under the stars and the following event happened....

The previous January 20th, at Boston in the Peter Bent Brigham Hospital, my mother had died of a spleen illness—the bone marrow stopped producing blood and the spleen took over and grew very large and they removed it and then she died. It had been a long illness and I had been with her through the week prior to her death and through it we had become extremely close. We had transcended mother-child and personalities and we had come into true contact. I spent days in the hospital just meditating. And I felt no loss when she died. Instead there was a tremendous continuing contact with her. And in fact, when I had been in Nepal, I had had a vision of her one night when I was going to bed. I saw her up on the ceiling and I was wondering whether to go to India or go on to Japan, and she had a look that was the look of "You damn fool—you're always getting into hot water, but go ahead, and I think that's great." She looked peeved-pleased. It was like there were two beings in my mother. She was a middle-class woman from Boston, who wanted me to be absolutely responsible in the most culturally acceptable fashion, and then there was this swinger underneath—this spiritual being underneath who said, "—go, baby." And I felt these two beings in that look which supported my going back into India.

This night I'm under the stars, and I hadn't thought about her at all since that time. I'm under the stars, urinating, and I look up and the stars are very close because it's very dark and I suddenly experience a presence of mother, and I'm thinking about her—not about how she died or anything about that, I just feel her presence. It's very very powerful. And I feel great love for her and then I go back to bed.

Of course, Bhagwan Dass is not the least interested in any of my life, so he'd be the last person I'd talk to about my thoughts or visions.

The next morning he says, "We've got to go to the mountains. I've got a visa problem. We've got to go see my guru."

Now the term "guru" had meant for me, in the West, a sort of high-grade teacher. There was a Life article about Allen Ginsberg—"Guru goes to Kansas"—and Allen was embarrassed and said, "I'm not really a guru." And I didn't know what a guru really was....

Bhagwan Dass also said we were going to borrow the Land Rover, which had been left with this sculptor, to go to the mountains. And I said, I didn't want to borrow the Land Rover. I'd just gotten out of that horrible blue box and I didn't want to get back into it, and I didn't want the responsibility. David had left it with this Indian sculptor and he wouldn't want to loan it to us anyway. I got very sulky. I didn't want to go see a guru—and suddenly I wanted to go back to America in the worst way.

I thought, "What am I doing? I'm following this kid and all he is..." But he says, "We've got to do this," and so we go to the town where the sculptor lives and within half an hour the sculptor says, "You have to go see your guru? Take the Land Rover!"

Well, that's interesting.

We're in the Land Rover and he won't let me drive. So I'm sitting there sulking. He won't let me drive and we are in the Land Rover which I don't want to have and I'm now really in a bad mood. I've stopped smoking hashish a few days before because I'm having all kinds of reactions to it, and so I'm just in a very, very uptight, negative paranoid state and all I want to do is go back to America and suddenly I'm following this young kid who wants to drive and all he wanted me for was to get the Land Rover and now the whole paranoid con world fills my head. I'm full of it.

We go about 80 or 100 miles and we come to a tiny temple by the side of the road in the foothills of the Himalayas. We're stopping and I think we're stopping because a truck's coming by, but when we stop, people surround the car, which they generally do, but they welcome him and he jumps out. And I can tell something's going to happen because as we go up into the hills, he's starting to cry.

We're singing songs and tears are streaming down his face, and I know something's going on, but I don't know what.

We stop at this temple and he asks where the guru is and they point up on a hill, and he goes running up this hill and they're all following him, so delighted to see him. They all love him so much.

I get out of the car. Now I'm additionally bugged because everybody's ignoring me. And I'm following him and he's way ahead of me and I'm running after him barefoot up this rocky path and I'm stumbling—by now my feet are very tough—but still his legs are very long and I'm running and people are ignoring me and I'm very bugged and I don't want to see the guru anyway and what the hell—

We go around this hill so that we come to a field which does not face on the road. It's facing into a valley and there's a little man in his 60s or 70s sitting with a blanket around him. And around him are eight or nine Hindu people and it's a beautiful tableau—clouds, beautiful green valley, lovely, lovely place—the foothills of the Himalayas.

And this fellow, Bhagwan Dass, comes up, runs to this man and throws himself on the ground, full-face doing "dunda pranam," and he's stretched out so his face is down on the ground, full-length and his hands are touching the feet of this man, who is sitting cross-legged. And he's crying and the man is patting him on the head and I don't know what's happening.

I'm standing on the side and thinking "I'm not going to touch his feet. I don't have to. I'm not required to do that." And every now and then this man looks up at me and he twinkles a little. But I'm so uptight that I couldn't care less. Twinkle away, man!

Then he looks up at me—he speaks in Hindi, of which I understand maybe half, but there is a fellow who's translating all the time, who hangs out with him, and the guru says to Bhagwan Dass, "You have a picture of me?"

Bhagwan Dass nods, "Yes."

"Give it to him," says the man, pointing at me.

"That's very nice, I think, giving me a picture of himself, and I smile and nod appreciatively. But I'm still not going to touch his feet!

Then he says, "You came in a big car?" Of course that's the one thing I'm really uptight about.

"Yeah."

So he looks at me and he smiles and says, "You give it to me?"

I started to say, "Wha..." and Bhagwan Dass looks up—he's lying there—and he says, "Maharaji (meaning 'great king'), if you want it you can have it—it's yours."

And I said, "No—now wait a minute—you can't give away David's car like that. That isn't our car..." and this old man is laughing. In fact, everyone is laughing...except me.

Then he says, "You made much money in America?"

"Ah, at last he's feeding my ego," I think.

So I flick through all of my years as a professor and years as a smuggler and all my different dramas in my mind and I said, "Yeah."

"How much you make?"

Well, I said, at one time—and I sort of upped the figure a bit, you know, my ego—$25,000.

So they all converted that into rupees which was practically half the economic base of India, and everybody was terribly awed by this figure, which was complete bragging on my part. It was phony—I never made $25,000. And he laughed again. And he said,

"You'll buy a car like that for me?"

And I remember what went through my mind. I had come out of a family of fund-raisers for the United Jewish Appeal, Brandeis, and Einstein Medical School, and I had never seen hustling like this. He doesn't even know my name and already he wants a $7,000 vehicle.

And I said, "Well, maybe..." The whole thing was freaking me so much.

And he said, "Take them away and give them food." So we were taken and given food—magnificent food—we were together still, and saddhus brought us beautiful food and then we were told to rest. Some time later we were back with the Maharaji and he said to me, "Come here. Sit." So I sat down and he looked at me and he said,

"You were out under the stars last night."

"Um-hum."

"You were thinking about your mother."

"Yes." ("Wow," I thought, "that's pretty good. I never mentioned that to anybody.")

"She died last year."

"Um-hum."

"She got very big in the stomach before she died."

Pause... "Yes."

He leaned back and closed his eyes and said, "Spleen. She died of spleen."

Well, what happened to me at that moment, I can't really put into words. He looked at me in a certain way at that moment, and two things happened—it seemed simultaneous. They do not seem like cause and effect.

The first thing that happened was that my mind raced faster and faster to try to get leverage—to get a hold on what he had just done. I went through every super CIA paranoia I've ever had:

"Who is he?" "Who does he represent?"

"Where's the button he pushes where the file appears?" and "Why have they brought me here?"

None of it would jell.

It was just too impossible that this could have happened this way. The guy I was with didn't know all that stuff, and I was a tourist in a car, and the whole thing was just too far out. My mind went faster and faster and faster.

Up until then I had two categories for "psychic experience." One was "they happened to somebody else and they haven't happened to me, and they were terribly interesting and we certainly had to keep an open mind about it." That was my social science approach. The other one was, "well, man, I'm high on LSD. Who knows how it really is? After all, under the influence of a chemical, how do I know I'm not creating the whole thing?" Because, in fact, I had taken certain chemicals where I experienced the creation of total realities. The greatest example I have of this came about through a drug called JB 318, which I took in a room at Millbrook. I was sitting on the third floor and it seemed like nothing was happening at all. And into the room walked a girl from the community with a pitcher of lemonade and she said, would I like some lemonade, and I said that would be great, and she poured the lemonade, and she poured it and she kept pouring and the lemonade went over the side of the glass and fell to the floor and it went across the floor and up the wall and over the ceiling and down the wall and under my pants which got wet and it came back up into the glass—and when it touched the glass the glass disappeared and the lemonade disappeared and the wetness in my pants disappeared and the girl disappeared and I turned around to Ralph Metzner and I said,

"Ralph, the most extraordinary thing happened to me," and Ralph disappeared!

I was afraid to do anything but just sit. Whatever this is, it's not nothing. Just sit. Don't move, just sit!

So I had had experiences where I had seen myself completely create whole environments under psychedelics, and therefore I wasn't eager to interpret these things very quickly, because I, the observer, was, at those times, under the influence of the psychedelics.

But neither of these categories applied in this situation, and my mind went faster and faster and then I felt like what happens when a computer is fed an insoluble problem; the bell rings and the red light goes on and the machine stops. And my mind just gave up. It burned out its circuitry...its need to have an explanation. I needed something to get closure at the rational level and there wasn't anything. There just wasn't a place I could hide in my head about this.

And at the same moment, I felt this extremely violent pain in my chest and a tremendous wrenching feeling and I started to cry. And I cried and I cried and I cried. And I wasn't happy and I wasn't sad. It was not that kind of crying. The only thing I could say was it felt like I was home. Like the journey was over. Like I had finished.

Well, I cried and they finally sort of spooned me up and took me to the home of devotee, K. K. Sah, to stay overnight. That night I was very confused. A great feeling of lightness and confusion.

At one point in the evening I was looking in my shoulder bag and came across the bottle of LSD.

"Wow! I've finally met a guy who is going to Know! He will definitely know what LSD is. I'll have to ask him. That's what I'll do. I'll ask him." Then I forgot about it.

The next morning, at eight o'clock a messenger comes. Maharaji wants to see you immediately. We went in the Land Rover. The three miles to the temple. When I'm approaching him, he yells out at me, "Have you got a question?"

And he's very impatient with all of this nonsense, and he says, "Where's the medicine?"

I got a translation of this. He said medicine. I said, "Medicine?" I never thought of LSD as medicine! And somebody said, he must mean the LSD. "LSD?" He said, "Ah-cha—bring the LSD."

So I went to the car and got the little bottle of LSD and I came back. "Let me see?"

So I poured it out in my hand—"What's that?"

"That's STP....That's librium and that's..." A little of everything. Sort of a little traveling kit.

He says, "Gives you siddhis?"

I had never heard the word "siddhi" before. So I asked for a translation and siddhi was translated as "power." From where I was at in relation to these concepts, I thought he was like a little old man, asking for power. Perhaps he was losing his vitality and wanted vitamin B 12. That was one thing I didn't have and I felt terribly apologetic because I would have given him anything. If he wanted the Land Rover, he could have it. And I said, "Oh, no, I'm sorry." I really felt bad I didn't have any and put it back in the bottle.

He looked at me and extended his hand. So I put into his hand what's called a "White Lightning." This is an LSD pill and this one was from a special batch that had been made specially for me for traveling. And each pill was 305 micrograms, and very pure. Very good acid. Usually you start a man over 60, maybe with 50 to 75 micrograms, very gently, so you won't upset him; 300 of pure acid is a very solid dose.

He looks at the pill and extends his hand farther. So I put a second pill—that's 610 micrograms—then a third pill that's 915 micrograms—into his palm.

That is sizeable for a first dose for anyone!

"Ah-cha."

And he swallows them! I see them go down. There's no doubt. And that little scientist in me says, "This is going to be very interesting!"

All day long I'm there, and every now and then he twinkles at me and nothing—nothing happens! That was his answer to my question. Now you have the data I have.

Ashtanga Yoga

I was taken back to the temple. It was interesting. At no time was I asked, do you want to stay? Do you want to study? Everything was understood. There were no contracts. There were no promises. There were no vows. There was nothing.

The next day Maharaji instructed them to take me out and buy me clothes. They gave me a room. Nobody ever asked me for a nickel. Nobody ever asked me to spread the word. Nobody ever did anything. There was no commitment whatsoever required. It was all done internally.

This guru—Maharaji—has only his blanket. You see, he's in a place called SAHAJ SAMADHI and he's not identified with this world as most of us identify with it. If you didn't watch him, he'd just disappear altogether into the jungle or leave his body, but his devotees are always protecting him and watching him so they can keep him around. They've got an entourage around him and people come and bring gifts to the holy man because that's part of the way in which you gain holy merit in India. And money piles up, and so they build temples, or they build schools. He will walk to a place and there will be a saint who has lived in that place or cave and he'll say, "There will be a temple here," and then they build a temple. And they do all this around Maharaji. He appears to do nothing.

As an example of Maharaji's style, I was once going through my address book and I came to Lama Govinda's name (he wrote *Foundations of Tibetan Mysticism* and *Way of the White Cloud*) and I thought, "Gee, I ought to go visit him. I'm here in the Himalayas and it wouldn't be a long trip and I could go and pay my respects. I must do that some time before I leave."

And the next day there is a message from Maharaji saying, "You are to go immediately to see Lama Govinda."

Another time, I had to go to Delhi to work on my visa and I took a bus. This was the first time after four months that they let me out alone. They were so protective of me. I don't know what they were afraid would happen to me, but they were always sending somebody with me.... They weren't giving me elopement privileges, as they say in mental hospitals.

But they allowed me to go alone to Delhi and I took a 12-hour bus trip. I went to Delhi and I was so high. I went through Connaught Place. And I went through that barefoot, silent with my chalkboard—I was silent all the time. At American Express, writing my words it was so high that not at one moment was there even a qualm or a doubt.

So after all day long of doing my dramas with the Health Department and so on, it came time for lunch. I had been on this very fierce austere diet and I had lost 60 lbs. I was feeling great—very light and very beautiful— but there was enough orality still left in me to want to have a feast. I'll have a vegetarian feast, I thought. So I went to a fancy restaurant and I got a table over in a corner and ordered their special deluxe vegetarian dinner, from nuts to nuts, and I had the whole thing and the last thing they served was vegetarian ice cream with two english biscuits stuck into it. And those biscuits...the sweet thing has always been a big part of my life, but I knew somehow, maybe I shouldn't be eating those. They're so far out from my diet. It's not vegetables—it's not rice. And so I was almost secretly eating the cookies in this dark corner. I was feeling very guilty about eating these cookies. But nobody was watching me. And then I went to a Buddhist monastery for the night and the next day took the bus back up to the mountain.

Two days later, we heard Maharaji was back—he had been up in the mountains in another little village. He travels around a lot, moves from place to place. I hadn't seen him in about a month and a half—I didn't see much of him at all. We all went rushing to see Maharaji and I got a bag of oranges to bring to him and I came and took one look at him, and the oranges went flying and I started to cry and I fell down and they were patting me. Maharaji was eating oranges as fast as he could, manifesting through eating food the process of taking on the karma of someone else.

Women bring him food all day long. He just opens his mouth and they feed him and he's taking on karma that way. And he ate eight oranges right before my eyes. I had never seen anything like that. And the principal of the school was feeding me oranges and I was crying and the whole thing was very maudlin, and he pulls me by the hair, and I look up and he says to me, "How did you like the biscuits?"

I'd be at my temple. And I'd think about arranging for a beautiful lama in America to get some money, or something like that. Then I'd go to bed and pull the covers over my head and perhaps have a very worldly thought; I would think about what I'd do with all my powers when I got them; perhaps a sexual thought. Then when next I saw Maharaji he would tell me something like, "You want to give money to a lama in America." And I'd feel like I was such a beautiful guy. Then suddenly I'd be horrified with the realization that if he knew that thought, then he must know that one, too... ohhhhh... and that one, too! Then I'd look at the ground. And when I'd finally steal a glance at him, he'd be looking at me with such total love.

Now the impact of these experiences was very profound. As they say in the Sikh religion—Once you realize God knows everything, you're free. I had been through many years of psychoanalysis and still I had managed to keep private places in my head—I wouldn't say they were big, labeled categories, but they were certain attitudes or feelings that were still very private. And suddenly I realized that he knew everything that was going on in my head, all the time, and that he still loved me. Because who we are is behind all that.

I said to Hari Dass Baba, my teacher at the time, "Why is it that Maharaji never tells me the bad things I think?" and he says, "It does not help your sadhana—your spiritual work. He knows it all, but he just does the things that help you."

The sculptor had said he loved Maharaji so much, we should keep the Land Rover up there. The Land Rover was just sitting around and so Maharaji got the Land Rover after all, for that time. And then one day, I was told we were going on an outing up in the Himalayas for the day. This was very exciting, because I never left my room in the temple. Now in the temple, or around Maharaji, there were eight or nine people. Bhagwan Dass and I were the only Westerners. In fact, at no time that I was there did I see any other Westerners. This is clearly not a Western scene, and in fact, I was specifically told when returning to the United States that I was not to mention Maharaji's name or where he was, or anything.

The few people that have slipped by this net and figured out from clues in my speech and their knowledge of India where he was and have gone to see him, were thrown out immediately...very summarily dismissed, which is very strange. All I can do is pass that information on to you. I think the message is that you don't need to go to anywhere else to find what you are seeking.

So there were eight or nine people and whenever there was a scene, I walked last. I was the lowest man on the totem pole. They all loved me and honored me and I was the novice, like in a karate or judo class, where you stand at the back until you learn more. I was always in the back and they were always teaching me.

So we went in the Land Rover. Maharaji was up in the front—Bhagwan Dass was driving. Bhagwan Dass turned out to be very high in this scene. He was very very highly thought of and honored. He had started playing the sitar; he was a fantastic musician and the Hindu people loved him. He would do bhajan—holy music—so high they would go out on it. So Bhagwan Dass was driving and I was way in the back of the Land Rover camper with the women and some luggage.

And we went up into the hills and came to a place where we stopped and were given apples, in an orchard and we looked at a beautiful view. We stayed about ten minutes, and then Maharaji says, "We've got to go on."

We got in the car, went farther up the hill and came to a forestry camp. Some of his devotees are people in the forestry department so they make this available to him.

So we got to this place and there was a building waiting and a caretaker—"Oh, Maharaji, you've graced us with your presence." He went inside with the man that is there to take care of him or be with him all the time—and we all sat on the lawn.

After a little while, a message came out, "Maharaji wants to see you." And I got up and went in, and sat down in front of him. He looked at me and said,

"You make many people laugh in America?"

I said, "Yes, I like to do that."

"Good...You like to feed children?"

"Yes. Sure."

"Good."

He asked a few more questions like that, which seemed to be nice questions, but...? Then he smiled and he reached forward and he tapped me right on the forehead, just three times. That's all.

Then the other fellow came along and lifted me and walked me out the door. I was completely confused. I didn't know what had happened to me—why he had done it—what is was about.

When I walked out, the people out in the yard said that I looked as if I were in a very high state. They said tears were streaming down my face. But all I felt inside was confusion. I have never felt any further understanding of it since then. I don't know what it was all about. It was not an idle movement, because the minute that was over, we all got back in the car and went home.

I pass that on to you. You know now, what I know about that. Just an interesting thing. I don't know what it means, yet.

Hari Dass Baba was my teacher. I was taught by this man with a chalkboard in the most terse way possible. I would get up early, take my bath in the river or out of a pail with a lota (a bowl). I would go in and do my breathing exercises, my pranayam and my hatha yoga, meditate, study, and around 11:30 in the morning, this man would arrive and with chalkboard he would write something down:

"If a pickpocket meets a saint, he sees only his pockets."

Then he'd get up and leave. Or he'd write,

"If you wear shoeleather, the whole earth is covered with leather."

These were his ways of teaching me about how motivation affects perception. His teaching seemed to be no teaching because he always taught from within...that is, his lessons aroused in me just affirmation...as if I knew it all already.

When starting to teach me about what it meant to be "ahimsa" or non-violent, and the effect on the environment around you of the vibrations—when he started to teach me about energy and vibrations, his opening statement was "Snakes Know Heart." "Yogis in jungle need not fear." Because if you're pure enough, cool it, don't worry. But you've got to be very pure.

So his teaching was of this nature. And it was not until a number of months later that I got hold of Vivekananda's book *Raja Yoga* and I realized that he had been teaching me Raja Yoga, very systematically—an exquisite scientific system that had been originally enunciated somewhere between 500 B.C. and 500 A.D. by Patanjali, in a set of sutras, or phrases, and it's called Ashtanga Yoga, or eight-limbed yoga—and also known as Raja or Kingly yoga. And this beautiful yogi was teaching me this wisdom with simple metaphor and brief phrase.

Now, though I am a beginner on the path, I have returned to the West for a time to work out karma or unfulfilled commitment. Part of this commitment is to share what I have learned with those of you who are on a similar journey. One can share a message through telling "our-story" as I have just done, or through teaching methods of yoga, or singing, or making love. Each of us finds his unique vehicle for sharing with others his bit of wisdom.

For me, this story is but a vehicle for sharing with you the true message... the living faith in what is possible.

Ram Dass, *Be Here Now*

→ Disciplines and Spiritual Practices ←

Largely through the teachings of gurus, swamis, and masters who have moved to North America and Europe and set up ashrams, centres, and schools, the Eastern spiritual disciplines of meditation and yoga are being incorporated into the everyday lives of many now in the West. We have come to recognize these ancient practices as unsurpassed in bridging the gap between the realities of the higher Self and the soul and the personality of the lower Self.

Yale Divinity School professor and author Henri J. M. Nouwen once wrote that "through a spiritual discipline we prevent the world from filling our lives to such an extent that there is no place left to listen." California psychologist Charles Tart's *Observations of a Meditation Practice* offers one of the most readable and humorous accounts of a battle with distractions.

Jewish philosopher Martin Buber writes: "In reality the main purpose of life is to raise everything that is profane to the level of the holy." This starts, particularly in the West, in the introduction of some prayerful techniques in our everyday lives. Thich Nhat Hanh, a Vietnamese Zen master, poet, and peace advocate who now lives in France, shows us how we can nurture the sacred within amid the stress and pressures from outside influences in his "A Day of Mindfulness."

Meditation techniques are for opening the heart, stilling the mind, and making them one, for grounding the soul in the body, for uniting the spirit in both. As witnessed earlier with Gopi Krishna's rigorous spiritual practice leading to his kundalini awakening, recognizing the sacredness of the body and of strengthening it to house the expanding soul are the requisites in yoga practice of combining mind and breath control with physical postures.

The beauty of the human body and its power of spiritual and creative expression is not always acknowledged in the Judeo-Christian tradition. But without the body's inclusion in expressing the spirit, through yoga, tai chi, dance, and tantric practices, all wilful efforts to achieve wholeness are tainted.

><

In spiritual practice in general—and asceticism in particular—the goal is always the recovery of wholeness. Today, I believe, the attainment of this goal requires great discretion in the use of physical means such as fasting and sleep deprivation. We need to recover, after thirteen centuries of Platonic dualism and three centuries of Cartesian dualism, a profoundly holistic understanding of ourselves as embodied spirit in the world, part of this world of bodies and open to Absolute Spirit or God.

> Thomas Matus, from Fritjof Capra, David Steindl-Rast
> with Thomas Matus, *Belonging to the Universe*

There is no halacha without agada, and no agada without halacha.* We must neither disparage the body, nor sacrifice the spirit. The body is the discipline, the pattern, the law; the spirit is inner devotion, spontaneity, freedom. The body without the spirit is a corpse; the spirit without the body is a ghost. Thus a mitsvah† is both a discipline and an inspiration, an act of obedience and an experience of joy, a yoke and a prerogative.

Our task is to learn how to maintain a harmony between the demands of halacha and the spirit of agada.

> Abraham Joshua Heschel, *God in Search of Man*

Good sailors in the storms of life use their own "I," their own ego, to discriminate in what situation to use their masculinity and in what situation to use their femininity. They build their ego strong enough to ride with the power of wind and wave. And that ego can only be strong enough if it is supported by the wisdom of the body whose messages are directly in touch with the instincts. Without that interplay between spirit and body, the spirit is always trapped. At the very moment when it could soar, it is undermined

---

* "Halacha" means "law" and "agada" means "lore."
† "Mitsvah" means "divine command."

by fear and lack of confidence because it cannot depend on its instinctual ground even for survival. Without that ground, the body is experienced as the enemy. Like a boat without a rudder whirling in panic-stricken circles, the sailor may be dragged into a vortex of paralysis or terror. If, on the other hand, spirit and body are attuned to each other, each complements the other with its own special wisdom.

Marion Woodman, *Addiction to Perfection*

You will know the wonders of the human body because there is nothing more wonderful. The next time you look into the mirror, just look at the way the ears rest next to the head; look at the way the hairline grows; think of all the little bones in your wrist. It is a miracle.

Martha Graham, *Blood Memory*

Your attitude toward your body should be pure, friendly, respectful, and affectionate. The body has been man's companion and friend through many births, through many different journeys of pain and happiness. The body is a fundamental necessity of *sadhana*. It is the ladder to the city of liberation; it is the great temple of the inner Self. In the innermost part of this bodily temple, God, the Lord of love, lives as the inner Self. Muktananda therefore says that, when a Siddha student achieves understanding of the body and sees that it is the temple of the inner Self, he will never do anything unfriendly to it nor involve it in anything degrading nor defile it through depraved or immoral acts.

Some people regard the body as a place of pleasure, like a club or a hotel or a cinema, and thus destroy its purity and lose their Shakti. In my opinion, they insult their bodies instead of honoring them and treating them justly. There are also some disturbed people who torture and repress their pure and friendly bodies in a way that is cruel and unnatural. Their hearts, which should be filled with love, are filled with lamentation. They hurt their bodies day and night. They constantly pray to the Lord to free them from the prison of the body. But the truth is that your body is without fault.

Swami Muktananda, *Play of Consciousness*

Like millions of trees which are all rooted in one and the same earth, so millions of human minds are rooted in one and the same universal being. Everything and every creature that is in the universe owes its own being to the undifferentiated Being, Mind. If then we declare that there is something godlike immanent in all men, we are not guilty of declaring an absurdity. It is not enough for anyone to look at his body and say he has seen a man. He must look also into the mysterious depths of his mind.

Paul Brunton, *The Spiritual Crisis of Man*

The Center Point Within Me

1. We are resting,
   Physically quiet,
   Breath and body
   In gentle harmony
   Holding the stillness within.

2. Holding the stillness within,
   Thoughts fit into place.
   No longer spinning,
   They come together;
   No longer disputing,
   Our thoughts
   Are friendly with each other.
   The quality of wholeness
   Replaces
   The discord of the mind.

3. Mind and body
   Together,
   Thoughts and emotions
   Revolving around
   A single center point.
   Varied movements
   Actively churning
   Form a quiet center.
   A quiet center forms
   In their midst.

4. We feel the center of our Self,
   The inner center of our Self,
   It is neither body
   Nor mind
   But a center point
   Not this, not that,
   A single center point,
   The inner center of the Self.

5. In the midst of activity
   Soft, slow breathing
   Sets a balance.
   An inward stillness
   Becomes present.
   The center point within me
   Establishes itself.

6. For each of us it is so.
   A center point within
   Forms itself.
   A center point is present
   Not in space
   But in our being.

7. A center point within me.
   My whole attention
   At that center point,
   Present there in the stillness,
   In the stillness of the Self.

8. Through this center point
   We move inward,
   Inward and downward
   Through a single straight shaft.
   It is as though we go
   Deep into the earth,
   But within our Self.
   Through the center point within
   We go inward,
   Deeper,
   Deeper inward.

9. My life
   Is like the shaft of a well.
   I go deep into it.
   The life of each of us
   Is a well.
   Its sources are deep,
   But it gives water on the surface.
   Now we go inward,

Moving through our center point,
Through our center point,
Deeply inward to explore
The infinities of our well.

10. Long enough
    We have been on the surface
    Of our life.
    Now we go inward,
    Moving through our center point
    Inward,
    Into the well of our Self,
    Deeply,
    Further inward
    Into the well of our Self.

11. We move away
    From the surface of things;
    We leave
    The circles of our thoughts,
    Our habits, customs.
    All the shoulds
    And the oughts
    Of our life
    We leave behind.

12. We leave them on the surface
    While we go inward,
    Into the depth of our life
    Moving through the center point
    Into the well of our Self
    As deeply
    As fully
    As freely as we can.
    Through the center point
    Exploring the deep places.
    Exploring the deep places
    In the Silence... In the Silence.

Ira Progoff, from "The Well and the Cathedral,"
in *The Practice of Process Meditation*

Breathing in, I calm body and mind.
Breathing out, I smile.
Dwelling in the present moment
I know this is the only moment.

Thich Nhat Hanh, Being Peace

A Day of Mindfulness

Every day and every hour, one should practice mindfulness. That's easy to say, but to carry it out in practice is not. That's why I suggest to those who come to the meditation sessions that each person should try hard to reserve one day out of the week to devote entirely to their practice of mindfulness. In principle, of course, every day should be your day, and every hour your hour. But the fact is that very few of us have reached such a point. We have the impression that our family, place of work, and society rob us of all our time. So I urge that everyone set aside one day each week. Saturday, perhaps.

If it is Saturday, then Saturday must be entirely your day, a day during which you are completely the master. Then Saturday will be the lever that will lift you to the habit of practicing mindfulness. Every worker in a peace or service community, no matter how urgent its work, has the right to such a day, for without it we will lose ourselves quickly in a life full of worry and action, and our responses will become increasingly useless. Whatever the day chosen, it can be considered as the day of mindfulness.

While still lying in bed, begin slowly to follow your breath—slow, long, and conscious breaths. Then slowly rise from bed (instead of turning out all at once as usual), nourishing mindfulness by every motion. Once up, brush your teeth, wash your face, and do all your morning activities in a calm and relaxing way, each movement done in mindfulness. Follow your breath, take hold of it, and don't let your thoughts scatter. Each movement should be done calmly. Measure your steps with quiet, long breaths. Maintain a half smile.

Spend at least a half hour taking a bath. Bathe slowly and mindfully, so that by the time you have finished, you feel light and refreshed. Afterward, you might do household work such as washing dishes, dusting and wiping off the tables, scrubbing the kitchen floor, arranging books on their shelves. Whatever the tasks, do them slowly and with ease, in mindfulness. Don't do any task in order to get it over with. Resolve to do each job in a relaxed way, with all your attention. Enjoy and be one with your work. Without this, the day of mindfulness will be of no value at all. The feeling that any task is a nuisance will soon disappear if it is done in mindfulness. Take the example of the Zen Masters. No matter what task or motion they undertake, they do it slowly and evenly, without reluctance.

For those who are just beginning to practice, it is best to maintain a spirit of silence throughout the day. That doesn't mean that on the day of mindfulness, you shouldn't speak at all. You can talk, you can even go ahead and sing, but if you talk or sing, do it in complete mindfulness of what you are saying or singing, and keep talking and singing to a minimum. Naturally, it is possible to sing and practice mindfulness at the same time, just as long as one is conscious of the fact that one is singing and aware of what one is singing. But be warned that it is much easier, when singing or talking, to stray from mindfulness if your meditation strength is still weak.

At lunchtime, prepare a meal for yourself. Cook the meal and wash the dishes in mindfulness. In the morning, after you have cleaned and straightened up your house, and in the afternoon, after you have worked in the garden or watched clouds or gathered flowers, prepare a pot of tea to sit and drink in mindfulness. Allow yourself a good length of time to do this. Don't drink your tea like someone who gulps down a cup of coffee during a workbreak. Drink your tea slowly and reverently, as if it is the axis on which the whole earth revolves—slowly, evenly, without rushing toward the future. Live the actual moment. Only this actual moment is life. Don't be attached to the future. Don't worry about things you have to do. Don't think about getting up or taking off to do anything. Don't think about "departing."

> Be a bud sitting quietly in the hedge
> Be a smile, one part of wondrous existence
> Stand here. There is no need to depart.
> This homeland is as beautiful as the homeland of our childhood
> Do not harm it, please, and continue to sing . . .
> ("Butterfly Over the Field of Golden Mustard Flowers")

In the evening, you might read scripture and copy passages, write letters to friends, or do anything else you enjoy outside of your normal duties during the week. But whatever you do, do it in mindfulness. Eat only a little for the evening meal. Later, around 10 or 11 o'clock, as you sit in meditation, you will be able to sit more easily on an empty stomach. Afterward you might take a slow walk in the fresh night air, following your breath in mindfulness and measuring the length of your breaths by your steps. Finally, return to your room and sleep in mindfulness.

Somehow we must find a way to allow each worker a day of mindfulness. Such a day is crucial. Its effect on the other days of the week is immeasurable. Ten years ago, thanks to such a day of mindfulness, Chu Van and our other sisters and brothers in the Tiep Hien Order were able to guide themselves through many difficult times. After only three months of observing such a day of mindfulness once a week, I know that you will see a significant change in your life. The day of mindfulness will begin to penetrate the other days of the week, enabling you to eventually live seven days a week in mindfulness. I'm sure you agree with me on the day of mindfulness's importance!

Thich Nhat Hanh, The Miracle of Mindfulness

Spiritual practice is not a mindless repetition of ritual or prayer. It works through consciously realizing the law of cause and effect and aligning our lives to it. Perhaps we can sense the potential of awakening in ourselves, but we must also see that it doesn't happen by itself. There are laws that we can follow to actualize this potential. How we act, how we relate to ourselves, to our bodies, to the people around us, to our work, creates the kind of world we live in, creates our very freedom or suffering.

Over the years and throughout various cultures, many techniques and systems of Buddhist practice have been developed to bring this aspiration to fruition, but the essence of awakening is always the same: to see clearly and directly the truth of our experience in each moment, to be aware, to be mindful. This practice is a systematic development and opening of awareness called by the Buddha the four foundations of mindfulness: awareness of the body, awareness of feelings, awareness of mental phenomena, and awareness of truths, of the laws of experience.

To succeed in the cultivation of mindfulness, said the Buddha, is the highest benefit, informing all aspects of our life. "Sandalwood and tagara are delicately scented and give a little fragrance, but the fragrance of virtue and a mind well trained rises even to the gods."

How are we to begin? The Path of Purification, an ancient Buddhist text and guide, was written in answer to a short poem:

The world is entangled in a knot.
Who can untangle the tangle?

It is to untangle the tangle that we begin meditation practice. To disentangle ourselves, to be free, requires that we train our attention. We must begin to see how we get caught by fear, by attachment, by aversion—caught by suffering. This means directing attention to our everyday experience and learning to listen to our bodies, hearts, and minds. We attain wisdom not by creating ideals but by learning to see things clearly, as they are.

Joseph Goldstein and Jack Kornfield, Seeking the Heart of Wisdom

The Adventure of Meditation

In this energetic era anyone who places a high or higher value on the practice of relaxation and meditation is likely to be thought either a fool or a fanatic. It is one of the chief delusions of modern men, caught in urban maelstroms, that if they were to make these daily pauses in life, they would lose something because of the time lost from their affairs. On the contrary, if the pause is real and sincere, they would gain something in the very sphere in which the supposed loss would occur. Simply to introduce short intervals of the fullest relaxation in the daily regime of personal activity is enough to yield markedly beneficial results. Under the pressures of modern civilization they are a biological need. Any man will do more and better work, will feel less fatigued and conserve more vitality if he replenishes his forces by such rearrangement of his hours. Thus he loses nothing in actuality by losing these few minutes from his labours and pleasures. Thought and feeling should welcome these brief beautiful deliverances from the burden of common existence. Yet the sad irony is that so many people are too preoccupied with worries to spare time for that which could help them better to bear their worries. It is to their own loss that they have no desire to relax or to meditate. And could they understand the deeper phases of spiritual life, they would understand that the common notion that no activity of the body means nothing done or gained, is falsified by the gratifying results of meditation. The less common notion that no activity of the intellect means the same profitless result is falsified by the unforgettable results of contemplation. Incidentally these two are not the same but lower and higher stages of the same practice.

We may now see what profound wisdom hid behind the ancient religious law givers' injunction to keep a weekly sabbatical day of rest. These wise men of antiquity considered ways and means of reminding man of his true purpose on earth. He was apt to become wholly entangled in earthly desires and physical matters, and to forget what should be his supreme desire—the discovery of, and communion with, his divine soul. This is why they instructed him to substitute spiritual affairs and transcendental business for them, why they instituted a special day in the week for the purpose. He was recalled every seventh day to the higher object of all this work, the ultimate end for which it was only a temporary means. He was to be serious and even grave, to put frivolity aside for this one day because death was an ever-present shadow. A day of rest let his depleted surface consciousness lie fallow only to be all the more fruitful later; it gave the deeper levels of mind a chance to present these intuitive knowledge and it turned thought towards the sacred ultimate purpose of all human life.

The same need or duty is even more urgent in this twentieth century of ours. For modern invention, which could be used to bestow more leisure for spiritual pursuits, is actually used to defeat this aim. With the aid of automobiles, trains and even airplanes, and with the facilities provided by amusement and sports places, the sabbath day is spent in transient pleasures. Such a day should be marked by the rededication of life to the loftiest accepted ideal and to the restatement of faith in its essentially spiritual character. It is the proper time to consider the future, to reflect upon the past and consequently to make advisable changes in thought, plan and practice. It is the time for a man to reinspire himself with basic attitudes. On that day he is to enter into prayer, think about ultimates, reflect about aims, remember aspirations, read inspired books and practice meditations. He is to re-estimate his worth as bearing something divine in his heart. He is, finally, to consider and become conscious of the relationship which exists between himself and God.

The flow of everyday living in work or leisure ordinarily distracts the mind from its higher purpose and keeps it moving from subject to subject. This continuous dissipation of the self's psychical energies and vital forces prevents any withdrawal of attention being concentrated in the endeavour to come to itself. The attempt to save a certain number of minutes out of the day's twenty-four hours for the sole purpose of reversing the flow of attention, turning it from restlessness to repose and from the senses to the soul, is the most important any man could engage in. He who excuses himself on the grounds that he cannot find even this short period, should ask his conscience whether all his ordinary activity in both work and leisure is really as necessary as it seems. If his conscience affirms that it is, if he can do no more, then it will be enough to maintain the right attitude towards external affairs and to keep constantly in the background of his mind the thought of the spiritual quest. Yet the truth is that few are really in such an unfortunate situation.

No man may rightly say that he has had a full experience of life if he has not had any spiritual experience during life. If he is to become better balanced, Western man should not only give himself to active life but also to contemplative life. Exercises in meditation should be given a definite and assured place in Euro-American habits. Mystical practices should no longer be confined to a few persons and therefore considered to be abnormal, eccentric or queer. They should be brought into use by a wider group. Whoever will devote a period of his day to them and will support them by an honest effort to reform his way of life, may one day feel within himself the presence of a purer individuality, a spiritual self. This daily habit of excluding the personal affairs from attention or detaching them from emotion, of holding the mind remote from the trivialities, the temptations and the frictions of the world, while letting it sink deeper into abstraction, leads it to get and enjoy a tranquillizing respite of freedom from the pressure of life, work and people.

The man who learns the art of retiring within himself to touch, not the darker strata of the ego's subconscious, but the deepest part of spiritual being, learns to possess both restfulness and happiness at his command. To the extent that he digs more deeply into his mind, he there finds benedictory powers of healing and pacification. A prefatory of such silent contemplation radiates its mood and spirit into the rest of his day.

The more interior degrees of the mind's own being are the degrees nearest to the Overself. It is because of this fact that the value of mystical meditation is unique. For it draws the meditator's consciousness more and more inward, more and more to the divine state that is its kernel. So long as the mind searches in regions alien to it, so long will the world's ultimate secret elude it. For the first step which the primordial cosmic Mind took was outward into world manifestation and this points out the inward direction in which our own last step must go: that is, within the mind itself.

The human mind is everlastingly curious. It wants to know more and more. Yet it can never finally slake this curiosity and satisfy this craving. All that it gathers is finite and limited, incomplete and insufficient—and must remain so. When at last it wakes up to this fact, it will sooner or later put itself upon the quest. Then, when it finally succeeds in turning around and gazing within it will be stilled in, and become questionless with, an infinite satisfaction.

We see things around us but not the light which renders the act of seeing possible. We experience the movement of thoughts but not that which renders this movement possible. For just as we must presuppose the existence of light in order to see a thing, so we must presuppose the existence of mind in order to know a thought. So long as the individual consciousness is entirely wrapped up in gazing at this pictorial presentation which it calls the "world," so long will it be unconscious of its own being, so long will it remain an undisclosed mystery to itself. We do not know that the same thoughts which make up the world of our transient experience, at the same time keep us from the world of eternal reality. This is why the need of mystic withdrawal from them is a paramount. The aim of meditation, when culminating in contemplation, is the stilling of all mental activity so that Mind itself, the source and condition of this activity, may be known in its original state. The practice ultimately leads the artist to find beauty and the mystic to find the godlike within himself. This is its highest purpose. Thus it leads them from materialism to mentalism, which teaches the truth about "matter" and unveils the reality behind its manifold appearances.

There is a Mind in man, immeasurably superior to his ordinary mind. If, in quiet moments and still moods, he will patiently wait its promptings and submit to them, if in these utterly relaxed reveries he will wait watchfully yet positively until the Overself reveals its presence to him, he may gain understanding, power and guidance immeasurably superior to what he ordinarily knows.

Strength runs wild without wisdom and calmness to direct it; the complementary truth is that knowledge is dumb unless it is put into action. The squatting figure of the yogi seated in tranquil meditation and resting under cooling palm-fronds, silent and motionless as a stone is fascinating to some harassed Westerners. He is a reflective witness and not an active player in the game of life, his eyes are set, half-closed in a still glance, and his mind is held fast in a world where there are not troublesome questions and no worrying problems. But can the yogi bring this same detachment into the same busy turbulent kind of life which the average Westerner must live?

That man comes nearer to sanity and a full balanced life who begins or punctuates or ends his day by sitting erect with folded palm or hands upon his knees, with quiet ordered breathing and with eyes half-open or closed, and who fixes his thoughts for as long as he can spare upon the Mind which is at once the sublime source and mysterious sustainer of his being; and who then deliberately draws moral strength and far-seeing vision from his moments of meditation in order to go about his daily business, be it in office or factory, law court or hospital, farm or ship, and if he seeks to do his work with efficient keenness and effective practicality, both he and the world will be gainers. He will have sufficient philosophic detachment to discern in the very midst of his external activities and earthly ambitions that they are as transient as foam. He will try to do his duty amid the world's bustle, and to do it well, but he will not neglect the higher duty which he learns from the stillness mystically hiding behind that bustle. He will discipline himself daily but the source of such discipline being the Overself, it will more and more arise spontaneously and without effort or seeking. By this regime it will eventually be possible for him to reach a state wherein the hurts and harms of everyday life possess but little power to wound. Even mistakes will be immediately converted into opportunities for growth.

Civilization will justify itself only when men of the world become mystics, and when at the same time mystics rediscover the world. In the kind of period in which we live today, dominated as it is by economics and politics by materialism and by violence, mysticism is inevitably separated from worldly life. The quieter minds react from its noisiness by withdrawal from the cities. The gentler spirits react from its violence by withdrawal into solitude. The intuitional minds react from its materialism by withdrawal into study and contemplation. Mysticism can find no standing ground for itself and allies itself with escapism. But although driven now to do this in self-defence, it will eventually be driven to reverse this process, following certain events. When the climax of violence passes, when materialism sinks exhausted, mysticism will have to return to active service and its leaders will begin to feel the urge and guidance to work in the outer world. Then they will find a place for themselves in a society which, in its old dispensation, had little use for them. Then public life will be inspired by its revelations.

When a fine Spanish contemplative, St. Theresa, finally penetrated the enchanting glamour of her own mystical experience, she remarked: "This is the end of that spiritual union, that there may be born of its working, *works*." What she found in the course of her own development foreshadowed what will be found eventually in our own century by intelligent mystics, as contrasted with self-centred neurotic ones. They will have to form precise and clear ideas as to the practical implications and social values of mysticism during a time of world upheaval.

The hour will indeed come for the extroverted man to get a fresh understanding of himself and at the same time to bring inner peace to his disrupted nerves. He has been questioning the whole universe for centuries, it is inevitable that he should also begin to question himself.

It is hard to say, precisely and accurately, how anyone begins to know that this sublime power, the Overself, exists within him: the revelation is a compounded one. It consists of a metaphysical certitude, an intuitive feeling, and a mystical experience—all pointing to an indescribable something which alone, of all things, exists by its own independent right; which has as its very nature, causeless, eternal and perfect being.

Take Jesus' statement that "The kingdom of heaven is within you." The meaning of his beautiful words is transparent. He who looks for something ecclesiastical behind them is wasting time. They plainly bid each man to listen in silent reverie to the sublime intimations of his hidden being, that is, to practise mental quiet and enter into contemplation. Once he recognizes that the Divine Mind, wherever else it may also be in this infinite universe, is certainly within himself too, he ceases to wander in darkness and starts walking in light. God is then no longer an alien and remote Being to be propitiated in abject fear or flattered in wheedling mendicancy but a sublime ever-presence to be sought in his own heart—and to be sought nobly in joy, reverence, humility and love. In the end, religious teachings about the soul must not only be founded on authentic personal experience of the leaders but must also lead to personal experience of the followers, or they will prove insufficient.

The soul, this mysterious entity who is wholly non-existent to many people and whose quest is a chimera to most people, will eventually prove to be the only one who remains when all others pass away. If a man's thought is always directed towards the objects of his experience and never diverted towards the consciousness which makes that experience possible, then it is inevitable that those objects shall assume a significance and reality in and for themselves alone. That is to say, he will become a materialist. Yet the Overself is that out of which his own consciousness has come. Ought he not to give himself the daily spiritual chance to come in contact with it, with his most intimate self?

He may travel the entire length and breadth of the five continents to commune with their cleverest scientists, but if he does not also travel within and commune with his own divine self, then the secret of life will still elude him. He misses what is most important if he misses going into the invisible temple of his own heart. There the soul abides, there the ray of God strikes the individual and there alone the satisfying discovery of what he really is may be made. This is the fundamental task—to become aware of the divine that is in him. All others are secondary and tertiary. He must establish himself in the consciousness of the Overself by and for himself. No other man can do it for him. And the Quest's labour in purification and meditation is indispensable for this purpose.

Paul Brunton, The Spiritual Crisis of Man

Devote one short hour every day
To serve your Maker and your Lord,
Do worship, meditate or pray
Or sow some seeds of Good abroad.

Do something, in His name, to show
That you are mindful of the debt
Which children to their parents owe
For all the gifts they freely get.

Do something noble, something fine
That has no colour of the self,
No shade of ego, me or mine,
No thought of honour, fame or pelf.

Do something good to benefit
The humble crowds surrounding you,
Whose minds not yet by Wisdom lit
Cannot decide what they should do.

Gopi Krishna, The Way to Self-Knowledge

Observations of a Meditation Practice

I had tried a little of various kinds of meditation years ago, with very poor results. My main practice was concentrative meditation, trying to focus just on the process of breathing, without thinking anything. My mind was too active to be stilled from thinking for more than a few seconds at a time, though, and I was too concerned with whether I was doing it correctly to be able to relax into the process. This was quite frustrating.

Some years ago I became involved in Transcendental Meditation (TM), which proved helpful on some levels but was ultimately unsatisfying. The following fourteen years were exceptionally rich in psychological insight, practice, struggle, and growth. They involved many years of practice of self-observation and self-remembering. Recently I have begun a new cycle of meditation practice, which has been both fruitful and frustrating. In this chapter I shall try an unusual experiment: I shall try to describe my own meditation practice by actually beginning to meditate as I sit in front of the word processor, interrupting the process to write descriptions.

This is ironic in a way, as one of the most common difficulties in meditation for me has always been the appearance of fascinating thoughts about how I would describe meditation if I were writing about it. I have always had to dismiss these as interruptions, but now the devil will get his due.

Beginning

I began meditation with a minute or two devoted to settling my body down to a comfortable, stable position that I can maintain for forty minutes or so without wiggling around. Sitting in my desk chair in front of the word processor is not my usual or optimal position, but it should be solid and comfortable enough for this session.

I start to settle my body and turn my attention more inward. I am very aware of sensations in my head and body. They are tense, "Go for it!" sorts of sensations. There is a tightness around my head, as if the skull and brain were pushing against my skin, as if they were hardened against the world, and a tension in my neck and shoulders, a straining forward.

One of the by-products of my meditation practice is that I pay more conscious attention to my psychophysiological state during my everyday activities. Consequently I recognize this as an all too common overexcitement that comes over me when I want to get something done. This is a frequent body pattern of mine, but since such physical tension is rarely required to actually accomplish anything effectively, I regard it as pathological: By analogy, I'm revving my engine when only a small touch is required on the gas pedal. My level of activation is much too high for the task at hand.

Even though writing about it has kept me from paying full attention to this tension pattern, some attention has gone to it and it has relaxed moderately. I say "it" because I didn't consciously choose to be this tense, nor does it instantly go away if I command it to. I generally find that conscious attention to tension patterns in my body relaxes them fairly quickly, though, even if I don't deliberately try to relax them. With more attention to or full consciousness of a useless tension pattern, I naturally perceive it as useless and relaxation comes pretty automatically. Now I shall stop writing a minute and deliberately pay full attention....

The first effect of fuller attention is a deeper understanding of how useless this tension is. Since useless tension is a dumb thing to have, this is a little upsetting to my self-image as a smart and efficient person. I know from past experience that insights that upset my self-image tend to make me resist looking inward, but I've also learned that such defensiveness gets me nowhere. So I'll just accept the feeling of dumbness and again get on with paying full attention to settle my body down for meditation.

Settling In

As I settle in a little more a specific component of the head tension stands out more clearly. I am still wearing my glasses. Even though I have closed my eyes, my eye muscles are still straining a little for "proper" focus through my glasses. They have become conditioned to the touch of the glasses upon my nose and ears.

I need my glasses to type. Since I don't want to keep taking them on and off I decide I will relax this sensation as much as I can and then ignore it. This involves setting up a sort of "background" intention during meditating. I won't keep thinking about it all the time, but I'll set up the intention to ignore this sensation, let the intention go, and hopefully only have to give the intention a second or so of attention once in a great while to keep it effective.

I have spent a long time describing the settling-in process and still haven't gotten very far. Such settling down processes are common for me in starting a meditation session.

As I again close my eyes and go inward the tension sensations relax and become a more general feeling of aliveness and awakeness, a pattern of sensations that is more generally spread through my body. I take this as a sign of success, for I have learned that this pattern means that the energy that was being automatically expressed as tension is now available to me for more conscious direction: I have acquired "fuel" to "burn" in the way I want.

Opening my eyes and writing interrupts the settling-down process and takes me back into the tension pattern. Rather than be upset about this I consider it a necessary price to pay in order to get a real-time account of the meditation experience. I have decided to bring mindfulness to this cycling in and out of meditation and so make it a part of the meditation process itself. Thus my process is not interrupted as deeply and I am settling down in a cyclical pattern, a little deeper each time, rather than settling down in a more linear pattern of steadily increasing relaxation.

Concentrative Meditation

My plan is to practice concentrative meditation at first, putting my attention as fully as possible on my breathing. I will feel the sensations associated with my belly moving in and out as my breathing goes on automatically. I will regard anything other than these sensations as a distraction.

This definition of what is appropriate experience (feeling the sensations of breathing) and what is not (anything else) is another of those intentions that will work in the background of consciousness to influence the course of the meditation process. I should not "fight" distractions—that just gives them more energy. Instead I should gently drop them from the focus of attention as soon as I become aware that I have drifted off.

I feel my body settling and relaxing. My breathing starts to become more prominent among the mass of body sensations, and I gently give myself the mind-set to gradually focus more and more on the motions of my belly, rather than forcibly concentrate on it all at once. This gentleness feels right: Being forcible in my intentions usually produces unnecessary tension.

The sensation/energy level is high throughout my body. I can feel my pulse beating all through it, my arms are tingling (my intellectual mind jumps in to "explain" that as a result of the activity of typing—my intellectual mind is addicted to explaining everything!), there is a constriction around my waist from my belt, a slight fullness in my stomach from breakfast an hour ago. I don't want to push away any of these nonbreathing sensations. I decide to be aware of them *from the perspective of the part of my belly that moves when I breathe.* Thus I put more attention into my breathing without actively rejecting anything else.

I also decide that since this is still the initial settling-in period it would be OK to loosen my belt, which I do. If I had been more than five minutes into this meditation I would regard loosening my belt as a kind of "cheating," since I believe I should be as still as possible once I've really gotten going. An older student of meditation who I respect once stated that the first five minutes is usually the squirming period, and I accept that.

I hear my wife, Judy, making a phone call just outside my study door. I'm annoyed. She is interrupting my meditation. She should have more consideration! She doesn't know I'm meditating, of course, but she does know I'm writing and that I don't want to be interrupted. These thoughts go on and on. Finally I call out to her, "Be quiet, I'm writing!" A long train of thoughts of annoyance with her, of annoyance with myself for being so petty, about how I ought to be able to be unaffected by such distractions, and so on, follows.

This long-winded thought-diversion event is all too typical of meditation for me when something external distracts me. I've learned that the best thing to do at this point is to drop the whole thing and get back to being focused on meditating.

Now I've focused on my breathing for a dozen breaths or so, with only occasional distractions. (That I can say "only occasional distractions" represents tremendous progress for me.) I am getting into this meditation. I can feel my body settling and relaxing more, with a kind of warm, heavy, comfortable sensation enveloping it. I sense this in the awareness that is peripheral to my primary focus on the sensation of my abdomen moving in breathing.

My mind is focused on my breathing sensations, but it is also getting more relaxed and contented. I'm getting deeper into my breathing. This warm, comfortable feeling in mind and body feels very like the one that occurs when I'm falling asleep. My meditation experience of these last months is that this is an almost certain indication that in a moment I am going to drift off into some hypnagogic fantasy and so totally lose my focus on my breathing for a period that might be moments or minutes in length. Since I don't think falling asleep into hypnagogic fantasies is the purpose of concentrative meditation, I must increase my level of alertness. In this case the desire to open my eyes and record this event is a very convenient way to increase my alertness, although I lose awareness of my breathing and stop meditation for the time it takes to write this.

An aside: Note that if I could learn to hover continuously at this point between clear focus on my breathing and starting to fall asleep, I would like it a lot. The pleasant body sensations, the calmness, the forgetting of troubles are very enjoyable. If my ordinary consciousness was usually a state of agitation and worry, I would regard this kind of meditative experience as a real "high" and use words like "peace," "bliss," and "tranquility" to describe it. Since I usually enjoy my ordinary state of consciousness, however, I find this particular aspect of meditation experience pleasant but not all that worthwhile; I want much more than that, so I don't want to learn to just hover there.

SEDUCTIVE THOUGHTS

Meditating again. For several breaths in a row I was calmly and strongly focused on my breathing. Suddenly I find that I am all wrapped up in a fascinating train of thought about how I might connect the two telephone lines running into the house together so that I could have conference calls with three people, whether this would damage the telephone system, how to try it using a resistor to test without allowing damage, where to mount the switch box for connecting the lines, and so on. I have been on this thought line for somewhere between thirty seconds and a minute or so. It has been a combination of thoughts and mild-intensity image—not as intense as hypnagogic imagery, but vivid enough in its own way. I don't know when I lost track of my breathing. That's my biggest problem with concentrative meditation: I seldom know when a thought is taking me away from concentration.

I love my thoughts. Almost every thought seduces me, charms me, casts its spell over me. It's as if I'm doing something boring when a beautiful woman walks in front of me, smiles, and beckons me to come with her. I instantly forget what I was doing. With a feeling of happiness and anticipation I automatically follow my enchantress. Every step of this journey is interesting, every step promises more pleasure with the next step, and on I go. When the part of my mind dedicated to meditating finally reactivates enough so I realize I have gone away on an enchanted journey, *I* suddenly reappear, the enchanted landscape fades. The mindful, present part that I call "I" is so real, so vivid at this moment, compared to the enchanted mind that I usually wonder, "Where have I been?" The real part of me exists now but it was gone, totally gone, disassembled, scattered to the breeze, under a fairy enchantment.

This part of meditation experience remains the biggest puzzle to me. I am so real, so vivid, when I am mindfully present, whether in concentrative meditation or insight meditation. During this existence as a vivid mindful *I*, I cannot conceive of giving it up voluntarily, of disappearing. Yet it happens all the time. Most of my life is spent on an enchanted journey in the Land of Thought and Fantasy, where this most real kind of "I" does not exist.

Back to meditation practice. I spend several minutes trying to re-center my awareness on my breathing. Miscellaneous thoughts come and go. Body sensations appear and disappear. A slight itch on my scalp appears, disappears, reappears, becomes very prominent, and "tempts" me: "I'm distracting you, there might be a real reason for this itch, like a bug or something, why don't you scratch me so I'll go away permanently? My background intention to ignore distractions and sit still is not enough and I have to remind myself in the foreground of my attention that I am not going to scratch this itch. Past experience reminds me that it will indeed be very satisfying if I scratch this itch, but a dozen new itches will spring up to replace it, each further tempting me to scratch it "one last time so you can settle down." Forget scratching the itch, go back to my breathing.

Now I have become sleepy. My mind drifts a lot. I seldom follow my breathing for more than a breath or two before drifting off on some train of thought. I want to focus, so I modify my concentration practice to try to compensate for excessive sleepiness: I begin counting each breath. I think "one" through the first inhalation and exhalation sensations, "two" through the next, and so on up through "ten," where I start again at "one." Since my automatic mind is addicted to thinking something, this is sort of an intellectual sop to it: Here, you can keep track of the count.

This is often, although not invariably, helpful. It doesn't help if I'm very sleepy. It is also somewhat tricky. I want the counting to be a *secondary* activity that helps me focus on the breathing sensations, but it is easy for the counting to become primary, with little attention on breathing. I have to monitor the balance of my attention: Is the actual sensation of my abdomen moving still primary? If not, make it primary.

This brings me to a constant problem I have with concentrative meditation. It seems to me that the point seems to be to become *totally* absorbed in the object of concentration—in this case, breathing. Every other sensation, thought, feeling, and so on, other than the concentration object, should cease to exist for the meditator with this degree of total absorption. But in my experience, moments when I start to become totally absorbed in my breathing, with everything else fading away, have always turned out to be moments when I either fell asleep or became enchanted by some thought train. When I am totally absorbed a dullness of mind occurs, and there is nothing or no one left to notice that I'm about to lose the concentration I do have.

I have not satisfactorily dealt with this conflict. Sometimes during concentrative meditation I think I should just keep trying to be totally focused and hope that someday a novel state of total absorption in my breathing that isn't falling asleep or being enchanted by a thought will occur. At other times it seems perfectly clear to me that you cannot literally be totally absorbed in the object of concentration. At least 1 percent has to be devoted to detecting the approach of a seductive thought or the sensations announcing that sleep is coming, and then initiating action to preserve the 99 percent concentration on the breath. I am inclined toward the latter view now, given my experience to date, but the idea of total absorption seems to be so clearly stated in the meditation literature that I remain open to the possibility that my understanding is quite incomplete. For the present I try to stay about 90 percent focused on my breathing and let the other 10 percent of my mind monitor my state and make little adjustments now and then.

Vipassana: Mindfulness Meditation

Usually I meditate for forty minutes. I devote the first twenty to concentration on my breathing, as described above, and the second twenty to *vipassana*, mindfulness meditation. I like to feel that I have gotten somewhere with the concentrative meditation before switching over when my timer sounds.

"Gotten somewhere" I now take as a criterion of at least ten breaths in a row where most of my attention was on my breathing and this attention was continuous, that is to say that even if part of my attention wandered elsewhere at least some part of it stayed aware of the abdominal sensations of breathing all the time. (This criterion of ten breaths is a major achievement for me.) If my concentrative meditation hasn't met this criterion I will do it more "forcibly" (even while trying to keep my concentration relaxed) toward the end of the first twenty minutes, or even continue into the mindfulness period until I've achieved it.

So now the particular form of mindfulness meditation I usually practice begins. My goal is to be completely attentive to whatever physical sensations come along. As a sensation arises in my body I will pay attention to it. I won't try to create or reject any particular sensations. I will pay attention to the sensation as it persists or changes. When it goes away by itself I let it go and turn my full attention to whatever replaces it.

I close my eyes. My attention broadens out from my abdomen, where it was focused in concentrative meditation, moving out to encompass my whole body. I notice a tightness in my head that I wasn't aware of a moment before, but which feels like a familiar tension pattern. Some of it is jaw and temple tightness, which partly relaxes as I perceive it more fully.

I recall that I'm not focusing on what's happening in my body in order to relax it or make it feel better; I'm just focusing on whatever is there. If it relaxes and feels better, that's fine. If it doesn't relax, that's also fine. My goal is to sense it completely and follow whatever happens by itself, not control it.

My mind fills with a sensation of "vibration" through my whole body. "Vibration" seems a grandiose sort of word, maybe tingling would be better. My intellectual mind cuts in: "Is this an *important* feeling? A *useful* sensation?" Realizing I'm not here to *think about* my sensations in this meditation, I let the thought go. Fortunately, I feel, it goes readily, without generating more thoughts.

More subtly my intellect slips in the thought, "But you should relax the obvious tensions; after all, you meditate to break through to profound experiences. You've felt muscle tension and tingling a million times already and they get in the way of the *real* experience, so take just a moment to deliberately relax and clear your mind." The thought catches me, and before I can think again about the purpose of my meditation I deliberately relax my body. The idea seems so sensible, after all. Then again, practically all the thoughts that distract me from meditating seem so sensible.

Well, I have relaxed, there's no point getting further distracted in thinking about whether I should have relaxed, so I'll just go back to sensing whatever sensations there are in my body.

"But remember that important, enjoyable phone call you want to remember to make to your friend?" whispers my intellect. Later. Back to sensing.

A sensation of fullness in my stomach fills my mind. As I watch it awareness of breathing through my whole chest and abdomen takes over. Then this fades and the tension in my temples becomes prominent again. But I am doing it: I am following the natural play of sensation.

EXPECTATIONS

My mind makes an interesting observation. After stopping to write the above paragraph I again close my eyes and automatically go back to the sensations in my head that were there when I stopped. I can't believe I really put the body's processes on "hold," since sensations usually change rapidly by themselves. Obviously my expectation that I should take up where I left off for the sake of this writing has influenced where my attention goes when I start again. Even though the intention wasn't conscious it played its part. How much do such background intentions and expectations guide all of meditation, even when I am supposedly being completely open to whatever happens by itself?

I hear the humming of the fans that cool my word processor, I feel a tingling in my body that seems to be associated with the humming. I frequently notice that the distinction between "outside sensations" and "inside" sensations of events in my body is not always that clear. Sounds and the like usually generate some distinctly localized and specific feelings somewhere in my body. The humming of the fans spreads through my torso, for example, as well as in a narrow, tubular channel running from each ear down into my torso. A heavy, distant rumbling sound, presumably from some distant truck, is associated with a delicate vibration in the central part of my neck. An airplane sound is like a ball of vibration in the bottom part of my neck.

My intellectual mind would like to construct an encyclopedia, a master map of just where every kind of sound vibrates in my body. Not now, though: I'm trying to meditate, not think up conceptual schemes. I don't want to build up expectations that sound X always is felt in body part Y, and so on. I'm here to fully experience the natural flow of things, not try to pin it down in some scheme. My seductive thoughts—so full of interest and implied promise—are my major distractions to being mindful of my body sensations. The kind of mindfulness meditation that calls for watching one's thoughts is almost impossible for me at this stage.

A small burp. I retaste the sandwich I had for lunch. It is enjoyable. "Ugh!" says the intellectual part of my mind, "What would someone think if they read that? How will you maintain any dignity? When are you going to have some interesting and uplifting experience to report, anyway?" I can get into an intellectual argument with myself about this, but it's better to just drop it and get on with meditating.

I regard drifting off into thought as a failure of my meditation: I already know what thinking is like and how I can drift with it. So I shall meditate without writing for a few minutes until a different kind of experience occurs. Although it doesn't sound *intellectually* convincing I must report that it is pleasing, at some level of my mind, to just clearly follow sensation after sensation. I am a very clear part of my consciousness while doing this and that's relaxing and gratifying. You will probably have to experience this yourself to fully understand what I mean.

PLEASURE AND PAIN

Now I have a kind of experience that is just beginning to happen to me. I slip into thinking about a novel I am reading, thinking how I would enjoy sitting on the living room couch with the sun shining on me, savoring the strange imagery of the novel. Although I am fairly (but not completely) lost in the thought, I notice that my body makes preparatory adjustments to get up and go read the novel, and that there is a feeling of enjoyment in my body at the anticipation of reading the novel.

Shinzen Young has told me that deep mindfulness meditation allows a realization that mental pleasures involve a pleasurable sensation in some part of the body, but this is one of the first times I have actually had some direct experience of this. What would happen if I looked even more directly at that pleasurable sensation in the body? What is behind pleasure?

Odd. I wanted to add, "What is behind pain?" as the last sentence of the previous paragraph but I stopped myself, thinking I wasn't experiencing any pain at the moment, so it wasn't representative of my ongoing experience to discuss pain, and it sounded too grandiose anyway. So I closed my eyes to go back to meditating by being mindful of my body sensations, and a second later I felt a sudden sharp pain in the ball of my left foot, like something had jabbed me. It was too fleeting to focus on closely. Perhaps it was a coincidence; or perhaps it resulted from the intentional set produced by thinking about pain, with a little help from some part of my mind then producing pain so I would be justified in reflecting on and writing about it. I hope it will return and last as I shut my eyes again and turn inward. I shouldn't be hoping for anything in particular, of course, if I'm going to do this meditation properly.

Pain is quite interesting, depending on its intensity. In my experience to date a mild pain coming along gives me "energy." If I have been drowsy it wakes me and helps me feel clearer. If I have been drifting off into thoughts a mild pain brings me back to my body. Then I can focus on the mild pain and it often becomes an interesting *sensation* instead of *pain*.

Some pains are more difficult to deal with, especially if they are the kind that seem to carry the inherent message, "This pain may represent a *real* problem, not just a painful sensation, so quick, move this part of your body and you'll feel more comfortable and prevent real damage!" I usually move automatically on these thoughts, and only afterward realize that most of these are not real dangers of any sort. My biological instincts to avoid pain are very strong and usually overcome my conscious decision to sit still and experience what is.

AWARENESS

I now notice that although I have not been thinking much, I haven't been very clearly present to sensation either. I've moved toward that pleasant but dull near-sleep state I described earlier. I don't want to be here. It is far more satisfying, in my experience, to be alert and relaxed in this meditation. Indeed the snatches of that simultaneously relaxed and alert state that come along are my main reward for doing mindfulness meditation.

Now, as in other meditation times, I reach a fairly quiet state of mind, following sensations for half a minute or so at a time before being distracted by a thought. I get intrigued with trying to follow or focus on my attention itself. What is it that is aware?

At first this makes me more aware of sensations of tension inside my head and in the back of my neck. But this does not satisfy me. Yes, I remember that I'm trying to focus on whatever is but I want something more than this, I want to "get behind" ordinary mind; I expect something unusual to happen but I don't know what that is. Surely "I," my basic awareness, is more than sensations of tension in my head? I reach some kind of barrier here that frustrates going beyond it. Or perhaps the idea that I must go beyond what is to something else creates the very barrier that frustrates me? This is one of the most interesting and frustrating aspects of my mindfulness meditation to date, the place where I am stuck. I go back to just observing whatever sensations there are, but with a feeling that someday I'll get around that "barrier," I'll find out something. So I end this meditation.

SATISFACTION

Given the expectation I brought to the practice of meditation when I first started years ago, this observation of my practice should strike me as examples of frustration. Nothing spectacular is happening, nothing obviously "spiritual." No visions, no revelations.

Yet I look forward to my next meditation period. There is a quiet satisfaction inherent in the moments of concentration and mindfulness in both the concentrative and mindfulness meditation practices that is very fulfilling. I usually meditate in the late afternoon, after I finish working, and most days I start anticipating the pleasure of meditation by early afternoon.

I am not very concerned about doing it "right" now, but somehow I suspect that by being less concerned about how I meditate I am indeed doing it better.

Ending Meditation Practice

My timer goes off, my formal meditation period is over. I feel relaxed and calm. I can destroy this feeling quite quickly if I overstimulate my mind with too many concerns of no real importance in the long run (this is called being normal), but I decide I will carry this calm, centered feeling with me into my daily activities.

Charles T. Tart, *Open Mind,*
Discriminating Mind

I am a dancer.

I believe that we learn by practice. Whether it means to learn to dance by practicing dancing or to learn to live by practicing living, the principles are the same. In each it is the performance of a dedicated precise set of acts, physical or intellectual, from which comes shape of achievement, a sense of one's being, a satisfaction of spirit. One becomes in some area an athlete of God.

Martha Graham, *Blood Memory*

Self-Portrait in Shoulder Stand

Old bag of bones
upside down,
what are you searching for
in poetry,
in meditation?

The mother you never had?

The child in you
that you did not conceive?

Death?

Ease from the fear of death?

Revelation?

Dwelling in the house of clouds
where you imagine
you once lived?

"Born alone,
we depart alone."
Someone said that
during meditation
& I nearly wept.

Oh melancholy lady
behind your clown face,
behind your wisecracks—
how heady it is
to let the ideas rush to your brain!

But even upside down,
you are sad.

Even upside down,
you think of your death.
Even upside down,
you curse the emptiness.

Meditating
on the immobile lotus,
your mind takes flight
like a butterfly
& dabbles in bloodred poppies
& purple heather.

Defying gravity,
defying death,
what makes you think
the body's riddle
is better solved
upside down?

Blood rushes to your head
like images that come too fast
to write.

After a life held in the double grip
of gravity & time,
after a headfirst birth
out of your mother's bowels
& into the earth,
you practice for the next.

You make your body light
so that in time,
feetfirst,
you will be born
into the sky.

Erica Jong, *At the Edge of the Body*

Free flight inwards.
Fleeing through all nights.
The realms of darkness in one taught throat.
Further into blackness
Razor sharp against the feathers.
Then out, naked.
It is called light, the brightness.
Blinding when one does not see the whiteness
In the light.
It is nothing
And yet, it is what all live by
the lucid darkness, relentless
silk and stone
feathers that fall
snow on eyelids
The ceiling of life opens slowly
I move upwards
And rotate out into nothing.
Oh—my dark flight
Towards the sea of freedom—so white:
not milk, not snow.

No, but the brightness of the light,
a body with white blood.
A glow that cannot be extinguished.
Lighthouse in the world.

Sun Axelsson,
Untitled from private collection

Can you explain to yourself what or who you are? What is the nature of this thinking, knowing, feeling entity in you which is conscious of the world around it and which is never able to answer the question whence it came and where it has to go.

Material progress is a preliminary step to spiritual awakening. In every civilization of the past, when the smoke and dust of the battle and struggles for supremacy died down, the eternal questions—Who am I and what is the mystery behind this creation?—began to agitate the more intelligent and evolved individuals of the populace.

The answers furnished by wise men among the Egyptians, Babylonians, Indo-Aryans, Chinese, Persians, Greeks, and Romans are still on record, and it is obvious that it is only this restless hunger of the soul to discover itself that has prompted most of man's mental, artistic, and scientific growth. In fact, at the beginning all knowledge originated from the pressures exerted by the religious thirst in man. There is nothing so erroneous as the opinions expressed by some scholars and men of science that religious experience is a pathological condition of the brain or an invasion from the unconscious. This irresponsible attitude destroys the very foundation of the precious urge responsible for the progress of mankind.

Yoga aims to give these momentous questions answers which cannot be furnished by skeptical denials, drug use, Asanas or mantras, breathing exercises, or meditation without other moral virtues. In order to be effective, Yoga must be practiced in the fullness of all its eight limbs or branches. Everyone who aspires to the supreme experience must strive for perfection; he must begin first with the development of his personality.

"I call him alone a Brahman, that is, a spiritually awakened person," says Buddha, "from whom lust, anger, pride, and envy have dropped off like a mustard seed from the point of a needle." Mere recitation of the well-known mantra, "Om Mani Padme Om," popular among the Buddhists in Tibet, or its rotation millions of times on prayer wheels, could not bear any fruit in one who did not follow the other teaching of Gotma the Buddha. The tragedy is that people do not often understand what "enlightenment" or "self-realization" means. It is a colossal achievement.

According to the records available, all the men who had the genuine experience through the whole course of history do not number more than a few hundred. They are far fewer in number than the men of talent and genius in all other branches of knowledge and art, but they created the revolutions in thought which continue to affect the world to this day. The spiritual-adept or religious genius is extremely rare for this reason: "Illumination" represents a transformation of consciousness, the opening of a new channel of perception within, by which the deathless and boundless universe is opened to the vision of the soul.

Just as every atom of matter represents a unit of basic energy forming the universe, every human soul represents a drop in an infinite ocean of consciousness which has no beginning and no end. The average man, oblivious to his own divine nature and unconscious of his own majesty, lives in permanent doubt because of the limitations of the human brain. He is overwhelmed by uncertainty and sorrow at the thought of death and identifies himself with the body from the first to the last. He does not realize that he has a glorious, unbounded, eternal existence of his own.

All the systems of Yoga and all religious disciplines are designed to bring about those psychosomatic changes in the body which are essential for the metamorphosis of consciousness. A new center—presently dormant in the average man and woman—has to be activated and a more powerful stream of psychic energy must rise into the head from the base of the spine to enable human consciousness to transcend the normal limits. This is the final phase of the present evolutionary impulse in man. The cerebrospinal system of man has to undergo a radical change, enabling consciousness to attain a dimension which transcends the limits of the highest intellect. Here reason yields to intuition and revelation appears to guide the steps of humankind.

The syllable "aum" represents the music of the soul. This melody is heard only when the Divine Power Center in man is roused to activity. Then a sublime radiation floods the brain like a stream of golden nectar, lighting what was dark before. As the luster spreads, the soul is filled with an inexpressible happiness and finds itself growing in dimension, extending outward like rays from the sun. It reaches all nearby objects, then spreads to the distant boundaries, including the horizon and the visible universe. There is no confusion or distortion as happens with drugs and no loss of memory as happens in hypnosis. The intellect remains unaffected, and there is no overlapping or aberration. The inner and outer worlds stand side by side, but with one momentous difference: From a point of consciousness the soul now seems to stretch from end to end, an ineffable and intangible intelligence present everywhere.

Gopi Krishna, from "The True Aim of Yoga,"
in *The Awakening of Kundalini*

✦ Consciousness, Transcendence ✦

"The longing for light is the longing of consciousness."

—C. G. JUNG

As we transcend towards our higher Selves, we also open to the expansion of our minds, that of becoming conscious of ourselves, of others, of the world, and of the divine. The term "consciousness" means awareness, receptivity, cognizance, being fully alive—nothing less than total awareness in all facets of our being. It can happen spontaneously in a sudden revelation, or a feeling of being part of our natural surroundings, belonging to them. Or it can happen through deliberate experimentation with various mind-expanding spiritual practices and breathing techniques. Becoming conscious—and remaining conscious—is an ever-evolving necessity on the journey of illumination. In his book *Science, Order & Creativity*, physicist David Bohm explains that consciousness' ground goes from "the relatively manifest on to ever greater subtlety."

In order to achieve consciousness, we must first acknowledge that God and the divine speak to us through our psyche, through the unconscious self. By trusting that God dwells in the darkness as well as the light, we overcome our fear of the unknown, and allow ourselves to transcend self-inflicted limitations and old ways of comprehending ourselves. Instead of fearing our dark side, or the darkness in the world, we need to embrace it as a part of the deep mystery of our being and our existence. Then transcendence can occur as the way to the unitive self—our beings joined with God. The bliss in the recognition and comprehension of the "all" consists of the folding together of all of the human being with the soul into the Source.

During the last fifty years, the unitive or transcendental experience has sometimes been induced with the assistance of psychedelics—LSD, for example, which has also been used in therapeutic processes. American psychiatrist Dr. Stanislav Grof's landmark account of his work in founding "transpersonal psychology" and finding the interconnection between psychotherapy and the soul, to a large degree, sums up what has been discovered about the unconscious. Through holotropic breath work (a technique involving breathing to the accompaniment of loud music), transcendental states have been achieved which are similar to those that are drug-induced. In so doing, Grof has paved a way to transcendental union and healing of the psyche through natural techniques, which, as you will read, Thomas Merton felt were necessary when he wrote to novelist and essayist Aldous Huxley.

Indian-born Jiddu Krishnamurti (1895–1986) has long been recognized as one of the world's foremost spiritual teachers. He was educated in England and spent much of his life in the West, especially in England, Switzerland,

and the United States. His piece on awareness and insight through his respect of our natural world is a consistent theme in all his writings. His descriptions of the messages that nature offers, of the necessity for us to see and experience, to be "attentive to all this, choicelessly aware," are, I believe, some of the most moving words on the gifts of our natural habitat.

><

To be conscious means to be aware, to know, to perceive, to observe. The content of consciousness is your belief, your pleasure, your experience, the particular knowledge that you have gathered, either through external experience or through your fears, attachments, pain, the agony of loneliness, sorrow, the search for something more than mere physical existence; all that is one's consciousness with its content. The content makes the consciousness. Without content there is not the consciousness as we know it. That consciousness, which is very complex, contradictory, with extraordinary vitality, is it yours? Is thought yours? Or is there only thinking, which is neither of the East nor the West? There is only thinking, which is common to all mankind, whether rich or poor. Technicians, with their extraordinary capacity, or the monks who withdraw from the world and consecrate themselves to an idea, are still thinking.

Is this consciousness common to all mankind? Wherever one goes, one sees suffering, pain, anxiety, loneliness, insanity, fear, the urge of desire. It is common, it is the ground on which every human being stands. Your consciousness is the consciousness of humanity, the rest of humanity. If one understands the nature of this—that you are the rest of mankind, though we may have different names, live in different parts of the world, be educated in different ways, be affluent or very poor—when you go behind the mask, you are like the rest of mankind: neurotic, aching, suffering loneliness and despair, believing in some illusion, and so on. Whether you go to the East or West, this is so. You may not like it; you may like to think that you are totally independent, free, individual. But when you observe very deeply, you are the rest of humanity.

J. Krishnamurti, *On Nature and the Environment*

Spiritual Energy

There is no concept more familiar to us than that of spiritual energy, yet there is none that is more opaque scientifically. On the one hand, the objective reality of psychical effort and work is so well established that the whole of ethics rests on it and, on the other hand, the nature of this inner power is so intangible that the whole description of the universe in mechanical terms has had no need to take account of it, but has been successfully completed in deliberate disregard of its reality.

The difficulties we still encounter in trying to hold together spirit and matter in a reasonable perspective are nowhere more harshly revealed. Nowhere either is the need more urgent of building a bridge between the two banks of our existence—the physical and the moral—if we wish the material and spiritual sides of our activities to be mutually enlivened.

To connect the two energies, of the body and the soul, in a coherent manner: science has provisionally decided to ignore the question, and it would be very convenient for us to do the same. Unfortunately, or fortunately, caught up as we are here in the logic of a system where the *within* of things has just as much or even more value than their *without*, we collide with the difficulty head on. It is impossible to avoid the clash: we must advance.

Naturally the following considerations do not pretend to be a truly satisfactory solution of the problem of spiritual energy. Their aim is merely to show by means of one example what, in my opinion, an integral science of nature should adopt as its line of research and the kind of interpretation it should follow.

The Problem of the Two Energies

Since the inner face of the world is manifest deep within our human consciousness, and there reflects upon itself, it would seem that we have only got to look at ourselves in order to understand the dynamic relationships existing between the *within* and the *without* of things at a given point in the universe.

In fact, to do so is one of the most difficult of all things.

We are perfectly well aware in our concrete actions that the two opposite forces combine. The motor works, but we cannot make out the method, which seems to be contradictory. What makes the crux—and an irritating one at that—of the problem of spiritual energy for our reason is the heightened sense that we bear without ceasing in ourselves that our action seems at once to depend on, and yet to be independent of, material forces.

First of all, the dependence. This is depressingly and magnificently obvious. "To think, we must eat." That blunt statement expresses a whole economy, and reveals, according to the way we look at it, either the tyranny of matter or its spiritual power. The loftiest speculation, the most burning love are, as we know only too well, accompanied and paid for by an expenditure of physical energy. Sometimes we need bread, sometimes wine, sometimes a drug or a hormone injection, sometimes the stimulation of a colour, sometimes the magic of a sound which goes in at our ears as a vibration and reaches our brains in the form of inspiration.

Without the slightest doubt *there is something* through which material and spiritual energy hold together and are complementary. In last analysis, *somehow or other*, there must be a single energy operating in the world. And the first idea that occurs to us is that the "soul" must be as it were a focal point of transformation at which, from all the points of nature, the forces of bodies converge, to become interiorised and sublimated in beauty and truth.

Yet, seductive though it be, the idea of the *direct* transformation of one of these two energies into the other is no sooner glimpsed than it has to be abandoned. As soon as we try to couple them together, their mutual independence becomes as clear as their interrelation.

Once again: "To think, we must eat." But what a variety of thoughts we get out of one slice of bread! Like the letters of the alphabet, which can equally well be assembled into nonsense as into the most beautiful poem, the same calories seem as indifferent as they are necessary to the spiritual values they nourish.

The two energies—of mind and matter—spread respectively through the two layers of the world (the *within* and the *without*) have, taken as a whole, much the same demeanour. They are constantly associated and in some way pass into each other. But it seems impossible to establish a simple correspondence between their curves. On the one hand, only a minute fraction of "physical" energy is used up in the highest exercise of spiritual energy; on the other, this minute fraction, once absorbed, results on the internal scale in the most extraordinary oscillations.

Pierre Teilhard de Chardin, The Phenomenon of Man

We always look from outside within; from knowledge we proceed to further knowledge, always adding and the very taking away is another addition. And our consciousness is made up of a thousand remembrances and recognitions, conscious of the trembling leaf, of the flower, of that man passing by, that child running across the field; conscious of the rock, the stream, the bright red flower, and the bad smell of a pigsty. From this remembering and recognizing, from the outward responses, we try to become conscious of the inner recesses, of the deeper motives and urges; we probe deeper and deeper into the vast depths of the mind. This whole process of challenges and responses, of the movement of experiencing and recognizing the hidden and the open activities, this whole is consciousness bound to time.

The cup is not only the shape, the colour, the design but also that emptiness inside the cup. The cup is the emptiness held within a form; without that emptiness there would be no cup nor form. We know consciousness by outer signs, by its limitations of height and depth, of thought and feeling. But all this is the outer form of consciousness; from the outer we try to find the inner. Is this possible? Theories and speculations are not significant; they actually prevent all discovery. From the outer we try to find the inner, from the known we probe hoping to find the unknown. Is it possible to probe from the inner to the outer? The instrument that probes from the outer we know, but is there such an instrument that probes from the unknown to the known? Is there? And how can there be? There cannot be. If there is one, it's recognizable and if it's recognizable, it's within the area of the known.

That strange benediction comes when it will, but with each visitation, deep within, there is a transformation; it is never the same.

J. Krishnamurti, *On God*

My first LSD session was an event that has in its consequences profoundly changed my professional and personal life. I experienced an extraordinary encounter and confrontation with my unconscious psyche, which instantly overshadowed my previous interest in Freudian psychoanalysis. This day marked the beginning of my radical departure from traditional thinking in psychiatry. I was treated to a fantastic display of colorful visions, some of them abstract and geometrical, others figurative and full of symbolic meaning. I also felt an amazing array of emotions with an intensity I did not know was possible. I could not believe how much I learned about my psyche in those few hours. One aspect of my first session deserves special notice, since its significance reached far beyond the level of psychological insights: my preceptor at the faculty was very interested in studying the electrical activity of the brain, and his favorite subject was the exploration of the influence of various frequencies of flashing light on the brain waves. I agreed to have my brain waves monitored by an electroencephalograph as part of the experiment.

I was exposed to a strong stroboscopic light between the third and fourth hour of my experience. At the scheduled time, a research assistant appeared and took me to a small room. She carefully pasted electrodes all over my scalp and asked me to lie down and close my eyes. Then she placed a giant stroboscopic light above my head and turned it on.

At this time, the effects of the drug were culminating, and that immensely enhanced the impact of the strobe. I was hit by a radiance that seemed comparable to the epicenter of an atomic explosion, or possibly to the light of supernatural brilliance that according to Oriental scriptures appears to us at the moment of death. This thunderbolt catapulted me out of my body. I lost first my awareness of the research assistant and the laboratory, then the psychiatric clinic, then Prague, and finally the planet. My consciousness expanded at an inconceivable speed and reached cosmic dimensions.

As the young assistant gradually shifted the frequency of the strobe up and down the scale, I found myself in the middle of a cosmic drama of unimaginable proportions. I experienced the Big Bang, passed through black and white holes in the universe, identified with exploding supernovas, and witnessed many other strange phenomena that seemed to be pulsars, quasars, and other amazing cosmic events.

There was no doubt that the experience I was having was very close to those I knew from reading the great mystical scriptures of the world. Even though my mind was deeply affected by the drug, I was able to see the irony and paradox of the situation. The Divine manifested itself and took me over in a modern laboratory in the middle of a serious scientific experiment conducted in a Communist country with a substance produced in the test tube of a twentieth-century chemist.

I emerged from this experience touched to the core and immensely impressed by its power. Not believing at that time, as I do today, that the potential for a mystical experience is the natural birthright of all human beings, I attributed everything to the effect of the drug. I felt strongly that the study of nonordinary states of mind in general, and those induced by psychedelics in particular, was by far the most interesting area of psychiatry and decided to make it my field of specialization.

I realized that, under the proper circumstances, psychedelic experiences—to a much greater degree than dreams, which play such a crucial role in psychoanalysis—are truly, in Freud's words, a "royal road into the unconscious." This powerful catalyst could help to heal the gap between the great explanatory power of psychoanalysis and its lack of efficacy as a therapeutic tool. I felt strongly that LSD-assisted analysis could deepen, intensify, and accelerate the therapeutic process and produce practical results matching the ingenuity of Freudian theoretical speculations.

Within weeks of my session, I joined a group of researchers comparing the effects of different psychedelic substances with naturally occurring psychoses. As I was working with experimental subjects, I could not get off my mind the idea of starting a project in which psychoactive drugs could be used as catalysts for psychoanalysis.

My dream came true when I won a position at the newly founded Psychiatric Research Institute in Prague. Its open-minded director appointed me principal investigator of a clinical study exploring the therapeutic potential of LSD psychotherapy. I initiated a research project using a series of sessions with medium dosages in patients with various forms of psychiatric disorders. On occasion, we included mental-health professionals, artists, scientists, and philosophers who were interested and had serious motivations for the experience, such as gaining a deeper understanding of the human psyche, enhancement of creativity, or facilitation of problem solving. The repeated use of such sessions became popular among European therapists under the name "psycholytic treatment"; its Greek roots suggest a process of dissolving psychological conflicts and tensions.

I began a fantastic intellectual, philosophical, and spiritual adventure that has now lasted more than three decades. During this time, my worldview has been undermined and destroyed many times by daily exposure to extraordinary observations and experiences. A most remarkable transformation has happened as a result of my systematic study of the psychedelic experiences of others as well as my own: under the unrelenting influx of incontrovertible evidence, my understanding of the world has gradually shifted from an atheistic position to a basically mystical one. What had been foreshadowed in a cataclysmic way by my first experience of cosmic consciousness has been brought to full fruition by careful daily work on the research data.

My initial approach to LSD psychotherapy was deeply influenced by the Freudian model of the psyche, which is limited to postnatal life history and the individual unconscious. Soon after I started working with different categories of psychiatric patients using repeated sessions, it became clear that such a conceptual framework was painfully narrow. While it might be appropriate for some forms of verbal psychotherapy, it was clearly inadequate for situations where the psyche was activated by a powerful catalyst. As long as we used medium dosages, many of the initial experiences of the series contained biographical material from the individual's infancy and childhood, as described by Freud. However, when the sessions were continued, each of the clients moved sooner or later into experiential realms that lay beyond this framework. When the dosages were increased, the same thing happened, but much earlier.

Once the sessions reached this point, I started witnessing experiences that were indistinguishable from those described in the ancient mystical traditions and spiritual philosophies of the East. Some of them were powerful sequences of psychological death and rebirth; others involved feelings of oneness with humanity, nature, and the cosmos. Many clients also reported visions of deities and demons from different cultures and visits to various mythological realms. Among the most astonishing occurrences were dramatic and vivid sequences that were subjectively experienced as past-incarnation memories.

I was not prepared to observe such phenomena in psychotherapeutic sessions. I knew about their existence from my studies of comparative religion, but my psychiatric training had taught me to consider them psychotic, not therapeutic. I was astonished by their emotional power, authenticity, and transformative potential. Initially, I did not welcome this unexpected development in my therapeutic venture. The intensity of the emotional and physiological manifestations of these states was frightening, and many of their aspects threatened to undermine my safe and reliable worldview.

However, as my experience and familiarity with these extraordinary phenomena increased, it became clear that they were normal and natural manifestations of the deeper domains of the human psyche. Their emergence from the unconscious followed upon the appearance of biographical material from childhood and infancy, which traditional psychotherapy considers a legitimate and desirable subject of exploration. Thus it would have been highly artificial and arbitrary to view childhood memories as normal and acceptable and attribute the experiences that followed them to a pathological process.

When the nature and content of these recesses of the psyche were fully revealed, they undoubtedly represented a significant source of difficult emotional and physical feelings. In addition, when these sequences were allowed to run their natural course, the therapeutic results transcended anything I had ever witnessed. Difficult symptoms that had resisted months and even years of conventional treatment often disappeared after experiences such as psychological death and rebirth, feelings of cosmic unity, and sequences that clients described as past-life memories.

My observations of others were in full agreement with those from my own psychedelic sessions: many states that mainstream psychiatry considers bizarre and incomprehensible are natural manifestations of the deep dynamics of the human psyche. And their emergence into consciousness, traditionally seen as a sign of mental illness, may actually be the organism's radical effort to free itself from the effects of various traumas, simplify its functioning, and heal itself. I realized that it was not up to us to dictate what the human psyche should be like in order to fit our scientific beliefs and worldview. Rather, it is important to discover and accept the true nature of the psyche and find out how we can best cooperate with it.

I attempted to map the experiential territories that were made available through the catalyzing action of LSD. For several years, I dedicated all of my time to psychedelic work with patients of various clinical diagnoses, keeping detailed records of my own observations and collecting their own descriptions of their sessions. I believed I was creating a new cartography of the human psyche. However, when I completed a map of consciousness that included the different types and levels of experiences I had observed in psychedelic sessions, it dawned on me that it was new only from the point of view of Western academic psychiatry. It became clear that I had rediscovered what Aldous Huxley called "perennial philosophy," an understanding of the universe and of existence that has emerged with some minor variations again and again in different countries and historical periods. Similar maps have existed in various cultures for centuries or even millennia. The different systems of yoga, Buddhist teachings, the Tibetan Vajrayana, Kashmir Shaivism, Taoism, Sufism, Kabbalah, and Christian mysticism are just a few examples.

The process I was witnessing in others and experiencing myself also had a deep similarity with shamanic initiations, rites of passage of various cultures, and the ancient mysteries of death and rebirth. Western scientists had ridiculed and rejected these sophisticated procedures, believing that they had successfully replaced them with rational and scientifically sound approaches. My observations convinced me that such modern fields as psychoanalysis and behaviorism had only scratched the surface of the human psyche and could bear no comparison to the depth and scope of such ancient knowledge.

In the early years of my research, I became enthusiastic about these exciting new observations and made several attempts to discuss them with my Czech colleagues. I quickly found that my scientific reputation would be at stake if I continued to do so. During the first decade of this work, much of my research was done in isolation, and I had to carefully censor my communications with other professionals. I found only a handful of friends with whom I could openly talk about my findings.

My situation started to change in 1967, when I was awarded a scholarship from a foundation for psychiatric research in New Haven, Connecticut. This made it possible for me to come to the United States and continue my psychedelic research at the Maryland Psychiatric Research Center in Baltimore. During my lectures in various American cities, I connected with many colleagues—consciousness researchers, anthropologists, parapsychologists, thanatologists, and others—whose work resulted in a scientific perspective that resembled or complemented my own.

One important event at this time was my encounter and friendship with Abraham Maslow and Anthony Sutich, the founders of humanistic psychology. Abe had conducted extensive research into spontaneous mystical states, or "peak experiences," and came to conclusions very similar to my own. Out of our joint meetings came the idea of launching a new discipline that would combine science and spirituality and incorporate the perennial wisdom concerning various levels and states of consciousness.

The new movement, which we called "transpersonal psychology," attracted many enthusiastic followers. As their numbers grew, I felt for the first time a sense of professional identity and belonging. However, one problem still remained: transpersonal psychology, although comprehensive and cohesive in its own right, seemed hopelessly separated from mainstream science.

Another decade passed before it became obvious that traditional science was itself undergoing a conceptual revolution of unprecedented proportions.

The radical changes that were introduced into the scientific worldview by Einstein's theories of relativity and quantum theory were followed by equally profound revisions occurring in many other disciplines. New connections were being established between transpersonal psychology and the emerging scientific worldview that has become known as the "new paradigm."

At present, we are still lacking a satisfactory synthesis of these developments, which are replacing old ways of thinking about the world. However, the impressive mosaic of new observations and theories that are already available suggest that in the future the old/new discoveries in regard to consciousness and the human psyche might become integral parts of a comprehensive scientific worldview.

Three decades of detailed and systematic studies of the human mind through observations of nonordinary states of consciousness in others and myself have led me to some radical conclusions. I now believe that consciousness and the human psyche are much more than accidental products of the physiological processes in the brain; they are reflections of the cosmic intelligence that permeates all of creation. We are not just biological machines and highly developed animals, but also fields of consciousness without limits, transcending space and time.

In this context, spirituality is an important dimension of existence, and becoming aware of this fact is a desirable development in human life.

Stanislav and Christina Grof, from
"God in the Laboratory: Stanislav's Story,"
in *The Stormy Search for the Self*

[The following is a letter to Aldous Huxley from Thomas Merton in response to Huxley's article "Drugs That Shape Men's Minds," which appeared in The Saturday Evening Post of October 1958. It is followed by Huxley's reply. Ed.]

November 27, 1958

Twenty years, or nearly that many, have gone by since a very pleasant exchange of letters took place between us. The other day, in correcting the proofs of a journal I kept then, and which is being published now, I was reminded of the fact. I shall send you the book when it appears. The final entries, in which you are mentioned, will testify to the gratitude and friendship with which I have continued to remember you since then.

Meanwhile, I am happy to open another discussion with you, and I intend to do so in a spirit which will, I hope, lead to something quite constructive. For I assure you that I have no wish whatever to enter into a silly argument, and that I approach you with none of the crudities or prejudices which I am sure annoy you in other clerics. I do not of course claim to be above the ordinary human failings of religious people, but I think I am at least relatively free of partisanship and fanaticism.

Your article in *The Saturday Evening Post* on drugs that help man to achieve an experience of self-transcendence has, you know, created quite a stir. We do not read *The Saturday Evening Post* here in the monastery, but a good lady sent me a copy of your article, together with a copy of a letter she sent to you advising you to read Fr. Garrigon Lagrange on contemplation. May God preserve you from such a fate.

I am in no position to dispute what you say about the effect of drugs. Though occasionally fortified by aspirin, and exhilarated by coffee, and even sometimes using a barbiturate to get to sleep (alas), I have no experience of the things you speak of. Perhaps I shall make a trial of them one of these days, so that I will know what I am talking about. But since I feel, as you do, that this is a matter which merits discussion and study, I would like to put forward the things that occur to me after my first encounter with the subject. I hope by this to *learn* rather than to teach and I can see that this is your attitude also. Therefore, if you will permit me, I would like to take up the implicit invitation you expressed in the article, and invite you still further, if you are interested, to go into this with us. If you are ever in this neighborhood perhaps you could come here and we could talk at leisure. Our mutual friends, Victor Hammer and his wife at Lexington, would gladly bring you over.

After this preamble, here are the questions I would like to raise:

1. Are you not endangering the whole concept of genuine mystical experience in saying that it is something that can be "produced" by a drug? I know, you qualify the statement, you say that a drug can induce a state in which mystical experience can be occasioned: a drug can remove obstacles in our ordinary everyday state of mind, and make a kind of latent mysticism come to the surface. But I wonder if this accords with the real nature of mystical experience?

I think this point must be studied carefully, and I suggest the following:

2. Ought we not to distinguish between an experience which is essentially *aesthetic and natural* from an experience which is *mystical and supernatural*? I would call aesthetic and natural an experience which would be an intuitive "tasting" of the inner spirituality of our own being—of an intuition of being as such, arrived at through an intuitive awareness of our own inmost reality. This would be an experience of "oneness" within oneself and with all beings, a flash of awareness of the transcendent reality that is within all that is real. This sort of thing "happens" to one in all sorts of ways and I see no reason why it should not be occasioned to the use of a drug. This intuition is very like the aesthetic intuition that precedes the creation of a work

of art. It is like the intuition of a philosopher who rises above his concepts and their synthesis to see everything at one glance, in all its length, height, breadth and depth. It is like the intuition of a person who has participated deeply in a liturgical act. (I think you take too cavalier an attitude toward liturgy, although I confess that I am irked by liturgical enthusiasts when they want to regiment others into their way of thinking.)

By the way, though I call this experience "natural," that does not preclude its being produced by the action of God's grace (a term that must be used with care). But I mean that it is not in its mode or in its content beyond the capacities of human nature itself. Please forgive me for glibly using this distinction between natural and supernatural as if I were quite sure where the dividing line came. Of course I am not.

What would I call a *supernatural and mystical* experience, then? I speak very hesitantly, and do not claim to be an authority. What I say may be very misleading. It may be the product of subjective and sentimental illusion or it may be the product of a rationalization superimposed on the experience described above. Anyway, here goes.

It seems to me that a fully mystical experience has in its very essence some note of a direct spiritual *contact of two liberties*, a kind of a flash or spark which ignites an intuition of all that has been said above, *plus* something much more which I can only describe as "personal," in which God is known not as an "object" or as "Him up there" or "Him in everything" nor as "the All" but as—the biblical expression—I AM, or simply AM. But what I mean is that this is not the kind of intuition that smacks of anything procurable because it is a presence of a Person and *depends on the liberty of that Person*. And lacking the element of a free gift, a free act of love on the part of Him Who comes, the experience would lose its specifically mystical quality.

3. But now, from the moment that such an experience can be conceived of as *dependent on* and *inevitably following from* the casual use of a material instrument, it loses the quality of spontaneity and freedom and transcendence which makes it truly mystical.

This then is my main question. It seems to me that for this reason, expressed lamely perhaps and without full understanding, real mystical experience would be more or less incompatible with the *consistent* use of a drug.

Here are some further thoughts: Supposing a person with a genuine vocation to mystical union. And supposing that person starts to use a drug. And supposing further that I am correct in the above estimate of what real mystical experience consists in: then the one using the drug can produce what I have called a "natural and aesthetic" experience. But at the same time his higher "conscience" (here I mean not merely a moral censor but his inmost spirit in its function of "judge" between what is real and what isn't) will inevitably reproach him for self-delusion. He will enjoy the experience for a moment, but it will be followed, not by the inner permanent strengthening of a real spiritual experience, but by lassitude, discouragement, confusion, and *an increased need for the drug*. This will produce a vicious circle of repeated use of the drug, renewed lassitude and guilt, greater need for the drug, and final complete addiction with the complete ruin of a mystical vocation, if not worse.

What I say here is based on suppositions, of course. I do not attempt to impose the analysis on you, but I would be very interested in your judgment of what I have said and your opinion in the matter.

I will not weary you by prolonging this letter, but will close here in the hope that we can go further into the matter later on.

May I add that I am interested in yoga and above all in Zen, which I find to be the finest example of a technique leading to the highest *natural* perfection of man's contemplative liberty. You may argue that the use of a koan to dispose one for satori is not different from the use of a drug. I would like to submit that there is all the difference in the world, and perhaps we can speak more of this later. My dear Mr. Huxley, it is a joy to write to you of these things. I hope you can reply. God bless you.

Thomas Merton, *The Hidden Ground of Love*

3276 Deronda Drive,
Los Angeles 28, Cal.
10 January, 1959

Dear Father Merton,

Thank you for your letter. The problems you raise are interesting and difficult, and their solution must be sought on the practical and factual level. A great deal of work has now been done on mescaline and lysergic acid, both by researchers and clinicians using the drugs therapeutically in such conditions as alcoholism and assorted neuroses. (One group now working on alcoholism in British Columbia, incidentally, is using lysergic acid within a religious, specifically Catholic, frame of reference, and achieving remarkable results, largely by getting patients to realize that the universe is profoundly different from what, on their ordinary, conditioned level of experience, it had seemed to be.) Statistically the results of all this experimentation are roughly as follows. About seventy percent of those who take the drug have a positive experience; the others have a negative experience, which may be really infernal. (A great many of the states experienced by the desert fathers were negative. See the thousands of pictures of the Temptations of St. Anthony.) All agree that the experience is profoundly significant. One finds again and again, in the reports written by subjects after the event, the statement that "this is the most wonderful experience I have ever had" and "I feel that my life will never be quite the same again." Among the positive experiences a certain proportion, on the first occasion of taking the drug, are purely aesthetic—transfiguration of the outer world so that it is seen as the young Wordsworth saw it and later described it in the "Ode on the Intimations of Immortality in Childhood": a universe of inconceivable beauty in which all things are full of life and charged with an obscure but immensely important meaning. Those who are congenitally good visualizers tend to see visions with the eyes closed, or even, projected upon the screen of the external world, with the eyes open. The nature of these visions is often paradisal and the descriptions of them remind one irresistibly of the description of the New Jerusalem in the Apocalypse or the Eden of Ezekiel, or the various paradises of other religions. Finally there are those whose experience seems to be much more than aesthetic and may be labeled as pre-mystical or even, I believe, mystical. In the course of the last five years I have taken mescaline twice and lysergic acid three or four times. My first experience was mainly aesthetic. Later experiences were of another nature and helped me to understand many of the obscure utterances to be found in the writings of the mystics, Christian and Oriental. An unspeakable sense of gratitude for the privilege of being born into this universe. ("Gratitude is heaven itself," says Blake—and I know now exactly what he was talking about.) A transcendence of the ordinary subject-object relationship. A transcendence of the fear of death. A sense of solidarity with the world and its spiritual principle and the conviction that, in spite of pain, evil and all the rest, everything is somehow all right. (One understands such phrases as, "Yea, though He slay me, yet will I trust in Him" and the great utterance, I can't quote it exactly, of Julian of Norwich.) Finally, an understanding, not intellectual, but in some sort total, an understanding with the entire organism, of the affirmation that God is Love. The experiences are transient, of course; but the memory of them, and the inchoate revivals of them which tend to recur spontaneously or during meditation, continue to exercise a profound effect upon one's mind. There seems to be no evidence in the published literature that the drug is habit forming or that it creates a craving for repetition. There is a feeling—I speak from personal experience and from word-of-mouth reports given me by others—that the experience is so transcendently important that it is in no circumstances a thing to be entered upon light-heartedly or for enjoyment. (In some respects, it is not enjoyable; for it entails a temporary death of the ego, a going-beyond.) Those who desire to make use of this "gratuitous grace," to co-operate with it, tend to do so, not by repeating the experiment at frequent intervals, but by trying to open themselves up, in a state of alert passivity, to the transcendent "isness," to use Eckhart's phrase, which they have known and, in some sort, *been*. Theoretically, there exists a danger that subjects would have a craving for constant repetition of the chemically induced experience. In practice this craving doesn't seem to manifest itself. A repetition every year, or every six months, is felt, most often, to be the desirable regimen.

A friend of mine, saved from alcoholism, during the last fatal phases of the disease, by a spontaneous theophany, which changed his life as completely as St. Paul's was changed by his theophany on the road to Damascus, has taken lysergic acid two or three times and affirms that his experience under the drug is identical with the spontaneous experience which changed his life—the only difference being that the spontaneous experience did not last so long as the chemically induced one. There is, obviously, a field here for serious and reverent experimentation.

With all good wishes, I am

Yours very sincerely,
Aldous Huxley

Aldous Huxley, *Letters of Aldous Huxley*

→ 6 ←

Archetypes, Myth, and Ritual

The eminent Swiss psychiatrist Carl Jung first laid bare the connection between psychology, spirituality, and religious and mythical symbolism. He provided evidence of ways that the unconscious communicates, connects, and is even shaped through symbols, metaphors, and archetypes. Through full comprehension of the archetypical world we can begin to understand the way spiritual energy manifests itself through humanity. "The instincts and archetypes together form the 'collective unconscious,'" Jung wrote. He calls it "collective" because it "is not made up of individual and more or less unique contents but of those which are universal and of regular occurrence." These supreme patterns and personalities in archetype are shaped by the collective human transcendent experience. They have existed from the earliest record of human spiritual history.

American educator and writer Joseph Campbell began his exploration into the mythical history of man by reading, studying, and thinking for many years in a cabin in the woods. He emerged as the foremost authority of our age on ancient mythical images, characters, and tales and how they connect us with our deepest and innermost longings and needs. Like Jung, Campbell also believes that we must recognize and acknowledge the archetypical world—that "no living system of symbols functioning for engagement can survive when it has lost contact with the actual conscious and unconscious worlds of its society." The acknowledgment of myth as more than an idea is the first step in keeping it a reality in our collective minds, but we can bring it to an even larger place in our lives through creativity. We can transform mythical and archetypal ideas through painting, writing, and performance. Modern dancer and choreographer Martha Graham, who used archetypes and myths as a basis of her work, left dance and movement notes which are like sparkling gems in a mythic labyrinth, a tapestry of mythic ideas.

Rituals and ceremonies formed and performed in belief and reverence become sanctifying acts in themselves. They bring the larger whole, the collective evolution of ourselves together in one moment and one place, thus ensuring its survival. This is why rituals are so powerful. Celebrating rites of passage, honouring and praying for the gifts of the gods, reenacting Christ's Last Supper in the Mass—are all ways of keeping the mythic alive and bestowing sacredness upon all of human life.

English biologist Rupert Sheldrake discovered that repetition of particular behaviours over time has an evolutionary effect upon a species—animals as well as humans. He writes that self-organizing systems of all levels of complexity—including molecules, crystals, cells, tissues, organisms, and societies of organisms—are organized by "morphic fields" and that these "morphic fields" extend to ability and knowledge among ourselves collectively. Once absorbed, this ability lives on in future generations of species. And so it is that worship and ritual brings with it the greater whole of the historic spiritual realm by acknowledging and honouring those who celebrated before.

In the pieces that follow, Michael Murphy, co-founder of The Esalen Institute in California, gives an account of his discovery of a divine presence in a ritual honouring Lord Shiva, and physicist Fritjof Capra becomes part of the archetypical world by witnessing a man offering candles in an Indian ceremony. Charlene Spretnak, a California eco-feminist, who has contributed towards raising the consciousness of women's spirituality in recent years, shares some ritualistic experiences among women. All together they show that there are ancient and traditional ways of transcending to the greater place in our spirituality, as well as ways in which we can create our own sacred spaces to welcome, petition, and celebrate the divine.

><

In addition to our immediate consciousness, which is of a thoroughly personal nature and which we believe to be the only empirical psyche (even if we tack on the personal unconscious as an appendix), there exists a second psychic system of a collective, universal, and impersonal nature which is identical in all individuals. This collective unconscious does not develop individually but is inherited. It consists of pre-existent forms, the archetypes, which can only become conscious secondarily and which give definite form to certain psychic contents.

C. G. Jung, *The Archetypes and the Collective Unconscious*

Science is tacitly convinced that a nonpsychic, transcendental object exists. But science also knows how difficult it is to grasp the real nature of the object, especially when the organ of perception fails or is lacking, and when the appropriate modes of thought do not exist or have still to be created. In cases where neither our sense organs nor their artificial aids can attest the presence of a real object, the difficulties mount enormously, so that one feels tempted to assert that there is simply no real object present. I have never drawn this overhasty conclusion, for I have never been inclined to think that our senses were capable of perceiving all forms of being. I have, therefore, even hazarded the postulate that the phenomenon of archetypal configurations—which are psychic events *par excellence*—may be founded upon a *psychoid* base, that is, upon an only partially psychic and possibly altogether different form of being. For lack of empirical data I have neither knowledge nor understanding of such forms of being, which are commonly called spiritual. From the point of view of science, it is immaterial what I may *believe* on that score, and I must accept my ignorance. But insofar as the archetypes act upon me, they are real and actual to me, even though I do not know what their real nature is. This applies, of course, not only to the archetypes but to the nature of the psyche in general. Whatever it may state about itself, it will never get beyond itself. All comprehension and all that is comprehended is in itself psychic, and to that extent we are hopelessly cooped up in an exclusively psychic world. Nevertheless, we have good reason to suppose that behind this veil there exists the uncomprehended absolute object which affects and influences us—and to suppose it even, or particularly, in the case of psychic phenomena about which no verifiable statements can be made. Statements concerning possibility or impossibility are valid only in specialized fields; outside those fields they are merely arrogant presumptions.

Prohibited though it may be from an objective point of view to make statements out of the blue—that is, without sufficient reason—there are nevertheless some statements which apparently have to be made without objective reasons. The justification here is a psychodynamic one, of the sort usually termed "subjective" and regarded as a purely personal matter. But that is to commit the mistake of failing to distinguish whether the statement really proceeds only from an isolated subject, and is prompted by exclusively personal motives, or whether it occurs generally and springs from a collectively present dynamic pattern. In that case it should not be classed as subjective, but as psychologically objective, since an indefinite number of individuals find themselves prompted by an inner impulse to make an identical statement, or feel a certain view to be a vital necessity. Since the archetype is not just an inactive form, but a real force charged with a specific energy, it may very well be regarded as the *causa efficiens* of such statements, and be understood as the subject of them. In other words, it is not the personal human being who is making the statement, but the archetype speaking through him. If these statements are stifled or disregarded, both medical experience and common knowledge demonstrate that psychic troubles are in store. These will appear either as neurotic symptoms or, in the case of persons who are incapable of neurosis, as collective delusions.

Archetypal statements are based upon instinctive preconditions and have nothing to do with reason; they are neither rationally grounded nor can they be banished by rational arguments. They have always been part of the world scene—*représentations collectives*, as Lévy-Bruhl rightly called them. Certainly the ego and its will have a great part to play in life; but what the ego wills is subject in the highest degree to the interference, in ways of which the ego is usually unaware, of the autonomy and numinosity of archetypal processes. Practical consideration of these processes is the essence of religion, insofar as religion can be approached from a psychological point of view.

C. G. Jung, *Memories, Dreams, Reflections*

Myths are not only mirrors, but corridors of mirrors. When we enter them, they become systems of thought branching towards the outer world and tunnels of enlightenment rooting towards the unconscious soul. We have constructed them to lead us back and forth from dream to vigil and from sensation to experience, and if we wilfully abandon them, we will be left, in the full meaning of the word, senseless.

Alberto Manguel, in a book review,
The Globe and Mail, Toronto, March 27, 1993

What did you do as a child
that created timelessness
that made you forget time?
There lies the myth to live by.
Joseph Campbell, *Reflections on the Art of Living*

It is no easy task for the contemporary Westerner to accept the validity of the mythic world. We are so accustomed to thinking of myths as fantasy that we often denigrate people to whom myth was and is an integral part of life. We tend to think of such people as ignorant and childlike, with no understanding of the physical universe.

The relegation of myth and fairy tale to childhood is a recent phenomenon. Before the twentieth century, myths and fairy tales were the repository of the wisdom of a whole culture. The people in such societies had a profound understanding and respect for the psychological forces symbolized by these tales, and that understanding enabled them to experience a living spiritual dimension in everyday life.

For the ancient Greeks the gods were real. A Greek who saw a thunderbolt was reminded of Zeus, and so reminded of another, simultaneous system of reality. In contrast, when we see a thunderbolt we see a weather pattern and are probably reminded to watch the six o'clock news for the weather report!

Robert A. Johnson, Ecstasy

What is basically required, and what is offered by literature functioning as myth in a bewildering and secular age, is to *imagine the real*. Not to avoid what *is*, by offering a substitute or a palliative, but to experience what exists so intensely that through the imagination it realizes its full potential. Just as Proustian memory not only recaptures the lost and forgotten moment but makes it more vivid than it had initially been, so imagination brings reality into its own: only through rivers running with wine do we really perceive, as if for the first time, the running waters of the time we live in. It is an act and an experience which restores that mythical significance to life without which it would simply flow through us, unobstructed and unperceived. Myth in literature creates the obstacle through which we recognize and acknowledge the existence both of ourselves and the world.

André Brink, Writing in a State of Siege:
Essays on Politics and Literature

In every age there is a structure of ideas, images, beliefs, assumptions, anxieties, and hopes which express the view of man's situation and destiny generally held at that time. I call this structure a mythology, and its units myths. A myth, in this sense, is an expression of man's concern about himself, about his place in the scheme of things, about his relation to society and God, about the ultimate origin and ultimate fate, either of himself or of the human species generally. A mythology is thus a product of human concern, of our involvement with ourselves, and it always looks at the world from a man-centred point of view. The early and primitive myths were stories, mainly stories about gods, and their units were physical images. In more highly structured societies they develop in two different but related directions. In the first place, they develop into literature as we know it, first into folktales and legends of heroes, thence into the conventional plots of fiction and metaphors of poetry. In the second place, they become conceptualized, and become the informing principles of historical and philosophical thought, as the myth of fall becomes the informing idea of Gibbon's history of Rome, or the myth of the sleeping beauty Rousseau's buried society of nature and reason. My first lecture dealt primarily with mythology in this sense, particularly with the so-called existential myths.

It seems to me that there have been two primary mythological constructions in Western culture. One was the vast synthesis that institutional Christianity made of its Biblical and Aristotelian sources. This myth is at its clearest in the Middle Ages, but it persisted for centuries later, and much of its structure, though greatly weakened by the advance of science, was still standing in the eighteenth century itself. The other is the modern mythology that began when the modern world did, in the later eighteenth century, but reached its more specifically modern shape a century later, and a century before now.

The older mythology was one that stressed two things in particular: the subject-object relation and the use of reason. Man was a subject confronting a nature set over against him. Both man and nature were creatures of God, and were united by that fact. There were no gods in nature: if man looked into the powers of nature to find such gods they would soon turn into devils. What he should look at nature for is the evidence of purpose and design which it shows as a complementary creation of God, and the reason can grasp this sense of design. The rational approach to nature was thus superior to the empirical and experimental approach to it, and the sciences that were most deductive and closest to mathematics were those that were first developed. Of all sciences, astronomy is the most dependent on the subject-object relationship, and in the Middle Ages particularly, astronomy was the science par excellence, the one science that a learned medieval poet, such as Dante or Chaucer, would be assumed to know.

In the pre-modern myth man's ultimate origin was of God, and his chief end was to draw closer to God. Even more important, the social discipline which raised him above the rest of creation was a divine ordinance. Law was of God; the forms of human civilization, the city and the garden, were imitations of divine models, for God planted the garden of Eden and had established his city before man was created; the ultimate human community was not in this world, but in a heaven closer to the divine presence. Philosophers recognized that the ordinary categories of the mind, such as our perception of time and space, might not be adequate at a purely spiritual level. It was possible, for example, that a spiritual body, such as an angel, did not occupy space or travel in space at all. The unfortunate wretch who attempted to put this question into a lively and memorable form by asking how many angels could stand on the point of a pin has become a byword for pedantic stupidity, a terrible warning to all instructors who try to make a technical subject interesting. But as far as popular belief and poetic imagery were concerned, the spiritual world was thought of as essentially another objective environment, to be described in symbols—city, temple, garden, streets—derived from human life, though the myth taught that human life had been derived from them. This mythology, relating as it did both man and nature to God, was a total one, so complete and far-reaching that an alternative world-picture was practically unthinkable. This is the real significance of Voltaire's familiar epigram, that if God did not exist it would be necessary to invent him, which was, in his day, a much more serious remark than it sounds. One could, theoretically, be an atheist; but even an atheist would find God blocking his way on all sides: he would meet the hypothesis of God in history, in philosophy, in psychology, in astronomy. As for morality, its standards were so completely assimilated to religious sanctions that even a century ago it was impossible for many people to believe that non-religious man could have any moral integrity at all.

In the eighteenth century there began to grow, slowly but irresistibly, the conviction that man had created his own civilization. This meant not merely that he was responsible for it—he had always been that—but that its forms of city and garden and design, of law and social discipline and education, even, ultimately, of morals and religion, were of human origin and human creation. This new feeling crystallized around Rousseau in the eighteenth century, and the assumptions underlying the American and French revolutions were relatively new assumptions. Liberty was no longer, as it had been for Milton, something that God gives and that man resists: it was something that most men want and that those who have a stake in slavery invoke their gods to prevent them from getting. Law was no longer, as it had been for Hooker, the reflection of divine order in human life, but in large part the reflection of class privilege in property rights. Art and culture were no longer, as they had been for the age of Shakespeare, the ornaments of social discipline: they took on a prophetic importance as portraying the forms of civilization that man had created. The Romantic movement brought in the conception of the "serious" artist, setting his face against society to follow his art, from which the modern antagonism of the artist to society…has descended.

A major principle of the older mythology was the correspondence of human reason with the design and purpose in nature which it perceives. This correspondence was still accepted even after God had dwindled into a deistic first cause, a necessary hypothesis and nothing more. The modern movement, properly speaking, began when Darwin finally shattered the old teleological conception of nature as reflecting an intelligent purpose. From then on design in nature has been increasingly interpreted by science as a product of a self-serving nature. The older view of design survives vestigially, as when religion tells us that some acts are "contrary to nature." But contemporary science, which is professionally concerned with nature, does not see in the ancient mother-goddess the Wisdom which was the bride of a superhuman creator. What it sees rather is a confused old beldame who has got where she has through a remarkable obstinacy in adhering to trial and error—mostly error—procedures. The rational design that nature reflects is in the human mind only. An example of the kind of thinking that Darwin has made impossible for the modern mind is: "If the Lord had intended us to fly, he'd have given us wings." The conception of natural functions as related to a personal and creative intention is no longer in our purview.

Modern mythology, at least with us, is naturally not as well unified as the earlier one, but it does possess some unity none the less. It reaches us on two main levels. There is a social mythology, which we learn through conversation and the contacts of family, teachers, and neighbours, which is reinforced by the mass media, newspapers, television, and movies, and which is based fundamentally on cliché and stock response. In the United States, elementary education, at least before the Sputnik revolution of 1957, consisted very largely of acquiring a stock-response mythology known as the American way of life. Canadian elementary teaching has been less obsessed by social mythology, as its children do not require the indoctrination that citizens of a great world power do, but it has its own kind, as in fact do all societies in all ages. Social mythology in our day is a faint parody of the Christian mythology which preceded it. "Things were simpler in the old days; the world has unaccountably lost its innocence since we were children. I just live to get out of this rat race for a bit and go somewhere where I can get away from it all." Yet there is a bracing atmosphere in competition and we may hope to see consumer goods enjoyed by all members of our society after we abolish poverty. The world is threatened with grave dangers from foreigners, perhaps with total destruction; yet if we dedicate ourselves anew to the tasks which lie before us we may preserve our way of life for generations yet unborn. One recognizes the familiar outlines of paradise myths, fall myths, exodus-from-Egypt myths, pastoral myths, apocalypse myths.

Northrop Frye, *The Modern Century*

Ancient myths are certainly not just a manifestation of archetypal images from man's collective unconsciousness. But they are undoubtedly that as well. Much of the mystery of being and of man, many of his dark visions, obsessions, longings, forebodings, much of his murky "pre-scientific" knowledge and many important metaphysical certainties are obviously encoded in old myths. Such myths, of course, transcend their creators: something higher spoke through them, something beyond their creators, something that not even they were fully able to understand and give a name to. The authority invested in old myths by people of ancient cultures indicates that this higher power, whatever it is, was once generally felt and acknowledged. If we go no further than Jung's interpretation of myths, it is obvious that they introduced a partial or temporary "order" into the complex world of those unconscious forebodings, unprovable certainties, hidden instincts, passions, and longings that are an intrinsic part of the human spirit. And they obviously exercised something like a "check" or "supervisory power" over those forces of the human unconscious.

The civilization of the new age has robbed old myths of their authority. It has put its full weight behind cold, descriptive Cartesian reason and recognizes only thinking in concepts.

I am unwilling to believe that this whole civilization is no more than a blind alley of history and a fatal error of the human spirit. More probably it represents a necessary phase that man and humanity must go through, one that man—if he survives—will ultimately, and on some higher level (unthinkable, of course, without the present phase), transcend.

Whatever the case may be, it is certain that the whole rationalistic bent of the new age, having given up on the authority of myths, has succumbed to a large and dangerous illusion: it believes that no higher and darker powers—which these myths in some ways touched, bore witness to, and whose relative "control" they guaranteed—ever existed, either in the human unconscious or in the mysterious universe. Today, the opinion prevails that everything can be "rationally explained," as they say, by alert reason. Nothing is obscure—and if it is, then we need only cast a ray of scientific light on it and it will cease to be so.

This, of course, is only a grand self-delusion of the modern spirit. For though it make that claim a thousand times, though it deny a thousand times

the "averted face" of the world and the human spirit, it can never eliminate
that face, but merely push it further into the shadows.

Vaclav Havel, from "Thriller," in *Living in Truth*

A Mad Gleam

Go back to Egypt and the Greeks,
Where the Wizard understood
The spectre haunted where man seeks
And spoke to ghosts that stood in blood.

Go back, go back to the old legend;
The soul remembers, and is true:
What has been most and least imagined,
No other, there is nothing new.

The giant Phantom is ascending
Toward its coronation, gowned
With music unheard, but unending:
Follow the flower to the ground.

New York, January 1949

Allen Ginsberg, *Collected Poems*

A serious science of mythology must take its subject matter with due seriousness, survey the field as a whole, and have at least some conception of the
prodigious range of functions that mythology has served in the course of
human history. It is dreamlike and, like dream, a spontaneous product of
the psyche; like dream, revelatory of the psyche and hence of the whole
nature and destiny of man; like dream—like life—enigmatic to the uninitiated ego; and, like dream, protective of that ego. In the simplest human
societies mythology is the text of the rites of passage; in the writings of the
Hindu, Chinese, and Greek philosophers (as of all who have ever read
them) mythology is the picture language of metaphysics. The first function
is not violated by the second but extended; both harmoniously bind man,
the growing animal, to his world, simultaneously in its visible and in its
transcendent aspects. Mythology is the womb of mankind's initiation to life
and death.

Today that corporeal world has vanished and another has taken its place: correlatively, that spiritual world has vanished and another has taken, or is taking, its place. But no living system of symbols functioning for engagement can survive when it has lost contact with the actual conscious and unconscious worlds of its society—when its references to the field of waking consciousness have been refuted and its notices to the seats of motivation are no longer felt. Like the signs referring to the known, so the symbols referring to the relatively unknown are functions of the knowledge of the time.

Joseph Campbell, *The Flight of the Wild Gander*

It is precisely the apparently merely "metaphysical" question about the nature of God, as discussed between East and West, precisely the question about the personal or nonpersonal nature of God, that decides what practical attitude toward him is possible: whether—to recall Heidegger—we can pray and offer sacrifice to him, kneel in awe before him, sing and dance before him.

Hans Küng, *Does God Exist?*

Feb. 18, 1950

Tonight in Deaths & Entrances while standing I suddenly knew what witchcraft is—in microcosm—It is the being within each of us—sometimes the witch, sometimes the real being of good—of creative energy—no matter in what area or direction of activity. The witches' sabbath is the anger we know at times. The sacrament is taken but the wine of life is the blood of death—It is the abomination which is partaken of rather than the essence of life—when I lose my temper it is like a witches' sabbath—the Black Mass—the world is given over to the powers of darkness & the rule of the blood—It is Kali in her terrible aspect—It is Shiva the destroyer—It is Lucifer—"as proud as Lucifer"—the obverse of God—

This, too, is what D & E. is about—only I did not know enough to quite see it through—

All the repentance is of no avail. It is "giving for" one mood the other state of consciousness—doing it quite consciously—in face of all temptation to do otherwise & to "ride the broom-stick." Strength comes from a use of the muscles—The athletes of God wrestled & grew strong. They chose, & they acted.

What I do must be done in full sunlight of awareness—I must learn a means of changing the mood—the state of consciousness—without double-mindedness or tho't of gain.

Martha Graham, *The Notebooks of Martha Graham*

Myth makes a connection between our waking consciousness and the mystery of the universe. It gives us a map or picture of the universe and allows us to see ourselves in relationship to nature, as when we speak of Father Sky and Mother Earth. It supports and validates a certain social and moral order. The Ten Commandments being given to Moses by God on Mount Sinai is an example of this. Lastly, it helps us pass through and deal with the various stages of life from birth to death. The first function of mythology is to sanctify the place you are in.

Joseph Campbell, *Reflections on the Art of Living*

Rituals and Morphic Resonance

All societies have their rituals, such as those of the seasonal festivals, the rituals of birth, marriage, and death, and the rituals that commemorate and reenact original events, charged with spiritual power, on which the social and religious group depends. For example, the Jewish feast of Passover recalls the original Passover dinner on the night when the firstborn of the Egyptians and their cattle were destroyed, after which the Jews began their journey out of bondage in Egypt. The Christian celebration of the Eucharist commemorates the last supper of Jesus with his disciples, itself a Passover dinner. The American national festival of Thanksgiving recalls the first thanksgiving dinner of the Pilgrims after their first harvests in the New World.

A general feature of all rituals is that they are intensely conservative. In order to work properly, they are supposed to be performed in the correct and customary manner. In many parts of the world, the very language of ritual is archaic, preserving the traditional form of words believed to be necessary for their efficacy. The liturgy of the Coptic church in Egypt is still carried out in the ancient Egyptian tongue; the Brahminic rituals of India, in Sanskrit.

Through this ritual participation, the past becomes present. The present participants are linked to all those who have gone before—to the ancestors, and ultimately to the primal creative moment the ritual commemorates. In Christianity, for example, this is the basis of the doctrine of the Communion of Saints. The sacred time of the mass is not only linked with that of preceding and following masses;

it can also be looked upon as a continuation of all the Masses which have taken place from the moment when the mystery of transubstanti-ation was first established until the present moment.... What is true of time in Christian worship is equally true of time in all religions, in magic, in myth and in legend. A ritual does not merely repeat the rit-ual that came before it (itself a repetition of an archetype), but is linked to it and continues it, whether at fixed periods or otherwise. (Mircea Eliade, 1958)

Why are rituals so conservative? And why do people all over the world believe that through ritual activities they are participating in a process that takes them out of ordinary secular time and somehow brings the past into the present? The idea of morphic resonance provides a natural answer to these questions. Through morphic resonance, ritual really can bring the past into the present. The present performers of the ritual indeed connect with those in the past. The greater the similarity between the way the ritual is per-formed now and the way it was performed before, the stronger the resonant connection between the past and present participants.

Rupert Sheldrake, *The Rebirth of Nature*

The Dance of Shiva

In South India, not far from Madras and Pondicherry, lies the Temple of Chidambaram, known to many as the original home of Natarajan, the danc-ing Shiva. The temple there is like a canyon-fort, with great walls enclosing smaller temples of varying shapes and sizes, all of them passageways to dif-ferent parts of Shiva's body. One without windows is black as night and houses the God's *akashic*, or etheric *Lingam*: in its dark recess Hindu women cover the black and tapering stone with melted butter, stroking it slowly until its shape is worn smooth. Another houses the great bell, which is struck to announce disappearances and renewals of the God. Around the com-pound there is a corridor with a thousand pillars, and near its southern gate there stands the pavilion with the famous figure. When the pavilion doors are open you can see the King of Dancers from any point—dancing on a pyramid of gods and demons in a prefiguration of His dance to bring the world down and end the cosmic cycle.

I visited the temple while I was at the Aurobindo ashram near the end of my journey around the world, passing through the outer gates in the wake of an American sadhu with orange robes and a devastating smile who said it had come to him in a dream that he should bring me here. The moment I crossed the threshold I felt the presence of the God. Not the excitement of anticipation merely or the strangeness of the place, but the overwhelming presence of Shiva, as tangible as the drum rolls and basso chanting one heard in the distance.

We walked in silence around the temple compound, past the candelit cave which housed the *Lingam* (women chanting as they rubbed its sides, being entered by its etheric substance for ether is the medium of sound, and this is its *Lingam*), past the temple bell, and smaller passages that showed you Shiva's many faces, down the thousand-pillared corridor to the edge of a crowd pressing round the dancing figure. Its flying arms and legs were perfect poise. It was glowing as if lit from within.

Ceremonies were beginning and the Brahmin priests of Tamilnad were seated around the statue in ascending banks, chanting Sanskrit mantras with a ringing power and hard, insistent beat—a beat to open nerveways of the densest mind, no one, no part to be left behind in this culminating act of worship. Then the sliding doors slammed shut. The God had disappeared.

The crowd pressed closer, and for a moment I was lost in the wavering space. Then the doors slid back. The God was covered high with flowers, a mountain of petals and blossoms where the statue had been, and the Sanskrit chant began to swell, hint of frenzy ordered by the mantra-beat, every white-robed figure bobbing now with growing passion.

They began to stroke the flowers away, to unveil Natarajan, the King of Dancers. Then the doors slammed shut.

Then opened to show a pile of rice, Shiva in the food of India.

Seven times the God was covered and revealed—Natarajan at the center of all the elements, dancing even in glowing stone. Each time the doors swung open the great bell rang and those hundreds in the pressing crowd saw Shiva at the heart of things.

In flowers, rice, bread, and stone; the Dance. His arms and legs the tendrils of exploding worlds, his eyes eternal stillness, his smile the ecstasy. The Dance was at the heart of every atom.

Michael Murphy, Golf in the Kingdom

On the very next evening I had another, no less extraordinary experience of Indian art, this time of movement, dance, and ritual. It was a performance of Odissi, one of the classical Indian dance forms. In India, dance has formed an integral part of worship from ancient times and is still one of the purest artistic expressions of spirituality. Every performance of classical dance is a dance drama in which the artist enacts well-known stories from Hindu mythology by communicating a series of emotions through *abhinaya*—an elaborate language of stylized body postures, gestures, and facial expressions. In Odissi dance, the classical poses are the same as those of the deities in the Hindu temples.

I went to the performance with a group of young people whom I had met after one of my lectures, one of them a student of Odissi dance herself. They told me very excitedly that the special attraction of that evening was not only to see Sanjukta Panigrahi, India's foremost Odissi dancer, but also her celebrated guru, Keluchara Mohaparta, who does not generally dance in public. This evening, however "Guruji," as everybody called him, would also dance.

Before the performance, my dancer friend and a fellow student of hers took me backstage to meet their dance teacher and, possibly, to see Guruji and Sanjukta prepare themselves for the performance. When the two young women encountered their teacher they bowed down and touched with their right hands first the teacher's feet and then their own foreheads. They did so with natural, flowing ease; their gestures hardly interrupted their movements and conversation. After I was introduced we were allowed to peek into an adjoining area where Sanjukta and Guruji were engaged in an intimate ritual. Fully dressed for the performance, they faced each other in prayer, whispering intensely and with closed eyes. It was a scene of utmost concentration, which ended with Guruji blessing his student and kissing her on the forehead.

I was amazed by Sanjukta's elaborate dress, makeup, and jewelry, but I was even more fascinated by Guruji. I saw a pouchy older man, half bald, with a delicate, strange, and compelling face that transcended conventional notions of male and female, young and old. He wore very little makeup and was dressed in some kind of ritualistic garment, which left his torso naked.

The performance was magnificent. The dancers evoked a ceaseless stream of emotions through a dazzling display of the most refined movements and gestures. Sanjukta's poses were fascinating. It seemed to me as if the ancient stone sculptures, which were so fresh in my memory, had suddenly come alive.

The most wondrous experience, however, was to see Guruji perform the initial invocation and offering, which begins every performance of classical Indian dance. He appeared at the left of the stage with a plate of burning candles in his hand, which he carried across the stage as an offering to a deity represented by a small statue. To see this oddly beautiful old man float across the stage in swirling, twisting, flowing movements, the candles flickering all about him, was an unforgettable experience of magic and ritual. I sat there spellbound, staring at Guruji as if he were some being from another world, a personification of archetypal movement.

Fritjof Capra, *Uncommon Wisdom*

The ritual acts of man are an answer and reaction to the action of God upon man; and perhaps they are not only that, but are also intended to be "activating," a form of magic coercion. That man feels capable of formulating valid replies to the overpowering influence of God, and that he can render back something which is essential even to God, induces pride, for it raises the human individual to the dignity of a metaphysical factor. "God and us"— even if it is only an unconscious *sous-entendu*—this equation no doubt underlies that enviable serenity of the Pueblo Indian. Such a man is in the fullest sense of the word in his proper place.

C. G. Jung, *Memories, Dreams, Reflections*

People ask me, "What can we have for rituals?" Well, what do you want to have a ritual for? You should have a ritual for your life. All a ritual does is concentrate your mind on the implications of what you are doing. For instance, the marriage ritual is a meditation on the step you are taking in learning to become a member of a duad, instead of one individual all alone. The ritual enables you to make the transit.

> *Ritual introduces you*
> *to the meaning of what's going on.*
>
> *Saying grace before meals*
> *lets you know that you're about to eat*
> *something that once was alive.*

When eating a meal, realize what you are doing. Hunting peoples thank the animal for having given itself. They feel real gratitude. The main rituals of mature hunting tribes, like those of the Americas, were addressed to the animal. On the Northwest Coast, the principle rites were when the first wave of salmon came in, and they were intended to thank the salmon.

> *The life of the animal that you've taken*
> *is given back when you recognize*
> *what you've done.*

And so, sitting down to eat, realize what you are doing: you are eating a life that has been given so that you might live.

> *...man, like no other animal, not only knows that he is killing when*
> *he kills but also knows that he too will die; and the length of his old*

*age, furthermore, is—like his infancy—a lifetime in itself, as long as
the entire span of many a beast.*

When I was working on the Gospel of Sri Ramakrishna, I had a lot of
meals with the monks. Their grace before meals is the most beautiful invocation. It goes like this: "Brahman is the cosmic, universal, life consciousness
energy of which we are all manifestations. Brahman is the sacrifice.
Brahman is the food that we are eating. Brahman is the consumer of the sacrifice. Brahman is the ladle that carries the sacrifice to the fire. Brahman is
the process of the sacrifice. He who recognizes that all things are Brahman is
on the way to realizing Brahman in himself."

The meaning of this grace is that taking food into your system is like
putting a libation into a sacrificial fire: the fire of your digestive apparatus
consumes what you eat, so eating is the counterpart of a sacrifice.

The communion ritual is an extension of this idea, a motif that came
into the world with the dawn of agriculture: "If the seed does not die, there
is no plant." It dies as seed and yields to the sprout. Now, since we are composed of spirit and matter—the two substances are what live in us—we need
two types of food. The food that nourishes our material part—vegetables,
animals, whatever it is we eat—is earthly food, but we must also have spiritual food, nourishment for our spiritual part. And communion, the eating of
Christ, is a symbolization of the imbibing of that spiritual nourishment, a
concretization of the idea of meditation. But in order to eat anything, it has
to be killed, so again we have the notion of the sacrifice.

*You should be willing
to be eaten also.
You are food body.*

Every ritual is of that order, properly putting your mind in touch with
what you really are doing. And so, we should realize that this event here and
now: our coming together to help each other in the realization is a beautiful,
beautiful ritual.

You can ritualize your entire life that way, and it's extremely helpful to
do so. The whole thing of compassion comes in there. What helped me was
waking up and thinking of my penny catechism: "to know, to love, to serve
God." I don't think of God as up there. I think of God as right here in whatever I'm knowing and loving and serving. "To be happy with Him forever in
heaven" means to recognize your own compassion, your own participation in
that creature or person you're with. That seems to be the goal of the journey.

Joseph Campbell, *Reflections on the Art of Living*

Gratitude

It is hard to feel a sense of gratitude for an inanimate, mechanical world proceeding inexorably in accordance with eternal laws of nature and blind chance. And this is a great spiritual loss, for it is through gratitude that we acknowledge the living powers on which our own lives depend; through gratitude we enter into a conscious relationship to them; through gratitude we can find ourselves in a state of grace.

All religions provide opportunities for giving thanks, both through simple everyday rituals, like saying grace before meals, and also in collective acts of thanksgiving. These customary expressions of gratitude help to remind us that we have much to be thankful for. Each religion has its own ways of recognizing the living powers on which we all depend and of establishing a relationship to these powers through thanksgiving.

For those for whom traditional religious practices seem empty and meaningless, there are three possibilities: first, to recognize no living power greater than humanity and hence to recognize neither a need for gratitude nor a means of expressing it; second, to feel such gratitude privately but with no means of public expression; third, to find new ways of expressing gratitude collectively and new conceptions of the life-giving powers to whom thanks are due.

Rupert Sheldrake, *The Rebirth of Nature*

Have I ever told you about the ritual in Kentucky where I had to give up seven things? It was one of the most interesting group experiences I've ever had. We were a group of about forty-nine people in one of those meetings of some society for the transformation of consciousness. Two couples from the University of Vermont, professors and their wives, had arranged a ritual that we were all going to undertake. We were divided into seven groups of seven and told to spend a day thinking of the seven things without which we'd not want to live: "What are the seven things for which you feel your life is worth living?" Then you were to gather seven little objects, small enough to hold in your hand, which were to represent your seven cherished things, and you were to know which was which.

In the evening we went down a wooded road in the dark to the mouth of a cave. The cave had a wooden door on it which could be opened. In front of the door was a man wearing the mask of a dog: Cerberus at the gate of hell. He put his hand out and said, "Give me that which you least cherish." When you gave him one of the little objects you were holding, he opened the door and allowed you to enter.

Then you proceeded forward through the cave, an enormous place, holding the six remaining things you most cherished. On five further occasions, you were asked to surrender that which you least cherished, until you were left with one object that represented what you treasured most. And you found out what it was, believe me. You really, really did. And the order in which you gave up your treasures was revelatory: you really knew what your order of values was. Then you came to an exit, where there were two people between whom you had to go. But before you could go through that guarded exit, you had to give up that which you most cherished.

I can tell you that ritual worked. All of the participants with whom I've talked had an actual experience of *moska*, "release," when they had given up their last treasure. One damned fool was the exception. He did not give up anything. That's how seriously this ritual was taken. When he was asked to give up something, he just stooped down, picked up a pebble, and handed that over. That's the refusal of the call.

> *...every failure to cope with a life situation must be laid, in the end, to a restriction of consciousness. Wars and temper tantrums are the makeshifts of ignorance; regrets are illuminations come too late.*

The exciting thing to me was the actual experience. It was a feeling of joyous participation. Watching your earlier bondages go really did change your feeling for the treasures you'd given up. It increased your love for them without the tenacity. I was amazed.

Joseph Campbell, *Reflections on the Art of Living*

In general, magical procedures seem to bear formal resemblance both to science and to religion. Magic may be a degenerate "applied" form of either. Consider such rituals as rain dances or the totemic rituals concerned with man's relationship to animals. In these types of ritual the human being invokes or imitates or seeks to control the weather or the ecology of wild creatures. But I believe that in their primitive state these are true religious ceremonials. They are ritual statements of unity, involving all the participants in an integration with the meteorological cycle or with the ecology of totemic animals. This is religion. But the pathway of deterioration from religion to magic is always tempting. From a statement of integration in some often dimly recognized whole, the practitioner turns aside to an appetitive stance. He sees his own ritual as a piece of purposive magic to make the rain come or to promote the fertility of the totemic animal or to achieve some other goal. The criterion that distinguishes magic from religion is, in fact, *purpose* and especially some extrovert purpose.

Introvert purpose, the desire to change the self, is a very different matter, but intermediate cases occur. If the hunter performs a ritual imitation of an animal to cause that animal to come into his net, that is surely magic; but if his purpose in imitating the animal is perhaps to improve his own empathy and understanding of the beast, his action is perhaps to be classed as religious.

Gregory Bateson and Mary Catherine Bateson,
Angels Fear: Towards an Epistemology of the Sacred

Human existence is not merely the space in which symbols and sacraments appear, and not merely the material with which they clothe themselves. The real existence of a human person can itself be symbol, itself be sacrament.

Martin Buber, *The Origin and Meaning of Hasidism*

It is my feeling that all humans mark their paths on trees, mark time with ceremony. That repetition and orderliness make for ritual. Etymologically, *rite* is from *ritual*, as is *arithmetic*. We want sums, constants. Rhythm is from the same root. Ritual is a collective experience, repeated and sanctified. We perform it to remind ourselves and one another that we are not alone, that we sing in chorus. We are historical, and what has happened to us is not an isolated instance. Birth has occurred before, and we women birth in a cave of women's experiences, when we are fortunate. Death has happened before, and we lament with others who have suffered losses.

Honoring Forms of Birthing

As exodus is universal, so is birthing, so is pairing, so is death. Women have always been present at birth, and women were there at the final exodus as the body dressers, keeners—gods of entrance and exit. Ceremony returns to ourselves as our bodies return to ourselves.

I have gone with Harriette Hartigan, a Detroit photographer, to watch a home delivery. There were no white-masked strangers, only friendly women, a child or two, and a father-to-be, who was massaging the laboring woman. Barbara was deep into her labor, and her lover rubbed her back low and to the sides when the contractions were full upon her. Barbara called to the life within: "Come down, baby." Her three-year-old, Lenay, asked, "What's Mommy doing?" Barbara said, "Mommy is working, Lenay." Lenay asked, "Why is Mommy making those sounds?" Barbara said, "Mommy is calling in a secret voice to the baby. Those are working and calling sounds." The child watched as the eye of the vagina opened wide in surprise, crowned with a head, with eyebrows, stuck on the nose. Barbara labored mightily and crooned and lullaby'd the life into birth. The midwife caught the baby. Barbara's body sweated like that of any road laborer; her hair was tangled and damp. She rose from the birthing bed, showered, and brushed her hair. I had brought champagne. We popped the cork, drank, and talked quietly about matters of birthing. We played the tape that we had made of Barbara calling to the baby, of Barbara calling out to her mother and to her lover. We were there to begin a new kind of ceremony.

I also participated in an old birthing ceremony. In January 1978, during a great snowstorm, I flew from Detroit to New York. It was Friday, the thirteenth, the day of the circumcision of Phyllis Chesler's son. Chesler knew the rabbi would speak of the son as if he were only of father born, grandfather connected, male ancestry descended, but would forget that the womb had held him. It was as we had anticipated. After the male ceremony, we women retrieved the baby and took him into the library. There we surrendered him with the magic circle of ourselves. I requested that we each bless him in our own voice, that we give him something useful and magical, a growing part of ourselves. I took out scissors and cut a lock of my hair. I taped it onto a sheet of red oaktag. Each woman present cut her hair—grey, black, blonde, brown hair. We lit candles and wished the baby courage to be the son of a feminist, courage to be lonely, to have laughter and friendship with his mother. We blew out the candles and presented the baby with this hairy card of great power. The storm had not abated, but I rose and flew through it back to Detroit.

> I bless you, I the priestess of you
> I, your mouth, your cry, your prayer, your pain,
> your connection, your separation...
> I am your scribe. I inscribe your pain.
> I am your collective soul...
> I am born through the tunnel of your collective bodies,
> yet I am old—your ancient, your memory, your ancestor.
> My tears fill cauldrons, brews, broths, seas, eyes,
> I am the mourner for you,
> I am your wake...
> I blow trumpets for you, I celebrate you,
> I laugh aloud for you...

Trust me for I am the ghost of you.
Look, in the shadows I walk behind you...
Spread your legs, my daughters,
let us give birth to one another.
Let us cry out in birthing pain.
Let us uncover our shame.
Let this ceremony, let these friendships be born.

E. M. Broner, from *Honor and Ceremony in Women's Rituals*

Awakening the Great Mother

Unseen fingers cool as hyacinth-roots
Dislimn the clay
Or soul's long-loved discarded mortal face:
She of graves,
Whose secret alchemy
Brings all our ends to her immaculate source.

—KATHLEEN RAINE

There is no doubt that the feminine spiritual energy of the archetype of the Great Mother, the feminine side of God, the all-powerful protector and creator of the world, is sweeping through the collective unconscious in our world today. As the patriarchal system, under which the world has been ruled for so long, breaks up, she returns after centuries of neglect. Joseph Campbell explains: "the world-generating spirit of the father passes into the manifold of earthly experience through a transforming medium—the mother of the World."

The Great Mother has many divine attributes. She is the creator of all creatures. She is the source of all life, "the lure that moved the Self-brooding Absolute to the act of creation" (Campbell). She is the evening star and "consort of the moon." She is wisdom. She is earth's mother, symbolized by a tree or the waters of the earth. Her awakening has been helped by the work of the feminists and the feminist theologians in the 1970s and the 1980s and the more recent rehonouring of the female in our rituals. Over the last twenty years we have been witness to the pains of this emergence—from the feminist message of the past, which projected the anger and frustration of the repressed masculine and feminine in women and promoted awareness of the inequality between the patriarchal and the matriarchal worlds, to the emerging archetype of the Mother, a powerful, yet gentle healing force who speaks to both women and men. Canadian Jungian analyst Marion Woodman speaks to this emerging feminine archetype in all her work and books. Single-handedly she has contributed more to the understanding of the embryonic stages of the reawakening to this archetype than any other woman writer in the last ten years.

In his Pondicherry Ashram in India, Sri Aurobindo, the Indian master, recognized the essential divine feminine by appointing The Mother as its manifestation. Born in Paris in 1878 as Mirra, she sailed to India at the age of thirty-six to meet Sri Aurobindo, who had for many years inwardly guided her. She joined his ashram in 1920 and was entrusted with its material and spiritual direction for more than fifty years. There, she and Sri Aurobindo both lived and taught together. He would bend to her and she to him, neither one without the other in a perfect harmony of the masculine and feminine divine essence. Sri Aurobindo was by far the most advanced of the recent spiritual masters to come out of India. He wrote profusely—his books number in the hundreds—on such diverse subjects as philosophy, yoga, and ancient scripture; his poems, sonnets, plays, and literary essays are of unique merit.

In this chapter, I have pinpointed the more prominent female archetypes who are finding favour today. The goddess as the overall female deity has many forms of revelation. In the Christian tradition, she is Mary; in the Buddhist, Kwan Yin or Tara; in Hinduism, Kali and Shakti. She is also coming alive in the better-known mystical teachers of our age, the divine women like Mata Amritanandamayi and Mother Meera, who impart wisdom, caring, healing, who embody her essence in their lives and in their teachings. And what is most exciting at this juncture in our evolution is the arrival of a new archetype, born from the old, born from the work of feminist theologians in the seventies and from the recent feminist spirituality movements. The Emerging Woman is not quite with us, she is still becoming, still being formed, but we can catch glimpses of her in the experiences of others, in the sharing of stories and of dreams. Her magnificence is appearing, piece by piece, and when she is here in full, she will guide us as true matriarch to the peace of her kingdom.

><

The sea organisms crawled up onto the land to commit ecstatic suicide, to escape triumphantly from existing, to return to infinite pure energy, motionless.

But life forced itself to flow through even the gasps they drank in of what they assumed was death: air. Despite themselves, they became air-breathing organisms. Every step taken toward nonexisting brings us closer toward existing.

It is the fault of something female.

Nature, we have heard, abhors a vacuum. Speaking then through male anguish at his own womb envy, nature discovered existential despair. But male anguish expressed this despair as misogyny. What else to feel when faced with this female endless birthing, this repeated insistence on life and life-giving and life-re-creation? What is this maddening tendency to bear and bear and bear, as if each woman were somehow somewhere in herself singing "I never met a universe I didn't like"?

He only wants her to understand his wretchedness. He persecutes her to make her understand why death is the answer, he tortures her to raise her consciousness to the suicidal, to make her as truly aware as he is. She won't despair. She won't die. She creates agriculture, domesticates animals. Culture is born.

He appropriates her gods, her whole cosmic space, to the merciless, negative, bleak, terror-filled void in which he is trapped. She curses his gods—but does not die. She calls to him. She sees his beauty writhing, contorted in pain. He sobs with longing to share what she is, sees, owns, the whole Earth as female, the solar system female, the universe female, all that he smells and touches and which holds him and bore him and will outlive him—female, eternally rutting and conceiving and laughing and producing.

For what? What is there to celebrate here, in this dimension? Is there no way to kill her out of this gross procreation? Can none of his entropy conquer her energy? If he cannot stop her, can he at least successfully pretend that he *insists* she do precisely what she is doing? Can he tell himself he *demands* she conceive? Rape is born, his own parthenogenetic child. Laws are written controlling her body's freedom. She creates pottery, baskets, songs. She investigates the power of herbs. Art and science are born.

Is there no way to stop her? Is there no way to evade this inexhaustible deathless pursuing consciousness? He devises nirvanas of escape. Oriental philosophies which pretend she is illusion, Occidental philosophies which pretend she is existentially meaningless. And all the while she smiles and conceives. Children. Grapefruits. The thimble. Barnacles. The printing press. City squirrels.

He is more and more trapped into his systems. He invents new and efficient ways of murdering what she produces—wars, chemicals, political systems which destroy her creations or treat them as products. He is consumed with self-loathing for having become the weapon of himself and never the victim in his global attempt to commit suicide. She weeps for him and gives birth to a new star, hoping its nova will divert him from his misery.

He invents names for her creatures, deliberately mixed around. He calls the human ones insects, vermin, pigs, cows. Then he kills them, and their animal namesakes, too. He forgets what and who and why he is killing. He knows only where he came from—that womb of Earth, and where he is going—that same insatiable womb with its infinite capacity for orgasm and for creation as it sucks him in and spews him out and laughs lovingly *lovingly* at him as if he were her plaything.

Only when he has totally forgotten who he is and why he hates her so; only when she herself has almost forgotten herself; only when his pain has at last infected her so that she almost has begun to listen, almost understand his message of nonexistence, his longing for peace and death and the silence of a collapsed nonwomb whose energy and matter are once and for all time separated—only then does she slowly rouse herself to remind him.

That time is now.

Robin Morgan, from "Metaphysical Feminism" in
Going Too Far: The Personal Chronicles of a Feminist

The Mother Archetype

Like any other archetype, the mother archetype appears under an almost infinite variety of aspects. I mention here only some of the more characteristic. First in importance are the personal mother and grandmother, stepmother and mother-in-law; then any woman with whom a relationship exists—for example, a nurse or governess or perhaps a remote ancestress. Then there are what might be termed mothers in a figurative sense. To this category belongs the goddess, and especially the Mother of God, the Virgin, and Sophia. Mythology offers many variations of the mother archetype, as for instance the mother who reappears as the maiden in the myth of Demeter and Kore; or the mother who is also the beloved, as in the Cybele-Attis myth. Other symbols of the mother in a figurative sense appear in things representing the goal of our longing for redemption, such as Paradise, the Kingdom of God, the Heavenly Jerusalem. Many things arousing devotion or feelings of awe, as for instance the Church, university, city or country, heaven, earth, the woods, the sea or any still waters, matter even, the underworld and the moon, can be mother-symbols. The archetype is often associated with things and places standing for fertility and fruitfulness: the cornucopia, a ploughed field, a garden. It can be attached to a rock, a cave, a tree, a spring, a deep well, or to various vessels such as the baptismal font, or to vessel-shaped flowers like the rose or the lotus. Because of the protection it implies, the magic circle or mandala can be a form of mother archetype. Hollow objects such as ovens and cooking vessels are associated with the mother archetype, and, of course, the uterus, *yoni*, and anything of a like shape. Added to this list there are many animals, such as the cow, hare, and helpful animals in general.

All these symbols can have a positive, favourable meaning or a negative, evil meaning. An ambivalent aspect is seen in the goddesses of fate (Moira, Graeae, Norns). Evil symbols are the witch, the dragon (or any devouring and entwining animal, such as a large fish or a serpent), the grave, the sar-cophagus, deep water, death, nightmares, and bogies (Empusa, Lilith, etc.). This list is not, of course, complete; it presents only the most important features of the mother archetype.

The qualities associated with it are maternal solicitude and sympathy; the magic authority of the female; the wisdom and spiritual exaltation that transcend reason; any helpful instinct or impulse; all that is benign, all that cherishes and sustains, that fosters growth and fertility. The place of magic transformation and rebirth, together with the underworld and its inhabitants, are presided over by the mother. On the negative side the mother archetype may connote anything secret, hidden, dark; the abyss, the world of the dead, anything that devours, seduces, and poisons, that is terrifying and inescapable like fate. All these attributes of the mother archetype have been fully described and documented in my book *Symbols of Transformation*. There I formulated the ambivalence of these attitudes as "the loving and the terrible mother." Perhaps the historical example of the dual nature of the mother most familiar to us is the Virgin Mary, who is not only the Lord's mother, but also, according to the medieval allegories, his cross. In India, "the loving and terrible mother" is the paradoxical Kali. Sankhya philosophy has elaborated the mother archetype into the concept of *prakṛti* (matter) and assigned to it the three *gunas* or fundamental attributes: *sattva*, *rajas*, *tamas*: goodness, passion, and darkness. These are three essential aspects of the mother: her cherishing and nourishing goodness, her orgiastic emotionality, and her Stygian depths. The special feature of the philosophical myth, which shows Prakṛti dancing before Purusha in order to remind him of "discriminating knowledge," does not belong to the mother archetype but to the archetype of the anima, which in a man's psychology invariably appears, at first, mingled with the mother-image.

C. G. Jung, *The Archetypes and the Collective Unconscious*

The unconscious per se is unknowable; it is a reality that is inferred from such things as spontaneous or involuntary body movement and dreams. Ultimately we may come to think of body movement or the dreaming state as a manifestation not of unconsciousness, but as a consciousness that operates upon us and within us. Certainly there are many who believe that what we now think of as the unconscious is equivalent to the traditional concept of God as an unsleeping Being within, an omniscient inner presence. Similarly, I speak of Sophia or of the Virgin because they are divine womanly beings associated with the feminine side of God. By locating them in the unconscious I am following the path of God from without to within, the path that characterizes the movement of consciousness itself. Moreover, I am suggesting that what we now call the unconscious is in psychological reality a consciousness that has simply been underground for too long. In alchemy there is the concept of the *deus absconditus* (male), the hidden god in matter. But the unconscious also includes the *dea abscondita*, the Black Madonna, the goddess who has chosen to hide herself in order to protect humanity from the devastating consequences of killing her. ,

Modern society, far more than we realize, is the offspring of Nietzsche's declaration, "God is dead." He is not dead, nor is the Goddess. They are merely hiding. Their hiding place is the unconscious. When it is no longer necessary for them to hide in order to protect man from destroying himself by destroying them, they, God and Goddess together, will re-emerge. And when they do we will see the unconscious for what it is: God's consciousness of his creation, which includes the body's consciousness of itself. That movement Nietzsche identified with Dionysus.

The return of God is one of the most ancient expectations of the human race. Every world religion has presented itself as preparing for his return. Every religion still awaits it. What does this expectation imply? We already know God in his outward manifestation, by his laws, his commands, his word. That is the Logos, the masculine side of God. What we await in the Second Coming is what we lack: God's inner dynamic or process. This— God in his creativeness rather than in his creation—is the essence of the feminine, traditionally enacted in the ancient Mysteries. The return is therefore the emergence of the feminine side of God, which has been gradually taking shape for centuries in what we call the unconscious. The time has now come when we can deal creatively with the concept of God as the union of opposites, and therefore see the feminine no longer darkly through a masculine glass, but face to androgynous face.

Marion Woodman, *Addiction to Perfection*

The Mother of God

A conscious and eternal Power is here
Behind unhappiness and mortal birth
And the error of Thought and blundering trudge of Time.
The Mother of God, his sister and his spouse,
Daughter of his wisdom, of his might the mate,
She has leapt from the Transcendent's secret breast
To build her rainbow worlds of mind and life.
Between the superconscient absolute Light

And the Inconscient's vast unthinking toil
In the rolling and routine of Matter's sleep
And the somnambulist motion of the stars
She forces on the cold unwilling Void
Her adventure of life, the passionate dreams of her lust.
Amid the work of darker Powers she is here
To heal the evils and mistakes of Space
And change the tragedy of the ignorant world
Into a Divine Comedy of joy
And the laughter and the rapture of God's bliss.
The Mother of God is master of our souls;
We are the partners of his birth in Time,
Inheritors we share his eternity.

       Sri Aurobindo, *Collected Poems*

Children, the mother who gave birth to you may look
after matters relating to this life, nowadays, even this is very rare.
But Mother's aim is to lead you in such a way that you can enjoy
bliss in all your future lives.

   Mata Amritanandamayi, from Swami Amritasvarupananda,
         Mata Amritanandamayi

→ The Goddess ←

As the Mother comes to us through a number of archetypical, mythical figures, goddesses and madonnas, we come to understand that many qualities and messages are revealed through her. The white witch Starhawk writes of the origins and the different guises of the goddess in her piece "The Consciousness of Immanence." Starhawk, who is a leading teacher of the cults of the goddess, brings to her writing a deep understanding of the Pagan pre-Christian principles. She says, "The Goddess Herself is not a belief or a dogma; She is a symbol for a transformative understanding of what is already here, what we know, what we can become. She is a real power, the name we give the binding force that holds together the universe."

→←

Night is the Time of the Goddess—
Day is the Time of the God—

Night is the Time one enters the regions
   of Demeter
     Persephone
     Isis
     Mary the Mother of God
     Hecate— the prostitute—

Death
change—
Renewal

The World of the Woman—
   where continuity is the dynamic

Martha Graham, *The Notebooks of Martha Graham*

If the simplest meaning of the Goddess symbol is an affirmation of the legitimacy and beneficence of female power, then a question immediately arises, "Is the Goddess simply female power writ large, and, if so, why bother with the symbol of Goddess at all? Or does the symbol refer to a Goddess 'out there' who is not reducible to a human potential?" The many women who have rediscovered the power of Goddess would give three answers to this question: (1) The Goddess is divine female, a personification who can be invoked in prayer and ritual; (2) the Goddess is symbol of the life, death, and rebirth energy in nature and culture, in personal and communal life; and (3) the Goddess is symbol of the affirmation of the legitimacy and beauty of female power (made possible by the new becoming of women in the women's liberation movement). If one were to ask these women which answer is the "correct" one, different responses would be given. Some would assert that the Goddess definitely is *not* "out there," that the symbol of a divinity "out there" is part of the legacy of patriarchal oppression, which brings with it the authoritarianism, hierarchicalism, and dogmatic rigidity associated with biblical monotheistic religions. They might assert that the Goddess symbol reflects the sacred power within women and nature, suggesting the connectedness between women's cycles of menstruation, birth, and menopause, and the life and death cycles of the universe. Others seem quite comfortable with the notion of Goddess as a divine female protector and creator and would find their experience of Goddess limited by the assertion that she is not *also* out there as well as within themselves and in all natural processes. When asked what the symbol of Goddess means, Starhawk, a feminist priestess, replied, "It all depends on how I feel. When I feel weak, She is someone who can help and protect me. When I feel strong, She is the symbol of my own power. At other times I feel Her as the natural energy in my body and the world." How are we to evaluate such a statement? Theologians might call these the words of a sloppy thinker. But my deepest intuition tells me they contain a wisdom that Western theological thought has lost.

Carol P. Christ, from "Why Women Need the Goddess," in
Judith Plaskow and Carol P. Christ, *Womanspirit Rising*

The Goddess is manifest not just in human life, but in the interwoven chain of relationships that link all forms of life. We are not given dominion over the birds of the air and the fish of the sea; rather, human life is recognized as part of the animal world. We are conscious, but consciousness itself is *of* nature, not separate from nature. And we do not have the right to damage or destroy other species in order to further purely human aims. Witches, of course, are not Jains, nor are most of us vegetarians. The Goddess in Her aspect as the Crone or Reaper and the God in His aspect of the Hunter embody the principle that all of life feeds on other life. Death sustains life. But the hunt, the harvest, the reaping of herbs—or of profits—must be practiced with respect for the balance of life and its continuation in the greatest possible richness and diversity of forms. The herds are culled, not obliterated. When herbs are cut, only a few are taken from each separate clump, so that they may grow back in future years. Human communities limit their numbers to what the land can support without straining its resources or displacing other species. We do not, for example, have the ethical right to destroy a species—even the lowly snail darter—in order to build a dam, regardless of how much money has already been invested in the project. When we consider ourselves as a true part of the fabric of life, then each time we irrevocably destroy an aspect of life we have destroyed an aspect of ourselves.

Diversity is highly valued—as it is in nature—in a polytheistic worldview which allows for many powers, many images of divinity. In ecological systems, the greater the diversity of a community, the greater is its power of resilience, of adaptation in the face of change, and the greater the chances for survival of its elements.

Diversity is also valued in human endeavors and creations. Ethics are concerned with fostering diversity rather than sameness, and they are not concerned with enforcing a dogma or a party line. Individual conscience—

itself a manifestation of the Goddess—is the final court of appeals, above codified laws or hierarchical proclamations.

Such a statement makes many people uneasy. If ethics are based on the individual's sense of right and wrong, then don't we open ourselves to the horrors of a Hitler, to crime, anarchy, and blind selfishness? Yes, if the individual self is seen out of context. But in Goddess religion, the individual self is never seen as a separate, isolated *object*: It is a nexus of interwoven relationships, an integral and inseparable part of the human and biological community. The Goddess is manifest in the self—but also in every other human self, and the biological world. We can not honor and serve the Goddess in ourselves unless we honor and serve Her in others.

Starhawk, from "Ethics and Justice in Goddess Religion,"
in Charlene Spretnak, *The Politics of Women's Spirituality*

Since the divine is understood to be immanent (dynamic creativity in the cosmic unfolding) as well as transcendent (as the sacred whole, or ultimate mystery), one approaches spiritual practice in this orientation as an awakening of possibilities. Engagement with myth and symbol, as participatory fields of relation rather than fixed artifacts, suggests a shaping of our continuity and groundedness while evoking a sense of our larger self, the fullness of our being. It is the aesthetic path to grace.

Many who follow this path assemble a home altar bearing symbols of the Goddess. It may be no more than a shelf in a bookcase covered with a cloth on which stand Goddess figurines, shells, stones, or other gifts of the Earthbody, but its affective power is remarkable. Even a passing glance at the symbolic forms of the Goddess reminds a woman that she is heir to a lineage of deeply grounded wisdom and inner strength and a weaver of the sacred whole. Sarasvati stands sensually poised on a lotus blossom, playing a sitar as She guides knowledge and the arts. Our Lady of Guadalupe stands on a crescent moon, clothed in a blue robe of the starry heavens and radiating a full-body aura of golden light. Yemaya, mother of the sea, the great womb of creation, stands draped in blue and white, a beautiful, dark woman of deep mystery. Quan Yin, smooth and serene, dispenses from her open hands the vast power of compassion. On many women's altars "the little snake Goddesses of Crete," their names long lost, stand as we moderns never could have imagined: planted firmly on the earth, baring breasts proudly, their outstretched arms hold writhing serpents, symbols of shedding and growth in endless regeneration. We sustain the mythic presence of the Goddess in our lives as She evokes our creativity and depth.

Charlene Spretnak, *States of Grace*

Mother-Goddess is reawakening, and we can begin to recover our primal birthright, the sheer, intoxicating joy of being alive. We can open new eyes and see that there is nothing to be saved *from*, no struggle of life *against* the universe, no God outside the world to be feared and obeyed; only the Goddess, the Mother, the turning spiral that whirls us in and out of existence, whose winking eye is the pulse of being—birth, death, rebirth—whose laughter bubbles and courses through all things and who is found only through love: love of trees, of stones, of sky and clouds, of scented blossoms and thundering waves; of all that runs and flies and swims and crawls on her face; through love of ourselves; life-dissolving world-creating orgasmic love of each other; each of us unique and natural as a snowflake, each of us our own star, her Child, her lover, her beloved, her Self.

Starhawk, from "Witchcraft as Goddess Religion,"
in Charlene Spretnak, *The Politics of Women's Spirituality*

⇥ Mary ⇤

Mary's separation from other women has been promoted by the need of the patriarchal Church to keep her the purified vessel for the incarnation of Christ, the son of God. As well as virgin, she is also known and acknowledged as daughter of God, Queen of Heaven, Star of the sea or Queen of the ocean, protector and guardian, and the bestower of miracles. She also carries a dual role as mother. She is mother of God, and also mother of the figurative Church.

Rosemary Radford Ruether, who teaches theology at a number of American universities, is undoubtedly the most informed and succinct of the Christian feminist theologians. She has introduced the concept of the Holy Spirit in the Trinity as the female power of gestation, birth, and nurturing, "female generative power that derives from the milk of the mothering breasts of God." This purely divine act involving the Virgin Mary elevates her to goddess status.

Personal associations with Mary are manifold. In this section, the late English novelist and essayist Angela Carter, provoked by a painting by Georges de La Tour, contemplates the Marys of the New Testament and of sacred womanhood. The late English novelist Graham Greene reveals Mary from a Catholic perspective. Somewhat sceptically, he notes her appearances in different guises through visions and miracles as a messenger of peace, as "the

Immaculate Conception." Then, transcending his own scepticism, he embraces her supposed resurrection as a significant sign of human redemption.

><

"You know, I always carry a tiny statue of our Lady in my pocket. At times, I give it away to some person for a very special reason. Then I get another one. The day I gave this one to Fulton Sheen, someone gave me another one, a very pretty one, in the afternoon.

"Our Lady is my companion on my tours. I call her my companion since the following fact happened. I had asked the father at Berhampur, after bringing my sisters there, to give me a big statue of the Miraculous Virgin with arms extended downward and palms open, sending graces to the world. He did so, packed it well in a large case, and I took it to the station. I had a railway pass for 'Mother Teresa and a companion.' They wanted me to pay for the freight of the case and the statue; but I refused. 'I have a pass for myself and a companion,' I said. 'Here is my companion. It is the statue of Mother Mary, and she travels with me as a companion.' They let me take her without paying extra for the freight of the box. Since then, I say that our Lady is my traveling companion. I am never alone."

Mother Teresa, from Edward Le Joly, *Mother Teresa of Calcutta*

The Wisdom of Solomon was written by an Alexandrian Jew of the second century B.C. It reflects both the mythical cultures of the Egyptian and Hellenistic world, which identified Goddesses with Wisdom, and also philosophical concepts that speak of an immanent power of divine truth and knowledge that comes forth from the transcendent world to found and guide the cosmos. The predominant imagery for Wisdom is drawn from light. Wisdom is like a spiritual effulgence that radiates from the divine source of light. As light, Wisdom both reveals the divine and illumines our knowledge of the divine. She is both the knowledge and the power of God immanent in our midst, for she is the power through which God creates the world.

She is the image of God for she translates into form the unspoken or unmanifest latency of transcendent divinity. As agent of creation, she translates divine potency into act in created beings. As revealer, she translates the search for God into clear forms of knowledge and divine precept. She is both the objective and subjective side of divine revelation for she not only manifests the latent power of God but enters into the seeker of truth and goodness and enables him to find knowledge and virtue.

This light imagery for Wisdom mingles with her description as feminine to suggest another modality of relationship. Wisdom is a love-object of the wise or "kingly" soul. Like the Goddess Isis, which probably has influenced the image of Wisdom here, she is a wise and beautiful woman whom the seeker after wisdom and virtue wishes to bring home as his bride. Like Isis, she is a model of faithful, wifely love. She is the ideal wife who can act as counselor, inspirer of virtue, and provider of peace and happiness to the man who comes home to her weary from the day's battles.

Thus, in spite of the image of female power conveyed in this Wisdom text, the interpretive stance of the writer is androcentric. One can assume that the Almighty from whom she arises is thought of as the patriarchal God of Judaism. Since Wisdom plays the same theological roles (except for incarnation) as the Logos of the New Testament, we might speak of her as "Daughter" of God. As such, she functions as a feminine mediator between the male God and humanity. Moreover, the seeker after Wisdom is thought of exclusively in male terms. As a "kingly" person, he is a male spiritual and social aristocrat. Thus Wisdom really provides no place where women can identify their own personhood as the center of agency and action. As in patriarchal culture generally, the femininity of Wisdom operates to mediate between male self and male self, in this case the transcendent Almighty as divine male self and the seeker after Wisdom as human male self. The femininity of Wisdom is containable in this androcentric culture precisely because it remains relative to and auxiliary to these male ego dramas rather than acting as a focus of female personhood in her own right.

Although an androgynous concept of the Trinity was repressed in Greco-Roman Christianity, Syriac Christianity carried on the Hebrew tradition of the feminine Wisdom and translated it into a feminine image of the Holy Spirit. This feminine Holy Spirit was thought of as mother and nurturer of the Christian. She was closely linked with baptism as the womb of rebirth and with regeneration imaged as breast-feeding of the reborn soul. There is a close parallelism between Christ, as one born from the womb of the Virgin Mary by the power of the Holy Spirit, and reborn Christians who likewise are to be virginal people through the gestating and birthing power of the Holy Spirit.

This kind of imagery of the Holy Spirit as the female power of gestation, birth, and nurturing is evident in the Syriac Ode of Solomon, No. 19. Here God is thought of as androgynous, containing breasts that burst with milk like a nursing mother's. The Holy Spirit is the power that milks these full breasts of the Father, and she herself is this full bosom of the Father. She bestows this milk of God upon Christians, giving them thereby regenerate life.

This milk from the breasts of God is thought of as the power of gestation and birth by which the Virgin Mary conceived and gave birth to Christ. Thus the belief that Mary "conceived through the power of the Holy Spirit" is not imaged as analogous to the male impregnating seed but as a female generative power that derives from the milk of the mothering breasts of God. Giving birth is itself seen not as a painful, much less a polluted, act but as both painless and powerful, a creative act that mirrors the generation or regeneration of the New Creation itself by God.

In a parallel Ode No. 36, this mothering Holy Spirit is thought of as lifting Christ (and the reborn Christian) from the earth to heaven, presenting him before the divine throne of perfection and glory. Thereby, Christ (and the Christian) become truly Son of Man, the image of divine perfection and glory. Again, as in the Wisdom text, the ultimate ego-center of the Transcendent God, as well as Christ and the reborn Christian, is seen as male. The birthing power of the Holy Spirit, however striking and powerful, mediates the power of this male God to the human male self and, in turn, exalts this male self to heaven to stand before the throne of the male God.

Although females were doubtless included among these virginal, reborn Christians of Syriac Christianity, the persona of the reborn Christian, like that of Christ, is normatively male. Female power remains auxiliary to this male-centered drama of mediation, rebirth, and transformation. The female person can relate to this text either by including herself, anomalously, as the reborn Christian or by imagining herself as playing an auxiliary role of birthgiver to a male offspring whose quest for redemption she supports and promotes through her motherly efforts.

Rosemary Radford Ruether,
from "The Divine Pleroma," in *Womanguides*

Mary's Assumption: Archetype of the Redeemed Cosmos and Church

The material world's completed redeemed state must also shine forth in Mary as Archetype of the Church. The essential point of view by which Mary is seen as the Type of the Church is as follows: Mary typifies the essence of the Church, a community of men and the Mystical Body of Christ, in whom the Divine Life of Christ dwells. This life is to be given to everyone who has been incorporated into this Body as a living member. The Church has performed her receptive co-redemption in Mary, her representative. It is in Mary that the Church has fully received her Redemption.

It follows, therefore, that the body must be seen in its perfected redeemed state in Mary. This does not mean that her body could have avoided
passing through the dark portal of death. Every human being assumes completely the work of Redemption and its fruits of grace when, by dying, he
gives his whole existence back to God the Father. Mary fulfilled this subjective, receptive and co-redeeming role of the Church when, by dying, she
made Christ's redemptive death her own and subjectively co-enacted it.

Mary died too, as Archetype of the co-redemptive Church. The Church
day by day has to make Christ's death her own. It is she who constantly, continually dies with Christ and therefore rises with Him to eternal life. Mary is
the perfect expression of the Church's co-redemptive work. Therefore it is
most fitting that she should have died as did her Redeemer, both by her constant moral affirmation and by a physical, bodily death.

At the same time the redeemed state of the physical cosmos at the end of
time shines forth in her body. In her body she co-enacted subjectively Christ's
death. In her, as Archetype, her body shows the Church's fully redeemed
body. Her body lights the way for the body of the Church and shows that the
transfiguration dwells like a seed within her corporeality.

Otto Semmelroth, from
"Mary, Archetype of the Church," in *Womanguides*

After it was all over, Mary, the mother of Jesus, together with the other Mary,
the mother of St. John, and the Mary Magdalene, the repentant harlot, went
down to the seashore; a woman named Fatima, a servant, went with them.
They stepped into a boat, they threw away the rudder, they permitted the sea
to take them where it wanted. It beached them near Marseilles. Don't run
away with the idea that the South of France was an easy option compared to
the deserts of Syria, of Egypt, or the wastes of Cappadocia, where other early
saints, likewise driven by the imperious need for solitude, found arid, inhos-
pitable crevices in which to contemplate the ineffable. There were clean,
square, white, modern cities all along the Mediterranean coast—everywhere
except the place the three Marys landed with their servant. They landed in
the middle of a malarial swamp. And there the two stern mothers and
Fatima—don't forget Fatima—set up a chapel, at the place we now call
Saintes-Maries-de-la-Mer. There they stayed. But the other Mary, the Magdalene, could not stop. Impelled by the demon of loneliness, she went off on her
own through the Camargue; then she crossed limestone hill after limestone
hill. Flints cut her feet, sun burned her skin. She ate fruit that had fallen
from the tree of its own accord, like a perfect Manichean. She ate dropped

berries. The black-browed Palestinian woman walked in silence, gaunt as famine, hairy as a dog.

She walked until she came to the forest of the Sainte-Baume. She walked until she came to the remotest part of the forest. There she found a cave. There she stopped. There she prayed. She did not speak to another human being, she did not see another human being, for thirty-three years, or so they say. Mary Magdalene, the Venus in sackcloth. Georges de La Tour's picture does not show a woman in sackcloth, but her chemise is coarse and simple enough to be a penitential garment, or, at least, the kind of garment that shows you were not thinking of personal adornment when you put it on. And even though the chemise is deeply open on the bosom, it does not seem to disclose flesh as such, but a flesh that has more akin to the wax of the burning candle, to the way the wax candle is irradiated by its own flame, and glows. So you could say that, from the waist up, this Mary Magdalene is on the high road to penitence, but, from the waist down, there is the question of her long, red skirt. Left-over finery? Was it the only frock she had, the frock she went whoring in, then repented in, then set sailing in? Did she walk all the way to the Sainte-Baume in this red skirt? It doesn't look travel-stained or worn or torn. It still has a luxurious, even a faintly scandalous air—a scarlet dress for a scarlet woman.

The Virgin Mary wears blue. Her preference has sanctified the colour. We think of a "heavenly" blue. But Mary Magdalene wears red, the colour of passion. The two women are twin paradoxes. One is not what the other is. One is a virgin and a mother; the other is a non-virgin, and childless. (Note how the English language doesn't contain a specific word to describe a woman who is grown-up, sexually mature and *not* a mother, unless such a woman is using her sexuality as her profession.)

Because Mary Magdalene is a woman and childless she goes out into the wilderness. The others, the mothers, stay and make a church, where people come. But why has she taken her pearl necklace with her? Look at it, lying in front of the mirror. And her long hair has been most beautifully brushed. Is she, yet, fully repentant?

In Georges de La Tour's painting, the Magdalene's hair is well-brushed. Sometimes the Magdalene's hair is as shaggy as a Rastafarian's. Sometimes her hair hangs down upon, is inextricably mixed up with, her furs. Mary Magdalene is easier to read when she is hairy, when, in the wilderness, she wears the rough coat of her own desires, as if the desires of her past have turned into the hairy shirt that torments her present, repentant flesh. Sometimes she wears only her hair, it never saw a comb, long, matted, unkempt, hanging down to her knees. She belts her own hair round her waist with the rope with which, each night, she lashes herself, making a rough tunic of it. On these occasions, the transformation from the young, lovely, voluptuous Mary Magdalene, the happy non-virgin, the party girl, the woman taken in adultery—on these occasions, the transformation is complete. She has turned into something wild and strange, into a female version of John the Baptist, a hairy hermit, as good as naked, transcending gender, sex obliterated, nakedness irrelevant. Now she is one with such pole-sitters as Simeon Stylites, and other solitary cave-dwellers who communed with beasts, like St. Jerome. She eats herbs, drinks water from the pool; she comes to resemble an even earlier incarnation of the "wild man of the woods" than John the Baptist. Now she looks like hairy Engidu, from the Babylonian epic of Gilgamesh. The woman who once, in her grand, red dress, was vice personified, has now retired to an existential situation in which vice simply isn't possible. In her new, resplendent animality, she is now beyond choice. Now she has no option but virtue.

But there is another way of looking at it. Think of Donatello's Magdalene, in Florence—she's dried-up by the suns of the wilderness, battered by wind and rain, anorexic, toothless, a body entirely annihilated by the soul. You can almost smell the odour of the kind of sanctity that reeks from her— it's rank, it's raw, it's horrible. By the ardour with which she has embraced the rigorous asceticism of penitence, you can tell how much she hated her early life of so-called pleasure. The mortification of the flesh comes naturally to her. When you learn that Donatello intended the piece to be, not black but gilded, that does not lighten its mood.

Nevertheless you can see the point that some anonymous Man of the Enlightenment on the Grand Tour made two hundred years ago—how Donatello's Mary Magdalene made him "disgusted with penitence."

Mary Magdalene can illustrate the point at which penitence becomes sado-masochism.

But it can also become kitsch. Consider the apocryphal story of Mary of Egypt. Who was a beautiful prostitute until she repented and spent the remaining forty-seven years of her life as a penitent in the desert, clothed only in her long hair and fed in perpetuity by the three loaves she had originally taken with her. This is a voluptuous image of eroticism and surprise. Mary of Egypt remains clean and fresh throughout. She remains miraculously unlined. She remains as untouched as the bread which she eats and which is not consumed. We imagine her sitting on a rock in the desert, combing her hair, like a lorelei whose water has turned to sand. She has turned penitence into kitsch.

Georges de La Tour's Mary Magdalene has not yet arrived at an ecstasy of repentance, evidently. Perhaps, indeed, he has pictured her as she is just about to repent—before her sea voyage, in fact, although I would prefer to think that this bare, bleak space, furnished only with the mirror, is that of her cave in the woods. But this is a woman who is still taking care of herself. Her long, black hair, sleek as that of a Japanese woman on a painted scroll— she must just have finished brushing it, reminding us that she is the patron saint of hairdressers. Her hair is the product of culture, not left as nature intended. Her hair shows she has just used the mirror as an instrument of worldly vanity. Her hair shows that, even as she meditates upon the candle flame, *this* world still has a claim upon her. Unless we are actually watching her as her soul is drawn out into the candle flame.

We meet Mary Magdalene in the gospels, doing something extraordinary with her hair. After she massaged Jesus' feet with her pot of precious ointment, she wiped them clean with her hair, an image so astonishing and erotically precise it is surprising it is represented so rarely in art, especially that of the seventeenth century, when religious excess and eroticism went so often together. Magdalene, using her hair, that beautiful net with which she used to snare men as well as a mop, a washcloth, a towel. And a slight element of the perverse about it, too. All in all, the kind of *gaudy gesture* a repentant prostitute *would* make.

She has brushed her hair, perhaps for the last time, and taken off her pearl necklace, also for the last time. Now she is gazing at the candle flame, which doubles itself in the mirror. Once upon a time, that mirror was the tool of her trade; it was within the mirror that she assembled all the elements of the femininity she put together for sale. But now, instead of reflecting her face, it duplicates the pure flame.

When I was in labour, I thought of a candle flame. I was in labour for nineteen hours. At first the pains came slowly and were relatively light; it was easy to ride them. But when they came more closely together, and grew more and more intense, then I began to concentrate my mind upon an imaginary candle flame.

Look at the candle flame as if it is the only thing in the world. How white and steady it is. At the core of the white flame is a cone of blue, transparent air; that is the thing to look at, that is the thing to concentrate on. When the pains came thick and fast, I fixed all my attention on the blue absence at the heart of the flame, as though it were the secret of the flame and, if I concentrated enough upon it, it would become *my* secret, too.

Soon there was no time to think of anything else. By then, I was entirely subsumed by the blue space. Even when they snipped away at my body, down below, to finally let the baby out the easiest way, all my attention was concentrated on the core of the flame.

Once the candle flame had done its work, it snuffed itself out; they wrapped my baby in a shawl and gave him to me.

Mary Magdalene meditates upon the candle flame. She enters the blue core, the blue absence. She becomes something other than herself.

The silence in the picture, for it is the most silent of pictures, emanates not from the darkness behind the candle in the mirror but from those two candles, the real candle and the mirror candle. Between them, the two candles disseminate light and silence. They have tranced the woman into enlightenment. She can't speak, won't speak. In the desert, she will grunt, maybe, but she will put speech aside, after this, after she has meditated upon the candle flame and the mirror. She will put speech aside just as she has put aside her pearl necklace and will put away her red skirt. The new person, the saint, is being born out of this intercourse with the candle flame.

But something has already been born out of this intercourse with the candle flame. See. She carries it already. She carries where, if she were a Virgin mother and not a sacred whore, she would rest her baby, not a living child but a *memento mori*, a skull.

Angela Carter, from "The Wrightsman Magdalene," in
American Ghosts and Old World Wonders

There is one saint in the calendar of the Church who has never been associated with the idea of punishment: even justice is alien to her, compared with the ideas of mercy and love. She is the one whom Catholics know as Our Lady.

Yet it is around this figure that the bitterest conflict has always been waged. No statues in Puritan England were more certain to be destroyed than hers, and the same was true in Spain in the 1930s. Ministers in their pulpits may question the divinity of Christ and cause no stir outside a few country rectories—but when the doctrine of the Assumption, which has been established as a feast of the Church for more than 1,000 years, is defined as a dogma, the Archbishops of Canterbury and York claim that the division of Christendom has been widened. They believe in the Resurrection of the dead—but to suggest that an actual resurrection has already taken place seems to them blasphemous. No storm was raised when, a hundred years ago, Newman wrote: "Original sin had not been found in her, by the wear of her senses, and the waste of her frame and the decrepitude of years, propagating death. She died, but her death was a mere fact, not an effect; and, when it was over, it ceased to be." Temporally there were other issues: the Protestant churches were worried by the idea of evolution, even the age of the earth was a cause of scandal because it was believed to contradict Genesis. But the conflict of science and religion always passes sooner or later: what remains is this mysterious savage war around the only figure of perfect human love.

What is the explanation? One theologian has explained it, for our generation, as a distrust of the concrete. We are so used to abstractions. Words like Democracy and Liberty can be used in quite opposite senses without arousing attention: they go in and out of our ears like air. So with religious belief. The Supreme Being, the Trinity, the Creator of all things, such phrases may once have excited thought, but they do so no longer. Even the concrete name Christ has become so diluted, into the Great Teacher, the First Communist, and the like, that only a small amount of opposition is raised by the idea that Christ is God—it is rather like saying Truth is God. But the statement that Mary is the Mother of God remains something shocking, paradoxical, physical.

But it is from that statement that all Christianity springs. To quote Newman again, "When once we have mastered the idea, that Mary bore, suckled, and handled the Eternal in the form of a child, what limit is conceivable to the rush and flood of thoughts which such a doctrine involves?" The flood of thoughts may sometimes have taken bizarre channels, but the Church is slow and careful: tales are allowed plenty of time to wither of themselves, and there is surely small sign of impetuosity in the proclamation in 1854 of the Immaculate Conception, which was already part of the accepted teaching of the Church, in the East and the West and in Africa, within a few years of the death of St. John. As for the Assumption, which even unguided human logic might detect as an essential effect of the Immaculate Conception, the Church has waited longer still.

Our opponents sometimes claim that no belief should be held dogmatically which is not explicitly stated in scripture (ignoring that it is only on the authority of the Church we recognise certain Gospels and not others as true). But the Protestant churches have themselves accepted such dogmas as the Trinity for which there is no such precise authority in the Gospels. St. John wrote, "There is much else besides that Jesus did; if all of it were put in writing I do not think the world itself would contain the books which would have to be written"; and it is our claim that Tradition alone—founded on the Apostles' teaching, analysed and reflected on through the ages by the Church, under the guidance of the Holy Spirit promised by Christ—illumines the full and true meaning of the Scriptures.

From the Scriptures themselves we know very little of Our Lady beyond the first appalling facts of the Annunciation and the Virgin Birth. St. Luke's Gospel is sometimes known as Our Lady's, for St. Luke gives details of the Visitation and the Birth that could only have come from Mary's account of them. St. Matthew's Gospel complements his account with the Flight into Egypt, St. John, with whom, so tradition declares, she spent the remainder of her life after the Crucifixion, tells us how Christ performed for her His first miracle at the wedding feast of Cana, how she stood at the foot of the Cross and how Christ entrusted her to the disciple whom He loved. From the Acts we learn that she was present with the Apostles in the upper room at Pentecost, and afterwards there is complete silence—a few legends, that is all. "Her departure made no noise in the world," Newman wrote. "The Church went about her common duties, preaching, converting, suffering; there were persecutions, there was fleeing from place to place, there were martyrs, there were triumphs; at length the rumour spread abroad that the Mother of God was no longer upon earth. Pilgrims went to and fro; they sought for her relics, but they found them not; did she die at Ephesus? or did she die at Jerusalem? Reports varied: but her tomb could not be pointed out, or if it was found it was open."

The Empty Tomb

Legend tells how the Apostles were suddenly gathered together round her deathbed, how they buried her and on the third day found her tomb empty, but the dogma of the Assumption does not demand that we should believe these details of her end. We are only asked to believe what the Church in historical memory has always believed, that, just as in her case the taint of original sin was never allowed to touch her ("our tainted nature's solitary boast," Wordsworth wrote), so the corruption of the body, which we believe is the effect of original sin, never occurred; she is soul and glorified body (whatever that may be) in heaven (wherever that can be found).

Scripture, tradition, legend—all these contribute either to our knowledge of Mary or to our knowledge of how men regarded her. In her case, unlike that of any other saint, there is another source; she alone has consistently, throughout history up to the present day, appeared to men. There has been an undrying flow of visions: she is a woman of a hundred geographical titles—Lourdes, La Salette, Carmel, Fatima, Guadalupe, Lima. The Church has never demanded that we should believe in any of these visions as an article of faith. Some of the visions, just as some of the legends, the Church has even condemned. Those regarded as worthy of credence are not confined to one continent or one race. Some go back beyond the period of proper investigation, like that of Our Lady of Walsingham in England whose shrine was visited barefoot one snowbound winter by Henry VIII and was afterwards destroyed by the same king's henchmen. The legend tells us that Our Lady appeared to a noble widow and commanded her to build a shrine after the style of her own house in Nazareth. The work went awry. During one night therefore Our Lady built the house herself with the help of angels. Of course we need give no credence to the legend as it has come down to us, but the persistence and purity of the devotion round this shrine—a devotion that touched even the sceptical Erasmus—which continues today in the pilgrimages to the restored shrine, suggests at least the possibility of some genuine vision behind the myth. Can one write so beautifully about a lie as the anonymous 16th century author of the *Lament over Walsingham*?

> Bitter bitter Oh to behold the grass to grow
> Where the walls of Walsingham so stately did show;
> Such were the works of Walsingham while she did stand:
> Such are the wrecks as now do show of that holy land.
> Level level with the ground the towers do lie
> Which with their golden glittering tops pierced once to the sky....
> Weep weep O Walsingham whose days and nights,
> Blessings turned to blasphemies, holy deeds to dispites.
> Sin is where Our Lady sat, Heaven turned to Hell,
> Satan sits where Our Lord did sway, Walsingham O farewell.

If the origin of Walsingham goes back into those deep medieval shadows that contrast with the clarity and lucidity of the primitive age, the vision of the Virgin of Guadalupe is established almost as exactly as the 19th century visions of Lourdes and La Salette, or the 20th century vision of Fatima. It was on Dec. 9, 1531, that Our Lady appeared to an Indian peasant called Juan Diego as he was climbing Tepayac Hill at the foot of which the shrine now stands, close to Mexico City. She told the Indian to carry a message to Bishop Zumarraga, that he was to build a shrine on the spot where she might watch and guard the Indians. Only two years before Mexico had fallen finally to Cortez, the country was not yet subdued, and the average Spanish adventurer would have given small welcome to an Indian peasant who said he had been addressed as "my child" by the Mother of God. Zumarraga himself refused to credit the story, and when the Virgin appeared again to the Indian at the same place, he asked her to send a Spaniard with her message whom the Bishop would trust. But the Virgin sent him back and this time the Bishop asked for a sign. For the third time Diego listened to the Virgin, who told him to return next day and she would give him the sign for which the Bishop asked. But next day Diego's uncle was very ill and he forgot—or more likely the immediate *fact* of the dying man seemed more important, more true, than a vision he may himself have discounted when the Bishop talked full of the wisdom and the slowness and the sane scepticism of the Church authority. On Tuesday, December 12, Diego had to return to Tlaltelolco to fetch a priest for his dying uncle, but he was afraid of that particular stony path he associated with his vision and took a different way. But he could not escape so easily. The Virgin blocked his new path too. She told him his uncle was already well and directed him to go to the top of the hill and gather roses from the rocks. He did as bidden, presenting the roses to Our Lady who, having touched them, returned them to him to take to the Bishop. Diego wrapped them in his serape, and when he opened it before Zumarraga the image of the Virgin was stamped on the cloth, just as it hangs above Guadalupe altar today.

I have described this vision in some detail because the legend, we are told by Mexican politicians, was invented by the Church to enslave the Indian mind. Their argument is a difficult one, for this Virgin, two years after the conquest, was claiming a church for the protection of her Indians from the Spanish conqueror. The legend gave the Indian self-respect: if it was a legend, it was a liberating and not an enslaving one. What would have been the future of the vision if it had been sent to the conqueror and not to the conquered? A rich shrine would have been built, and eventually it would have been closed like other churches during the persecution of the 1920s. This shrine, because it was Indian, remained open and helped to break the career of the only man who threatened it. When Garrido Canabal, the dictator of Tabasco, arrived in the capital with his private army of Red Shirts to take his seat as minister of agriculture in Cardenas' cabinet, he gave secret orders that the shrine was to be destroyed by dynamite. But the orders became known and the Indians guarded the shrine night and day until eventually Garrido, who had so successfully eliminated every church in Tabasco, was driven into exile.

The Virgin of Guadalupe has the features of an Indian. We know nothing of a resurrected body save that it has substance (St. Thomas put his hand in Our Lord's wounds) and yet can pass through the wall of a room, that Christ after His resurrection was sometimes recognised immediately by the disciples and yet sometimes could walk beside them unknown. The Virgin appeared to Bernadette as a girl little older than herself, to the children of Fatima as a woman, to an Indian as an Indian.

While many cases of reported visions will never even reach the stage of Church investigation, others are investigated and condemned. Two years ago a case so condemned was that of the moving statue in Assisi. The stone statue stands above the main door of the Church of Santa Maria degli Angeli at the foot of Assisi hill. One night somebody noticed that the statue seemed to breathe and move her arms. The story spread rapidly and at weekends thousands would come to see the "miracle." When I went with a companion it was in the middle of the week and only a small group stood in the forecourt singing and praying. But there were two busloads of pilgrims from towns nearby, who sat in their buses eating sandwiches and hard-boiled eggs and occasionally dipping their heads to take a look at the statue through the windows—a miracle from a Pullman seat. My companion and I were both sceptics, but from the first glance we took the statue seemed to move, sometimes the breast, sometimes the hands, sometimes the whole statue seemed on the point of toppling into the square. It was probably, we thought, the movement of our own heads that produced the illusion, so we lay flat on our backs on the gravel and shut our eyes and rested them. We opened our eyes and immediately the statue breathed and moved above us. The illusion may have been caused by the bright lights of the halo. In any case the "miracle" was a little too timely, for the elections were only a few weeks off. After the bishop's condemnation the pilgrimages would soon have ceased if the Communist mayor of Assisi had left well enough alone. But he came down to the church and attacked Our Lady in an address to the crowd and had a paralytic stroke then and there. Even with that assistance the legend is dying out. Its death is one more support for the legends that do not die. We are forced to ask ourselves: is there any explanation but that some are true?

In spite of the miracles of Lourdes, attested by a sceptic like Zola and a scientist like Alexis Carrel, we are apt to think of this an an unmiraculous age. The miracles of Lourdes are cures—we can persuade ourselves that science will one day explain them (Carrel, who witnessed the instantaneous cure of a girl dying of tubercular peritonitis, tried unsuccessfully to persuade himself that his diagnosis had been at fault). But this is an age of visions as well as cures: if we are entering a new Dark Age we are being given the same consolations as our ancestors. Since the defeat of the Turks at Lepanto the battle for Christianity has never been more critical, and sometimes it seems as though the supernatural were gathering its forces for our support, and whom should we expect in the vanguard but Our Lady? For the attack on the Son has always come through the Mother. She is the keystone of Christian doctrine. If you wish to discredit the divinity of Christ you discredit the Virgin Birth; if you wish to discredit the manhood of Christ you discredit the motherhood of Our Lady.

One vision which is likely to be regarded as credible by the Church (let me emphasise again that no Catholic is bound to believe even in the vision of St. Bernadette, for a Saint can be deceived) is that of the Tre Fontane, a cave on a hillside near Rome opposite a Trappist monastery that is said to be the scene of St. Paul's execution. Now a rough path made by pilgrims runs along the slope of the hill among the low eucalyptus trees to a small clearing and a cave sparkling with votive offerings. Cripples sell candles along the way, and when I was last there dozens of children from a war orphanage, each child without a leg or an arm, were helping each other across the clearing to where women knelt and scooped into their handkerchiefs the earth they believed had been pressed by Mary's feet. On April 12, 1947, a Roman bus inspector, Bruno Cornacchiola, a Communist and renegade Catholic, was walking in these woods with his three children: he was preparing a speech attacking the title of the Mother of God. His children called to him to help them find their ball. "I went over," he said. "What do I see? Gianfranco on his knees at the entrance to the grotto, his hands joined. He murmurs, 'Beautiful lady, beautiful lady.' I call Isola. 'Come here. What is your brother saying? What is there in there?' 'It's nothing,' says the child and at the same moment there she is on the ground in the same attitude, saying the same words as Gianfranco. I understand nothing. 'Carlo, tell me what is this and what are you playing at?' 'I don't know,' replies the child, and there he is on his knees too. 'Beautiful lady, beautiful lady,' he says. I am astounded, and it is as though two hands are passed over my eyes; a veil has fallen. A great light illuminates the grotto, and in the middle there appears..."

Message to Bernadette

I quote no more because, as so often in such cases, the human description of the vision becomes unreal, stilted, academic. (We judge its authenticity partly by its effect on the family concerned.) If St. John of the Cross fails to convey his vision, how can a child or a bus inspector convey theirs? They are forced back on trite words, pious phrases, "I am She who lies in the bosom of the Divine Trinity," and the like. To me almost the only convincing words any of these visions have spoken were those reported by the child Bernadette. There had been many sermons and much talk on the new dogma of the Immaculate Conception and she had no idea of its meaning, until that girl of about her own age appeared to her in the Pyrenean cave and explained, "*I am the Immaculate Conception*," as much as to say, "This doctrine of the Second Eve which theologians have been discussing for 1,600 years is as simple as that—it is me, whom you know, that's all." We can look for no enlargements of knowledge from these visions. But there is a common feature in all her appearances, the appeal for prayer and yet more prayer. Her message is as simple as that, and it may seem unimportant unless we have some realisation of the terrible force of prayer, the mysterious untapped power able to move mountains.

What a strange distance, like a stellar space, cold and incomprehensible, separates the child Bernadette or the boy Francesco at Fatima from indignant theologians who deplore the dogma of the Assumption as "an added difficulty to reunion" of all Christian churches. It may be "a difficulty," but these children have *seen* the glorified body, and you will not persuade them to suppress their vision because it is tactless, because it may offend a few dignitaries of an alien faith. If the dogma had not been proclaimed now it would still one day have been proclaimed. The Church has waited nearly twelve hundred years since the feast of the Assumption was appointed by the Synod of Salzburg in 800, and the Synod had waited several centuries since the first written reference to the common belief. We might have waited another thousand years, but the Church has decided otherwise.

It is legitimate, of course, to speculate why this precise moment in history has been chosen. I can write only as an uninstructed Catholic. Because the doctrines of Christ's nature as God and Man are walled about by the doctrine of the Annunciation and the Virgin Birth, so that it is not too much to say that the whole of Christianity to this day lies in Our Lady's womb, it is to her that recourse has always been had in times of crisis. So it was through all the terrible storms of the 16th century when the Turks seemed on the point of conquering Europe: appropriately Pius V instituted the feast day of the Most Holy Rosary in thanksgiving for the great victory of Lepanto. And now, when a yet heavier threat lies upon our borders, perhaps the proclamation of the new dogma will help the devotion of millions. Devotion means simply an expression of love, and if we love enough, even in human terms, we gain courage.

This would be no argument, of course, for proclaiming a novel belief, but a dogma is only a definition of an old belief. It restricts the area of truth at the expense of legend or heresy, and the greatest definitions of the Church, accepted alike by Protestants and Catholics—the nature of Christ, the doctrine of the Trinity—were definitions drawn up to exclude heresies within the Church itself.

In our day there are no obvious signs of heretical beliefs within the Church concerning the Assumption of Our Lady and therefore it was believed by some Catholics that to proclaim the dogma was unnecessary. But Catholics today cannot remain quite untouched by the general heresy of our time, the unimportance of the individual. Today the human body is regarded as expendable material, something to be eliminated wholesale by the atom bomb, a kind of anonymous carrion. After the First World War, crosses marked the places where the dead lay, allied and enemy: lights burned continually in the capitals of Europe over the graves of the unknown warriors. But no crosses today mark the common graves into which the dead of London and Berlin were shovelled, and Hiroshima's memorial is the outline of a body photographed by the heat flash on asphalt. The definition of the Assumption proclaims again the doctrine of our Resurrection, the eternal destiny of each human body, and again it is the history of Mary which maintains the doctrine in its clarity. The Resurrection of Christ can be regarded as the Resurrection of a God, but the Resurrection of Mary foreshadows the Resurrection of each one of us.

> Graham Greene, from "The Conflict Round the Dogma,"
> in *The Story of Mary*

⇥ Kuan Yin ⇤

Kuan Yin (sometimes spelled Kwan Yin or Quan Yin) of the Buddhist tradition is the female form of the Bodhisattva of compassion, Avalokiteshvara, which means "the Lord Looking Down in Pity." She is the yin to his yang, and is celebrated as the goddess/madonna of the Orient (Tibet, China, and Japan) who is prayed to as the sustainer, as the gentle mother who performs miracles, much as Mary does in the West. Kuan Yin is found in the tao of the natural elements, in the rushing waters (the tears of Buddha), in the form of a young girl, or a bejewelled icon in the temples, and she moves in all our senses. She crosses the boundaries of culture and devotion and appears in Thomas Merton's dreams and in John Blofeld's pilgrimage, where a young Christian sees her manifestation in a combination of Eastern and Western deity. Kuan Yin is active and alive in all of us in the form of the lotus and the heart as feminine divinity, compassion, love, and virtue.

⇥⇤

Thus the woman is the original seeress, the lady of the wisdom-bringing waters of the depths, of the murmuring springs and fountains, for the "original utterance of seerdom is the language of water." But the woman also understands the rustling of the trees & all the signs of nature, with whose life she is so closely bound up.

> Martha Graham, *Notebooks of Martha Graham*

Creation and Creator art Thou,
Thou art Energy and Truth,
O Goddess, O Goddess, O Goddess!

Creator of the Cosmos art Thou,
And Thou art the beginning and end...

The Essence of the individual soul art Thou, and
Thou art the five elements as well....

Mata Amritanandamayi, from Swami Amritasvarupananda,
Mata Amritanandamayi

I have a wonderful story about Kuan-yin, one of the personifications of the great Mahāyāna Bodhisattva Avalokiteshvara, the embodiment of compassion.

It seems that Kuan-yin realized that in a certain part of China, out in the rural areas, nobody had ever heard of enlightenment. They were all interested in horse racing and all this macho stuff. So she turns herself into a gloriously beautiful girl, comes into town with fresh fish from the river to sell, and when her basket is empty, she disappears. Early the next day, this beautiful fish-selling girl is there again, and then once again she disappears. This daily pattern continues, and soon all of the men have become enchanted by her.

One morning, when she appears, about ten or twenty of them surround her and say, "You have to marry one of us." "Well," she says, "I cannot marry twenty men, but tomorrow morning, if one of you can recite by heart the Sutra of the Compassionate Kuan-yin, I will marry that man." The next morning, a dozen men know the entire sutra by heart, so she says, "Well, I cannot marry all of you, but I will marry the one who can interpret this sutra to me tomorrow."

The next day, there are four men who can interpret the sutra, so now she says, "I am only one woman, and I can't marry four men, but if one of you has *experienced* the meaning of this sutra three days from now, then I will marry that man."

Three days later, there is but one man waiting for her. Now she says, "My little house is down by the bend in the river. Come there this evening, and you will be my husband."

So that evening, he goes to where the shore bends and comes to a little house. An old couple is standing outside, and the old man says, "Oh, we've been waiting a long, long time for you. Our daughter is inside." But when he goes into the room, it's empty. She isn't there. So he looks out the window and sees footprints, which he follows down to the river, where he finds a little pair of shoes at the water's edge, but no girl.

Then, as he's standing there, with the reeds blowing and so forth, he realizes that all the reeds and everything else is she. Through her allure and charm, which is what the female figure represent in these Mahāyāna images, he realizes the nirvānic grace of beauty in the universe. Having understood the sutra, he knew what he was experiencing, and he received illumination.

Joseph Campbell, *Reflections on the Art of Living*

Last night I had a haunting dream of a Chinese princess which stayed with me all day. ("Proverb" again.) This lovely and familiar and archetypal person. (No "object" yet how close and real, and how elusive.) She comes to me in various mysterious ways in my dreams. This time she was with her "brothers," and I felt overwhelmingly the freshness, the youth, the wonder, the truth of her; her complete reality, more real than any other, yet unobtainable. Yet I deeply felt the sense of her understanding, knowing and loving me, in my depths—not merely in my individuality and everyday self, yet not as if this self were utterly irrelevant to her. (Not rejected, not accepted either.)

Thomas Merton, *A Vow of Conversation*

Some Manifestations

> To hear her name and see her form
> Delivers beings from every woe.
> —LOTUS SŪTRA

The embassy of the boat-women to Kuan Yin's temple well exemplifies how peasants in China and neighbouring countries conceive of her. Seeing her as a benevolent goddess into whose nature it would be discourteous to enquire, they rejoice because she is lovely in herself and generous in heeding supplications. This uncomplicated attitude is not limited to illiterate followers of ancient folk-religions, for even among the general run of Buddhists in China and Japan, the distinction between deities and celestial Bodhisattvas is blurred. However, more erudite Buddhists see her otherwise. The following account of an experience significant to me personally prefaces two other stories that will serve as a preview of some of the ways in which Kuan Yin is conceptualised. One, though it does just touch upon the Mind Only doctrine lying at the root of the celestial Bodhisattva concept, reveals her in a guise very similar to that of a goddess, whereas the other carries us to a high metaphysical level.

One of the three main annual festivals of Kuan Yin, Hearer-of-Cries, falls on the nineteenth day of the sixth lunar month (about July). For centuries it has been celebrated by gatherings in her honour, some of which assemble on the twelfth of the month and spend no less than seven days on rites and contemplative meditation centred on Kuan Yin. Alas, in recent years the ranks of her followers have been thinned. For all I know, such festivals still take place in Japan, Korea and Singapore, but hardly in China or Viet-Nam.

Quite soon after my arrival in China, while staying at a monastery nestling among clumps of lychee-trees on the sunny side of a minor sacred mountain, I heard that "Kuan Yin's Birthday" was going to be celebrated that evening at a neighbouring temple over which she presided, so at sunset I set off in that direction. By the time I arrived, night had fallen. Scudding clouds obscured the moon, but peach-shaped lanterns suspended from the temple gateway's elegantly curving roof cast a pool of crimson light that could be seen from a distance. Beyond lay a courtyard thronged with worshippers whose faces were illumined by the rays of perhaps a hundred candles streaming through the shrine-hall's wide-flung doors. Most were lay-people, but a sprinkling of bald pates showed that some monks and nuns from neighbouring monasteries were among them. All were craning their heads towards the shrine where Kuan Yin's statue rose behind a lavishly carved and gilded altar where stood innumerable candle-sticks, a great bronze incense tripod and an array of porcelain vessels piled with offerings of fruit and flowers. No animal flesh or cups of wine were to be seen, for even the peasants had some inkling of the difference between Kuan Yin and the more gluttonous local deities; besides, the keepers of the shrine would have rejected such offerings as impure and displeasing to the Bodhisattva—though not monks, they would hardly have accepted them even for themselves.

The night air, drenched with the mingled perfumes of burning sandalwood and of jasmine and champak flowers, quivered as the mallet thudded upon a large hollowed block known as the wooden-fish drum; its throb was punctuated by the clang and tinkle of bronze and silver instruments used to mark the rhythm of the chant. Though the same few words, *Namu tatzû tapei Kuan Shih Yin P'u-Sa* (Homage to the greatly compassionate, greatly merciful Kuan Shih Yin Bodhisattva)! were intoned repeatedly, the ardour of those taking part and frequent subtle changes in the rhythm dispelled monotony, so that the music lifted me into a realm of beauty and enchantment.

Taller than the wiry southerners pressing all about me, I had an unobstructed view. The Bodhisattva was depicted as a gracious young lady with smoothly rounded cheeks and chin, sitting very informally upon a rock-like throne, one knee raised so high that the elegant little slipper peeping from beneath her robe was on a level with the other knee. One slender hand toyed with a willow sprig, the other held a vase of "sweet dew" symbolising the nectar of compassion. To either side, wrought on a smaller scale, stood her attendants—Shan Ts'ai, a smiling boy, and Lung Nü, the Dragon Maiden, who was holding out a giant pearl. These statues can hardly have been the work of local artists; they were finely sculpted and had a pleasing liveliness, though I could have wished them less ornate. But for her distinctive posture and the nature of the symbols in her hands, the splendidly robed and bejewelled figure could almost have been mistaken for that of Mary arrayed as Queen of Heaven in the manner of South Europe. Superficially at least, her robes and ornaments resembled artifacts from Byzantium. Struck by this lavish costume, I wondered how this empress-like being could be made to fit in with the gently austere teaching of the Buddha; for I had still to learn that the external forms taken by Buddhism in different countries, though strikingly varied, entail no real departures from its doctrines.

Presently a gust of wind sent incense-smoke billowing upwards in heavy clouds that momentarily blurred the Bodhisattva's features, creating the illusion of a living being whose expression now altered and took on unimaginable beauty. As though chiding my churlishness in the matter of her costume, she seemed to fix me with her eyes and gently shake her head.

Aware that this was no miracle, I was nevertheless entranced and tried hard to believe that the goddess had taken notice of me. What is more, there seemed to hover just beyond the threshold of my mind a teasing recollection of something or someone once greatly loved but long faded from my memory. The effect was so poignant that I wanted both to laugh and to cry. I am convinced that it was this elusive recollection rather than the trick wrought by the incense smoke that produced what seems in retrospect a magical effect; in that moment I conceived a reverence for the Compassionate One which, far from fading with the years, was destined to intensify, although for a long time it remained no more than a pleasant whimsy. In those days I had not the wisdom to reconcile deep devotion to a deity with the knowledge that deities are not!

I was too moved to pay attention to what followed. No doubt the long period of invocation gave place to recitation of the P'u Mên chapter of the Lotus Sūtra or of Kuan Yin's Dhāranī of Great Compassion. The rite must have ended with an inspiring crescendo of cymbals and drums succeeded by an eerie silence as the officiants prostrated themselves; but by then I had slipped away to begin my walk through the darkness to the monastery where I lodged. To this day I recall my pleasure in the cool night air so free from cloying scents, the creek of bamboos swaying in the wind and the scurrying of small creatures in the undergrowth. Throughout the walk I indulged the poetic fancy that the goddess had wished to remind me of something immensely important to my happiness. Such a mood is not difficult to sustain while strolling by moonlight on the slopes of a mountain where immortal beings have been worshipped since before the dawn of history; the very atmosphere is vibrant with intimations of their presence. To a part of my mind which told me I was being absurd, I put up strenuous resistance, being loath to return to an ugly world which, even in those days, was fast coming under the domination of monsters disguised as inventors and technicians. Having disposed of cavilling logic, my mind soared, leading me to a state bordering on ecstasy. I had a foretaste of the wisdom born of full realisation that only mind is real; the demons of duality were temporarily vanquished so that it became possible to entertain simultaneously two opposing facets of truth.

Back at the monastery, while waiting for the sleepy porter to admit me, I became aware of a delicious fragrance which I supposed to have a supernatural origin until, looking up, I saw that the gateway was overhung by the boughs of a tree called in Chinese *yeh-lai-hsiang* (night fragrance) which pours out its perfume during the first watches of the night. The great courtyard was in darkness, the monks being still away celebrating the festival or else retired to their cells to sleep or meditate until summoned for the morning rite an hour before dawn. Noticing that lamps still glimmered in the deserted shrine-hall, I felt a sudden impulse to enter and make my way round behind the Buddha statues to where it was customary in Chinese monasteries to house a statue of Kuan Yin. There she was, standing upon a shelf at about the level of my chest. It was an image of fine bronze some three feet high, with the right hand raised in benediction, the elongated eyes half closed in contemplative bliss. The stumps of votive candles still guttered at her feet, whereas the incense sticks lit in her honour had burnt down to the stubs leaving behind a sour staleness. It seems sad that deities have to endure this odour when their worshippers have retired for the night. Perhaps the truth is that it is the worshippers themselves who enjoy temple offerings. Lighting fresh incense, I stood before her in silence until, suddenly carried away by exaltation, I whispered, "Compassionate One, be pleased to speak and convince me of your reality!"

How foolish this must sound and how ashamed I should be to write of it, were it not for the sequel. Even with the words upon my lips I reflected that a sane man should know better than to attempt holding converse with a statue! Yet perhaps I had some excuse; for, apart from being then in a special state of mind, I had recently spent much time in the company of certain Chinese Buddhists who, despite being men of obvious good sense and erudition, would have found nothing surprising in such conduct. As it turned out, no justification was needed, for the plain truth is that the statue answered me at once, saying: "Look not for my reality in the realm of appearances or in the Void. Seek it in your own mind. There only it resides."

I wish I could make the story even more extraordinary by affirming that the bronze lips moved, that the beautifully moulded throat gave forth melodious sounds. It was not so. No sound or movement stirred the silence. The enigmatic words entered my consciousness as thought-forms, but so palpably that not even sound itself could have made the effect more electrifying or their sequence more precise. It is hard to believe that, at a time when my knowledge of Mahayana Buddhism was so slight, I could have summoned such a pronouncement from within myself. I did not really know then what the first sentence meant. I felt sure I had received an intimation that Kuan Yin exists—to the extent that "exists" is a fitting description of her subtle nature. Using the word thus is perhaps to overstate the case, just as to say that she does not exist would be to understate it. My experience was not imaginary. Such intuitive perceptions are too direct, too penetrating to be mistaken for ordinary imaginings. Yet for years I hesitated to speak of it, except to my Chinese friends, who understood its nature; but now I have come to recognise that no good purpose is served by concealing marvels merely because people nowadays are apt to disbelieve them. In truth, such a marvel is not magical to those who recognise mind's sovereign power over phenomena of every kind whatsoever.

> *Chrysanthemums* are *gold*
> *To those who see them so.*
> *Red gold is just a metal*
> *Till thought-forms give it worth.*

There is a modern short story about a timid knight who, armed with a magic word to make him invulnerable, slew fifty dragons as easily as cock- roaches. Unfortunately, while engaged in slaying the fiftieth, he suddenly realised that he had been tricked by his teacher into putting faith in a made- up nonsense-word. Needless to say, his fifty-first dragon gobbled him up in no time at all! Yet can one say that the magic wrought by his faith in that nonsense-word was not real? It stood him in far better stead than his "real" armour and "objectively existing" sword!

A British-educated Chinese friend of mine once told me a story that fully bears out this view of reality.

"As you know, though my mother was a Buddhist, I received all my pre-university education at Catholic schools, was baptised at sixteen and later took a Catholic wife. For years I was as devout a convert as could rea- sonably be expected of a man like me, a geologist. Then came the war which sent so many of us fleeing westward before the Japanese advance. My native city suffered cruelly from indiscriminate rape and slaughter. I could not think of my old home without tears. My work for a government prospecting enterprise took me to some wild and lonely places in Kweichow province and once I was sent to look for wolfram in a mountainous region six or seven days walk from the nearest motor-road. One day, an hour before our usual stop for midday rice, I mistook a mule-track for the path we were following and wandered far away from the men carrying my luggage and equipment. Knowing I was lost, but hungry and convinced by occasional fresh piles of mule dung that the track must lead to human habitations, I pressed forward.

Upward and upward I went until clouds were swirling about me and I could hear what sounded like the weird cries of gibbons high up in the trees. At every turn I hoped in vain to come upon at least a woodsman's hovel, but I had wandered too far by then to feel it wise to turn back. I needed food and some local man to guide me to where my porters were likely to be found.

"An icy wind came tearing down from the high peaks and dusk was closing in. Eerie sounds were all about me, some recognisable as the voices of wind and stream, others inexplicable and mournful as the cries of wandering ghosts. With each step I grew more afraid and the mists swirling among the rocks grew denser and more opaque. Fears of wild beasts rose to haunt me; as for bandits, of whom the local people had told me sinister tales, I longed to meet a fellow-human being, bandit or not. At last terror brought me to my knees beside the path and, teeth chattering, I poured out a prayer to my patron saint, St. Bernadette, begging that sweet child (as I thought of her) to appear and lead me to a place of safety. By what light remained, my eyes sought for her among the rocks. I believed that if she did not come, I should lose my sanity, if not my life!

"Then she was there, standing on a small flat rock, her flimsy blue robe hardly ruffled by the fierce and bitterly cold wind. She was smiling, as I could see well, for around her glowed a nimbus of soft light. Gradually I took in that there was something unexpected about her face. Then I realised what it was—she was a *Chinese* Bernadette! Her high-swept hair, the jewelled ornaments clasped about her throat, the white silk trousers peeping through a blue robe slit to the thigh were those of a noble Chinese maiden many centuries ago.

"'Come, Elder Brother,' she said, speaking melodious Mandarin in a childish voice too young to have belonged to Bernadette even at the time of her first meeting with the Holy Virgin, 'I shall show you a place where you can rest safely and tomorrow all will be very well.'

"She led me a short distance to a shallow cave well protected from the wind. Its floor was as soft as the softest of beds and I am nearly sure I caught sight of a silken *pei-wo* (quilt) stuffed no doubt with warm silk-floss, just as I fell asleep in the very act of lying down at her command.

"The next day I awoke, after a long, deep sleep, to find the sun high in the sky. There was no sign of bedding and the floor of the cave, far from being soft, was rugged and strewn with pebbles, but I had slept as well and warmly as in the room I once shared with my mother in my beloved native place, now a thousand *li* away. While I was washing in a nearby stream, a train of mules came down the track, driven by three mounted *lo-fu*. I easily persuaded one of these mule-drivers to sell me some cold steamed bread—

he would have given it without payment, I am sure—and, with his help, I was able to rejoin my party by noon the following day.

"For more than a year I believed I had been saved by St. Bernadette, though I could not account for her extreme youthfulness and Chinese appearance. Then, one day, I happened to take shelter from the rain in a disused temple not far from Chengtu and there, in a small chapel, I came upon a faded fresco showing Kuan Yin clad in a simple robe of blue cotton without her usual ornaments. Seated by the ocean, she was attended as usual by Shan Ts'ai and Lung Nü. In great astonishment, I recognised in Lung Nü my 'Bernadette'! Even the blue dress and white trousers were the same, but now there were no jewels clasped about her throat. Thinking about those jewels roused a memory of a similar picture that used to hang in my mother's bedroom, showing both Kuan Yin and Lung Nü adorned with splendid ornaments. So that was it! You could say that the lady who saved my life on that freezing night was neither Bernadette nor Lung Nü, just a childhood memory lighting up a fear-crazed mind. And you would be right—partly! Still, childish memories do not guide people to unknown caves, make rocks and pebbles become fine mattresses, conjure *pei-wos* from the air or drive away deadly cold.

"Yes, in a way you would be right. It *was* that memory. It was also Lung Nü herself, sent out of pity by Kuan Yin. Having since then studied the profound Mahayana doctrine of Mind Only, I accept no contradiction between those two. Driven to the edge of a reason, I sought divine aid, and divine aid came *instantly*—in a form that accorded with the contents of my mind. It was as a mental apparition that Lung Nü appeared and brought from my mind the warmth and comfort that made me physically able to withstand great cold. Would you dare say that was not a miracle wrought by the Bodhisattva I had worshipped as a child? All miracles are so—working through mind. True, the Bodhisattva did not come herself. Having too much delicacy to appear before someone calling on a foreign goddess, she sent Lung Nü who could be taken for the child saint I was expecting. Attributing my good fortune to the marvellous workings of my own mind and accepting it as the intervention of the Bodhisattva are two ways of expressing the same truth."

I have often pondered on the mineralogist's wisdom-opening experience. His penetrating understanding of it explains many similar occurrences, bridging the gap between magical and psychological. Years later, I chanced to hear—at second hand—another story, different in purport, but also illustrating the identity of miraculous intervention from "within" and "without" the mind. To understand what the narrator tells us, one must know that, whereas Kuan Yin, though often depicted as a member of a trinity with the celestial Buddha Amitābha in the centre and Kuan Yin and Ta Shih-Chih Bodhisattvas standing on either hand, is also worshipped independently by millions, this is not the case with Ta Shih-Chih. The latter seems to have faded from human consciousness, being rarely invoked in his own right. I am told the narrator was a very old gentleman called Mr. Ch'ên, who had spent the last forty years of his life as a recluse.

"In my young days, preparing for the imperial civil service examinations was, for cultivated youths, the most important thing in life. Everything depended on success—not just rank and wealth, but the honour brought to one's family and the power to serve society effectively. You cannot imagine how hard we used to work at the ancient classics, straining our eyes through reading late into the night by the pitiful glimmer of a wick floating in a saucer of oil. No wonder so many of us became stooped early in life with all that poring over books! For me and my four brothers it was especially bad. My father, who loved the Buddhist sutras even more than the Confucian classics, made us spend much time on those as well! I do not know whether we grudged the extra burden more or less than we came to love the splendour, vastness and depth of their philosophy. 'You must,' my father often said, 'pursue these studies until the meaning of the four characters FEI K'UNG CHIH K'UNG (voidness of the non-void) is as clear to you as the orb of the sun blazing down from a cloudless autumn sky.'

"On some nights when I was especially weary, I liked to imagine that the compassionate Kuan Yin appeared before me in the library in a blaze of light. This never failed to wipe away my fatigue, making me as alert as in the mornings. Afterwards I could read the sutras quickly, easily and with greater understanding. I do not say that I truly saw her, unless dimly with my mind's eye, but I knew when and how sweetly she smiled or when she was displeased with a feeling I sometimes had that reading so many sutras was an intolerable chore. My fourth brother, who was sickly and the only one of us to fail the examinations, was extremely fond of me. When we were alone, we put aside the formality that had to be shown in public by juniors to seniors, even brothers almost of an age. Once when I had been describing what I liked to call the Bodhisattva's personal manifestations to me, he said, laughing: 'How you flatter yourself, Second Brother. Such things don't happen. If they do, why is it always Kuan Yin and never Ta Shih-Chih who appears? The picture in our shrine-room contains both of them; they get the same amount of incense, bowing and the rest. Why doesn't Ta Shih-Chih do his share of healing you? It is because you forget him that he plays no part in your imagination—for it *is* imagination, whatever you say.'

"His words set me thinking. I did not agree with his main point, but he had made me feel guilty towards Ta Shih-Chih Bodhisattva, to whom none of us paid reverence except as one of three. I began offering him special prayers. For several months I never went to sleep at night without first sitting cross-legged on my bed and visualising Ta Shih-Chih. But when I invoked him instead of Kuan Yin, there was no result. Never any result at all. At last I spoke of this to my father. Unable to explain, he sent me off to a monastery lying a few *li* beyond the city wall and overlooking a stream bordered with ancient willows—Kuan Yin's emblem. On learning why I had come, the elderly Tripitaka Master who presided there smiled and said: 'You alone cannot evoke him.'

"'You mean, Venerable, that the Bodhisattvas are merely forms in people's minds?' I protested, full of wonder to hear a monk speak so. Seeing him vigorously shake his head, I went on: 'If they are real, what need of many minds to give them power to appear?'

"'What an ignorant young scholar you must be!' he answered, laughing. 'Surely you know there *are* not many minds—just Mind. All the Buddhas and Bodhisattvas, all the myriad objects exist in this one Mind. How could it be otherwise? What is in your mind is naturally in Mind itself; even so, until you have dissipated the great mountains of obscurations constructed by karma earned in previous lives, you will not have the power to call forth a response to the feeble thoughts you put there. With Kuan Yin, the case is otherwise because so many millions of beings invoke her. Now do you understand?'

"'Venerable Sir, this worthless disciple can catch something of the profound purport of your enlightening teaching,' I answered formally, though by no means sure I did. Satisfied, he raised his tea-cup in dismissal.

"That night I sat up later than any of my brothers. The little library-boy, who had orders from my father to stay within call until the last of us had handed him the books that needed putting away, replenished my tea-pot three times before I remembered to tell him to go off to bed, promising to put the flimsy volumes very carefully away in their blue boxes with my own hands. No sooner had the child walked off sleepily than the far end of the dimly lit library was illumined by a softly brilliant radiance and, as I fell to my knees, a slim, majestically tall, richly garbed figure, whom I took to be Kuan Yin was manifested in the centre of that circle of very bright but not dazzling light. The garments of the two Bodhisattvas being similar except for the head-dress, it took me a few moments to recognise Ta Shih-Chih encircled by a nimbus of golden flame.

"'Old Two,' he announced in a thrillingly beautiful voice, but addressing me informally by the nickname used by my father and uncles, 'the Venerable Tripitaka Master erred. Know that your mind is in itself immeasurable, the container of a myriad myriad universes, each of them vast beyond your comprehension. All the illimitable power that exists in those myriads of universes would be yours in full, if you had wisdom enough to use it. The same is true of every sentient being. Because your faith in me was not well developed, I have come to you always as Kuan Yin—not as I am now. Can you suppose we are two? Two in the great Mind where no two exist? Can a Bodhisattva feel wounded by neglect for as long as any other Bodhisattva is called upon? Not to speak of Bodhisattvas, when a single bee sucks honey, all beings in the myriad myriad universes suck honey; when a worm is crushed, all beings in those universes are crushed. Remember the source of all power lies within yourself and cease this foolish longing to behold mere manifestations.'

"The lovely vision faded and was gone. Since then, I have never dared to call upon such beings, except as it should be done during meditation. Seeking from them power beyond the infinite power of our own mind, which is limited only by our own dark karmic obstructions, is like what the sutras call 'looking for a head upon your head'! When, at those previous times, Kuan Yin assuaged my fatigue, it was because my mind willed that fatigue away, but needed the stimulation of the Bodhisattva's presence to function thus.

"Believe me, the Bodhisattvas are as real as earth and sky and have infinite power to aid beings in distress, but they exist within our common mind, which, to speak the truth, is itself the *container* of earth and sky."

Both the mineralogist's story and old Mr. Ch'ên's illustrate a concept not easy to grasp and perhaps not fully graspable until Enlightenment is won; but they do make it clear that, when Kuan Yin is regarded by some as a mental creation and by others as a being hardly distinguishable from a goddess, there is no question of the one view being right, the other wrong. She is both an abstraction and a goddess; how one sees her depends upon one's expectation and attitude of mind. All such mental attitudes, though one may think of them as "higher" or "lower" in the sense of exhibiting more or less wisdom and understanding, are probably so far from the ultimate truth that differences in one's level of wisdom becomes negligible. Nor is it certain that to perceive a Bodhisattva as a god- or goddess-like being does in fact demonstrate a lower degree of wisdom. All talk of high and low, except in relative and provisional contexts, is beside the point.

> To the frogs in a temple pool
> The lotus-stems are tall;
> To the Gods of Mount Everest
> An elephant is small.

John Blofeld, *In Search of the Goddess of Compassion*

✦ Divine Mothers ✦

"Mother Divine, grant that today may bring to us a completer consecration to thy Will, a more integral gift of ourselves to thy work, a more total forgetfulness of self, a greater illumination, a purer love. Grant that in a communion growing ever deeper, more constant and entire we may be united always more and more closely to thee and become thy servitors worthy of Thee. Remove from us all egoism, root out all petty vanity, greed and obscurity. May we be all ablaze with thy divine Love; make us thy torches in the world."

— SRI AUROBINDO

There are many modern-day saintly women who, by embodying the principles of the great mother, become for us human examples of her. She is brought to life through their lives. These women are the "torches in the world" as Sri Aurobindo wrote in his prayer above. Some of these women are Mother Teresa, with her devotion and service to the poorest of the poor; The Mother, who lived, worked, and taught the precepts of divine motherhood with Sri Aurobindo in his Pondicherry Ashram; and many young and old Indian women saints who mentor and guide their disciples.

Saintly women become divine because they live the message they teach, because they bestow grace and healing energy to those in their presence. The three Indian women introduced here are internationally acclaimed as living saints and teachers in the guru/disciple tradition and as manifestations of the divine mother, bestowing the spirituality of the all-protective Great Mother of God upon those who seek her.

Mata Amritanandamayi is described by Swami Amritasvarupananda as "a mystic accessible to anyone and everyone, with whom you can converse and in whose presence you can feel God. She is humble but firm as the Earth. She is simple yet beautiful like the full moon. She is Love, she is Truth, she is the embodiment of Renunciation and self-sacrifice. She not only teaches but does. She is a giver of everything and a receiver of nothing. She is soft like a flower but hard like a diamond. She is a Great Master and a Great Mother." Mata Amritanandamayi has many followers. Her centre is in the Kerala region of southern India and she travels extensively in the West, making personal appearances in many prominent cities.

In his *Autobiography of a Yogi*, one of the leading and most revealing spiritual memoirs of our age, Paramahansa Yogananda introduces the young

Ananda Moyi Ma (Joy-Permeated Mother), on his visit to her in Ranchi, India, and Oxford Fellow Andrew Harvey, in his enlightened book *Hidden Journey: A Spiritual Awakening*, recounts his meeting with his guru, the Divine Mother, Meera, at the Pondicherry Ashram. Mother Meera was born in 1960 in a village in southern India and now lives in Germany. Most of her devotees visit her there to receive *darshan* (a bestowal of grace and light).

Mother Teresa, who is founder and head of her order of The Missionaries of Charity, lives her example of divine motherhood through loving the poor in action. For this reason, I introduce her through her work later in this volume, in the chapter "Doing for God."

※

The Divine Servant

Mother is the servant of servants. She has no special place to dwell. She dwells in your heart.

Mata Amritanandamayi, from Swami Amritasvarupananda,
Mata Amritanandamayi

The Bengali
"Joy-Permeated Mother"

"Sir, please do not leave India without a glimpse of Nirmala Devi. Her sanctity is intense; she is known far and wide as Ananda Moyi Ma (Joy-Permeated Mother)." My niece, Amiyo Bose, gazed at me earnestly.

"Of course! I want very much to see the woman saint." I added, "I have read of her advanced state of God-realization. A little article about her appeared years ago in *East-West*."

"I have met her," Amiyo went on. "She recently visited my own small town of Jamshedpur. At the entreaty of a disciple, Ananda Moyi Ma went to the home of a dying man. She stood by his bedside; as her hand touched his forehead, his death-rattle ceased. The disease vanished at once; to the man's glad astonishment, he was well."

A few days later I heard that the Blissful Mother was staying at the home of a disciple in the Bhowanipur section of Calcutta. Mr. Wright and I set out immediately from my father's Calcutta home. As the Ford neared the Bhowanipur house, my companion and I observed an unusual street scene.

Ananda Moyi Ma was standing in an open-topped automobile, blessing a throng of about one hundred disciples. She was evidently on the point of departure. Mr. Wright parked the Ford some distance away, and accompanied me on foot toward the quiet assemblage. The woman saint glanced in our direction; she alit from her car and walked toward us.

"Father, you have come!" With these fervent words (in Bengali) she put her arm around my neck and her head on my shoulder. Mr. Wright, to whom I had just remarked that I did not know the saint, was hugely enjoying this extraordinary demonstration of welcome. The eyes of the hundred *chelas* were also fixed with some surprise on the affectionate tableau.

I had instantly seen that the saint was in a high state of *samadhi*. Oblivious to her outward garb as a woman, she knew herself as the changeless soul; from that plane she was joyously greeting another devotee of God. She led me by the hand into her automobile.

"Ananda Moyi Ma, I am delaying your journey!" I protested.

"Father, I am meeting you for the first time in this life,* after ages!" she said. "Please do not leave yet."

We sat together in the rear seats of the car. The Blissful Mother soon entered the immobile ecstatic state. Her beautiful eyes glanced heavenward and, half-opened, became stilled, gazing into the near-far inner Elysium. The disciples chanted gently: "Victory to Mother Divine!"

I had found many men of God-realization in India, but never before had I met such an exalted woman saint. Her gentle face was burnished with the ineffable joy that had given her the name of Blissful Mother. Long black tresses lay loosely behind her veiled head. A red dot of sandalwood paste on her forehead symbolized the spiritual eye, ever open within her. Tiny face, tiny hands, tiny feet—a contrast to her spiritual magnitude!

I put some questions to a nearby woman *chela* while Ananda Moyi Ma remained entranced.

"The Blissful Mother travels widely in India; in many parts she has hundreds of disciples," the *chela* told me. "Her courageous efforts have brought about many desirable social reforms. Although a *Brahmin*, the saint recognizes no caste distinctions. A group of us always travels with her, looking after her comforts. We have to mother her; she takes no notice of her body. If no one gave her food, she would not eat or make any inquiries. Even when meals are placed before her, she does not touch them. To prevent her

---

* Ananda Moyi Ma was born in 1896 in the village of Kheora in the Tripura District of east Bengal.

disappearance from this world, we disciples feed her with our own hands. For days together she often stays in the divine trance, scarcely breathing, her eyes unwinking. One of her chief disciples is her husband, Bholanath. Many years ago, soon after their marriage, he took the vow of silence."

The *chela* pointed to a broad-shouldered, fine-featured man with long hair and hoary beard. He was standing quietly in the midst of the gathering, his hands folded in a disciple's reverential attitude.

Refreshed by her dip in the Infinite, Ananda Moyi Ma was now focusing her consciousness on the material world.

"Father, please tell me where you stay." Her voice was clear and melodious.

"At present, in Calcutta or Ranchi; but soon I shall be returning to America."

"America?"

"Yes. An Indian woman saint would be sincerely appreciated there by spiritual seekers. Would you like to go?"

"If Father can take me, I will go."

This reply caused her nearby disciples to start in alarm.

"Twenty or more of us always travel with the Blissful Mother," one of them told me firmly. "We could not live without her. Wherever she goes, we must go."

Reluctantly I abandoned the plan, as possessing an impractical feature of spontaneous enlargement!

"Please come at least to Ranchi, with your devotees," I said on taking leave of the saint. "As a divine child yourself, you will enjoy the little ones in my school."

"Whenever Father takes me, I will gladly go."

A short time later the Ranchi Vidyalaya was in gala array for the saint's promised visit. The youngsters looked forward to any day of festivity—no lessons, hours of music, and a feast for the climax!

"Victory! Ananda Moyi Ma, *ki jai!*" This reiterated chant from scores of enthusiastic little throats greeted the saint's party as it entered the school gates. Showers of marigolds, tinkle of cymbals, lusty blowing of conch shells and beat of the *mridanga* drum! The Blissful Mother wandered smilingly over the sunny Vidyalaya grounds, ever carrying within her heart the portable paradise.

"It is beautiful here," Ananda Moyi Ma said graciously as I led her into the main building. She seated herself with a childlike smile by my side. The closest of dear friends, she made one feel, yet an aura of remoteness was ever around her—the paradoxical isolation of Omnipresence.

"Please tell me something of your life."

"Father knows all about it; why repeat it?" She evidently felt that the factual history of one short incarnation was beneath notice.

I laughed, gently repeating my request.

"Father, there is little to tell." She spread her graceful hands in a deprecatory gesture. "My consciousness has never associated itself with this temporary body. Before I* came on this earth, Father, 'I was the same.' As a little girl, 'I was the same.' I grew into womanhood; still 'I was the same.' When the family into which I had been born made arrangements to have this body married, 'I was the same.' And, Father, in front of you now, 'I am the same.' Ever afterward, though the dance of creation change around me in the hall of eternity, 'I shall be the same.'"

Ananda Moyi Ma sank into a deep meditative state. Her form was statue-still; she had fled to her ever calling kingdom. The dark pools of her eyes appeared lifeless and glassy. This expression is often present when saints remove their consciousness from the physical body, which is then hardly more than a piece of soulless clay. We sat together for an hour in the ecstatic trance. She returned to this world with a gay little laugh.

"Please, Ananda Moyi Ma," I said, "come with me to the garden. Mr. Wright will take some pictures."

"Of course, Father. Your will is my will." Her glorious eyes retained an unchanging divine luster as she posed for many photographs.

Time for the feast! Ananda Moyi Ma squatted on her blanket-seat, a disciple at her elbow to feed her. Like an infant, the saint obediently swallowed the food after the *chela* had brought it to her lips. It was plain that the Blissful Mother did not recognize any difference between curries and sweetmeats!

As dusk approached, the saint left with her party amidst a shower of rose petals, her hands raised in blessing on the little lads. Their faces shone with the affection she had effortlessly awakened.

"Thou shalt love the Lord thy God with all thy heart, and with all thy soul, and with all thy mind, and with all thy strength," Christ has proclaimed; "this is the first commandment."†

Casting aside every inferior attachment, Ananda Moyi Ma offers her sole allegiance to the Lord. Not by the hair-splitting distinctions of scholars but by the sure logic of faith, the childlike saint has solved the only problem in human life—establishment of unity with God.

---

* Ananda Moyi Ma does not refer to herself as "I"; she uses humble circumlocutions like "this body" or "this little girl" or "your daughter." Nor does she refer to anyone as her "disciple." With impersonal wisdom she bestows equally on all human beings the divine love of the Universal Mother.

† Mark 12:30.

Man has forgotten this stark simplicity, now befogged by a million issues. Refusing a monotheistic love to the Creator, nations try to disguise their infidelity by punctilious respect before the outward shrines of charity. These humanitarian gestures are virtuous, because for a moment they divert man's attention from himself; but they do not free him from his prime responsibility in life, referred to by Jesus as the "first commandment." The uplifting obligation to love God is assumed with man's earliest breath of an air freely bestowed by his only Benefactor.†

On one other occasion after her visit to the Ranchi school I had opportunity to see Ananda Moyi Ma. She stood with a group some months later on the Serampore station platform, waiting for the train.

"Father, I am going to the Himalayas," she told me. "Some kind persons have built for us a hermitage in Dehra Dun."

As she boarded the train, I marveled to see that whether amidst a crowd, on a train, feasting, or sitting in silence, her eyes never looked away from God.

Within me I still hear her voice, an echo of measureless sweetness:

"Behold, now and always one with the Eternal, 'I am ever the same.'"

Paramahansa Yogananda, *Autobiography of a Yogi*

Early the next morning I read for the first time these words in Aurobindo: "Love is a passion and it seeks for two things, eternity and intensity, and in the relation of the lover and the Beloved the seeking for eternity and for intensity is instinctive and self-born.... Passing beyond desire for possession, which means a difference, it is a seeking for oneness, of two souls merging into each other."

I wrote Aurobindo's words down in the yellow notebook I had with me, realizing I had been given them as a sign and a task. I had recognized something none of the lies or evasions of the years to come could entirely efface; recognized, as if by the light of one of those lightnings that had broken from her body, that She was my soul's Beloved, and that the meaning of my life lay in love for Her.

On the walk to Ma's house next morning I wondered how she would next appear. She was sitting on the veranda, shelling peas with Adilakshmi. Her hair was down, and she was rubbing her eyes a little sleepily.

† "Many feel the urge to create a new and better world. Rather than let your thoughts dwell on such matters, you should concentrate on That by the contemplation of which there is hope of perfect peace. It is man's duty to become a seeker after God or Truth."—Ananda Moyi Ma

I sat down by them. After a while Ma went in, and Adilakshmi and I went on shelling the peas. That morning we had our first long conversation. Adilakshmi is a stately, radiant woman, then in her middle thirties. She wore a deep gold sari and gold bangles on both wrists, which made her very beautiful. I told her so.

"Mother is the beautiful one," she said, looking down.

I asked her if she ever wanted to marry.

"No," she answered. "I always wanted to live with the Divine, even as a child. I always knew I would. I used to dream of living on an ashram. As a young girl I used to dream of living with a god."

She smiled at my astonishment.

"We in India do not think the gods are far. They are all around us. They walk our streets; they come to us in dreams. I always had to find God, or die."

We went on shelling peas. "When I was twenty-five, after getting a philosophy degree, I just left home. I took a train, saying to myself that if God existed he would look after me!"

"You mean to tell me that you, a daughter of a good family—"

"Very good family," Adilakshmi corrected me.

"You mean to tell me you just got onto a train to look for God?"

"Yes," Adilakshmi said. "With one hundred rupees and no saris. I have always been mad. If I had not been mad, I would never have left home. If I had never left home, I would not have found her. So madness is a good thing, no?"

I nodded helplessly.

"In the train I saw myself protected by lions and tigers."

I started to laugh.

"And where were you going on this heroic train journey protected by lions and tigers?"

"What did it matter where I was going! The important thing was to leave home. The *most* important thing was to find God. Actually I was going to Pandaripur, a pilgrimage center for Krishna. Suddenly, instead of asking for a ticket to Pandaripur, I said, 'Pondicherry.' I arrived in Pondy, went to the ashram, and the first person I met was Mr. Reddy. He was standing at the ashram gate. He had made a mistake about the time of a class he was giving (he used to teach Telugu). I looked at him and thought, This man is the person I am searching for: He will take me to God."

I stared at Adilakshmi.

"Just like that?"

"Just like that. Mr. Reddy took me to his home, where his wife gave me a sari, and then I came back to the samadhi, the tomb of Aurobindo, where I had a very, very beautiful experience." Adilakshmi smiled at the memory.

"I knelt by the tomb and saw clearly a beautiful old man with long white hair and a fractured leg in splints come toward me and embrace me."

"You did not know that Aurobindo at the end of his life had a broken leg?"

"Of course not. I knew nothing about Aurobindo. Sometime later he gave me vision after vision of the inner meaning of 'Savitri,' his poem about the Mother. He would tell me to look up line so-and-so after the vision, and there I would see everything I had seen written."

Adilakshmi spoke with the same unnerving directness and simplicity as did Mr. Reddy.

"Sweet Mother accepted me into the ashram in 1969. I loved her very much. I was very depressed when she left the body in 1973. Then Mr. Reddy told me about Mother Meera." Adilakshmi gazed down at the floor.

"Mr. Reddy is a wonderful man," she said. "He has saved my life many, many times. Through him I met Ma in 1974.

"The first time I saw Meera I loved her. She was fourteen, so thin and elegant and smartly dressed. She had such big open eyes. I had always wanted to give myself to God; I recognized the Divine in her and so decided to offer her everything. At that time Ma was staying with Mr. Reddy in Pondy. Every day we would see each other.

"How beautiful those days were! When I wasn't teaching—I taught English at the ashram—I would be with Mr. Reddy and her. She was only fourteen, and yet she had the calm and presence of mind of an old man. Whatever she did she did perfectly. And she was so kind. I felt her greatness immediately; but it was her humility that made me love her."

Adilakshmi's eyes filled with tears, which she brushed away with her gold sleeve. "To have so much power and be so humble? How is it possible?"

Her tears fell.

"I met Ma again in 1976. When I saw her that time she was wearing a blue dress. Immediately, with open eyes, I saw her as Krishna."

"Krishna?" I said, surprised, remembering the experience in Ladakh.

"All forms are the Mother. The Divine Mother has the whole universe in her." Adilakshmi opened her arms very wide. "All the gods are in her. Where would the male gods be without the Shakti, the female power that creates everything? Many people have seen Ma in different forms. Some as Sri Aurobindo, some as the Virgin Mary. It is normal."

"Normal?" I laughed.

"Yes," said Adilakshmi firmly. "One day all the things that seem so wild and strange to you now will seem normal."

She stood up to go in.

"Isn't it hard, Adilakshmi, to worship Ma? I, too, have seen some small parts of her power, but how to connect that with the young girl we see every day, sewing, shopping, walking in the drive?"

Adilakshmi burst out laughing.

"But that is the mystery, isn't it?"

"How do you worship Ma?"

"As she is. Simply as she is."

She turned and was about to leave when I said: "You realize how the world could view you and Mr. Reddy?"

"Oh, yes," she said, turning back to face me. "They would see us as mad fantasists. Two people with a divine dream projecting it onto a small, innocent girl. Something stupid like that."

"But how do you know that Ma is divine?" I said in my rational "Oxford" voice.

Adilakshmi clapped her hands. "How do I know? By continual living experience. How else? I live with Ma; I see her sometimes twenty-two hours of the day. I know she is absolutely unlike me. The more I know her, the deeper I wonder at her. I am not a stupid love-drunk person. I watch; I observe. Do you imagine I would give up my life to her had I not known? Would I and Mr. Reddy have risked everything, given up respectability, money, position, the ashram, our whole world, had we not been certain?" She paused. "Andrew, I never try to convince anyone of anything. The great mysteries have to be experienced. They have to be lived. The only way to reach anyone really is to offer your life. That is what Ma is doing. She is not talking, justifying. She is giving herself completely, at every second, in every way. Just giving herself. Those with eyes to see will see. Those who dare to know will know. I try to offer my life also."

She paused. "And now I must go in and make lunch."

I thought, after Adilakshmi had left, of the old woman I had seen at Mahabalipuram worshipping the lingam as the sea poured over her. The joy on her face and on Adilakshmi's were the same joy—that of surrender. Adilakshmi and Mr. Reddy had given all they had to Ma. By their love and its mad courage they had both crossed over into a dimension of humble happiness.

Mr. Reddy and Adilakshmi were both whole human beings. Their sacrifice—if that was the right word—had not made them narrow or unaware of the world. Adilakshmi's beauty, exuberance, and wit were not at all characteristic of the shriveled ashramite women I had seen. Nothing seemed extinguished in her. And although Mr. Reddy was sick, his whole being emanated peace.

Seeing their delight so clearly made me sad. Adilakshmi and Mr. Reddy were so Indian—Indian in their spiritual passion, their daring, their exultation in renunciation of the world for God. My Indian childhood made me understand them intuitively; but my Western training and ambition distanced me from their innocence. I realized that my road to Ma would be crooked; it would not have the honest straightness I admired in theirs.

I said this later to Mr. Reddy.

He laughed. "A zigzag path gets there in the end, no? And the best police, you know, are reformed thieves."

He tickled my neck. "Don't always be so serious. *Some* seriousness is good. But remember to play with the Mother also."

He whispered, "I am doing nothing but playing with Ma. Is that a serious thing for a dignified old man to be doing? Oh, and I used to be so very serious."

Ma came in and Mr. Reddy said something to her in Telugu. She answered and then retired.

"What did you say?" I asked.

"I said to Ma, 'You have made a very happy small boy out of a serious and dignified old man.'"

"And what did Ma say?"

"If I was not always a child, I would never have found the Mother."

"So Ma wins?"

"Ma always wins. In the great Divine Game, the one who loves most wins. And who loves more than the Mother?"

Ma reentered and stood by his chair. "Ma," he said, "Ma, give me the words to tell this young man how loving you are. Give me words beautiful enough."

That night, back at the hotel, I fell quickly into deep sleep. All night in dreams, the image of a sculpture I had loved in a temple in Mahabalipuram—of the goddess Durga slaying Mahisasura, the Buffalo demon—kept coming back to me, and with such insistence I knew I was being told something. When I woke, I remembered what I had read in the local guidebook; this sculpture is the illustration of the "Devi Mahatmyam," an epic poem about the Goddess, which I had made a note of to read. I looked all over Kakinada for a copy of the work and at last, in the most unlikely and grimy of bookshops, I found one. It was the last copy, the man said, that he would ever have in stock. "I am going out of business," he said. "No one reads now."

The "Devi Mahatmyam" is a glorification of the Divine Mother and an account of her creation and conquest of the supreme asura and demon of destruction, who threatens the creation.

I sat out in the noisy street and opened it at random.

"By you this universe is borne, by you this world is created. By you it is protected, O Devi, and you always consume it in the end."

I saw Ma sitting with the whole horizon blazing behind her.

I opened the book again. The gods are told that Mahisasura has usurped the functions and powers of many of their number and is threatening the cosmos:

Having thus heard the words of the devas, Vishnu was angry and also Shiva, and their faces became fierce with frowns.
Then issued forth a great light from the face of Vishnu, who was full of intense anger, and from that of Brahma and Shiva, too. From the bodies of Indra and other devas also sprang forth a very great light. And all this light united together.
The devas saw there a concentration of light like a mountain blazing excessively, *pervading all the quarters with its flames. Then that unique light, produced from the bodies of all the devas, pervading the three worlds with its luster, combined into one and became a female form.*

Sitting in the dirt, with bicycles ringing around me and car horns blaring, I felt my body fill with bliss. Then with extreme urgency messages came.

Mahisasura is the madness of the human mind without God — the mind that is destroying the planet; the mind that made and used the atomic bomb; the mind that is everywhere creating a wrecked, starved world in its own psychic image.

The gods have created me, the Mother, out of all their different lights so this evil can be destroyed. Destroyed not with cruelty but with the power of love and gnosis.

I tried to get up three times, but my legs buckled under me. I found myself, my head in my hands, saying over and over the different names of the Divine Mother that I knew, Brahmani, Mahesvari, Virgin Mary, Fatima, Neit, Isis, Saraswati, Kali, Meera.

I am above all names and all worlds and all forms. Open the book again.
I opened to: "Whenever trouble arises...I shall incarnate and destroy all enemies."

Again I saw Ma: face and body on the roof, the sky on fire behind her. This time she was smiling with the same triumphant passion as she had in the doorway in Pondicherry.

Next day I woke up determined to ask Ma for an interview. I had to talk to her. I had only two days left before I went back to Oxford. I asked Mr. Reddy to ask Ma for me.

He went into the room where Ma was and returned. "Ma will talk to you this afternoon."

I felt sick to the stomach at myself, at all the doubts and fears I knew still accompanied my love for her. I felt weak, so I sat down in a chair and put my face in my hands.

Mr. Reddy sat down on the sofa beside me and took my hand.

"All this is very bewildering to the mind," I said. "I've been given so much. Why can't I give myself completely?"

I stared at the dark green marble floor, awash in sunlight.

"To give yourself completely to the Mother is complete realization," Mr. Reddy whispered. "It can take many lives."

"Everything has to be changed, doesn't it?—every habit, every way of thinking."

"Yes." He smiled. "It is a long work. But it is the only real work. And Ma is here to help you. She is *here*. She is in the other room as we speak, cooking lunch. Follow her and she will be your Master, your Mother, your Beloved, your Friend. She will become everything to you as she has become everything to me. And when she is everything to you, you will know her in everything."

He started to cough and looked suddenly frail. He saw me looking at him with concern and looked back mischievously.

"This illness, too, is only Ma's play, her maya."

Either this man is mad, I thought, or he is illumined. There is no other possible explanation.

"I am not illumined completely," Mr. Reddy said out loud, reading my thought. "But Ma has lit some lamps in my brain that nothing can put out."

The hours before seeing her I spent in prayer. I remembered something Thuksey Rinpoche had once said: "The great enemy to spiritual progress is the belief you know already. Knowledge is unfolded. Pray to be willing, at every stage to be ignorant, so you can be really taught."

How would I learn *that* ignorance rather than rely on the learned ignorance of years of habit, assumption, intellectual formulation?

Mr. Reddy, Adilakshmi, and I waited for Ma in the drawing room. A late red-gold light filled the room.

She came in silently in a white sari, not smiling, and sat in the chair opposite me, gazing down. I had thought I was calm, until she entered, but her beauty and her majesty made me tremble.

"Ma," I began.

"Andrew," she said, looking up.

As she said my name for the first time a sob arose in me and shook my entire body. I tried to control it, but my whole being started to weep before her. The grief of my life's loneliness, guilt, and sexual pain seemed to seize me and pour itself out at her feet.

I wept for a long time. Slowly, in the huge and healing silence of her presence, I began to feel calm.

"I came before you with questions. But now I understand I only wanted to weep before you and sit with you."

Mr. Reddy translated.

Ma smiled.

Another long silence began, golden this time with the light that was filling the room, covering the chairs, Ma's hands, the floor between me and her. I knew I should not speak, just open and wait.

Ma gazed at the pearl ring on her right hand.

A calm bliss filled my body.

The tears began again. This time they were tears of relief and joy, with no grief in them at all.

I began to speak haltingly.

"You have always been guiding me, haven't you?"

"Yes."

"You were in Pondicherry living quietly with Mr. Reddy when I first came here. It was you who, with Aurobindo, opened my mind; it was you who prepared me to meet you."

"Yes."

"In these last weeks I feel you have been revealing to me your divine Self. Is this true?"

"Yes."

"Can I receive your Light?"

"You are receiving it. One day you will see it."

I trembled. "You have come to save the world, haven't you?"

"Yes. There are others working here, too."

"What can I do to help your work?"

"Realize yourself."

There was nothing else to say. I sat gazing at Ma with astonishment, and she gazed calmly back. After one last long silence she smiled and rose.

I went over and knelt at her feet.

Andrew Harvey, *Hidden Journey:*
A Spiritual Awakening

⇥ The Emerging Woman ⇤

"In our approaches to woman, and when we come into contact
with her, we are enveloped in a sort of indistinct glow of illumination—the instinctive feeling that a new world awaits us and is
about to develop in the depths of matter—if only we fold the
wings of spirit, and surrender ourselves to it."

— PIERRE TEILHARD DE CHARDIN

Carl Jung wrote: "A primordial image
is determined as to its content only when it has become conscious and is
therefore filled out with the material and conscious experience."

In this section, I have gathered material that shows the divine feminine
as it is manifested in its many different forms as we prepare for her coming
in our daily lives. Her time is near as she appears in dreams and visions, and
in collective experiences like the feminist struggle of the last twenty-five
years. Feminist spirituality is closely linked to the feminist movement itself,
in that it isn't only about the recognition of sexism or about rebelling against
restraints of patriarchy, of societal rules, about being angry and about trying
to be understood, but it is also about discovering and sharing. The scholarship of Christian women theologians as well as feminist activists has brought
a new awareness and interpretation of the scriptures as well. For example,
after reviewing the language of the Bible, they have prompted gender
change in traditional prayers. All this has contributed to a united sisterhood
to promote the cause of the feminine, given hope, brought maturity, forgiveness, and finally a peaceful purpose.

In the opening piece, a clear and captivating example of an archetype
being awakened from her subconscious, Sherry Ruth Anderson describes a
dream she had in 1984 which precipitated a move of home and the beginnings of work on a book called *The Feminine Face of God* (co-authored with
Patricia Hopkins). Rosemary Radford Ruether charts the historical course of
the emerging feminine divinity from its origins, in the subjugation of the
female body, to its flourishing in the archetype of the feminine side of God.
Judith Plaskow offers a new look at the ancient archetype of Eve, while
Charles Tart addresses the inner self and anger. Charlene Spretnak explores
the sense of the dual powers of woman (e.g., the warrior woman and the sensitive goddess) and Germaine Greer the united sisterhood and true liberation. All together they show that reverence for the sacredness of womanhood
is a part of the preparation for the Emerging Woman. Through women celebrating women in spiritual camaraderie and through rituals, we can find

the strength and the purpose to become mothers of the twenty-first century—purified, powerful, and able to uphold the divinity of the feminine in mind, body, and spirit.

>+<

The Question That Wouldn't Go Away

Shekhinah. Shekhinah. The word simply popped into my mind like an uninvited guest and wouldn't go away. At times it seemed to disappear, but then it would come again, quietly, this strange word—*Shekhinah*. It seemed to be waiting patiently for me to pay attention to it. After hearing it in my mind for three days I tried saying it out loud. "Shekhinah." It had an interesting sound. And when I said it, I felt a soft tug somewhere deep inside.

I began to ask my friends if they knew what it meant. It sounded as if it could be Hebrew, but although I knew some Hebrew, it was not familiar to me. When my husband and friends were unable to help, I tried the library in our small town but found no answer there either. Shekhinah. Shekhinah. It was becoming more insistent now, demanding my attention.

Still puzzling over what it could mean, I was sitting in my bedroom one morning when my friend Joan hurried through the door. She strode across the room and thrust a book into my hands. "Let's try this," she said. I glanced down at the blue cover on which the word Kabbalah was written, and turned to the index. Running my finger quickly down the S column, I read, "Shekhinah: the feminine face of God."

The words sent shock waves rippling down my spine and goose flesh bristling on my bare arms because I realized at once that the Shekhinah was not an uninvited guest at all. She had been announced to me with great ceremony in a powerful dream a full month earlier.

In the dream, I happily soar high above the clouds on a great golden dragon until I wonder, "Is this all there is?" The dragon immediately descends to earth, alighting at the side of a jewellike temple on a large body of water. I want to enter the temple, but I'm afraid to go in alone. I turn back to the dragon, hoping it will come and protect me. But this temple is human-sized and the dragon will not fit through the door.

I begin to climb the stairs to the entrance anyway, and now I see a ferocious temple guardian with bulging eyes looming menacingly in the doorway. Black dogs snarl on either side of him. With uncharacteristic bravery I continue walking, and as I stride through the door the guardian and his dogs evaporate as if made of fog.

Once I'm inside the doorway, an old man with long robes and a white beard emerges from an inner hallway to greet me. Without actually speaking, he lets me know that his name is Melchizedek. He is wearing a handsome dagger with a handle of turquoise and jade, and as soon as I notice this he presents me with a matching dagger, indicating that I am to wear it on my right side. Then he motions me ahead of him. It is clear that he expects me to lead the way.

I step into a long hallway with a high ceiling and red tiles on the floor. Walking slowly, we eventually come to a pair of polished wooden doors at the end of the corridor. I open them silently and lead the way into a large, empty room. A plain wooden stage is set against the far wall. At the back of the stage is a built-in cabinet. I approach the cabinet and pull open the doors.

I am dumbfounded by what I see. Rolled onto finely carved wooden poles is the most sacred object in Judaism, the Torah. I learned as a child that the Torah contains the five books of Moses written on parchment by an Orthodox scribe, and that if even one letter has been written incorrectly, the Torah cannot be used. I have never actually seen a Torah close up or held one, since these privileges were permitted only to men when I was growing up. But now I lift this Torah carefully out of its cabinet and cradle it to me tenderly as if it were a baby.

Then I notice something unusual. Instead of a mantle of velvet covering the scrolls, or a simple ribbon holding them closed, the Torah has been sealed shut by a dark round blot of red wax. I look at Melchizedek. "This is a very special Torah," he says. Pulling out his dagger, he breaks the seal and rolls open the scrolls. They are absolutely blank. "The Torah is empty," he says, "because what you need to know now is not written in any book. You already contain that knowledge. It is to be unfolded from within you."

"What is this Torah for?" I ask.

My question seems to set in motion the next sequence of events. Without speaking Melchizedek lifts the Torah and lightly places it inside my body, from my shoulders to my knees. I accept this gratefully, feeling my body as a sacred vessel.

At once, a great commotion breaks out behind us. Spinning around, I see that the room is now filled with long-bearded patriarchs wearing black coats and trousers. They're holding hands, laughing, singing, and dancing jubilantly around the room. They pull me into their celebration. As I dance I seem to see Moses, King David, and King Solomon, and Abraham, Isaac, and Jacob. They, too, are dressed in black coats and trousers, dancing with such heartfelt abandonment that I catch their joy and am filled with it. Ecstatically we whirl round and round the room, laughing.

Finally the dancing stops and I ask, "What is this all about?" Melchizedek answers, "We are celebrating because you, a woman, have consented to accept full spiritual responsibility in your life. This is your initiation as one who will serve the planet."

As I wonder what this means, he continues, "And you are not the only one. Many, many women are coming forward now to lead the way."

"But who will be our teachers?" I protest.

"You will be teachers for each other. You will come together in circles and speak your truth to each other. The time has come for women to accept their spiritual responsibility for our planet."

"Will you help us?" I ask the assembled patriarchs.

"We are your brothers," they answer, and with that the entire room is flooded with an energy of indescribable kindness. I am absolutely confident in this moment that they *are* our brothers. I feel their love without any question. They say then, "We have initiated you and we give you our whole-hearted blessings. But we no longer know the way. Our ways do not work anymore. You women must find a new way."

Sherry Ruth Anderson and Patricia Hopkins,
The Feminine Face of God

Woman/Body/Nature: The Icon of the Divine

Layer by layer we must strip off the false consciousness that alienates us from our bodies, from our roots in the earth, sky, and water. Layer by layer we expose the twisted consciousness that has distorted our relationships and turned them to their opposite. But in so doing we discover that the Big Lie has limited power. Earth is not mocked. She brings her judgment, and this judgment can no longer be confined to the ghettos and the reservations of the poor.

The stench of it, the floating poison, the underground rumblings begin to reach out to the suburbs of affluence, signaling the beginning of the end of a way of life, a question mark over a social system. But also the possibility of asking the question, the question of new relations: simpler, more harmonious, more just, more beautiful patterns of life. Woman/body/nature, no longer as the icon of carnality, sin, and death, but as the icon of the divine, the divine *Shekinah*, the Wisdom of God manifest, alive in our midst as the true center that holds us all together.

The First Level: Control Over the Womb

The first subjugation of woman is the subjugation of her womb, the subjugation of access to her body, so that she should not choose her own beloved or explore the pleasures of her own body but that her body and its fruits should belong first to her father, who would sell or trade her to her husband. She must be delivered as undamaged goods, duly inspected, any signs of previous use punished by death. Only the male to whom she has been legally handed over may put his seed in her body, so that he can be sure that the children that emerge from her body belong to him, pass on his name, inherit his property. Boy children are preferred. Too many girl children bring shame, perhaps expulsion, for the errant mother.

Philosophers minimize her contribution to the acts of conception and birth. Aristotle proclaims through two thousand years of teachers that woman is a misbegotten male, that the male seed alone provides the form of the child, the woman is only the passive receptacle for man's active power.

Moses teaches that the male is the original human model. The woman was created second, out of man's rib, to be his helpmate. Man gives birth to woman, she is his offspring and creature, formed from his side to serve him in lowliness. In these ways the power of her motherhood is stolen from her, and she is reduced to an instrument of his virility.

The Christian Church teaches that birth is shameful, that from the sexual libido the corruption of the human race is passed on from generation to generation. Only through the second birth of baptism, administered by the male clergy, is the filth of mother's birth remedied and the offspring of the woman's womb made fit to be a child of God. Woman is taught that the worst of sins, the worst of crimes, is to deflect the male seed from its intended course in her womb. This is more sinful than rape, for the rape of a woman does not interfere with the purposes of the seed, while contraception wastes the precious seed and defeats its high purposes. Anatomy is destiny, the psychologists teach. Woman must subject herself to necessity, for this is the divine will. She must obediently accept the effects of these holy male acts upon her body, must not seek to control their effects, must not become a conscious decision maker about the destiny of her own body.

The Second Level: Exploited Labor

The control of woman's womb means the subjugation of her person. From person she becomes property to be bought and sold, passed from father to husband for the price of two good plow oxen. To violate her is to offend the property rights of her husband. If she does not resist to the death, she can be divorced, perhaps even killed by her outraged male relatives. Girl children are expendable; perhaps they are exposed on hillsides at birth or sold into slavery.

Her labor belongs to him. To labor from before dawn to after dusk in his household is her purpose for existence. She has no need to read and write, no need to learn, to travel, to dream. Her sphere is defined, confined; she must not stray from it. Each generation of daughters must have its wings clipped early to be fed back into the treadmill. For him she sets her maid-servants spinning and weaving before dawn. She considers a field and buys it, plants it with her own hands, harvests it, sells its produce. Her lamp does not go out at night. Her labor frees him for the momentous tasks of war and politics. He is known at the gates. She is not be known in public. She is to remain invisible. When he returns in the evening, his food shall be ready, his clothes in order, his couch prepared. In this way her history is stolen from her. It is said that she did nothing. It is his achievements that we read about in books; his laws, his wars, his power, his mayhem. He is the achiever, carried about on the backs of the laborers. The laborers who carry him have done nothing; they are invisible, silent. No scrolls testify to their experience. No monuments mark the places of their sufferings and deaths. Their laboring hands and backs hold him up to the light of history, and they sink down into the dark earth again.

Woman, the nonachiever, becomes woman the nonworker, the ornament of conspicuous consumption, the object of pride of ownership and economic prowess. Her furs testify to her husband's success. She adorns his household, displaying dainty feet that cannot walk, polished nails that cannot work. The pinnacle of his success is to no longer need her work, to possess her only as a toy and a plaything. Black women, brown women, immigrant women toil silently in the background, supporting the display, polishing the cage of the songbird. The wife herself must conceal the signs of her own toil, ease the lines of suffering from her face, the marks of labor from her hands, keep up appearances. Women are set at enmity with each other while collaborating in his service.

Early in the morning the army of chars, waitresses, secretaries, nurses, librarians, and teachers march from their houses. The morning chores are rushed, the children pressed through breakfast and off to school so that women can get to work at the same time as men whose women do these chores for them. On the job the women service male work: clean the offices, prepare the food, type the letters, answer the phones, research the studies. Upon this pyramid of female labor the executive arises, seemingly imbued with superhuman wisdom and magnified power drawn from the combined force of a vast, invisible reservoir; he stands upon it commanding, pronouncing, deciding. . . .

At five o'clock the army of women scatter to markets, nurseries, and kitchens to prepare the home, so that, when the men return, the children are already fetched, the food bought and cooked, the house cleaned. The men linger to consolidate the networks that advance them on the ladder. Women, it is said, just can't compete; they lack what it takes, the drive, the ambition. . . .

The Third Level: The Rape of the Earth
and Its Peoples

The labor of dominated bodies, dominated peoples—women, peasants, workers—mediate for those who rule the fruits of the earth. The toil of laboring bodies provides the tools through which the earth is despoiled and left desolate. Through the raped bodies the earth is raped. Those who enjoy the goods distance themselves from the destruction.

The gold wrestled from the mines of Mexico and Peru is carried across the oceans in Spanish galleons, stolen by fast ships of Dutch and English merchants, and ends up in banks in Amsterdam and London. The Indians who mined it die of starvation. The pineapple and banana plantations ship their succulent fruits to adorn the tables of Yankees whose own soil is stony, whose climate is cold and damp. But those who are blessed with warm suns and rich soil cannot afford to taste their own fruits. The strip mines of Appalachia do not despoil the golf courses and parks of the mine owners. No, they despoil the rocky hillsides of the dirt farmers. The detergents flow through the streams where Indians live. The fish upon whom the Indian depends for food floats belly up in the soapy water.

It is said that these people are lazy, backward, that they are poor because they have few resources and no energy…that we have gained a head start because of our hard work. If we help them, maybe they can catch up. So we ship down armies of technologists and allow the poor to mortgage their future on loans for development.

The development displaces the poor from the countryside and gives the land to the plantation owners. The industries of the nation are bought by the multinationals. The peasants who come to the city for work shine shoes and sell chewing gum. They multiply like festering sores around the glittering steel and glass monuments to development. The mood grows ugly. We send their governments population-control experts and counterinsurgency police. We finance the hardware of repression, and we call it the Alliance for Progress. Armies of teenage girls in border towns assemble electronic systems by day for a few dollars, return home at night to cook beans in shanty kitchens. The electronic assemblies are shipped back across the border to add to the fame and fortune of Yankee ingenuity.

On the backs, through the hands of vast toiling masses in Asia, Africa, Latin America, the affluent colonizers arise, congratulate themselves on their progress, and wonder at the poverty and ingratitude of those whose bananas, gold, oil they have consumed. A bomb crashes through the plate-glass window, blowing a hole in the dream of progress.

The Fourth Level: The Big Lie

Those who rule pay their professors to proliferate lies, to generate a mental universe that turns everything upside down. The Big Lie makes those who toil appear to be idle, while those who speak into dictaphones appear to be the hard workers. It makes women appear the offspring of males, and males the primary creators of babies. It makes matter the final devolution of the mind, and mind the original source of all being. It regards the body as an alien tomb of the soul, and the soul as growing stronger the more it weakens the body. It abstracts the human from the earth and God from the cosmos, and says that that which is abstracted is the original, and the first, and can exist alone and independent.

The Big Lie tells us that we are strangers and sojourners on this planet, that our flesh, our blood, our instincts for survival are our enemies. Originally we lived as disincarnate orbs of light in the heavenly heights. We have fallen to this earth and into this clay through accident or sin. We must spend our lives suppressing our hungers and thirsts and shunning our fellow beings, so that we can dematerialize and fly away again to our stars.

It is said that mothers particularly are the enemy, responsible for our mortal flesh. To become eternal and everlasting we must flee the body, the woman, and the world. She is the icon of the corruptible nature, seduced by the serpent in the beginning. Through her, death entered the world. Even now she collaborates with devils to hold men in fast fetters to the ground. A million women twisted on the rack, smoldered in burning fagots to pay homage to this Lie.

It is said that enlightened man must drive the devils and witches from the world, restore order, put himself in charge, reduce nature to his control. With numbers and formulas he can search out her innermost secrets, learn all the laws of her ways, become her lord and master. The cosmos is reduced to elements, molecules, atoms, positive and negative charges, infinitely manipulatable, having no nature of her own, given to him to do with what he will. He will mount upon her with wings, fly away to the moon, blow her up in the flash of atomic energy, live forever in a space capsule, entombed in plastic, dining on chemicals.

The Collapse of the House of Cards: The Disclosure of Divine Wisdom

The facade starts to crumble. We discover buried histories. "We Shall Overcome." "Sisterhood Is Powerful." "Viva la Huelga." "Bury My Heart at Wounded Knee." We begin to understand the hidden costs. "Hello, carbon dioxide; the air, the air is everywhere." Carcinogens in our health food, strontium 90 in mother's milk. Atomic fallout in our swimming pool. Threats to generations yet unborn. We are held hostage by the colonized, blackmailed by the poor rich in raw materials. The Petroleum Age starts to run out of gas.

Through the fissures of the system we glimpse the forgotten world of our homeland. We learn to walk again; to watch sunsets; to examine leaves; to plant seeds in soil. Turn off the TV; talk to each other to ease the frenetic pace; get in touch with our circulatory system, with the rhythms of our menstrual cycle that link us to the pull of the moon and tides of the sea.

The scales begin to fall from our eyes, and all around us we see miracles. Babies grow in wombs without help from computers. The sun rises every day. Con Ed sends no bill for sunshine. The harmony is still there, persisting, supporting, forgiving, preserving us in spite of ourselves. Divine Grace keeps faith with us when we have broken faith with her. Through the years of alien madness, she did not abandon us; she kept the planets turning, the seasons recurring, even struggled to put the upside down rightside up, to cleanse the channels of the garbage, to blow the smog out to sea.

To return Home: to learn the harmony, the peace, the justice of body, bodies in right relation to each other. The whence we have come and whither we go, not from alien skies but here, in the community of earth. Holy One, Thy Kingdom come, Thy will done on earth. All shall sit under their own vines and fig trees and none shall be afraid. The lion will lay down with the lamb and the little child will lead them. A new thing is revealed; the woman will encompass the warrior. Thou shalt not hurt, thou shalt not kill in all my holy mountain.

The Shalom of the Holy; the disclosure of the gracious *Shekinah*; Divine Wisdom; the empowering Matrix; She, in whom we live and move and have our being—She comes; She is here.

Rosemary Radford Ruether, *Sexism and God-Talk*

We are coming to the end of the line personally and globally through our rejection of the feminine side of God. Addicts manifest an extreme form of this desecration in our culture, but they are also potential catalysts for the rebirth of the feminine. Not only are they individuals carrying the unconscious of their forebears. As human beings in the history of mankind they are also living out what is unconscious in the social environment. We can remain blind to our personal shadow until we look into the starving eyes of an anorexic or alcoholic we love; we can also remain blind to the collective shadow until we turn on television and look into the eyes of a starving child.

In a technological civilization geared up for its own heady destruction, we are destined to become the victims of an outworn patriarchal consciousness so long as we collude in equating femininity with biological identity. That kind of consciousness is propelling not only individuals but the whole planet into an addiction to power and perfection which, viewed from the perspective of nature, can lead only to suicide. Feminine consciousness dare not be limited to unredeemed matter or unconscious mother. The realization that a neurosis has a creative purpose applies globally as well as personally, and surely, in an age addicted to power and the acquisition of material possessions, the creative purpose must have something to do with the one thing that can save us—love for the earth, love for each other—the wisdom of the Goddess. Responsibility belongs in the individual home, in the individual heart, in the energy that holds atoms together rather than blows them apart.

Marion Woodman, *The Pregnant Virgin*

Recently I heard a great spiritual leader, the Dalai Lama, talk about promoting world peace. I was very moved by his lecture, for he spoke from his heart as well as his mind. He stressed the many ways that external conflicts between people and nations stem from internal conflicts within ourselves, rather than arising only from external sources. We have to work on the external reasons for conflict, but if we want lasting external peace, we must work for it from a solid, inner foundation of personal peace.

There were several other speakers at this meeting. Immediately following His Holiness's talk, a woman commented from a feminist perspective on peace. She spoke of the way women have been mistreated in our own and other cultures, the ways in which war is a masculine activity that hurts women, and the need for women to use their power to stop war. Her analysis of the way sexism supports war opened new understandings to me. Intellectually, I agreed with all the points she made. They were clear, incisive, and very practical.

Emotionally, though, it was a different story. "Illogically," I found myself growing increasingly angry at her and everything she represented. My wife felt the same way, as did every other person in the audience with whom we later spoke. I was disturbed at feeling angry, as I knew it was both irrational and contrary to my own positive feelings toward feminist perspectives.

Through self-examination I realized that while the conceptual content of what she said was fine, indeed noble, the emotional tone of her talk was angry and aggressive, and aroused an automatic emotional opposition. Conditioned emotional reactions were aroused in spite of intellectual acceptance.

She illustrated, unfortunately, His Holiness's main point. If you don't have peace within yourself, your attempts to create peace in the outer world can backfire, and may create even more hostility than if you hadn't done anything.

The fact that I and others automatically grew angry illustrates another aspect of the horror of the human situation, of course. We are far too automatic; indeed, we are automatons....

We are "asleep," compared with what we could be. We are dreaming. We are entranced. We are automatized. We are caught in illusions while thinking we are perceiving reality. The woman who spoke after the Dalai Lama's talk was asleep, dreaming, entranced, unaware that parts of her self contradicted and sabotaged other parts. Her condition is our condition. We need to awaken to reality, the reality of the problems caused by our fragmented selves, so we can discover our deeper selves and the reality of our world, undistorted by our entranced condition.

Charles T. Tart, *Waking Up*

A Litany of Deliverance

From Patriarchy's dualism,
From Patriarchy's proneness to self-pity,
From Patriarchy's sentimentalism,
From Patriarchy's violence,
From Patriarchy's lack of imagination,
From Patriarchy's intellectual laziness,
From Patriarchy's lack of authentic curiosity,
From Patriarchy's separation of head from body,
From Patriarchy's separation of body from feelings,
From Patriarchy's preoccupation with sex,
From Patriarchy's fear of intimacy,
From Patriarchy's reptilian brain,
From Patriarchy's anthropocentrism,
From Patriarchy's cosmic loneliness,
From Patriarchy's crucifixion of Mother Earth,
From Patriarchy's envy and manipulation of children,
From Patriarchy's abuse of women,
From Patriarchy's homophobia,
From Patriarchy's righteousness,
From Patriarchy's idolatry of nationhood and national security,
From Patriarchy's forgetfulness of beauty and art,
From Patriarchy's impotence to heal,

From Patriarchy's sado-masochism,
From Patriarchy's parental cannibalism and devouring of its
    children,
From Patriarchy's lack of balance,
From Patriarchy's savaging of the earth,
From Patriarchy's quest for immortality,
From Patriarchy's ego,
From Patriarchy's waste of talent and resources, human and earth,
From Patriarchy's human chauvinism,
From Patriarchy's compulsion to go into debt to finance its bloated
    lifestyles,
From Patriarchy's matricide, spare us O Divine One.

Matthew Fox, *The Coming of the Cosmic Christ*

A Jewish Feminist Midrash on Lilith and Eve

In the beginning the Lord God formed Adam and Lilith from the dust of the ground and breathed into their nostrils the breath of life. Created from the same source, both having been formed from the ground, they were equal in all ways. Adam, man that he was, didn't like this situation, and he looked for ways to change it. He said, "I'll have my figs now, Lilith," ordering her to wait on him, and he tried to leave to her the daily tasks of life in the garden. But Lilith wasn't one to take any nonsense; she picked herself up, uttered God's holy name, and flew away. "Well, now, Lord," complained Adam, "that uppity woman you sent me has gone and deserted me." The Lord, inclined to be sympathetic, sent his messengers after Lilith, telling her to shape up and return to Adam or face dire punishment. She, however, preferring anything to living with Adam, decided to stay right where she was. And so God, after more careful consideration this time, caused a deep sleep to fall upon Adam, and out of one of his ribs created for him a second companion, Eve.

For a time Eve and Adam had quite a good thing going. Adam was happy now, and Eve, though she occasionally sensed capacities within herself that remained undeveloped, was basically satisfied with the role of Adam's wife and helper. The only thing that really disturbed her was the excluding closeness of the relationship between Adam and God. Adam and God just seemed to have more in common, being both men, and Adam came to identify with God more and more. After a while that made God a bit uncomfortable too, and he started going over in his mind whether he might not have made a mistake in letting Adam talk him into banishing Lilith and creating Eve, in light of the power that had given Adam.

Meanwhile Lilith, all alone, attempted from time to time to rejoin the human community in the garden. After her first fruitless attempt to breach its walls, Adam worked hard to build them stronger, even getting Eve to help him. He told her fearsome stories of the demon Lilith who threatens women in childbirth and steals children from their cradles in the middle of the night. The second time Lilith came she stormed the garden's main gate, and a great battle between her and Adam ensued, in which she was finally defeated. This time, however, before Lilith got away, Eve got a glimpse of her and saw she was a woman like herself.

After this encounter, seeds of curiosity and doubt began to grow in Eve's mind. Was Lilith indeed just another woman? Adam had said she was a demon. Another woman! The very idea attracted Eve. She had never seen another creature like herself before. And how beautiful and strong Lilith had looked! How bravely she had fought! Slowly, slowly, Eve began to think about the limits of her own life within the garden.

One day, after many months of strange and disturbing thoughts, Eve, wandering around the edge of the garden, noticed a young apple tree she and Adam had planted, and saw that one of its branches stretched over the garden wall. Spontaneously she tried to climb it, and struggling to the top, swung herself over the wall.

She had not wandered long on the other side before she met the one she had come to find, for Lilith was waiting. At first sight of her, Eve remembered the tales of Adam and was frightened, but Lilith understood and greeted her kindly. "Who are you?" they asked each other, "What is your story?" And they sat and spoke together, of the past and then of the future. They talked not once, but many times, and for many hours. They taught each other many things, and told each other stories, and laughed together, and cried, over and over, till the bond of sisterhood grew between them.

Meanwhile, back in the garden, Adam was puzzled by Eve's comings and goings, and disturbed by what he sensed to be her new attitude toward him. He talked to God about it, and God, having his own problems with Adam and a somewhat broader perspective, was able to help him out a little—but he, too, was confused. Something had failed to go according to plan. As in the days of Abraham, he needed counsel from his children. "I am who I am," thought God, "but I must become who I will become."

And God and Adam were expectant and afraid the day Eve and Lilith returned to the garden, bursting with possibilities, ready to rebuild it together.

Judith Plaskow, from "The Coming of Lilith," in *Womanguides*

Garden of Eden—expulsion
1st step toward maturity

gospel of Eve—
    Struggle toward a maturity of being—
    Struggle to return to that "bright nature" which was lost.
    Struggle to acquire the "bright nature" of faith—

The Summons to the stage of one's most inner being—
The Summons to appear in the garden before the god—
    To show the treasures of one's inheritance—

    Fan
bridal wreath
veil of sorrow
cloak

an accounting to Eve—Mary—Magdalene—you—of a woman's
inheritance

Her care of her treasures that she may achieve the "bright nature"
which is hers—her maturity—

Temptation
Ordeal—

From the hands of the Mother (Eve) from the tree in the garden—
    Terror—sorrow
    bridal—love—happiness—
Enter into tree—receive dress from within—
    a shrine
    a symbol of Eden— Yew Tree
some device when she is within—
    ringing of bells—
    darkness—
    fluttering on the strings
        magical—supernatural
        moment of deeply felt terror—beauty—

                garden in the desert—
                    an oasis of hope—faith
                    symbol of re-birth—
                        continuity of life—

Martha Graham, *The Notebooks of Martha Graham*

What Is Feminist Spirituality?

There are in the North American world at the present moment two primary contenders for the definition of feminist spirituality. These two contenders appear, from the perspective of this writer, to fall into two different patterns, which might be characterized as the "aesthetic" and the "ethical" understandings of feminist theology. The aesthetic position assumes that there is a preexisting harmony between all parts of reality. Yin and yang, male and female, spirit and flesh, humans and nature, nature and the divine, all are parts of one primal rhythm. The breaking of this harmony into contraries is an illusion. Sin and evil do not really exist. It is a lie foisted upon us by anti-natural civilization. One has only to escape from civilization back to nature to reembrace the primal harmony. Rituals and chants disenchant the false world of contraries and put us back in union with the primal harmony.

This primal harmony lies under the sign of the primacy of the mother. The original deity of humanity was the Mother Goddess, representing this primal rule of the mother. The advent of father rule broke the primal harmony and subjugated the mother. Bliss and harmony will be restored by escaping from father culture in all its forms, especially its religious forms, and reembracing the religion of the Mother Goddess, either as groups of women exclusively or as groups which include males, but only those who accept the integration of maleness *under* mother rule.

This religion of primary harmony under the Mother Goddess is presumed to reflect both the actual religion and the actual sociology of prepatriarchal matriarchal cultures. They correspond to "original paganism" before its distortion by patriarchy and suppression by Judaism, Christianity, and Islam. Feminist religion necessarily involves a root and branch repudiation of biblical religion in favor of goddess religion.

The "ethical" or "liberation" perspective on feminist theology also believes in original harmony as a symbol of the authentic ground and potential of human life. But it takes more seriously the broken relations between self and body, self and others, self and nature, self and God, as creating not just false images, but also broken and distorted existence. It sees this brokenness as generating a massive historical counterreality, a system of evil relationships that divides all reality from its authentic potential. This corruption does not leave either side uncorrupted. One cannot imagine that maleness and fathering stand for falsehood, but femaleness and motherhood stand for unbroken harmony; that civilization stands for corruption, but uncultivated nature stands for unbroken harmony; that reason is distorted, but spontaneous bodily appetites connect us with harmony and goodness.

If patriarchal theology sacralized the lie of distorted relations by making the male side of the dualism good and the female evil, goddess religion is in danger of simply reversing the same dualisms. Liberation feminism does not believe that one can banish the contradictions by cultural methods of identifying with the maternal pole against the paternal pole of the traditional dualism. Rather, it calls for an ethical struggle to transform both the self and the social system that supports exploitative relations. Females as well as males, nature as well as civilization, bodiliness as well as rationality, have been distorted by sinful existence. Both sides need to be transformed into a new whole.

Liberation feminist spirituality finds this tradition of critical judgment and transformation at the base of the Jewish and Christian prophetic tradition. It cannot deny that it learned this pattern of thought from biblical religion and that biblical religion taught this tradition to modern liberation movements. Thus while it repudiates the patriarchy of biblical religion, it nevertheless claims this underlying prophetic base of biblical religion. Feminist theology should not fall back on biblical exclusivism over against "paganism." It should not call for biblical religion as the "true" foundation of feminism over against non-Christian traditions. Rather it should raise questions about all religious exclusivism, including the reversed use of exclusivism by goddess religion to repudiate biblical religion.

Many of the theses of goddess religion are problematic. It is not clear that female symbols of God point to original matriarchy. Moreover, it does not appear that the joint worship of gods and goddesses in ancient cultures represented the dualisms of the feminine against the masculine, nature against civilization. These are modern dualisms generated by post-Christian culture out of and against inherited Christian patterns. Indeed what may be a positive resource of ancient paganism is that both male and female symbols of the divine represented divine sovereignty in a way that united natural and social powers.

Feminist theology seeks to transcend the dichotomy of biblical exclusivism or a reversed exclusivism that would call for the rejection of biblical religion in favor of a "goddess religion." Instead, it should seek to recapitulate the religious journey of the Near Eastern, Mediterranean, and Western worlds in a way that could embrace both non-Christian and Christian traditions, both suppressed and dominant traditions—in Mary Wakeman's words, "By reaching back and encompassing, we point forward to a new synthesis."

Rosemary Radford Ruether, *Feminist Theology
and Spirituality*

There is no point in growing old unless you can be a witch, and accumulate spiritual power in place of the political and economic power that has been denied you as a woman. Witches are descended from the sibyls and female saints; their lineage is noble and no woman need be ashamed to call herself a witch. This does not mean that she has to dress up and babble meaningless formulae in cellars and crypts. The wild white witches live outdoors and hobnob with the lower orders.

The object of facing up squarely to the fact of the climacteric is to acquire serenity and power. If women on the youthful side of the climacteric could glimpse what this state of peaceful potency might be, the difficulties of making the transition would be less. It is the nature of the case that life beyond the menopause is as invisible to the woman who has yet to struggle through the change as the top of any mountain is invisible from the valley below. Calm and poise do not simply happen to the postmenopausal woman; she has to fight for them. When the fight is over her altered state might look to a younger woman rather like exhaustion, when in reality it is anything but. The dependent woman is obliged to believe that only her turmoil of passion, fear, rage, expectancy and disappointment is living and that when she is no longer tormented by desire, insecurity, jealousy and the rest of the paraphernalia of romance she will be as dead as a spent match. The difference between her clamorous feelings and the feelings of the silent, apparently withdrawn older woman is the difference between the perception of the sea of someone tossing upon the surface, and of one who has plunged so deep that she has felt death in her throat. The older woman's love is not love of herself, nor of herself mirrored in a lover's eyes, nor is it corrupted by need. It is a feeling of tenderness so still and deep and warm that it gilds every grassblade and blesses every fly. It includes the ones who have a claim on it, and a great deal else besides. I wouldn't have missed it for the world.

Germaine Greer, The Change

In my own life, for instance, I know intellectually that the perception of time as a linear continuum with three neat divisions of past, present, and future is merely an artifice, a mental device; I have read the words of the physicists and the Eastern metaphysicians explaining that all time (and space) is of one essence, is now. But I never *felt* that knowledge as an experiential truth until I encountered women's spirituality and discovered that temporal boundaries can be rather simply dissolved by the female mind's propensity for empathetic comprehension and bonding. Through ritual moments and countless meditations, through absorbing the sacred myths of our prepatriarchal foremothers and passing them on to my daughter, through experiencing in my own daughter/mother mind and body the mysteries celebrated in the ancient rites, I have come to know, to *feel*, oneness with all the millions of women who have lived, who live, and who will live. I contain those millions. Each of us does. Every moment. Such a power cannot be stopped.

> CHARLENE SPRETNAK
> Berkeley
> November 9980*

Charlene Spretnak, *The Politics of Women's Spirituality*

In the contemporary renaissance of Goddess spirituality, women have formed ritual groups in order to mark passages in their lives, to affirm their emotional and other mind/body experiences, to heal and to celebrate, to explore new possibilities of being, to empower their efforts and desires, to renew commitment to ongoing social-change work, to enrich their spiritual lives, and to strengthen bonds of communion in this fragmented, atomized society. At times these rituals are wrenching, raucous, or sweetly rapturous. In my own life I have participated in many rituals over the years with a rather fluid configuration of sisterly ritualists: an intimate group of four, a larger group of a dozen or so, and a full tribal gathering of both sexes who assemble irregularly for solstice, equinox, wedding, and funeral rituals that include a multiplicity of friends and relations.

Although it is impossible to convey the experience of ritual on the printed page, I offer brief accounts of two ceremonies that may serve as examples of affirming the female dimension of being even in the midst of

---

* In "9978: Repairing the Time Warp and Other Related Realities" (*Heresies*, no. 5, Sept. 1978), Merlin Stone pointed out that Christian dating skews time in a manner that makes the A.D. era the "real" time and the B.C. era, which is enormously larger, "a vast emptiness of the unknown or unreal." The truly momentous event for the human race was the development of agriculture [by women, who had been the gatherers of plants, seeds, and roots] during the Proto-Neolithic period, 9000–7000 B.C. Since that radical shift in our ancestors' way of living, there has been a continuous, though not always wise or truly progressive, development of technology and culture. Stone proposes that we acknowledge the midpoint of the Proto-Neolithic period, 8000 B.C., as the actual beginning of our cultural history, after the long hunter-gatherer stage. Counting the years by the A.D.A. system (After the Development of Agriculture) brings us now to 9980 and, asserts Stone, makes us aware of that important part of our heritage.

diffuse cultural mechanisms that degrade it. The first is a menarche ritual, the second a bride's prenuptial ritual. (This selection is not intended to slight other rites of passage; I look forward to attending lots of truly great menopause rituals in the future!)

Some months after the daughters of two of us had their first menstrual periods, seven women plus the two adolescents spend a weekend at a hexagon-shaped house in the country with an open deck in the center. On Saturday afternoon the mothers prepare an altar in the womblike round enclosure, a cloth on which they set red candles and a pot of big red Gerber daisies, along with Goddess figurines, pine cones, an abalone shell filled with dried cypress needles, and other favorite objects that people had brought. The group silently drifts toward the circle from various doors and is seated on cushions. We listen as the order of the ceremony is explained. We begin by lighting the dried needles and passing the shell around the circle, breathing in the purifying smoke and fanning it gently to surround each body. We invoke the presence of the four directions and sing a melodic chant: *We all come from the Goddess and to Her we shall return like a drop of rain flowing to the ocean*. We tell the girls about some of the many, many cultural responses to menses as a visitation of transformative power, a sacred time set apart from the mundane. We tell them of the cultural degradation of women's procreative power to potential danger and then shameful uncleanliness. We tell them of the invention of counting, the Paleolithic bone-calendars etched with twenty-eight marks, the cycle of women's blood and the moon. We read them a poetic myth of Hera, goddess of women and the powers of fecundity, who draws forth the lunar blood. We sing again: *She changes everything She touches, and everything She touches changes*. Then, one by one, the women tell the story of their menarche, that first visitation of Hera—the excitement, the embarrassment, the confusion, the family's response. After each story, the speaker receives a crescent moon painted with berry juice on her forehead. Some women also speak of their first sexual experiences, of how they hope the girls might think about their bodies and their womanhood. The girls tell their stories last, tales of red blood on white slacks during the middle of movies! The circle is filled with laughter and tears, blessings and hope. We sing a final song, *Listen, listen, listen to my heart's song....* Then the women stand and form a birth canal, an archway with our upraised arms. The two mothers stand at the far end of the passageway, near the opening of the deck into the outer world. One at a time the girls pass through our arch of arms as we chant their names and kiss their cheeks. As they emerge as women, the mothers paint a crimson moon on their foreheads and hug them. Then come gifts and feasting. That was my daughter's menarche ritual.

When two women in our group married in recent years, we created a prenuptial ritual that draws on the ancient association of women and water. In pre-Olympian mythology, the goddess Hera returned each year for her ritual bath of renewal at the spring called Kanathos, just as the goddess Aphrodite returned to the sea at Paphos. They renewed their sense of virginity, which originally meant one-in-herself, independent, and self-directed. In our ritual the women form a circle, seated around a low table that has been transformed into a visual feast with flowers, candles, Goddess figurines, shells, and other favorite objects. We begin by invoking the presence of the four directions and passing a large shell containing smoldering sage sprigs for purification. We ask the blessing of the waters that love might flow, the blessing of fire that passion might burn, the blessing of the air to cleanse a new beginning, and the blessing of earth that the lovers might stay grounded and sure. We sing a chant of the Goddess's names: *Isis, Astarte, Diana, Hecate, Demeter, Kali, Inanna*. We invoke the spirit of Hera and Aphrodite. Each woman offers a blessing for the bride, the union, and her new state of being. We close our eyes as one of us leads us on an inner journey of transformation in which one's old identity, as old clothes, is sloughed off on the bank of a stream one crosses to enter a bower of eros. Someone reads from the myth of Aphrodite about her return to Paphos for her sacred bath of renewal: *"There She was attended by Her Graces: Flowering, Growth, Beauty, Joy, and Radiance. They crowned Her with myrtle and lay a path of rose petals at Her feet. . . . "* Then we crown the bride with laurels and lay a path of rose petals before her as, humming a chant, we lead her to the grotto, that is, the transformed bathroom, filled with a profusion of flowers, numerous candles, and fragrant incense. Her warm bath of water and scented oils is sprinkled with petals, and she is left alone to immerse as gently lilting music plays. When she rejoins us, the bride reclines and we encircle her, massaging oil into her warm, soft body while we take turns reading favorite poems of eros softly near her ear, poems of opening one's heart and mind and body to the beloved. Then we dress the bride in our gift, an extravagantly beautiful sleeping gown. With still more blessings and radiance, we break the circle. We eat voluptuous fruits and cake.

I was given that ritual before my remarriage. The following day, still enveloped with the glow of grace and transformation, I thought back to the bridal showers I had attended during my college years and just after: ladies in cheery frocks playing parlor games, partaking of tea and cake, chatting of just about anything on the eve of a marriage except the elemental bounteousness of the female, skimming on the surface of our lives.

Charlene Spretnak, *States of Grace*

Woman dancing with hair
on fire, woman writhing in the
cone of orange snakes, glowering
into crackling lithe vines:
Woman
you are not the bound witch
at the stake, whose broiled alive
agonized screams
thrust from charred flesh
darkened Europe in the nine millions.
Woman
you are not the madonna impaled
whose sacrifice of self leaves her
empty and mad as wind,
or whore crucified
studded with nails.
Woman
you are the demon of a fountain of energy
rushing up from the coal hard
memories in the ancient spine,
flickering lights from the furnace in the solar
plexus, lush scents from the reptilian brain,
river that winds up the hypothalamus
with its fibroids of pleasure and pain
twisted and braided like rope,
like the days of our living,
firing the lanterns of the forebrain
till they glow blood red.

You are the fire sprite
that charges leaping thighs,
that whips the supple back on its arc
as deer leap through the ankles:
dance of a woman strong
in beauty that crouches
inside like a cougar in the belly
not in the eyes of others measuring.

You are the icon of woman sexual
in herself like a great forest tree
in flower, liriondendron bearing sweet tulips,

cups of joy and drunkenness.
You drink strength from your dark fierce roots
and you hang at the sun's own fiery breast
and with the green cities of your boughs
you shelter and celebrate
woman, with the cauldrons of your energies
burning red, burning green.

Marge Piercy, "The Window of the Woman Burning," in
The Twelve-Spoked Wheel Flashing

→ III ←

Trials

"Not everything is immediately good to those who seek God; but everything is capable of becoming good."

—PIERRE TEILHARD DE CHARDIN

Those who seek the spirit and have discovered an exciting new reality through various forms of revelation hardly ever escape God's tests—the challenges that must be overcome in order to strengthen the Self even more and make ready for the truth.

The first revelations are unitive; they make us feel special, part of something greater. Then the polarity emerges: we are pulled to a place of doubt, insecurity, loneliness, and disbelief about what happened to us in revelation. We fear the loss of the old self before revelation occurred. The burning question becomes "Where now?"

No one—not even the saints—is immune. It is through the ways we behave in suffering or torment and learn from loss, grief, or sickness that the verdict for our spiritual future is given. The experiences themselves are about breaking down and conquering the old ways of being and about finding more meaning in the present, as well as some faith and hope in the future. In myths and fairy tales, the hero or heroine must overcome the biggest obstacle—demon or monster—before he or she is rewarded. And so it is that the self is challenged and the physical, mental, and emotional effort needed to overcome the challenge is usually great. The spiritual battle begins in recognizing the existence of the powers of darkness and of overcoming and absorbing these presences and energies. Trials form a training ground for God. Without recognizing darkness, one cannot see light; without living in doubt, find faith. Doubt necessitates the course of conclusion; in order to embrace the new we need to be strong, certain that we can live up to the responsibilities the spiritual life requires. Through such disciplines as prayer, meditation, yoga, and therapy, we have been given the means to strengthen ourselves. We become able to face evil, to become familiar with the dark side, the demons in the world and in ourselves. We can recognize the powers of darkness even when they parade in the guise of light.

To understand the necessity of suffering is to surrender to the purpose of change. And this is the way to truth and a deeper, more open relationship with God. And through this comes the greatest revelation—the liberation and freedom of truth—the reward of love.

→ 8 ←

The Struggle with Evil

It is not my intention to dwell too much on the existence of evil as an individual and collective compulsion, that would take a book in itself, but to ignore its very arresting power in our world and throughout the last fifty years would be a disservice to the spiritual seeker and to humanity as a whole.

It is a common pitfall to those who find spiritual nourishment through a haphazard picking of available disciplines that they seek only the good, see the light, and then fear the darkness. Yet the darkness never goes away. It is there until acknowledged; there until disarmed. Gary Zukav in his piece from *The Seat of the Soul* says that evil is "an absence." An absence of light, warmth, goodness, completeness.

Evil, threatened by the powers of illumination, rears its head when the sacred has been revealed. It seems to "smother the light," as Marion Woodman explains.

There are few nonfiction writers who describe the manifestation of evil among individuals with real clarity and focus. And they are usually the therapists or spiritual counsellors who have witnessed evil people from their unique vantage points. One such counsellor is South African–born Martin Israel, a priest of the Church of England as well as a practising physician. Israel warns of the irrational and dangerous meddling in psychic and occult practices, which opens doors to all spirits, good and bad, and invites invasion, disorder, and confusion. American psychiatrist M. Scott Peck, whose groundbreaking book *People of the Lie* documents his experience with people who are totally evil—people who lack the basic understanding of love and of sharing and are instead possessed by a sinister, cold, suffering disposition—suggests that evil be designated a disease. If it is thus recognized, then we might be driven to find a cure for what he terms "the greatest problem of mankind."

This greatest problem has been in evidence at the collective as well as the individual level. Since World War II, the major battles of the world have been fought over differences of religious beliefs and practices or to deter the spread of communism. I have chosen two pieces about the murder of the Polish priest Jerzy Popieluszko—one by Mary Craig and one by Vaclav Havel—because this act in itself is sadly representative of our time with the contending elements of religion and communism. Popieluszko was executed on charges of giving Black masses of anticommunism. In his wise piece from his book *Living in Truth*, Vaclav Havel dissects the irrationality behind the Marxist murderers of a Catholic priest, noting the irony of murderers becoming the upholders of truth and the good. As Havel concludes: "The demons have been turned loose and go about, grotesquely pretending to be honourable 20th-century men who do not believe in evil spirits."

Evil is also bent on destroying significant spiritual relationships and the growing interest of the sexes to unite in equality. Canadian novelist and playwright Patricia Joudry and American psychoanalyst Maurie D. Pressman illustrate how most of us are prevented from finding the complementary "other" in this world—our twin soul—because of disbelief, doubt, negativity, and fear of intimacy—all representations of the powers of darkness that we all carry within ourselves. This darkness is referred to as "the shadow." We cannot eliminate it, we can only learn to identify it, find a relationship with it and then integrate it into our spiritual beings. Shakti Gawain, the American writer and counsellor who has proven that New Age concepts such as visualization and affirmations can change individuals' life patterns, writes that we need to take responsibility for our darker sides. We need to own the parts of ourselves that we find hateful, fear, and do not want to accept. Only by seeing and acknowledging the evil within ourselves, do we recognize its power—and its weakness—and truly protect ourselves from its influence.

Pierre Teilhard de Chardin writes that from the first fall from Paradise, God will make good his purpose "by making evil itself serve the higher good of His faithful." Behind all things, however awful, God is present, and it is only through the dreadful, humbling experience itself are we given the revelation of that great purpose.

❧

Is anything more obvious than the presence of evil in the universe? Its nagging, prehensile tentacles project into every level of human existence. We may debate the origin of evil, but only a victim of superficial optimism would debate its reality. Evil is stark, grim, and colossally real.

Within the wide arena of everyday life we see evil in all of its ugly dimensions. We see it expressed in tragic lust and inordinate selfishness. We see it in high places where men are willing to sacrifice truth on the altars of their self-interest. We see it in imperialistic nations crushing other people with the battering rams of social injustice. We see it clothed in the garments of calamitous wars which leave men and nations morally and physically bankrupt.

In a sense, the history of man is the story of the struggle between good and evil. All of the great religions have recognized a tension at the very core of the universe. Hinduism, for instance, calls this tension a conflict between illusion and reality; Zoroastrianism, a conflict between the god of light and the god of darkness; and traditional Judaism and Christianity, a conflict between God and Satan. Each realizes that in the midst of the upward thrust of goodness there is the downward pull of evil.

Christianity clearly affirms that in the long struggle between good and evil, good eventually will emerge as victor. Evil is ultimately doomed by the powerful, inexorable forces of good. Good Friday must give way to the triumphant music of Easter. Degrading tares choke the sprouting necks of growing wheat for a season, but when the harvest is gleaned the evil tares will be separated from the good wheat. Caesar occupied a palace and Christ a cross, but the same Christ so split history into A.D. and B.C. that even the reign of Caesar was subsequently dated by his name. Long ago biblical religion recognized what William Cullen Bryant affirmed, "Truth crushed to earth will rise again," and what Thomas Carlyle wrote, "No lie you can speak or act but it will come, after longer or shorter circulation, like a bill drawn on Nature's Reality, and be presented there for payment—with the answer, No effects."

Martin Luther King, Jr., *Strength to Love*

I have been repeatedly aware of a realm or dimension of reality that has transcended but never occluded the material base of everyday existence. It has usually been of solemn hue (if one may be permitted to transcribe inner emotional impressions into the symbols of colour), but occasionally sharply accentuated around the atmosphere of certain individuals as a dark aura. I have known intuitively, even as a child, that such people were unwholesome—and sometimes a similarly unwholesome atmosphere has pervaded a house in which they lived or even had visited for a short time. In childhood I was aware of the terrible evil festering in Germany and the tortures committed on Jews and others detested by the Nazi regime. The pain was at times almost too severe to bear, but then an atmosphere of light penetrated the gloom, and the path of hope was shown again. Faith was the prerequisite for traversing that path when the radiance waned and I was on the solitary trail once more. In this gloom I was aware of presences whose origin I could not define. Some were probably the unquiet spirits of the dead, but a few had a darker, more forbidding emanation. These filled me with terror, but by holding fast to God, whom I had known from an amazingly early period of my childhood, I was supported and guided in this uncharted terrain of dark radiance. All this is, as already stated, an essentially private testimony, but the experience was to play an important part in my later work in the ministry of healing and deliverance, especially after I had submitted to the authority of the Church and received ordination as a priest. Priestly orders were to confer on me a spiritual authority that I lacked as a layman, even though I had been much involved in conducting retreats and in the ministry of counselling and healing for quite a number of years before I entered into the ordained ministry.

Almost at once, in my first parochial attachment, I was consulted by a man of artistic temperament but employed in the financial world, who had suffered from repeated bouts of severe depression which his doctors could only partially control with drugs. He came to me in a state of near-suicidal darkness, and suddenly I was aware of a malign presence overshadowing him. I asked him whether anyone close to him had recently died, and was told that, indeed, a colleague had just lost his life in distinctly unusual circumstances, so that suicide could not be excluded. This colleague had held a position of authority over the man, and had always behaved tyrannically towards him, making his life at work a constant misery. One would have expected his death to have come as something of a relief, but instead the depression intensified to near-suicidal proportions. There was certainly no question of grief for the dead man, nor any unresolved feeling of guilt about the unsatisfactory relationship in the past. It came upon me as a thundering shock that the dead man was obsessing (or infesting) the psyche of his sensitive colleague, with the intention of driving him also to suicide. The evil of the situation was overwhelming. I bade the "spirit" of the deceased one to depart forthwith into the protective custody of God, and at once the suicidal depression lifted from the sensitive man. He attained a balanced emotional frame very rapidly, and was able to leave the church in a state of calm relief. It later transpired that he was a natural sensitive, and he had to be instructed in the proper control of the psychic faculty. The depression, it must be admitted, did occasionally recur, but there was never again so terrible an episode that suicide was threatened. He was above all now in control of his life, and he subsequently left the world of finance for that of art.

This is a prototype example of the work that has subsequently been thrust upon me. I have been shown that bad relationships between parents and their children do not automatically terminate with the death of the former. On some occasions the "spirit" of the parent has hovered around the child's psyche and caused distress and even accidents, until once more the unquiet deceased were kindly, but with uncompromising authority, told to quit the earth-bound plane and move on to the greater life beyond death, to that place that God in his infinite mercy had prepared for their reception and healing. In some other instances, the disturbing entity has been a sibling or a more distant relative. Sometimes a sibling who has died in early childhood, even shortly after birth, has caused the disturbance. I would emphasize that this type of situation is not common, at least in my experience. I say this advisedly, lest a picture of the after-death state be painted in which all the recently deceased "spirits" hang around the living and cause unpleasant psychological disturbances. Fortunately, this is the exception rather than the rule: the penitent departed move to their apportioned place for further service and growth. We are accepted by God's grace, but we have to accept that grace whose full nature is love. It cannot be thrust upon us in such a way that our own inviolate will is outraged, a point not always appreciated by fervent revivalists who are hell-bent on saving the souls of all unbelievers. Yes, indeed, their heaven is too close to hell for the comfort of any perceptive individual, because the power of private judgement is overwhelmed in a seething emotional barrage of threats. The situation shades imperceptibly into the ways of the dictators of our time. In respect of the very young who have died and then obsessed the personalities of their siblings or other near relatives, their problem seems to be one of ignorance or else resentment that their lives have been cut short so summarily. In all these instances a Requiem Mass said for the dead can help to settle their souls, but often a word of command is also necessary. This has, indeed, been my experience.

All this is to be clearly distinguished from the practices of spiritualism. Here there is a willed attempt to communicate with the deceased through the agency of mediums, or sensitives. The impetus is nearly always the need of those who are bereaved or the curiosity of those dabbling in occult, potentially dangerous matters for the sake of new experiences. The results of this type of attempted contact are seldom satisfactory, since the issue is invariably clouded by the possibility of fraud on the part of the medium or else unconscious telepathic contact with the mind of the sitter. Even if what appears to be a genuine contact is made, the communication is very likely to be coloured by the personality of the medium. Furthermore, there is always the possibility of interference by mischievous entities from the vast intermediate psychic realm, some of which may well be of demonic nature. This is why willed communication by the agency of mediums is to be deprecated. But the phenomenon of mediumship is worthy of investigation by qualified research workers. These may, at the very least, gain new insights into the range of the human mind: the fruits of these studies are extensions of normal psychology (parapsychology). They shed new light on the mechanisms of life. Those who depend on communication through mediums with their dead loved ones tend to be drawn ineluctably into a prison of past associations which they then project into the present. Instead of growing through loss into a life of greater relationships with humanity at large, they remain stuck in past attitudes. By not letting go of the past, they remain trapped in it, and quite possibly restrict their loved ones on the other side of death.

The person who is naturally sensitive psychically is in possession of a gift that is both serviceable to others and wounding to himself. It must be used with reverence, and the call is from God, not man. If mediumship is indeed a valid means of communication with deceased souls, its purpose is to help those who are earth-bound on their journey to the light, and the operative work is prayer. It is conceivable that such entities are closer to the earth they once knew than to the "heavens" (using the term in a collective sense rather than one of spiritual distinction) they are to inhabit in their new form. And so their earthly helpers may assist the greater communion of saints in liberating them from past associations. Then the work is continued by that great communion, which surely includes the ministry of angels too. Such a sensitive person is, as I have already indicated from my own experience, vulnerable to the less desirable influences of the intermediate dimension (between solid earth and the heaven of the blessed departed), and needs constant protection. This is afforded by a life of humble submission to God in prayer, worship, service, and a chaste style of living. Furthermore, there should be unfailing prayer support from a devoted community: religious orders have an important place in this work, especially the contemplative communities whose life is centred on prayer. In this way the psychic faculty is sanctified. In the spiritualistic way it tends to be sensationalized, cheapened and brought into ridicule, at least among people with intelligence and spiritual discernment. All this is very sad, because the psychic mode is one of intimate communication between people and between the divine and the human.

On some occasions I have been aware of a powerful, more concentrated and malign source of disturbance around a person who is in severe difficulties. He may be aware of a destructive force around him that threatens his security, or there may be dangerous accidents, or simply an atmosphere of general disquiet. In these circumstances I have had little doubt that a demonic agency has been at work, rather than simply the unquiet soul of a deceased person. Sometimes the fallen angel, which is the usual identity of the demonic presence, has attached itself to a deceased person, so that the two appear to work in collaboration. Occasionally a decidedly evil deceased person may gain control over a neutral angelic presence on the lower grades of the hierarchy and use it for destructive purposes. All this, needless to say, is a purely private, subjective judgement which follows a personal encounter with a focus of evil. But the course of action is the same—to banish the entity, however it may be described, from the reaches of the earth and despatch it to the place in the greater world beyond death which God has prepared for it. It is essential to direct the demonic entity to a place of reception and not simply to leave it unattended in the darkness. Not only would this be very unloving, but it could also leave the entity free to continue its disturbing work among us all.

Some readers, disturbed enough by this account of obsessing demonic agents, would raise their eyebrows in incredulous horror at the suggestion of love being expended on such a vile entity. But we have, as Jesus once taught us, to love our enemies, and not only those who are well-disposed to us. Only the spirit of love can start the work of redemption. What God has in store for his errant creatures—remembering that he alone is the universal creator—is not our business, but it is surely not out of place to look for a final healing of all that is aberrant and unclean, whether human or angelic. Such must be the measure of divine love, of which human sacrificial love is a reflection in our little world. Such a universalistic hope does not in any way excuse, let alone overlook, the evil of the creature, which is to be expiated in full measure. But it can nevertheless envisage the sinner's final repentance, absolution and reception into the body of saints who are perpetually about their Father's business.

If we accept the thesis that there are agents of evil in the intermediate psychic realm, whether discarnate humans or fallen angels, can we postulate a personality of supreme evil, the devil? I believe we are entitled to do so, even if we cannot define the nature of the ultimate destructive power with precision. It may be a powerful fallen angel, or demon, or else the summation of all the evil power that has accumulated in the cosmos from the time of creation, especially since the Fall of the angels which was succeeded by the Fall of man in the mythological guise of Adam and Eve. Whatever may be the answer, it feels right to deal with the devil as a personal entity with whom we can attain a finite relationship, albeit a destructive one. This way seems better than being submerged in a vast ocean of darkness, floundering in dire panic. Since the devil strikes at the very root of the human personality, it seems not misguided to accept an element of the personal in its constitution. But more we cannot say. Personal experience often sheds light on dark areas of existence that far outdistance the dogmas of the rationalist.

A number of questions rise to mind. If there is indeed a vast nexus of cosmic evil (involving both the astronomical universe and the intermediate psychic realm), why does it appear to strike people so arbitrarily? The answer seems to lie in part in variations of individual sensitivity, especially where there is no protection by prayer in the lives of vulnerable people, like the man who was assailed by his dead colleague. Other people lay themselves open through unwise practices such as the use of the ouija board or their attendance at spiritualistic seances (these should be reserved for psychical research workers who know what they are doing, and certainly not be patronized by the general public). Again there are other people who, like Faust, deliberately give themselves over to the devil, just as spiritual aspirants dedicate their lives to God. Satanism itself is an evil cult that has always been part of the depraved mass of society, but is currently on the increase. Satanists believe that the Creator God has withdrawn from the world, never intervening anymore in its affairs, and that the Son of God who has been given control of the earth in the Creator's absence is Satan, the god of this world (described in 2 Corinthians 4:4 as the god of this passing age). Jesus tried to destroy Satan's plan for the world, but it is, according to their belief, Satan that will attain the final victory. They participate in depraved rites and through psychic practices open themselves to the influence of satanic powers. The motives of its practitioners are mixed. Most are mentally or emotionally unbalanced, some are frankly evil people, while others get drawn into the scene as curious bystanders. These may later be the victims of blackmail.

I have no doubt that the practitioners of Satan worship are soon assaulted by evil forces, an infestation that shows itself in a progressive deterioration of the person's character. Deceitfulness, perverse sexual behaviour, stealing, and increasing destructiveness are typical features of this breakdown of the personality. To the rationalist all these changes can easily be attributed to fear and the general atmosphere of perversion that lies around zealous practitioners, but in practice there is usually a more concentrated focus of psychic assault in such cases, in addition to the psychological confusion that is drawn to the surface by the eruption of fear and hatred. It is certain that mentally balanced people do not espouse satanism, nor do they get involved in strange cults. It is the social misfit and emotional cripple who are attracted to bizarre activities of this kind. They are sad specimens of disordered humanity who seek power to affirm their shaky confidence. What they are really seeking is understanding and affection, but there are not many agencies who provide these needs, at least in a form that accepts the person as he is without imposing a rationalistic or a sectarian religious style of thinking upon him.

Martin Israel, *The Dark Face of Reality*

The evil deny the suffering of their guilt—the painful awareness of their sin, inadequacy, and imperfection—by casting their pain onto others through projection and scapegoating. They themselves may not suffer, but those around them do. They cause suffering. The evil create for those under their dominion a miniature sick society.

In reality, we exist not merely as individuals but as social creatures who are integral component parts of a larger organism called society. Even if we were to insist upon suffering in the definition of illness, it is neither necessary nor wise to conceive of illness solely in terms of the individual. It may be that the parents described were not themselves suffering, but their families were. And the symptoms of family disorder—depression, suicide, failing grades, and theft—were attributable to their leadership. In terms of "systems theory," the suffering of the children was symptomatic not of their own sickness but of that of their parents. Are we to consider individuals healthy simply because they are not in pain—no matter how much havoc and harm they bring to their fellow human beings?

Finally, who is to say what the evil suffer? It is consistently true that the evil do not *appear* to suffer deeply. Because they cannot admit to weakness or imperfection in themselves, they must appear this way. They must appear to themselves to be continually on top of things, continually in command. Their narcissism demands it. Yet we know they are not truly on top of things. No matter how competent the parents described thought themselves, we know that in fact they were incompetent in their parental role. Their appearance of competence was just that: an appearance. A pretense. Rather than being in command of themselves, it was their narcissism that was in command, always demanding, whipping them into maintaining their pretense of health and wholeness.

Think of the psychic energy required for the continued maintenance of the pretense so characteristic of the evil! They perhaps direct at least as much energy into their devious rationalizations and destructive compensations as the healthiest do into loving behavior. Why? What possesses them, drives them? Basically, it is fear. They are terrified that the pretense will break down and they will be exposed to the world and to themselves. They are continually frightened that they will come face-to-face with their own evil. Of all emotions, fear is the most painful. Regardless of how well they attempt to appear calm and collected in their daily dealings, the evil live their lives in fear. It is a terror—and a suffering—so chronic, so interwoven into the fabric of their being, that they may not even feel it as such. And if they could, their omnipresent narcissism will prohibit them from ever acknowledging it. Even if we cannot pity the evil for their inevitably ghastly old age or for the state of their souls after death, we can surely pity them for the lives they live of almost unremitting apprehension.

Whether the evil suffer or not, the experience of suffering is so subjective, and the meaning of suffering so complex, I think it best not to define illness and disease in its terms. Instead, I believe that illness and disease should be defined as *any defect in the structure of our bodies or our personalities that prevents us from fulfilling our potential as human beings.*

Admittedly, we may have some differences of opinion as to what exactly constitutes the human potential. Nonetheless, there are a sufficient number of men and women in all cultures and at all times who have achieved in their full adulthood a kind of gracefulness of existence so that we can generally say of them: "They have become truly human." By which we mean their lives seem almost to touch on the divine. And we can study these people and examine their characteristics. Briefly, they are wise and aware; they enjoy life with gusto, yet face and accept death; they not only work productively but creatively, and they obviously love their fellow human beings, whom they lead with a benignity of both intent and result.

Most people, however, are so crippled in body and spirit that they cannot possibly ever attain such a lofty condition even through their best efforts without massive therapeutic assistance. Among these crippled legions—the mass of suffering humanity—the evil reside, perhaps the most pitiable of all.

I said there were two other reasons one might hesitate to label evil an illness. They can be countered more briefly. One is the notion that someone who is ill must be a victim. We tend to think of illness as something that befalls us, a circumstance over which we have no control, an unfortunate accident visited on us by meaningless fate, a curse in the creation of which we did not participate.

Certainly many illnesses seem like this. But many others—perhaps the majority—do not conform to such a pattern at all. Is the child who runs out on the street, when he has been told not to, and gets hit by a car, a victim? How about the driver of a car who gets in an "accident" when he is racing well above the speed limit to meet an appointment for which he is late? Or let us examine the enormous variety of psychosomatic illnesses and diseases of stress. Are people who suffer tension headaches because they don't like their jobs victims? Of what? A woman has an asthmatic attack every time she is in a situation in which she feels ignored, isolated, and uncared for. Is she a victim? One way or another, to some extent, all these people and a host of others victimize themselves. Their motives, failures, and choices are deeply and intimately involved in the creation of their injuries and diseases. Although they all have a certain degree of responsibility for their condition, we still consider them ill.

Most recently this issue has been debated in reference to alcoholism—some vigorously insisting that it is a disease and others insisting that because it appears to be self-inflicted, it is not. Not only physicians but courts and legislatures have been involved in this debate, and have reached the conclusion that alcoholism is indeed a disease, despite the fact that the alcoholic may sometimes seem nobody's victim except his or her own.

The issue of evil is similar. An individual's evil can almost always be traced to some extent to his or her childhood circumstances, the sins of the parents and the nature of their heredity. Yet evil is always also a choice one has made—indeed, a whole series of choices. The fact that we are all responsible for the state of health of our souls does not mean that a poor state of health is something other than disease. Once again, I believe we are on safest and soundest ground when we do not define disease in terms of victimization or responsibility but instead hold onto the definition already offered: An illness or disease is any defect in the structure of our bodies or personalities that prevents us from fulfilling our potential as human beings.

The final argument against labeling evil an illness is the belief that evil is a seemingly untreatable condition. Why designate as a disease a condition for which there is neither known treatment nor cure? Had we an elixir of youth in our doctor's black bag, it might make good sense to consider old age a disease, but we do not generally or currently think of it so. We accept old age as an inevitable part of the human condition, a natural process that is our lot and against which we are fools to rage.

This argument, however, ignores the fact that there are a whole host of disorders, from multiple sclerosis to mental deficiency, for which there is no treatment or cure but which we don't hesitate to call diseases. Perhaps we call them diseases because we hope to find the means to combat them. But is this not the case with evil? It is true that we do not currently possess any generally feasible or effective form of treatment to heal the thoroughly evil of their hatred and destructiveness. Indeed, the analysis of evil presented thus far reveals several reasons just why it is an extraordinarily difficult condition to approach, much less cure. But is a cure possible? Are we to simply throw up our hands in the face of this difficulty and sigh, "It's beyond us"? Even when it is the greatest problem of mankind?

Rather than being an effective argument against it, the fact that we currently do not know how to treat evil in the human individual is the best reason to designate it a disease. For the label of disease implies that the disorder is not inevitable, that healing should be possible, that it should be studied scientifically and methods of treatment should be sought. If evil is an illness, it should then become an object for research like any other mental illness, be it schizophrenia or neurasthenia. It is the central proposition of this book that the phenomenon of evil can and should be subjected to scientific scrutiny. We can and should move from our present state of ignorance and helplessness toward a true psychology of evil.

The designation of evil as a disease also obligates us to approach the evil with compassion. By their nature the evil inspire in us more of a desire to destroy than to heal, to hate than to pity. While these natural reactions serve to protect the uninitiated, they otherwise prevent any possible solution. I do not think we shall come any closer than we are today to understanding and, I hope, curing human evil until the healing professions name evil as an illness within the domain of their professional responsibility.

There is a wise old priest retired to the mountains of North Carolina who has long done battle with the forces of darkness. After he had done me the favor of reviewing a draft of this book he commented: "I am glad that you have labeled evil an illness. It is not only a disease; it is the ultimate disease."

M. Scott Peck, *People of the Lie*

The three poisons: craving,
hatred,
ignorance.
Thomas Merton, *The Asian Journals of Thomas Merton*

Jerzy Popieluszko

The ten days which followed the news of Jerzy Popieluszko's abduction were filled with uncertainty and anxious speculation. The churches—particularly St. Stanislaw Kostka—were packed night and day, and throughout Poland Masses were said for his safe return. A banner outside St. Stanislaw Kostka proclaimed: WHEREVER YOU ARE, JUREK,* CHRIST IS WITH YOU, AND OUR PRAYERS. Many workers wanted to organise strikes or protest marches, in order to relieve their pent-up emotions. Solidarity, however, urged caution. As tension and fear grew steadily, the bishops appealed

* A diminutive form of Jerzy.

to the authorities to find the missing priest with all possible speed. Uniformed and plainclothes police scoured the country, using helicopters and sniffer dogs in the search. General Jaruzelski denounced the kidnapping and suggested that it was a move on the part of hard-line Communists (backed by the Soviet Union) to undermine his authority and portray him as incapable of keeping order. Solidarity was inclined to think so too.

On 27 October, the day before the usual monthly Mass for Poland was due to take place, General Kiszczak, the Minister for Internal Affairs, announced on TV that "sadly" the authors of this "revolting crime" were three officials from his own Ministry. They had been arrested, he said, and would suffer severe penalties for their crime. Next day, 80,000 people from all over the country attended the Mass for Poland, for the first time without Jerzy Popieluszko. The mood was sombre and fearful.

Then, on 30 October, after an announcement that a search was taking place in the Wloclawek dam, the grisly tragedy moved towards its inevitable end. At eight o'clock, as the evening Mass was finishing, a priest brought the news: "Brothers and sisters, today in the waters of the Wloclawek dam, they found our priest...." A howl of agony arose and continued for many minutes, growing in intensity as it was reinforced by the tolling of the bells. "Outside," wrote a British journalist who was present, "the people...were visibly stunned and helpless. They stood with pale, shut faces, with forgotten, folded hands." By midnight, the fence surrounding the church was ablaze with flowers and candles.

Some attempt was made to pressurise Jerzy's parents into having him buried in his home village away from the glare of publicity. But his mother would have none of it. "Years ago," she said, "I gave my son to the Church. I am not going to take him back now." Eventually, it was agreed that he should be buried in Warsaw and—after much argument—in the grounds of his own beloved church of St. Stanislaw Kostka.

On 2 November, the family and friends of the murdered priest went to the Institute of Forensic Medicine in Bialystok to collect the body. The full horror of his dying was at last apparent. The body was covered with brownish-grey bruises; the nose and eyes were blackened, the fingers dark red, the feet grey. It seemed as though much of his hair had been pulled out and large areas of the skin on his legs had been rubbed away. Where his tongue had once been there was only a piece of mangled pulp. The doctor who was present said that in all his experience he had never examined a corpse with so much external damage.

Outside the church and in the surrounding streets tens of thousands awaited the arrival of the body at about six-thirty in the evening. Waldemar Chrostowski was one of the pallbearers:

Amid the tolling of the bells and the overwhelming sobbing of thousands of people, the coffin containing Jerzy's body was lowered to the ground in front of the church. With the others I took it on my shoulder and carried it into the church. I wanted to stay with Jerzy as long as I could. I turned my face towards the coffin, thinking of all that he had suffered before he died. Thinking too that when his time had come to die, those he loved were far away; that in those last fateful moments there was no one to protect him from the hatred of his attackers. Tears poured down my cheeks—I kept asking myself the same question over and over—why had I not stayed with him till the end?

In that regret he was not alone. Among the many farewell notes pinned to the perimeter fence was one from Solidarity: "We could not protect the one we loved best," it mourned. Another, from a group of non-believers, promised that they too would be joining in the all-night vigil around Fr. Jerzy's coffin. And a third simply proclaimed the words by which Jerzy had lived: FORGIVE US OUR TRESPASSES AS WE FORGIVE THOSE WHO TRESPASS AGAINST US and FATHER, FORGIVE THEM, THEY KNOW NOT WHAT THEY DO.

There were steel-workers, medical workers, actors, teachers, film-makers, printers, students, writers, priests, nuns and many others who filed slowly past the coffin to pay their last respects to Poland's best-loved son. They stayed in the church until five o'clock next morning when the church was cleared of its mourners. By seven they had returned, their numbers swollen now by delegations representing the banned Solidarity movement from all over Poland.

When the funeral Mass began (celebrated by Cardinal Glemp, six bishops and six priests on the exterior balcony, and over a thousand other priests inside and outside the church), a wreath of thorns lay on the catafalque. Between 300,000 and 350,000 mourners were in attendance, and their self-discipline was astonishing. In the overpowering silence, it was as if the whole assembly had been, as one woman put it, "touched by a visible wave of grace."

Anguish broke through afterwards, in the farewell speeches which followed the Mass. "Jurek," cried one of the Warsaw steel-men, his voice hoarse with grief. "Jurek, our friend, can you hear the bells tolling for freedom? Can you hear us praying? Your ark, the good ship Solidarity of Hearts drifts along carrying more and more of us on board....You have already conquered Christ...and that was the victory you most longed for."

When the coffin was sealed, it was carried to the grave outside. The flowers, wreaths and candles enveloping not only the grave-site but the church, the forecourt and the squares and streets beyond, bore witness to the fact that Poland had acquired a new martyr and the pilgrims had come already to his shrine. That Christmas, the crib at St. Stanislaw Kostka would be not a manger but a car boot filled with straw on which lay the mangled body of a young man. The Poles understand about martyrdom; it has for so long been part of their living experience.

In the short term, Jerzy's death heralded a new wave of repression aimed principally, as the Minister for Religious Affairs said, at "priests who deliver sermons which violate the laws." 1985 saw a spate of attacks against the clergy and Solidarity. There were more "disappearances." Stones were thrown at the car of Fr. Kazimierz Jancarz, for example, as he drove from Gdańsk to attend a Mass for Poland in Warsaw. In April a twenty-nine-year-old priest, Tadeusz Zaleski, was attacked in his parents' house, immobilised by a chemical spray and burned on his hands, face and chest with V-shaped burns. The authorities claimed that the priest was mentally disturbed and had inflicted the burns on himself. But two separate commissions of doctors found this proposition unlikely in the extreme, particularly as they found no evidence of instability in the young man.

Jerzy Popieluszko's murderers were put on trial in Torun four months after his death—an event unique in the annals of Communist Eastern Europe, in that for the first time the secret police were being forced to account for their actions. But the event itself was a travesty in which the victim himself rather than the accused seemed to be on trial. One defendant, ex-Captain Piotrowski, was allowed to utter an impassioned tirade against the Church and to blame Father Popieluszko for all the social unrest in Poland. Ex-Colonel Adam Pietruszka said that Popieluszko was one of a number of priests in Poland "who wear a cross on their chests and carry hatred in their hearts." The State Prosecutor suggested that it was "the extremism" of Father Popieluszko which had given rise to an unfortunate matching "extremism" on the part of his murderers. Mr. Olszewski, the Prosecutor representing the Church, was dumbfounded by all this. "This is supposed to be the trial of the murderers of Father Popieluszko," he bitterly reminded the court. "I never thought I should have to stand in court and defend the innocent victim of the crime." Waldemar Chrostowski, whose testimony the State Prosecutor had done everything in his power to discredit, said the trial had been used "to spit upon the Church."

The trial lasted twelve days. In his summing-up, the Judge said there was no question of a death penalty since the accused had not acted "from base motives" but only out of excessive zeal in eliminating an "enemy of the State." Nevertheless, he conceded, a crime had been committed and he sentenced Pietruszka and Piotrowski to twenty-five years' imprisonment (with ten years' loss of civil rights). Pekala was sentenced to fifteen years, and Chmielewski to fourteen.

To counter the trauma induced by the Torun trial and its own loss of face, the government unleashed a barrage of propaganda against both Solidarity and the Church. "We are faced with propaganda terrorism," said the Solidarity leader, Lech Walesa, in March. "They have practically declared civil war on us." Bishops were asked to remove outspoken priests to country parishes where they could do no harm. Not that bishops themselves were immune from attack. The new bishop of Gdańsk was attacked in front of his own cathedral. He managed to reach his car and the attacker ran straight into the police station dropping his identification papers as he ran. Two young girls, witnesses to the incident, picked up the papers and took them to the clergy-house. As they left, they were detained, charged with prostitution and locked up. They were released when the policeman's identity papers were handed over, but no explanation or apology was offered for their treatment.

But in spite of the regime doing its worst, an indefinable change had come over Poland. The fear had gone, and in its place had come a deep contempt. With hindsight it is possible to say that with the death of Jerzy Popieluszko, the Communists finally lost the battle for Poland—and, by extension, for the world. The murder dispelled any lingering doubts the Poles might have had about the possibility of co-existing with the regime. It was obvious that no accommodation was possible with people who would stop at nothing—not even murder—to stamp out opposition to its policies. As long as they remained in power, the nation would continue without hope.

A new hymn, popularly attributed to the pen of Fr. Popieluszko, expressed this combination of anguish and determination. Sung at every Mass, it began with a lament: "Oh my country, how long you have suffered. How deep are your wounds to-day!" But it ended on a note of hope. The white eagle of Poland, chained now by the foot, would break its chain "when the freedom bell shall ring." Meanwhile, "Mary, Queen of Poland, grant us freedom, peace and loving hearts, that we may always be true to you and to your Son." In those trying days, it was a chokingly sad but uplifting experience to hear them sing these words. In spite of their spiritual fervour, one had little hope that their Freedom bell would ever ring.

In a farcical show-trial of Solidarity activists in May 1985 the defendants were prevented from stating their case, defence lawyers were not allowed to question police witnesses and all embarrassing questions were disallowed. On the other hand, free rein was given to prosecuting counsel and police witnesses. It was, said Lech Walesa, "an insult to justice. The law in Poland has been trodden underfoot and its place taken by brute force." Yet the trial was probably Communism's last gasp. "Whatever sentence is passed on us," wrote one of the defendants, Adam Michnik, in his diary, "it will be a sentence on Jaruzelski and his cohorts rather than on us. They will incur the odium of the world for their lawlessness; whereas they will have offered us the priceless gift of dignity, which is inseparable from faithfulness.... The functionaries think that by gagging us they have deprived us of our dignity. But that is the one thing they cannot do." Jaruzelski's totalitarian regime in Poland was, wrote Michnik in his prison cell, in its death throes. Totally deprived of popular support, it was "Communism with its teeth knocked out."

Adam Michnik's insight proved right. Four years later, on 4 June 1989, the first post-war, non-Communist government came to power without bloodshed in Poland. It was headed by a Catholic, Tadeusz Mazowiecki. Not only in Poland, but throughout Eastern Europe, Communism was in disarray. The Freedom bell was ringing at last.

Mary Craig, Candles in the Dark

To this day, we cannot understand how a great, civilized nation—or at least a considerable part of it—could, in the twentieth century, succumb to its fascination for a single, ridiculous, complex-ridden, *petit bourgeois*; could fall for his pseudo-scientific theories and in their name exterminate nations, conquer continents, and commit unbelievable cruelties. Positivistic science, Marxism included, offers a variety of scientific explanations for this mysterious phenomenon, but instead of eliminating the mystery, they tend rather to deepen it. For the cold, "objective" reason that speaks to us from these explanations in fact only underlines the disproportion between itself—a power that claims to be the decisive one in this civilization—and the mass insanity that has nothing in common with any form of rationality.

Yes, when traditional myth was laid to rest, a kind of "order" in the dark region of our being was buried along with it. And what modern reason has attempted to substitute for this order, has consistently proved erroneous, false, and disastrous, because it is always in some way deceitful, artificial, rootless, lacking in both ontology and morality. It may even border on the ludicrous, like the cult of the "Supreme Being" during the French Revolution, the collectivist folklore of totalitarian systems, or their "realist," self-celebrating art. It seems to me that with the burial of myth, the barn in which the mysterious animals of the human unconscious were housed over thousands of years has been abandoned and the animals turned loose—or, the tragically mistaken assumption that they were phantoms—and that now they are devastating the countryside. They devastate it, and at the same time they make themselves at home where we least expect them to—in the secretariats of modern political parties, for example. These sanctuaries of modern reason lend them their tools and their authority so that ultimately the plunder is sanctioned by the most scientific of world views.

Generally, people do not begin to grasp the horror of their situation until too late: that is, until they realize that thousands of their fellow humans have been murdered for reasons that are utterly irrational. Irrationality, hiding behind sober reason and a belief that the inexorable march of history demands the sacrifice of millions to assure a happy future for billions, seems essentially more irrational and dangerous than the kind of irrationality that, in and through myth, admits to its own existence, comes to terms with the "positive powers" and, at most, sacrifices animals. The demons simply do what they want while the gods take diffident refuge in the final asylum to which they have been driven, called "human conscience." And so at last bloodlust, disguised as the most scientific of the world's views (which teaches, by the way, that conscience must submit to historical necessity) throws a twentieth-century John of Nepomuk into the Vistula. And the nation immediately canonizes its martyr in spirit.

In the events which chance tossed together in a single newscast, and juxtaposed with Agrippa's *Occult Philosophy*, I begin to see a sophisticated collage that takes on the dimensions of a symbol, an emblem, a code. I do not know what message is hidden in that unintentional artefact, which might be called "Thriller," after Michael Jackson's famous song. I only feel that chance—that great poet—is stammering an indistinct message about the desperate state of the modern world.

First, Marxist demonologists in the Polish papers label Popieluszko a practitioner of black magic who, with the assistance of the Devil, serves the black mass of anti-communism in the church of St. Stanislav Kostka; then, other scientific Marxists waylay him at night, beat him to death and throw him into the Vistula; and finally, still other "scientists" on one-sixth of the earth's surface claim that the Devil in disguise—the CIA, in other words—is behind it. It is all pure medieval history. Except that the actors are scientists, people shielded by science, possessing an allegedly scientific world view. Of course that makes the whole thing so much more powerful. The demons have been turned loose and go about, grotesquely pretending to be honourable twentieth-century men who do not believe in evil spirits. The Sikhs do not even need to masquerade as men of science. Confronting this modern world with modern machine guns in their hands, they believe themselves to be instruments of providence: after all, they are merely meting out punishment in accordance with the ancient prophecy about the desecrator of their Golden Temple. The Hindus then turn around and murder Sikhs, burning them alive, as though all Sikhs, to the last man, had taken part in Mrs. Gandhi's murder. How can this happen in the century of science and reason? How can science and reason explain it? How does it relate to colonizing the Moon and making ready an expedition to Mars? How does it relate to an age capable of transplanting the heart of a baboon into a person? Could we be getting ready to go to Mars in the secret hope of leaving our demons behind on the earth and so disposing of them? And who, in fact, has a baboon heart: that little girl in California—or the Marxist government of Ethiopia, building its mausoleums in a time of famine; or the Polish police; or the Sikhs in the personal bodyguard of the Indian prime minister who died—thanks to their belief in ancient prophecies—like an antique emperor at the hands of his own servants?

It seems to me that man has what we call a human heart, but that he also has something of the baboon within him. The modern age treats the heart as a pump and denies the presence of the baboon within us. And so again and again, this officially non-existent baboon, unobserved, goes on the rampage, either as the personal bodyguard of a politician, or wearing the uniform of the most scientific police force in the world.

Modern man, that methodical civil servant in the great bureaucracy of the world, mildly frustrated by the collapse of his "scientific" world view, finally switches on his video recorder to watch Michael Jackson playing a vampire in "Thriller," the best-selling video cassette in the history of the world, then goes into the kitchen to remove from a thermos flask—behind the backs of all animal welfare societies—the still warm heart of a hoopoe. And he swallows it, hoping to have the gift of prophecy conferred upon him.

Vaclav Havel, from "Thriller," in *Living in Truth*

The reality of evil is a well-kept secret, guarded by the dark forces themselves; for they thrive on concealment. In contrast, the forces of Light wish always to be known. The power of Light increases as it is brought to consciousness. Darkness loses its power when revealed, for we are then able to see it in action, recognize its purpose, and employ it so that it no longer employs us.

Fascism, racism, and religious wars have all demonstrated how the dark powers foment hatred among human beings. The war between modern feminism and the male gender is another example. This is our present and immediate concern.

Each forward thrust of evolution evokes an equal and opposite reaction from the opposing tide. The liberation of women from ancient repression holds the prospect—indeed the eventual certainty—of improved relations between the sexes. The spirit of the Eternal Feminine will be free to soar and inspire to new heights the Eternal Masculine, the other side of itself. The masculine spirit, also, has long been separated from its true nature, despite apparent male supremacy in the world.

Men have had no real joy in their power, for joy comes through other channels. Men are seeking their joy now, as they struggle toward spirituality. But they are like creatures caught in an oil spill, struggling to be free of the sticky tar, the same tar that blackened their ancestors and continues to blacken the minds of undeveloped individuals today.

The seeds of war were planted early, as far back as the first man and the first woman. From the beginning of human history, men have possessed the power in this world. They did not seize it; it was accorded them in the Plan of things. By his nature, unevolved man was fully yang, aggressive and self-assertive. Thousands of years would elapse before his tempering yin would unfold within him. The undeveloped woman was his total opposite. She was all yin, entirely passive, lacking any of the strength that would later flower to equal and parallel that of her partner. Primitive man and primitive woman were a natural fit, and for a long time the arrangement caused no trouble. They were preoccupied enough with remaining alive.

Civilization advanced and every advance was met with opposition from the mounting wave of evil emanating from the dark psychic pool of the world. Men abused their power and perpetrated cruelties on men and women alike. Men of old are not to be excused for their acts, but neither should the blame be placed on men of today, many of whom are working toward the next step in liberation—the freeing of *all* persons from the down-pulling tide.

If blame there must be, let it be placed where it belongs—at the door of the hidden powers of evil, the forces opposing life and growth, willing the destruction of the world, and dedicated to maintaining and increasing the separateness of souls. Separateness prolongs the life and usefulness of evil entities; the ultimate reunion of all will spell their dissolution. We shall call them the Separatists; for their every impulse is divisive, as opposed to the guiding agencies of Light, ever urging to union.

The Separatists laid the groundwork well for the uprising of women and their demands for equality. Then they delivered their master stroke, which was to fan the flames of women's anger to a place far past the point of usefulness.

The purpose of the feminist movement was the righting of ancient imbalances between the sexes. In a reactive imbalance, men now carry the weight of blame for all of history's crimes and misdemeanors against women;

hence their anger. There is the danger that feminism, wrongly used, could go the way of past masculine dominance. Female individual and collective power is now being awakened. Disunity arises when the radical aspect of feminism is carried too far, obscuring the need for men and women to communicate and love and be intimate with each other. Masculinity has paraded as patriarchy in the past. There is the possibility that feminism (not femininity) could become a matriarchy, a patriarchy in disguise.

No person is blameless in the matter of dark inspiration. Influences from the collective shadow seek access through human temptation. They gain entry through the shadow area of temptation, which exists in each individual's unconscious mind. The great challenge that faces us is to withstand such temptation, to understand and recognize the forces that are playing upon us, so that we may reject the lower and embrace the higher.

Freud's discovery of the interior of the mind underscored the fact that early experiences shape and influence later ones. The former function like color filters in front of camera lenses. They do not change the picture; rather, they modify, it, lending their affective influence to those experiences that occur later in life. Studies documented by Sigmund Freud, John Bowlby, Margaret Mahler, and many other psychoanalytic investigators, demonstrate that a person's earliest experiences at the mother's breast produce feelings of either optimism or pessimism that will last throughout life. Rings of influence, or shapers, are created in tandem at other crucial developmental periods, notably that of adolescence. Further shapers are continually at work, such as the astronomical and astrological forces, which lend their influence to gravity and to the newly entered individual. Similarly, influences of darkness and light surround us in mutual contention. The shifting light and shadow from these powerful antagonists falls over the rings within rings already coloring the events and the characters, the feelings and the expressions, of every human being.

Yet we are not helpless before these influences. The directing center is the spiritual will, the essential Self, which chooses between the lower and the higher. To make informed choices we need to become familiar with the superordinant, those spiritual realms that have been described in the ancient mysteries and the core religions. Those realms surround us, exchange with us and receive from us. Like stalactite meeting stalagmite, the upper and the lower grow toward each other. The surrounding forces of darkness and light approach each other too, reaching out to draw unto themselves human beings of like mind.

Dark forces are easily attracted to the neurotic and psychotic aspects of the individual. This is because the earlier and more primitive fixations, contained within psychosis and neurosis, come from an earlier and more primitive place in ontogenetic development. That which is more primitive is more selfish and cruel, more divisive, more secretive, more separate and destructive. And so it is that evil forces draw to themselves those with under-developed personalities, the proclivities and desires to exercise cruelty and victimize their fellows.

At the far end of the scale, we can discern the satanic power enthroned in the caverns of the psychic underworld, ruling over the Black Lodge. The Black Lodge is that collection of satanic spirits who are opposed to the Light and have directed the massive crimes of history. In the day-to-day course of events, their lesser servants—evil spirits of the lower astral—attach them-selves to individuals of every kind, male and female, inspiring acts of child abuse, racial hatred, and the many perversions that cripple the human spirit. In a less noticeable way they invade the minds of intelligent, well-intentioned persons to sow seeds of separatism in every patch of likely soil within the unconscious mind.

It is in the relation between the sexes that the dark force counts its proudest gains, in suffering imposed and evolution delayed; for the realm of love is where it could be most seriously threatened. Any blossoming of love draws the attention of the opposition. If the love is of a high order, the oppo-sition intensifies and continues to intensify until it either wins the day or is vanquished by the force of love itself. The outcome is clear-cut in every case: there is no middle way; either love or evil triumphs. It is a pattern we watch for in all our love stories, for we see in it the working of a cosmic truth.

Long before Oedipus appeared, the dark spiritual agencies that seek to foster separation recognized love relationships as fertile ground for human conflict. There is scarcely anyone who has not some aspect, stemming from childhood insecurity or trauma, that can be manipulated into hostility toward the sexual partner or the entire opposite gender. At this root the dark forces strike for their avowed purpose: to obstruct the course of love on earth. Love between man and woman is the very basis of human life and the springboard to cosmic union. Schisms created in these vital centers impede the work of the Universe itself.

The deep schism between male and female created by the women's movement was predictable. The higher forces expected it to be transitional, however, and so it will be. But the transition has been slowed by the Separ-atists, whose tactic is to spread confusion about what constitutes feminine and masculine identity.

The twin union can be realized only between a man complete and cer-tain in his manhood and a woman strong and joyous in her womanhood. What is it to be a woman? What is it to be a man? Are the two simply the same, anatomy aside? The Separatists would have us think so, for to remain in this limbo would nullify the polarity that moves life forward. Alternatively they offer us the simpleminded slogan of divisiveness: Woman is passive, man is aggressive.

Woman was passive long ago, in the early stages of her evolution. She can be wholly passive still, when the shadow influence has her in its grip. But in its developed state, passivity becomes receptivity, that which takes in, gestates, nurtures, brings to birth, and provides a clear channel for the intuition, the direct line to God and creativity itself. It is the yin energy of the Eternal Feminine, and it is not her treasure alone but shared with man. Similarly, the aggressiveness of early man, or man in the shadow, transmutes to creative initiative as he grows into his fuller stature and is revealed in light.

The creative power of the Eternal Masculine resides also in woman, to be employed in her unique way, flowing back to him refined and beautified. These are the conditions of true equality, the kind that need not be fought for; they are built into the soul, needing only to come to recognition and maturity. Such fine distinctions are urged upon us by the guiding forces of Light, while the retrogressive powers work to bind us to the simplistic stereotypes and social myths that breed resentment of those we are fated to greatly love.

To be a woman or to be a man, therefore, is to stand on the ground of our gendered self, allowing it to color the contra-gender within, so that they become as one. A man is yang-based with yin rising; a woman is yin-based with yang rising. They are each within each, and the balances and proportions are the measure of their maturity and gender strength. A truly strong woman is strong in her femininity, as well as in her secondary masculine character; a fully masculine man exhibits all the best of his yang qualities along with yin sensitivities in high degree. When a self-actualized man and self-actualized woman meet and bond, their gender characteristics become shared, flowing in harmonious exchange.

They do not become homogeneous. Male/female energies are separate and distinct; they can be recognized at work within us, and, recognizing them, we can employ them creatively, bringing them into balance and hastening our progress toward the completing union.

In Eastern philosophy yang and yin are defined as follows: yang is the initiating impulse, which divides and delineates; yin is the responsive impulse, which nurtures and reunites. Without yang nothing would come into being; without yin all that comes into being would die. Yang is mental activity in its forceful aspect, yin the imaginative and poetic, exalting the merely mental to the beautiful. Yang goes ahead with things, yin contains things within herself and knows their nature without effort. Yang does, yin is. Yang in his givingness bestows the gifts; yin in her being receives, preserves, enhances, and redistributes them.

Yang constructs, yin instructs; yang implements, yin complements; yang is strength, yin endurance; yang is knowledge, yin the mystery that reveals itself and becomes knowledge. Yang is the discoverer, yin lures toward greater discovery. Yang is the self-developer, inspired by yin, the self-dedicator, for her development and his dedication. Yang is the lover, and therefore beloved; yin is the beloved and the source of love. Yang is will and yin is wisdom, and one without the other is neither, and together they are joy. Yang is as the day, turning into night, and yin the night preceding the day; the one is the force that drives the waves of the ocean forward, the other the force that draws them back so that they may go forward again.

Male and female, yang and yin, are the principles that rule the Universe, demonstrating the separation of a unity into opposites. On the physical level the opposites are experienced as sex. Sex is the ruling force in the world. It is the urge that brings the opposites together to create a vessel for the incoming soul, and thus populates the earth. As a palliative for the loneliness of separation, it rules supreme. And sex is unmatched in the opportunities it offers for the expression of love and of hate. At its finest it allows a glimpse of higher soul states in its ecstatic orgasmic moments. The craving for that ecstasy is what goads the darkened mind in its acts of depravity.

But there comes at last a new balance of forces, a point at which the lower powers begin to lose ground to the higher. People are fond of saying that nothing or no one is all black or white. This is true; it is the condition of our world. But ultimately, in the course of our incarnations, one force gains supremacy over the other. It is boldly stated in saintly beings such as Mother Teresa and Albert Schweitzer, and on the other side, in such as Hitler and Stalin. Thus is depicted the love energy winning or losing the battle for the individual soul.

That separation is paralleled on the inner planes of existence. The struggle begins in the astral, which is closest to the earth. The astral world has several levels, the lowest of which is of near material substance. The inhabitants of the lower astral are those who have held too strongly to the material and selfish pleasures of life, who could not yield them during physical existence and must therefore cling to them for a long time yet. These are the creatures who would inhabit the physical bodies of susceptible persons to continue to play out their selfish motives. Their sexual desires also crave a physical outlet. Many of these individuals have passed over with sadistic impulses unchecked, and they prowl the psychic aura of the earth hunting for suitable human instruments through whom to express themselves.

But other souls, those capable of love, pass quickly to the higher astral after shedding the physical body. In this, the emotional world, the higher emotions become spiritualized and infused with light, while the lower sink from their own weight. Sexuality, the urge for union between gender opposites, continues in transcendent form throughout the heights. Eternally, masculine and feminine will exchange in love and the creative expansion of love that issues from it. In the finer vehicles of the spirit, that which manifested as physical sex finds expression befitting a higher plane.

In the purer stages of the astral, spirit bodies unite in ways more loving and more ecstatic than anything known to mortals. The unions are between male and female souls yearning toward the twin, as they did on earth. This is where the twins find each other if they have not done so in physical life.

They then move as one to the next higher plane, the mental. This is the domain of pure mind. The only emotion remaining is love: mental love, the love of souls, embracing all feelings, purified and ennobled. Here the spirit finds itself clothed in a body of exquisite lightness, sensitivity and power of expression. It is also more substantial, being closer to the Ultimate Reality. The soul is always embodied, but in finer and finer substance with greater capacity for rapture as it ascends.

Union between beings composed of mind-stuff would be bliss uncontainable, were it not that love passes beyond containment into group love. And this is the beginning of the greater reunions lifting toward the transcendental states beyond our conceiving.

How can we know that such states exist? Because flashes of this higher consciousness have always come down to us, transmitted to those advanced persons who are open to receive them. Cosmic consciousness, the direct, existential knowledge of the Divine inclusiveness and bliss of realized union, has consistently descended upon advanced men and women over the centuries. The mystical experience is of this nature. It is also the experience of twin-soul lovers who, by the intensity of their reach, have managed to break through into other dimensions and engage in ecstatic communion while still in their physical bodies, perhaps thousands of miles apart.

In all of this, evil as we know it is left behind. From the great heights of the spirit, the diabolical force is seen for what it is—a manifestation of cosmic darkness, which came into being with the first stirring of Creation. God willed that there be light, and light came forth from the void, and darkness with it. This was the fundamental duality of polar opposites, which existed thereafter on all planes below.

Patricia Joudry and Maurie D. Pressman, Twin Souls

> ... The world is not a vacuum.
> Either we make it an altar for God
> or it is invaded by demons.

There can be no neutrality.
Either we are ministers of the sacred
or slaves of evil.

Abraham Joshua Heschel, *Man's Quest for God*

The devil is no fool. He can get people feeling about heaven the way they ought to feel about hell. He can make them fear the means of grace the way they do not fear sin. And he does so, not by light but by obscurity, not by realities but by shadows; not by clarity and substance, but by dreams and the creatures of psychosis.

Thomas Merton, *The Seven Storey Mountain*

The devil believes in God but he has no God. The Lord is not *his* God. To be at enmity with life is to have nothing to live for. To live forever without life is everlasting death: but it is a living and wakeful death without the consolation of forgetfulness. Now the very essence of this death is the absence of hope. The damned have confirmed themselves in the belief that they cannot hope in God. We sometimes think of the damned as men who think of only themselves as good, since all sin flows from pride that refuses to love. But the pride of those who live as if they believed they were better than anyone else is rooted in a secret failure to believe in their own goodness. If I can see clear enough to realize that I am good because God has willed me to be good, I will at the same time be able to see more clearly the goodness of other men and of God. And I will be more aware of my own failings. I cannot be humble unless I first know that I am good, and know that what is good in me is not my own, and know how easy it is for me to substitute an evil of my own choice for the good that is God's gift to me.

Thomas Merton, No Man Is an Island

Unfortunately there can be no doubt that man is, on the whole, less good than he imagines himself or wants to be. Everyone carries a shadow, and the less it is embodied in the individual's conscious life, the blacker and denser it is. If an inferiority is conscious, one always has a chance to correct it. Furthermore, it is constantly in contact with other interests, so that it is continually subjected to modifications. But if it is repressed and isolated from consciousness, it never gets corrected, and is liable to burst forth suddenly in a moment of unawareness. At all events, it forms an unconscious snag, thwarting our most well-meant intentions.

We carry our past with us, to wit, the primitive and inferior man with his desires and emotions, and it is only with an enormous effort that we can detach ourselves from this burden. If it comes to a neurosis, we invariably have to deal with a considerably intensified shadow. And if such a person wants to be cured it is necessary to find a way in which his conscious personality and his shadow can live together.

C. G. Jung, *Psychology and Religion: West and East*

Evil needs to be understood for what it is: the dynamic of the absence of Light. It is not something that one should prepare to battle, to run from or to outlaw. Understanding evil as the absence of Light automatically requires that we reach for this thing called Light.

Conscious Light is equal to Divinity, to Divine Intelligence. Where there is an absence of Divine Intelligence, that darkness itself maneuvers. It is simply that there is darkness, and we stumble in the darkness. The existence in darkness is not permanent. Every soul will eventually be fully enLightened. A soul with no Light will always come to know Light because there is so much assistance provided to each soul at all times. There is much Light, as we shall see, that is continually surrounding such a soul even though it may not be able to directly penetrate it, and there is much assistance for souls that insist upon living in darkness. The encouragement to take even one thought into Light is always available. Eventually, they always do.

Understanding that evil is the absence of Light does not mean that it is inappropriate to respond to evil.

What is the appropriate response to evil?

The remedy for an absence is a presence. Evil is an absence and, therefore, it cannot be healed with an absence. By hating evil, or one who is engaged in evil, you contribute to the absence of Light and not to its presence. Hatred of evil does not diminish evil, it increases it.

The absence of Light causes the personality to suffer. There is pain. When you hate, you bring the same suffering upon yourself. Hatred of evil affects the one who hates. It makes him or her a hateful person, a person who also has absented himself or herself from Light.

Understanding evil as the absence of Light does not require becoming passive, or disregarding evil actions or evil behavior. If you see a child being abused, or a people being oppressed, for example, it is appropriate that you do what you can to protect the child, or to aid the people, but if there is not compassion in your heart also for those who abuse and oppress—for those who have no compassion—do you not become like them? Compassion is being moved to and by acts of the heart, to and by the energy of love. If you strike without compassion against the darkness, you yourself enter the darkness.

Understanding that evil is the absence of Light challenges the perception of power as external. Can an absence be defeated? An evil person can be arrested, but can evil be arrested? An evil group can be imprisoned, but can evil be imprisoned? A compassionate heart is more effective against evil than an army. An army can engage another army, but it cannot engage evil. A compassionate heart can engage evil directly—it can bring Light where there was no Light.

Understanding evil as the absence of Light requires you to examine the choices that you make each moment in terms of whether they move you toward Light or away from it. It allows you to look with compassion upon those who engage in evil activities, even as you challenge their activities, and thus protects you from the creation of negative karma. It permits you to see that the place to begin the task of eliminating evil is within yourself. This is the appropriate response to evil.

Gary Zukav, *The Seat of the Soul*

Facing Our Shadow

One of the most important aspects of healing ourselves and the earth is the willingness to face our "shadow"—the feelings and parts of ourselves that we have rejected, repressed, or disowned. Our society has tremendous prohibitions against feeling too much. We are afraid to feel too much fear, hurt, sadness, or anger, and oftentimes we are also afraid to feel too much love, passion, or joy! And we're definitely afraid of our natural sensuality and sexuality.

As children we learn to reject and repress these unacceptable feelings and parts of ourselves. Most of us are encouraged either to repress our vulnerable feelings and become strong and powerful, or to repress our power and aggression and be gentle and vulnerable. Or we may repress both vulnerability and power (as well as sexuality, of course) and become nice, safe, middle-of-the-roaders. In any case we lose not only major parts of our personality and being, but an enormous amount of our life force.

The feelings and parts of ourselves that we have repressed do not go away just because we don't want them. They are necessary parts of us, parts we actually need for our survival. If they are not allowed their natural expression, they go underground and fester inside of us, building up steam, needing eventual release. If we do not find ways to express them, they begin to "leak out" in distorted ways, or they begin to lead us into life situations which will give them a chance to emerge. For example, if you have repressed your power, you will have anger building up inside of you. If you don't find a way to express your anger in a direct, constructive way, it will leak out as indirect, covert hostility, or it will eventually burst forth as explosive rage or violence. It might well attract you toward angry people, with the unconscious intention of triggering your own anger.

If attempts to find expression fail or are blocked, the repressed feelings will eventually make your body sick. It is my belief that most illnesses are caused by repressed or disowned energies within us.

Personal healing on all levels—physical, emotional, mental, and spiritual—comes when we get in touch with our disowned energies. As we begin to accept them as vital parts of ourselves, we begin to find safe, constructive modes of expression. Once we get to know these parts of ourselves, we find they are not as scary as we had imagined. In fact, when they are expressed and integrated, they take their place as important facets of our nature. Through integrating all aspects of ourselves, we become whole.

Everything in the universe, including every part of ourselves, wants love and acceptance. Anything in life that we don't accept will simply make trouble for us until we make peace with it. Once we do, the trouble is over.

Here is an image I have found useful to illustrate this point: Suppose you lived in a large mansion, but only occupied a few of the rooms. These rooms are bright, clean, and nicely furnished and decorated. You lead a reasonably good life in them. However, you never enter any of the other rooms in the mansion because you have been told there may be frightening things in them. You keep all the doors in the unoccupied part of the house locked and spend a lot of time worrying about what might escape from the dark part of the house into your safe area. At night you imagine all kinds of noises. A great deal of your life energy is taken up with worrying and defending yourself.

Finally you become tired of living this way, and decide to take control of the situation and examine some of the rooms. Perhaps you ask a trusted friend or two to come with you, so you will feel safer. You take a big, bright lantern and venture into the first unknown room. You find some unattractive, old-fashioned furniture, cobwebs, and a few beautiful antiques. Once you clean up the room, give away the things you don't need, and decorate it to enhance the treasures you've found, you have another unique and beautiful room in your home. When you are ready, you can proceed to the next room. Eventually, you will find yourself living in a large, beautiful, well-lighted mansion. Since you no longer have to spend your time defending yourself against the unknown darkness, you can turn your energy to more creative things.

In order to become "enlightened," we must shine the light of consciousness into any dark places that we have not yet explored. This is true on a planetary level as well as a personal one. Just as we individuals have repressed aspects of ourselves, the mass consciousness has disowned much of its energy. So we have a large collective shadow to explore.

In modern society, much of what has been repressed involves the energies related to the earth—our primal selves. We have identified too frequently with the masculine rational, active, work-oriented, orderly principles and denied the more feminine emotional, intuitive, sensual aspects. I believe this is why we are having an overwhelming epidemic of drug addiction—drugs release those disowned energies. These energies have to be expressed somehow, or we would not survive. The healing for our drug problems will come as we find more natural and constructive ways for society to support all of us, and young people in particular, in expressing energies that have been restricted, such as intuition, artistic creativity, sexuality, playfulness, and just "being."

We are also having difficulty right now dealing with our natural aggressive energy. In previous times, societies channeled this energy through great numbers of men engaging in warfare. In modern times, this is increasingly dangerous and unacceptable. Aggression is frowned upon in civilized society, except in a few sanctioned ways—through sports or business. So we have our leaders toying frustratedly with their weapons systems, not daring to use them but not willing to give them up, either, and we have increasing outbreaks of violence in our cities as well. We need to find constructive ways for all of us, men *and* women, to channel our natural aggressive energy creatively.

Many people, especially those in the spiritual and new age movements, believe that we can bring peace and light to the world by focusing on the light, trying to be unconditionally loving, visualizing peace, and so forth. There is a fundamental misunderstanding here. By trying to focus only on the things we deem "positive" and ignoring or repressing the rest, we are simply perpetuating the polarization of light and dark forces. Ironically, this further distorts and empowers the very energies we are trying to avoid.

We must deeply recognize that there is no split between "spiritual" and "unspiritual," good and bad. All aspects of life are elements of the life force and facets of the divine. True healing comes from owning and accepting all of life's energies within ourselves.

Ultimately, the collective healing of our planet can only come through the personal commitment of us all as individuals, in exploring and embracing the shadow in our own lives.

Shakti Gawain, *Return to the Garden: A Journey of Discovery*

Recognition of the reality of evil necessarily relativizes the good, and the evil likewise, converting both into halves of a paradoxical whole.

C. G. Jung, *Memories, Dreams, Reflections*

The Problem of Good and Evil

The moralist enjoins the practice of virtue by laying down the dictum that good must create good and evil must create evil in accordance with the law that like creates like. "Do unto others as you would be done by," he says, because then they will indeed so do to you. The strict pacifist, for example, would never admit the use of violence or a resort to war in any circumstances whatsoever on the ground that violence leads always to further violence. Does any such strict rule of moral return prevail in actual life?

The rule is true to a certain extent in tendency and works sometimes well enough and the prudential intelligence of man takes some account of it in action, but it is not true all the way and all the time. It is evident enough that hatred, violence, injustice are likely to create an answering hatred, violence and injustice and that I can only indulge these propensities with impunity if I am sufficiently powerful to defy resistance or so long as I am at once strong and prudent enough to provide against their natural reactions. It is true also that by doing good and kindness I create a certain good-will in others and can rely under ordinary or favourable circumstances not so much on gratitude and return in kind as on their support and favour. But this good and this evil are both of them movements of the ego, and on the mixed egoism of human nature there can be no safe or positive reliance. An egoistic selfish strength, if it knows what to do and where to stop, even a certain measure of violence and injustice, if it is strong and skilful, cunning, fraud, many kinds of evil, do actually pay in man's dealing with man hardly less than in the animal's with the animal, and on the other hand the doer of good who counts on a return or reward finds himself as often as not disappointed of his bargained recompense.

Why is this so?

It is because the weakness of human nature worships the power that tramples on it, does homage to successful strength, can return to every kind of strong or skilful imposition, belief, acceptance, obedience: it can crouch and fawn

and admire even amidst movements of hatred and terror; it has singular loy-
alties and unreasoning instincts. And its disloyalties too are as unreasoning or
light and fickle: it takes just dealing and beneficence as its right and forgets or
cares not to repay. And there is worse; for justice, mercy, beneficence, kindness are often enough rewarded by their opposites and ill-will an answer to
good-will is a brutally common experience. If something in the world and in
man returns good for good and evil for evil, it as often returns evil for good
and, with or without a conscious moral intention, good for evil. And even an
unegoistic virtue or a divine good and love entering the world awakens hostile reactions. Attila and Jenghiz on the throne to the end, Christ on the cross
and Socrates drinking his potion of hemlock are not very clear evidence for
any optimistic notion of a law of moral return in the world of human nature.

If not in human nature, does this law operate in the action of the
larger world measures?

There is little more sign of its sure existence in the world measures. Actually
in the cosmic dispensation evil comes out of good and good out of evil and
there seems to be no exact correspondence between the moral and the vital
measures. All that we can say is that good done tends to increase the sum and
total power of good in the world and the greater this grows, the greater is
likely to be the sum of human happiness, and that evil done tends to increase
the sum and total power of evil in the world and the greater this grows, the
greater is likely to be the sum of human suffering and, eventually, man or
nation doing evil has in some way to pay for it, but not often in any intelligi-
bly graded or apportioned measure and not always in clearly translating
terms of vital good fortune and ill fortune.

Sri Aurobindo, in Kisher Gandhi's *Lights on Life Problems*

Good and Evil are the two-forked trunk of the Tree of Life, sprung from a
single Seed. Each fork alike has its support in the root-system of the One
Tree. The same sap flows to and nourishes both forks equally.

Or Good and Evil may be viewed as being like twins, offspring of one
Father-Mother. They are compensatory, the one to the other, like the right
and left ventricles of the heart. They are the two hands doing the work of the
Cosmic Body, the two feet by which humanity traverses the Highway of Life
leading to the City of *Nirvāṇa*. If either be amputated, there is crippling.
Virtue of itself leads to good results, vice to evil results. The Sage who knows
both Good and Evil to be one and inseparable is transcendent over both. It is

only in the *Sangsāra* that opposition is operative. In the Beyond-Nature, in the Voidness, there is but the Unmodified, the Primordial, the Unformed, the Unmade, the Unborn, the All-Embracing Womb whence comes forth into being the manifested Universe. The *Dharma*, or the Supra-mundane Law of the Cosmos, enthroned upon the Immutable Throne of *Karma*, crowned with the Double Crown of the Two Opposites, holding the Sceptre of At-one-ment, robed in the gold and purple robes of Justice, guides all sentient creatures to Understanding and Wisdom by means of Good and Evil.

This Section, which is necessarily the longest and in some respects the most important part of this Introduction, will be fittingly concluded by summarizing in a tenfold category the essentialities of the moral standard of the Oriental Sages, by which alone the Great *Guru* should be judged:

(1) Good and Evil, when viewed exoterically, are a duality, neither member of which is conceivable or capable of mentally existing independently of the other. Being thus inseparable, Good and Evil, when viewed esoterically, are intrinsically a unity.

(2) A thing is considered to be either good or evil in accordance with the mental state in which it is viewed, the state itself being determined by racial, social, or religious environment and heredity. Otherwise stated, as by Shakespeare, "there is nothing either good or bad, but thinking makes it so."*

(3) There being nothing which has other than an illusory existence in the mundane mind, nothing can be said to be either good or evil *per se*.

(4) Inasmuch as it is the motive and intent initiating an act which determines its character, no act, in itself, can be either good or evil; for the same act when performed independently by two persons, one with altruistic the other with selfish motive and intent, becomes both good and evil.

(5) There being nothing which is good *per se* or evil *per se*, Good and Evil, like all dualities, are hallucinatory concepts of the *sangsārically* constituted mind of their percipient. As such, like the world of appearances (which is merely a conglomerate of *sangsāric* concepts), they have only a relative, not an absolute, or true, existence.

(6) Hence, doctrines concerning a state of absolute evil called Hell and a state of absolute good called Heaven, being based entirely upon *sangsārically* born concepts, are also entirely relative and illusory; *Nirvāṇa* is beyond good and evil.

* Cf. Hamlet, ii. ii. 245.

(7) Accordingly, all standards of morality founded upon any such doctrines are unstable; and, like the *Sangsāra* itself, by which they are circumscribed, from which they arise, and upon which they are dependent for their illusoriness, they are ever-changing and transitory, like the mundane mind of their creators and advocates, and, therefore, unsatisfactory and unfixable.

(8) Not until mankind shall transcend dualism and phenomenal appearances, and realize the natural at-one-ment of all living creatures, will they be able to formulate a sound standard of morality.

(9) Such a standard will be based entirely, not partially, as are prevailing standards of morality, upon worldwide *Bodhisattvic* altruism.

(10) Its Golden Rule may be stated thus: "Do unto others and to yourself only that which fosters Divine Wisdom and will guide every sentient being to the *Bodhi* Path of transcendence over the *Sangsāra* and to the Final Goal of Deliverance from Ignorance."*

C. G. Jung, General Introduction to
The Tibetan Book of the Great Liberation

In a sermon on the Day of Atonement, the Rabbi of Ger warned against self-torture:

"He who has done ill and talks about it and thinks about it all the time does not cast the base thing he did out of his thoughts, and whatever one thinks, therein one is, one's soul is wholly and utterly in what one thinks, and so he dwells in baseness. He will certainly not be able to turn, for his spirit will grow coarse and his heart stubborn, and in addition to this he may be overcome by gloom. What would you? Rake the muck this way, rake the muck that way—it will always be muck. Have I sinned, or have I not sinned—what does Heaven get out of it? In the time I am brooding over it I could be stringing pearls for the delight of Heaven. That is why it is written: 'Depart from evil and do good'—turn wholly away from evil, do not dwell upon it, and do good. You have done wrong? Then counteract it by doing right." [Way, 36-37]

Martin Buber, *To Hallow This Life*

* The teaching, that men should do unto others what they would that others should do unto them, is capable of misconstruction, or misapplication, notwithstanding that its intent is obviously right. For so long as men are fettered to the *Sangsāra* and misled by its delusive glamorous mirages, and thus in bondage to Ignorance, they are quite incapable of knowing in what right action, either to themselves or to others, consists.

The One Self

All are deceived, do what the One Power dictates,
    Yet each thinks his own will his nature moves;
The hater knows not 'tis himself he hates,
    The lover knows not 'tis himself he loves.

In all is one being many bodies bear;
    Here Krishna flutes upon the forest mood,
Here Shiva sits ash-smeared, with matted hair.
    But Shiva and Krishna are the single God.

In us too Krishna seeks for love and joy,
    In us too Shiva struggles with the world's grief.
One Self in all of us endures annoy,
    Cries in his pain and asks his fate's relief.

My rival's downfall is my own disgrace;
I look on my enemy and see Krishna's face.

Sri Aurobindo, *Collected Poems*

The problem of evil, that is to say the reconciling of our failures, even the purely physical ones, with creative goodness and creative power, will always remain one of the most disturbing mysteries of the universe for both our hearts and our minds. A full understanding of the suffering of God's creatures (like that of the pains of the damned) presupposes in us an appreciation of the nature and value of "participate being" which, for lack of any point of comparison, we cannot have. Yet this much we can see: on the one hand, the work which God has undertaken in uniting Himself intimately to created beings presupposes in them a slow preparation in the course of which they (*who already exist, but are not yet complete*) cannot of their nature avoid the risks (aggravated by an original fault) involved in the imperfect organisation of the multiple principle in them and around them; and on the other hand, because the final victory of good over evil can only be completed in the total organisation of the world, our infinitely short individual lives cannot hope to benefit here below from access to the Promised Land. We are like soldiers who fall during the assault which leads to peace. God does not therefore suffer a preliminary defeat in our defeat because, although we appear to succumb individually, the world, in which we shall live again, triumphs in and through our deaths.

But this first aspect of His victory, which is enough to assure us of His omnipotence, is completed by another manifestation—possibly more direct and in any case more immediately palpable for each of us—of His universal authority. In virtue of His very perfections, God cannot ordain that the elements of a world in the course of growth—or at least of a fallen world in the process of rising again—should avoid shocks and diminishments, even moral ones: *necessarium est ut scandala eveniant*. But God will make it good— He will take His revenge, if one may use the expression—by making evil itself serve the higher good of His faithful, the very evil which the present state of creation does not allow Him to suppress immediately. Like an artist making use of a fault or an impurity in the stone he is sculpting or the bronze he is casting so as to produce more exquisite lines or a more beautiful tone, God, without sparing us the partial deaths, nor the final death, which form an essential part of our lives, transfigures them by integrating them in a better plan—*provided we trust lovingly in Him*. Not only our unavoidable ills but our faults, even our most deliberate ones, can be embraced in that transformation, provided always we repent of them. Not everything is immediately good to those who seek God; but everything is capable of becoming good: *omnia convertuntur in bonum*.

Pierre Teilhard de Chardin, *The Divine Milieu*

✢ 9 ✢

The Hidden Face of God

"Where is God?"

It is at a time of greatest suffering that this question is asked. It was inscribed on a wall at Auschwitz and beneath it someone had scratched "Where is man?"

The following pieces are categorized under the subjects of imprisonment, illness, loss, loneliness, and grief and show where man has found God in a landscape of unmitigated despair.

Through the voices of concentration camp survivors, the horrors of the Holocaust still unfold before us. But along with a comprehension of the full scope of such evil, come accounts of the transcending power of faith and hope. Jewish writer Martin Buber, asks: "In this our own time, one asks again and again: how is a Jewish life still possible after Auschwitz? I would like to frame this question more correctly: how is life with God still possible in a time in which there is an Auschwitz?" and later answers by acknowledging the "cruel and merciful Lord."

In one of the most detailed and vivid accounts of life in a prison camp, Viktor Frankl, a survivor of four years at Auschwitz, shows how the inner strength his faith and love gave him helped him to survive and led him to see the hidden face of God. It's a lesson in believing and knowing that the suffering was part of God's work. The victims of evil who were not broken by it, absorbed it, lived it. M. Scott Peck suggests that when this happens, "there is a slight shift in the balance of power in the world." This healing of evil by suffering it and surviving it promotes the sufferer to a deeper relationship with God. It shows us that we do not really know what the greater purpose is, nor particularly at the time of our greatest suffering what our role is in promoting it. A common assumption is that we know the way it should or shouldn't be; a leap of faith would be to acknowledge that God's purpose is hardly ever revealed in straight clear lines. But there is humility in *not* understanding the levels of God's lessons, but accepting them as they are.

Sickness also offers spiritual gifts, for it is how we suffer, how we receive and communicate and love as sufferers, which is the true trial. Canadian writer Michael Ignatieff's sensitive piece is taken from his novel *Scar Tissue*, a son's study in understanding his mother's affliction with Alzheimer's disease. It is a simple example of how knowledge and wisdom are bestowed upon the sufferer. It also reveals how illness becomes a gift to the visitor; the ill by becoming conscious of the greatness of the gift of suffering open "the gates of truth."

A benevolent God is frequently called to question when we experience loss. How could this happen to me? Again, "Where is God?" Thomas Merton wrote: "Suffering is wasted if we suffer alone." It is by accepting aloneness and believing in loss as a gift that we join in the aloneness of God. Krishnamurti wrote: "One can truly communicate only when there is aloneness." God calls us to him when the noise within has stopped, when we are quiet enough to listen.

> "I muse this blessed morning
> Sad in solitude yet somehow not alone."
> —DOROTHY LIVESAY

><

→ Imprisonment ←

The Bible knows of God's hiding His face, of times when the contact between heaven and earth seems to be interrupted. God seems to withdraw Himself utterly from the earth and no longer to participate in its existence. The space of history is then full of noise, but empty of the divine breath. For one who believes in the living God, who knows about Him, and is fated to spend his life in a time of His hiddenness, it is very difficult to live.

There is a psalm, the 82nd, in which life in a time of God's hiddenness is described in a picture of startling cruelty. It is assumed that God has entrusted the government of mankind to a host of angels and commanded them to realize justice on earth and to protect the weak, the poor, and the helpless from the encroachments of the wrongdoers. But they "judge unjustly" and "respect the persons of the wicked." Now the Psalmist envisions how God draws the unfaithful angels before His seat, judges them, and passes sentence upon them: they are to become mortal. But the Psalmist awakes from his vision and looks about him: iniquity still reigns on earth with unlimited power. And he cries to God: "Arise, O God, judge the earth!"

This cry is to be understood as a late, but even more powerful, echo of that bold speech of the patriarch arguing with God: "The judge of all the earth, will He not do justice?!" It reinforces and augments that speech; its implication is: Will He allow injustice to reign further? And so the cry transmitted to us by Scripture becomes our own cry, which bursts from our hearts and rises to our lips in a time of God's hiddenness. For this is what the biblical word does to us: it confronts us with the human address as one that in spite of everything is heard and in spite of everything may expect an answer.

In this our own time, one asks again and again: How is a Jewish life still possible after Auschwitz? I would like to frame this question more correctly: how is a life with God still possible in a time in which there is an Auschwitz? The estrangement has become too cruel, the hiddenness too deep. One can still "believe" in the God who allowed those things to happen, but can one still speak to Him? Can one still hear His word? Can one still, as an individual and as a people, enter at all into a dialogic relationship with Him? Can one still call to Him? Dare we recommend to the survivors of Auschwitz, the Job of the gas chambers: "Give thanks unto the Lord, for He is good; for His mercy endureth forever"?

But how about Job himself? He not only laments, but he charges that the "cruel" God (30:21) has "removed his right" from him (27:2) and thus that the judge of all the earth acts against justice. And he receives an answer from God. But what God says to him does not answer the charge; it does not even touch upon it. The true answer that Job receives is God's appearance only, only this that distance turns into nearness, that "his eye sees Him" (42:5), that he knows Him again. Nothing is explained, nothing adjusted; wrong has not become right, nor cruelty kindness. Nothing has happened but that man again hears God's address.

The mystery has remained unsolved, but it has become his, it has become man's.

And we?

We—by that is meant all those who have not got over what happened and will not get over it. How is it with us? Do we stand overcome before the hidden face of God like the tragic hero of the Greeks before faceless fate? No, rather even now we contend, we too, with God, even with Him, the Lord of Being, whom we once, we here, chose for our Lord. We do not put up with earthly being; we struggle for its redemption, and struggling we appeal to the help of our Lord, who is again and still a hiding one. In such a state we await His voice, whether it comes out of the storm or out of a still-ness that follows it. Though His coming appearance resemble no earlier one, we shall recognize again our cruel and merciful Lord.

Martin Buber, On Judaism

By Degrees

...Awareness of God does not come by degrees:
from timidity to intellectual temerity;
   from guesswork, reluctance, to certainty;
it is not a decision reached at the crossroads of doubt.
It comes when, drifting in the wilderness,
   having gone astray,
we suddenly behold the immutable polar star.
Out of endless anxiety,
out of denial and despair,
the soul bursts out in speechless crying.

Abraham Joshua Heschel, Man Is Not Alone

Experiences in a Concentration Camp

In spite of all the enforced physical and mental primitiveness of the life in a concentration camp, it was possible for spiritual life to deepen. Sensitive peo-ple who were used to a rich intellectual life may have suffered much pain (they were often of a delicate constitution), but the damage to their inner selves was less. They were able to retreat from their terrible surroundings to a life of inner riches and spiritual freedom. Only in this way can one explain the appar-ent paradox that some prisoners of a less hardy make-up often seemed to sur-vive camp life better than did those of a robust nature. In order to make myself clear, I am forced to fall back on personal experience. Let me tell what hap-pened on those early mornings when we had to march to our work site.

There were shouted commands: "Detachment, forward march! Left-2-3-4! Left-2-3-4! Left-2-3-4! Left-2-3-4! First man about, left and left and left and left! Caps off!" These words sound in my ears even now. At the order "Caps off!" we passed the gate of the camp, and searchlights were trained upon us. Whoever did not march smartly got a kick. And worse off was the man who, because of the cold, had pulled his cap back over his ears before permission was given.

We stumbled on in the darkness, over big stones and through large puddles, along the one road leading from the camp. The accompanying guards kept shouting at us and driving us with the butts of their rifles. Anyone with very sore feet supported himself on his neighbor's arm. Hardly a word was spoken; the icy wind did not encourage talk. Hiding his mouth behind his upturned collar, the man marching next to me whispered suddenly: "If our wives could see us now! I do hope they are better off in their camps and don't know what is happening to us."

That brought thoughts of my own wife to mind. And as we stumbled on for miles, slipping on icy spots, supporting each other time and again, dragging one another up and onward, nothing was said, but we both knew: each of us was thinking of his wife. Occasionally I looked at the sky, where the stars were fading and the pink light of the morning was beginning to spread behind a dark bank of clouds. But my mind clung to my wife's image, imagining it with an uncanny acuteness. I heard her answering me, saw her smile, her frank and encouraging look. Real or not, her look was then more luminous than the sun which was beginning to rise.

A thought transfixed me: for the first time in my life I saw the truth as it is set into song by so many poets, proclaimed as the final wisdom by so many thinkers. The truth—that love is the ultimate and the highest goal to which man can aspire. Then I grasped the meaning of the greatest secret that human poetry and human thought and belief have to impart: *The salvation of man is through love and in love.* I understood how a man who has nothing left in this world still may know bliss, be it only for a brief moment, in the contemplation of his beloved. In a position of utter desolation, when man cannot express himself in positive action, when his only achievement may consist in enduring his sufferings in the right way—an honorable way—in such a position man can, through loving contemplation of the image he carries of his beloved, achieve fulfillment. For the first time in my life I was able to understand the meaning of the words, "The angels are lost in perpetual contemplation of an infinite glory."

In front of me a man stumbled and those following him fell on top of him. The guard rushed over and used his whip on them all. Thus my thoughts were interrupted for a few minutes. But soon my soul found its way back from the prisoner's existence to another world, and I resumed talk with my loved one: I asked her questions, and she answered; she questioned me in return, and I answered.

"Stop!" We had arrived at our work site. Everybody rushed into the dark hut in the hope of getting a fairly decent tool. Each prisoner got a spade or a pickaxe.

"Can't you hurry up, you pigs?" Soon we had resumed the previous day's positions in the ditch. The frozen ground cracked under the point of the pickaxes, and sparks flew. The men were silent, their brains numb.

My mind still clung to the image of my wife. A thought crossed my mind: I didn't even know if she were still alive. I knew only one thing—which I have learned well by now: Love goes very far beyond the physical person of the beloved. It finds its deepest meaning in his spiritual being, his inner self. Whether or not he is actually present, whether or not he is still alive at all, ceases somehow to be of importance.

I did not know whether my wife was alive, and I had no means of finding out (during all my prison life there was no outgoing or incoming mail); but at that moment it ceased to matter. There was no need for me to know; nothing could touch the strength of my love, my thoughts, and the image of my beloved. Had I known then that my wife was dead, I think that I would still have given myself, undisturbed by that knowledge, to the contemplation of her image, and that my mental conversation with her would have been just as vivid and just as satisfying. "Set me like a seal upon thy heart, love is as strong as death."

This intensification of inner life helped the prisoner find a refuge from the emptiness, desolation and spiritual poverty of his existence, by letting him escape into the past. When given free rein, his imagination played with past events, often not important ones, but minor happenings and trifling things. His nostalgic memory glorified them and they assumed a strange character. Their world and their existence seemed very distant and the spirit reached out for them longingly: In my mind I took bus rides, unlocked the front door of my apartment, answered my telephone, switched on the electric lights. Our thoughts often centered on such details, and these memories could move one to tears.

As the inner life of the prisoner tended to become more intense, he also experienced the beauty of art and nature as never before. Under their influence he sometimes even forgot his own frightful circumstances. If someone had seen our faces on the journey from Auschwitz to a Bavarian camp as we beheld the mountains of Salzburg with their summits glowing in the sunset, through the little barred windows of the prison carriage, he would never have believed that those were the faces of men who had given up all hope of life and liberty. Despite that factor—or maybe because of it—we were carried away by nature's beauty, which we had missed for so long.

In camp, too, a man might draw the attention of a comrade working next to him to a nice view of the setting sun shining through the tall trees of the Bavarian woods (as in the famous watercolor by Dürer), the same woods in which we had built an enormous, hidden munitions plant. One evening, when we were already resting on the floor of our hut, dead tired, soup bowls in hand, a fellow prisoner rushed in and asked us to run out to the assembly grounds and see the wonderful sunset. Standing outside we saw sinister clouds glowing in the west and the whole sky alive with clouds of ever-changing shapes and colors, from steel blue to blood red. The desolate gray mud huts provided a sharp contrast, while the puddles on the muddy ground reflected the glowing sky. Then, after minutes of moving silence, one prisoner said to another, "How beautiful the world *could* be!"

Another time we were at work in a trench. The dawn was gray around us; gray was the sky above; gray the snow in the pale light of dawn; gray the rags in which my fellow prisoners were clad, and gray their faces. I was again conversing silently with my wife, or perhaps I was struggling to find the *reason* for my sufferings, my slow dying. In a last violent protest against the hopelessness of imminent death, I sensed my spirit piercing through the enveloping gloom. I felt it transcend that hopeless, meaningless world, and from somewhere I heard a victorious "Yes" in answer to my question of the existence of an ultimate purpose. At that moment a light was lit in a distant farmhouse, which stood on the horizon as if painted there, in the midst of the miserable gray of a dawning morning in Bavaria. *"Et lux in tenebris lucet"*— and the light shineth in the darkness. For hours I stood hacking at the icy ground. The guard passed by, insulting me, and once again I communed with my beloved. More and more I felt that she was present, that she was with me; I had the feeling that I was able to touch her, able to stretch out my hand and grasp hers. The feeling was very strong: she was *there*. Then, at that very moment, a bird flew down silently and perched just in front of me, on the heap of soil which I had dug up from the ditch, and looked steadily at me.

Viktor E. Frankl, *Man's Search for Meaning*

The healing of evil—scientifically or otherwise—can be accomplished only by the love of individuals. A willing sacrifice is required. The individual healer must allow his or her own soul to become the battleground. He or she must sacrificially *absorb* the evil.

Then what prevents the destruction of that soul? If one takes the evil itself into one's heart, like a spear, how can one's goodness still survive? Even if the evil is vanquished thereby, will not the good be also? What will have been achieved beyond some meaningless trade-off?

I cannot answer this in language other than mystical. I can say only that there is a mysterious alchemy whereby the victim becomes the victor. As C. S. Lewis wrote: "When a willing victim who had committed no treachery was killed in a traitor's stead, the Table would crack and Death itself would start working backwards."

I do not know how this occurs. But I know that it does. I know that good people can deliberately allow themselves to be pierced by the evil of others—to be broken thereby yet somehow not broken—to even be killed in some sense and yet still survive and not succumb. Whenever this happens there is a slight shift in the balance of power in the world.

M. Scott Peck, *People of the Lie*

The more we believe that God hurts only to heal, the less we can believe that there is any use in begging for tenderness. A cruel man might be bribed— might grow tired of his vile sport—might have a temporary fit of mercy, as alcoholics have fits of sobriety. But suppose that what you are up against is a surgeon whose intentions are wholly good. The kinder and more conscientious he is, the more inexorably he will go on cutting. If he yielded to your entreaties, if he stopped before the operation was complete, all the pain up to that point would have been useless. But is it credible that such extremities of torture should be necessary for us? Well, take your choice. The tortures occur. If they are unnecessary, then there is no God or a bad one. If there is a good God, then these tortures are necessary. For no even moderately good Being could possibly inflict or permit them if they weren't.

Either way, we're for it.

What do people mean when they say "I am not afraid of God because I know He is good?" Have they never even been to a dentist?

C. S. Lewis, *A Grief Observed*

Suffering is a great gift of God;
those who accept it willingly,
those who love deeply,
those who offer themselves
know its value.

Mother Teresa, in Edward Le Joly,
Mother Teresa of Calcutta

In moments of weakness and distress it is good to tread closely in God's footsteps.

Alexander Solzhenitsyn

✦ Illness ✦

"I was consoling a little girl who was sick and had much pain," said Mother. "I told her, 'You should be happy that God sends you suffering, because your sufferings are a proof that God loves you much. Your sufferings are kisses from Jesus.' 'Then, Mother,' answered the little girl, 'please ask Jesus not to kiss me so much.'"

Mother Teresa, in Edward Le Joly,
Mother Teresa of Calcutta

Every night at about eleven o'clock, it started up again. First came the tears. Gradually they increased in intensity. The rhythm became more accelerated and developed into a series of rattles which cascaded through the dividing wall. A ten-year-old Muslim boy was dying of osteotuberculosis in the hovel next door. His name was Sabia.

"Why this agony of an innocent in a place already scarred by so much suffering?" protested an indignant Kovalski.

During the first few evenings the priest had succumbed to cowardice. He had stopped up his ears with cotton so that he would not hear. "I was like Job on the brink of revolt," he was to explain. "In vain I scoured the Scriptures by the light of my oil lamp. I could not find a satisfactory explanation for the idea that God could let such a thing happen. Who could ever venture to say to a child like that, writhing in pain: 'Blessed are the poor, for theirs is the Kingdom of Heaven; blessed are the sorrowful, for they shall find consolation; blessed are those who thirst, for they shall be satisfied?' The prophet Isaiah tried hard to justify the suffering of the innocent. It was *our* suffering that the boy was enduring, Isaiah affirmed, and he would help to save us from our sins. The idea that the suffering of one human being could help to save the world was certainly very alluring, but how could I concede that the suffering of my little neighbor was part of that redemptive process? Everything in me rebelled against the idea."

It took several nights before Stephan Kovalski could accept the experience of listening to Sabia's cries and several more for him to listen to them not only with his ears but also with his heart. He was torn between his religious faith and his very human feelings of revolt. Had he any right to be happy, to sing praises to God while that intolerable torment was going on right next to him? Every night when his young neighbor began to groan again, he emptied himself and prayed. Then he ceased to hear the tears, the cries, the noises; he ceased to notice the rustle of the rats in the darkness; he no longer smelled the stench of the blocked drain outside his door. He entered into what he described as a state of "weightlessness."

"In the beginning my prayer was exclusively concerned with young Sabia's agony. I begged the Lord to alleviate his suffering, to lessen his sacrifice. And if, in his judgment, this trial was really useful for the redemption of the sins of mankind, then I asked him, the Father who had not hesitated to sacrifice his own son, to let me assume a part of it, to let me suffer instead of that child." Night after night, his eyes turned in the darkness toward the picture of the Sacred Shroud, Stephan Kovalski prayed until the groans were still. Tirelessly he prayed and pleaded: "You who died on the Cross to save mankind, help me to understand the mystery of suffering. Help me to transcend it. Help me, above all, to fight against its causes, against the lack of love, against hatred and against all the injustices that give rise to it."

The illness of his young neighbor grew worse and the sounds of his agony increased. One morning the priest caught the bus to the nearest hospital.

"I need a syringe and a dose of morphine. It's very urgent," he said to the attendant in charge of the hospital pharmacy, handing him thirty rupees.

"Since his illness was incurable and my prayer had proved abortive," he would later say to justify himself, "Sabia should at least be able to die in peace."

Helped by her three daughters, aged eleven, eight, and five, Sabia's mother spent her days squatting in the alleyway, making paper bags out of old newspapers. She was a widow and this activity represented the only income with which she could support her family. A hundred times a day she had to get up and clear everything out of the way to allow a cycle-car or cart to pass. Yet Stephan Kovalski had noticed that her smile never deserted her.

Hostile gazes beset him as soon as he stopped outside Sabia's hovel. Why did this infidel want to visit the little Muslim who was dying? Was he going to try to convert the boy to his religion? Tell him that Allah was not the true God? There were many in the area who mistrusted the priest. So many stories were told about the zeal of Christian missionaries, about their diabolical capacity to wheedle their way in anywhere. Wasn't it merely to reduce their vigilance that this particular one wore trousers and sneakers instead of a cassock? Nevertheless, Sabia's mother welcomed him with her remarkable smile. She sent her eldest daughter to fetch him a cup of tea from the old Hindu and invited the priest to come in. The smell of putrid flesh caused him to hesitate for a few seconds on the threshold. Then he plunged into the half-light.

The little Muslim boy was lying on a mattress of rags, his arms crossed, his skin pitted with sores, crawling with lice, his knees half bent back over his fleshless torso. Stephan Kovalski drew nearer to him and the boy opened his eyes. His gaze lit up with a spark of joy. Kovalski was totally overwhelmed.

"How could I believe my own eyes? How could so much serenity radiate from that little martyred frame?" His fingers tightened on the vial of morphine.

"Salaam, Sabia," he murmured, smiling.

"Salaam, *Daddah*," responded the child cheerfully. "What have you got in your hand? Sweets?"

Startled, Stephan Kovalski dropped the vial which shattered as it fell. "Sabia had no need of morphine. His features were imbued with a peace that quite disarmed me. Bruised, mutilated, crucified as he was, he remained undefeated. He had just given me the most precious gift of all: a secret reason never to despair, a light in the darkness."

Dominique Lapierre, *The City of Joy*

Enduring Pain

From youth until old age Rabbi Yitzhak Eisik suffered from an ailment which was known to involve very great pain. His physician once asked him how he managed to endure such pain without complaining or groaning. He replied: "You would understand that readily enough if you thought of the pain as scrubbing and soaking the soul in a strong solution. Since this is so, one cannot do otherwise than accept such pain with love and not grumble. After a time, one gains the strength to endure the present pain. It is always only the question of a moment, for the pain which has passed is no longer present, and who would be so foolish as to concern himself with future pain!"

Martin Buber, *Tales of the Hasidim*

He said he had someone he wanted me to meet. "A teacher," he said, as we eased into the morning rush-hour traffic on the cross-town expressway. "Like you."

The patient had come in with symptoms of numbness and pain in his muscles and joints. That was five years ago. He had ordered some tests, but they were just to be sure. He knew right away.

"Classic presentation. ALS."

My brother spelled it out for me, "Amyotrophic lateral sclerosis, also known as motor neurone disease."

"Stephen Hawking's disease?"

My brother nodded. "Radical and irreversible deterioration of the nerve centres responsible for muscular and autonomic function."

It had never occurred to me before that my brother had to tell people they were going to die.

"How did you tell him?"

My brother signalled and pulled off the expressway ramp at the Charlestown exit and he said, "I'm always giving people the good news. His name, by the way, is Moe."

In the lobby of the St. Mary's Extended Care Centre, the wheelchair cases are lined up against the walls; some are moaning, some intoning private mantras, some asleep with their mouths open, and some staring out at the heat shimmer above the lawn. Moe's room is near the lobby and his door is open.

Moe is lying on his side, facing a computer terminal and a printer, and there is a tube taped to the side of his pillow. My brother pats his arm in greeting and Moe gives a deep gargling sound by way of reply. I say hello and position myself in Moe's eyeline. He is a big man, with a full strong chest covered in dark curly black hair. His diminished thighs and legs lie concealed beneath a white sheet. He purses his lips round the tube and I can see his cheeks puffing out and his forehead wrinkling with effort. Slowly the words tap out on the computer screen: "It is good of U to come." The computer department at Moe's school had come up with the software and the hospital technical department had devised the straw and the keyboard. Moe can't move or talk but he can communicate with the world by blowing through a straw to activate the keyboard.

There are pictures of his wife and children on the walls, some of their drawings from school, a poster of a Greek Orthodox icon, and a sign saying, Nuclear Free Zone: No Enemas Here, and another one saying: If Choking or Gagging, Sit Me Upright.

I ask him what he thinks of his doctor, and Moe purses his lips together to send a message to the screen.

"He does what I tell him."

Both of them grin. "Any problems?" my brother asks and the nurse explains that he is having trouble with his bedsores. Moe blows into his straw. The word "Ouch!" comes up on the screen.

With an expert, gentle touch, my brother lifts the sheet and turns Moe over. His hip and his right shoulder are inflamed where his body weight presses him against the sheets. His legs are frighteningly thin and emaciated. While my brother is telling the nurses to change the bedsore ointment, Moe winks at me.

My brother leaves me to look in on another patient and I tell him I wouldn't mind staying and talking to Moe for a while. Moe must think I am a strange kind of visitor, pressing into the domains of intimacy so quickly because I sit down on the bottom of the bed and ask him, right away, how much pain he is having. One by one, the words come up on the screen:

*i cant sit up because i cant hold my head up and to support it makes me
gag. so my days are now spent lying on my side.*
*there is no pain attributable directly to als although the deterioration
of the organ in the brainstem which controls body temperature and frequent choking spells have led to some very traumatic moments. eating
has become a hazardous occupation. as well my hips often hurt from
lying that way.*
*i have had much time to ponder and reflect and to try to understand
what is happening. i write almost every day.*
it has been 4 years since i could hold a pen.

It takes him many minutes to get this on to the screen and when he fin-
ishes he has to lie back and rest. Words matter to this man. Filling a screen
with words is equal to a whole day's teaching in the classroom for me.

What I want to know is why he isn't more angry.

Letter by letter the words appear on the screen:

*i was angry for about three years. it ate me up. Then i stopped being
angry. now i pray to jesus christ.*

I have no right to object to this, but I do, strenuously. I tell him that I
will not pray to someone who makes him suffer like this. His mischievous
eyes do not lose their sense of humour. Letter by letter, more words emerge
on the green screen.

*i lie here; i cannot move; however, i can listen, think, pray. how is it i
    feel love? and where is it coming from?*

I am sitting on his bed by this time, awkwardly laying my hand on his
shoulder, wondering if he is able to feel it there.

I tell him it isn't my business to come all this way to try to turn him into
an atheist. He smiles and then indicates his water bottle with his eyes. I help
him drink his water through a straw. After that he goes to sleep almost
immediately, his mouth open, his face blank with exhaustion.

His wife comes by, and we eat a sandwich in the corridor together
while Moe is sleeping. She is a nurse herself with a full-time job and three
kids to raise on her own, yet she manages to get down to the hospital every
day to visit him. Five years spent in the company of illness have refined her
pretty face into something grave and fine.

"Your brother has been good to Moe," she says. "Not like some of the
other doctors."

"Moe says my brother does what he tells him to."

"It wasn't that way at the beginning, I can tell you. Your brother wanted Moe to do this and that, wanted him to fight this right down to the wire, and Moe went along for some time, and then I said, This is crazy, you know. We're talking about disease here, not some sports event, not some competition you can win or make a good showing in or anything like that. I think that woke Moe up some. He isn't like that any more."

"Neither is my brother," I say.

"I think he learned that from Moe. Accepting things."

She leaves and says I can stay until he wakes up again. When Moe comes to, I put my hand on his shoulder and say I had better be going. He makes one of those gargling sounds and I figure out that he wants the tube placed in his mouth. A word comes up on the screen.

"stay."

When the nurses have changed his catheter and sponge-bathed his body, I ask him how he feels about the future. He doesn't seem to mind being asked. I put the tube between his lips and stand behind him to watch the words slowly come up on the screen.

feel that i have to choose to live even now which is hard for someone so tired when i do this he takes care of meee mi fear and anxieti so hoping that i can be conscious for the move.

"Conscious for the move." The words glow on the screen and at first I don't understand them. Moe lies next to the screen, some of its green pallor reflected on his face, his eyes shut, the tube resting on his open lips.

Then I realise what he is trying to say. He wants to see everything, to feel everything, to hold on to his awareness of life until the very last moment; and to him this consciousness—whatever its desolation—is worth fighting for to the last instant. I have never met anyone before who values the ordinary state of human awareness so keenly.

It goes dark and the fluorescent lights come on overhead. A nurse comes in and puts a visor on Moe's forehead to shield him from the light and to allow him to see the computer screen better. I tell him he looks like the dealer at a crap game in a gangster movie. He smiles.

Then I ask him, as I might have asked a priest if I had one, what I should think about my mother's illness. His eyes remain shut for a long time, then his lips close around the tube and letter by letter, pause by pause, space by space, over twenty-five minutes, words begin to emerge onto the screen.

consider the following now
1) illness. not the beginning of the end but the beginning of THE
beginning. to be honest i did not FEEL this very strongly till about 6
months ago. nevertheless, i lived every day since my diagnosis to the
fullest knowing the physical exertion would speed the progression of the
illness. to sit back however, would have only robbed me of moments
with my family and friends.
thus, i continue. only now i sense if i had become a stoic or a fighter, i
would probably be gone by now. rather, i face each day with a prayer.
i try to be completely open to whatever christ brings.

The word "stoic" gives me the idea that he might have read my lecture. It made sense after all. I had sent it to my brother, though he'd never told me what he thought about it. While Moe is having another rest, I get talking to one of the nurses and she tells me that my brother had come in one day and plastered some sheets all around the room—because Moe couldn't hold anything in his hand—and then my brother got the nurses to wheel Moe's bed round from sheet to sheet so that he could read the whole lecture. I feel ridiculously pleased, as if all the shame attendant upon that lecture had suddenly been wiped away.

When Moe wakes up, I tell him how angry the lecture had made my wife. Up on the screen come the words,

anger is a waste of time.

I tell him that a friend of mine once said you don't get any smarter or wiser as you get older. All that happens is that you understand the true meaning of clichés. Like: "Take it day by day." Or "As long as you've got your health." Or that cliché about anger: "You can't get beyond it, until you've gone through it." Words come up quickly on the screen,

so get through it.

I ask him what he thought about my lecture. His answer takes twenty minutes to appear on the screen. More and more often he has to stop and rest.

better to know and grow from the experience than to remain aloof and
have no basis for wisdom. stoicism. not much of a motivator. perhaps
the unsung reason for searching out one's spirituality.

"Not much of a motivator." It had turned out that I wasn't much into stoicism either, whatever I had said in that lecture. I was more of a rage rage type, actually. He winks when I say that.

I stroke his shoulder and want to say, though I can't get it right, that what I had learned from him and from Mother was that when you strip us right down, when illness pares us back to our core, we remain creatures of the word. Nothing can save us but the word, the messages we send from deep in the shaft of sickness.

Letters came up very slowly, one by one, on the screen.

believe in the word.

I tell him that my father had said she was on a voyage away from us, and that there were times when we all wished we could follow her. She couldn't tell us what it was like, I say, but you can.

a journey, yes.

It takes minutes for him to get it down, his face sweating with the effort. I can hardly bear to watch.

away from my body away from family and the world I know,

I walk up and down the room, so I won't have to look, feeling ashamed of the effortlessness of my own body and my speech, while he lies there underneath a sheet in a darkened room, struggling to report back from unvisitable terrain:

into the heart of life.

I can't ask any more of him. He lies still, eyes shut, beneath his visor, sweating, emaciated, exhausted. I want to thank him, but it seems altogether too lightweight a gesture to do that, as if I had come for advice or a consultation or something, so I just say goodbye and stroke his inert arm again and add, "we're not finished with each other," feeling foolish that I have said it. A thin, tired cry issues from this throat.

A nurse comes in and sends a command to the printer which prints out his part of our conversation. As I leave, I turn back. The computer screen is glowing green and empty. Before it lies a big tapering shape under a sheet, framed between the steel bars of a hospital bed. The green visor is still shading his eyes but he is asleep.

In a cab on the way back to my brother's place, I unroll the computer paper and discover that, at the end of what he had said to me, the nurse had printed out a poem of his:

5NO
what is happening?
what are these flashes crashing noiselessly from side to side in my
    mind? spells of brownouts follow ozone cinders down the
    unknown path
the child within calls out how much farther, dad?

When I got back to my brother's place, he was sitting in a pool of light at the table, eating dinner. The glow of the city rose over the horizon and above that there was a sky full of stars. He was wearing a dressing gown over a T-shirt and sweat pants, and in that dressing gown, in the pool of light, he looked solitary and grand, like some abbot in a mountain monastery. "I kept some for you," he said, and we ate the rest of his Indian takeout together. When I told him I had spent the whole day with Moe, he said, "I figured you might." I asked him how long he gave him.

"Three months, maybe four at the outside."

"Does he know?"

"Of course."

I wondered about friendship between a doctor and a patient, between a man who knows what it is like to die, second by second, and another man who knows everything about that death—down to the molecular structure of cell decay—except what it feels like. He knew the meaning of those dark regions of Mother's scans, the hidden logic of the sequence of numbers in her test scores. What he didn't know was what it was like to be her. It struck me then that his science was the form of love he understood best.

I was thinking about this when he said, "ALS accelerates if you move; slows down if you keep still. Every time Moe communicates it speeds up the deterioration. Further proof, if need there be, for the existence of a merciful creator—as I always say to Moe."

"And what does Moe say to that?"

"He says mind your own damned business."

My brother pushed back his chair. "I use Moe in my medical ethics classes. I ask them whether a certain neurologist is entitled to allow an ALS patient to hook up to a computer system, if the doctor knows that using it will shorten the patient's life."

"So why did you?"

My brother gave a small laugh. "My students always say the doctor shouldn't. Then I take them to meet Moe. He changes their minds in half an hour. What conclusion do we draw? I ask them."

"Speech can matter more than life itself," I said.

"Exactly," my brother said and lit a cigarette. "The word. Believe in the word."

My brother cleared away the boxes of takeout and went to the fridge and got out a beer for each of us.

"I also give my class a thought experiment. If you had to choose, which would you prefer: to lose your mind but keep your body, or to lose your body but keep your mind?"

"I don't like games like that," I said.

"Thought experiments."

"I don't care what the hell they're called."

He ignored me. "Asking this question is a way of exploring the value human beings place on self-awareness."

"It's voyeuristic," I said.

"Come on," he said. "We're all moral tourists here. Illness is another country. None of us has any idea. That's what thought experiments are for. My students, by the way, are all sure. Until they meet Moe."

"And then?"

"He tells them about the choking spells or watching his legs wasting away, and then," my brother smiled, "they're not so sure. He's great with students."

"You must make a hell of a team," I said.

My brother went over and sat on the sofa. "Mother can only suffer. She can't give her experience any meaning. That's the worst thing about it for her."

I didn't know why he was so sure about this, but I let him go on.

"Moe, on the other hand, can shape his experience. He sees it in a Christian light—which I can't stand—but that is what keeps him holding on. I nearly counted him out twice before this, you know. Respiratory infections. Each time he pulls himself back from the edge."

"Positive mental attitude," I said. I didn't know what name to give to that fierce thing which made Moe refuse his fate, but whatever its name, even desperation, it was life, and my "stoicism" now seemed to me nothing more than surrender.

My brother walked across the darkened room and stood looking out at the blue lights of the runways at Logan. "I used to think, because of Mother, that consciousness was the most precious thing of all, and oblivion the thing to be resisted at all costs. Now I'm not so sure. Now I see what Moe is going through, how he sees his own linguistic powers disintegrating, his own words and sentences unravelling on the screen. I'm not so sure I could stand it."

I wasn't sure why he was telling me all this, but I was glad he was. Finally he said, "It's all a question of how much awareness a human being can stand." He glanced back at me from the window. "I know what you think, but believe me, it's good that Mother doesn't know."

"She's still suffering. It's not over. She still knows what's happening."

"Sure?" he said.

"Sure," I said. "After all, she still recognises you. As long as she does, she can still suffer."

I wanted to tell my brother about the night when I had lain beside my mother in the dark and watched her sleep, lying on her back with her mouth open, how I had imagined taking the pillow and holding it over her face. I wanted to confess the shame of that to someone, to unburden myself of that memory and the rage it contained. Then, just as quickly as those feelings came over me again, I found myself thinking how absurd they were. Why had I ever wanted to do such a thing? Her awareness, that fragile and damaged thing, suddenly seemed infinitely precious to me, like a painted egg I might have crushed in my hands and now saw for the thing that it was.

I didn't say any of this to my brother. Instead I told him about an evening a few nights before when Mother and I had been sitting there in her room, watching the people waiting at the bus stop in the rain opposite her window, and she had seemed faded and blurred and ebbing away, and I told her that I felt like going down to Boston to pay him a visit. Out of the stillness of the room, she said, "I see him."

"What do you see?"

Long pause. She looked me straight in the eye.

"I see him walking through the gates of truth."

My brother went still. I knew he could see himself as she saw him: a small child, between two ruined columns reaching up into the sky, among the flames and smoke of some great destruction, a child frozen between the weight of the columns, unable to move, within the gates of truth. I knew he saw her—as I did—standing on the other side of the gates, beckoning us both to follow.

Michael Ignatieff, *Scar Tissue*

A man who was afflicted with a terrible disease complained to Rabbi Israel that his suffering interfered with his learning and praying. The rabbi put his hand on his shoulder and said: "How do you know, friend, what is more pleasing to God, your studying or your suffering?"

Martin Buber, *Tales of the Hasidim*

→ Loss, Loneliness, and Grief ←

Having no butter and milk to offer to Thee, I will offer Thee a little of my pain. O Kanna, at Thy Feet I will offer the pearl drops of my tears.

Mata Amritanandamayi, in Swami Amritasvarupananda,
Mata Amritanandamayi

It's not true that I'm always thinking of H. Work and conversation make that impossible. But the times when I'm not are perhaps my worst. For then, though I have forgotten the reason, there is spread over everything a vague sense of wrongness, of something amiss. Like in those dreams where nothing terrible occurs—nothing that would sound even remarkable if you told it at breakfast-time—but the atmosphere, the taste, of the whole thing is deadly. So with this. I see the rowan berries reddening and don't know for a moment why they, of all things, should be depressing. I hear a clock strike and some quality it always had before has gone out of the sound. What's wrong with the world to make it so flat, shabby, worn-out looking? Then I remember.

This is one of the things I'm afraid of. The agonies, the mad midnight moments, must, in the course of nature, die away. But what will follow? Just this apathy, this dead flatness? Will there come a time when I no longer ask why the world is like a mean street, because I shall take the squalour as normal? Does grief finally subside into boredom tinged by faint nausea?

Feelings, and feelings, and feelings. Let me try thinking instead. From the rational point of view, what new factor has H's death introduced into the problem of the universe? What grounds has it given me for doubting all that I believe? I knew already that these things, and worse, happened daily. I would have said that I had taken them into account. I had been warned—I had warned myself—not to reckon on worldly happiness. We were even promised sufferings. They were part of the programme. We were even told "Blessed are they that mourn" and I accepted it. I've got nothing that I hadn't bargained for. Of course it is different when the thing happens to oneself, not to others, and in reality, not in imagination. Yes; but should it, for a sane man, make quite such a difference as this? No. And it wouldn't for a man whose faith had been real faith and whose concern for other people's sorrows had been real concern. The case is too plain. If my house has collapsed at one blow, that is because it was a house of cards. The faith which "took these things into account" was not faith but imagination. The taking them into account was not real sympathy. If I had really cared, as I thought I did, about the sorrows of the world, I should not have been so overwhelmed when my own sorrow came. It has been an imaginary faith playing with innocuous counters labelled "Illness," "Pain," "Death" and "Loneliness." I thought I trusted the rope until it mattered to me whether it would bear me. Now it matters, and I find I didn't.

Bridge-players tell me that there must be some money on the game "or else people won't take it seriously." Apparently it's like that. Your bid—for God or no God, for a good God or the Cosmic Sadist, for eternal life or nonentity—will not be serious if nothing much is staked on it. And you will never discover how serious it was until the stakes are raised horribly high; until you find that you are playing not for counters or for sixpences but for every penny you have in the world. Nothing less will shake a man—or at any rate a man like me—out of his merely verbal thinking and his merely notional beliefs. He has to be knocked silly before he comes to his senses. Only torture will bring out the truth. Only under torture does he discover it himself.

C. S. Lewis, *A Grief Observed*

It may help us, in those times of trouble, to remember that love is not only about relationship, it is also an affair of the soul. Disappointments in love, even betrayals and losses, serve the soul at the very moment they seem in life to be tragedies. The soul is partly in time and partly in eternity. We might remember the part that resides in eternity when we feel despair over the part that is in life.

Thomas Moore, *Care of the Soul*

The Well of Grief

Those who will not slip beneath
 the still surface on the well of grief

turning downward through its black water
 to the place we cannot breathe

will never know the source from which we drink,
 the secret water, cold and clear,

nor find in the darkness glimmering
 the small round coins
  thrown by those who wished for something else.

David Whyte, *Where Many Rivers Meet*

At times we may feel that we do not need God, but on the day when the storms of disappointment rage, the winds of disaster blow, and the tidal waves of grief beat against our lives, if we do not have a deep and patient faith our emotional lives will be ripped to shreds. There is so much frustration in the world because we have relied on gods rather than God. We have genuflected before the god of science only to find that it has given us the atomic bomb, producing fears and anxieties that science can never mitigate. We have worshipped the god of pleasure only to discover that thrills play out and sensations are short-lived. We have bowed before the god of money only to learn that there are such things as love and friendship that money cannot buy and that in a world of possible depressions, stock market crashes, and bad business investments, money is a rather uncertain deity. These transitory gods are not able to save us or bring happiness to the human heart.

Only God is able. It is faith in him that we must rediscover. With this faith we can transform bleak and desolate valleys into sunlit paths of joy and bring new light into the dark caverns of pessimism. Is someone here moving toward the twilight of life and fearful of that which we call death? Why be afraid? God is able. Is someone here on the brink of despair because of the death of a loved one, the breaking of a marriage, or the waywardness of a child? Why despair? God is able to give you the power to endure that which cannot be changed. Is someone here anxious because of bad health? Why be anxious? Come what may, God is able.

As I come to the conclusion of my message, I would wish you to permit a personal experience. The first twenty-four years of my life were years packed with fulfillment. I had no basic problems or burdens. Because of concerned and loving parents who provided for my every need, I sallied through high school, college, theological school, and graduate school without interruption. It was not until I became a part of the leadership of the Montgomery bus protest that I was actually confronted with the trials of life. Almost immediately after the protest had been undertaken, we began to receive threatening telephone calls and letters in our home. Sporadic in the beginning, they increased day after day. At first I took them in my stride, feeling that they were the work of a few hotheads who would become discouraged after they discovered that we would not fight back. But as the weeks passed, I realized that many of the threats were in earnest. I felt myself faltering and growing in fear.

After a particularly strenuous day, I settled in bed at a late hour. My wife had already fallen asleep and I was about to doze off when the telephone rang. An angry voice said, "Listen, nigger, we've taken all we want from you. Before next week you'll be sorry you ever came to Montgomery."

I hung up, but I could not sleep. It seemed that all of my fears had come down on me at once. I had reached the saturation point.

I got out of bed and began to walk the floor. Finally, I went to the kitchen and heated a pot of coffee. I was ready to give up. I tried to think of a way to move out of the picture without appearing to be a coward. In this state of exhaustion, when my courage had almost gone, I determined to take my problem to God. My head in my hands, I bowed over the kitchen table and prayed aloud. The words I spoke to God that midnight are still vivid in my memory. "I am here taking a stand for what I believe is right. But now I am afraid. The people are looking to me for leadership, and if I stand before them without strength and courage, they too will falter. I am at the end of my powers. I have nothing left. I've come to the point where I can't face it alone."

At that moment I experienced the presence of the Divine as I had never before experienced him. It seemed as though I could hear the quiet assurance of an inner voice, saying, "Stand up for righteousness, stand up for truth. God will be at your side forever." Almost at once my fears began to pass from me. My uncertainty disappeared. I was ready to face anything. The outer situation remained the same, but God had given me inner calm.

Three nights later, our home was bombed. Strangely enough, I accepted the word of the bombing calmly. My experience with God had given me a new strength and trust. I knew now that God is able to give us the interior resources to face the storms and problems of life.

Let this affirmation be our ringing cry. It will give us courage to face the uncertainties of the future. It will give our tired feet new strength as we continue our forward stride toward the city of freedom. When our days become dreary with low-hovering clouds and our nights become darker than a thousand midnights, let us remember that there is a great benign Power in the universe whose name is God, and he is able to make a way out of no way, and transform dark yesterdays into bright tomorrows. This is our hope for becoming better men. This is our mandate for seeking to make a better world.

Martin Luther King, Jr., *Strength to Love*

> I have fled you down the nights and days,
> down the labyrinth ways of my mind.
> —"THE HOUND OF HEAVEN," FRANCIS THOMPSON

Francis Thompson's poem, a favorite of mine since my freshman year in college, had taken on a personal quality as I reached my late forties. I was nagged by the notion that I was on the last leg of my life and had yet to do something that could give it meaning. As my fiftieth birthday approached, I had begun careening from one thing to another, always lured by the possibility that the new path would be the answer, the direction for which I seemed to be searching.

I never acknowledged the possibility that I might simply be scared by the thought of dying. It was much easier to find fault with people and circumstances I felt certain were shackling my potential, stifling my growth. I was "choking." I needed "air, space in which to grow."

I believed I had earned the opportunity. I had been the dutiful father, husband, and loyal corporate executive. I had demonstrated further vigor with a turn as an entrepreneur and had even rounded out my profile as the ultimate sportsman, a superior competitive surf fisherman who could wrest achievement from Mother Nature's grasp. I had even prayed at the altar of psychoanalysis for five years and, freed from all my hang-ups, I had finally sought fulfillment as a free-lance journalist.

At that point, there seemed to be only one obstacle remaining between me and meaning. Though I could not have survived without my wife's patience and support (she went back to work when the struggling "artiste" didn't earn enough to pay the mortgage), I began thinking that maybe the problem was my marriage: that after twenty-eight years and five children, it was time for a change—the kind that many "sensible, mature" adults seemed to be making.

That was as far as my script had taken me when it began to undergo changes that were clearly beyond my control. The first of these took place early Friday morning, 8 June 1984. At that particular moment in time, I was busy being the dedicated professional. I had to take the quintessential photograph of Monticello, Thomas Jefferson's home, as it glistened in the slanting rays of a rising sun.

My wife, Marie, and I were both working on newspaper features and I was convinced that sunrise would provide exceptional photographs of the home, which stands on a Virginia mountaintop. Since the gates at the base of the mountain didn't open until seven o'clock, I decided to get there before dawn. I would hike to the top and begin to photograph while Marie patiently waited in our van camper for the caretaker to open up.

Our work had earned us special permission to park in one of the four spaces that were built into a shelf in front of the cottage/gift shop alongside the mansion. The mountain dropped off about twenty feet from that point to the plateau where Jefferson had once farmed an experimental garden. That is where a security guard found our camper. It had rolled away on its own from the space where Marie had parked it. It had rolled until it went over the edge of the shelf, tumbling until it came to rest in Jefferson's garden.

The fall bent the wheels, shattered all the windows, and crumpled every side. The interior had undergone an implosion that heaped it with all the equipment, cans, and clothing we had carefully squeezed into the van's storage spaces. All of it was salted with broken glass.

As a tow truck took us and the sad-looking wreck into nearby Charlottesville, Marie remarked, "This has to be the worst day of my life." We also realized it could have been her last. After she parked that morning, she had altered her usual schedule and gone to see how I was doing. She had foregone the luxury of staying inside the camper and going back to sleep as she regularly did when I went out on an early morning shoot.

Michael, the youngest of our five children, was going to be disappointed, I thought. I had promised that he and a high school buddy could take the camper on a trip west after their high school graduation, which was just two weeks away. The camper would not be making many—if any—more trips.

A few minutes before noon that day, Marie and I were sitting in the office of an auto repair shop, making arrangements to fly home to Long Island. A tall, well-built man in a shirt and tie walked in. The pistol holstered on his hip caught my attention even before he asked if anyone knew where he could find the owner of the wrecked camper resting outside.

He was the sheriff, he told me when I identified myself. "You have an emergency back home," he said. "It might be best if you called there immediately."

Emergency, I scoffed to myself as I dialed. What could possibly be worse than what had already happened? The phone only rang once before twenty-one-year-old Jimmy, the middle child of our three sons and two daughters, answered. His "hello" was alarmingly solemn.

"Michael's had an accident, Dad," he said. "Is he okay?" I asked, half-hoping for confirmation. Jimmy paused for a long moment, and said, "Dad," before pausing again. He choked trying to repeat "Dad" and began to cry, but not so much that I couldn't hear him say, "We've lost him, Dad. Michael's dead."

Only part of me listened as Jimmy told me that Michael was apparently headed back to our house during the break after his first early morning class. For reasons that will never be known, his Volkswagen Beetle had swerved on a curve and collided head-on with a heavy equipment truck. He had died instantly, at approximately 8:30 a.m., about an hour after our camper had made its own final journey.

I remember putting my arms around Marie after I told her what had happened. "Please stay close to me," she said. "I really need you now." I nodded in assurance, but inside I wondered where the strength would come from. I was already drowning in my own grief.

No one can ever be said to be ready for such a blow, but I could not have been less prepared. Whereas Marie could find a measure of solace in her faith, I had no such resource. Though I had been born and raised a Catholic and had even studied for the priesthood, God had become another encumbrance in my sophisticated search for fulfillment. At best I was an agnostic.

Michael's death got me off that fence. I blamed God for our son's death and I directed all my hurt and anger at him. What right did he have to take my son? Michael was one of the most generous human beings I had ever known, happiest when he could help someone, a gifted entertainer who would do anything to bring a smile to an otherwise unhappy face. If God needed to take somebody, why hadn't it been one of the many useless bastards who seemed to live off everybody's misery?

In those pain-filled first days, I could hardly restrain my anger when well-meaning people tried to console me by explaining the "good" reasons why God might have taken Michael, or how much better off he was than the rest of us still living. I was not about to let God off the hook that easily.

I had never hurt so badly. I saw reminders of Michael everywhere. But I drew a blank every time I tried to recall him to mind. Loss is death's principle trauma and I was terrified that mine seemed to be so total. Michael's living presence had been torn away and memories that might have consoled me had disappeared. I could not believe God would be that cruel and I became even more bitter.

Things were not much better a year later. Although the loss had made me more appreciative of my wife and family, I still suffered amnesia so far as any memory of Michael was concerned. Shortly after the first anniversary of his death, Marie and I went south again to research assignments in Bardstown, Kentucky. We considered it a bonus when we learned that a Trappist abbey was only a few miles away from where we were working, and that the monks produced food products to support themselves. That sounded like a feature opportunity for Marie.

I had first learned about the Trappists when I was a Maryknoll Missionary seminarian. The monks were the elite strike force in the spiritual life— penitents who never spoke, fasted, and chanted liturgy in a way that evoked an angelic chorus.

They had swallowed a fellow seminarian who had slept on the bunk beneath mine. Tom Barrett, who was probably the most outgoing member of our class, had vanished between the moment one bell rang for "lights out" and another woke us the next morning.

"Hear about Barrett?" a classmate had whispered, his voice mixing awe and disbelief. "The Trappists. Can you believe it? Barrett, the guy they must have vaccinated with a phonograph needle. Him, silent? He'll never last."

Apparently, he hadn't. The last I heard, he had stayed a few years and then left. Another example of misplaced idealism, I thought, as Marie and I parked our car by Gethsemani's front gate at about half past five on a July morning in 1985.

The monastery was very plain-looking, the kind of architecture institutions choose when utility is the only priority. White stuccoed walls met at a wooden gate that was wide enough to drive a car through. The words *pax intrantibus* (peace to all who enter) were chiseled in the arch above and formed a semicircle around a statue of the Virgin Mary standing in a niche. The three-story quadrangle behind the wall replicated classic monastic form that dated to the fifth century.

That form positioned the abbey's church on the highest point of land on the north side of the quadrangle. Inside, Gethsemani's founders had deeply struck the mortar when they laid the bricks—which they had first made from clay at the site. That pattern gave a warm texture to walls which might have otherwise appeared antiseptic beneath their stiff coat of white paint.

The tapestry of white masonry peaked in a roof whose wooden buttresses were about fifty feet above the floor. These seemed to sit atop the narrow windows that had been slit into the walls, translucent fingers of stained glass through which first and last light pierced the interior. The church was not designed to be admired. It was a place where man could speak with God, free from distractions.

There was a balcony across the rear, where guests attended the monastic liturgy. A handful of locals came faithfully, even at three in the morning, when the monks chanted their first office of the day. Retreatants and other more casual visitors used the same facility.

When Marie and I entered, about fifty white- and black-robed monks were already in their choir stalls directly below. Five minutes later, they were standing, facing forward, when a knock signaled them to begin.

I do not recall particular words or phrases from the liturgy that followed. I know I was struck by the monks' genuine reverence. They were not mouthing rituals. They were singing carefully, slowly, as one disciplined voice. They were talking to someone. I did not doubt that any more than I would doubt the presence of a catcher if I were watching a pitcher winding up.

I glanced around the church, looking for that catcher. But the tabernacle was not glowing. Nor was the crucifix over the altar moving. And the light streaming through the stained-glass windows did not alter a bit. No, everything was perfectly normal. With one exception. For the first time since he had died, memories of Michael began to flood my mind.

I could see him vividly. A happy smile wreathed his handsome face. I could actually hear him. "Dad, it's OK. It's me, Mikey." He was so real. So alive. I reached out, just to hold him, just once more. And then I began to cry because I knew I couldn't. Not ever again.

The experience absorbed me completely for however long it took the monks to finish their office and celebrate mass, a bit more than an hour. As they disappeared into the cloister, Michael and his memory seemed to go with them, leaving me heartsick, alone again with my loss.

During the summer months that followed, I received additional newspaper and magazine assignments that required me to visit two other Trappist monasteries to do research and take photographs. Each time, the experience was the same. My memory of Michael would be restored from the moment I entered any church where Trappist monks were praying. I could remember him until they had finished. Then a curtain would fall.

God seemed to be tantalizing me, holding my memories hostage. I resented being forced to go to church. But, strangely, I found myself growing envious of the monks, who, like Marie, drew obvious nourishment from a faith I had once shared. I began to feel confused. Michael's death was no less a painful mystery for which I still held God responsible. But why could I only remember my dead son in circumstances that I believed had nothing whatsoever to do with him?

My involvement with Trappists did not end when I finished the assignments. On the contrary, the subject had aroused an editor's interest in a possible book. But in order to write a proposal, I would have to spend some time actually living among the Trappists and following their routine.

I arranged to spend a week living at Holy Cross Abbey in Berryville, Virginia. I had mixed feelings about the visit. On the one hand, I was curious to get to know the monks and to learn about their way of life. On the other, I was uneasy.

I was a Catholic in name only. Given my antipathy and alienation, how could I go through the motions of worship—which I felt was necessary if I was to learn firsthand about the monks? Besides, all my previous visits had been brief and I had only been an observer. What would happen when I remained for a lengthy period of time and began to participate in the routine that had been so powerful a trigger for my emotions?

I was quite nervous when, on the first evening of my visit, I joined the monks as they sang the prayers and psalms for vespers at 5:30 P.M. When they came to the Lord's Prayer, I went no further than the first two words before my lips froze. I would not acknowledge as my Father, the agent of my son's death. I wanted no bread, needed no forgiveness, and swore against doing the will of a God who had put a knife in my heart. I stood stiffly, anger chilling any appreciation I might have had for the prayers the monks recited with obvious feeling and sincerity.

In the period after vespers, the monks go individually to the refectory for a light supper, usually fruit augmented by the leftovers from lunch, their principal meal of the day. My insides were so knotted that I could not think of food. I wanted to leave by morning and began planning to do so.

First, though, I would have to get through compline, the final choir office of the day, at 7:30 P.M. The church was dimly lit as the monks began reciting the prayers by heart. They moved slowly through Psalm four, which cites God's love for the steadfast heart, and then to Psalm number ninety. When I heard the words, my bitterness dissolved into tears. Psalm ninety is the substance of "On Eagle's Wings," the hymn that was sung at Michael's funeral mass.

The words forced me back to that moment. Marie was kneeling next to me in the front pew. All that remained of our youngest son lay uncharacteristically still in the aisle in front of us, sealed forever in a polished wooden coffin. If I put my arm out, I could have touched it.

"You who dwell in the shelter of the Lord," the hymn promised,

> who abide in his shadow for life.
> Say to the Lord, my refuge, my rock in whom I trust.
> And He will raise you up on eagle's wings.
> Bear you on the breath of dawn.
> Make you to shine like the sun,
> and hold you in the palm of his hand.

The words were a mockery. Michael's coffin, so close, so frighteningly final, was by no means the wings of eagles. I had watched his two brothers, tears streaming down their faces, help carry it into the church. It was their hands and their hearts that were visible. I saw nothing of God's palm. I didn't want to see him anywhere near that box.

As that scene flickered through my mind, reopening painful memories, I began to pray. "Please," I pleaded, "don't make me cry in front of these people. Why are you doing this to me? You took my son. Isn't that enough? Leave me alone. Please, go away. What have I done to make you want to hurt me like this?" Even if I wanted to sing with the monks, I couldn't. I had all to do to keep from sobbing aloud.

I don't remember anything until the monks stopped singing and silence brought me back to the moment at hand. All lights had been turned off, save for a single spot that illuminated a statue of the Virgin Mary in a niche above the main altar.

Turning in their stalls, the monks faced the statue and began to sing the Salve Regina, as monks have done every evening since the Middle Ages. They called on Mary, "our advocate…our queen…our life, our sweetness, and our hope. To you do we send up our sights, mourning and weeping in this vale of tears."

I felt tears on my face as I listened, recognizing the bond I shared with that poor woman. The pain that Michelangelo had carved into the *Pietà* was knifing into my heart. I knew how Mary must have felt when they took the broken body of her son from the cross and laid him, lifeless, in her arms. Sweet Mother of God, I said to myself without thinking, how I know.

The notes of the hymn ranged high, yet there was no audible straining as the two choirs, one soft voice, easily scaled the register, holding notes, caressing words, polishing the phrases of petition. Their tenderness had the special quality love acquires when strong men expose their vulnerability by its confession. They ended their goodnight gently, crooning its last words, "O, clement. O, loving. O, sweet Virgin Mary."

The monastery bell began slowly tolling the angelus as they finished and stood silently, heads bowed. The clanging quickened and the monks beckoned to me to join them as they filed from the stalls and walked in two lines to a point where the abbot stood with a holy-water sprinkler. Each monk came before him, bowed, and was sprinkled with the water before leaving the church. In a minute or two, the ceremony was over and I found myself standing outside in the cloister.

As the monks walked by me on their way to their rooms, I was startled to hear my name whispered. Turning around, I came face to face with my old seminary classmate, Tom Barrett, now known as Father Daniel. He was thinner than he had been when he had once emphatically dumped me with a cross-body block during a football game. But I felt the raw strength in the arm he threw around my shoulders, as he squeezed and half-carried me along into the preau, a small garden that formed the core of the monastery quadrangle.

He responded immediately to my shaken appearance and asked what was the matter. The pain pushed aside any bravado and in a rush I told him about Michael's death, the experiences I'd had in other abbeys, and what had just taken place inside the church. Tom had been standing in front of me with his arms folded, listening. When I finished, he nodded and said, "He's after you." Then, nodding again, as though saying the words had made him more certain of his conclusion, he repeated, "He's after you."

I said nothing in reply. The thought made me sick. Tom continued, explaining how he believed God never stops trying to draw us close to him. "If we resist," he said, "he finds ways to get through our barriers. I'm positive he's reaching out to you, and your experience just now is an example. I'm just as certain that your continued involvement with us is no coincidence. I think he brought you here for a very special reason."

I remained silent at first, even though I was tempted to tell Tom that if God was trying to reach me, I was not interested. While I was glad to regain access to my memories of Michael, they did not offset his loss. That thought finally overrode any desire I had to be polite and I blurted out, "Screw the sadistic son of a bitch. If he really did care about me, then why did he take my son?"

"He didn't take your son," Tom answered very calmly, "no more than he could be blamed for your death if someone shot and killed you. That tragedy would be the result of whatever reasons brought you and the gunman to the same place and time.

"We're not windup toys. We call the shots. Not God. He offers us options, opportunities—graces, as we call them—to grow into the unique individuals he created us to be. But we call the shots. Did you forget your Baltimore catechism? Remember what it gave as the reason for our creation?

"'God made us to know him, to love him and to serve him in this world and so earn happiness in the next.' You can't love under duress. To love is to choose, and to choose, you must have free will."

Tom's logic left me nothing to say. He was right. God was no more the agent of Michael's death than I was. Michael had chosen to be driving that road at the moment when something caused his car to veer into that particular truck's path. Had the truck come one minute sooner or later ... had the drivers stopped for coffee ... or skipped a break ... the accident might never have happened.

I needed to think, I told Tom, who then nodded in the direction of the church. As I began walking toward it, he called softly, and when I turned, he came over to me, hugged me tightly and said, "I'm so sorry, old buddy. Look, take it easy in there. Give God a chance. Listen. I think that's what's most important now. Just listen."

God did not kill my son, I thought as I sat in the church. Then if there is a God, I asked, where did he fit in all of this? Something told me, "love." That was God's most dominant characteristic, an all-encompassing, unqualified love—one that included every possible variety and expression.

If that was true, then God had to "feel" the love I had for Michael. It had to be part of his experience. And he had to know my pain. He knew it as intensely as he knew the loss of love that caused it. If he did, he had to feel as badly as any friend. At least that much. He had been as much a part of Michael's creation as had Marie and I. He knew the joy that had been Michael. The pain had to cut him deeply. As deeply as it did me. He had to be grieving my—our—loss, sorrowing as Christ's own mother must have sorrowed.

All this was happening in minutes, one thought after another, pulling and then sweeping me along. The God I had reviled and rejected had been waiting to mourn with me, burdened with sorrow he would share with me. I felt so ashamed. I had been so wrong, for so long. Yet God had never given up on me. The Hound of Heaven had kept following me, his arms open, no matter what I had said or done.

Then, without warning, the experience of Michael's death began to replay in my mind, but as though for the first time. I could sense it surging up inside me, a mass of agony and pain, and I wanted to get up and run. But something told me there was no need to be afraid. I heard the words, "I know. I know. As you did, as you still do, I love him too. I know."

I stayed put, weeping, as the pain poured out. But not alone. Not unconsoled. This time I wept in the arms of my God, whom I finally allowed to hold me in that monastery church.

And so, I stopped running. God had finally brought me to ground in the silence of Trappists and I knew it was there I had to listen.

Frank Bianco, *Voices of Silence*

I climb the trembling, twisted stair into the belfry. The darkness stirs with a flurry of wings high above me in the gloomy engineering that holds the steeple together. Nearer at hand the old clock ticks in the tower. I flash the light into the mystery which keeps it going, and gaze upon the ancient bells.

I have seen the fuse box. I have looked in the corners where I think there is some wiring. I am satisfied that there is no fire in this tower which would flare like a great torch and take the whole abbey up with it in twenty minutes. . . .

And now my whole being breathes the wind which blows through the belfry, and my hand is on the door through which I see the heavens. The door swings out upon a vast sea of darkness and of prayer. Will it come like this, the moment of my death? Will You open a door upon the great forest and set my feet upon a ladder under the moon, and take me out among the stars?

The roof glistens under my feet, this long metal roof facing the forest and the hills, where I stand higher than the treetops and walk upon shining air.

Mists of damp heat rise up out of the fields around the sleeping abbey. The whole valley is flooded with moonlight and I can count the southern hills beyond the water tank, and almost number the trees of the forest to the north. Now the huge chorus of living beings rises up out of the world beneath my feet: life singing in the watercourses, throbbing in the creeks and the fields and the trees, choirs of millions and millions of jumping and flying and creeping things. And far above me the cool sky opens upon the frozen distance of the stars.

I lay the clock upon the belfry ledge and pray cross-legged with my back against the tower, and face the same unanswered question.

Lord God of this great night: Do You see the woods? Do You hear the rumor of their loneliness? Do You behold their secrecy? Do You remember their solitudes? Do You see that my soul is beginning to dissolve like wax within me?

Clamabo per diem et non exaudies, et nocte et non ad insipientiam mihi!

Do You remember the place by the stream? Do You remember the top of the Vineyard Knob that time in autumn, when the train was in the valley? Do You remember McGinty's hollow? Do You remember the thinly wooded hillside behind Hanekamp's place? Do You remember the time of the forest fire? Do You know what has become of the little poplars we planted in the spring? Do You observe the valley where I marked the trees?

There is no leaf that is not in Your care. There is no cry that was not heard by You before it was uttered. There is no water in the shales that was not hidden there by Your wisdom. There is no concealed spring that was not concealed by You. There is no glen for a lone house that was not planned by You for a lone house. There is no man for that acre of woods that was not made by You for that acre of woods.

But there is greater comfort in the substance of silence than in the answer to a question. Eternity is in the present. Eternity is in the palm of the hand. Eternity is a seed of fire, whose sudden roots break barriers that keep my heart from being an abyss.

The things of Time are in connivance with eternity. The shadows serve You. The beasts sing to You before they pass away. The solid hills shall vanish like a worn-out garment. All things change, and die and disappear. Questions arrive, assume their actuality, and also disappear. In this hour I shall cease to ask them, and silence shall be my answer. The world that Your love created, that the heat has distorted, and that my mind is always misinterpreting, shall cease to interfere with our voices.

Minds which are separated pretend to blend in one another's language. The marriage of souls in concepts is mostly an illusion. Thoughts which travel outward bring back reports of You from outward things: but a dialogue with You, uttered through the world, always ends by being a dialogue with my own reflection in the stream of time. With You there is no dialogue unless You choose a mountain and circle it with cloud and print Your words in fire upon the mind of Moses. What was delivered to Moses on tables of stone, as the fruit of lightning and thunder, is now more thoroughly born in our own souls as quietly as the breath of our own being.

The hand lies open. The heart is dumb. The soul that held my substance together, like a hard gem in the hollow of my own power, will one day totally give in.

Although I see the stars, I no longer pretend to know them. Although I have walked in those woods, how can I claim to love them? One by one I shall forget the names of individual things.

You, Who sleep in my breast, are not met with words, but in the emergence of life within life and of wisdom within wisdom. You are found in communion: Thou in me and I in Thee and Thou in them and they in me: dispossession within dispossession, dispassion within dispassion, emptiness within emptiness, freedom within freedom. I am alone. Thou art alone. The Father and I are One.

Thomas Merton, The Sign of Jonas

Loneliness, with its fear and ache, is isolation, the inevitable action of the self. This process of isolation, whether expansive or narrow, is productive of confusion, conflict and sorrow. Isolation can never give birth to aloneness; the one has to cease for the other to be. Aloneness is indivisible and loneliness is separation. That which is alone is pliable and so enduring. Only the alone can commune with that which is causeless, the immeasurable. To the alone, life is eternal; to the alone there is no death. The alone can never cease to be.

J. Krishnamurti, Commentaries on Living

⊰ 10 ⊱

Liberation

"Why would you not perceive it as a release from suffering to learn that you are free? Why would you not acclaim the truth instead of looking on it as an enemy?"

—A COURSE IN MIRACLES ®

A Course in Miracles is one of the most edifying of recent spiritual texts. First published in 1976, the three-volume work was written by Helen Schucman and William Thetford, two professors of medical psychology at Columbia University's College of Physicians and Surgeons in New York City, as a treatise for a more enlightened way of living and working. It is now used as a teaching tool for many educators, psychologists, and groups seeking new methods for achieving spiritual well-being. The underlying promise of the Christian-based work rests in the notion that the lessons of pain and suffering are the gifts to be passed on in love and understanding. God "has laid them at your feet, and asks you now that you will look on them and take them for your own." This is the service to humanity. We become like gods through the awfulness of our own suffering, as theologian Hans Küng came to realize by reminding himself of the suffering of Christ.

With suffering comes a liberation from the limits of our previous existence. Through sickness we get to know our body as something different, tender, special, not purely functioning without notice. We find that our old life was not altogether complete. Everything continually grows and is stretched towards knowledge; all experiences are lessons towards this attainment. God jostles us and rearranges us into a new order. Through the hardships we may question His motives. We are liberated when we recognize them. And this recognition of God's ways is the gift, the reward.

When Irish poet Derek Mahon writes of his liberation in "Matthew V, 29-30," he describes a total clearing out of mind, body, environment, and attitude. Only then is he ready for human society. We are never empty forever. At the end of our trial we wait for what Paul Brunton calls the "cycle of new growth." Brunton writes that by embracing the suffering we become masters of our own life. "Every fresh experience will then become like oil to the flame of his growing understanding."

This is where the ancient concept of karma comes into play, that we experience what we need to learn in this life and how we experience it determines the future of our souls. The early Indian teachings, the Upanishads, offers the various forms that karma can take, but the general understanding is that when the self has transcended the ego and action takes place through service to others, then we are released from any binding of the past which could have been negative or harmful.

Realignment in our attitude is necessary after any personal suffering. Stephen Levine explains this realignment in his piece about constant change. He wrote: "We relearn the ability to experience life as it unfolds, to play lightly without force or judgement."

><

The Coming of the Guest

Why would you not perceive it as a release from suffering to learn that you are free? Why would you not acclaim the truth instead of looking on it as an enemy? Why does an easy path, so clearly marked it is impossible to lose the way, seem thorny, rough and far too difficult for you to follow? Is it not because you see it as the road to hell instead of looking on it as a simple way, without a sacrifice or any loss, to find yourself in Heaven and in God? Until you realize you give up nothing, until you understand there is no loss, you will have some regrets about the way that you have chosen. And you will not see the many gains your choice has offered you. Yet though you do not see them, they are there. Their cause has been effected, and they must be present where their cause has entered in.

You have accepted healing's cause, and so it must be you are healed. And being healed, the power to heal must also now be yours. The miracle is not a separate thing that happens suddenly, as an effect without a cause. Nor is it, in itself, a cause. But where its cause is must it be. Now is it caused, though not as yet perceived. And its effects are there, though not yet seen. Look inward now, and you will not behold a reason for regret, but cause indeed for glad rejoicing and for hope of peace.

It has been hopeless to attempt to find the hope of peace upon a battleground. It has been futile to demand escape from sin and pain of what was made to serve the function of retaining sin and pain. For pain and sin are one illusion, as are hate and fear, attack and guilt but one. Where they are causeless their effects are gone, and love must come wherever they are not. Why are you not rejoicing? You are free of pain and sickness, misery and loss, and all effects of hatred and attack. No more is pain your friend and guilt your god, and you should welcome the effects of love.

Your Guest *has* come. You asked Him, and He came. You did not hear Him enter, for you did not wholly welcome Him. And yet His gifts came with Him. He has laid them at your feet, and asks you now that you will look on them and take them for your own. He needs your help in giving them to all who walk apart, believing they are separate and alone. They will be healed when you accept your gifts, because your Guest will welcome everyone whose feet have touched the holy ground whereon you stand, and where His gifts for them are laid.

You do not see how much you now can give, because of everything you have received. Yet He Who entered in but waits for you to come where you invited Him to be. There is no other place where He can find His host, nor where His host can meet with Him. And nowhere else His gifts of peace and joy, and all the happiness His Presence brings, can be obtained. For they are where He is Who brought them with Him, that they might be yours. You cannot see your Guest, but you can see the gifts He brought. And when you look on them, you will believe His Presence must be there. For what you now can do could not be done without the love and grace His Presence holds.

Such is the promise of the loving God; His Son have life and every living thing be part of him, and nothing else have life. What you have given "life" is not alive, and symbolizes but your wish to be alive apart from life, alive in death, with death perceived as life, and living, death. Confusion follows on confusion here, for on confusion has this world been based, and there is nothing else it rests upon. Its base does not change, although it seems to be in constant change. Yet what is that except the state confusion really means? Stability to those who are confused is meaningless, and shift and change become the law on which they predicate their lives.

The body does not change. It represents the larger dream that change is possible. To change is to attain a state unlike the one in which you found yourself before. There is no change in immortality, and Heaven knows it not. Yet here on earth it has a double purpose, for it can be made to teach opposing things. And they reflect the teacher who is teaching them. The body can appear to change with time, with sickness or with health, and with events that seem to alter it. Yet this but means the mind remains unchanged in its belief of what the purpose of the body is.

Sickness is a demand the body be a thing that it is not. Its nothingness is guarantee that it can *not* be sick. In your demand that it be more than this lies the idea of sickness. For it asks that God be less than all He really is. What, then, becomes of you, for it is you of whom the sacrifice is asked? For He is told that part of Him belongs to Him no longer. He must sacrifice your self, and in His sacrifice are you made more and He is lessened by the loss of you. And what is gone from Him becomes your god, protecting you from being part of Him.

The body that is asked to be a god will be attacked, because its nothingness has not been recognized. And so it seems to be a thing with power in itself. As something, it can be perceived and thought to feel and act, and hold you in its grasp as prisoner to itself. And it can fail to be what you demanded that it be. And you will hate it for its littleness, unmindful that the failure does not lie in that it is not more than it should be, but only in your failure to perceive that it is nothing. Yet its nothingness is your salvation, from which you would flee.

As "something" is the body asked to be God's enemy, replacing what He is with littleness and limit and despair. It is His loss you celebrate when you behold the body as a thing you love, or look upon it as a thing you hate. For if He be the Sum of everything, then what is not in Him does not exist, and His completion is its nothingness. Your savior is not dead, nor does he dwell in what was built as a temple unto death. He lives in God, and it is this that makes him savior unto you, and only this. His body's nothingness releases yours from sickness and from death. For what is yours cannot be more or less than what is his.

Helen Schucman and William Thetford, *A Course in Miracles* ®

Only the man who has had to face despair is really convinced that he needs mercy. Those who do not want mercy never seek it. It is better to find God on the threshold of despair than to risk our lives in a complacency that has never felt the need of forgiveness. A life that is without problems may literally be more hopeless than one that always verges on despair.

Thomas Merton, *No Man Is an Island*

Matthew V, 29-30

Lord, mine eye offended
So I plucked it out.
Imagine my chagrin

When the offence continued.
So I plucked out
The other, but

The offence continued.
In the dark now, and
Working by touch, I shaved

My head. The offence continued.
Removed an ear,
Another, dispatched the nose,

The offence continued.
Imagine my chagrin.
Next, in long strips, the skin—

Razored the tongue, the toes,
The personal nitty-gritty.
The offence continued.

But now, the thing
Finding its own momentum,
The more so since

The offence continued,
I entered upon
A prolonged course

Of lobotomy and vivisection.
Reducing the self
To a rubble of organs,

A wreckage of bones
In the midst of which, somewhere,
The offence continued.

Quicklime, then, for the
Calcium, paraquat
For the unregenerate offal,

A spreading of topsoil,
A ploughing of this
And a sowing of it with barley.

Paraffin for the records
Of birth, flu
And abortive scholarship.

For the whimsical postcards,
The cheques
Dancing like hail,

The surviving copies
Of poems published
And unpublished. A scalpel

For the casual turns
Of phrase engraved
On the minds of others.

A chemical spray
For the stray
Thoughts hanging in the air,

For the people
Who breathed them in.
Sadly, therefore, deletion

Of the many people
From their desks, beds,
Breakfasts, buses,

Tandems and catamarans.
Deletion of their
Machinery and architecture,

All evidence whatever
Of civility and reflection
Of laughter and tears.

Destruction of all things on which
That reflection fed,
Of vegetable and bird,

Erosion of all rocks
From the holiest mountain
To the least stone,

Evaporation of all seas,
The extinction of heavenly bodies—
Until, at last, offence

Was not to be found
In that silence without bound.
Only then was I fit for human society.

Derek Mahon, *Poems 1962–1978*

If one purpose of human life upon this earth is to unfold spiritually and if a section of humanity is driven by the pressures of crisis and the sufferings of war to seek such unfoldment, why should not the World Mind permit these drastic happenings? The same Nature which gives us mild balmy summers also gives us arctic cold winters. The same universal laws which bring the sunlight of noon also bring the midnight of darkness. The same Power which is bringing infant humanity through its first fumbling steps towards self-realization, is also permitting it to fall and bruise itself because only so will humanity ever learn to walk. Who can deny that at least one section of humanity needs the whip of suffering to act as a lesson in its moral education or as punishment for its blind sins or as stimulant to awaken it from stagnation into evolutionary movement? Those who will take the trouble to look deep beneath appearances for realities may even see in these very same world happenings the vindication of the World Mind's care for humanity and a demonstration of Its presence in the world.

Paul Brunton, *The Spiritual Crisis of Man*

The hour is here for us to associate ourselves *consciously* with the two laws of compensation and evolution. We may base our general policy of living on selfish interest, on upsurges of emotion, on calculating cunning or on idle drifting with the tide of circumstances. In consequence, we may find momentary benefits but we shall not find permanent ones. Or we may base it on philosophy. If we do so, we desert the old game in trial, error and suffering and begin to live by *understanding*. In that case, it is not the unexpected but the expected which will happen to us. If a man can look impersonally at his own present life and analytically at his own past history, comprehension will begin to be born and later, out of that, mastery. He to whom the pursuit of moral excellence and practical wisdom is something more than a phrase, will find both in the fortunes and misfortunes of existence help to achieve his aims. He will see the mistakes he has made, what psychological causes led up to them and what external consequences they themselves led to; and seeing, he will suffer. If this suffering engraves a new and higher attitude upon his mind, it will not be regarded as something to be avoided but rather as something to be accepted. If, perceiving this, he co-operates consciously and deliberately in the gestation process, he will triumph over it. Out of the suffering, thus properly regarded, he will draw a heightened power to control his lower self and a heightened capacity to understand it. Every fresh experience will then become like oil to the flame of his growing understanding.

This result is arrived at only because he changes his attitude to that of an eager learner and rejects the egotist interpretation of life for the impersonal one. To others, suffering merely brings dulled consciousness but to such a man it brings a cycle of new growth. Whatever severe anguish enters his life for the first time or the fourth time, be it the unheralded turn of fortune for the worse or the unanticipated anxiety of surprising events, be it the wrongdoing of a human being or the tragic news of a written letter, be it a painful illness or a tremendous failure, he instinctively asks himself such questions as: "Why has this come to me?" or "Why has this person entered my life?" and then reflects impartially, coolly and slowly, until he can discover its physical or inward significance. For life would not have brought it into his experience if it were not his due, which means if he had not earned it or needed it. Such philosophical analysis often shows him that causes within himself are responsible for many external happenings. Awakened by suffering to remove defects or to cultivate needed qualities and thus improve himself, he transmutes it into an asset. Every defect in character or deficiency in judgment is seen to lead in the end to a deficit in happiness. The problem of making right choices or wise decisions is no easy one.

Men can help change the course of their destiny by changing the shape of their character, intelligence and talent, or the form, energy, health and condition of their body. If they inertly accept themselves as they are, they must also accept the fulfillment of their destiny. When the law of recompense lays out this destiny with hard living conditions or unwanted misfortune, they are dissatisfied with its harshness. If, instead, while trying to relieve the conditions or remove the misfortunes they gracefully accepted the law as a just one, they would demonstrate wisdom and shorten the period of suffering.

Where a sufferer finds that he cannot mend a bad environment or cannot undo a tangle of bad karma, then he should mend the way in which he views them. Where he cannot quickly adjust his outer circumstances, he can and must adjust his inner self. When he cannot extricate himself from a disharmonious environment by the integral use of intense endeavor and inspired imagination, he must learn to look on it with new eyes. It is the use that he makes of his sufferings that determines their values for him. With the recognition that his faults punish him and his weaknesses betray him, with a wise and impersonal attitude toward his troubles—whatever his personal feelings may be—he can turn them into assets. But if he lets those feelings sweep him away into bitterness, hatred, resentment, malice, fear or selfishness, they will remain as debits. It is not only unscrupulous conduct and injury of others that brings eventual retribution. Bitter thoughts and resentful feelings, negative ideas and unbalanced emotions will affect not only the quality of a man's character but, if strong and prolonged enough, also the quality of his fortunes. Troubles may come to him which would not otherwise have come to him. Enmities may be created or kept alive which would not have touched him or, touching, would have died down. If his experience of life has soured him, he may be sure that his thinking about life has something to do with the unhappy result.

When the mind's negatives reach a certain degree of strength, a certain depth of intensity, or when their repetition extends over a sufficient period of time, a physical manifestation may eventually follow. A man's actions are largely predetermined and his fortunes largely predestined by no other power or creature than himself. Both arise out of his own nature. He may take a misfortune as a final defeat and sink by the wayside of despair. Or he may take it as a first challenge and rise to the summit of determination. In the end, it is his *thought* about it that matters. His attitude toward these happenings is not less important than the happenings themselves. The creative thought comes first; its visible results will come later.

Paul Brunton, *The Spiritual Crisis of Man*

One day, a few days after the liberation, I walked through the country past flowering meadows, for miles and miles, toward the market town near the camp. Larks rose to the sky and I could hear their joyous song. There was no one to be seen for miles around; there was nothing but the wide earth and sky and the larks' jubilation and the freedom of space. I stopped, looked around, and up to the sky—and then I went down on my knees. At that moment there was very little I knew of myself or of the world—I had but one sentence in mind—always the same: "I called to the Lord from my narrow prison and He answered me in the freedom of space."

How long I knelt there and repeated this sentence memory can no longer recall. But I know that on that day, in that hour, my new life started. Step for step I progressed, until I again became a human being.

The way that led from the acute mental tension of the last days in camp (from that war of nerves to mental peace) was certainly not free from obstacles. It would be an error to think that a liberated prisoner was not in need of spiritual care any more. We have to consider that a man who has been under such enormous mental pressure for such a long time is naturally in some danger after his liberation, especially since the pressure was released quite suddenly. This danger (in the sense of psychological hygiene) is the psychological counterpart of the bends. Just as the physical health of the caisson worker would be endangered if he left his diver's chamber suddenly (where he is under enormous atmospheric pressure), so the man who has suddenly been liberated from mental pressure can suffer damage to his moral and spiritual health.

During this psychological phase one observed that people with natures of a more primitive kind could not escape the influences of the brutality which had surrounded them in camp life. Now, being free, they thought they could use their freedom licentiously and ruthlessly. The only thing that had changed for them was that they were now the oppressors instead of the oppressed. They became instigators, not objects, of willful force and injustice. They justified their behavior by their own terrible experiences. This was often revealed in apparently insignificant events. A friend was walking across a field with me toward the camp when suddenly we came to a field of green crops. Automatically, I avoided it, but he drew his arm through mine and dragged me through it. I stammered something about not treading down the young crops. He became annoyed, gave me an angry look and shouted, "You don't say! And hasn't enough been taken from us? My wife and child have been gassed—not to mention everything else—and you would forbid me to tread on a few stalks of oats!"

Only slowly could these men be guided back to the commonplace truth that no one has the right to do wrong, not even if wrong has been done to them. We had to strive to lead them back to this truth, or the consequences would have been much worse than the loss of a few thousand stalks of oats. I can still see the prisoner who rolled up his shirt sleeves, thrust his right hand under my nose and shouted, "May this hand be cut off if I don't stain it with blood on the day when I get home!" I want to emphasize that the man who said these words was not a bad fellow. He had been the best of comrades in camp and afterwards.

Apart from the moral deformity resulting from the sudden release of mental pressure, there were two other fundamental experiences which threatened to damage the character of the liberated prisoner: bitterness and disillusionment when he returned to his former life.

Bitterness was caused by a number of things he came up against in his former home town. When, on his return, a man found that in many places he was met only with a shrug of the shoulders and with hackneyed phrases, he tended to become bitter and to ask himself why he had gone through all that he had. When he heard the same phrases nearly everywhere—"We did not know about it," and "We, too, have suffered," then he asked himself, have they really nothing better to say to me?

The experience of disillusionment is different. Here it was not one's fellow man (whose superficiality and lack of feeling was so disgusting that one finally felt like creeping into a hole and neither hearing nor seeing human beings any more) but fate itself which seemed so cruel. A man who for years had thought he had reached the absolute limit of all possible suffering now found that suffering has no limits, and that he could suffer still more, and still more intensely.

When we spoke about attempts to give a man in camp mental courage, we said that he had to be shown something to look forward to in the future. He had to be reminded that life still waited for him, that a human being waited for his return. But after liberation? There were some men who found that no one awaited them. Woe to him who found that the person whose memory alone had given him courage in camp did not exist any more! Woe to him who, when the day of his dreams finally came, found it so different from all he had longed for! Perhaps he boarded a trolley, traveled out to the home which he had seen for years in his mind, and only in his mind, and pressed the bell, just as he has longed to do in thousands of dreams, only to find that the person who should open the door was not there, and would never be there again.

We all said to each other in camp that there could be no earthly happiness which could compensate for all we had suffered. We were not hoping for happiness—it was not that which gave us courage and gave meaning to our suffering, our sacrifices and our dying. And yet we were not prepared for unhappiness. This disillusionment, which awaited not a small number of prisoners, was an experience which these men have found very hard to get over and which, for a psychiatrist, is also very difficult to help them overcome. But this must not be a discouragement to him; on the contrary, it should provide an added stimulus.

But for every one of the liberated prisoners, the day comes when, looking back on his camp experiences, he can no longer understand how he endured it all. As the day of his liberation eventually came, when everything seemed to him like a beautiful dream, so also the day comes when all his camp experiences seem to him nothing but a nightmare.

The crowning experience of all, for the homecoming man, is the wonderful feeling that, after all he has suffered, there is nothing he need fear any more—except his God.

Viktor E. Frankl, *Man's Search for Meaning*

Once someone asked a well-known Thai meditation master, "In this world where everything changes, where nothing remains the same, where loss and grief are inherent in our very coming into existence, how can there be any happiness? How can we find security when we see that we can't count on anything being the way we want it to be?" The teacher, looking compassionately at this fellow, held up a drinking glass which had been given to him earlier in the morning and said, "You see this goblet? For me, this glass is already broken. I enjoy it, I drink out of it. It holds my water admirably, sometimes even reflecting the sun in beautiful patterns. If I should tap it, it has a lovely ring to it. But when I put this glass on a shelf and the wind knocks it over or my elbow brushes it off the table and it falls to the ground and shatters, I say, 'Of course.' But when I understand that this glass is already broken, every moment with it is precious. Every moment is just as it is and nothing need be otherwise."

When we recognize that, just as that glass, our body is already broken, that indeed we are already dead, then life becomes precious and we open to it just as it is, in the moment it is occurring. When we understand that all our loved ones are already dead—our children, our mates, our friends—how precious they become. How little fear can interpose, how little doubt can estrange us. When you live your life as though you're already dead, life takes on new meaning. Each moment becomes a whole lifetime, a universe unto itself.

When we realize we are already dead, our priorities change, our heart opens, our mind begins to clear of the fog of old holdings and pretendings. We watch all life in transit and what matters becomes instantly apparent: The transmission of love, the letting go of obstacles to understanding, the relinquishment of our grasping, of our hiding from ourselves. Seeing the mercilessness of our self-strangulation, we begin to come gently into the light we share with all beings. Taking each teaching, each loss, each gain, each fear, each joy as it arises and experiencing it fully, life becomes workable. We are no longer "a victim of life." And then every experience, even the loss of our dearest one, becomes another opportunity for awakening.

If our only spiritual practice were to live as though we were already dead, relating to all we meet, to all we do, as though it were our final moments in the world, what time would there be for old games or falsehoods or posturing? If we lived our life as though we were already dead, as though our children were already dead, how much time would there be for self-protection and the re-creation of ancient mirages? Only love would be appropriate, only the truth.

Stephen Levine, Who Dies?

I received a call not long ago from a woman I have known for some years who has been a prostitute and heroin addict. She had been involved in this life for about twelve years, until her best friend died in her arms of an overdose of heroin two years before. She said she just couldn't hide any more. The pain was too great, and she decided not to pull back, but to go right to the edge of her holding and play it for all it was worth. She moved out of downtown San Francisco and found an apartment in the suburbs where she got a job in a large office and began, as someone put it, "to take herself apart, bone by bone," not to let anything go by unexamined.

Now this kind of fierceness, which attempts to compensate for years of hiding, also has a tendency to breed certain qualities of self-judgment, which she discovered too had to be worked with, had to be seen as an edge, had to be let go of.

Her commitment is so great, because the pain in her life has been so intense. She has been brought to a place where she is willing to stop deadening the pain with temporary satisfactions so she can go to the root of what or who is suffering. She said that she had to come to a point where there was no place to turn, except inward.

So, the unexpected or unwanted brings each of us to the edge of our pain. But we begin to investigate what causes the pain and posturing. We come to the fear, the doubt, the anger that we usually withdraw from, and gently enter into it. We often find that we don't know what anger is or guilt is or fear is. Because we have always pushed these qualities away or compulsively acted them out, with very little awareness of what was happening. We don't know what these qualities of mind are because as we have approached our edge we have withdrawn into the drowsy blindness of a life only partially lived. We have judged these qualities as unworthy of our fantasy of our imagined self. And, in order to protect that mirage of some separate worthy solidity, instead of using the signal of our attachment, our pain, as a notice to go beyond our cage, we have withdrawn from the edge of life. We have postponed our life in the same way we are attempting to postpone our death.

A friend, taking robes as a Buddhist monk in Thailand, went to study with one of the great meditation masters. When he met with the teacher, the teacher said, "I hope you are not afraid to suffer." Because if you want to find the truth, you cannot allow your resistance to continually motivate you. We are constantly hiding and posturing, inventing an acceptable reality, instead of meeting with the pain and resistance which so cloud understanding. We continually elude our liberation because of an unwillingness to open to the stuff which has been locked in by years of postponing life. All the encrustations of the heart, all the mercilessness to ourselves, all our fear of letting go of who we think we are.

And this is the condition we find ourselves in. It's not something to judge. It's just something to notice. Here we all are, with so many unwanted states of mind. And we pull back. Our reaction limits our openness to what comes next. Fear arises, we close. Doubt arises, we close. Anger arises, we close. Death arises, we close.

To some, this encouragement to acknowledge the blockages of the heart and the confusion of the mind may seem quite negative. But actually what we are speaking about is the path of joy. The acknowledgment of the stuff which closes us allows a softening, a melting away at the edges. And the spaciousness which results illuminates that which has always been there, our original nature shining through, the joy of pure being, the stillness of the underlying reality we all share.

Indeed, the mind is always dreaming itself. So we start coming to the edge of the dream, start cultivating the compassion to let go. We relearn the ability to experience life as it unfolds, to play lightly without force or judgment. It is not a war. It is at last a kindness to ourselves, which gives rise in time, with constancy, to a spacious participation in the flow of change, beyond ideas of loss and gain, beyond ideas of life and death; opening into just this much, the vastness of what is.

We begin to open to awareness itself, threatened by nothing, withdrawing from nothing, becoming one with life. Perfectly prepared for death, knowing that nothing can separate us from our true nature and that only our forgetfulness can obscure it.

Stephen Levine, *Who Dies?*

What is important is to live a life without effort, without a single problem. You can live without a problem if you understand the nature of effort and see very clearly the whole structure of desire. Most of us have a thousand problems, and to be free of problems we must be able to end each problem immediately as it arises. It is absolutely necessary for the mind to have no problems at all, and so live a life without effort. Surely such a mind is the only religious mind, because it has understood sorrow and the ending of sorrow. It is without fear, and is therefore a light unto itself.

J. Krishnamurti, *On God*

The Yellow Mustard

Cabined beneath low vaults of cloud,
Sultry and still, the fields do lie,
Like one wrapt living in his shroud,
Who stifles silently.

Stripped of all beauty not their own—
The gulfs of shade, the golden bloom—
Grey mountain-heaps of slag and stone
Wall in the silent tomb.

I, through this emblem of a mind
Dark with repinings, slowly went,
Its captive, and myself confined
In like discouragement.

When, at a winding of the way,
A sudden glory met my eye,
As though a single, conquering ray
Had rent the cloudy sky

And touched, transfiguringly bright
In that dull plain, one luminous field;
And there the miracle of light
Lay goldenly revealed.

And yet the reasons for despair
Hung dark, without one rift of blue;
No loophole to the living air
Had let the glory through.

In their own soil those acres found
The sunlight of a flowering weed;
For still there sleeps in every ground
Some grain of mustard seed.

Aldous Huxley, *Huxley and God*

→ IV ←

Surrender

⬩ Birth of the New ⬩

Surrendering the old self to make way for the new is not easy; it requires relinquishing our power, our expectations, and our independence to make way for humility, guidance, awareness, consciousness, grace, and simplicity. Although we are sometimes forced to surrender through suffering and illness, conscious surrender to the greater good can be a celebration of belonging to God. To live in a state of surrender is to let go of our concept of time, of form, of a beginning, middle, and end of the course of life and to live solely in the present. It is about believing that everything continues as it is meant to be in every moment. One of my favourite Buddhist sayings aptly describes this: "When in doubt about where you are meant to be, look down at your feet."

Surrender requires an active will of faith, a healthy positivism—it requires going forward with confidence. Then there is little room for lingering doubt or fear. Sometimes it requires our doing nothing but waiting for a sign from God. The patience needed to do this may in itself be the lesson. Or it may require us to go further still and *be* nothing, a void waiting. Ram Dass explores this nonbeing, nondoing concept in his piece "Nobody's Special" from *Grist for the Mill*.

Hans Küng suggests that "man should live his humanity at all levels and in all dimensions," and it is in the state of surrender that these dimensions become familiar.

The revelations that the spiritual experience has brought, through nature, prayer, and meditation and through trials and suffering, have led to an unfolding of the heart, a freeing of the soul from its fragile boundaries, and a sense of fundamental trust that all is well in oneself, in others, and around us, as it always was before we were taught to believe otherwise.

And so we become wholly ourselves, perhaps for the first time. We encompass all the parts of which we are made—dark and light, angry, sad, hopeful, fragile, weak, forgiving, and strong. By accepting ourselves as we are—not egotistically but with humility and gratitude—we become more unusual yet more usual at the same time. Krishnamurti says, "The tree is nothing to itself. It exists. And in its very existence it is the most beautiful thing."

The surrendered self therefore becomes more united with the whole environment. The responsibility that goes with this cannot be denied—if our life is meaningless to us, then it will become so for others. If we live in tune with our surroundings, in touch with our destiny, then we share in the joy of God, and become as Krishnamurti said, "a light to oneself; this light is the law."

This part is divided into five sections to illustrate the path of surrender. There is the beginning itself—"The Way" of contemplation and silence which leads us to the way of life, the "Being for God"—that is living in the present, building a relationship through prayer and thought. This leads to action and compassion, the "Doing for God" in our world. As the first three sections look at how a person must serve God in surrender, the last two focus on what God gives in return—the help from the right people who act like signposts on the road—"The Guides" and the enormous spiritual gifts of love, grace, creativity, bliss, peace, and happiness which are generously bestowed.

II

The Way

The Way is toward the "relationship that has no end" (Martin Israel) between our own soul and our own God. One begins it in silence and solitude. In silence and solitude we find "peace with God" (Merton). We find a deeper and subtler way of communicating with the divine by listening in silence. We are healed in silence and also through the natural sounds of our world, the music of nature. Krishnamurti's piece on page 391 is like a long drink for the thirsty, his observations in his own silence of nature and his surroundings, bring home the need we all have to relish what is. It is in solitude that the word is passed to us, the message is given. We become conscious of all things, see divinity in all beings, even the unseemly. And from this place, intuition, our inner wisdom, is fine-tuned.

⊁⊰

When all within is dark,
and former friends misprise;
from them I turn to you,
and find love in Your eyes.

When all within is dark,
and I my soul despise;
from me I turn to You,
and find love in Your eyes.

When all Your face is dark,
and Your just angers rise;
From You I turn to You,
and find love in Your eyes.

Israel Abrahams, based on Ibi Gabirol,
in *The Oxford Book of Prayer*

One has to be a light to oneself; this light is the law. There is no other law. All the other laws are made by thought and so fragmentary and contradictory. To be a light to oneself is not to follow the light of another, however reasonable, logical, historical, and however convincing. You cannot be a light to yourself if you are in the dark shadows of authority, of dogma, of conclusion. Morality is not put together by thought; it is not the outcome of environmental pressure; it is not of yesterday, of tradition. Morality is the child of love and love is not desire and pleasure. Sexual or sensory enjoyment is not love.

High in the mountains there were hardly any birds; there were some crows, there were deer and an occasional bear. The huge redwoods, the silent ones, were everywhere, dwarfing all other trees. It was a magnificent country and utterly peaceful, for no hunting was allowed. Every animal, every tree and flower was protected. Sitting under one of those massive redwoods, one was aware of the history of man and the beauty of the earth. A fat red squirrel passed by most elegantly, stopping a few feet away, watching and wondering what you were doing there. The earth was dry, though there was a stream nearby. Not a leaf stirred and the beauty of silence was among the trees. Going slowly along the narrow path, round a bend was a bear with four cubs as large as big cats. They rushed off to crawl up trees and the mother faced one without a movement, without a sound. About fifty feet separated us; she was enormous, brown, and prepared. One immediately turned one's back on her and left. Each understood that there was no fear and no intention to hurt, but all the same one was glad to be among the protecting trees, squirrels and the scolding jays.

Freedom is to be a light to oneself; then it is not an abstraction, a thing conjured up by thought. Actual freedom is freedom from dependency, attachment, from the craving for experience. Freedom from the very structure of thought is to be a light to oneself. In this light all action takes place and thus it is never contradictory. Contradiction exists only when that law, light, is separate from action, when the actor is separate from action. The ideal, the principle, is the barren movement of thought and cannot coexist with this light; one denies the other. This light, this law, is separate from you;

where the observer is, this light, this love, is not. The structure of the observer is put together by thought, which is never new, never free. There is no "how," no system, no practice. There is only the seeing which is the doing. You have to see, not through the eyes of another. This light, this law, is neither yours nor that of another. There is only light. This is love.

J. Krishnamurti, Krishnamurti's Journal

Best Society

When I was a child, I thought,
Casually, that solitude
Never needed to be sought.
Something everybody had,
Like nakedness, it lay at hand,
Not specially right or specially wrong,
A plentiful and obvious thing
Not at all hard to understand.

Then, after twenty, it became
At once more difficult to get
And more desired—though all the same
More undesirable; for what
You are alone has, to achieve
The rank of fact, to be expressed
In terms of others, or it's just
A compensating make-believe.

Much better stay in company!
To love you must have someone else,
Giving requires a legatee,
Good neighbours need whole parishfuls
Of folk to do it on—in short,
Our virtues are all social; if,
Deprived of solitude, you chafe,
It's clear you're not the virtuous sort.

Viciously, then, I lock my door.
The gas-fire breathes. The wind outside
Ushers in evening rain. Once more
Uncontradicting solitude
Supports me on its giant palm;

And like a sea-anemone
Or simple snail, there cautiously
Unfolds, emerges, what I am.

Philip Larkin, *Collected Poems*

If you live alone, you probably spend a large part of your time in solitude. Solitude does not mean that you are really living alone, even if you *seem* to be living alone. You know that when you shut the door and darken the room and look within that the door is open, the light is on, and, "Someone is in your room...darkness like a dark bird, flies away...flies away."

Ram Dass, "Sadhana If You Live Alone,"
from *Be Here Now*

Silence is something extraordinary; it's not the silence between two noises. Peace is not between two wars. Silence is something that comes naturally when you are watching, when you are watching without motive, without any kind of demand, just to watch, and see the beauty of a single star in the sky, or to watch a single tree in a field, or to watch your wife or husband, or whatever you watch. To watch with a great silence and space. Then in that watching, in that alertness, there is something that is beyond words, beyond all measure.

We use words to measure the immeasurable. So one must be aware also of the network of words, how words cheat us, how words mean so much: *communism*, to a capitalist, means something terrible. Words become extraordinarily important. But to be aware of those words and to live with the word *silence*, knowing that the word is not silence, but to live with that word and see the weight of that word, the content of that word, the beauty of that word! So one begins to realize, when thought is quiet, watching, that there is something beyond all imagination, doubt, and seeking. And there is such a thing—at least for the speaker. But what the speaker says has no validity to another. If you listen, learn, watch, be totally free from all the anxieties of life, then only is there a religion that brings about a new, totally different culture. We are not cultured people at all. You may be very clever in business, you may be extraordinarily capable technologically, be a doctor or a professor; but we are still very limited.

The ending of the self, the "me": to be nothing. The word *nothing* means "not a thing." Not a thing created by thought. To be nothing; having no image of yourself. But we have a great many images of ourselves. To have no image of any kind, no illusion, to be absolutely nothing. The tree is nothing to itself. It exists. And in its very existence it is the most beautiful thing, like those hills: they exist. They don't become something, because they can't. Like a seed of an apple tree, it is apple; it doesn't try to become the pear, or another fruit—it is.

J. Krishnamurti, On Nature and the Environment

Words stand between silence and silence: between the silence of things and the silence of our own being. Between the silence of the world and the silence of God. When we have really met and known the world in silence, words do not separate us from the world nor from other men, nor from God, nor from ourselves, because we no longer trust entirely in language to contain reality.

    Truth rises from the silence of being to the quiet, tremendous presence of the Word. Then, sinking again into silence, the truth of words bears us down into the silence of God. Or rather God rises out of the sea like a treasure in the waves, and when language recedes his brightness remains on the shores of our own being.

Thomas Merton, "Thoughts in Solitude"

Silence demands space, space in the whole structure of consciousness. There is no space in the structure of one's consciousness as it is, because it is crowded with fears—crowded, chattering, chattering. When there is silence, there is immense, timeless space; then only is there a possibility of coming upon that which is the eternal, sacred.

J. Krishnamurti, The Wholeness of Life

September 15, 1973

It is good to be alone. To be far away from the world and yet walk its streets is to be alone. To be alone walking up the path beside the rushing, noisy mountain stream full of spring water and melting snows is to be aware of that solitary tree, alone in its beauty. The loneliness of a man in the street is the pain of life; he's never alone, far away, untouched and vulnerable. To be full of knowledge breeds endless misery. The demand for expression, with its frustrations and pains, is that man who walks the streets; he is never alone. Sorrow is the movement of that loneliness.

    That mountain stream was full and high with the melting snows and the rains of early spring. You could hear big boulders being pushed around by the force of on-rushing waters. A tall pine of fifty years or more crashed into the water; the road was being washed away. The stream was muddy, slate coloured. The fields above it were full of wild flowers. The air was pure and there was enchantment. On the high hills there was still snow, and the glaciers and the great peaks still held the recent snows; they will still be white all the summer long.

It was a marvellous morning and you could have walked on endlessly, never feeling the steep hills. There was a perfume in the air, clear and strong. There was no one on that path, coming down or going up. You were alone with those dark pines and the rushing waters. The sky was that astonishing blue that only the mountains have. You looked at it through leaves and the straight pines. There was no one to talk to and there was no chattering of the mind. A magpie, white and black, flew by, disappearing into the woods. The path led away from the noisy stream and the silence was absolute. It wasn't the silence after the noise; it wasn't the silence that comes with the setting of the sun, nor that silence when the mind dies down. It wasn't the silence of museums and churches but something totally unrelated to time and space. It wasn't the silence that mind makes for itself. The sun was hot and the shadows were pleasant.

He only discovered recently that there was not a single thought during these long walks, in the crowded streets or on the solitary paths. Ever since he was a boy it had been like that, no thought entered his mind. He was watching and listening and nothing else. Thought with its associations never arose. There was no image-making. One day he was suddenly aware how extraordinary it was; he attempted often to think but no thought would come. On these walks, with people or without them, any movement of thought was absent. This is to be alone.

Over the snow peaks clouds were forming, heavy and dark; probably it would rain later on but now the shadows were very sharp with the sun bright and clear. There was still that pleasant smell in the air and the rains would bring a different smell. It was a long way down to the chalet.

J. Krishnamurti, Krishnamurti's Journal

Today, more than ever, we need to recognize that the gift of solitude is not ordered to the acquisition of strange contemplative powers, but, first of all, to the recovery of one's deep self, and to the renewal of an authenticity which is presently twisted out of shape by the pretentious routines of a disordered togetherness.

Thomas Merton, from Contemplation in a World of Action

Where is silence? Where is solitude? Where is Love? Ultimately, these cannot be found anywhere except in the ground of our own being. There, in the silent depths, there is no more distinction between the I and the Not-I. There is perfect peace because we are grounded in infinite creative and redemptive Love.

Thomas Merton, preface to Japanese edition of *Thoughts in Solitude*

Silence Is All

1

Silence is all, say the sages.
Silence watches the work of the ages;
In the book of Silence the cosmic Scribe has written his cosmic
  pages;
Silence is all, say the sages.

2

What then of the word, O speaker?
What then of the thought, O thinker?
Thought is the wine of the soul and the word is the beaker;
Life is the banquet-table—the soul of the sage is the drinker.

3

What of the wine, O mortal?
I am drunk with the wine as I sit at Wisdom's portal,
Waiting for the Light beyond thought and the Word immortal.
Long I sit in vain at Wisdom's portal.

4

How shalt thou know the Word when it comes, O seeker?
How shalt thou know the Light when it breaks, O witness?
I shall hear the voice of the God within me and grow wiser and
  meeker;
I shall be the tree that takes in the light as its food, I shall drink
  its nectar of sweetness.

Sri Aurobindo, *Collected Poems*

In a tent on the Desert of Time we have a tryst—
This tent is the tabernacle of our own being—
The Tryst is with the God which is our being—

In a tent on the Desert of Time each keeps a Tryst—
A Tryst with the God of his being—
This Trysting tent is the abode, the dwelling place of God.
This Trysting Tent is all we are—
    Our body, our heart, our imagination, our mind.
    It is the inner chamber of love,
    It is the tabernacle of The Holy One
    Its servants are our thoughts—

What takes place in this Trysting Tent—
Whom do we meet there
        The Discovery of the Self

Martha Graham, "The Trysting Tent,"
in *Notebooks of Martha Graham*

In actuality, God is not far from the seeker, nor is it impossible to see Him. He is like the sun, which is ever shining right above you. It is you who have held over your head the umbrella of your variegated mental impressions which hide Him from your view. You have only to remove the umbrella and the Sun is there for you to see. It does not have to be brought there from anywhere. But such a tiny and trivial thing as an umbrella can deprive you of the sight of such a stupendous fact as the Sun.

Meher Baba, *Life at Its Best*

✦ 12 ✦

Being for God

At this point in the act of surrender, being for God means being true in all possible ways. It means accepting the way of being that is best expressed by the words "I am"—I am wholly myself in all that I am, or, as in the Zen Buddhist tradition, I am nothing, and therefore am one with everything. By surrendering the Self to this depth of existence, God can begin to dwell within us. As Thomas Merton explains so succinctly, "He asks for ourselves."

By not forcing our intent upon anything or anyone, by not being a "somebody" (as Ram Dass says), we begin to live every moment perfectly in the "here and now." This more Eastern view of being is sometimes very foreign to Westerners, as Alan Watts points out. We in the West are far more used to action, to the "doing" side of being. Being is clearly not about doing. It is just being. In the process of being we learn the steps to heightened conscious awareness. Carlos Castaneda writes of his experience when, as a pupil of don Juan (an Yaqui Indian shaman), he is led to experience the "luminous body" in this heightened state. The more open we become in surrender, the lighter and brighter we are in spirit. We begin to feel the glow of God.

Many of us have been brought up to believe we are unworthy of God's love. But Nancy Ore's poem provides a lovely example of surrender as the "giving up" of self-imposed expectations, of throwing the senses of inadequacy, guilt, and hopelessness to the wind. It is at this point that spiritual ascension occurs. We begin to experience pure joy and freedom. From this freedom comes love; the love of Self expands into the love of others and of God, from which come all things—love, liberty, and light. This love from God brings a feeling of perfect harmony, warmth, peace, and security.

Part of building this ongoing relationship with God is to learn to communicate with Him in open intimacy. To love what Bulgarian master Omraam Mikhaël Aïvanhov calls "the infinity, eternity or perfection of God," we need to come from the most silent place of our being, the most fragile and sometimes most lost place that is our own souls' dwelling and this process is prayer itself. Finding the time, then the peace, and lastly the words with which to pray is not an easy task in this world. Many have difficulty, but Thomas Merton offers down-to-earth advice when he describes the meaning and stages of prayer and its importance in maintaining the "deep and vital contact" with God that brings us to "a high perfection." Prayer is powerful—it has its purpose at many levels—in supplication, in petition, discourse, and worship and in celebration and thanksgiving. And its effects are manifold. Perhaps, most importantly, it brings "God back into the world, to establish His Kingship for a second at least." To pray means "to expand His presence" (Abraham Joshua Heschel).

※

Man is man because something divine is at stake in his existence. He is not an innocent bystander in the cosmic drama. There is in us more kinship with the divine than we are able to believe.

Abraham Joshua Heschel,
The Insecurity of Freedom

If I am to know the will of God, I must have the right attitude toward life. I must first of all know what life is, and to know the purpose of my existence.

It is all very well to declare that I exist in order to save my soul and give glory to God by doing so. And it is all very well to say that in order to do this I obey certain commandments and keep certain counsels. Yet knowing this much, and indeed knowing all moral theology and ethics and canon law, I might still go through life conforming myself to certain indications of God's will without ever fully giving myself to God. For that, in the last analysis, is the real meaning of His will. He does not need our sacrifices, He asks for our selves.

Thomas Merton, *No Man Is an Island*

The Sound of Rain

This is all there is;
the path comes to an end
among the parsley.

Perhaps I can express this Buddhist fascination for the mystery of nothingness in another way. If we get rid of all wishful thinking and dubious metaphysical speculations, we can hardly doubt that—at a time not too
distant—each one of us will simply cease to be. It won't be like going into
darkness forever, for there will be neither darkness, nor time, nor sense of
futility, nor anyone to feel anything about it. Try as best you can to imagine
this, and keep at it. The universe will, supposedly, be going on as usual, but
for each individual it will be as if it had never happened at all; and even that
is saying too much, because there won't be anyone for whom it never happened. Make this prospect as real as possible: the one total certainty. You will
be as if you had never existed, which was, however, the way you were before
you did exist—and not only you but everything else. Nevertheless, with such
an improbable past, here we are. We begin from nothing and end in nothing.
You can say that again. Think it over and over, trying to conceive the fact of
coming to never having existed. After a while you will begin to feel rather
weird, as if this very apparent something that you are is at the same time
nothing at all. Indeed, you seem to be rather firmly and certainly grounded
in nothingness, much as your sight seems to emerge from that total blankness
behind your eyes. The weird feeling goes with the fact that you are being
introduced to a new common sense, a new logic, in which you are beginning
to realize the identity of *ku* and *shiki*, void and form. All of a sudden it will
strike you that this nothingness is the most potent, magical, basic, and reliable
thing you ever thought of, and that the reason you can't form the slightest
idea of it is that it's yourself. But not the self you thought you were.

Alan Watts, *In My Own Way*

Paradoxical as it may seem, the purposeful life has no content, no point. It
hurries on and on, and misses everything. Not hurrying, the purposeless life
misses nothing, for it is only when there is no goal and no rush that the
human senses are fully open to receive the world. Absence of hurry also
involves a certain lack of interference with the natural course of events, especially when it is felt that the natural course follows principles which are not
foreign to human intelligence. For, as we have seen, the Taoist mentality

makes, or forces, nothing but "grows" everything. When human reason is seen to be an expression of the same spontaneous balance of *yang* and *yin* as the natural universe, man's action upon his environment is not felt as a conflict, an action from outside. Thus the difference between forcing and growing cannot be expressed in terms of specific directions as to what should or should not be done, for the difference lies primarily in the quality and feeling of the action. The difficulty of describing these things for Western ears is that people in a hurry cannot feel.

Alan Watts, *The Way of Zen*

For Zen, as Suzuki exemplified it, was spontaneously intelligent living, without calculation, and without rigid conceptual distinctions between self and other, knower and known. He used the force of gravity as a sailor uses the wind.

Alan Watts, *In My Own Way*

For our first *not-doing*, Silvio Manuel constructed a wooden crate big enough to house la Gorda and me, if we sat back-to-back with our knees up. The crate had a lid made of lattice-work to let in a flow of air. La Gorda and I were to climb inside it and sit in total darkness and total silence, without falling asleep. He began by letting us enter the box for short periods; then he increased the time as we got used to the procedure, until we could spend the entire night inside it without moving or dozing off.

The Nagual woman stayed with us to make sure that we would not change levels of awareness due to fatigue. Silvio Manuel said that our natural tendency under unusual conditions of stress is to shift from the heightened state of awareness to our normal one, and vice versa.

The general effect of the *not-doing* every time we performed it was to give us an unequaled sense of rest, which was a complete puzzle to me, since we never fell asleep during our nightlong vigils. I attributed the sense of rest to the fact that we were in a state of heightened awareness, but Silvio Manuel said that the one had nothing to do with the other, that the sense of rest was the result of sitting with our knees up.

The second *not-doing* consisted of making us lie on the ground like curled-up dogs, almost in the fetal position, resting on our left sides, our foreheads on our folded arms. Silvio Manuel insisted that we keep our eyes closed as long as possible, opening them only when he told us to shift positions and lie on our right sides. He told us that the purpose of this *not-doing* was to allow our sense of hearing to separate from our sight. As before, he gradually increased the length of time until we could spend the entire night in auditory vigil.

Silvio Manuel was then ready to move us to another area of activity. He explained that in the first two *not-doings* we had broken a certain perceptual barrier while we were stuck to the ground. By way of analogy, he compared human beings to trees. We are like mobile trees. We are somehow rooted to the ground; our roots are transportable, but that does not free us from the ground. He said that in order to establish balance we had to perform the third *not-doing* while dangling in the air. If we succeeded in channeling our *intent* while we were suspended from a tree inside a leather harness, we would make a triangle with our *intent*, a triangle whose base was on the ground and its vertex in the air. Silvio Manuel thought that we had gathered our attention with the first two *not-doings* to the point that we could perform the third perfectly from the beginning.

One night he suspended la Gorda and me in two separate harnesses like strap chairs. We sat in them and he lifted us with a pulley to the highest large branches of a tall tree. He wanted us to pay attention to the awareness of the tree, which he said would give us signals, since we were its guests. He made the Nagual woman stay on the ground and call our names from time to time during the entire night.

While we were suspended from the tree, in the innumerable times we performed this *not-doing*, we experienced a glorious flood of physical sensations, like mild charges of electrical impulses. During the first three or four attempts, it was as if the tree were protesting our intrusion; then after that the impulses became signals of peace and balance. Silvio Manuel told us that the awareness of a tree draws its nourishment from the depths of the earth, while the awareness of mobile creatures draws it from the surface. There is no sense of strife in a tree, whereas moving beings are filled to the brim with it.

His contention was that perception suffers a profound jolt when we are placed in states of quietude in darkness. Our hearing takes the lead then, and the signals from all the living and existing entities around us can be detected—not with our hearing only, but with a combination of the auditory and visual senses, in that order. He said that in darkness, especially while one is suspended, the eyes become subsidiary to the ears.

He was absolutely right, as la Gorda and I discovered. Through the exercise of the third *not-doing*, Silvio Manuel gave a new dimension to our perception of the world around us.

He then told la Gorda and me that the next set of three *not-doings* would be intrinsically different and more complex. These had to do with learning to handle the other world. It was mandatory to maximize their effect by moving our time of action to the evening or predawn twilight. He told us that the first not-doing of the second set had two stages. In stage one we had to bring ourselves to our keenest state of heightened awareness so as to detect the wall of fog. Once that was done, stage two consisted of making that wall stop rotating in order to venture into the world between the parallel lines.

He warned us that what he was aiming at was to place us directly into the second attention, without any intellectual preparation. He wanted us to learn its intricacies without rationally understanding what we were doing. His contention was that a magical deer or a magical coyote handles the second attention without having any intellect. Through the forced practice of journeying behind the wall of fog, we were going to undergo, sooner or later, a permanent alteration in our total being, an alteration that would make us accept that the world between the parallel lines is real, because it is part of the total world, as our luminous body is part of our total being.

Carlos Castaneda, *The Eagle's Gift*

Nobody's Special

We are in training to be nobody special. And it is in that nobody-specialness that we can be anybody. The fatigue, the neurosis, the anxiety, the fear, all come from identifying with the somebody-ness. But we have to start somewhere. It does seem that we have to be somebody before we can become nobody. If we started out being nobody at the beginning of this incarnation, we probably wouldn't have made it this far. Blue babies are examples of nobody special; they just don't have the will to breathe or eat or live. For it's that force of somebody-ness that develops the social and physical survival mechanisms. It's only now, having evolved to this point, that we learn to put that somebody-ness, that whole survival kit, which is called the ego, into perspective.

When I was a Harvard professor, I would spend all my time thinking. I was paid for that. I would have clipboards and tape recorders to collect all my thoughts. Now I'm becoming more and more simple as I quiet. Sometimes there seems to be no one in there at all, and I just sit. Then, when something needs to happen, it happens, even thinking or speaking, and I just witness it.

It's very far out when we begin not to think, or the thinking is going by, and we're not identified with being the thinker. At first we really "think" we've lost something. It's a while before we can appreciate the peace that comes from the simplicity of no-mind, of just emptiness, of not having to be somebody all the time. We've been somebody long enough. We spent the first half of our lives becoming somebody. Now we can work on becoming nobody, which is really somebody.

For when we become nobody, there is no tension, no pretense, no one trying to be anyone or anything, and the natural state of the mind shines through unobstructed. The natural state of the mind is pure love, which is not other than pure awareness. Can you imagine when we become that place we've only touched through our meditations? When we *are* love. We've finally acknowledged who we really are. We've cleared away all of the mind trips that kept us being who we thought we were. Now, everybody we look at we're in love with. We experience the exquisiteness of being in love with everybody and not having to do anything about it—because we've developed compassion. The compassion is to let people be as they need to be without coming on to them. The only time we come on to people is when their actions are limiting the opportunities for other human beings to be free. And then the way in which we come on is very mindfully and open heartedly. For if we are somebody coming on to change someone, we're just creating more anger. If we are nobody special, but it is our dharma to come on about injustice, then it is merely an act of the Dharma. And not for a moment do we lose that total love for the other person who is not other than us. For being nobody, there is nobody we're not.

Had we sufficient discipline, we could pursue the steepest of paths to get rid of all the ways we cling to models of ourselves. We could just sit—Zen Buddhism—and every thought that comes by, that creates another reality, we would let it go. And clinging to none, we would know enlightenment. Or we might pursue the path of Ramana Maharshi—Vicharya Atman, "Who am I?" We simply ask, "Who am I?" "Who am I?" And slowly we watch ourselves be other than all the ways in which we identify ourselves—as bodies, organs, emotions, social roles—we see it all. We keep dissociating from it until we are left with the thought of "I." "I am the thought 'I.'" This path takes incredible discipline, for as we have freed ourselves from our bodies and our emotions, and we're just about to drop this last thought of "I," our body grabs us again. And we're back in our habitual thoughts about our bodies, our identities.

Most of the time when we watch our mind we find it keeps grabbing at things and making them the foreground. And everything else becomes the background. When we're reading, we're not listening. When we're listening, we're not seeing. When we're remembering, we forget where we're at. But can we function when the world is all background and awareness itself is foreground?

When awareness is identified with thoughts we only exist in a certain time/space dimension. But when awareness goes behind thought, we are able to be free of time and see thoughts appearing and disappearing, just watching thought forms come into existence, exist, and pass away in a millisecond. And when the intensity of concentration allows us to see the space between two thoughts, we see eternity. There is no thought there. We realize that thoughts exist against the backdrop of no thought. Against the backdrop of emptiness, of nothing, we exist. And there we are at the edge of perceiving who we are. Then we face one of the greatest fears we will ever confront: the fear of our own extinction. The fear of ceasing to exist—not just as a body, but even as a soul. It is similar to the statement made by Huang Po about people approaching this point: that they become fearful to enter into what they consider "the void," distressed that once they let go into it they will drop unendingly, that there will be nothing to stay their fall, not realizing the Void is the Dharma itself.

But as we're ready for the ultimate mystic doorway, the inner door of the seventh temple, we say, "I am not this thought." We let go of even the great fear of non-existence. The senses are just working by themselves. There is hearing occurring, but there is no listener. There is seeing but there is no see-er. The senses are just all doing their thing, but there's nobody home. If the mind thinks, "I am aware," that is recognized as just another thought, a part of the show passing by. It's not awareness itself. Thoughts are going by like a river, and awareness simply is. When we become just awareness, there is no more "me" being aware.

By letting go of even the thought "I," what is left? There is nowhere to stand, and no one to stand there. No separation anywhere. Pure awareness. Neither this, nor that. Just clarity and being.

Ram Dass, *Grist for the Mill*

The living by Zen means to remain itself, to be complete by itself, and therefore it is always self-working; it gives out what it has, and never tries or contrives to be other than itself. With Zen every morning is a good morning, every day a fine day, no matter how stormy. Morality always binds itself with the ideas of good and evil, just and unjust, virtuous and unvirtuous, and cannot go beyond them; for if it goes, it will no longer be itself; it is its own nature that it cannot be free and self-independent. Zen is, however, not tied up with any such ideas; it is as free as the bird flying, the fish swimming, and the lilies blooming.

Daisetz Teitaro Suzuki, *Living by Zen*

"You Are Enough!"
A Woman Seminarian's Story

It is not enough
said her father
that you
    get all A's each quarter
    play Mozart for your kinfolk
    win starred-firsts in contest
you must
come home on your wedding night.

It is not enough
said her mother
that you
    smile at Auntie Lockwood
    take cookies to the neighbors
    keep quiet while I'm napping
you must
cure my asthma.

It is not enough
said her husband
that you
    write letters to my parents
    fix pumpkin pie and pastry
    forget your name was Bauer
you must
always
you must
never.

It is not enough
said her children
that you
    make us female brownies
    tend our friends and puppies
    buy us Nike tennies
you must
let us kill you.

It is not enough
said her pastor
that you
    teach the second graders
    change the cloths and candles
    kneel prostrate at the altar
as long as there are starving children in the world
you must
not eat
without guilt.

It is not enough
said her counselor
that you
    struggle with the demons
    integrate your childhood
    leave when time is over
you must
stop crying
clarify your poetic symbols
and
not feel
that you are
not enough.

I give up
she said
I am not enough
and laid down
into the deep blue pocket
of night
to wait
for death.

She waited...

and
finally
her heart exploded
her breathing stopped

They came with stretcher
took her clothes off
covered her with linen
then went away
and left her locked
in deep blue pocket tomb

The voice said
   YOU ARE ENOUGH

      naked
      crying
      bleeding
      nameless
      starving
      sinful
YOU ARE ENOUGH

And the third day
she sat up
   asked for milk and crackers
   took ritual bath with angels
   dressed herself with wings
and flew away.

               Nancy Ore, in Rosemary Radford Ruether,
                              Womanguides

Love sails me around the house. I walk two steps on the ground and four steps in the air. It is love. It is consolation. I don't care if it is consolation. I am not attached to consolation. I love God. Love carries me all around. I don't want to *do* anything but love.

And when the bell rings, it is like pulling teeth to make myself shift because of that love, secret love, hidden love, obscure love, down inside me and outside me, where I don't care to talk about it. Anyway, I don't have the time or the energy to discuss such matters. I have only time for eternity, which is to say, for love, love, love.

Maybe Saint Teresa would like to have me snap out of it, but it is pure, I tell you: I am not attached to it (I hope) and it is love, and it gives me soft punches all the time in the center of my heart. Love is pushing me around the monastery, love is kicking me all around, like a gong, I tell you. Love is the only thing that makes it possible for me to continue to tick.

Thomas Merton, *"The Sign of Jonas"*

Let God be the object of all your senses. Tukaram says that the man whose one enjoyment is Narayana sees the world filled with love.

Love is your very nature. It is your *sadhana* and your highest attainment. Love is God; love is the universe. God has appeared as the universe—the universe is no different; it is a manifestation of the divine Shakti. Love is a complete *sadhana* for the realization of God. Without love He cannot be attained.

Love is a great inner experience. Seek it within. You will see the divine Shakti darting with the speed of electricity through your whole body, through all its fluids, blood, prana. As you experience this Shakti, you will know what love is.

The activity inside you always goes on. It never stops. Your nerves, muscles, and blood cells are constantly performing their functions. You should also do your work with love, enthusiasm, and determination, whether you are at home, in an ashram, or elsewhere.

Man should love his Self, which is all-embracing. He should have complete faith in it. Love turns man into an ocean of happiness, an image of peace, a temple of wisdom. Love is man's very Self, his true beauty, and the glory of his human existence. Muktananda says, "First love yourself, then your neighbors, and then the whole world."

Swami Muktananda, *Play of Consciousness*

A Christian is a tabernacle of the living God. He created me, he chose me, he came to dwell in me, because he wanted me. Now that you have known how much God is in love with you, it is but natural that you spend the rest of your life radiating that love.

Mother Teresa, *A Gift for God*

What I cry out for, like every being, with my whole life and all my earthly passion, is something very different from an equal to cherish: it is a God to adore.

To adore... that means to lose oneself in the unfathomable, to plunge into the inexhaustible, to find peace in the incorruptible, to be absorbed in

defined immensity, to offer oneself to the fire and the transparency, to anni-
hilate oneself in proportion as one becomes more deliberately conscious of
oneself, and to give of one's deepest to that whose depth has no end.

Pierre Teilhard de Chardin,
Love and Happiness

If you ask a sage to describe God he will say nothing; his only response will
be silence, for silence alone can express the essence of the Deity. Yes, to say
what God is is not enough; and to say what He is not is not enough either. It
is true to say that God is love, wisdom, power and goodness, but it is also true
to say that these words fall far short of the divine reality; they are incapable
of encompassing anything of the infinity, eternity or perfection of God. We
cannot know God by talking or hearing others talk about Him; we can only
know Him by plunging into the depths of our own being and entering that
innermost region: the region that is silence.

Omraam Mikhaël Aïvanhov, *The Path of Silence*

All help is given to you always, but you must learn to receive it in the silence
of your heart and not through external means. It is in the silence of your heart
that the Divine will speak to you and will guide you and will lead you to your
goal. But for that you must have full faith in the Divine Grace and Love.

18 January 1962

The Mother, *Words of the Mother*, Part Two

All sincere prayers are granted, but it may take some time to realise materially.

The Mother, *Words of the Mother*, Part Two

Prayer obviously produces results, otherwise millions wouldn't pray.

J. Krishnamurti, *On God*

We do not step out of the world when we pray; we merely see the world in
a different setting. The self is not the hub, but the spoke of the revolving
wheel. In prayer we shift the center of living from self-consciousness to self-
surrender. God is the center toward which all forces tend. He is the source,
and we are the flowing of His force, the ebb and flow of His tides.

Prayer takes the mind out of the narrowness of self-interest, and enables us to see the world in the mirror of the holy. For when we betake ourselves to the extreme opposite of the ego, we can behold a situation from the aspect of God.

Abraham Joshua Heschel, *Man's Quest for God*

"While walking I would repeat the Divine Name with each and every step. Always the next step was made only after chanting the mantra. If ever I forgot to chant the mantra while taking a step, immediately I would step backwards. Having withdrawn the step, I would repeat the mantra. Only then would I proceed. If I happened to be engaged in any external activity, I would decide beforehand to chant the mantra a certain number of times before finishing the work. While bathing in the river, before plunging into the water, I would resolve to chant the mantra a set number of times before coming to the surface of the water. I never had a Guru, nor was I ever initiated by anyone and given a particular mantra. The mantra which I used to chant was 'Amma, Amma.'"

Mata Amritanandamayi, in Swami Amritasvarupananda,
Mata Amritanandamayi

The peculiar value of mental prayer...is that it is completely personal and favors a spiritual development along lines dictated by our own particular needs. The interior life demands of us a heroic struggle to practice virtue and to detach ourselves from inordinate love of temporal, created things. We cannot possibly bring our souls to renounce our most powerful natural desires unless we somehow have a real and conscious appreciation of our contact with something better. The love of God remains a cold and abstract thing unless we can bring ourselves to realize its deeply intimate and personal character.

Thomas Merton, "Spiritual Direction and Meditation," in
Robert E. Daggy, *The Honourable Reader*

Worry

A hasid told the rabbi of Kotzk about his poverty and troubles.

"Don't worry," advised the rabbi. "Pray to God with all your heart, and the merciful Lord will have mercy upon you."

"But I don't know how to pray," said the other.

Pity surged up in the rabbi of Kotzk as he looked at him. "Then," he said, "you have indeed a great deal to worry about."

Martin Buber, Tales of the Hasidim

I had to touch on the subject of prayer, and while that is still fresh in your mind and my own, I should like to deal with a difficulty that some people find about the whole idea of prayer. A man put it to me by saying "I can believe in God all right, but what I cannot swallow is the idea of Him attending to several hundred million human beings who are all addressing Him at the same moment." And I have found that quite a lot of people feel this.

Now, the first thing to notice is that the whole sting of it comes in the words *at the same moment*. Most of us can imagine God attending to any number of applicants if only they came one by one and He had an endless time to do it in. So what is really at the back of this difficulty is the idea of God having to fit too many things into one moment of time.

Well that is of course what happens to us. Our life comes to us moment by moment. One moment disappears before the next comes along: and there is room for very little in each. That is what Time is like. And of course you and I tend to take it for granted that this Time series—this arrangement of past, present and future—is not simply the way life comes to us but the way all things really exist. We tend to assume that the whole universe and God Himself are always moving on from past to future just as we do. But many learned men do not agree with that. It was the Theologians who first started the idea that some things are not in Time at all: later the Philosophers took it over: and now some of the scientists are doing the same.

Almost certainly God is not in Time. His life does not consist of moments following one another. If a million people are praying to Him at ten-thirty tonight, He need not listen to them all in that one little snippet which we call ten-thirty. Ten-thirty—and every other moment from the beginning of the world—is always the Present for Him. If you like to put it that way, He has all eternity in which to listen to the split second of prayer put up by a pilot as his plane crashes in flames.

C. S. Lewis, Mere Christianity

Prayer is inspired by God in the depth of our own nothingness. It is the movement of trust, of gratitude, of adoration, or of sorrow that places us before God, seeing both Him and ourselves in the light of His infinite truth, and moves us to ask Him for the mercy, the spiritual strength, the material help that we all need. The man whose prayer is so pure that he never asks

God for anything does not know who God is, and does not know who he is himself: for he does not know his own need of God.

All true prayer somehow confesses our absolute dependence on the Lord of life and death. It is, therefore, a deep and vital contact with Him Whom we know not only as Lord but as Father. It is when we pray truly that we really *are*. Our being is brought to a high perfection by this, which is one of its most perfect activities. When we cease to pray, we tend to fall back into nothingness. True, we continue to exist. But since the main reason for our existence is the knowledge and love of God, when our conscious contact with Him is severed we sleep or we die. Of course, we cannot always, or even often, remain clearly conscious of Him. Spiritual wakefulness demands only the habitual awareness of Him which surrounds all our actions in a spiritual atmosphere without formally striking our attention except at certain moments of keener perception. But if God leaves us so completely that we are no longer disposed to think of Him with love, then we are spiritually dead.

Most of the world is either asleep or dead. The religious people are, for the most part, asleep. The irreligious are dead. Those who are asleep are divided into two classes, like the Virgins in the parable, waiting for the Bridegroom's coming. The wise have oil in their lamps. That is to say they are detached from themselves and from the cares of the world, and they are full of charity. They are indeed waiting for the Bridegroom, and they desire nothing else but His coming, even though they may fall asleep while waiting for Him to appear. But the others are not only asleep: they are full of other dreams and other desires. Their lamps are empty because they have burned themselves out in the wisdom of the flesh and in their own vanity. When He comes, it is too late for them to buy oil. They light their lamps only after He has gone. So they fall asleep again, with useless lamps, and when they wake up they trim them to investigate, once again, the matters of a dying world.

There are many levels of attention in prayer.

First of all, there is purely exterior attention. We "say prayers" with our lips, but our hearts are not following what we say although we think we would like to mean what we are saying. If we do not cultivate something better than this, we will seldom really pray. If we are quite content to pray without paying attention to our prayer or to God, it shows we have not much idea of who God is, and that we do not really appreciate the grace and the privilege of being able to speak to Him in prayer. For prayer is a gift of God, a gift which is by no means given to all men. Perhaps it is given to few because so few desire it, and of those who have received it so few have received it with gratitude.

At other times, we think of God in prayer but our thoughts of Him are not concerned with prayer. They are thoughts about Him that do not establish any contact with Him. So, while we pray, we are speculating about God and about the spiritual life, or composing sermons, or drawing up theological arguments. These thoughts are all right in their place, but if we take prayer seriously we will not call them prayer. For such thoughts cannot satisfy the soul that desires to find God in prayer. On the contrary, they leave it with a feeling of emptiness and dissatisfaction. At the same time, when one is really a man of prayer, speculative thoughts about God in the time of study or of intellectual work can often lead into prayer and give place to it; but only on condition that prayer is more to him than speculation.

Again, in prayer we are distracted by our practical difficulties, the problems of our state of life, the duties we have to face. It is not possible to avoid such distractions all the time, but if we know what prayer means, and know Who God is, we will be able to turn these thoughts themselves into motives of prayer. But we will not be satisfied with such prayer as this. It is good, indeed, to turn distractions into material for petition, but it is better not to be distracted, or at least not to be drawn away from God by our distractions.

Then there is the prayer that is well used: words or thought serve their purpose and lead our minds and hearts to God, and in our prayer we receive light to apply these thoughts to our own problems and difficulties, to those of our friends, or to those of the Church. But sometimes this prayer, which is, of course, valid, leaves our hearts unsatisfied because it is more concerned with our problems, with our friends, and ourselves, than it is with God. However, if we are humble men, we will be grateful for ever so little light in our prayer, and will not complain too much, for it is a great thing to receive even a little light from so great a God.

There is a better way of prayer, a greater gift from God, in which we pass through our prayer to Him, and love Him. We taste the goodness of His infinite mercy. We know that we are indeed His sons, although we know our unworthiness to be called the sons of God. We know His infinite mercy in Jesus, and we know the meaning of the fact that we, who are sinners, indeed have a Savior. And we learn what it is to know the Father in this Savior, Jesus, His Son. We enter thus into a great mystery which cannot be explained, but only experienced. But in this prayer we still remain conscious of ourselves, we can reflect upon ourselves, and realize that we are the subjects of this great experience of love, as well as the objects of God's love.

In the beginning this reflexive quality in our prayer does not disturb us. But as we mature in the spiritual life it begins to be a source of unrest and dissatisfaction. We are ashamed to be so much aware of ourselves in our prayer. We wish we were not in the way. We wish our love for God were no longer spoiled and clouded by any return upon ourselves. We wish we were no longer aware that we rejoiced in His love, for we fear that our rejoicing might end in selfishness and self-complacency. And although we are grateful for the consolation and the light of His love, we wish we ourselves could disappear and see only Jesus. These two moments of prayer are like the two phases of the Apostles' vision of the Transfigured Christ on Mount Thabor. At first Peter, James, and John were delighted with the vision of Jesus, Moses, and Elias. They thought it would be a fine thing to build three tabernacles and stay there on the mountain forever. But they were overshadowed by a cloud, and a voice came out of the cloud striking them with fear, and when they regained their vision they saw no one but Jesus alone.

So too there is another stage in our prayer, when consolation gives place to fear. It is a place of darkness and anguish and of conversion: for here a great change takes place in our spirit. All our love for God appears to us to have been full of imperfection, as indeed it has. We begin to doubt that we have ever loved Him. With shame and sorrow we find that our love was full of complacency, and that although we thought ourselves modest, we overflowed with conceit. We were too sure of ourselves, not afraid of illusion, not afraid to be recognized by other men as men of prayer. Now we see things in a different light, for we are in the cloud, and the voice of the Father fills our hearts with unrest and fear, telling us that we must no longer see ourselves: and yet, to our terror, Jesus does not appear to us and all that we see is—ourselves. Then what we find in our souls becomes terrible to us. Instead of complacently calling ourselves sinners (and secretly believing ourselves just) we begin to find that the sins of our past life were really sins, and really *our* sins—and we have not regretted them! And that since the time when we were grave sinners, we have still sinned without realizing it, because we were too sure we were the friends of God, and we have taken His graces lightly, or taken them to ourselves, and turned them to our own selfish profit, and used them for our own vanity, and even exploited them to lift ourselves above other men, so that in many ways we have turned the love of God into selfishness and have reveled in His gifts without thanking Him or using them for His glory.

Then we begin to see that it is just and right that we be abandoned by God, and left to face many and great temptations. Nor do we complain of these temptations, for we are forced to recognize that they are only the expression of the forces that were always hiding behind the façade of our supposed virtues. Dark things come out of the depths of our souls, and we have to consider them and recognize them for our own, and then repudiate them, lest we be saddled with them for eternity. Yet they return, and we cannot escape them. They plague us in our prayer. And while we face them, and cannot get rid of them, we realize more clearly than ever before our great need for God, and the tremendous debt we owe His honor, and we try to pray to Him and it seems that we cannot pray. Then begins a spiritual revaluation of all that is in us. We begin to ask ourselves what is and is not *real* in our ideals!

This is the time when we really learn to pray in earnest. For now we are no longer proud enough to expect great lights and consolations in our prayer. We are satisfied with the driest crust of supernatural food, glad to get anything at all, surprised that God should even pay the slightest attention. And if we cannot pray (which is a source of concern) yet we know more than ever before how much we desire to pray. If we could be consoled at all, this would be our only consolation.

The man who can face such dryness and abandonment for a long time, with great patience, and asks nothing more of God but to do His holy will and never offend Him, finally enters into pure prayer. Here the soul goes to God in prayer without any longer adverting either to itself or to its prayer. It speaks to Him without knowing what it is saying because God Himself has distracted the mind from its words and thoughts. It reaches Him without thoughts because, before it can think of Him, He is already present in the depths of the spirit, moving it to love Him in a way it cannot explain or understand. Time no longer means anything in such prayer, which is carried on in instants of its own, instants that can last a second or an hour without our being able to distinguish one from another. For this prayer belongs less to time than to eternity.

This deep interior prayer comes to us of its own accord, that is, by the secret movement of the Spirit of God, at all times and in all places, whether we be praying or not. It can come at work, in the middle of our daily business, at a meal, on a silent road, or in a busy thoroughfare, as well as at Mass, or in Church, or when we recite the psalms in choir. However, such prayer draws us naturally to interior and even exterior solitude. It does not depend on exterior conditions, but it has effected such an interior isolation and solitariness in our own souls that we naturally tend to seek silence and solitude for our bodies as well as for our souls. And it is good for the soul to be in solitude for a great part of the time. But if it should seek solitude for its own comfort and consolation, it will have to endure more darkness and more anguish and more trial. Pure prayer only takes possession of our hearts for good when we no longer desire any special light or grace or consolation for ourselves, and pray without any thought of our own satisfaction.

Finally, the purest prayer is something on which it is impossible to reflect until after it is over. And when the grace has gone we no longer seek to reflect on it, because we realize that it belongs to another order of things, and that it will be in some sense debased by our reflecting on it. Such prayer desires no witness, even the witness of our own souls. It seeks to keep itself entirely hidden in God. The experience remains in our spirit like a wound, like a scar that will not heal. But we do not reflect upon it. This living wound may become a source of knowledge, if we are to instruct others in the ways of prayer; or else it may become a bar and an obstacle to knowledge, a seal of silence set upon the soul, closing the way to words and thoughts, so that we can say nothing of it to other men. For the way is left open to God alone. This is like the door spoken of by Ezechiel, which shall remain closed because the King is enthroned within.

Thomas Merton, No Man Is an Island

It is not sufficient to place yourself daily under God. What really matters is to be *only* under God: the slightest division of allegiance opens the door to day-dreaming, petty conversation, petty boasting, petty malice—all the petty satellites of the death-instinct.

"But how, then, am I to love God?" "You must love Him as if He were a Non-God, a Non-Spirit, a Non-Person, a Non-Substance: love Him simply as the One, the pure and absolute Unity in which is no trace of Duality. And into this One, we must let ourselves fall continually from being into non-being. God helps us to do this."

Dag Hammerskjold, Markings

Introit

This morning,
on entering the cold chapel,

    I looked first
to the sun, as the pagan does;
not for any reason
in particular, but because

    I too, as creature,
sense man's primitive emotion:
his need to praise.
And so, like priest or pagan,

according
as the sun moves, I perform
this ancient ritual.
And though not always able

to approach,
often, effaced in light, I stand
before this
chalice of the morning,

I break this
ordinary bread as something holy.

Paul Murray, *Ritual Poems*

Come Then to Prayers

Come then to prayers
And kneel upon the stone,
For we have tried
All courages on these despairs,
And are required lastly to give up pride,
And the last difficult pride in being humble.

Draw down the window-frame
That we may be unparted from the darkness,
Inviting to this house
Air from a field, air from a salt grave,
That questions if we have
Concealed no flaw in this confessional,
And, being satisfied,
Lingers, and troubles, and is lightless,
And so grows darker, as if clapped on a flame,
Whose great extinguishing still makes it tremble.

Only our hearts go beating towards the east.
Out of this darkness, let the unmeasured sword
Rising from sleep to execute or crown
Rest on our shoulders, as we then can rest

On the outdistancing, all-capable flood
Whose brim touches the morning. Down
The long shadows were undriven the dawn
Hunts light into nobility, arouse us noble.

13 May 1946

Philip Larkin, *Collected Poems*

In addition to saying his prayers, the Journalist discovers that they are indeed answered; not always in the way he might hope for or expect, but still answered. He finds it extraordinary that they should be so answered, just by waiting for a response, which, when it comes, is perfectly adjusted to the request. In the deeply troubled times he is living through he grieves that he should be expending all his energies on following what is going on— reading the newspapers, and otherwise heeding the Media, arguing and declaiming. Then a kind of passion takes possession of him, and all sorts of apprehensions gather round, so that he cannot sleep, or, waking in the night, he is troubled by the thought of work undone, commitments made and not fulfilled, an overwhelming sense of his total inadequacy. Somehow he spells out the Lord's Prayer, and asks to be taken over so that his remaining days or months or even years may be wholly taken over by our Creator, or by Jesus on behalf of our Creator. Nothing happens; he continues to be lost and hopeless, until, hours later, the answer comes in the shape of illumination, enabling him to understand perfectly that history is to mankind precisely what the experience of living is to an individual—that is to say, a drama to be lived through. We do not write the script, nor do we choose our allotted parts; what is required of us is to speak our lines, make our entrances and our exits, until the curtain falls and our role is for the time being exhausted.

Malcolm Muggeridge, *Conversion*

Prayer begins where expression ends. The words that reach our lips are often but waves of an overflowing stream touching the shore. We often seek and miss, struggle and fail to adjust our unique feelings to the patterns of texts. Where is the tree that can utter fully the silent passion of the soil? Words can only open the door, and we can only weep on the threshold of our incommunicable thirst after the incomprehensible.

Abraham Joshua Heschel, *Man's Quest for God*

The true motivation for prayer is not, as it has been said, the sense of being at home in the universe, but rather the sense of not being at home in the universe.

Is there a sensitive heart that could stand indifferent and feel at home in the sight of so much evil and suffering, in the face of countless failures to live up to the will of God? On the contrary, the experience of not being at home in the world is a motivation for prayer.

That experience gains intensity in the amazing awareness that God himself is not at home in the universe. He is not at home in a universe where His will is defied and where His kingship is denied. God is in exile; the world is corrupt. The universe itself is not at home.

To pray means to bring God back into the world, to establish His kingship for a second at least. To pray means to expand His presence.

Abraham Joshua Heschel, *The Insecurity of Freedom*

Let me try that. We spoke about this sense of belonging. All the religions of the world would admit that this is our basic common ground. This is the experiential ground. So we have now established something that we could call God, if you want to use that term for the reference point of our ultimate belonging. God is the one to whom we ultimately belong.

Expressed in this way, this insight presupposes a long journey of exploration into God. It already presupposes the recognition that the reference point of our belonging must be personal. If I am personal, then the one to whom I belong must be personal. But of course God must not be restricted by any of the limitations we associate with being a person. One of those limitations is, for instance, that being me, I cannot at the same time be another. This does not apply to God. In other words, God must have all the perfection of being a person and none of the limitations.

Now, from there, it is again a long journey of exploration until we come to see that God freely allows us to belong, gives us this belonging. Up to this point, it was a sort of territory I was exploring, God-territory. But now all of a sudden I experience Yes! I am doing the exploring, but it isn't just my exploring, it is at the same time God's unveiling Godself. In the process of religious history, which stretches over millennia, this is a milestone. Yet every one of us can relive this experience. To explore into God is prayer, not in the conventional sense, but in the sense that theology is prayer. As we explore the God-territory prayerfully, we suddenly reach a point where we discover that it gives itself to us. God and the whole universe are giving themselves continuously to us.

David Steindl-Rast, from Fritjof Capra, David Steindl-Rast
with Thomas Matus, *Belonging to the Universe*

The End of Prayers

At the close of the seventy-second psalm are the words: "And let the whole earth be filled with His glory. Amen, and Amen. The prayers of David the son of Jesse are ended."

Concerning this Rabbi Levi Yitzhak said: "All prayers and hymns are a plea to have His glory revealed throughout the world. But if once the whole earth is, indeed, filled with it, there will be no further need to pray."

Martin Buber, Tales of the Hasidim

✦ 13 ✦

Doing for God

"God is hiding in the world and our task is to let the divine emerge from our deeds."

—ABRAHAM JOSHUA HESCHEL

"Prayer in action is love. Love in action is service."

—MOTHER TERESA

When we surrender to God, we begin to accept all that happens in our lives as God's will; we feel compassionate and grateful and, as Elisabeth Kübler-Ross says, we "learn the lesson of unconditional love." In surrendering ourselves, we become less and therefore can be more to others. And this ability is joined with an urgent need to heal the unhappiness, the distress, the destruction around us with understanding, solace, fairness, and the newfound joy that have become part of our lives.

Through prayer and contemplation comes clarity in action. Every moment of our life becomes an act of surrender, of giving completely the gift of ourselves and our talents. In becoming servants for God, service to others is what calls us and what nourishes us.

I have concentrated much of this section on Mother Teresa of Calcutta. Through her devotion to Jesus Christ and the Christian principles, she is a living example of complete surrender to God. She has taught the world much about compassion and love in action, and also of how we can live in holiness, in commitment to God. She is a rare combination of the transcended soul and the grounded being; through prayer she says she can strike "the proper balance between earth and heaven." Her service to Calcutta's poor, sick, and dying and now to thousands who have benefitted from her homes in over 120 countries, is phenomenal. Desmond Doig describes the everyday running of her most famous home, Nirmal Hriday; his vivid description transports us to Mother Teresa's "Place of the Pure Heart" and gives an example of the purity of her work.

✦

I always say I am a little pencil in the hands of God. He does the thinking, He does the writing, He does everything.

All of us are but his instruments, who do our little bit and pass by.

Mother Teresa, from Franca Zanbonini, Teresa of Calcutta

We ourselves feel that what we are doing is just a drop in the ocean. But if that drop was not in the ocean I think that ocean will be less because of that missing drop.

Mother Teresa, from Mary Craig, Mother Teresa

When she came to Cambridge for the convocation at which she was to receive an honorary doctorate in divinity from Prince Philip, the chancellor of the university, Mother went to the convent around midday. People came to meet her there, including members of the press. A reporter asked her, "What made you start your work, what inspired you and kept you going during so many years?"

Mother answered, "Jesus."

The reporter looked disappointed; he must have expected long explanations, but was told only one word. For Mother one word sufficed to sum up her whole life, to explain her faith, enterprise, courage, love, devotion, efficiency, single-mindedness: Jesus. Everything was due to him, every effort and sacrifice made for him. Mother expressed it again forcefully when she said, "Father, tell them: we do it for Jesus." The sentence has become her motto, her watchword, the explanation she gives of the activity and the success of the sisters, "We do it for Jesus," everything, all the time.

Edward Le Joly, Mother Teresa of Calcutta

The Place of the Pure Heart

Kalighat, on the banks of a brown, sacred stream in south Calcutta, is named after the ancient temple to Kali, a powerful Hindu goddess. It is one of the most congested areas in an overcrowded city. One of its oldest. A labyrinth of narrow lanes, middle-class boxes, slums, shops, pilgrims' rest-houses and *ghats* where the dead are cremated. The temple itself, built in the sugar-loaf style of medieval Bengal, reaches above the congestion like a flower for sunlight. Its precincts swarm. Rich and poor. A millionaire family bearing expensive gifts in gold tissue. Devotees in white cotton leading goats to sacrifice.

Saffron-robed *yogis* with piled hair and extravagant caste marks vermilioned on their foreheads. Beggars. Tourists. Troubadours singing devotional songs, plaintive, like sighs set to music. Balloon-men almost airborne. Skeins of students. Mendicants. And now, strangely, nuns in blue-bordered white saris.

There is always a festive confusion about Kalighat, particularly in its shanty shops which sell everything from fruit and carved wood to brass cooking pots and images; from gaudy flowers and toys to religious prints, fresh fish and caged birds. Over all is the blue mist of funeral pyres, and the smell of incense mingles with the smell of death. Boisterous life and a calm acceptance of death is characteristic of Kalighat. Numerous funeral processions nudge shoppers and high-spirited children playing in the road.

Just below the grey walls of the temple is a long, low whitewashed building that is Mother Teresa's Home for dying destitutes. A board at the entrance carries the name, Nirmal Hriday, the Place of the Pure Heart. There are no doors; it is always open. One enters directly into a reception area of sorts which is part of the men's ward and is more often than not occupied by patients. The first impression, as one's eyes grow accustomed to the gloom, is of tiers of closely packed litters, a colourless, slow moving of people and a nameless smell that antiseptic cannot overpower. Then, individuals take shape: gauntly emerging from the anonymity of the hopelessly ill, or moving silently about their work. A boy carrying a bed-pan and soiled bandages. A Sister hurrying to a bedside. Two young men crouched over a prostrate form, tenderly dressing a wound. Daylight shafts through the barred windows like rays of hope that fade and grow bright and dim and disappear.

A board hanging from a pillar has chalked on it the number of inmates, men and women. Through a doorway, past a nun with her sleeves rolled up, and some helpers toiling around vast vessels of food, is the women's ward, larger than the men's and suffused with the same quiet. There is no horror. The mind, shocked for a moment, easily accepts this new dimension. Here are people no longer tormented by fear, loneliness, degradation, abandonment, but people cared for, loved and at peace. On the streets they would be objects of pity or revulsion, but under the sheltering roof of Nirmal Hriday, which is more truly the sheltering umbrella of the Missionaries of Charity, are old people, scarred people, critically ill people, but people. Without conscious effort, without a second thought, you can suddenly find yourself helping to do things you would never imagine you could do. Or would dare do under ordinary circumstances.

My many visits to Nirmal Hriday have been kaleidoscoped into a powerful image of incandescent serenity, a peace that really does pass understanding and of a beauty as mysterious as death itself. Mother Teresa tells of how the dying destitute, without anything to give and with a past of horror that should, understandably, embitter him for all time, will smile and say thank you and then die.

Perhaps the beauty, the strange radiance that one encounters in Nirmal Hriday is a coming to terms with death. A completely natural acceptance of the inevitable. Mother Teresa calls it going home. "Nirmal Hriday," she says, "is really the treasure house of Calcutta. These people go to God straight away and when they go they tell Him about us. We help them to die with God. We help them to say sorry to God. To make peace with God according to their faith." My own wavering faith has never allowed me to accept death as a going home or an adventure into some other life, possibly in some other form. I have met, particularly on the northern borders of India, people who are recognized and accepted as reincarnates, people who speak intelligently about their previous lives. The Bardo of Mahayana, the Paradise of Christianity, and the Swarg of Hinduism hold out for me neither the terror nor the promise of life everlasting. To me, death is the closing of a book, the fading of a flower. But in Nirmal Hriday, I can feel something: something, perhaps, as negative as an absence of fear, which could be the stirring of a belief itself.

There was the morning when we set out for Nirmal Hriday via the Mother House. I had woken depressed and in one of those frustrated bad tempers that come with the heat and the humidity of the monsoon. Mother was away somewhere and I was tempted to call it a day and go home. My photographer friend, Kalyan, persisted, and as we neared Kalighat I was driven to one of those excesses of self-pity that has one bordering on hysteria. It was no good. If I saw another dying destitute, another slum, experienced another bout of nose-rubbing ghastliness, I would revolt and abandon the entire project of the book. Suddenly there were the grey walls and silver roofs of Kalighat temple looming above us and, as we parked the car, a siege of beggars and near-naked children. I wanted to explode with anger. To get the hell out of there and go home to a bath and clean clothes. To the security of my familiar, upper-class surroundings.

Then there was the enveloping smell of the subterranean gloom of the Home for dying destitutes and a quite inexplicable falling away of all pressures. Someone, something, was draining me of all poison. I felt relaxed, secure. We were immediately drawn into the women's ward, though it is more usual to visit the men's ward first, since that is where one enters. A Sister was bending over an old woman who was refusing to eat or drink. Looking despairingly at us she said, "She won't eat." So I tried, noticing as I knelt beside the pathetic figure that there was no flesh, just skin papered to the bones. She kept her lips tightly clamped and the reason was in her eyes—an unblinking defiance prompted by some deep, insoluble hurt. There was nothing I could do to soften the pain. The Sisters, busy with other imperative calls upon their time and strength, returned and tried again. We all tried. But there was no response. I have often wondered since what became of her because, immediately afterwards, I was distracted by a quite unexpected voice that said in a very crisp British accent, "I say, do you have a fag?"

I looked around at the patients, most of them lying spent and beyond talking, or crouched silently staring at nothing in particular. Nearest me was an old woman brown and crumpled like a raisin, with cropped white hair and eyes rimmed with age who sat holding her bleached nightdress about her as if she had been taken unawares by a man in her boudoir. "I beg your pardon?" I found myself saying inanely, and once again there was that very English voice asking if I had a fag. I have never smoked in my life, but there I was, searching my pockets in a hopeless endeavour to be helpful. My companions, who smoke like chimneys, were out of cigarettes, but hastened to get some. All the while she sat there with a composure that would have done a *grande dame* justice.

"You know," she said very earnestly, "they don't give one fags here, but I do like the occasional one." Amazed as I was, I tried to look my casual best and began by introducing myself formally. "And I am Miss Murray," she said. "I am a nurse. I was trained in Edinburgh, that's Scotland, you know." While I found myself groping for something to say, she leaned forward as if to impart a confidence and said, "It's all right here, my dear, but, frankly, I don't like the food. Too much oil. I'm not complaining, of course, they are wonderful people. They're doing extraordinary things. And that woman's a saint, a saint, I tell you. But I would like some good grub and a fag now and then. One does get a bit tired, you know."

A packet of cigarettes arrived and was handed over. Miss Murray received it with almost ritualistic graciousness, and then, crossing her legs and lighting a cigarette with studied care, took a first exaggerated puff. We had seen it before: Marlene Dietrich in *The Blue Angel*, we decided later. "Aahh!" she said, "that's good."

I wondered what string of tragedies had brought the likes of Miss Murray into a home for dying destitutes. She might have heard me thinking because she said, "I was living in this small room down there," and she pointed way through the walls and her memories, "when I had this stupid collapse." A long pause then, "Are you a doctor?" she asked suddenly. When I replied in the negative she said, "Well, come closer. Look at me. Do you notice anything? I'm blind, you know, quite blind. I can see shadows, shapes, that's all. But that doesn't do, does it?" She puffed reflectively and added, "It's good to be here with other people. It can be lonely, you know. And when the time comes, one needs people." I asked her if there was anything we might do for her and she said, "No, this is good enough," holding up the packet of cigarettes and then, once again, as if to reassure us of her well-being she said, "That Mother Teresa is a saint. She does such wonderful work." It was difficult to leave her but we promised to return, knowing full well that when we did Miss Murray would have gone home.

My first memory of Nirmal Hriday is of Mother Teresa, with whom I went, personally admitting a man who lay dying on the steps outside. He had hardly been taken in when a Sister came and called Mother away. I followed, and there was the man from outside. Stripped of his rags he was one appalling wound alive with maggots. Mother sank down beside him and, with quiet efficiency, began to clean him as she talked to him caressingly in Bengali. A young man, very slight and with the beginnings of a beard, joined Mother and, without a word being said, handed her forceps, swabs and whatever she seemed to need from a kidney-bowl. I shall never forget the look on the man's face: pain changing to amazement and unashamed love. A Sister came hurriedly to Mother, whispered; Mother handed over to the young man and left, one gathered, in answer to a more urgent call. I remember I was surprised to find myself helping the young man and, eventually, when the dressing was done, I asked him who he was. There were no Brothers then. In a voice so gentle I hardly heard it, he said that he was a co-worker of Mother Teresa and that his name was Christo Das. Then he told me what I was to discover later is one of the most powerful motivating forces of the Missionaries of Charity: "When I cleanse the wounds of the poor, I am cleansing the wounds of Christ."

There was a service held in Nirmal Hriday that morning at which Christo Das and a few helpers like him received the Sacrament from a Jesuit priest. It was an extraordinary act of worship seen from where I knelt beside a dying man: the priest in white, a few patients propped up in prayer, framed by the tiers of litters and lit by a shaft of sunlight. Mother Teresa and her Sisters were far too occupied to join the service. They did not even genuflect when they passed the impromptu altar.

Once I accompanied Rahu Rai to take photographs at Nirmal Hriday. I went squirming with embarrassment since one is always conscious of being healthy and well fed in the company of these unfortunate people. To photograph them seemed an impossible outrage. But something incredible happened. The atmosphere of quiet understanding that prevails in Nirmal Hriday accepts even the probing eye of the camera. A woman sat sobbing soundlessly on her bed and Raghu Rai advanced slowly towards her, taking photographs as he went. I was beginning to think him distinctly callous, when he dropped his camera and took hold of the gnarled hands held out towards him. "Why do you cry, Mother?" he asked, sitting beside her. Immediately she stopped crying and looking intently at him asked, "Is it you, my son?"

"Yes, Mother, it is I."

"You've been a long time. I thought you would never come."

"Now I am here. Don't worry any more."

"Are you married?"

"Yes, and I have children. I tell them about you."

The old lady smiled toothlessly and reaching her hands towards Raghu's neck touched his forehead to hers. "God bless you, my son," she said. "Now I can die happy."

In the car returning from Nirmal Hriday, Raghu impetuously told Mother Teresa, "I did not believe much in God and things. But today, Mother, I do." The quiet smile she gave in answer was a thankful prayer. I could almost hear her saying, "They have so little but they give so much."

I had occasion to take a visiting English Lord to Nirmal Hriday. He has asked to see the "real" Calcutta and expressed a wish to be shown what positive steps were being taken to combat poverty and suffering. It was winter and he was wearing a three-piece suit. We had hardly entered the building when a Sister unceremoniously asked us to move back because the dead were being brought out. Even as what she said sank into our astonished minds, a file of people carrying pathetically small bundles of white cloth brushed past. My guest was visibly shocked. He was silent for most of the time while we were in Nirmal Hriday but, as we were about to enter the magnificent limousine provided by the local British High Commission, he told me with genuine sincerity that he wished he was less clad and fed. "This suit burns me," he said.

The extraordinary spirit of Nirmal Hriday now reaches out to wherever the Missionaries of Charity work. One morning, we accompanied two Sisters to their small dispensary and feeding centre near the busy Sealdah Station. Sealdah has resisted several shock waves of refugees coming from what was East Pakistan, now Bangladesh. But the refugees have invariably won by occupying every lane and sidewalk and open space in the vicinity. For months on end in the past they have lived on the platforms of the busy station while officialdom fought desperately to find ways and means to rehabilitate them. It has been an almost unending battle since 1947, and one that the world has failed to recognize but has often criticized.

Imagine Charing Cross or Grand Central or the Gare du Nord beset every day by thousands upon thousands of starving, homeless refugees. Occupying kiosks, benches, lounges, restaurants and raising hovels on the platforms, cooking, bathing and defecating there. Relief organizations fling themselves into action distributing food and clothing, providing limited shelter for a lucky few. Newspapers scream in headlines and editorials. TV watches with baleful eyes. But they keep coming, spilling out of the station to settle where they can. The relief organizations call up reserves. Urgent appeals go out. The law is dismayed into taking no action because what action can it take? Charge every unfortunate man, woman and child with vagrancy? Unlawful occupation of land? Loitering? So the gaols are filled, the hospitals are filled, the homes for the poor are filled. And they keep coming, hungry and homeless. What then? Friends near and far send clothes, blankets, food and toys—yes, toys. They keep coming. They have nothing. Nothing to lose. And a city's resources are inadequate. A country's means too small. A world's conscience too fazed or its will too politically influenced.

In her own small way Mother Teresa has tried to help by sending her Sisters to feed the starving and administer to the sick at Sealdah. As Father Henry would say, "Theirs has been an infiltration of love."

Opposite the dispensary, something of a small settlement has grown up where the very poor wait to be fed and treated. Some of them have even been pressed into collecting green coconut shells for Prem Daan, so there is a great pile of shells near by on which very small children play.

We watched a queue forming for medicines and then accompanied one of the Sisters to the nearby station where she felt there must be one or two people in need of urgent help. We found a man crouching just outside the entrance, so spent he could not even speak when the Sister talked to him. So she summoned a passing rickshaw, but when the rickshaw puller saw his intended fare he began protesting that he could not possibly pick up someone so filthy and so ill. The Sister and a growing crowd prevailed; someone came forward to lift the man into the rickshaw and they were soon lost in a sea of people. I walked into the station and strolled half the length of a shadowy platform before returning to the dispensary. A Sister was pulling a white sheet over a prone figure in the queue of patients as I approached, and I knew instinctively that it was the man who had been rescued just minutes before.

"He's got his ticket; we never say people die," said a Sister joyfully. "I'm sure he went straight to heaven. It was lucky we found him. He died so peacefully. We just made him comfortable, gave him some water and he smiled and was gone. I'm sure he got his ticket straight to heaven."

The shock I should have felt at finding someone dead in a queue of living did not register. There was no fuss, no remorse, no fear. People sitting next to the corpse hardly noticed. The work of examination and dispensing medicine went on. Had the man lived a little longer he would have been sent to Nirmal Hriday. Had he not been found by the good Sisters he would have died unloved and unattended on a city street.

It is difficult to believe now, when moving about with the Missionaries of Charity, that they were once resented and faced considerable opposition. Sister Bernard, with whom we visited the leper colony at Titagarh, remembers how "People would even threaten to kill Mother, but she would just walk through the crowds. She was never frightened. Then, when it was seen that so much good was being done to all people, regardless of caste or creed, they began to accept us. Soon people who had been against us in Kalighat were coming to Nirmal Hriday with small gifts of food. It was usually on festival days when they were going to offer puja at the Kali temple. It was an outlet for their charity and it brought happiness and consolation to our people."

There was a time when it was thought that Mother Teresa and her Missionaries were converting the dying to Christianity. But it needs only a glance at the records that are kept to see that Christians are in the minority at Nirmal Hriday. I remember being present once as an old man died in the Home for dying destitutes. He was a Hindu. I can still see a Brother crouched over him, wetting his lips with water from the sacred Ganges. I have asked Mother about this and she has made it abundantly clear that those who die in her Homes are given whatever comfort they ask and it is possible to give according to their beliefs. Sister Bernard told us how arrangements are made for Muslim burials and Hindu cremations through religious agencies. This, of course, does not prevent the good Missionaries from adding their own dimension of love and devotion. Sister Bernard recalls how quite recently Sister Luke, who is very devoted, received lots of flowers on her Feast Day, and yet she had none. So we asked her what had happened to the flowers and she said that there had been about twelve deaths in Nirmal Hriday during the day and no one had come to remove the bodies. So, she garlanded them with her flowers because she was sad that there was no one to mourn them because no one had tears for them.

Father Henry remembers how a young Anglo-Indian girl used to press him for a job. According to him, "She looked a shy, miserable creature." Quite hopeless for any work he had to give. Then, one day, Mother Teresa asked him to send her a Bengali woman to help in Nirmal Hriday. "The Anglo-Indian girl comes to me and I have a wicked thought," said Father Henry. "I'll send her to Nirmal Hriday and in two days' time she'll run away and I'll get rid of her." So he sent her and a few days later he had a report that there had seldom been anyone who had worked so hard and so devotedly. She remained not for the expected two days but for six months and then asked Mother Teresa if she might join the Order. And she was gladly accepted. "For those who love God," added Father Henry, "everything finally takes a good turn. Even your weak side. Even your stupidity."

Another person who came and stayed at Nirmal Hriday was a young boy, abandoned and very sick, whom some Brothers picked up at Howrah Station and sent to the Home for dying destitutes. Miraculously, he recovered but refused to leave. Instead he remained to help care for those he had learned to love, living and eating with the patients and finding time to go first to school, and later to college.

Just inside the entrance to Nirmal Hriday, is a small illuminated glass case in which reposes a statue of the Virgin Mary, quite unlike any other in that it wears the ribbon and medal of the Padmashree, the Indian Order of the Lotus. Mother Teresa was given the award in 1962, the first non-Indian ever to receive it. She became an Indian citizen in 1948.

In the twenty-seven years since she left the shelter of Loreto Convent, Mother Teresa has received several awards: the Nehru Award (1969), the Magsaysay Award (1962), the Pope John XXIII Peace Prize (1971) and the Templeton Award (1973), in recognition of her crusade among the world's deprived. A very different kind of award was a limousine presented to Mother Teresa by Pope Paul VI at the conclusion of the Eucharistic Congress in Bombay in 1964. It was no ordinary limousine and no ordinary presentation. The car, a 1964 Ford Lincoln, had been especially designed and manufactured, just one of its kind, and was a gift to the Pope from the American people. When, after using it for a brief few hours he presented it to Mother Teresa, he did so, in his own words, "To share in her universal mission of love."

No one knowing Mother Teresa could imagine her or her Missionaries driving around in a sleek, cruiser-sized, white car. It was clearly meant as a gift to raise funds for her rapidly expanding mission. An outright sale would have raised a useful lakh of rupees (£7500). Mother Teresa had a better idea. She sought, and received, permission from the Government to raffle the car, and that in a unique way: every donation of one hundred rupees (about £13) or more, to her Mission, was acknowledged with a numbered receipt. The target was four thousand such donations, but in the time it took to close the raffle, it was oversubscribed. And so the Pope's limousine, aptly named the "People's Car," raised almost five lakhs of rupees (£37,500) and was won by a young Indian chartered accountant studying at the time in Britain.

A charming recollection attaches to this raffle. Several people who made donations promised Mother Teresa that if they won the car they would return it to her to re-raffle. Among them was the then Governor of West Bengal. Mother admitted to having prayed that one of these generous souls would be the lucky winner but then, in her extraordinary matter-of-fact way she said cheerfully that the Lord must have wished otherwise. As it was she had raised the money she required to start one of her most cherished ventures— Shantinagar, the Home for lepers.

It was while returning from Shantinagar with Mother Teresa in her old pickup van that she disarmingly talked about the possibility of her being awarded the Nobel Peace Prize: the news of her name being included in the final short list of nominees had been making the front page in all Indian newspapers. If she did get it, the money would be spent in founding new Homes for dying destitutes, abandoned children, alcoholics, drug addicts, lepers and generally for her people, the poorest of the poor, in whichever part of the world they might be. She told me that Mrs. Ghandhi had very generously allowed her, in the past, to keep some of the money she received by way of foreign awards abroad, so it could be used for her Missions outside India.

"You know," she continued, as disarmingly, "these awards are not for me, they are for my people. That is why they don't affect me at all. Because I know they are not for me. It is for the poor people who are being recognized. They are becoming wanted. Loved. The whole world is beginning to know about it. The very fact that so much is being written means the people are getting involved."

Desmond Doig, *Mother Teresa*

On Love

"The poor must know that we love them, that they are wanted. They themselves have nothing to give but love. We are concerned with how to get this message of love and compassion across. We are trying to bring peace to the world through our work. But the work is the gift of God, eh?

"People today are hungry for love, for understanding love which is much greater and which is the only answer to loneliness and great poverty. That is why we are able to go to countries like England and America and Australia where there is no hunger for bread. But there, people are suffering from terrible loneliness, terrible despair, terrible hatred, feeling unwanted, feeling helpless, feeling hopeless. They have forgotten how to smile, they have forgotten the beauty of the human touch. They are forgetting what is human love. They need someone who will understand and respect them.

"The poor are not respected. People do not think that the poor can be treated as people who are lovable, as people like you and I.

"You know, the young are beginning to understand. They want to serve with their hands, and to love with their hearts. To the full, not superficially.

"Love can be misused for selfish motives. I love you, but at the same time I want to take from you as much as I can, even the things that are not for me to take. Then there is no true love any more. True love hurts. It always has to hurt. It must be painful to love someone, painful to leave them, you might have to die for them. When people marry they have to give up everything to love each other. The mother who gives birth to her child suffers much. It is the same for us in religious life. To belong fully to God we have to give up everything. Only then can we truly love. The word 'love' is so misunderstood and so misused.

"A young American couple told me once, 'You know a lot about love; you must be married.' And I said, 'Yes, but sometimes I find it difficult to smile at Him.'"

Desmond Doig, Mother Teresa

How the Rabbi of Sasov Learned How to Love

Rabbi Moshe Leib told this story:

"How to love men is something I learned from a peasant. He was sitting in an inn along with other peasants, drinking. For a long time he was as silent as all the rest, but when he was moved by the wine, he asked one of the men seated beside him: 'Tell me, do you love me or don't you love me?' The other replied: 'I love you very much.' But the first peasant replied: 'You say that you love me, but you do not know what I need. If you really loved me, you would know.' The other had not a word to say to this, and the peasant who had put the question fell silent again.

"But I understood. To know the needs of men and to bear the burden of their sorrow—that is the true love of men."

Martin Buber, Tales of the Hasidim

> For as long as space endures,
> And for as long as living beings remain,
> Until then may I, too, abide
> To dispel the misery of the world.

The Dalai Lama, Freedom in Exile

Asanga was one of the most famous Indian Buddhist saints, and lived in the fourth century. He went to the mountains to do a solitary retreat, concentrating all his meditation practice on the Buddha Maitreya, in the fervent hope that he would be blessed with a vision of this Buddha and receive teachings from him.

For six years Asanga meditated in extreme hardship, but did not even have one auspicious dream. He was disheartened and thought he would never succeed with his aspiration to meet the Buddha Maitreya, and so he abandoned his retreat and left his hermitage. He had not gone far down the road when he saw a man rubbing an enormous iron bar with a strip of silk. Asanga went up to him and asked him what he was doing. "I haven't got a needle," the man replied, "so I'm going to make one out of this iron bar." Asanga stared at him, astounded; even if the man were able to manage it in a hundred years, he thought, what would be the point? He said to himself: "Look at the trouble people give themselves over things that are totally absurd. You are doing something really valuable, spiritual practice, and you're not nearly so dedicated." He turned around and went back to his retreat.

Another three years went by, still without the slightest sign from the Buddha Maitreya. "Now I know for certain," he thought, "I'm never going to succeed." So he left again, and soon came to a bend in the road where there was a huge rock, so tall it seemed to touch the sky. At the foot of the rock was a man busily rubbing it with a feather soaked in water. "What are you doing?" Asanga asked.

"This rock is so big it's stopping the sun from shining on my house, so I'm trying to get rid of it." Asanga was amazed at the man's indefatigable energy, and ashamed at his own lack of dedication. He returned to his retreat.

Three more years passed, and still he had not even had a single good dream. He decided, once and for all, that it was hopeless, and he left his retreat for good. The day wore on, and in the afternoon he came across a dog lying by the side of the road. It had only its front legs, and the whole of the lower part of its body was rotting and covered with maggots. Despite its pitiful condition, the dog was snapping at passersby, and pathetically trying to bite them by dragging itself along the ground with its two good legs.

Asanga was overwhelmed with a vivid and unbearable feeling of compassion. He cut a piece of flesh off his own body and gave it to the dog to eat. Then he bent down to take off the maggots that were consuming the dog's body. But he suddenly thought he might hurt them if he tried to pull them out with his fingers, and realized that the only way to remove them would be on his tongue. Asanga knelt on the ground, and looking at the horrible festering, writhing mass, closed his eyes. He leant closer and put out his tongue.... The next thing he knew, his tongue was touching the ground. He opened his eyes and looked up. The dog was gone; there in its place was the Buddha Maitreya, ringed by a shimmering aura of light.

"At last," said Asanga, "why did you never appear to me before?"

Maitreya spoke softly: "It is not true that I have never appeared to you before. I was with you all the time, but your negative karma and obscurations prevented you from seeing me. Your twelve years of practice dissolved them slightly, so that you were at last able to see the dog. Then, thanks to your genuine and heartfelt compassion, all those obscurations were completely swept away, and you can see me before you with your very own eyes. If you don't believe that this is what happened, put me on your shoulder and try and see if anyone else can see me."

Asanga put Maitreya on his right shoulder and went to the market-place, where he began to ask everyone: "What have I got on my shoulder?" "Nothing," most people said, and hurried on. Only one old woman, whose karma had been slightly purified, answered: "You've got the rotting corpse of an old dog on your shoulder, that's all." Asanga at last understood the boundless power of compassion that had purified and transformed his karma, and so made him a vessel fit to receive the vision and instruction of Maitreya. Then the Buddha Maitreya, whose name means "loving kind-ness," took Asanga to a heavenly realm, and there gave him many sublime teachings that are among the most important in the whole of Buddhism.

Sogyal Rinpoche, *The Tibetan Book of Living and Dying*

It is very important to recognize the basic nature of humanity and the value of human qualities. Whether one is educated or uneducated, rich or poor, or belongs to this nation or that nation, this religion or that religion, this ide-ology or that ideology, is secondary and doesn't matter. When we return to this basis, all people are the same. Then we can truly say the words *brother*, *sister*; then they are not just nice words—they have some meaning. That kind of motivation automatically builds the practice of kindness. This gives us inner strength.

What is my purpose in life, what is my responsibility? Whether I like it or not, I am on this planet, and it is far better to do something for humanity. So you see that compassion is the seed or basis. If we take care to foster com-passion, we will see that it brings the other good human qualities. The topic of compassion is not at all religious business; it is very important to know that it is human business, that it is a question of human survival, that is not a question of human luxury. I might say that religion is a kind of luxury. If you have religion, that is good. But it is clear that even without religion we can manage. However, without these basic human qualities we cannot sur-vive. It is a question of our own peace and mental stability.

The Dalai Lama, *A Policy of Kindness*

Real compassion and love will come only by practicing spirituality. We must have a high ideal in our life. We must be ready to sacrifice everything to uphold that ideal. This is genuine spirituality. Simply providing food will not solve anyone's problems either. Again one will be in want of food. So the best way is to help others both externally and internally, i.e., feed them and at the same time make them aware of the necessity to develop internally as well. This is possible only through spiritual education. This kind of service will help one to lead a happy and balanced life in any circumstance even if one is starving. In reality spirituality is that which teaches us how to lead a perfect life in the world. Son, everything depends on the mind. If the mind is calm and tranquil even the lowest hell will become an abode of happiness but if the mind is agitated even the highest of heavens will become a place of tremendous suffering. That is what one gets from spirituality and spiritual masters, peace and tranquility without which one cannot live.

Mata Amritanandamayi, in Swami Amritasvarupananda,
Mata Amritanandamayi

Over and above personal problems, there is an objective challenge to over-come inequity, injustice, helplessness, suffering, carelessness, oppression. Over and above the din of desires there is a calling, a demanding, a waiting, an expectation. There is a question that follows me wherever I turn. What is expected of me? What is demanded of me?

What we encounter is not only flowers and stars, mountains and walls. Over and above all things is a sublime expectation, a waiting for. With every child born a new expectation enters the world.

This is the most important experience in the life of every human being: something is asked of me. Every human being has had a moment in which he sensed a mysterious waiting for him. Meaning is found in responding to the demand, meaning is found in sensing the demand.

Abraham Joshua Heschel, *Who Is Man?*

There is a type of faith quite essential in daily living. It is the courage and tenacity to proceed with the work in hand despite the discouraging wisdom of both the bystanders and our own critical mind.

Martin Israel, *Night Thoughts*

The spiritual effectivity of work of course depends on the inner attitude. What is important is the spirit of offering put into the work. If one can in addition remember the Mother in the work or through a certain concentra-tion feel the Mother's presence or force sustaining or doing the work, that carries the spiritual effectivity still farther.

Sri Aurobindo, *The Words of Sri Aurobindo*

Let us work as we pray, for indeed work is the body's best prayer to the Divine.

The Mother, *Words of The Mother*, Part Two

"Have you any financial problems?"

"Money? I never give it a thought. It always comes. We do all our work for our Lord; he must look after us. If he wants something to be done, he must give us the means. If he does not provide us with the means, then it shows that he does not want that particular work. I forget about it."

To the same question put to her some fifteen years earlier, she had given exactly the same answer. So that was truly a part of her attitude in life, her trust in God, her assurance that he looked after this small society. She took our Lord at his word in this matter of material means. Thus a great source of worry and anxiety was removed from her mind, allowing her perfect freedom of thought and action. Having put her full trust in God, she abandoned herself to his holy guidance in all she did, thought, said, and taught.

Edward Le Joly, *Mother Teresa of Calcutta*

⇝ 14 ⇜

The Guides

"If one is not oneself a sage or saint, the best thing one can do is
to study the works of those who were."

—ALDOUS HUXLEY

I believe that the fascinating first-person
accounts of some famous modern-day saints illuminate and exemplify the
simplicity and humility in daily life. I have included here His Holiness the
Dalai Lama's own very intimate account of his normal day, Indian saint Mata
Amritanandamayi's (introduced in "Divine Women") devotion to Lord
Krishna and the gifts of her enlightenment (she is referred to by her young
name, Sudhamani), and writer John Cornwell's first encounter with the Irish
healing nun Sister Briege. And I have also included a short humorous piece
by Gary Kowalski, expounding the spiritual qualities of his pet dog.

A common step on the spiritual path, in the Eastern religions in particular, is to be a disciple, to learn the practices of a committed spiritual life
from those who have the wisdom and the experience. In all religions there
are teachers, prophets, gurus, and helpers, like the zaddik in the Hasidic tradition, the rabbi, the Zen or Sufi master, the Christian priest or minister, the
Hindu guru or swami, the Muslim mullah or imam. Martin Buber writes:
"the teacher kindles the souls of his disciples and they surround him and
light his life with the flame he has kindled." The German philosopher
Eugen Herrigel, whose famous understanding of and conversion to Zen was
recorded in his book *Zen in the Art of Archery*, writes of a master's gift to his
pupil as being a "wealth of spiritual power which only one who has experienced it possesses, and which—logically—is not his own."

Russian-born Irina Tweedie is a woman who, through the premature
death of her husband in England in 1954, began searching for consolation and
meaning in her life. This search led her to India, where she met a Sufi master
who was to become her divine teacher. In *The Chasm of Fire*, a modern classic
compiled in diary form, she documents her conversion, what she refers to as
her "spiritual training." The excerpt from this book provides insight into the

[435]

surrender necessary for the fulfilment of the true love partnership between teacher and disciple.

Here also is Carl Jung's meeting with Shri Ramana, at which he witnessed a full integration of spiritual values in one person, and Alan Watts' discourse about "Brahman" (the highest form of God) with Swami Prabhavananda, who lived and taught in California and had such distinguished followers as Aldous Huxley and English playwright Christopher Isherwood.

One of the most moving accounts of the deep love between a guru and disciple is in Yogananda's *Autobiography of a Yogi*. I have selected the account of the actual meeting between Yogananda's future guru, Swami Sri Yukteswar Giri, and himself—a meeting of destiny, of joyous discovery, that was the beginning of a life-long commitment to service and devotion. And as Jesus Christ is "Our Lord" the divine teacher to Christians, Hans Küng offers the idea of discipleship with Christ today.

It was during the 1960s and the emergence of the Beat Movement and hippie culture that spiritual practices, transcendental meditation, and the following of a guru or master teacher became a trend in Western cultures. American poet Allen Ginsberg, a literary rebel, openly homosexual, Jewish with a commitment to Buddhism and pro-hallucinogenics and the peace movement, was part of this trend. While his poem "Thoughts on a Breath" suggests this movement provided the basis for genuine spiritual liberation and wisdom, it also bred a number of what Alan Watts terms "Trickster" gurus, who were caught up in pursuits of power and wealth in the guise of truth. Watts' "The Trickster Guru" sums up the tricky situation perfectly. It's a warning to those in search of a teacher, and an example of what to avoid.

✦

Solitude is necessary to become established in the Self, but masters then return to the world to serve it. Even saints who engage in no outward work bestow, through their thoughts and holy vibrations, more precious gifts on the world than can be given by the most strenuous humanitarian activities of unenlightened men. The great ones, each in his own way and often against bitter opposition, strive selflessly to inspire and uplift their fellows.

Paramahansa Yogananda, *Autobiography of a Yogi*

"For the 'seeker after Truth' only meetings with very great masters and very great sages can be really interesting. It is better to seek, seek, and seek again a real sage, a truly liberated sage, and spend perhaps no more than a single day with him, than to dissipate one's efforts in encounters and conversations with less representative persons, or persons who are in any case further from true Realisation. It is no longer a matter of talking to Tibetans who have the title lama; it is a matter of meeting masters."

Arnaud Desjardins, *The Message of the Tibetans*

A Life in the Day: The Dalai Lama
AS TOLD TO VANYA KEWLEY

When I wake at four o'clock, I automatically start reciting the *Ngagjhinlab* mantra. It's a prayer that dedicates everything I do, my speech, my thoughts, my deeds, my whole day, as an offering, a positive way to help others. Like all monks, I obey a vow of poverty, so there are no personal possessions. My bedroom has just a bed and the first thing I see when I wake is the face of the Buddha on a holy seventeenth-century statue from Kyirong, one of the very few that escaped the Chinese desecration. It's cold when I wake, as we are at 7000 feet, so I do some exercises, wash and dress quickly.

I wear the same maroon robe as all the monks. It's not of good quality, and it's patched. If it was of good material and in one piece, you could sell it and gain something. This way you can't. This reinforces our philosophy of becoming detached from worldly goods. I meditate until five-thirty and make prostrations. We have a special practice to remind ourselves of our misdeeds and I make my confession and recite prayers for the well-being of all sentient beings.

Then at daybreak, if the weather is fine, I go into the garden. This time of day is very special to me. I look at the sky. It's very clear and I see the stars and have this special feeling—of my insignificance in the cosmos. The realization of what we Buddhists call impermanence. It's very relaxing. Sometimes I don't think at all and just enjoy the dawn and listen to the birds.

Then Penjor or Loga, monks from Namgyal monastery who have been with me for 28 years, bring my breakfast. It's a half-Tibetan, half-Western mixture. Tsampa—roasted barley flour—and porridge. While I have breakfast, my ears are very busy listening to the news on the BBC World Service.

Then at about six, I move into another room and meditate until nine. Through meditation, all Buddhists try and develop the right kind of motivation—compassion, forgiveness and tolerance. I meditate six or seven times a day.

From nine until lunch I read and study our scriptures. Buddhism is a very profound religion and, although I have been studying all my life, there is still so much to learn.

Unfortunately nearly all our ancient books and manuscripts have been destroyed by the Chinese. It's as though all the Gutenberg bibles and Domesday books in the world had been destroyed. No record. No memory. Before the Chinese invasion, we had over six thousand functioning monasteries and temples. Now there are only thirty-seven.

I also try and read Western masters. I want to learn more about Western philosophy and science. Especially nuclear physics, astronomy and neurobiology. Often Western scientists come and discuss the relationship between our philosophy and theirs, or compare their work on the brain function and Buddhist experience of different levels of consciousness. It is an absorbing exchange, for all of us!

I often get up and go and fiddle with things. Charge batteries for the radio, repair something. From childhood I have been fascinated with mechanical things—toys, small cars, airplanes—things I could explore with my hands. We had an old movie projector in Lhasa that belonged to the Thirteenth Dalai Lama. It was looked after by an ancient Chinese monk. But when he died, no one else knew how to make it work. So I learnt how to make it go, but it was trial and error, as I couldn't read the instructions. I only spoke Tibetan. So now sometimes I work in my workshop repairing things like watches or blocks. Or planting things in the greenhouse. I love plants, especially delphiniums and tulips, and love to see them grow.

At twelve-thirty I have lunch, usually non-vegetarian, though I prefer vegetarian. I eat what I'm given. Sometimes thupka—soup with noodles, occasionally momo—steamed dumplings with meat—and skabakleb—deep-fried bread with meat inside.

The afternoon is taken up with official meetings with the *Bka'zhag* (Tibetan cabinet in exile), or deputies from the Assembly of Tibetan People's Deputies. But there are always people who come from Tibet, with or without the permission of the Chinese. Mostly without—brave people who escape over 17,000-foot Himalayan passes.

It is very painful for me. They all have sad stories and cry. Practically everyone tells me the names of relatives who have been killed by the Chinese, or died in Chinese prisons or labor camps. I try to give them encouragement and see how I can help them practically, as they arrive here destitute and in very bad health.

Very often they bring their children here. They tell me it is the only way they can learn our language, faith and culture. We put the younger ones in the Tibetan Children's Village here or in Mussoorie. Older ones who want to be monks we send for training in our monasteries in South India.

Although Tibetans want me to return, I get messages from *inside* not to return under the present circumstances. They don't want me to be a Chinese puppet like the Panchen Lama. Here, in the free world, I am more useful to my people as a spokesman. I can serve them better from outside.

Sometimes Pema, my youngest sister, who runs the Tibetan Children's Village for orphans here, comes and discusses problems. Like all monks, I don't see much of my family; my parents are dead. My elder brother, Norbu, is Professor of Tibetan studies in Bloomington, Indiana. Thondup, a businessman, lives in Hong Kong.

Unfortunately my middle brother, Lobsang Samden, died two years ago. We were very close. He lived and studied with me in the Potala where we used to get up to all sorts of mischief. Before his death, he worked here at the medical center. I miss him very much.

At six I have tea. As a monk, I have no dinner. At seven it is television time, but unfortunately they transmit discussion programs. And as one is from Amritsar and the other from Pakistan, and I don't know Punjabi or Urdu, it's all talk to me. But occasionally there is a film in English. I liked the BBC series on Western Civilization, and those wonderful nature programs.

Then it's time for bed and more meditation and prayers and by eight-thirty or nine I fall asleep. But if there is a moon, I think that it is also looking down on my people imprisoned in Tibet. I give thanks that, even though I am a refugee, I am free here, free to speak for my people. I pray especially to the patron deity of Tibet, Avalokitesvara, for them. There is not one waking hour when I don't think of the plight of my people, locked away in their mountain fastness.

The Dalai Lama, *Sunday Times Magazine*,
London. December 4, 1988.

The saint then seeks not his own glory but the glory of God. And in order that God may be glorified in all things, the saint wishes himself to be nothing but a pure instrument of the divine will. He wants himself to be simply a window through which God's mercy shines on the world. And for this he strives to be holy. He strives to practice virtue heroically, not in order to be known as a virtuous and holy man, but in order that the goodness of God may never be obscured by any selfish act of his.

Thomas Merton, *Life and Holiness*

Sudhamani stood there captured by the moment and appeared to be intently listening to the singing. Suddenly her mood changed dramatically. The bundle of grass fell from her head as the little one ran to the spot and stood in the midst of the devotees who were gathered there. Overwhelmed with divine bliss, her inner identification with the Lord overflowed into her external being transforming her features and movements into that of Sri Krishna Himself!

The devotees, for the most part, believed that Sri Krishna had come there temporarily in the form of this village girl in order to bless them. Sudhamani asked one amongst the devotees to bring some water and sprinkled it on everyone as sacred water. News about Sudhamani's Divine Manifestation spread quickly and soon a big crowd had gathered. There were skeptics in the crowd who raised an objection to the little one's sudden Divine Mood saying, "If you are really Lord Krishna, then you should be able to show us some proof of it through a miracle. Otherwise, how is it possible for us to believe?" Straight away came the reply,

"An object which does not already exist cannot be brought into existence. All things are really only the projection of the mind. Having the Real Gem within you, why do you crave for an imitation? Even though the Pure Being is within you, ignorance is veiling It!"

Unable to grasp this sublime truth uttered by one established in that Pure Being, they pressed her again and again to show a miracle. Sudhamani replied,

"I am least interested to make somebody a believer by showing a miracle. It is not my intention to show miracles. My goal is to inspire people with the desire for Liberation through Realization of their Eternal Self. Miracles are illusory. That is not the essential principle behind spirituality. Not only that, once a miracle is shown you will desire and demand to see it again and again. I am not here to create desire, but to remove it."

The skeptics insisted, "No, we won't demand again, show a miracle once, we won't insist again!" At last, conceding to their insistent demand, Sudhamani told, "In order to inculcate faith in you I will do it once, but never again approach me with such desires. Those who doubt, let them come to this same place on the day of the next Srimad Bhagavatam discourse."

When the next Bhagavatam discourse was held, a huge crowd gathered inside and outside the house. The non-believers even climbed the trees and perched on the rooftops hoping to expose any fraud. Revealing her oneness with Krishna, Sudhamani called one of the doubting Toms to bring a pitcher of water. As before, this was sprinkled on the devotees as sacred water. Then Sudhamani asked the same man to dip his fingers in the remaining water. To everyone's amazement the water had become pure milk! This was then distributed among the crowd as a holy offering from God. Then Sudhamani called another skeptic and asked him to dip his fingers in the pitcher. The milk in the pot had turned into a sweet and fragrant pudding (panchamritam) made of milk, bananas, raw sugar, raisins, rock sugar. All present raised a cry, "O God! O God!" and believed themselves to indeed be in the Divine Presence of Lord Krishna. The panchamritam was distributed among more than a thousand people who had gathered, yet the pot remained full to the brim. Some people who were sitting at a distance near a small banyan tree at the seaside also received the sweet pudding, but still the vessel's contents did not diminish. A few skeptics were not satisfied and they declared the whole incident a feat of mesmerism insisting that the panchamritam would vanish within a few seconds. Much to their disappointment it did not vanish and the sweet scent remained on everyones' hands for several days. This event greatly increased the faith of the villagers and they all firmly believed in Sudhamani's divinity.

Referring to the advent of Krishna, Bhava Sudhamani explained,

"In the early days I used to dance in bliss and move about alone, persisting in Krishna Bhava, but no one knew. One day I strongly felt the urge to get absorbed in that Supreme Being once and for all. Then I heard a voice from within, 'Thousands and thousands of people in the world are steeped in misery. I have a lot to be done by you who are one with Me."

It was after hearing this voice that Sudhamani manifested her inner identity with Lord Krishna to the villagers. Sudhamani further continued,

"I was able to know everything concerning everyone. I was fully conscious that I myself was Krishna, not only during that particular time of manifestation, but at all other times as well. I did not feel, 'I am great.' When I saw the people and knew their sufferings, I felt immense pity for them. I was conscious of devotees offering salutations to me and addressing me as 'Lord.' I could understand the grievances of the devotees even without being told."

From that time onwards, Sudhamani regularly revealed Krishna Bhava near a small banyan tree growing on the western side of Idamannel near the seashore path. Around the tree there were quite a few flowering plants as well. On the whole it looked like a bush. A few years earlier the villagers had planned to construct a temple there. To inaugurate the temple site, some of the village youth had united and planted another banyan tree as well as lighting a sacred oil lamp.

Mata Amritanandamayi, in Swami Amritasvarupananda,
Mata Amritanandamayi

On the evening of my arrival at All Hallows, Barbara, the retreat administrator, came to fetch me after supper and took me to Briege.

She was waiting in a ground-floor parlor at the back of the building. There were a dozen armchairs set in a circle, as if for a conference. She did not get up when I entered the room; she asked me to come and sit next to her.

She looked tired; there was a weary edge to her voice. She chatted amiably for a while, telling me about a recent trip to Nigeria. I could not take my eyes off the marked gap in her front teeth that gave her face a sort of street-urchin appearance when she smiled. I was wondering, once again (unworthy thought!), what she would do if she fell in love with one of her priests. But she unnerved me by suddenly stopping and looking at me curiously.

I said, almost without thinking, "How do you get through life—loving Christ, a figment of history?"

Even as I said it, I hated the superficial question and I braced myself for a pious answer. I should, by now, have known her better. She merely laughed.

Then she said gently, "The only way any of us are going to discover God's love in life is through the love of human beings. Christ's love comes through you and me as loving people."

We were silent for a while; I was looking out towards the playing fields and the lines of horse-chestnut trees on the perimeter.

Suddenly she leaned forward and, before I could utter a word or resist, she took my hand and said, "Just before we go, John, I'd like to say a prayer with you."

To my embarrassment she immediately began to pray out loud, in short impromptu sentences, as if she were seeking guidance as she went along. I had seen evangelicals praying in this way on American television. There were occasional pauses for a breathless "praise you Jesus...Praise you..." She was thanking God for the opportunity to talk with me, praising Jesus, asking for guidance and grace. I was seized with a mixture of outrage and curiosity. I wanted to tear my hand away and tell her to stop, but fascination kept me rooted to the chair. Every so often she paused again, as if inviting me to praise Jesus.

I could not. I would not.

She stopped suddenly. I stole a look at her face; her eyes were shut tight with concentration and her lips were pursed. She seemed to hold on to me tighter, with both hands. Then she said, "I see an image, John. You are sitting in a chapel. You are all by yourself, in complete solitude. On the chair next to you is a Bible. You pick it up and open on a certain page. I see that page open."

I had heard this tone of voice before—the fortune-teller gazing into the palm of the credulous client. I wanted to giggle, and yet I was consumed with curiosity as to what she was going to say next.

Her eyes were still shut tight. Her concentration seemed immense, her face almost in pain. "I can see the heading of the Book of Wisdom, Chapter Nine," she said. "I feel that the Lord has a special word for you in Wisdom, Chapter Nine."

She was finished. She seemed to jump up out of her seat. She was smiling and pulling me to my feet as well. "God bless you, John," she said, "and now let me kiss you."

With this she gave me a tight hug and kissed me on both cheeks.

As I left her at the door, I said, "Sister, what's in this Wisdom, Chapter Nine?"

"I've no idea," she replied. "I don't ever recollect reading it."

A snack of biscuits and tea was provided for the retreatant priests at ten o'clock. I escaped the jovial clerical throng and went out of the grounds in search of a pub.

The Cat and the Fiddle on the Drumcondra Road welcome me into its roaring bosom with an hour to closing time. I was standing sipping a glass of Guinness, trying to put my thoughts in order, when I felt a finger on my shoulder. I turned to find a stocky little man with pale, thinning hair and spectacles. I recognised him as one of the priests from All Hallows.

"You've escaped too," he said, toasting me with his glass.

We sat ourselves down in a corner.

"So what do you make of Briege, Father?" he said.

He was surprised to discover that I was not a priest.

"She's great, but a bit manipulative," I said.

"Rubbish!" said the priest. "If you had an inkling of the problems she's sorting out among those priests you wouldn't say that."

"So?"

"There are a lot of priests go off the rails; for some of them she's the only answer. Take me. I'm a chaplain in the Irish Army: my milieu is the NCO's mess, not a nun's apron-strings. I was out in Beirut, being shelled. Some of our youngsters copped it. There's not an ounce of sentimentality in me, I can tell you. That woman put a finger on a deep-rooted problem I've had for ten years. She shocked the life out of me. She knew the effect she had, she's been keeping an eye on me. Several times she's looked across at me, and just the eye contact is enough."

"Do you believe that she has special powers?" I asked.

"I do," said the priest.

"But why *her*?"

"I don't know."

"And how does it work?"

"I don't know," said the priest. "It's a mystery. And I'll tell you another thing…" He was looking me directly in the eye. "Your coming here is no idle coincidence in your life; when you get mixed up with Briege it's for a reason." The priest could see that he had embarrassed me. He guffawed to himself and took a draught of his stout.

He looked around the pub as if searching for a change of focus. Then he said, "Briege can be a bit of holy terror, you know. When she was a novice she got hold of one of these fox furs that women used to wear—from the wardrobe of abandoned clothes from when they entered the convent. She ran this thing under the tap and put it at the bottom of the bed of the Mother Superior. They heard the screams all over Newry...."

I woke with a start and saw by my watch that it was two in the morning. I had fallen asleep on the bed after returning from the pub, and I was still fully dressed.

I felt restless, hungry. I wondered if I might find some biscuits in the room where the priests had gathered for their night collation. On tiptoe I went down the granite staircase to the ground floor, but everything had been cleared away in the common room and there wasn't a crumb to be found.

On the way back I stopped at the oratory door. It was open and a light was still on. I went in and sat down in sight of the Blessed Sacrament tabernacle.

I must have sat there for thirty minutes in the stillness of the night, thinking about faith and its relationship to evidence. Could faith be acquired by a sceptic who had merely been granted a small shred of evidence? Or did faith only feed on faith?

Sitting there gazing at the flickering sanctuary lamp, I began to wonder again whether it was possible to pray without faith. Did it make sense for an agnostic to seek guidance and help from God? Surely it was no more unreasonable, I thought, than the act of someone adrift at night on the ocean, who cries for help or fires a signal that may never be seen. What was the prayer of the agnostic, if it wasn't a cry for help?

Just at that point I noticed a Bible on the chair next to me, and I remembered Sister Briege's "vision" that afternoon. "I see you sitting in solitude in a chapel," she had said. I picked it up and turned to Wisdom, Chapter Nine. It began with the passage:

> *God of our ancestors, Lord of mercy,*
> *who by your word has made the universe...*
> *grant me Wisdom, consort of your throne,*
> *and do not reject me from the number of your children,*
> *For I am your servant, son of your serving maid,*
> *a feeble man, with little time to live,*
> *with small understanding of justice and the laws...*
> *What human being indeed can know the intentions of God?...*
> *It is hard enough to work out what is on earth,*
> *laborious to know what lies within our reach;*
> *who, then, can discover what is in the heavens?*

And who could ever have known your will, had you not given
  Wisdom?
who has learned thy counsel, unless
you sent your holy Spirit from above?

Had I been made especially susceptible by my mood, by an indefinable sense of hunger and restlessness? Or was it one or two drinks too many in the Cat and Fiddle on the Drumcondra Road? Whatever the case, in the solitude and silence of the oratory the words opened my mind and my heart; and the phrase "do not reject me from the number of your children" echoed the yearnings I had felt when face to face with the rejected religion of my childhood and youth in my American dream. I wanted to believe this, and I was moved to tears by the force of the appropriateness of the words I had read.

I lost all sense of time, until the tall windows captured the first pale light of day. I felt that I had found an acceptable prayer to pray, and in the silence and stillness of this moment I was even prepared to believe it possible that my tears were a token of the "loving-kindness of the heart of our God," who gives "light to those in darkness."

John Cornwell, *Powers of Darkness, Powers of Light*

An authentically empowered person is humble. This does not mean the false humility of one who stoops to be with those who are below him or her. It is the inclusiveness of one who responds to the beauty of each soul, who sees in each personality and in the actions of each personality the soul incarnate upon the Earth. It is the harmlessness of one who treasures and honors and reveres life in all its forms.

Gary Zukav, *The Seat of the Soul*

Everyone needs a spiritual guide: a minister, rabbi, counselor, wise friend, or therapist. My own wise friend is my dog. He has deep knowledge to impart. He makes friends easily and doesn't hold a grudge. He enjoys simple pleasures and takes each day as it comes. Like a true Zen master, he eats when he's hungry and sleeps when he's tired. He's not hung up about sex. Best of all, he befriends me with an unconditional love that human beings would do well to imitate.

"I think I could turn and live with the animals, they're so placid and self-contained," wrote the poet Walt Whitman. "I stand and look at them long and long." He goes on:

They do not sweat and whine about their condition,
They do not lie awake in the dark and weep for their sins,
They do not make me sick discussing their duty to God,
Not one is dissatisfied, not one is demented with the mania of owning
*   things,*
Not one kneels to another, nor to his kind that lived thousands of
*   years ago,*
Not one is respectable or unhappy over the whole earth.

My dog does have his failings, of course. He's afraid of firecrackers and hides in the clothes closet whenever we run the vacuum cleaner, but unlike me he's not afraid of what other people think of him or anxious about his public image. He barks at the mail carrier and the newsboy, but in contrast to some people I know he never growls at the children or barks at his wife.

So my dog is a sort of guru. When I become too serious and preoccupied, he reminds me of the importance of frolicking and play. When I get too wrapped up in abstractions and ideas, he reminds me of the importance of exercising and caring for my body. On his own canine level, he shows me that it might be possible to live without inner conflicts or neuroses: uncomplicated, genuine, and glad to be alive.

Mark Twain remarked long ago that human beings have a lot to learn from the Higher Animals. Just because they haven't invented static cling, ICBMs, or television evangelists doesn't mean they aren't spiritually evolved.

But what does it mean for an animal (including the human animal) to be spiritually evolved? In my mind, it means many things: the development of a moral sense, the appreciation of beauty, the capacity for creativity, and the awareness of one's self within a larger universe as well as a sense of mystery and wonder about it all. These are the most precious gifts we possess, yet there is nothing esoteric or otherworldly about such "spiritual" capabilities. Indeed, my contention is that spirituality is quite natural, rooted firmly in the biological order and in the ecology shared by all life.

Gary A. Kowalski, *The Souls of Animals*

The Fool and the Sage

Rabbi Bunam once said:

"If I were to set out to give learned and subtle interpretations of the Scriptures, I could say a great many things. But a fool says what he knows, while a sage knows what he says."

Martin Buber, *Tales of the Hasidim*

Most of the world's wickedness arises out of the tragic ignorance of men and not out of the repulsive badness of men. This ignorance arises, in turn, out of their habitual identification of self with the body alone, utterly ignoring its larger and diviner self. The separation which exists in consciousness between the ego and Overself is a fatal one. It is the root of all man's sins, ignorance, woes and evils. To counteract this ignorance and gradually to remove it, religious, mystical and philosophic teachers are in very truth sent by God to enlighten the three different strata of the human race. Left to themselves without the guidance of spiritual instructors and divine awakeners, men would lie in the torpor of ignorance and die in the baseness of animalism. It is not enough for experience alone to form their characters and sharpen their intelligence. Their experience must be explained to them— something of its inner significance must be revealed to them. Their suffering must be solaced by compassionate words and their vaguely felt faith supported by given instruction.

In the appearance from time to time of a spiritual teacher, a religious prophet or a divine healer, we may see one source of such instruction. Out of the divine silence there intermittently issues forth The Word. It is spoken, not by the sky but by the lips of a man. It is not only a heard sound or written document; it is also a creative and transforming power. He who speaks or writes The Word becomes the founder of a new religion, the prophet of a new uplift. His part is carefully to decode, if it may be put in that way, a message received in trans-human cypher and to fit language to it. Such is the supreme intelligence which holds the world within its grip, that its operations help mankind by bringing about his birth as, when, and where he is needed. Sometimes he comes here, as Jesus came, from a higher evolved planet. Such an individual is like a general in the war against evil. He works for its defeat. His appearance among us at periodical intervals is as wise as it is necessary. Neither this nor the eventual spread of his influence is accidental or dependent on anyone's personal choice. Both are divinely ordained through the forces guiding human evolution and the law of universal recompense.

Paul Brunton, *The Spiritual Crisis of Man*

For Christians, Jesus is certainly a teacher, but also essentially more. As crucified and raised to life, he is in person the living, authoritative embodiment of his cause: the cause of God and the cause of man. This living Christ in particular does not call for ineffective adoration, still less to mystical union. But neither does he call for mere imitation. What he does is to call for personal *discipleship, for response and correlation*; he calls me to commit myself to him wholly and entirely, while going my own way—each has his own way—

according to his directions. This is a great opportunity, which was regarded from the very beginning not as what must be done but as what might be done, as an unexpected chance and true gift, a genuine grace. A grace that presupposes nothing more than this one thing: that we seize on it with trust and faith and adapt our life to it; a new attitude to life, which consequently makes possible a new lifestyle.

Hans Küng, *Does God Exist?*

A helper is needed, a helper for both body and soul, for both earthly and heavenly matters. This helper is called the zaddik. He can heal both the ailing body and the ailing soul, for he knows how one is bound up with the other, and this knowledge gives him the power to influence both. It is he who can teach you to conduct your affairs so that your soul remains free, and he can teach you to strengthen your soul, to keep you steadfast beneath the blows of destiny. And over and over he takes you by the hand and guides you until you are able to venture on alone. He does not relieve you of doing what you have grown strong enough to do for yourself. He does not lighten your soul of the struggle it must wage in order to accomplish its particular task in this world. And all this also holds for the communication of the soul with God. The zaddik must make communication with God easier for his hasidim, but he cannot take their place. This is the teaching of the Baal Shem and all the great hasidim followed it; everything else is distortion and the signs of it appear relatively early. The zaddik strengthens his hasid in the hours of doubting, but he does not infiltrate him with truth, he only helps him conquer and reconquer it for himself. He develops the hasid's own power for right prayer, he teaches him how to give the words of prayer the right direction, and he joins his own prayer to that of his disciple and therewith lends him courage, an increase of power—wings. In hours of need, he prays for his disciple and gives all of himself, but he never permits the soul of the hasid to rely so wholly on his own that it relinquishes independent concentration and tension, in other words, that striving-to-God of the soul without which life on this earth is bound to be unfulfilled. Not only in the realm of human passions does the zaddik point over and over to the limits of counsel and help. He does this also in the realm of association with God; again and again he emphasizes the limits of mediation. One man can take the place of another only as far as the threshold of the inner sanctum.

Both in the hasidic teachings and in the tales, we often hear of zaddikim who take upon themselves the sorrow of others, and even atone for others by sacrificing their own lives. But on the very rare occasions (as in the case of Rabbi Nahman of Bratzlav) when we read that the true zaddik can accomplish the act of turning to God for those nearest and dearest to him, the author immediately adds that this act done in place of the other, facilitates the hasid's own turning to God. The zaddik helps everyone, but he does not relieve anyone of what he must do for himself. His helping is a delivery. He even helps the hasid through his death; those near him in the hour of his death receive "a great illumining."

Within these limits the zaddik has the greatest possible influence not only on the faith and mind of the hasid, but on his active everyday life, and even on his sleep, which he renders deep and pure. Through the zaddik, all the senses of the hasid are perfected, not through conscious directing, but through bodily nearness. The fact that the hasid looks at the zaddik perfects his sense of sight, his listening to him, his sense of hearing. Not the teachings of the zaddik but his existence constitute his effectiveness; and not so much the circumstance that he is present on extraordinary occasions as that he is there in the ordinary course of days, unemphatic, undeliberate, unconscious; not that he is there as an intellectual leader but as the complete human being with his whole worldly life in which the completeness of the human being is tested. As a zaddik once said: "I learned the Torah from all the limbs of my teacher." This was the zaddik's influence on his true disciples. But his mere physical presence did not, of course, suffice to exert influence on the many, on the people at large, that influence which made hasidism a popular movement. To achieve this, he had to work with the people until they were ready to receive what he had to give them, to present his teachings in a form the people could accept as their own, he must "participate in the multitude." He had to mix with the people and, in order to raise them to the rung of what perfection they were capable of, he had to descend from his own rung. "If a man falls into the mire," says the Baal Shem, "and his friend wants to fetch him out, he must not hesitate to get himself a little dirty."

One of the great principles of hasidism is that the zaddik and the people are dependent on one another. Again and again, their relationship is compared to that between substance and form in the life of the individual, between body and soul. The soul must not boast that it is more holy than the body, for only in that it has climbed down into the body and works through its limbs can the soul attain to its own perfection. The body, on the other hand, may not brag of supporting the soul, for when the soul leaves, the flesh falls into decay. Thus the zaddikim need the multitude, and the multitude need the zaddikim. The realities of hasidic teaching depend on this interrelationship. And so the "descending from the rung" is not a true descent. Quite the contrary: "If the zaddik serves God," says Rabbi Nahman of Bratzlav, "but does not take the trouble to teach the multitude, he will descend from his rung."

Rabbi Nahman himself, one of the most spiritual of all the zaddikim, felt a deep and secret sense of union between himself and "simple men." This union is the point of departure for his strange utterances about two months before he died. At first he was in a state of such spiritual exhaustion that he declared he was nothing but a "simple man." But when this state suddenly went over into the loftiest elation of spirit, he said that in such periods of descending, the zaddik was infused with vital strength which poured out from him into all the "simple men" in the world, not only those of Israel, but of all people. And the vital strength which flowed into him, hailed from "the treasure trove of gratuitous gifts" stored up in the land of Canaan from time immemorial, time before Israel, and this treasure trove, he added, consists of that secret substance which is also accorded to the souls of simple men and makes them capable of simple faith.

Here we come to the very foundation of hasidism, on which the life between those who quicken, and those who are quickened, is built up. The quintessence of this life is the relationship between the zaddik and his disciples, which unfolds the interaction between the quickener and the quickened in complete clarity. The teacher helps his disciples find themselves, and in hours of desolation the disciples help their teacher find himself again. The teacher kindles the souls of his disciples and they surround him and light his life with the flame he has kindled. The disciple asks, and by his manner of asking unconsciously evokes a reply, which his teacher's spirit would not have produced without the stimulus of the question.

Two "miracle tales" will serve to demonstrate the lofty function of discipleship.

Once, at the close of the Day of Atonement, the Baal Shem is greatly troubled because the moon cannot pierce the clouds and so he cannot say the Blessing of the New Moon, which in this very hour, an hour when Israel is threatened with grave danger, was to have a particularly salutary effect. In vain he strains his soul to alter the state of the sky. Then his hasidim, who know nothing of all this, begin to dance just as every year at this time, in joyful elation at the service performed by their master, a service like that of the high priest in the Temple of Jerusalem. First they dance in the outer room of the Baal Shem's house, but in their elation they enter his room and dance around him. At last, at the peak of ecstasy, they beg him to join the dance and draw him into the circle. And then the moon breaks through the heavy clouds and shines out, a marvel of flawless light. The joy of the hasidim has brought about what the soul of the zaddik, straining to the utmost of its power, was not able to effect.

Among the disciples of Rabbi Dov Baer the Great Maggid, the greatest disciple of the Baal Shem, Rabbi Elimelekh was the man who kept alive the core of the tradition and preserved the school as such. Once, when his soul rose up to heaven, he learned that with his holiness he was rebuilding the ravaged altar in the sanctuary of heavenly Jerusalem, which corresponds to the sanctuary of Jerusalem on this earth. At the same time, he learned that his disciples were helping him in this task of restoration. In a certain year, two of these were absent from the Festival of Rejoicing in the Law, Rabbi Jacob Yitzhak, later the rabbi of Lublin (the "Seer"), and Rabbi Abraham Joshua Heshel, later the rabbi of Apt. Heaven had told Elimelekh that Jacob Yitzhak would bring the Ark into the sanctuary, and that Abraham Joshua Heshel would bring the tables of the law. Yet now they were both missing! Then the zaddik said to his son: "Eighteen times over I can cry: 'Rise up, O Lord!' (as Israel, in the days of old, called toward the Ark, which was to precede them into battle)—and it will be of no use."

In this second story, the disciples participate in the work of the zaddik as individuals, in the first they take part in it as a "holy community." This form of collective effect is undoubtedly the more significant, though we have many and varied tales concerning the participation of individuals. The community of hasidim who belong to a zaddik, especially the close-knit circle of those who are constantly with him, or   at least   visit him regularly, is felt as a powerful dynamic unit. The zaddik unites with this circle both in prayer and in teaching. They are his point of departure in praying, for he does not pray merely as one speaking for them, but as their focus of strength in which the blaze of the community-soul is gathered, and from which this blaze is borne aloft fused with the flame of his own soul. On the sabbath when, at the third meal, he expounds the Scriptures and reveals what is hidden, his teaching is directed toward them: they are the field of force in which his words make manifest the spirit in expanding circles, like rings widening on the waters. And this meal itself! We can approach an understanding of its tension and bliss only when we realize that all—each giving himself utterly— are united into an elated whole, such as can only form around an elated center, which through its very being, points to the divine center of all being. This is a living connection which sometimes expresses itself strangely and even grotesquely, but the grotesque in itself is so genuine that it bears witness to the genuineness of the impulses. For hasidism must not be interpreted as an esoteric movement but one charged with primitive vitality which—as all primitive vitality—sometimes vents itself rather crudely. It is this very vitality which lends peculiar intensity to the relationship of one hasid toward another. Their common attachment to the zaddik and to the holy life he embodies binds them to one another, not only in the festive hours of common prayer, and of the common meal, but in all the hours of everyday living. In moments of elation, they drink to one another, they sing and dance together, and tell one another abstruse and comforting miracle tales. But they help one another too. They are prepared to risk their lives for a comrade, and this readiness comes from the same deep source as their elation. Everything the true hasid does or does not do mirrors his belief that, in spite of the intolerable suffering men must endure, the heartbeat of life is holy joy, and that always and everywhere, one can force a way through to that joy—provided one devotes one's self entirely to his deed.

Martin Buber, Tales of the Hasidim

"Well, at least we've got over the worst," I said to the Master, when he announced one day that we were going on to some new exercises. "He who has a hundred miles to walk should reckon ninety as half the journey," he replied, quoting the proverb. "Our new exercise is shooting at a target."

What had served till now as a target and arrow-catcher was a roll of straw on a wooden stand, which one faced at a distance of two arrows laid end to end. The target, on the other hand, set up at a distance of about sixty feet, stands on a high and broadly based bank of sand which is piled up against three walls, and, like the hall in which the archer stands, is covered by a beautifully curved tile roof. The two halls are connected by high wooden partitions which shut off from the outside the space where such strange things happen.

The Master proceeded to give us a demonstration of target-shooting: both arrows were embedded in the black of the target. Then he bade us perform the ceremony exactly as before, and, without letting ourselves be put off by the target, wait at the highest tension until the shot "fell." The slender bamboo arrows flew off in the right direction, but failed to hit even the sandbank, still less the target, and buried themselves in the ground just in front of it.

"Your arrows do not carry," observed the Master, "because they do not reach far enough spiritually. You must act as if the goal were infinitely far off. For master archers it is a fact of common experience that a good archer can shoot further with a medium-strong bow than an unspiritual archer can with the strongest. It does not depend on the bow, but on the presence of mind, on the vitality and awareness with which you shoot. In order to unleash the full force of this spiritual awareness, you must perform the ceremony differently: rather as a good dancer dances. If you do this, your movements will spring from the center, from the seat of right breathing. Instead of reeling off the ceremony like something learned by heart, it will then be as if you were creating it under the inspiration of the moment, so that dance and dancer are one and the same. By performing the ceremony like a religious dance, your spiritual awareness will develop its full force."

I do not know how far I succeeded in "dancing" the ceremony and thereby activating it from the center. I no longer shot too short, but I still failed to hit the target. This prompted me to ask the Master why he had never yet explained to us how to take aim. There must, I supposed, be a relation of sorts between the target and the tip of the arrow, and hence an approved method of sighting which makes hitting possible.

"Of course there is," answered the Master, "and you can easily find the required aim yourself. But if you hit the target with nearly every shot you are nothing more than a trick archer who likes to show off. For the professional who counts his hits, the target is only a miserable piece of paper which he shoots to bits. The "Great Doctrine" holds this to be sheer devilry. It knows nothing of a target which is set up at a definite distance from the archer. It only knows of the goal, which cannot be aimed at technically, and it names this goal, if it names it at all, the Buddha." After these words, which he spoke as though they were self-evident, the Master told us to watch his eyes closely as he shot. As when performing the ceremony, they were almost closed, and we did not have the impression that he was sighting.

Obediently we practiced letting off our shots without taking aim. At first I remained completely unmoved by where my arrows went. Even occasional hits did not excite me, for I knew that so far as I was concerned they were only flukes. But in the end this shooting into the blue was too much for me. I fell back into the temptation to worry. The Master pretended not to notice my disquiet, until one day I confessed to him that I was at the end of my tether.

"You worry yourself unnecessarily," the Master comforted me. "Put the thought of hitting right out of your mind! You can be a Master even if every shot does not hit. The hits on the target are only the outward proof and confirmation of your purposelessness at its highest, of your egolessness, your self-abandonment, or whatever you like to call this state. There are different grades of mastery, and only when you have made the last grade will you be sure of not missing the goal."

"That is just what I cannot get into my head," I answered. "I think I understand what you mean by the real, inner goal which ought to be hit. But how it happens that the outer goal, the disk of paper, is hit without the archer's taking aim, and that the hits are only outward confirmations of inner events—that correspondence is beyond me."

"You are under an illusion," said the Master after awhile, "if you imagine that even a rough understanding of these dark connections would help you. These are processes which are beyond the reach of understanding. Do not forget that even in Nature there are correspondences which cannot be understood, and yet are so real that we have grown accustomed to them, just as if they could not be any different. I will give you an example which I have often puzzled over. The spider dances her web without knowing that there are flies who will get caught in it. The fly, dancing nonchalantly on a sunbeam, gets caught in the net without knowing what lies in store. But through both of them 'It' dances, and inside and outside are united in this dance. So, too, the archer hits the target without having aimed—more I cannot say."

Much as this comparison occupied my thoughts—though I could not of course think it to a satisfactory conclusion—something in me refused to be mollified and would not let me go on practicing unworried. An objection, which in the course of weeks had taken on more definite outline, formulated itself in my mind. I therefore asked: "Is it not at least conceivable that after all your years of practice you involuntarily raise the bow and arrow with the certainty of a sleepwalker, so that, although you do not consciously take aim when drawing it, you must hit the target—simply cannot fail to hit it?"

The Master, long accustomed to my tiresome questions, shook his head. "I do not deny," he said after a short silence, "that there may be something in what you say. I do stand facing the goal in such a way that I am bound to see it, even if I do not intentionally turn my gaze in that direction. On the other hand I know that this seeing is not enough, decides nothing, explains nothing, for I see the goal as though I did not see it."

"Then you ought to be able to hit it blindfolded," I jerked out.

The Master turned on me a glance which made me fear that I had insulted him and then said: "Come to see me this evening."

I seated myself opposite him on a cushion. He handed me tea, but did not speak a word. So we sat for a long while. There was no sound but the singing of the kettle on the hot coals. At last the Master rose and made me a sign to follow him. The practice hall was brightly lit. The Master told me to put a taper, long and thin as a knitting needle, in the sand in front of the target, but not to switch on the light in the target-stand. It was so dark that I could not even see its outlines, and if the tiny flame of the taper had not been there, I might perhaps have guessed the position of the target, though I could not have made it out with any precision. The Master "danced" the ceremony. His first arrow shot out of dazzling brightness into deep night. The second arrow was a hit, too. When I switched on the light in the target-stand, I discovered to my amazement that the first arrow was lodged full in the middle of the black, while the second arrow had splintered the butt of the first and plowed through the shaft before embedding itself beside it. I did not dare to pull the arrows out separately, but carried them back together with the target. The Master surveyed them critically. "The first shot," he then said, "was no great feat, you will think, because after all these years I am so familiar with my target-stand that I must know even in pitch darkness where the target is. That may be, and I won't try to pretend otherwise. But the second arrow which hit the first—what do you make of that? I at any rate know that it is not 'I' who must be given credit for this shot. 'It' shot and 'It' made the hit. Let us bow to the goal as before the Buddha!"

The Master had evidently hit me, too, with both arrows: as though transformed overnight, I no longer succumbed to the temptation of worrying about my arrows and what happened to them. The Master strengthened me in this attitude still further by never looking at the target, but simply keeping his eye on the archer, as though that gave him the most suitable indication of how the shot had fallen out. On being questioned, he freely admitted that this was so, and I was able to prove for myself again and again that his sureness of judgment in this matter was no whit inferior to the sureness of his arrows. Thus, through deepest concentration, he transferred the spirit of his art to his pupils, and I am not afraid to confirm from my own experience, which I doubted long enough, that the talk of immediate communication is not just a figure of speech but a tangible reality. There was another form of help which the Master communicated to us at that time, and which he likewise spoke of as immediate transference of the spirit. If I had been continually shooting badly, the Master gave a few shots with my bow. The improvement was startling: it was as if the bow let itself be drawn differently, more willingly, more understandingly. This did not happen only with me. Even his oldest and most experienced pupils, men from all walks of life, took this as an established fact and were astonished that I should ask questions like one who wished to make quite sure. Similarly, no master of swordsmanship can be moved from his conviction that each of the swords fashioned with so much hard work and infinite care takes on the spirit of the swordsmith, who therefore sets about his work in ritual costume. Their experiences are far too striking, and they themselves far too skilled, for them not to perceive how a sword reacts in their hands.

One day the Master cried out the moment my shot was loosed: "It is there! Bow down to the goal!" Later, when I glanced towards the target—unfortunately I couldn't help myself—I saw that the arrow had only grazed the edge. "That was a right shot," said the Master decisively, "and so it must begin. But enough for today, otherwise you will take special pains with the next shot and spoil the good beginning." Occasionally several of these right shots came off in close succession and hit the target, besides of course the many more that failed. But if ever the least flicker of satisfaction showed in my face the Master turned on me with unwonted fierceness. "What are you thinking of?" he would cry. "You know already that you should not grieve over bad shots; learn now not to rejoice over the good ones. You must free yourself from the buffetings of pleasure and pain, and learn to rise above them in easy equanimity, to rejoice as though not you but another had shot well. This, too, you must practice unceasingly—you cannot conceive how important it is."

During these weeks and months I passed through the hardest schooling of my life, and though the discipline was not always easy for me to accept, I gradually came to see how much I was indebted to it. It destroyed the last traces of any preoccupation with myself and the fluctuations of my mood. "Do you now understand," the Master asked me one day after a particularly good shot, "what I mean by 'It shoots,' 'It hits'?"

"I'm afraid I don't understand anything more at all," I answered, "even the simplest things have got in a muddle. Is it 'I' who draw the bow, or is it the bow that draws me into the state of highest tension? Do 'I' hit the goal, or does the goal hit me? Is 'It' spiritual when seen by the eyes of the body, and corporeal when seen by the eyes of the spirit—or both or neither? Bow, arrow, goal and ego, all melt into one another, so that I can no longer separate them. And even the need to separate has gone. For as soon as I take the bow and shoot, everything becomes so clear and straightforward and so ridiculously simple...."

"Now at last," the Master broke in, "the bowstring has cut right through you."

Eugen Herrigel, Zen in the Art of Archery

23 November

I lay down on my bed for a short rest this afternoon. Listening within I noticed a vibration. It was like a motor going inside me, vibrating in the whole of the body; or rather, perhaps, like a soundless, supersonic "sound," or like the feeling one gets after a row; a strong tension, an excitement without excitement. Parallel with it was a tremendous longing for it, for that which is nameless. And in this longing was peace; only infinite peace. I know it sounds rather complicated, but it is the best I can do when trying to describe it.

When L. came back from the post office, she told me that it is the famous Mystical Sound and it is called *Dzikr*. It is the preliminary step to dhyana. I was fascinated. Was watching it going inside me; such a new experience.

In the evening a man was sitting opposite the guru telling him his troubles of which he had many. When he left, the guru began to sing. I was sitting there, the "sound" going on inside me, with a tremendous longing; but for what? I was not quite sure... Waited for an opportunity to ask. He sang in Urdu and translated it:

I will come to you in the shape of a nightingale,
Many branches are on a tree, on each branch I will Be,
The nightingale is here, there, everywhere,
When you will hear it, you will know that I am here,
The nightingale who at all times is everywhere…

The room was dark, full of peace, filled with his voice. It seemed to me that he was singing it for me. I have to love him, I thought. The shishya has to love the guru; one can only progress through love. And love for the guru is love for God. He began another song:

I am here and I am there and I show myself in different shapes.
And you may wonder what or who am I and you will not under-
*   stand.*
But in time the answer is given.
I am here and I am there and it is all the same,
Everywhere all the time, am I alone…

This one I did not understand and was pondering over it when he began another song:

There must be a complete surrender, even physically,
Surrender of everything without reserve and without regret,
If you want to see the Real Shape of the Guru.
Either the Guru has to come down to you,
Or you must go to him, but a complete surrender is needed,
If you want to see the Real Shape of the Guru!

"Did you get the idea?" he asked. Perhaps it was the answer to my request the other day, to let me see him as he really is, I ventured.

"Yes; either you are a guest on my plane, or I am on yours; but at first a complete surrender is essential, complete surrender, beginning from the physical body and on all the levels."

Told him that I understood, and even told L. a few days ago, that my physical body was going to be subjected to much strain, and I was quite prepared for it, ready for everything which might be necessary to be "taken in gallop" (his own expression).

"Don't say that you are ready for it; rather say that you are trying to do it; it is better."

"Yes, Bhai Sahib," I answered, and my heart was so full of gratitude.

"If one is pledged, pledged for spiritual life and work, there is no reserve, a complete surrender on all the planes, when one enters the arena. What is a pledge? It is a promise; never to be broken, never."

"It lasts for ever and ever and ever," I said softly.

Irina Tweedie, *The Chasm of Fire*

Perhaps I should have visited Shri Ramana. Yet I fear that if I journeyed to India a second time to make up for my omission, it would fare with me just the same: I simply could not, despite the uniqueness of the occasion, bring myself to visit this undoubtedly distinguished man personally. For the fact is, I doubt his uniqueness; he is of a type which always was and will be. Therefore it was not necessary to seek him out. I saw him all over India, in the pictures of Ramakrishna, in Ramakrishna's disciples, in Buddhist monks, in innumerable other figures of the daily Indian scene, and the words of his wisdom are the *sous-entendu* of India's spiritual life. Shri Ramana is, in a sense, a *hominum homo*, a true "son of man" of the Indian earth. He is "genuine," and on top of that he is a "phenomenon" which, seen through European eyes, has claims to uniqueness. But in India he is merely the whitest spot on a white surface (whose whiteness is mentioned only because there are so many surfaces that are just as black). Altogether, one sees so much in India that in the end one only wishes one could see less: the enormous variety of countries and human beings creates a longing for complete simplicity. This simplicity is there too; it pervades the spiritual life of India like a pleasant fragrance or a melody. It is everywhere the same, but never monotonous, endlessly varied. To get to know it, it is sufficient to read an *Upanishad* or any discourse of the Buddha. What is heard there is heard everywhere; it speaks out of a million eyes, it expresses itself in countless gestures, and there is no village or country road where that broad-branched tree cannot be found in whose shade the ego struggles for its own abolition, drowning the world of multiplicity in the All and All-Oneness of Universal Being. This note rang so insistently in my ears that soon I was no longer able to shake off its spell. I was then absolutely certain that no one could ever get beyond this, least of all the Indian holy man himself; and should Shri Ramana say anything that did not chime in with this melody, or claim to know anything that transcended it, his illumination would assuredly be false. The holy man is right when he intones India's ancient chants, but wrong when he pipes any other tune. This effortless drone of argumentation, so suited to the heat of southern India, made me refrain, without regret, from a visit to Tiruvannamalai.

Nevertheless, the unfathomableness of India saw to it that I should encounter the holy man after all, and in a form that was more congenial to me, without my seeking him out: in Trivandrum, the capital of Travancore, I ran across a disciple of the Maharshi. He was an unassuming little man, of a social status which we would describe as that of a primary-school teacher, and he reminded me most vividly of the shoemaker of Alexandria who (in Anatole France's story) was presented to St. Anthony by the angel as an example of an even greater saint than he. Like the shoemaker, my little holy man had innumerable children to feed and was making special sacrifices in order that his eldest son might be educated. (I will not enter here into the closely allied question as to whether holy men are always wise, and conversely, whether all wise men are unconditionally holy. In this respect there is room for doubt.) Be that as it may, in this modest, kindly, devout, and childlike spirit I encountered a man who had absorbed the wisdom of the Maharshi with utter devotion, and at the same time had surpassed his master because, notwithstanding his cleverness and holiness, he had "eaten" the world. I acknowledge with deep gratitude this meeting with him; nothing better could have happened to me. The man who is only wise and only holy interests me about as much as the skeleton of a rare saurian, which would not move me to tears. The insane contradiction, on the other hand, between existence beyond Māyā in the cosmic Self, and that amiable human weakness which fruitfully sinks many roots into the black earth, repeating for all eternity the weaving and rending of the veil as the ageless melody of India—this contradiction fascinates me; for how else can one perceive the light without the shadow, hear the silence without the noise, attain wisdom without foolishness? The experience of holiness may well be the most painful of all. My man—thank God—was only a little holy man; no radiant peak above the dark abysses, no shattering sport of nature, but an example of how wisdom, holiness, *and* humanity can dwell together in harmony, richly, pleasantly, sweetly, peacefully, and patiently, without limiting one another, without being peculiar, causing no surprise, in no way sensational, necessitating no special post-office, yet embodying an age-old culture amid the gentle murmur of the coconut palms fanning themselves in the light sea wind. He has found a meaning in the rushing phantasmagoria of Being, freedom in bondage, victory in defeat.

> C. G. Jung, *Psychology and Religion: West and East*

All these factions were somehow represented at a tea party gathered by Swami Prabhavananda, a few days after my lecture, in his apartment at the Vedanta Temple—in a room which had so many doors that it seemed like a setting for a French farce. As the guests assembled, the various doors kept opening to admit young women who identified themselves as Sister Radha,

Sister Parvati, Sister Shaktidevi, Sister Indira, and Sister Anandamaya (I am just making up the names), and we were joined by Huxley, Isherwood, and many of the Swami's distinguished lay disciples. Very soon it became apparent that I had been put on the path of the razor's edge: that on the one hand, the Swami wanted to demonstrate the error of my views, and that on the other, I did not want to embarrass him in front of his disciples.

The trouble started when one of the sisters said, rather too innocently, "Oh Mr. Watts, I'd be so interested to know what you think about Krishnamurti."

"Well," I replied, "I must say that I find his work very fascinating, because I think he's one of the few people who have come to grips with such basic problems of the spiritual life as trying to make oneself unselfish."

"Yes, Krishnamurti is a very fine man," the Swami chipped in. "I don't think any of us can doubt the greatness of his character. But his teaching is very misleading. I mean, he seems to be saying that one can attain realization without any kind of yoga or spiritual method, and of course that isn't true."

"No indeed," I countered, "if in fact there is something to be attained. Your *Upanishads* say very plainly, *Tat tvam asi*, 'You *are* That,' so what is there to attain?"

"Oh no, no!" the Swami protested. "There's all the difference in the world between being merely informed, in words, that this is so and realizing it truly, between understanding it intellectually and really knowing it. It takes a great deal of work to go from one state to the other."

"But so far as I can see," I went on, "the more people consider themselves to have made progress in such work, the greater their spiritual pride. They are putting legs on a snake—congratulating themselves for bringing about, by their own efforts, a state of affairs which already *is*."

"Well, I wonder," mused Aldous, "isn't it rather curious that there has always been a school of thought in religion which attributes salvation or realization to an unmerited gift of divine grace rather than personal effort?"

"Of course," said the Swami, "there are those exceptional cases of people who seem to be born—or suddenly endowed—with realization. But we mustn't leave out of account the work that must have gone into it in their former lives."

"But that virtually cuts out the principle of grace altogether," I said. "When Christians say that something comes about by the grace of God, Hindus and Buddhists say that it is so already and always has been. The self, *atman*, is the Godhead, Brahman. It has always been so from the very beginning, so that your very *trying* to realize it is pushing it away, refusing the gift, ignoring the fact."

"But this is ridiculous," the Swami objected. "That amounts to saying that an ordinary ignorant and deluded person is just as good, or just as realized, as an advanced yogi."

"Exactly," I said. "And what advanced yogi would deny it? Doesn't he see the Brahman everywhere, and in all people, all beings?"

"You are saying," said the Swami, "that you yourself, or just any other person, can realize that you are the Brahman just as you are, without any spiritual effort or discipline at all!"

"Just so. After all, one's very not realizing is, in its turn, also the Brahman. According to your own doctrine, what else is there, what else is real other than the Brahman?"

"Oh!" he exclaimed. "There was someone who came to Sri Ramakrishna with such talk. He said, 'If that is your Brahman, I spit on it!' Don't fool me. If you were truly one with the Brahman and truly in *samadhi*, you would be beyond suffering. You would not be able to feel a pinch."

"You mean that the Brahman can't feel a pinch?"

"Of course not!"

At that moment I had one of the great temptations of my life, and resisted it. Instead, I said something like, "Well I don't think your Brahman is very sensitive," laughed, and changed the subject. Yet, in a way, I regretted it. I felt, in retrospect, that I should have honored the Swami by going the whole way, pinching him hard, and seeing what he would have done, for although he may be shrugged off by those who see him as representing the idle romanticism of Hollywood Swami-Land, he has nonetheless given thousands of people that startling and disquieting question: "Who, what, do you think you really are? Absolutely, basically, deeply within?"

Alan Watts, *In My Own Way*

Together Habu and I set out for a distant marketplace in the Bengali section of Banaras. The ungentle Indian sun was not yet at zenith as we made our purchases in the bazaars. We pushed our way through the colorful medley of housewives, guides, priests, simply clad widows, dignified *Brahmins*, and ubiquitous holy bulls. As Habu and I moved on, I turned my head to survey a narrow, inconspicuous lane.

A Christlike man in the ocher robes of a swami stood motionless at the end of the lane. Instantly and anciently familiar he seemed; for a trice my gaze fed hungrily. Then doubt assailed me.

"You are confusing this wandering monk with someone known to you," I thought. "Dreamer, walk on."

After ten minutes, I felt heavy numbness in my feet. As though turned to stone, they were unable to carry me farther. Laboriously I turned around; my feet regained normality. I faced the opposite direction; again the curious weight oppressed me.

"The saint is magnetically drawing me to him!" With this thought, I heaped my parcels into the arms of Habu. He had been observing my erratic footwork with amazement, and now burst into laughter.

"What ails you? Are you crazy?"

My tumultuous emotion prevented any retort; I sped silently away.

Retracing my steps as though wing-shod, I reached the narrow lane. My quick glance revealed the quiet figure, steadily gazing in my direction. A few eager steps and I was at his feet.

"Gurudeva!" The divine face was the one I had seen in a thousand visions. These halcyon eyes, in a leonine head with pointed beard and flowing locks, had oft peered through the gloom of my nocturnal reveries, holding a promise I had not fully understood.

"O my own, you have come to me!" My guru uttered the words again and again in Bengali, his voice tremulous with joy. "How many years I have waited for you!"

We entered a oneness of silence; words seemed the rankest superfluities. Eloquence flowed in soundless chant from the heart of master to disciple. With an antenna of irrefragable insight I sensed that my guru knew God and would lead me to Him. The obscuration of this life disappeared in a fragile dawn of prenatal memories. Dramatic time! Past, present, and future are its cycling scenes. This was not the first sun to find me at these holy feet!

My hand in his, my guru led me to his temporary residence in the Rana Mahal section of the city. His athletic figure moved with firm tread. Tall, erect, about fifty-five at this time, he was active and vigorous as a young man. His dark eyes were large, beautiful with plumbless wisdom. Slightly curly hair softened a face of striking power. Strength mingled subtly with gentleness.

As we made our way to the stone balcony of a house overlooking the Ganges, he said affectionately:

"I shall give you my hermitages and all I possess."

"Sir, I come for wisdom and God-realization. Those are your treasure troves I am after!"

The swift Indian twilight had dropped its half-curtain before my master spoke again. His eyes held unfathomable tenderness.

"I give you my unconditional love."

Precious words! A quarter-century elapsed before I had another auricular proof of his love. His lips were strange to ardor; silence suited his oceanic heart.

"Will you give me the same unconditional love?" He gazed at me with childlike trust.

"I will love you eternally, Gurudeva!"

"Ordinary love is selfish, darkly rooted in desires and satisfactions. Divine love is without condition, without boundary, without change. The flux of the human heart is gone forever at the transfixing touch of pure love." He added humbly, "If ever you find me falling from a state of God-realization, please promise to put my head on your lap and help to bring me back to the Cosmic Beloved we both worship."

He rose then in the gathering darkness and guided me to an inner room. As we ate mangoes and almond sweetmeats, he unobtrusively wove into his conversation an intimate knowledge of my nature. I was awe-struck at the grandeur of his wisdom, exquisitely blended with an innate humility.

"Do not grieve for your amulet. It has served its purpose." Like a divine mirror, my guru apparently had caught a reflection of my whole life.

"The living reality of your presence, Master, is joy beyond any symbol."

"It is time for a change, inasmuch as you are unhappily situated in the hermitage."

I had made no references to my life; they now seemed superfluous! By his natural, unemphatic manner, I understood that he wished no astonished ejaculations at his clairvoyance.

"You should go back to Calcutta. Why exclude relatives from your love of humanity?"

His suggestion dismayed me. My family was predicting my return, though I had been unresponsive to many pleas by letter. "Let the young bird fly in the metaphysical skies," Ananta had remarked. "His wings will tire in the heavy atmosphere. We shall yet see him swoop toward home, fold his pinions, and humbly rest in our family nest." This discouraging simile fresh in my mind, I was determined to do no "swooping" in the direction of Calcutta.

"Sir, I am not returning home. But I will follow you anywhere. Please give me your address, and your name."

"Swami Sri Yukteswar Giri. My chief hermitage is in Serampore, on Rai Ghat Lane. I am visiting my mother here for only a few days."

I wondered at God's intricate play with His devotees. Serampore is but twelve miles from Calcutta, yet in those regions I had never caught a glimpse of my guru. We had had to travel for our meeting to the ancient city of Kashi (Banaras), hallowed by memories of Lahiri Mahasaya. Here too the feet of Buddha, Shankaracharya, and many other Yogi-Christs had blessed the soil.

"You will come to me in four weeks." For the first time, Sri Yukteswar's voice was stern. "Now that I have told you of my eternal affection and have shown my happiness at finding you, you feel free to disregard my request.

The next time we meet, you shall have to reawaken my interest. I won't easily accept you as a disciple: there must be complete surrender by obedience to my strict training."

I remained obstinately silent. My guru quickly penetrated my difficulty.

"Do you think your relatives will laugh at you?"

"I will not return."

"You will return in thirty days."

"Never."

The controversial tension unrelieved, I bowed reverently at his feet and departed. Walking in the midnight darkness toward the hermitage, I wondered why the miraculous meeting had ended on an inharmonious note. The dual scales of *maya*, that balance every joy with a grief! My young heart was not yet malleable to the transforming fingers of my guru.

The next morning I noticed increased hostility in the attitude of the hermitage members. They spiked my days with invariable rudeness. Three weeks passed; Dayananda then left the ashram to attend a conference in Bombay. Pandemonium broke over my hapless head.

"Mukunda is a parasite, accepting hermitage hospitality without making proper return." Overhearing this remark, I regretted for the first time that I had obeyed the request to send back my money to Father. With heavy heart, I sought out my sole friend, Jitendra.

"I am leaving. Please convey my respectful regrets to Dayanandaji when he returns."

"I will leave also! My attempts to meditate here meet with no more favor than your own." Jitendra spoke with determination.

"I have met a Christlike saint. Let us visit him in Serampore."

And so the "bird" prepared to "swoop" perilously close to Calcutta!

Paramahansa Yogananda, *Autobiography of a Yogi*

On intellect of body back & Cock whose red neck
supports the S&M freaks of Government
    police & Fascist Monopolies—
Kissinger bare assed & big buttocked
    with a whip, in leather boots
scrawling on a memo to Chile "No more
    civic lectures please"
When the ambassador complained about Torture
    methods used in the Detention Stadium!
And I ride the planes that Rockefeller gassed
    when he paid off Kissinger!

Stony Burns sits in jail, in a stone cell in
     Huntsville
and breathes his news to solitude.
                              Homage
to the Gurus, Guru om! Thanks to the teachers
     who taught us to breathe,
to watch our minds revolve in emptiness,
     to follow the rise & fall of thoughts,
Illusions big as empires flowering &
     Vanishing on a breath!
Thanks to aged teachers whose wrinkles
     read our minds' newspapers &
     taught us not to Cling to yesterday's
     thoughts,
nor thoughts split seconds ago, but
     let cities vanish on a breath—
Thanks to teachers who showed us behold
     Dust motes in our own eye,
     anger our own hearts,
emptiness of Dallases where we
     sit thinking knitted brows—
Sentient beings are numberless I vow
     to liberate all
Passions unfathomable I vow to
     release them all
Thought forms limitless I vow to
     master all
Awakened space is endless I vow to
     enter it forever.

Dallas, December 4, 1974

Allen Ginsberg, from
"Thoughts on a Breath," in *Collected Poems: 1947–1980*

I have often thought of writing a novel, similar to Thomas Mann's *Confessions of Felix Krüll*, which would be the life story of a charlatan making out as a master guru—either initiated in Tibet or appearing as the reincarnation of Nagarjuna, Padmasambhava, or some other great historical sage of the Orient. It would be a romantic and glamorous tale, flavored with the scent of pines in Himalayan valleys, with garden courtyards in obscure parts of

Alexandria, with mountain temples in Japan, and with secretive meetings and initiations in country houses adjoining Paris, New York, and Los Angeles. It would also raise some rather unexpected philosophical questions as to the relations between genuine mysticism and stage magic. But I have neither the patience nor the skill to be a novelist, and thus can do no more than sketch the idea for some more gifted author.

The attractions of being a trickster guru are many. There is power and there is wealth, and still more the satisfactions of being an actor without need for a stage, who turns "real life" into a drama. It is not, furthermore, an illegal undertaking such as selling shares in non-existent corporations, impersonating a doctor, or falsifying checks. There are no recognized and official qualifications for being a guru, though now that some universities are offering courses in meditation and Kundalini Yoga it may soon be necessary to be a member of the U.S. Fraternity of Gurus. But a really fine trickster would get around all that by the one-upmanship of inventing an entirely new discipline outside and beyond all known forms of esoteric teaching.

It must be understood from the start that the trickster guru fills a real need and performs a genuine public service. Millions of people are searching desperately for a true father-Magician,* especially at a time when the clergy and the psychiatrists are making rather a poor show, and do not seem to have the courage of their convictions or of their fantasies. Perhaps they have lost nerve through too high a valuation of the virtue of honesty—as if a painter felt bound to give his landscapes the fidelity of photographs. To fulfill his compassionate vocation, the trickster guru must above all have nerve. He must also be quite well-read in mystical and occult literature, both that which is historically authentic and sound in scholarship, and that which is somewhat questionable—such as the writings of H. P. Blavatsky, P. D. Ouspensky, and Aleister Crowley. It doesn't do to be caught out on details now known to a wide public.

After such preparatory studies, the first step is to frequent those circles where gurus are especially sought, such as the various cult groups which pursue oriental religions or peculiar forms of psychotherapy, or simply the intellectual and artistic milieux of any great city. Be somewhat quiet and solitary. Never ask questions, but occasionally add a point—quite briefly—to what some speaker has said. Volunteer no information about your personal life, but occasionally indulge in a little absent-minded name-dropping to suggest that you have traveled widely and spent time in Turkestan. Evade

---

* And there have also been such effective mother-magicians as Mary Baker Eddy, Helena Blavatsky, Aimie McPherson, Annie Besant, and Alice Bailey.

close questioning by giving the impression that mere travel is a small matter hardly worth discussing, and that your real interests lie on much deeper levels. Such behavior will soon provoke people into asking your advice. Don't come right out with it, but suggest that the question is rather deep and ought to be discussed at length in some quiet place. Make an appointment at a congenial restaurant or cafe—not at your home, unless you have an impressive library and no evidence of being tied down with a family. At first, answer nothing, but without direct questioning, draw the person out to enlarge on his problem and listen with your eyes closed—not as if sleeping, but as if attending to the deep inner vibrations of his thoughts. Conclude the interview with a slightly veiled command to perform some rather odd exercise, such as humming a sound and then suddenly stopping. Carefully instruct the person to be aware of the slightest decision to stop before actually stopping, and indicate that the point is to be able to stop without any prior decision. Make a further appointment for a report on progress.

To carry this through, you must work out a whole series of unusual exercises, both psychological and physical. Some must be rather difficult tricks which can actually be accomplished, to give your student the sense of real progress. Others must be virtually impossible—such as to think of the words *yes* and *no* at the same instant, repeatedly for five minutes, or with a pencil in each hand, to try to hit the opposite hand—which is equally trying to defend itself and hit the other. Don't give all your students the same exercises but, because people love to be types, sort them into groups according to their astrological sun signs or according to your own private classifications, which must be given such odd names as grubers, jongers, milers, and trovers.

A judicious use of hypnosis—avoiding all the common tricks of hand-raising, staring at lights, or saying "Relax, relax, while I count up to ten" will produce pleasant changes of feeling and the impression of attaining higher states of consciousness.

First, describe such a stage quite vividly—say, the sense of walking on air—and then have your students walk around barefooted trying not to make the slightest sound and yet giving their whole weight to the floor. Imply that the floor will soon feel like a cushion, then like water, and finally like air. Indicate a little later that there is reason to believe that something of this kind is the initial stage of levitation.

Next, be sure to have about thirty or forty different stages of progress worked out, giving them numbers, and suggest that there are still some extremely high stages beyond those numbered which can only be understood by those who have reached twenty-eight—so no point in discussing them now. After the walking-on-air gambit, try for instance having them push out hard with their arms as if some overwhelming force were pulling them.

Reverse the procedure. This leads quickly to the feeling that one is not doing what one is doing and doing what one is not doing. Tell them to stay in this state while going about everyday business.

After a while let it be known that you have a rather special and peculiar background—as when some student asks, "Where did you get all this?" Well, you just picked up a thing or two in Turkestan, or "I'm quite a bit older than I look," or say that "Reincarnation is entirely unlike what people suppose it to be." Later, let on that you are in some way connected with an extremely select in-group. Don't brashly claim anything. Your students will soon do that for you, and, when one hits on the fantasy that pleases you most, say, "I see you are just touching stage eighteen."

There are two schools of thought about asking for money for your services. One is to have fees just like a doctor, because people are embarrassed if they do not know just what is expected of them. The other, used by the real high-powered tricksters, is to do everything free with, however, the understanding that each student has been personally selected for his or her innate capacity for the work (call it that), and thus be careful not to admit anyone without first putting them through some sort of hazing. Monetary contributions will soon be offered. Otherwise, charge rather heavily, making it clear that the work is worth infinitely more to oneself and to others than, say, expensive surgery or a new home. Imply that you give most of it away to mysterious beneficiaries.

As soon as you can afford to wangle it, get hold of a country house as an *ashram* or spiritual retreat, and put students to work on all the menial tasks. Insist on some special diet, but do not follow it yourself. Indeed, you should cultivate small vices, such as smoking, mild boozing, or, if you are very careful, sleeping with the ladies, to suggest that your stage of evolution is so high that such things do not affect you, or that only by such means can you remain in contact with ordinary mundane consciousness.

On the one hand, you yourself must be utterly free from any form of religious or parapsychological superstition, lest some other trickster should outplay you. On the other hand, you must eventually come to believe in your own hoax, because this will give you ten times more nerve. This can be done through religionizing total skepticism to the point of basic incredulity about everything—even science. After all, this is in line with the Hindu-Buddhist position that the whole universe is an illusion, and you need not worry about whether the Absolute is real or unreal, eternal or non-eternal, because every idea of it that you could form would, in comparison with living it up in the present, be horribly boring. Furthermore, you should convince yourself that the Absolute is precisely the same as illusion, and thus not be in the least ashamed of being greedy or anxious or depressed. Make it clear that we are ultimately God, but that you *know* it. If you are challenged to perform wonders, point out that everything is already a fabulous wonder, and to do something bizarre would be to go against your own most perfect scheme of things. On the other hand, when funny coincidences turn up, look knowing and show no surprise, especially when any student has good fortune or recovers from sickness. It will promptly be attributed to your powers, and you may be astonished to find that your very touch becomes healing, because people really believe in you. When it doesn't work, you should sigh gently about lack of faith, or explain that this particular sickness is a very important working out of Karma which will have to be reckoned with some day, so why not now.

The reputation for supernormal powers is self-reinforcing, and as it builds up you can get more daring, such that you will have the whole power of mass self-deception working for you. But always remember that a good guru plays it cool and maintains a certain aloofness, especially from those sharpies of the press and TV whose game is to expose just about everyone as a fraud. Always insist, like the finest restaurants, that your clientele is exclusive. The very highest "society" does not deign to be listed in the Social Register.

As time goes on, allow it more and more to be understood that you are in constant touch with other centers of work. Disappear from time to time by taking trips abroad, and come back looking more mysterious than ever. You can easily find someone in India or Syria to do duty as your colleague, and take a small and select group of students on a journey which includes a brief interview with this Personage. He can talk any kind of nonsense, while you do the "translating." When traveling with students, avoid any obvious assistance from regular agencies, and let it appear that your secret fraternity has arranged everything in advance.

Now a trickster guru is certainly an illusionist, but one might ask "What else is art?" If the universe is nothing but a vast Rorschach blot upon which we project our collective measures and interpretations, and if past and future has no real existence, an illusionist is simply a creative artist who changes the collective interpretation of life, and even improves on it. Reality is mostly what a people or a culture conceives it to be. Money, worthless in itself, depends entirely on collective faith for its value. The past is held against you only because others believe in it, and the future seems important only because we have conned ourselves into the notion that surviving for a long time, with painstaking care, is preferable to surviving for a short time with no responsibility and lots of thrills. It is really a matter of changing fashion.

Perhaps, then, a trickster may be one who actually liberates people from their more masochistic participations in the collective illusion, on the homeopathic principle of "The hair of the dog that bit you." Even genuine gurus set their disciples impossible psychological exercises to demonstrate the unreality of the ego, and it could be argued that they too, are unwitting tricksters, raised as they have been in cultures without disillusioning benefits of "scientific knowledge," which, as ecologists note, isn't working out too well. Perhaps it all boils down to the ancient belief that God himself is a trickster, eternally fooling himself by the power of *maya* into the sensation that he is a human being, a cat, or an insect, since no art can be accomplished which does not set itself certain rules and limitations. A fully infinite and boundless God would have no limitations, and thus no way of manifesting power or love. Omnipotence must therefore include the power of self-restriction—to the point of forgetting that it is restricting itself and thus making limitations seem real. It could be that genuine students and gurus are on the side of being fooled, whereas the phony gurus are the foolers—and one must make one's choice.

I am proposing this problem as a kind of Zen *koan*, like "Beyond positive and negative, what is reality?" How will you avoid being either a fool or a fooler? How will you get rid of the ego-illusion without either trying or not trying? If you need God's grace to be saved, how will you get the grace to get grace? Who will answer these questions if yourself is itself an illusion? Man's extremity is God's opportunity.

> *The cock crows in the evening;*
> *At midnight, the brilliant sun.*

Alan Watts, "The Trickster Guru," in *The Essential Alan Watts*

☞ 15 ☜

The Gifts

By embracing the surrendered state we become a receptacle to divine manifestations. Being open to God in all things means living life in a new kind of reality. One of St. Francis of Assisi's most popular prayers begins with the line "Lord, Make me an instrument of your peace." By surrendering we become like a flute for God, open, clear, pure, beautiful, and, as Irish poet Brendan Kennelly writes, "vulnerable new."

In surrendering to God, we let go of the old ways, the old skins, the old scripts, the old family/societal rules and laws of the old self, to prepare for a more transcendent life. Eugen Herrigel mentions that we are helped by the "immediate transference of the spirit." And this transference of the spirit comes through the Gifts. In this section I have collected descriptions of what surrender actually feels like when we receive these gifts of the spirit—gifts that do not nourish without partnership. For when we surrender, all sorts of tunes are played through us. We discover love, grace, creativity, bliss, peace, and happiness—all of which lead to our own perfect way of being and doing for God. The Gifts are there to help us unite with one another. It is at this point that we gain a full understanding of what God intends the members of the human race to be; a full understanding of what the purpose of life is, and its sanctity. We become profoundly grateful.

☞☜

...reality gives itself, unveils itself to us *deliberately*. And we are awestruck with this gift. It is available to everybody, to every human being. That is the main thing, the world gives itself to us. It gives itself freely to us, if we just allow it. It showers us with gifts.

David Steindl-Rast, in Fritjof Capra, David Steindl-Rast with Thomas Matus, *Belonging to the Universe*

When we do not desire the things of this world for their own sake, we become able to see them as they are. We see at once their goodness and their purpose, and we become able to appreciate them as we never have before. As soon as we are free of them, they begin to please us. As soon as we cease to rely on them alone, they are able to serve us. Since we depend neither on the pleasure nor on the assistance we get from them, they offer us both pleasure and assistance, at the command of God.

Thomas Merton, *No Man Is an Island*

Five breaths pray in me: sun moon
Rain wind and fire
Five seated Buddhas reign in the breaths
Five illusions
One universe:
The white breath, yellow breath,
Green breath, blue breath,
Red fire breath. Amitabha
Knowledge and Desire
And the quiescence
Of Knowledge and Desire.

Thomas Merton, *The Asian Journals of Thomas Merton*

It takes courage
to do what you want.

Other people
have a lot of plans for you.

Nobody wants you to do
what you want to do.

They want you to go on their trip,
but you can do what you want.

I did. I went into the woods
and read for five years.

> Joseph Campbell, *Reflections on the Art of Living*

When Music was needed Music sounded
When a Ceremony was needed a Teacher appeared
When Students were needed Telephones rang.
When Cars were needed Wheels rolled in
When a Place was needed a Mansion appeared
When a Fire was needed Wood appeared
When an Ocean was needed Waters rippled waves
When Shore was needed Shore met Ocean
When Sun was needed the Sun rose east

> *Rolling Thunder Stones*

> Sunrise Ceremony Verse
> Improvised with Australian Aborigine Song-Sticks
> at Request of Medicine Man Rolling Thunder
> November 5, 1975

> Allen Ginsberg, from "Rolling Thunder Stones II,"
> in *Collected Poems*

The joy and consolation of our life is realizing that what we have cannot be lost because it is God's.

> Thomas Merton, *The Springs of Contemplation*

What does that feel like? Coming out of a ten-day silent meditation retreat, not necessarily with full liberation, one is taken by surprise. Waves of gratitude arise in the mind at unexpected moments for all that is wholesome and beautiful in one's life: the richness of parental love, the blessing of a child, the pleasure of good friends, the bounty of the erotic. One is amazed at how precisely one can see—the vibrancy of flowers and the hundred shades of green, the wing bars on a goldfinch, the exquisite grain in a piece of wood, the shading in the clouds.

Charlene Spretnak, *States of Grace*

Good Souls, to Survive

Things inside things endure
Longer than things exposed;
We see because we are blind
And should not be surprised to find
We survive because we're enclosed.

If merit is measured at all,
Vulnerability is the measure;
The little desire protection
With something approaching passion,
Will not be injured, cannot face error.

So the bird in astonishing flight
Chokes on the stricken blood,
The bull in the dust is one
With surrendered flesh and bone,
Naked on chill wood.

The real is rightly intolerable,
Its countenance stark and abrupt,
Good souls, to survive, select
Their symbols from among the elect—
Articulate, suave, corrupt.

But from corruption comes the deep
Desire to plunge to the true;
To dare is to redeem the blood,
Discover the buried good,
Be vulnerably new.

Brendan Kennelly, *Irish Poets 1924–1974*

A Tale of Two Birds

The whole of the Vedanta Philosophy is in this story:

Two birds of golden plumage sat on the same tree. The one above, serene, majestic, immersed in his own glory; the one below restless and eating the fruits of the tree, now sweet, now bitter. Once he ate an exceptionally bitter fruit, then he paused and looked up at the majestic bird above; but he soon forgot about the other bird and went on eating the fruits of the tree as before. Again he ate a bitter fruit, and this time he hopped up a few boughs nearer to the bird at the top. This happened many times until at last the lower bird came to the place of the upper bird and lost himself. He found all at once that there had never been two birds, but that he was all the time that upper bird, serene, majestic, and immersed in his own glory.

Swami Vivekananda, *Meditations and Its Methods*

Stranger

When no one listens
To the quiet trees
When no one notices
The sun in the pool
Where no one feels
The first drop of rain
Or sees the last star

Or hails the first morning
Of a giant world
Where peace begins
And rages end:

One bird sits still
Watching the work of God:
One turning leaf,
Two falling blossoms,
Ten circles upon the pond.

One cloud upon the hillside,
Two shadows in the valley

And the light strikes home.
Now dawn commands the capture
Of the tallest fortune,
The surrender
Of no less marvelous prize!

Closer and clearer
Than any wordy master,
Thou inward Stranger
Whom I have never seen,

Deeper and cleaner
Than the clamorous ocean,
Seize up my silence
Hold me in Thy Hand!

Now act is waste
And suffering undone
Laws become prodigals
Limits are torn down
For envy has no property
And passion is none.

Look, the vast Light stands still
Our cleanest Light is One!

Thomas Merton, *The Collected Poems*

In Buddhism, knowledge is regarded as an obstacle to understanding, like a block of ice that obstructs water from flowing. It is said that if we take one thing to be the truth and cling to it, even if truth itself comes in person and knocks at our door, we won't open it. For things to reveal themselves to us, we need to be ready to abandon our views about them.

The Buddha told a story about this. A young widower, who loved his five-year-old son very much, was away on business, and bandits came, burned down his whole village, and took his son away. When the man returned, he saw the ruins, and panicked. He took the charred corpse of an infant to be his own child, and he began to pull his hair and beat his chest, crying uncontrollably. He organized a cremation ceremony, collected the ashes and put them in a very beautiful velvet bag. Working, sleeping, eating, he always carried the bag of ashes with him.

One day his real son escaped from the robbers and found his way home. He arrived at his father's new cottage at midnight, and knocked at the door. You can imagine at that time, the young father was still carrying the bag of ashes, and crying. He asked, "Who is there?" And the child answered, "It's me Papa. Open the door, it's your son." In his agitated state of mind the father thought that some mischievous boy was making fun of him, and he shouted at the child to go away, and he continued to cry. The boy knocked again and again, but the father refused to let him in. Some time passed, and finally the child left. From that time on, father and son never saw one another. After telling this story, the Buddha said, "Sometime, somewhere you take something to be the truth. If you cling to it so much, when the truth comes in person and knocks at your door, you will not open it."

Guarding knowledge is not a good way to understand. Understanding means to throw away your knowledge. You have to be able to transcend your knowledge the way people climb a ladder. If you are on the fifth step of a ladder and think that you are very high, there is no hope for you to climb to the sixth. The technique is to release. The Buddhist way of understanding is always letting go of our views and knowledge in order to transcend. This is the most important teaching. That is why I use the image of water to talk about understanding. Knowledge is solid; it blocks the way of understanding. Water can flow, can penetrate.

Thich Nhat Hanh, *Being Peace*

Keishu, the monk, asked Ungo-chi about the meaning of the dictum considered to characterize the teaching of Zen. "By seeing into one's own Nature (or Being) one becomes a Buddha."

Ungo-chi gave this answer: "The Nature is primarily pure, absolutely tranquil, altogether free from disturbances, does not belong to the category of being and non-being, purity and defilement, longness and shortness, attachment and detachment; it is serenity itself. When one has a clear insight of it, one is said to have seen into one's own Nature. The Nature is the Buddha, and the Buddha is the Nature. Hence seeing into the Nature is becoming the Buddha."

The monk: "If the Nature is pure in essence and has no attribute, either being or non-being, how can there be any seeing at all?"

Chi: "Though there is the seeing, there is nothing seen."

Monk: "If there is nothing seen, how can there be any seeing?"

Chi: "The seeing itself is not."

Monk: "In this kind of seeing, whose seeing is it?"

Chi: "There is no seer either."

Monk: "Where are we then?"

Chi: "Do you know that the idea of being is the product of false thinking? Because of this there is subject and object, which we call an error. When there is a seeing (dualistically conceived), difference of opinion arises, and one falls into birth-and-death. It is not so with the one who has a clear seeing. He sees all day, and yet he sees nothing. The seeing has neither substance nor manifestation; action and reaction are both lacking in it; therefore it is called seeing into the Nature."

Monk: "Is the Nature present everywhere?"

Chi: "Yes, there is nowhere it is not present."

Monk: "Are plain-minded people supplied with it also?"

Chi: "I have already said that there is nowhere the Nature is not present, and why not in the plain-minded people too?"

Monk: "Why is it, then, that while Buddhas and Bodhisattvas are not bound up by birth-and-death, plain ordinary people are to undergo its bondage? Does this not go against the omnipresence?"

Chi: "The trouble is that the latter imagine, in spite of the Nature's being absolutely pure, the opposition of action and reaction in it, and this makes them fall into birth-and-death. Buddhas and great souls are fully cognizant of the truth that there is no distinction between being and non-being in the purity of the Nature, and therefore action and reaction does not take place."

Monk: "If so, some are completed, while others are not?"

Chi: "There is no completion to talk about, how much less the completed one!"

Monk: "What is the ultimate truth?"

Chi: "To state briefly, you should think of this: in the Nature absolutely pure there are neither plain-minded people nor wise men, neither the completed nor the not-completed. The plain-minded or the wise—they are names. When your understanding is based on names, you fall into birth-and-death. When you know that names are provisional and have no reality, you find that there are no personalities corresponding to names."

Chi said again: "This is the ultimate position we come to, and if we here say 'I am the completed one but they are not,' we commit a great error. And another great error is to think that in the seeing there is (the distinction of) pure and defiled, common and wise. But if we take the view that there are no differences of understanding between the common people and the wise, this will be ignoring the law of causation. Further, it is a great error to consider that in the absolutely pure Nature there is a place for abiding.

"It is great error, too, to hold that this is not a place for abiding. While there is nothing moving and disturbing in the absolutely pure Nature, it is furnished with measures and activities which never cease to work, and whereby love and compassion are set to work. Where these workings take place there is the fulfilment of the absolutely pure Nature. This is the seeing into one's Nature and becoming the Buddha."

Daisetz Teitaro Suzuki, *Living By Zen*

Generic Buddha

Like the unnamed official
who opens Harlem fire hydrants
offers cool mist to sweltering
confused nigger children, barefoot
on August Manhattan tarmacs,
generic Buddha
ultimate product
you can be found anywhere

Unnamed and plain wrapped
that inconceivable combination
of new-old ingredients
Oh what a feeling!
you do not Toyota with us
you drive the vehicle
not designed for California highways
vehicle that knows the unknown terrain,
to travel the fresh path you continually uncover
I would cut all credit cards

Like Gleem itself
you clean and conquer in two ways
polish the inner enamel
purify both breath and breathing
morning noon and night,
ultimate Lifesaver that never dissolves
natural deodorant that never diminishes
generic Buddha
ultimate product
to wash in the rain of purity you provide,
I would drain the entire Tide of samsara

No plop plop, fizz fizz
no bizmo or gizmo
no roto rooter, no draino
no extra vapour power
can bloom those flowers that appear
after you clear and rout
the clogged channels of memory and sense

Available on every shelf of every self
Universal Product Code itself
product beyond the concept of products
yet ultimate product
generic Buddha
I would empty all pockets
and purge all sockets of purchase-attachment
to simply walk the aisles
of that magical market
while you alone
gently proclaim the Dharma

Peter Livingston, from private collection

An Epilogue

I have seen flowers come in stony places
And kind things done by men with ugly faces,
And the gold cup won by the worst horse at the races,
So I trust, too.
John Masefield, *The Faber Book of Epigrams and Epitaphs*

⇥ Love ⇤

Love is the basis of all union—with each other, our surroundings, and with God. Pierre Teilhard de Chardin calls love "the great union of the universe" and "the blood of spiritual evolution." In spiritual terms love is not a human need that wants fulfilment but a personal gift to others. Love is about giving unconditionally, about living in this state of unconditional love with no expectations of reciprocity. This is love in maturity, love in its fullness and the ultimate spiritual goal. And it is through the experiences received in return for love given that God's guidance and God's nourishment are revealed.

Love as a word and deed, especially in sexual expression, has been misused and abused over time, and particularly in the last twenty years since the sexual liberation movement. The threat of AIDS has dampened the spirit of "free love," and contributed to the revival of a more conservative morality. The growing interest in Tantric sexual practices hails a return to sexual monogamy with the added ingredient of spirituality, leading to a more spiritual physical partnership.

In the following section, Bede Griffiths asserts that the separateness—the otherness—of the male and female sexes exists to bring us together. Psychologist Abraham H. Maslow explains the necessity of recognizing and honouring the very human, imperfect aspects of the other, that we love and serve the profane as well as the sacred. Gary Zukav explains further the idea of service in a committed relationship. We no longer need to unite in partnership in order to survive, or build a future for ourselves but to "reflect spiritual consciousness."

Many today are searching for the paradisiacal state of union, the "heaven on earth" that God created for Adam and Eve before the Fall. These unions are based upon spiritual values and commitment to God and are comprised of twin souls. Omraam Mikhaël Aïvanhov explains who and what these are. (We have heard a lot of talk about soul mates lately—some books, like Thomas Moore's more recent work, addressed them specifically—but the twin soul is different.) The twin soul is the perfect contra-gender; the glove of the hand of the other, the gender complement to the soul. Every soul searches for its other half, all relationships are an attempt at finding him or her. The sharing with the twin is more perfect than anyone could ever expect to find through the similarity of type of work, attitude, service, and interest in spiritual subjects and practices and the longing for God. The twin soul is a reward from God. When the twin soul arrives, all loneliness is ended forever—the search has been completed. Patricia Joudry and Maurie Pressman have studied twin souls in relationship in their book *Twin Souls: A Guide to Finding Your True Spiritual Partner*. The relationship can be sexual if both people are free to express this—and are not married to others when they meet. Joudry and Pressman's description of Alexander and Leroy, who live far from each other and only meet physically very infrequently, reveals sexual union on a spiritual plane. This spiritual love is a transcendent experience, and can bring, as one of the many divine gifts, great insight, great peace, great nourishment, and great life energy—the manifestations of high love.

✦

...Love is the most universal, the most tremendous and the most mysterious of the cosmic forces. After centuries of tentative effort, social institutions have externally diked and canalized it. Taking advantage of this situation, the moralists have tried to submit it to rules. But in constructing their theories they have never got beyond the level of an elementary empiricism influenced by out-of-date conceptions of matter and the relics of old taboos. Socially, in science, business and public affairs, men pretend not to know it, though under the surface it is everywhere. Huge, ubiquitous and always unsubdued—this wild force seems to have defeated all hopes of understanding and governing it. It is therefore allowed to run everywhere beneath our civilization. We are conscious of it, but all we ask of it is to amuse us, or not to harm us. Is it truly possible for humanity to continue to live and grow without asking itself how much truth and energy it is losing by neglecting its incredible power of love?

From the standpoint of spiritual evolution, which we here assume, it seems that we can give a name and value to this strange energy of love. Can we not say quite simply that in its essence it is the attraction exercised on each unit of consciousness by the center of the universe in course of taking shape? It calls us to the great union, the realization of which is the only process at present taking place in nature. By this hypothesis, according to which (in agreement with the findings of psychological analysis) love is the primal and universal psychic energy, does not everything become clear around us, both for our minds and our actions? We may try to reconstruct the history of the world from outside by observing this play of atomic, molecular or cellular combinations in their various processes. We may attempt, still more efficaciously, this same task from within by following the progress made by conscious spontaneity and noting the successive stages achieved. The most telling and profound way of describing the evolution of the universe would undoubtedly be to trace the evolution of love.

In its most primitive forms, when life is scarcely individualized, love is hard to distinguish from molecular forces; one might think of it as a matter of chemisms or tactisms. Then little by little it becomes distinct, though still *confused* for a very long time with the simple function of reproduction. Not till hominization does it at last reveal the secret and manifold virtues of its violence. "Hominized" love is distinct from all other love, because the "spectrum" of its warm and penetrating light is marvelously enriched. No longer only a unique and periodic attraction directed to material fertility; but an unbounded and continuous possibility of contact through spirit much more than through body; the play of countless subtle antennae seeking one another in the light and darkness of the soul; the pull toward mutual sensibility and completion, in which preoccupation with preserving the species gradually dissolves in the greater intoxication of two people consummating a world. It is in reality the universe that is pressing on, through woman, toward man. The whole question (the vital question for the earth) is that they shall recognize one another.

If man fails to recognize the true nature, the true object of his love, the confusion is vast and irremediable. Bent on assuaging a passion intended for the All on an object too small to satisfy it, he will strive to compensate a fundamental imbalance by materialism or an ever increasing multiplicity of experiments. His efforts will be fruitless—and in the eyes of one who can see the inestimable value of the "spiritual quantum" of man, a terrible waste. But let us put aside any sentimental feelings or virtuous indignation. Let us look very coolly as biologists or engineers, at the lurid atmosphere of our great towns at evening. There, and everywhere else as well, the earth is continually dissipating its most marvelous power. This is pure loss. Earth is burning away, wasted on the empty air. How much energy do you think the spirit of the earth loses in a single night?

If only man would turn and see the reality of the universe shining in the spirit and through the flesh. He would then discover the reason for what has hitherto deceived and perverted his powers of love. Woman stands before him as the lure and symbol of the world. He cannot embrace her except by himself growing, in his turn, to a world scale. And because the world is always growing and always unfinished and always ahead of us, to achieve his love man is engaged in a limitless conquest of the universe and himself. In this sense, man can only attain woman by consummating a union with the universe. Love is a sacred reserve of energy; it is like the blood of spiritual evolution. This is the first revelation we receive from the sense of the earth.

Pierre Teilhard de Chardin, from "Love and Happiness"

Of all the worn, smudged, dog's-eared words in our vocabulary, "love" is surely the grubbiest, smelliest, slimiest. Bawled from a million pulpits, lasciviously crooned through hundreds of millions of loud-speakers, it has become an outrage to good taste and decent feeling, an obscenity which one hesitates to pronounce. And yet it has to be pronounced, for, after all, Love is the last word.

Aldous Huxley, from "Adonis and the Alphabet," in *Collected Essays*

We use the word "love" but we have no more understanding of love than we do of anger or fear or jealousy or even joy, because we have seldom investigated what that state of mind is. What are the feelings we so quickly label as love? For many what is called love is not lovely at all but is a tangle of needs and desires, of momentary ecstasies and bewilderment—moments of unity, of intense feelings of closeness, occur in a mind so fragile that the least squint or sideways glance shatters its oneness into a dozen ghostly paranoias. When we say love we usually mean some emotion, some deep feeling for an object or a person, that momentarily allows us to open to another. But in such emotional love, self-protection is never far away. Still there is "business" to the relationship: clouds of jealousy, possessiveness, guilt, intentional and unintentional manipulation, separateness and the shadow of all previous "loves" darken the light of oneness. But what I mean by love is not an emotion, it is a state of being. True love has no object. Many speak of their unconditional love for another. But in truth one does not have unconditional love for another. Unconditional love is the experience of being, there is no "I" and "other" and anyone or anything it touches is experienced in love. You cannot unconditionally love someone. You can only *be* unconditional love. It is not a dualistic emotion. It is a sense of oneness with all that is. The experience of love arises when we surrender our separateness into the universal. It is a feeling of unity. You don't love another, you *are* another. There is no fear because there is no separation. It is not so much that "two are as one" so much as it is "the One manifested as two." In such love there can be no unfinished business.

Stephen Levine, Who Dies?

Laila was the daughter of a king, and Majnu was the son of a laborer. They were very much in love but could not get married because of the difference in their social status. This, however, did not prevent them yearning for each other with deep love. Their love increased every day until they became almost mad thinking about each other. Laila would climb to a room high up in the palace and call, "Majnu, Majnu." Majnu would wander through the streets of the city, crying "Laila, Laila." He had only one ambition—to be united with Laila. She was his only desire, his only succor, his only hope. Majnu was not promiscuous for a moment; he did not think of anything but Laila. When Majnu's father saw his son's madness, he was very frightened, thinking that the king would punish Majnu. But Majnu himself was not frightened, for true love does not care about anything.

The king, Laila's father, was also very worried when he saw his daughter's condition. He called doctors, magicians, astrologers, and experts in mantras and *tantras*, but nothing had any effect on her. He would suggest a visit to the theater to divert her, but she would only say, "Will Majnu be there?"

He would say, "Let us travel far away into a cool and beautiful land."

She would reply, "Majnu is not there. I don't want to go." Thus Majnu and Laila pined for each other. Muktananda says: If you long for something, long for it like this, otherwise don't. To pursue something for selfish ends is of no use and cannot lead you to God.

Because they thought about each other and meditated on each other all the time, Laila and Majnu completely lost themselves. Laila thought about Majnu so much that she became Majnu, and Majnu thought about Laila so much that he became Laila. If a meditator withholds a part of himself and does not lose himself completely, he is a thief; he is stealing what he holds back. A poem I once heard describes Majnu's state exactly:

khatakā nahīm hai khāne kā chintā nahīm hai pāne kī
mamatā nahīm hai deha kī paravāha nahīm hai prānon kī

He is not worried about his food nor anxious for any gain;
He is not attached to his body, nor does he cling to life itself.

Majnu had only one hope—that he might attain Laila. He wandered around completely forgetful of himself. The people of the city took him for a lunatic. Seeing Majnu in this state, the king felt pity for him, for he became convinced that Majnu's love for his daughter was true. Majnu had ceased to exist as Majnu and had offered himself to Laila, like earrings melting into gold. He saw Laila everywhere he looked. There was no more "you and I"; only Laila remained. The king ordered a proclamation in the town: "Majnu is not well. His love for Laila has made him helpless. Give him food and drink and clothes, and send the bills to the royal treasury." Everywhere in the town it was heard that Majnu, because he had thought about nothing but Laila, was to receive everything he wanted from the king. All the destitute, lazy, and needy people in the town—all the parasites—realized that it would be a good plan to pretend to be Majnu, and so every day a new Majnu appeared. The number of new Majnus increased.

All the new Majnus got shoes, clothes, and food from the shopkeepers, and the bills were sent to the treasury. The king noticed that Majnu's bills were running into thousands, and he had inquiries made. He discovered that there were over a thousand Majnus in the town. "Because I had pity this misfortune has come," he thought to himself, wondering what to do next. He had a very clever minister in his service and this minister said, "Your Majesty, if you delegate full authority to me, I shall handle the matter." The king agreed, and the minister sent the crier around to proclaim: "Exactly one week from today, at 12:00 noon, Majnu will be hanged, for he has fallen in love with the princess and this is against the law." The effect of this proclamation was startling. All the Majnus threw away their clothes and shoes and hats and ran as far away as they could. They found jobs in offices and houses and factories. They all did their best to hide their identities since if they were discovered they would be hanged. All of them disappeared. Only the real Majnu remained. He was quite ready to be speared to death or burned alive, for he had no desire to keep his life. His only desire was for Laila. He had lost himself in Laila. Only the real Majnu had a genuine desire, and only he was left. And it was the real Majnu who found his Laila.

Dear students of meditation! Your worth can only be ascertained when you are put through a test, and there is a test for meditation, just as there is for anything else. The one who proves to be a true Majnu, a true meditator, will find his Laila, which is God. The rest will throw off their clothes and shoes and hats and run away.

Swami Muktananda, *Play of Consciousness*

Within the human mass there floats a certain power of development, represented by the forces of love, which infinitely surpasses the power absorbed in the necessary concern for the reproduction of the species. The old doctrine of chastity assumed that this drive could and should be diverted directly toward God, with no need of support from the creature. In this there was a failure to see that such an energy, still largely potential (as are all the other spiritual powers of matter), also required a long period of development in its natural plane. In the present state of the world, man has not yet, in reality, been completely revealed to himself by woman, nor is the reciprocal revelation complete. In view, therefore, of the evolutive structure of the universe, it is impossible for one to be separated from the other while their development is still continuing. It is not in isolation (whether married or unmarried), but in paired units, that the two portions, masculine and feminine, of nature are to rise up toward God. The view has been put forward that there can be no sexes in spirit. This arises from not having understood that their duality was to be found again in the composition of divinized being.

Pierre Teilhard de Chardin, *Toward the Future*

An Example of B-Analysis

Any woman can be seen under the aspect of eternity, in her capacity as a symbol, as a goddess, priestess, sibyl, as mother earth, as the eternal flowing breasts, as the uterus from which life comes, and as the life-giver, the life-creator. This can also be seen operationally in terms of the Jungian archetypes which can be recovered in several ways. I have managed to get it in good introspectors simply by asking them directly to free associate to a particular symbol. The psychoanalytic literature, of course, has many such reports. Practically every deep case history will report such symbolic, archaic ways of viewing the woman, both in her good aspects and her bad aspects. (Both the Jungians and the Kleinians recognize the great and good mother and the witch mother as basic archetypes.) Another way of getting at this is in terms of the artificial dream that is suggested under hypnosis. It can also probably be investigated by spontaneous drawings, as the art therapists have pointed out. Still another possibility is the George Klein technique of two cards very rapidly succeeding each other so that symbolism can be studied. Any person who has been psychoanalyzed can fairly easily fall into such symbolic or metaphorical thinking in his dreams or free associations or fantasies or reveries. It is possible then to see the woman under the aspect of her Being. Another way of saying this is that she is to be seen in her sacred, rather than the profane, aspects; or under the holy or pious aspects; or from the point of view of eternity or infinity; from the point of view of perfection; from the point of view of the ideal end-goal; from the point of view of what in principle any woman could have become. This fits in with the self-actualization theory that any new-born baby in principle has the capacity to become perfect or healthy or virtuous although we know very well that in actuality most of them won't.

On the other hand, the woman seen in her D-aspect, in the world of deficiencies, of worries and bills and anxieties and wars and fears and pains, is profane rather than sacred, momentary rather than eternal, local rather than infinite, etc. Here we see in women what is equally true: they can be bitches, selfish, empty-headed, stupid, foolish, catty, trivial, boring, mean, whorish. The D-aspect and B-aspect are equally true.

The general point is: we must try to see *both* or else bad things can happen psychologically. For one thing, if the woman is seen *only* as a goddess, as the madonna, as unearthly beauty, as on a pedestal, as in the sky or in Heaven, then she becomes inaccessible to the male—she can't be played with or made love to. She isn't earthy or fleshy enough. In the critical situations in which this actually happens with men, i.e., where they identify women with the madonna or with the mother, they often become sexually impotent and find it impossible to have sexual intercourse with such a woman. This is good neither for his pleasure nor for her pleasure either, especially since making madonnas out of some women is apt to go along with making prostitutes out of other women. And then the whole madonna-prostitute complex which is so familiar to the clinician comes up, in which sex is impossible with good and noble and perfect women, but is possible only with dirty or nasty or low women. Somehow it is necessary to be able to see the B-woman, the actually noble and wonderful goddess-woman, and also the D-woman, who sometimes sweats and stinks and who gets belly aches, and with whom one can go to bed.

On the other hand, we have very considerable clinical information about what happens when men can see women only in their D-aspect and are unable to see them as beautiful and noble and virtuous and wonderful as well. This breeds what Kirkendall in his book on sex has called the exploitative relationship. It can get very ugly both for men and for women and can deprive them both of the really great pleasures of life. Certainly it can deprive them of all the love pleasures, which means also most of the major sex pleasures (because the people who can't love don't get the same kind of thrill out of sex as the people who can love and who can get romantic). The men who think of women merely as sexual objects—and who call them by purely sexual names—thereby depersonalize the woman as if she were not person enough to be called a human being. This is obviously bad for her—but in a more subtle way it is also very bad for him, in the sense that every exploiter is damaged by being an exploiter. The possibility of being friends across such exploitative lines is practically zero, which means that men and women, the two halves of the human species, are cut off from one another. They can never learn the delights of being fused with each other, of being friendly, affectionate, loving partners, or the like. To sum this up, it means that there are horrors in seeing the woman only in the B-way, and there are horrors in seeing her only in a D-way, and clearly the psychologically healthy goal is for these to be combined or to alternate or to be fused in some way.

It is this fusion that I can use as an example of the more general problem of fusing the B-psychology and the D-psychology, the sacred and the profane, the eternal and the temporal, the infinite and the local, the perfect and the defective, and so on.

Seeing the man in a B-way means seeing also his ultimate, ideal possibilities, in Marion Milner's case, as God the Father, as all-powerful, as the one who created the world and who rules the world of things, the world outside, the world of nature, and who changes it and masters it and conquers it. Also at this deep level, Milner, and probably many other women, will identify the noble man, the B-man, as the spirit of rationality, the spirit of intelligence, of probing and exploring, of mathematics, and the like. The male as a father image is strong and capable, fearless, noble, clean, not trivial, not small, a protector of the weak, the innocent, children and orphans and widows, the hunter and bringer of food, and so on. Secondly, he can be seen archaically as the master and the conqueror of nature, the engineer, the carpenter, the builder, which the woman is generally not. It is quite probable that women, when they get into the eternal mood, or into the B-attitude, must see men in this ideal way even if they can't see their own particular man in this way. The very fact that a woman is dissatisfied with her own man may be an indication that she has some other image or imago or ideal in mind to which he doesn't measure up. I think that investigation would show that this ideal was as Milner expressed it and as it is seen also in the direct investigations of schizophrenics of the sort that John Rosen did. Clearly any woman who could not see her man (or some man anyhow) in this way could not use men, would have to disrespect them, might need a man in the D-world, but deep down would be contemptuous because he didn't measure up to the B-realm.

(I should mention that we already have a kind of precursor, a model of the B-woman and the B-man in the child's attitude toward his mother and father. Through his eyes they can be seen as perfect and godlike and so on. This attitude can be retained by any child who has the good fortune of having a good enough mother and a good enough father so as to permit such attitudes to be formed, i.e., to give him some notion of what the ideally good woman and of what the ideally good man could be.)

The D-man, in the world of trivialities, the world of striving, etc. may not be able to induce the B-attitude in his woman, but this seems to be a necessity if she is to be able to love a man fully. At this deep level, it's necessary for her to be able to adore a man, to look up to him as once she looked up to her father, to be able to lean on him, to be able to trust him, to feel him to be reliable, to feel him to be strong enough so that she can feel precious, delicate, dainty, and so that she can trustfully snuggle down on his lap and let him take care of her and the babies, and the world, and everything else outside the home. This is especially so when she's pregnant, or when she's raising small infants and children. Then she most needs a man around to take care of her, to protect her, and to mediate between her and the world, to go out and hunt the deer and get the food, to chop the wood, and so on. If she cannot see her man (or *any* man) in a B-way, then such looking up to, respect, adoration, perhaps surrender, giving in to him, fearing him a bit, trying to please him, loving him, all of this becomes in principle impossible. She may make a good arrangement with him, but at a very profound level she will be deprived. If she cannot perceive in him the ultimate, eternal, B-masculine qualities, either because he hasn't got enough of them or because she is incapable of perceiving in a B-way (either one can happen), then, in effect, she has no man at all. She may have a boy, a son, a child, a neuter of some sort, a hermaphrodite, but she has no man in the ultimate sense. Therefore, she must be profoundly and deeply unhappy as any woman without a man must be. In the same way, any man without a woman in the B-sense must be profoundly unhappy, stunted, missing something, deprived of a very basic experience, a basic richness in life.

If the woman (like the prostitutes and call girls that the psychoanalysts have been writing about recently) can have toward men only a D-attitude (because of the defects in their own relations with their fathers), then such women have a hopeless future so far as happiness is concerned. In the same way, the D-men who see women only in a D-way can have only a half-life. The D-woman or the woman who can see men only in a D-way can have no relationship to a man except to exploit him, and this will make for the expected consequences of enmity and hatred across the sex lines.

If the woman can see her man *only* as B-man, then she too can't sleep with him, or at least not be able to enjoy him sexually, because this would be like sleeping with her own father or a god, etc. He must be sufficiently down to earth so that she isn't too awed by him. He must be homey, so to speak, part of the actual world and not some ethereal, angelic figure who will never have an erection and who won't have sexual impulses, etc. I may say also that a woman whose strong impulse is to see man, her man, only in the B-way is shocked every time such a man behaves in the normal, natural, human, everyday D-way, i.e., if he goes to the toilet, if he shows himself to have faults, or if he's not perfect. Since she is apt to be horrified, shocked, disillusioned, and disappointed by his D-behavior, this means that she can never live with any man (*any* man would shock her and disillusion her, because no man is *only* a B-man).

The good man, the most desirable we know, is a combination of the B and the D. The same is true for the good woman who is a combination of the B and the D. She must be able to be a madonna, partly; she must be able to be motherly; she must be able to be holy; she must be able to strike awe into the heart of the man, at times; but also, she must come down to earth, and he must be able to see her come down to earth without getting shocked. The truth is she also goes to the toilet, and she also sweats and also has belly aches and gets fat and so on. She is of the earth; and if he has any need to make her of the sky only, then trouble is inevitable.

Now the truth is that any woman, especially to the perceptive eye, to the sensitive man, to the more aesthetic man, to the more intelligent man, to the more healthy man, can be seen in a B-way, with B-cognition, however horrible or dirty or ugly or bitchy or however much a prostitute or a psychopath or a gold digger or a hateful murderess or a witch she may be. The truth is that at some moments she will suddenly flip into her goddesslike aspect, most especially when she's fulfilling those biological functions that men see as basically female: nursing, feeding, giving birth, taking care of children, cleaning the baby, being beautiful, being sexually exciting, etc. It would take a pretty stunted and diminished man not to be able to see this ever. (Can a man who is reduced to the concrete see a woman in a B-way?) The man who is conscious only of the D-characteristics of women is not living the unitive life, is not seeing Heaven on earth, is not seeing the eternal characteristics which exist all around him. To put it bluntly, such a man is being blind to certain aspects of the real world.

This kind of analysis should teach people to see *generally* in a more unitive or B-cognitive fashion. Not only should men see the B-aspects of women, but women themselves should occasionally feel their own B-aspects, i.e., they should feel like priestesses at certain moments, feel symbolic as they give the breast to the baby, or nurse the wounded soldier, or bake bread. Once we become fully conscious of this twofold nature of people, we should more often see a woman setting out dinner on the table for her family as going through some kind of ritual or ceremony like a ritual or ceremonial dance in some religious place (ritual in the very strict sense that she is not only shoving a lamb chop into his mouth or feeding his gut but is reenacting, in a dramatic fashion, in a symbolic fashion, in a poetic fashion, the eternal relation between man and woman). Symbolically this is almost as if she were giving her husband the breast out of which comes milk and food and life and nourishment. It can be seen in this way, and she can take on the noble proportions of a priestess in some ancient religion.

So also, with this sensitizing, should it become possible for us to see the man coming home with his pay check as acting out an ancient ritual of bringing home a food animal that he has killed in a hunt and that he tosses down with a lordly air for his wife and children and dependents, while they look on with admiration because they can't do it and he can. Now it certainly is true that it is harder to see the B-man in this aspect of hunter and provider in a man who is actually a bookkeeper in an office with three thousand other bookkeepers. Yet the fact remains that he can be seen so and should be. So also for the awesome way in which he willingly takes on his shoulders the responsibility for supporting his family; this too can be seen in a B-way, as an ancient and holy act. The right kind of education may actually help women to realize these basic, symbolic, archaic, ritual, ceremonial aspects of their husbands and make the husband also feel a slightly pious or holy thrill as he goes through the ancient ritual of entering his wife sexually, or of taking food from her, or of having her disrobe before him freely, or of being awestruck and pious and worshipful as he comes into the hospital where she has just delivered a baby, or perhaps even with the ceremony of menstruation. To pay a bill with money that he has earned, perhaps in some unexciting way, e.g., selling shoes, is actually in a straight biological line with the cavemen and their caring for their families.

Rather than being a local and temporary nuisance, menstruation can be seen as a biological drama that has to do with the very profound biological rhythm of reproduction and life and death. Each menstruation, after all, represents a baby that could have been. This may be seen strictly as a mystery by the man because it is something he doesn't experience, something he doesn't know about, something which is altogether woman's secret. Menstruation has been called the weeping of a disappointed uterus; this puts it squarely in the B-realm, and makes of it a holy ceremony rather than a messy accident or "curse."

For practically all primitives, these matters that I have spoken about are seen in a more pious, sacred way, as Eliade has stressed, i.e., as rituals, ceremonies, and mysteries. The ceremony of puberty, which we make nothing of, is extremely important for most primitive cultures. When the girl menstruates for the first time and becomes a woman, it is truly a great event and a great ceremony; and it is truly, in the profound and naturalistic and human sense, a great religious moment in the life not only of the girl herself but also of the whole tribe. She steps into the realm of these who can carry on life and those who can produce life; so also for the boy's puberty; so also for the ceremonies of death, of old age, of marriage, of the mysteries of women, the mysteries of men. I think that an examination of primitive or preliterate cultures would show that they often manage the unitive life better than we do, at least as far as relations between the sexes are concerned and also as between adults and children. They combine better than we do the B and the D, as Eliade has pointed out. He defined primitive cultures as different from industrial cultures because they have kept their sense of the sacred about the basic biological things of life.

We must remember, after all, that all these happenings are in truth mysteries. Even though they happen a million times, they are still mysteries. If we lose our sense of the mysterious, or the numinous, if we lose our sense of awe, of humility, of being struck dumb, if we lose our sense of good fortune, then we have lost a very real and basic human capacity and are diminished thereby.

Perceiving in this way can also be a powerful self-therapy. Again the truth of the matter is that any woman, any girl, any man, any boy, any child, is in *fact* a mysterious, wonderful, ceremonial, and ritual B-object. Practically every simple culture make a big fuss over the woman and her childbearing function and everything that has anything to do with it. Now, of course, their ceremonies over the placenta, the umbilical cord, or menstrual blood, and their various cleansing ceremonies may look ridiculous and superstitious to us. Yet the fact remains that they keep the whole area mythological (archaic, poetic, symbolic); by these methods, they keep it all sacred. Even where the woman is severely disadvantaged by, e.g., menstrual huts—where every menstruating woman must hide from all human contacts for a whole week, and must then take ritual baths, etc.—perhaps even this has certain advantages over just taking the whole matter for granted. Such a woman must think that her menstruation and her menstrual blood can be powerful and dangerous. She must, therefore, think of herself as a pretty powerful person who is capable of being dangerous. She matters, she's important. My guess is that this does something for her self-esteem as a woman. (I remember James Thurber's very funny and yet very touching cartoon, uncaptioned, of a lady with four cute children strung out behind her, meeting a dog with four cute puppies strung out behind her. The two mothers are caught turning back to look each other in the eye, sympathetically, with understanding, with fellow feeling, like two sisters.)

The same thing could be true for the man also, if all his mysteries were taken as true mysteries, e.g., the fact that he can produce erections and ejaculate spermatozoa, that these live, that they swim, that in some mysterious way they can penetrate the ovum and make a baby to grow, etc., etc. There are many myths in which the man in sexual intercourse with his wife is seen as a farmer, as a man with a plow, or as a man who is sowing seeds, or as a man who puts something into the earth. His ejaculation is not then just some casual spilling out of something: it becomes as much a ceremony, a mysterious, awe-inspiring, piety-producing ceremony as any high religious ceremony like the Mass, the Sun Dance, etc. Similarly, it might be desirable if we could teach our young men to think of their penises, for instance, as phallic worshipers do, as beautiful and holy objects, as awe inspiring, as mysterious, as big and strong, possibly dangerous and fear inspiring, as miracles which are not understood. If we can teach our young men this, not to mention our young women, then every boy will become the bearer of a holy thing, of a sceptre, of something given to him by nature which no woman can ever have. We supply him thereby with an ultimate and irreducible self-esteem which is his simply by virtue of being a male, a man with a penis and testicles, which should at times awe the woman and the man himself as well. This B-attitude should help him to maintain a sense of the holy or the sacred whenever he has an ejaculation, and should help him to think of his orgasm in the same way that the Tantrists and other religious sects do, i.e., as a unifying experience, a holy experience, a symbol, as a miracle, and as a religious ceremony.

Any woman who is at all sensitive to the philosophical must occasionally be awed by the great storms of sexuality that she can arouse in her man, and also by her power to allay and quiet these storms. This can be seen as goddesslike power, and therefore may be used as one basis for her profound biological self-esteem as a woman. Something similar can be true for male self-esteem, to the extent that he is able to arouse and to calm sexual storms in his wife.

Such perceptions and awarenesses should be able to help any male and any female to experience the transcendent and unitive, both in oneself and in the other. In this way, the eternal becomes visible *in* and *through* the particular, the symbolic and platonic can be experienced *in* and *through* the concrete instance, the sacred can fuse with the profane, and one can transcend the universe of time and space while being of it.

Abraham H. Maslow, *Religions, Values, and Peak-Experiences*

Sex is the sacrament of love. It is the means which nature has contrived for the expression of love, first in the plant and animal world, then in man. It is the outward and visible sign of the mystery of love, which lies at the heart of the universe. But it belongs essentially to this world of signs and appearances; it is the shadow of love, and has therefore always to be transcended. Not only the physical expression of love, but also the psychic division of man into male and female, are stages in the evolution of man, through which we have to pass before we can realize the mystery of love. Every man and woman is both male and female. The division of the sexes is the means which nature has contrived for developing these characteristics in separation, so that they may eventually be reunited. The man has to find his feminine side in the woman, and the woman her masculine side in the man. Then only is human nature fully achieved, where the marriage of the male and the female has taken place in each person. The exterior marriage is for the sake of the interior marriage, in which man and woman recover their original unity. In heaven, we are told, there is neither marrying nor giving in marriage, and in Christ there is neither male nor female. So also the god Siva unites in himself the male and the female; in the final state Siva and Sakti are one.

Bede Griffiths, *Return to the Centre*

The underlying premise of a spiritual partnership is a sacred commitment between the partners to assist each other's spiritual growth. Spiritual partners recognize their equality. Spiritual partners are able to distinguish personality from soul, and, therefore, they are able to discuss the dynamics between them, their interactions, on a less emotionally bound ground than husbands and wives. That ground does not exist within the consciousness of marriage. It exists only within the consciousness of spiritual partnership because spiritual partners are able to see clearly that there is indeed a deeper reason why they are together, and that that reason has a great deal to do with the evolution of their souls.

Because spiritual, or sacred, partners can see from this perspective, they engage in a very different dynamic than do husbands and wives. The conscious evolution of the soul is not part of the structural dynamic of marriage. It does not exist within that evolution because when the evolutionary archetype of marriage was created for our species, the dynamic of conscious spiritual growth was far too mature a concept to be included. What makes a spiritual, or sacred, partnership is that the souls within the partnership understand that they are together in a committed relationship, but the commitment is not to physical security. It is rather to be with each other's physical lives as they reflect spiritual consciousness.

The bond between spiritual partners exists as real as it does in marriage, but for significantly different reasons. Spiritual partners are not together in order to quell each other's financial fears or because they can produce a house in the suburbs and that entire conceptual framework. The understanding or consciousness that spiritual partners bring to their commitment is dynamically different. The commitment of spiritual partners is to each other's spiritual growth, recognizing that that is what each of them is doing on Earth, and that everything serves that.

Spiritual partners bond with an understanding that they are together because it is appropriate for their souls to grow together. They recognize that their growth may take them to the end of their days in this incarnation and beyond, or it may take them to six months. They cannot say that they will be together forever. The duration of their partnership is determined by how long it is appropriate for their evolution to be together. All of the vows that a human being can take cannot prevent the spiritual path from exploding through and breaking those vows if the spirit must move on. It is appropriate for spiritual partners to remain together only as long as they grow together.

Spiritual partnership is a much freer and more spiritually accurate dynamic than marriage because spiritual partners come together from a position of spirit and consciousness. How spiritual partners merge and move their concept of partnership is a matter of free will. So long as they recognize that they bring the consequences of their choices into their partnership, and know the full extent of their choices, that is what influences the manner and direction that the partnership goes.

Spiritual partners commit to a growing dynamic. Their commitment is truly a promise toward their own growth, to their own spiritual survival and enhancement, and not to their physical.

The archetype of spiritual partnership is new to the human experience. Because there is not yet a social convention for spiritual partnership, spiritual partners may decide that the convention of marriage, reinterpreted to meet their needs, is the most appropriate physical expression of their bond. These souls infuse the archetype of marriage with the energy of the archetype of spiritual partnership, as do marriage partners who have discovered in their togetherness that their bond is actually one of commitment to mutual spiritual growth rather than to physical survival or security or comfort.

Just as external power is no longer appropriate to our evolution, the archetype of marriage is no longer appropriate. This does not mean that the institution of marriage will disappear overnight. Marriages will continue to exist, but marriages that succeed will only succeed with the consciousness of spiritual partnership. The partners in these marriages contribute through their participation in them to the archetype of spiritual partnership.

When you bring the consciousness of your soul to your intention-setting process, when you choose to align yourself with your soul instead of with your personality, you create a reality that reflects your soul rather than your personality. When you look upon the experiences of your life as karmic necessities, when you react to your experiences as the products of an impersonal energy dynamic rather than the products of particular interactions, you bring the wisdom of your soul into your reality. When you choose to respond to life's difficulties with compassion and love instead of fear and doubt, you create a "heaven on Earth"—you bring the aspects of a more balanced and harmonious level of reality into physical being.

Gary Zukav, The Seat of the Soul

The Twin-Soul

Every human being has a twin-soul. When man leapt like a spark from the bosom of his Creator he was two in one, and these two parts complemented each other perfectly, each was the other's twin. These two halves became separated, they took different directions, and they have evolved separately. If they come to recognize each other at any point during their evolution, it is because each carries the image of the other in the depth of his being, each has put his seal on the other. Thus, each one carries the image of his twin-soul within. The image may be blurred but it is there. For this reason, everyone who comes on earth has a vague hope that he will meet somewhere a soul who will be everything he needs, and that with this soul he will find indescribable harmony and perfect fusion.

Twin-souls complete each other, no other person in the world can so complete them. Thus, all the beings you have met since the beginning of your multiple incarnations, all the husbands and wives you've had, all the lovers or mistresses, have all left you, because they were not for you. Perhaps you were together for a short while, like a pot with a lid that doesn't match. Whereas two souls whom God has created together are absolutely made one for the other, and nothing can separate them; they have no fear of being separated. In a married couple, when one or the other is afraid that someone may rob him of his partner (and nothing can keep this from happening) it is because that partner was not really the beloved, not the true beloved, the twin-soul. A woman loves a man, he leaves her for another. A man loves a woman, she abandons him . . . but twin-souls, on the contrary, recognize each other with absolute certainty and can never leave one another.

Omraam Mikhaël Aïvanhov, Love and Sexuality

The complete union that is possible to spirit bodies is that for which everyone yearns, and seeks in the joinings of the flesh. This explains the disappointment and letdown that so often follow the physical act of sex. The soul carries the vision but the body does not fulfill it, despite its moment or two of glory.

In contrast, let us listen to Alexandra as she described for Leroy one of their spiritual love meetings, encounters that occurred weekly, or several times a week, over many years:

> *It is always different, new, original, creative, like each new day. I have learned to be completely open and receptive and allow you to set the tone. At the beginning there is the breeze on my face, intensifying around the mouth, often felt inside it, or around my feet underneath the covers—sometimes in the bath! Yes, the breeze under the water! How thrilling it is to see natural laws broken by themselves. But even before the breeze there is a knowing, a certainty of your presence, slow-gathering in my mind. It expands my heart and sends warmth flowing through my veins. It is high, high excitement, yet a peaceful excitement with no tension in it. Always there comes the quiet seizure in the throat. It is your speech to mind, your creative soul speaking a thousand words a second, all of them beautiful with love.*

Then your spirit body acts on me in ways so thrilling, so varied and creative, that I hold my breath! Breath stops, the way it does in meditation, or so it seems. I sink into the feelings and observe them all at once. It rouses in me an attentiveness *so acute that I think Nature must feel like this in bringing round the sun!*

Sometimes you lift my spirit right out of me; I feel you lifting it, so tenderly, like a mother gently raising a child up from its cradle. As this happens I become keenly aware of your spirit body, its racing vibrations, its brilliant colors. Then all of these stream into me, passing through and through me in waves of rapture. And I respond with the passion of my liberated spirit. We engage each other, ah, how we engage!...like foamings of the sea or the sparkling, tumbling waters of a fountain. I will never get used to the passage of time as this happens, two hours or more as a rule, never less than two. When I finally glance at the clock I can't believe what it is telling me, for I have been in timelessness, in eternity. The hours have passed like minutes. And I am hungry! I get up and make some tea and sit a long time sipping it, watching the snow or the rain or the moon through the french windows, remembering...unable to sleep and not wanting to.

As we go on, you refine the methods. Last night you introduced a variation on one which you have used before and which I love...but this time with a stroke of genius. Immediately on coming to me, gradually but swiftly you moved into me, filling me up completely with your being. I felt your life within me, very still, as though waiting. Then came the faintest stirring in the solar plexus, and after that a touch, a whispering touch, traveling slowly, infinitely slowly down the center of my legs, lightly, like the delicate etchings of frost on windowpanes. These fragile sensations entered each of my toes in turn, going to the very tip of each, then appeared in my arms, down through hands and fingers, the thrillingness gathering through the very delicacy of it. This went on all through my body, and when it reached my head I even had the feeling it was being drawn along each separate hair! And when every inch had been covered with this infinitely gentle, loving touch, then...then your power surged! You became a flowing, pulsing radiance within me, all of your magnetism compressed into my exact shape and size. You became my very life; I was like someone who had been only a shell, an empty skin, and had now leapt to livingness.

That livingness we shared was pure ecstasy, an almost unbearable ecstasy. I spoke your name and cried out my love, my body twisting and moving. I felt it graceful like a joyous creature of the wild. I was part of the cosmic movement, all the actions of love concentrated in me. I

*became truly aware, for the first time, of the absolute oneness of our
souls. No longer were we two lovers acting upon one another, two beings
consorting together, but one bliss weaving back and forth within itself.*

*This is the true experience of heaven. You have brought me to it.
How can I speak my adoration? It's the adoration of God, God in thee,
and of the sure promise that it will be like this for everyone. In my joy
I feel some of the joy of everyone, the joy locked up within them as it
used to be in me, but present, even now all present!—simply waiting,
as I waited for you and you for me.*

*Let me describe it more from this earthly perspective. It is impossi-
ble to convey, and yet it must be attempted, I feel. This is not just an
ecstasy of mind! This is thoroughly physical, a sensation as of pure
golden sunlight spreading open all the fibers of the body and filling
them up with pleasure—something beyond pleasure, the very source
of pleasure. It emits rays of itself into the cosmos and receives them
back in a swoon of gratitude. It is subtly, excruciatingly orgiastic, as if
the entire physical structure trembles on the very edge of that
precipice. This is because it is being experienced in the body as well as
engaging all the other finer vehicles. It is total. It wants nothing but
to remain, to be, to continue; it is sufficient to itself. It is perfect peace
and being-ness.*

Patricia Joudry and Maurie D. Pressman,
from "Sex as Transcendence," in *Twin Souls*

⇥ Grace and Creativity ⇤

Grace nourishes the spiritual life from
within. It has been associated with the symbol of a fountain—"a fountain of
grace"—which spontaneously replenishes itself through prayer, through the
practice of surrender and of humility. As Aldous Huxley exclaims, it is "Not
I, but God in me." It is a gift of the spirit, the holy spirit, Shakti, God's power.
Sri Aurobindo calls grace "a fact of spiritual experience"; Hans Küng says it
is as "important for life as the air we breathe." Charlene Spretnak describes
it as "God's saving love" and explains that the "Amazing Grace," which is so
frequently sung about, touches "the ultimate truth." A powerful presence,
grace reveals itself to the world through our actions, our deeds, and our creative works. Creativity is the divine afflatus, the muse, the fire, the beauty of

expression. Joseph Campbell believes that "art really is worship," a product or form we create to give to each other, to share together in celebration of the talents we have been given. I have chosen some more familiar artistic forms here, like painting, writing, dancing, and lifestyles, to show that all individual creativity expressed is a gift to oneself and others. Gandhi once said that life is your own creation, and Bede Griffiths' account of his experiment with a particular way of life—a rustic, spiritual simplicity in the countryside of England—proves Gandhi's point by showing how living life itself can be an art which nourishes the heart and soul.

Sri Aurobindo's answers to his disciples' questions in "Art and Spirituality" brilliantly sum up the spiritual force of creativity. We are all made to be messengers of expression, to carve out an icon of our existence in this world. Thomas Merton calls the creative force or conaturality "the living law that rules the universe."

><

Strength has a value for spiritual realisation, but to say that it can be done by strength only and by no other means is a violent exaggeration. Grace is not an invention, it is a fact of spiritual experience. Many who would be considered as mere nothings by the wise and strong have attained by Grace; illiterate, without mental power or training, without "strength" of character or will, they have yet aspired and suddenly or rapidly grown into spiritual realisation, because they had faith or because they were sincere. I do not see why these facts which are facts of spiritual history and of quite ordinary spiritual experience should be discussed and denied and argued as if they were mere matters of speculation.

Strength, if it is spiritual, is a power for spiritual realisation; a greater power is sincerity; the greatest power of all is Grace.

Sri Aurobindo, *Words of Sri Aurobindo,* First Series

It is beautiful to see God's grace working in people. The most beautiful thing about it is to see how the desires of the soul, inspired by God, so fit in and harmonize with grace that holy things seem natural to the soul, seem to be part of its very self. That is what God wants to create in us—that marvelous spontaneity in which his life becomes perfectly ours and our life his, and it seems inborn in us to act as his children, and to have his light shining out of our eyes.

Thomas Merton, *The Sign of Jonas*

Perceptible and yet not perceptible, invisible and yet powerful, real like the energy-charged air, the wind, the storm, as important for life as the air we breathe: this is how people in ancient times frequently imagined the "Spirit" and God's invisible working. According to the beginning of the creation account, "spirit" (Hebrew *ruah*, Greek *pneuma*) is the "roaring," the "tempest" of God over the waters. "Spirit" as understood in the Bible means—as opposed to "flesh," to created, perishable reality—the *force or power proceeding from God*: that invisible force of God and power of God that is effective, creatively or destructively, for life or judgment, in creation and history, in Israel and later in the Church. It comes upon man powerfully or gently, stirring up individuals or groups to ecstasy, often producing extraordinary phenomena, active in great men and women, in Moses and the "judges" of Israel, in warriors and singers, kings, prophets and prophetesses.

This Spirit is not—as the word itself might suggest—the spirit of man. He is the Spirit of God, who as the *Holy* Spirit is distinguished from the unholy spirit of man and his world. In the light of the New Testament, he is not—as often in the history of religion—he is not any sort of magic, substance-like, mysterious, supernatural aura of a dynamistic character or a magical being of an animistic kind. The Spirit is *no other than God himself*. He is God himself close to man and the world, as the comprehending but not comprehensible, the bestowing but not controllable, the life-creating but also judging, power and force.

This is important. The Holy Spirit is not a third party, not a thing between God and men, but God's personal closeness to men.

Hans Küng, *Does God Exist?*

The Cord of Grace

Rabbi Yitzhak Eisik of Zhydatchov, Rabbi Hirsh's nephew, was an only son. Once when he was little more than a boy, his father asked him: "How do you interpret the words of our sages: 'Whoever occupies himself with the Torah by night, around him God strings a cord of grace by day.' Do we not always rise at midnight to occupy ourselves with the Torah, and are we not in need and trouble by day notwithstanding? So where does the cord of grace come in?"

The boy answered: "Father, the fact that we rise midnight after midnight, and occupy ourselves with the Torah, without heeding our troubles— that in itself is the cord of grace."

Martin Buber, *Tales of the Hasidim*

It is not hard to stand behind one's successes. But to accept responsibility for one's failures, to accept them unreservedly as failures that are truly one's own, that cannot be shifted somewhere else or onto something else, and actively to accept—without regard for any worldly interests, no matter how well disguised, or for well-meant advice—the price that has to be paid for it: that is devilishly hard! But only thence does the road lead—as my experience, I hope, has persuaded me—to a renewal of sovereignty over my own affairs, to a radically new insight into the mysterious gravity of my existence as an uncertain enterprise, and to its transcendental meaning. And only this kind of inner understanding can ultimately lead to what might be called true "peace of mind," to that highest delight, to genuine meaningfulness, to that endless "joy of Being." If one manages to achieve that, then all one's worldly privations cease to be privations, and become what Christians call grace.

Vaclav Havel, Letters to Olga

Good actions and thoughts produce consequences which tend to neutralize, or put a stop to, the results of evil thoughts and actions. For as we give up the life of self (and note that, like forgiveness, repentance and humility are also special cases of giving), as we abandon what the German mystics called "the I, me, mine," we make ourselves progressively capable of receiving grace. By grace we are enabled to know reality more completely, and this knowledge of reality helps us to give up more of the life of selfhood—and so on, in a mounting spiral of illumination and regeneration.

Aldous Huxley, Huxley and God

We are dependent on grace; but we do not do God's will when we take it upon ourselves to begin with grace instead of beginning with ourselves. Only our beginning, our having begun, poor as it is, leads us to grace. God made no tools for Himself, He needs none; He created for Himself a partner in the dialogue of time and one who is capable of holding converse.

Martin Buber, To Hallow This Life

Human grace comes to us either from persons, or from social groups, or from our own wishes, hopes and imaginings projected outside ourselves and persisting somehow in the psychic medium in a state of what may be called second-hand objectivity. We have all had experience of the different types of human grace. There is, for example, the grace which, during childhood, comes from mother, father, nurse or beloved teacher. At a later stage we experience the grace of friends; the grace of men and women morally better and wiser than ourselves; the grace of the *guru*, or spiritual director. Then there is the grace which comes to us because of our attachment to country, party, church or other social organization—a grace which has helped even the feeblest and most timid individuals to achieve what, without it, would have been the impossible. And finally there is the grace which we derive from our ideals, whether low or high, whether conceived of in abstract terms or bodied forth in imaginary personifications. To this last type, it would seem, belong many of the graces experienced by the pious adherents of the various religions. The help received by those who devotedly adore or pray to some personal saint, deity or Avatar is often, we may guess, not a genuinely spiritual grace, but a human grace, coming back to the worshipper from the vortex of psychic power set up by repeated acts (his own and other people's) of faith, yearning and imagination.

Spiritual grace cannot be received continuously or in its fullness, except by those who have willed away their self-will to the point of being able truthfully to say, "Not I, but God in me." There are, however, few people so irremediably self-condemned to imprisonment within their own personality as to be wholly incapable of receiving the graces which are from instant to instant being offered to every soul. By fits and starts most of us contrive to forget, if only partially, our preoccupation with "I," "me," "mine," and so become capable of receiving, if only partially, the graces which, in that moment, are being offered us.

Spiritual grace originates from the divine Ground of all being, and it is given for the purpose of helping man to achieve his final end, which is to return out of time and self-hood to that Ground. It resembles animal grace in being derived from a source wholly other than our self-conscious, human selves; indeed, it is the same thing as animal grace, but manifesting itself on a higher level of the ascending spiral that leads from matter to the Godhead. In any given instance, human grace may be wholly good, inasmuch as it helps the recipient in the task of achieving the unitive knowledge of God; but because of its source in the individualized self, it is always a little suspect and, in many cases, of course, the help it gives is help towards the achievement of ends very different from the true end of our existence.

Aldous Huxley, *The Perennial Philosophy*

The Experience of Grace

When we experience consciousness of the unity in which we are embedded, the sacred whole that is in and around us, we exist in a state of grace. At such moments our consciousness perceives not only our individual self, but also our larger self, the self of the cosmos. The gestalt of unitive existence becomes palpable.

The term *grace* comes from the Christian tradition, but the unitive experiences it names are common to spiritual practice in all the wisdom traditions. Catholic and Protestant theologies disagree over whether the Christian notion of grace, the infusion of "God's saving love," is gained through sincere participation in the sacraments (baptism, eucharist, confirmation, penance, matrimony, ordination, and last rites) or directly through active faith. St. Augustine comprehended grace almost entirely in terms of sin and redemption, a private matter in which no external elements are relevant. Unfortunately, his view has shaped much of Western thinking on grace. In contrast, the formative theologians of Eastern Orthodox Christianity perceived divine grace diffused throughout nature. More recently, the Protestant theologian Paul Tillich defined grace as "the impact of the Spiritual Presence," an unexacted gift that is present within this life. The Jesuit theologian Karl Rahner rejected the Roman Catholic church's teaching, following the Council of Trent, that grace is a supernatural structure above humanity's conscious, spiritual, and moral life, a view he called extrinsicalness at its worst. Instead, he perceived nature as enveloped in grace and grace bearing upon our inmost reality.

Grace is considered by nearly all theologians to be a gift that is given to humans by the divine, in whose image we are made. If our image is a clue to the nature of the divine, however, why should we settle on an interpretation that stops at surface perceptions: why should our "image" denote only physical human form and behavior rather than our composition of vibratory flux, subatomic dynamism and creativity, and inherent relatedness? What if the divine is comprehended not as a godhead outside the universe, but as the diffused "mind," or process of subjectivity, that informs the alternatives chosen trillions of times per second at the subatomic level, that makes possible the self-organizing behavior throughout the cosmos, and that informed the evolution of our own form such that we are able to perceive and reflect on all those workings of divine creativity, cosmic subjectivity, or God? Then we see clearly that we are indeed created in the "image" of the participatory universe. We are of it—not by projecting our type of mental processes onto the universe, but by realizing that the human mind participates in the processes of the larger "mind." We are not apart from the dynamic cosmos.

Experiencing grace involves the expansion of consciousness of self to all of one's surroundings as an unbroken whole, a consciousness of awe from which negative mindstates are absent, from which healing and groundedness result. For these reasons grace has long been deemed "amazing." Sometimes the consciousness of grace comes on quite suddenly and so intensely that the moment is never forgotten. More frequently, we experience slight versions of it, as in the act of group singing when the alignment of vibrations evokes in us awareness of the vibratory ocean of flux and form in and around us. Touching the ultimate truth in that way, and many others, brings us joy, release, connection, and peace.

Since ritual has the potential to bring forth the experience of grace in the consciousness of participants, it is easy to understand why Catholicism urged, even to the point of requiring, participation in sacramental rituals. On the other hand, Luther's insistence that grace can be experienced without benefit of institutional rituals is also correct, especially if we understand grace in a cosmological sense, extending beyond denominational faith. Many people vividly recall from childhood unexpected moments of perceiving the grand unity. Some experience the grace of interbeing on extended trips into the deep silence of wilderness. Some know a version of it in the postorgasmic state. Some have reported that such "altered" consciousness occurs suddenly in mundane circumstances. It seems to persist even through our deeply ingrained habits of seeing only separateness and fragmentation.

Persons adept at spiritual practice—meditation, contemplative prayer, or ritual, for instance—experience graced consciousness for extended periods. Perhaps traditional native peoples who regard every act throughout the day as ceremonial practice, or right living, know a certain sense of graced consciousness at all times. That such a possibility is within human reach, even if fitfully, has been the message of the mystics and many poets and artists. It was for Henri Matisse apparently an informing desire. Late in his life, when he agreed to design the stained-glass windows for a chapel, he was angrily confronted by Picasso. He reminded Matisse that they had spent their entire professional lives championing the new, the modern, the progressive, the liberated. How, he demanded, could Matisse now further such a backward cause as the church? Matisse replied calmly that they had both been trying their whole lives to regain through art the inner "atmosphere" of their First Communion, a state of grace.

Experiencing grace is only one aspect of spiritual practice, but it is particularly important for a culture that has validated only perceptions of separateness and fragmentation.

Charlene Spretnak, *States of Grace*

The goal of life is rapture.
Art is the way we experience it.

Joseph Campbell, *Reflections on the Art of Living*

When Matisse was asked whether he believed in God, his response was, "Yes, when I'm working."

Marion Woodman, *Conscious Femininity*

There Will Be a Talking...

there will be a talking of lovely things,
there will be cognizance of the seasons,
there will be men who know the flights of birds,
in new days there will be love for women:
we will walk the balance of artistry.
and things will have a middle and an end,
and be loved because being beautiful.
who in a walk will find a lasting vase
depicting dance and hold it in his hands
and sell it then? no man on the new earth
will barter with malice nor make of stone
a hollowed riddle: for art will be art,
the freak, the rare no longer commonplace:
there will be a going back to the laws.

Michael Hartnett, *Selected Poems*

It is right in principle that those should be the best loved who have contributed most to the elevation of the human race and human life. But, if one goes on to ask who they are, one finds oneself in no inconsiderable difficulties. In the case of political, and even of religious, leaders, it is often very doubtful whether they have done more good or harm. Hence I most seriously believe that one does people the best service by giving them some elevating work to do and thus indirectly elevating them. This applies most of all to the great artist, but also in a lesser degree to the scientist. To be sure, it is not the fruits of scientific research that elevate a man and enrich his nature, but the urge to understand, the intellectual work, creative or receptive. It would surely be absurd to judge the value of the Talmud, for instance, by its intellectual fruits.

Albert Einstein, *The World As I See It*

Beauty is a transcendental, a perfection in things which transcends things and attests their kinship with the infinite, because it makes them fit to give joy to the spirit. It is a reflection in things of the Spirit from which they proceed, and it is a divine name: God is subsistent Beauty, and "the being of all things derives from the divine beauty." Knowing this, we realize that it is impossible that the artist, devoted as he is to created beauty which is a mirror of God, should not tend at the same time—but by a more profound and more secret urge than all that he can know of himself—toward the principle of beauty.

Jacques Maritain, "The Ways of the Practical Intellect,"
in *Approaches to God*

The solidarity of poets is an elemental fact like sunlight, like the seasons, like the rain. It is something that cannot be organized, it can only happen. It can only be "received." It is a gift to which we must remain open.

Thomas Merton, *"Raids on the Unspeakable"*

> The Gods have meant
> That I should dance
> And in some mystic hour
> I shall move to unheard rhythms
> Of the cosmic orchestra of heaven,
> And you will know the language
> Of my wordless poems
> And will come to me,
> For that is why I dance.

Ruth St. Denis, in Martha Graham, *Blood Memory*

When you are alone and in your own place, you are dancing for the god and identifying with it. This whole idea is basic to Tantra: to worship a god, you must become that god. No matter what you call the god or think it is, the god you worship is the one you are capable of becoming.

The power of a deity is that it personifies a power that is in Nature and in your nature. When you find that level, then you are in play. That is the work of art in general, because art really is a worship.

Joseph Campbell, *Reflections on the Art of Living*

Community is a necessary part of the Sun Dance. The dancers need the presence of the community to sustain them in their sacrifice and their brave prayer. The community offers spiritual support and often dances with the

Sun Dancers. After all, the community is the purpose of the gift the sun dancers give—they dance so that the people might live. Solidarity is experienced and formed when the community worships richly and deeply together. It includes mutual laughter and feasting as well as fasting and sweating. "Being-with" is integral to community support and sustenance. To be with one another in deep, sacrificial prayers of thanksgiving is a highpoint in the community's year. The Indian Sun Dance is folk mysticism. It is for the people and by them. It does not conceal their pain—rather, it dives into the pain. The Sun Dance is an ultimate group expression of what Rank calls the "irrational" dimension of life that is so essential to a living mysticism. The left brain will never grasp or possess the work of the Spirit occurring therein. The Sun Dance awakens the collective right brain, the mystical energy of the community.

Matthew Fox, The Coming of the Cosmic Christ

One example of artists of lifestyles in Western culture have been the founders of religious orders. Benedict, Francis, and Dominic—to name three such artists—responded creatively to a yearning for lifestyles of substance in a time of spiritual vacuity. A lifestyle is an art form. It brings life and wonder, joy and hope to persons otherwise condemned to superficial living. Our times call for the creation of lifestyles of spiritual substance.

Matthew Fox, The Coming of the Cosmic Christ

An Experiment in Common Life

It was in April 1930 that we set out upon our adventure. It was a time of crisis when to others beside ourselves our civilisation seemed to be in danger of collapse. The movement of parties to the extreme Left and the extreme Right was beginning, and many of our contemporaries at Oxford were turning to Communism. But for us politics offered no solution to the problem. The political parties, whether of the Left or the Right, were concerned only with the organisation of civilised life; but we were concerned with the very nature of our civilisation. Communism, as we saw it evolving in Russia, was working more and more for the mechanisation of life and therefore for that inhumanity which we believed must necessarily follow, though we were not then aware of the extent of the inhumanity to which it would lead. Our purpose was to escape from industrialism altogether, from the whole system of mechanisation which we felt to be the cause of the trouble. There was no doubt an element of escapism in our attitude, and there was certainly a radical inconsistency. For we were going to live on money which was derived from the system which we repudiated and we were dependent on it in a hundred ways which we could not escape. But though we were not unaware of the inconsistency of our position, we were determined to do what was in our power at least to escape from the evil influence. Whatever may be said for it in theory, in practice it was an experience which taught us a lesson in life which nothing else could have done. It not only forced us to face the fundamental problems of human life, of food and clothing and shelter, in their most elementary nature, but it also brought us into contact with a mode of life very close to that in which man has been compelled to live for the greater part of his history, and made a corresponding change in our own outlook. We passed at a single bound from the complexities of twentieth-century civilisation to a life which was primeval in its simplicity.

We began by buying a cottage in the small village of Eastington, about two miles from Northleach. It was a four-roomed cottage built of solid Cotswold stone with Cotswold tiling but without water, drainage or lighting of any sort. It was attached to another cottage of the same style, and we bought them both for £500. The second cottage was occupied by a young man, Jim Holtom, and his wife, who proved themselves among our best friends. Jim was driving a coal lorry at the time, but he had farming in his blood and spent all his spare time working on a small holding. His father was the shepherd of the farm on the hill above us and his brother was working on another farm. Jim soon agreed to work in with us and we bought some land and a couple of cows, and soon we were able to supply the whole village with milk. There were not more than twenty people altogether in the village, and all lived in small cottages like our own with Cotswold tiles, except for one, which had had the tiles stripped and sold to make money, and replaced by a hideous asbestos roof. We thus had always before our eyes an example of greed and industrialism bringing disharmony and ugliness into the ordered beauty of life.

The village had nothing particularly picturesque about it. It was a plain little village at the bottom of a valley with a small stream running through it, but it had the simple beauty of everything which is in harmony with nature. It will give some idea of the cost of living in these conditions if I say that the rent of most of these cottages was not more than three or four shillings a week, and yet each of them had a small garden and often a solid stone pig-sty as well. Jim Holtom's father, the shepherd, had brought up his family of five on a wage of twelve and six a week, and they had never lacked for any of the necessities of life. There were others living on the old-age pension who, with the vegetables from their garden, a sow and perhaps some bees, could live in considerable comfort. They always welcomed us with a glass of home-made wine and would never take money for the vegetables which they gave us.

Our next-door neighbours were three brothers, one of whom was a devout Methodist, whose favourite books were the Bible, *Pilgrim's Progress* and Foxe's *Book of Martyrs*; but he was an epileptic, and it was a shock one day to find him, when I went to draw the water at the village tap, lying on his cabbage patch in a fit. Another brother was said to be an atheist. They lived in separate houses and it was said that they had never spoken to one another in twenty years. The inhabitants of the cottage with the asbestos roof were unmarried and had a bad reputation, which sometimes caused a disturbance in the village. But generally the life was very peaceful and we made friends of all.

There was no water laid on in the village and we all went to the village tap to draw water. Twenty years before, it was said, there had been no tap even and the villagers had gone to fetch their water from the spring. It was my job to fill the water-pots every morning, and often in the winter one would go out in the early morning before it was yet light and find the tap frozen; but we soon learned to light a straw fire underneath it on these occasions so as to thaw it. We had our own garden which Hugh used to work, and very soon we were able to grow most of our own vegetables. The only form of sanitation was an earth closet outside, and one of my first jobs was to clean this out and spread the contents on the garden for manure. We were thus faced from the start with the most primitive conditions of life, but it was exactly what we wanted. We were up by six o'clock every morning, and each of us learned to milk, so that our lives fell into the regular rhythm of the country. We had not to get up to see the dawn; it was there waiting for us when we went out to draw the water or to milk the cows, and morning and evening in winter we could watch the constellations moving round the sky.

Inside, the cottage was as bare and simple as we could make it. There were four rooms, a kitchen which we used also as a living-room, and another room, which we used as a study, downstairs; and two bedrooms upstairs, one of which we made into a dormitory and the other we kept as a spare room for our friends. The walls we had whitewashed and for ceiling there were the oak rafters stained with creosote. We picked up a kitchen table and some old wheel-back chairs second-hand, and apart from them we had no furniture. On the floor we had coconut-matting. Our beds were made of wood by the local carpenter and we had mattresses stuffed with straw from a neighbouring farm. We had no curtains or coverlets or cushions or anything to relieve the bare simplicity. All this was a matter of long discussion and often of argument between us, as we were not all alike in our tastes and it took time to work out the principles on which we wished to live. Our aim was to do without all products of the industrial revolution as far as it was humanly possible. At first we compromised in many things, but gradually we found that it was possible to go further than we had ever imagined. For instance, we had bought to begin with an oil lamp, but we later found a blacksmith who was willing to make us an iron candelabrum, and to our delight we discovered that it was possible to get tallow dips for candles, which had once been a local industry. We found, moreover, that the four candles gave a perfect light for reading; and we learned from this one of the great lessons of our life. Our purpose in using the tallow dips had been simply to do without the products of industrialism, but we found that the light of these candles, reflected on the bare white walls and against the dark oak rafters, created an atmosphere of indescribable beauty. Thus we were able to prove in our own lives that when the simple, natural means are used for any natural end, however humble, they will inevitably produce an effect of beauty.

Another problem which presented itself was that of crockery. There was an ironmonger's van which used to call each week in the village with oil which we bought at first for our oil lamp, and also with a stock of cheap modern ware. We thought at first that we should have to buy some of this, but when we asked the man he told us that there was a pottery at Winchcombe where we could get hand-made pots. The next day, therefore, I rode over to Winchcombe and was met at the pottery by an old man who, I discovered, was called Elijah Comfort. He told me that "the master" was inside and I went in, expecting to see another old man like himself. But I was met by a young man not much older than myself, who had been a contemporary at Oxford and had given up academic life in order to devote his life to the revival of the old English type of pottery known as slip-ware. This was Michael Cardew, whose work was already becoming well known and was afterwards exhibited at the Victoria and Albert Museum as some of the finest work of modern craftsmanship. But his desire was not to produce pots for exhibition but for the ordinary use of the house.

He soon became one of our closest friends and was ready to provide us with anything which we wanted and to make special pots for us if it was necessary. In this way we obtained all the crockery we needed, made out of the local clay and fashioned with the kind of instinctive beauty of the homely old English ware. Among other things he made us two superb pitchers for fetching the water from the village tap, which were large enough to last, when filled, for the whole day. Michael was a great admirer of Chinese pottery and culture, to such an extent that he had learned the language in order to be able to study the *Analects* of Confucius in Chinese. We found in him, therefore, a link with the whole of that traditional culture which had existed all over the world before the Industrial Revolution came to destroy it. He was also a musician and had learned to play the recorder, and sometimes when he was staying with us he would entertain us with airs from Purcell or Palestrina.

We allowed ourselves no modern books or newspapers or gramophone or wireless in the cottage, but for recreation we learned some old English rounds which we used to sing sitting together round the table. I remember one in particular by William Byrd made on the words of the psalm, *"Non nobis Domine non nobis, sed nomini tuo da gloriam."* We sang it for the beauty of the melody and the counterpoint, but the words nevertheless made a deep impression on me and like so much else in our life were prophetic of events which were to come. Our reading was all in the literature of the sixteenth and seventeenth centuries or earlier, and even the books, as time went on, were mostly early editions and folios. In this way we soaked ourselves in the traditions of the past and the modern world became more and more remote. I used sometimes to go and stand by the main road not two miles away and watch the cars going by, and it seemed as far removed from our life as ancient Rome or Babylon.

We used to travel at first on a bicycle but after a short time we decided to give this up and buy a horse. We all learned to ride simply by jumping on the horse's back and riding bare-back round a field, and soon we were able to ride for quite long distances. When we went home, as we did from time to time, we would never go by train, as the train stood for us above all things as the symbol of that which had destroyed the peace and order of the countryside. At first I would go by bicycle, but when we had given up the bicycle I decided to walk. It was, I think, about seventy or eighty miles and I could just manage it by staying at two places on the way. Every departure from the village thus became an adventure, which was often tiring but which gave one a deep sense of belonging to the country.

Our food was always very simple and we soon settled into a regular routine. For breakfast we had porridge which we cooked in an iron cauldron over-night and put in a hay-box until the morning. For dinner we had a vegetable stew which we prepared after breakfast and again put in the hay-box until dinner-time. With this we had cheese from a great round of "Double-Gloster" Cheese, which had once been the ordinary cheese of the locality. For supper we had eggs from four Khaki-Campbell ducks which we left to forage round the village all day and which laid four eggs without fail every morning. Our bread was baked for us by a baker at Bibury. We had wholemeal stone-ground floor from the old mill at Winchcombe, which was said to have been working since the Norman Conquest, and it was baked in an old brick oven heated by faggots.

In many ways like this, we found that the customs of former ages still survived in one or two places, though it is probable that they have now died out. I was told that twenty years before the old flour mills had been working in all the villages down the little river valleys, whereas now all the corn was sent to Cirencester to be ground by machinery. We were thus witnessing the death of a great cultural inheritance. For all around us in the Cotswold villages and towns we could see the remains of a local culture of authentic beauty. It had grown out of the country and developed century by century until it had formed a closely woven pattern of economic life, in which all the native skill of craftsmanship was able to reveal itself. It was a culture based on local custom and tradition, centred in small towns and villages, which were largely independent of the outside world, and which therefore had its own unique, distinctive character. The new world of the industrial towns was steadily destroying it, but at least we were able to learn some of the secrets of that way of life, which had sustained its existence for so many centuries.

We tried to live as far as possible without the use of anything which could not be obtained in the locality. Thus we had no tea or coffee or sugar or tobacco, but drank milk from the cows and used honey with which one of our neighbours supplied us for sweetening. We even tried to get our bread made from Cotswold wheat and our porridge from Cotswold oats. Of course, we were not pretending that it was possible to go back altogether to those earlier conditions of life, but we wanted to test for ourselves what life under such conditions was like. At least it taught us one lesson of permanent value. We found that the cost of living was lower than we could ever have imagined. We reckoned after some experiment that the three of us could live on an income of £100 a year altogether, allowing not only for food and clothing and all household expenses but also for books. On the other hand, if we went home for two or three days we would spend more in a day than would have kept us in the necessities of life for a week or a fortnight.

From this we learned that modern civilisation is not concerned primarily with providing the necessities of life any more than with producing those things which make for its beauty and dignity, but above all in extending the quantity of material conveniences. This served us as a criterion to distinguish between civilisation and culture. For while a civilisation is concerned with the continual extension of material luxury, often at the cost of the health and happiness of those who work for it, a culture like that of the Cotswolds, in which we were living, is based first of all on the necessities of human life, on the need for food and clothing and shelter. On this basis it builds up a network of human industry, in which the skill of men's hands is employed in co-operation with nature. The ploughing of the earth and the sowing and reaping of the corn; the tending of cattle and sheep for meat and leather and wool; the brewing of malt and baking of bread; the spinning and weaving for clothes; the quarrying of stone for building and the felling of timber for the carpenter's shop—all these were part of an age-long ritual in which it was understood that man's well-being was to be found. It was on this basis that the great cultures of antiquity had grown, of China and India no less than of Greece and Rome. Upon this basis the arts of architecture, sculpture, painting, poetry, music and dancing could develop, all in vital relationship with the common life of the town and village. A culture was an organic growth in which man and nature worked together in a profound harmony which satisfied the deepest instincts of the human heart....

In the meantime we had already begun to practise our own religion. It was Hugh who first suggested that we should begin to pray as well as to read the Bible, but the step was almost inevitable. I had not prayed since I had been at school, but the change which had now taken place in my mind made it seem natural to do so, and the Book of Common Prayer offered a perfect method of prayer. The Psalms and the Canticles of the Gospel in Coverdale's version came to me as poetry in a way that made the transition to prayer almost imperceptible. I had gone to the poetry of Wordsworth, Shelley and Keats in my early days at school in order to find my experience of the mystery and beauty of nature renewed and enlarged; for poetry is the means by which the feelings and the imagination are educated and their powers developed. Then my vision of human life and especially of its underlying tragedy had been extended by Shakespeare and Sophocles and by the great novelists. Now my horizon was being enlarged and the mystery of God's dealings with humanity and with the individual soul became apparent to me through my reading of the Bible. But it was the same path of imaginative experience which I had been following all the time; and now I found that the words of the Psalms came to me like pure poetry awaking the sense of God's power over nature and His providence over the human soul, and I prayed the Psalms almost without realising it.

Nevertheless a definite break was made in our lives when we began to pray on our knees. We used to kneel on the bare stone floor, not in the kitchen but out in the cold at the back of the house, and the words seemed to pierce the soul. Our life had already become extremely ascetic in many ways, not so much from any deliberate choice, but simply as the result of the way of life which we had adopted. Now we began to think of practising some deliberate austerity. Again, it was Hugh who suggested that we should fast on Fridays. This we did by taking nothing but some dry bread and cold milk throughout the day. There is no doubt that this was very unwise. We were none of us really prepared for such a penance and it imposed a great strain upon us. I myself began to read also the Imitation of Christ, which we had in a beautiful edition of the Early English Text Society. It was typical of our attitude that we read it first as an example of medieval prose; but its message made itself felt none the less, and I began to feel a desire for some kind of mortification; but it was very feeble and I could not stand up to any real privation.

By this time, however, our life had begun to develop along lines which none of us had envisaged, and a division began to take place among us. Hugh, though naturally religious, was of a very sociable character, and the austerity of the life told on him more than on any of us. He was the first to break away and to declare after his return from home at Christmas that he intended to get married. He later returned to Oxford to take his degree and then took a job as a schoolmaster. But he afterwards joined his wife's father on his farm and has remained a farmer ever since, bringing up his family on his own farm.

While we were together at Eastington two little children came to stay with us, a girl and a boy. The girl afterwards became Martyn's wife, and he also went to live on a farm taking Jim Holtom and his family with him. Thus in different ways our adventure at Eastington was the decisive event in all our lives. It only lasted for less than a year, but it taught us the lessons of a life-time. Our attitude to life had been radically changed, and we each of us drew from it the experience which was to shape our lives for the future, however far apart they might be.

Bede Griffiths, The Golden String

Intellectual and Spiritual Value of Art

Since the aim of Art is to reveal beauty and yield delight, it is maintained that it can be of no use in the training and development of our intellectual faculty which is concerned with the seeking of rational truth. Is this true?

Our intellectual activity has a double character divided between the imaginative, creative and sympathetic or comprehensive intellectual centres on the one side and the critical, analytic and penetrative on the other. The latter are best trained by science, criticism and observation, the former by art, poetry, music, literature and the sympathetic study of man and his creations. These make the mind quick to grasp at a glance, subtle to distinguish shades, deep to reject shallow self-sufficiency, mobile, delicate, swift, intuitive. Art assists in this training by raising images in the mind which it has to understand not by analysis, but by self-identification with other minds; it is a powerful stimulator of sympathetic insight. Art is subtle and delicate, and it makes the mind also in its movements subtle and delicate. It is suggestive, and the intellect habituated to the appreciation of art is quick to catch suggestions, mastering not only, as the scientific mind does, that which is positive and on the surface, but that which leads to ever fresh widening and subtilising of knowledge and opens a door into the deeper secrets of inner nature where the positive instruments of science cannot take the depth or measure. This supreme intellectual value of Art has never been sufficiently recognised. Men have made language, poetry, history, philosophy agents for the training of this side of intellectuality, necessary parts of a liberal education, but the immense educative force of music, painting and sculpture has not been duly recognised. They have been thought to be by-paths of the human mind, beautiful and interesting, but not necessary, therefore intended for the few. Yet the universal impulse to enjoy the beauty and attractiveness of sound, to look at and live among pictures, colours, forms ought to have warned mankind of the superficiality and ignorance of such a view of these eternal and important occupations of the human mind. The impulse, denied proper training and self-purification, has spent itself on the trivial, gaudy, sensuous, cheap or vulgar instead of helping man upward by its powerful aid in the evocation of what is best and highest in intellect as well as in character, emotion and the aesthetic enjoyment and regulation of life and manners. It is difficult to appreciate the waste and detriment involved in the low and debased level of enjoyment to which the artistic impulses are condemned in the majority of mankind.

> Beyond the intellect is the spirit; can Art be of any help in the discovery and expression of the spirit in life which is the highest of all human endeavours?

Beyond and above this intellectual utility of Art, there is a higher use, the noblest of all, its service to the growth of spirituality in the race. European critics have dwelt on the close connection of the highest developments of art with religion, and it is undoubtedly true that in Greece, in Italy, in India, the greatest efflorescence of a national Art has been associated with the employment of the artistic genius to illustrate or adorn the thoughts and fancies or the temples and instruments of the national religion. This was not because Art is necessarily associated with the outward forms of religion, but because it was in the religion that men's spiritual aspirations centred themselves. Spirituality is a wider thing than formal religion and it is in the service of spirituality that Art reaches its highest self-expression. Spirituality is a single word expressive of three lines of human aspiration towards divine knowledge, divine love and joy, divine strength, and that will be the highest and most perfect Art which, while satisfying the physical requirements of the aesthetic sense, the laws of formal beauty, the emotional demand of humanity, the portrayal of life and outward reality, as the best European Art satisfies these requirements, reaches beyond them and expresses inner spiritual truth, the deeper not obvious reality of things, the joy of God in the world and its beauty and desirableness and the manifestation of divine force and energy in phenomenal creation. This is what Indian Art alone attempted thoroughly and in the effort it often dispensed, either deliberately or from impatience, with the lower, yet not negligible perfections which the more material European demanded. Therefore Art has flowed in two separate streams in Europe and Asia, so diverse that it is only now that the European aesthetic sense has so far trained itself as to begin to appreciate the artistic conventions, aims and traditions of Asia. Asia's future development will unite these two streams in one deep and grandiose flood of artistic self-expression perfecting the aesthetic evolution of humanity.

> But can Art, which even at its highest is an activity of the limited
> human mind, possibly express the eternal and infinite Truth,
> Love, Joy and Power of the Spirit?

Art can express eternal truth, it is not limited to the expression of form and appearance. So wonderfully has God made the world that a man using a simple combination of lines, an unpretentious harmony of colours, can raise this apparently insignificant medium to suggest absolute and profound truths with a perfection which language labours with difficulty to reach. What Nature is, what God is, what man is can be triumphantly revealed in stone or on canvas.

Behind a few figures, a few trees and rocks the supreme Intelligence, the supreme Imagination, the supreme Energy lurks, acts, feels, is, and, if the artist has the spiritual vision, he can see it and suggest perfectly the great mysterious Life in its manifestations brooding in action, active in thought, energetic in stillness, creative in repose, full of a mastering intention in that which appears blind and unconscious. The great truths of religion, science, metaphysics, life, development, become concrete, emotional, universally intelligible and convincing in the hands of the master of plastic Art, and the soul of man, in the stage when it is rising from emotion to intellect, looks, receives the suggestion and is uplifted towards a higher development; a diviner knowledge.

So it is with the divine love and joy which pulsates throughout existence and is far superior to alloyed earthly pleasure. Catholic, perfect, unmixed with repulsion, radiating through all things, the common no less than the high, the mean and shabby no less than the lofty and splendid, the terrible and the repulsive no less than the charming and attractive, it uplifts all, purifies all, turns all to love and delight and beauty. A little of this immortal nectar poured into a man's heart transfigures life and action. The whole flood of it pouring in would lift mankind to God. This too Art can seize on and suggest to the human soul, aiding it in its stormy and toilsome pilgrimage. In that pilgrimage it is the divine strength that supports. *Sakti*, Force, pouring through the universe supports its boundless activities, the frail and tremulous life of the rose no less than the flaming motions of sun and star. To suggest the strength and virile unconquerable force of the divine Nature in man and in the outside world, its energy, its calm, its powerful inspiration, its august enthusiasm, its wildness, greatness, attractiveness, to breathe that into man's soul and gradually mould the finite into the image of the Infinite is another spiritual utility of Art. This is its loftiest function, its fullest consummation, its most perfect privilege.

Sri Aurobindo, in Kisher Gandhi,
Lights on Life Problems

A young hunter, thirsty from wandering through the bush, stops at a pool and bends over to drink. In his stooped position he suddenly glimpses the reflection of a great white bird in the water, the most beautiful creature he has ever seen in his life. When he looks up, the bird has disappeared from the sky; but having seen that brilliant reflection he knows it exists. And from that moment he spends the rest of his life in search of the great white bird. Many years pass; and at last, when he is very old and close to death, he is directed to a high and perpendicular cliff rumoured to be the home of the white bird of truth. It appears unscalable; yet mustering his last strength he starts climbing. For days on end he struggles up the sheer face of the cliff until, too weak to continue, he sinks down on a narrow ridge where he lies staring up, through breaking eyes, at the forever unreachable summit. And suddenly a single white feather comes fluttering down and lands on his breast before he dies.

I know of no more moving symbol of the quest of the writer who, through the imagination, makes the real more vibrantly real than before, and deepens fact into mythical truth.

André Brink, "Imagining the Real," in *Writing in a State of Siege*

If the Church has emphasized the function of art in her public prayer, it has been because she knew that a true and valid aesthetic formation was necessary for the wholeness of Christian living and worship. The liturgy and the chant and Church art are all supposed to form and spiritualize man's consciousness, to give him a tone and a maturity without which his prayer cannot normally be either very deep or very wide or very pure.

There is only one reason why this is completely true: art is not an end in itself. It introduces the soul into a higher spiritual order, which it expresses and in some sense explains. Music and art and poetry attune the soul to God because they induce a kind of contact with the Creator and Ruler of the Universe. The genius of the artist finds its way by the affinity of creative sympathy, or conaturality, into the living law that rules the universe. This law is nothing but the secret gravitation that draws all things to God as to their center. Since all true art lays bare the action of this same law in the depths of our own nature, it makes us alive to the tremendous mystery of being, in which we ourselves, together with all other living and existing things, come forth from the depths of God and return again to Him. An art that does not produce something of this is not worthy of its name.

Thomas Merton, *No Man Is an Island*

The poet, the painter, the artist, is always in touch with this transcendent Mystery—in so far as he is an authentic poet—however much he may be enclosed in the world of the senses and the imagination. He may write of nature or war or human love and passion; he may paint a landscape or a portrait without any "sacred" character: but it is the presence of the sacred Mystery in his work which makes it poetry. Raïssa Maritain has written well of this when she says that poetry is conceived in "those depths of the soul where intelligence and desire, intuition and sensibility, imagination and love, have their common source." Poetry and mysticism both derive from a common source, the ground or depth of the soul, where the Mystery of Being is experienced. But the poet is always driven to "symbolize" his experience, to express it in words or in paint or in music. The mystic seeks the experience in itself, beyond words or sounds or images.

Bede Griffiths, *Return to the Centre*

→ Mystical Experiences ←

Unlike the transcendent experiences recorded earlier in "Revelation," which were spontaneous and sometimes completely unexpected, the joyful mystical experience occurs when a more conscious union with the divine is formed. Through what theologian Paul Tillich calls "a close personal intercourse with God," we can achieve a state of ultimate bliss, even ecstasy, for which surrender was preparation. This mystical state exists without fragmentation; it is beyond struggle—even beyond determination.

The true mystical experience is rarely recorded well in literature, which is why, when it is done, it usually becomes a spiritual classic—such as "The Interior Castle" by the sixteenth-century saint Teresa of Avila and the writings of St. John of the Cross. In contemporary times, particularly during the last fifty-year period, accounts of mystical unions are even rarer.

I've included here a section from German writer Hermann Broch's novel *The Death of Virgil* as an example of how to put into words the *feelings* of the soul, its thirst for unity with the All—the creator and the creation, its real hunger for the ultimate homecoming that is its destiny.

Abraham H. Maslow explains that "the peak experience," as a powerful, mystical rapture, is sometimes likened to "a single glimpse of heaven"—a glimpse that can validate the meaning of existence, help in curing suicidal tendencies, ease feelings of hopelessness, and the fear of death.

Because the mystical tradition itself has been lost in the Western religious tradition (since the sixteenth century), we need to turn to the East for insight—to Buddhism for the practice necessary to attain nirvana, to Zen for satori, the experience of Truth. Japanese Zen Buddhist teacher and writer Dr. Daisetz Teitaro Suzuki aptly explains this state as "enlightenment" in one of the most important books ever written on Zen *Living by Zen* (1950). He shows how when one becomes enlightened after having experienced satori, one must use it to advance self-knowledge and spiritual wisdom. By uniting with all creation, by living in the eternity of time, God's greatness and goodness are revealed in the largest and widest of conscious experiences, and in the smallest, simplest of tasks at hand.

><

Mystical identification transcends the aristocratic virtue of courageous self-sacrifice. It is self-surrender in a higher, more complete, and more radical form. It is the perfect form of self-affirmation.

Paul Tillich, *The Courage to Be*

In all mysticism that springs from the soil of the so-called "theistic" religions, there is an additional factor to which a special, specifically religious significance is to be accorded. Here the mystic knows of a close personal intercourse with God. This intercourse has as its goal, certainly, a union with God, a union that not seldom is felt and presented in images of earthly eros. But in erotic intercourse between being and being as in the intercourse between man and God it is still just the duality of these beings which is the elementary presupposition of what passes between them. It is not the duality of subject and object: neither is to the other a mere object of contemplation that does not itself participate in the relation. It is the duality of I and Thou, both entering into the reciprocity of the relation. No matter how absolute God is comprehended as being, He is here, nonetheless, not the whole but the Facing One. He is the One standing over against this man; He is what this man is not and is not what this man is. It is precisely on this duality that the longing for union can base itself. In other words, in this close intercourse that the mystic experiences, God, no matter how infinite he is comprehended as being, is still Person and remains Person. And even if the mystic wants to be merged in Him, he means none other than Him whom he knows in this intercourse, just this Person. The I of the mystic seeks to lose itself in the Thou of God, but this Thou of God, or, after the I of the mystic has been merged in Him, this absolute I of God, cannot pass away. The "I am" of man must vanish so that the "I am" of God alone remains. "Between me and thee," goes one of the sayings of al-Hallaj, the great martyr of Islamic mysticism, "there is an 'I am' that torments me. Ah! Through thy 'I am' take away my 'I am' from between us both." The mystic never thinks of calling into question the personal character of this divine "I am." "I call thee," says al-Hallaj, "...no, it is thou who callest me to thee! How could I have said to thee, 'It is thou,' if thou hadst not whispered to me, 'It is I.'" The I of the revealing God, the I of the God who grants to the mystic the intercourse with Him, and the I of God in which the human is merged are identical. In the realm of the intercourse with God the mystic remains what he was in the realm of revelation, a theist.

It is otherwise when mysticism, stepping beyond the realm of experienced intercourse, dares to deal with God as He is in Himself, that is, outside His relation to man, indeed outside His relationship to the created world.

Martin Buber, *The Origin and Meaning of Hasidim*

—, oh homecoming in that deed which signifies love, is only the serving helpful deed, in that it bestows the name and fulfills the empty form of fate, is stronger than fate itself—

—, not quite here but yet at hand! And it was knowledge at the heart of an inconceivable loving distance that was buried in the innermost heart of the dream, it was awareness of the similarity in that tidal flood, the heart of this side and the heart of the beyond pulsing and beating within each other, the divine symbol kindled in the human being to a common language, the language of the divine-human pledge of allegiance, the language of everlasting creation in prayer and more prayer, mounting and subsiding in creative images; and it was the knowledge of this language of the redeeming deed, of this language of loving sacrifice, which floated as far above every human offering as the envoiced other-worldliness of the one voice floated over the babble of voices on earth, as the loving other-worldliness floated above every love that operates from man to man, the divine-human heart contained in divinity and humanity, containing both god and man; but it was likewise an awareness of him who—because the voice to be credible on earth must have an announcer—was destined to be the bearer of the creative deed, the deed and the doer born into earthly life from an unearthly conception, for only he who in his very origin is already exempt from chance is able to reunite chance with the miracle of that ultimate lawfulness to which fate itself is subjected; for only he who originates from a destiny beyond fate and who, despite this, drains the destined calamity to the last drop, only he is given grace to turn calamity into salvation again and to become the bearer of salvation; oh to him and only to him, the divinely conceived figure in heroic human form, is it permitted to carry the father across the fires of iniquity, and he alone is entrusted with the rescue of the father, he is allowed to carry the one who conceived him, taking him on his shoulders and bearing him off to the ship and to the homecoming flight into a new country, into the land of promise that has always been the homeland of the father. Not quite here, but yet at hand! That land lay before him in the knowledge of the enjoining, name-giving father-summons which embodies the divine in the human and inspirits the human into the divine; it lay before him in radiation and counter-radiation, it lay before him in the knowledge of the salvation-bearer and in the salvation-bearer's knowledge, full of humanity, full of divinity, the brands of iniquity changed to pure sacrificial flames, the rigidity shattered, the gravestone of the middle lifted, good and evil parted and purified, god and man enlarged to a resurrected creation, the prophecy reclaimed in a future in the name of the father, forever sanctified in the name of the son, forever affianced in the spirit, not quite here but yet at hand, the promised one. Was that which he perceived already recognition? was it only the recognition in dream? was it already the awakening? Oh, it was still this side of the boundary, but even though the dream palpitated against it, it had not broken through the border; the vision was not to be grasped, it was not recognition, it was only awareness, a dream-awareness, a dream-recollection, a distant memory of the never-heard, ever-resounding voice of a Once, the furthest recollection of the never-encountered land beyond the border, through which he had always wandered, a land enlarged by distance, reduced by distance, the source, the estuary; it was the memory-strengthened approach to the border, but it was still a spellbound quivering, a throbbing, expectant illumination. And just for that reason, even in this peering knowledge, in this extremely transparent blindness, that without being recognition was a form of recognition, a transparent bandage over his eyes, yes, for that reason, although sunk into the dream-meadows and overgrown by their bracken, he found himself placed abruptly on the peak of a very high mountain, as if he had been ordered there so that he might look beyond the border, he a beholder, but still not an announcer, placed there and held there by a gentle-unyielding hand, held into a future yet always existent actuality, beat upon by the throbbing of a heart that though enshrined in him yet enshrined him by being greater than himself; breathing with reality and animated by this throbbing, he was enabled to release his arms from the crystalline transparency and to stretch them upward, upward toward the luminous dome wherein the stars were shining and great suns were beginning to revolve, a single star above them all: he gazed out over the fields of dream, over the fields of those countries predestined to be the theater of the deed, the theater of his vision, beyond touch, beyond tread, yet his own from the very start; he gazed out, spellbound, dreambound here as he was, unable to part from or to be removed from his dream, gazing out over the landscape in which, though it was beyond his touch and tread, he was stretched out with his own dream radiation and his own dream illumination and, surveying both the landscape and the dream, he saw that they were reciprocally merged, he saw amidst the landscape all the crystalline formations, the light-cubes, the light-circles, the light-pyramids, the light-clusters of the dream; he saw, stretched out and imbedded in the dreamy confluence and boundless radiation of its light-paths, the landscape, made rich, transparent and magical through memory; indeed, it was imbedded in the dream with all its night-times and day-times, vacillating between light and darkness, inflating and deflating under the twofold dusk of morning and evening, filled with every possible kind of earthly shape, filled with a motley crowd of all creaturehood, filled with the roaring medley of all earthly voices, filled with intoxication, with torment, with yearning, filled with the created and the developing creation, filled with the silence of beaches, of undulating meadows and of fading mountain summits,—the heights bearing loneliness and the plains bearing cities,—filled with the peaceful glow of human life and living but also filled by the rustling and crackling of the evil flames, endless, endless, endless; everything there was to be wandered through, nothing could be trodden, dream and landscape imbedded one into the other, shining into and shading out into each other, joined in expectation, joined in yearning, joined in a readiness for awakening, waiting to receive him who would stride through them, bringing the voice of the awakening. And he too was waiting; with uplifted arms he waited with dream and landscape, he gazed over the still pastures on which the cattle were grazing without motion, he perceived the muteness of the motionlessly burning brands, and no bird-flight moved across the pavilion of the air; the flames rose higher into the immobility, the confusion of the manifold voices increased in the unbreakable silence, the yearning became deeper and deeper, the suns stood still and the throbbing of the heart beat more and more heavily against the walls of the boundlessness within and without—, oh when was the end to be? where was the end to be found? when would the desecration be quaffed to the last drop? Was there a nethermost stage to this deepening silence? And then it seemed to him that just such an ultimate silence had now been achieved. For he saw the mouths of men gaping at each other full of terror, no sound wrenched itself from the dry clefts and no one understood the other. It was the last step of silence on earth, it was the ultimate silencing of men; and beholding this his mouth also yearned to open in a last mute cry of horror. Still while seeing it, almost before he had really seen it, he no longer saw anything. For the visible had vanished into most abrupt darkness, the light of dream quenched, the landscape disappeared, the flames quelled, the people evaporated, the mouths abolished, this was night, timeless, spaceless, wordless, toneless, the most empty blackness, an empty night without form and without content; empty and black became the waiting, even the throbbing died down, sucked up by emptiness. The bottom of existence had been reached. He stood at the boundary, he stood at the edge of destiny, at the border of chance, he stood at the boundary with blank expectation, with blank listening, with blank looking, with blank wisdom, yet drained as he was and in this blankness he knew that the borderline would be opened. This began to happen very softly as if not to alarm him. It began as a whisper that he had heard once before, it began in his innermost ear, in his innermost soul, in his innermost heart, yet simultaneously surrounding him and penetrating him, stemming from the uttermost darkness, streaming in and out of the night; it was the same quietly great power of the tone to which once before he had had to submit in repentance, swelling out now as then, fulfilling him, enwrapping him, although it was no longer the accord of many voices; it was not the accord of the voice-herds, it was not the accord of any voice-multiplicity, instead it was far rather a single voice, making itself more and more solitary, a voice of such great loneliness that it glowed like a single star in the darkness, nevertheless an invisible one shining in the invisible, for as the summons grew greater and more distinct, it was subsumed not less greatly into the infinite and inscrutable, which is inaudible because it is mute: what took place here was beyond the visible and the audible, it was beyond the reach of every sense-perception, it happened obscurely and for all that it was of a most compelling, perceptible clarity; it happened in a realm of shadows, yet included the forms of every essence, oh, it occurred as equilibrium, it was manifested as an infinite, inconceivably balanced order, giving meaning, content and name, comprised of all being and all memory, including the iron booming of seas as well as the silver susurrus of autumn, the celesta-stroke of the stars as well as the warm breathing of flocks, the flutetone of the moon even as the dew on the sunny hedges of childhood; it was a beholding of the unbeholdable, a listening into the inaudible, and he flooded in darkness, the world's diversity and entity likewise held in balance within the flood of darkness, in this last command to equilibrium which is the only reality and which annuls chance, he heard, no he did not hear, he saw the voice which brought this to pass; and it was not one of those voices which, belonging to the world, insert themselves into the structure of world-facts in order to turn them into a symbol, symbolizing one thing by another but also symbolizing the word by the word, this was not the voice of worldly truth, neither one of them nor the summation of all such truths, no, it was unterrestrially, inaudibly, invisibly beyond the world; it was the extra-worldly agent of truth, the extra-worldly agent of equilibrium, it was the essence of the outside, bringing near all the strength and all the amplitude of the outside as it brought itself nearer, comprehending all that is within in order to be comprehended by it, the all-embracing receptacle of the spheres; and thus he realized it, hearing by seeing, seeing by hearing the voice in the shadow of whose word peace and homeland are ever to be found, the voice of timelessness and of the everlasting creation, the judgment-voice of the beginning and the end, the equilibrating voice outside the dream, the voice of safe-keeping; its tone was brazen and crystal and flute-like in one; it was thunder and the preponderance of silence, and it was all sounds and yet a single sound, commanding and gentle, forgiving and discerning, a single lightning-flash, oh, an unspeakably gentle blinding, quiet because consummate; oh, thus it disclosed itself, grace fused with the pledge, disclosing itself not as word, not as speech, far rather as symbol of a word, as symbol of all speech, as symbol of every voice, as the arch-image of them all, overcoming fate in the form of the holy father-summons; it revealed itself as the tone-picture of the annunciating deed: "Open your eyes to Love!"

Hermann Broch, *The Death of Virgil*

The mystical courage to be lasts as long as the mystical situation. Its limit is the state of emptiness of being and meaning, with its horror and despair, which the mystics have described. In these moments the courage to be is reduced to the acceptance of even this state as a way to prepare through darkness for light, through emptiness for abundance. As long as the absence of the power of being is felt as despair, it is the power of being which makes itself felt through despair. To experience this and to endure it is the courage to be of the mystic in the state of emptiness. Although mysticism in its extreme positive and extreme negative aspects is a comparatively rare event, the basic attitude, the striving for union with ultimate reality, and the corresponding courage to take the nonbeing which is implied in finitude upon oneself are a way of life which is accepted by and has shaped large sections of mankind.

Paul Tillich, *The Courage to Be*

There is no doubt that great insights and revelations are profoundly felt in mystic or peak-experiences, and certainly some of these are, *ipso facto*, intrinsically valid as *experiences*. That is, one can and does learn from such experiences that, e.g., joy, ecstasy, and rapture do in fact exist and that they are in principle available for the experiencer, even if they never have been before. Thus the peaker learns surely and certainly that life *can* be worthwhile, that it *can* be beautiful and valuable. There *are* ends in life, i.e., experiences which are so precious in themselves as to prove that not everything is a means to some end other than itself.

Another kind of self-validating insight is the experience of being a real identity, a real self, of feeling what it is like to feel really oneself, what in fact one is—not a phony, a fake, a striver, an impersonator. Here again, the experiencing itself is the revelation of a truth.

My feeling is that if it were never to happen again, the power of the experience could permanently affect the attitude toward life. A single glimpse of heaven is enough to confirm its existence even if it is never experienced again. It is my strong suspicion that even one such experience might be able to prevent suicide, for instance, and perhaps many varieties of slow self-destruction, e.g., alcoholism, drug-addiction, addiction to violence, etc. I would guess also, on theoretical grounds, that peak-experiences might very well abort "existential meaninglessness," states of valuelessness, etc., at least occasionally. (These deductions from the nature of intense peak-experiences are given some support by general experience with LSD and psilocybin. Of course these preliminary reports also await confirmation.)

This then is one kind of peak-knowledge of whose validity and usefulness there can be no doubt, no more than there could be with discovering for the first time that the color "red" exists and is wonderful. Joy exists, can be experienced and feels very good indeed, and one can always hope that it will be experienced again.

Perhaps I should add here the paradoxical result—for some—that death may lose its dread aspect. Ecstasy is somehow close to death-experience, at least in the simple, empirical sense that death is often mentioned during reports of peaks, *sweet* death that is. After the acme, only less is possible. In any case, I have occasionally been told, "I felt that I could willingly die," or, "No one can ever again tell me death is bad," etc. Experiencing a kind of "sweet death" may remove its frightening aspect. This observation should, of course, be studied far more carefully than I have been able to. But, the point is that the experience itself is a kind of knowledge gained (or attitude changed) which is self-validating. Other such experiences, coming for the first time, are true simply because experienced, e.g., greater integration of the organism, experiencing physiognomic perception, fusing primary and secondary-process, fusing knowing and valuing, transcending dichotomies, experiencing knowing as being, etc., etc. The widening and enriching of consciousness through new perceptual experiences, many of which leave a lasting effect, is a little like improving the perceiver himself.

More frequently, however, peak-knowledge *does* need external, independent validation (70) or at least the request for such validation is a meaningful request; for instance, falling in love leads not only to greater care, which means closer attention, examination, and, therefore, greater knowledge, but it may also lead to affirmative statements and judgments which may be untrue however touching and affecting they may also be, e.g., "my husband is a genius."

The history of science and invention is full of instances of validated peak-insights and also of "insights" that failed. At any rate, there are enough of the former to support the proposition that the knowledge obtained in peak-insight-experiences *can* be validated and valuable.

This is also true sometimes for the awe-inspiring, poignant insights (both of peak type and also of the desolation type) or revelations that can come in psychotherapy—even though not very frequently. This falling of the veils can be a valid perception of what has not been consciously perceived before.

Abraham H. Maslow, *Religions, Values, and
Peak-Experiences*

Note that in Buddhism also the highest development of consciousness is that by which the individual ego is completely emptied and becomes identified with the enlightened Buddha, or rather finds itself to be in reality the enlightened Buddha mind. Nirvana is not the consciousness of an ego that is aware of itself as having crossed over to "the other shore" (to be on "another shore" is the same as not having crossed over), but the Absolute Ground-Consciousness of the Void, in which there are no shores. Thus the Buddhist enters into the self-emptying and enlightenment of Buddha as the Christian enters into the self-emptying (crucifixion) and glorification (resurrection and ascension) of Christ. The chief difference between the two is that the former is existential and ontological, the latter is theological and personal. But "person" here must be distinguished from "the individual empirical ego."

Thomas Merton, *Zen and the Birds of Appetite*

Satori

To understand Zen, it is essential to have an experience known as Satori, for without this one can have no insight into the truth of Zen, which, as we have already seen, is generally paradoxically expressed:

"When snow covers all the mountains white, why is one left uncovered (literally, not white)?"

"The ascetic, pure in heart, does not enter Nirvana (i.e. Paradise); the monk violating the Precepts does not fall into Hell."

"What I know, you do not know; what you know, I know all."

"While the post is moving around all day, how is it that I do not know?"

"How is it that a man of great strength cannot lift his legs?"

All these statements defy being fitted into the frame of logical reasonableness. To make them intelligible satori is needed. They are in fact purposely set forth by Zen masters to confuse those minds whose field of operation cannot go beyond our everyday common-sense experience. When satori is attained the irrationalities cease to be such; they fall back on the level of logic and common-sense. The hunger is said not to know the mountains because he is right in them. He has to be up in the air to see the whole range of the undulations.

Satori achieves this feat; it detaches a man from his environment, and makes him survey the entire field. But this does not mean that satori keeps him away from the field where it operates. This is a dualistic way of interpreting satori, for a genuine satori is at once transcendent and imminent. It becomes really operative at the point where subject is object and object is subject. Or we can say that unless this identity is effected there is no satori. In satori what is imminent is transcendent and what is transcendent is imminent. The hunter is at once out of the mountains and in them, for he has never gone one step away from them.

We must remember, however, that satori is not a mere intellectual discipline; nor is it a kind of dialectic whereby contradictoriness becomes logically tenable and turns into a reasonable proposition. Satori is existential and not dialectical, as Kierkegaard may say. It does not work with logical formulas and abstractions. It is a concrete fact in itself. When it states that the waters do not flow but the bridge does, it is, to men of satori, not a paradox but a direct statement of their living existential experience. Kierkegaard says that faith is an existential leap. So is satori. Faith has a Christian ring, while satori is specifically Zen. In my view both are experientially identifiable.

What is given us primarily, immediately, is a continuum which is not divisible into atoms; but as we "experience" it, it divides itself into an infinity of atoms. This is due to our sense limitations and to the construction of consciousness. We do not ordinarily reflect on this fact and go on with our daily life, taking sensual-intellectual facts of experience for finalities. Those who reflect, however, build up a world of concepts, and postulate a continuum. But as this is the result of intellectual deliberation the continuum is not apprehended as such by most of us.

To us, therefore, God is not an object of immediate experience. He is inferred by logical process. He is thought of, he is not seen. From thinking to seeing is not a continuous process, it is a leap. For however much we multiply our atomic experiences of parts, no continuum as a concrete whole will be experienced. The concrete whole is to be intuited as such. The whole is not to be apprehended by accumulations; a whole thus arrived at is no more than parts added, and however far we may carry this addition it goes on *ad infinitum*. An all-embracing whole must be directly grasped as a whole complete in itself. But if it is grasped in the way in which parts, atomic parts, are grasped, it ceases to be a whole, it turns to be a part of the whole which, as an infinitely expansible totality, for ever eludes our prehension, which is postulationally conditioned.

Therefore, the continuum, undivided, indivisible, infinitely cumulative, and yet a concrete object of apprehension, cannot belong to the world of particulars. It belongs to another order of existence; it constitutes a world by itself, and it is attainable only by transcending our everyday experience of sense-intellect, that is, by an existential leap. This is satori.

It is thus seen that satori is the apprehending of the continuum as such, as not subject to differentiation and determination. But the continuum thus apprehended as the object, as it were, of satori experience ought not to be judged as standing against particular objects of our daily experience. When this way of thinking is cherished, satori is no more satori; it turns to be one of sense-experiences, and creates a new continuum over the one we already have, and we shall have to repeat this process indefinitely.

Another important thing to remember is that satori takes in the continuum not only as undifferentiated and undetermined but as infinitely divided and determinated. This means that satori is never in conflict with the world of sense-intellect, it never negates its experiences. When it declares that the spade is in my hands and yet I am empty-handed, it does not mean to contradict the fact of the spade's actually being in the hands, but it only means that each single fact of experience is to be related to the totality of things, for thereby it gains for the first time its meaning.

The negating by satori of our everyday facts of experience is to make us thereby realize that God's hands are also holding the spade. When satori makes us conscious of the spade being held in God's hands and not in my hands which I imagine to be my own, each movement I perform becomes directly connected with the one who is more than myself, and reflects his will. Hence the Christian saying, "Let thy will be done, not mine." Christians are more ethical and do not speak about negating our common-sense experience. Satori in this respect reflects the general characteristic of Buddhist teaching, especially that of Prajna philosophy.

The Prajna begins its thinking with denying everything; the idea, however, is not to build up a system of philosophy, but to free us from all our egoistic impulses and the idea of permanency, for these are the source of human miseries, are not intellectually tenable and are spiritually altogether unsound. They are the outgrowth of Ignorance (*avidya*), declares the Buddha. Satori is enlightenment (*sambodhi*), just the opposite of ignorance and darkness. Enlightenment consists in spiritually elucidating facts of experience and not in denying or abnegating them. The light whereby satori illuminates the continuum also illuminates the world of divisions and multitudes. This is the meaning of the Buddhist dictum: *Shabetsu* (difference) and *Byodo* (sameness) are identical.

Daisetz Teitaro Suzuki, *Living by Zen*

Now, I think, we can fairly well characterize what Zen satori is:

It is to be with God before he cried out, "Let there be light."

It is to be with God when his spirit moved to give this order.

It is to be with God and also with the light so created.

It is even to be God himself, and also to be his firmament, his earth, his day and night.

Satori is God's coming to self-consciousness in man—the consciousness all the time underlining human consciousness, which may be called super-consciousness.

Satori is not knowledge in its commonly understood sense.

Satori goes beyond knowledge. It is absolute knowledge in the sense that in satori there is neither the knowledge of subject nor the object of knowledge.

Satori is not a higher unity in which two contradictory terms are synthesized. When a staff is not a staff and yet it is a staff, satori obtains.

When the bridge flows and the water does not, there is satori.

Satori is not an act of intuition as long as there are traces in it of a dualistic conception.

Satori is intuition dynamically conceived. When you move with a moving object, when you are identified with it, and yet when you are not moving at all, a certain state of consciousness—super-consciousness—prevails, which is satori.

When an individual monad is perceived reflecting eternity or as eternity itself, there is satori.

Every moment we live is, therefore, eternity itself. Eternity is no other than this instant. They are mutually merged and identical. This state of perfect interpenetration is the content of satori.

Satori does not perceive eternity as stretching itself over an infinite number of unit-instants but in the instant itself, for every instant is eternity.

Satori may be defined as dynamic intuition.

Psychologically speaking, satori is super-consciousness, or consciousness of the Unconscious. The Unconscious is, however, not to be identified with the one psychologically postulated. The Unconscious of satori is with God even prior to his creation. It is what lies at the basis of reality; it is the cosmic Unconscious.

This Unconscious is a metaphysical concept, and it is through satori that we become conscious of the Unconscious.

Satori is Ummon's light possessed by each one of us. And as he says, when we want to lay hands on it there is utter darkness. Satori refuses to be brought on to the surface of our relative consciousness. This, however, does not mean that satori is altogether isolated. To *satoru* means to become conscious of the Unconscious, and this Unconscious is all the time along with consciousness.

Satori makes the Unconscious articulate. And the articulated Unconscious expresses itself in terms of logic incoherently, but most eloquently from the Zen point of view. This "incoherency," indeed, is Zen.

The cosmic Unconscious in terms of space is "Emptiness" (*sunyata*). To reach this Emptiness is satori. Therefore, when things are surveyed from the satori point of view, Mount Sumeru conceals itself in one of the innumerable pores on the skin. I lift a finger and it covers the whole universe.

Daisetz Teitaro Suzuki, *Living by Zen*

Bliss of Identity

All Nature is taught in radiant ways to move,
All beings are in myself embraced.
O fiery boundless Heart of joy and love,
How art thou beating in a mortal's breast!

It is Thy rapture flaming through my nerves
And all my cells and atoms thrill with Thee;
My body Thy vessel is and only serves
As a living wine-cup of Thy ecstasy.

I am a centre of Thy golden light
And I its vast and vague circumference;
Thou art my soul great, luminous and white
And Thine my mind and will and glowing sense.

Thy spirit's infinite breath I feel in me;
My life is a throb of Thy eternity.

Sri Aurobindo, *Collected Poems*

Joy is prayer—Joy is strength—Joy is love—Joy is a net of love by which you can catch souls.

Mother Teresa, *A Gift for God*

But this joy must not be the goal toward which you strive. It will be vouch-safed you if you strive to "give joy to God." Your personal joy will rise up when you want nothing but the joy of God—nothing but joy in itself.

Martin Buber, *Tales of the Hasidim*

It is God's love that warms me in the sun and God's love that sends the cold rain. It is God's love that feeds me in the bread I eat and God that feeds me also by hunger and fasting.

It is the love of God that sends the winter days when I am cold and sick, and the hot summer when I labor and my clothes are full of sweat: but it is God who breathes on me with light winds off the river and in breezes out of the wood.

His love spreads the shade of the sycamore over my head and sends the water-boy along the edge of the wheatfield with a bucket from the spring, while the laborers are resting and the mules stand under the tree.

It is God's love that speaks to me in the birds and streams, and all these things are seeds sent to me from his will. If these seeds would take root in my liberty, and if his will would grow from my freedom, I would become the love that he is, and my harvest would be his glory and my own joy.

Thomas Merton, *New Seeds of Contemplation*

The Eternal Image

Her angel looked upon God's face
As eagles gaze upon the sun,
Fair in the everlasting place.

And saw that everything is one
And moveless, in the eternal light:
Never completed, not begun.

She on the earth, with steadfast sight,
Stood like an image of the Muse
Amid the falling veils of night:

Her feet were silvered in the dews,
Dew fell upon her darkling tree,
And washed the plain with whitish hues.

Standing so still, what does she see?
She sees the changeless creature shine
Apparelled in eternity:

She knows the constancy divine;
The whole of life sees harvested,
And frozen into crystalline

And final form, the quick, the dead,
All that has ever seemed to change,
Possess at once the pale and red:

All that from birth to death may range
Newborn and dead she sees, nor says
The vision to be sad or strange.

How may this serve her mortal ways?
Truly it cannot buy her bread
Nor ease the labour of her days:

But calm her waking, quiet her bed,
For she has seen the perfect round
That binds the infant to the dead,

And one by one draws underground
All men; and still, and one by one,
Into the air the living bound,

Never completed, not begun.
With burning hair, with moveless grace,
As eagles gaze against the sun

Her angel looks upon God's face.

Ruth Pitter, *Poems 1926–1966*

✣ Peace and Happiness ✣

What ultimately arrives as part of the
gifts of surrender is what we humans need more than anything—peace and
happiness. The peace that emerges from within is the sign of God's presence
within. The silence in which we seek Him at the onset of surrender is the
silence in which we find Him now inside, always, like a healing, sweet, perpetual balm—the "breath of human existence" (Henri Nouwen). When
there is peace inside, it pervades the outside and affects the energy of our
environment. It also happens in reverse—like a connective thread, peace
weaves its way into a healing circle. Omraam Mikhaël Aïvanhov writes of
the "true silence" being "inhabited by countless beings" and speaks of awareness of *all* spirits in nature, of communing with them, of learning and experiencing fulfilment from our surroundings. This is what most of the Native

American Indians believe and honour, that all living things, trees, flowers, all matter in nature have their own spiritual life, which is connected with ours; everything is "living, intelligent souls" (Aïvanhov).

The place of ultimate peace is at infinity, yet how to get there? How to *be* there? Argentinian novelist and essayist Jorge Luis Borges suggests that we embrace "something infinite" we have lost by finding it in the signs of daily life, or deep within "the labyrinth of dreams." In glimpsing this infinite life, in believing that our souls belong there, that we are beyond death on this journey, we come to know of this promised, eternal peace.

><

There in the silence I love the green grass. The tortured gestures of the apple trees have become part of my prayer. I look at the shining water under the willows and listen to the sweet songs of all the living things that are in our woods and fields. So much do I love this solitude that when I walk out along the road to the old barns that stand alone, far from the new buildings, delight begins to overpower me from head to foot and peace smiles even in the marrow of my bones.

Thomas Merton, *The Sign of Jonas*

We all need silence. We particularly need the silence of nature, for that is where our roots lie: in nature. Sometimes, when one is alone in a forest or up in the mountains, one feels as though one were being carried back into a distant past, into an era in which human beings were in communion with the forces and the spirits of nature. And if the call of a bird or the sound of a waterfall is heard, it is as though these very sounds were part of the silence: rather than destroying it, they emphasize and contribute to it. For, quite often, we are not even conscious of silence; we don't notice it. It takes the sound of a twig snapping, a bird singing or a pebble falling to awaken us suddenly to an acute perception of the silence around us. Even the subdued roaring of the waves cannot destroy the profound silence of the oceans.

Many people confuse silence with solitude. That is why they are afraid of silence: they are afraid of loneliness. The truth is, though, that silence is inhabited. If you want to ensure that you will never be poor and lonely, seek silence, for true silence is inhabited by countless beings. The Lord has populated the whole of creation; in the forests, lakes, and oceans, in the mountains and even in the depths of the earth dwell living beings. Even fire has its inhabitants. Yes, even the ether and the stars; everything is inhabited.

Unfortunately, the noise of civilization, that is gradually invading every corner of the earth, and the increasingly materialistic and prosaic lives of most human beings have created conditions that are far from conducive to the presence amongst them of entities from the invisible world. On the contrary, these entities are forced to shun their company. Not that they have an aversion for human beings; but how can they stay in places that are constantly disturbed and desecrated by men's lack of respect, by their crudeness and violence? Is there any wonder that these spirits are more and more inclined to withdraw into places that are inaccessible to men? I have already seen evidence of this for myself. In the Yosemite National Park in the United States, for instance, there are some 4,000-year-old trees. I have seen them and they are magnificent but they are no longer inhabited. The trees and this whole glorious region have been abandoned by their devas because all the tourists and holiday-makers bring in so much noise and turmoil. In almost every tree that grows there is a living creature but here, in this park, these gigantic trees are no longer alive or expressive because they are no longer inhabited. Just as human sages escape from the noise and agitation of unconscious human beings by going off and taking refuge in the solitude of the desert, a mountain or a cave, the luminous spirits of nature take refuge in places that human beings have not yet managed to spoil. Perhaps you are thinking, "They must be terrible weaklings if they can't put up with a little noise!" Well, you are free to think what you like.

In most mythological traditions, mountains are seen as the home of the gods. This can be understood symbolically, of course, but it is also a reality: the peaks of high mountains are antennae which put the earth in contact with Heaven. This is why they are the home of very pure and very powerful entities. When you climb a mountain, the higher you go the deeper the silence, and in this silence you discover the origin of all things, you become one with the First Cause, you are plunged into the ocean of divine light.

Nowadays, unfortunately, with the constant improvements in the means of transport, mountains have become fashionable resorts and more and more people flock to them for winter sports. They amuse themselves on the ski slopes all day and spend their evenings boasting about their skiing or climbing exploits. Instead of respecting the silence of the mountains and allowing it to influence them and lead them to the discovery of higher states of consciousness, they behave as they are accustomed to behaving everywhere else. With their bottles of wine, their hams, their cigarettes and their cacophonous music, their raucous shouts and jokes and arguments, how could any shreds of silence survive? As though there were not plenty of other places they could go to for their rowdy parties! No wonder the luminous inhabitants of these regions are driven away by such disruptive behavior.

Nobody ever tells people that their lack of attention and respect destroys the atmosphere and distresses these invisible beings. In fact, if the commotion goes on for too long, they simply go away and find somewhere where they can enjoy true silence, somewhere that is virtually inaccessible to human beings. And this is a great pity for, when their ancient dwelling places are deserted, their mystery and their aura of sacredness is lost; the light and all the spiritual currents that impregnated them gradually fade and disappear.

Let this be quite clear, therefore: if you are not in the right frame of mind when you go for a holiday in the mountains, the invisible creatures that inhabit them will guard against you by disappearing and you will receive nothing from them. When you go home you will be as indigent and as limited as ever. In fact, even your physical health will not really benefit from your stay, because your physical health depends to a great extent on your psychic state.

What is the use of going up into the mountains if you are no purer, no stronger, no nobler and no healthier when you come down? What is the use if you have not understood that the ascension of a physical mountain symbolizes the ascension of a spiritual mountain? To climb up and then to come down . . . To climb up is to free yourself, little by little, from all that burdens and restricts you until you attain silence, purity, light and immensity and can feel divine order flowing into you. I hardly need to explain in detail what it means to come down again; you all understand that: it is to come back to the noise of your thoughts and feelings, to your habitual inner state of turmoil, disorder and conflict. Yes, this is just one example of how to read the great Book of Nature by learning to interpret its various manifestations.

Wherever you go, whether it be up in the mountains, in the depths of a forest, by the shores of lakes or oceans, if you want to manifest yourselves as children of God who aspire to a subtler, more luminous life, you must be conscious of the presence of the etheric inhabitants of that place. Approach them with an attitude of respect and reverence; begin by greeting them, by expressing friendship and love for them and then ask them for their blessing. They will be so delighted with your attitude that, when they see you coming, they will prepare their gifts of peace, light and pure energy and pour them into your heart. You will feel yourself bathed in the love and delight of these spiritual beings and, when you come back into the valley or the town, you will bring all these treasures with you. And you will also bring back revelations and more open, vaster, broader ideas.

And then, of course, there is the joy you get from knowing that your attitude contributes to causing these celestial beings to stay in those regions or even to persuading others to come and dwell there. Yes, you must never forget that it is only in silence that you can prepare conditions conducive to the manifestation of divine entities. These entities need silence and they are always waiting for the rare occasions when human beings provide the conditions they need. Henceforth, therefore, learn to love this silence; try to surround yourself with an atmosphere of spiritual silence and harmony so as to prepare for the coming of powerful, luminous beings.

Omraam Mikhaël Aïvanhov, *The Path of Silence*

What struck me most was the silence. It was a great silence, unlike any I have encountered on Earth, so vast and deep that I began to hear my own body: my heart beating, my blood vessels pulsing, even the rustle of my muscles moving over each other seemed audible. There were more stars in the sky than I had expected. The sky was deep black, yet at the same time bright with sunlight.

The Earth was small, light blue, and so touchingly alone, our home that must be defended like a holy relic. The Earth was absolutely round. I believe I never knew what the word round meant until I saw Earth from space.

Aleksei Leonov, *The Home Planet*

There is only one true flight from the world; it is not an escape from conflict, anguish, and suffering, but the flight from disunity and separation, to unity and peace in the love of other men.

What is the "world" that Christ would not pray for, and of which He said that His disciples were in it but not of it? The world is the unquiet city of those who live for themselves and are therefore divided against one another in a struggle that cannot end, for it will go on eternally in hell. It is the city of those who are fighting for possession of limited things and for the monopoly of goods and pleasures that cannot be shared by all.

But if you try to escape from this world merely by leaving the city and hiding yourself in solitude, you will only take the city with you into solitude; and yet you can be entirely out of the world while remaining in the midst of it, if you let God set you free from your own selfishness and if you live for love alone.

For the flight from the world is nothing else but the flight from self-concern. And the man who locks himself up in private with his own selfishness has put himself into a position where the evil within him will either possess him like a devil or drive him out of his head.

That is why it is dangerous to go into solitude merely because you like to be alone.

Thomas Merton, *New Seeds of Contemplation*

Even after all these years, I still remember certain experiences I had when I was young, in Bulgaria. In the summer, when the Master Peter Deunov and the members of the Brotherhood camped in the Rila Mountains, I would sometimes climb up and spend the night at the top of Mount Musallah. I would wrap myself up in several blankets and, stretching out on my back, I would gaze up at the starry sky and try to link myself to the cosmic forces and entities of which the stars are only the physical aspect. I could not understand all that they said to me, but I loved them; my whole soul glowed with the wonder of them while I lay and looked at them until, without realizing it, I finally fell asleep. Sometimes it would snow a little during the night and I would wake up to find myself under a light covering of snow. But that never worried me: I was happy!

Those were the years in which I discovered the extraordinary peace that floods one's being when one spends the night on a mountain. I found myself transported to regions in which I felt and understood that the only activity that really matters in life is to become one with the cosmic Spirit that animates the universe. The slightest little thing in the everyday lives of human beings torments them and sets them at each others' throats. Their consciousness has such a narrow field of vision that they think there is nothing more important than their petty cares, ambitions, love affairs and quarrels. They cannot see the immensity, the infinite reaches of the heavens over their heads which, if only they would lift their eyes to it, would permit them to break the bonds that restrict them and breathe a purer air. Don't be like that; don't deprive yourself of all the different opportunities that arise to lighten the burden of daily life.

Reflecting on infinity and eternity, you will begin to feel that you are floating above all contingencies, that nothing can touch you any more. Distress, sorrow and bereavement no longer have the power to trouble you, for a new consciousness awakens within you and enables you to feel and judge things differently. This state of consciousness which is new to you is that of the Initiates and great Masters: whatever happens to them, whether they are deprived of their rights, betrayed or injured, none of it really affects them; they are above it all. Unfortunately, most human beings cannot understand this; they are accustomed to stagnating on the lowest levels of thoughts and feelings and it is this that makes them so weak. Not knowing how to disentangle themselves, they are perpetually victimized by the negative conditions that they themselves have allowed to take root in them.

Believe me, it is important to learn to use all possible occasions to rise above such a terribly mediocre life. And the star-filled sky in the silence of the night is one such occasion which invites us to forget our earthly affairs for a few minutes and think of other worlds in which other, more highly evolved creatures live in harmony and splendour. All the things we worry so much about mean nothing to them; they are too tiny, too insignificant. You will say, "What? Are you saying that famine and mass murder and all the other cataclysms we experience are insignificant? But they're frightful!" Yes, they are frightful but, in the eyes of Cosmic Intelligence, they are hardly worth mentioning. In the eyes of Cosmic Intelligence, the only events that matter are those that affect the soul and the spirit.

When the sky is clear at night, therefore, get into the habit of gazing at the stars and drinking in the peace that flows so sweetly from a starry sky. Put yourself in touch with each star and you will find that they respond and speak to you like living, intelligent souls. Try to pick out one with which you feel a special affinity and link yourself to it, imagine that you go and talk to it or that it comes and talks to you. The stars are very highly evolved souls. If you listen to them, you will find the solution to many of your problems and feel more peaceful and enlightened.

All the great Initiates learned by contemplating the night sky; when their souls were in communion with the stars, these powerhouses of inexhaustible forces, they received messages from them which they then transmitted to men. We have to learn to read the stars as though we were learning to decipher a sacred scripture of which the stars are the letters. And this cannot be done all at once; it is only after a long time that we begin, little by little, to understand what they have revealed. In fact, even I am only now beginning to understand some of the things that the starry skies whispered to me in the silence of the night. My soul received and recorded those messages and they have been stored safely away ever since.

When I watched the twinkling of the stars, sending signals of light through space to each other, it seemed to me, too, that they were at war with each other—but a war of light and love. And now I know that war will always exist in the universe, for the principle of Mars will always be there (that is, the need to compete, the need to prove oneself stronger than others), but the nature of war and its manifestations will be different. Weapons of death and destruction will be replaced by weapons that shoot rays of light and love. This is what the stars taught me: that it is possible to fight a war of love and light.

Omraam Mikhaël Aïvanhov, *The Path of Silence*

Paradiso, XXXI, 108

Diodorus Siculus tells the story of a god, broken and scattered abroad. What man of us has never felt, walking through the twilight or writing down a date from his past, that he has lost something infinite?

Mankind has lost a face, an irretrievable face, and all have longed to be that pilgrim—imagined in the Empyrean, beneath the Rose—who in Rome sees the Veronica and murmurs in faith, "Lord Jesus, my God, true God, is this then what Thy face was like?"

Beside a road there is a stone face and an inscription that says, "The True Portrait of the Holy Face of the God of Jaén." If we truly knew what it was like, the key to the parables would be ours and we would know whether the son of the carpenter was also the Son of God.

Paul saw it as a light that struck him to the ground; John, as the sun when it shines in all its strength; Teresa de Jesús saw it many times, bathed in tranquil light, yet she was never sure of the color of His eyes.

We lost those features, as one may lose a magic number made up of the usual ciphers, as one loses an image in a kaleidoscope, forever. We may see them and know them not. The profile of a Jew in the subway is perhaps the profile of Christ; perhaps the hands that give us our change at a ticket window duplicate the ones some soldiers nailed one day to the cross.

Perhaps a feature of the crucified face lurks in every mirror; perhaps the face died, was erased, so that God may be all of us.

Who knows but that tonight we may see it in the labyrinth of dreams, and tomorrow not know we saw it.

Jorge Luis Borges, Dreamtigers

Song of One Who Goes On

ABOVE MANANG

What I have left behind
has not left me.
Those I have failed
have not failed me,
and those I have not loved
will love me
even in my worst.

What I have not seen
or failed to see
I leave as gift.

The lands I have not walked
will offer their paths as I sleep.

This earth I have not loved
will hold me
even as I am laid beneath it.

To everything that is
I give everything I am not.

To the life through which
I have walked blindfold,
I give it the sight of my weakness.

To life I give thanks for this:—
one strength through great failure
with marvellous opportunity for all.

David Whyte, *Where Many Rivers Meet*

→ V ←

Death and the Eternal Life

✤ 16 ✦

Death

Krishnamurti wrote that "Death is always there watching, waiting. But the one who dies each day is beyond death." This "dying each day" is a more advanced practice of surrender; we let go of things that are transient, including memory, and empty ourselves in order to live at a higher level—one that touches the infinite.

As we grow older and our bodies age, our minds and our souls expand towards infinity. This letting go of what we have grown into being makes way for the next phase in the evolution of our spirit. It is a challenge to live our lives in preparation for our death, yet we cannot escape it; when others die we partly die too—we are pushed from our conception of mortal life towards the broader perception of immortality, as is illustrated herein with some firsthand accounts.

Thomas Merton points out that if we have chosen life as our code of living, accepting what is and giving to life totally—as opposed to being only half alive, living in death, waiting begrudgingly for the end—then our death becomes just an overture to a further life, a joyful experience beyond. The recent masters of spiritual teaching instruct us to be grateful for the miraculous gift of all life. They tell us to be mindful of the soul's journey towards its destination, of surrendering the self and the body on its way home, of having faith. Endings are always followed by beginnings—we have so much evidence of this, in nature as well as in our own lives. We also have the examples set forth by many masters' lives—the most familiar perhaps being Christ's, with His suffering, death, and resurrection and His promise of eternal life for all in this world.

Death is not free of fear and darkness. Today we have what Thomas Merton terms "a huge inscrutable quantity" of death, through witnessing images of war, of mass murders, of holocausts, violence. We hear about death almost daily in the news. Merton explains that fear of death taken to the extreme becomes hate—and then murder. Fear annihilates faith and hope. It is a hindrance to love, a barrier that keeps us from moving towards new beginnings. If we fear, we believe in only the manifestation of fear. But if we believe in redemption and love, they will be manifested. So, how do we befriend death, how do we transform our fear of it? The fear of death is primarily the fear of the unknown—or as Krishnamurti suggests, "losing the known." Martin Buber writes that what we fear is looking back at our own lives, that moment in the Judaic and Christian faiths known as the Day of Judgement, when we examine our lives, our consciences, and whether or not we have lived the way we wanted to live, or more precisely followed our life purpose.

In this section, I have selected material by people who have spent some time pondering the subject, experiencing the death of others, or who have otherwise advanced spiritual awareness and compassion. One of the most poignant death experiences I have read in my research was that of American psychologist Ken Wilber's devotion to his dying wife, Treya, an extraordinary, eclectic spiritual woman who had suffered cancer for most of their five-year marriage. In his account, Wilber includes Treya's thoughts, poems, and diary entries written during her long sickness and her final surrender, and in doing so he offers a beautiful description of the death process itself, and of a great soul surrendering to the All. Treya's was a conscious death, and her husband's compassion, love, and appreciation of the gift of her life and death is an example of true twin soulship—a relationship never ending.

Alan Watts writes: "By holding his breath, he loses it. By letting go he finds it." We will never know, or even begin to know the great kingdom we go to when we die, but as Hans Küng writes, God is "calling us home." This is the place for our souls to travel to, and we need to yield the breath of this life, to find it.

><

Our whole life should be a meditation of our last and most important decision: the choice between life and death.

We must all die. But the dispositions with which we face death make of our death a choice either of death or of life.

If, during our life we have chosen life, then in death we will pass from death to life. Life is a spiritual thing, and spiritual things are silent. If the spirit that kept the flame of physical life burning in our bodies took care to nourish itself with the oil that is found only in the silence of God's charity, then when the body dies, the spirit itself goes on burning the same oil, with its own flame. But if the spirit has burned all along with the base oils of passion or egoism or pride, then when death comes the flame of the spirit goes out with the light of the body because there is no more oil in the lamp.

We must learn during our lifetime to trim our lamps and fill them with charity in silence, sometimes speaking and confessing the glory of God in order to increase our charity by increasing the charity of others, and teaching them also the ways of peace and of silence.

Thomas Merton, *No Man Is an Island*

Be grateful, in your final hour, for life. Not for your life alone, but for the fact of life: for everything that is.

After all is said and done, I know I will have no answers. None. I don't expect to have them. What I will have, and all I have now, is questions. What I have done—what I have tried to do—is frame those questions—not with question marks—but in the paragraphs of books.

> *... then I Daniel looked and saw—*
> *but what do you care for the grief*
> *of what I Daniel understood by*
> *books the number of the years of desolation?*
> *Confusion of faces, yours among them,*
> *the poetry tangled, no vision of my own to speak of.*
>
> *The hand moved along the wall.*
> *I was able to read, that's all.*

I am still—and will always be—myself alone. But, as myself, I know, now, I am not alone.

Timothy Findley, *Inside Memory*

So to live before death is to live with death; which means that one is living in a timeless world. One is living a life in which everything that one acquires is constantly ending, so that there is always a tremendous movement, one is not fixed in a certain place. This is not a concept. When one invites death, which means the ending of everything that one holds, dying to it, each day, each minute, then one will find—[not "one" there is then no oneself finding it,

because one has gone]—then there is that state of a timeless dimension in
which the movement we know as time, is not. It means the emptying of the
content of one's consciousness so that there is no time; time comes to an end,
which is death.

J. Krishnamurti, *Wholeness of Life*

A Letter from Brooklyn

An old lady writes me in a spidery style,
Each character trembling, and I see a veined hand
Pellucid as paper, travelling on a skein
Of such frail thoughts its thread is often broken;
Or else the filament from which a phrase is hung
Dims to my sense, but caught, it shines like steel,
As touch a line, and the whole web will feel.
She describes my father, yet I forget her face
More easily than my father's yearly dying;
Of her I remember small, buttoned boots and the place
She kept in our wooden church on those Sundays
Whenever her strength allowed;
Grey haired, thin voiced, perpetually bowed.

"I am Mable Rawlins," she writes, "and know both your
    parents";
He is dead, Miss Rawlins, but God bless your tense:
"Your father was a dutiful, honest,
Faithful and useful person."
For such plain praise what fame is recompense?
"A horn-painter, he painted delicately on horn,
He used to sit around the table and paint pictures."
The peace of God needs nothing to adorn
It, nor glory nor ambition.
"He is twenty-eight years buried," she writes, "he was
    called home,
And is, I am sure, doing greater work."

The strength of one frail hand in a dim room
Somewhere in Brooklyn, patient and assured,
Restores my sacred duty to the Word.
"Home, home," she can write, with such short time to live,

Alone as she spins the blessings of her years;
Not withered of beauty if she can bring such tears,
Nor withdrawn from the world that breaks its lovers so;
Heaven is to her the place where painters go,
All who bring beauty on frail shell or horn,
There was all made, thence their *lux-mundi* drawn,
Drawn, drawn, till the thread is resilient steel,
Lost though it seems in darkening periods,
And there they return to do work that is God's.

So this old lady writes, and again I believe,
I believe it all, and for no man's death I grieve.

Derek Walcott, *Collected Poems 1948–1984*

"Death is going home, yet people are afraid of what will come so they do not want to die. If we do, if there is no mystery, we will not be afraid. There is also the question of conscience 'I could have done better.' Very often as we live, so we die. Death is nothing but a continuation of life, the completion of life. The surrendering of the human body. But the heart and the soul live for ever. They do not die. Every religion has got eternity—another life; this life is not the end; people who believe it is, fear death. If it was properly explained that death was nothing but going home to God, then there would be no fear."
Mother Teresa, in Desmond Doig, *Mother Teresa*

What Is Death?

One has known of thousands of deaths—the death of someone very close or the death of masses through the atomic bomb—Hiroshima and all the horrors that man has perpetrated on other human beings in the name of peace and in the pursuit of ideologies. So, without any ideology, without any conclusion, one asks: What is death? What is the thing that dies—that terminates? One sees that if there is something that is continuous it becomes mechanical. If there is an ending to everything there is a new beginning. If one is afraid then one cannot possibly find out what this immense thing called death is. It must be the most extraordinary thing. To find out what death is one must also enquire into what life is before death. One never does that. One never enquires what living is. Death is inevitable; but what is living? Is this living, this enormous suffering, fear, anxiety, sorrow, and all the rest of it—is this living? Clinging to that one is afraid of death. If one does not know what living is one cannot know what death is—they go together. If one can find out what the full meaning of living is, the totality of living, the wholeness of living, then one is capable of understanding the wholeness of death. But one usually enquires into the meaning of death without enquiring into the meaning of life.

When one asks: What is the meaning of life?—one immediately has conclusions. One says it is this; one gives it a significance according to one's conditioning. If one is an idealist, one gives life an ideological significance; again, according to one's conditioning, according to what one has read and so on. But if one is not giving a particular significance to life, if one is not saying life is this or something else, then one is free, free of ideologies, of systems, political, religious or social. So, before one enquires into the meaning of death one is asking what living is. Is the life one is living, living? The constant struggle with each other? Trying to understand each other? Is living according to a book, according to some psychologists, according to some orthodoxy, living?

If one banishes all that, totally, then one will begin with "what is." "What is" is that our living has become a tremendous torture, a tremendous battle between human beings, man, woman, neighbour—whether close or far. It is a conflict in which there is occasional freedom to look at the blue sky, to see something lovely and enjoy it and be happy for a while; but the cloud of struggle soon returns. All this we call living; going to church with all the traditional repetition, or the new English reception, accepting certain ideologies. This is what one calls living and one is so committed to it one accepts it. But discontentment has its significance—real discontent. Discontent is a flame and one suppresses it by childish acts, by momentary satisfactions; but discontent when you let it flower, arise, it burns away everything that is not true.

Can one live a life that is whole, not fragmented?—a life in which thought does not divide as the family, the office, the church, this and that and death so divided off that when it comes one is appalled by it, one is shocked by it so that one's mind is incapable of meeting it because one has not lived a total life.

Death comes and with that one cannot argue; one cannot say: "Wait a few minutes more"—it is there. When it comes, can the mind meet the end of everything while one is living, while one has vitality and energy, while one is full of life? When one's life is not wasted in conflicts and worries one is full of energy, clarity. Death means the ending of all that one knows, of all one's attachments, of one's bank accounts, of all one's attainments—there is a complete ending. Can the mind, while living, meet such a state? Then one will understand the full meaning of what death is. If one clings to the idea of "me," that me which one believes must continue, the me that is put together by thought, including the me in which one believes there is the higher consciousness, the supreme consciousness, then one will not understand what death is in life.

Thought lives in the known; it is the outcome of the known; if there is not freedom from the known one cannot possibly find out what death is, which is the ending of everything, the physical organism with all its ingrained habits, the identification with the body, with the name, with all the memories it has acquired. One cannot carry it all over when one goes to death. One cannot carry there all one's money; so, in the same way one has to end in life everything that one knows. That means there is absolute aloneness; not loneliness but aloneness, in the sense there is nothing else but that state of mind that is completely whole. Aloneness means all one.

J. Krishnamurti, Wholeness of Life

Death is a silent yet eloquent teacher of truth. Death is a teacher that speaks openly and yet is [not] easily heard. Death is very much present in our modern world: and yet it has become an enigma to that world. Instead of understanding death, it would seem that our world simply multiplies it. Death becomes a huge, inscrutable *quantity*. The mystery of death, more terrible and sometimes more cruel than ever, remains incomprehensible to men who, though they know they must die, retain a grim and total attachment to individual life as if they could be physically indestructible.

Perhaps it is this failure to understand and to face the fact of death that helps beget so many wars and so much violence. As if men, attached to individual bodily life, thought they could protect themselves against death by inflicting it on others.

Death cannot be understood without *compassion*. Compassion teaches me that when my brother dies, I too die. Compassion teaches me that my brother and I are one. That if I love my brother, then my love benefits my own life as well, and if I hate my brother and seek to destroy him, I destroy myself also. The desire to kill is like the desire to attack another with an ingot of red hot iron: I have to pick up the incandescent metal and burn my own hand while burning the other. Hate itself is the seed of death in my own heart, while it seeks the death of the other. Love is the seed of life in my own heart when it seeks the good of the other.

Thomas Merton, Preface to the Vietnamese edition
of No Man Is an Island

The process of dying seems to be an expansion beyond the forms in which it has always been measured. The following is a scenario for the physical experience of dying as based on the ancient concepts of the body being composed of the four elements of earth, water, fire, and air, as felt within the aggregate of form:

> As death approaches the earth element, the feeling of the solidity and hardness of the body, begins to melt. The body seems very heavy. The boundaries of the body, its edge, are less solid. There is not so much a feeling of being "in" the body. One is less sensitive to impressions and feelings. One can no longer move the limbs at will. Peristalsis slows, the bowels no longer move without aid. The organs begin to shut down. As the earth element continues to dissolve into the water element there is a feeling of flowingness, a liquidity, as the solidity that has always intensified identification with the body begins to melt, a feeling of fluidity.
>
> As the water element begins to dissolve into the fire element, the feeling of fluidity becomes more like a warm mist. The bodily fluids begin to slow, the mouth and eyes become dry, circulation slows, blood pressure drops. As the circulation begins to thicken and stop, blood settles in the lowest extremities. A feeling of lightness ensues.
>
> As the fire element dissolves into the air element, feelings of warmth and cold dissipate, physical comfort and discomfort no longer have meaning. The body temperature drops until it reaches a stage where the body begins to cool and becomes pale. Digestion stops. A feeling of lightness, as of heat rising, becomes predominant. A feeling of dissolving into yet subtler and subtler boundarylessness.
>
> As the air element dissolves into consciousness itself there is a feeling of edgelessness. The out breath having become longer than the in breath has dissolved into space and there is no longer the experience of bodily form or function but just a sense of vast expanding airiness, a dissolving into pure being.

It will be noticed that each stage is accompanied by less solidity, the edges less defined; less external input is received and there is an increasing feeling of boundarylessness. Death or the process or dying seems to be accompanied by a sense of expanding beyond oneself, of dissolving out of form, of melting into the undifferentiated.

But imagine attempting to resist this dissolution, this feeling of edges melting away. Imagine trying to hold on to the solidity as it melts into the fluidity. Of trying to push against that liquidity, to grasp back at something solid, only to experience the fluidity become lighter and more flowing as it dissolves into the fire element, feeling the temperatures of the body cool and, like heat dissipating, to melt into the vastness of space as the air element and the energy expand and dissolve into consciousness itself. Imagine trying to push against this, trying to halt the incessant progression of this process. If you go with it, opening into it, there is an experience of expansion, a melting out of solidity, a dissolving into the underlying reality. Imagine trying to hold on to that which is melting away. Perhaps this is what some call purgatory. The hellish holding back from the next unfolding, resistance to what is?

All apparently come to a point where they are evaporating out of the body and the body must be left behind. All experience the elements merging into their essential energy. Their separate qualities of solidity, fluidity, temperature, and flow are no longer predominant and there is just consciousness floating free. For a few moments, awareness shines more brilliantly than a thousand suns and there is the experience of the one reality out of which all creation arises. The duration of the experience of the light seems to vary for different people, perhaps depending upon the willingness to open into the truth and the trust and reverence in which you hold your original nature.

Stephen Levine, *Who Dies?*

Death is not at all what you believe it to be. You expect from death the natural quietness of an unconscious rest. But to obtain that rest you must prepare for it.

When you die you lose only your body and at the same time the possibilities of relation with and action on the material world. But all that belongs to the vital world does not disappear with the material substance; all your desires, attachments, cravings persist with the sense of frustration and disappointment, and all that prevents you from finding the expected peace. To enjoy a peaceful and eventless death you must prepare for it. And the only effective preparation is the abolition of desires.

So long as we have a body we have to act, to work, to do something: but if we do it simply because it has to be done, without seeking for the result or wanting it to be like this or like that, we get progressively detached and thus prepare ourselves for a restful death.

The Mother, *Words of the Mother*, Part Two

If you are mindful of death, it will not come as a surprise—you will not be anxious. You will feel that death is merely like changing your clothes. Consequently, at that point you will be able to maintain your calmness of mind.

The Dalai Lama, *A Policy of Kindness*

In the Eastern tradition, the state of your consciousness at the last moment of life is so crucial that you spend your whole life preparing for that moment. We've had many assassinations in our culture, and we wonder what it was like for Bobby Kennedy or Jack Kennedy—if they had any thought, and what those thoughts might have been. "Oh, I've been shot!" or "He did it," or "Goodbye," or "Get him," or "Forgive him." Mahatma Gandhi walked out into a garden to give a press conference when a gunman shot him three or four times, but as he was falling, the only thing that came out of his mouth was, "Ram...." The name of God. He was ready!

At the moment of death if we let go lightly, we go out into the light, towards the One, towards God. The only thing that died, after all, was another set of thoughts of who we were this time around.

Ram Dass, Grist for the Mill

Death does not mean an end of all effort. The Eternal Law which we term God will be a mockery, if death were the end of such an effort. "Hereafter" is a mystery into which we may not peep. We should have enough faith to know that death, after life truly lived, is but a prelude to a better and richer life.

Now for Ram Rajya. It can be religiously translated as Kingdom of God on Earth; politically translated, it is perfect democracy in which, inequalities based on possession and non-possession, colour, race or creed or sex vanish; in it, land and State belong to the people, justice is prompt, perfect and cheap and, therefore, there is freedom of worship, speech and the Press—all this because of the reign of the self-imposed law of moral restraint.

Such a State must be based on truth and non-violence and must consist of prosperous, happy and self-contained villages and village communities. It is a dream that may never be realized. I find happiness in living in that dreamland, ever trying to realize it in the quickest way.

Mahatma Gandhi, from "The Hindu," June 12, 1945,
in Gandhi in India, 1944–1948

For a Radiant Star

> Dazed, uncertain, hesitating,
> Wings still damp, bent, unfolded,
> As if still molded
> By darkness, change, confusion,
> Bound still
> In the emptied chrysalis.

The air stirs.
I tremble,
Feel still within that mold,
Shaped by a form I now
Vaguely sense
Is hollow, empty, spent,
Its work complete.

I only need to move—
One step, another, tentative,
And wait.

Feel the air dry this strange new form,
Watch tissue thin patterns of gold, black, orange,
Unfold into readiness,
Unfurl into openness,
As the air takes me,
Lifts me
Into surprise.

I know not what to do
Yet giddy with instinct
Throw myself out,
Caught by a current unseen,
Swoop low, glide high, dive
Into surrender.

A chrysalis stands now empty,
Drying in the sun,
Constraints forgotten by the life once served.

One day, perhaps, a child will come,
Will ask its mother,
"What strange creature one day lived
In such a tiny home?"

(Treya, 1974)

And so began the most extraordinary forty-eight hours of our life together. Treya had decided to die. There was no medical reason for her to die at this point. With medication and modest supports, her doctors felt she could live another several months at least, albeit in a hospital, and yes, then she would die. But Treya had made up her mind. She was not going to die like that, in a hospital, with tubes coming out of her and continuous IV morphine drip and the inevitable pneumonia and slow suffocation—all the horrible images that had gone through my mind at Drachenfels. And I had the strangest feeling that, whatever else her reasons, Treya was going to spare all of us that ordeal. She would simply bypass all that, thank you very much, and die peacefully now. But whatever her reasons, I knew that once Treya had made up her mind, then it was done.

I put Treya in bed that evening, and sat down next to her. She had become almost ecstatic. "I'm going, I can't believe it, I'm going. I'm so happy, I'm so happy, I'm so happy." Like a mantra of final release, she kept repeating, "I'm so happy, I'm so happy...."

Her entire countenance lit up. She glowed. And right in front of my eyes her body began to change. Within one hour, it looked to me as if she lost ten pounds. It was as if her body, acquiescing to her will, began to shrink and draw in on itself. She began to shut down her vital systems; she began to die. Within that hour, she was a different being, ready and willing to leave. She was very determined about this, and she was very happy. Her ecstatic response was infectious, and I found myself sharing in her joy, much to my confusion.

Then, rather abruptly, she said, "But I don't want to leave you. I love you so much. I can't leave you. I love you so much." She began crying, sobbing, and I began crying, sobbing, as well. I felt like I was crying all the tears of the past five years, deep tears I had held back in order to be strong for Treya. We talked at length of our love for each other, a love that had made both of us—it sounds corny—a love that had made both of us stronger, and better, and wiser. Decades of growth had gone into our care for each other, and now, faced with the conclusion of it all, we were both overwhelmed. It sounds so dry, but it was the tenderest moment I have ever known, with the only person with whom I could ever have known it.

"Honey, if it's time to go, then it's time to go. Don't worry, I'll find you. I found you before, I promise I'll find you again. So if you want to go, don't worry. Just go."

"You promise you'll find me?"

"I promise."

I should explain that, during the last two weeks, Treya had almost obsessively been going over what I had said to her on the way to our wedding ceremony, five years earlier. I had whispered in her ear: "Where have you been? I've been searching for you for lifetimes. I finally found you. I had to slay dragons to find you, you know. And if anything happens, I will find you again." She looked profoundly at peace. "You promise?" "I promise."

I have no conscious idea why I said that; I was simply stating, for reasons I did not understand, exactly how I felt about our relationship. And it was to this exchange that Treya returned time and again during the last weeks. It seemed to give her a tremendous sense of safety. The world was OK if I kept my promise.

And so she said, at that point, "You promise you'll find me?"

"I promise."

"Forever and forever?"

"Forever and forever."

"Then I can go. I can't believe it. I'm so happy. This has been much harder than I ever thought. It's been so hard. Honey, it's been so hard." "I know, sweetheart, I know." "But now I can go. I'm so happy. I love you so much. I'm so happy."

That night I slept on the acupuncture table in her room. It seems to me that I dreamt of a great luminous cloud of white light, hovering over the house, like the light of a thousand suns blazing on a snowcapped mountain. I say "it seems to me," because now I'm not sure whether it was a dream or not.

When I looked at her early the next morning (Sunday), she had just awoken. Her eyes were clear, she was very alert, and she was very determined: "I'm going. I'm so happy. You'll be there?"

"I'll be there, kid. Let's do it. Let's go."

I called the family. I don't remember exactly what I said, but it was something like, please come as soon as you can. I called Warren, the dear friend who had been helping Treya with acupuncture for the last few months. Again, I don't remember what I said. But I think that my tone said, It's dying time.

The family began arriving fairly early that day, and each member had a chance to have a last open talk with Treya. What I remember most was her saying how much she loved her family; how incredibly fortunate she felt to have each of them; how they were the best family anyone could want. It was as if Treya were determined to "come clean" with every single family member; she was going to burn as clean as ashes, with no unspoken lines left in her body, with no guilt and no blame. As far as I can tell, she succeeded.

We put her to bed that night—Sunday night—and again I slept on her acupuncture table so I could be there if anything happened. Something extraordinary seemed to be going on in that house, and we all knew it.

About 3:30 that morning, Treya awoke abruptly. The atmosphere was almost hallucinogenic. I awoke immediately, and asked how she was. "Is it morphine time?" she said with a smile. In her entire ordeal with cancer, except for surgery, Treya had taken a sum total of four morphine tablets.

"Sure, sweetie, whatever you want." I gave her a morphine tablet and a mild sleeping pill, and we had our last conversation.

"Sweetie, I think it's time to go," she began.

"I'm here, honey."

"I'm so happy." Long pause. "This world is so weird. It's just so weird. But I'm going." Her mood was one of joy, and humor, and determination.

I began repeating several of the "pith phrases" from the religious traditions that she considered so important, phrases that she had wanted me to remind her of right up to the end, phrases she had carried with her on her flash cards.

"Relax with the presence of what is," I began. "Allow the self to uncoil in the vast expanse of all space. Your own primordial mind is unborn and undying; it was not born with this body and it will not die with this body. Recognize your own mind as eternally one with Spirit."

Her faced relaxed, and she looked at me very clearly and directly.

"You'll find me?"

"I promise."

"Then it's time to go."

There was a very long pause, and the room seemed to me to become entirely luminous, which was strange, given how utterly dark it was. It was the most sacred moment, the most direct moment, the simplest moment I have ever known. The most obvious. The most perfectly obvious. I had never seen anything like this in my life. I did not know what to do. I was simply present for Treya.

She moved toward me, trying to gesture, trying to say something, something she wanted me to understand, the last thing she told me. "You're the greatest man I've ever known," she whispered. "You're the greatest man I've ever known. My champion..." She kept repeating it: "My champion." I leaned forward to tell her that she was the only really enlightened person I had ever known. That enlightenment made sense to me because of her. That a universe that had produced Treya was a sacred universe. That God existed because of her. All these things went through my mind. All these things I wanted to say. I knew she was aware how I felt, but my throat had closed in on itself; I couldn't speak; I wasn't crying, I just couldn't speak. I croaked out only, "I'll find you, honey, I will...."

Treya closed her eyes, and for all purposes, she never opened them again.

My heart broke. Da Free John's phrase kept running through my mind: "Practice the wound of love... practice the wound of love." Real love hurts; real love makes you totally vulnerable and open; real love will take you far beyond yourself; and therefore real love will devastate you. I kept thinking, if love does not shatter you, you do not know love. We had both been practicing the wound of love, and I was shattered. Looking back on it, it seems to me that in that simple and direct moment, we both died.

It was at that moment that I began to notice that the atmosphere had become very turbulent. It took me several minutes to realize that it wasn't my distress or my grief that seemed to be so disturbing. It was the wind blowing wildly outside the house. And not just blowing. The wind began whipping up a ferocious storm; our ordinarily rock-solid house was shaking and rattling in the gale-force winds that hammered the house at exactly that moment. In fact, the newspapers reported the next day that at exactly four o'clock that morning, record-breaking winds—reaching up to an incredible 115 miles an hour—began to whip through Boulder (though inexplicably, no place else in Colorado). The winds overturned cars—and even an airplane!—all of which was duly reported in the headlines of the papers the next day.

The winds, I suppose, were coincidence. Nonetheless, the constant rattling and shaking of the house simply added to the feeling that something unearthly was happening. I remember trying to go back to sleep, but the house was rattling so hard I got up and put some blankets around the windows in the bedroom, fearing they would shatter. I finally drifted off, thinking, "Treya is dying, nothing is permanent, everything is empty, Treya is dying...."

The next morning, Treya settled into the position in which she would die—propped up on pillows, arms at her sides, mala in her hand. The night before she had begun repeating silently to herself "Om Mani Padme Hung," the Buddhist mantra of compassion, and "Surrender to God," her favorite Christian prayer. I believe she continued to do so.

We had invited a member of the Hospice movement to come by and work with us, and in due course—around eleven that morning—Claire arrived. I personally had wanted a Hospice member to come by because I wanted to make sure that we were doing everything possible to ensure that Treya could die painlessly and in peace, in her own bed, in her own way.

Claire was perfect. Looking very like a beautiful and peaceful angel (so beatific that Kati unconsciously kept referring to her as "Grace Dawn"), she entered the room and announced to Treya that, if it was OK with her, she was going to take her vital signs. "Treya," she said, "is it all right if I take your blood pressure?" I don't think Claire thought Treya would actually answer. The point, rather, was that Hospice members are taught that the dying person can hear quite clearly everything you say right up to the end, and perhaps beyond, so Claire extended this elemental courtesy to Treya. Treya herself had not really spoken anything for several hours. But when Claire asked that simple question, Treya abruptly turned her head (eyes still closed) and very clearly said, "Sure." From that point on, everybody knew that Treya, "unconscious" as she was, was in fact fully aware of everything that was happening.

(At one point, Kati, who like all of us had assumed Treya was "unconscious," looked at me and said, "Ken she is so beautiful." Treya said very clearly, "Thank you." Those were her last words—"Thank you.")

The wind continued to howl, rattling the house severely. The family members maintained their vigil. Sue, Rad, Kati, Tracy, David, Mary Lamar, Michael, Warren—all touched Treya and many whispered final words to her.

Treya held her mala, a mala she had gotten at a meditation retreat with Kalu Rinpoche, a retreat in which she had taken a vow to practice compassion as her path to enlightenment. The spiritual name given to her at that time, by Kalu himself, was "Dakini Wind" (which means, "the wind of enlightenment").

By two o'clock that afternoon (Monday), Treya had ceased to respond overtly to any stimuli. Her eyes were closed; her breathing was following a pattern of apnea (shallow gasps with long pauses); her limbs had become cold. Claire took us aside and said that she thought Treya would die very soon, possibly within hours. She said she would return if at all necessary, and with the kindest of wishes, left us.

The afternoon stretched on; the winds continued rattling the house and contributing to the eeriest atmosphere. For hours I held Treya's hand and kept whispering in her ear: "Treya, you can go now. Everything here is complete and finished. Just let go, just let it happen. We're all here, honey, just let it happen."

(Then, uncontrollably, I began laughing to myself, thinking: "Treya has never done anything anybody ever told her to do. Maybe I should quit saying all this; she'll never let go if I don't shut up.")

I continued with her favorite pith phrases: "Move toward the Light, Treya. Look for the five-pointed cosmic star, luminous and radiant and free. Hold to the Light, sweetheart, just hold to the Light. Let go of us, hold to the Light."

I should mention that, in the year of Treya's fortieth birthday, a teacher of both of us, Da Free John, began saying that the ultimate enlightened vision was when one saw the five-pointed cosmic star, or cosmic mandala, pure and white and radiant, utterly beyond all finite limitations. Treya didn't know this was said at that time, but nonetheless that is exactly when she changed her name from Terry to Estrella, or Treya, which is Spanish for star. And it is held that, at the precise moment of death, the great five-pointed cosmic star, or the clear light void, or simply great Spirit or luminous Godhead, appears to every soul. It is my own belief that this vision had appeared to Treya some three years earlier—it had done so in a dream she told me of, right after an empowerment with the Very Venerable Kalu Rinpoche—the vision was unmistakable, and accompanied by all the classic signs, though she told no one of it. She did not change her name to "Treya" because Free John had talked about this ultimate vision; she had simply had this vision, of the luminous cosmic star, in a very real and direct way. Thus upon actual death, I thought to myself, Treya would simply be seeing her own Original Face, and not for the first time. She would simply be experiencing, once again, her own true nature as luminosity, as radiant star.

The only piece of jewelry she really valued was the five-pointed gold star pendant that Sue and Rad had made for her (based on a drawing Treya had made of exactly that vision). I thought to myself, about that star pendant, that it was, in the words of a Christian mystic, "The outward and visible sign of an inward and invisible grace." She died with it on.

I think everybody realized that their letting go of Treya was crucial to the process, and in their own individual ways, each person released her. I would like to report what transpired in those moments, as family members touched Treya, and softly talked to her, because everybody acted with such dignity and grace. I think that Treya would want me at least to say that Rad,, who was beside himself with grief, touched her ever so gently on the forehead, and said, "You are the best daughter I could ever want." And Sue: "I love you so much."

I stepped out to get a drink of water, and suddenly Tracy was there, saying, "Ken, get up there immediately." I ran upstairs, jumped on the bed, grabbed Treya's hand. The entire family—every single member, and good friend Warren—made it into the room. Treya opened her eyes, looked very softly at everybody there, looked directly at me, closed her eyes, and quit breathing.

Everybody in the room was completely there and present for Treya. Then the entire room began to cry. I was holding her hand, with my other hand over her heart. My body began to shake violently. It had finally happened. I could not stop shaking. I whispered in her ear the few key phrases from the Book of the Dead ("Recognize the clear light as your own primordial Mind, recognize you are now one with Enlightened Spirit"). But mostly we all cried.

The best, the strongest, the most enlightened, the most honest, the most beautiful, the most inspiring, the most virtuous, the most cherished person I had ever known, had just died. Somehow, I felt that the universe would never be the same.

Exactly five minutes after her death, Michael said, "Listen. Listen to that." The gale-force winds had completely ceased blowing, and the atmosphere was a perfect calm.

This, too, was dutifully noted in the next day's papers, right to the exact minute. The ancients have a saying: "When a great soul dies, the winds go wild." The greater the soul, the greater the wind necessary to carry it away. Perhaps it was all coincidence, but I couldn't help thinking: A great, great soul had died, and the wind responded.

In the last six months of her life, it was as if Treya and I went into spiritual overdrive for each other, serving each other in every way that we could. I finally quit the bitching and moaning that is so normal for a support person, a bitching and moaning that came from the fact that I had, for five years, set aside my career in order to serve her. I just dropped all that. I had absolutely no regrets; I had only gratitude for her presence, and for the extraordinary grace of serving her. And she quit the bitching and moaning about how her cancer had "wrecked" my life. For the simple fact was, we together had made a pact, on some profound level, to see her through this ordeal, come what may. It was a profound choice. We were both very, very, very clear about this, particularly during the last six months. We simply and directly served each other, exchanging self for other, and *therefore* glimpsing that eternal Spirit which transcends both self and, other, both "me" and "mine."

"I've always loved you," she began on an occasion about three months before she died, "but recently you have changed in very profound ways. Have you noticed?"

"Yes."

"What is it?"

There was a long pause. This was the period right after I had come back from the Dzogchen retreat, but that wasn't the main cause for the change she had noted. "I don't know, kid. I love you, so I'm serving you. It seems very straightforward, don't you think?"

"There's an awareness about you that has kept me going for months. What is it?" She kept repeating, as if it were very important, "What is it?" And I had the strangest feeling that it wasn't a question, really, but more of a test, which I did not understand.

"I think it's just that I'm here for you, sweetheart. I'm here."

"You're why I'm alive," she finally said, and it wasn't a comment about me. The point was that we kept each other going, and we became each other's teacher during those last extraordinary months. My continued service to Treya generated in her almost overwhelming feelings of gratitude and kindness, and the love she had for me in return began to saturate my being. I became completely full because of Treya. It was as if we were mutually generating in each other the enlightened compassion that we had both studied for so long. I felt like years, maybe lifetimes, of karma was being burned out of me in my continued response to her needs. And in her love and compassion for me, Treya also became completely full. There were no empty places in her soul, no corners left untouched by love, not a shadow in her heart.

I'm no longer sure exactly what "enlightenment" means. I prefer to think in terms of "enlightened understanding" or "enlightened presence" or "enlightened awareness." I know what that means, and I think I can recognize that. And it was unmistakable in Treya. I'm not saying this simply because she is gone. That is *exactly* how I came to see it, over those last few months, when she met suffering and death with a pure and simple presence, a presence that outshone her pain, a presence that clearly announced what she was. I saw that enlightened presence, unmistakably.

And those who were with her in those last few months, they saw it, too.

I had arranged for Treya's body to remain undisturbed for twenty-four hours. About an hour after her death, we all left the room, mostly to compose ourselves. Because Treya had propped herself up for the last twenty-four hours, her mouth had hung open for almost a day. Consequently, due to insipient rigor, her jaw was locked in an open position. We tried to close her jaw before we left, but it wouldn't shut; it was locked tight. I continued whispering "pith sayings" to her, then we all left the room.

About forty-five minutes later, we went back into the room, only to be met with a stunning vision: Treya had closed her mouth, and there appeared instead on her face an extraordinary smile, a smile of utter contentment, peace, fulfillment, release. Nor was it a standard "rigor smile"—the lines were entirely and totally different. She looked exactly like a beautiful Buddha statue, smiling the smile of complete release. The lines that had been deeply etched on her face—lines of suffering and exhaustion and pain—had all completely disappeared. Her face was pure, smooth, without wrinkles or lines of any sort, radiant, glowing. It was so profound that we were all taken aback. But there she was, smiling, glowing, radiant, content. I couldn't help it, I kept saying out loud, as I gently leaned over her body, "Treya, look at you! Treya, honey, look at you!"

That smile of contentment and release remained on her face for the entire twenty-four hour period that she was left in her bed. Her body was finally moved, but I think that smile is etched on her soul for eternity.

Everybody went up and said goodbye to her that evening. I stayed up that night and read to her until three that morning. I read her favorite religious passages (Suzuki Roshi, Ramana Maharshi, Kalu, St. Teresa, St. John, Norbu, Trungpa, the *Course*); I repeated her favorite Christian prayer ("Surrender to God"); I performed her favorite sadhana or spiritual practice (Chenrezi, the Buddha of compassion); and most of all I read to her the essential pointing-out instructions from the Book of the Dead. (These I read to her forty-nine times. The essence of these instructions is that, to put it in Christian terms, the time of death is the time that you shed your physical body and individual ego, and become one with absolute Spirit or God. Recognizing the radiance and luminosity that naturally dawns at the time of death is thus to recognize your own awareness as eternally enlightened, or one with Godhead. You simply repeat these instructions to the person, over and over again, with the very likely assumption that their soul can still hear you. And so this I did.)

I may be imagining all this, but I swear that, on the third reading of the essential instructions for recognizing that your soul is one with God, something audibly clicked in the room. I actually ducked. I had the distinct and palpable feeling, at that utterly dark 2:00 a.m., that she directly recognized her own true nature and burned clean. In other words, that she acknowledged, upon hearing, the great liberation or enlightenment that had always been hers. That she had dissolved cleanly into All Space, mixing with the entire universe, just like in her experience as a thirteen-year-old, just like in her meditations, just like she hoped she would upon final death.

I don't know, maybe I'm imagining this. But knowing Treya, maybe I'm not.

Some months later I was reading a highly revered text of Dzogchen which describes the stages of dying. And it listed two physical signs that indicated that the person had recognized their own True Nature and had become one with luminous Spirit—that they had dissolved cleanly into All Space. The two signs?

> *If you remain in the Ground Luminosity,*
> *As a sign of that, your complexion will be nice...*
> *And it is taught also that your mouth will be smiling.*

I stayed in Treya's room that night. When I finally fell asleep, I had a dream. But it wasn't a dream, it was more of a simple image: a raindrop fell into the ocean, thus becoming one with the all. At first I thought that this meant Treya had become enlightened, that Treya was the drop that had become one with the ocean of enlightenment. And that made sense.

But then I realized it was more profound than that: I was the drop, and Treya the ocean. She had not been released—she was *already* so. Rather, it was I who had been released, by the simple virtue of serving her.

And there, there it was: that was exactly why she had so insistently asked me to promise that I would find her. It wasn't that she needed me to find her;

it was that, through my promise to her, she would therefore find me, and help me, yet again, and again, and again. I had it all backwards: I thought my promise was how I would help her, whereas it was actually how she would reach and help me, again, and again, and forever again, as long as it took for me to awaken, as long as it took for me to acknowledge, as long as it took for me to realize the Spirit that she had come so clearly to announce. And by no means just me: Treya came for all her friends, for her family, and especially for those stricken with terrible illness. For all of this, Treya was present.

Twenty-four hours later, I kissed her forehead, and we all said goodbye. Treya, still smiling, was taken for cremation. But "goodbye" is the wrong word. Perhaps *au revoir*—"till we meet again"—or *aloha*—"goodbye/hello" —would be better.

Rick Fields, a good friend of both Treya and myself, wrote a very simple poem upon hearing of her death. Somehow, it seemed to say it all:

First we're not here
Then we are
Then we're not

You looked into
Our coming and going
Face to Face

Longer than most of us
With more courage and grace
Than I have ever seen

And you smiled
All the way—

This is no hyperbole, it is a simple statement of fact: I have never known anyone who knew Treya who did not think that she had more integrity and honesty than any person they had ever known. Treya's integrity was absolute, unimpeachable by even the meanest of circumstances, and overwhelming to virtually all who knew her.

I don't think any of us will ever actually meet Treya again. I don't think it works that way. That's much too concrete and literal. Rather, it is my own deepest feeling that every time you and I—and any who knew her—that every time we act from a position of integrity, and honesty, and strength, and compassion: every time we do that, now and forever, we unmistakenly meet again the mind and soul of Treya.

So my promise to Treya—the only promise that she made me repeat over and over—my promise that I would find her again really meant that I had promised to find my own enlightened Heart.

And I know, in those last six months, that I did so. I know that I found the cave of enlightenment, where I was married, by grace, and where I died, by grace. This was the change that had come over me that Treya had noticed, and about which she kept saying, "What is it?" The fact is, she knew exactly what it was. She simply wanted to know if I did. ("And as for the Heart, it is Brahman, it is All. And the couple, now one, having died to themselves, live life eternal.")

And I know, in those last few moments of death itself, and during the night that followed, when Treya's luminosity overwhelmed my soul, and outshone the finite world forever, that it all became perfectly clear to me. There are no lies left in my soul, because of Treya. And Treya, honey, dear sweet Treya, I promise to find you forever and forever and forever in my Heart, as the simple awareness of what is.

Treya's ashes came back to us, and we had a simple passing-over ceremony.

Ken McLeod read passages on the development of compassion, which Treya had studied under Kalu's guidance. Roger Walsh read selections on forgiveness from *A Course in Miracles*, which Treya had practiced daily. These two themes—compassion and forgiveness—had become the path that Treya most valued as the way to express her own enlightenment.

Then Sam performed the final ceremony, during the course of which a picture of Treya was burned, representing a final letting-go. Sam (or as Treya called him, "dearest Sammy") was the only person that Treya had wanted to perform this ceremony.

Some there spoke final words of remembrance about Treya, and some remained in silence. Twelve-year-old Chloe, Steve and Linda's daughter, wrote this for the ceremony:

> *Treya, my guardian angel, you were a star on earth and gave us all warmth and light, but every star must die to be born again, this time in the heavens above, dwelling with the eternal lightness of the soul. I know you are dancing upon the clouds right now, and I'm lucky enough to feel your joy, feel your smile. I look at the sky and I know you're shining, with your brilliant, radiant soul.*
>
> *I love you Treya and I know I'll miss you here, but I'm so happy for you! You have shed your body and your pains, and are able to dance the dance of true life, and that is the life of the soul. I can dance with you in my dreams, and in my heart. So, you are not dead, your soul still lives, lives on a higher plane, and in your loved ones' hearts.*

You've taught me the most important lesson, what life and love is.
Love is complete and sincere respect for another being...
It is the ecstasy of the true self...
Love extends beyond all planes and is limitless....
After a million lives, and a million deaths it still lives...
And it only dwells in the heart and soul...
Life is of the soul, and of nothing else...
Love and laughter ride with it, but so do pain and anguish...

WHEREVER I GO
AND WHATEVER I SEE
IN MY HEART AND SOUL
YOU'LL ALWAYS BE WITH ME

I looked at Sam, and I found myself saying to those assembled:

"Not many people remember that it was here in Boulder that I proposed to Treya. We were living in San Francisco at the time, but I brought Treya here to meet Sam, to see what he thought. After meeting with Treya for just a few minutes, Sam laughed and said something like, Not only do I approve, I'm worried about her getting shortchanged. I proposed to Treya that night, and she said only, 'If you didn't ask me, I was going to ask you.' And so, in a very special sense, our life together began here, in Boulder, with Sammy, and it ended here, in Boulder, with Sammy."

We would eventually have a memorial for Treya in San Francisco—with remembrances spoken by Vicky Wells, Roger Walsh, Frances Vaughan, Ange Stephens, Joan Steffy, Judith Skutch, and Huston Smith—and in Aspen—with eulogies by Steve and Linda and Chloe Conger, Tom and Cathy Crum, Amory Lovins, Father Michael Abdo, and the monks from Snowmass Monastery. But somehow Sam summarized it all in just two sentences that day:

"Treya was the strongest person I have ever known. She taught us how to live, and she taught us how to die."

In the following days, letters began to arrive. What struck me most was how many of them reported essentially the same events that I have recorded here. It seemed to me, perhaps in my grief, that maybe hundreds of people had participated in the remarkable events of those last two days.

Here is a letter from my family—a poem, actually, that an aunt had sent to me. ("This is a favored poem and symbolic of Treya we think, and one day we will all be reunited. Of this we are absolutely sure.")

I found, in all the letters, a repeating of the words "wind," and "radiance," and "sunlight," and "star." I kept thinking: How did they know?

The "favored poem . . . symbolic of Treya," my aunt had sent to me, was very simple:

> Do not stand at my grave and weep;
> I am not there. I do not sleep.
> I am a thousand winds that blow;
> I am the diamond glints on snow.
> I am the sunlight on ripened grain;
> I am the gentle autumn's rain.
> When you awake in morning's hush,
> I am the swift uplifting rush
> Of quiet birds in circled flight.
> I am the soft star that shines at night.
> Do not stand at my grave and cry,
> I am not there . . . .

Here is a letter, from a woman who had met Treya only once, a woman who was nonetheless overwhelmed by her presence (I kept thinking: This is so typical, because all you had to do was meet Treya *once*)—

"The dream came on Monday night the 9th, before I knew Treya was in the last hours of her life.

"As with most everyone, I felt so much the presence of her great soul and have carried it, like the light that was all around her, with me since then. The only other time I've seen and felt that kind of light around people was in the presence of Kalu Rinpoche."

(When Kalu learned of her death, he performed a special prayer for Treya. For Dakini Wind.)

"Maybe that's why the path was open to dream of her 'out of nowhere' that night. She touched so many of us so deeply.

"In the dream, Treya was lying—floating—on air. . . . As I looked on, a great sound came, and soon I realized that it was the wind coming. It blew all around her body, and as it did, her body began to stretch out, becoming finer, until it became translucent and took on a soft glow. The wind kept blowing around her and through her with a sound that was also somehow music. Her body became more and more transparent and then began slowly bending into the snows on the side of the mountain . . . then up and up with the wind into that fire, crystalline powder that 'smokes' off the mountaintop to become a trillion stars, and eventually the sky itself.

"I woke up crying that morning, filled with awe and beauty. . . ."

So the letters went.

After the passing-over ceremony, we all watched the video of Treya speaking at Windstar. And an image went through my mind, the most difficult image I will ever have, an image that will never leave me: When we first received this video from Windstar, I played it for Treya. She was sitting there, in her chair, too tired to move, hooked to oxygen, in much discomfort. I played the video, the video of her speaking so straightforwardly and so strongly, just a few months ago, the video in which she had said, so clearly, "Because I can no longer ignore death, I pay more attention to life." The speech that had made grown men weep and people clap with joy.

I looked at Treya. I looked at that video. I saw both images together in my mind. The strong Treya, and then the Treya crippled by this cruel disease. And then Treya said to me, through her great discomfort: "Did I do all right?"

I have seen, in this lifetime, in this body, the great five-pointed cosmic star, the radiant star of final release, the star whose name will always be, for me... "Treya."

Aloha, and Godspeed, my dearest Treya. I will always, already, find you.

"You promise?" she whispered yet again to me.

"I promise, my dearest Treya."

I promise.

Ken Wilber, *Grace and Grit*

Death is the epitome of the truth that in each moment we are thrust into the unknown. Here all clinging to security is compelled to cease, and wherever the past is dropped away and safety abandoned, life is renewed. Death is the unknown in which all of us lived before birth.

Nothing is more creative than death, since it is the whole secret of life. It means that the past must be abandoned, that the unknown cannot be avoided, that "I" cannot continue, and that nothing can be ultimately fixed. When a man knows this, he lives for the first time in his life. By holding his breath, he loses it. By letting it go he finds it.

> *Und so lang du das nicht hast,*
> *Dieses: stirb und werde,*
> *Bist du nur ein trüber Gast*
> *Auf der dunklen Erde.**

Alan Watts, *The Wisdom of Insecurity*

---

* Goethe, West-östlicher Divan. "As long as you do not know how to die and come to life again, you are but a sorry traveler on this dark earth."

With twenty-five fertile acres at our disposal, the students, teachers, and I enjoyed daily periods of gardening and other outdoor work. We had many pets, including a young deer that was fairly idolized by the children. I, too, loved the fawn so much that I allowed it to sleep in my room. At the light of dawn the little creature would toddle over to my bed for a morning caress.

One day, because some business would require my attention in the town of Ranchi, I fed the pet earlier than usual. I told the boys not to feed the fawn until my return. One lad was disobedient and gave it a large quantity of milk. When I came back in the evening, sad news greeted me: "The fawn is nearly dead, through overfeeding."

In tears, I placed the apparently lifeless pet on my lap. I prayed piteously to God to spare its life. Hours later, the small creature opened its eyes, stood up, and walked feebly. The whole school shouted for joy.

But a deep lesson came to me that night, one I can never forget. I stayed up with the fawn until two o'clock, when I fell asleep. The deer appeared in a dream, and spoke to me:

"You are holding me back. Please let me go; let me go!"

"All right," I answered in the dream.

I awoke immediately, and cried out, "Boys, the deer is dying!" The children rushed to my side.

I ran to the corner of the room where I had placed the pet. It made a last effort to rise, stumbled toward me, then dropped at my feet, dead.

According to the mass karma that guides and regulates the destinies of animals, the deer's life was over, and it was ready to progress to a higher form. But by my deep attachment, which I later realized was selfish, and by my fervent prayers, I had been able to hold it in the limitations of the animal form from which the soul was struggling for release. The soul of the deer made its plea in a dream because, without my loving permission, it either would not or could not go. As soon as I agreed, it departed.

All sorrow left me; I realized anew that God wants His children to love everything as a part of Him, and not to feel delusively that death ends all. The ignorant man sees only the unsurmountable wall of death, hiding, seemingly forever, his cherished friends. But the man of unattachment, he who loves others as expressions of the Lord, understands that at death the dear ones have only returned for a breathing space of joy in Him.

Paramahansa Yogananda, *Autobiography of a Yogi*

For if God really exists and if this existing God is really God, then he is not the God only of the beginning but also the God of the end, he is not only alpha but also omega, he is both my Creator and my Finisher. I can therefore rely with absolutely reasonable confidence on dying—like Jesus of Nazareth—in death, with death, out of death, into God; or—better—on being taken up by him. For death is my affair; raising up to life can only be God's affair. It is by God himself that I am taken up, called, brought home into him as the incomprehensible, comprehensive, last and first reality, and thus finally accepted and saved. All this occurs in death or—better—out of death, as an event of my own, based on God's deed and fidelity. This is the hidden, unimaginable, new creative deed of him who calls into existence the things that are not. And for this reason—and not as a supernatural "intervention" contrary to the laws of nature—it is for me a genuine gift and a true miracle.

Hans Küng, *Does God Exist?*

The Fear of Death

The rabbi of Ger once said:
    "Why is man afraid of dying? For does he not then go to his Father! What man fears is the moment he will survey from the other world everything he has experienced on this earth."

Martin Buber, *Tales of the Hasidim*

The Mask of Death

From the hospital bed
you look back on the world of life
and already the only words you speak
are the ones rehearsed by heart.

And the face rising
from the white sheets around your feet
is the face for which you have waited.
Its lips are strong and its eyes are empty
and the cheek bones are dark and still.

It is the face of all you have not known
staring through the strange hollow inside you
that refused before to know the pain.

Yes you are chilled
and the small child you were a moment before
slips his frightened eyes beneath the sheets.

But with the small gesture of love
that is left to you,
slip your left arm around the frail child's shoulder
and with the other
raise yourself slowly toward those eyes.

And when you feel through the distance
that cannot make you falter
the bones of his cheeks as yours
and your empty eyes turn inward
on the griefs you would not know

you will want no other vision
and find, on your own lips
the first smile on the face of death
that will lead you to your joy.

David Whyte, *Where Many Rivers Meet*

I

Death, I repent
Of these hands and feet
That for forty years
Have been my own
And I repent
Of flesh and bone,
Of heart and liver,
Of hair and skin—
Rid me, death,
Of face and form,
Of all that I am.

And I repent
Of the forms of thought,
The habit of mind
And heart crippled

By long-spent pain,
The memory-traces
Faded and worn
Of vanished places
And human faces
Not rightly seen
Or understood
Rid me, death,
Of the words I have used.

Not this or that
But all is amiss,
That I have done,
And I have seen
Sin and sorrow
Befoul the world—
Release me, death,
Forgive, remove
From place and time
The trace of all
That I have been.

Kathleen Raine, "Two Invocations of Death,"
from *Collected Poems 1956*

Is This the End

Is this the end of all that we have been,
  And all we did or dreamed,—
A name unremembered and a form undone,—
  Is this the end?

A body rotting under a slab of stone
  Or turned to ash in fire,
A mind dissolved, lost its forgotten thoughts,—
  Is this the end?

Our little hours that were and are no more,
  Our passions once so high
Being mocked by the still earth and calm sunshine,—
  Is this the end?

Our yearnings for the human Godward climb
    Passing to other hearts
Deceived, while smiles towards death and hell the world,—
    Is this the end?

Fallen is the harp; shattered it lies and mute;
    Is the unseen player dead?
Because the tree is felled where the bird sang,
    Must the song too hush?

One in the mind who planned and willed and thought,
    Worked to reshape earth's fate,
One in the heart who loved and yearned and hoped,
    Does he too end?

The Immortal in the mortal is his Name;
    An artist Godhead here
Ever remoulds himself in diviner shapes,
    Unwilling to cease

Till all is done for which the stars were made,
    Till the heart discovers God
And the soul knows itself. And even then
    There is no end.

Sri Aurobindo, *Collected Poems*

I know nothing of death, but I know that God is eternity, and I know this, too, that he is my God. Whether what we call time remains to us beyond our death becomes quite unimportant to us next to this knowing, that we are God's—who is not immortal, but eternal. Instead of imagining ourselves living instead of dead, we shall prepare ourselves for a real death which is perhaps the final limit of time but which, if that is the case, is surely the threshold of eternity.

Martin Buber, *A Believing Humanism*

Those who die go no further from
us than God, and God is very near.

Anon

→ 17 ←

The Gate of Life

That there is another existence, that this life is not the end, is a common belief among some of the greatest religions. As American best-selling author Erica Jong writes in her poem "The Buddha in the Womb," "Flesh is merely a lesson. We learn it and pass on."

In the advanced practice of yoga, many prepare to consciously leave their bodies by helping the spirit exit upwards through the seven chakras (energy centres in the body), which are located at the sacrum, spleen, solar plexus, heart, throat, forehead, and crown. It is common for great ascetics, swamis, and gurus to be buried in circular graves sitting in the lotus position, their bodies just a shell they left behind. Many times the bodies do not immediately decompose, because of the advanced soul they once contained. I've included here the postscript from Yogananda's autobiography, which describes this phenomenon.

There have been numerous instances of people who have passed through the gate to the other side and returned, and these experiences are commonly referred to as "near-death experiences" or NDEs. I have chosen just two examples here: Carl Jung's own experience after suffering a heart attack, and a woman's experience after a car accident, described by Stanislav and Christina Grof.

The Buddhists believe that there is a special place we go after the death of the body, a sort of departure region called Bardo (similar in fact to the Catholic purgatory). Joel L. Whitton and Joe Fisher describe it in the section from their book *Life Between Life*. It is a common belief that those who die go to this intermediary place, where they can still be a part of this world before moving on to vaster realms. There have been many examples of those who have recently died communicating with loved ones and friends after their deaths. Two of them being C. S. Lewis's deceased wife, H., and the American Presbyterian minister Frederick Buechner's friend, whom Buechner meets in his dream and of whom he finds evidence on wakening. One of the most comprehensive and articulate accounts of what life is about in the higher realms of the life beyond is given to Yogananda by his deceased guru Sri Yukteswar, who appeared to Yogananda in a resurrected form of his previous body. He confirms that how we live our lives in this world, certainly affects our future in the next.

><

The Buddha in the Womb

Bobbing in the waters of the womb,
little godhead, ten toes, ten fingers
& infinite hope,
sails upside down through the world.

My bones, I know, are only a cage
for death.
Meditating, I can see my skull,
a death's hand,
lit from within
by candles
which are possibly the suns
of other galaxies.

I know that death
is a movement toward light,
a happy dream
from which you are loath to awaken,
a lover left
in a country
to which you have no visa,
& I know that the horses of the spirit
are galloping, galloping, galloping
out of time
& into the moment called NOW.

Why then do I care
for this upside-down Buddha
bobbling through the world,

his toes, his fingers
alive with blood
that will only sing & die?

There is a light in my skull
& a light in his.
We meditate on our bones only
to let them blow away
with fewer regrets

Flesh is merely a lesson.
We learn it
& pass on.

Erica Jong, *At the Edge of the Body*

Paramahansa Yogananda: A Yogi in Life and Death

Paramahansa Yogananda entered *mahasamadhi* (a yogi's final conscious exit from the body) in Los Angeles, California, on March 7, 1952, after concluding his speech at a banquet held in honor of H. E. Binay R. Sen, Ambassador of India.

The great world teacher demonstrated the value of yoga (scientific techniques for God-realization) not only in life but in death. Weeks after his departure his unchanged face shone with the divine luster of incorruptibility.

Mr. Harry T. Rowe, Los Angeles Mortuary Director, Forest Lawn Memorial-Park (in which the body of the great master is temporarily placed), sent Self-Realization Fellowship a notarized letter from which the following extracts are taken:

"The absence of any visual signs of decay in the dead body of Paramahansa Yogananda offers the most extraordinary case in our experience.... No physical disintegration was visible in his body even twenty days after death.... No indication of mold was visible on his skin, and no visible desiccation (drying up) took place in the bodily tissues. This state of perfect preservation of a body is, so far as we know from mortuary annals, an unparalleled one.... At the time of receiving Yogananda's body, the Mortuary personnel expected to observe, through the glass lid of the casket, the usual progressive signs of bodily decay. Our astonishment increased as day followed day without bringing any visible change in the body under observation. Yogananda's body was apparently in a phenomenal state of immutability....

"No odor of decay emanated from his body at any time.... The physical appearance of Yogananda on March 27th, just before the bronze cover of the casket was put into position, was the same as it had been on March 7th. He looked on March 27th as fresh and as unravaged by decay as he had looked on the night of his death. On March 27th there was no reason to say that his body had suffered any visible physical disintegration at all. For these reasons we state again that the case of Paramahansa Yogananda is unique in our experience."

Paramahansa Yogananda, *Autobiography of a Yogi*

Visions

At the beginning of 1944 I broke my foot, and this misadventure was followed by a heart attack. In a state of unconsciousness I experienced deliriums and visions which must have begun when I hung on the edge of death and was being given oxygen and camphor injections. The images were so tremendous that I myself concluded that I was close to death. My nurse afterward told me, "It was as if you were surrounded by a bright glow." That was a phenomenon she had sometimes observed in the dying, she added. I had reached the outermost limit, and do not know whether I was in a dream or an ecstasy. At any rate, extremely strange things began to happen to me.

It seemed to me that I was high up in space. Far below I saw the globe of the earth, bathed in a gloriously blue light. I saw the deep blue sea and the continents. Far below my feet lay Ceylon, and in the distance ahead of me the subcontinent of India. My field of vision did not include the whole earth, but its global shape was plainly distinguishable and its outlines shone with a silvery gleam through that wonderful blue light. In many places the globe seemed colored, or spotted dark green like oxydized silver. Far away to the left lay a broad expanse—the reddish-yellow desert of Arabia; it was as though the silver of the earth had there assumed a reddish-gold hue. Then came the Red Sea, and far, far back—as if in the upper left of a map—I could just make out a bit of the Mediterranean. My gaze was directed chiefly toward that. Everything else appeared indistinct. I could also see the snow-covered Himalayas, but in that direction it was foggy or cloudy. I did not look to the right at all. I knew that I was on the point of departing from the earth.

Later I discovered how high in space one would have to be to have so extensive a view—approximately a thousand miles! The sight of the earth from this height was the most glorious thing I had ever seen.

After contemplating it for a while, I turned around. I had been standing with my back to the Indian Ocean, as it were, and my face to the north.

Then it seemed to me that I made a turn to the south. Something new entered my field of vision. A short distance away I saw in space a tremendous dark block of stone, like a meteorite. It was about the size of my house, or even bigger. It was floating in space, and I myself was floating in space.

I had seen similar stones on the coast of the Gulf of Bengal. They were blocks of tawny granite, and some of them had been hollowed out into temples. My stone was one such gigantic dark block. An entrance led into a small antechamber. To the right of the entrance, a black Hindu sat silently in lotus posture upon a stone bench. He wore a white gown, and I knew that he expected me. Two steps led up to this antechamber, and inside on the left, was the gate to the temple. Innumerable tiny niches, each with a saucer-like concavity filled with coconut oil and small burning wicks, surrounded the door with a wreath of bright flames. I had once actually seen this when I visited the Temple of the Holy Tooth at Kandy in Ceylon; the gate had been framed by several rows of burning oil lamps of this sort.

As I approached the steps leading up to the entrance into the rock, a strange thing happened: I had the feeling that everything was being sloughed away; everything I aimed at or wished for or thought, the whole phantasmagoria of earthly existence, fell away or was stripped from me — an extremely painful process. Nevertheless something remained; it was as if I now carried along with me everything I had ever experienced or done, everything that had happened around me. I might also say: it was with me, and I was it. I consisted of all that, so to speak. I consisted of my own history, and I felt with great certainty: this is what I am. "I am this bundle of what has been, and what has been accomplished."

This experience gave me a feeling of extreme poverty, but at the same time of great fullness. There was no longer anything I wanted or desired. I existed in an objective form; I was what I had been and lived. At first the sense of annihilation predominated, of having been stripped or pillaged; but suddenly that became of no consequence. Everything seemed to be past; what remained was a *fait accompli*, without any reference back to what had been. There was no longer any regret that something had dropped away or been taken away. On the contrary: I had everything that I was, and that was everything.

Something else engaged my attention: as I approached the temple I had the certainty that I was about to enter an illuminated room and would meet there all those people to whom I belong in reality. There I would at last understand—this too was a certainty—what historical nexus I or my life fitted into. I would know what had been before me, why I had come into being, and where my life was flowing. My life as I lived it had often seemed to me like a story that has no beginning and no end. I had the feeling that I was a historical fragment, an excerpt for which the preceding and succeeding text was missing. My life seemed to have been snipped out of a long chain of events, and many questions had remained unanswered. Why had it taken this course? Why had I brought these particular assumptions with me? What had I made of them? What will follow? I felt sure that I would receive an answer to all these questions as soon as I entered the rock temple. There I would learn why everything had been thus and not otherwise. There I would meet the people who knew the answer to my question about what had been before and what would come after.

While I was thinking over these matters, something happened that caught my attention. From below, from the direction of Europe, an image floated up. It was my doctor, Dr. H.—or, rather, his likeness—framed by a golden chain or a golden laurel wreath. I knew at once: "Aha, this is my doctor, of course, the one who has been treating me. But now he is coming in his primal form, as a *basileus* of Kos.* In life he was an avatar of this *basileus*, the temporal embodiment of the primal form, which has existed from the beginning. Now he is appearing in that primal form."

Presumably I too was in my primal form, though this was something I did not observe but simply took for granted. As he stood before me, a mute exchange of thought took place between us. Dr. H. had been delegated by the earth to deliver a message to me, to tell me that there was a protest against my going away. I had no right to leave the earth and must return. The moment I heard that, the vision ceased.

I was profoundly disappointed, for now it all seemed to have been for nothing. The painful process of defoliation had been in vain, and I was not to be allowed to enter the temple, to join the people in whose company I belonged.

In reality, a good three weeks were still to pass before I could truly make up my mind to live again. I could not eat because all food repelled me. The view of city and mountains from my sickbed seemed to me like a painted curtain with black holes in it, or a tattered sheet of newspaper full of photographs that meant nothing. Disappointed, I thought, "Now I must return to the 'box system' again." For it seemed to me as if behind the horizon of the cosmos a three-dimensional world had been artificially built up, in which each person sat by himself in a little box. And now I should have to convince myself all over again that this was important! Life and the whole world struck me as a prison, and it bothered me beyond measure that I

---

* Basileus = king. Kos was famous in antiquity as the site of the temple of Asklepios, and was the birthplace of Hippocrates.—A. J.

should again be finding all that quite in order. I had been so glad to shed it all, and now it had come about that I—along with everyone else—would again be hung up in a box by a thread. While I floated in space, I had been weightless, and there had been nothing tugging at me. And now all that was to be a thing of the past!

I felt violent resistance to my doctor because he had brought me back to life. At the same time, I was worried about him. "His life is in danger, for heaven's sake! He has appeared to me in his primal form! When anybody attains this form it means he is going to die, for already he belongs to the 'greater company'!" Suddenly the terrifying thought came to me that Dr. H. would have to die in my stead. I tried my best to talk to him about it, but he did not understand me. Then I became angry with him. "Why does he always pretend he doesn't know he is a basileus of Kos? And that he has already assumed his primal form? He wants to make me believe that he doesn't know!" That irritated me. My wife reproved me for being so unfriendly to him. She was right; but at the time I was angry with him for stubbornly refusing to speak of all that had passed between us in my vision. "Damn it all, he ought to watch his step. He has no right to be so reckless! I want to tell him to take care of himself." I was firmly convinced that his life was in jeopardy.

In actual fact I was his last patient. On April 4, 1944—I still remember the exact date—I was allowed to sit up on the edge of my bed for the first time since the beginning of my illness, and on this same day Dr. H. took to his bed and did not leave it again. I heard that he was having intermittent attacks of fever. Soon afterward he died of septicemia. He was a good doctor; there was something of the genius about him. Otherwise he would not have appeared to me as a prince of Kos.

During those weeks I lived in a strange rhythm. By day I was usually depressed. I felt weak and wretched, and scarcely dared to stir. Gloomily, I thought, "Now I must go back to this drab world." Toward evening I would fall asleep, and my sleep would last until about midnight. Then I would come to myself and lie awake for about an hour, but in an utterly transformed state. It was as if I were in an ecstasy. I felt as though I were floating in space, as though I were safe in the womb of the universe—in a tremendous void, but filled with the highest possible feeling of happiness. "This is eternal bliss," I thought. "This cannot be described; it is far too wonderful!"

Everything around me seemed enchanted. At this hour of the night the nurse brought me some food she had warmed—for only then was I able to take any, and I ate with appetite. For a time it seemed to me that she was an old Jewish woman, much older than she actually was, and that she was preparing ritual kosher dishes for me. When I looked at her, she seemed to have a blue halo around her head. I myself was, so it seemed, in the Pardes Rimmonim, the garden of pomegranates,* and the wedding of Tifereth with Malchuth was taking place. Or else I was Rabbi Simon ben Jochai, whose wedding in the afterlife was being celebrated. It was the mystic marriage as it appears in the Cabbalistic tradition. I cannot tell you how wonderful it was. I could only think continually, "Now this is the garden of pomegranates! Now this is the marriage of Malchuth with Tifereth!" I do not know exactly what part I played in it. At bottom it was I myself: I was the marriage. And my beatitude was that of a blissful wedding.

Gradually the garden of pomegranates faded away and changed. There followed the Marriage of the Lamb, in a Jerusalem festively bedecked. I cannot describe what it was like in detail. These were ineffable states of joy. Angels were present, and light. I myself was the "Marriage of the Lamb."

That, too, vanished, and there came a new image, the last vision. I walked up a wide valley to the end, where a gentle chain of hills began. The valley ended in a classical amphitheater. It was magnificently situated in the green landscape. And there, in this theater, the *hierosgamos* was being celebrated. Men and women dancers came onstage, and upon a flower-decked couch All-father Zeus and Hera consummated the mystic marriage, as it is described in the *Iliad*.

All these experiences were glorious. Night after night I floated in a state of purest bliss, "thronged round with images of all creation."† Gradually, the motifs mingled and paled. Usually the visions lasted for about an hour; then I would fall asleep again. By the time morning drew near, I would feel: Now gray morning is coming again; now comes the gray world with its boxes! What idiocy, what hideous nonsense! Those inner states were so fantastically beautiful that by comparison this world appeared downright ridiculous. As I approached closer to life again, they grew fainter, and scarcely three weeks after the first vision they ceased altogether.

It is impossible to convey the beauty and intensity of emotion during those visions. They were the most tremendous things I have ever experienced. And what a contrast the day was: I was tormented and on edge; everything irritated me; everything was too material, too crude and clumsy, terribly limited both spatially and spiritually. It was all an imprisonment, for reasons

---

* *Pardes Rimmonim* is the title of an old Cabbalistic tract by Moses Cordovero (sixteenth century). In Cabbalistic doctrine Malchuth and Tifereth are two of the ten spheres of divine manifestation in which God emerges from his hidden state. They represent the female and male principles within the Godhead.
† *Faust*, Part Two.

impossible to divine, and yet it had a kind of hypnotic power, a cogency, as if it were reality itself, for all that I had clearly perceived its emptiness. Although my belief in the world returned to me, I have never since entirely freed myself of the impression that this life is a segment of existence which is enacted in a three-dimensional boxlike universe especially set up for it.

There is something else I quite distinctly remember. At the beginning, when I was having the vision of the garden of pomegranates, I asked the nurse to forgive me if she were harmed. There was such sanctity in the room, I said, that it might be harmful to her. Of course she did not understand me. For me the presence of sanctity had a magical atmosphere; I feared it might be unendurable to others. I understood then why one speaks of the odor of sanctity, of the "sweet smell" of the Holy Ghost. This was it. There was a *pneuma* of inexpressible sanctity in the room, whose manifestation was the *mysterium coniunctionis*.

I would never have imagined that any such experience was possible. It was not a product of imagination. The visions and experiences were utterly real; there was nothing subjective about them; they all had a quality of absolute objectivity.

We shy away from the word "eternal," but I can describe the experience only as the ecstasy of a non-temporal state in which present, past, and future are one. Everything that happens in time had been brought together into a concrete whole. Nothing was distributed over time, nothing could be measured by temporal concepts. The experience might best be defined as a state of feeling, but one which cannot be produced by imagination. How can I imagine that I exist simultaneously the day before yesterday, today, and the day after tomorrow? There would be things which would not yet have begun, other things which would be indubitably present, and others again which would already be finished—and yet all this would be one. The only thing that feeling could grasp would be a sum, an iridescent whole, containing all at once expectation of a beginning, surprise at what is now happening, and satisfaction or disappointment with the result of what has happened. One is interwoven into an indescribable whole and yet observes it with complete objectivity.

I experienced this objectivity once again later on. That was after the death of my wife. I saw her in a dream which was like a vision. She stood at some distance from me, looking at me squarely. She was in her prime, perhaps about thirty, and wearing the dress which had been made for her many years before by my cousin the medium. It was perhaps the most beautiful thing she had ever worn. Her expression was neither joyful nor sad, but, rather, objectively wise and understanding, without the slightest emotional reaction, as though she were beyond the mist of affects. I knew that it was not she, but a portrait she had made or commissioned for me. It contained the beginning of our relationship, the events of fifty-three years of marriage, and the end of her life also. Face to face with such wholeness one remains speechless, for it can scarcely be comprehended.

The objectivity which I experienced in this dream and in the visions is part of a completed individuation. It signifies detachment from valuations and from what we call emotional ties. In general, emotional ties are very important to human beings. But they still contain projections, and it is essential to withdraw these projections in order to attain to oneself and to objectivity. Emotional relationships are relationships of desire, tainted by coercion and constraint; something is expected from the other person, and that makes him and ourselves unfree. Objective cognition lies hidden behind the attraction of the emotional relationship; it seems to be the central secret. Only through objective cognition is the real *coniunctio* possible.

After the illness a fruitful period of work began for me. A good many of my principal works were written only then. The insight I had had, or the vision of the end of all things, gave me the courage to undertake new formulations. I no longer attempted to put across my own opinion, but surrendered myself to the current of my thoughts. Thus one problem after the other revealed itself to me and took shape.

Something else, too, came to me from my illness. I might formulate it as an affirmation of things as they are: an unconditional "yes" to that which is, without subjective protests—acceptance of the conditions of existence as I see them and understand them, acceptance of my own nature, as I happen to be. At the beginning of the illness I had the feeling that there was something wrong with my attitude, and that I was to some extent responsible for the mishap. But when one follows the path of individuation, when one lives one's own life, one must take mistakes into the bargain; life would not be complete without them. There is no guarantee—not for a single moment—that we will not fall into error or stumble into deadly peril. We may think there is a sure road. But that would be the road of death. Then nothing happens any longer—at any rate, not the right things. Anyone who takes the sure road is as good as dead.

It was only after the illness that I understood how important it is to affirm one's own destiny. In this way we forge an ego that does not break down when incomprehensible things happen; an ego that endures, that endures the truth, and that is capable of coping with the world and with fate. Then, to experience defeat is also to experience victory. Nothing is disturbed—neither inwardly nor outwardly, for one's own continuity has withstood the current of life and of time. But that can come to pass only when one does not meddle inquisitively with the workings of fate.

I have also realized that one must accept the thoughts that go on within oneself of their own accord as part of one's reality. The categories of true and false are, of course, always present; but because they are not binding they take second place. The presence of thoughts is more important than our subjective judgment of them. But neither must these judgments be suppressed, for they also are existent thoughts which are part of our wholeness.

C. G. Jung, *Memories, Dreams, Reflections*

During the several seconds that my car was in motion, I had an experience that seemed to span centuries. I rapidly moved from sheer terror and overwhelming fear for my life to a profound knowledge that I would die. Ironically, with that knowledge came the deepest sense of peace and serenity that I have ever encountered. It was as though I had moved from the periphery of my being—the body that contained me—to the very center of myself, a place that was imperturbable, totally quiet and at rest. The mantra that I had previously been using in meditation sprang into my consciousness and revolved automatically, with an ease I had never before known. Time seemed to have disappeared as I watched sequences from my life passing before me like a movie, quite rapidly, but with amazing detail. When I reached the point of death, it seemed that I was facing an opaque curtain of some kind. The momentum of the experience carried me, still completely calm, through the curtain and I realized that it had not been a point of termination, but rather of transition. The only way that I can describe the next sensation is to say that every part of me, whatever I was at that moment, felt without question a far-reaching and encompassing continuum beyond what I had previously thought of as death. It was as though the force that had moved me toward death and then past it would endlessly continue to carry me, through ever-expanding vistas.

It was at this point that my car hit a truck with a great impact. As it came to rest, I looked around and realized that by some miracle I was still alive. And then, an amazing thing happened. As I sat in the midst of the tangled metal, I felt my individual boundaries begin to melt. I started to merge with everything around me—with the policemen, the wreck, the workers with crowbars trying to liberate me, the ambulance, the flowers on a nearby hedge, and the television cameramen. Somewhere, I could see and feel my injuries, but they did not seem to have anything to do with me; they were merely part of a rapidly expanding network that included much more than my body. The sunlight was unusually bright and golden and the entire world seemed to shimmer with a beautiful radiance. I felt blissful and exuberant, even in the middle of the drama around me, and I remained in that state for several days in the hospital. The accident and the experience that accompanied it totally transformed my world-view and my way of understanding existence. Previously, I had not had much interest in spiritual areas and my concept of life was that it was contained between birth and death. The thought of death had always frightened me. I had believed that "we walk across life's stage but once," and then—nothing. Consequently I had been driven by the fear that I would not have a chance to do all that I wanted to accomplish during my life. Now, the world and my place in it feel completely different. I feel that my self-definition transcends the notion of a limited physical body existing in a limited time frame. I know myself to be part of a larger, unrestricted, creative network that could be described as divine.

Stanislav and Christina Grof, *Beyond Death*

The faint stars said,
"Our distances of night,
These wastes of space,
Sight can in an instant cross,

But who has passed
On soul's dark flight
Journeys beyond
The flash of our light."

I said, "Whence he is travelling
Let no heart's grief of mine
Draw back a thought
To these dim skies,

Nor human tears
Drench those wings that pass,
Freed from earth's weight
And the wheel of stars."

7 September 1969
Kathleen Raine, *On a Deserted Shore*

Through self-revelation, the life between life places physical being in its proper perspective. Metaconsciousness tells us, above all, that the subtle and the spiritual in man—our essence—is beyond destruction. At death we leave behind our chosen vehicle of flesh and bones so that another stage of life may begin.

The next world, being our natural home, brings awakening and remembrance and the restoration of clarity. And in seeing ourselves as we truly are, we are able to learn from the last expedition into earthly reality, assess our progress, and eventually plan the next incarnation according to our needs.

If all the world's a stage, the *bardo* is life in the wings where the props, pulleys, prompt cards, and all else that make a theatrical production possible have been brought together ready for use. Well performed or shoddily executed, the "performance" of life incarnate goes on once the decision making, rehearsing, and preparatory work have taken place. Each script is written, directed, and produced by the performer, many scripts being required for the acting out of many lifetimes. Only through a relentless succession of exits and entrances can learning and growth be achieved.

Carefully or haphazardly, we choose our earthly circumstances. The message of metaconsciousness is that the life situation of every human being—whether a victim of AIDS, an aborted child, a movie star, a legless newspaper vendor, or the President of the United States—is neither random nor inappropriate. Seen objectively from the interlife, every human experience is simply another lesson in the cosmic classroom. The more we learn from each lesson, the faster we evolve. Opportunities to love and serve are always sought in interlife planning and, consequently, they must be seen as fundamental to self-development. As restful and rejuvenating as the experience of solitude might be from time to time, karmic unfoldment demands human interaction.

Human existence only becomes comprehensible when the tiny segment between birth and death—our current reality—is placed in a cosmic context. No longer just a name given to a religious concept which may or may not have validity, life eternal is suddenly a reality and the overriding meaning and purpose of existence become dazzlingly clear, if difficult to convey in language. The interlife panorama is breathtaking to behold: no space, no time...awesome infinity forever.

All our lives and interlives lie within that infinity, as do the karmic patterns which shape personal evolutionary development. And just as the most microscopic detail of our past-life actions and interlife experience is open to inspection from this state, so are we granted an overview of the journey thus far...the unspeakably long odyssey that weaves in and out of incarnation. Awareness of this greater reality subjects earthbound values, attitudes, and preoccupations to rigorous revision by revealing that death is merely a transition. Conscious immortality cannot help but lead to personal reformation. As Carl Jung wrote in *Memories, Dreams, Reflections*: "Only if we know that the thing which truly matters is the infinite can we avoid fixing our interest upon futilities."

Joel L. Whitton and Joe Fisher, *Life Between Life*

Some of the living are already half-dead. Many of the dead are very much alive.
The Mother, *Words of the Mother*, Part Two

Lord, are these your real terms? Can I meet H. again only if I learn to love you so much that I don't care whether I meet her or not? Consider, Lord, how it looks to us. What would anyone think of me if I said to the boys, "No toffee now. But when you've grown up and don't really want toffee you shall have as much of it as you choose?"

If I knew that to be eternally divided from H. and eternally forgotten by her would add a greater joy and splendour to her being, of course I'd say "Fire ahead." Just as if, on earth, I could have cured her cancer by never seeing her again, I'd have arranged never to see her again. I'd have had to. Any decent person would. But that's quite different. That's not the situation I'm in.

When I lay these questions before God I get no answer. But a rather special sort of "No answer." It is not the locked door. It is more like a silent, certainly not uncompassionate, gaze. As though He shook His head not in refusal but waiving the question. Like, "Peace, child; you don't understand."

Can a mortal ask questions which God finds unanswerable? Quite easily, I should think. All nonsense questions are unanswerable. How many hours are there in a mile? Is yellow square or round? Probably half the questions we ask—half our great theological and metaphysical problems—are like that.

And now that I come to think of it, there's no practical problem before me at all. I know the two great commandments, and I'd better get on with them. While she was alive I could, in practice, have put her before God; that is, could have done what she wanted instead of what He wanted; if there'd been a conflict. What's left is not a problem about anything I could *do*. It's all about weights of feelings and motives and that sort of thing. It's a problem I'm setting myself. I don't believe God set it [for] me at all.

The fruition of God. Re-union with the dead. These can't figure in my thinking except as counters. Blank cheques. My idea—if you can call it an idea—of the first is a huge, risky extrapolation from a very few and short experiences here on earth. Probably not such valuable experiences as I think. Perhaps even of less value than others that I take no account of. My idea of the second is also an extrapolation. The reality of either—the cashing of either cheque—would probably blow all one's ideas about both (how much more one's ideas about their relations to each other) into smithereens.

The mystical union on the one hand. The resurrection of the body, on the other. I can't reach the ghost of an image, a formula, or even a feeling, that combines them. But the reality, we are given to understand, does. Reality the iconoclast once more. Heaven will solve our problems, but not, I think, by showing us subtle reconciliations between all our apparently contradictory notions. The notions will all be knocked from under our feet. We shall see that there never was any problem.

And, more than once, that impression which I can't describe except by saying that it's like the sound of a chuckle in the darkness. The sense that some shattering and disarming simplicity is the real answer.

It is often thought that the dead see us. And we assume, whether reasonably or not, that if they see us at all they see us more clearly than before. Does H. now see exactly how much froth or tinsel there was in what she called, and I call, my love? So be it. Look your hardest, dear. I wouldn't hide if I could. We didn't idealize each other. We tried to keep no secrets. You knew most of the rotten places in me already. If you now see anything worse, I can take it. So can you. Rebuke, explain, mock, forgive. For this is one of the miracles of love; it gives—to both, but perhaps especially to the woman—a power of seeing through its own enchantments and yet not being disenchanted.

To see, in some measure, like God. His love and His knowledge are not distinct from one another, nor from Him. We could almost say He sees because He loves, and therefore loves although He sees.

Sometimes, Lord, one is tempted to say that if you wanted us to behave like the lilies of the field you might have given us an organization more like theirs. But that, I suppose, is just your grand experiment. Or no; not an experiment, for you have no need to find things out. Rather your grand enterprise. To make an organism which is also a spirit; to make that terrible oxymoron, a "spiritual animal." To take a poor primate, a beast with nerve-endings all over it, a creature with a stomach that wants to be filled, a breeding animal that wants its mate, and say, "Now get on with it. Become a god."

I said, several notebooks ago, that even if I got what seemed like an assurance of H.'s presence, I wouldn't believe it. Easier said than done. Even now, though, I won't treat anything of that sort as evidence. It's the *quality* of last night's experience—not what it proves but what it was—that makes it worth putting down. It was quite incredibly unemotional. Just the impression of her *mind* momentarily facing my own. Mind, not "soul" as we tend to think of soul. Certainly the reverse of what is called "soulful." Not at all like a rapturous re-union of lovers. Much more like getting a telephone call or a wire from her about some practical arrangement. Not that there was any "message"—just intelligence and attention. No sense of joy or sorrow. No love even, in our ordinary sense. No un-love. I had never in any mood imagined the dead as being so—well, so business-like. Yet there was an extreme and cheerful intimacy. An intimacy that had not passed through the senses or the emotions at all.

If this was a throw-up from my unconscious, then my unconscious must be a far more interesting region than the depth psychologists have led me to expect. For one thing, it is apparently much less primitive than my consciousness.

Wherever it came from, it has made a sort of spring cleaning in my mind. The dead could be like that; sheer intellects. A Greek philosopher wouldn't have been surprised at an experience like mine. He would have expected that if anything of us remained after death it would be just that. Up to now this always seemed to me a most arid and chilling idea. The absence of emotion repelled me. But in this contact (whether real or apparent) it didn't do anything of the sort. One didn't need emotion. The intimacy was complete—sharply bracing and restorative too—without it. Can that intimacy be love itself—always in this life attended with emotion, not because it is itself an emotion, or needs an attendant emotion, but because our animal souls, our nervous systems, our imaginations, have to respond to it in that way? If so, how many preconceptions I must scrap! A society, a communion, of pure intelligences would not be cold, drab and comfortless. On the other hand it wouldn't be very like what people usually mean when they use such words as "spiritual," or "mystical," or "holy." It would, if I have had a glimpse, be—well, I'm almost scared at the adjectives I'd have to use. Brisk? cheerful? keen? alert? intense? wide-awake? Above all, solid. Utterly reliable. Firm. There is no nonsense about the dead.

When I say "intellect" I include will. Attention is an act of will. Intelligence in action is will *par excellence*. What seemed to meet me was full of resolution.

Once very near the end I said, "If you can—if it is allowed—come to me when I too am on my death bed." "Allowed!" she said. "Heaven would have a job to hold me; and as for Hell, I'd break it into bits." She knew she was speaking a kind of mythological language, with even an element of comedy in it. There was a twinkle as well as a tear in her eye. But there was no myth and no joke about the will, deeper than any feeling, that flashed through her.

But I mustn't, because I have come to misunderstand a little less completely what a pure intelligence might be, lean over too far. There is also, whatever it means, the resurrection of the body. We cannot understand. The best is perhaps what we understand least.

Didn't people dispute once whether the final vision of God was more an act of intelligence or of love? That is probably another of the nonsense questions.

How wicked it would be, if we could, to call the dead back! She said not to me but to the chaplain, "I am at peace with God." She smiled, but not at me. *Poi si torno all'eterna fontana.*

C. S. Lewis, A Grief Observed

Exactly a year ago tomorrow, the fifth of March, 1986, a very good friend of mind died. He was an Englishman—a witty, elegant, many-faceted man. One morning in his sixty-eighth year he simply didn't wake up. Which was about as easy a way as he could possibly have done it. But it wasn't easy for the people he left behind because it gave us no chance to say good-bye, either in words, if we turned out to be up to that, or in some unspoken way if we weren't. A couple of months later my wife and I were staying with his widow overnight in Charleston, South Carolina, when I had a short dream about him, which I want to tell you about.

I dreamed that he was standing there in the dark guest room, where my wife and I were asleep, looking very much the way he always did in the navy blue jersey and white slacks that he often wore, and I told him how much we missed him and how glad I was to see him again, and so on. He acknowledged that somehow. Then I said, "Are you really there, Dudley?" I meant was he there in fact and truth, or was I merely dreaming that he was? His answer was that he was really there. And then I said, "Can you prove it?" "Of course," he said. Then he plucked a strand of blue wool out of his jersey and tossed it to me, and I caught it between my index finger and my thumb, and the feel of it was so palpable and so real that it woke me up. That's all there was to the dream. But it was as if he had come on purpose to do what he had done and then left. When I told that dream at breakfast the next morning, I had hardly finished when my wife spoke. She said she had noticed the strand of wool on the carpet when she was getting dressed. She was sure it hadn't been there the night before. I thought I was losing my mind, and I rushed upstairs to see, and there it was—a little tangle of navy blue wool that I have in my wallet as I stand here today.

Another event was this. I went into a bar in an airport not long ago to fortify myself against my least favorite means of moving around the world. It was an off hour, so I was the only customer and had a choice of a whole row of empty barstools. And on the counter in front of each barstool there was a holder with a little card stuck in it, advertising the drink of the day, or something like that. I noticed that the one in front of me had an extra little bit of metal stuck on top of the card. It wasn't on any of the others, so I took a look at it. It turned out to be one of those tie clips that men used to wear. It had three letters engraved on it, and the letters were C.F.B. Those are my initials.

Lastly, this. I was receiving communion in an Episcopal church early one morning. The priest was an acquaintance of mine, and I could hear him moving along the rail from person to person as I knelt there waiting for my turn. The body of Christ, he said, the bread of heaven. The body of Christ, the bread of heaven. When he got to me he put in another word. The word was my name. "The body of Christ, Freddy, the bread of heaven."

The dream I had about my friend may very well have been just another dream, and you certainly don't have to invoke the supernatural to account for the thread on the carpet. The tie clip I find harder to explain away; it seems to me that the mathematical odds against its having not just one or two but all three of my initials and in the right order must be astronomical. But I suppose that too could be just a coincidence. On the other hand, in both cases there is also the other possibility. Far out or not, I don't see how any open-minded person can *a priori* deny it. And it's that other possibility that's at the heart of everything I want to say here on this Ash Wednesday night.

Maybe my friend really did come in my dream, and the thread was a sign to me that he had. Maybe it's true that by God's grace the dead are given back their lives and that the doctrine of the resurrection of the body is not just a doctrine. My friend couldn't have looked more substantial, less ecto-plasmic, standing there in the dark, and it was such a crisp, no-nonsense exchange that we had. There was nothing surreal or wispy about it.

As to the tie clip, it seemed so extraordinary that for a moment I almost refused to believe that it had happened. Even though I had the thing right there in my hand, with my initials on it, my first inclination was to deny it—for the simple reason that it was so unsettling to my whole common-sense view of the way the world works that it was easier and less confusing just to shrug it off as a crazy fluke. We're all inclined to do that. But maybe it was-n't a fluke. Maybe it was a crazy little peek behind the curtain, a dim little whisper of providence from the wings. I had been expected, I was on sched-ule, I was taking the right journey at the right time. I was not alone.

What happened at the communion rail was different. There was noth-ing extraordinary about the priest knowing my name—I knew he knew it—and there was nothing extraordinary about his using it in the service because he evidently did that kind of thing quite often. But the effect on *me* was extraordinary. It caught me off guard. It moved me deeply. For the first time in my life, maybe, it struck me that when Jesus picked up the bread at his last meal and said, "This is my body which is for you," he was doing it not just in a ritual way for humankind in general, but in an unthinkably personal way for every particular man or woman or child who ever existed or some-day would exist. Most unthinkable of all: maybe he was doing it for me. At that holiest of feasts we are known not just by our official name but by the names people use who have known us the longest and most intimately. We are welcomed not as the solid citizens that our Sunday best suggests we are, but in all our tackiness and tatteredness that nobody in the world knows bet-ter than each of us knows it about ourselves—the bitterness and the phoni-ness and the confusion and the irritability and the prurience and the half-heartedness. The bread of heaven, *Freddy*, of all people. Molly? Bill?

Ridiculous little So-and-so? Boring old What's-his-name? Extraordinary. It seemed a revelation from on high. Was it?

Maybe all that's extraordinary about these three little events is the fuss I've made about them. Things like that happen every day to everybody. They're a dime a dozen; they mean absolutely nothing.

Or, things like that are momentary glimpses into a mystery of such depth, power and beauty that if we were to see it head on, in any way other than in glimpses, I suspect we would be annihilated. If I had to bet my life and my children's lives, my wife's life, on one possibility or the other, which one would I bet it on? If you had to bet your life, which would you bet it on? On "Yes, there is God in the highest," or, if that language is no longer viable, "There is mystery and meaning in the deepest"? Or on "No, there is whatever happens to happen, and it means whatever you choose it to mean, and that's all there is"?

Of course we can bet Yes this evening and No tomorrow morning. We may know we're betting; we may not know. We may bet one way with our lips, our minds, even our hearts, and another way with our feet. But we all of us bet, and it's our lives themselves we're betting with, in the sense that the betting is what shapes our lives. And of course we can never be sure we bet right because the evidence both ways is fragmentary, fragile, ambiguous. A coincidence, as somebody said, can be God's way of remaining anonymous, or it can be just a coincidence. Is the dream that brings healing and hope just a product of wishful thinking? Or is it a message maybe from another world? Whether we bet Yes or No is equally an act of faith.

There's a famous section in the Epistle to the Hebrews where the author, whoever it was, says that "faith is the substance of things hoped for, the evidence of things not seen." Marvelous definition. Noah, Abraham, Sarah, all the rest, it goes on to say, all died in faith, not having received what was promised but having seen it and greeted it from afar, and having acknowledged that they were strangers and pilgrims on the earth. For such people make it clear that they're seeking a homeland. Wonderful passage.

In other words, faith, it seems to me, is distinctly different from other aspects of religious life and not to be confused with them, even though we often use the word "faith" to mean religious belief in general, as in the phrase "What faith are you?" Faith is different from theology because theology is disorderly and intermittent and full of surprises. Faith is different from mysticism because mystics in their ecstasy become one with what faith can at most see only from afar, as that passage from Hebrews says. Faith is different from ethics because ethics is primarily concerned not, like faith, with our relationship with God but with our relationship with each other. I think maybe faith is closest to worship because, like worship, it is essentially a response to God.

It involves the emotions and the physical senses as well as the mind. But worship is consistent, structured, single-minded and seems to know what it's doing, while faith is a stranger, an exile on the earth, and doesn't know for certain about anything. Faith is homesickness. Faith is a lump in the throat. Faith is less a position *on* than a movement *toward*—less a sure thing than a hunch. Faith is waiting. Faith is journeying through space and time.

Frederick Buechner, *Faith and Fiction*

↛ *"Resurrection" means* a life that bursts through the dimensions of space
and time in God's invisible, imperishable, incomprehensible domain.
*This is what is meant by "heaven"—not the heaven of the astronauts, but
God's heaven. It means going into reality, not going out.*

Hans Küng, *Does God Exist?*

The Resurrection of Sri Yukteswar

"Lord Krishna!" The glorious form of the avatar appeared in a shimmering blaze as I sat in my room at the Regent Hotel in Bombay. Shining over the roof of a high building across the street, the ineffable vision had suddenly burst on my sight as I gazed out of my tall open third-story window.

The divine figure waved to me, smiling and nodding in greeting. When I could not understand the exact message of Lord Krishna, he departed with a gesture of blessing. Wondrously uplifted, I felt that some spiritual event was presaged.

My Western voyage had, for the time being, been canceled. I was scheduled for several public addresses in Bombay before leaving on a return visit to Bengal.

Sitting on my bed in the Bombay hotel at three o'clock in the afternoon of June 19, 1936—one week after the vision of Krishna—I was roused from my meditation by a beatific light. Before my open and astonished eyes, the whole room was transformed into a strange world, the sunlight transmuted into supernal splendour.

Waves of rapture engulfed me as I beheld the flesh and blood form of Sri Yukteswar!

"My son!" Master spoke tenderly, on his face an angel-bewitching smile.

For the first time in my life I did not kneel at his feet in greeting, but instantly advanced to gather him hungrily in my arms. Moments of moments! The anguish of past months was a toll I counted weightless against the torrential bliss now descending.

"Master mine, beloved of my heart, why did you leave me?" I was incoherent in an excess of joy. "Why did you let me go to the *Kumbha Mela*? How bitterly have I blamed myself for leaving you!"

"I did not want to interfere with your happy anticipation of seeing the pilgrimage spot where first I met Babaji. I left you only for a little while; am I not with you again?"

"But is it *you*, Master, the same Lion of God? Are you wearing a body like the one I buried beneath the cruel Puri sands?"

"Yes, my child, I am the same. This is a flesh and blood body. Though I see it as ethereal, to your sight it is physical. From cosmic atoms I created an entirely new body, exactly like that cosmic-dream physical body which you laid beneath the dream-sands at Puri in your dream-world. I am in truth resurrected—not on earth but on an astral planet. Its inhabitants are better able than earthly humanity to meet my lofty standards. There you and your exalted loved ones shall someday come to be with me."

"Deathless guru, tell me more!"

Master gave a quick, mirthful chuckle. "Please, dear one," he said, "won't you relax your hold a little?"

"Only a little!" I had been embracing him with an octopus grip. I could detect the same faint, fragrant, natural odor which had been characteristic of his body before. The thrilling touch of his divine flesh still persists around the inner sides of my arms and in my palms whenever I recall those glorious hours.

"As prophets are sent on earth to help men work out their physical karma, so I have been directed by God to serve on an astral planet as a savior," Sri Yukteswar explained. "It is called Hiranyaloka or 'Illumined Astral Planet.' There I am aiding advanced beings to rid themselves of astral karma and thus attain liberation from astral rebirths. The dwellers on Hiranyaloka are highly developed spiritually; all of them had acquired, in their last earth-incarnation, the meditation-given power of consciously leaving their physical bodies at death. No one can enter Hiranyaloka unless he has passed on earth beyond the state of *sabikalpa samadhi* into the higher state of *nirbikalpa samadhi*.*

---

* In *sabikalpa samadhi* the devotee has attained realization of his oneness with Spirit but cannot maintain his cosmic consciousness except in the immobile trance state. By continuous meditation he reaches the superior state of *nirbikalpa samadhi*, in which he may move freely in the world without any loss of God-perception.

In *nirbikalpa samadhi* the yogi dissolves the last vestiges of his material or earthly karma. Nevertheless, he may still have certain astral and causal karma to work out, and therefore takes astral and then causal reembodiments on high-vibrational spheres.

"Hiranyaloka inhabitants have already passed through the ordinary astral spheres, where nearly all beings from earth must go at death; there they destroyed many seeds of karma connected with their past actions in astral worlds. None but advanced devotees can perform such redemptive work effectively in the astral spheres.* Then, in order to free their souls fully from all traces of astral karma, these aspirants were drawn by cosmic law to be reborn in new astral bodies on Hiranyaloka, the astral sun or heaven, where I am present to help them. There are also nearly perfect beings on Hiranyaloka who have come from the superior causal world."

My mind was now in such perfect attunement with my guru's that he was conveying his word-pictures to me partly by speech and partly by thought transference. I was thus quickly receiving his idea-tabloids.

"You have read in the scriptures," Master went on, "that God encased the human soul successively in three bodies—the idea, or causal, body; the subtle astral body, seat of man's mental and emotional natures; and the gross physical body. On earth a man is equipped with his physical senses. An astral being works with his consciousness and feelings and a body made of lifetrons.† A causal-bodied being remains in the blissful realm of ideas. My work is with those astral beings who are preparing to enter the causal world."

"Adorable Master, please tell me more about the astral cosmos." Though I had slightly relaxed my embrace at Sri Yukteswar's request, my arms were still around him. Treasure beyond all treasures, my guru who had laughed at death to reach me!

"There are many astral planets, teeming with astral beings," Master began. "The inhabitants use astral planes, or masses of light, to travel from one planet to another, faster than electricity and radioactive energies.

"The astral universe, made of various subtle vibrations of light and color, is hundreds of times larger than the material cosmos. The entire physical creation hangs like a little solid basket under the huge luminous balloon of the astral sphere. Just as many physical suns and stars roam in space, so there are also countless astral solar and stellar systems. Their planets have astral suns and moons, more beautiful than the physical ones. The astral luminaries resemble the aurora borealis—the sunny astral aurora being more

---

* Because most persons, enjoying the beauty of the astral worlds, do not see any necessity for strenuous spiritual effort.

† Sri Yukteswar used the word *prana*; I have translated it as lifetrons. The Hindu scriptures refer not only to the *anu*, "atom," and to the *paramanu*, "beyond the atom," finer electronic energies, but also to *prana*, "creative lifetronic force." Atoms and electrons are blind forces; prana is inherently intelligent. The pranic lifetrons in the spermatozoa and ova, for instance, guide the development of the embryo according to a karmic design.

dazzling than the mild-rayed moon-aurora. The astral day and night are longer than those of earth.

"The astral world is infinitely beautiful, clean, pure, and orderly. There are no dead planets or barren lands. The terrestrial blemishes—weeds, bacteria, insects, snakes—are absent. Unlike the variable climates and seasons of the earth, the astral planets maintain the even temperature of an eternal spring, with occasional luminous white snow and rain of many-colored lights. Astral planets abound in opal lakes and bright seas and rainbow rivers.

"The ordinary astral universe—not the subtler astral heaven of Hiranyaloka—is peopled with millions of astral beings who have come, more or less recently, from the earth, and also with myriads of fairies, mermaids, fishes, animals, goblins, gnomes, demigods, and spirits, all residing on different astral planets in accordance with karmic qualifications. Various spheric mansions or vibratory regions are provided for good and evil spirits. Good ones can travel freely, but the evil spirits are confined to limited zones. In the same way that human beings live on the surface of the earth, worms inside the soil, fish in water, and birds in air, so astral beings of different grades are assigned to suitable vibratory quarters.

"Among the fallen dark angels, expelled from other worlds, friction and war take place with lifetronic bombs or mental mantric* vibratory rays. These beings dwell in the gloom-drenched regions of the lower astral cosmos, working out their evil karma.

"In the vast realms above the dark astral prison, all is shining and beautiful. The astral cosmos is more naturally attuned than the earth to the divine will and plan of perfection. Every astral object is manifested primarily by the will of God, and partially by the will-call of astral beings. They possess the power of modifying or enhancing the grace and form of anything already created by the Lord. He has given His astral children the freedom and privilege of changing or improving at will the astral cosmos. On earth a solid must be transformed into liquid or other form through natural or chemical processes, but astral solids are changed into astral liquids, gases, or energy solely and instantly by the will of the inhabitants.

"The earth is dark with warfare and murder in the sea, land, and air," my guru continued, "but the astral realms know a happy harmony and equality. Astral beings dematerialize or materialize their forms at will. Flowers

---

* Adjective of *mantra*, chanted seed-sounds discharged by the mental gun of concentration. The *Puranas* (ancient *shastras* or treatises) describe these mantric wars between *devas* and *asuras* (gods and demons). An *asura* once tried to slay a *deva* with a potent chant. Because of mispronunciation the mental bomb acted as a boomerang and killed the demon.

or fish or animals can metamorphose themselves, for a time, into astral men. All astral beings are free to assume any form, and can easily commune together. No fixed, definite, natural law hems them round—any astral tree, for example, can be successfully asked to produce an astral mango or other desired fruit, flower, or indeed any other object. Certain karmic restrictions are present, but there are no distinctions in the astral world about desirability of various forms. Everything is vibrant with God's creative light.

"No one is born of woman; offspring are materialized by astral beings through the help of their cosmic will into specially patterned, astrally condensed forms. The recently physically disembodied being arrives in an astral family through invitation, drawn by similar mental and spiritual tendencies.

"The astral body is not subject to cold or heat or other natural conditions. The anatomy includes an astral brain, or the thousand-petaled lotus of light, and six awakened centers in the *sushumna*, or astral cerebrospinal axis. The heart draws cosmic energy as well as light from the astral brain, and pumps it to the astral nerves and body cells, or lifetrons. Astral beings are able to effect changes in their forms by lifetronic force and by holy mantric vibrations.

"In most cases the astral body is an exact counterpart of the last physical form. The face and figure of an astral person resemble those of his youth in his previous earthly sojourn. Occasionally someone, like myself, chooses to retain his old-age appearance." Master, emanating the very essence of youth, chuckled merrily.

"Unlike the spacial, three-dimensional physical world cognized only by the five senses, the astral spheres are visible to the all-inclusive sixth sense—intuition," Sri Yukteswar went on. "By sheer intuitional feeling, all astral beings see, hear, smell, taste, and touch. They possess three eyes, two of which are partly closed. The third and chief astral eye, vertically placed on the forehead, is open. Astral beings have all the outer sensory organs—ears, eyes, nose, tongue, and skin—but they employ the intuitional sense to experience sensations through any part of the body; they can see through the ear, or nose, or skin. They are able to hear through the eyes or tongue, and can taste through the ears or skin, and so forth.*

"Man's physical body is exposed to countless dangers, and is easily hurt or maimed; the ethereal astral body may occasionally be cut or bruised but is healed at once by mere willing."

"Gurudeva, are all astral persons beautiful?"

---

* Examples of such powers are not wanting even on earth, as in the case of Helen Keller and other rare beings.

"Beauty in the astral world is known to be a spiritual quality, and not an outward conformation," Sri Yukteswar replied. "Astral beings therefore attach little importance to facial features. They have the privilege, however, of costuming themselves at will with new, colorful, astrally materialized bodies. Just as worldly men don new array for gala events, so astral beings find occasions to bedeck themselves in specially designed forms.

"Joyous astral festivities on the higher astral planets like Hiranyaloka take place when a being is liberated from the astral world through spiritual advancement, and is therefore ready to enter the heaven of the causal world. On such occasions the Invisible Heavenly Father, and the saints who are merged in Him, materialize Themselves into bodies of Their own choice and join the astral celebration. In order to please His beloved devotee, the Lord takes any desired form. If the devotee worshipped through devotion, he sees God as the Divine Mother. To Jesus, the Father-aspect of the Infinite One was appealing beyond other conceptions. The individuality with which the Creator has endowed each of His creatures makes every conceivable and inconceivable demand on the Lord's versatility!" My guru and I laughed happily together.

"Friends of other lives easily recognize one another in the astral world," Sri Yukteswar went on in his beautiful, flutelike voice. "Rejoicing at the immortality of friendship, they realize the indestructibility of love, often doubted at the time of the sad, delusive partings of earthly life.

"The intuition of astral beings pierces through the veil and observes human activities on earth, but man cannot view the astral world unless his sixth sense is somewhat developed. Thousands of earth-dwellers have momentarily glimpsed an astral being or an astral world.*

"The advanced beings on Hiranyaloka remain mostly awake in ecstasy during the long astral day and night, helping to work out intricate problems of cosmic government and the redemption of prodigal sons, earthbound souls. When the Hiranyaloka beings sleep, they have occasional dreamlike astral visions. Their minds are usually engrossed in the conscious state of highest *nirbikalpa* bliss.

"Inhabitants in all parts of the astral worlds are still subject to mental agonies. The sensitive minds of the higher beings on planets like Hiranyaloka

---

* On earth pure-minded children are sometimes able to see the graceful astral bodies of fairies. Through drugs or intoxicating drink, whose use is forbidden by all scriptures, a man may so derange his consciousness that he perceives the hideous forms in astral hells.

feel keen pain if any mistake is made in conduct or perception of truth. These advanced beings endeavor to attune their every act and thought with the perfection of spiritual law.

"Communication among the astral inhabitants is held entirely by astral telepathy and television; there is none of the confusion and misunderstanding of the written and spoken word which earth-dwellers must endure. Just as persons on the cinema screen appear to move and act through a series of light pictures, and do not actually breathe, so the astral beings walk and work as intelligently guided and coordinated images of light, without the necessity of drawing power from oxygen. Man depends upon solids, liquids, gases, and energy for sustenance; astral beings sustain themselves principally by cosmic light."

"Master mine, do astral beings eat anything?" I was drinking in his marvelous elucidations with the receptivity of all my faculties—mind, heart, soul. Superconscious perceptions of truth are permanently real and changeless, while fleeting sense experiences and impressions are never more than temporarily or relatively true, and soon lose in memory all their vividness. My guru's words were so penetratingly imprinted on the parchment of my being that at any time, by transferring my mind to the superconscious state, I can clearly relive the divine experience.

"Luminous raylike vegetables abound in the astral soils," he answered. "The astral beings consume vegetables, and drink a nectar flowing from glorious fountains of light and from astral brooks and rivers. Just as invisible images of persons on the earth can be dug out of the ether and made visible by a television apparatus, later being dismissed again into space, so the God-created, unseen astral blueprints of vegetables and plants floating in the ether are precipitated on an astral planet by the will of its inhabitants. In the same way, from the wildest fancy of these beings, whole gardens of fragrant flowers are materialized, returning later to the etheric invisibility. Although dwellers on the heavenly planets like Hiranyaloka are almost freed from any necessity of eating, still higher is the unconditioned existence of almost completely liberated souls in the causal world, who eat nothing save the manna of bliss.

"The earth-liberated astral being meets a multitude of relatives, fathers, mothers, wives, husbands, and friends, acquired during different incarnations on earth,* as they appear from time to time in various parts of the astral realms. He is therefore at a loss to understand whom to love especially; he

---

* Lord Buddha was once asked why a man should love all persons equally. "Because," the great teacher replied, "in the very numerous and varied life-spans of each man, every other being has at one time or another been dear to him."

learns in this way to give a divine and equal love to all, as children and individualized expressions of God. Though the outward appearance of loved
ones may have changed, more or less according to the development of new
qualities in the latest life of any particular soul, the astral being employs his
unerring intuition to recognize all those once dear to him in other planes of
existence, and to welcome them to their new astral home. Because every atom
in creation is inextinguishably dowered with individuality,* an astral friend
will be recognized no matter what costume he may don, even as on earth an
actor's identity is discoverable by close observation despite any disguise.

"The span of life in the astral world is much longer than on earth. A
normal advanced astral being's average life period is from five hundred to one
thousand years, measured in accordance with earthly standards of time. As
certain redwood trees outlive most trees by millenniums, or as some yogis live
several hundred years though most men die before the age of sixty, so some
astral beings live much longer than the usual span of astral existence. Visitors
to the astral world dwell there for a longer or shorter period in accordance
with the weight of their physical karma, which draws them back to earth
within a specified time.

"The astral being does not have to contend painfully with death at the
time of shedding his luminous body. Many of these beings nevertheless feel
slightly nervous at the thought of dropping their astral form for the subtler
causal one. The astral world is free from unwilling death, disease, and old
age. These three dreads are the curse of earth, where man has allowed his
consciousness to identify itself almost wholly with a frail physical body
requiring constant aid from air, food, and sleep in order to exist at all.

"Physical death is attended by the disappearance of breath and the disintegration of fleshly cells. Astral death consists of the dispersement of
lifetrons, those manifest units of energy which constitute the life of astral
beings. At physical death a being loses his consciousness of flesh and becomes
aware of his subtle body in the astral world. Experiencing astral death in due
time, a being thus passes from the consciousness of astral birth and death to
that of physical birth and death. These recurrent cycles of astral and physical encasement are the ineluctable destiny of all unenlightened beings.
Scriptural definitions of heaven and hell sometimes stir man's deeper-than-
subconscious memories of his long series of experiences in the blithesome
astral and disappointing terrestrial worlds."

---

* The eight elemental qualities that enter into all created life, from atom to man, are
earth, water, fire, air, ether, sensory mind (*manas*), intelligence (*buddhi*), and individuality or ego (*ahamkara*). (Cf. Bhagavad Gita: VII:4.)

"Beloved Master," I asked, "will you please describe more in detail the difference between rebirth on the earth and in the astral and causal spheres?"

"Man as an individualized soul is essentially causal-bodied," my guru explained. "That body is a matrix of the thirty-five *ideas* required by God as the basic or causal thought forces from which He later formed the subtle astral body of nineteen elements and the gross physical body of sixteen elements.

"The nineteen elements of the astral body are mental, emotional, and lifetronic. The nineteen components are intelligence; ego; feeling; mind (sense-consciousness); five instruments of *knowledge*, the subtle counterparts of the senses of sight, hearing, smell, taste, touch; five instruments of *action*, the mental correspondence for the executive abilities to procreate, excrete, talk, walk, and exercise manual skill; and five instruments of *life force*, those empowered to perform the crystallizing, assimilating, eliminating, metabolizing, and circulating functions of the body. This subtle astral encasement of nineteen elements survives the death of the physical body, which is made of sixteen gross chemical elements.

"God thought out different ideas within Himself and projected them into dreams. Lady Cosmic Dream thus sprang out decorated in all her colossal endless ornaments of relativity.

"In thirty-five thought categories of the causal body, God elaborated all the complexities of man's nineteen astral and sixteen physical counterparts. By condensation of vibratory forces, first subtle, then gross, He produced man's astral body and finally his physical form. According to the law of relativity, by which the Prime Simplicity has become the bewildering manifold, the causal cosmos and causal body are different from the astral cosmos and astral body; the physical cosmos and physical body are likewise characteristically at variance with the other forms of creation.

"The fleshly body is made of the fixed, objectified dreams of the Creator. The dualities are ever present on earth: disease and health, pain and pleasure, loss and gain. Human beings find limitation and resistance in three-dimensional matter. When man's desire to live is severely shaken by disease or other causes, death arrives; the heavy overcoat of the flesh is temporarily shed. The soul, however, remains encased in the astral and causal bodies.* The cohesive force by which all three bodies are held together is desire. The power of unfulfilled desires is the root of all of man's slavery.

"Physical desires are rooted in egotism and sense pleasures. The compulsion or temptation of sensory experience is more powerful than the desire-force connected with astral attachments or causal perceptions.

---

* "Body" signifies any soul encasement, whether gross or subtle. The three bodies are cages for the Bird of Paradise.

"Astral desires center around enjoyment in terms of vibration. Astral beings enjoy the ethereal music of the spheres and are entranced by the sight of all creation as exhaustless expressions of changing light. The astral beings also smell, taste, and touch light. Astral desires are thus connected with an astral being's power to precipitate all objects and experiences as forms of light or as condensed thoughts or dreams.

"Causal desires are fulfilled by perception only. The nearly free beings who are encased only in the causal body see the whole universe as realizations of the dream-ideas of God; they can materialize anything and everything in sheer thought. Causal beings therefore consider the enjoyment of physical sensations or astral delights as gross and suffocating to the soul's fine sensibilities. Causal beings work out their desires by materializing them instantly.* Those who find themselves covered only by the delicate veil of the causal body can bring universes into manifestation even as the Creator. Because all creation is made of the cosmic dream-texture, the soul thinly clothed in the causal has vast realizations of power.

"A soul, being invisible by nature, can be distinguished only by the presence of its body or bodies. The mere presence of a body signifies that its existence is made possible by unfulfilled desires.*

"So long as the soul of man is encased in one, two, or three body-containers, sealed tightly with the corks of ignorance and desires, he cannot merge with the sea of Spirit. When the gross physical receptacle is destroyed by the hammer of death, the other two coverings—astral and causal—still remain to prevent the soul from consciously joining the Omnipresent Life. When desirelessness is attained through wisdom, its power disintegrates the two remaining vessels. The tiny human soul emerges, free at last; it is one with the Measureless Amplitude."

I asked my divine guru to shed further light on the high and mysterious causal world.

"The causal world is indescribably subtle," he replied. "In order to understand it, one would have to possess such tremendous powers of concentration that he could close his eyes and visualize the astral cosmos and the physical cosmos in all their vastness—the luminous balloon with the solid basket—as existing in ideas only. If by this superhuman concentration one succeeded in converting or resolving the two cosmoses with all their

---

* "And he said unto them, Wheresoever the body is, thither will the eagles be gathered together."—Luke 17:37. Wherever the soul is encased in the physical body or in the astral body or in the causal body, there the eagles of desires—which prey on human sense weaknesses, or on astral and causal attachments—will also gather to keep the soul a prisoner.

complexities into sheer ideas, he would then reach the causal world and stand on the borderline of fusion between mind and matter. There one perceives all created things—solids, liquids, gases, electricity, energy, all beings, gods, men, animals, plants, bacteria—as forms of consciousness, just as a man can close his eyes and realize that he exists, even though his body is invisible to his physical eyes and is present only as an idea.

"Whatever a human being can do in fancy, a causal being can do in reality. The most colossal imaginative human intelligence is able, in mind only, to range from one extreme of thought to another, to skip mentally from planet to planet, to tumble endlessly down a pit of eternity, or soar rocketlike into the galaxied canopy, or scintillate like a searchlight over milky ways and the starry spaces. But beings in the causal world have a much greater freedom, and can effortlessly manifest their thoughts into instant objectivity, without any material or astral obstruction or karmic limitation.

"Causal beings realize that the physical cosmos is not primarily constructed of electrons, nor is the astral cosmos basically composed of lifetrons—both in reality are created from the minutest particles of God-thought, chopped and divided by *maya*, the law of relativity that apparently intervenes to separate creation from its Creator.

"Souls in the causal world recognize one another as individualized points of joyous Spirit; their thought-things are the only objects that surround them. Causal beings see the difference between their bodies and thoughts to be merely ideas. As a man, closing his eyes, can visualize a dazzling white light or a faint blue haze, so causal beings by thought alone are able to see, hear, smell, taste, touch; they create anything, or dissolve it, by the power of cosmic mind.

"Both death and rebirth in the causal world are in thought. Causal-bodied beings feast only on the ambrosia of eternally new knowledge. They drink from the springs of peace, roam on the trackless soil of perceptions, swim in the ocean-endlessness of bliss. Lo! see their bright thought-bodies zoom past trillions of Spirit-created planets, fresh bubbles of universes, wisdom-stars, spectral dreams of golden nebulae on the skyey bosom of Infinity!

"Many beings remain for thousands of years in the causal cosmos. By deeper ecstasies the freed soul then withdraws itself from the little causal body and puts on the vastness of the causal cosmos. All the separate eddies of ideas, particularized waves of power, love, will, joy, peace, intuition, calmness, self-control, and concentration melt into the ever-joyous Sea of Bliss. No longer does the soul have to experience its joy as an individualized wave of consciousness, but is merged in the One Cosmic Ocean, with all its waves—eternal laughter, thrills, throbs.

"When a soul is out of the cocoon of the three bodies it escapes forever from the law of relativity and becomes the ineffable Ever-Existent.* Behold the butterfly of Omnipresence, its wings etched with stars and moons and suns! The soul expanded into Spirit remains alone in the region of lightless light, darkless dark, thoughtless thought, intoxicated with its ecstasy of joy in God's dream of cosmic creation."

"A free soul!" I ejaculated in awe.

"When a soul finally gets out of the three jars of bodily delusions," Master continued, "it becomes one with the Infinite without any loss of individuality. Christ had won this final freedom even before he was born as Jesus. In three stages of his past, symbolized in his earth-life as the three days of his experience of death and resurrection, he had attained the power to fully arise in Spirit.

"The undeveloped man must undergo countless earthly and astral and causal incarnations in order to emerge from his three bodies. A master who achieves this final freedom may elect to return to earth as a prophet to bring other human beings back to God, or like myself he may choose to reside in the astral cosmos. There a savior assumes some of the burden of the inhabitants' karma† and thus helps them to terminate their cycle of reincarnation in the astral cosmos and go on permanently to the causal spheres. Or a freed soul may enter the causal world to aid its beings to shorten their span in the causal body and thus attain the Absolute Freedom."

"Resurrected One, I want to know more about the karma which forces souls to return to the three worlds." I could listen forever, I thought, to my omniscient Master. Never in his earth-life had I been able at one time to assimilate so much of his wisdom. Now for the first time I was receiving a clear, definite insight into the enigmatic interspaces on the checkerboard of life and death.

"The physical karma or desires of man must be completely worked out before his continued stay in astral worlds becomes possible," my guru elucidated in his thrilling voice. "Two kinds of beings live in the astral spheres.

---

* "Him that overcometh will I make a pillar in the temple of my God, and he shall go no more out (i.e., shall reincarnate no more). . . . To him that overcometh will I grant to sit with me in my throne, even as I also overcame, and am set down with my Father in this throne."—Revelation 3:12, 21.

† Sri Yukteswar was signifying that, even as in his earthly incarnation he had occasionally assumed the weight of disease to lighten his disciples' karma, so in the astral world his mission as a savior enabled him to take on certain astral karma of dwellers on Hiranyaloka, and thus hasten their evolution into the higher causal world.

Those who will have earthly karma to dispose of and who must therefore reinhabit a gross physical body in order to pay their karmic debts could be classified, after physical death, as temporary visitors to the astral world rather than as established residents.

"Beings with unredeemed earthly karma are not permitted after astral death to go to the high causal sphere of cosmic ideas, but must shuttle to and fro from the physical and astral worlds only, conscious successively of their physical body of sixteen gross elements, and of their astral body of nineteen subtle elements. After each loss of his physical body, however, an undeveloped being from the earth remains for the most part in the deep stupor of the death-sleep and is hardly conscious of the beautiful astral sphere. After the astral rest, such a man returns to the material plane for further lessons, gradually accustoming himself, through repeated journeys, to the worlds of subtle astral texture.

"Normal or long-established residents of the astral universe, on the other hand, are those who, freed forever from all material longings, need return no more to the gross vibrations of earth. Such beings have only astral and causal karma to work out. At astral death these beings pass to the infinitely finer and more delicate causal world. At the end of a certain span, determined by cosmic law, these advanced beings then return to Hiranyaloka or a similar high astral planet, reborn in a new astral body to work out their unredeemed astral karma.

"My son, you may now comprehend more fully that I am resurrected by divine decree," Sri Yukteswar continued, "as a savior of astrally reincarnating souls coming back from the causal sphere, in particular, rather than of those astral beings who are coming up from the earth. Those from the earth, if they still retain vestiges of material karma, do not rise to the very high astral planets like Hiranyaloka.

"Just as most people on earth have not learned through meditation-acquired vision to appreciate the superior joys and advantages of astral life and thus, after death, desire to return to the limited, imperfect pleasures of earth, so many astral beings, during the normal disintegration of their astral bodies, fail to picture the advanced state of spiritual joy in the causal world and, dwelling on thoughts of the more gross and gaudy astral happiness, yearn to revisit the astral paradise. Heavy astral karma must be redeemed by such beings before they can achieve after astral death an unbroken stay in the causal thought-world, so thinly partitioned from the Creator.

"Only when a being has no further desires for experiences in the pleasing-to-the-eye astral cosmos, and cannot be tempted to go back there, does he remain in the causal world. Completing there the work of redeeming all causal karma or seeds of past desires, the confined soul thrusts out the last of the three corks of ignorance and, emerging from the final jar of the causal body, commingles with the Eternal.

"Now do you understand?" Master smiled so enchantingly!

"Yes, through your grace. I am speechless with joy and gratitude."

Never from song or story had I ever received such inspiring knowledge. Though the Hindu scriptures refer to the causal and astral worlds and to man's three bodies, how remote and meaningless those pages compared with the warm authenticity of my resurrected Master! For him indeed existed not a single "undiscover'd country from whose bourn no traveller returns"!*

"The interpenetration of man's three bodies is expressed in many ways through his threefold nature," my great guru went on. "In the wakeful state on earth a human being is conscious more or less of his three vehicles. When he is sensuously intent on tasting, smelling, touching, listening, or seeing, he is working principally through his physical body. Visualizing or willing, he is working mainly through his astral body. His causal being finds expression when man is thinking or diving deep in introspection or meditation; the cosmical thoughts of genius come to the man who habitually contacts his causal body. In this sense an individual may be classified broadly as 'a material man,' 'an energetic man,' or 'an intellectual man.'

"A man identifies himself about sixteen hours daily with his physical vehicle. Then he sleeps; if he dreams, he remains in his astral body, effortlessly creating any object even as do the astral beings. If man's sleep be deep and dreamless, for several hours he is able to transfer his consciousness, or sense of I-ness, to the causal body; such sleep is revivifying. A dreamer is contacting his astral and not his causal body; his sleep is not fully refreshing."

I had been lovingly observing Sri Yukteswar while he gave his wondrous exposition.

"Angelic Guru," I said, "your body looks exactly as it did when last I wept over it in the Puri ashram."

"O yes, my new body is a perfect copy of the old one. I materialize or dematerialize this form any time at will, much more frequently than I did while on earth. By quick dematerialization, I now travel instantly by light express from planet to planet or, indeed, from astral to causal or to physical cosmos." My divine guru smiled. "Though you move about so fast these days, I had no difficulty in finding you at Bombay!"

"O Master, I was grieving so deeply about your death!"

"Ah, wherein did I die! Isn't there some contradiction?" Sri Yukteswar's eyes were twinkling with love and amusement.

---

* *Hamlet* (Act III, Scene 1).

"You were only dreaming on earth; on that earth you saw my dream-body," he went on. "Later you buried that dream-image. Now my finer fleshly body—which you behold and are even now embracing rather closely!—is resurrected on another finer dream-planet of God. Someday that finer dream-body and finer dream-planet will pass away; they too are not for-ever. All dream-bubbles must eventually burst at a final wakeful touch. Differentiate, my son Yogananda, between dreams and Reality!"

This idea of Vedantic resurrection struck me with wonder. I was ashamed that I had pitied Master when I had seen his lifeless body at Puri. I comprehended at last that my guru had always been fully awake in God, perceiving his own life and passing on earth, and his present resurrection, as nothing more than relativities of divine ideas in the cosmic dream.

"I have now told you, Yogananda, the truths of my life, death, and res-urrection. Grieve not for me; rather broadcast everywhere the story of my resurrection from the God-dreamed earth of men to another God-dreamed planet of astrally garbed souls! New hope will be infused into the hearts of misery-made, death-fearing dreamers of the world."

"Yes, Master!" How willingly would I share with others my joy at his resurrection!

Paramahansa Yogananda, *Autobiography of a Yogi*

The Benediction

The Sabbath candles
my mother blesses
burn brightly

The flames dance
like little old men,
their visages
crumpled up with joy

To what music?
Or is it the silence
my mother
        has just shut the door on?

Souls are the candleflames'
blue centre
burning stilly;

I gaze entranced
at those of long departed
rabbinical ancestors
lecherous great-uncles
murdered kin
famed disputants in seminaries

Their shadows
linked as one
flicker
on the Friday-white tablecloth

While all the little old men
dance joyfully
in their orbits

Irving Layton, *Fortunate Exile*

⇾ 18 ⇽

Rebirth

"If we understand and feel that here in this life we already have a
link with the infinite, desires and attitudes change."

—C. G. JUNG

There is a lot of truth in the idea that
in our eternal life we are reborn into this world, reincarnated, to make good
the actions of the past, or to find answers to the questions of our forebears.
We are connected at this moment of time with the present world's population and are a part of the collective purpose of its people.

Leading Buddhist teacher and writer Jack Kornfield and his co-writer
Joseph Goldstein say of understanding our karma that we need "the basis for
a very straight-forward development of the wisdom to know whether our
actions will lead to happiness and freedom, or to further suffering."

A most unusual example of the reincarnated soul is that of the four-
teenth Dalai Lama. His own humble—sometimes even humorous—story
of his recruitment, after he recognizes the possessions and associates of the
late thirteenth Dalai Lama, recounts the restoration of the lineage of one
reincarnated high soul. It is believed that this soul is the manifestation of
Avalokiteshvara or Chenrezig, the Bodhisattva of Compassion.

All the masters, including The Mother here, write of the necessity of
the soul not to dwell on the past but to be fully aware in the present of the
great gift of opportunity that is life. We live in a technological and scientific
period in the evolution of the world, and we are moving towards the marrying of the knowledge gained from the past with superconscious wisdom in
an exciting metaphysical and spiritual environment.

⇾⇽

On Earth, immersion in lives of war, disease, crime, affluence, motherhood,
confinement, fame, guilt, hunger, disillusionment, and much, much more
serves to spur the growth of knowledge, wisdom, compassion, and all else

that prepares us for the elevated state beyond the pull of earthly incarnation. To say that perfection takes a long, long time would be an understatement. The journey would be intolerable without the constant change of scene and sustenance that comes from cycling in and out of incarnation. Earth life is not only difficult, it's myopic—we rarely see beyond the desires and imperfections of our physical frames and the flux of circumstances into which we cast ourselves. Yet at death we regain the grander vision of the disembodied state in order to rest, evaluate, and acquire further learning in readiness for the next round of rebirth. Then, having filled our sights with the life to come, we plunge once more into the crucible of earthly existence where deeds determine destiny.

Joel L. Whitton and Joe Fisher, *Life Between Life*

Sri Aurobindo told us last week that this Nature was following an ascending progression in order to manifest more and more the divine consciousness contained in all forms. So, with each new form that it produces, Nature makes a form capable of expressing more completely the spirit which this form contains. But if it were like this, a form comes, develops, reaches its highest point and is followed by another form; the others do not disappear, but the individual does not progress. The individual dog or monkey, for instance, belongs to a species which has its own peculiar characteristics; when the monkey or the man arrives at the height of its possibilities, that is, when a human individual becomes the best type of humanity, it will be finished; the individual will not be able to progress any farther. He belongs to the human species, he will continue to belong to it. So, from the point of view of terrestrial history there is a progress, for each species represents a progress compared with the preceding species; but from the point of view of the individual, there is no progress: he is born, he follows his development, dies and disappears. Therefore, to ensure the progress of the individual, it was necessary to find another means; this one was not adequate. But within the individual, contained in each form, there is an organisation of consciousness which is closer to and more directly under the influence of the inner divine Presence, and the form which is under this influence—this kind of inner concentration of energy—has a life independent of the physical form—this is what we generally call the "soul" or the "psychic being"—and since it is organised around the divine centre it partakes of the divine nature which is immortal, eternal. The outer body falls away, and this remains throughout every experience that it has in each life, and there is a progress from life to life, and it is the progress of the *same* individual. And this movement complements the other, in the sense that instead of a species which progresses relative to other species, it is an individual who passes through all the stages of progress of these species and can continue to progress even when the species have reached the limit of their possibilities and...stay there or disappear—it depends on the case—but they cannot go any farther, whereas the individual, having a life independent of the purely material form, can pass from one form to another and continue his progress *indefinitely*. That makes a double movement which completes itself. And that is why each individual has the possibility of reaching the utmost realisation, independent of the form to which he momentarily belongs.

There are people—there used to be and there still are, I believe—who say they remember their past lives and recount what happened when they were dogs or elephants or monkeys, and tell you stories in great detail about what happened to them. I am not going to argue with them, but anyway this illustrates the fact that before being a man, one could have been a monkey—perhaps one doesn't have the power to remember it, that's another matter—but certainly, this inner divine spark has passed through successive forms in order to become more and more conscious of itself.

The Mother, Life Divine, The Mother's Talks

People sometimes wonder whether reflecting upon the law of karma will lead to feelings of guilt for past unwholesome actions. Guilt is a manifestation of condemnation or aversion toward oneself, which does not understand the changing transformative quality of mind. It solidifies a sense of self by being nonforgiving. Understanding the law of karma leads us to reflect wisely on the skillfulness or unskillfulness of our actions. In the infinite time of our births, through all the realms of existence, we have done so many different kinds of actions, wholesome and unwholesome. In view of karmic law, guilt is an inappropriate feeling, and a rather useless burden. It simply creates more unwholesome results. Coming to an understanding of karma is the basis for a very straightforward development of the wisdom to know whether our actions will lead to happiness and freedom, or to further suffering. When we understand this, it allows us to take responsibility for past actions with an attitude of compassion, appreciating that a particular act may have been unwholesome or harmful, and strongly determining not to repeat it. Guilt is a manifestation of condemnation, wisdom an expression of sensitivity and forgiveness.

Joseph Goldstein and Jack Kornfield,
Seeking the Heart of Wisdom

The Soul

On the Day of Atonement, when Rabbi Abraham Yehoshua would recite the Avodah, the prayer that repeats the service of the high priest in the Temple of Jerusalem, and would come to the passage: "And thus he spoke," he would never say those words, but would say: "And thus I spoke." For he had not forgotten the time his soul was in the body of a high priest of Jerusalem, and he had no need to learn from the outside how they had served in the Temple.

Once he himself related: "Ten times have I been in this world. I was a high priest, I was a prince, I was a king, I was an exilarch. I was ten different kinds of dignitary. But I never learned to love mankind perfectly. And so I was sent forth again and again in order to perfect my love. If I succeed this time, I shall never return again."

Martin Buber, *Tales of the Hasidim*

Is it necessary to know what I was in my previous life?
If it is necessary you will know it.

The Mother, *Words of the Mother*, Part Two

The whole purpose of reincarnation is to facilitate the continuity of a being's work.

The Dalai Lama, *Freedom in Exile*

Of course, no one had any idea that I might be anything other than an ordinary baby. It was almost unthinkable that more than one *tulku* could be born into the same family and certainly my parents had no idea that I would be proclaimed Dalai Lama. My father's recovery from illness was auspicious, but it was not taken to be of great significance. I myself likewise had no particular intimation of what lay ahead. My earliest memories are very ordinary. Some people put great emphasis on a person's first recollections, but I do not. Amongst mine I remember, for example, observing a group of children fighting and running to join in with the weaker side. I also remember the first time I saw a camel. These are quite common in parts of Mongolia and occasionally they were brought over the border. It looked huge and majestic and very frightening. I also recall discovering one day that I had worms—a common affliction in the East.

One thing that I remember enjoying particularly as a very young boy was going into the hen coop to collect the eggs with my mother and then staying behind. I liked to sit in the hens' nest and make clucking noises. Another favorite occupation of mine as an infant was to pack things in a bag as if I was about to go on a long journey. "I'm going to Lhasa, I'm going to Lhasa," I would say. This, coupled with my insistence that I be allowed always to sit at the head of the table, was later said to be an indication that I must have known that I was destined for greater things. I also had a number of dreams as a small child that were open to a similar interpretation, but I cannot say categorically that I knew of my future all along. Later on, my mother told me several stories which could be taken as signs of high birth. For example, I never allowed anyone but her to handle my bowl. Nor did I ever show fear of strangers.

Before going on to tell about my discovery as Dalai Lama, I must first say something about Buddhism and its history in Tibet. The founder of Buddhism was an historical figure, Siddhartha, who came to be recognised as the Buddha Shakyamuni. He was born more than 2,500 years ago. His teachings, now known as the *Dharma*, or Buddhism, were introduced to Tibet during the fourth century A.D. They took several centuries to supplant the native Bon religion and become fully established, but eventually the country was so thoroughly converted that Buddhist principles governed all society, at every level. And whilst Tibetans are by nature quite aggressive people and quite warlike, their increasing interest in religious practice was a major factor in bringing about the country's isolation. Before then, Tibet possessed a vast empire, which dominated Central Asia with territories covering large parts of northern India, Nepal and Bhutan in the south. It also included much Chinese territory. In 763 A.D., Tibetan forces actually captured the Chinese capital, where they extracted promises of tribute and other concessions. However, as Tibetans' enthusiasm for Buddhism increased, Tibet's relations with her neighbours became of a spiritual rather than a political nature. This was especially true of China, where a "priest-patron" relationship developed. The Manchu Emperors, who were Buddhists, referred to the Dalai Lama as "King of Expounding Buddhism."

The fundamental precept of Buddhism is Interdependence or the Law of Cause and Effect. This simply states that everything which an individual being experiences is derived through action from motivation. Motivation is thus the root of both action and experience. From this understanding are derived the Buddhist theories of consciousness and rebirth.

The first holds that, because cause gives rise to effect which in turn becomes the cause of further effect, consciousness must be continual. It flows on and on, gathering experiences and impressions from one moment to the next. At the point of physical death, it follows that a being's consciousness contains an imprint of all these past experiences and impressions, and the actions which preceded them. This is known as *karma*, which means "action." It is thus consciousness, with its attendant *karma*, which then becomes "reborn" in a new body—animal, human or divine.

So, to give a simple example, a person who has spent his or her life mistreating animals could quite easily be reborn in the next life as a dog belonging to someone who is unkind to animals. Similarly, meritorious conduct in this life will assist in a favourable rebirth in the next.

Buddhists further believe that because the basic nature of consciousness is neutral, it is possible to escape from the unending cycle of birth, suffering, death and rebirth that life inevitably entails, but only when all negative *karma* has been eliminated along with all worldly attachments. When this point is reached, the consciousness in question is believed to attain first liberation and then ultimately Buddhahood. However, according to Buddhism in the Tibetan tradition, a being that achieves Buddhahood, although freed from *Samsara*, the "wheel of suffering," as the phenomenon of existence is known, will continue to return to work for the benefit of all other sentient beings until such time as each one is similarly liberated.

Now in my own case, I am held to be the reincarnation of each of the previous thirteen Dalai Lamas of Tibet (the first having been born in 1351 A.D.), who are in turn considered to be manifestations of Avalokiteshvara, or Chenrezig, Bodhisattva of Compassion, holder of the White Lotus. Thus I am believed also to be a manifestation of Chenrezig, in fact the seventy-fourth in a lineage that can be traced back to a Brahmin boy who lived in the time of Buddha Shakyamuni. I am often asked whether I truly believe this. The answer is not simple to give. But as a fifty-six-year-old, when I consider my experiences during this present life, and given my Buddhist beliefs, I have no difficulty accepting that I am spiritually connected both to the thirteen previous Dalai Lamas, to Chenrezig and to the Buddha himself.

When I was not quite three years old, a search party that had been sent out by the Government to find the new incarnation of the Dalai Lama arrived at Kumbum monastery. It had been led there by a number of signs. One of these concerned the embalmed body of my predecessor, Thupten Gyatso, the Thirteenth Dalai Lama, who had died aged fifty-seven in 1933. During its period of sitting in state, the head was discovered to have turned from facing south to north-east. Shortly after that the Regent, himself a senior lama, had a vision. Looking into the waters of the sacred lake, Lhamoi Lhatso, in southern Tibet, he clearly saw the Tibetan letters *Ah*, *Ka* and *Ma* float into view. These were followed by the image of a three-storeyed monastery with a turquoise and gold roof and a path running from it to a hill. Finally, he saw a small house with strangely shaped guttering. He was sure that the letter *Ah* referred to Amdo, the north-eastern province, so it was there that the search party was sent.

By the time they reached Kumbum, the members of the search party felt that they were on the right track. It seemed likely that if the letter *Ah* referred to Amdo, then *Ka* must indicate the monastery at Kumbum—which was indeed three-storeyed and turquoise-roofed. They now only needed to locate a hill and a house with peculiar guttering. So they began to search the neighbouring villages. When they saw the gnarled branches of juniper wood on the roof of my parents' house, they were certain that the new Dalai Lama would not be far away. Nevertheless, rather than reveal the purpose of their visit, the group asked only to stay the night. The leader of the party, Kewtsang Rinpoché, then pretended to be a servant and spent much of the evening observing and playing with the youngest child in the house.

The child recognised him and called out "Sera lama, Sera lama." Sera was Kewtsang Rinpoché's monastery. Next day they left—only to return a few days later as a formal deputation. This time they brought with them a number of things that had belonged to my predecessor, together with several similar items that did not. In every case, the infant correctly identified those belonging to the Thirteenth Dalai Lama saying, "It's mine. It's mine." This more or less convinced the search party that they had found the new incarnation. However, there was another candidate to be seen before a final decision could be reached. But it was not long before the boy from Taktser was acknowledged to be the new Dalai Lama. I was that child.

Needless to say, I do not remember very much of these events. I was too small. My only real recollection is of a man with piercing eyes. These turned out to belong to a man named Kenrap Tenzin, who became my Master of the Robes and later taught me to write.

As soon as the search party had concluded that the child from Taktser was the true incarnation of the Dalai Lama, word was sent back to Lhasa informing the Regent. It would be several months before official confirmation was received. Until then, I was to remain at home. In the meantime, Ma Bufeng, the local Governor, began to make trouble. But eventually I was taken by my parents to Kumbum monastery, where I was installed in a ceremony that took place at dawn. I remember this fact particularly as I was surprised to be woken and dressed before the sun had risen. I also remember being seated on a throne.

The Dalai Lama, *Freedom in Exile*

In rebirth it is not the external being, that which is formed by parents, environment and circumstances—the mental, the vital and the physical—that is born again: it is only the psychic being that passes from body to body. Logically, then, neither the mental nor the vital being can remember past lives or recognise itself in the character or mode of life of this or that person. The psychic being alone can remember; and it is by becoming conscious of our psychic being that we can have at the same time exact impressions about our past lives.

Besides, it is much more important for us to fix our attention upon what we want to become than upon what we have been.

The Mother, *Words of the Mother*, Part Two

"The Soul falls from her native place in the Highest Heaven, thru the Heavenly Spheres, to her first incarnation on Earth. By means of a series of sojourns in Hades and reincarnations on Earth...she is purified from the taint of the flesh. Then, at last, she returns to her native place in the Highest Heaven, passing, in the upward flight of her Chariot, thru the Heavenly Spheres, as thru *Stations or Doors*."

Martha Graham, *Notebooks of Martha Graham*

❖ VI ❖

Awe

"Awe is what moves us forward"
— JOSEPH CAMPBELL

Through awareness, expanded consciousness, and the wisdom that comes from pain and suffering and the trials of the journey, a vast land of eternal beauty unfolds before us. It's a place we recognize from deep within our souls, an awesome mystery of which we are a part. As the first stages of the journey towards illumination end, a joyous existence in the greater spaces begins. And it begins here on earth, in our more loosely defined home. We are globes moving on a globe; we are all related, all part of it. Our existence contributes to its energy, and it to ours, and this energy extends further to the heavens and the stars, who become like friends, with special messages for us, special hope. At the same time, the largest message is delivered in the smallest, simplest way—through incidents that reveal the connected truth, through rites of passage or events that signify the larger meaning in the everyday. When we are born into this awesome land of mystery and miracles, we know deep inside us that a shift has happened: we are partakers of divine energy, we have finally developed, trained, progressed, and learnt the lessons to arrive at the place where we are enfolded into the everlasting heart and mind of God.

><

Awe is an intuition for the dignity of all things, a realization that things not only are what they are but also stand, however, remotely, for something supreme.

Awe is a sense for the transcendence, for the reference everywhere to mystery beyond all things. It enables us to perceive in the world intimations of the divine,...to sense the ultimate in the common and the simple; to feel in the rush of the passing the stillness of the eternal. What we cannot comprehend by analysis, we become aware of in awe.

Abraham Joshua Heschel, *Who Is Man?*

✦ 19 ✦

The Life Divine

"The 'I,' however, is this initially pure unity which relates itself to itself—not immediately, but in that it abstracts from all determinateness and content, and goes back to the freedom of its unrestricted self-equality. Thus the 'I' is 'universitality,' but it is 'individuality' just as immediately."

— MARTIN HEIDEGGER

When we fully realize that we are one with the All and the All is one with us, all things in our own individual life collect in a reverential peace. God's gifts—love, grace, creativity, mysticism, peace, joy—are revealed from our own selves, and when they come, they do not again depart. Once the gifts are recognized as the nourishment of our existence and lived and revealed through our work, our study, our creativity, our relationships, then we become at one with the Tao, the invisible thread of life with which we are connected, at one with the divine energy, absorbed into the eternal essence of the life without end.

In this section, I have included Raymond M. Smullyan's exceptional dialogue between God and mortal "Is God a Taoist?" as it encapsulates an understanding of God as the tao, the one who is "everywhere and nowhere" (Thomas Merton). Smullyan illustrates the struggle that the modern human being has in trying to understand the God who is so flexible, who has given us free will. It might be that since Adam and Eve took liberties with this free will, we have a reason to misunderstand and mistrust it. By providing the discussion the way he has, Smullyan paints a clear picture of the transcended place of the tao, the truth of the world.

✦

Tao of Self

Nature shall live to manifest secret God,
The Spirit shall take up the human play,
This earthly life become the Life Divine.

Sri Aurobindo, *Savitri*

The world in which we are born is brutal and cruel, and at the same time of divine beauty. Which element we think outweighs the other, whether meaninglessness or meaning, is a matter of temperament. If meaninglessness were absolutely preponderant, the meaningfulness of life would vanish to an increasing degree with each step in our development. But that is—or seems to me—not the case. Probably, as in all metaphysical questions, both are true: Life is—or has—meaning and meaninglessness. I cherish the anxious hope that meaning will preponderate and win the battle.

When Lao-tzu says: "All are clear, I alone am clouded," he is expressing what I now feel in advanced old age. Lao-tzu is the example of a man with superior insight who has seen and experienced worth and worthlessness, and who at the end of his life desires to return into his own being, into the eternal unknowable meaning. The archetype of the old man who has seen enough is eternally true. At every level of intelligence this type appears, and its lineaments are always the same, whether it be an old peasant or a great philosopher like Lao-tzu. This is old age, and a limitation. Yet there is so much that fills me: plants, animals, clouds, day and night, and the eternal in man. The more uncertain I have felt about myself, the more there has grown up in me a feeling of kinship with all things. In fact it seems to me as if that alienation which so long separated me from the world has become transferred into my own inner world, and has revealed to me an unexpected unfamiliarity with myself.

C. G. Jung, Memories, Dreams, Reflections

The environmental is not a world—it is an individual thing.

A spiritual atmosphere is more important than outer conditions; if one can get that and also create one's own spiritual air to breathe in and live in it, that is the true condition of progress.

Sri Aurobindo, Words of Sri Aurobindo, Third Series

Eternity is not a timeless state in the sense that events that take place in time will simply have ceased to be, but rather in the sense that time is fulfilled, that the events have reached their consummation. The whole of the past will be present to me, not in its dispersion in time, in its state of becoming, but in its fullness, its complete being. Eternity is *"tota et simul"*—the total and simultaneous enjoyment of unending life. Everyone and everything will be totally and simultaneously present to everyone and everything. All the multiplicity of creation will be there, but it will be there in its unity. When we think of unity, we lose sight of the multiplicity; when we think of multiplicity, we lose sight of the unity. But in eternity the many are contained in the One without losing their individuality. Each human being is a focus of the divine Light which shines through all equally, but each receives it according to its capacity. Each is conscious only of the divine Light itself and loses itself in its radiance; each is filled to capacity and knows no difference, yet the distinctions and the differences remain. The experience is of "non-duality," of immersion in the divine Being, Knowledge and Bliss, yet no two souls are the same and the experience of each is unique. This was the very purpose of creation—that each unique, individual being should participate in its own way in the divine Being, should realize its eternal "idea" in God, should "become" God by participation, God expressing himself through that unique being.

Bede Griffiths, *Return to the Centre*

To be and to be fully is Nature's aim in us; but to be fully is to be wholly conscious of one's being: unconsciousness, half consciousness or deficient consciousness is a state of being not in possession of itself; it is existence, but not fullness of being. To be aware wholly or integrally of oneself and of all the truth of one's being is the necessary condition of true possession of existence.

But also, since consciousness carries in itself the force of existence, to be fully is to have the intrinsic and integral force of one's being; it is to come into possession of all one's force of self and of all its use. To be merely, without possessing the force of one's being or with a half-force or deficient force of it, is a mutilated or diminished existence; it is to exist, but it is not fullness of being....

Lastly, to be fully is to have the full delight of being. Being without delight of being, without an entire delight of itself and all things is something neutral or diminished; it is existence, but it is not fullness of being. This delight too must be intrinsic, self-existent, automatic; it cannot be dependent on things outside itself: whatever it delights in, it makes part of itself, has the joy of it as part of its universality. All undelight, all pain and suffering are a sign of imperfection, of incompleteness; they arise from a division of being, an incompleteness of consciousness of being, an incompleteness of the force of being. To become complete in being, in consciousness of being, in force of being, in delight of being and to live in this integrated completeness is the divine living.

But, again, to be fully is to be universally. To be in the limitations of a small restricted ego is to exist, but it is an imperfect existence.... All being is one and to be fully is to be all that is. To be in the being of all and to include all in one's being, to be conscious of the consciousness of all, to be integrated in force with the universal force...to feel all selves as one's own self, to feel all delight of being as one's own delight of being is a necessary condition of the integral divine living.

But thus to be universally in the fullness and freedom of one's universality, one must be also transcendentally. The spiritual fullness of the being is eternity; if one has not the consciousness of timeless eternal being, if one is dependent on body or embodied mind or embodied life, or dependent on this world or that world or on this condition of being or that condition of being, that is not the reality of self, not the fullness of our spiritual existence....

But one must transcend not only the individual formula but the formula of the universe, for only so can either the individual or the universal existence find its own true being and a perfect harmonisation; both are in their outer formulation incomplete terms of the Transcendence, but they are that in their essence, and it is only by becoming conscious of that essence that individual consciousness or universal consciousness can come to its own fullness and freedom of reality. Otherwise the individual may remain subject to the cosmic movement and its reactions and limitations and miss his entire spiritual freedom. He must enter into the supreme divine Reality, feel his oneness with it, live in it, be its self-creation: all his mind, life, physicality must be converted into terms of its Supernature; all his thoughts, feelings, actions must be determined by it and be it, its self-formation.

Sri Aurobindo, *Words of Sri Aurobindo*, First Series

What Is Enlightenment?

A part of my mind is highly amused that I plan to write about the nature of enlightenment. What presumption! Isn't enlightenment something possessed and understood only by superhuman beings? What in the world can a Western psychologist have to say about it?

As I will elaborate later, many of the most important aspects of enlightenment are nonverbal in nature. Words cannot capture the essence of this knowledge. Further, enlightenment involves certain kinds of knowledge, *state-specific knowledge*, that cannot be adequately comprehended in our ordinary state of consciousness, a point that I will also elaborate upon later. Here we are, right now, using words in our ordinary state of consciousness. It certainly is silly, in one sense, to use words about enlightenment. Nevertheless, words in our ordinary state can be useful in thinking about enlightenment, *especially if we are careful not to confuse the words with the realities*. With this caution in mind, let us go on and consider some aspects of what enlightenment is, and later see how altered states fit in with it.

To begin with, I find it helpful to think about enlightenment as a *continuum* of development rather than an all-or-none state. Just seeing it as a totally-incomprehensible-to-us end point, with no intermediate steps, does make it difficult to talk about, and difficult to do anything about. Compared to the rest of us, a pilot is enlightened about flying airplanes, but he didn't get that way in a single magical act; he studied for a long time, moving along a continuum from being completely unenlightened about flying to knowing more and more about it. When we think about enlightenment on a continuum, we can see it as a process, not just a final state.

Within this overall continuum of enlightenment there are "jumps," though, created by the functioning of altered states, and this is where state-specific knowledge becomes important.

The phenomenon of state-specific knowledge is important in understanding why complete enlightenment must involve access to altered states of consciousness. In a particular state of consciousness you may have access to and/or deeper understanding of certain kinds of knowledge that you cannot adequately comprehend in other states of consciousness. Thus, if you cannot enter a certain state, you can never fully understand certain things. Insofar as these items of state-specific knowledge are important, your life without them is impoverished: you have to settle for partial and often distorted understanding of them based on others' descriptions.

Consider a person with no musical training or talent hearing a symphony for the first time. It may have a strong emotional impact on him, and afterward he may tell his friends that the symphony was beautiful or deeply moving or full of sound. That sort of description is like someone else telling you that in an altered state "I directly experienced the Infinite Love at the core of the universe!" It's impressive-sounding but not very specific or useful if your goal is to reproduce the sounds of the symphony.

Now consider a trained musician hearing the same symphony. In addition to being moved by it, the musician can describe it (at least to other musicians) in quite precise terms of notes, keys, and movements, and even write it out in a musical notation so precise that other musicians can re-create the symphony almost exactly as it was originally played. The musician has far greater understanding (of a specialized kind) of the symphony than the untrained listener. The musician's knowledge is analogous to state-specific knowledge. Similarly, the person who has directly experienced certain kinds of knowledge in an altered state has much more understanding of it than the person whose mind has never functioned in that mode. Reading a retrospective philosophical analysis of a mystical experience of union with the universe, for example, may be intellectually stimulating, but it hardly provides a new foundation for your life the way the experience of union probably did for the person who had the actual experience.

Charles T. Tart, Waking Up

Is God a Taoist?

MORTAL: And therefore, O God, I pray thee, if thou hast one ounce of mercy for this thy suffering creature, absolve me of *having* to have free will!

GOD: You reject the greatest gift I have given thee?

MORTAL: How can you call that which was forced on me a gift? I have free will, but not of my own choice. I have never freely chosen to have free will. I have to have free will, whether I like it or not!

GOD: Why would you wish not to have free will?

MORTAL: Because free will means moral responsibility, and moral responsibility is more than I can bear!

GOD: Why do you find moral responsibility so unbearable?

MORTAL: Why? I honestly can't analyze why; all I know is that I do.

GOD: All right, in that case suppose I absolve you from all moral responsibility but leave you still with free will. Will this be satisfactory?

MORTAL (*after a pause*): No, I am afraid not.

GOD: Ah, just as I thought! So moral responsibility is not the only aspect of free will to which you object. What else about free will is bothering you?

MORTAL: With free will I am capable of sinning, and I don't want to sin!

GOD: If you don't want to sin, then why do you?

MORTAL: Good God! I don't know why I sin, I just do? Evil temptations come along, and try as I can, I cannot resist them.

GOD: If it is really true that you cannot resist them, then you are not sinning of your own free will and hence (at least according to me) not sinning at all.

MORTAL: No, no! I keep feeling that if only I tried harder I could avoid sinning. I understand that the will is infinite. If one wholeheartedly wills not to sin, then one won't.

GOD: Well now, you should know. Do you try as hard as you can to avoid sinning or don't you?

MORTAL: I honestly don't know! At the time, I feel I am trying as hard as I can, but in retrospect, I am worried that maybe I didn't!

GOD: So in other words, you don't really know whether or not you have been sinning. So the possibility is open that you haven't been sinning at all!

MORTAL: Of course this possibility is open, but maybe I have been sinning, and this thought is what so frightens me!

GOD: Why does the thought of your sinning frighten you?

MORTAL: I don't know why! For one thing, you do have a reputation for meting out rather gruesome punishments in the afterlife!

GOD: Oh, that's what's bothering you! Why didn't you say so in the first place instead of all this peripheral talk about free will and responsibility? Why didn't you simply request me not to punish you for any of your sins?

MORTAL: I think I am realistic enough to know that you would hardly grant such a request!

GOD: You don't say! *You* have a realistic knowledge of what requests I will grant, eh? Well, I'll tell you what I'm going to do! I will grant you a very, very special dispensation to sin as much as you like, and I give you my divine word of honor that I will never punish you for it in the least. Agreed?

MORTAL: (*in great terror*): No, no, don't do that!

GOD: Why not? Don't you trust my divine word?

MORTAL: Of course I do! But don't you see, I don't want to sin! I have an utter abhorrence of sinning, quite apart from any punishments it may entail.

GOD: In that case, I'll go you one better. I'll remove your abhorrence of sinning. Here is a magic pill! Just swallow it, and you will lose all *abhorrence* of sinning. You will joyfully and merrily sin away, you will have no regrets, no abhorrence and I still promise you will never be punished by me, or yourself, or by any source whatever. You will be blissful for all eternity. So here is the pill!

MORTAL: No, no!

GOD: Are you not being irrational? I am even removing your abhorrence of sin, which is your last obstacle.

MORTAL: I still won't take it!

GOD: Why not?

MORTAL: I believe that the pill will indeed remove my future abhorrence for sin, but my present abhorrence is enough to prevent me from being willing to take it.

GOD: I command you to take it!

MORTAL: I refuse!

GOD: What, you refuse of your own free will?

MORTAL: Yes!

GOD: So it seems that your free will comes in pretty handy, doesn't it?

MORTAL: I don't understand!

GOD: Are you not glad now that you have the free will to refuse such a ghastly offer? How would you like it if I forced you to take this pill, whether you wanted it or not?

MORTAL: No, no! Please don't!

GOD: Of course I won't; I'm just trying to illustrate a point. All right, let me put it this way. Instead of forcing you to take the pill, suppose I grant your original prayer of removing your free will—but with the understanding that the moment you are no longer free, then you *will* take the pill.

MORTAL: Once my will is gone, how could I possibly choose to take the pill?

GOD: I did not say you would choose it; I merely said you would take it. You would act, let us say, according to purely deterministic laws which are such that you would as a matter of fact take it.

MORTAL: I still refuse.

GOD: So you refuse my offer to remove your free will. This is rather different from your original prayer, isn't it?

MORTAL: Now I see what you are up to. Your argument is ingenious, but I'm not sure it is really correct. There are some points we will have to go over again.

GOD: Certainly.

MORTAL: There are two things you said which seem contradictory to me. First you said that one cannot sin unless one does so of one's own free will. But then you said you would give me a pill which would deprive me of my own free will, and then I could sin as much as I liked. But if I no longer had free will, then, according to your first statement, how could I be capable of sinning?

GOD: You are confusing two separate parts of our conversation. I never said the pill would deprive you of your free will, but only that it would remove your abhorrence of sinning.

MORTAL: I'm afraid I'm a bit confused.

GOD: All right, then let us make a fresh start. Suppose I agree to remove your free will, but with the understanding that you will then commit an enormous number of acts which you now regard as sinful. Technically speaking, you will not then be sinning since you will not be doing these acts of your own free will. And these acts will carry no moral responsibility, nor moral culpability, nor any punishment whatsoever. Nevertheless, these acts will all be of the type which you presently regard as sinful; they will all have this quality which you presently feel as abhorrent, but your abhorrence will disappear; so you will not *then* feel abhorrence toward the acts.

MORTAL: No, but I have present abhorrence toward the acts, and this present abhorrence is sufficient to prevent me from accepting your proposal.

GOD: Hm! So let me get this absolutely straight. I take it you no longer wish me to remove your free will.

MORTAL (*reluctantly*): No, I guess not.

GOD: All right, I agree not to. But I am still not exactly clear as to why you now no longer wish to be rid of your free will. Please tell me again.

MORTAL: Because, as you have told me, without free will I would sin even more than I do now.

GOD: But I have already told you that without free will you cannot sin.

MORTAL: But if I choose now to be rid of free will, then all my subsequent evil actions will be sins, not of the future, but of the present moment in which I choose not to have free will.

GOD: Sounds like you are pretty badly trapped, doesn't it?

MORTAL: Of course I am trapped! You have placed me in a hideous double bind! Now whatever I do is wrong. If I retain free will, I will continue to sin, and if I abandon free will (with your help, of course), I will now be sinning in so doing.

GOD: But by the same token, you place me in a double bind. I am willing to leave you free will or remove it as you choose, but neither alternative satisfies you. I wish to help you, but it seems I cannot.

MORTAL: True!

GOD: But since it is not my fault, why are you still angry with me?

MORTAL: For having placed me in such a horrible predicament in the first place!

GOD: But, according to you, there is nothing satisfactory I could have done.

MORTAL: You mean there is nothing satisfactory you can now do, but that does not mean that there is nothing you could have done.

GOD: Why? What could I have done?

MORTAL: Obviously you should never have given me free will in the first place. Now that you have given it to me, it is too late—anything I do will be bad. But you should never have given it to me in the first place.

GOD: Oh, that's it! Why would it have been better had I never given it to you?

MORTAL: Because then I never would have been capable of sinning at all.

GOD: Well, I'm always glad to learn from my mistakes.

MORTAL: What!

GOD: I know, that sounds sort of self-blasphemous, doesn't it? It almost involves a logical paradox! On the one hand, as you have been taught, it is morally wrong for any sentient being to claim that I am capable of making mistakes. On the other hand, I have the right to do anything. But I am also a sentient being. So the question is, Do I or do I not have the right to claim that I am capable of making mistakes?

MORTAL: That is a bad joke! One of your premises is simply false. I have not been taught that it is wrong for any sentient being to doubt your omniscience, but only for a mortal to doubt it. But since you are not mortal, then you are obviously free from this injunction.

GOD: Good, so you realize this on a rational level. Nevertheless, you did appear shocked when I said, "I am always glad to learn from my mistakes."

MORTAL: Of course I was shocked. I was shocked not by your self-blasphemy (as you jokingly called it), not by the fact that you had no right to say it, but just by the fact that you did say it, since I have been taught that as a matter of fact you don't make mistakes. So I was amazed that you claimed that it is possible for you to make mistakes.

GOD: I have not claimed that it is possible. All I am saying is that *if* I make mistakes, I will be happy to learn from them. But this says nothing about whether the *if* has or ever can be realized.

MORTAL: Let's please stop quibbling about this point. Do you or do you not admit it was a mistake to have given me free will?

GOD: Well now, this is precisely what I propose we should investigate. Let me review your present predicament. You don't want to have free will because with free will you can sin, and you don't want to sin. (Though I still find this puzzling; in a way you must want to sin, or else you wouldn't. But let this pass for now.) On the other hand, if you agreed to give up free will, then you would now be responsible for the acts of the future. Ergo, I should never have given you free will in the first place.

MORTAL: Exactly!

GOD: I understand exactly how you feel. Many mortals—even some theologians—have complained that I have been unfair in that it was I, not they, who decided that they should have free will, and then I hold *them* responsible for their actions. In other words, they feel that they are expected to live up to a contract with me which they never agreed to in the first place.

MORTAL: Exactly!

GOD: As I said, I understand the feeling perfectly. And I can appreciate the justice of the complaint. But the complaint arises only from an unrealistic understanding of the true issues involved. I am about to enlighten you as to what these are, and I think the results will surprise you! But instead of telling you outright, I shall continue to use the Socratic method.

To repeat, you regret that I ever gave you free will. I claim that when you see the true ramifications you will no longer have this regret. To prove my point, I'll tell you what I'm going to do. I am about to create a new universe—a new space-time continuum. In this new universe will be born a mortal just like you—for all practical purposes, we might say that you will be reborn. Now, I can give this new mortal—this new you—free will or not. What would you like me to do?

MORTAL (*in great relief*): Oh, please! Spare him from having to have free will!

GOD: All right, I'll do as you say. But you do realize that this new *you* without free will, will commit all sorts of horrible acts.

MORTAL: But they will not be sins since he will have no free will.

GOD: Whether you call them sins or not, the fact remains that they will be horrible acts in the sense that they will cause great pain to many sentient beings.

MORTAL (*after a pause*): Good God, you have trapped me again! Always the same game! If I now give you the go-ahead to create this new creature with no free will who will nevertheless commit atrocious acts, then true enough he will not be sinning, but I again will be the sinner to sanction this.

GOD: In that case, I'll go you one better! Here, I have already decided whether to create this new *you* with free will or not. Now, I am writing my decision on this piece of paper and I won't show it to you until later. But my decision is now made and is absolutely irrevocable. There is nothing you can possibly do to alter it; you have no responsibility in the matter. Now, what I wish to know is this: Which way do you hope I have decided? Remember now, the responsibility for the decision falls entirely on my shoulders, not yours. So you can tell me perfectly honestly and without any fear, which way do you hope I have decided?

MORTAL (*after a very long pause*): I hope you have decided to give him free will.

GOD: Most interesting! I have removed your last obstacle! If I do not give him free will, then no sin is to be imputed to anybody. So why do you hope I will give him free will?

MORTAL: Because sin or no sin, the important point is that if you do not give him free will, then (at least according to what you have said) he will go around hurting people, and I don't want to see people hurt.

GOD (*with an infinite sigh of relief*): At last! At last you see the real point!

MORTAL: What point is that?

GOD: That sinning is not the real issue! The important thing is that people as well as other sentient beings don't get hurt!

MORTAL: You sound like a utilitarian!

GOD: I am a utilitarian!

MORTAL: What!

GOD: Whats or no whats, I am a utilitarian. Not a unitarian, mind you, but a utilitarian.

MORTAL: I just can't believe it!

GOD: Yes, I know, your religious training has taught you otherwise. You have probably thought of me more like a Kantian than a utilitarian, but your training was simply wrong.

MORTAL: You leave me speechless!

GOD: I leave you speechless, do I! Well, that is perhaps not too bad a thing— you have a tendency to speak too much as it is. Seriously, though, why do you think I ever did give you free will in the first place?

MORTAL: Why did you? I never have thought much about why you did; all I have been arguing for is that you shouldn't have! But why did you? I guess all I can think of is the standard religious explanation: Without free will, one is not capable of meriting either salvation or damnation. So without free will, we could not earn the right to eternal life.

GOD: Most interesting! *I* have eternal life; do you think I have ever done anything to merit it?

MORTAL: Of course not! With you it is different. You are already so good and perfect (at least allegedly) that it is not necessary for you to merit eternal life.

GOD: Really now? That puts me in a rather enviable position, doesn't it?

MORTAL: I don't think I understand you.

GOD: Here I am eternally blissful without ever having to suffer or make sacrifices or struggle against evil temptations or anything like that. Without any of that type of "merit," I enjoy blissful eternal existence. By contrast, you poor mortals have to sweat and suffer and have all sorts of horrible conflicts about morality, and all for what? You don't even know whether I really exist or not, or if there really is any afterlife, or if there is, where you come into the picture. No matter how much you try to placate me by being "good," you never have any real assurance that your "best" is good enough for me, and hence you have no real security in obtaining salvation. Just think of it! I already *have* the equivalent of "salvation"—and have never had to go through this infinitely lugubrious process of earning it. Don't you ever envy me for this?

MORTAL: But it is blasphemous to envy you!

GOD: Oh come off it! You're not now talking to your Sunday school teacher, you are talking to *me*. Blasphemous or not, the important question is not whether you have the right to be envious of me but whether you are. Are you?

MORTAL: Of course I am!

GOD: Good! Under your present world view, you sure should be most envious of me. But I think with a more realistic world view, you no longer will be. So you really have swallowed the idea which has been taught you that your life on earth is like an examination period and that the purpose of providing you with free will is to test you, to see if you merit blissful eternal life. But what puzzles me is this: If you really believe I am as good and benevolent as I am cracked up to be, why should I require people to merit things like happiness and eternal life? Why should I not grant such things to everyone regardless of whether or not he deserves them?

MORTAL: But I have been taught that your sense of morality—your sense of justice—demands that goodness be rewarded with happiness and evil be punished with pain.

GOD: Then you have been taught wrong.

MORTAL: But the religious literature is so full of this idea! Take for example Jonathan Edwards's "Sinners in the Hands of an Angry God." How he describes you as holding your enemies like loathsome scorpions over the flaming pit of hell, preventing them from falling into the fate that they deserve only by dint of your mercy.

GOD: Fortunately, I have not been exposed to the tirades of Mr. Jonathan Edwards. Few sermons have ever been preached which are more misleading. The very title "Sinners in the Hands of an Angry God" tells its own tale. In the first place, I am never angry. In the second place, I do not think at all in terms of "sin." In the third place, I have no enemies.

MORTAL: By that do you mean that there are no people whom you hate, or that there are no people who hate you?

GOD: I meant the former although the latter also happens to be true.

MORTAL: Oh come now, I know people who have openly claimed to have hated you. At times *I* have hated you!

GOD: You mean you have hated your image of me. That is not the same thing as hating me as I really am.

MORTAL: Are you trying to say that it is not wrong to hate a false conception of you, but that it is wrong to hate you as you really are?

GOD: No, I am not saying that at all; I am saying something far more drastic! What I am saying has absolutely nothing to do with right or wrong. What I am saying is that one who knows me for what I really am would simply find it psychologically impossible to hate me.

MORTAL: Tell me, since we mortals seem to have such erroneous views about your real nature, why don't you enlighten us? Why don't you guide us the right way?

GOD: What makes you think I'm not?

MORTAL: I mean, why don't you appear to our very senses and simply tell us that we are wrong?

GOD: Are you really so naive as to believe that I am the sort of being which can *appear* to your senses? It would be more correct to say that I *am* your senses.

MORTAL (*astonished*): You are my senses?

GOD: Not quite, I am more than that. But it comes closer to the truth than the idea that I am perceivable by the senses. I am not an object; like you, I am a subject, and a subject can perceive, but cannot be perceived. You can no more see me than you can see your own thoughts. You can see an apple, but the event of your seeing an apple is itself not seeable. And I am far more like the seeing of an apple than the apple itself.

MORTAL: If I can't see you, how do I know you exist?

GOD: Good question! How in fact do you know I exist?

MORTAL: Well, I am talking to you, am I not?

GOD: How do you know you are talking to me? Suppose you told a psychiatrist, "Yesterday I talked to God." What do you think he would say?

MORTAL: That might depend on the psychiatrist. Since most of them are atheistic, I guess most would tell me I had simply been talking to myself.

GOD: And they would be right!

MORTAL: What? You mean you don't exist?

GOD: You have the strangest faculty of drawing false conclusions! Just because you are talking to yourself, it follows that *I* don't exist?

MORTAL: Well, if I think I am talking to you, but I am really talking to myself, in what sense do you exist?

GOD: Your question is based on two fallacies plus a confusion. The question of whether or not you are now talking to me and the question of whether or not I exist are totally separate. Even if you were not now talking to me (which obviously you are), it still would not mean that I don't exist.

MORTAL: Well, all right, of course! So instead of saying "if I am talking to myself, then you don't exist," I should rather have said, "if I am talking to myself, then I obviously am not talking to you."

GOD: A very different statement indeed, but still false.

MORTAL: Oh, come now, if I am only talking to myself, then how can I be talking to you?

GOD: Your use of the word "only" is quite misleading! I can suggest several logical possibilities under which your talking to yourself does not imply that you are not talking to me.

MORTAL: Suggest just one!

GOD: Well, obviously one such possibility is that you and I are identical.

MORTAL: Such a blasphemous thought—at least had *I* uttered it!

GOD: According to some religions, yes. According to others, it is the plain, simple, immediately perceived truth.

MORTAL: So the only way out of my dilemma is to believe that you and I are identical?

GOD: Not at all! This is only one way out. There are several others. For example, it may be that you are part of me, in which case you may be talking to that part of me which is you. Or I may be part of you, in which case you may be talking to that part of you which is me. Or again, you and I might partially overlap, in which case you may be talking to the intersection and hence talking both to you and to me. The only way your talking to yourself might seem to imply that you are not talking to me is if you and I were totally disjoint—and even then, you could conceivably be talking to both of us.

MORTAL: So you claim you do exist.

GOD: Not at all. Again you draw false conclusions! The question of my existence has not even come up. All I have said is that from the fact that you are talking to yourself one cannot possibly infer my nonexistence, let alone the weaker fact that you are not talking to me.

MORTAL: All right, I'll grant your point! But what I really want to know is *do* you exist?

GOD: What a strange question!

MORTAL: Why? Men have been asking it for countless millennia.

GOD: I know that! The question itself is not strange; what I mean is that it is a most strange question to ask of *me*!

MORTAL: Why?

GOD: Because I am the very one whose existence you doubt! I perfectly well understand your anxiety. You are worried that your present experience with me is a mere hallucination. But how can you possibly expect to obtain reliable information from a being about his very existence when you suspect the nonexistence of the very same being?

MORTAL: So you won't tell me whether or not you exist?

GOD: I am not being willful! I merely wish to point out that no answer I could give could possibly satisfy you. All right, suppose I said, "No, I don't exist." What would that prove? Absolutely nothing! Or if I said, "Yes, I exist." Would that convince you? Of course not!

MORTAL: Well, if you can't tell me whether or not you exist, then who possibly can?

GOD: That is something which no one can tell you. It is something which only you can find out for yourself.

MORTAL: How do I go about finding this out for myself?

GOD: That also no one can tell you. This is another thing you will have to find out for yourself.

MORTAL: So there is no way you can help me?

GOD: I didn't say that. I said there is no way I can tell you. But that doesn't mean there is no way I can help you.

MORTAL: In what manner then can you help me?

GOD: I suggest you leave that to me! We have gotten sidetracked as it is, and I would like to return to the question of what you believed my purpose to be in giving you free will. Your first idea of my giving you free will in order to test whether you merit salvation or not may appeal to many moralists, but the idea is quite hideous to me. You cannot think of any nicer reason—any more humane reason—why I gave you free will?

MORTAL: Well now, I once asked this question of an Orthodox rabbi. He told me that the way we are constituted, it is simply not possible for us to enjoy salvation unless we feel we have earned it. And to earn it, we of course need free will.

GOD: That explanation is indeed much nicer than your former but still is far from correct. According to Orthodox Judaism, I created angels, and they have no free will. They are in actual sight of me and are so completely attracted by goodness that they never have even the slightest temptation toward evil. They really have no choice in the matter. Yet they are eternally happy even though they have never earned it. So if your rabbi's explanation were correct, why wouldn't I have simply created only angels rather than mortals?

MORTAL: Beats me! Why didn't you?

GOD: Because the explanation is simply not correct. In the first place, I have never created any ready-made angels. All sentient beings ultimately approach the state which might be called "angelhood." But just as the race of human beings is in a certain stage of biologi-evolution, so angels are simply the end result of a process of Cosmic Evolution. The only difference between the so-called *saint* and the so-called *sinner* is that the former is vastly older than the latter. Unfortunately it takes countless life cycles to learn what is perhaps the most important fact of the universe—all the alleged reasons why people *shouldn't* commit evil acts—simply pale into insignificance in light of the one basic truth that *evil is suffering*.

No, my dear friend, I am not a moralist. I am wholly a utilitarian. That I should have been convinced in the role of a moralist is one of the great tragedies of the human race. My role in the scheme of things (if one can use this misleading expression) is neither to punish nor reward, but to aid the process by which all sentient beings achieve ultimate perfection.

MORTAL: Why did you say your expression is misleading?

GOD: What I said was misleading in two respects. First of all it is inaccurate to speak of my role in the scheme of things. I *am* the scheme of things.

Secondly, it is equally misleading to speak of my aiding the process of sentient beings attaining enlightenment. I *am* the process. The ancient Taoists were quite close when they said of me (whom they called "Tao") that I do not *do* things, yet through me all things get done. In more modern terms, I am not the cause of Cosmic Process, I am Cosmic Process itself. I think the most accurate and fruitful definition of me which man can frame—at least in his present state of evolution—is that I am the very process of enlightenment. Those who wish to think of the devil (although I wish they wouldn't!) might analogously define him as the unfortunate length of time the process takes. In this sense, the devil is necessary; the process simply does take an enormous length of time, and there is absolutely nothing I can do about it. But, I assure you, once the process is more correctly understood, the painful length of time will no longer be regarded as an essential limitation or an evil. It will be seen to be the very essence of the process itself. I know this is not completely consoling to you who are now in the finite sea of suffering, but the amazing thing is that once you grasp this fundamental attitude, your very finite suffering will begin to diminish—ultimately to the vanishing point.

MORTAL: I have been told this, and I tend to believe it. But suppose I personally succeed in seeing things through your eternal eyes. Then I will be happier, but don't I have a duty to others?

GOD (*laughing*): You remind me of the Mahayana Buddhists! Each one says, "I will not enter Nirvana until I first see that all other sentient beings do so." So each one waits for the other fellow to go first. No wonder it takes them so long! The Hinayana Buddhist errs in a different direction. He believes that no one can be of the slightest help to others in obtaining salvation; each one has to do it entirely by himself. And so each tries only for his own salvation. But this very detached attitude makes salvation impossible. The truth of the matter is that salvation is partly an individual and partly a social process. But it is a grave mistake to believe—as do many Mahayana Buddhists—that the attaining of enlightenment puts one out of commission, so to speak, for helping others. The best way of helping others is by first seeing the light oneself.

MORTAL: There is one thing about your self-description which is somewhat disturbing. You describe yourself essentially as a *process*. This puts you in such an impersonal light, and so many people have a need for a personal God.

GOD: So because they need a personal God, it follows that I am one?

MORTAL: Of course not. But to be acceptable to a mortal a religion must satisfy his needs.

GOD: I realize that. But the so-called *personality* of a being is really more in the eyes of the beholder than in the being itself. The controversies which have raged about whether I am a personal or an impersonal being are rather silly because neither side is right or wrong. From one point of view, I am personal, from another, I am not. It is the same with a human being. A creature from another planet may look at him purely impersonally as a mere collection of atomic particles behaving according to strictly prescribed physical laws. He may have no more feeling for the personality of a human than the average human has for an ant. Yet an ant has just as much individual personality as a human to beings like myself who really know the ant. To look at something impersonally is no more correct or incorrect than to look at it personally, but in general, the better you get to know something, the more personal it becomes. To illustrate my point, do you think of me as a personal or impersonal being?

MORTAL: Well, I'm talking to you, am I not?

GOD: Exactly! From that point of view, your attitude toward me might be described as a personal one. And yet, from another point of view—no less valid—I can also be looked at impersonally.

MORTAL: But if you are really such an abstract thing as a process, I don't see what sense it can make my talking to a mere "process."

GOD: I love the way you say "mere." You might just as well say that you are living in a "mere universe." Also, why must everything one does make sense? Does it make sense to talk to a tree?

MORTAL: Of course not!

GOD: And yet, many children and primitives do just that.

MORTAL: But I am neither a child nor a primitive.

GOD: I realize that, unfortunately.

MORTAL: Why unfortunately?

GOD: Because many children and primitives have a primal intuition which the likes of you have lost. Frankly, I think it would do you a lot of good to talk to a tree once in a while, even more good than talking to me! But we seem always to be getting sidetracked! For the last time, I would like us to try to come to an understanding about why I gave you free will.

MORTAL: I have been thinking about this all the while.

GOD: You mean you haven't been paying attention to our conversation?

MORTAL: Of course I have. But all the while, on another level, I have been thinking about it.

GOD: And have you come to any conclusion?

MORTAL: Well, you say the reason is not to test our worthiness. And you disclaimed the reason that we need to feel that we must merit things in order to enjoy them. And you claim to be a utilitarian. Most significant of all, you appeared so delighted when I came to the sudden realization that it is not sinning itself which is bad but only the suffering which it causes.

GOD: Well of course! What else could conceivably be bad about sinning?

MORTAL: All right, you know that, and now I know that. But all my life I unfortunately have been under the influence of those moralists who hold sinning to be bad in itself. Anyway, putting all these pieces together, it occurs to me that the only reason you gave free will is because of your belief that with free will, people will tend to hurt each other—and them-selves—less than without free will.

GOD: Bravo! That is by far the best reason you have yet given! I can assure you that had I *chosen* to give free will, that would have been my very reason for so choosing.

MORTAL: What! You mean to say you did not choose to give us free will?

GOD: My dear fellow, I could no more choose to give you free will than I could choose to make an equilateral triangle equiangular. I could choose to make or not to make an equilateral triangle in the first place, but having chosen to make one I would then have no choice but to make it equi-angular.

MORTAL: I thought you could do anything!

GOD: Only things which are logically possible. As St. Thomas said, "It is a sin to regard the fact that God cannot do the impossible, as a limitation on His powers." I agree, except that in place of his using the word *sin* I would use the term *error*.

MORTAL: Anyhow, I am still puzzled by your implication that you did not choose to give me free will.

GOD: Well, it is high time I inform you that the entire discussion—from the very beginning—has been based on one monstrous fallacy! We have been talking purely on a moral level—you originally complained that I gave you free will, and raised the whole question as to whether I should have. It never once occurred to you that I had absolutely no choice in the matter.

MORTAL: I am still in the dark!

GOD: Absolutely! Because you are only able to look at it through the eyes of a moralist. The more fundamental *metaphysical* aspects of the question you never even considered.

MORTAL: I still do not see what you are driving at.

GOD: Before you requested me to remove your free will, shouldn't your first question have been whether as a matter of fact you *do* have free will?

MORTAL: That I simply took for granted.

GOD: But why should you?

MORTAL: I don't know. Do I have free will?

GOD: Yes.

MORTAL: Then why did you say I shouldn't have taken it for granted?

GOD: Because you shouldn't. Just because something happens to be true, it does not follow that it should be taken for granted.

MORTAL: Anyway, it is reassuring to know that my natural intuition about having free will is correct. Sometimes I have been worried that determinists are correct.

GOD: They are correct.

MORTAL: Wait a minute now, do I have free will or don't I?

GOD: I already told you you do. But that does not mean that determinism is incorrect.

MORTAL: Well, are my acts determined by the laws of nature or aren't they?

GOD: The word *determined* here is subtly but powerfully misleading and has contributed so much to the confusions of the free will versus determinism controversies. Your acts are certainly in accordance with the laws of nature, but to say they are *determined* by the laws of nature creates a totally misleading psychological image which is that your will could somehow be in conflict with the laws of nature and that the latter is somehow more powerful than you, and could "determine" your acts whether you liked it or not. But it is simply impossible for your will to ever conflict with natural law. You and natural law are really one and the same.

MORTAL: What do you mean that I cannot conflict with nature? Suppose I were to become very stubborn, and I *determined* not to obey the laws of nature. What could stop me? If I became sufficiently stubborn, even you could not stop me!

GOD: You are absolutely right! *I* certainly could not stop you. Nothing could stop you. But there is no need to stop you, because you could not even start! As Goethe very beautifully expressed it, "In trying to oppose Nature, we are, in the very process of doing so, acting according to the laws of nature!" Don't you see that the so-called *laws of nature* are nothing more than a description of how in fact you and other beings *do* act? They are merely a description of how you act, not a prescription of how you should act, not a power or force which compels or determines your acts. To be valid a law of nature must take into account how in fact you do act, or, if you like, how you choose to act.

MORTAL: So you really claim that I am incapable of determining to act against natural law?

GOD: It is interesting that you have twice now used the phrase "determined to act" instead of "chosen to act." This identification is quite common.

Often one uses the statement "I am determined to do this" synonymously with "I have chosen to do this." This very psychological identification should reveal that determinism and choice are much closer than they might appear. Of course, you might well say that the doctrine of free will says that it is *you* who are doing the determining, whereas the doctrine of determinism appears to say that your acts are determined by something apparently outside you. But the confusion is largely caused by your bifurcation of reality into the "you" and the "not you." Really now, just where do you leave off and the rest of the universe begin? Or where does the rest of the universe leave off and you begin? Once you can see the so-called *you* and the so-called *nature* as a continuous whole, then you can never again be bothered by such questions as whether it is you who are controlling nature or nature who is controlling you. Thus the muddle of free will versus determinism will vanish. If I may use a crude analogy, imagine two bodies moving toward each other by virtue of gravitational attraction. Each body, if sentient, might wonder whether it is he or the other fellow who is exerting the "force." In a way it is both, in a way it is neither. It is best to say that it is the configuration of the two which is crucial.

MORTAL: You said a short while ago that our whole discussion was based on a monstrous fallacy. You still have not told me what this fallacy is.

GOD: Why, the idea that I could possibly have created you without free will! You acted as if this were a genuine possibility, and wondered why I did not choose it! It never occurred to you that a sentient being without free will is no more conceivable than a physical object which exerts no gravitational attraction. (There is, incidentally, more analogy than you realize between a physical object exerting gravitational attraction and a sentient being exerting free will!) Can you honestly even imagine a conscious being without free will? What on earth could it be like? I think that one thing in your life that has so misled you is your having been told that I gave man the *gift* of free will. As if I first created man, and then as an afterthought endowed him with the extra property of free will. Maybe you think I have some sort of "paint brush" with which I daub some creatures with free will and not others. No, free will is not an "extra"; it is part and parcel of the very essence of consciousness. A conscious being without free will is simply a metaphysical absurdity.

MORTAL: Then why did you play along with me all this while discussing what I thought was a moral problem, when, as you say, my basic confusion was metaphysical?

GOD: Because I thought it would be good therapy for you to get some of this moral poison out of your system. Much of your metaphysical confusion was due to faulty moral notions, and so the latter had to be dealt with first.

And now we must part—at least until you need me again. I think our present union will do much to sustain you for a long while. But do remember what I told you about trees. Of course, you don't have to literally talk to them if doing so makes you feel silly. But there is so much you can learn from them, as well as from the rocks and streams and other aspects of nature. There is nothing like a naturalistic orientation to dispel all these morbid thoughts of "sin" and "free will" and "moral responsibility." At one stage of history, such notions were actually useful. I refer to the days when tyrants had unlimited power and nothing short of fears of hell could possibly restrain them. But mankind has grown up since then, and this gruesome way of thinking is no longer necessary.

It might be helpful to you to recall what I once said through the writings of the great Zen poet Seng-Ts'an:

If you want to get the plain truth,
Be not concerned with right and wrong.
The conflict between right and wrong
Is the sickness of the mind.

I can see by your expression that you are simultaneously soothed and terrified by these words! What are you afraid of? That if in your mind you abolish the distinction between right and wrong you are more likely to commit acts which are wrong? What makes you so sure that self-consciousness about right and wrong does not in fact lead to more wrong acts than right ones? Do you honestly believe that so-called *amoral* people, when it comes to action rather than theory, behave less ethically than moralists? Of course not! Even most moralists acknowledge the ethical superiority of the behavior of most of those who theoretically take an amoral position. They seem so surprised that without ethical *principles* these people behave so nicely! It never seems to occur to them that it is by virtue of the very lack of moral principles that their good behavior flows so freely! Do the words "The conflict between right and wrong is the sickness of the human mind" express an idea so different from the story of the Garden of Eden and the fall of Man due to Adam's eating of the fruit of knowledge? This knowledge, mind you, was of ethical principles, not ethical feelings—these Adam already had. There is much truth in this story, though I never commanded Adam not to eat the apple, I merely advised him not to. I told him it would not be good for him. If the damn fool had only listened to me, so much trouble could have been avoided! But no, he thought he knew everything! But I wish the theologians would finally learn that I am not punishing Adam and his descendants for the act, but rather that the fruit in question is poisonous in its own right and its effects, unfortunately, last countless generations.

And now really I must take leave. I do hope that our discussion will dispel some of your ethical morbidity and replace it by a more naturalistic orientation. Remember also the marvelous words I once uttered through the mouth of Lao-tse when I chided Confucius for his moralizing:

All this talk of goodness and duty, these perpetual pin-pricks unnerve and irritate the hearer—You had best study how it is that Heaven and Earth maintain their eternal course, that the sun and moon maintain their light, the stars their seried ranks, the birds and beasts their flocks, the trees and shrubs their station. This you too should learn to guide your steps by Inward Power, to follow the course that the Way of Nature sets; and soon you will no longer need to go round laboriously advertising goodness and duty.... The swan does not need a daily bath in order to remain white.

MORTAL: You certainly seem partial to Eastern philosophy!
GOD: Oh, not at all! Some of my finest thoughts have bloomed in native American soil. For example, I never expressed my notion of "duty" more eloquently than through the thoughts of Walt Whitman:

I give nothing as duties,
What others give as duties, I give as living impulses.

Raymond M. Smullyan, *The Tao Is Silent*

The important difference between the Tao and the usual idea of God is that whereas God produces the world by making (*wei^h*), the Tao produces it by "not-making" (*wu-wei^i*)—which is approximately what we mean by "growing." For things made are separate parts put together, like machines, or things fashioned from without inwards, like sculptures. Whereas things grown divide themselves into parts, from within outwards. Because the natural universe works mainly according to the principles of growth, it would seem quite odd to the Chinese mind to ask how it was made. If the universe were made, there would of course be someone who knows *how* it is made—who could explain how it was put together bit by bit as a technician can explain in one-at-a-time words how to assemble a machine. But a universe which grows utterly excludes the possibility of knowing how it grows in the clumsy terms of thought and language, so that no Taoist would dream of asking whether the Tao knows how it produces the universe. For it operates according to spontaneity, not according to plan.

Alan Watts, *The Way of Zen*

As soon as one is convinced that there is a living and real Truth seeking to express itself in an objective universe, the only thing that seems to have any importance or value is to come into contact with this Truth, to identify one-self with it as perfectly as possible, and to no longer be anything but a means of expressing it, making it more and more living and tangible so that it may be manifested more and more perfectly. All theories, all principles, all meth-ods are more or less good according to their capacity to express that Truth; and as one goes forward on this path, if one goes beyond all the limits of the Ignorance, one becomes aware that the *totality* of this manifestation, its wholeness, its integrality is necessary for the expression of that Truth, that *nothing* can be left out, and perhaps that there is nothing more important or less important. The one thing that seems necessary is a harmonisation of everything which puts each thing in its place, in its true relation with all the rest, so that the total Unity may manifest harmoniously.

If one comes down from this level, according to me one no longer understands anything and all arguments are of equal worth in the narrow-ness and limitation which take away all their real value.

Each thing in its place, in harmony with all the rest, and then one can begin to understand and to live.

The Mother, *The Life Divine, The Mother's Talks*

✦ Gaia ✦

With consciousness of the All comes a necessary commitment to the sacredness of our planet. Through advanced technology, like satellite and space travel, we have witnessed the Earth's beauty from afar. We recognize its diversity and above all its fragility for over the last three decades, in which time industrial and scientific growth have been unsurpassed in the world, we have managed to cause radical dam-age to our Earth in the names of progress and commerce.

English scientist James Lovelock is one of the most prominent re-searchers and writers on Gaia, which Rupert Sheldrake calls the "soul of the earth." Lovelock reminds us that the majority of people are trapped in the world of cities and "all too often as spectators, not players." It is through the natural world—in the air and the waters—that we hear the word of God. We see the brilliant colours of God's creation in the changing seasons, in the sun and the moon, the stars, and in their interplay with us. In the Shamanic beliefs and rituals of the North American Indians, the first nations people, all nature is sacred, all beings, including trees, rocks, flowers, and streams, are spirits. With the growing threat we pose to our environment, many are returning to the Shamanic ideas and rituals in order to honour our Earth again, and in order to receive her guidance.

This section is divided into two parts. In the first are selected writings by those who are close to nature, who have a deep reverence and awe for her gifts. They are Krishnamurti, Thomas Merton, American traveller and writer Barry Lopez, biologist Rupert Sheldrake, English poets Philip Larkin and David Whyte, and American poet Maya Angelou. These people have slowed down to the tempo of the tao and the energies and heartbeat of Gaia, to bear witness to the miracles that she reveals through the living water and the seas and to the connection she has to our spirit and our survival.

The second part is about the commitment to serve the community of our Earth. Rosemary Ruether terms this commitment a new religion, "ecology spirituality." As the urgency of preserving our natural world intensifies, the old ways of Shamanism and petition to the Christian patron saint of ecology, St. Francis of Assisi, the Great Mother, and Gaia herself, become the only new solution. Ruether recommends that this new religion be built on three premises: the transcience of selves, the living interdependency of all things, and the value of the personal in communion with the "infinite creativity" of nature, cycles, and rituals of the seasons, the budding, the blossoming, the shedding, the letting go, the death.

David Quammen brings this idea of the new religion of ecology spirituality to life in his piece on the inner and outer landscapes, and explains the practice of "storytelling" in Native American cultures as an example not only of experiencing the inner and outer encounter but of how sharing it heals and nurtures the spirit in both.

><

Suddenly from behind the rim of the moon, in long, slow-motion moments of immense majesty, there emerges a sparkling blue and white jewel, a light, delicate sky-blue sphere laced with slowly swirling veils of white, rising gradually like a small pearl in a thick sea of black mystery.

It takes more than a moment to fully realize this is Earth...home.

Edgar Mitchell, *The Home Planet*

How can we revere the living world if we can no longer hear the bird song through the noise of traffic, or smell the sweetness of fresh air? How can we wonder about God and the Universe if we never see the stars because of the city lights? If you think this to be exaggeration, think back to when you last lay in a meadow in the sunshine and smelt the fragrant thyme and heard and saw the larks soaring and singing. Think back to the last night you looked up into the deep blue black of a sky clear enough to see the Milky Way, the congregation of stars, our Galaxy.

The attraction of the city is seductive. Socrates said that nothing of interest happened outside its walls and, much later, Dr. Johnson expressed his view of country living as "One green field is like another." Most of us are trapped in this world of the city, an everlasting soap opera, and all too often as spectators, not players. It is something to have sensitive commentators like Sir David Attenborough bring the natural world with its visions of forests and wilderness to the television screens of our suburban rooms. But the television screen is only a window and only rarely clear enough to see the world outside; it can never bring us back into the real world of Gaia. City life reinforces and strengthens the heresy of humanism, that narcissistic devotion to human interests alone. The Irish missionary Sean McDonagh wrote in his book, *To Care for the Earth*: "The 20 billion years of God's creative love is either seen simply as the stage on which the drama of human salvation is worked out, or as something radically sinful in itself and needing transformation."

The heartlands of the great religions are now in the last bastions of rural existence, in the Third World of the tropics. Elsewhere God and Gaia that once were joined and respected are now divorced and of no account. We have, as a species, almost resigned from membership in Gaia and given to our cities and our nations the rights and responsibilities of environmental regulation. We struggle to enjoy the human interactions of city life yet still yearn to possess the natural world as well. We want to be free to drive into the country or the wilderness without polluting it in so doing; to have our cake and eat it. Human and understandable such striving may be, but it is illogical. Our humanist concerns about the poor of the inner cities or the Third World, are our near-obscene obsession with death, suffering, and pain as if these were evil in themselves—these thoughts divert the mind from our gross and excessive domination of the natural world. Poverty and suffering are not sent; they are the consequences of what we do. Pain and death are normal and natural; we could not long survive without them. Science, it is true, assisted at the birth of technology. But when we drive our cars and listen to the radio bringing news of acid rain, we need to remind ourselves that we, personally, are the polluters. We, not some white-coated devil figure, buy the cars, drive them, and foul the air. We are therefore accountable, person-ally, for the destruction of the trees by photochemical smog and acid rain. We are responsible for the silent spring that Rachel Carson predicted.

There are many ways to keep in touch with Gaia. Individual humans are densely populated cellular and endosymbiont collectives, but clearly also identities. Individuals interact with Gaia in the cycling of the elements and in the control of the climate, just like a cell does in the body. You also inter-act individually in a spiritual manner through a sense of wonder about the natural world and from feeling a part of it. In some ways this interaction is not unlike the tight coupling between the state of the mind and the body. Another connection is through the powerful infrastructures of human com-munication and mass transfer. We as a species now move a greater mass of some materials around the Earth than did all the biota of Gaia before we appeared. Our chattering is so loud that it can be heard to the depths of the Universe. Always, as with other and earlier species within Gaia, the entire development arises from the activity of a few individuals. The urban nests, the agricultural ecosystems, good and bad, are all the consequences of rapid positive feedback starting from the action of an inspired individual.

A frequent misunderstanding of my vision of Gaia is that I champion complacence, that I claim feedback will always protect the environment from any serious harm that humans might do. It is sometimes more crudely put as "Lovelock's Gaia gives industry the green light to pollute at will." The truth is almost diametrically opposite. Gaia, as I see her, is no doting mother toler-ant of misdemeanors, nor is she some fragile and delicate damsel in danger from brutal mankind. She is stern and tough, always keeping the world warm and comfortable for those who obey the rules, but ruthless in her destruction of those who transgress. Her unconscious goal is a planet fit for life. If humans stand in the way of this, we shall be eliminated with as little pity as would be shown by the micro-brain of an intercontinental ballistic nuclear missile in full flight to its target.

James Lovelock, *The Ages of Gaia*

The nature which surrounds us—sun, moon, stars, day and night, the sea-sons, the waters, mountains, forests and flowers—is a kind of primordial Revelation; now these three things—nature, light and breath—are pro-foundly linked with one another. Breathing should be linked with the remembrance of God; we should breathe with reverence, with the heart so to speak. It is said that the Spirit of God—the Divine Breath—was "over the waters" and that it was by breathing into it that God created the soul, as it is also said that man, who is "born of the Spirit," is like the wind; "thou hearest the sound thereof, but canst not tell whence it cometh, and whither it goeth."

Frithjof Schuon, *Understanding Islam*

"It is harder for us today to feel near to God among the streets and houses of the city than it is for country folk. For them the harvested fields bathed in the autumn mists speak of God and his goodness far more vividly than any human lips."

Albert Schweitzer, *Reverence for Life*

The glory of God, then, is closer to the sense of "What a glorious sunset!" That luminosity which illuminates the whole landscape, ourselves included.

Thomas Matus, from Fritjof Capra, David Steindl-Rast with Thomas Matus, *Belonging to the Universe*

Nature is part of our life. We grew out of the seed, the earth, and we are part of all that, but we are rapidly losing the sense that we are animals like the others. Can you have a feeling for that tree? Look at it, see the beauty of it, listen to the sound it makes; be sensitive to the little plant, to the little weed, to that creeper that is growing up the wall, to the light on the leaves and the many shadows. You must be aware of all this and have that sense of communion with nature around you. You may live in a town but you do have trees here and there. A flower in the next garden may be ill-kept, crowded with weeds, but look at it, feel that you are part of all that, part of all living things. If you hurt nature you are hurting yourself.

You know all this has been said before in different ways, but we don't seem to pay much attention. Is it that we are so caught up in our own network of problems, our own desires, our own urges of pleasure and pain, that we never look around, never watch the moon? Watch it. Watch with all your eyes and ears, your sense of smell. If you can do that, you are seeing that tree, that bush, that blade of grass for the first time. Then you can see your teacher, your mother and father, your brother and sister for the first time. There is an extraordinary feeling about that: the wonder, the strangeness, the miracle of a fresh morning that has never been before, never will be. Be really in communion with nature, not verbally caught in the description of it, but be a part of it, be aware, feel that you belong to all that, be able to have love for all that, to admire a deer, the lizard on the wall, that broken branch lying on the ground. Look at the evening star or the new moon, without the word, without merely saying how beautiful it is and turning your back on it, attracted by something else, but watch that single star and new delicate moon as though for the first time. If there is such communion between you and nature then you can commune with man, with the boy sitting next to you, with your educator, or with your parents. We have lost all sense of relationship in which there is not only a verbal statement of affection and concern but also this sense of communion that is not verbal. It is a sense that we are all together, that we are all human beings, not divided, not broken up, not belonging to any particular group or race, or to some idealistic concepts, but that we are all human beings, we are all living on this extraordinary, beautiful earth.

J. Krishnamurti, *On Nature and the Environment*

A spring morning alone in the woods. Sunrise: the enormous yoke of energy spreading and spreading as if to take over the entire sky. After that: the ceremonies of the birds feeding in the wet grass. The meadowlark, feeding and singing. Then the quiet, totally silent, dry, sun-drenched mid-morning of spring, under the climbing sun.

April is not the cruelest month. Not in Kentucky. It was hard to say Psalms. Attention would get carried away in the vast blue arc of the sky, trees, hills, grass, and all things. How absolutely central is the truth that we are, first of all, part of nature, though we are a very special part, that which is conscious of God.

One has to be alone, under the sky, before everything falls into place and one finds his own place in the midst of it all. We have to have the humility to realize ourselves as part of nature. Denial of this results only in madness and cruelties. One can be part of nature, surely, without being Lady Chatterly's lover.

It was one good morning. A return in spirit to the first morning of the world.

Thomas Merton, *Conjectures of a Guilty Bystander*

By the reading of Scripture, I am so renewed that all nature seems renewed around me and with me.

The sky seems to be a pure, a cooler blue, the trees a deeper green, light is sharper on the outlines of the forest and the hills, and the whole world is charged with the glory of God, and I feel fire and music in the earth under my feet.

Thomas Merton, *The Sign of Jonas*

Breathe it with me, sweet heart, breathe this blessed air, let it roll over us with its salt cleanliness and the negative-ioned green of cedar, Douglas firs, redwood and sky-reaching pines of every kind. Here is the earth in all its honesty, true and beautiful as your own, and the rushing water as though it rushed through the veins of God and gave him greater life. Here, right here, is where all the grossness and the slag of the world is bought into balance, giving equal weight to God's right hand and his left, showing us that though men are out of kilter, he is not. And you and I who are his devoted servants, are not either, but are wholly blessed, baptized afresh with the mists floating down from the mountains and the perfume afloat on the sea.

Patricia Joudry, private letter

He had picked it up, he said, on a beach; it was a piece of sea-washed wood in the shape of a human head. It was made of hard wood, shaped by the waters of the sea, cleansed by many seasons. He had brought it home and put it on the mantelpiece; he looked at it from time to time and admired what he had done. One day, he put some flowers round it and then it happened every day; he felt uncomfortable if there were not fresh flowers every day and gradually that piece of shaped wood became very important in his life. He would allow no one to touch it except himself; they might desecrate it; he washed his hands before he touched it. It had become holy, sacred, and he alone was the high priest of it; he represented it; it told him of things he could never know by himself. His life was filled with it and he was, he said, unspeakably happy.

J. Krishnamurti, *Krishnamurti's Journal*

Whenever I walk with a child, I think how much I have seen disappear in my own life. What will there be for this person when he is my age? If he senses something ineffable in the landscape, will I know enough to encourage it?—to somehow show him that, yes, when people talk about violent death, spiritual exhilaration, compassion, futility, final causes, they are drawing on forty thousand years of human meditation on *this*—as we embrace Douglas firs, or stand by a river across whose undulating back we skip stones, or dig out a camas bulb, biting down into a taste so much wilder than last night's potatoes.

The most moving look I ever saw from a child in the woods was on a mud bar by the footprints of a heron. We were on our knees, making handprints beside the footprints. You could feel the creek vibrating in the silt and sand. The sun beat down heavily on our hair. Our shoes were soaking wet. The look said: I did not know until now that I needed someone much older to confirm this, the feeling I have of life here. I can now grow older, knowing it need never be lost.

The quickest door to open in the woods for a child is the one that leads to the smallest room, by knowing the name each thing is called. The door that leads to the cathedral is marked by a hesitancy to speak at all, rather to encourage by example a sharpness of the senses. If one speaks it should only be to say, as well as one can, how wonderfully all this fits together, to indicate what a long, fierce peace can derive from this knowledge.

Barry Lopez, *Crossing Open Ground*

April 1, 1975

Even so early in the morning the sun was hot and burning. There wasn't a breeze and not a leaf was stirring. In the ancient temple it was cool and pleasant; the bare feet were aware of the solid slabs of rocks, their shapes and their unevenness. Many thousands of people must have walked on them for a thousand years. It was dark there after the glare of the morning sun and in the corridors there seemed to be few people that morning and in the narrow passage it was still darker. This passage led to a wide corridor which led to the inner shrine. There was a strong smell of flowers and the incense of many centuries. And a hundred Brahmanas, freshly bathed, in newly washed white loin cloths, were chanting. Sanskrit is a powerful language, resonant with depth. The ancient walls were vibrating, almost shaking to the sound of a hundred voices. The dignity of the sound was incredible and the sacredness of the moment was beyond the words. It was not the words that awakened this immensity but the depth of the sound of many thousand years held within these walls and in the immeasurable space beyond them. It was not the meaning of those words, nor the clarity of their pronunciation, nor the dark beauty of the temple but the quality of sound that broke walls and the limitations of the human mind. The song of a bird, the distant flute, the breeze among the leaves, all these break down the walls that human beings have created for themselves.

J. Krishnamurti, *Krishnamurti's Journal*

The Spirits of Places

Different places on the face of the earth have different vital effluence, different vibration, different chemical exhalation, different polarity with different stars: call it what you like. But the spirit of place is a great reality. (D. H. Lawrence)

The qualities of places are traditionally conceived of in terms of the *genius loci*, the "spirit of the place." In this context, the word *spirit* has two connected meanings: a feeling, atmosphere, or character; and an invisible entity or being, with its own soul and personality. It is difficult to disentangle these meanings, for the second could be thought of as a personification of the first. But then some people claim to experience the presence of beings in particular places. Are these simply psychological projections? Or are they an intuitive way of relating to the living quality of the place, which may indeed have a kind of personality?

Places traditionally associated with the presence of nature spirits are not distributed equally across the landscape. They are concentrated in particular areas, such as waterfalls, springs, streams, and rivers; in and around various trees; in caves and grottoes; and in parts of woodland, desert, moorland, mountains, and seashore. The nature spirits of such places were given generic names in classical mythology: naiads were water spirits; dryads, the spirits of trees and woodland; oreads, mountain spirits; nereids, sea spirits. Comparable categories of nature spirits are recognized in many traditional cultures throughout the world. What are we to make of them?

One suggestion, proposed by the archaeologist T. C. Lethbridge, is that they are not conscious entities as much as kinds of fields. The qualities and character associated with waterfalls, for example, he attributed to "naiad fields." At first glance, this simply seems to involve a vague new terminology as obscure as the traditional one. But I think it is an idea worth pursuing. Fields are regions of influence, and in this general sense, the term is appropriate. But then what kinds of fields could the field of places be? They are obviously not reducible to the known fields of conventional physics, though electromagnetic fields no doubt contribute something to the quality of the place. However, it might make sense to think of the fields of places as *morphic fields*. Such fields are associated with self-organizing systems at all levels of complexity, and they are ordered in nested hierarchies. If particular places do indeed have morphic fields, then these fields must be embedded within larger fields, such as the fields of river systems and mountain chains, and these in turn within the fields of islands, archipelagos, and continents, and ultimately within the morphic fields of Gaia and the entire solar system.

When I first began to think along these lines, I was reluctant to extend the concept of fields to places because this seemed to be stretching the idea too far. But then I realized that the field concept itself is grounded in the idea of place. It involves a metaphorical extension of the everyday sense of fields as places of activity—as in cornfields, battlefields, football fields, and coalfields. The wider sense of fields as areas or spheres of action, operation, or investigation—as in the "field of trade" or "field of view"—predates by centuries the technical use of this term in physics. When the word was adopted by Faraday in the 1830s for his field theory of magnetism and electricity, he inevitably drew on these already-established usages, which go back to the Old English *feld* and *folde*, "earth" or "land." Thus, a field theory of places recalls the fact that fields *are* places.

The idea of the spirits of places as morphic fields implies that particular places are subject to morphic resonance from similar places in the past. The generic qualities of places, traditionally expressed in terms of the various classes of nature spirits, will indeed have a kind of collective character and memory. Moreover, particular places will have their own memories by self-resonance with their own past. Morphic resonance takes place on the basis of similarity; hence the patterns of activity of the place in the summer will tend to resonate most specifically with those in previous summers, the winter patterns with previous winter patterns, and so on.

Memory also plays a part in the responses of animals and of people to the particular place. Obviously when people enter the place, their memory of their previous experience in the place or in similar places will tend to affect their present experience. But in addition to individual memory, through morphic resonance there will also be a component of collective memory through which a person can tune in to the past experiences of other people in the same place. Of course, not all such experiences are good. For instance, throughout the world it is widely believed that places where people have been murdered, executed, or tortured are inauspicious if not actually haunted.

Thus, in the context of morphic resonance, the experience of a particular place involves both a memory inherent in the place itself and a memory of previous experiences of the same individual and similar individuals in the place. The quality or atmosphere of the place does not depend just on what is happening there now but on what has happened there before and on the way it has been experienced. These principles are quite general, but take on a special significance in relation to places traditionally regarded as sacred.

Rupert Sheldrake, *The Rebirth of Nature*

The Willingness to Rest

In my tiredness
and willingness to rest
I slipped so far down

I felt the earth
embraced me
and knew me once again.

I became
    compressed by earth
        a single drop of water

Slipping through
    small crumbs of soil
        to an earthy darkness

        where my breath unbound.

In those deep
    soils of rest
        I fell again

unbinding more
    to those strange
        pathways

where many waters
    meet in slow descent
        to the place in meeting

where we rise again
    becoming in the spiral rise
        this longing for the surface

Out of shallow springs
    I float into the first
        hours of night.

Becoming as I leave
    slow streams and ponds,
        haunt of lilies, and so become

again the unknown child
    looking for a gift
        to give his mother.

All night I work,
    dreaming, hands in the water,
        harvesting the white flowers of sleep.

David Whyte, *Where Many Rivers Meet*

I came up here from the monastery last night, sloshing through the cornfield, said Vespers, and put some oatmeal on the Coleman stove for supper. It boiled over while I was listening to the rain and toasting a piece of bread at the log fire. The night became very dark. The rain surrounded the whole cabin with its enormous virginal myth, a whole world of meaning, of secrecy, of silence, of rumor. Think of it: all that speech pouring down, selling nothing, judging nobody, drenching the thick mulch of dead leaves, soaking the trees, filling the gullies and crannies of the woods with water, washing out the places where men have stripped the hillside! What a thing it is to sit absolutely alone, in the forest, at night, cherished by this wonderful, unintelligible, perfectly innocent speech, the most comforting speech in the world, the talk that rain makes by itself all over the ridges, and the talk of the watercourses everywhere in the hollows!

Thomas Merton, Raids on the Unspeakable

Living Water

The human body consists mainly of water. So does a cucumber. So does the surface of the Earth. An odorless, tasteless liquid, say the scientific encyclopedias, abundant and widely distributed throughout the planet; built with simple elegance from two hydrogen atoms and an oxygen; essential in plant and animal nutrition; constituent of the crystals of many minerals; blue when encountered in thick layers: water. You can't get away from the stuff, and if you could, you wouldn't want to. It is an exaggeration to say that "Water is life," an exaggeration of the ubiquitousness, and perhaps the importance, certainly the durability, of life. Water came first, necessarily. Without life, there would still be water. Without water, no life.

The first primitive form of life was probably born about 3 1/2 billion years ago, when a bolt of lightning striking the primordial sea water delivered an energy jolt that spurred dissolved amino acids to cluster into self-interested coalitions of protein. The protein clusters began to grow into droplets, to pull water molecules up around themselves like cell walls, to compete with each other for the recruitment of further dissolved molecules—and the process of organic evolution was under way. But by that time it had already been raining on Earth, the seas had been rising and falling, the rivers had been flowing, for over a billion years.

Of all the types of hydrological features into which this planet's water has arranged itself—oceans, polar ice, glaciers, groundwater, fresh and salt lakes, soil moisture, atmospheric vapor—the least imposing, judged by volume, are rivers. Only one millionth part of our total water, as it turns out, is at this

moment moving within the banks of rivers. Don't be fooled: They are important, in the history of life, in the history of man, far beyond their size. Rivers
have served as crucibles of evolution, pathways of colonization, sources of
power, and inspiration, and topsoil. They not only provide, they deliver.
Glaciers come and go, lakes fill up and disappear, but rivers continue to follow
their chosen routes with exceptional permanence, changing character gradually, maturing, cutting tight canyons and then wide valleys, shifting about restlessly within their domains, always wandering, always leaving, never gone;
offering to their living inhabitants that one crucial element that survival by
evolution demands: time. Just recently—say within the last 7,000 years—the
great early flowerings of human culture appeared, surely by no accident, in the
Nile Valley, along the Indus, between the Tigris and the Euphrates, on the
banks of the Hwang Ho. The sea is where we came from. Rivers are how we
got here.

Every river on Earth is a symphony of elaborate and ordered entangle-
ments—physical factors entangled with chemical factors entangled with biological ones—and as sure as the *Jupiter* symphony is not the *Pastorale*, every
river is different from all others. But one thing remains common by definition, and represents the central, dominating fact to be coped with by the creatures that make their lives in rivers: The water never stops moving. The
pressure of current never relents. The river, as Roderick Haig-Brown has
said, never sleeps. To the plants and animals involved, the current brings food,
oxygen and all the other nutrients they need for survival; it also, that very
same current, threatens every moment to sweep them downstream into drastically different habitats where they will quickly die. The current giveth, the
current taketh away, the current has the power of a god. Because of this harsh
reality, a river is perhaps the most challenging of ecosystems. It is also one of
the most complicated and—thanks to that complexity—one of the most rich.

Current velocity is a variable factor, interdependent with a number of
other physical variables, including source of the water, slope of the streambed,
depth of the channel, width of the channel, and total volume of the water
being moved. When one of those factors changes, the others make compensatory adjustments, and the path and shape of a river reflect their compro-
mise. For instance, if the source of a river is snow-melt from high
mountainsides, the volume of discharge generally rises to a torrential peak in
late spring or early summer, carrying sediments and pushing boulders, back-
cutting by erosion to flatten the slope of the streambed, dismantling riffles and
rebuilding them, widening and deepening the channel on the outside of the
bends, sometimes gouging entirely new channels, shortcuts, that may become
permanent when the flooding subsides. If the source is a glacier, the pulse of

high water comes later, in midsummer, and is less extreme, simply because ice melts more slowly than snow. If the source is a spring, there is no annual flood, little erosion, greater permanence to the shape of the channel. And if the source is groundwater seepage, the river is actually lowered in springtime, when riverside trees leaf out and begin competing to suck away moisture. Most rivers, of course, have a combination of sources and a mixture of these flow regimens. The whole system of discharge and channel adjustment tends, as the scientists say, toward conservative dynamic equilibrium. In other words: The water looks for the laziest way of getting itself fastest to the sea.

In times of normal flow, a streambed composed of rocks and large boulders retards current velocity, holding the water back by friction, while a sandy bottom offers little resistance. A wide and deep channel also entails less friction—which is why broad lower stretches of a river like the Mississippi, despite the gentle slope, despite the sluggish appearance, despite what we expect, may well be flowing faster than many steep mountain rivers. Whatever its size or shape, a river with current velocity of four to six feet per second is moving quite swiftly. At eight feet per second, it is roaring. Very few creatures, even among those adapted to river habitats, can survive against such a constant force. So they have found and invented ways, not to live in the current, but to live out of it. The most important of those little secrets is called the boundary layer.

Current speed at any point in a channel is inversely related to depth, with the surface water in midstream moving fastest, other water moving slower beneath the surface and nearer the banks, and the deep water moving slower still; but a point is reached, about one to three millimeters above the streambed, where the water is not moving at all. Brought to a full stop by friction, this boundary layer of still water allows a huge variety of small animals, mainly insects, to live and flourish along stream bottoms in even the stretches of heaviest current. It also explains why most river insects are shaped more like alligators than like giraffes: They are adapted for life in the boundary layer, where it is a mortal necessity to keep your head down.

Also necessary to support life on the stream bottom are a variety of dissolved gases and solids, especially oxygen, carbon dioxide, calcium, potassium, nitrate, phosphate, and silica. Unless oxygen is present to the level of four or five parts per million, animals such as stoneflies and trout, with great respiratory needs, will suffocate. Under conditions of high temperature, the same animals may require twice as much oxygen—yet as the water temperature rises above 70°F., oxygen will be forced out of solution and lost from the river. It is stirred back in by any turbulent movement, over riffles, down cascades, and replaced during daylight by the photosynthetic activity of green plants. At night the concentration tends to fall again, with photosynthesis shut down for lack of light, and both animals and plants using oxygen for respiration. The decomposition of dead plant tissue, a massive continuing enterprise, conducted in rivers by bacteria and fungi, also consumes oxygen. Rivers are constantly depleting their oxygen, and constantly—unless they are dammed—replacing it. A river must tumble, must thrash, must dance along freely, or it goes blue in the face.

Meanwhile, the plants breathe in the carbon dioxide that the animals have exhaled. Thick layers of moss spread like green terry cloth over rocks in the shady areas where carbon dioxide is plentiful, and provide habitat for tiny species of insects, crustaceans, and fleas. Dissolved carbon dioxide also nourishes algae (which serve as fodder for many insects), and allows calcium to remain in solution as calcium bicarbonate, an important mineral salt. This available calcium salt balances the acidity of the river's water, encourages algal growth, helps fish to breathe more efficiently, and provides snails, mussels, and crayfish with building material for their shells. It is precious useful stuff, calcium bicarbonate.

Potassium, nitrate, and phosphate are all essential plant nutrients, natural fertilizers, and even silica evidently spurs the growth of diatoms, those microscopic algae that coat stream boulders in a smooth slime and turn wading fishermen into riotously comic spectacles. Nitrate and phosphate enter a river mainly through rainfall, runoff from the land surface and bank erosion. Nitrate also arrives, like a sprinkling of compost to help the river plants burgeon, in the dead foliage dropped on the water by streamside trees—particularly a common species of alder, which concentrates in its leaves exceptionally high levels of nitrate, and vastly enriches the food cycle of any river into which those leaves fall.

Fallen leaves, in fact, are the single chief source of fuel for the river ecosystem. The chain of river life begins—in an important sense, the sense of energy transfer and the construction of living matter—in autumn, at just the time when life on land is closing down for the winter hiatus. Yellowed alder leaves, aspen and willow and cottonwood, drift onto the water and float for a while, then sink, to become wedged between rocks; bacteria and fungi climb aboard and begin feasting, digesting, causing decay; the leaves crumble to a fine mulch that sails away on the current. Downstream, the larvae of caddisflies, blackflies, and mayflies scoop in the mulch with all manner of ingenious nets and filters, and devour it like a chef's salad, bacteria and fungi included. Where the mixture falls to rest in dead water, where half-decayed fragments catch in crannies, stonefly nymphs waddle up to browse, hungry crayfish appear, and those delicate shrimplike scudders, the amphipods. Eaten once, passed once through a gut, the same stuff is taken again further downstream by other insects and shellfish, passed again through a gut, and still again after that, until all food value has been extracted. It's a system that brooks no waste. This nutritious vegetable bounty is called detritus: the granola of rivers.

Other species of mayfly, stonefly, and caddisfly, as well as midge larvae and snails, satisfy themselves grazing algae off rocks. The common blackfly larva, bizarre of design and flexible of habit, hangs backward from hooked feet with its head swinging downstream, straining the current with bristly mustaches for detritus and floating diatoms, and then occasionally, for variety, bends over to scrape its foothold clear of algae. A few stoneflies and caddisflies also raid the moss gardens. All of these pacific invertebrates— grazing and cropping and savoring their tangy mulch—are the primary consumers in the river ecosystem, the creatures responsible for turning vegetables into meat. After them, in hot pursuit, come their natural enemies, the small carnivores. Most of these, too, are insects.

The dragonfly nymph is a formidable hunter, with a wildly improbable lower lip that springs out under hydraulic pressure, snags a tiny victim in its hooked teeth, and then, on retrieve, slaps the food straight back into the dragonfly's mouth, brisk and indelicate as a chimp stealing peaches. Making it even more deadly, the nymph has a pair of large compound eyes that achieve their binocular focus at precisely the point before its nose where the lip structure reaches full extension: Any morsel seen with both eyes is a morsel perfectly targeted. One type of caddisfly larva builds a conical silken net facing open to the current, then lurks at the narrow end and, when a smaller animal is swept in, rushes out like a spider to pounce on it. Large nymphs from a branch of the stonefly clan are also estimable predators, as are both the larvae and adults of some water beetles, and even a few species of mayfly. On their best days, these secondary consumers rule as lords of the stream-bottom jungle; one bad day, one mistake, one loss of footing, and they are in the belly of a trout.

Thousands of bad days for millions of cold-water insects, and the result is what we often call, with some narrowness of vision, a good trout stream. But a good trout stream must first be an excellent insect stream, a superior haven for algae and fungi and bacteria, a prime dumping ground for dead leaves, a surpassing reservoir of oxygen and calcium. It will then also, and thereby, be a good osprey stream, a favorite among otters, a salvation to dippers and kingfishers and bank swallows and heron, mergansers and Canada geese and water shrews, mink and muskrat and beaver. Not to mention the occasional grizzly bear. And who knows but that, sometime, a human might want to drink.

The essence of vitality for any ecosystem is complexity and balance. In a free-flowing mountain river, the physical, chemical, and biological conditions that constitute habitat for a single living creature change drastically over short distances in all directions—upstream, downstream, shallower, deeper, in front of a rock, behind it, under it. This heterogeneity makes for spectacular diversity of species, comparable to an ocean shelf, or the heart of an equatorial rainforest. And that diversity in its turn makes for great complexity of interlocking relationships, great richness of life, and balance.

But the balance, in a river, is especially precarious, especially delicate: because the water never stops moving. The pressure never relents. The boundary between life and death is measured in millimeters. There is no room for error.

David Quammen, Natural Acts

The Dolphin*

Wherever the dolphin jumps
(the sea is his kingdom,
they say, from the Ocean
to the Mediterranean) there
you can see the spring of God
which appears and disappears, joyous
acrobat with a witty beak.

He is the juggler of our
restless fate—the emblem
of the Other we eagerly
seek, and that
(the dolphin is lively—he is the happy
companion to all navigation)
he enjoys himself (he urges us)
mixing negation
(a submarine dive—a flight
elegant and improvised
in a white of foam)
with a cry of affirmation.

Giorgio Caproni, in Greg Gatenby,
Whales: A Celebration

* Translated from the Italian by Gabriel del Re

We're told that we must never anthropomorphize
when we are writing about animals, or "creatures"
as we'd prefer to say; nor are we now allowed,
of course, to speak of "all God's creatures" either,
since there are few today who can believe
that He exists and once created them and us.
To write a poem about whales or dolphins, then,
presents a challenge to all those who see
in the great whale the dread Leviathan
which Scripture teaches man should look upon
as the huge proof of the Creator's mightiness,
the ruler of the deeps, and in the guise
of the White Whale of Melville's *Moby Dick*
a mighty symbol of both Death and Mystery;
or who, as I do, see in the dolphin's face
the look both of the cherubim and of the unborn child
safe in its mother's womb, with the angelic, innocent
smile worn by all the creatures of God's Paradise.
Many the myths about the dolphin. *Dauphin* means,
or used to, dolphin and also "first-born"; and
a boy upon a dolphin's back is such an old
image, it surely tells us men have always sensed
some sort of kinship that the reason can't explain
between the amphibious being and our own.
Then there's the recent question or new myth
about the dolphin's sort of speech: a mystery
indeed! Poets and thinkers are increasingly
concerned with the great problems language sets.
A poem should avoid abstraction and all forms
of private declaration of belief; yet I must state
that I'm convinced by what is called the Fall of Man.
We've been turned out of Paradise; we've made the world
into a shambles and a slaughter-house; we've lost
the primal *Urspräch* which may once have been
also an aid in our communion with the beasts
we now exploit and prey upon. Polluted earth,
polluted souls: Now finally, perhaps too late,
we try to care, if not to pray, for some Salvation.
A poet friend of mine* wrote lately that: "We live

* Kathleen Raine

in the mind of God, here, now and always, for there is
no other place." And R. Buckminster Fuller wrote
in nineteen sixty-three: "Stop 'calling names'
names that are meaningless; / you can't suppress God
by killing off people which are, physically,
only transceiver mechanisms through which God
is broadcasting." And too: "The more man becomes man,
the more it will be needful for him to,
and to know how to, worship": thus the Père
Teilhard de Chardin. I do not digress.
If you have faith you may not have it every day
but somehow you believe that we shall not destroy
ourselves and God's creation; though we can
"kill off people" and, be it added, species like
the direly menaced whales and dwindling dolphins.
Now "the light of the public darkens everything."†
But still the animal kingdom and the world of nature can
remind us of our long-lost innocence. All things shall be
made new. Let chaos come. The mortal must first die.
Yet even an atheist poet‡ could write: "The rose
tells that the aptitude to be regenerated has
no limit"; and "what selectivity there can occur,
only just in time, and succeed in imposing its law
in spite of everything. Man sees this pinion tremble
which in every language is the first great letter of
the word Resurrection." Redemption. Paradise Regained.
God's Kingdom here on earth. Absurd, discarded dreams?
 Not only fools can still believe and fight for faith
and meaning: to preserve our innate, obstinate capacity
for love, for wonder at the miracle of life:
to speak out even if the words one's forced to use
seem worn nearly to death, and say: "Yes, we can still
do what we can to preserve not only such rare things
as whales and dolphins, but the eternal Mystery of which
they are both emblem and incarnate form.

David Gascoyne, "Whales and Dolphins," in
Greg Gatenby *Whales: A Celebration*

† Martin Heidegger
‡ André Breton

Across the wall of the world,
A River sings a beautiful song,
It says, come, rest here by my side.

Each of you a bordered country,
Delicate and strangely made, proud,
Yet thrusting perpetually under siege.
Your armed struggles for profit
Have left collars of waste upon
My shore, currents of debris upon my breast.
Yet today I call you to my riverside,
If you will study war no more. Come,
Clad in peace and I will sing the songs
The Creator gave to me when I and the
Tree and the rock were one.
Before cynicism was a bloody sear across your
Brow and when you yet know you still
Knew nothing.
The River sang and sings on.

Maya Angelou, *On the Pulse of Morning*

⤳ Eco Consciousness ⤶

Consciousness is one type of highly intense experience of life, but there are
other forms present in other species, sometimes with capacities that humans
lack, as in fish that can hear ranges of sound or animals that can see ranges of
light not possible to our ears and eyes. Nor can we simply draw a line between
us, together with large-brained mammals, and other beings, as a distinction
of "living persons" and "dead bodies." For plants too are living organic beings
that respond to heat, light, water, and sound as organisms, and even chemical
aggregates are dancing centers of energy.

Human consciousness, then, should not be what utterly separates us
from the rest of "nature." Rather, consciousness is where this dance of energy
organizes itself in increasingly unified ways, until it reflects back on itself in
self-awareness. Consciousness is and must be where we recognize our kinship with all other beings. The dancing void from which the tiniest energy

events of atomic structures flicker in and out of existence and self-aware thought are kin along a continuum of organized life-energy.

Our capacity for consciousness, which allows us to roam through space and time, remembering past ages, exploring the inner workings of all other existing beings on earth or on distant planets, also makes us aware of the ephemeral nature of our "self." Our capacity for consciousness is sustained by a complex but fragile organism. Cut that organism at its vital centers, in the brain or in the heart, and the light of consciousness goes out, and with it our "self."

It is this juxtaposition of the capacity of consciousness to roam through space and time, and its utter transience in its dependence on our mortal organisms, that has generated much of the energy of what has been called "religion" in the past. Much of this religious quest has sought to resolve this contradiction by denying it, imagining that consciousness was not really dependent on the mortal organism. The mental self could survive, and even be "purified" and strengthened, by the demise of the body. This concept of the "immortal self," survivable apart from our particular transient organism, must be recognized, not only as untenable, but as the source of much destructive behavior toward the earth and other humans.

An ecological spirituality needs to be built on three premises: the transience of selves, the living interdependency of all things, and the value of the personal in communion. Many spiritual traditions have emphasized the need to "let go of the ego," but in ways that diminished the value of the person, undercutting particularly those, like women, who scarcely have been allowed individuated personhood at all. We need to "let go of the ego" in a different sense. We are called to affirm the integrity of our personal center of being, in mutuality with the personal centers of all other beings across species and, at the same time, accept the transience of these personal selves.

As we accept both the value and the transience of the self, we can also be awakened to a new sense of kinship with all other organisms. Like humans, the animals and the plants are living centers of organic life who exist for a season. Then each of our roots shrivels, the organic structures that sustain our life fail, and we die. The cutting of the life center also means that our bodies disintegrate into organic matter, to enter the cycle of decomposition and recomposition as other entities.

The material substances of our bodies live on in plants and animals, just as our own bodies are composed from minute to minute of substances that once were parts of other animals and plants, stretching back through time to prehistoric ferns and reptiles, to ancient biota that floated in the primal seas of earth. Our kinship with all earth creatures is global, linking us to the whole living Gaia today. It also spans the ages, linking our material substance with all the beings that have gone before us on earth and even to the dust of exploding stars. We need new psalms and meditations to make this kinship vivid in our communal and personal devotions.

But, even as we take into our spirituality and ethical practice the transience of selves, relinquishing the illusion of permanence, and accepting the dissolution of our physical substance into primal energy, to become matter for new organisms, we also come to value again the personal center of each being. My eye catches the eye of a bird as it turns its head toward me on the side of the tree, and then continues its tasks. Brendan spies me coming up the path, and with flashing red fur is at the door, leaping in circles with unfeigned delight. My body, stretching in the sun, notices a tiny flower pushing up through the soil to greet the same sun. As we know our kinship as I and Thou, saluting one another as fellow persons.

Compassion for all living things fills our spirits, breaking down the illusion of otherness. At this moment we can encounter the matrix of energy of the universe that sustains the dissolution and recomposition of matter as also a heart that knows us even as we are known. Is there also a consciousness that remembers and envisions and reconciles all things, as the Process theologians believe? Surely, if we are kin to all things and offspring of the universe, then what has flowered in us as consciousness must also be reflected in that universe as well, in the ongoing creative Matrix of the whole.

As we gaze in the void of our future extinguished self and dissolving substance, we encounter there the wellspring of life and creativity from which all things have sprung and into which they return, only to well up again in new forms. But we also know this as the great Thou, the personal center of the universal process, with which all the small centers of personal being dialogue in the conversation that continually creates and re-creates the world. The small selves and the Great Self are finally one, for as She bodies forth in us, all the beings respond in the bodying forth of their diversive creative work that makes the world.

The dialogue can become truncated. We can seek to grasp our ego centers of being in negation of others, proliferating our existence by diminishing that of others, and finally poisoning the wellspring of the life process itself. Or we can dance gracefully with our fellow beings, spinning out our creative work in such a way as to affirm theirs and they ours as well.

Then, like bread tossed on the water, we can be confident that our creative work will be nourishing to the community of life, even as we relinquish our small self back into the great Self. Our final gesture, as we surrender ourself into the Matrix of life, then can become a prayer of ultimate trust: "Mother, into your hands I commend my spirit. Use me as you will in your infinite creativity."

Rosemary Radford Ruether, Gaia and God

I think of two landscapes—one outside the self, the other within. The external landscape is the one we see—not only the line and color of the land and its shading at different times of the day, but also its plants and animals in season, its weather, its geology, the record of its climate and evolution. If you walk up, say, a dry arroyo in the Sonoran Desert you will feel a mounding and rolling of sand and silt beneath your foot that is distinctive. You will anticipate the crumbling of the sedimentary earth in the arroyo bank as your hand reaches out, and in that tangible evidence you will sense a history of water in the region. Perhaps a black-throated sparrow lands in a paloverde bush—the resiliency of the twig under the bird, that precise shade of yellowish-green against the milk-blue sky, the fluttering whir of the arriving sparrow, are what I mean by "the landscape." Draw on the smell of creosote bush, or clack stones together in the dry air. Feel how light is the desiccated dropping of the kangaroo rat. Study an animal track obscured by the wind. These are all elements of the land, and what makes the landscape comprehensible are the relationships between them. One learns a landscape finally not by knowing the name or identity of everything in it, but by perceiving the relationships in it—like that between the sparrow and the twig. The difference between the relationships and the elements is the same as that between written history and a catalog of events.

The second landscape I think of is an interior one, a kind of projection within a person of a part of the exterior landscape. Relationships in the exterior landscape include those that are named and discernible, such as the nitrogen cycle, or a vertical sequence of Ordovician limestone, and others that are uncodified or ineffable, such as winter light falling on a particular kind of granite, or the effect of humidity on the frequency of a blackpoll warbler's burst of song. That these relationships have purpose and order, however inscrutable they may seem to us, is a tenet of evolution. Similarly, the speculations, intuitions, and formal ideas we refer to as "mind" are a set of relationships in the interior landscape with purpose and order; some of these are obvious, many impenetrably subtle. The shape and character of these relationships in a person's thinking, I believe, are deeply influenced by where on this earth one goes, what one touches, the patterns one observes in nature—the intricate history of one's life in the land, even a life in the city, where wind, the chirp of birds, the line of a falling leaf, are known. These thoughts are arranged, further, according to the thread of one's moral, intellectual, and spiritual development. The interior landscape responds to the character and subtlety of an exterior landscape; the shape of the individual mind is affected by land as it is by genes.

In stories like those I heard at Anaktuvuk Pass about wolverine, the relationship between separate elements in the land is set forth clearly. It is put in a simple framework of sequential incidents and apposite detail. If the exterior landscape is limned well, the listener often feels that he has heard something pleasing and authentic—trustworthy. We derive this sense of confidence I think not so much from verifiable truth as from an understanding that lying has played no role in the narrative. The storyteller is obligated to engage the reader with a precise vocabulary, to set forth a coherent and dramatic rendering of incidents—and to be ingenuous.

When one hears a story one takes pleasure in it for different reasons— for the euphony of its phrases, an aspect of the plot, or because one identifies with one of the characters. With certain stories certain individuals may experience a deeper, more profound sense of well-being. This latter phenomenon, in my understanding, rests at the heart of storytelling as an elevated experience among aboriginal peoples. It results from bringing two landscapes together. The exterior landscape is organized according to principles or laws or tendencies beyond human control. It is understood to contain an integrity that is beyond human analysis and unimpeachable. Insofar as the storyteller depicts various subtle and obvious relationships in the exterior landscape accurately in his story, and insofar as he orders them along traditional lines of meaning to create the narrative, the narrative will "ring true." The listener who "takes the story to heart" will feel a pervasive sense of congruence within himself and also with the world.

Among the Navajo and, as far as I know, many other native peoples, the land is thought to exhibit a sacred order. That order is the basis of ritual. The rituals themselves reveal the power in that order. Art, architecture, vocabulary, and costume, as well as ritual, are derived from the perceived natural order of the universe—from observations and meditations on the exterior landscape. An indigenous philosophy—metaphysics, ethics, epistemology, aesthetics, and logic—may also be derived from a people's continuous attentiveness to both the obvious (scientific) and ineffable (artistic) orders of the local landscape. Each individual, further, undertakes to order his interior landscape according to the exterior landscape. To succeed in this means to achieve a balanced state of mental health.

I think of the Navajo for a specific reason. Among the various sung ceremonies of this people—Enemyway, Coyoteway, Red Antway, Uglyway—is one called Beautyway. In the Navajo view, the elements of one's interior life— one's psychological makeup and moral bearing—are subject to a persistent principle of disarray. Beautyway is, in part, a spiritual invocation of the order of the exterior universe, that irreducible, holy complexity that manifests itself as all things changing through time (a Navajo definition of beauty, hózhóó). The purpose of this invocation is to re-create in the individual who is the subject of the Beautyway ceremony that same order, to make the individual again a reflection of the myriad enduring relationships of the landscape.

I believe story functions in a similar way. A story draws on relationships in the exterior landscape and projects them onto the interior landscape. The purpose of storytelling is to achieve harmony between the two landscapes, to use all the elements of story—syntax, mood, figures of speech—in a harmonious way to reproduce the harmony of the land in the individual's interior. Inherent in story is the power to reorder a state of psychological confusion through contact with the pervasive truth of those relationships we call "the land."

These thoughts, of course, are susceptible to interpretation. I am convinced, however, that these observations can be applied to the kind of prose we call nonfiction as well as to traditional narrative forms such as the novel and the short story, and to some poems. Distinctions between fiction and nonfiction are sometimes obscured by arguments over what constitutes "the truth." In the aboriginal literature I am familiar with, the first distinction made among narratives is to separate the authentic from the inauthentic. Myth, which we tend to regard as fictitious or "merely metaphorical," is as authentic, as real, as the story of a wolverine in a man's lap. (A distinction is made, of course, about the elevated nature of myth—and frequently the circumstances of myth-telling are more rigorously prescribed than those for the telling of legends or vernacular stories—but all of these narratives are rooted in the local landscape. To violate *that* connection is to call the narrative itself into question.)

The power of narrative to nurture and heal, to repair a spirit in disarray, rests on two things: the skillful invocation of unimpeachable sources and a listener's knowledge that no hypocrisy or subterfuge is involved. This last simple fact is to me one of the most imposing aspects of the Holocene history of man.

We are more accustomed now to thinking of "the truth" as something that can be explicitly stated, rather than as something that can be evoked in a metaphorical way outside science and Occidental culture. Neither can truth be reduced to aphorism or formulas. It is something alive and unpronounceable. Story creates an atmosphere in which it becomes discernible as a pattern. For a storyteller to insist on relationships that do not exist is to lie. Lying is the opposite of story. (I do not mean to confuse ignorance with deception, or to imply that a storyteller can perceive all that is inherent in the land. Every storyteller falls short of a perfect limning of the landscape—perception and language both fail. But to make up something that is not there, something which can never be corroborated in the land, to knowingly set forth a false relationship, is to be lying, no longer telling a story.)

Because of the intricate, complex nature of the land, it is not always possible for a storyteller to grasp what is contained in a story. The intent of the storyteller, then, must be to evoke, honestly, some single aspect of all that the land contains. The storyteller knows that because different individuals grasp the story at different levels, the focus of his regard for truth must be at the primary one—with who was there, what happened, when, where, and why things occurred. The story will then possess similar truth at other levels—the integrity inherent at the primary level of meaning will be conveyed every-where else. As long as the storyteller carefully describes the order before him, and uses his storytelling skill to heighten and emphasize certain relation-ships, it is even possible for the story to be more successful than the storyteller himself is able to imagine.

I would like to make a final point about the wolverine stories I heard at Anaktuvuk Pass. I wrote down the details afterward, concentrating especially on aspects of the biology and ecology of the animals. I sent the information on to my friend living with the Cree. When, many months later, I saw him, I asked whether the Cree had enjoyed these insights of the Nunamiut into the nature of the wolverine. What had they said?

"You know," he told me, "how they are. They said, 'That could happen.'"

In these uncomplicated words the Cree declared their own knowledge of the wolverine. They acknowledged that although they themselves had never seen the things the Nunamiut spoke of, they accepted them as accurate observations, because they did not consider story a context for misrepresen-tation. They also preserved their own dignity by not overstating their confi-dence in the Nunamiut, a distant and unknown people.

Whenever I think of this courtesy on the part of the Cree I think of the dignity that is ours when we cease to demand the truth and realize that the best we can have of those substantial truths that guide our lives is metaphori-cal—a story. And the most of it we are likely to discern comes only when we accord one another the respect the Cree showed the Nunamiut. Beyond this— that the interior landscape is a metaphorical representation of the exterior landscape, that the truth reveals itself most fully not in dogma but in the para-dox, irony, and contradictions that distinguish compelling narratives—beyond this there are only failures of imagination: reductionism in science; funda-mentalism in religion; fascism in politics.

Our national literatures should be important to us insofar as they sus-tain us with illumination and heal us. They can always do that so long as they are written with respect for both the source and the reader, and with an understanding of why the human heart and the land have been brought together so regularly in human history.

Barry Lopez, *Crossing Open Ground*

This is that story
   The heaving high seas were laden with scum
   The dull sky glowed red
   Dust and ashes drifted in the wind circling the earth
   The burdened seas slanted this way, and that, flooding
the scorched land under a daylight moon
   A black oily rain rained
   No one was there

At the end, after the thermonuclear war between the Djanks and Druzhkies, in consequence of which they had destroyed themselves, and, madly, all other inhabitants of the earth. God spoke through a glowing crack in a bulbous black cloud to Calvin Cohn, the paleologist, who of all men had miraculously survived in a battered oceanography vessel with sails, as the swollen seas tilted this way and that;

Saying this:

"Don't presume on Me a visible face, Mr. Cohn, I am not that kind, but if you can, imagine Me. I regret to say it was through a minuscule error that you escaped destruction. Though mine, it was not a serious one; a serious mistake might have jammed the universe. The cosmos is so conceived that I myself don't know what goes on everywhere. It is not perfection although I, of course, am perfect. That's how I arranged my mind.

"And that you, Mr. Cohn, happen to exist when no one else does, though embarrassing to Me, has nothing to do with your once having studied for the rabbinate, or for that matter, having given it up.

"That was your concern, but I don't want you to conceive any false expectations. Inevitably, my purpose is to rectify the error I conceived.

"I have no wish to torment you, only once more affirm cause and effect. It is no more than a system within a system, yet I depend on it to maintain a certain order. Man, after failing to use to a sufficient purpose his possibilities, and my good will, has destroyed himself; therefore, in truth, so have you."

Cohn, shivering in his dripping rubber diving suit, complained bitterly:

"After Your first Holocaust You promised no further Floods. 'Never again shall there be a Flood to destroy the earth.' That was Your Covenant with Noah and all living creatures. Instead, You turned the water on again. Everyone who wasn't consumed in fire is drowned in bitter water, and a Second Flood covers the earth."

God said this: "All that was pre-Torah. There was no such thing as Holocaust, only cause and effect. But after I had created man I did not know how he would fail Me next, in what matter of violence, corruption, blasphemy, beastliness, sin beyond belief. Thus he defiled himself. I had not foreseen the extent of it.

"The present Devastation, ending in smoke and dust, comes as a consequence of man's self-betrayal. From the beginning, when I gave them the gift of life, they were perversely greedy for death. At last I thought, I will give them death because they are engrossed in evil.

"They have destroyed my handiwork, the conditions of their survival: the sweet air I gave them to breathe; the fresh water I blessed them with, to drink and bathe in; the fertile green earth. They tore apart my ozone, carbonized my oxygen, acidified my refreshing rain. Now they affront my cosmos. How much shall the Lord endure?

"I made man to be free, but his freedom, badly used, destroyed him. In sum, the evil overwhelmed the good. The Second Flood, this that now subsides on the broken earth, they brought on themselves. They had not lived according to the Covenant.

"Therefore I let them do away with themselves. They invented the manner; I turned my head. That you went on living, Mr. Cohn, I regret to say, was no more than a marginal error. Such things may happen."

"Lord," begged Calvin Cohn, a five-foot-six man in his late thirties, on his wet knees. "It wasn't as though I had a choice. I was at the bottom of the ocean attending to my work when the Devastation struck. Since I am still alive it would only be fair if You let me live. A new fact is a new condition. Though I deeply regret man's insult to a more worthy fate, still I would consider it a favor if You permit me to live."

"That cannot be my intent, Mr. Cohn. My anger has diminished but my patience is not endless. In the past I often forgave them their evil; but I shall not now. No Noah this time, no exceptions, righteous or otherwise. Though it hurts Me to say it, I must slay you; it is just. Yet because of my error, I will grant you time to compose yourself, make your peace. Therefore live quickly —a few deep breaths and go your way. Beyond that lies nothing for you. These are my words."

"It says in Sanhedrin," Cohn attempted to say, "He who saves one life, it is as if he saved the world," He begged for another such favor.

"Although the world was saved it could not save itself. I will not save it again. I am not a tribal God; I am Master of the Universe. That means more interrelated responsibilities than you can imagine."

Cohn then asked for a miracle.

"Miracles," God answered, "go only so far. Once you proclaim it, a miracle is limited. Man would need more than a miracle."

The Lord snapped the crack in the cloud shut. He had been invisible, light from which a voice extruded; no sign of Godcrown, silverbeard, peering eye—the image in which man had sought his own. The bulbous cloud sailed imperiously away, vanishing.

A dark coldness descended. Either the dust had thickened or night had fallen. Calvin Cohn was alone, forlorn. When he raised his head the silence all but cracked his neck.

As he struggled to stand, he lifted his fist at the darkened sky. "God made us who we are."

He danced in a shower of rocks; but that may have been his imagining. Yet those that hit the head hurt.

Cohn fell to his knees, fearing God's wrath. His teeth chattered; he shivered as though touched on the neck by icy fingers. Taking back his angry words, he spoke these: "I am not a secularist although I have doubts. Einstein said God doesn't dice with the universe; if he could believe it maybe I can. I accept Your conditions, but please don't cut my time too short."

The rusty, battered vessel with one broken mast drifted on slanted seas. Of all men only Calvin Cohn lived on, passionate to survive.

Bernard Malamud, *God's Grace*

Building Communities of Celebration and Resistance

How do we carry on a struggle to heal the world and to build a new biospheric community in the face of this intransigent system of death? It is my belief that those who want to carry on this struggle in a sustained way must build strong base communities of celebration and resistance. By "base communities" I mean local face-to-face groups with which one lives, works, and prays. I do not mean that all these functions would necessarily come together for most people in one base community. Most people will find these different forms of support in a variety of groups and networks, although it is important that these many groups recognize their interconnections in one unified struggle.

There are three interrelated aspects of the work of such local communities. One is shaping the personal therapies, spiritualities, and corporate liturgies by which we nurture and symbolize a new biophilic consciousness. Second, there is the utilization of local institutions over which we have some control, our homes, schools, churches, farms, and locally controlled businesses, as pilot projects of ecological living. Third, there is the building of organizational networks that reach out, regionally, nationally, and internationally, in a struggle to change the power structures that keep the present death system in place.

We must start by recognizing that *metanoia*, or change of consciousness, begins with us. This does not happen all at once, but is an ongoing process. We all have been shaped to misname evil, to seek invulnerable power, or else to capitulate to such power demands in the hands of male authorities. We are tied to present systems of consumption and can hardly imagine alternatives to them that might give us greater peace and wholeness, even though the scramble to "keep up" in the present systems leaves us ever more insecure, anxious, and exhausted.

We need healing therapies and spiritualities of inner growth to let go of fears and open up to each other and to the world around us, to learn how to *be*, rather than to *strive*. The struggle to change the death system must be deeply rooted in joy in the goodness of life. Making healing and inner growth available to us all means unhooking them from professionalized "help," which comes with credentials and high price tags. Although there is a place for skilled people, most of what we need is fairly simple and "free."

We can survey ideas from a few good books, gather a group on a regular basis to discuss the ideas from "experts," and then begin to open up to each other and learn to become good "ears" for hearing each other's story. We also need to recover our body-psyche-spirit nexus, to learn to breathe again, to feel our life energy. Small groups can learn, perhaps with initial expert advice, and teach each other techniques of breathing, biofeedback, meditation, and massage.

We need to take the time to sit under trees, look at water, and at the sky, observe small biotic communities of plants and animals with close attention, get back in touch with the living earth. We can start to release the stifled intuitive and creative powers of our organism, to draw and to write poetry, and to know that we stand on holy ground.

In addition to personal therapies and spirituality, we need corporate liturgies as well, to symbolize and express our altered consciousness. Unfortunately most of our institutional forums of worship are tied to alienated, patriarchal consciousness. Much of their worship is literally "deadly," although some are open to partial transformation. Thus communities of new being and consciousness need to become their own liturgists. They need to learn to shape corporate liturgies to mourn together for violated lives, to midwife healing and new birth, and to taste a new creation already present.

Such communities can also learn to carry liturgy to the streets, in protest marches and demonstrations that cry out against the death system and visualize renewed life in ways that can catch the imagination of others who participate with them or watch them. We can call on all the arts—song and music, dance and mime, posters and banners, costumes and puppetry—to shape the public liturgies of biospheric politics. The Vermont-based Bread and Puppet Theatre is a model for such public liturgies of transformed consciousness.

Another essential work of local communities is to begin to live now an ecologically healthful life. We can see our own homes and other institutions over which we have some control, such as schools or churches, as "pilot projects." We can form a local committee and study a basic manual of ecological living, such as Jeremy Rifkin's *Green Lifestyle Handbook: 1001 Ways You Can Heal the Earth*. We can systematically check different aspects of our lives in this structure, our energy use in heating, cooling, and lighting, toxic cleaners, waste products, land use and transportation, and begin to implement some changes that bring our home or other institutions up to ecological "code."

Such efforts can only be pilot projects and will function as learning and consciousness-raising processes. As we try to implement some changes, it will become quickly evident that our church, school, and workplace, and even our home, are not autonomous. They are dependent parts of larger systems that operate, to a large extent, to tie them to present wasteful ways of functioning. As we try, for example, to implement recycling of household wastes, we run into city waste-disposal systems and resistance to new forms of trash collection that are integrated into recycling industries. We begin to recognize these systems in their local and regional expressions, and even beyond, and to put names to those who control the decisions.

This leads us to the third role of local communities, to become political bases of organizing and action. Here again it is useful to start locally, where we can be concrete and where there is often some possibilities of real change. When our group has formulated some clear policy changes, for example, toward a recycling center coordinated with city waste collection, we can network with other groups in the city. We can form a larger organizational base, attend town council meetings, eventually run candidates for local office. We can find ways to pressure local business, both negatively through boycotts and positively through petitions and discussion.

Such local organizing efforts will also reveal the extent to which local government and business really have local control and the extent to which they too are dependent parts of national and international political and economic systems. This is a part of a learning process in which we put names to links in the chains of control, and imagine ways to put pressure for change on the weak links in those chains. Local "green committees" begin to link up with one another across the country.

We ultimately have to think and also act globally, as well as locally. We need to become knowledgeable about parallel movements in Western and Eastern Europe, Asia, Africa, and Latin America, and also the distinct problems of different regions and their interconnection with our own lives. This global consciousness plays two roles. It makes us constantly aware that our local efforts are part of a global struggle, and we are all interdependent in that struggle. It also allows us, at times, to link up with movements internationally that have political forums through the United Nations and other international organizations.

We need to amend the famous slogan of René Dubos: "Think globally and act locally." We need to think both locally and globally and act both locally and globally. The struggle for local changes will lack depth unless it understands itself as an integral part of a global new consciousness. This needs to be more than an abstraction. We need to read about, and sometimes visit, groups who are organizing in other parts of the world and learn from what they are doing. We need to find ways to link up concretely in international forums where the defense of the global commons of forests, oceans, and atmosphere is being carried out against their corporate abusers.

The time is short for major changes, if we are to save much of the biotic system of the earth that is in danger. The Worldwatch Institute estimates that we have about forty years for major global shifts to be carried out voluntarily (until 2030). After that time major disasters of famine and collapse of life systems, under the pressures of exploitative use, will take place, and there could well be very dangerous militarist and totalitarian responses from threatened elites, as indeed is already happening.

In speaking about the urgency of the situation before audiences, I am often asked if I am "optimistic" about the possibilities for change. The assumption behind this question seems to be that we have two ideational stances toward these crises: optimism or pessimism. But I am inclined to think that both these stances get us off the hook. If we are "optimistic," it suggests that change is inevitable and will happen in the "natural" course of things, and so we need not make much effort ourselves. Someone else will take care of it. If we are "pessimistic," change is impossible, and therefore it is useless to try. In either case we have the luxury, as critical but comfortable elites in the United States, to question the present system without being responsible for it.

What we need is neither optimism nor pessimism, in these terms, but committed love. This means that we remain committed to a vision and to concrete communities of life no matter what the "trends" may be. Whether we are immediately "winning" or "losing" cannot shake our rooted understandings of what biophilic life is and should be, although we need to adapt our strategies to the changing fortunes of the struggle. We also remain clear that life is not made whole "once and for all," in some static millennium of the future. It is made whole again and again, in the renewed day born from night and in the new spring that rises from each winter.

Being rooted in love for our real communities of life and for our common mother, Gaia, can teach us patient passion, a passion that is not burnt out in a season, but can be renewed season after season. Our revolution is not just for us, but for our children, for the generations of living beings to come. What we can do is to plant a seed, nurture a seed-bearing plant here and there, and hope for a harvest that goes beyond the limits of our powers and the span of our lives.

Rosemary Radford Ruether, *Gaia and God*

To me the closest concept to sustainability I can think of in spiritual traditions is the concept of karma. I can imagine a traditional Buddhist or Hindu telling us, even five hundred years ago, that if we dump toxic waste, this is bad karma. This means that eventually it will come back to us. Karma, of course, implies time only in the context of "future lives," but our children, in a sense, are our future lives. Future generations are our future lives. So karma to me is a very ecological concept.

Fritjof Capra, in Fritjof Capra, David Steindl-Rast
with Thomas Matus, *Belonging to the Universe*

The Spiritual Age

W e stand upon the threshold of a changing world, a world whose values have become contraspiritual, fraught with anger and violence, exhaustion and disillusionment. Paul Brunton writes: "the only cure for the newest chaos in which the whole world has fallen is also the oldest one"—commitment to the self, to the inner life, to individual growth, to surrender and service to the divine within the self and others, and the pursuit of the divine in all things, to live in truth, to be, as Paul Brunton puts it "more spiritualized."

We have strived for the spiritual in our everyday from the outset of our quest, even if we were not readily aware of the fact. And, as outlined earlier in "Trials," we are sometimes individually forced into silence when we encounter obstacles. Now that our world's natural resources are threatened to the point of no return, we need to gather together in silence. Then we might hear the direction we need to take, to hear God's instruction. Carl Jung emphasizes that through the understanding of the symbolic astrology of our times, the word of God is revealed. In recent years, there has been a steadily increasing participation in psychotherapy and dream analysis as we have tried to understand more about ourselves and each other's makeup and purpose. This collective searching for the ways forward has been referred to as "New Age," a term that has not always been positive. We are, however, in a time of great change and transition as we enter the third millennium, and a new code of living and being is forced upon us.

In this section, Bede Griffiths describes the communion needed between us, the spiritual values necessary to integrate a "whole new reality," and of the necessity of honouring the transcendent forms of human life. Shakti Gawain provides her views on the evolution of this New Age, of the unity of the masculine and feminine which is taking place, the healing and teaching and communicating which is leading us to a new consciousness. And Charles Tart culminates this new tenet in his Transpersonal Creed.

✠

Man's Need of a Higher Power

Everywhere today we see that the human being has misunderstood itself and misconceived the World-Mind's will for it in this era. And because there is a price to be paid for all mistakes, everywhere we also see human distress and human suffering. The way out of these afflictions is being desperately sought but seldom found...for it is being sought in the wrong direction. There is only one proper way out, and that is to correct the misunderstanding and to remove the misconception. This needs a dramatic change of moral attitude, a large renunciation of materialist outlook and a quick reversal of spiritual indifference. A change in thinking is the first way to ensure a change in the world's condition. In changing himself, man takes the first step to changing his environment and in changing his environment he takes the second step toward changing himself. For the first step of self-change must be a mental, not a physical one. Therefore he will profit best in these difficult days by subduing pride and being perfectly frank with himself, even to the point of putting on mental sackcloth and emotional ashes. His mental attitude must effect an about-face. He must heed that inspired bidding, *"Repent—and be saved."* This has been the divine message for all such times but it is especially applicable to the present time. He has lived a materialistic life which is but a half-life.

The only cure for the newest chaos in which the whole world has fallen is also the oldest one. Those who wait for the announcement of miracle-working prescriptions wait in vain. The truth that is around the corner is as old as mankind, only the face it shows is fresh and the clothes it wears are styled to the century itself. Some thousands of years ago India's sacred writing, The Bhagavad Gita, proclaimed that there is peace and prosperity on the earth for those who will learn and follow the laws of the inner life.

To say that the higher powers have created a crisis of human destiny in order to compel human beings to face the inner challenge is true. To say that human history and conduct have themselves created it is also true. These two halves must be put together to get the whole truth about the dark events which have overtaken humanity. Every attempt to save itself that is only an external attempt and not also an internal one, is foredoomed to failure. This needs to be remembered by all peoples because all peoples have been caught in the world's challenging situation, even though their particular responsibility is less in some cases, more in others. It is not the Europeans and Americans who are alone being challenged today by their creations, but also the Indians and the Chinese, inheritors of the oldest civilizations on the planet. We are not of those who eulogize the Orient as the sole abode of spirituality, and titter at the Occident as the polluted abode of materiality. Each hemisphere has its own special faults to set right, each has strayed from the path ordained by God for it and consequently both are being involved in the crisis. All peoples, all races, have reached a point where the road traveled can no longer be traveled, where going forward and retreating backward are both impossible. What then are they to do? The obvious and only correct answer is to get off the wrong road and get on to a new one.

The ultimate destiny of the world—as apart from its immediate destiny—is to become more spiritualized and not less. Every man who believes this will understand that society is as good or as bad as the individuals who compose it, and there is no magic which can make a good civilization out of bad individuals, a golden new order out of the leaden old characters. He will consequently believe in the need of fine character to guide a people, rather than in cheap slogans. He will look for guidance from men who believe it too, not from those who believe in the materialism which darkly shadows everything. This is why philosophy points to the need of human reformation for any durable reformation of society. This is why there is no nobler task today than diffusing that knowledge about man himself, which at least possesses and most needs. This is an even more valuable service than reforming the society in which he lives, although that is perfectly proper and absolutely necessary in its place. The task is not only to reaffirm that under the law of compensation we get back the results of our own good or evil doing, not only to advertise to an ignorant blinded world that the Overself exists and is the supreme value; not only to show that it is an experienceable reality and not an imagined fancy or a speculative concept, but also to advocate to an indifferent complacent world that the Overself's life must be brought into its own practical everyday life.

In the end, humanity will be driven to have recourse to its true spiritual teachers, after all other guides have led it into material ruin and mutual destruction. No other refuge is left for stricken humanity than this one. The notion that their teaching is of no use to men of the world, versed in the facts of life, and aware of the compromises involved in business and political affairs, is a delusion which dates the origin of man's unnecessary and avoidable sufferings. It is indeed the greatest of errors to regard such guides as impractical visionaries. Their vision of what is happening around them is never circumscribed by petty personal considerations. Having rid themselves of narrow views and parochial prejudices, having learned to think of human affairs in large terms and through long vistas of times, having transcended the limitations of a merely intellectual approach and entered into an intuitive one, they are in a good position to understand the course of past history and to discern meaning behind the veils of present events. They can satisfy the deep-rooted need of the human mind to discover some worthier significance in life today. Hence their philosophy is not irrelevant to the purposeful activities and practical interests of men. They know the true causes of humanity's distress and the true remedies.

The declaration of eternal laws and revelation of universal patterns must be made anew. The sooner we discover that there are spiritual laws which cannot be outwitted, the better for us. Never before did the function which the philosophic sage, the religious prophet and the mystical seer could perform in society be so needed yet remain so neglected. We have no worship for their wisdom, revelation or guidance, only for the engineer's mechanical skill, the tradesman's fortune-making capacity, the entertainer's escape-providing talent. The old spiritual teachers with their keen penetration into the inner side of things, and their certainty about truth only because it was their experience and not their opinion, gave merely moral injunctions against all the ugly emotions and passions, especially hate. Today the scientific laws of the power of thought must be given out to explain these injunctions, and to warn us that negative mental-emotional states reflect themselves in physical strife, war, trouble, sickness and even misfortune. When, for instance, a man so easily loses his balance as to fall into a wrathful state at the smallest provocation, he is exposed to many dangers—such as fights, sickness, accidents and loss of friends.

The war was a warning to begin afresh and a reminder that the Day of Judgment is at hand. Yet out of its definite evil there arose a certain good. In such hours of tragic need which the universal conflict so often brought, a number of those who had lived empty, frivolous or materialistic lives were driven by hitherto suppressed instincts to seek outside help or transhuman support. Today humanity is reaching a dead end where on its own admission, its problems have expanded to almost insoluble proportions. Its wiser leaders begin to confess that it needs help from sources beyond itself, that human power unaided by spiritual wisdom and strength, is not sufficient to deal with such wide and explosive problems. It has come to witness in its own time how a rapidly developing civilization unillumined by spiritual content, must end in tragedy. The painful contradictions which were always inherent in materialism came glaringly to the surface during the wartime climax of world crisis. They forced many to look beyond their own resources for guidance and strength. Where else could they look except to religion, mysticism or philosophy? Events opened a passage into their hearts through which a spiritual impulse could enter less obstructed by the obstacles which formerly blocked the way. A world in crisis has found that without higher guidance there is only perplexity. These are critical and momentous times. Spiritual values alone stand out as the really worthwhile and enduring things today. There is no other hope for present-day humanity than this earnest repentant effort to lift itself. We have to find a more spiritual way of looking at life, or pay the penalty for failure to do so. There can be no standing still. The world has fought long enough against the truth, but in the end it will find no other way out of its troubles than by accepting it.

The divinity within us, the Overself, is always there even when we disbelieve in it and its presence is the secret why sooner or later there must be a reaction in human life toward spiritual values. Only after we realize vividly our human insufficiency and our human inadequacy are we likely to turn toward it for help, sustenance and strength. When we feel deeply how imperfect is our knowledge, how uncertain and limited our happiness, how weak and sinful our character, we may become sufficiently humbled to turn our faces imploringly and devotedly toward our higher selves for relief. It is thus that we are really able to progress. The need to progress from an inferior to a superior kind of life was never more urgent than today. We must take the lesson of the prodigal son deeply into our mind and come, like penitent sinners, to prayer before the higher power.

When contemporary man looks outward on the contemporary scene he is distressed by its violence. When he looks inward for the soul's comfort, he is bewildered by its silence. To the objector who says: "We know nothing about a Higher Power and we have lost the capacity for simple faith in it," the answer is that there is a way whereby he may discover by his own inner experience the truth about its existence. But he must follow this way and practice its methods. "Knock and it shall be opened unto you," does not mean that a single act is enough. Rather does it involve a whole series of acts. Nor does it mean that knocking in the wrong way or at the wrong door will bring about the desired opening. This single sentence of Jesus, put plainly out of his deep insight into universal laws, embodies a whole course of instructions.

Faith which humbly acknowledges the existence of a higher power is a true instinct planted in the heart of humanity. It is supported by the proper use of Reason although it may be throttled by the unbalanced use of intellect. Let no one be ashamed to kneel in prayer, or irked to sit in meditation. Because a man professes such a faith or practices communion with his soul, it does not mean he thereby discloses feeble intelligence. Why should the modern man leave religious faith and mystical practice to women? Have not an innumerable galaxy of historical stars in the past been men who drew the power for great needs from these deeper sources? Rightly understood, such faith and practice do not enfeeble men or narcotize their minds; it is only superstitious religion and false mysticism that do so. Rather do they exalt the mind and calm the heart. The reverent worship of, or inward communion with, a higher power is indispensable to the fuller human life.

A great and holy mystery lies enshrined in the world's blatant failure and heavy crisis. When humanity finds itself with its back to an impassable wall, when it seems to reach the utmost limit of disasters, when the agony of utter helplessness crushes it down, it stands close, very close, to the Gate. If in such moments it will reorient its thoughts in sincerest self-surrender to the Divine and in fullest humility of the ego; if too it will calmly accept the dis-valuation of all earthly things which truthful reflection upon its situation should yield—then the climax of its outer suffering and inner defeat will be reached. If, with patience, repentance, reform and acceptance of life's higher purpose accompanying its prayers, it will stretch forth its arms into the dark-ness and plead that Peace may come forth again, it will not plead in vain. The higher Self will take a hand in the game, taking possession of the con-scious mind at the same time for some memorable moments at least. Relief will mysteriously appear and rescuing hands will move toward it. Courage will arise and the strength to support what is unchangeable will be given, thus promising a tranquil heart even in the midst of a troubled life.

Paul Brunton, *The Spiritual Crisis of Man*

I do not imagine that in my reflections on the meaning of man and his myth I have uttered a final truth, but I think that this is what can be said at the end of our aeon of the Fishes, and perhaps must be said in view of the coming aeon of Aquarius (the Water Bearer), who has a human figure and is next to the sign of the Fishes. This is a *coniunctio oppositorum* composed of two fishes in reverse. The Water Bearer seems to represent the self. With a sovereign gesture he pours the contents of his jug into the mouth of *Piscis austrinus*,* which symbolizes a son, a still unconscious content. Out of this unconscious content will emerge, after the passage of another aeon of more than two thousand years, a future whose features are indicated by the symbol of Capricorn: an *aigokeros*, the monstrosity of the Goat-Fish,† symbolizing the

---

* Constellation of the "Southern Fish." Its mouth is formed by Fomalhaut (Arabic for "mouth of the fish") below the constellation of the Water Bearer.

† The constellation of Capricorn was originally called the "Goat-Fish."

mountains and the depths of the sea, a polarity made up of two undifferentiated animal elements which have grown together. This strange being could easily be the primordial image of a Creator-god confronting "man," the Anthropos. On this question there is a silence within me, as there is in the empirical data at my disposal—the products of the unconscious of other people with which I am acquainted, or historical documents. If insight does not come by itself, speculation is pointless. It makes sense only when we have objective data comparable to our material on the aeon of Aquarius.

We do not know how far the process of coming to consciousness can extend, or where it will lead. It is a new element in the story of creation, and there are no parallels we can look to. We therefore cannot know what potentialities are inherent in it. Neither can we know the prospects for the species Homo sapiens. Will it imitate the fate of other species, which once flourished on the earth and now are extinct? Biology can advance no reasons why this should not be so.

The need for mythic statements is satisfied when we frame a view of the world which adequately explains the meaning of human existence in the cosmos, a view which springs from our psychic wholeness, from the co-operation between conscious and unconscious. Meaninglessness inhibits fullness of life and is therefore equivalent to illness. Meaning makes a great many things endurable—perhaps everything. No science will ever replace myth, and a myth cannot be made out of any science. For it is not that "God" is a myth, but that myth is the revelation of a divine life in man. It is not we who invent myth, rather it speaks to us as a Word of God. The Word of God comes to us, and we have no way of distinguishing whether and to what extent it is different from God. There is nothing about this Word that could not be considered known and human, except for the manner in which it confronts us spontaneously and places obligations upon us. It is not affected by the arbitrary operation of our will. We cannot explain an inspiration. Our chief feeling about it is that it is not the result of our own ratiocinations, but that it came to us from elsewhere. And if we happen to have a precognitive dream, how can we possibly ascribe it to our own powers? After all, often we do not even know, until some time afterward, that the dream represented foreknowledge, or knowledge of something that happened at a distance.

The Word happens to us; we suffer it, for we are victims of a profound uncertainty: with God as a *complexio oppositorum*, all things are possible, in the fullest meaning of the phrase. Truth and delusion, good and evil, are equally possible. Myth is or can be equivocal, like the oracle of Delphi or like a dream. We cannot and ought not to repudiate reason; but equally we must cling to the hope that instinct will hasten to our aid—in which case God is supporting us against God, as Job long ago understood. Everything through which the "other will" is expressed proceeds from man—his thinking, his words, his images, and even his limitations. Consequently he has the tendency to refer everything to himself, when he begins to think in clumsy psychological terms, and decides that everything proceeds out of his intentions and out of himself. With childlike naïveté he assumes that he knows all his own reaches and knows what he is "in himself." Yet all the while he is fatally handicapped by the weakness of his consciousness and the corresponding fear of the unconscious. Therefore he is utterly unable to separate what he has carefully reasoned out from what has spontaneously flowed to him from another source. He has no objectivity toward himself and cannot yet regard himself as a phenomenon which he finds in existence and with which, for better or worse, he is identical. At first everything is thrust upon him, everything happens to him, and it is only by great effort that he finally succeeds in conquering and holding for himself an area of relative freedom.

Only when he has won his way to this achievement, and then only, is he in a position to recognize that he is confronting his instinctive foundations, given him from the beginning, which he cannot make disappear, however much he would like to. His beginnings are not by any means mere pasts; they live with him as the constant substratum of his existence, and his consciousness is as much molded by them as by the physical world around him.

C. G. Jung, Memories, Dreams, Reflections

The New Age

There is a general feeling today that we are at the end of an age, an age which began three centuries ago with the discoveries of Galileo and Newton and resulted in the gradual development of a materialist philosophy and a mechanistic model of the universe. This has in the course of time affected our whole society. The present industrial system and modern technology are the direct result of this mechanistic concept of the universe. The whole social, political and economic system of the West is governed by it, and even art, morality and religion are affected by it. So we live in a world which came into being in the last three centuries, and has come to a head only in the last century.

The basic principle of this world is its materialistic philosophy. This materialism is explicit in Marxism but it is implicit practically everywhere and it governs people's attitudes of mind and behaviour. Its basic principle is reductionism; it is the reduction of everything to certain material principles and to its material base. To take a simple example, all music can be reduced to vibrations on strings or in a pipe, mere vibrations in the air, and those vibrations may then be treated as being what music is, without concern for any other value which belongs to it. Fritjof Capra has shown convincingly in *The Turning Point* (1982) how this mechanistic system has come to dominate every aspect of science and of practical life today. He shows how modern physics was at first an attempt to explain everything in terms of atoms, where everything was reduced to material particles which obeyed mechanical laws and could be known by mathematical calculations. So the whole physical world came to be reduced to a machine. In biology the attempt still continues to explain all life in terms of physics and chemistry, and to believe that living beings are simply more complicated machines. More seriously for practical purposes, in medicine the human body is conceived from a biological point of view as a mechanical system obeying physical and chemical laws, and to be treated simply as a physical entity and manipulated by genetic engineering, without relation to the psyche or to the whole human person.

Psychology is obviously less amenable to reductionism than medicine. Nevertheless many of its methods are conspicuously reductionistic. Behaviourism, for instance, is a serious attempt to reduce the human psyche to the status of a machine by analysing it only in terms of external behaviour. Another example is the psychoanalysis of Freud and the tremendously influential method based on his work, where the attempt is made to explain the whole human personality in the light of the unconscious, which is seen in terms of repressed appetites, instincts and desires. In Freudian psychology all the higher levels of consciousness, the motives of the heart, morality and religion are explained in terms of the unconscious. This is typical of the whole method. It is an attempt to explain the higher in terms of the lower and to reduce the higher to the level of the lower, so that, to take a glaring example, religion is regarded as repressed sex.

In sociology the attempt is made to reduce society to individual persons who are either left free to seek their own advantage or have to be organised by the state. From this arises capitalism and communism, in both of which systems society is reduced to a multitude of individuals. Finally, in economics this principle is most obvious where the whole aim is to conceive society simply in terms of production and distribution. In Marxism society is deliberately reduced to the economic base, which is conceived as determining the whole. In capitalism society is judged in terms of monetary value so that the prosperity of a nation is evaluated in terms of its gross national product, by the money which is being circulated in it and the way it is being used.

This is a drastic system by which everything is reduced to the material level, and it has had extraordinary success. Scientifically it has led to great discoveries being made and it has undoubtedly produced an impressive system of technology. On a social scale it has produced states with tremendous power building up influence all over the world. But at the same time it is gradually producing inevitable evil effects, rapidly exhausting material resources, polluting the environment and leading to the build-up of armaments which threatens to lead to a nuclear war capable of destroying our entire civilisation and the whole planet. All this is the result of three centuries of materialism building up to its height in the first part of this century.

In the second part of this century we have begun to discover what has been taking place and in what we are involved, and a new movement has begun which is the opposite of all this. We are beginning now to be able to replace the mechanistic system and mechanistic model of the universe with an organic model. This is the beginning of a return to the traditional wisdom, the wisdom by which human beings have lived over thousands and thousands of years and with which the great societies of the past have been built up. In this ancient traditional wisdom the order of the universe is seen always to be three-fold, consisting not only of a physical dimension but also of a psychological and a spiritual world. The three worlds were always seen as interrelated and interdependent. This understanding of the three orders of being and of their interdependence is what is known as the perennial philosophy.

Materialism is correct in so far as it recognises the material basis of reality, and science has explored this basis further than has ever been done before. This is a positive achievement. The rational, logical mind has been used in the analysis of matter, and this has led to the organisation of matter to such an extent that it is hoped that by this means all human needs can be satisfied. This is why many people think that this age is in advance of any previous age. But it is only in this respect that the present age is in advance of others. In all other respects it is to be judged as being far below. A little exaggeratedly perhaps, Coomaraswami once made the remark, "From the stone age to the twentieth century, what a descent!" There is something in this. The perennial philosophy was present in the stone age and human beings lived by that. In this view, as has been said, there was the order of nature, the physical world, then the psychological, social world and, highest of all, the divine spiritual world, and all three were seen as interdependent and integrated. If we want to see the decline of the modern world we cannot do better than to compare stages in the development of art.

Looking back on the history of art from the stone age onwards, you see how the ancient wisdom was embodied in every form of art. In the early stages art in whatever form was the expression of the religious instinct, the sense of the sacred. Everything in nature was held to be sacred, because it was pervaded by the universal Spirit. Art, whether in the form of stone implements, or burial places, or roughly carved figures, or paintings as in the paleolithic caves, or pottery or clothing, was a way of expressing the sense of the sacred, of enacting the sacred mystery which pervaded human life. When the great civilisations arose in Egypt and Babylon, the temple became the centre of civilised life and all the arts were used to adorn the temple and to provide for human needs. Agriculture and pottery and weaving were no less sacred than the service of the temple. All alike were ways of expressing and manifesting the all-pervading mystery.

When the great awakening took place in the first millennium to the transcendence of the mystery with the Upanishads, the Buddha, the Hebrew prophets, art was less conspicuous. The Israelites were forbidden to make any image of their God and the early Buddhists made no image of the Buddha. The Hindu temple also had not yet come into being. But as these religions became established and as Christianity with its doctrine of incarnation emerged from Judaism, there was a flowering of art in every form over all the ancient world, in China, India, Persia, Greece and Rome. In Greece, Athens was leading the way already in the fifth century before Christ and Greek influence seems to have been responsible for the development of Buddhist sculpture. Gradually throughout all these regions a marvellous synthesis of art and poetry and philosophy was achieved, which gave rise to Hindu sculpture and architecture, Buddhist painting and sculpture, the Chinese art of every kind and the cathedrals of Europe with their sculpture and stained glass and the painting of the icons in Eastern orthodoxy. Everywhere art expressed the mystery of religion, the sacred mystery revealed in the Scriptures and embodied in every form of art and poetry, music and dancing, and even the simple articles of daily use. Even Islam, which had rejected all images, developed a style of architecture of the utmost refinement.

It was this period then, between AD 500 and 1500, that saw the great flowering of art and culture which took place all over the civilised world. After that the hold of the perennial philosophy with its holistic vision began to loosen. Individual geniuses arose but the sense of a cosmic vision and a cosmic whole was gradually lost and art and culture became more and more fragmented. Today we inherit this fragmented universe and we are as far as possible from the sacred universe of earlier times. The present system of industrialisation which emerged in the nineteenth century marked the death knell of traditional art. Yet, as we have seen, a renewal is taking place. As the cosmic vision of the new science and philosophy takes over we may hope that there will be a renewal of art, not merely in the sense of the fine arts, but in all the humble daily expressions of a sense of beauty, which is also a sense of the sacred in human life. We may therefore look forward to a new birth, another renaissance of art and culture in the New Age.

Many people today anticipate a great advance in humanity and I think that is perfectly right, as we shall see. In many respects we can look forward to a great advance but I think we also have to look back. We have to recognise that the summit was achieved in those centuries before Christ, and that with the coming of Christ the final fulfilment of this experience of ultimate Reality was reached. In other respects great developments took place and they can also take place again in the future. So there we have the perennial philosophy, with the physical base, the psychological development and the spiritual order transcending all and integrating all. We need to remember that it is the spiritual that integrates the whole reality.

We go on now to ask, what will the pattern of the new age be like? What can we discern in the light of our present understanding of the universe and of the knowledge which we have of Eastern mysticism and spiritual experience? How in our time can we look forward in the light of our present knowledge of what science has done both for good and for evil, and what are we to make of the past, its art and philosophy, its religion and its mythical experience?

The first thing is that human society will be based on a new relationship to the world of nature, arising from an organic understanding of nature in place of a mechanistic view of the universe. This is a major change which is taking place. We have to learn to see ourselves as part of the physical organism of the universe. We need to develop the sense of the cosmic whole and of a way of relating to the world around us as a living being which sustains and nourishes us and for which we have responsibility. This will give rise to a new understanding of our environment and will put an end to this age of the exploitation of nature. At the present moment the whole movement of economics and politics is characterised and marred by the exploitation of nature at every level. The material resources of the universe are being grossly exploited in order to create more material prosperity for relatively few human beings, no matter at what cost that is done. That trend would be reversed by the new understanding that we are all parts of this universe, of this natural world, that we are integral elements in it and that we have to respect it. This would involve a new attitude to the earth and to the natural resources of the earth, to the sea and all the creatures in it, to the animal world as a whole, to the question of vivisection and the treatment of animals in general, and to our attitude to outer space, whether we try to exploit it for human gain or whether we look on it in another way.

Secondly, the sense of communion with an encompassing reality will replace the attempt to dominate the world. The different understanding of ecology and a greater sensitivity to its realities would revolutionise our understanding of nature and of the world in which we live. This would lead to a new kind of technology based on the new understanding of science, and an appropriate or intermediate technology as Schumacher conceived it, answering the needs of the vast majority of people in Asia, Africa and South

America who live in rural communities. The present system of technology has been built up on the basis of mechanistic science and it savagely and indiscriminately exploits the world of nature. This has produced the terrible situation in which we find ourselves with its material conveniences for a minority but with its disastrous consequences of global injustice and destruction. We are looking for a new technology which Schumacher speaks of as appropriate or intermediate technology which builds up from the villages. It would build upon the economy of the village instead of destroying it. There would be respect for the basic crafts of spinning, weaving, pottery, carpentry, metal work and of course all forms of gardening and agriculture. This is very important. All these crafts were evolved in the millennia before Christ, from roughly the fourth millennium onwards, and they represent a summit of human achievement in this sphere. When we look back on the past and see the weaving, the clothing, pottery, woodwork and metalwork of the past ages, we put them in museums as something to marvel at because of their beauty. And that was the ordinary work of the people of those times. To discard those abilities in favour of the progress of the mechanistic system is to degrade civilisation and human life.

Respect for the basic crafts enables human persons to live in harmony with nature and with the world around them. Their art and their work express this harmony and therefore it is beautiful. Beauty is always due to this harmony with nature. When we have that harmony the products of our hands are beautiful, and when we do not have harmony the products may be useful and very helpful in other ways but they lose their beauty.

Thirdly, these new values would give rise to a new type of human community. This would be a decentralised society drawing people from large cities to smaller towns and villages where a much more total and integrated human life would be possible. I do not see any future for the huge cities of the present world, London, New York, Tokyo, Bombay and Calcutta. In such cities all over the world in every continent the population may be over ten million. Cities of millions of people do not provide a human mode of existence and depend on a whole economic system which will eventually collapse, for such societies cannot sustain their economies. So we have to look back beyond these industrialised cities to find some kind of norm of human existence. Here I would like to quote from Lewis Mumford, where in his book *The Myth of the Machine* he describes the neolithic village. This is a village the like of which lasted for thousands of years, all over the world, and still exists to some extent to the present day. This is how he describes it. "Where the seasons are marked by holiday festivals and ceremonies; where the stages of life are punctuated by family and communal rituals; where eating and drinking and sexual play constitute the central core of life, where work, even hard work, is rarely divorced from rhythm, song, human companionship and aesthetic delight; where vital activity is considered as great a reward of labour as the product; where neither power nor profit has precedence over life; where the family, the neighbour and the friend are all parts of a visible, tangible, face-to-face community. There the neolithic culture in its essential elements is still in existence." That is to my mind a model of wholesome human existence. All these elements were present in the villages of India until recently and are still basically there although they are being undermined daily. That Indian village life and culture which existed for millennia is being systematically destroyed, year by year.

Mumford's description of the neolithic village remains a model for a human community. Science and appropriate technology, building on that, may introduce improvements, especially forms of transport and communication which may link up the different human centres, but these will be based on natural sources of energy, particularly the sun. Fritjof Capra considers that the new age will be the solar age. The sun provides all the energy that is conceivably necessary for human existence. Such a society would be decentralised. It does not require huge conglomerations of people in cities. The sun is available everywhere and the energy can be made available. Also, of course, water and the wind are appropriate sources of energy. The new society would certainly exclude all forms of nuclear energy which is perhaps the supreme example of this mechanistic system and the most destructive form of it.

Education in the new society would be basic education, as understood for instance by Mahatma Gandhi. It would be an integral education of body, soul and spirit, relating each person to the world in an organic way and developing their personal capacities. Perhaps, following Rudolf Steiner's understanding, such education would centre first on emotional growth. Steiner held that during the first seven years the child has primarily to grow at the level of the emotions and the education given should foster this emotional development. During the next seven years the growth of the imagination predominates and education centres on music, art, dance and poetry. Only in the third seven years, from fourteen onwards, should the rational, logical mind be trained to develop seriously. To some extent obviously it is functioning before this but in the Steiner system the emphasis on it only begins there. The result of acting on these principles is an integrated education of the whole person, emotional, imaginative and rational, where each level, emotions, imagination and rationality, is properly developed, consolidated and stabilised. This is in marked contrast to our usual method of education, which concentrates on developing the rational, logical mind as early as five and so often loses out on these other aspects of human personality.

In medicine, rather than making use almost entirely of modern allopathic methods, there will be a turn to alternative methods such as homeopathy, acupuncture, Ayurvedic and Tibetan medicine and herbal medicine in general, all of which are concerned with the health of the whole person. These forms of treatment always relate the body to the soul and the spirit and never regard it as something that can be treated in isolation. The human person is conceived as an integral whole, and it is seen that health, wholeness and holiness, being derived from the same root, are totally interrelated. The health of the body, the wholeness of the person and holiness itself are all aspects of the same reality and they cannot be separated.

This leads to the third aspect. We have considered first the physical, material growth of the world and secondly its psychological and social growth. Now we turn to the spiritual order and the place of religion. This involves a return to the perennial philosophy, the ancient wisdom which underlies all religion from the earliest times. It will involve a respect for the traditional wisdom of primitive people, the Australian Aborigines, the American Indians and the tribal peoples of Asia and Africa. More and more today we are discovering the wisdom of these people, the harmony they have achieved in their lives and the very profound understanding they have of how human life is related to the natural world about them and to the world of spirits beyond them. Generally such people evidence an integrated, holistic view of life.

Then we turn to the great religious traditions, Hindu, Buddhist, Jain, Sikh, Taoist, Confucian, Shinto, Zoroastrian, Judaic, Muslim and Christian. These are systems of religion which had their origin during the first millennium before Christ. All are based on the perennial philosophy, developed under different situations and in different circumstances, and all embody in their different ways the ancient wisdom and the wholeness of life. These different traditions will all be seen as interrelated and interdependent, each giving a particular and unique insight into ultimate truth and reality. In fact, of course, they all grew up apart and mostly without contact with each other for many centuries. When they did make contact there was often rivalry, acrimony and conflict, and as a result we have the disastrous divisions of religion today. But we are learning, and we shall continue to learn, that all the different religious traditions, from the most primitive to the most advanced, are interrelated and interdependent, and that each has its own particular insights. For the Semitic religions in particular, Judaism, Christianity and Islam, it is important that they give up the exclusive claims which characterise them. This would free them to recognise the action of God in all humanity from the beginnings of history. For the Semitic religions this is a particularly difficult problem. All three tend to extreme exclusivism and on that account have brought so much conflict into the world.

For Christianity this enlargement of its horizons would involve a recognition of the limited character of its original revelation, coming as it did from within a Semitic culture in the limited world and thought-forms of the Ancient Near East. Emerging from that world it spread through the Roman Empire from Palestine through Greece to Rome. For centuries the whole sphere of Christianity was simply the Roman Empire centred around the Mediterranean and completely without contact with the greater part of Asia, Africa, America and Australia. Yet we have seen that Christianity is a unique revelation of God in Jesus Christ and that, although it was conditioned by the circumstances of its origin, this revelation has a unique message for the whole world. The Christian church began as a Jewish sect and only gradually realised its vocation as a universal religion. It developed its structures from the second century onwards entirely in the context of Graeco-Roman culture, with an extension which must not be overlooked in the Syrian East, in Egypt and Ethiopia. The doctrine of the church remains essentially based on a Semitic foundation developed by the Greek genius in terms of Greek philosophy, while the organisation of the church remains a Roman structure built on the foundation of the original Jewish community.

In the course of the centuries these structures within Christianity have expanded and a whole system of theology, philosophy and morality, a sacramental order and an ecclesiastical hierarchy, have developed, Though it derives from Jesus and the apostles in the first century, the Christian church as such received its definitive structure in the second century, its evolution in the Roman Empire being determined by the circumstances of the time. All these structures which we have inherited are Western structures built on the foundation of the original Semitic revelation. These structures of doctrine, discipline and sacrament are thus historically conditioned. They are integral elements in a historical development which has taken place gradually over many centuries. In the course of its history—and this is the great tragedy— the Asian and African churches were separated from the main body. In Asia, where St. Paul conducted his missions, the churches which were centred on Antioch were separated in the fifth century, while the churches of Africa, based on Egypt and Alexandria, were also separated. The result was that by the fifth century Asia and Africa were lost to the church. Then in the eleventh century Eastern Europe, centred on Byzantium, separated from Rome which was the centre of the Western church. Finally, at the Reformation the churches of Northern Europe were separated from Rome. It is this tragically divided church that we have inherited. The separations which have accumulated over the centuries are all still present today. It will be one of the tasks of the new age to see the reconciliation of these divided churches as each recognises the other as a particular expression of Christian faith and worship, and as each seeks to reconcile the differences. There are valid elements in every Christian church. Each is a way of expressing Christian faith and worship. There are obvious limitations and obvious differences in each but today we seek to discern the differences and overcome the divisions, in contrast to previous times when we were engaged in dividing from one another and in asserting our own values at the expense of those of others.

Reconciliation within the Christian church will involve recognition of different ministries. The present ministries of the different churches all derive from the second century or later. In the New Testament there is neither papacy, episcopacy nor priesthood. The only priesthood, properly speaking, in the New Testament is that of Christ himself and of the people, which St. Peter describes as a "holy priesthood." It would be necessary to reconsider the different ministries in this light.

The present system of the papacy dates from the Gregorian reform of the twelfth century. It is important to recognise that this movement had its value at the time. One must consider that the Holy Spirit was present in each development of the church but each was limited to its particular historic horizon. It was only when the Eastern church separated from the Western that the papacy began to develop its present structure. It would be necessary to go behind the present structure of the papacy to the fifth century if a reconciliation is to be found with the Eastern churches. The Eastern church will never be reconciled with the present system of papacy which is an evolution of the last ten centuries. In the fifth century there were five patriarchates: Jerusalem, Antioch, Alexandria, Constantinople and Rome. Already in the fifth century the primacy of the Pope, St. Leo, was fully recognised but he was *primus inter pares*, the first among equals, and he normally never interfered in the affairs of the Eastern churches. There was a right of appeal to Rome and the right of intervention in grave necessity was recognised, but the patriarchs were responsible for the liturgy, theology and the whole conduct of their churches just as the Pope, as patriarch of the West, was responsible for the Western churches. At that time the Pope only appointed bishops in his own patriarchate. So this was a very different structure of the church from that of later centuries, and yet it was a unified church which recognised the primacy of the Pope. So we could go back to that point as a model for the reorganisation of the church today, particularly in the light of the Eastern churches.

With regard to the other churches apart from the Eastern church, it will be necessary to go even further back for a model. The person to go to is St. Irenaeus, that great theologian and churchman of the second century. He was the most representative figure in the Catholic church at the time, being a bishop in Gaul, coming originally from Asia and being in close touch with Rome. He shows the Roman church at that time as the centre of Christendom. He speaks of it as being founded by the chief of the apostles, Peter and Paul, not Peter alone, notice, and he uses a very important phrase, *potiorem principalitatem*. This may mean "more powerful presidency" or perhaps "more powerful origin." The original was written in Greek and we only have the Latin translation so we cannot be quite sure of the meaning. But because the Roman church was founded by Peter and Paul it has a kind of primacy without a doubt. Then Irenaeus says in a very important sentence, "With this church it is necessary that every church should agree, or come together (*convenire* in Latin), every church, that is, the faithful from all parts (*eos qui sunt undeque fideles*)." This is an excellent model of the Roman church as a centre of unity to which people come from all parts. It seems to me that we have a model, there in the second century, of Rome seen as the seat of Peter and Paul, as a centre of unity to which people come from all parts and where the true faith is always preserved. That was St. Irenaeus's point. It is to be noticed that the emphasis is on the church itself, rather than on the bishop. The bishop became more important in the course of time but at this point it was the church that was important. This brings out further the function of Rome which is that it should be a centre of unity rather than a centre of power. Today many people in all churches see the possibility of a papacy which would be a centre of unity, of the Pope as exercising a ministry of unity on behalf of the whole church. This would mean that Rome would no longer be the centre of power and domination which it had become in the Middle Ages.

This character of the Roman church is brought out further by St. Ignatius writing in the second century to the Roman church, again not to the bishop but to the church. He speaks of the church as "presiding over the charity" (*prothestos tes agapes*) or, perhaps, "presiding in charity." Again it is a difficult phrase to translate, let alone know the exact meaning of, but it looks as though the church herself is considered as a charity, a school of love. The Pope has this function of "presiding over the charity" or "presiding in charity." The point is that it is a presidence of love rather than of power. That takes us back to the second century. But now we have to go further back still, because Irenaeus speaks always in terms of episcopacy, which was fully developed by this time in the second century. But when we go back to the New Testament there is neither episcopacy nor priesthood in the usual sense. On the other hand we find a great many other different ministries. St. Paul speaks of apostles and prophets but also of evangelists, pastors and teachers, helpers and administrators. So that was the structure of the church in the New Testament and it seems that we have to go back to the New Testament itself to restructure the ministries of the church. In that light the ministries of other churches which have no bishops could be reconciled with the church as a whole. We should also be aware that in the New Testament women played a very considerable part in the ministry of the church, and any attempt at renewing the structures of the ministry of the church would involve women having ministries in equality with men. That would be the normal development that we would expect. So this is how the development of the ministries in the church could be envisaged, while remembering, of course, that in the New Testament the position of Peter among the apostles still remains a valid and unquestionable fact which has meaning for the church today just as it had then.

When the church has been opened in this way to a more universal structure of ministry it would be much more possible for her to open herself to the cultures of Asia and Africa and to answer the needs of the people in the Third World. So far the church has had a European structure. In its liturgy, theology, canon law and organisation it is a totally Western structure. We are only today beginning to discover the possibilities of structuring the church, not in the light of Europe, but in the light of Asia, Africa and South America. That is clearly where the future lies.

It may be that the basic communities in South America, particularly in Brazil, could provide a model for the church in the Third World. In these communities lay people, men and women, meet regularly to study the Scriptures, to celebrate the Eucharist, and to reflect on their life and experience in the light of the Bible and the Eucharist. They also relate their political and socio-economic problems to their experience of the Bible and the Eucharist and try to develop these aspects of their lives within this context. These basic communities, in Brazil in particular where there are tens of thousands of them, are all in communion with the bishops and the clergy, but they are lay communities. This kind of involved and committed community may well be the model for a renewed Christian church. Such commodities could be compared to the monastic communities at the break-up of the Roman Empire. In many respects we seem to be entering a period not unlike that of the Roman Empire in the fifth century when the entire structure began to collapse. It was monastic communities, integrated communities with a physical, social base and a religious character, which were the sources from which the new civilisation emerged. As economic, social and political tensions increase in the present world there will be an ever stronger need for small communities, based on the new vision of life, which could in time form the basis of a new civilisation, like the monasteries in the Middle Ages. These communities would be communities of men and women, married and single, basically Christian but also open to people of other religious traditions and of other understandings also, where a new culture would gradually be formed.

Along with this a new theology would be developed, particularly as the church comes into contact with the religious cultures of Asia and Africa. Again we must remember that our present theology was first built up entirely in contact with Greek philosophy. The whole system was based on divine revelation in the Scriptures interpreted in the light of Greek philosophy. Today theology has drawn on modern philosophy, especially existentialism, but nowhere until the present time has the church succeeded in evolving a theology based on the experience and the wisdom of Asia and of Africa. Our present theology was evolved in Europe and we have to look forward to a theology which would evolve in contact with Hindu, Buddhist, Taoist and Confucian thought and at the same time a liturgy which would develop from contact with the art, music and dance of Asian and African peoples. It would be an assimilation first of the culture of the Greeks and the Romans and then of all the "barbarian" peoples of Europe. That was how the church emerged in the Middle Ages. It brought its original Semitic wisdom, religion and faith and interpreted it in the light of the Greek and the Roman world. Then later it assimilated the "barbarian" peoples with their wonderful gifts, creating that great church of the Middle Ages which we have inherited.

In this way we can envision the emergence of a new world culture as the present materialist and mechanistic system breaks down under the continued crisis of economic, social and political conflict. One of the characteristics of this new culture would be its feminine aspects. For three thousand years the world has been dominated by patriarchal cultures which overcame the ancient matriarchal cultures of the earlier ages. We have now reached the limit of this masculine culture with its aggressive, competitive, rational, analytic character. We are moving now into an age where the feminine principle will be valued, the *yin* in contrast to the *yang*. In the Chinese understanding *yang* is the masculine principle, *yin* is the feminine and as the *yang* reaches its limit it begins to move back again to the *yin*. We have now reached the limit of the *yang*, the masculine culture, and we are moving inevitably back to the feminine. The feminine will sooner or later begin to take its proper place with its characteristics of intuition, empathy and co-operation, and with its holistic approach. This will necessarily affect not only the economic, social and political orders but also spirituality and religion. The Christian religion has developed an entirely masculine concept of God. We always speak of God as Father, and of the incarnation of the Son. Even the Holy Spirit, which is neuter in Greek but masculine in Latin, we have conceived normally in masculine terms. In the Old Testament, however, the Spirit, the *ruach*, is feminine and in the Syrian church this same word was used of the Holy Spirit when they spoke of "our Mother, the Holy Spirit." That is found in the second and third centuries but it does not seem to have survived after that. The masculine character of the Godhead has always prevailed since then. There was however a feminine aspect in God in the Old Testament and to some extent in the New, and in the Christian tradition we have particularly Julian of Norwich, who speaks of Jesus as our Mother. St. Anselm of Canterbury does the same. So apart from a few exceptions the masculine character of God has strongly prevailed in the West. By contrast, in India God is conceived both as Father and Mother. Obviously theologically God may be conceived as both Father and Mother. Being neither masculine nor feminine he can be represented as either Father or Mother, or both, in masculine and feminine terms. In the Tantric tradition, which derives from the ancient matriarchal culture, the mother aspect of God is dominant. In that tradition the whole universe is seen to derive from the Mother and all worship is offered to the Mother. That is precisely the opposite of the Judaeo-Christian tradition. We may expect therefore a corresponding development in Christian theology recognising the feminine aspect of God and the place of women in the ministry of the church. There is of course no question of a return to a matriarchal society. It is a matter of the recovery of feminine values and the reconciliation of the masculine and the feminine.

It should be added that in Catholicism the feminine aspect is entirely centred on the Virgin Mary. It is the only way a Catholic, or indeed a Christian, can find a feminine figure in relation to God. So devotion to the feminine archetype centres on the Virgin Mary, but we should recognise that there is a feminine aspect of God himself and that the Virgin Mother is a manifestation of this. This means, in other words, that devotion to the Mother has its origin in God.

It is possible that the transition from a mechanistic to an organic society will come about gradually, without too much conflict. But it is more likely that there will be a general catastrophe as the economic, social and political structures of the present civilisation break down. We must remember, and this is important, that the conflicts of the present world do not derive merely from human failings and miscalculations. There has been a reversal of human values, a spiritual breakdown, which has brought into play forces beyond the material and the human. The present crisis has been prepared by the whole system of science and philosophy, affecting religion and leading to atheism. This is a systematic development where the previous spiritual values have been broken down and the materialistic system discussed earlier has prevailed. This has released forces beyond the material and the human. If a nuclear war takes place it will not be because anyone desires it but because people are being driven by forces of the unconscious which they cannot control. As St. Paul says, "We are not contending with flesh and blood, but against the principalities, against the powers, against the world rulers of this present darkness." When the truth of the transcendent order of reality is rejected we do not remain neutral. We become exposed to the hostile forces of the subtle world of which we have been speaking, forces which work in the unconscious and bring destruction upon humankind. Western Europe rejected the perennial philosophy at the Renaissance and has been led step by step to the materialistic philosophy which rejects fundamental human values and exposes humankind to the contrary forces at work in the universe. The only way of recovery is to rediscover the perennial philosophy, the traditional wisdom, which is found in all ancient religions and especially in the great religions of the world. But those religions have in turn become fossilised and have each to be renewed, not only in themselves but also in relation to one another, so that a cosmic, universal religion can emerge, in which the essential values of Christian religion will be preserved in living relationship with the other religious traditions of the world. This is a task for the coming centuries as the present world order breaks down and a new world order emerges from the ashes of the old.

Bede Griffiths, A New Vision of Reality

The Garden
(A Short History of the World)

Once, in a place beyond time and space, a consciousness existed in a state of oneness and bliss. This consciousness came to realize it also wanted to experience twoness, or duality. In this way it could experience the excitement of splitting into opposite polarities, and the ecstasy of merging back into one.

So original consciousness (which we can call Spirit, or God, or Source), while still remaining one, also created itself into two opposite energies which we can call yin and yang, or female and male, or dark and light, or spirit and form. The yang, or masculine force, would always pull toward action, individuation, separation, difference. The yin, or feminine force, would always pull toward being, merging, union, oneness. Life became the dance of the continuous pulsation between these energies. Each time the male and female energies met, a new creation was born.

From this dance physical form was created. The pull of the masculine force toward individuation created a dense physical world in which each form was separate and distinct from every other form. Of course, all the forms were created out of the same original energy, so the feminine force constantly pulled them back toward experiencing the energetic vibration of their oneness. The yang pushed toward constant birth of new forms, the yin moved toward death of form and surrender back into the whole.

The physical world that was created from this dance of energies was astounding. There was a vast cosmos filled with blazing suns and countless planets. One small planet, which would become known as Earth, was unbelievably rich and beautiful. She was a lush, magical garden with vast, deep oceans, dense jungles, green forests, and white deserts. Spirit had created itself into many wondrous forms of plants and other living creatures on Earth.

The yin and yang energies began to create two separate kinds of forms—male and female. Each form contained both energies, but outwardly manifested more of the qualities of one than the other. The male forms expressed more aggressive, outward-moving energies. The female forms expressed more receptive, inward-moving energies. When the two united, a new being was created.

All kinds of new and interesting creatures developed. Some of the older forms remained undifferentiated male and female all in one, but many of the newer types were divided into males and females. The garden flourished and was abundant with millions of species of plants, insects, fish, and animals, all living in balance and harmony in an explosion of creativity.

Then a new kind of creature developed, known as a human being. The one who represented the male polarity was called Man; the one who represented the female polarity was called Woman. As a whole, their species had a stronger male energy than any previous creature, and because of this they had a new feature—a rational mind that could make all kinds of distinctions and separations.

For a while, Man and Woman dwelt happily in the garden in a childlike state of innocence and wonder. They lived spontaneously in each moment, experiencing life deeply and fully and with great feeling. They loved each other passionately, for each recognized in the other a mirror of the opposite polarity they carried within themselves. Man knew he contained a female aspect with him and Woman was aware of the male aspect of herself. They realized they were expressions of the two aspects of God, and they delighted in their own beauty and power. They spent their days frolicking with the other creatures in the garden, loving each other, and learning about existence. But a strange fate awaited them.

One day a beautiful and wise creature known as Snake came to Woman. He told her that humankind had a powerful and unique destiny. Through them, the Universal Source would explore the farthest limits of the masculine polarity—the principle of individuation and separation. Snake said that Spirit needed to develop its masculine principle of action and individuality as strongly as it had already developed its feminine principle of being and oneness. Only with an equally strong male and female could the universe eventually make love to itself in endless ecstatic union.

Snake said that Man and Woman would have to leave their innocent, delightful life in the garden, and venture deeper into the physical world. They needed to explore physical existence to the fullest. In order to do so they would have to temporarily forget their spiritual selves and become almost totally lost in and preoccupied with the material world. He told her that the physical plane would come to feel much more real than the spiritual. Man and Woman and their descendants would become the masters of the material world. The knowledge and power they would gain from their experiences would be incredible. The danger was that they would eventually have the power of destruction to match the power of creation they already had, gaining the ability to destroy themselves and the entire physical world.

If they were able to meet their challenges successfully, the wisdom and maturity they would gain would be invaluable. They would become fully integrated, balanced spiritual/physical beings, channeling the full creative power of the universe into the physical world. They would re-create life in the garden on Earth, more beautiful than ever. They would return to the garden of innocence, love, and wonder, but this time with the wisdom of experience and the power to protect it and take care of it forever.

Snake told Woman that the journey would be hard and long and a great challenge, but the rewards could be equally great. They would have to leave the garden and find their own way. He said all the other creatures on Earth would be helping them, although Man and Woman would not remember that. Then he pointed to a certain tree known as the Tree of Knowledge. It had beautiful juicy-looking fruit, but for some reason no one had ever eaten any of it. Snake told Woman she must convince Man to eat some. Then he disappeared.

Woman was heavy-hearted, intuitively sensing what lay before her. But she knew she must do as advised. She had no trouble convincing Man to eat the fruit. He loved and trusted her completely, knowing her to truly be the reflection of the female energy within himself, so he ate the delicious fruit as she suggested.

Immediately, everything shifted.

Man and Woman no longer felt the bliss and safety of the magical garden. Suddenly their minds felt very sharp, and they began to question everything. "Where am I? Why am I here?" Rather than living in just the present moment, they became vividly aware of the past and the future. "Where have I been? What should I do next?" They began to question and analyze everything and to notice all kinds of distinctions and differences.

Although their surroundings remained the same, they saw and felt everything differently. Their world seemed duller, as if their senses were perceiving less vividly. Nothing looked quite perfect anymore. They felt frightened and alone.

Worst of all they felt differently about themselves and each other. They became very self-conscious. Instead of feeling like natural godlike beings, they now felt inadequate and foolish. Instead of loving and trusting each other as aspects of themselves, they noticed how different they were and felt suspicious of one another. Once they realized they were physically different, they felt embarrassed about being naked, and made clothes out of leaves and put them on.

They felt hungry and worried about how they were going to survive, so they set out to find food and shelter. Although they vaguely remembered life in the Garden, the memory gradually faded as they became preoccupied with learning about survival in this new reality. They forgot that they were God's spirit in physical form, and began to think of God as someone very far away who might or might not help them in their struggles. They created some rituals which momentarily brought back the blissful feeling of being one with God, but most of the time they felt separate and alone.

Still, they became fascinated with the task of learning to live in the physical world. They learned how to gather fruits and nuts and hunt animals for food. The climate had changed when they left the Garden, and because it was often very cold, they discovered how to use animal skins for clothing, and caves for shelter.

Man and Woman began to divide their tasks. Since Man was physically stronger he went out to hunt, while Woman gathered and prepared food and maintained their shelter.

While being conscious of their differences made them feel uncomfortable with each other, at the same time their polarization made them very attracted to each other. They had forgotten that they were each whole within themselves. Each felt the other had something he or she lacked, and needed desperately. Their need for one another frightened them. They didn't like the feeling that each one had so much power over the other, so they tried to hide their feelings. They became distrustful of each other, yet they couldn't help longing to be close.

The only way they knew how to express this yearning toward one another was through sexual union. When they had sex, they felt that old familiar ecstatic feeling they used to experience continuously when they lived in the Garden. The feeling passed quickly, however, and their attention turned once again to important matters of survival.

One fascinating result of their sexual experiences was that they began to have children! It was amazing and exciting to discover that they had the power together to create new human beings similar to themselves. Yet it was worrisome, too, because it meant more mouths to feed and more responsibilities.

Their children grew up and had children. Man and Woman discovered that their physical bodies were changing—they were slowly wearing out! As their bodies grew slower and more tired, and their grown children took over most of the work, they found more leisure time. They took walks in the forest, and sat together and watched the sunset. It stirred ancient memories of their joyous time together in the Garden. The everyday concerns of the world no longer seemed so important. In fact, they began to forget a lot of irrelevant details, like the names of all their children, or what year it was. They loved being with their little grandchildren, though. In their innocent young faces, so filled with spontaneous feeling in each moment, Man and Woman saw the mirror of their own souls, which they had long forgotten. Through the beauty of nature and the reflection from their children's children, they found and reunited with the pure essence of their beings. Soon, their souls passed from their physical forms and moved to another level of reality.

The grandchildren of Man and Woman grew up and lost their innocence, as they, too, faced the cares and challenges of the world. With each succeeding generation it was the same. For a brief time in infancy, it was as if each being dwelt momentarily in the Garden, and perceived the world with fresh new eyes of love and wonder and oneness with all life. And then each person set about to define him- or herself as a separate and unique human being, and to discover how to survive and grow in what often came to seem like an unfriendly and difficult world.

Many hundreds and thousands of generations passed, and despite countless difficulties and disasters, humankind as a whole developed and prospered and spread all over Earth. They learned to grow food and developed more and more efficient ways to farm. They discovered better and better ways to make tools and weapons so that they could defend their territory or take over someone else's. They built bigger and fancier shelters; eventually some were so huge that they were taller than any tree and could hold hundreds of people!

True to Snake's prediction, after many, many centuries, human beings had become masters of the physical world. They had created a sophisticated technology that could accomplish all kinds of amazing and seemingly magical feats. They could propel human beings from Earth into space and return them safely (most of the time). They had ships that could dive into the depths of the ocean and return safely to the surface (most of the time). A human being on one side of Earth could speak to a human being on the other side of Earth just by talking into a little gadget called a telephone (unless they got "a bad connection").

People could talk or play music and millions of others all over the world could see and hear them on a box called a television. And people could travel hundreds or thousands of miles in a few minutes or hours in strange creatures called automobiles and airplanes, which gulped strong-smelling liquids and then bellowed out fumes.

As Snake had promised Woman, the plants, animals, and other creatures on Earth helped humanity in its endeavors. Certain species of plants and animals had even sacrificed themselves to become food, companions, and workers for the human race. Unfortunately, most human beings did not recognize or appreciate this. They had become extremely arrogant, almost blind in their relationship to Earth and her other creatures, and they saw themselves as superior to everyone and everything else on Earth. They felt it their duty and their right to conquer and control everything around them. In their quest for mastery of the physical universe, they had completely lost touch with many of the simple, natural laws of Earth that had kept everything functioning harmoniously.

As a result, Earth's systems became severely out of balance and life on earth for human beings and all other creatures deteriorated rapidly. Humans had proliferated so greatly that there were just too many of them to live comfortably on the planet. A great number of humans lived in crowded concrete jungles of buildings, called cities, where there was little contact with the nurturing, comforting elements of nature. Life was dreary and often dangerous and violent in these jungles. The air and the food were filled with poisons, so people were actually destroying themselves as they breathed and ate!

Vast amounts of Earth's resources—land and water all over the world— were used to grow feed for animals who were then slaughtered to feed the wealthiest people in small areas of the world. These people sometimes destroyed large amounts of food to keep things in what they called "economic balance." Meanwhile, increasing numbers of poor people in these same areas, and even more all over the world, were actually starving to death!

Ultimately, large areas of Earth became polluted. Many rivers and lakes and even the vast oceans were being destroyed by chemicals used routinely by humans in their farming and manufacturing endeavors.

Many species of plants and animals were destroyed by man's activities. Many other magnificent creatures grew close to extinction as human civilization expanded heedlessly into previously pristine areas.

Even the weather on Earth began to change dramatically, altered by human beings' experiments on earth and in space, and by the destruction of the tropical rain forests.

As Snake had warned, the human species had indeed developed the power of destruction. Not only were they destroying Earth through their careless lack of attunement to one another and to Earth as a whole, they actually set about to create the most violent, destructive weapons they could, and succeeded extremely well at the task. They had systems in which a few people could push buttons that would instantly unleash enough power to destroy the entire Earth and all her living creatures!

Like small boys playing with their Christmas toys, the humans experimented with the first versions of these powerful weapons, and they destroyed many other people and scared themselves quite a bit in the process. So they put the weapons on the shelf, but kept building bigger and stronger ones and putting those on the shelf as well. They loved to threaten each other with them, and were always trying to figure out who had the most potential destructive power.

The human beings were in a sad state spiritually and emotionally. As Snake had predicted, humans had gone so deeply into the consciousness of the physical plane that they had become lost in that reality. They had forgotten their origin as divine, loving, powerful spiritual beings.

Because they had disconnected themselves from the power of Spirit, at their emotional core they felt helpless, frightened, and alone. They became preoccupied with trying to gain material power in the world, thinking this would make them feel safe and secure. Many of them became obsessed with money, success, status, and political influence.

Because human beings were disconnected from the fullness of Spirit, feeling empty and dissatisfied, they became engrossed in trying to find some kind of fulfillment in external things. They became addicted to food, alcohol and other drugs, sex, or other pursuits that could give them a temporary feeling of pleasure or satisfaction.

Because they had lost touch with their own inner nature, and with the natural world around them, they lost much of their intuitive understanding about relating to one another. And since many humans were so emotionally deprived and out of balance, they had great difficulty raising their children in a healthy way. The environments they had created were not very conducive to the nurturing of children, either.

Many young humans were not getting their emotional needs met, and were growing up frightened, sad, angry, frustrated, or emotionally numb. They, in turn, passed these qualities on to their children.

Throughout the ages there had always been a few human beings who retained their connection to Spirit, and who recognized the imbalances in the world. Some of them had tried to bring awareness to others, in various ways and with varying degrees of success. Now, because of the increasing severity of the situation, more people were becoming aware of the problems and were searching for solutions. Many were seeking truth through exploring the creative arts. Some explored human psychology in order to heal themselves and each other emotionally. Others worked on political and environmental issues.

And some, in search of spiritual answers, turned toward ancient teachings, reinterpreted them for modern times, and shared them with others.

Many of these truthseekers found that their lives were improving. Their spiritual practices helped them feel more and more connected with their Source and they began to feel the power of God moving through them to heal some of the problems in their lives and in the world. Sometimes they observed miraculous things happening through this creative power they channeled.

The psychological work they did helped them clear away a lot of the old misconceptions and emotional patterns that had been handed down through generations. Those who had the courage to face their greatest fear and pain moved through their deepest darkness and found the light.

They began to love and accept themselves and each other again. They learned to accept and enjoy their human feelings and emotions, and to communicate with each other more honestly. This helped them find more of the closeness and intimacy they needed in their relationships with each other. Some men started to realize that the women in their lives mirrored the female energy within themselves, while some women began to recognize the men in their lives as the reflection of their own inner male energies.

All of this helped them to appreciate each other more. As they gained more confidence in the wholeness within themselves, they felt less powerless and less frightened of each other. They became more comfortable with the tremendous attraction they felt between them, recognizing it as the natural dance between the female and male polarities of the universe. Once they felt better about themselves and each other, they were more able to love and nurture the children they gave birth to. They began to recognize in their children the innocent, spontaneous essence they had lost touch with in themselves, and they allowed their children to teach them about reuniting with their own inner selves.

In turn, they were finally able to model for their children how to live effectively and happily in the physical world. The new beings being born into bodies no longer had to go through the pain of forgetting who they were and feeling lost, but were recognized from conception and birth as spiritual beings, and encouraged to live and express their truth. Open and clear, channeling a great deal of creative power, many of them seemed to know their life purpose and began to move toward it at a young age.

The truthseekers tried to solve some of the political, social, and environmental problems around them. A few of them were even elected or appointed to political office. Others wrote books and articles or created movies or television programs to try to wake people up. Many simply worked hard to deal with individual problems in their communities. In some cases, wonderful progress was made; other times it was discouraging.

The number of truthseekers was small though steadily growing, but overall conditions on Earth were becoming worse for most people. There was increasing violence and insanity among humans. Most of the political leaders, reflecting the masses, were still trying to do things in the same old way. Pollution and ecological destruction were rampant. The Earth herself was angry and upset, and demonstrated her desire for respect through earthquakes, volcanoes, floods, climactic change, and other means at her disposal.

The souls of many humans and other creatures, recognizing the degree of transformation that was called for and not desiring to go through all the effort, chose to go through the transition called "death," and departed from their physical bodies. They went on to experience another level of existence for a while, some of them feeling that perhaps they would come back to this physical reality again later on when it got a little easier or more pleasurable.

Those who remained, whether or not they were consciously aware of it, were determinedly adventurous types who wanted to be part of the dramatic change that was taking place.

As outward conditions continued to grow darker, increasing numbers of humans were driven inward, looking for some light. They were forced out of their numb state of denial, and began facing their fear and pain. More and more of them became truthseekers.

The new teachings spread, through speakers, books, movies, and even television (the bastion of the old reality). People began to gather into small groups everywhere on Earth, sharing their fears and problems and giving each other support and inspiration. They realized that none of them could solve their difficulties alone—they needed each other's assistance and love. From these gatherings new tribes gradually formed, made up of people who realized their spiritual connection to one another and their mission together. Different tribes worked in different ways but they shared a similar purpose—to serve God by saving themselves and the planet.

Some of these tribes of truthseekers found themselves drawn to certain powerful places on the earth. They migrated and settled in these special power spots. Here they recognized Earth herself as their mother and their greatest teacher. They surrendered their lives to her, and asked her to guide them in learning to live naturally, in truth and harmony.

Thus humankind, which had fulfilled its destiny to carry the polarity of male energy to its extreme of individuation and separation, was coming full circle. Once again humans were returning to the power of the feminine principle and embracing her.

Earth responded like any loving mother to her children, embracing the humans with an abundance of nurturing, love, and wisdom. She began to talk to them in many ways and teach them everything they needed to know. They began to practice rituals of meditation, singing, and dancing to attune themselves to Earth. With her support they reconnected with the ancient wisdom they carried in their souls. Step by step, Earth taught them how to live naturally and in a balanced way. They found healing for their bodies, emotions, minds, and spirits. They lived in increasing honesty and acceptance with themselves and one another. They grew and ate food that was natural and nourishing to them in ways that followed Earth's natural laws. They built shelters that were comfortable, beautiful, and that blended with the surrounding environment. They created schools that were fun and exciting for their children and taught them all the things they needed to know about living. They reformed local political systems and elected leaders who upheld their values. They committed themselves to solving local ecological and environmental problems, while also working to influence larger world issues.

They also created healing and teaching centers. Many people came from all over the world to receive personal healing on all levels and to learn all aspects of this new way of life. They would stay for a certain period of time, undergo great personal transformation, and then return to their homes to teach and heal others. In this way, the new way was carried from the power spots to many places on Earth.

Certain people who came for healing were very powerful in the old world. Some of them were influential in the media, and once they realized the transformation that was possible, they began to send the message out to the world. They created some popular television programs that carried the message in an interesting and entertaining way, and since millions of people were plugged into the global network of television, the vision of a new way of life was effectively spread everywhere. New leaders were elected who were committed to their own personal transformation and to the creation of a new world. With guidance from the Higher Power and support from the people and all the creatures of Earth, they dissolved or changed the old institutions that were no longer working and created new ones that worked effectively for the highest good of all.

The human species stopped polluting and destroying the earth. They learned to live on her in balance and love. Gradually, Earth began flourishing again and grew more beautiful than ever before.

Human beings lived spontaneously, finding in each moment the pleasure and fulfillment of growth, change, and aliveness. They felt a part of the Great Spirit that unified all life and all existence. At the same time they appreciated their individual differences and loved themselves, including their human limitations. They looked at the world with innocent freshness in each moment, yet remembered their past pain. Their experience brought them the wisdom and strength to protect and care for themselves and for the Earth.

Men and women loved each other passionately and were not afraid to feel the intensity of their love. They saw the beauty and power of the entire universe reflected in one another, and in their children. They lived in harmony with the Earth, with all the Earth's creatures and with all the rhythms of nature.

Humankind had returned to the Garden.

Shakti Gawain, *Return to the Garden*

A Transpersonal Creed

I BELIEVE that the universe is spiritual as well as material, and that what happens to us is controlled by a combination of both physical and spiritual laws.

I AFFIRM that human beings are part of an integrated Order of life; that we have considerable potential to evolve toward higher levels of this Order; and that seeking to evolve toward this Order is one of the highest values of human life.

I MAINTAIN that there are higher spiritual beings and enlightened humans. Life and consciousness seek to evolve toward these higher, non-physical manifestations, even though currently rooted in the physical. Like the rest of life, my life and my consciousness share this purpose and destiny.

I BELIEVE that while some judgments, values, and moralities are subjective and personal, some are based on a valid intuition of higher possibilities. Satisfactory personal values and morality must be based on a continual dedication to understanding and living my and others' higher possibilities. Those who help me understand and develop these higher possibilities are my friends and teachers; those who hinder me should be helped as much as possible. Insofar as all Life may be one Being, in a real and transpersonal sense, we should seek to maximize our love of and minimize our harm to all Life.

I AFFIRM that churches or other transpersonally oriented activities may sometimes be useful for aiding my and others' spiritual evolution; that there are actions that are objectively wrong, which we should avoid committing once we understand their nature; that there is a real and objective sense in which harming others harms myself and life; that the universe is lawful on mental and transpersonal levels as well as physical levels, so all acts have consequences that must eventually be faced. Virtue for me is loving and helping myself and others, so I and Life may evolve.

I MAINTAIN that the death of the body may not be the death of the mind. While hope of an afterlife can be a rationalization for lack of evolutionary effort in this life, the probable reality of transpersonal levels of existence not dependent on a physical body may mean that individual life is much greater than physical life.

Charles T. Tart, *Open Mind, Discriminating Mind*

✣ East and West ✣

One of the most exciting and evolutionary challenges in this period of the world's history is the movement of the West to the spiritual wisdom of the East, and the movement of the East to the scientific economy of the West. Emerging from this exchange comes an enquiry into the habits of the other, and an exploration of the diverse traditions and laws of existence and meaning that each brings. Hans Küng explains that the similarities outweigh dissimilarities when we meet on the ground of the spiritual; that whatever our differences, whatever name we give to the Almighty Creator, we are at one in our belief in the nature of deity. This "oneness" is again the wholeness and unity which we are striving to achieve collectively as well as individually. The ecumenical movement of the 1960s began the surge of a more catholic view and interest in other religions and beliefs. Now we are more actively pursuing the methods of many of the Eastern traditional religions and finding ways of marrying them with the Western ways of worship.

The writers in this section have all contributed largely to the understanding of East and West by their work and their writings—theologian Hans Küng, from his ecumenical Christian base; Alan Watts, from his knowledge of Zen Buddhism and Taoism; Pierre Teilhard de Chardin, with his cosmic understanding of evolution; and David Bohm, for his connecting consciousness with physics.

✣

"I believe that by openness to Buddhism, to Hinduism, and to these great Asian traditions, we stand a wonderful chance of learning more about the potentiality of our own traditions.... The combination of the natural techniques and the graces and the other things that have been manifested in Asia, and the Christian liberty of the gospel should bring us all at last to that full and transcendent liberty which is beyond mere cultural differences and mere externals....

Thomas Merton, *The Asian Journals of Thomas Merton*

The *God of the religions is not nameless*. For the religions were always more than philosophy, more than a doctrine of God, a theory of God, a thinking of God. Religions do not emerge from conceptual reflection, still less from strictly argued rational proof. And certainly not—as former historians of religion thought—from the purely irrational, unintellectual strata of the human psyche. No, they are rooted—and there is a large measure of agreement on this—in the experiential unity of knowing, willing and feeling, which, however, should not be understood as one's own achievement, but as an answer: an answer to an encounter with or an experience of God (or the Absolute), whatever form it may have taken. Most religions appeal to an illumination or a manifestation of God (or the Absolute), who is in himself hidden and ambivalent.

But, despite all convergences among the religions, there are fundamental differences; despite all similarities, far too many contradictions. The God of the religions has *many names*. In view of the innumerable gods of the religions in history and at the present time, in view of the divine natural forms and natural forces, of plant, animal and human gods, of deities equal in rank or arranged in hierarchies, the question is thrust upon us inescapably: Which is the true God? Is he to be found in the original, primitive religions or in the highly developed? In those which have grown slowly or in those which have been instituted? In the mythological or in the enlightened religions? Are there many gods: polytheism? Or a single supreme god among many gods: henotheism? Or even one sole god: monotheism? Is God above or outside everything: deism? Or is God everything: pantheism? Or all in all: panentheism? Distinctions and decisions cannot be avoided. It is not, however, a question of an arbitrary decision, but of a decision of faith justified at the bar of reason. For we cannot simply "make" a religion. With all respect for the other religions, we have stated the reasons why we decide for the God of Israel, the God of the Bible, and this will become still clearer later.

> ✢ The understanding of God on the part of the religions as a whole is definite but not coherent.
> The gods of the religions display many contrasts in names and natures. They contradict and refute one another; it is impossible to believe in all of them at the same time.
> A rationally justifiable decision is required.
> ✢ The biblical faith in God is in itself coherent, is also rationally justifiable and has proved itself historically over many thousands of years.
> The God of Israel is for believers the one, sole God who has no other gods beside him.
> He bears unmistakably the one name of Yahweh; man is to believe in him alone.

And yet the religions—if not the nature religions, then at least the ethical higher religions—start out from the *same unending questions* of man that open up behind the visible and palpable and behind any individual's span of life: Where does the world and its order come from, why are we born and why must we die, what decides the fate of the individual and of mankind, what is the explanation of moral consciousness and the existence of ethical norms? And all religions seek to go beyond the interpretation of the world in order to make possible a *practical way* to salvation out of distress and torment. Do they not all regard lying, theft, adultery and murder as culpable? Do they not uphold a universally valid practical criterion something like a "golden rule" (do not do to others what you would not have done to yourself)? Were, then, Buddha, K'ung-fu-tse, Lao-tse, Zarathustra, Mohammed, not concerned with the same great ultimate questions and hopes?

It cannot be denied that in the other world religions also it is known that the Deity, however close, is remote and hidden and must itself bestow closeness, presence and manifestness. In the world religions also it is known that man cannot approach God quite naturally assuming his own innocence, that he needs purification and reconciliation, that sacrifice is needed to wipe out sin, that he reaches life only by passing through death, in fact, that man, in the last resort, cannot redeem and liberate himself but is dependent on God's all-embracing love. Hence, in virtue of what we have now said about the God of the Fathers and formerly about the salvation of pagans, it must be observed:

- ✦ Not only Muslims in Allah, but also Hindus in Brahma, Buddhists in the Absolute, Chinese in heaven or in the Tao, are seeking one and the same absolutely first, absolutely last reality, which for Jews and Christians is the one true God.
- ✦ The religions of the world can perceive not only the alienation, enslavement and need of redemption on man's part but also the goodness, mercy and graciousness of the one God.
- ✦ Because of this truth—despite many untruths, despite polytheism, magic, natural forces and superstition—people in the world religions can gain eternal salvation.

In that sense, the other world religions can also be ways of salvation. *The question of salvation must therefore be distinguished from the question of truth.* And if the question of salvation is settled positively, this by no means renders superfluous the question of truth. For, however much truth can be seen in detail in the world religions that can be accepted by Jews and Christians, they do not provide *the* truth for Jews and Christians. Only the one true God of Israel, known by faith, is *the* truth for Jews and Christians. Neither Jew

nor Christian could claim that he might just as well be a Muslim, or even a
Buddhist, Hindu or Confucian.

Hans Küng, Does God Exist?

Since the latter part of the nineteenth century there has been an enormous
growth of Western interest in the philosophical and spiritual traditions of
Asia. Today this interest seems to be widening in such a way as to amount to
a major "cultural invasion," so that it is possible for so serious a historian as
Arnold Toynbee to speak of the future growth of religion in terms of a fusion
of Christianity and Buddhism.

Much of this popular interest in Asian spirituality has been focussed
upon those aspects of it which have to do with parapsychology, with the
development of what are called in Sanskrit *siddhi*, or supernormal powers. By
no means all of this interest in *siddhi* is at the unfortunate level of those so-
called yogis who give public instruction in Raja or Hatha Yoga in the great
metropolitan cities.

The studies and experiments which have been made in this area by
such people as Pitirim Sorokin of Harvard, Mircea Eliade, C. G. Jung, Roger
Godel, and others less well-known are of a serious and sober character.
Nonetheless, it is an area fraught with misunderstanding, especially as concerns the relationship of parapsychology to the primary purposes of such
ways of life as Buddhism, the Vedanta, and Taoism.

One must remember that a great deal of Western interest in Asian philosophy stems from the wide influence exercised by the Theosophical movement in the early part of this century, by the work of H. P. Blavatsky, Annie
Besant, Rudolph Steiner, G. R. S. Mead, and many others. Although, at the
present time, Theosophy has little of its former prestige, it did much to lay
down the general lines of Western interest in Asian spirituality, where this
interest was not of a purely academic nature. But in so doing it propagated
some serious confusions. For its sources of information about these matters
were principally the labors of Western scholars who had, as then, hardly
come to grips with the subject, and who had confused communication
between East and West with—perhaps inevitably—misleading dictionaries
of Sanskrit, Chinese, and Tibetan.

The main misunderstanding which emerged from this early interest
had to do with the kind of knowledge which, in Buddhism or the Vedanta,
would be called "supreme knowledge," "enlightenment," or "awakening"—
or sometimes even "omniscience" (*sarvajnana*). This is the kind of knowledge
which the Oriental philosophies hold to be characteristic of the highest form
of man, of a Buddha or "awakened one," or of a *jivan-mukta*—one who is

liberated from bondage to the conventional world of ordinary perception. Perhaps the chief reason for the misunderstanding was that this type of knowledge was confused with the omniscience and consequent omnipotence attributed to God in Christian theology.

For when we think about omniscience in the context of Christian theology, we tend to think of a knowledge which is infinitely encyclopedic and of power which is infinitely magical or "technological." We think of God as being exhaustively informed about all facts and events whatsoever, and as being in conscious and voluntary control of absolutely everything which happens. Consequently God has a conscious and technical mastery of the world of nature such that he can at any moment alter its normal and expected course by performing miracles. Such miracles are not violations of nature, but actions which proceed, like those of the scientist, from an extraordinary knowledge of its processes.

With such ideas of omniscience in mind, it is easy to see how Western people might credit the "divine men" of Asia with powers like those of the Christian God. To complicate the problem—this is by no means a purely Western misconception. All over the world, men's minds are fascinated by prospects of unusual power. To complicate it still more—there are Hindus and Buddhists who train themselves in disciplines which do, in fact, produce some quite extraordinary psychophysical powers. But this latter fact must not be considered out of context.

We must begin by showing the difference between Western and Eastern ideas of omniscience and omnipotence. A Chinese Buddhist poem says:

> *You may wish to ask where the flowers come from,*
> *But even the God of Spring doesn't know.*

A Westerner would expect that, of all people, the God of Spring would know exactly how flowers are made. But if he doesn't know, how can he possibly make them? A Buddhist would answer that the question itself is misleading since flowers are grown, not made. Things which are made are either assemblages of formerly separate parts (like houses) or constructed by cutting and shaping from without inwards (like pots of clay or images). But things which are grown formulate their own structure and differentiate their own parts from within outwards.

Thus it would be absurd, in a Buddhist's view, to ask, "Who made the world?" because the world as a whole is not considered as an artifact, a structure made by putting formerly distinct pieces together—pieces which were originally shaped by an external agency from some kind of material. No analogy is felt to exist between natural growth and human manufacture.

If, then, the God of Spring does not make the flowers, how *does* he produce them? The answer is that he does so in the same way that you and I
grow our hair, beat our hearts, structure our bones and nerves, and move our
limbs. To us, this seems a very odd statement because we do not ordinarily
think of ourselves as actively growing our hair in the same way that we move
our limbs. But the difference vanishes when we ask ourselves just *how* we
raise a hand, or just how we make a mental decision to raise a hand. For we
do not know—or, more correctly, we do know but we cannot describe how it
is done in words.

To be more exact: the process is so innate and so *simple* that it cannot be
conveyed by anything so complicated and cumbersome as human language,
which has to describe everything in terms of a linear series of fixed signs. This
cumbersome way of making communicable representations of the world
makes the description of certain events as complicated as trying to drink water
with a fork. It is not that these actions or events are complicated in themselves:
the complexity lies in trying to fit them into the clumsy instrumentality of language, which can deal only with one thing (or "think") at a time.

Now the Western mind identifies what it knows with what it can
describe and communicate in some system of symbols, whether linguistic or
mathematical—that is, with what it can think about. Knowledge is thus primarily the content of thought, of a system of symbols which make up a very
approximate model or representation of reality. In somewhat the same way, a
newspaper photograph is a representation of a natural scene in terms of a fine
screen of dots. But as the actual scene is not a lot of dots, so the real world is
not in fact a lot of things or "thinks."

The Oriental mind uses the term *knowledge* in another sense besides
this—in the sense of knowing how to do actions which cannot be explained.
In this sense, we know how to breathe and how to walk, and even how to
grow hair, because that is just what we do!

This kind of "knowing how" does not apply to voluntary acts alone.
Buddhist psychology does not admit our rather rigid distinction between the
voluntary and the involuntary. For if voluntary acts are those preceded by a
decision or choice, is decision itself voluntary? Were it so, every decision would
have to be preceded by a decision to decide, and so on in an infinite regression.

This is not to say that all acts are involuntary. The point is that an act is
voluntary or involuntary, not in itself, but according to the point of view
from which it is regarded. In itself, every act is said to be happening *shizen*
or *mushin*, that is, spontaneously. This is expressed in the poem:

> *The wild geese do not intend to cast their reflection;*
> *The water has no mind to retain their image*

We are now in a position to see what Buddhism might mean by the *siddhi* or marvelous power of omnipotence. So long as I identify myself with my conscious, intentional, and voluntary mind, I feel that I am in control of relatively few events. But I can realize that this identification is after all a matter of opinion, of social convention, of an acquired way of describing myself to myself. Both Buddhist and Hindu disciplines of spiritual growth (i.e., meditation or yoga), consist primarily in exploring the question, "What am I?"

This leads to the discovery that the accepted way of conceiving myself—as this consciousness, this body, or this particular series of experiences—is simply conventional, just one among many possible ways of describing myself. Then what am I in reality? The answer, from one side, is "no-thing" or "nothing special" (*muji*). But since it is written that "between the All and the Void is only a difference of name," it appears possible to identify myself as all, as the total process of *shizen*, or "things-happening-spontaneously-by-themselves."

In this sense, I feel that "I" am shining the stars and blowing the clouds above my head in just the same way that "I" am growing my hair, breathing, and walking. This is omniscience and omnipotence, but as the God of Spring does not know where the flowers come from, so "I" cannot, or rather, words cannot describe how all this is done.

We are now in a position to discuss the production of psychophysical acts which are out of the ordinary. In the first place it must be understood that such acts are no more necessarily connected with Buddhist "omniscience" than any ordinary feat of scientific or artistic skill. Qualitatively, telepathy is not different from acquiring the knack of wiggling one's ears or shooting a bow and arrow, and one of the best discussions of this whole problem in a Buddhist setting is Eugen Herrigel's marvelous little book *Zen in the Art of Archery* (Pantheon Books, New York)—in which he relates how he learned to let the bowstring go *shizen*, by itself. It took him five years to learn the knack, five years to overcome the obsession that decisive motions of this nature must be felt as forced choices, and not as happening by themselves.

However, as soon as he learned the feeling of his hand releasing the bowstring by itself, he discovered the clue to an extraordinary and indeed supernormal mastery of the art of archery. Similarly, when one learns the feeling of thoughts and mental impressions coming and going of themselves, one has discovered the clue to a mastery of the mental art which could, if so desired, be applied to experiments in parapsychology.

But such experiments would be a sideline, having no more intrinsic connection with Buddhist wisdom than any other type of scientific or artistic research. To be aware of phenomena on "higher planes of vibration" is, in principle, no different from visiting Australia or the moon. One who is a fool here will also be a fool on the moon, and a fool in the sensible world will likewise be a fool in the suprasensible world, and a very dangerous fool by consequence.

The connection between the *shizen* feeling and the acquisition of supernormal skills is simply that the ordinary, egocentric way of feeling our actions arouses tensions which block and hinder their efficiency. For example, I am late in catching a train, so I try as hard as possible to hurry. But the effortful tension hinders my freedom and elasticity of movement in such a way that I stumble and fumble. My anxiety not to be late makes me tremble and dither in such a way that I get later and later and thus still more anxious, creating a vicious circle which deprives me of freedom of movement. To act in this way sets up all kinds of unnecessary limitations to the possibilities of human action, but that we do not know what the human organism might achieve if it behaved otherwise.

Just as there is no fixed and necessary reason why man should regard himself as identical with his conscious will or his body, there is likewise no reason other than habit and convention why he should regard his human nature as having rigidly circumscribed possibilities of thought and activity.

But a Western approach to Oriental wisdom based largely on the peculiarly Western urge for the extension of human power will neglect the main thing which this wisdom has to offer, and of which we stand so tremendously in need—and that is deliverance from the egocentric way of feeling the world, from our titanic anxiety to control everything and to obliterate the limits of time and space, from that will-to-power which makes our culture such a menace to life on this planet.

Alan Watts, "Oriental Omnipotence," in *The Essential Alan Watts*

The Confluence of East and West

"The whole spiritual mass of the East once more under way": I would like to conclude the evidence offered here with that great possibility or even, I would say—if my judgement is correct—that great event.

An ever-increasing number of persons is concerned with this much-canvassed question of a convergence of East and West; they are apt to picture it to themselves by the idea of two complementary blocs, or two conflicting principles, which are merging into one: another example of Chinese Tao's *yin* and *yang*. To my mind, if the meeting is effected—as soon or later *must* happen—the phenomenon will come about as the result of a different mechanism, one much more akin to that by which a number of streams pour simultaneously through a breach opened by one of them in a common retaining barrier.

As it happens, and through a complex of historical factors which it would not be difficult to analyse, the honour and the opportunity of opening the road for a new surge of human consciousness have fallen, I repeat, to the West. But while there can no longer be any doubt about the correct approach, or even about whether the breach has been made, we are still a long way from the final target; nor can we be certain of success. In one sense, the real battle for spirit is only beginning in our world; and if we are to win it, all the available forces must be brought into action.

Pierre Teilhard de Chardin, *Toward the Future*

Résumé of Discussion on Western and Eastern Forms of Insight into Wholeness

In the very early phases of the development of civilization, man's views were essentially of wholeness rather than of fragmentation. In the East (especially in India) such views still survive, in the sense that philosophy and religion emphasize wholeness and imply the futility of analysis of the world into parts. Why, then, do we not drop our fragmentary Western approach and adopt these Eastern notions which include not only a self-world view that denies division and fragmentation but also techniques of meditation that lead the whole process of mental operation non-verbally to the sort of quiet state of orderly and smooth flow needed to end fragmentation both in the actual process of thought and in its content?

To answer such a question, it is useful to begin by going into the difference between Western and Eastern notions of measure. Now, in the West the notion of measure has, from very early times, played a key role in determining the general self-world view and the way of life implicit in such a view. Thus among the Ancient Greeks, from whom we derive a large part of our fundamental notions (by way of the Romans), to keep everything in its right measure was regarded as one of the essentials of a good life (e.g., Greek tragedies generally portrayed man's suffering as a consequence of his going beyond the proper measure of things). In this regard, measure was not looked on in its modern sense as being primarily some sort of comparison of an object with an external standard or unit. Rather, this latter procedure was regarded as a kind of outward display or appearance of a deeper "inner measure," which played an essential role in everything. When something went beyond its proper measure, this meant not merely that it was not conforming to some external standard of what was right but, much more, that it was inwardly out of harmony, so that it was bound to lose its integrity and break up into fragments. One can obtain some insight into this way of thinking by considering the earlier meanings of certain words. Thus, the Latin *mederi* meaning "to cure" (the root of the modern "medicine") is based on a root meaning "to measure." This reflects the view that physical health is to be regarded as the outcome of a state of right inward measure in all parts and processes of the body. Similarly, the word "moderation," which describes one of the prime ancient notions of virtue, is based on the same root, and this shows that such virtue was regarded as the outcome of a right inner measure underlying man's social actions and behaviour. Again, the word "meditation," which is based on the same root, implies a kind of weighing, pondering, or measuring of the whole process of thought, which could bring the inner activities of the mind to a state of harmonious measure. So, physically, socially and mentally, awareness of the inner measure of things was seen as the essential key to a healthy, happy, harmonious life.

It is clear that measure is to be expressed in more detail through proportion or ratio; and "ratio" is the Latin word from which our modern "reason" is derived. In the ancient view, reason is seen as insight into a totality of ratio or proportion, regarded as relevant inwardly to the very nature of things (and not only outwardly as a form of comparison with a standard or unit). Of course, this ratio is not necessarily merely a numerical proportion (though it does, of course, include such proportion). Rather, it is in general a qualitative sort of universal proportion or relationship. Thus, when Newton perceived the insight of universal gravitation, what he saw could be put in this way: "As the apple falls, so does the moon, and so indeed does everything." To exhibit the form of the ratio yet more explicitly, one can write:

$$A : B :: C : D :: E : F$$

where A and B represent successive positions of the apple at successive moments of time, C and D those of the moon, and E and F those of any other object.

Whenever we find a theoretical reason for something, we are exemplifying this notion of ratio, in the sense of implying that as the various aspects are related in our idea, so they are related in the thing that the idea is about. The essential reason or ratio of a thing is then the totality of inner proportions in its structure, and in the process in which it forms, maintains itself, and ultimately dissolves. In this view, to understand such ratio is to understand the "innermost being" of that thing.

It is thus implied that measure is a form of insight into the essence of everything, and that man's perception, following on ways indicated by such insight, will be clear and will thus bring about generally orderly action and harmonious living. In this connection, it is useful to call to mind Ancient

Greek notions of measure in music and in the visual arts. These notions emphasized that a grasp of measure was a key to the understanding of harmony in music (e.g., measure as rhythm, right proportion in intensity of sound, right proportion in tonality, etc.). Likewise, in the visual arts, right measure was seen as essential to overall harmony and beauty (e.g., consider the "Golden Mean"). All of this indicates how far the notion of measure went beyond that of comparison with an external standard, to point to a universal sort of inner ratio or proportion, perceived both through the senses and through the mind.

Of course, as time went on, this notion of measure gradually began to change, to lose its subtlety and to become relatively gross and mechanical. Probably this was because man's notion of measure became more and more routinized and habitual, both with regard to its outward display in measurements relative to an external unit and to its inner significance as universal ratio relevant physical health, social order, and mental harmony. Men began to learn such notions of measure mechanically, by conforming to the teachings of their elders or their masters, and not creatively through an inner feeling and understanding of the deeper meaning of the ratio or proportion which they were learning. So measure gradually came to be taught as a sort of rule that was to be imposed from outside on the human being, who in turn imposed the corresponding measure physically, socially, and mentally, in every context in which he was working. As a result, the prevailing notions of measure were no longer seen as forms of insight. Rather, they appeared to be "absolute truths about reality as it is," which men seemed always to have known, and whose origin was often explained mythologically as binding injunctions of the Gods, which it would be both dangerous and wicked to question. Thought about measure thus tended to fall mainly into the domain of unconscious habit and, as a result, the forms induced in perception by this thought were now seen as directly observed objective realities, which were essentially independent of how they were thought about.

Even by the time of the Ancient Greeks, this process had gone a long way and, as men realized this, they began to question the notion of measure. Thus Protagoras said: "Man is the measure of all things," thus emphasizing that measure is not a reality external to man, existing independently of him. But many who were in the habit of looking at everything externally also applied this way of looking to what Protagoras said. Thus, they concluded that measure was something arbitrary, and subject to the capricious choice or taste of each individual. In this way they of course overlooked the fact that measure is a form of insight that has to fit the overall reality in which man lives, as demonstrated by the clarity of perception and harmony of action to which it leads. Such insight can arise properly only when a man works with seriousness and honesty, putting truth and factuality first, rather than his own whims or desires.

The general rigidification and objectification of the notion of measure continued to develop until, in modern times, the very word "measure" has come to denote mainly a process of comparison of something with an external standard. While the original meaning still survives in some contexts (e.g., art and mathematics) it is generally felt as having only a secondary sort of significance.

Now, in the East the notion of measure has not played nearly so fundamental a role. Rather, in the prevailing philosophy in the Orient, the immeasurable (i.e., that which cannot be named, described, or understood through any form of reason) is regarded as the primary reality. Thus, in Sanskrit (which has an origin common to the Indo-European language group) there is a word "matra" meaning "measure," in the musical sense, which is evidently close to the Greek "metron." But then there is another word "maya" obtained from the same root, which means "illusion." This is an extraordinarily significant point. Whereas to Western society, as it derives from the Greeks, measure, with all that this word implies, is the very essence of reality, or at least the key to this essence, in the East measure has now come to be regarded commonly as being in some way false and deceitful. In this view the entire structure and order of forms, proportions, and "ratios" that present themselves to ordinary perception and reason are regarded as a sort of veil, covering the true reality, which cannot be perceived by the senses and of which nothing can be said or thought.

It is clear that the different ways the two societies have developed fit in with their different attitudes to measure. Thus, in the West, society has mainly emphasized the development of science and technology (dependent on measure), while in the East, the main emphasis has gone to religion and philosophy (which are directed ultimately toward the immeasurable).

If one considers this question carefully, one can see that in a certain sense the East was right to see the immeasurable as the primary reality. For, as has already been indicated, measure is an insight created by man. A reality that is beyond man and prior to him cannot depend on such insight. Indeed, the attempt to suppose that measure exists prior to man and independently of him leads, as has been seen, to the "objectification" of man's insight, so that it becomes rigidified and unable to change, eventually bringing about fragmentation and general confusion in the way described in this chapter.

One may speculate that perhaps in ancient times, the men who were wise enough to see that the immeasurable is the primary reality were also wise enough to see that measure is insight into a secondary and dependent but nonetheless necessary aspect of reality. Thus they may have agreed with the Greeks that insight into measure is capable of helping to bring about order and harmony in our lives, while at the same time, seeing perhaps more deeply, that it cannot be what is most fundamental in this regard.

What they may further have said is that when measure is identified with the very essence of reality, *this* is illusion. But then, when men learned this by conforming to the teachings of tradition, the meaning became largely habitual and mechanical. In the way indicated earlier, the subtlety was lost and men began to say simply: "measure is illusion." Thus, both in the East and in the West, true insight may have been turned into something false and misleading by the procedure of learning mechanically through conformity to existent teachings, rather than through a creative and original grasp of the insights implicit in such teachings.

It is of course impossible to go back to a state of wholeness that may have been present before the split between East and West developed (if only because we know little, if anything, about this state). Rather, what is needed is to learn afresh, to observe, and to discover for ourselves the meaning of wholeness. Of course, we have to be cognizant of the teachings of the past, both Western and Eastern, but to imitate these teachings or to try to conform to them would have little value. For, as has been pointed out in this chapter, to develop new insight into fragmentation and wholeness requires a creative work even more difficult than that needed to make fundamental new discoveries in science, or great and original works of art. It might in this context be said that one who is similar to Einstein in creativity is not the one who imitates Einstein's ideas, nor even the one who applies these ideas in new ways, rather, it is the one who learns from Einstein and then goes on to do something original, which is able to assimilate what is valid in Einstein's work and yet goes beyond this work in qualitatively new ways. So what we have to do with regard to the great wisdom from the whole of the past, both in the East and in the West; is to assimilate it and to go on to new and original perception relevant to our present condition of life.

In doing this, it is important that we be clear on the role of techniques, such as those used in various forms of meditation. In a way, techniques of meditation can be looked on as measures (actions ordered by knowledge and reason) which are taken by man to try to reach the immeasurable, i.e., a state of mind in which he ceases to sense a separation between himself and the whole of reality. But clearly, there is a contradiction in such a notion, for the immeasurable is, if anything, just that which cannot be brought within limits determined by man's knowledge and reason.

To be sure, in certain specifiable contexts, technical measures, understood in a right spirit, can lead us to do things from which we can derive insight if we are observant. Such possibilities, however, are limited. Thus, it would be a contradiction in terms to think of formulating techniques for making fundamental new discoveries in science or original and creative works of art, for the very essence of such action is a certain freedom from dependence on others, who would be needed as guides. How can this freedom be transmitted in an activity in which conformity to someone else's knowledge is the main source of energy? And if techniques cannot teach originality and creativity in art and science, how much less is it possible for them to enable us to "discover the immeasurable"?

Actually, there are no direct and positive things that man can do to get in touch with the immeasurable, for this must be immensely beyond anything that man can grasp with his mind or accomplish with his hands or his instruments. What man *can* do is to give his full attention and creative energies to bring clarity and order into the totality of the field of measure. This involves, of course, not only the outward display of measure in terms of external units but also inward measure, as health of the body, moderation in action, and meditation, which gives insight into the measure of thought. This latter is particularly important because, as has been seen, the illusion that the self and the world are broken into fragments originates in the kind of thought that goes beyond its proper measure and confuses its own product with the same independent reality. To end this illusion requires insight, not only into the world as a whole, but also into how the instrument of thought is working. Such insight implies an original and creative act of perception into all aspects of life, mental and physical, both through the senses and through the mind, and this is perhaps the true meaning of meditation.

As has been seen, fragmentation originates in essence in the fixing of the insights forming our overall self-world view, which follows on our generally mechanical, routinized and habitual modes of thought about these matters. Because the primary reality goes beyond anything that can be contained in such fixed forms of measure, these insights must eventually cease to be adequate, and will thus give rise to various forms of unclarity or confusion. However, when the whole field of measure is open to original and creative insight, without any fixed limits or barriers, then our overall world views will cease to be rigid, and the whole field of measure will come into harmony, as fragmentation within it comes to an end. But original and creative insight within the whole field of measure *is* the action of the immeasurable. For when such insight occurs, the source cannot be within ideas already contained in the field of measure but rather has to be in the immeasurable, which contains the essential formative cause of all that happens in the field of measure. The measurable and the immeasurable are then in harmony and indeed one sees that they are but different ways of considering the one and undivided whole.

When such harmony prevails, man can then not only have insight into the meaning of wholeness but, what is much more significant, he can realize the truth of this insight in every phase and aspect of his life.

As Krishnamurti has brought out with great force and clarity, this requires that man gives his full creative energies to the inquiry into the whole field of measure. To do this may perhaps be extremely difficult and arduous, but since everything turns on this, it is surely worthy of the serious attention and utmost consideration of each of us.

David Bohm, *Wholeness and the Implicate Order*

Apology to Native Congregations— United Church of Canada

Submitted by the United Church of Canada General Council to Native Elders and accepted by the Same on August 15, 1986:

Long before my people journeyed to this land
your people were here, and you received from
your elders an understanding of creation, and of the
Mystery that surrounds us all that was deep, and rich and
* to be treasured.*
We did not hear you when you shared your vision.
In our zeal to tell you of the good news of Jesus Christ
we were closed to the value of your spirituality.
We confused western ways and culture with the depth and breadth
* and length and height of the gospel of Christ.*
We imposed our civilization as a condition of accepting the Gospel.
We tried to make you be like us and in so doing
we helped to destroy the vision that made you what you were.
As a result you, and we, are poorer and the image of the Creator
* in us is twisted, blurred and we are not what we are meant*
* by God to be.*
We ask you to forgive us and we ask you to walk with us
* in the spirit of Christ so that our peoples may be blessed*
* and God's creation healed.*

Prayers were offered in four languages—Mohawk, Cree, Kwaquilth, and English—and a native dance of victory was held. Pledges of commitment and solidarity with native people and their needs were exchanged.

Matthew Fox, *The Coming of the Cosmic Christ*

✣ 21 ✣

Emerging World

We are all part of the emerging world of the twenty-first century. The emergence of any change, of any new creation, is usually painful and not always clearly understood. As though in the hands of the Hindu god, Lord Shiva, who represents the destroyer—the older ways of being are in many cases radically demolished. Much suffering, turmoil, and destruction seems to be taking place as the old world transforms into the new. There is little choice than to change in order to survive, and we in the West have started to review the quest for materialistic riches and comfort, started to review a way of being that has for so long been devoid of awareness of community, of poverty, pain, and violence in the world around us.

Each individual is alive here and now for the purpose of contributing to the world. And just as we are necessary, we are also responsible for doing our part within this changing time. Ram Dass, who takes us through seven steps for new creation in "The Evolutionary Cycle," speaks of a "humanizing society" in the making. In our pursuit of more meaningful lives, lives that have an impact on change, we are helping to build a new spiritual order, a race of people who work for the common good. In doing so we move nearer to God, the creator and orchestrator of this change, and through this we learn to trust and surrender to the greater plan for us on this planet.

In this section, Sri Aurobindo answers questions about the re-creation of a spiritual society, and E. P. Schumacher, in his piece on Buddhist economics, addresses the Buddhist principle of "the middle way"—working between "materialistic needlessness" and "traditionalist immobility." Omraam Mikhaël Aïvanhov goes further by noting that we are all bridges between "two opposite banks of the river"—these being east and west, feminine and masculine, above and below. He explains our connection with the Cosmic

Moral Law—how we should strive to live "on earth as it is in heaven" and how our work, as part of our lives and our actions, needs to be for the purpose of the collective whole, and not for individual gratification. This is what American psychotherapist and yoga teacher Bonnie Greenwell, who has specialized in kundalini research and written about her findings in *Energies of Transformation*, terms the "Collective Awakening." She believes, as do so many others, that a collective kundalini awakening is taking place in the world, to complement the individual experiences, like that described earlier by Gopi Krishna. This awakened kundalini energy is the spiritual energy necessary for change; it reveals itself through the natural disasters and earthquakes and floods of the earth, and in our own individual lives through rumblings, reshifts, and extreme changes.

⊹

This world is a perfect reflection of God. The Vedantic teaching: *sarvam khalvidam brahma*—"All this is indeed the Absolute"—is the ultimate truth. Everything is God. All countries, all holy places, all names are God's. Only in the eyes of men are there differences of high and low. Truly, all the regions of this earth are holy places of the Lord. All bodies of water are holy rivers of God. All the shapes and forms of the world contain the very sound of God's name. Endless is the glory, endless are the names, endless is the sport of the Infinite. There is no end to God. However much you read, there is something left to study. However many holy places you visit, there are still more left to see. However far you see, there is always more ahead. Such is the pervasiveness of the divine principle, the divine vastness; more divine than the divine is His glory.

Swami Muktananda, *Play of Consciousness*

The past decade has been a most exciting one. In spite of the tensions and uncertainties of our age something profoundly meaningful has begun. Old systems of exploitation and oppression are passing away and new systems of justice and equality are being born. In a real sense ours is a great time in which to be alive. Therefore I am not yet discouraged about the future. Granted that the easygoing optimism of yesterday is impossible. Granted that we face a world crisis which often leaves us standing amid the surging murmur of life's restless sea. But every crisis has both its dangers and its opportunities. Each can spell either salvation or doom. In a dark, confused world the spirit of God may yet reign supreme.

Martin Luther King, Jr., "A Testament of Hope"

A world has vanished. All that remains is a sanctuary hidden in the realm of spirit. We of this generation are still holding the key. Unless we remember, unless we unlock it, the holiness of ages will remain a secret of God. We of this generation are still holding the key—the key to the sanctuary which is also the shelter of our own deserted souls. If we mislay the key, we shall elude ourselves.

Abraham Joshua Heschel, The Earth Is the Lord's

It is not a question of who has the greatest military might, but rather it is man against man, man who has put together ideologies, and these ideologies, which man has made, are against each other. Until these ideas, ideologies, end and man becomes responsible for other human beings, there cannot possibly be peace in the world.

J. Krishnamurti, Krishnamurti to Himself

All the same, the faith in modern man's omnipotence is wearing thin. Even if all the "new" problems were solved by technological fixes, the state of futility, disorder and corruption would remain. It existed before the present crises became acute, and it will not go away by itself. More and more people are beginning to realise that "the modern experiment" has failed. It received its early impetus by what I have called the Cartesian revolution, which, with implacable logic, separated man from those Higher Levels that alone can maintain his humanity. Man closed the gates of Heaven against himself and tried, with immense energy and ingenuity, to confine himself to the Earth. He is now discovering that the Earth is but a transitory state, so that a refusal to reach for Heaven means an involuntary descent into Hell.

It may conceivably be possible to live without churches; but it is not possible to live without religion, that is without systematic work to keep in contact with and develop towards Higher Levels than those of "ordinary life," with all its pleasure and pain, sensation and gratification, refinement or crudity—whatever it may be. *The modern experiment to live without religion has failed*, and once we have understood this, we know what our "post-modern" tasks really are. Significantly, a large number of young people (of varying ages!) are looking in the right direction. They feel it in their bones that the ever more successful solution of convergent problems is of no help at all—it may even be a hindrance—in learning how to cope, to grapple with, the divergent problems that are the stuff of real life.

The art of living is always to make a good thing out of a bad thing. Only if we *know* that we have actually descended into infernal regions where nothing awaits us "but the cold death of society and the extinguishing of all civilised relations," can we summon the courage and imagination needed for a "turning around," a *metanoia*. This then leads to seeing the world in a new light, namely as a place where the things modern man continuously talks about and always fails to accomplish can actually be done. The generosity of the Earth allows us to feed all mankind; we know enough about ecology to keep the Earth a healthy place; there is enough room on the Earth, and there are enough materials, so that everybody can have adequate shelter; we are quite competent enough to produce sufficient supplies of necessities so that no one need live in misery. Above all, we shall then see that the economic problem is a convergent problem that has been solved already: we know how to provide enough, and do not require any violent, inhuman, aggressive technologies to do so. There is no economic problem and, in a sense, there never has been. But there is a moral problem, and moral problems are not convergent, capable of being solved so that future generations can live without effort; no, they are divergent problems, which have to be understood and transcended.

Can we rely on it that a "turning around" will be accomplished by enough people quickly enough to save the modern world? This question is often asked, but whatever answer is given to it will mislead. The answer "Yes" would lead to complacency; the answer "No" to despair. It is desirable to leave these perplexities behind us and get down to work.

E. F. Schumacher, *A Guide for the Perplexed*

Man's self-realization, his becoming human and the humanizing of society are possible only on the basis of a positive attitude in principle to the uncertain reality of world and man. Only if man's self-realization and the humanizing of society are regarded as equally urgent tasks will this attitude be more than a congenial ideology hostile to change. The acceptance of autonomous norms of the human is thus the ethical expression of fundamental trust in the identity, significance and especially the value of the uncertain reality of world and man. Without this fundamental trust, autonomous ethical norms cannot be accepted as meaningful and justified.

Hans Küng, *Does God Exist?*

The Evolutionary Cycle

Back in the sixties when we gathered we were confused as to whether we were psychotic or spiritual. We needed to gather in order to reassure ourselves that if we were psychotic at least there were a lot of us. We were freeing ourselves from a cultural model of a reality that had been considered absolute. And as we started to break free there was much melodrama: violence, anger, confusion, as well as bliss and delight. Some of the confusion came because we kept trying to make the outside different as a reflection of the fact that the inside was changing. Part of that was pure in the sense that the new inner being was manifesting a new outer being, and part of it was impure because our faith was still flickering and we needed new symbols in order to reassure ourselves that we were in fact different. Some may recall the period when men started to grow their hair long and the power of that symbol, along with communal statements and alternative economics. During the sixties we were confused between internal freedom and external freedom, between revolution and evolution, because we didn't have models in our heads that would allow us to appreciate the grandeur of the change that we were undergoing. So we kept reducing its implications and seeing it as a social, psychological, or political change.

During the late sixties and early seventies there was a period of fanaticism in our spiritual involvement. We were importing models from the East at a great rate and trying very hard to convert ourselves, but, consistent with our tradition of doing things from the outside in, although we were taking on a lot of the symbols and accoutrements and might have looked like Buddha from outside, from inside we were just somebody who was trying to look like Buddha. We were very confused about vows and commitments, the relationship to teachers, the whole concept of Guru, and what the journey was about. In the sixties the word God was still taboo, so we talked about "altered states of consciousness."

Implicit in all that we were doing was still an attachment to the fact that *we* could do it, that who we were or who we thought we were could change ourselves and become whatever it was that Buddha was or Christ was. That is, we were living in a culture in which humans ruled nature, within obvious boundaries, and we were so addicted to the rational mind and its power that we assumed we could think our way out of any predicament, we could figure out a new way to be through our thoughts and through our doing. But the predicament is that enlightenment is not an achievement; enlightenment is a transformation of being. And the achiever goes as well as the achievement.

Most of us didn't bargain for the implications of the journey we found ourselves on. We started to understand that it might have something to do with what had been talked about as "God" or a "coming to God" or, if you would rather deal with the unmanifest, the state of Nirvana. And we didn't really want them, we wanted to want them. That's a different level of the game. For most of us it has been quite enough to want to want God or to want to want enlightenment. That keeps us cool, safe, secure, with a feeling that we're moving in the right direction. It gets a little scary when you start to disappear into the Void. In *Be Here Now* we referred to it as "the crisp trip."

Now the strength in us lies in our honesty with ourselves about our predicament. We have tasted of something, we are drawn to it as a moth toward a flame, we recognize our own fear. There is less melodrama and dramatic histrionics, and we are patiently and insistently doing the purification of being necessary for this transformation to occur. Realizing that we can't grab it—we tried that—nor can we ignore it, we all tried that. We try to grab it and up we go and down we come, another high to add to our collection of moldering butterflies. We try to push it away and go back to not remembering that there is something else, and we can't do it. As we're in the middle of our intense sensual enjoyment—which we would like to get lost back into, there is always the voice which says, "You are now in the middle of your intense sensual enjoyment." We can't get in, we can't get out. And here we are.

The melodrama is passing away. We recognize now that we are bringing our external world genuinely and honestly into harmony with our inner perceptions, and we don't need to try so hard to create an external space to prove anything. We're learning not to overkill with our intellect, to think our way into holiness, because it just ends up being another prison, and we get caught pretending we're something we're not.

We are developing a deeper philosophical understanding of the predicament we are in as mutants, as evolving beings. We're listening inside to see what it is that is keeping us from that place or space or realization or connection that we have touched, tasted, felt, or somehow known about, and we are starting to find the methods to get on with the work. We have begun to understand that, though we gather as a group and listen to one another, each of us is in a unique predicament, and that we must listen to our own hearts to hear what we need; we can't imitate anybody else's journey.

To characterize these individual differences in terms of evolution, let me share with you a model that is just a model. Imagine an evolutionary clock. At twelve o'clock there is perfect harmony, "the Tao" as the Chinese say, "the Way" Christ talks about. The perfect balance, the interrelationship of all things with nothing separate, each in its proper place. The tree is the perfect tree, the river is the perfect river, the human being is the perfect human being. All is in its perfection.

At one minute after twelve, something is separate. At twelve it was the Garden of Eden: perfect harmony and balance. Then came a bite of the apple, and suddenly they're wearing fig leaves, and God is asking, "Who told you you were naked?" Where did shame come from? It came from self-consciousness. And where did self-consciousness come from? It came from identifying with our thinking mind and thus experiencing ourselves as separate from that which we think about. At 12:01 duality has been created: subject/object, thinker and that which is thought. Separateness.

From 12:01 to 6:00 there is a continuous attempt to solidify, protect, and increase the power of our position as separate entities, to create security, gratification, power over the world around us, to re-create the feeling of well-being that existed when we weren't, but now we are. Who I am talking about is us; you understand what I'm saying?

Let's just imagine that 12:00 is a sort of total perfection; although it's obviously unlabelable, we'll call it "God" but since it really is unlabelable maybe we better just call it "G-d" so we won't get confused. Now G-d has within its perfection the freedom for any entity, such as a human entity, to pit its will against the total will, or G-d's will. So at first there were beings pitting themselves against the system, against the harmony, then everybody was "us," and "them" were the forces of nature, the storms and so on. But between 12:01 and 6:00 a bizarre thing happened. Slowly "them" started to become others of us. Our tribe was "us" and other tribes were "them." Then within tribe there was the family, and pretty soon it was "our family" and everybody else was "them." And then, within the family, Uncle Dave screwed us on that business deal, so he was sort of "them"; we couldn't really even trust the greater family that much; "us" had to be our immediate family. That's around 4:30 or 5:00. Then there was a generation gap—we can't trust elders or youth—so maybe it's just me and my wife or me and my husband. And then there's a sex difference, so I can't fully consider my spouse as "us," then I'm "us" and everything else in the universe is "them." "I'm very strong, I've got my protection, I know where I am, see?" You think it would end there. But that's about 5:45. In the final fifteen minutes is what now is called the total alienation of an individual. From whom? From himself. So, finally we're looking at ourselves from outside and we don't even trust ourselves, so we're "them," too.

And what was the greatest power we had to work with in this journey from twelve to six, what was the greatest siddhi or power, that was available to us as long as we were attached to our senses and our thinking mind? It was our intellect. Look at what our intellect has done. Look at this illusion. Look at the awesome impact of technology. They are all extensions of the human mind. At the moment I'm living in Manhattan, where, except for Central Park, there isn't anything you see that hasn't been run through a human mind. It's living inside human intellect actually. And the power of the human intellect is based on discrimination, individual differences; if we can tell the difference between this and that, and we can do it better than anybody else, we get paid more. And this intellect, which now decided that it could do anything, started to create models of what it had to do in order to get into that space it remembered somewhere inside of itself as that perfect feeling of at-AUM-ness, perfect well-being. It developed a number of strategies. The most obvious one in our culture is "more is better."

Most of us have been on that journey, haven't we? On the supersensual astral planes. "Have you heard that new record by the blups? Yeah, but have you heard it when you're in the bathtub—with somebody else? Have you heard it when you're in the bathtub with somebody else by candlelight? On a good stereo set? There's an incredible wine; put it at the side of the tub: musk oil in the bath, the incense, the candlelight, the wine, the other being and the bath water is just right and on the stereo...Oh...Oh..." More is better. The obvious predicament that the intellect has a difficult time with is the sneaking realization that more is never enough. Or, more is maybe enough for a moment but it doesn't last.

If we watch the patterns of our desire systems and minds, the end of our day goes something like: "I think I'll take a nap. Gee, I'd like a cup of tea. How about a cigarette with that? I'm gonna listen to that music. What are we gonna have for dinner? What do you want for dessert, ice cream? I'm gonna have some coffee. What's on television? No, let's go bowling. Bicycle? Great. Ice cream soda? Let's go home. Okay. Want to go to bed? Okay. Ah, that's great. Got a cigarette?" On and on and in the middle of the main course, we're already thinking about what we'll have for dessert. The way we deal with this game is by constantly keeping the things going by fast, like a sleight-of-hand trick. Knowing that none of them will last, we figure that enough of them with small enough spaces in between will keep the rush going. Rush after rush after rush. But it's like building a house on sand—and we can't stop, because it gets a little frightening if we stop. If those spaces in between get too big, there is depression, confusion, disorientation, anger, loneliness, self-pity, unworthiness. Such stuff! Yech! So keep it coming, Ma. More and more and more.

But it turns out that Christ was right when he said, "Lay not up your treasures where moth and rust doth corrupt and thieves break in." Buddha was right when he said, "The cause of suffering is craving," craving after things that are not permanent, and nothing is permanent. If we cling to anything which is in form we're going to suffer. That was Buddha's point. What is blue chip, that we can invest in, that we can stop feeling frightened about? Our bodies? Our bodies are decaying at this very minute. Even the youngest person here is decaying. Fifty or sixty years from now, you know where your body will be, what it will look like? And your intellect? All the knowledge that you've collected? Did you ever see a skull and consider what's been eaten away and who ate it? And do you know what that emptiness is? That's everything you think you know. No wonder we're frightened. If we're thinking that we're our thinking mind, or that we're our body, it's panic.

From 12:00 to 6:00 is the increasing hope that we can get it all together, get it to feel just right. But there's a scariness, because we're trying to do it in a dimension that exists in time where everything changes, we're going to lose everything. At the very least we're going to die. As philosophical materialists—not materialists in gold Cadillacs, but those who are attached to the senses and intellect, and what we can think about—we are afraid because when we're dead, we're dead. As we get close to dying, we start to get very frightened and we start to push pretty hard. We say, "Doctor, you've got new pills, use them, do anything, save me, freeze-dry me, do anything, I don't want to die," and grab and hold the bedsheets and pay more and more and get more and more hysterical and get into intensive care units and keep alive even if they have to transplant everything. But no matter how hard we try, suddenly we're dead.

And then a voice says to us, "Hello." If we're philosophical materialists, this leads us to say, "I guess I didn't die." To which the voice replies, "Oh yes, you did." Just as an example, at one point Buddha with his clear vision looked back and saw his last ninety-nine thousand incarnations. And that was only a trivial amount of them. Birth-death-rebirth-redeath, on and on.

Now, in the early period, say between 12:00 and 3:00, every time we die, we're so caught in our own attachments to our senses and our minds, we're so deep in the illusion, that when somebody says we're dead, we deny it and stay in total confusion until we get sent into the next round. Which is all, as we will see, perfectly designed. Later, as we get on with this round of births and deaths, we realize our predicament. We are under the veil of illusion of the birth—we don't want to die; then we're dead, and we say, "Far out, there goes another one." At this point we look around and we see all our old mothers and fathers and friends. "Oh, my, you were my wife this time, last time you were my brother."

When we're more conscious, we share in the understanding of where we are situated on the clock, in the round of births and deaths. We begin to see exactly what the next birth has to do from a karmic point of view, what it has to work out. And when we design the next birth, we say, "Well, I think I should be born into the lower middle class in New York City, and then around ten I think I should get raped, that would be useful for that particular samskara, that deeply imbedded mental impression, that I've been working out from four thousand births back. Let's see. I'll have my first child when I'm eighteen," and on and on. We design it all the way through—up until how we'll die. We've run it all through the computer, the right parents come together, the right combinations have come up, comes the moment of birth. And there we go. We dive back down in.

Some beings enter into this trip at the moment of conception, others at the moment of birth. You can tell those babies that entered at the moment of birth—the baby comes into the world and has that kind of stoned-out look, like what the hell am I doing here? Like an old lama who has been born, say, in the Bronx, and he would like to bless everybody, but he can't get it to work. The ones that entered in at the moment of conception are busy being babies already. "Waaaaaa, give me." Those that come in bliss, because the veil hasn't shut down yet, are most of the time around parents who are busy inside the veil saying, "You're a baby, you're a baby. Goo-goo, look at the little baby." Pretty soon you buy it, and there you are again. On and on and on and on. Until something interesting happens at six o'clock, or one minute past six. Up until then, in every birth we've gone back into the illusion that we are this body, we are this thinking mind, we are these senses. Everything we think we could get is what we can sense and think about; we're grabbing, looking out and down. Grabbing and grabbing and grabbing, and then suddenly at one birth there is a moment when the veil parts—albeit for just a second—and we stick our noses through, and we say, "Wow, it isn't how I thought it was at all." Maybe the veil parted for a millisecond, but that was all it took if we were ready. The veil is parting all the time for everybody, but most of the time our karma is so heavy, and we're so used to the veil, that we're not ready, so that the minute we do see through, we immediately deny it or push it away as hard as we can. Some years back, I read in the *New York Times* magazine an article on "Mysticism in America," which said that two-fifths of the population of the United States has had a genuine mystic transcendent experience, which means they saw through the veil. In sampling that two-fifths of the population, eighty-five percent said, "It was the greatest experience of my life, but I never want to have it again." Of course not, because look at how it upsets the apple cart. If we've built a whole universe around being somebody, and suddenly we see that that isn't who we are at all, what then?

But what is the condition necessary so that the moment comes when we see through the veil in a way that changes everything from then on, so that from 6:01 to 12:00 our whole journey changes its meaning? The condition necessary for that to happen is that despair, the realization that everything we think we can do to create perfection isn't going to be enough, that who we are and who we think we are is where the problem lies. It leads to a deep despair that seems to be a necessary condition for us to awaken at that moment. Once we have seen and know we have seen, we can never totally go back to sleep again. Even though we may forget for moments—and we will go through many, many more births from 6:01 to 12:00—we can never fully forget. We are starting to be drawn back to twelve o'clock.

I'm talking about a clock of births and deaths which is all in time, which is all an illusion or relatively real, but we're just workings with this metaphor for a moment. The nature of the beings in tune with these words are by definition after six o'clock. Otherwise there'd be no reason for you to have read this far. Maybe you're a 4:13, but why would you put up with this long rap then when you could be out getting more which is better. But you know something, and you're trapped in what you know, and look at what it's led you to. And it gets worse; that's what's so extraordinary about it: Once we start at one minute past six the return journey to 12:00, we're trying to grab at experiences that are going to get us back. We're going to collect new experiences that are called "getting high." We come down from something and we treat that down as the time between the last time we got high and the next time when once again we'll get on with our journey to God or back to 12:00 or whatever we want to call it. As the experiential clock ticks on, we keep developing in our understanding of how it's all working, and we begin to recognize a peculiar phenomenon that, as C. S. Lewis points out, "You don't see the center of the universe because it's all center." That we, in fact, are the center of a universe which has been designed perfectly in order to awaken us out of the illusion and that every experience we have is equally valid as grist for the mill of awakening. Our whole incarnation is the teaching.

Next we begin to realize that although they are all equal in teaching quality, some of our experiences seem to shake us more than others, that the model which we are stuck in, sometimes so subtly we don't even know it, is shaken by pain and suffering and all the negative qualities. At that point we recognize the bizarre phenomenon that suffering is grace. Now that's heavy, because up until that time, we've been trying to optimize pleasure and minimize pain. When we realize that in its fullest dimension, we may still live to optimize pleasure and minimize pain, but whatever comes down the pike is all right. "Boy, am I depressed." Now, there's depression. Until finally "There's pleasure." "There's pain." "I just made a thousand dollars. Wow." Or, "Oh, I just got robbed." And the "Wow" and the "Oh" and the "Ah" and the "Uhh," all of these alternatives are just more stuff, beautiful, delightful stuff. This incarnation is the absolutely optimal one which we must be in now in order to do what needs to be done, or have done through us what needs to be done, in order to bring us home, bring us Aum, or out or in. It's happening whether we know it or not. But as we know it, it changes it, that's part of it, that's all karma, too.

Along around 10:00 or 11:00, we're going into other planes of reality in our meditation, and they are equally as real as the plane that we started this incarnation in. We don't quite understand where we are. Sometimes we get confused. It's very uneven and complicated work. But if we're really aiming at perfected truth, we move at a rate at which we can keep it all perfectly together. We work for the perfect balance of the different planes. At one minute past six we started to awaken and got so fascinated with what we started to see we couldn't take our eyes off it, and forgot to look down and we fell on our faces. We started to study the "absolute truths of God," and got so fascinated with the impersonal perfection of the universe beyond all polarities, we were so involved in the icy cold impersonality of it all that we kept stepping on things and we looked and said, "Well so what, it's all perfect." But we learn the simple rule of the game is that as long as we push away one plane to grab another, we're still off balance. Ultimately, we understand that the truth must be balanced with the caring, with the honoring of this incarnation. That's when we start to develop the capacity to look up and to look down at the same moment. To look in and to look out.

When we look at pure truth, we can see the grace that suffering is. From our point of view, when we're suffering, "Fine, I'm suffering, that's interesting." At the same moment if we are looking down and honoring our incarnation, we're working to alleviate suffering. Let me give you an example. Somebody says, "I want to study yoga with you. I want to fast." And you say, "All right, fast for nine days." At the end of the seventh day they say, "I've fasted for seven days." And you say, "Wonderful, wonderful. You've got two more days to go." Then you walk outside the building and somebody comes up to you and says, "Hey man, you got a quarter, I haven't eaten in seven days." You don't say, "Wonderful, wonderful, you have two more days to go." It's not an appropriate response, because for that being, suffering isn't grace, suffering is a drag.

When that discipline is developed to allow us to look up and look down simultaneously, we have the absolute clarity of the pure white snow on the Himalayan peaks, the exquisite clarity, raw truth, the impersonal perfection which includes everything—Vietnam, Cambodia, Bangladesh, Biafra, persecution in our cities, inequality, violence, as well as all the bliss and love and compassion and kindness—the entire mosaic. In the icy peaks of the Himalayas, we see the perfection of it all in the evolutionary journey of beings. And at the same moment the caring part of us is like the bleeding heart of Jesus and we look down and see the blood on the snow. We keep both of those in mind at every moment, so we can help beings that are suffering in the way they need to be helped.

If we are really going to help them get out of the illusion, we ourselves must not get lost in the illusion. We must continue to keep our eyes fixed on absolutely clear truth. We love without clinging; we help without being identified as the helper; we protest without getting lost in our protests; we care for our children remembering that, behind it all, here we are: the truth, the caring. We honor our bodies; we honor our society; we honor our whole game; we change it in the way it needs to be changed. We listen to hear what our particular karmic predicaments are in this round, and we find our dharma, the way to live this life in perfect harmony with the forces inside and outside of us in order to bring us home.

If we get greedy and try to push or pull, we're going to fall on our faces. If we go up to sit in a cave, we'll become so holy that light will be pouring out of our heads, everybody will be falling at our feet, and we'll have great powers. But we try coming into New York City and we will see that there are little seeds inside of us, as Ramakrishna talks about, that never quite got cooked. It's an interesting point of view when we say, "Hey, I can't stand to live in the city, I've got to live out in the country." All we're saying is, "I can't stand those things in myself that the city fans." Believe me, if there's nothing that we want, the city is the same as the Himalayan peak. All the city is showing us is stuff in ourselves that we wish we didn't have.

As we get further along in this journey, the pull of twelve o'clock gets so fierce and we want to get done so bad that we can taste it, and, at that point, we say, "Give me the fire. I want a hot fire. Make it hotter, hotter. Come on, give it to me." Then, when somebody gets us furious, we know that the only reason we got angry is because we have a secret hidden model of how we think it ought to be that we're holding on to. We realize that the person that got us angry is a teaching, and in our minds we thank him. We get so eager to root out the stuff in us that's keeping us from getting on, from awakening, that we start to look for situations to force us to do it.

A couple of years ago I spent nine days in a seshin, a Zen Buddhist retreat. It was without doubt a miserable, horrible, cruel, sadistic experience....I got sick. I was paranoid. They sucked me in, they seduced me on my ego, making me feel like I could do it. Then, I got there and they didn't even give me a reward of saying, "Ram Dass, welcome." A guy met me with a clipboard and said, "Dass, Ram; you'll be in the upper bunk in Cabin Three. Here is your robe. Report to the zendo in five minutes." There was a fellow with a stick, and unless you sat in perfect form—which was really uncomfortable—you got beaten. And I was paying money for this! If you tilted, this really fierce character would come up and he'd bow to you, then you'd bow to him, and then you'd lean over to the side and he'd beat you on one shoulder and then you'd lean over the other way and he'd beat you on the other shoulder, and you'd thank him and he'd thank you. Five times a day, you'd go in to see the Roshi, a tough Japanese fellow, bald headed. He had a bell and a stick and he'd ask you ridiculous questions like, "How do you know your Buddha-nature from the sound of clapping hands?" And you'd answer something or other which you'd been thinking about the whole time you were sitting there, knowing you had four more to go yet today. And he'd say, "Oh, Doctor, you're not doing it right at all. Maybe we should give you your money back, you leave. I had great hopes for you. You're very important, people know you, you're very famous, but you don't seem to understand this, I think you'd better forget it."

Then he rings his bell and you leave and you're crushed. Not only are you crushed but you have to run back to the place to sit up so as not to get beaten. This goes on from two in the morning until ten at night. There's no edge. I spent five days plotting how to be called away on an emergency, some face-saving device. I even tried to hide in the bathroom, but they checked the bathroom. There was simply no place to hide.

Finally, by the fifth day, I didn't give a damn about the Roshi or the whole scene. I went in kind of slouching, thinking "The hell with it, let them throw me out," and he said, "Doctor, how do you know your Buddha-nature through clapping hands?" And I said, "Good morning, Roshi." He said, "AH!!" He was delighted, and smiled and then, lest it go to my head, he said, "Now you are becoming a beginning student of Zen!"

Well, it was interesting because just before that, just as I was walking up the path and saying "Screw it," fire started to pour out of all the bushes and the whole sky became radiant, and I went into this other state. It was like I had been released from this incredible sickness and tension and I went in and I was having a satori experience. And he kept asking me koan after koan and the answers kept coming right out. I was right in the moment and there were no models in my mind. And we just went higher and higher together and we were both just spinning out.

From then on the rest of the nine days was ecstasy. The sittings were beautiful and I was just floating. Suddenly, the perfection of the emptiness of the forms and the impersonality, became my freedom. Had I come to the seshin and had they said, "Oh, Ram Dass, we're so happy," and had I known who everybody was, it would have occupied my mind in a way that I was freed from by the total impersonality of the whole scene.

It's just like any meditation when it's not all bliss and light and we're uncomfortable and it's hot and we're bored and our butts hurt and all that. It's all the same as that seshin. But we do it because there's something we want bad enough to go through it, to struggle against the forces in us that just want "more." That's what the *Bhagavad Gita* is about, the battle inside between those two forces. Right until the very end it's hell. It doesn't get any better, it gets worse because the fire gets hotter and hotter.

You see, once we decide that we really want to go for broke, for per-fected truth, once we're being pulled that way in our guts and we finally say, "I don't want anything else, I just want to go" (which is usually a lie, but we're still saying it), that pull, that reaching, draws down upon us all kinds of forces which help that thing happen. That's called grace. There are many beings, both on this plane and on other planes, that are available to guide us and help us, but they don't come unless we want them. Our reaching elicits their help.

The teaching gets fiercer, the fire gets hotter, we start to do it to ourselves because the pull of God is deeper and deeper. At that point just before twelve on our evolutionary clock the entire universe is within us and we experience all of the suffering that is connected with form on any plane of existence. We are one with it. By that time, we have worked out all our personal karma or clinging. Now we're aware of the collective nature of the karma. Right at that moment the pull to twelve o'clock is incredible. To go into twelve o'clock means that we merge back in, we as consciously separate entities cease. Everything that went on from one minute past twelve until 11:59 was designed for this moment of choice. If we want to be God at this moment, we can merge back in, but it doesn't matter what choice we make. That may be scary because we wanted it to matter. Most of us are so caught in righteousness we're afraid of truth. Righteousness would say it matters at 11:59 but truth says it doesn't matter. At 11:59 we have the choice of going back into God, in which case, if we had left bodies, they would just sort of disintegrate because there was nobody in them, or we can stay back in form on this or another plane. Why would we do it? This is free will in the true sense of free will, not the illusion of free will that we have, for there is no individual karma in this. The only reason a totally free being would choose to stay within the illusion is in order to relieve the suffering of all beings. This is the time when the vow that's known as "the Bodhisattva Vow" is taken. This is the only moment it's real. Up until then it's phony—it's our karma working out. The moment we choose to come back, we have to push against that force that is drawing us in to merge. We are pushing against God. That is the sacrifice. The sacrifice that Christ made is not the crucifixion. The chance for a conscious being to leave his body is bliss. The sacrifice was leaving the Father in the first place and becoming the Son. Free beings, realized perfected beings, have that free choice. They are here only because of us, and I mean us, because otherwise we wouldn't meet them. Anybody they meet is by design part of what they're doing to relieve suffering. They are here only as instruments to bring through that non-clinging, non-attached truth, to create a mirror against which we can see where we're holding our secret stash of stuff that is keeping us from being perfected also. These are the beings that bestow the grace. They are the Gods and Goddesses and Gurus on all planes. Everyone has one of these helpers specifically designed for his or her karma, but most never meet them in this lifetime because they never reach out.

Every night Buddha would look over all the realms, the Buddha-fields, to see who was ready, who looked up, who was reaching, who said, "I want to get out," who says "Know me, let me out, I'm ready, let's go." Not wanting to want, not phony wanting, but wanting. If we don't reach out, nothing happens. For whom is the despair deep enough?

This game is designed so that within the illusion where we think there is free will, we've got to reach for it. And we only reach for it when our karma allows us to reach for it. See the predicament? The only real free will there was in the whole clock was at twelve o'clock to one minute past twelve—the free will to go against the system—and at 11:59 to go back into the system. Otherwise all of it was determined by law.

Keep in mind the entire clock is in the realm of metaphor, or relative reality. At twelve o'clock we never were, nothing has happened, nobody is. To answer the question of why did it all begin, one of the answers is it never did. It's just a play of mind, just a play of mind. People who have come this far in this transmission are everywhere between one minute past six and 11:59 and because of the nature of our attachments we can only see what we can see. We might be sitting next to an 11:59er, and we wouldn't know it, because he doesn't have a sign on him, and the ones that do have signs on them usually aren't, because they wrote them themselves. It might turn out that your Aunt Thelma was Buddha. She was cooking chicken soup and you went to India and Tibet for forty years looking for somebody that looked like Buddha. You got totally despairing and in the despair you gave up all your hope and all your models. You came home and you walked in and there she was. You look and you fall on your face before this brilliant light and she says, "Have some soup." The pure Buddha, the mind that is clear of attachment, exists anywhere in perfect harmony with all the forces around it.

And to complete this clock image I might add that for some of us it has become time to awaken and for others it's later than we think.

Ram Dass, *Grist for the Mill*

Conditions for the Coming of a Spiritual Age

Like all other great changes the change from the mental and vital
to the spiritual order of life must come first in an individual or a
limited number of individuals and then in a great and growing
number of individuals.

Therefore if the spiritual change of which we have been speaking is to be effected, it must unite two conditions which have to be simultaneously satisfied but are most difficult to bring together. There must be the individual and the individuals who are able to see, to develop, to re-create themselves in the image of the Spirit and to communicate both their idea and its power to the mass. And there must be at the same time a mass, a society, a communal mind or at the least the constituents of a group-body, the possibility of a group-soul which is capable of receiving and effectively assimilating, ready to follow and effectively arrive, not compelled by its own inherent deficiencies, its defect of preparation to stop on the way or fall back before the decisive change is made. Such a simultaneity has never yet happened, although the appearance of it has sometimes been created by the ardour of a moment. That the combination must happen some day is a certainty, but none can tell how many attempts will have to be made and how many sediments of spiritual experience will have to be accumulated in the subconscient mentality of the communal human being before the soil is ready. For the chances of success are always less powerful in a difficult upward effort affecting the very roots of our nature than the numerous possibilities of failure. The initiator himself may be imperfect, may not have waited to become entirely the thing that he has seen. Even the few who have the apostolate in their charge may not have perfectly assimilated and shaped it in themselves and may hand on the power of the Spirit still further diminished to the many who will come after them. The society may be intellectually, vitally, ethically, temperamentally unready, with the result that the final acceptance of the spiritual idea by the society may be also the beginning of its debasement and distortion and of the consequent departure or diminution of the Spirit. Any or all of these things may happen, and the result will be, as has so often happened in the past, that even though some progress is made and an important change effected, it will not be the decisive change which can alone re-create humanity in a diviner image.

> What is needed is the preparedness of the common mind of man.
> And here the first essential sign would be the growth of the subjective idea of life which, again, is not sufficient.

A subjective age may stop very far short of spirituality; for the subjective turn is only a first condition, not the thing itself, not the end of the matter. The search for the Reality, the true self of man, may very easily follow out the natural order described by the Upanishad in the profound apologue of the seekings of Bhrigu, son of Varuna. For first the seeker found the ultimate reality to be Matter and the physical, the material being, the external man our only self and spirit. Next he fixed on Life as the Reality and the vital being as the self and spirit; in the third essay on Mind and the mental being;

only afterwards could he get beyond the superficial subjective through the supramental Truth-Consciousness to the eternal, the blissful, the ever creative Reality of which these are the sheaths. But humanity may not be as persistent or as plastic as the son of Varuna, the search may stop short anywhere.

The true secret can only be discovered if in the third stage, in an age of mental subjectivism, the idea becomes strong of the Mind itself as no more than a secondary power of the Spirit's working and of the Spirit as the great Eternal, the original and, in spite of the many terms in which it is both expressed and hidden, the sole reality, *ayam ātmā brahma*. Then only will the real, the decisive endeavour begin and life and the world be studied, known, dealt with in all directions as the self-finding and self-expression of the Spirit. Then only will a spiritual age of mankind be possible. To attempt any adequate discussion of what that would mean, and in an inadequate discussion there is no fruit, would need another volume or two of essays; for we should have to examine a knowledge which is rare and nowhere more than initial. It is enough to say that a spiritual human society would start from and try to realise three essential truths of existence which all Nature seems to be an attempt to hide by their opposites and which therefore are as yet for the mass of mankind only words and dreams, God, freedom, unity. Three things which are one, for you cannot realise freedom and unity unless you realise God, you cannot possess freedom and unity unless you possess God, possess at once your highest self and the self of all creatures. The freedom and unity which otherwise go by that name, are simply attempts of our subjection and our division to get away from themselves by shutting their eyes while they turn somersaults around their own centre. When man is able to see God and to possess him, then he will know real freedom and arrive at real unity, never otherwise. And God is only waiting to be known, while man seeks for him everywhere and creates images of the Divine, but all the while truly finds, effectively erects and worships images only of his own mind-ego and life-ego. When this ego pivot is abandoned and this ego-hunt ceases, then man gets his first real chance of achieving spirituality in his inner and outer life. It will not be enough, but it will be a commencement, a true gate and not a blind entrance.

A spiritualised society would live like its spiritual individuals, not in the ego, but in the spirit, not as the collective ego, but as the collective soul. This freedom from the egoistic standpoint would be its first and most prominent characteristic. But the elimination of egoism would not be brought about, as it is now proposed to bring it about, by persuading or forcing the individual to immolate his personal will and aspirations and his precious and hard-won individuality to the collective will, aims and egoism of the society, driving him like a victim of ancient sacrifice to slay his soul on the altar of that huge and shapeless idol. For that would be only the sacrifice of the smaller to the larger egoism, larger only in bulk, not necessarily greater in quality or wider or nobler, since a collective egoism, result of the united egoisms of all, is as little a god to be worshipped, as flawed and often an uglier and more barbarous fetish than the egoism of the individual. What the spiritual man seeks is to find by the loss of the ego the Self which is one in all and perfect and complete in each and by living in that to grow into the image of its perfection,—individually, be it noted, though with an all-embracing universality of his nature and its conscious circumference. It is said in the old Indian writings that while in the second age, the age of Power, Vishnu descends in the King, and in the third, the age of balance, as the legislator or codifier, in the age of the Truth he descends as Yajna, that is to say, as the Master of works manifest in the heart of his creatures. It is this kingdom of God within, the result of the finding of God not in a distant heaven but within ourselves, of which the state of society in an age of the Truth, spiritual age, would be the result and the external figure.

Therefore a society which was even initially spiritualised, would make the revealing and finding of the divine Self in man the whole first aim of all its activities, its education, its knowledge, its science, its ethics, its art, its economical and political structure. As it was to some extent in the ancient Vedic times with the cultural education of the higher classes, so it would be then with all education. It would embrace all knowledge in its scope, but would make the whole trend and aim and the permeating spirit not mere worldly efficiency, but this self-developing and self-finding. It would pursue physical and psychical science not in order merely to know the world and Nature in her processes and to use them for material human ends, but to know through and in and under and over all things the Divine in the world and the ways of the Spirit in its masks and behind them. It would make it the aim of ethics not to establish a rule of action whether supplementary to the social law or partially corrective of it, the social law that is after all only the rule, often clumsy and ignorant, of the biped pack, the human herd, but to develop the divine nature in the human being. It would make it the aim of Art not merely to present images of the subjective and objective world, but to see them with the significant and creative vision that goes behind their appearances and to reveal the Truth and Beauty of which things visible to us and invisible are the forms, the masks or the symbols and significant figures.

A spiritualised society would treat in its sociology the individual, from the saint to the criminal, not as units of a social problem to be passed through some skilfully devised machinery and either flattened into the social mould or crushed out of it, but as souls suffering and entangled in a net and to be rescued, souls growing and to be encouraged to grow, souls grown and from whom help and power can be drawn by the lesser spirits who are not yet

adult. The aim of its economics would be not to create a huge engine of production, whether of the competitive or the co-operative kind, but to give to
men—not only to some but to all men each in his highest possible measure—
the joy of work according to their own nature and free leisure to grow
inwardly, as well as a simply rich and beautiful life for all. In its politics it
would not regard the nations within the scope of their own internal life as
enormous State machines regulated and armoured with man living for the
sake of the machine and worshipping it as his God and his larger self, content at the first call to kill others upon its altar and to bleed there himself so
that the machine may remain intact and powerful and to be made ever
larger, more complex, more cumbrous, more mechanically efficient and
entire. Neither would it be content to maintain these nations or States in
their mutual relations as noxious engines meant to discharge poisonous gas
upon each other in peace and to rush in times of clash upon each other's
armed hosts and unarmed millions, full of belching shot and men missioned
to murder like hostile tanks in a modern battlefield. It would regard the peoples as group-souls, the Divinity concealed and to be self-discovered in its
human collectivities, group-souls meant like the individual to grow according to their own nature and by that growth to help each other, to help the
whole race in the one common work of humanity. And that work would be
to find the divine Self in the individual and the collectivity and to realise spiritually, mentally, vitally, materially, its greatest, largest, richest and deepest
possibilities in the inner life of all and their outer action and nature.

For it is into the Divine within each man and each people that the man
and the nation have to grow; it is not an external idea or rule that has to be
imposed on them from without. Therefore the law of a growing inner freedom is that which will be most honoured in the spiritual age of mankind.
True it is that so long as man has not come within measurable distance of self-
escape from the law of external compulsion and all his efforts to do so must
be vain. He is and always must be, so long as that lasts, the slave of others, the
slave of his family, his caste, his clan, his Church, his society, his nation; and
he cannot but be that and they too cannot help throwing their crude and
mechanical compulsion on him, because he and they are the slaves of their
own ego, of their own lower nature. We must feel and obey the compulsion
of the Spirit if we would establish our inner right to escape other compulsion;
we must make our lower nature the willing slave, the conscious and illumined instrument or the ennobled but still self-subjected portion, consort or
partner of the divine Being within us, for it is that subjection which is the condition of our freedom, since spiritual freedom is not the egoistic assertion of
our separate mind and life but obedience to the Divine Truth in ourself and
our members and in all around us. But we have, even so, to remark that God

respects the freedom of the natural members of our being and that he gives them room to grow in their own nature so that by natural growth and not by self-extinction they may find the Divine in themselves. The subjection which they finally accept, complete and absolute, must be a willing subjection of recognition and aspiration to their own source of light and power and their highest being. Therefore even in the unregenerated state we find that the healthiest, the truest, the most living growth and action is that which arises in the largest possible freedom and that all excess of compulsion is either the law of a gradual atrophy or a tyranny varied or cured by outbreaks of rabid disorder. And as soon as man comes to know his spiritual self, he does by that discovery, often even by the very seeking for it, as ancient thought and religion saw, escape from the outer law and enter into the law of freedom.

A spiritual age of mankind will perceive this truth. It will not try to make man perfect by machinery or keep him straight by tying up all his limbs. It will not present to the member of the society his higher self in the person of the policeman, the official and the corporal, nor, let us say, in the form of a socialistic bureaucracy or a Labour Soviet. Its aim will be to diminish as soon and as far as possible the element of external compulsion in human life by awakening the inner divine compulsion of the Spirit within and all the preliminary means it will use will have that for its aim. In the end it will employ chiefly if not solely the spiritual compulsion which even the spiritual individual can exercise on those around him,—and how much more should a spiritual society be able to do it,—that which awakens within us in spite of all inner resistance and outer denial the compulsions of the Light, the desire and the power to grow through one's own nature into the Divine. For the perfectly spiritualised society will be one in which, as is dreamed by the spiritual anarchist, all men will be deeply free, and it will be so because the preliminary condition will have been satisfied. In that state each man will be not a law to himself, but *the* law, the divine Law, because he will be a soul living in the Divine and not an ego living mainly if not entirely for its own interest and purpose. His life will be led by the law of his own divine nature liberated from the ego.

Nor will that mean a breaking up of all human society into the isolated action of individuals; for the third word of the Spirit is unity. The spiritual life is the flower not of a featureless but a conscious and diversified oneness. Each man has to grow into the Divine within himself through his own individual being, therefore is a certain growing measure of freedom a necessity of the being as it develops and perfect freedom the sign and the condition of the perfect life. But also, the Divine whom he thus sees in himself, he sees equally in all others and as the same Spirit in all. Therefore too is a growing inner unity with others a necessity of his being and perfect unity the sign and condition of the perfect life. Not only to see and find the Divine in oneself, but to see and find the Divine in all, not only to seek one's own individual liberation or perfection, but to seek the liberation and perfection of others is the complete law of the spiritual being. If the divinity sought were a separate godhead within oneself and not the one Divine, or if one sought God for oneself alone, then indeed the result might be a grandiose egoism, the Olympian egoism of a Goethe or the Titanic egoism imagined by Nietzsche, or it might be the isolated self-knowledge or asceticism of the ivory tower or the Stylites pillar. But he who sees God in all, will serve freely God in all with the service of love. He will, that is to say, seek not only his own freedom, but the freedom of all. He will not feel his individuality perfect except in the largest universality, nor his own life to be full life except as it is one with the universal life. He will not live either for himself or for the State and society, for the individual ego or the collective ego, but for something much greater, for God in himself and for the Divine in the universe.

The spiritual age will be ready to set in when the common mind of man begins to be alive to these truths and to be moved or desire to be moved by this triple or triune Spirit. That will mean the turning of the cycle of social development which we have been considering out of its incomplete repetitions on a new upward line towards its goal. For having set out, according to our supposition, with a symbolic age, an age in which man felt a great Reality behind all life which he sought through symbols, it will reach an age in which it will begin to live in that Reality, not through the symbol, not by the power of the type or of the convention or of the individual reason and intellectual will, but in our own highest nature which will be the nature of that Reality fulfilled in the conditions—not necessarily the same as now—of terrestrial existence. This is what the religions have seen with a more or less adequate intuition, but most often as in a glass darkly, that which they called the kingdom of God on earth,—his kingdom within in men's spirit and therefore, for the one is the material result of the effectivity of the other, his kingdom without in the life of the peoples.

> *A change of this kind, the change from the mental and vital to the spiritual order of life, must necessarily be accomplished in the individual and in a great number of individuals before it can lay any effective hold upon the community. The Spirit in humanity discovers, develops, builds into form in the individual man: it is through the progressive and formative individual that it offers the discovery and the chance of a new self-creation to the mind of the race.*

Sri Aurobindo, *Human Unity and the Spiritual Age*

Buddhist Economics

"Right Livelihood" is one of the requirements of the Buddha's Noble Eight-fold Path. It is clear, therefore, that there must be such a thing as Buddhist economics.

Buddhist countries have often stated that they wish to remain faithful to their heritage. So Burma: "The New Burma sees no conflict between religious values and economic progress. Spiritual health and material well-being are not enemies: they are natural allies." Or: "We can blend successfully the religious and spiritual values of our heritage with the benefits of modern technology." Or: "We Burmans have a sacred duty to conform both our dreams and our acts to our faith. This we shall ever do."

All the same, such countries invariably assume that they can model their economic development plans in accordance with modern economics, and they call upon modern economists from so-called advanced countries to advise them, to formulate the policies to be pursued, and to construct the grand design for development, the Five-Year Plan or whatever it may be called. No one seems to think that a Buddhist way of life would call for Buddhist economics, just as the modern materialist way of life has brought forth modern economics.

Economists themselves, like most specialists, normally suffer from a kind of metaphysical blindness, assuming that theirs is a science of absolute and invariable truths, without any presuppositions. Some go as far as to claim that economic laws are as free from "metaphysics" or "values" as the law of gravitation. We need not, however, get involved in arguments of methodology. Instead, let us take some fundamentals and see what they look like when viewed by a modern economist and a Buddhist economist.

There is universal agreement that a fundamental source of wealth is human labour. Now, the modern economist has been brought up to consider "labour" or work as little more than a necessary evil. From the point of view of the employer, it is in any case simply an item of cost, to be reduced to a minimum if it cannot be eliminated altogether, say, by automation. From the point of view of the workman, it is a "disutility"; to work is to make a sacrifice of one's leisure and comfort, and wages are a kind of compensation for the sacrifice. Hence the ideal from the point of view of the employer is to have output without employees, and the ideal from the point of view of the employee is to have income without employment.

The consequences of these attitudes both in theory and in practice are, of course, extremely far-reaching. If the ideal with regard to work is to get rid of it, every method that "reduces the work load" is a good thing. The most potent method, short of automation, is the so-called division of labour and the classical example is the pin factory eulogised in Adam Smith's *Wealth of Nations*. Here it is not a matter of ordinary specialisation, which mankind has practised from time immemorial, but of dividing up every complete process of production into minute parts, so that the final product can be produced at great speed without anyone having had to contribute more than a totally insignificant and, in most cases, unskilled movement of his limbs.

The Buddhist point of view takes the function of work to be at least threefold: to give a man a chance to utilise and develop his faculties; to enable him to overcome his egocentredness by joining with other people in a common task; and to bring forth the goods and services needed for a becoming existence. Again, the consequences that flow from this view are endless. To organise work in such a manner that it becomes meaningless, boring, stultifying, or nerve-racking for the worker would be little short of criminal; it would indicate a greater concern with goods than with people, an evil lack of compassion and a soul-destroying degree of attachment to the most primitive side of this worldly existence. Equally, to strive for leisure as an alternative to work would be considered a complete misunderstanding of one of the basic truths of human existence, namely that work and leisure are complementary parts of the same living process and cannot be separated without destroying the joy of work and the bliss of leisure.

From the Buddhist point of view, there are therefore two types of mechanisation which must be clearly distinguished: one that enhances a man's skill and power and one that turns the work of man over to a mechanical slave, leaving man in a position of having to serve the slave. How to tell the one from the other? "The craftsman himself," says Ananda Coomaraswamy, a man equally competent to talk about the modern west as the ancient east, "can always, if allowed to, draw the delicate distinction between the machine and the tool. The carpet loom is a tool, a contrivance for holding warp threads at a stretch for the pile to be woven round them by the craftsmen's fingers; but the power loom is a machine, and its significance as a destroyer of culture lies in the fact that it does the essentially human part of the work." It is clear, therefore, that Buddhist economics must be very different from the economics of modern materialism, since the Buddhist sees the essence of civilisation not in a multiplication of wants but in the purification of human character. Character, at the same time, is formed primarily by a man's work. And work, properly conducted in conditions of human dignity and freedom, blesses those who do it and equally their products. The Indian philosopher and economist J. C. Kumarappa sums the matter up as follows:

"If the nature of the work is properly appreciated and applied, it will stand in the same relation to the higher faculties as food is to the physical body. It nourishes and enlivens the higher man and urges him to produce the best he is capable of. It directs his free will along the proper course and disciplines the animal in him into progressive channels. It furnishes an excellent background for man to display his scale of values and develop his personality."

If a man has no chance of obtaining work he is in a desperate position, not simply because he lacks an income but because he lacks this nourishing and enlivening factor of disciplined work which nothing can replace. A modern economist may engage in highly sophisticated calculations on whether full employment "pays" or whether it might be more "economic" to run an economy at less than full employment so as to ensure a greater mobility of labour, a better stability of wages, and so forth. His fundamental criterion of success is simply the total quantity of goods produced during a given period of time. "If the marginal urgency of goods is low," says Professor Galbraith in *The Affluent Society*, "then so is the urgency of employing the last man or the last million men in the labour force." And again: "If...we can afford some unemployment in the interest of stability—a proposition, incidentally, of impeccably conservative antecedents—then we can afford to give those who are unemployed the goods that enable them to sustain their accustomed standard of living."

From a Buddhist point of view, this is standing the truth on its head by considering goods as more important than people and consumption as more important than creative activity. It means shifting the emphasis from the worker to the product of work, that is, from the human to the sub-human, a surrender to the forces of evil. The very start of Buddhist economic planning would be a planning for full employment, and the primary purpose of this would in fact be employment for everyone who needs an "outside" job: it would not be the maximisation of employment nor the maximisation of production. Women, on the whole, do not need an "outside" job, and the large-scale employment of women in offices or factories would be considered a sign of serious economic failure. In particular, to let mothers of young children work in factories while the children run wild would be as uneconomic in the eyes of a Buddhist economist as the employment of a skilled worker as a soldier in the eyes of a modern economist.

While the materialist is mainly interested in goods, the Buddhist is mainly interested in liberation. But Buddhism is "The Middle Way" and therefore in no way antagonistic to physical well-being. It is not wealth that stands in the way of liberation but the attachment to wealth; not the enjoyment of pleasurable things but the craving for them. The keynote of Buddhist economics, therefore, is simplicity and non-violence. From an economist's point of view, the marvel of the Buddhist way of life is the utter rationality of its pattern—amazingly small means leading to extraordinarily satisfactory results.

For the modern economist this is very difficult to understand. He is used to measuring the "standard of living" by the amount of annual consumption, assuming all the time that a man who consumes more is "better off" than a man who consumes less. A Buddhist economist would consider this approach excessively irrational: since consumption is merely a means to human well-being, the aim should be to obtain the maximum of well-being with the minimum of consumption. Thus, if the purpose of clothing is a certain amount of temperature comfort and an attractive appearance, the task is to attain this purpose with the smallest possible effort, that is, with the smallest annual destruction of cloth and with the help of designs that involve the smallest possible input of toil. The less toil there is, the more time and strength is left for artistic creativity. It would be highly uneconomic, for instance, to go in for complicated tailoring, like the modern west, when a much more beautiful effect can be achieved by the skilful draping of uncut material. It would be the height of folly to make material so that it should wear out quickly and the height of barbarity to make anything ugly, shabby, or mean. What has just been said about clothing applies equally to all other human requirements. The ownership and the consumption of goods is a means to an end, and Buddhist economics is the systematic study of how to attain given ends with the minimum means.

Modern economics, on the other hand, considers consumption to be the sole end and purpose of all economic activity, taking the factors of production—land, labour, and capital—as the means. The former, in short, tries to maximise human satisfactions by the optimal pattern of consumption, while the latter tries to maximise consumption by the optimal pattern of productive effort. It is easy to see that the effort needed to sustain a way of life which seeks to attain the optimal pattern of consumption is likely to be much smaller than the effort needed to sustain a drive for maximum consumption. We need not be surprised, therefore, that the pressure and strain of living is very much less in, say, Burma than it is in the United States, in spite of the fact that the amount of labour-saving machinery used in the former country is only a minute fraction of the amount used in the latter.

Simplicity and non-violence are obviously closely related. The optimal pattern of consumption, producing a high degree of human satisfaction by means of a relatively low rate of consumption, allows people to live without great pressure and strain and to fulfil the primary injunction of Buddhist teaching: "Cease to do evil; try to do good." As physical resources are everywhere limited, people satisfying their needs by means of a modest use of resources are obviously less likely to be at each other's throats than people depending upon a high rate of use. Equally, people who live in highly self-sufficient local communities are less likely to get involved in large-scale violence than people whose existence depends on world-wide systems of trade.

From the point of view of Buddhist economics, therefore, production from local resources for local needs is the most rational way of economic life, while dependence on imports from afar and the consequent need to produce for export to unknown and distant peoples is highly uneconomic and justifiable only in exceptional cases and on a small scale. Just as the modern economist would admit that a high rate of consumption of transport services between a man's home and his place of work signifies a misfortune and not a high standard of life, so the Buddhist economist would hold that to satisfy human wants from faraway sources rather than from sources nearby signifies failure rather than success. The former tends to take statistics showing an increase in the number of ton/miles per head of the population carried by a country's transport system as proof of economic progress, while to the latter—the Buddhist economist—the same statistics would indicate a highly undesirable deterioration in the *pattern* of consumption.

Another striking difference between modern economics and Buddhist economics arises over the use of natural resources. Bertrand de Jouvenel, the eminent French political philosopher, has characterised "western man" in words which may be taken as a fair description of the modern economist:

"He tends to count nothing as an expenditure, other than human effort; he does not seem to mind how much mineral matter he wastes and, far worse, how much living matter he destroys. He does not seem to realise at all that human life is a dependent part of an ecosystem of many different forms of life. As the world is ruled from towns where men are cut off from any form of life other than human, the feeling of belonging to an ecosystem is not revived. This results in a harsh and improvident treatment of things upon which we ultimately depend, such as water and trees."

The teaching of the Buddha, on the other hand, enjoins a reverent and non-violent attitude not only to all sentient beings but also, with great emphasis, to trees. Every follower of the Buddha ought to plant a tree every few years and look after it until it is safely established, and the Buddhist economist can demonstrate without difficulty that the universal observation of this rule would result in a high rate of genuine economic development independent of any foreign aid. Much of the economic decay of southeast Asia (as of many other parts of the world) is undoubtedly due to a heedless and shameful neglect of trees.

Modern economics does not distinguish between renewable and non-renewable materials, as its very method is to equalise and quantify everything by means of a money price. Thus, taking various alternative fuels, like coal, oil, wood, or water-power: the only difference between them recognised by modern economics is relative cost per equivalent unit. The cheapest is automatically the one to be preferred, as to do otherwise would be irrational and "uneconomic." From a Buddhist point of view, of course, this will not do; the essential difference between non-renewable fuels like coal and oil on the one hand and renewable fuels like wood and water-power on the other cannot be simply overlooked. Non-renewable goods must be used only if they are indispensable, and then only with the greatest care and the most meticulous concern for conservation. To use them heedlessly or extravagantly is an act of violence, and while complete non-violence may not be attainable on this earth, there is nonetheless an ineluctable duty on man to aim at the ideal of non-violence in all he does.

Just as a modern European economist would not consider it a great economic achievement if all European art treasures were sold to America at attractive prices, so the Buddhist economist would insist that a population basing its economic life on non-renewable fuels is living parasitically, on capital instead of income. Such a way of life could have no permanence and could therefore be justified only as a purely temporary expedient. As the world's resources of non-renewable fuels—coal, oil, and natural gas—are exceedingly unevenly distributed over the globe and undoubtedly limited in quantity, it is clear that their exploitation at an ever-increasing rate is an act of violence against nature which must almost inevitably lead to violence between men.

This fact alone might give food for thought even to those people in Buddhist countries who care nothing for the religious and spiritual values of their heritage and ardently desire to embrace the materialism of modern economics at the fastest possible speed. Before they dismiss Buddhist economics as nothing better than a nostalgic dream, they might wish to consider whether the path of economic development outlined by modern economics is likely to lead them to places where they really want to be. Towards the end of his courageous book *The Challenge of Man's Future*, Professor Harrison Brown of the California Institute of Technology gives the following appraisal:

"Thus we see that, just as industrial society is fundamentally, unstable and subject to reversion to agrarian existence, so within it the conditions which offer individual freedom are unstable in their ability to avoid the conditions which impose rigid organisation and totalitarian control. Indeed, when we examine all of the foreseeable difficulties which threaten the survival of industrial civilisation, it is difficult to see how the achievement of stability and the maintenance of individual liberty can be made compatible."

Even if this were dismissed as a long-term view there is the immediate question of whether "modernisation," as currently practised without regard to religious and spiritual values, is actually producing agreeable results. As far as the masses are concerned, the results appear to be disastrous—a collapse of the rural economy, a rising tide of unemployment in town and country, and the growth of a city proletariat without nourishment for either body or soul.

It is in the light of both immediate experience and long-term prospects that the study of Buddhist economics could be recommended even to those who believe that economic growth is more important than any spiritual or religious values. For it is not a question of choosing between "modern growth" and "traditional stagnation." It is a question of finding the right path of development, the Middle Way between materialist heedlessness and traditionalist immobility, in short, of finding "Right Livelihood."

E. F. Schumacher, Small Is Beautiful

We Must Not Sever the Link Between the World Below and the World Above

You must not think that I continually feel obliged to attack the glory and prestige of scientists; on the contrary, there is only one point on which I criticize them, and that is the fact that they have cut the link between the external world of matter, which is their particular field of action, and the inner world of the soul and of consciousness. This is where they are at fault and this is where I quarrel with them. Only when the link between the spiritual world and the physical, mechanical, material world is restored, will true progress become possible. Perhaps you feel like asking, "But why do you attach so much importance to this link? Surely it doesn't change things all that much?" This is precisely what saddens me, the fact that nobody recognizes the importance of this link. If it were not vitally important, I would not waste my time and energies on it. I insist on it because, as long as this link is severed, nothing in life will ever be clear and comprehensible.

Hermes Trismegistus said, "That which is below is like to that which is above," and this precept has constantly guided my research. Let me give you an example. When a doctor auscultates a patient, he may discover a deficiency in one of his organs which is upsetting the balance of the whole system, and then he will use all the means at his disposal to correct that imbalance. But the point is that we should go beyond the purely physiological question and let the human organism teach us how to solve the problems of mankind as a whole. An organ is composed of cells; the cells are composed of particles, and the particles, themselves, are composed of even smaller particles (in fact, today, no one knows just how far the analysis of the infinitely small can be taken). A multitude of cells, therefore, forms an organ; many organs form a unit, a human body, and the body, in turn, represents one minute particle in relation to the whole universe. Of course, you all know this.

But if this unit is to be healthy and to eat, move about, speak and think, etc., its organs must all be in good working order and this is possible only if each one works for all the others. The stomach digests food, but it does not keep it all for itself, it distributes it to the rest of the body. The heart does not keep all the blood for itself, it pumps it through the blood vessels. And the eyes do not see or the ears hear only for themselves. They are all at the service of the whole organism; their job is to feed or protect or warn or guide or transport the whole. None of them works exclusively in its own interests, to ensure its own livelihood or wealth, or to establish its pre-eminence over the others. They all obey the law of self-sacrifice, disinterestedness or brotherliness—call it what you will—and when a person falls ill, it means that microbes, viruses or impurities of some kind are preventing one of his organs from carrying on its divine work of selflessness.

From all this we can draw the conclusion that there is a higher Intelligence who has established certain laws and that every breach of these laws, that is to say, every manifestation of egoism or disorder, leads to illness and death. Human beings have known all this for thousands of years: why have they never seen what it meant? Since that which is below is like that which is above—and this means, too, that that which is small is like that which is big—we can conclude that what is true for the individual is also true for the collectivity. Mankind is an organism and each country is an organ which, in turn, is made up of the individual cells that live and work there. But the organs of mankind are not animated by the same spirit of disinterestedness, the same love, as the organs of the body. Each one seeks its own interest and works exclusively for its own welfare, to the detriment of its neighbours.

The human body functions according to laws conceived by a Sublime Intelligence, whereas the "body" of mankind functions according to rules laid down by human minds. This is why it is not functioning properly: the body is ill, so ill, in fact, that it is in danger of death. If mankind is to be restored to health, we must take the human body built by nature as our example, see how it functions and what makes it healthy or sick, and apply the same rules to the whole of humanity.

I know what your objections will be. You will say that it can't be done because human beings are still like animals, they are still too narrow-minded, selfish and cruel. I know better than you why things are as they are today, but that is not the point. The elite, the leaders are in a position to intervene and change things, but they do nothing. All of them work for only one organ whereas each organ should work for all the others; if they did this, the whole of mankind would live in prosperity and peace.

When a body is healthy, all its cells benefit. When your brain is lucid and your heart is beating regularly, without tension, even your feet are comfortable—you can actually feel that your feet and even your toes are happy! Have you ever noticed? On the other hand, when your feet are cold, you start to sneeze; it is your feet that suffer from the cold and your nose that reacts by sneezing. I don't need to give you more examples. It is obvious that when one organ is comfortable, all the others benefit and feel comfortable, too, and when one organ is in a tight spot, all the others feel the pinch. Human beings are the only creatures that rejoice when someone else, another country, is in a tight spot, and that is because they have severed the link.

Human beings have broken the link that connects them to each other, and that break is called hatred, hostility, revenge or spite. You only have to look at Israel and the Arab countries, or the United States and Vietnam. Perhaps you will say, "But they haven't broken off relations; on the contrary, they are fighting each other." That is true. On the physical plane, at least, the link has not been broken, they are continually at each other's throats. But the link I am talking about is the spiritual bond and it is this that has been broken—and the breaking of this bond is called war. Of course, there is a link of a kind there, too. There is certainly a link between two people who loathe each other and who are locked in a struggle to the death; they could hardly be closer! And others, too, even if they are thousands of miles apart, may be joined by a very strong bond. My understanding of the link, the connection, is that of a mechanic or an electrician faced with the problem of a machine that is not working because one little bit of wire is missing. If he can just replace that length of wire, the connection will be restored and the machine can function again. It is the link that is all-important.

Once men have really understood that that which is below is like that which is above, the groundwork will have been done and it will be possible to establish the Kingdom of God on earth. The vital thing is to understand that there is a link, a bond between Heaven and earth. At the moment, it is obvious that this link has been severed, for even scientists and philosophers claim that nature is neither intelligent nor conscious. But if they continue to divide matter into smaller and smaller particles, they will eventually discover the intelligence that rules these particles. And, let me tell you, there are three categories of particles, just as there are three categories of men.

The first category of men includes those who are content with the laws as they exist. They are the respectable, law-abiding citizens. A second category includes those who are not content with the present state of things and want to get humanity to rise to a higher state, to the divine, angelic state. These are all the great Initiates who have come to earth and tried to help man to free himself from the condition of an animal and rise to a higher plane where there is greater justice and love. And, finally, there is a third category, and these are the destroyers, the anarchists, who have appeared at different moments of history in order to lay waste and introduce their pernicious philosophies. Thus, there are three categories, one of which respects the established order, and two of which want to change it. One of these wants to change it for a divine order and the other for a diabolical order. These three categories can also be found in atoms. The question is, what is the Intelligence that commands these particles, these three categories of particles?

But scientists have never accepted the system of correspondences which would have enabled them to draw a parallel between the life of man in the family and society, and the life of atoms. It was a blow to their hopes and expectations when, in spite of themselves, they discovered that the atom was built on the same pattern as the solar system. Many of them were shaken by the discovery because it upset some of their theories. But, whether they liked it or not, it was so obvious that they were obliged to recognize it. And one day, in their studies of the atom, they are going to find some "comets," some foreign particles that are not part of the system, and this is going to puzzle them very much, for they will not understand where they have come from. In other words, scientists are going to find so many things that surprise them that, in the end, they will have to give in and recognize the law of correspondences. In the meantime, they have been misleading mankind because, once you sever the link between Heaven and earth, true morality begins to break down.

When human beings cease to believe in the existence of a Supreme Intelligence that presides over all that exists, they lose their faith in the meaning of life. And once faith is shaken, love also begins to wane, for faith and love are linked. As I have said: "Believe in someone and he will love you; love someone and he will believe in you." If you believe in nothing, why should you love your neighbour? What is the point of trying to do good? Surely it would be more logical and more profitable to do just the opposite and take advantage of others, to do them down or even assassinate them, if need be, in order to get them out of your way.

This shows how the mere fact of severing the link between Heaven and earth, between the great and the small, between the inner consciousness and the outer world, has led to an upheaval in behaviour and attitudes. The present situation is a result of this rupture for which scientists and philosophers are largely responsible. They failed to foresee that, by destroying the two pillars of faith and love on which the whole edifice depended, it would all come crashing down. And, today, the situation has reached catastrophic proportions, and nobody knows what to do about it. You will say, "But these people were very sincere." True, but they were blind, they did not possess the light. This is why, in spite of all their discoveries and inventions, I have to criticize them. They should have foreseen the disastrous consequences that their theories would lead to; they should have understood that there is a connection between what a man believes and what he does. They thought that even if he no longer believed in God or Cosmic Intelligence, man would continue to be virtuous, honest, noble and disinterested. But this is one more link that they cut in failing to see the connection between the two things. I have always insisted on that connection—always!

Philosophy and science have destroyed man's faith in something reasonable, in something with meaning, only to drive him to believe in something senseless, in chance, in the absurd. Could the unutterably complex arrangement of the atoms and molecules that go to make up an intelligent being have happened by accident? Are we to believe that intelligence is the outcome of chance, of the absurd? What strange reasoning that is! The fact is that everything in nature flatly contradicts that idea, for a seed cannot produce something that does not correspond to its own nature. Even the alchemists used to say that one cannot manufacture gold if one does not have at least one particle of gold to begin with. But now, because scientists and philosophers proclaim that it was mindless chance that gave birth to an intelligent being, everything becomes monstrous.

The link. I can never insist enough on the importance of the link, and life will prove how right I am, events will vindicate me. The other day I heard a so-called thinker talking on the television, explaining that he was in favour of disorder. But what kind of men are these who claim to instruct mankind? He was in love with disorder! I can assure you, if I could meet that man face to face he would have a very bad time of it! I would say, "Ah, so you love disorder do you? Then, of course, I presume that you are perfectly willing to suffer from cancer?" "No, no, certainly not." "Well, that is the disorder you appreciate so much, cancer. Since you like disorder around you, you must accept its presence within you as well. And, I promise you, when that happens you will see what disorder really is. You are an imbecile; you don't know what you are saying!" And to think that it is people like this that are welcomed with open arms on television programmes.

If human beings sincerely want to work for good they must first realize that they will never manage to do so as long as each one works for himself; never! Everything may go smoothly for a time, they may become rich and powerful, but nothing can save them from being attacked and destroyed by others. No one who works exclusively for himself can ever be safe. True safety is to be found by working, first and foremost, for others. If you work for others, you need never fear that someone might attack you, because everyone will love you.

This tendency on the part of human beings, which is so widespread today, to work only for themselves, for their own safety and well-being, will never bring them the fruits they hope for. They must get rid of that idea. Individuals will be in safety only when all members of the collectivity are linked together to form one mind and one conscience. Once again, we can see this mirrored in the human body: the different organs don't consume each other. I have never heard of a stomach attacking the heart or liver and devouring it. To be sure, there are cases of men whose hand has picked up a revolver and blown their brains out, but that is abnormal. In normal human beings one organ never tries to harm another. On the contrary, if your head aches or you have a pain somewhere, consciously or unconsciously, your hand will go to the spot that hurts to soothe and warm it. Our different organs help and collaborate with each other.

In the long run, a philosophy which urges men to work exclusively for their own country can only bring misfortune. History gives us ample proof of this. Look at how many powerful kingdoms have disappeared—and other powers are doomed to disappear, one day. What will become of England, France, America and Russia if they continue to cultivate a jealously separative spirit. Ours is the only philosophy that can lead mankind to happiness and fulfilment. The great need, now, is to find intelligent men and women in government who will understand and decide to apply it. To understand it is not difficult; it is the practical application of it that is difficult. Political leaders will say, "It is not possible to put it into practice yet. We represent a country and it is our duty to work only for that country. Apart from that, we absolutely agree with you. Clearly, what you say, is quite true." Thus, even the heads of State are not free.

Mankind has such powerful means at its disposal today, that, if this philosophy were accepted, the Kingdom of God would very soon be established on earth. All the means and possibilities we need are there, but there is still something missing in the minds of men. All that is needed is for those at the top to decide to form a world government that would ensure peace for all men. Then, as it would no longer be necessary to spend billions on weapons and defence systems, all that money could be used to ensure a better life for each individual.

When you hear me denouncing scientists you always wonder what I have against them. Nothing; I have absolutely nothing against scientists. It is their mentality that I am opposed to. I would like to destroy their attitude and put a different one in its place, but they themselves are magnificent, wonderful people. I would like to embrace them all! What I am fighting is an idea, but the scientists themselves are very precious people for, while spiritualists,* mystics and the religious do nothing at all, scientists work very hard, so we must take care of them. If only they would restore the link between the physical world and the moral, spiritual world! If they did that, they would be so useful, so necessary and admirable, that everybody would embrace them and serenade them—by moonlight, perhaps! It is this link, therefore, that matters, this tiny wire that needs to be put back where it belongs so that the current can flow, once again, between Heaven and earth, between the world above and the world below.

When Hermes Trismegistus, speaking of the force of Telesma, says, "It doth ascend gently from Earth to Heaven. Again it doth descend to Earth, and uniteth in itself the force from things superior and things inferior," he was referring to this communication, this contact between the divine and the physical worlds. This force is life, the current that flows between Heaven and earth. Everything is connected. Outwardly, everything seems to be disconnected but, in reality, everything is tied in to everything else.

All the power of magic is here, in this one thing, the link. A magic wand is simply a rod that links the two worlds and he who wishes to be a magus must possess this little rod within himself. If he does not possess it, if all he has is the wand he is holding in his hand, he will be incapable of setting in motion the forces of nature or of working magic of any kind, because it means that he has not understood that the only true magic wand is this living link which allows the current to flow between the two worlds, the plug that must be connected to the mains. The function of a magic wand is to close the circuit so that energy can flow from one world to the other. If you want your lamps to light up you have to connect them to the electric current from the power station, and a magic wand is the plug that makes this connection.

When a magus possesses this wand in his head and his heart, therefore, and, in addition, he holds a physical magic wand as a symbol of this connecting rod, he is able to trigger the flow of current from the divine world to the physical world. I realize that this is new to you; in fact, I am convinced that it is also new for most occultists, who often have rather vague ideas on the subject. They use various props but without understanding what they mean or how they should be used and, as long as they fail to understand this, as long as there is no little "fuse wire" within them to ensure the connection between the two worlds, there can be no spark of magic. This is what a magic wand is, a fuse wire.

---

* The word "spiritualist," in the language of Omraam Mikhaël Aïvanhov, simply means one who looks at things from a spiritual point of view, whose philosophy of life is based on belief in a spiritual reality.

No matter what I tell you, it seems that you still do not see the importance of this thread that links the two worlds. You say, "He keeps talking about a thread, a connection, that science has cut. Pooh. Who needs it?" You do! Without this thread you will never get anywhere. For my part, I have this thread, but I am the only one who can use it. I cannot lend it to you, everybody has to have it for themselves, it is not something that you can borrow and plug in, mechanically. Each individual must understand what it is and accept and agree to it in order to plug it in for himself. For my part, I have already done this; but we are not talking about me, we are talking about you and all the others like you. Believe me, all the misfortunes of mankind stem from the fact that this connection has been cut. Of course, everyone explains these misfortunes in his own way; economists see them as a result of economic factors; politicians explain them in terms of politics; the clergy will say that it is because people have stopped going to Mass, and doctors will say that it is because people refuse to take their advice. But I am telling you that all the misery in the world is a consequence of the rupture of this link. It now remains to restore the connection, to rebuild it with wisdom, intelligence and skill.

Hermes Trismegistus said something else, too. He said, "You shall separate the subtle from the gross with great diligence." Why must they be separated? And what must we do with them once we have separated them? The answer is simple: we must break our bonds and separate ourselves from all that is dense, obscure and mindless, and bind ourselves to all that is subtle, luminous and intelligent. When one cuts one's ties with Cosmic Intelligence, as contemporary scientists and thinkers have done, one establishes ties with the absurd. To detach oneself from one thing always implies an attachment to something else. If you detach yourself from the Lord you will inevitably attach yourself to demons. If you move farther away from the light you will be closer to darkness. Nobody has ever envisaged this broader application of the words of Hermes Trismegistus. The precept, "You shall separate the subtle from the gross" implies the underlying notion that this separation is followed by an attachment, that when one detaches oneself from an object or being, one inevitably attaches oneself to another object or being.

Perhaps you understand, now, that if I am always scolding scientists and philosophers, it is not that I believe myself to be any better than they are, but because my point of view is superior to theirs. I am like a child who, from his perch at the top of a tree, can see things that those on the ground cannot see. When I was very young, about four or five, I had four passions which I have kept to this very day—although in a different form, of course. I loved to climb trees, light fires, collect threads and bits of string—it may seem very stupid, but I was fascinated by threads—and watch running water. In the village of Macedonia, where I was born, at the foot of the Babuna Planina (the Grandmother Mountain), there were some very big trees, mostly poplars, and I loved to climb up as high as possible into the branches of those trees and stay there a long time. When my mother called me—she always knew where to find me—I would get down by sliding down the trunk and, as I never wore a shirt in summer, the skin of my tummy became as tough as leather! How I loved those trees. I could stay there for hours, perched up in the highest branches.

As for my love of threads, I remember that, one day, when I was only five or six years old and not fully conscious of what I was doing, it caused something of a tragedy. One of the women in our family was a weaver and, one day, when I saw her loom standing there, with all the threads so beautifully arranged on it... Well, I don't know what got into me, but I wanted those threads so badly that I cut them all off her loom and took them. There, now I have confessed my sin of destruction to you. Of course, I was duly punished, but what a tragedy! I can still see everybody running round in circles in a panic while I looked on, wondering why they were so upset. I had cut everything off the loom just because I wanted the threads! And what did I do with them when I had got them? Nothing. Why did I want those threads? It was only much later that I began to understand my fascination with threads and, also, with fire and running water.

I did quite a bit of mischief with fire, too. I used to light a fire anywhere I could, just for the joy of watching it burn and, one day, it was my parents' barn that burned down! I could not understand, on that occasion, either, why everybody was in such a panic and rushed to put it out. I thought it was so beautiful. The flames were so bright.

Water, also, had the same enchantment for me. I shall never forget the little spring that bubbled up from the ground quite near where we lived; I would sit there for hours, watching it, entranced by that pure, crystal-clear water flowing out of the ground. To this day, I have a vivid picture in my mind of the pure, transparent waters of that spring. And ever since then, all my life long, I have had this constant preoccupation with water and fire. That is why the very first lecture I gave here, in France, was about fire and water and the relationship between the masculine principle (fire) and the feminine principle (water). None of this was accidental: something within me, something from the past, drew me to these two elements and allowed me to discover a whole new world in them.

Even my passion for threads can be explained. Why was I never interested in needles? All I was interested in was the threads; needles held no attraction for me. What did that mean? Needles did not interest me because they represented the masculine principle and I already possessed that. What I needed was the feminine principle, matter, the thread with which to weave my cloth. Eventually, after a great deal of hard work, God gave me the threads I needed, so now I have them. But I can see that you have never looked for threads; you have never cut all the threads off a loom, as I have. It was a crime, I admit, but I made reparation for it, later on. A few years ago, I returned to the village where I was born (it is now in the part of Macedonia which belongs to Yugoslavia), and the people who were there at the time of my "crime" were very old but they were still there, so I was able to give them something to atone for the disaster I had inflicted on them. We must never leave things unfinished. Sooner or later, we have to pay all our debts.

As for my passion for climbing trees, it was an early indication of my determination to see everything from above, from very high up. God did not give me the intellectual faculties that I see in today's scientists and philosophers. Their intellectual capacity is truly phenomenal. I do not have that, but I am the little boy who loves to climb up to the top of a tree. His father, who has doctorates from several universities is downstairs, in his study, reading or writing, and he hears his son calling out, "Dad, Uncle is coming. I can see him at the bottom of the road." "What else can you see?" asks his father. "Aunty is with him." "What else?" "He's carrying a big basket..." etc. Thus the son can explain certain things to his father because he can see a long way from his vantage point at the top of the tree. He may be ignorant, that little boy, but, thanks to his viewpoint, he can see things at a great distance, whereas his father, for all his brainpower and his numerous degrees, sees nothing, because he is too low down. There, that is my explanation. I am not as proud or conceited as I may seem. I know how limited I am, but I also know that I have been placed on a summit from which I can see a great deal farther afield than all those who have much greater intellectual ability.

You never imagined that my passion for threads could lead me such a long way, did you? But a magic wand is a thread, a wire. Even in our own bodies we see examples of this: what are muscles, nerve fibres, blood vessels? They are threads. And plants and trees? Threads again. And rays of sunlight are also threads which come all the way down to earth so that we can tie ourselves to the sun with them. You see? The ramifications are endless. Isn't life itself a fabric of interwoven threads? Nature works with threads. Indeed, all human beings also work with threads, particularly women, when they sew, embroider or knit. Nowadays, even in industry, in the manufacture of plastics, for instance, we see nothing but threads, threads and still more threads.

How could I have sensed the significance of threads at the age of five or six? Obviously, at that age, it was unconscious, but there was certainly a hidden intelligence behind it. It was given to me in order to show me that nothing happens by chance for, as soon as I began to examine my seemingly strange childhood passions, I discovered the existence of a marvellous, extraordinary world. Life itself is a tissue of threads. Chromosomes are threads and the character, heredity and structure of a living being are all contained in these threads. And telephones, radios, computers—they are all threads, a mass of interwoven threads. You could say that everything that exists consists of threads. Isn't it extraordinary?

Human beings constantly work with threads but they have cut the one thread that matters, the one I am talking about, the one that I am working to restore in order to restore the connection between the two worlds. This is the only true magic. Can you define magic? I was very young, about fifteen, and still living in Bulgaria, when I first read a definition of magic. I had got hold of a book about chiromancy by Desbarolles in which, amongst many other interesting things, I found this definition of magic: "Magic is a comparison between the two worlds." This definition made a great impression on me, although, as you can imagine, I was too young to understand it. At fifteen, after all, one cannot be expected to grasp the full significance of such a profound thought. I imagined that magic was the ability to command the spirits and work miracles. But, even so, that phrase stuck in my mind, I kept thinking about it and, later, when I studied it and reflected about these things, I realized that it expressed a very important truth. You cannot compare two things unless there is a link between them. That is what a comparison is, therefore, first and foremost, a connection. True magic is the comparison between the divine and the physical worlds which is made possible by the link between them. Without this link there can be no magic.

This is what I understood and this explains why, for years, now, I have been so insistent about this question of the link. The whole of my philosophy is based on this little thread, the fragile link between the two worlds. Do away with this link and, not long after, it is all over: nothing has any sense any more, you find yourself floundering in the absurd, everything is confused and disorganized. But as soon as the link is restored, things become clear and simple once again. When it gets dark, you plug in your lamp and, at once, the light comes on and you can see everything as clear as day.

Instead of speaking of a link you might prefer to speak of a bridge, for it amounts to the same thing. A bridge joins the two opposite banks of a river, if there is no bridge you cannot cross to the other side. In wartime, the opposing forces try to destroy all the bridges so as to disrupt the enemy's progress. And highways? Roads, paths, highways are also links. The destruction of all its bridges and roads is a disaster for a country because the cessation of all traffic and communication spells inevitable ruin. An exact parallel can be seen in the physical body: if an artery is cut, the organ that depended on it dies, for its supply of nourishment is cut off. And yet human beings think that they can cut their link with Heaven with impunity, that nothing will be changed, that they will continue to receive nourishment, happiness and fulfilment. Good God, how stupid they are! Fortunately there are still some links that they have not managed to cut. The fact that they are still alive means that they have not cut the silver cord that links them to their physical body. And they still have their links to air, water and food. Many of them still retain their links with society and their families, also. But they have severed the link that joined them to their Heavenly Father and, gradually, if they don't change their attitude, they will destroy all their other links as well.

We can find the equivalent of the word "link" in other contexts, too. Why do we speak of a "liaison" between a man and woman? The coming of a child into the world is the result of a link between the father and mother. This is a good example of the magic of it: a man and woman form a bond, a link, and the result is this child that we see walking and talking and playing! It is always a question of a rod, a magic wand that has to be plugged in, inserted into something so that the current can circulate. Every man possesses this wand, but if he does not "plug it in," there can be no child. Men and women do this all the time, but without understanding the first thing about what they are doing. There is no higher magic than to restore the link, restore contact between the two worlds: between the feminine and the masculine worlds, between the world below and the world above, between the receptive and the emissive worlds. Where will you find a more significant event than the birth of a child? Everything else pales in comparison.

But the conception of a child is not a phenomenon that takes place only on the physical plane between a man and woman. There are other realms in which a child can be conceived, and this is the vital work that is waiting for you.

Sèvres, January 14, 1968

Omraam Mikhaël Aïvanhov, *Cosmic Moral Law*

Collective Awakening

Many mystics and teachers suggest that the increased reports of Kundalini awakening at this time in history suggest a larger purpose at work, a universal planetary movement. The earth appears to be trembling in the foreboding presence of major upheavals as we approach the 21st century. There are dire predictions of cataclysmic environmental changes, along with the ever-present annihilating threat of nuclear war and the continual pressures of war, oppression, starvation, crime and economic collapse in every sector of the hemisphere. We have watched with astonishment the collapse of Communism and the emergence of freedom in Eastern Europe. This is a radical upheaval, to a remarkable extent non-violent, coming from the core of millions of people who have long felt trapped in an unresponsive political system. For decades the possibility of such enormous shifts in ideology was inconceivable. That this kind of shift can occur so rapidly offers hope for all of the stuck places on the planet—ideologies that hold many in the throes of poverty, starvation, guerrilla wars, and criminal activities.

Perhaps such spontaneous movements, impacting the entire world, are part of the universal aspect of Kundalini. Certainly great confusion and chaos will reign for some years as the countries of Eastern Europe struggle to create a new economic and political system, and the entire continent moves to form the United States of Europe. The possibilities in Europe have far surpassed any previous predictions, and no one can say what will eventually emerge. Even more desperate upheavals are underway in Africa, Burma, Haiti and hundreds of other countries at this time.

Not only politically, but environmentally, monumental and inconceivable adaptations may lie in our immediate future. At every level we are poisoning the environment, from the ocean to the ozone layer to storage within the earth of deadly gases. Major earthquakes, shifting of the earth plates, and weather changes that promote drought are only a few of the predicted disasters psychics say may herald the "New Age." If these predictions should ever come to pass human life will only continue because of human beings with strong characters, flexibility, creativity, cooperative attitudes, inner resources, values which promote communal survival above individual acquisition, and the inner strength that is nourished by engaging that which is divine in us. Spiritual communities are emerging around the globe at this time, and individuals in many unlikely places are having Shamanic visions, Kundalini awakenings, psychic intuitions and a passion for teaching what they know to others. Slowly the vision of what it means to be human and divine is changing, merging, awakening, and teaching us more about our capacities and potentialities.

Perhaps the individuals engaging in the tumultuous event of spiritual awakening are prototypes for what the planetary consciousness must ultimately face:

—purification of the unconscious patterns that allow us to destroy, abuse and violate one another;

—awareness there is one humanity and one planet with one set of resources we all share that could only be connected to one spiritual source;

—reawakening of our capacity to connect psychically and experientially with that source and experience bliss and joy and wisdom directly;

—and willingness to live in moderation and nurture our planet in healthy ways which sustain all life.

There are numerous patterns with which to identify the human microcosm with the planetary macrocosm, for universally our thought forms as a species create the quality of life on this fragile sphere hurtling through space, sustained by the same pranic sources on which we all depend.

Kundalini awakening is awakening into awareness of this energy which can be used to heal, transform, energize and evolve higher levels of consciousness. Once we are fully alive as a spiritual species we will know how to sustain change and develop from within us a quality of life that can cooperate with the forces of nature to nurture our planet for future generations. We do not yet know what is possible and can only play with imagination to visualize a healthier and saner planet, peopled by a wise and loving species in touch with the natural ecstasy of the inner being. Such changes are unlikely to be the consequence of following one great teacher, many of whom we have known already. They will result when many individuals are willing to turn their egos inside out and plunge deeply into the more firmly rooted core of the Self, in order to activate the fundamental values of human existence. This is the long-term potential of such awakenings, whether they occur after great disciplined effort, or spontaneously. They teach of the possibilities inherent in transformational change which we need to understand in order to move to the next stage of planetary development.

This does not mean that all who have awakened Kundalini energies are already so wise. Universal energy/consciousness has always been neutral, has the capacity to be used for better or worse purposes by an individual who does not have the strength to go completely through the purifying process it offers. There are always forces in human consciousness that tempt us with power, greed, envy, sloth and all the seven deadly sins. These "sins" are human failings, our shadows, which keep us in ignorance because we cannot go all the way through this process as long as we actively focus our attention on them. And everyone fails, over and over. At this stage of development it is prudent to acknowledge with compassion and love who we are, where we are weak, where we can become stronger.

As we push toward awakening, and try to engage in activities that sustain and deepen it, we may possibly become more than we were. When we break into the ecstasy of pure awareness, at those moments we cannot be anything else but light, but how impossible it seems to live there all the time, and how natural to fall back into our ordinary imperfections. Never underestimate the difficulties of such a process—for individuals, for the planet.

The lessons are all around us. It is in the Christianity that became the Inquisition, in the Islam that killed infidels, in the failed guru who betrayed his followers, in governments ruled by special interests, in corruption that follows in the footsteps of good intentions. No matter how noble our ideals and purposes, we slide repeatedly into destruction and inhumane choices, in order to protect our position, our desires, our points of view. Spiritual awakening does not prevent this, at least not in the early stages with which we are primarily involved here: it simply gives us an added incentive to transform those renegade elements of our psyches, which keep us from being in the peace and ecstasy that is hidden inside our deepest core.

The more I open myself to observe the true condition of the planet, the depth of the pain that is the norm for much of the human species, and the portents for the future, the less surprised I am at the growing number of individuals who are "awakening," and going through ordeals much like ancient initiations which shift their consciousness. Perhaps all of us need this experience, and need it quickly. Or perhaps the earth is being seeded for something to come in the distant future, and we are only being asked to experiment and to study spiritual processes at this moment in time. Whatever the purpose, we cannot afford to allow psychology, philosophy, science or religion to ignore or reject these processes. We need to develop tolerance, respect, understanding and support for souls who are pioneering these uncharted territories. We are all learning together, we share a common destiny, and we are winding hand-in-hand through the labyrinthine energy fields that will ultimately lead us into the sacred light and purpose of the human soul.

Bonnie Greenwell, Energies of Transformation

INVENTIONS	WHAT COULD SOON BE	WHAT WILL EVENTUALLY BE
Airplanes and Automobiles	Ravine Jumps	Full Flight in True Gravity
Telephones	Urgent Telepathic Messages	The Divine Silence
Radio	Sensitive Listening	Universal Clairvoyance and Psychic Mobility
Heating Systems	The Tumo of Tibetan Golfers	The Primal Fire in the Living Soul
Clothes	A Lovely Body	The Power of Emanation and Invisibility

Food Industries	Little Need for Food	Constant Energy Interchange
Newspapers	Intuition of the World's State	Omniscience and Self-existent Delight
Orchestras	Melodies in the Inner Ear	The Music of the Spheres
Hospitals and Medicine	Bodily Harmony	The Luminous Body
Atom Smashers	Baffing Spoons	Knowledge of the Cracks in Space-Time
Rocket Ships	Astral Flight	Materialization in Another Place
X-Rays	Body Reading	Universal Transparency
Hydrogen Bombs	Psychokinetic Blasts	Explosions of Ecstasy

Shiva Irons, from "History of the Western World,"
in Michael Murphy, *Golf in the Kingdom*

❖ Science and Religion ❖

"If modern science wanted to proceed with methodical irre-
proachability it necessarily had to leave out God, for he cannot be
empirically verified and analyzed like other objects."

— HANS KÜNG

At this juncture of the world's evolu-
tion, we are a scientific people. Through enquiry, we've discovered and
invented, and through these inventions nothing seems to surprise us. We are
constantly looking to attain more and more knowledge, but to what end?
This is Teilhard de Chardin's question. Do these discoveries and inventions
pose a new problem for God? Abraham Maslow says that the need to have
God revealed to us, as proof, like the result of scientific research, is not about
surrender and humility (the real path to evidence, as Christ taught), but
about control and power. Alan Watts says "a zeal and reverence for facts"
and the skill of surrendering are both required to lead us to true answers.
Through deciphering scientific principles, like the atom and physics, we

begin to comprehend God's magnitude, His greatness, as we never have before. By acknowledging God's scientific self, we bring the God of our own past, of our religions, to this new place in evolution, a new God of science, a God who loves all people, who serves all, individually and collectively, and continues to create and destroy as He has always done.

In progressing towards higher knowledge, we also discover the restrictions of the finite and the vastness of the infinite. The mind is familiar with the finite, and the soul with the infinite. The purpose is to know the difference. There can be no fusion between the scientific and spiritual realms without the presence of the soul. Without it something would always be missing, and that something is at the centre of all things—unity with God. Alan Watts suggests that we adopt the reality of God, we acknowledge that God is all around us and plain to see. To do this, he suggests that through "a correction of mind" we change in how we view reality.

And so it is at this exciting moment in time as we move to the place God planned for us, a new theology is emerging; a theology of truth, of eco-consciousness, of wholeness; a theology composed by the Super Mind of science and religion; a theology with no boundaries formed by what Albert Einstein terms "cosmic religious feeling."

❋

One could say that the nineteenth-century atheist had burnt down the house instead of remodeling it. He had thrown out the religious questions with the religious answers, because he had to reject the religious answers. That is, he turned his back on the whole religious enterprise because organized religion presented him with a set of answers which he could not intellectually accept—which rested on no evidence which a self-respecting scientist could swallow. But what the more sophisticated scientist is now in the process of learning is that though he must disagree with most of the answers to the religious questions which have been given by organized religion, it is increasingly clear that the religious questions themselves—and religious quests, the religious yearnings, the religious needs themselves—are perfectly respectable scientifically, that they are rooted deep in human nature, that they can be studied, described, examined in a scientific way, and that the churches were trying to answer perfectly sound human questions. Though the answers were not acceptable, the questions themselves were and are perfectly acceptable, and perfectly legitimate.

Abraham H. Maslow, *Religions, Values
and Peak-Experiences*

Some Reflections on the Spiritual Repercussions
of the Atom Bomb

One early dawn in the "bad lands" of Arizona, something over a year ago, a dazzling flash of light, strangely brilliant in quality, illumined the most distant peaks, eclipsing the first rays of the rising sun. There followed a prodigious burst of sound.... The thing had happened. For the first time on earth an atomic fire had burned for the space of a second, industriously kindled by the science of Man.

But having thus realised his dream of creating a new thunderclap, Man, stunned by his success, looked inward and sought by the glare of the lightning his own hand had loosed to understand its effect upon himself. His body was safe; but what had happened to his soul?

I shall not seek to discuss or defend the essential morality of this act of releasing atomic energy. There were those, on the morrow of the Arizona experiment, who had the temerity to assert that the physicists, having brought their researches to a successful conclusion, should have suppressed and destroyed the dangerous fruits of their invention. As though it were not every man's duty to pursue the creative forces of knowledge and action to their uttermost end! As though, in any event, there exists any force on earth capable of restraining human thought from following any course upon which it has embarked!

Neither shall I here attempt to examine the economic and political problems created by the intrusion of nuclear energy upon human affairs. How is the use of this terrifying power to be organised and controlled? This is for the worldly technicians to answer. It is sufficient for me to recall the general condition which is necessary for the solution of the problem: it must be posed on an international scale. As the American journal *The New Yorker* observed with remarkable penetration on August 18th, 1945: "Political plans for the new world, as shaped by statesmen, are not fantastic enough. The only conceivable way to catch up with atomic energy is with political energy directed to a universal structure."

The aim of these reflections—more narrowly concerned with our separate souls, but for that reason perhaps going deeper—is simply to examine, in the case of the atomic bomb, the effects of the invention upon the inventor, arising out of the fact of the invention. Each of our actions, and the more so the more novel the action, has its deep-seated repercussions upon our subsequent inner orientation. To fly, to beget, to kill for the first time—these, as we know, suffice to transform a life. By the liberation of atomic energy on a massive scale, and for the first time, man has not only changed the face of the earth, he has by the very act set in motion at the heart of his being a long chain of reactions which, in the brief flash of an explosion of matter, has made of him, virtually at least, a new being hitherto unknown to himself.

Let me try, in a first approximation, to distinguish the main links in this chain.

At that crucial instant when the explosion was about to happen (or not happen) the first artificers of the atom bomb were crouched on the soil of the desert. When they got to their feet after it was over, it was Mankind who stood up with them, instilled with a *new* sense of power. Certainly the power was of a kind which Man had many times felt emanating from himself, in great pulsations, during the course of his history. He had felt it, for example, in the darkness of the paleolithic age when for the first time he ventured to put fire to his own use, or accidentally discovered how to produce it; in neolithic times when he found that by cultivating thin ears of grass he could turn them into rice and millet and corn; and much later, at the dawn of our industrial era, when he found that he could tame and harness not only animals but the tireless energies of steam and electricity. Each of these new conquests signified extensively and intensively, for Man and for the earth, a total rearrangement of life, a change of epoch; but when all is said they did not bring about any essential *change of plane* in the depths of human consciousness. For in all these cases (even the most beneficial, that of electricity), what did the discovery lead to except the control and utilisation of forces already at liberty in the surrounding world? They called for ingenuity and adaptiveness rather than any act of creation; they were no more, in each case, than a new sail hoisted to catch a new wind. But the discovery and liberation of atomic power bears quite another aspect and in consequence has had a very different effect upon Man's soul. Here it is no longer a question of laying hands upon existing forces freely available for his use. This time a door has been decidedly forced open, giving access to a new and supposedly inviolable compartment of the universe. Hitherto Man was using matter to serve his needs. Now he has succeeded in seizing and manipulating the sources commanding the very origins of matter—springs so deep that he can release for his own purposes what seemed to be the exclusive property of the sidereal powers, and so powerful that he must think twice before committing some act which might destroy the truth. In the glow of this triumph how can he feel otherwise than exalted as he has never been since his birth; the more so since the prodigious event is not the mere accidental product of a futureless chance but the long-prepared outcome of intelligently concerted action?

Therefore, a new sense of power: but even more, the sense of a power capable of development *to an indefinite extent*. What gripped the throats of those bold experimenters in Arizona, in that minute before the explosion, must surely have been far less the thought of the destruction it might lead to than of the critical test which the pyramid of calculation and hypothesis culminating in this solemn moment was about to undergo. The quicker ending of the war, the vast sums of money spent—what did such things matter when the very worth of science itself was on trial? That vast and subtle edifice of equations, experiments, inter-woven calculations put together little by little in the laboratories, would it survive the test of this culminating experiment which would make of it, in everyday terms, something tangible, efficacious, unanswerable? Was it a dream or reality? This was the moment of truth. In a few instants they would know....

And the flame truly sprang upwards at the place and time prescribed, energy did indeed burst forth from what, to ordinary perception, was inert, non-inflammable matter. Man at that moment found himself endowed not merely with his existing strength but with a method which would enable him to master all the forces surrounding him. For one thing he had acquired absolute and final confidence in the instrument of mathematical analysis which for the past century he had been forging. Not only could matter be expressed in terms of mathematics, it could be subjugated by mathematics. Perhaps even more important, he had discovered, in the unconsidered unanimity of the act which circumstances had forced upon him, another secret pointing the way to his omnipotence. For the first time in history, through the non-fortuitous conjunction of a world crisis and an unprecedented advance in means of communication, a planned scientific experiment employing units of a hundred or a thousand men had been successfully completed. And very swiftly. In three years a technical achievement had been realised which might not have been accomplished in a century of isolated efforts. This greatest of Man's scientific triumphs happens also to be the one in which the largest number of brains were enabled to join together in a single organism, the most complex and the most centrated, for the purpose of research. Was this simply coincidence? Did it not rather show that in this as in other fields nothing in the universe can resist the converging energies of a sufficient number of minds sufficiently grouped and organised?

Thus considered, the fact of the release of nuclear energy, overwhelming and intoxicating though it was, began to seem less tremendous. Was it not simply the first act, even a mere prelude, in a series of fantastic events which, having afforded us access to the heart of the atom, would lead us on to overthrow, one by one, the many other strongholds which science is already besieging? The vitalisation of matter by the creation of super-molecules. The re-modelling of the human organism by means of hormones. Control of heredity and sex by the manipulation of genes and chromosomes. The readjustment and internal liberation of our souls by direct action upon springs gradually brought to light by psycho-analysis. The arousing and harnessing of the unfathomable intellectual and effective powers still latent in the human mass....Is not every kind of effect produced by a suitable arrangement of matter? And have we not reason to hope that in the end we shall be able to arrange every kind of matter, following the results we have obtained in the nuclear field?

It is thus, step by step, that Man, pursuing the flight of his growing aspirations, taught by a first success to be conscious of his power, finds himself impelled to look beyond any purely mechanical improvement of the earth's surface and increase of his external riches, and to dwell upon the *growth and biological perfection of himself*. A vast accumulation of historical research and imaginative reconstruction already existed to teach him this. For millions of years a tide of knowledge has risen ceaselessly about him through the stuff of the cosmos; and that in him which he calls his "I" is nothing other than this tide atomically turning inward upon itself. This he knew already, but without knowing to what extent he could render effective aid to the flood of life pouring through him. But now, after that famous sunrise in Arizona, he can no longer doubt. He not only can but, of organic necessity, he *must* for the future assist in his own becoming. The first phase was the creation of mind through the obscure, instinctive play of vital forces. The second phase is the rebounding and acceleration of the upward movement through the reflexive play of mind itself, the only principle in the world capable of combining and using for the purposes of Life, *and on the planetary scale*, the still-dispersed or slumbering energies of matter and of thought. It is broadly in these terms that we are obliged henceforth to envisage the grand scheme of things of which, by the fact of our existence, we find ourselves a part.

So that today there exists in each of us a man whose mind has been opened to the meaning, the responsibility and the aspirations of his cosmic function in the universe; a man, that is to say, who whether he likes it or not has been transformed into another man, in his very depths.

The great enemy of the modern world, "Public Enemy No. 1," is *boredom*. So long as Life did not think, and above all did not have *time* to think—that is to say, while it was still developing and absorbed with the immediate struggle to maintain itself and advance—it was untroubled by questions as to the value and interest of action. Only when a margin of leisure for reflection came to intervene between the task and its execution did the workman experience the first pangs of *taedium vitae*. But in these days the margin is immeasurably greater, so that it fills our horizon. Thanks to the mechanical devices which we increasingly charge with the burden not only of production but also of calculation, the quantity of unused human energy is growing at a disturbing rate both within us and around us; and this phenomenon will reach its climax in the near future, when nuclear forces have been harnessed to useful work. I repeat: despite all appearances, Mankind is bored. Perhaps this is the underlying cause of all our troubles. We no longer know what to do with ourselves. Hence in social terms the disorderly turmoil of individuals pursuing conflicting and egoistical aims; and, on the national scale, the chaos of armed conflict in which, for want of a better object, the excess of accumulated energy is destructively released... "Idleness, mother of all vices."

But these lowering storm clouds are what the Sense of Evolution, arising in human consciousness, is destined to disperse. Whatever may be the future economic repercussions of the atom bomb, whether over- or underestimated, the fact remains that in laying hands on the very core of matter we have disclosed to human existence a supreme purpose: the purpose of pursuing even further, to the very end, the forces of Life. In exploding the atom we took our first bite at the fruit of the great discovery, and this was enough for a taste to enter our mouths that can never be washed away: the taste for super-creativeness. It was also enough to ensure that the nightmare of bloody combat must vanish in the light of some form of growing unanimity. We are told that, drunk with its own power, mankind is rushing to self-destruction, that it will be consumed in the fire it has so rashly lit. To me it seems that thanks to the atom bomb it is war, not mankind, that is destined to be eliminated, and for two reasons. The first, which we all know and long for, is that the very excess of destructive power placed in our hands must render all armed conflict impossible. But what is even more important, although we have thought less about it, is that war will be eliminated at its source in our hearts because, compared with the vast field for conquest which science has disclosed to us, its triumphs will soon appear trivial and outmoded. Now that a true objective is offered us, one that we can only attain by striving with all our power in a concerted effort, our future action can only be convergent, drawing us together in an atmosphere of sympathy. I repeat, sympathy, because to be ardently intent upon a common object is inevitably the beginning of love. In affording us a biological, "phyletic" outlet directed upwards, the shock which threatened to destroy us will have the effect of re-orienting us, of instilling a new dynamic and finally (within certain limits) of making us one whole. The atomic age is not the age of destruction but of union in research. For all their military trappings, the recent explosions at Bikini herald the birth into the world of a Mankind both inwardly and outwardly pacified. They proclaim the coming of the *Spirit of the Earth*.

We are at the point where, if we are to restore complete equilibrium to the state of psychic disarray which the atomic shock has induced in us, we must sooner or later (sooner?) decide upon our attitude to a fundamental choice;

the point where our conflicts may begin again, and fiercely, but by other means and on a different plane.

I spoke of the Spirit of the Earth. What are we to understand by that ambiguous phrase?

Is it the Promethean or Faustian spirit: the spirit of autonomy and solitude; Man with his own strength and for his own sake opposing a blind and hostile Universe; the rise of consciousness concluding in an act of possession?

Is it the Christian spirit, on the contrary: the spirit of service and of giving; Man struggling like Jacob to conquer and attain a supreme centre of consciousness which calls to him; the evolution of the earth ending in an act of union?

Spirit of force or spirit of love? Where shall we place true heroism, where look for true greatness, where recognise objective truth?

It would take too long, and it is outside the scope of this paper, to discuss the comparative worth of two opposed forms of adoration, the first of which may well have attracted poets, but only the second of which, I think, presents itself to the reflective mind as capable of conferring upon a universe in motion its full spiritual coherence, its total substance beyond death, and finally its whole message for our hearts.*What does matter here is to note that Mankind cannot go much further along the road upon which it has embarked through its latest conquests without having to settle (or be divided intellectually on) the question of which summit it must seek to attain.

In short, the final effect of the light cast by the atomic fire into the spiritual depths of the earth is to illumine within them the over-riding question of the ultimate end of Evolution—that is to say, the problem of God.

Études, September 1946.

Pierre Teilhard de Chardin, *The Future of Man*

The Age of Anxiety

By all outward appearances our life is a spark of light between one eternal darkness and another. Nor is the interval between these two nights an unclouded day, for the more we are able to feel pleasure, the more we are vulnerable to pain—and, whether in background or foreground, the pain is always with us. We have been accustomed to make this existence worth-while by the belief that there is more than the outward appearance—that we live for

---

* Witnesses of that experiment in Arizona found, in the anguish of the last instants, that in the depths of their hearts they were *praying.*

a future beyond this life here. For the outward appearance does not seem to make sense. If living is to end in pain, incompleteness, and nothingness, it seems a cruel and futile experience for beings who are born to reason, hope, create, and love. Man, as a being of sense, wants his life to make sense, and he has found it hard to believe that it does so unless there is more than what he sees—unless there is an eternal order and an eternal life behind the uncertain and momentary experience of life-and-death.

I may not, perhaps, be forgiven for introducing sober matters with a frivolous notion, but the problem of making sense out of the seeming chaos of experience reminds me of my childish desire to send someone a parcel of water in the mail. The recipient unties the string, releasing the deluge in his lap. But the game would never work, since it is irritatingly impossible to wrap and tie a pound of water in a paper package. There are kinds of paper which won't disintegrate when wet, but the trouble is to get the water itself into any manageable shape, and to tie the string without bursting the bundle.

The more one studies attempted solutions to problems in politics and economics, in art, philosophy, and religion, the more one has the impression of extremely gifted people wearing out their ingenuity at the impossible and futile task of trying to get the water of life into neat and permanent packages.

There are many reasons why this should be particularly evident to a person living today. We know so much about history, about all the packages which have been tied and which have duly come apart. We know so much detail about the problems of life that they resist easy simplification, and seem more complex and shapeless than ever. Furthermore, science and industry have so increased both the tempo and the violence of living that our packages seem to come apart faster and faster every day.

There is, then, the feeling that we live in a time of unusual insecurity. In the past hundred years so many long-established traditions have broken down—traditions of family and social life, of government, of the economic order, and of religious belief. As the years go by, there seem to be fewer and fewer rocks to which we can hold, fewer things which we can regard as absolutely right and true, and fixed for all time.

To some this is a welcome release from the restraints of moral, social, and spiritual dogma. To others it is a dangerous and terrifying breach with reason and sanity, tending to plunge human life into hopeless chaos. To most, perhaps, the immediate sense of release has given a brief exhilaration, to be followed by the deepest anxiety. For if all is relative, if life is a torrent without form or goal in whose flood absolutely nothing save change itself can last, it seems to be something in which there is "no future" and thus no hope.

Human beings appear to be happy just so long as they have a future to which they can look forward—whether it be a "good time" tomorrow or an everlasting life beyond the grave. For various reasons, more and more people find it hard to believe in the latter. On the other hand, the former has the disadvantage that when this "good time" arrives, it is difficult to enjoy it to the full without some promise of more to come. If happiness always depends on something expected in the future, we are chasing a will-o'-the-wisp that ever eludes our grasp, until the future, and ourselves, vanish into the abyss of death.

As a matter of fact, our age is no more insecure than any other. Poverty, disease, war, change, and death are nothing new. In the best of times "security" has never been more than temporary and apparent. But it has been possible to make the insecurity of human life supportable by belief in unchanging things beyond the reach of calamity—in God, in man's immortal soul, and in the government of the universe by eternal laws of right.

Today such convictions are rare, even in religious circles. There is no level of society, there must even be few individuals, touched by modern education, where there is not some trace of the leaven of doubt. It is simply self-evident that during the past century the authority of science has taken the place of the authority of religion in the popular imagination, and that skepticism, at least in spiritual things, has become more general than belief.

The decay of belief has come about through the honest doubt, the careful and fearless thinking of highly intelligent men of science and philosophy. Moved by a zeal and reverence for facts, they have tried to see, understand, and face life as it is without wishful thinking. Yet for all that they have done to improve the conditions of life, their picture of the universe seems to leave the individual without ultimate hope. The price of their miracles in this world has been the disappearance of the world-to-come, and one is inclined to ask the old question, "What shall it profit a man if he gain the whole world and lose his soul?" Logic, intelligence, and reason are satisfied, but the heart goes hungry. For the heart has learned to feel that we live for the future. Science may, slowly and uncertainly, give us a better future—for a few years. And then, for each of us, it will end. It will all end. However long postponed, everything composed must decompose.

Despite some opinions to the contrary, this is still the general view of science. In literary and religious circles it is now often supposed that the conflict between science and belief is a thing of the past. There are even some rather wishful scientists who feel that when modern physics abandoned a crude atomistic materialism, the chief reasons for this conflict were removed. But this is not at all the case. In most of our great centers of learning, those who make it their business to study the full implications of science and its methods are as far as ever from what they understand as a religious point of view.

Nuclear physics and relativity have, it is true, done away with the old materialism, but they now give us a view of the universe in which there is even less room for ideas of any absolute purpose or design. The modern scientist is not so naive as to deny God because he cannot be found with a telescope, or the soul because it is not revealed by the scalpel. He has merely noted that the idea of God is logically unnecessary. He even doubts that it has any meaning. It does not help him to explain anything which he cannot explain in some other, and simpler, way.

He argues that if everything which happens is said to be under the providence and control of God, this actually amounts to saying nothing. To say that everything is governed and created by God is like saying, "Everything is up,"—which means nothing at all. The notion does not help us to make any verifiable predictions, and so, from the scientific standpoint, is of no value whatsoever. Scientists may be right in this respect. They may be wrong. It is not our purpose here to argue this point. We need only note that such skepticism has immense influence, and sets the prevailing mood of the age.

What science has said, in sum, is this: We do not, and in all probability cannot, know whether God exists. Nothing that we do know suggests that he does, and all the arguments which claim to prove his existence are found to be without logical meaning. There is nothing, indeed, to prove that there is no God, but the burden of proof rests with those who propose the idea. If, the scientists would say, you believe in God, you must do so on purely emotional grounds, without basis in logic or fact. Practically speaking, this may amount to atheism. Theoretically, it is simple agnosticism. For it is of the essence of scientific honesty that you do not pretend to know what you do not know, and of the essence of scientific method that you do not employ hypotheses which cannot be tested.

The immediate results of this honesty have been deeply unsettling and depressing. For man seems to be unable to live without myth, without the belief that the routine and drudgery, the pain and fear of this life have some meaning and goal in the future. At once new myths come into being—political and economic myths with extravagant promises of the best of futures in the present world. These myths give the individual a certain sense of meaning by making him part of a vast social effort, in which he loses something of his own emptiness and loneliness. Yet the very violence of these political religions betrays the anxiety beneath them—for they are but men huddling together and shouting to give themselves courage in the dark.

Once there is the suspicion that a religion is a myth, its power has gone. It may be necessary for man to have a myth, but he cannot self-consciously prescribe one as he can mix a pill for a headache. A myth can only "work" when it is thought to be truth, and man cannot for long knowingly and intentionally "kid" himself.

Even the best modern apologists for religion seem to overlook this fact. For their most forceful arguments for some sort of return to orthodoxy are those which show the social and moral advantages of belief in God. But this does not prove that God is a reality. It proves, at most, that believing in God is useful. "If God did not exist, it would be necessary to invent him." Perhaps. But if the public has any suspicion that he does not exist, the invention is in vain.

It is for this reason that most of the current return to orthodoxy in some intellectual circles has a rather hollow ring. So much of it is more a belief in believing than a belief in God. The contrast between the insecure, neurotic, educated "modern" and the quiet dignity and inner peace of the old-fashioned believer, makes the latter a man to be envied. But it is a serious misapplication of psychology to make the presence or absence of neurosis the touchstone of truth, and to argue that if a man's philosophy makes him neurotic, it must be wrong. "Most atheists and agnostics are neurotic, whereas most simple Catholics are happy and at peace with themselves. Therefore the views of the former are false, and of the latter true."

Even if the observation is correct, the reasoning based on it is absurd. It is as if to say, "You say there is a fire in the basement. You are upset about it. Because you are upset, there is obviously no fire." The agnostic, the skeptic, is neurotic, but this does not imply a false philosophy; it implies the discovery of facts to which he does not know how to adapt himself. The intellectual who tries to escape from neurosis by escaping from the facts is merely acting on the principle that "where ignorance is bliss, 'tis folly to be wise."

When belief in the eternal becomes impossible, and there is only the poor substitute of belief in believing, men seek their happiness in the joys of time. However much they may try to bury it in the depths of their minds, they are well aware that these joys are both uncertain and brief. This has two results. On the one hand, there is the anxiety that one may be missing something, so that the mind flits nervously and greedily from one pleasure to another, without finding rest and satisfaction in any. On the other, the frustration of having always to pursue a future good in a tomorrow which never comes, and in a world where everything must disintegrate, gives men an attitude of "What's the use anyhow?"

Consequently our age is one of frustration, anxiety, agitation, and addiction to "dope." Somehow we must grab what we can while we can, and drown out the realization that the whole thing is futile and meaningless. This "dope" we call our high standard of living, a violent and complex stimulation of the senses, which makes them progressively less sensitive and thus in need of yet more violent stimulation. We crave distraction—a panorama of sights, sounds, thrills, and titillations into which as much as possible must be crowded in the shortest possible time.

To keep up this "standard" most of us are willing to put up with lives that consist largely in doing jobs that are a bore, earning the means to seek relief from the tedium by intervals of hectic and expensive pleasure. These intervals are supposed to be the real *living*, the real purpose served by the necessary evil of work. Or we imagine that the justification of such work is the rearing of a family to go on doing the same kind of thing, in order to rear another family... and so *ad infinitum*.

This is no caricature. It is the simple reality of millions of lives, so commonplace that we need hardly dwell upon the details, save to note the anxiety and frustration of those who put up with it, not knowing what else to do.

But what *are* we to do? The alternatives seem to be two. The first is, somehow or other, to discover a new myth, or convincingly resuscitate an old one. If science cannot *prove* there is no God, we can try to live and act on the bare chance that he may exist after all. There seems to be nothing to lose in such a gamble, for if death is the end, we shall never know that we have lost. But, obviously, this will never amount to a vital faith, for it is really no more than to say, "Since the whole thing is futile anyhow, let's pretend it isn't." The second is to try grimly to face the fact that life is "a tale told by an idiot," and make of it what we can, letting science and technology serve us as well as they may in our journey from nothing to nothing.

Yet these are not the only solutions. We may begin by granting all the agnosticism of a critical science. We may admit, frankly, that we have no scientific grounds for belief in God, in personal immortality, or in any absolutes. We may refrain altogether from trying to believe, taking life just as it is, and no more. From this *point of departure* there is yet another way of life that requires neither myth nor despair. But it requires a complete revolution in our ordinary, habitual ways of thinking and feeling.

The extraordinary thing about this revolution is that it reveals the truth behind the so-called myths of traditional religion and metaphysic. It reveals, not beliefs, but actual realities corresponding—in an unexpected way—to the ideas of God and of eternal life. There are reasons for supposing that a revolution of this kind was the original source of some of the main religious ideas, standing in relation to them as reality to symbol and cause to effect. The common error of ordinary religious practice is to mistake the symbol for the reality, to look at the finger pointing the way and then to suck it for comfort rather than follow it. Religious ideas are like words—of little use, and often misleading, unless you know the concrete realities to which they refer. The word "water" is a useful means of communication amongst those who know water. The same is true of the word and the idea called "God."

I do not, at this point, wish to seem mysterious or to be making claims to "secret knowledge." The reality which corresponds to "God" and "eternal life" is honest, above-board, plain, and open for all to see. But the seeing requires a correction of mind, just as clear vision sometimes requires a correction of the eyes.

The discovery of this reality is hindered rather than helped by belief, whether one believes in God or believes in atheism. We must here make a clear distinction between belief and faith, because, in general practice, belief has come to mean a state of mind which is almost the opposite of faith. Belief, as I use the word here, is the insistence that the truth is what one would "lief" or wish it to be. The believer will open his mind to the truth on condition that it fits in with his preconceived ideas and wishes. Faith, on the other hand, whatever it may turn out to be. Faith has no preconceptions; it is a plunge into the unknown. Belief clings, but faith lets go. In this sense of the word, faith is the essential virtue of science, and likewise of any religion that is not self-deception.

Most of us believe in order to feel secure, in order to make our individual lives seem valuable and meaningful. Belief has thus become an attempt to hang on to life, to grasp and keep it for one's own. But you cannot understand life and its mysteries as long as you try to grasp it. Indeed, you cannot grasp it, just as you cannot walk off with a river in a bucket. If you try to capture running water in a bucket, it is clear that you do not understand it and that you will always be disappointed, for in the bucket the water does not run. To "have" running water you must let go of it and let it run. The same is true of life and of God.

The present phase of human thought and history is especially ripe for this "letting go." Our minds have been prepared for it by this very collapse of the beliefs in which we have sought security. From a point of view strictly, if strangely, in accord with certain religious traditions, this disappearance of the old rocks and absolutes is no calamity, but rather a blessing. It almost compels us to face reality with open minds, and you can only know God through an open mind just as you can only see the sky through a clear window. You will not see the sky if you have covered the glass with blue paint.

But "religious" people who resist the scraping of the paint from the glass, who regard the scientific attitude with fear and mistrust, and confuse faith with clinging to certain ideas, are curiously ignorant of laws of the spiritual life which they might find in their own traditional records. A careful study of comparative religion and spiritual philosophy reveals that abandonment of belief, of any clinging to a future life for one's own, and of any attempt to escape from finitude and mortality, is a regular and normal stage in the way of the spirit. Indeed, this is actually such a "first principle" of the spiritual life that it should have been obvious from the beginning, and it seems, after all, surprising that learned theologians should adopt anything but a cooperative attitude towards the critical philosophy of science.

Surely it is old news that salvation comes only through the death of the human form of God. But it was not, perhaps, so easy to see that God's human form is not simply the historic Christ, but also the images, ideas, and beliefs in the Absolute to which man clings in his mind. Here is the full sense of the commandment, "Thou shalt not make to thyself any graven image, nor the likeness of anything that is in heaven above;...thou shalt not bow down to them, nor worship them."

To discover the ultimate Reality of life—the Absolute, the eternal, God—you must cease to try to grasp it in the forms of idols. These idols are not just crude images, such as the mental picture of God as an old gentleman on a golden throne. They are our beliefs, our cherished preconceptions of the truth, which block the unreserved opening of mind and heart to reality. The legitimate use of images is to express the truth, not to possess it.

This was always recognized in the great Oriental traditions such as Buddhism, Vedanta, and Taoism. The principle has not been unknown to Christians, for it was implicit in the whole story and teaching of Christ. His life was from the beginning a complete acceptance and embracing of insecurity. "The foxes have holes, and the birds of the air have nests, but the Son of Man hath not where to lay his head."

The principle is yet more to the point if Christ is regarded as divine in the most orthodox sense—as the unique and special incarnation of God. For the basic theme of the Christ-story is that this "express image" of God becomes the source of life in the very act of being destroyed. To the disciples who tried to cling to his divinity in the form of his human individuality he explained, "Unless a grain of corn fall into the ground and die, it remains alone. But if it dies, it brings forth much fruit." In the same vein he warned them, "It is expedient for you that I go away, for if I go not away the Paraclete (the Holy Spirit) cannot come unto you."

These words are more than ever applicable to Christians, and speak exactly to the whole condition of our times. For we have never actually understood the revolutionary sense beneath them—the incredible truth that what religion calls the vision of God is found in giving up any belief in the idea of God. By the same law of reversed effort, we discover the "infinite" and the "absolute," not by straining to escape from the finite and relative world, but by the most complete acceptance of its limitations. Paradox as it may seem, we likewise find life meaningful only when we have seen that it is without purpose, and know the "mystery of the universe" only when we are convinced that we know nothing about it at all. The ordinary agnostic, relativist, or materialist fails to reach this point because he does not follow his line of thought consistently to its end—an end which would be the surprise of his life. All too soon he abandons faith, openness to reality, and lets his mind harden into doctrine. The discovery of the mystery, the wonder beyond all wonders, needs no belief, for we can only believe in what we have already known, preconceived, and imagined. But *this* is beyond any imagination. We have but to open the eyes of the mind wide enough, and "the truth will out."

Alan Watts, *The Wisdom of Insecurity*

We can't judge God by the limits of our knowledge of natural beings.

Flannery O'Connor, *The Habit of Being*

Parallels Between Physics and Mysticism

When I first learned about the Eastern traditions I discovered parallels between modern physics and Eastern mysticism almost immediately. I remember reading a French book about Zen Buddhism in Paris from which I first learned about the important role of paradox in mystical traditions. I learned that spiritual teachers in the East would often use paradoxical riddles in a very skillful way to make their students realize the limitations of logic and reasoning. The Zen tradition, in particular, developed a system of non-verbal instruction through seemingly nonsensical riddles, called koans, which cannot be solved by thinking. They are designed precisely to stop the thought process and thus to make the student ready for the nonverbal experience of reality. All koans, I read, have more or less unique solutions which a competent master recognizes immediately. Once the solution is found, the koan ceases to be paradoxical and becomes a profoundly meaningful statement made from the state of consciousness that it has helped to awaken.

When I first read about the koan method in Zen training, it had a strangely familiar ring to me. I had spent many years studying another kind of paradox that seemed to play a similar role in the training of physicists. There were differences, of course. My own training as a physicist certainly had not had the intensity of Zen training. But then I thought about Heisenberg's account of the way in which physicists in the 1920s experienced the quantum paradoxes, struggling for understanding in a situation where nature alone was the teacher. The parallel was obvious and fascinating and, later on, when I learned more about Zen Buddhism, I found that it was indeed very significant. As in Zen, the solutions to the physicists' problems were hidden in paradoxes that could not be solved by logical reasoning but had to be understood in terms of a new awareness, the awareness of the atomic reality. Nature was their teacher and, like the Zen masters, she did not provide any statement; she just provided the riddles.

The similarity of the experiences of quantum physicists and of Zen Buddhists was very striking to me. The descriptions of the koan method all emphasized that the solving of such a riddle demands a supreme effort of concentration and involvement from the student. The koan, it is said, grips the student's heart and mind and creates a true mental impasse, a state of sustained tension in which the whole world becomes an enormous mass of doubt and questioning. When I compared this description to the passage from Heisenberg's book that I remembered so well, I felt very strongly that the founders of quantum theory experienced exactly the same situation:

> *I remember discussions with Bohr which went through many hours till very late at night and ended almost in despair; and when at the end of the discussion I went alone for a walk in the neighboring park I repeated to myself again and again the question: Can nature possibly be so absurd as it seemed to us in these atomic experiments?*

Later on, I also came to understand why quantum physicists and Eastern mystics were faced with similar problems and went through similar experiences. Whenever the essential nature of things is analyzed by the intellect, it will seem absurd or paradoxical. This has always been recognized by mystics but has become a problem in science only very recently. For centuries, the phenomena studied in science belonged to the scientists' everyday environment and thus to the realm of their sensory experience. Since the images and concepts of their language were abstracted from this very experience, they were sufficient and adequate to describe the natural phenomena.

In the twentieth century, however, physicists penetrated deep into the submicroscopic world, into realms of nature far removed from our macroscopic environment. Our knowledge of matter at this level is no longer derived from direct sensory experience, and therefore our ordinary language is no longer adequate to describe the observed phenomena. Atomic physics provided the scientists with the first glimpses of the essential nature of things. Like the mystics, physicists were now dealing with a nonsensory experience of reality and, like the mystics, they had to face the paradoxical aspects of this experience. From then on, the models and images of modern physics became akin to those of Eastern philosophy.

The discovery of the parallel between the Zen koans and the paradoxes of quantum physics, which I would later call "quantum koans," greatly stimulated my interest in Eastern mysticism and sharpened my attention. In subsequent years, as I became more involved in Eastern spirituality, I would again and again encounter concepts that would be somewhat familiar to me from my training in atomic and subatomic physics. The discovery of these similarities was at first not much more than an intellectual exercise, albeit a very exciting one, but then, one late afternoon in the summer of 1969, I had a powerful experience that made me take the parallels between physics and mysticism much more seriously. The description of this experience that I gave on the opening page of *The Tao of Physics* is still the best I can find:

> *I was sitting by the ocean one late summer afternoon, watching the waves rolling in and feeling the rhythm of my breathing, when I suddenly became aware of my whole environment as being engaged in a gigantic cosmic dance. Being a physicist, I knew that the sand, rocks, water, and air around me were made of vibrating molecules and atoms, and that these consisted of particles which interacted with one another by creating and destroying other particles. I knew also that the earth's atmosphere was continually bombarded by showers of "cosmic rays," particles of high energy undergoing multiple collisions as they penetrated the air. All this was familiar to me from my research in high-energy physics, but until that moment I had only experienced it through graphs, diagrams, and mathematical theories. As I sat on that beach my former experiences came to life; I "saw" cascades of energy coming down from outer space, in which particles were created and destroyed in rhythmic pulses; I "saw" the atoms of the elements and those of my body participating in this cosmic dance of energy; I felt its rhythm and I "heard" its sound, and at that moment I knew that this was the Dance of Shiva, the Lord of Dancers worshiped by the Hindus.*

At the end of 1970, my American visa expired and I had to return to Europe. I was not sure where I wanted to continue my research, so I planned to visit the best research institutes in my field, in each case making contact with people I knew, with a view to obtaining a fellowship or some other position. My first stop was London, where I arrived in October, still a hippie at heart. When I entered the office of P. T. Matthews, a particle physicist I had met in California and who was then the head of the theory division at Imperial College, the first thing I saw was a giant poster of Bob Dylan. I took this as a good omen and decided on the spot that I would stay in London, and Matthews told me that he would be very happy to offer me hospitality at Imperial College. I have never regretted this decision, which resulted in my staying in London for four years, even though the first few months after my arrival were, perhaps, the hardest in my life.

The end of 1970 was a difficult time of transition for me. I was at the beginning of a long series of painful separations from my wife that would eventually end in divorce. I had no friends in London, and I soon found out that it was impossible for me to get a research grant or academic position because I had already begun my search for the new paradigm and was not willing to give it up and accept the narrow confines of a full-time academic job. It was during these first weeks in London, when my spirits were at the lowest they had ever been, that I made the decision that gave my life a new direction.

Shortly before leaving California I had designed a photomontage—a dancing Shiva superimposed on tracks of colliding particles in a bubble chamber—to illustrate my experience of the cosmic dance on the beach. One day I sat in my tiny room near Imperial College and looked at this beautiful picture, and suddenly I had a very clear realization. I knew with absolute certainty that the parallels between physics and mysticism, which I had just begun to discover, would someday be common knowledge; I also knew that I was best placed to explore these parallels thoroughly and to write a book about them. I resolved there and then to write that book, but I also decided that I was not yet ready to do so. I would first study my subject further and write a few articles about it before attempting the book.

Encouraged by this resolution I took my photomontage, which for me contained a profound and powerful statement, to Imperial College to show it to an Indian colleague of mine with whom I happened to share an office. When I showed him the photomontage, without any comment, he was deeply moved and spontaneously began reciting sacred verses in Sanskrit which he remembered from his childhood. He told me that he had grown up as a Hindu but had forgotten everything about his spiritual heritage when he became "brainwashed," as he put it, by Western science. He himself would never have thought of the parallels between particle physics and Hinduism, he said, but upon seeing my photomontage they immediately became evident to him.

Over the next two and a half years I undertook a systematic study of Hinduism, Buddhism, and Taoism, and of the parallels I saw between the basic ideas of those mystical traditions and the basic concepts and theories of modern physics. During the sixties I had tried various techniques of meditation and read a number of books on Eastern mysticism without really engaging myself to follow any of their paths. But now, as I studied the Eastern traditions more carefully, I was most attracted to Taoism.

Among the great spiritual traditions, Taoism offers, in my view, the most profound and most beautiful expressions of ecological wisdom, emphasizing both the fundamental oneness of all phenomena and the embeddedness of individual and societies in the cyclical processes of nature. Thus Chuang Tzu:

*In the transformation and growth of all things, every bud and feature
has its proper form. In this we have their gradual maturing and decay,
the constant flow of transformation and change.*

And Huai Nan Tzu:

Those who follow the natural order flow in the current of the Tao.

The Taoist sages concentrated their attention fully on the observation
of nature in order to discern the "characteristics of the Tao." In doing so they
developed an attitude that was essentially scientific; only their deep mistrust
of the analytic method of reasoning prevented them from constructing
proper scientific theories. Nevertheless, their careful observation of nature,
combined with a strong mystical intuition, led them to profound insights
which are confirmed by modern scientific theories. The deep ecological wisdom, the empirical approach, and the special flavor of Taoism, which I can
best describe as "quiet ecstasy," were enormously attractive to me, and so
Taoism quite naturally became the way for me to follow.

Castaneda, too, exerted a strong influence on me in those years, and his
books showed me yet another approach to the spiritual teachings of the East.
I found the teachings of the American Indian traditions, expressed by the
legendary Yaqui sage Don Juan, very close to those of the Taoist tradition,
transmitted by the legendary sages Lao Tzu and Chuang Tzu. The awareness of being embedded in the natural flow of things and the skill to act
accordingly are central to both traditions. As the Taoist sage flows in the current of the Tao, the Yaqui "man of knowledge" needs to be light and fluid to
"see" the essential nature of things.

Taoism and Buddhism are both traditions that deal with the very essence
of spirituality, which is not bound to any particular culture. Buddhism, in particular, has shown throughout its history that it is adaptable to various cultural
situations. It originated with the Buddha in India, then spread to China and
Southeast Asia, ending up in Japan and, many centuries later, jumping across
the Pacific to California. The strongest influence of the Buddhist tradition on
my own thinking has been the emphasis on the central role of compassion in
the attainment of knowledge. According to the Buddhist view, there can be no
wisdom without compassion, which means for me that science is of no value
unless it is accompanied by social concern.

Although the years 1971 and 1972 were very difficult for me, they also
were very exciting. I continued my life as part-time physicist and part-time
hippie, doing research in particle physics at Imperial College while also pur-

suing my larger research in an organized and systematic way. I managed to get several part-time jobs—teaching high-energy physics to a group of engineers, translating technical texts from English into German, teaching mathematics to high school girls—which made enough money for me to survive but did not allow for any material luxury. My life during those two years was very much like that of a pilgrim; its luxuries and joys were not those of the material plane. What carried me through this period was a strong belief in my vision and a conviction that my persistence would eventually be rewarded. During those two years I always had a quote from the Taoist sage Chuang Tzu pinned to my wall: "I have sought a ruler who would employ me for a long time. That I have not found one shows the character of the time."

Fritjof Capra, *Uncommon Wisdom*

It would be a mistake to assume that theological reflection is concerned with the inner experience while science reflects on the outer. No, both science and theology are concerned with reality as a whole. But theology looks at reality under the aspect of our relationship to God, the Horizon, while science narrows its focus to what is contained within our horizon.

David Steindl-Rast, from Fritjof Capra, David Steindl-Rast
with Thomas Matus, *Belonging to the Universe*

Religion and Science

Everything that the human race has done and thought is concerned with the satisfaction of felt needs and the assuagement of pain. One has to keep this constantly in mind if one wishes to understand spiritual movements and their development. Feeling and desire are the motive forces behind all human endeavour and human creation, in however exalted a guise the latter may present itself to us. Now what are the feelings and needs that have led man to religious thought and belief in the widest sense of the words? A little consideration will suffice to show us that the most varying emotions preside over the birth of religious thought and experience. With primitive man it is above all fear that evokes religious notions—fear of hunger, wild beasts, sickness, death. Since at this stage of existence understanding of causal connexions is usually poorly developed, the human mind creates for itself more or less analogous beings on whose wills and actions these fearful happenings depend. One's object now is to secure the favour of these beings by carrying out actions and offering sacrifices which, according to the tradition handed down from generation to generation, propitiate them or make them well disposed towards a mortal. I am speaking now of the religion of fear. This, though not created, is in an important degree stabilized by the formation of a special priestly caste which sets up as a mediator between the people and the beings they fear, and erects a hegemony on this basis. In many cases the leader or ruler whose position depends on other factors, or a privileged class, combines priestly functions with its secular authority in order to make the latter more secure; or the political rulers and the priestly caste make common cause in their own interests.

The social feelings are another source of the crystallization of religion. Fathers and mothers and the leaders of larger human communities are mortal and fallible. The desire for guidance, love, and support prompts men to form the social or moral conception of God. This is the God of Providence who protects, disposes, rewards, and punishes, the God who, according to the width of the believer's outlook, loves and cherishes the life of the tribe or of the human race, or even life as such, the comforter in sorrow and unsatisfied longing, who preserves the souls of the dead. This is the social or moral conception of God.

The Jewish scriptures admirably illustrate the development from the religion of fear to moral religion, which is continued in the New Testament. The religions of all civilized peoples, especially the peoples of the Orient, are primarily moral religions. The development from a religion of fear to moral religion is a great step in a nation's life. That primitive religions are based entirely on fear and the religions of civilized peoples purely on morality is a prejudice against which we must be on our guard. The truth is that they are all intermediate types, with this reservation, that on the higher levels of social life the religion of morality predominates.

Common to all these types is the anthropomorphic character of their conception of God. Only individuals of exceptional endowments and exceptionally high-minded communities, as a general rule, get in any real sense beyond this level. But there is a third state of religious experience which belongs to all of them, even though it is rarely found in a pure form, and which I will call cosmic religious feeling. It is very difficult to explain this feeling to anyone who is entirely without it, especially as there is no anthropomorphic conception of God corresponding to it.

The individual feels the nothingness of human desires and aims and the sublimity and marvellous order which reveals themselves both in nature and in the world of thought. He looks upon individual existence as a sort of prison and wants to experience the universe as a single significant whole. The beginnings of cosmic religious feeling already appear in earlier stages of development—e.g., in many of the Psalms of David and in some of the

Prophets. Buddhism, as we have learnt from the wonderful writings of Schopenhauer especially, contains a much stronger element of it.

The religious geniuses of all ages have been distinguished by this kind of religious feeling, which knows no dogma and no God conceived in man's image; so that there can be no Church whose central teachings are based on it. Hence it is precisely among the heretics of every age that we find men who were filled with the highest kind of religious feeling and were in many cases regarded by their contemporaries as Atheists, sometimes also as saints. Looked at in this light, men like Democritus, Francis of Assisi, and Spinoza are closely akin to one another.

How can cosmic religious feeling be communicated from one person to another, if it can give rise to no definite notion of a God and no theology? In my view, it is the most important function of art and science to awaken this feeling and keep it alive in those who are capable of it.

We thus arrive at a conception of the relation of science to religion very different from the usual one. When one views the matter historically one is inclined to look upon science and religion as irreconcilable antagonists, and for a very obvious reason. The man who is thoroughly convinced of the universal operation of the law of causation cannot for a moment entertain the idea of a being who interferes in the course of events—that is, if he takes the hypothesis of causality really seriously. He has no use for the religion of fear and equally little for social or moral religion. A God who rewards and punishes is inconceivable to him for the simple reason that a man's actions are determined by necessity, external and internal, so that in God's eyes he cannot be responsible, any more than an inanimate object is responsible for the motions it goes through. Hence science has been charged with undermining morality, but the charge is unjust. A man's ethical behaviour should be based effectually on sympathy, education, and social ties; no religious basis is necessary. Man would indeed be in a poor way if he had to be restrained by fear and punishment and hope of reward after death.

It is therefore easy to see why the Churches have always fought science and persecuted its devotees. On the other hand, I maintain that cosmic religious feeling is the strongest and noblest incitement to scientific research. Only those who realize the immense efforts and, above all, the devotion which pioneer work in theoretical science demands, can grasp the strength of the emotion out of which alone such work, remote as it is from the immediate realities of life, can issue. What a deep conviction of the rationality of the universe and what a yearning to understand, were it but a feeble reflection of the mind revealed in this world, Kepler and Newton must have had to enable them to spend years of solitary labour in disentangling the principles of celestial mechanics! Those whose acquaintances with scientific research is derived chiefly from its practical results easily develop a completely false notion of the mentality of the men who, surrounded by a sceptical world, have shown the way to those like-minded with themselves, scattered through the earth and the centuries. Only one who has devoted his life to similar ends can have a vivid realization of what has inspired these men and given them the strength to remain true to their purpose in spite of countless failures. It is cosmic religious feeling that gives a man strength of this sort. A contemporary has said, not unjustly, that in this materialistic age of ours the serious scientific workers are the only profoundly religious people.

Albert Einstein, The World As I See It

First, as to creation: if a human mind can directly influence matter not merely within, but even outside its body, then a divine mind, immanent in the universe or transcendent to it, may be presumed to be capable of imposing forms upon a pre-existing chaos of formless matter, or even, perhaps, of thinking substance as well as forms into existence.

Aldous Huxley, The Perennial Philosophy

The Involved and Evolving Godhead

The involution of a superconscient Spirit in inconscient Matter is the secret cause of this visible and apparent world. The key-word of the earth's riddle is the gradual evolution of a hidden illimitable consciousness and power out of the seemingly inert yet furiously driven force of insensible Nature. Earth-life is one self-chosen habitation of a great Divinity and his aeonic will is to change it from a blind prison into his splendid mansion and high heaven-reaching temple.

The nature of the Divinity in the world is an enigma to the mind, but to our enlarging consciousness it will appear as a presence simple and inevitable. Freed, we shall enter into the immutable stability of an eternal existence that puts on this revealing multitude of significant mutable forms. Illumined, we shall become aware of the indivisible light of an infinite consciousness that breaks out here into multiform grouping and detail of knowledge. Sublimated in might, we shall share the illimitable movement of an omnipotent force that works out its marvels in self-imposed limits. Fixed in griefless bliss, we shall possess the calm and ecstasy of an immeasurable Delight that creates for ever the multitudinous waves and rhythms and the ever increasing outward-going and inward-drawing intensities of its own creative and communicative world-possessing and self-possessing bliss. This, since we are inwardly souls of that Spirit, will be the nature of our fourfold experience when the evolving Godhead will work here in its own unveiled movement.

If that full manifestation had been from the beginning, there would be no terrestrial problem, no anguish of growth, no baffled seeking out of mind and will and life and body towards knowledge and force and joy and an immortal persistence. But this Godhead, whether within us or outside in things and forces and creatures, started from an involution in inconscience of Nature and began by the manifestation of its apparent opposites. Out of a vast cosmic inconscience and inertia and insensibility, an initial disguise that is almost non-existence, the Spirit in Matter has chosen to evolve and slowly shape, as if in a grudging and gradually yielding material, its might and light and infinity and beatitude.

The significance of the terrestrial evolution lies in this slow and progressive liberation of some latent indwelling Spirit. The heart of its mystery is the difficult appearance, the tardy becoming of a divine Something or Someone already involved in physical Nature. The Spirit is there with all its potential forces in a first formal basis of its own supporting, yet resistant substance. Its greater subsequent and deliberately emerging movements, life and mind and intuition and soul and supermind and the light of the Godhead are already there, locked up and obscurely compressed into the initial power and first expressive values of Matter.

Before there could be any evolution, there must needs be this involution of the Divine All that is to emerge. Otherwise there would have been not an ordered and significant evolution, but a successive creation of things unforeseeable, not contained in their antecedents, not their inevitable consequences or right followers in sequence.

This world is not an apparent order fortuitously managed by an inexplicable Chance. Neither is it a marvellous mechanism miraculously contrived by a stumblingly fortunate unconscious Force or mechanical Necessity. It is not even a structure built according to his fancy or will by an external and therefore necessarily a limited Creator. Mentally conceivable, each of these solutions can explain one side or appearance of things; but there is a greater truth that can alone successfully join all the aspects and illumine all the facts of the enigma.

If all were indeed a result of cosmic Chance, there would be no necessity of a new advance; nothing beyond mind need appear in the material world,— as indeed there was then no necessity for even mind to arise at all out of the meaningless blind material whirl. Consciousness itself would be only a fortuitous apparition, a strange hallucinating reflection or ghost of Matter.

Or if all were the work of a mechanical Force, then too mind need not have appeared at all as part of the huge grinding engine; there was no indispensable call for this subtler and yet less competent groping mechanic contrivance. No frail thinking brain should have been there to labour over the quite sufficient cogs and springs and pistons of the first unerring machine. A supermind added on this brilliant and painful complication would be still more a superfluity and a luminous insolence; it could be nothing more than a false pretension of transitory consciousness to govern and possess the greater inconscient Force that is its creator.

Or if an experimenting, external and therefore limited Creator were the inventor of the animal's suffering life and man's fumbling mind and this huge mainly unused and useless universe, there was no reason why he should not have stopped short with the construction of a mental intelligence in his creatures, content with the difficult ingenuity of his labour. Even if he were all-powerful and all-wise, he might well pause there; for if he went farther, the creature would be in danger of rising too near to the level of his Maker.

But if this is the truth of things that an infinite Spirit, an eternal Divine Presence and Consciousness and Force and Bliss is involved and hidden here and slowly emerges, then is it inevitable that its powers or the ascending degrees of its one power should emerge too one after the other till the whole glory is manifested, a mighty divine Fact embodied and dynamic and visible.

All mental ideas of the nature of things are inconclusive considerations of our insufficient logical reason when it attempts in its limited light and ignorant self-sufficiency to weigh the logical probabilities of a universal order which after all its speculation and discovery must remain obscure to it still and an enigma. The true witness and discoverer is our growing consciousness; for that consciousness is itself the sign and power of the evolving Divine, and its growth out of the apparent inconscience of the material universe is the fundamental, the one abiding, progressive index event of the long earth-story.

Only when this evolving consciousness can grow into its own full divine power will we directly know ourselves and the world instead of catching at tags and tail ends of an insufficient figure of knowledge. This full power of the consciousness is supermind or gnosis,—supermind because to reach it we have to pass beyond and turn upon mind, as the mind itself has passed and turned upon life and inconscient matter and gnosis because it is eternally self-possessed of Truth and in its very stuff and nature it is dynamic substance of knowledge.

The true knowledge of things is denied to our reason, because that is not our spirit's greatest essential power but only an expedient, a transitional instrument meant to deal with the appearance of things and their phenomenal process. True knowledge commences only when our consciousness can pass beyond its present normal limit in man: for then it becomes directly aware of its self and of the Power in the world and begins to have at least an initial knowledge by identity which is the sole true knowledge. Henceforward it knows and sees, no longer by the reason groping among external data, but by an ever increasing and always more luminous self-illumining and all-illuminating experience. In the end it will become a conscious part of the Divine revealing itself in the world; its life will be a power for the conscious evolution of that involved Divine which is still unmanifested in the material universe.

Sri Aurobindo, The Hour of God

→ 22 ←

The Universal Force

Over the centuries, a universal force has been revealed to us through prayer, through miraculous and synchronistic events, through mystical experiences and transformatory episodes, and through the messages received in our bodies and psyches. God reveals Himself through the invisible energies which are a part of the universe in which we dwell, and these energies have been called by different names— tao, Holy Spirit, prana, chi, and the Great Spirit of the Shamans. With scientific knowledge, we are able to grasp and accept some of the theories and facts which make up the force of our environment, and in doing so, we can recognize how much more there is to know of this force of infinite life.

At the beginning of this book, when we contemplated God and where He might be, we were searching for a personal deity to heed as we embarked upon the human spiritual quest. Now, through our experiencing and understanding the other religions and science, we have broadened our perspective, and our knowledge. We have moved to the greater place where God is in the All, the supreme intelligence, the loving Universal force that is present simultaneously in everything everywhere. We have discovered the broader perspective, the broader knowledge to surrender in order to allow this universal force—this All—to work through us. We can empty ourselves in order to join with our fellow human beings.

There is much evidence already that we are moving towards becoming a super-race of people that will be able to communicate beyond all borders, languages, and creeds. We will be able to look to the future and beyond. Divinity will be manifested in all our experiences. However, to grow securely into this way of being—to be one with the All at all times, to be part of this divine evolution—we must always act from our hearts, remain conscious in mind and body, surrender to intuition as our inner guide, and know that what we all do and can become is connected to the greater whole, the greater purpose.

The subjects in this chapter, evolution and cosmology among them, are awesome in their ramifications and possibly difficult to comprehend. However, I feel that as a result of the very recent partnerships between Eastern and Western philosophies and science and religion, this material is exciting and revolutionary, and will eventually lead to the new theology and way of being. This theology is still very much in the making, being explored through all the elements here, especially cosmology, where the concepts of creation, destruction, and transformation are viewed in a galactical context. For the first time in our history, theology is emerging from scientific knowledge. The Universal Force of God eternally creates and renews the face of the earth, and we are all affected.

>‹

→ Evolution ‹

"Evolution, the way out towards something that escapes total death, is the hand of God gathering us back to himself."
— PIERRE TEILHARD DE CHARDIN

The evolution of the spirit in the universal force comes through the play of polarities and dualities. Pierre Teilhard de Chardin writes of the evolution of two faiths, faith in God and faith in man, and speculates which is to guide us on this mission forward. Rupert Sheldrake writes of the evolutionary creativity of the planet, and the ways that the partnerships of dualities, for example mother and father and below and above, are the principles of dualities in creativity and reflect the dual situation of "with God and without God." The universe unfolds in such duality according to Sheldrake, and he suggests that it originates at one point of unity and then returns to it.

Here we sit between the two knowns of our own duality in the world's evolution—the scientific knowledge of matter of the universe on the one hand, the experiences of mysticism on the other. In the middle is the void, which contains the mystery, the cosmic chaos, and there, in this place, is the movement and formation of new life.

꙳

It is inevitable that under the influence of the almost magical powers that science gives him of controlling the progress of evolution, modern man should feel himself tied to the future, to the progress of the world, by a sort of religion which is often (wrongly, I believe) treated as neo-paganism. Faith in some evolutionary continuation of the world at variance with the gospel faith in a creative and personal God; a neo-humanist mysticism of an *Ahead* clashing with the Christian mysticism of the *Above*: in this apparent conflict between the old faith in a transcendent God and a youthful "faith" in an immanent universe—it is precisely there, if I am not mistaken, that we shall find, *in its twofold form, scientific and social*, what is really essential in the modern religious crisis. Faith in God, and faith in man or in the world. The whole progress of the Kingdom of God, I am convinced, is today tied up with the problem of reconciling (not superficially but organically) these two currents. "The problem of the two faiths." What method should we follow in attacking it? And who should be given the task, the "mission" of solving it?

Pierre Teilhard de Chardin, *Science and Christ*

Nature Without God

In a mechanistic world, nature worship makes no sense. There is no point in trying to form a personal relationship with blind mechanical processes or with blind chance. All that matters is to try to understand nature so that it can be controlled for human ends. By contrast, in a living world, nature contains living powers far greater than human powers. In the cosmic evolutionary process and in the evolution of life on earth, she is vastly more creative than man. She is the source of life, and she brings forth its myriad forms with inexhaustible creativity. She is all material processes; she is the cosmic flow of energy; she is in all physical fields; she is chance and merciless necessity. Indeed, if there is no God, she is everything.

The trouble is that if nature is the Great Mother and there is no Father, the feminine principle is entirely predominant. An image of the Great Mother as all-powerful is just as unbalanced as an all-powerful Great Father. Some radical feminists and some male chauvinists may like the idea of the cosmic primacy of their own gender, but the metaphors of motherhood and fatherhood inevitably work against a one-sided view. When some people claim that everything comes from the Mother and others claim that everything comes from the Father, there is another obvious possibility: everything comes from both. This is in fact the traditional view in most parts of the world. If the earth is the realm of the Mother, the heavens are the realm of the Father, and all life depends on their relationship. Or if the feminine principle is the cosmic flux of power and energy, the masculine is the source of form and order, like Shakti and Shiva in Indian Tantrism. Or, as in the Taoist view, there is a continuous interplay of the feminine and masculine principles, yin and yang, throughout all nature. And there are many other ways of modeling polarities in terms of female and male, mother and father.

The image of nature as the Great Mother has been associated for millennia with sky-gods. If this male principle is suppressed, if God is eliminated from the picture, he is likely to live on in an unconscious form. This is the case in the mechanistic worldview, where nature is governed by eternal laws that transcend the physical world, laws that are the ghost of the rational, mathematical God of the world-machine. If nature is to be conceived of without God, and without God-substitutes in the form of disembodied laws, then nature must include both male and female principles within herself— or, rather, *itself*. For if nature is all and everything, it cannot be just female or just male but must include and embrace all polarities.

Everywhere we look in the realm of nature we find polarities, such as electrical and magnetic polarities. These can, if we like, be modeled in terms of gender; for example, positive electrical charge is associated with dense, relatively immobile atomic nuclei, a bit like eggs; negative charge is associated with the smaller electrons, moving in swarms, a bit like sperm. But sexual gender is only one of many kinds of natural polarity and only one of the ways we experience polarity in our own lives. Others include the polarities of up and down, in and out, front and back, right and left, past and future, sleeping and waking, friend and foe, sweet and sour, hot and cold, pleasure and pain, good and bad.

On the cosmological level, the primary polarity is between the expansive impulse that underlies the growth of the universe and the contractive field of gravitation that holds everything together. If the centrifugal force is predominant, the universe will expand indefinitely; if the centripetal, the universe will sooner or later stop growing and begin to contract until everything is annihilated in the Big Crunch. No one knows what will happen. But in the meantime, the interplay between these expansive and contractive principles underlies the processes of cosmic evolution.

As the newborn universe expanded and cooled, the primal unified field gave rise to the fundamental fields of gravitation, the quantum fields of material particles, and the electromagnetic field. With further expansion and cooling, galaxies and stars came into being under the influence of gravitation, and within the stars the evolution of the chemical elements continued. Later still, when matter ejected from exploding stars aggregated gravitationally into planets, a great variety of molecular and crystalline forms arose, and liquids, such as water, appeared for the first time. Then life emerged, at least on earth, and biological evolution began. The creative processes of evolution continue to this day and are expressed in our own collective and personal lives. Creativity was inherent in the universe from the beginning. What is the nature of this evolutionary creativity?

Evolutionary Creativity

The cosmic evolutionary process has a direction, an arrow of time. This arrow ultimately depends on the expansive impulse inherent in the cosmos since its birth. But because the growth of the universe has been accompanied by the development of fields, particles, atoms, galaxies, stars, planets, molecules, crystals, and biological life, the arrow of time has a cumulative developmental quality as well. Just as an embryo passes through a series of stages, each of which forms the foundation for the next, so does the evolutionary cosmos. There could be no biological life until there were planets, no planets until there were galaxies and stars, no galaxies and stars until there were atoms of matter, and no atoms of matter until their constituent particles had first come into being.

According to the hypothesis of formative causation, each new pattern of organization (a molecule, a galaxy, a crystal, a fern, or an instinct) involves the appearance of a new kind of morphic field. Through repetition, these new patterns of organization become increasingly habitual. Because of this habit-memory inherent in nature, the evolutionary process is cumulative; new patterns of organization come into being in the context of the existing habits of nature and through repetition in turn become habitual. But if evolutionary creativity—the appearance of new patterns of organization—involves the coming into being of new kinds of morphic fields, where do these fields come from? Here we come back to the mystery of creativity, and as so often happens, there are three kinds of theory.

According to the first theory, all creativity emerges from the mother principle: it is inherent in nature, and emerges from blind, unconscious processes such as the workings of chance. It wells up from material activities. New patterns of organization, new morphic fields, spring into being spontaneously.

The second theory proposes that all creativity comes from the father principle. It descends into the physical world of space and time from a "higher," transcendent level that is mindlike. In the Platonic tradition, this eternal intelligence is the source and abode of the ideas reflected in the world of nature; for Christian Platonists it is none other than the mind of God. For Pythagoreans, this transcendent mindlike realm is mathematical. From mathematical principles, everything is governed. Insofar as new kinds of fields come into being, they are governed by field equations that exist eternally in the transcendent mathematical reality, irrespective of whether they are reified in the physical world or not. Evolutionary creativity involves the manifestation in physical form of mathematical structures that have always existed, or rather that are beyond time altogether.

Third, there is the theory that all creativity comes from an interplay between the mother and the father principle, or, more abstractly, from below and above. It depends on chance, conflict, and necessity, the mother of invention. It arises in particular environments, at particular places and times; it is rooted in the ongoing processes of nature. But at the same time it occurs within the framework of higher systems of order. For example, new species arise within ecosystems; new ecosystems within Gaia; Gaia within the solar system; the solar system within the galaxy; the galaxy within the growing cosmos. At every level of organization, there is a higher level that includes it, right up to the level of the cosmos. Many theoretical physicists now think that the fundamental fields of physics arose from a higher and more inclusive field, the primal unified field of the universe; in the same way, at every level of organization, new morphic fields may arise within and from higher-level fields. Creativity occurs not just upward from the bottom, with new forms arising from less complex systems by spontaneous jumps; it also proceeds downward from the top, through the creative activity of higher-level fields.

The same principles apply to human creativity. It depends on accidents, conflicts, and needs, and is rooted in particular bodily, psychological, cultural, and environmental processes. At the same time, new inventions, new insights, new works of art, come into being in the context of ecologies, societies, cultures, and religions, and ultimately in the context of Gaia, the solar system, the galaxy, and the cosmos—and, as many creative people have themselves thought, God. Traditional theories of human creativity ascribe it to inspiration from a higher source working through the creative individual, who acts as a channel. The same conception underlies the notion of genius; originally the genius was not the person himself but his presiding god or spirit.

As with all polarities and dualities, when we try to conceive of how they are unified or held together, sooner or later we arrive at the idea that they are aspects of a higher unity. And indeed, according to the Big Bang theory, fields and energy arose together within the original cosmic singularity. All physical phenomena—such as sunlight, molecules, trees, and stars—have both a field aspect and an energy aspect. The wave and particle aspects of light, for example, are not two separate things but two aspects of the same structure of activity. So are the field and energy aspects of everything else, including ourselves.

A view of nature without God must account not only for the many kinds of polarity inherent in the world and our experience but also for the higher form of unity that includes these poles. Indeed, since the universe is a unity by definition, there must be a unitary principle that includes all nature. What is the nature of this unity? It is not enough to conceive of it as static, for the universe is evolving. Somehow the underlying unity of nature has to give rise spontaneously to new kinds of organisms and new patterns of behavior, which are themselves unities, wholes, or holons.

Thus a view of nature without God must include a creative unitary principle that includes the entire cosmos and unites the polarities and dualities found throughout the natural realm. But this is not far removed from views of nature *with* God.

Creative Trinities

An understanding of evolutionary creativity in terms of the interaction of two principles, such as fields and energy, inevitably implies a third, unifying principle of which they are both aspects. This unity is implied in the sexual metaphor; the generative power of father and mother depends on their union, and their offspring unite aspects of both parents. This is expressed in the most direct way in Indian tantric images of Shakti and Shiva in sexual embrace; in a more abstract manner in the Taoist representation of yin and yang intertwined and interpenetrating within a circle unifying both, the Tao.... In other trinities, the polarity of gender is replaced by different principles, as in trinities of goddesses and gods such as the Hindu trinity of Brahma the creator, Vishnu the preserver, and Shiva the destroyer. Here Vishnu could represent the organizing fields of nature, Shiva the cosmic flux of energy, and Brahma the creative unity that includes both.

The Christian conception of God is as a creative trinity: the Father, Son, and Holy Spirit. The mystery of the Holy Trinity has traditionally been considered in a variety of ways. One is the psychological model, favored by St. Augustine. Here the Father is the knower, the Son the known, and the Spirit the relationship between them, the bliss of knowing. Another model is implicit in the identification of the Son with the Word, or Logos. Clearly this biblical concept of the Word relates to the spoken rather than the written word and thus implies not only a vibratory pattern of physical activity but also an unfolding pattern of meaning. And just as human speech involves imposing an ordered pattern of vibrations on the outward flow of the breath, so the creative Word of God works together with the breath of God, the onward and outward movement of the Spirit. The Spirit is the principle of flow and change. The traditional images of the Spirit include breath, wind, life, flames, and the flying dove. Its movement is free and unpredictable:

"The wind blows where it wills, you hear the sound of it; but you do not know where it comes from or where it is going" (John 3:8).

In the doctrine of the Holy Trinity in the Orthodox churches, the Spirit plays a richer and fuller role than it does in most Western theology and gives a much stronger sense of the immanence of nature in the divine:

> *The creative energies of God did not merely produce the created world from without like a builder or engineer, but are the ever-present, indwelling and spontaneous causes of every manifestation of life within it, whatever form this may take. [This understanding] depends, in other words, upon the recognition of the continuing, vitalizing activity of the Holy Spirit in the world, animating these energies—luminous uncreated radiations of the divine—in the very heart of every existing thing.*

In the context of evolutionary cosmology, the Spirit underlies the onward flow of energy and the expansive impulse of the universe; the Word is in the patterns of activity and meaning expressed through fields. God the Father is the speaker, the conscious source of both Word and Spirit who transcends both. Thus, the energy and fields of the evolutionary cosmos have a common source, a unity. And not just a unity but a conscious unity.

If the fields and energy of nature are aspects of the Word and Spirit of God, then God must have an evolutionary aspect, evolving along with the cosmos, with biological life and humanity. God is not remote and separate from nature, but immanent in it. Yet at the same time, God is the unity that transcends it. In other words, God is not just immanent in nature, as in pantheist philosophies, and not just transcendent, as in deist philosophies, but both immanent and transcendent, a philosophy known as *panentheism*. As the fifteenth-century mystic Nicholas of Cusa put it: "Divinity is the enfolding and unfolding of everything that is. Divinity is in all things in such a way that all things are in divinity."

The creative polarity of Spirit and Word, like other creative polarities, can be modeled in terms of gender, but in an ambiguous manner. If we think of the feminine principle as active, like Shakti, then the Spirit is feminine, the Word masculine. The word for "spirit" in Hebrew, *ruah*, is indeed feminine. (In Greek, the corresponding word, *pneuma*, is neuter; in Latin it is masculine, *spiritus*.) Alternatively, taking the masculine principle as active, then the Spirit is masculine and the Word feminine. This is an unfamiliar way of thinking, given the identification of the Word with the Son. But there is no doubt that the biblical concept of the Word of God has much in common with the feminine divine Wisdom, Sophia. In the Book of Proverbs, she speaks of herself as follows:

The Lord created me in the beginning of his works
before all else that he made, long ago.
Alone, I was fashioned in times long past,
at the beginning, long before earth itself....
When he set the heavens in their place I was there...
when he prescribed the limits for the sea
and knit together earth's foundations.
Then I was at his side each day,
his darling and delight,
playing in his presence continually,
playing on the earth, when he had finished it,
while my delight was in mankind.
(Proverbs 8:22–3, 27, 29–31)

In the prologue to St. John's Gospel, the Word is very like Wisdom:

In the beginning the Word already was. The Word was in God's pres-
ence, and what God was, the Word was. He was with God at the
beginning, and through him all things came to be; without him no cre-
ated thing came into being. In him was life, and that life was the light
of mankind.
(John 1:1–5)

The Gender of God

When God is conceived of in relation to Mother Earth or Mother Nature, he
is male. The Father and the Mother create together. In the first chapter of the
Book of Genesis, the primal mother principle is the void or the deep, coexistent with God from the start. From this womb everything ultimately comes
forth, through a series of divisions made by God: the light from the darkness,
the day from the night, the heaven from the earth, the seas from the dry land.
The power to give birth is implicit in the primal void or deep, and present in
the earth and the seas. When God calls forth plants and animals, he does not
create them directly; they are born from the earth and the waters, from the
womb of the Mother.

But when God is conceived of as creating everything from nothing, as in
the theology of St. Thomas Aquinas, the mother principle has to come forth
from God or be inherent within God. In this sense, God is both Mother and
Father, male and female. We have already seen how this male-female polarity can be expressed in terms of the Word and the Spirit within the Holy
Trinity. But then is God the Father also God the Mother? Is the Godhead, the
source of the Holy Trinity itself, masculine, feminine, or neuter?

The earliest Hebrew name for God was *elohim*, a plural word of obscure origins that could mean "goddesses" and "gods," and was also used to mean the "spirits of the ancestors." Nevertheless, by convention, God is treated as masculine, and so it is both surprising and illuminating to encounter the feminine imagery employed by medieval mystics such as Meister Eckhart. "God lies in the maternity bed, like a woman who has given birth, in every good soul which has abandoned its self-centeredness and received the indwelling of God." The hermitess Julian of Norwich wrote of the maternal aspect of the Godhead enclosing us in "the deep Wisdom of the Trinity [who] is our Mother."

Just as an all-powerful nature cannot be simply female, neither can an all-powerful God be simply male. Either we have to think of the male-female polarity as coexistent from the start, or we have to derive them both from a common source that transcends the polarity between them. Even if we want to try to conceive of the universe in purely scientific terms, the same questions arise. Science, like religion, is pervaded by a strong sense of a fundamental unity. This intuition underlay Einstein's search for a unified field theory and currently inspires attempts to conceive of the primal field of the cosmos and the primal source of energy. Here science meets theology; for if fields and energy have a common source that transcends both, we find ourselves back in the field of creative trinities. And as theology meets science, a new evolutionary conception of the creative trinity is coming into being; theology itself is evolving.

An Evolutionary God

In a Christian context, fields can be thought of as an aspect of the Word and energy as an aspect of the Spirit. If the Word and Spirit of God are immanent in the realm of nature and immanent in the creative process, then God must be evolving along with nature. At the same time, God somehow gives this process its overall purpose, which the evolutionary mystic Teilhard de Chardin conceived of as the Omega Point, the state of unity toward which everything is developing. Such a conception is necessarily obscure since it goes beyond anything that has happened so far, beyond our limited powers of thought. This is how Teilhard described it:

> *By its structure Omega, in its ultimate principle, can only be a distinct Center radiating at the core of a system of centers; a grouping in which the personalization of the All and personalizations of the elements reach their maximum, simultaneously and without merging, under the influence of a supremely autonomous focus of union.*

New forms of theology have recently been developing in an attempt to conceive of the God of a living, evolutionary cosmos. Evolutionary theology involves a radical break with traditional theological ideas of God as timeless, uninfluenced by events in the world, acting on it but not really interacting with it. However, the God of the Bible was intimately involved with the history of the world and humanity. This remote, impassive image is not biblical but developed in the early church under the influence of Greek philosophy. In the spirit of Platonism, the mind of God was identified with the transcendent realm of eternal Forms; under the influence of Aristotle, God was conceived of as the unmoved mover.

By contrast, in the new, evolutionary view of God,

> like all living things, God not only acts on others, but also takes account of others in the divine self-constitution.... God is not the world, and the world is not God. But God includes the world, and the world includes God. God perfects the world and the world perfects God. There is no world apart from God, and there is no God apart from some world. Of course there are differences. Whereas no world can exist without God, God can exist without this world. Not only our planet but the whole universe may disappear and be superseded by something else, and God will continue. But since God, like all living things, only perfectly, embodies the principle of internal relations, God's life depends on there being some world to include. (C. Birch and J. B. Cobb, 1981)

Mystery

Each of us, faced with the mystery of our existence and experience, has to try to find some way of making sense of it. We have a choice of philosophies: the mechanistic theory of nature and of human life, with God as an optional extra; the theory of nature as alive but without God; or the theory of a living God together with living nature. Each of these views can be elaborated intellectually, each can be defended on rational grounds, and each is held with deep conviction by many people. In the end, we have to choose between them on the basis of intuition. Our choice is influenced by our acknowledgment of mystery and in turn affects our tolerance of it. Those with the lowest mystery-tolerance thresholds are drawn to the mechanistic-atheistic worldview, which as a matter of principle denies the existence of mysterious entities like souls and God, and portrays a disenchanted, unmagical reality proceeding entirely mechanically. Those who acknowledge the life of evolutionary nature admit the mystery of life and creativity. And those who acknowledge the life of God are consciously open to the mystery of divine consciousness, grace, and love.

Rupert Sheldrake, The Rebirth of Nature

It is thus that the age of science will open for the world. And science, in all probability, will be progressively more impregnated by mysticism (*not* in order *to be directed*, but in order *to be animated, by it*). Impelled by the logic of effort and the hidden dynamism of matter towards ever more universal hopes—realising, with pitiless clarity, the absurdity of carrying on with a human task that has no future—that portion of mankind that is following the upward road will concentrate continually more exclusively on the search for, and the anticipation of, a God; and never will Christ have found in Creation a more magnificent capacity for either loving or hating him. The truth is that forced against one another by the increase in their numbers and the multiplication of their interrelations—compressed together by the activation of a common force and the awareness of a common distress—the men of the future will form, in some way, but one single consciousness; and since, once their initiation is complete, they will have gauged the strength of their associated minds, the immensity of the universe, and the straitness of their prison, this consciousness will be truly adult and of age. May we not imagine that at that moment, a truly and totally human act will be effected for the first time, in a final option—the yes or no as an answer to God, pronounced individually by beings in each one of whom the sense of human freedom and responsibility will have reached its full development?

It is by no means easy to picture to ourselves what sort of event the end of the world could be. A sidereal catastrophe would be a fitting counterpart to our individual deaths, but it would entail the end of the earth rather than that of the cosmos—and it is the cosmos that has to disappear.

The more I think about this mystery, the more it appears to me, in my dreams, as a "turning-about" of consciousness—as an eruption of interior life—as an ecstasy. There is no need to rack our brains to understand how the material vastness of the universe will ever be able to disappear. Spirit has only to be reversed, to move into a different zone, for the whole shape of the world immediately to be changed.

Pierre Teilhard de Chardin, Science and Christ

Whether or not we choose to admit that the evolution of the cosmic organism is purposive, the very idea that other universes are possible raises the question of not only why this particular universe has the quantitative features that it does but how its particular features are maintained. The eternal realm of mathematics imagined by Platonists presumably contains the mathematical laws of all possible universes, so how was this subset of mathematical possibilities brought into relation to the newborn universe in the first place and maintained thereafter?

Again, God could provide one kind of answer: He designed this universe, skillfully selecting the values of the numerical constants of nature, and he then maintained them by remembering them. Alternatively, the "constants" could be remembered within nature herself rather than by a mind transcending nature. Once particular patterns were established—however they came into being in the first place—they could become increasingly habitual through repetition. Perhaps the numerical constants of physics and the properties of the known physical fields are in fact long-established habits. They could have been different, but only a universe that developed these particular habits could hang together as ours does and allow the evolution of habits of chemical, biological, cultural, and mental organization within it.

Natural Selection of the Habits of Nature

If nature is organized by eternal transcendent mathematical laws, they have to be framed with the greatest precision. The exact values of all numerical "constants" have to be specified precisely from the outset. The designing mind of a mathematical God is still there in the background. By contrast, if nature is organized habitually, the regularities of nature can grow up within the developing cosmos by an organic evolutionary process. Not all new patterns of organization that come into being in the physical, chemical, biological, cultural, and mental realms are viable. Only those that are in harmony with their environment can survive, and only through survival and repetition can they become habitual.

The evolution of habits—such as the way protein molecules fold up, crystals form, or plants develop; or the instincts of animals; or human cultural and mental habits—involves a two-stage process. First, the new pattern has to come into being by a creative leap or synthesis; second, it is subject to natural selection.

You are probably familiar with this two-stage process from your own experience. New ideas, for example, or new ways of doing things generally arise suddenly by a creative jump or insight. Then they are subject to a process of selection. Some are so successful that they become habitual; others are rejected, die out, or fade away. The same is true of biological evolution. New bodily forms can arise suddenly, for example, as a result of genetic mutations or unusual environmental conditions, and so can new patterns of behavior. These are then subject to natural selection, and the successful oft-repeated patterns become increasingly habitual. According to the hypothesis of formative causation, this happens not only because of genetic inheritance but also because of morphic resonance from previous similar organisms.

Creative jumps also occur in the chemical realm. Many new kinds of molecules and crystals are still coming into being for the first time through the activities of synthetic chemists; they are new material forms, new patterns, new syntheses. Indeed, all existing molecules and crystals, such as the benzene molecule or the mica crystal, must likewise have come into being for the first time at some stage in the past; even atoms did not always exist. Their present forms and properties may just be successful habits. Natural selection may be operating in the atomic, molecular, and crystalline realms, just as it is in the biological realm. And if molecules and crystals do indeed inherit a memory from previous ones of their kind by morphic resonance, it should be possible to study the building-up of habits by means of experiments with newly synthesized chemicals and crystals.

Galaxies and stars also represent repetitive patterns of organization, falling into distinct types with characteristic life cycles. Perhaps these too are habitual; successful patterns of galactic and stellar organization have, through repetition, become increasingly probable. The same may be true of planetary systems and planets. Perhaps there are other planets elsewhere of the same species as Venus, say, or Jupiter, or earth. This raises the mind-boggling possibility that our own planet may be in morphic resonance with similar planets elsewhere in the universe. The evolutionary process on earth may have been following a habitual pattern already established on other similar planets. Or perhaps ours is the first planet to follow this kind of developmental path, and there are others tagging along behind.

Rupert Sheldrake, *The Rebirth of Nature*

The search of reason ends at the shore of the known; on the immense expanse beyond it only the sense of the ineffable can glide. It alone knows the route to that which is remote from experience and understanding. Neither of them is amphibious: reason cannot go beyond the shore, and the sense of the ineffable is out of place where we measure, where we weigh.

We do not leave the shore of the known in search of adventure or suspense or because of the failure of reason to answer our questions. We sail because our mind is like a fantastic seashell, and when applying our ear to its lips we hear a perpetual murmur from the waves beyond the shore.

Citizens of two realms, we all must sustain a dual allegiance: we sense the ineffable in one realm, we name and exploit reality in another. Between the two we set up a system of references, but we can never fill the gap. They are as far and as close to each other as time and calendar, as violin and melody, as life and what lies beyond the last breath.

Abraham Joshua Heschel, *Man Is Not Alone*

Blessed are those who take a leap towards the Future.

The Mother, *Words of the Mother*, Part Two

✦ The Cosmic Sense ✦

"It is cosmic religious feeling that gives a man strength. . . . According to Einstein, it is the function in particular of art and science 'to awaken this feeling and keep it alive in those who are capable of it.'"

—HANS KÜNG

Within the void of cosmic chaos mentioned in the last section and lying between the relative view (the scientific theory of relativity of the polarities), and the "absolute knowledge" of the mystic, is a third dimension of the cosmic whole of virtual reality. David Bohm and Mark Edwards write of the three basic dimensions of the life of a human being (individual, collective, and cosmic); Sri Aurobindo also discusses the three levels of consciousness, explaining the cosmic element inherent in us.

This apocalyptical awareness of our own place in this third dimension is one of ultimate joy in belonging to the universe—of throwing ourselves completely outside our old world and into the galaxy, to a place of great magnificence. This awareness is described and revealed in two poems here, Allen Ginsberg's cosmic sense of his self as a rocketing star, "one united ray," followed by Yogananda's blissful samadhi in the Cosmic sea.

➤◄

I see science and mysticism as two complementary manifestations of the human mind; of its rational and intuitive faculties. The modern physicist experiences the world through an extreme specialization of the rational mind; the mystic through an extreme specialization of the intuitive mind. The two approaches are entirely different and involve far more than a certain view of the physical world. However, they are complementary, as we have learned to say in physics. Neither is comprehended in the other, nor can either of them be reduced to the other, but both of them are necessary, supplementing one another for a fuller understanding of the world. To paraphrase an old Chinese saying, mystics understand the roots of the *Tao* but not its branches; scientists understand its branches but not its roots. Science does not need mysticism and mysticism does not need science; but man needs both. Mystical experience is necessary to understand the deepest nature of things, and science is essential for modern life. What we need, therefore, is not a synthesis but a dynamic interplay between mystical intuition and scientific analysis.

So far, this has not been achieved in our society. At present, our attitude is too *yang*—to use again Chinese phraseology—too rational, male and aggressive. Scientists themselves are a typical example. Although their theories are leading to a world view which is similar to that of the mystics, it is striking how little this has affected the attitudes of most scientists. In mysticism, knowledge cannot be separated from a certain way of life which becomes its living manifestation. To acquire mystical knowledge means to undergo a transformation; one could even say that the knowledge *is* the transformation. Scientific knowledge, on the other hand, can often stay abstract and theoretical. Thus most of today's physicists do not seem to realize the philosophical, cultural and spiritual implications of their theories. Many of them actively support a society which is still based on the mechanistic, fragmented world view, without seeing that science points beyond such a view, towards a oneness of the universe which includes not only our natural environment but also our fellow human beings. I believe that the world view implied by modern physics is inconsistent with our present society, which does not reflect the harmonious interrelatedness we observe in nature. To achieve such a state of dynamic balance, a radically different social and economic structure will be needed: a cultural revolution in the true sense of the word. The survival of our whole civilization may depend on whether we can bring about such a change. It will depend, ultimately, on our ability to adopt some of the *yin* attitudes of Eastern mysticism; to experience the wholeness of nature and the art of living with it in harmony.

Fritjof Capra, *The Tao of Physics*

In the Eastern view then, as in the view of modern physics, everything in the universe is connected to everything else and no part of it is fundamental. The properties of any part are determined, not by some fundamental law, but by the properties of all the other parts. Both physicists and mystics realize the resulting impossibility of fully explaining any phenomenon, but then they take different attitudes. Physicists, as discussed before, are satisfied with an approximate understanding of nature. The Eastern mystics, on the other hand, are not interested in approximate, or "relative" knowledge. They are concerned with "absolute" knowledge involving an understanding of the totality of Life. Being well aware of the essential interrelationship of the universe, they realize that to explain something means, ultimately, to show how it is connected to everything else.

Fritjof Capra, *The Tao of Physics*

But of course we must not overlook the fact that the individual human being as a whole has his or her own peculiar features, even though many of these are chosen out of the collective pool. These include the body of that person, and also the brain and nervous system. Moreover, each person has certain unique potentialities, based not only on special talents and a particular inherited constitution but also on what has been learned from experiences that are, in some ways at least, different from those of anyone else. But then there is something much deeper that really belongs in a much more essential way to the individual. I would say this involves the possibility of a connection with what I would call the cosmic dimension of life.

I think that the life of a human being has three basic dimensions: the individual, the collective, and the cosmic. We have already discussed the first two to some extent. However, since ancient times, people have had a regard for something greater, the whole, cosmic. Perhaps in early times people felt very close to nature. Under these conditions nature can be felt as something that gives a sense of the whole that goes far beyond the individual or the collective.

David Bohm and Mark Edwards, *Changing Consciousness*

The Three Levels of Consciousness

The spiritual consciousness is that in which we enter into the awareness of Self, the Spirit, the Divine and are able to see in all things their essential reality and the play of forces and phenomena as proceeding from that essential Reality.

The cosmic consciousness is that in which the limits of ego, personal mind and body disappear and one becomes aware of a cosmic vastness which is or filled by a cosmic spirit and aware also of the direct play of cosmic forces, universal mind forces, universal life forces, universal energies of Matter, universal overmind forces. But one does not become aware of all these together; the opening of the cosmic consciousness is usually progressive. It is not that the ego, the body, the personal mind disappear, but one feels them as only a small part of oneself. One begins to feel others too as part of oneself or varied repetitions of oneself, the same self modified by Nature in other bodies. Or, at the least, as living in the larger universal self which is henceforth one's own greater reality. All things in fact begin to change their nature and appearance; one's whole experience of the world is radically different from that of those who are shut up in their personal selves. One begins to know things by a different kind of experience, more direct, not depending on the external mind and the senses. It is not that the possibility of error disappears, for that cannot be so long as mind of any kind is one's instrument for transcribing knowledge, but there is a new, vast and deep way of experience, seeing, knowing, contacting things; and the confines of knowledge can be rolled back to an almost unmeasurable degree. The thing one has to be on guard against in the cosmic consciousness is the play of a magnified ego, the vaster attacks of the hostile forces—for they too are part of the cosmic consciousness—and the attempt of the cosmic Illusion (Ignorance, Avidya) to prevent the growth of the soul into the cosmic Truth. These are things that one has to learn from experience; mental teaching or explanation is quite insufficient. To enter safely into the cosmic consciousness and to pass safely through it, it is necessary to have strong unegoistic sincerity and to have the psychic being, with its divination of truth and unfaltering orientation toward the Divine, already in front in the nature.

The ordinary consciousness is that in which one knows things only or mainly by the intellect, the external mind and the senses and knows forces etc. only by their outward manifestations and results and the rest by inference from these data. There may be some play of mental intuition, deeper psychic seeing or impulsions, spiritual intimations, etc.—but in the ordinary consciousness these are incidental only and do not modify its fundamental character.

Sri Aurobindo, *Words of Sri Aurobindo*, Third Series

A mere factual truth (it is raining this morning) is less elevated in the scale of truth than a scientific truth such as the law of falling bodies. So physical truths are less elevated in the scale of truth than either mathematical truths or metaphysical truths, both of which are eternal, that is to say that their object is beyond time. The idea of number is drawn from sense experience, but once it has been disengaged by the intellect, it places the intellect itself in the presence of an objective world, a world which exists, no doubt, only in the mind, but which nevertheless exists as a universe set out for itself and independent of us, consistent and inexhaustible. It is not a world constructed by us; we penetrate into it as best we can through those central openings which are our axioms and postulates.

Jacques Maritain, *Approaches to God*

If all metaphysics thinks of Being as eternity and independence of time, it means precisely this: the idea of beings sees them as in their Being independent of time, the idea of time sees time in the sense of a passing away. What must pass away cannot be the ground of the eternal. To be properly beings in their Being means to be independent of time in the sense of a passing away. But what about that definition, here left unattended, of Being itself as being present, even as the enduring presence? What about Being as the being-present, in whose light time was conceived as a passing away, and even eternity as the present "now"? Is not this definition of Being ruled by the view of presence, the present—ruled, that is, by the view of time, and of a time of such a nature as we could never surmise, let alone think, with the help of the traditional time concept? What about Being and Time, then? Must not one as much as the other, Being as much as Time—must not both become questionable in their relatedness, first questionable and finally doubtful? And does not this show, then, that something was left unthought at the very core of the definition which is regarded as guiding all Western metaphysics—something essential in the essential nature of Being? The question "Being and Time" points to what is unthought in all metaphysics. Metaphysics consists of this unthought matter; what is unthought in metaphysics is therefore not a defect of metaphysics. Still less may we declare metaphysics to be false, or even reject it as a wrong turn, a mistake, on the grounds that it rests upon this unthought matter.

Martin Heidegger, *What Is Called Thinking?*

The way in which we *interpret* mystical experience must be plausible. That is to say, it must fit in with and/or throw light upon the best available knowledge about life and the universe. As we enter the latter half of the twentieth century, there seem to me to be three main trends in scientific thought which are at once three ways of expressing the same idea, and three ways of *describing* the identity of things or events as the mystic *feels* them.

The first is the growing recognition that causally connected or related events are not separate events, but aspects of a single event. To describe a causal relation is a fumbling way of recognizing that cause A and effect B go together in the same way as the head and the tail of a cat. This implies that earlier events may often depend in some way upon later events, somewhat as an electric impulse will not depart from the positive pole until the negative pole is established or connected, or as the meaning of a word in a sentence is determined by words that follow. Compare, "That is the bark of a tree," with, "That is the bark of a dog." The sentence as a whole is the event which determines the function and meaning of the "separate" words. Perhaps the best illustration of this way of understanding causality is that the event *rainbow* does not occur without the simultaneous presence of sun, atmospheric moisture, and an observer—all in a certain angular configuration. If any one of the three is absent, there is no rainbow. This may be difficult to understand in the case of the absence of an observer unless one remembers that every observer sees the rainbow in a different place. Where, then, *is* the rainbow? A little consideration will show that something of the same kind must be true of *all* experiences, not only of flimsy and transparent luminescences, but also of such apparently solid things as mountains.

The second is the tendency to think of the behavior of things and objects as the behavior of *fields*—spatial, gravitational, magnetic or social. The reason is that careful and detailed description of the behavior or movement of a body must *also* involve description of the behavior of its environment or surrounding space. Where, then, does the behavior start? Inside the body, or outside it in the surrounding space? The answer is in both and neither, because it is best to abandon the body *and* the space for a new descriptive unit, the body-space, the organism-environment, the figure-ground. It is important to distinguish this way of looking at things from old-fashioned environmental determinism, which describes the organism as moved *by* the environment rather than moving *with* it.

The third, long familiar to biologists, is what Ludwig von Bertelannfy has called Systems Theory. This is approximately that the structure and behavior of any system is only partially accounted for by analysis and description of the smaller units that allegedly "compose" it. For what any of these units is and does depends upon its place in and its relation to the system as a whole. Thus blood in a test tube is not the same thing as blood flowing in veins. For an organism disposes itself in and as various parts; it is not composed of them as one puts together tubes, wires, dials and condensers to make a radio.

These are, then, three ways of approaching the world as a unitary and relational system which are highly useful in the sciences but strangely unfamiliar to common sense. For the latter derives from political, constructionist and mechanical models of nature which, in turn, strongly influence our sensation of the person as an enclosed unit of life excluded from the world outside. But these unitary, relational and "fieldish" ways of thinking in the sciences give immense plausibility to non-dualist or pantheist (to be frightfully exact, "pan*en*theist") types of metaphysic, and to theories of the self more-or-less akin to the "multisolipsism" of the Hindu *atman-is-Brahman* doctrine.

When, for example, we consider the full implications of the way in which we see the rainbow, and realize that this is *also* the way in which we perceive the clouds, the sun, the earth and the stars, we find ourselves strangely close to the "idealism" of Mahayana Buddhism, Berkeley, and Bradley—but with the great advantage of being able to describe the situation in physical and neurological terms, and no gobbledy-gook about "minds" and "souls" to offend the prejudices of the tough-minded or (should I say?) hard-headed. And to such as these the subjective experiences of the mystics are always suspect, for might they not be *distortions* of consciousness brought about by stress, self-hypnosis, fasting, hyperoxygenation or drugs? There is, then, a more structural and objective foundation for that leap of faith in which a man may dare to think that he is not a stranger in the universe, nor a solitary and tragic flash of awareness in endless and overwhelming darkness. For in the light of what we now know in physical terms, it is not unreasonable to wager that deep down at the center "I myself" is "It"—as in "as *it* was in the beginning, is now and ever shall be, world without end."

If this is a hope, or a fervent belief, Krishnamurti is right in saying that it should be challenged and tested with the question, "Why do you want to believe that? Is it because you are afraid of dying, of coming to an end? Is this identification with the cosmic Self the last desperate resort of your ego to continue its game?" Indeed, if this Supreme Identity is, for me, a belief to which I am clinging, I am in total self-contradiction. Not only is there no sense in clinging to what I am; the very act of clinging also implies that I do not really know that I *am* it! Such belief is merely doubt dressed up. The final meaning of negative theology, of knowing God by unknowing, of the abandonment of idols both sensible and conceptual, is that ultimate faith is not in or upon anything at all. It is complete letting go. Not only is it beyond theology; it is also beyond atheism and nihilism. Such letting go cannot be attained. It cannot be acquired or developed through perseverance and exercises, except insofar as such efforts prove the impossibility of acquiring it. Letting go comes only through desperation. When you know that it is beyond you—beyond your powers of action as beyond your powers of relaxation. When you give up every last trick and device for getting it, including this "giving up" as something that one might *do*, say, at ten o'clock tonight. That you cannot by any means do it—that IS it! *That* is the mighty self-abandonment which gives birth to the stars.

Alan Watts, Beyond Theology

"It is your story that is being told, you are part of it all." So the shift from the part to the whole also involves the realization that I belong to the whole universe, not as if I were a negligible phenomenon on a small planet in a minor solar system but as a vital participant in the living cosmos. This realization is both the context and the condition of God's self-disclosure.

Thomas Matus, in Fritjof Capra, David Steindl-Rast
with Thomas Matus, *Belonging to the Universe*

```
          *
       *     *
   POEM
   Rocket
       .       .
       .       .
       .       .
       .       .
     . . . . . . . .
   **************
```

"Be a Star-screwer!" — GREGORY CORSO

Old moon my eyes are new moon with human footprint
no longer Romeo Sadface in drunken river Loony Pierre
    eyebrow, goof moon
O possible moon in Heaven we get to first of ageless
    constellations of names
as God is possible as All is possible so we'll reach another life.

Moon politicians earth weeping and warring in eternity
tho not one star disturbed by screaming madmen from
    Hollywood
oil tycoons from Romania making secret deals with flabby
    green Plutonians—
slave camps on Saturn Cuban revolutions on Mars?
Old life and new side by side, will Catholic church find Christ
    on Jupiter

Mohammed rave in Uranus will Buddha be acceptable on the
    stolid planets

or will we find Zoroastrian temples flowering on Neptune?
What monstrous new ecclesiastical design on the entire
    universe unfolds in the dying Pope's brain?
Scientist alone is true poet he gives us the moon
he promises the stars he'll make us a new universe if it
    comes to that
O Einstein I should have sent you my flaming mss.
O Einstein I should have pilgrimaged to your white hair!

O fellow travellers I write you a poem in Amsterdam in
    the Cosmos
where Spinoza ground his magic lenses long ago
I write you a poem long ago
already my feet are washed in death
Here I am naked without identity
with no more body than the fine black tracery of pen mark
    on soft paper
as star talks to star multiple beams of sunlight all the same
    myriad thought
in one fold of the universe where Whitman was
and Blake and Shelley saw Milton dwelling as in a starry temple
brooding in his blindness seeing all—
Now at last I can speak to you beloved brothers of an unknown
    moon
real Yous squatting in whatever form amidst Platonic Vapors
    of Eternity
I am another Star.
Will you eat my poems or read them
or gaze with aluminum blind plates on sunless pages?
do you dream or translate & accept data with indifferent
    droopings of antennae?
do I make sense to your flowery green receptor eyesockets?
    do you have visions of God?
Which way will the sunflower turn surrounded by millions
    of suns?

This is my rocket my personal rocket I send up my message
    Beyond
Someone to hear me there
My immortality

without steel or cobalt basalt or diamond gold or mercurial fire
without passports filing cabinets bits of paper warheads
without myself finally
pure thought
message all and everywhere the same
I send up my rocket to land on whatever planet awaits it
preferably religious sweet planets no money
fourth dimensional planets where Death shows movies
plants speak (courteously) of ancient physics and poetry itself
    is manufactured by the trees
the final Planet where the Great Brain of the Universe sits
    waiting for a poem to land in His golden pocket
joining the other notes mash-notes love-sighs complaints-
    musical shrieks of despair and the million unutterable
    thoughts of frogs
I send you my rocket of amazing chemical
more than my hair my sperm or the cells of my body
the speeding thought that flies upward with my desire as
    instantaneous as the universe and faster than light
and leave all other questions unfinished for the moment to
    turn back to sleep in my dark bed on earth.

Amsterdam 1958

Allen Ginsberg, *Kaddish and
Other Poems 1958–1960*

Cosmos, Eros and Logos

For actually there is a cosmos for man only when the universe becomes his
home, with its holy hearth whereon he offers sacrifice; there is Eros for man
only when beings become for him pictures of the eternal, and community is
revealed along with them; and there is Logos for man only when he
addresses the mystery with work and service for the spirit.

    Form's silent asking, man's loving speech, the mute proclamation of the
creature, are all gates leading into the presence of the Word.

    But when the full and complete meeting is to take place, the gates are
united in one gateway of real life, and you no longer know through which
you have entered.   [I and Thou, 102]

Martin Buber, *I and Thou*

Samadhi

Vanished the veils of light and shade,
Lifted every vapor of sorrow,
Sailed away all dawns of fleeting joy,
Gone the dim sensory mirage.
Love, hate, health, disease, life, death:
Perished these false shadows on the screen of duality.
The storm of *maya* stilled
By magic wand of intuition deep.
Present, past, future, no more for me,
But ever-present, all-flowing I, I, everywhere.
Planets, stars, stardust, earth,
Volcanic bursts of doomsday cataclysms,
Creation's molding furnace,
Glaciers of silent X-rays, burning electron floods,
Thoughts of all men, past, present, to come,
Every blade of grass, myself, mankind,
Each particle of universal dust,
Anger, greed, good, bad, salvation, lust,
I swallowed, transmuted all
Into a vast ocean of blood of my own one Being.
Smoldering joy, oft-puffed by meditation
Blinding my tearful eyes,
Burst into immortal flames of bliss,
Consumed my tears, my frame, my all.
Thou art, I am Thou,
Knowing, Knower, Known, as One!
Tranquilled, unbroken thrill, eternally living, ever-new peace.
Enjoyable beyond imagination of expectancy, *samadhi* bliss!
Not an unconscious state
Or mental chloroform without willful return,
Samadhi but extends my conscious realm
Beyond limits of the mortal frame
To farthest boundary of eternity
Where I, the Cosmic Sea,
Watch the little ego floating in Me.
Mobile murmurs of atoms are heard,
The dark earth, mountains, vales, lo! molten liquid!
Flowing seas change into vapors of nebulae!
Aum blows upon vapors, opening wondrously their veils,

Oceans stand revealed, shining electrons,
Till, at the last sound of the cosmic drum,*
Vanish the grosser lights into eternal rays
Of all-pervading bliss.
From joy I came, for joy I live, in sacred joy I melt.
Ocean of mind, I drink all creation's waves.
Four veils of solid, liquid, vapor, light,
Lift aright.
I, in everything, enter the Great Myself.
Gone forever: fitful, flickering shadows of mortal memory;
Spotless is my mental sky—below, ahead, and high above;
Eternity and I, one united ray.
A tiny bubble of laughter, I
Am become the Sea of Mirth Itself.

> Paramahansa Yogananda, *Autobiography of a Yogi*

When I picture this vulnerable little ball turning in the universe and I study the thrust of the dreams people bring me, I'm convinced that consciousness is trying to move from power to love. If we're going to be a global village, members of that large community, receiving each other with all our differences, we need to accept ourselves as imperfect human beings. That involves a whole new understanding of what love is.

> Marion Woodman, from "The Conscious Feminine,"
> in *Conscious Femininity*

A common faith in a future of the earth is a frame of mind, perhaps even the only frame of mind, that can create the psychic atmosphere required for a spiritual convergence of all human consciousness: but can that common faith, in its merely natural form, constitute a religion that will be permanently satisfactory?...In other words, is not *something more* required to maintain the evolutive effort of hominization unimpaired and unfaltering to its final term, and to love it: does it not call for the manifest appearance and explicit intervention of the ultimate focus of biological involution? I believe that it does; and it is here that Christic faith comes in to take over from and to consummate faith in man.

> Pierre Teilhard de Chardin, *Toward the Future*

---

* Aum, the creative vibration that externalizes all creation.

⇻ The Cosmic Christ ⇺

Out of the void of the strong cosmic revolution of change emerges a new archetype to transform and to lead the way. Many Christians, especially those involved in the cosmological spirit, like the American priest Matthew Fox who leads the theory of the Cosmic Christ, believe that the global renaissance heralds the coming about "in our times" of a living cosmology and the prophetic message of the second coming is upon us. And this guiding spirit is accessible not just to Christians but to people of all religions.

Time and space, history and mystery, prophecy and mysticism— Matthew Fox explains that the Cosmic Christ "awakens us to the lessons of interpretation" between them all. He is not only the loving teacher, the intellectual philosopher, the Godhead evolving, but the scientist and metaphysician, the one who gathers us all together, to make whole our parts and the particles around us. Christ, it seems, continues to grow, to change, to form again. He is, as always, the anointed and the anointer, the saviour who redeems us, the mediator, the advocate, the good shepherd, the light, the true vine. He is incarnate in us all. He is the Logos, the word made flesh, and now in the cosmic sense he is the truth, the "pattern that connects" (Matthew Fox) essence and matter. In portraying the figure of this Cosmic Christ, Carl Jung writes that the *anima mundi* is green gold in colour and the *filius macrocosmi* shows the "alchemical conception of Christ as a union of spiritually alive and physically dead matter," while British poet Edith Sitwell offers a more severe view of the new Christ, when she suggests that He is coming to judge us. David Steindl-Rast confirms that Christ lives within us as the spirit, for Christ Himself said, "I am with you even to the end of the age."

Some yogis believe Christ is one of the highest divine souls ever incarnated, and their regard for Him is growing and becoming broader. Christ is fulfilment (as Pierre Teilhard de Chardin points out). He comes at a time when God has prepared the way. According to Rosemary Ruether, Christ returns as a sister, as contributor to human liberation. "He aggregates to himself the total psychism of the earth" (de Chardin). The Cosmic Christ is our transformer to the All as Stephen Mitchell explains, and refers to Him as "a magnetic field." Hans Küng says that we are moving beyond organized religion, beyond all separate worship, to honour the spiritual essence of our age.

⇻⇺

...when we find the truth that shapes our lives we have found more than an idea. We have found a Person. We have come upon the actions of One Who is still hidden, but Whose work proclaims Him holy and worthy to be adored. And in Him we also find ourselves.

Thomas Merton, *No Man Is an Island*

The Shadow of Cain

TO C. M. BOWRA

Under great yellow flags and banners of the ancient Cold
Began the huge migrations
From some primeval disaster in the heart of Man.

There were great oscillations
Of temperature.... You knew there had once been warmth;

But the Cold is the highest mathematical Idea...the Cold is Zero—
The Nothing from which arose
All Being and all variation....It is the sound too high for our hearing,
　　the Point that flows

Till it becomes the line of Time...an endless positing
Of Nothing, or the Ideal that tries to burgeon
Into Reality through multiplying. Then Time froze

To immobility and changed to Space.
Black flags among the ice, blue rays
And the purple perfumes of the polar Sun
Freezing the bone to sapphire and to zircon—
These were our days.

And now in memory of great oscillations
Of temperature in that epoch of the Cold,
We found a continent of turquoise, vast as Asia
In the yellowing airs of the Cold: the tooth of a mammoth;
And there, in a gulf, a dark pine-sword

To show there had once been warmth and the gulf stream in our veins
Where only the Chaos of the Antarctic Pole
Or the peace of its atonic coldness reigns.

And sometimes we found the trace
Of a bird's claw in the immensity of the Cold:
The trace of the first letters we could not read:
Some message of Man's need,

And of the slow subsidence of a Race;
And of great heats in which the Pampean mud was formed,
In which the Megatherium Mylodon
Lies buried under Mastodon-trumpetings of leprous Suns.

The Earth had cloven in two in that primal disaster.
But when the glacial period began
There was still some method of communication
Between Man and his brother Man—
Although their speech
Was alien, each from each
As the Bird's from the Tiger's, born from the needs of our opposing
    famines.

Each said "This is the Race of the Dead . . . their blood is cold. . . .
For the heat of those more recent on the Earth
Is higher . . . the blood-beat of the Bird more high
Than that of the ancient race of the primeval Tiger":
The Earth had lived without the Bird

In that Spring when there were no flowers like thunders in the air.
And now the Earth lies flat beneath the shade of an iron wing.
And of what does the Pterodactyl sing—
"Of what red buds in what tremendous Spring?"

The thunders of the Spring began. . . . We came again
After that long migration
To the city built before the Flood by our brother Cain.

And when we reached an open door
The Fate said "My feet ache."
The Wanderers said "Our hearts ache."
There was great lightning
In flashes coming to us over the floor:
The Whiteness of the Bread—

The Whiteness of the Dead—
The Whiteness of the Claw—
All this coming to us in flashes through the open door.

There were great emerald thunders in the air
In the violent Spring, the thunders of the sap and the blood in the
    heart
—The Spiritual Light, the physical Revelation.

In the streets of the City of Cain there were great Rainbows
Of emeralds: the young people, crossing and meeting.

And everywhere
The great voice of the Sun in sap and bud
Fed from the heart of Being, the panic Power,
The sacred Fury, shouts of Eternity
To the blind eyes, the heat in the winged seed, the fire in the blood.

And through the works of Death,
The dust's aridity, is heard the sound
Of mounting saps like monstrous bull-voices of unseen fearful mimes:
And the great rolling world-wide thunders of that drumming under-
    ground

Proclaim our Christ, and roar "Let there be harvest!
Let there be no more Poor—
For the Son of God is sowed in every furrow!"

We did not heed the Cloud in the Heavens shaped like the hand
Of Man.... But there came a roar as if the Sun and Earth had come
    together—
The Sun descending and the Earth ascending
To take its place above... the Primal Matter
Was broken, the womb from which all life began.
Then to the murdered Sun a totem pole of dust arose in memory of
    Man.

The cataclysm of the Sun down-pouring
Seemed the roar
Of those vermilion Suns the drops of the blood

That bellowing like Mastodons at war
Rush down the length of the world—away—away—

The violence of torrents, cataracts, maelstroms, rains
That went before the Flood—
These covered the earth from the freshets of our brothers' veins;

And with them, the forked lightnings of the gold
From the split mountains,
Blasting their rivals, the young foolish wheat-ears
Amid those terrible rains.

The gulf that was torn across the world seemed as if the beds of all the
    Oceans
Were emptied....Naked, and gaping at what once had been the Sun,
Like the mouth of the Universal Famine
It stretched its jaws from one end of the Earth to the other.

And in that hollow lay the body of our brother
Lazarus, upheaved from the world's tomb.
He lay in that great Death like the gold in the husk
Of the world...and round him, like spent lightnings, lay the Ore—
The balm for the world's sore.

And the gold lay in its husk of rough earth like the core
In the furred almond, the chestnut in its prickly
Bark, the walnut in a husk green and bitter.

And to that hollow sea
The civilisation of the Maimed, and, too, Life's lepers, came
As once to Christ near the Sea of Galilee.

They brought the Aeons of Blindness and the Night
Of the World, crying to him, "Lazarus, give us sight!
O you whose sores are of gold, who are the new Light
Of the World!"
           They brought to the Tomb
The Condemned of Man, who wear as stigmata from the womb
The depression of the skull as in the lesser
Beasts of Prey, the marks of Ape and Dog,
The canine and lemurine muscle...the pitiable, the terrible,

The loveless, whose deformities arose
Before their birth, or from a betrayal by the gold wheatear.
"Lazarus, for all love we knew the great Sun's kiss

On the loveless cheek. He came to the dog-fang and the lion-claw
That Famine gave the empty mouth, the workless hands.
He came to the inner leaf of the forsaken heart—
He spoke of our Christ, and of a golden love....
But our Sun is gone...will your gold bring warmth to the loveless lips,
   and harvest to barren lands?"

Then Dives was brought....He lay like a leprous Sun
That is covered with the sores of the world...the leprosy
Of gold encrusts the world that was his heart.

Like a great ear of wheat that is swoln with grain,
Then ruined by white rain,
He lay....His hollow face, dust white, was cowled with a hood of
   gold:
But you saw there was no beat or pulse of blood—
You would not know him now from Lazarus!

He did not look at us.
He said "What was spilt still surges like the Flood.
But Gold shall be the Blood
Of the world....Brute gold condensed to the primal essence
Has the texture, smell, warmth, colour of Blood. We must take

A quintessence of the disease for remedy. Once hold
The primal matter of all gold—
From which it grows
(That Rose of the World) as the sharp clear tree from the seed of the
   great rose,

Then give of this, condensed to the transparency
Of the beryl, the weight of twenty barley grains:
And the leper's face will be full as the rose's face
After great rains.

It will shape again the Shadow of Man. Or at least will take
From all roots of life the symptoms of the leper—

And make the body sharp as the honeycomb,
The roots of life that are left like the red roots of the rose-branches."

But near him a gold sound—
The voice of an unborn wheat-ear accusing Dives—
Said "Soon I shall be more rare, more precious than gold."

There are no thunders, there are no fires, no suns, no earthquakes
Left in our blood.... But yet like the rolling thunders of all the fires in
    the world, we cry
To Dives: "You are the shadow of Cain. Your shade is the primal
    Hunger."
"I lie under what condemnation?"
"The same as Adam, the same as Cain, the same as Sodom, the same
    as Judas.

"And the fires of your Hell shall not be quenched by the rain
From those torn and parti-coloured garments of Christ, those rags
That once were Men. Each wound, each stripe,
Cries out more loudly than the voice of Cain—
Saying 'Am I my brother's keeper?'" Think! When the last clamour
    of the Bought and Sold
The agony of Gold
Is hushed.... When the last Judas-kiss
Has died upon the cheek of the Starved Man Christ, those ashes that
    were men
Will rise again
To be our Fires upon the Judgment Day!
And yet—who dreamed that Christ has died in vain?
He walks again on the Seas of Blood, He comes in the terrible Rain.

Edith Sitwell, "The Shadow of Cain,"
in *Collected Poems of Edith Sitwell*

In Jesus myth and history meet. Myth reveals the ultimate meaning and significance of life, but it has no hold on history and loses itself in the world of imagination. History of itself, as a mere succession of events, has no meaning. It is the record of events which reveal their meaning only by the significance which the historian finds in them. When historical events are seen to reveal the ultimate significance of life, then myth and history meet. Such are the virgin birth, the resurrection and the ascension. They are historical events, whose records date back to contemporary sources—unlike, for instance, the records of the life of the Buddha, which are so late that fact and fiction can no longer be separated. Yet these events are wholly mythical—they are symbols of ultimate Reality, of the eternal Mystery manifest in space and time, of the new birth by which man becomes God, of the deliverance from sin and death and the achievement of immortality, of man's ascent to the divine, of the return to the One. At this point, history—the world of sensible and psychological appearances—becomes wholly meaningful. Nature reveals the meaning and purpose of her existence, which had been hidden from the beginning of time. Man discovers his real nature and knows himself as a son of God. The divine and the human meet "without separation and without confusion."

There is no need to "demythologize" the New Testament, or the Old Testament for that matter. On the contrary, it is precisely the mythical element that reveals the universal significance of the events. Of themselves the events recorded in the Old and the New Testaments would have a very limited importance; it is the myth that relates them to the eternal drama of man's salvation. Paradise and the Fall, the Exodus and the Promised Land, the Messiah and his kingdom, Jerusalem, the City of God, the new heaven and the new earth—these are the great "myths" which transform the history of a small people in the Middle East into a symbol of the destiny of man. In the same way, it is the virgin birth, the sacrificial death, the resurrection and the ascension which transform the life of Christ from that of a local prophet and reformer into a symbol of the divine Mystery, a revelation of the plan of God for man's salvation. If it were myth alone, it would be no more than other myths of virgin birth, death and resurrection and ascension to heaven, which are found all over the world. It would be a reflection in the human psyche of the divine Mystery; it would be deeply significant, but it would be poetry, not fact. It would not be an event that has transformed the world. But if it were only an event, if it were simply a case of parthenogenesis, of a man appearing alive after his death, of a body being levitated and disappearing from sight—these would be remarkable phenomena, but they would have a very limited interest. It is the combination of myth and history, of meaning and event, that makes them a revelation of the ultimate meaning and purpose of life.

Bede Griffiths, *Return to the Centre*

The apocalyptic vision, in which the body of Christ is the metaphor holding together all categories of being in an identity, presents us with a world in which there is only one knower, for whom there is nothing outside of or objective to that knower, hence nothing dead or insensible. This knower is also the real consciousness in each of us. In the center of our table is the identification of the body and blood of the animal world, and the bread and wine that are the human forms of the vegetable kingdom, with the body of Christ. This identification forms the basis of the Eucharist rite instituted by Jesus at the Last Supper. The statements about this in the New Testament are too explicit for historical Christianity to avoid the question of what identity means in these categories and in that context. But there is a recurrent tendency in Christianity to ignore or even resist the extension of such a sense of identity beyond the specific rite.

Isaac Watts, in the eighteenth century, has a poem on the metaphors attached to Christ in Scripture, and his phrasing makes it clear that for him as many as possible of these metaphors are to be regarded as "just" metaphors, rhetorical expressions of pious emotion but not of the meaning of the Bible. The New Testament itself is rather reserved in its metaphorical language, and it is interesting to note that the scattered sayings of Jesus recorded outside it are sometimes more uninhibited in expression. One of them reads "He who is near to me is near unto the fire," and the Oxyrhynchus Papyri represent him as saying: "Raise the stone and thou shalt find me; cleave the wood and I am there."

Northrop Frye, *The Great Code*

I had been thinking a great deal about the *Anima Christi*, one of the meditations from the *Spiritual Exercises*. The vision came to me as if to point out that I had overlooked something in my reflections: the analogy of Christ with the *aurum non vulgi* and the *viriditas* of the alchemists. When I realized that the vision pointed to this central alchemical symbol, and that I had had an essentially alchemical vision of Christ, I felt comforted.

The green gold is the living quality which the alchemists saw not only in man but also in inorganic nature. It is an expression of the life-spirit, the *anima mundi* or *filius macrocosmi*, the Anthropos who animates the whole cosmos. This spirit has poured himself out into everything, even into inorganic matter; he is present in metal and stone. My vision was thus a union of the Christ-image with his analogue in matter, the *filius macrocosmi*. If I had not been so struck by the greenish-gold, I would have been tempted to assume that something essential was missing from my "Christian" view—in other words, that my traditional Christ-image was somehow inadequate and that I still had to catch up with part of the Christian development. The emphasis on the metal, however, showed me the undisguised alchemical conception of Christ as a union of spiritually alive and physically dead matter.

I took up the problem of Christ again in Aion. Here I was concerned not with the various historical parallels but with the relation of the Christ figure to psychology. Nor did I see Christ as a figure stripped of all externalities. Rather, I wished to show the development, extending over the centuries, of the religious content which he represented. It was also important to me to show how Christ could have been astrologically predicted, and how he was understood both in terms of the spirit of his age and in the course of two thousand years of Christian civilization. This was what I wanted to portray, together with all the curious marginal glosses which have accumulated around him in the course of the centuries.

As I delved into all these matters the question of the historical person, of Jesus the man, also came up. It is of importance because the collective mentality of his time—one might also say: the archetype which was already constellated, the primordial image of the Anthropos—was condensed in him, an almost unknown Jewish prophet. The ancient idea of the Anthropos, whose roots lie in Jewish tradition on the one hand and in the Egyptian Horus myth on the other, had taken possession of the people at the beginning of the Christian era, for it was part of the Zeitgeist. It was essentially concerned with the Son of Man, God's own son, who stood opposed to the deified Augustus, the ruler of this world. This idea fastened upon the originally Jewish problem of the Messiah and made it a world problem.

It would be a serious misunderstanding to regard as "mere chance" the fact that Jesus, the carpenter's son, proclaimed the gospel and became the savior of the world. He must have been a person of singular gifts to have been able so completely to express and to represent the general, though unconscious, expectations of his age. No one else could have been the bearer of such a message; it was possible only for this particular man Jesus.

In those times the omnipresent, crushing power of Rome, embodied in the divine Caesar, had created a world where countless individuals, indeed whole peoples, were robbed of their cultural independence and of their spiritual autonomy. Today, individuals and cultures are faced with a similar threat, namely of being swallowed up in the mass. Hence in many places there is a wave of hope in a reappearance of Christ, and a visionary rumor has even arisen which expresses expectations of redemption. The form it has taken, however, is comparable to nothing in the past, but is a typical child of the "age of technology." This is the worldwide distribution of the UFO phenomenon (unidentified flying objects).

C. G. Jung, Memories, Dreams, Reflections

What is specific to Christianity is the person of Jesus and the event of his life, death, and resurrection. And then the radiation of this historical person through the community of those who believe in him and who try to live as he did, a life of self-sacrificing love.

In my own personal experience, I find that the very nature of this mystery of Jesus is such that it cannot be monopolized by the Church. In fact many Hindus, Buddhists, and others are now seeking to understand Jesus in terms of their own traditions; some have arrived at a deep understanding of him. I consider this highly significant from a theological viewpoint. The mystery of Jesus is specific to Christianity, but it cannot be monopolized by Christian believers, because it is universal.

> Thomas Matus, in Fritjof Capra, David Steindl-Rast
> with Thomas Matus, *Belonging to the Universe*

And since the time when Jesus was born, when He finished growing and died and rose again, *everything has continued to move because Christ has not yet completed His own forming*. He has not yet gathered in to Himself the last folds of the Garment of flesh and love which His disciples are making for him. *The mystical Christ has not yet attained His full growth*. In the pursuance of this engendering is situated the ultimate spring of all created activity... Christ is the Fulfilment even of the natural evolution of beings.

> Pierre Teilhard de Chardin, *The Future of Man*

Who would dare to speak of a renaissance in our times? Is it a bourgeois dream of an armchair theologian, a romantic cop-out from an academician? Who in their right mind would look at the suffering in today's world and suggest that the human race is, in fact, on the verge of a vast, global renaissance? I suppose it is the mystic in me that dares to suggest such a vision. And why? Because the mystic teaches us to trust all bottoming out, all emptying, all nothingness experiences as the matrix and patrix of new birth. It is precisely the despair of our times that convinces me that a renaissance is right around the corner, that a renaissance is the only answer to the depths of our dilemma. It is either renaissance or planetary extinction. There is no middle ground.

How might this renaissance happen? By the paradigm shift that is possible when a living cosmology bursts on the scene. Consider a new paradigm to be a new wineskin. One does not harvest a new crop of grapes, crush them, and pour them into old, dried-up wineskins. Rather, one seeks a new wineskin that is supple and soft, giving and forgiving, flexible and eager to be made wet, one that welcomes newness and creativity. Such a wineskin is the living cosmology being blended from three rich vineyards: science, from which we derive a universal creation story today; mysticism, from which we awaken the human psyche's powers for unity, wholeness, and imagination; and art, from which the Good News of a living cosmology is born into the hearts, dreams, imaginations, and bodies of persons, and even into the institutions of the culture.

We thus find ourselves at the threshold of naming the paschal mystery anew for the third millennium of Christianity: matricide, mysticism, and the Cosmic Christ name the Paschal story we have understood as the death, resurrection, and second coming of Jesus the Christ. The death of Mother Earth (matricide) and the resurrection of the human psyche (mysticism) and the coming of the Cosmic Christ (a living cosmology) name the mystery of the divine cycle of death and rebirth and the sending of the Spirit in our time. Were the human race to believe anew in this mystery, a renaissance would surely occur.

Matthew Fox, *The Coming of the Cosmic Christ*

The past one hundred years of science have reawakened the human race to the power and dimension of time. Surely our dawning awareness of evolution and our gradual appreciation of the vast distances of time represented by the age of the earth (four and a half billion years) and the universe (about twenty billion years) fill us with a new awe at the mystery of our origins. All things are in flux; all things evolve; all things come and go; all things are in time and birthing in their time. Time and history are integral to all mystery. This is a cosmic law.

A deep connection exists between the time consciousness of today's science and the time consciousness of Jesus Christ. One of Jesus' essential contributions, like that of the Jewish prophets before him, is the call to the human to celebrate one's time, one's lifetime, one another's lifetimes—and not to take time for granted. We are called to give birth in our times to "fruit that will last" (John 15:16) and to the Cosmic Christ who, as "the pattern that connects," connects all time.

Another contribution of this "pattern that connects" who is Jesus the Christ is the connection of time and space. The West has indeed awakened its time consciousness through the work of science this past century, but our space consciousness remains dormant. Just as I understand our time consciousness to be our prophetic soul, so I see our space consciousness as our mystical soul or psyche. And our civilization is not in touch with its mystical powers. The Cosmic Christ awakens us precisely to this dimension that sleeps fitfully within us. The mystical experience is invariably one of the suspension

of time—"Where did the time go?" we ask after undergoing such an experience. Space takes over, spacefulness—with emphasis on the *fullness*, the
pleroma. That space is filled by divine experience, by the eternal now, by forgetfulness of all but the glory—the beautiful presence of the divine loved one.
The Cosmic Christ travels not just in time but also in space. Our space-full
moments are precious and memorable—they ought to be the grounding
point for all morality and decision making. Eckhart says God is *spatiosissimus*,
the most spacious thing there is. Here we are all given permission—at last—
to celebrate our spacefulness. Jesus dares to confuse the space known as
heaven with the space known as earth—"thy will be done on earth as it is in
heaven." The resurrection is nothing if not a conquest of time and place
(death on Golgotha) by space—that is by an empty (space-filled) tomb where
sadness and death no longer are granted place. Where grief comes to an end.
Where life, new but mysterious, is resurrected against all odds and all pessimism and all cynicism and all sadness. Where a return to the land of the living (walking, talking, and eating at Emmaus) and to the origin of the cosmos
(ascension) and the sending of the spirit (Pentecost) is accomplished.

Without a healthy sense of space and mysticism, time becomes idola-
trous—either the idolatry of time that a culture of "progress" has been heralding for one hundred years (years that have culminated in at least as much
degradation as progress), or an idolatry of guilt and apocalyptic shouting that
deadens all space consciousness and therefore all powers of imagination and
creativity to resurrect the human spirit and thus redeem the times. Today
some scientists are sounding as pessimistic as some fundamentalist preachers.
Both camps lack mysticism and a sense of the Cosmic Christ who, like every
mystic, operates paradoxically and snatches hope from despair, light from
darkness, life from death, and youthfulness from oldness. All who are in this
Christ, Paul declares, are themselves a "New Creation" (2 Cor. 15:17).

On today's spiritual scene we see two distortions (in addition to funda-
mentalism which is not mature enough to be called a spirituality). One distortion occurs in certain trends in the New Age movement which are all
space and no time; all consciousness and no conscience; all mysticism and no
prophecy; all past life experiences, angelic encounters, untold bliss, and no
critique of injustice or acknowledgment of the suffering and death that the
toll of time takes. In short, no body. To these movements the Cosmic Christ
says, "Enter time. Behold my wounds. Love your neighbor. Set the captives
free." A second distortion occurs among good-intentioned persons working
intensely and sacrificing much for peace and justice—in other words, struggling to right the times, to see the messianic times happen, to taste the
promise of peace and justice flowing like waters, as the prophets promised.
The danger is too much time consciousness cut off from mysticism or space

consciousness embroils and attaches one to the struggle of time that leads to burn out, pessimism, lack of creativity, spirit, and imagination. To these persons the Cosmic Christ says, "Behold the universe. Behold its fulsome mysteries. Behold its glory which is that of my Creator. Behold your universe within, your ever-expanding psyche, your powers of creativity, wetness, rebirth, generativity, youthfulness. Behold your connection to all things, great and small. Beauty abounds. Partake of it. You are of it. 'Be still and know that I am God' (Ps. 46:10). And you are too."

Technology has refashioned drastically our notions of space. "Space" has now emerged as a term denoting another frontier for human exploration and conquest, as in the common phrase, "conquer space." While technology has allowed us to exult in the vast awe and wonder of our planet floating in space, to visit other stars, and to stretch our telescopes and thus ears and eyes into the very moment of the origins of time and space, it has also brought the human shadow into space. What we call Star Wars is an example of exporting our militarism into outer space. We lack the inner, psychic space of mysticism that would allow us to let go of war, dualism, and unresolved oppressions. To this distorted attitude toward space the Cosmic Christ says, "Let your compulsion to conquer go. Let your militarism go. Listen to your inner space for the divine and project *that*—its glory and beauty, its hope and justice—into other spaces. Cease making space over into your own image and start reimaging yourselves in light of space. Do unto space what you would have space do unto you. And love space as yourself."

By uniting time and space the Cosmic Christ challenges twentieth- and twenty-first-century citizens to get on with the deep work of the universe. Just as Einstein alerted our century to the interconnectivity of time and space, the Cosmic Christ awakens us to the lessons of interpenetration between the experiences of history and mystery, of prophecy and mysticism, of time and space.

Matthew Fox, *The Coming of the Cosmic Christ*

Christ is not necessarily male, nor is the redeemed community only women, but a new humanity, female and male. We need to think in terms of a dynamic, rather than a static, relationship between redeemer and redeemed. The redeemer is one who has been redeemed, just as Jesus himself accepted the baptism of John. Those who have been liberated can, in turn, become paradigmatic, liberating persons for others.

Christ, as redemptive person and Word of God, is not to be encapsulated "once-for-all" in the historical Jesus. The Christian community continues Christ's identity. As vine and branches, Christic personhood continues in our sisters and brothers. In the language of early Christian prophetism, we can encounter Christ *in the form of our sister*. Christ, the liberated humanity, is not confined to a static perfection of one person two thousand years ago. Rather, redemptive humanity goes ahead of us, calling us to yet incompleted dimensions of human liberation.

Rosemary Radford Ruether, *Sexism and God-Talk*

The Cosmic Christ can be both female and male, heterosexual and homosexual.

Matthew Fox, *The Coming of the Cosmic Christ*

In what ways do women need such an appearance of a WomanChrist? Do men also need a WomanChrist, and how would their need for Her be different or similar to that of women today? Do we all today, in one way or another, really "know that we will all die unless a WomanChrist pops up from somewhere (like a rabbit out of a hat)" to break apart the weapons of global destruction and spill their seeds on the ground to renew the earth?

Rosemary Radford Ruether, *Womanguides*

Christ, principle of universal vitality because sprung up as man among men, put himself in the position (maintained ever since) to subdue under himself, to purify, to direct and superanimate the general ascent of consciousness into which he inserted himself. By a perennial act of communion and sublimation, he aggregates to himself the total psychism of the earth. And when he has gathered everything together and transformed everything, he will close in upon himself and his conquests, thereby rejoining, in a final gesture, the divine focus he has never left.

Pierre Teilhard de Chardin, *The Phenomenon of Man*

The Cosmic Christ calls us to renewed worship: "Come to me all you who are burdened by lack of praise, lack of beauty, lack of vision in your lives. Look about you at the starry heavens and the deep, deep sea; at the amazing history that has birthed a home for you on this planet; at the surprise and joy of your existence. Gather together—you and your communities—in the context of this great, cosmic community to rejoice and give thanks. To heal and let go. To enter the dark and deep mysteries, to share the news, to break the bread of the universe and drink blood of the cosmos itself in all its divinity. Be brave.

Let your worship make you strong and great again. Never be bored again. Create yourselves, re-create your worlds, by the news you share and the visions you celebrate. Bring your sense of being microcosm in a vast macrocosm; bring your bodies; bring your play; bring your darkness and your pain. Gather and do not scatter. Learn not to take for granted and learn this together. Become a people. Worship together."

Matthew Fox, *The Coming of the Cosmic Christ*

But whither, some will ask, *will all this lead?* History is open toward the future, and open-ended too is interreligious dialogue, which—unlike interdenominational dialogue—has only just begun. What the future of the Christian religion, which is for me the true one, will bring, we do not know. Nor do we know what the future will bring to the other, non-Christian religions. Who knows what the Christology, the Qur'anology, or the Buddhology, like the Church, the *Umma*, the *Sangha*, of the year 2087, will look like?

As far as the future goes, only one thing is certain: At the end both of human life and the course of the world, Buddhism and Hinduism will no longer be there, nor will Islam nor Judaism. Indeed, in the end Christianity will not be there either. In the end no religion will be left standing, but the one Inexpressible, to whom all religions are oriented, whom Christians will only then completely recognize—when the imperfect gives way before the perfect—even as they themselves are recognized: *the* truth face to face. And in the end there will no longer be standing between the religions a figure that separates them, no more prophet or enlightened one, not Muhammad and not the Buddha. Indeed even Christ Jesus, whom Christians believe in, will no longer stand here as a figure of separation. But he, to whom, Paul says, all powers (including death) are subjected, "subjects himself, then, to God" so that God *himself* (*ho theos*)—or however he may be called in the East—may truly be not just in all things but *"everything to everyone"* (1 Cor 15:28).

Hans Küng, *Theology for the Third Millennium*

To believe in this "pattern that connects" is to start connecting once again. For all belief is about practice, not just theory. Belief is not belief if it is not launched into *praxis*. The practice of making and seeking connections, and of seeking even "the pattern that connects," can now begin in earnest. This enterprise will require those "new wineskins" or "new paradigms" that a living cosmology represented by the Cosmic Christ ushers in. These wineskins will offer themselves as vessels for the Spirit rising afresh among the young in all institutions of church and society; making new connections between world religions; reconnecting our lifestyles to our capacities for creativity, imagination, play, suffering, sexuality, knowledge, and wisdom itself. Embracing the Cosmic Christ will demand a paradigm shift, and it will empower us for that shift:

A shift	
from anthropocentrism	to a living cosmology
from Newton	to Einstein
from parts-mentality	to wholeness
from rationalism	to mysticism
from obedience as a prime moral virtue	to creativity as a prime moral virtue
from personal salvation	to communal healing, i.e., compassion as salvation
from theism (God outside us)	to panentheism (God in us and us in God)
from fall-redemption religion	to creation-centered spirituality
from the ascetic	to the aesthetic.

Consider how the right-hand column that represents the new paradigm is all about "patterns that connect"—cosmology; Einstein; wholeness; mysticism; creativity; compassion; panentheism; creation-centered spirituality; beauty—each new wineskin is a connecting wineskin. Truly the Cosmic Christ ushers in an era of connection making.

The Cosmic Christ is the *divine* pattern that connects in the person of Jesus Christ (but by no means is limited to that person). The divine pattern of connectivity *was made flesh and set up its tent among us* (John 1:14). In a special way the "us" includes the dispossessed—those least connected, those least established and least part of the connections that "the establishment" has to offer. Jesus offered connections to the dispossessed in particular: to the lepers, women, slaves, sinners, and outcasts of society. He connected with them not only by conversation and scandalous associations at meals but by undergoing the death of the unconnected, the death of the dispossessed on Golgotha. The historical person of Jesus offers a "pattern that connects" substantially different from the *anima mundi* ("soul of the world") tradition of Platonism, which lacks all concern and therefore connection with the *anawim*, the little and forgotten ones, the oppressed victims of social injustice. The Cosmic Christ liberates all persons and thus, like Moses of old, leads a new exodus from the bondage and pessimistic news of a Newtonian, mechanistic universe so ripe with competition, winners and losers, dualisms, anthropocentrism, and the boredom that comes when our exciting universe is pictured as a machine bereft of mystery and mysticism. The Cosmic Christ is local and historical, indeed intimate to human history. The Cosmic Christ might be living next door or even inside one's deepest and truest self. The reign of God may well be among us after all.

Matthew Fox, *The Coming of the Cosmic Christ*

What *is* the gospel according to Jesus? Simply this: that the love we all long for in our innermost heart is already present, beyond longing. Most of us can remember a time (it may have been just a moment) when we felt that everything in the world was exactly as it should be. Or we can think of a joy (it happened when we were children, perhaps, or the first time we fell in love) so vast that it was no longer inside us, but we were inside it. What we intuited then, and what we later thought was too good to be true, isn't an illusion. It is real. It is realer than the real, more intimate than anything we can see or touch, "unreachable," as the Upanishads say, "yet nearer than breath, than heartbeat." The more deeply we receive it, the more real it becomes.

Like all the great spiritual Masters, Jesus taught one thing only: presence. Ultimate reality, the luminous, compassionate intelligence of the universe, is not somewhere else, in some heaven light-years away. It didn't manifest itself any more fully to Abraham or Moses than to us, nor will it be any more present to some Messiah at the far end of time. It is always right here, right now. That is what the Bible means when it says that God's true name is *I am*.

There is such a thing as nostalgia for the future. Both Judaism and Christianity ache with it. It is a vision of the Golden Age, the days of perpetual summer in a world of straw-eating lions and roses without thorns, when human life will be foolproof, and fulfilled in an endlessly prolonged finale of delight. I don't mean to make fun of the messianic vision. In many ways it is admirable, and it has inspired political and religious leaders from Isaiah to Martin Luther King, Jr. But it is a kind of benign insanity. And if we take it seriously enough, if we live it twenty-four hours a day, we will spend all our time working in anticipation, and will never enter the Sabbath of the heart. How moving and at the same time how ridiculous is the story of the Hasidic rabbi who, every morning, as soon as he woke up, would rush out his front door to see if the Messiah had arrived. (Another Hasidic story, about a more mature stage of this consciousness, takes place at the Passover seder. The rabbi tells his chief disciple to go outside and see if the Messiah has come. "But Rabbi, if the Messiah came, wouldn't you know it in here?" the disciple says, pointing to his heart. "Ah," says the rabbi, pointing to his own heart, "but in here, the Messiah has already come.") Who among the now-middle-aged doesn't remember the fervor of the Sixties, when young people believed that love could transform the world? "You may say I'm a dreamer," John Lennon sang, "but I'm not the only one." The messianic dream of the future may be humanity's sweetest dream. But it is a dream nevertheless, as long as there is a separation between inside and outside, as long as we don't transform ourselves. And Jesus, like the Buddha, was a man who had awakened from all dreams.

When Jesus talked about the kingdom of God, he was not prophesying about some easy, danger-free perfection that will someday appear. He was talking about a state of being, a way of living at ease among the joys and sorrows of *our* world. It is possible, he said, to be as simple and beautiful as the birds of the sky or the lilies of the field, who are always within the eternal Now. This state of being is not something alien or mystical. We don't need to earn it. It is already ours. Most of us lose it as we grow up and become self-conscious, but it doesn't disappear forever; it is always there to be reclaimed, though we have to search hard in order to find it. The rich especially have a hard time reentering this state of being; they are so possessed by their possessions, so entrenched in their social power, that it is almost impossible for them to let go. Not that it is easy for any of us. But if we need reminding, we can always sit at the feet of our young children. They, because they haven't yet developed a firm sense of past and future, accept the infinite abundance of the present with all their hearts, in complete trust. Entering the kingdom of God means feeling, as if we were floating in the womb of the universe, that we are being taken care of, always, at every moment.

All spiritual Masters, in all the great religious traditions, have come to experience the present as the only reality. The Gospel passages in which "Jesus" speaks of a kingdom of God in the future can't be authentic, unless Jesus was a split personality, and could turn on and off two different consciousnesses as if they were hot- and cold-water faucets. And it is easy to understand how these passages would have been inserted into the Gospel by disciples, or disciples of disciples, who hadn't understood his teaching. Passages about the kingdom of God as coming in the future are a dime a dozen in the prophets, in the Jewish apocalyptic writings of the first centuries B.C.E., in Paul and the early church. They are filled with passionate hope, with a desire for universal justice, and also, as Nietzsche so correctly insisted, with a festering resentment against "them" (the powerful, the ungodly). But they arise from ideas, not from an experience of the state of being that Jesus called the kingdom of God.

The Jewish Bible doesn't talk much about this state; it is more interested in what Moses said at the bottom of the mountain than in what he saw at the top. But there are exceptions. The most dramatic is the Voice from the Whirlwind in the Book of Job, which I have examined at length elsewhere. Another famous passage occurs at the beginning of Genesis: God completes the work

of creation by entering the Sabbath mind, the mind of absolute, joyous serenity; contemplates the whole universe and says, "Behold, it is very good."

The kingdom of God is not something that will happen, because it isn't
something that *can* happen. It can't appear in a world or a nation; it is a condition that has no plural, but only infinite singulars. Jesus spoke of people
"entering" it, said that children were already inside it, told one particularly
ardent scribe that he, the scribe, was not "far from" it. If only we stop looking forward and backward, he said, we will be able to devote ourselves to
seeking the kingdom of God, which is right beneath our feet, right under
our noses; and when we find it, food, clothing, and other necessities are given
to us as well, as they are to the birds and the lilies. Where else but here and
now can we find the grace-bestowing, inexhaustible presence of God? In its
light, all our hopes and fears flitter away like ghosts. It is like a treasure
buried in a field; it is like a pearl of great price; it is like coming home. When
we find it, we find ourselves, rich beyond all dreams, and we realize that we
can afford to lose everything else in the world, even (if we must) someone we
love more dearly than life itself.

The portrait of Jesus that emerges from the authentic passages in the
Gospels is of a man who has emptied himself of desires, doctrines, rules—all
the mental claptrap and spiritual baggage that separate us from true life—and
has been filled with the vivid reality of the Unnamable. Because he has let go
of the merely personal, he is no one, he is everyone. Because he allows God
through the personal, his personality is like a magnetic field. Those who are
drawn to him have a hunger for the real; the closer they approach, the more
they can feel the purity of his heart.

What is purity of heart? If we compare God to sunlight, we can say that
the heart is like a window. Cravings, aversions, fixed judgments, concepts,
beliefs—all forms of selfishness or self-protection—are, when we cling to
them, like dirt on the windowpane. The thicker the dirt, the more opaque
the window. When there is no dirt, the window is by its own nature perfectly
transparent, and the light can stream through it without hindrance.

Or we can compare a pure heart to a spacious, light-filled room. People or
possibilities open the door and walk in; the room will receive them, however
many they are, for as long as they want to stay, and will let them leave when
they want to. Whereas a corrupted heart is like a room cluttered with valuable
possessions, in which the owner sits behind a locked door, with a loaded gun.

One last comparison, from the viewpoint of spiritual practice. To grow
in purity of heart is to grow like a tree. The tree doesn't try to wrench its
roots out of the earth and plant itself in the sky, nor does it reach its leaves
downward into the dirt. It needs both ground and sunlight, and knows the
direction of each. Only because it digs into the dark earth with its roots is it
able to hold its leaves out to receive the sunlight.

For every teacher who lives in this way, the word of God has become flesh, and there is no longer a separation between body and spirit. Everything he or she does proclaims the kingdom of God. (A visitor once said of the eighteenth-century Hasidic rabbi Dov Baer, "I didn't travel to Mezritch to hear him teach, but to watch him tie his shoelaces.")

People can feel Jesus' radiance whether or not he is teaching or healing; they can feel it in proportion to their own openness. There is a deep sense of peace in his presence, and a sense of respect for him that far exceeds what they have felt for any other human being. Even his silence is eloquent. He is immediately recognizable by the quality of his aliveness, by his disinterestedness and compassion. He is like a mirror for us all, showing us who we essentially are.

Stephen Mitchell, The Gospel According to Jesus

Reverence is one's response to an *awesome* experience. Reverence is integral to a cosmological spirituality in which awe names the mystical experience known as the *via positiva*, the first of the four paths of Creation Spirituality. A morality of reverence will also be a morality of responsibility—not a responsibility based on duty and fear of disobedience but a responsibility based on *care for what we cherish and revere*.

Matthew Fox, The Coming of the Cosmic Christ

Prayer to the Ever-Greater Christ

Because, Lord, by every innate impulse and through all the hazards of my life I have been driven ceaselessly to search for you and to set you in the heart of the universe of matter, I shall have the joy, when death comes, of closing my eyes amidst the splendour of a universal transparency aglow with fire...

It is as if the fact of bringing together and connecting the two poles, tangible and intangible, external and internal, of the world which bears us onwards had caused everything to burst into flames and set everything free.

In the guise of a tiny babe in its mother's arms, obeying the great law of birth, you came, Lord Jesus, to swell in my infant soul; and then, as you re-enacted in me—and in so doing extended the range of—your growth through the Church, that same humanity which once was born and dwelt in Palestine began now to spread out gradually everywhere like an iridescence of unnumbered hues through which, without destroying anything, your presence penetrated—and endued with supervitality—every other presence about me.

And all this took place because, in a universe which was disclosing itself to me as structurally convergent, you, by right of your resurrection, had assumed the dominating position of all-inclusive Centre in which everything is gathered together.

A fantastic molecular swarm which—either falling like snow from the inmost recesses of the Infinitely Diffuse—or on the other hand surging up like smoke from the explosion of some Infinitely Simple—an awe-inspiring multitude, indeed, which whirls us around in its tornado!...It is in this terrifying granular Energy that you, Lord—that so I may be able the better to touch you, or rather, who knows? to be more closely embraced by you—have clothed yourself for me: nay, it is of this that you have formed your very Body. And for many years I saw in it no more than a wonderful contact with an already completed Perfection...

Until that day, and it was only yesterday, when you made me realize that when you espoused Matter it was not merely its Immensity and its Organicity that you had taken on: what you did was to absorb, concentrate, and make entirely your own, its unfathomable reserves of spiritual energies.

So true is this that ever since that time you have become for my mind and heart much more than He who was and who is; you have become *He who shall be*.

For some of your servants, Lord, the World, our New World—the world of nuclei, of atoms and genes—has become a source of constant anxiety: because it seems to us now so mobile, so irresistible, and so big! The increasing probability (to which we conspire to close our eyes) of other thinking planets in the firmament...the unmistakable rebound of an evolution that has become capable, through planetary effort, of governing its own direction and speed...the rising over our horizon, as an effect of ultra-reflection, of an Ultra-human...all this seems frightening to a man who, as he still shrinks from flinging himself into the great ocean of Matter, is afraid that he may see his God burst asunder in the acquisition of a new dimension...

Yet can anything, Lord, in fact do more for my understanding and my soul to make you an object of love, the only object of love, than to see that you—the Centre ever opened into your own deepest core—continue to grow in intensity, that there is an added glow to your lustre, at the same pace as *you pleromize yourself* by gathering together the Universe and subjecting it ever more fully at the heart of your being ("until the time for returning, You and the World in You, to the bosom of Him from whom you came")?

The more the years go by, Lord, the more I believe that I can see that in myself and in the world around me the most important though unvoiced concern of modern Man is much less a struggle for the possession of the World than a search for a way of escaping from it. The agony of feeling that one is imprisoned in the cosmic Bubble, not so much spatially as ontologically! The fretful hunt for a way out for Evolution—or, more exactly, for its point of focus! In the modern world, that is the sorrow, the price to be paid for a growing planetary Reflection, that lies heavy, but as yet hardly recognized, on the soul of both Christian and Gentile.

As mankind emerges into consciousness of the movement that carries it along, it has a continually more urgent need of a Direction and a Solution ahead and above, to which it will at last be able to consecrate itself.

Who, then is this God, no longer the God of the old Cosmos but the God of the new Cosmogenesis—so constituted precisely because the effect of a mystical operation that has been going on for two thousand years has been to disclose in you, beneath the Child of Bethlehem and the Crucified, the moving Principle and the all-embracing Nucleus of the World itself? Who is this God for whom our generation looks so eagerly? Who but you, Jesus, who represent him and bring him to us?

Lord of consistence and union, you whose *distinguishing mark* and *essence* is the power indefinitely to grow greater, without distortion or loss of continuity, to the measure of the mysterious Matter whose Heart you fill and all whose movements you ultimately control—Lord of my childhood and Lord of my last days—God, complete in relation to yourself and yet, for us, continually being born—God, who, because you offer yourself to our worship as "evolver" and "evolving," are henceforth the only being that can satisfy us—sweep away at last the clouds that still hide you—the clouds of hostile prejudice and those, too, of false creeds.

Let your universal Presence spring forth in a blaze that is at once Diaphany and Fire.

O ever-greater Christ!

Pierre Teilhard de Chardin, *The Heart of Matter*

✢ The Kingdom of God ✦

"Heaven does not stand in opposition to earth: it is born from the conquest and transformation of earth."

—PIERRE TEILHARD DE CHARDIN

The words that appear throughout this book by individuals who have experienced deeply enough, have conviction strong enough, have faith infallible enough, have pondered and contemplated long enough to share their spiritual wisdom, all deliver a common lesson: that the peace, the joy, and the love which we seek, the paradise where God dwells, can be found within ourselves, here, at this time in our existence. For while the kingdom of God is not of this earth, we can secure "a relatively bearable life" here (Vaclav Havel) beyond the burden of everyday problems and necessities, by relating to existence in eternity, the place in which our souls dwell and know as home. By choosing the infinite as the place of belonging, "our souls are purified of Time by Time" (Allen Ginsberg).

At every level of discovery and experience in the search for God, life becomes richer and more awesome as we step closer and closer to the infinite. We know we have arrived when, without fear, without question, our souls are at peace. At the threshold of the Kingdom of God, all there is left to do is to offer gratitude for the gifts and the lessons of life, joyfully celebrate our own existence and that of others, and sincerely worship and devote the rest of our lives to creation and our creator.

⊷⊶

"If you listen you will hear the sound of the kingdom of God in the air as no generation ever could before."

Albert Schweitzer, Reverence for Life

We are, as the aborigines say, just learning how to survive in infinity.

Michael Talbot, The Holographic Universe

Imagine a time without beginning or end; imagine that there was nevertheless absolutely nothing necessary, either in time or above time: It is then impossible that there *always* was being, for that for which there is *no necessity* cannot have been always.

Jacques Maritain, Approaches to God

The roots of heaven are of great emptiness, for in emptiness there is energy, incalculable, vast and profound.

J. Krishnamurti, Krishnamurti to Himself

Only one reality seems to survive and be capable of succeeding and spanning the infinitesimal and the immense: energy—that floating, universal entity from which all emerges and into which all falls back as into an ocean; energy, the new spirit; the new god.

Pierre Teilhard de Chardin, The Phenomenon of Man

...*reality* includes both the past and the future, but *existence* includes only the present and is totally dependent on the reality of past and future universes. Without them there is no existence now.

Fred Alan Wolf, Parallel Universes

I think that religious archetypes accurately mirror the dimensions of this ambiguous essence of humanity—from the idea of paradise, that "recollection" of a lost participation in the integrity of Being, the idea of a fall into the world as an act of "separation" (is not the apple of knowledge in fact the "knowledge of the self" that separates us?), the idea of the last judgment as our confrontation with the absolute horizon of our relating, right down to the idea of salvation as supreme transcendence, that "quasi-identification" with the fullness of Being, to which humanity is constantly aspiring. And the fact that all the short-circuited attempts of fanaticism to organize a "heaven on earth" inevitably lead to an earthly hell is more than clearly expressed in the reminder that the kingdom of God is not "of this earth." Indeed: a relatively bearable life on this earth can only be secured by a humanity whose orientation is "beyond" this world, a humanity that—in each of its "heres" and each of its "nows"—relates to infinity, to the absolute and to eternity. An unqualified orientation to the "here" and "now," however bearable that may be, hopelessly transforms that "here" and "now" into desolation and waste and ultimately colors it with blood.

Yes: man is in fact nailed down—like Christ on the cross—to a grid of paradoxes: stretched between the horizontal of the world and the vertical of Being; dragged down by the hopelessness of existing-in-the-world on the one hand, and the unattainability of the absolute on the other, he balances between the torment of not knowing his mission and the joy of carrying it out, between nothingness and meaningfulness. And like Christ, he is in fact victorious, but by virtue of his defeats: through perceiving absurdity, he once again finds meaning; through personal failure, he once more discovers responsibility; through the defeat of several prison sentences, he gains a victory—at the very least—over himself (as an object of worldly temptations); and through death—his last and greatest defeat—he finally triumphs over his fragmentation; by completing, for all time, his outline in the "memory of

Being," he returns at last—having rejected nothing of his "otherness"—to the womb of integral Being.

Vaclav Havel, Letters to Olga

The universe is not solely an ethical proposition, a problem of the antinomy of the good and the evil; the Spirit of the universe can in no way be imagined as a rigid moralist concerned only with making all things obey the law of moral good, or a stream of tendency towards righteousness attempting, hitherto with only a very poor success, to prevail and rule, or a stern Justicer rewarding and punishing creatures in a world that he has made or has suffered to be full of wickedness and suffering and evil. The universal Will has evidently many other and more supple modes than that, an infinity of interests, many other elements of its being to manifest, many lines to follow, many laws and purposes to pursue. The law of the world is not this alone that our good brings good to us and our evil brings evil, nor is its sufficient key the ethical-hedonistic rule that our moral good brings to us happiness and success and our moral evil brings to us sorrow and misfortune. There is a rule of right in the world, but it is the right of the truth of Nature and of the truth of the Spirit, and that is a vast and various rule and takes many forms that have to be understood and accepted before we can reach either its highest or its integral principle.

Sri Aurobindo, Kisher Gandhi, in
Lights on Life Problems

One of my views is that it will be possible to have experiences of the future. We already know of the existence of "psychics" and seers, and many of us scoff at the idea while others have no difficulty in accepting them.

So if time is present and unredeemable, might it be possible to observe a future parallel universe?

The only way to have time unredeemable is to have it exist as a maze of parallel universes. Perhaps a better image is the hologram of parallel universes.

What one sees when viewing the hologram depends on the viewpoint one takes. And that viewpoint alters the hologram because it alters the probabilities by moving in time.

After all, if the hologram is constructed from transacting quantum waves moving in all time directions, then who assigns the possibilities? Somehow a field of consciousness must illuminate the hologram and *IT* assigns the probabilities.

There must be a conscious observer. In my view this observer is ourselves—a spill from the giant ocean of thought that is God, temporarily trapped by the hologram, but also unredeemable and unchanging....

The human mind is the laboratory of the new physics. It already is tuned to the past and the future, making existential certainties out of probable realities. It does this by simply observing. Observing oneself in a dream. Observing oneself in this world when awake. Observing the action of observing. If we are brave enough to venture into this world with consciousness as our ally, through our dreams and altered states of awareness, we may be able to alter the hologram by bringing more conscious "light" to the hell worlds that also exist side-by-side with our own.

Indeed what with our bent toward constantly "defending ourselves," this parallel world already is a hell world. It is time to speed up the process of illuminating the hologram, time to bring in the big laser of consciousness. Evolution is our business too. It is time to know this universe-place for the first time ever.

Fred Alan Wolf, Parallel Universes

Our destiny is to go on beyond everything, to leave everything, to press forward to the End and find in the End our Beginning, the ever-new Beginning that has no End.

Thomas Merton, Conjectures of a Guilty Bystander

Adam

I wish we could go back
to the beginning

When there were no hospitals
and no churches dispensing
the analgesics of religion,
not even the famous eye-tingling one
in Milan, the *Duomo*;
no typewriters furiously clicking out
for the jocoseness of cherubs and angels
our latest humiliation and impotency;
when there were no circus freaks
Fellini freaks, speedfreaks, Jesusfreaks
no Seventh-Day Adventists, Scientologists
apocalyptics, epileptics, eupeptics, and sceptics

and no bloated greedyguts
stuffing their diseased bladders
with paper money and gold,
no courtesans lining their perfumed orifices
with expensive many-hued crystals
amassed at Cusy's

Before the human larynx acquired
its tinge of querulous dissatisfaction
and mind became a forever open wound
of militant self-serving cynicism and doubt

Before Caesar crossed the Rubicon
because there was no Rubicon to cross
and no Alexander the Dardanelles
because there was no Dardanelles
and no Alexander handsome and mad;
no Darius, no Sarpedon, no Xerxes
no Pharaohs, no Baals, no Astarte
no Chinese dynasties or ideograms
nurturing in their mysterious script
Maoism and the Long March

There's only God and myself
in the cool first evening in Eden
discussing his fantastic creation,
the moon and the stars,
and the enveloping stillness.
About the woman
he has in mind for me
we talk softly and for a long time
and very, very carefully.

Irving Layton, *Fortunate Exile*

Psalm II

Ah, still Lord, ah, sweet Divinity
Incarnate in our grave and holy substance,
Circumscribed in this hexed endless world
Of Time, that turns a triple face, from Hell,

Imprisoned joy's incognizable thought,
To mounted earth, that shudders to conceive,
Toward angels, borne unseen out of this world,
Translate the speechless stanzas of the rose
Into my poem, and I vow to copy
Every petal on a page; perfume
My mind, ungardened, and in weedy earth;
Let these dark leaves be lit with images
That strike like lightning from eternal mind,
Truths that are not visible in any light
That changes and is Time, like flesh or theory,
Corruptible like any clock of meat
That sickens and runs down to die
With all those structures and machinery
Whose bones and bridges break and wash to sea
And are dissolved into green salt and coral.

A Bird of Paradise, the Nightingale
I cried for not so long ago, the poet's
Phoenix, and the erotic Swan
Which descended and transfigured Time,
And all but destroyed it, in the Dove
I speak of now are here, I saw it here,
The Miracle, which no man knows entire,
Nor I myself. But shadow is my prophet,
I cast a shadow that surpasses me,
And I write, shadow changes into bone,
To say that still Word, the prophetic image
Beyond our present strength of flesh to bear,
Incarnate in the rain as in the sea,
Watches after us out of our eyes.
What a sweet dream! to be some incorruptible
Divinity, corporeal without a name,
Suffering metamorphosis of flesh.

Holy are the visions of the soul
The visible mind seeks out for marriage,
As if the sleeping heart, agaze, in darkness,
Would dream her passions out as in the Heavens.
In flesh and flesh, imperfect spirits join
Vision upon vision, image upon image,

All physical and perishing, till spirit
Driven mad by Time, a ghost still haunted
By his mortal house, goes from the tomb
And drops his body back into the dirt.
I fear it till my soul remembers Heaven.
My name is Angel and my eyes are Fire!
O wonder, and more than wonder, in the world!
Now I have built my Love a sepulchre
Of whitened thoughts, and sat a year in ash,
Grieving for the lost entempled dead,
And Him who appeared to these dead eyes,
And Him my wakened beating mind remembered,
And Love that moved in substance clear as bone,
With beautiful music, at the fatal moment,
And clock stopped by its own, or hidden, hand.
These are the hollow echoes of His word.

Ah, but to have seen the Dove of still
Divinity come down in silken light of summer sun
In ignorance of the body and bone's madness.
Light falls and I fail! My youth is ending,
All my youth, and Death and Beauty cry
Like horns and motors from a ship afar,
Half heard, an echo in the sea beneath,
And Death and Beauty beckon in the dawn,
A presage of the world of whitening shadows
As another pale memorial.
Ah! but to have seen the Dove, and then go blind.

I will grow old a grey and groaning man,
Hour after hour, with each hour a thought,
And with each thought the same denial. Am I to spend
My life in praise of the idea of God?
Time leaves no hope, and leaves us none of love;
We creep and wait, we wait and go alone.
When will the heart be weary of its own
Indignity? Or Time endured destroy
The last such thoughts as these, the thoughts of Dove?
Must ravenous reason not be self-consumed?
Our souls are purified of Time by Time,
And ignorance consumes itself like flesh.

Bigger and bigger gates, Thou givest, Lord,
And vaster deaths, and deaths not by my hand,
Till, in each season, as the garden dies,
I die with each, until I die no more
Time's many deaths, and pass toward the last gates,
Till come, pure light, at last to pass through pearl.
Take me to thy mansion, for I house
In clay, in a sad dolor out of joy.

Behold thy myth incarnate in my flesh
Now made incarnate in Thy Psalm, O Lord.

New York, March 1949

Allen Ginsberg, *Collected Poems*

Epilogue

Forget not once this journey is begun the end is certain. Doubt along the way will come and go and go to come again. Yet is the ending sure? No one can fail to do what God appointed him to do. When you forget, remember that you walk with Him and with His Word upon your heart. Who could despair when Hope like this is his? Illusions of despair may seem to come, but learn how not to be deceived by them. Behind each one there is reality and there is God. Why would you wait for this and trade it for illusions, when His Love is but an instant farther on the road where all illusions end? The end is sure and guaranteed by God. Who stands before a lifeless image when a step away the Holy of the Holies opens up an ancient door that leads beyond the world?

You *are* a stranger here. But you belong to Him Who loves you as He loves Himself. Ask but my help to roll the stone away, and it is done according to His Will. We *have* begun the journey. Long ago the end was written in the stars and set into the Heavens with a shining ray that held it safe within eternity and through all time as well. And holds it still; unchanged, unchanging and unchangeable.

Be not afraid. We only start again an ancient journey long ago begun that but seems new. We have begun again upon a road we travelled on before and lost our way a little while. And now we try again. Our new beginning has the certainty the journey lacked till now. Look up and see His Word among the stars, where He has set your name along with His. Look up and find your certain destiny the world would hide but God would have you see.

Let us wait here in silence, and kneel down an instant in our gratitude to Him Who called to us and helped us hear His Call. And then let us arise and go in faith along the way to Him. Now we are sure we do not walk alone. For God is here, and with Him all our brothers. Now we know that we will never lose the way again. The song begins again which had been stopped only an instant, though it seems to be unsung forever. What is here begun will grow in life and strength and hope, until the world is still an instant and forgets all that the dream of sin had made of it.

Let us go out and meet the newborn world, knowing that Christ has been reborn in it, and that the holiness of this rebirth will last forever. We had lost our way but He has found it for us. Let us go and bid Him welcome Who returns to us to celebrate salvation and the end of all we thought we made. The morning star of this new day looks on a different world where God is welcomed and His Son with Him. We who complete Him offer thanks to Him, as He gives thanks to us. The Son is still, and in the quiet God has given him enters his home and is at peace at last.

Helen Schucman and William Thetford, *A Course in Miracles*®

But this joy must not be the goal toward which you strive. It will be vouch-safed to you if you strive to "give joy to God." Your personal joy will rise up when you want nothing but the joy of God—nothing but joy in itself.

Martin Buber, *The Early Masters*

And now in all your doings be you blessed.
God turns to you for help to save the world.
Teacher of God, His thanks He offers you,
And all the world stands silent in the grace
You bring from Him. You are the Son He loves,
And it is given you to be the means
Through which His Voice is heard around the world,
To close all things of time; to end the sight
Of all things visible; and to undo
All things that change. Through you is ushered in
A world unseen, unheard, yet truly there.
Holy are you, and in your light the world
Reflects your holiness, for you are not
Alone and friendless. I give thanks for you,
And join your efforts on behalf of God,

Knowing they are on my behalf as well,
And for all those who walk to God with me.

AMEN

Helen Schucman and William Thetford,
A Course in Miracles®

Cloud-Hidden

This chapter is closed now,
not one word more
until we meet some day
and the voices rising
to the window
take wing and fly.

Open the old casement
to the lands we have forgotten,
look
to the mountains and ridgeways
and the steep valleys,
quilted by green,
here, as the last words fall away,
the great and silent rivers of life
are flowing into the oceans,
and on a day like any other
they will carry you again,
abandoned,
on the currents you have fought,
to the place you did not know
you belonged.

And just as you came into life
surprised
you go out again,
lifted,
cloud-hidden

from one unknown
to another
and fall and turn
and appear again in the mountains

not remembering
how in the beginning
you refused
to join,
could not speak of,
did not even know
you were that
deep
calm
welling
almost forgotten
spring
of eternal presence.

David Whyte, *Where Many Rivers Meet*

...there is not a world without God.
Hans Küng, *Does God Exist?*

⇸ Acknowledgements ⇷

For their generous sharing of insight and wisdom and for the many authors and books they have introduced to me during the research and compilation of this anthology, I wish to acknowledge and thank Lee Davis Creal and Michael Creal, Richard Gonda, Patricia Joudry, Yvonne Kason, Keith Kirts, Sarah Krzeczunowicz, Alberto Manguel, Maurie D. Pressman, Lorne Rubenstein, Craig Stephenson, Melissa Vardey, Marion Woodman, and Catherine Yolles.

I am very grateful to my American publisher, Marty Asher, who has had faith in me from the start; to Louise Dennys, my Canadian publisher, for her friendship, guidance, and assistance in steering this book to conclusion; and to my editor, Jenna Laslocky, for her intelligence, sensitivity, and care in helping me through the pages of this journey. To my agents and my friends Carolyn Brunton, Jane Gelfman, and Jill Hickson, thank you; and my thanks also to Jonathan Burnham, Sonny Mehta, Catherine Hammond and Miguelita Costes, Marilyn Schulz, Othelia Wegner and Carol Welch at the Queen/Saulter Library in Toronto.

I could not have found the conviction of the spiritual life or the challenge to embrace other disciplines without the love, care, and teachings of my friends at Prem Anandham Ashram, and I would still be in the dark if I had not experienced the brilliance of the work of Paul Rebillot. I would have floundered in my task without the encouragement, love, and support of my cherished husband, John Dalla Costa. And my heartfelt, eternal gratitude to my dear friend Carol Mark, who has assisted me at every moment over the last three years with tracking down authors and titles, setting up systems, phoning, faxing, enquiring, supporting, encouraging, advising, and sharing, at the deepest level, the spirit of God in all worlds.

✦ About the Editor ✦

Lucinda Vardey was born in England in 1949 and was educated as a Catholic. She has been in the book business for thirty years, working in England and in Canada as a publisher and later as a literary agent. Her previous book was *Belonging: A Questioning Catholic Comes to Terms with the Church*, published in 1988. Her interest in Eastern philosophy and religions was spurred by her practice of yoga, and she now teaches Kripalu yoga, runs personal development retreats in Canada and in her centre in Tuscany, Italy. She also practises as a spiritual counsellor and is a writer and reviewer of spiritual and religious subjects. She is presently training at the North American School of Gestalt and Experiential Teaching in California.

Lucinda divides her time between her homes in Toronto, Canada, and Tuscany, Italy.

☀ Permissions Acknowledgements ☀

Every effort has been made to ensure that permissions for all material were obtained. The editor cannot take responsibility for any errors and omissions, but would be grateful for notification and corrections. Those sources not formally acknowledged here will be included in all future editions of this book.

Grateful acknowledgment is made to the following for permission to reprint previously published and unpublished material:

ABRAHAMS, ISRAEL, based on Ibin Gabirol. *Forms of Prayer for Jewish Worship*, Vol. 1: *Daily Sabbath and Occasional Prayerbook*. Copyright © 1977 by Israel Abrahams, London. Reprinted by permission of the Reform Synagogues of Great Britain.

AÏVANHOV, OMRAAM MIKHAËL. *Cosmic Moral Law* (Original title: *Les Lois de la Morale Cosmique*). Copyright © Editions Prosveta SA 1989. Complete Works, Volume 12. *Love and Sexuality*. Copyright © Editions Prosveta. Volume 14-15. *The Path of Silence* (Original title: *La Voie du Silence*). Copyright © Prosveta SA 1990. Collection No. 229 (All of the above reprinted by permission of Editions Prosveta).

SWAMI AMRITASVARUPANANDA. *Mata Amritanandamayi, Her Life and the Experiences of Her Devotees*. Copyright © 1988 by Mata Amritanandamayi; Mission Trust. Reprinted by permission of the Mata Amritanandamayi Centers, San Ramon, CA.

ANDERSON, SHERRY, and PATRICIA HOPKINS. *The Feminine Face of God*. Copyright © 1991 by Sherry Anderson and Patricia Hopkins. Reprinted by permission of Bantam Books, a division of Bantam Doubleday Dell Publishing Group, Inc.

ANGELOU, MAYA. *On the Pulse of Morning*. Copyright © 1993 by Maya Angelou. Reprinted by permission of Random House, Inc., and Virago Press.

AUROBINDO, SRI. *Human Unity and the Spiritual Age*, edited by Shyamsunder Jhunijhunwala; *Lights on Life-Problems*; *Sonnets*; *Collected Poems*; *The Hour of God*; *Savitri*; *Words of Sri Aurobindo*, First Series & Third Series. Reprinted by kind permission of Sri Aurobindo Ashram Trust.

AXELSSON, SUN. "Free Flight Inwards." Reprinted by kind permission of Sun Axelsson.

BABA, MEYER. *Life at Its Best*. Copyright © 1957 by Sufism Reoriented Inc. Copyright renewed. Reprinted by permission of HarperCollins Publishers, Inc.

BATESON, GREGORY, and MARY CATHERINE BATESON. *Angels Fear: Towards an Epistemology of the Sacred*. Copyright © 1987 by The Estate of Gregory Bateson and Mary Catherine Bateson. Reprinted by permission of Macmillan Publishing Company and the kind permission of Mary Catherine Bateson and the Estate of Gregory Bateson.

BIANCO, FRANK. *Voices of Silence: Lives of the Trappists Today*. Copyright © 1991 by Frank Bianco. Reprinted by permission of Paragon House Publishers and Frank Bianco.

BLOFELD, JOHN. *In Search of the Goddess of Compassion: The Mystical Cult of Kuan Yin*. Copyright © 1977 by John Blofeld. (Originally published as *Compassion Yoga* by George Allen & Unwin in 1977.)

BOHM, DAVID. *Wholeness and the Implicate Order*. Copyright © 1980 by David Bohm. Reprinted by permission of Routledge & Kegan Paul Ltd.

BOHM, DAVID, and MARK EDWARDS. *Changing Consciousness*. Copyright © 1991 by David Bohm and Mark Edwards. Reprinted by permission of HarperCollins Publishers, Inc.

BOHM, DAVID, and DAVID PEAT. *Science, Order and Creativity*. Copyright © 1987 by David Bohm and David Peat. Reprinted by permission of Bantam Books, a division of Bantam Doubleday Dell Publishing Group, Inc.

BORGES, JORGE LUIS. "Paradiso, XXXI 108" reprinted from *Dreamtigers*, translated by Mildred Boyer and Harold Morland. Copyright © 1964 by Jorge Luis Borges. Reprinted by permission of University of Texas Press.

BRINK, ANDRÉ. *Writing in a State of Siege*. Copyright © 1983 by André Brink. Reprinted by permission of Simon & Schuster, Inc., and Aitken, Stone & Wylie, Ltd.

BROCH, HERMANN. *The Death of Virgil*. Copyright © 1945 by Pantheon Books, Inc. Reprinted by permission of Vintage Books, a division of Random House, Inc.

BRONER, E. M. "Honor and Ceremony in Women's Rituals" from *Politics of Women's Spirituality*, edited by Charlene Spretnak (Published by Anchor Books in 1982).

his books and tapes is available from the Hanuman Foundation, 524 San Anselmo Avenue, #203, San Anselmo, CA 94960 (tel: 415-457-8570).

DASS, RAM, and STEPHEN LEVINE. *Grist for the Mill.* Copyright © 1976, 1987 by Ram Dass and Stephen Levine. Reprinted by permission of Celestial Arts, P.O. Box 7327, Berkeley, CA 94707.

DESJARDINS, ARNAUD. *The Message of the Tibetans*, translated from the French by R. H. Ward and Vega Stewart (Published in London by Stuart & Watkins in 1969).

DOIG, DESMOND. *Mother Teresa: Her People and Her Work.* Copyright © Nachiketa Publications 1976. Reprinted by permission of HarperCollins Religious, an imprint of HarperCollins Publishers Ltd.

DURRELL, LAWRENCE. "The Reckoning," from *Collected Poems 1931-1974.* Edited by James A. Brigham. Copyright © 1971 by Lawrence Durrell. Reprinted by permission of Faber and Faber Ltd., Viking Penguin, a division of Penguin Books USA Inc., and Curtis Brown, Ltd.

EINSTEIN, ALBERT. *The World As I See It*, translated by Alan Harris. Copyright © 1956, 1984 by The Estate of Albert Einstein. Reprinted by permission of The Carol Publishing Group.

EVERSON, WILLIAM. *Birth of a Poet.* Copyright © 1982 by William Everson. Reprinted by permission of Black Sparrow Press.

FINDLEY, TIMOTHY. *Inside Memory.* Copyright © 1990 by Timothy Findley. Reprinted by permission of HarperCollins Publishers, Canada.

FISHER, JOE, and JOEL WHITTON. *Life Between Life.* Copyright © 1986 by Joe Fisher and Joel Whitton. Reprinted by permission of Doubleday, a division of Bantam Doubleday Dell Publishing Group, Inc.

FOX, MATTHEW. *The Coming of the Cosmic Christ.* Copyright © 1988 by Matthew Fox. Reprinted by permission of HarperCollins Publishers, Inc.

FRANKL, VIKTOR. *Man's Search for Meaning.* Copyright © 1959, 1963, 1984, 1992 by Viktor Frankl. Reprinted by permission of Beacon Press. *The Unheard Cry for Meaning: Psychotherapy and Humanism.* Copyright © 1978 by Viktor E. Frankl. Reprinted by permission of Simon & Schuster, Inc.

FRYE, NORTHROP. *The Great Code.* Copyright © 1982, 1981 by Northrop Frye. Reprinted by permission of Harcourt Brace & Company. *The Modern Century*, New Edition. Copyright © 1991 by Oxford University Press, Canada. Reprinted by permission of Oxford University Press, Canada.

GANDHI, KISHOR. *Lights on Life-Problems.* Copyright © 1987 by Sri Aurobindo Ashram Trust. Reprinted by kind permission of Sri Aurobindo Ashram Trust.

GASCOYNE, DAVID. "Whales and Dolphins" reprinted from *Whales: A Celebration*, edited by Greg Gatenby. Copyright © 1983 by Greg Gatenby. Reprinted by kind permission of David Gascoyne.

GAWAIN, SHAKTI. *Return to the Garden: A Journey of Discovery.* Copyright © 1989 by Shakti Gawain. Reprinted by permission of Nataraj Publishing.

GINSBERG, ALLEN. "A Mad Gleam" and "Psalm II" from *Collected Poems (1947-1980).* Copyright © 1948, 1949 by Allen Ginsberg. Copyright renewed. Reprinted by permission of HarperCollins Publishers, Inc., and Viking 1985. (First published in *The Gates of Wrath: Rhymed Poems, 1948-1951.*) "Poem Rocket" from *Collected Poems (1947-1980).* Copyright © 1957 by Allen Ginsberg. Copyright renewed. Reprinted by permission of HarperCollins Publishers, Inc. Copyright © 1961, 1984. Viking 1985, first published in *Kaddish and Other Poems 1958-1960.* "Rolling Thunder Stones II" from *Collected Poems (1947-1980).* Copyright © 1975 by Allen Ginsberg. Copyright renewed. Reprinted by permission of HarperCollins Publishers, Inc. Copyright © 1975, 1984. Viking 1985, first published in *Mind Breaths.* "Thoughts on a Breath" from *Collected Poems (1947-1980).* Copyright © 1974 by Allen Ginsberg. Reprinted by permission of HarperCollins Publishers, Inc. Copyright © 1974, 1984. Viking 1985, first published in *Poems All Over the Place.*

GOLDSTEIN, JOSEPH, and JACK KORNFIELD. *Seeking the Heart of Wisdom: The Path of Insight Meditation.* Copyright © 1987 by Joseph Goldstein and Jack Kornfield. Reprinted by permission of Shambhala Publications, Inc., P.O. Box 308, Boston, MA 02117.

GRAHAM, MARTHA. *Blood Memory.* Copyright © 1991 by The Estate of Martha Graham. Reprinted by permission of Doubleday, a division of Bantam Doubleday Dell Publishing Group, Inc. *The Notebooks of Martha Graham.* Copyright © 1973 by Martha Graham. Reprinted by permission of Harcourt Brace & Company and The Barbara Hogenson Agency.

GREEN, MARTIN (ed.) *Gandhi in India: In His Own Words*, edited by Martin Green. Copyright © 1987. Reprinted by permission of Navajivan Trust.

GREENE, GRAHAM. *The Glory of Mary.* Copyright © Graham Greene. Reprinted by permission of David Higham Associates, London.

GREENWELL, BONNIE. *Energies of Transformation.* Copyright © 1990 by Bonnie Greenwell. Reprinted by kind permission of Bonnie Greenwell, Shakti River Press, 22375 Rolling Hills Road, Saratoga, CA 95070 ($15.95) ISBN: 0-9627327-0-2.

GREER, GERMAINE. *The Change: Women, Aging and Menopause.* Copyright © 1991 Germaine Greer. Reprinted by permission of Hamish Hamilton Ltd. and Aitken, Stone & Wylie, Ltd.

GRIFFITHS, BEDE. *A New Vision of Reality.* Copyright © 1989 by Bede Griffiths. Reprinted by permission of HarperCollins Publishers, Ltd., and Templegate

JONG, ERICA. "Self-Portrait in Shoulder Stand" and "The Buddha in the Womb" from *At the Edge of the Body* (Published by Holt, Rhinehart and Winston). Copyright © 1979, 1993 by Erica Mann Jong. Reprinted by permission of HarperCollins Publishers, Inc., and Kenneth David Burrows.

JOUDRY, PATRICIA. Part of a private letter. Reprinted by kind permission of the author.

JOUDRY, PATRICIA, and MAURIE D. PRESSMAN. *Twin Souls.* Copyright © 1993 by Patricia Joudry and Maurie D. Pressman. Reprinted by kind permission of Somerville House Publishing, Toronto.

JUNG, C. G. *Memories, Dreams, Reflections*, recorded and edited by Aniela Jaffe. Translation copyright © 1961, 1962, 1963 by Random House, Inc. Copyright renewed © 1989, 1990, 1991 by Random House, Inc. Reprinted by permission of Pantheon Books, a division of Random House, Inc., and HarperCollins Publishers, Ltd. *Psychology and Religion: West and East*, translated by R. F. C. Hull, *The Bollingen Series* xx. Copyright © 1958 by The Bollingen Foundation Inc., New York, NY. Reprinted by permission of Princeton University Press and Routledge. *The Archetypes and the Collective Unconsciousness*, translated by R. F. C. Hull, *The Bollingen Series* xx. Copyright © 1959 by The Bollingen Foundation Inc., New York, NY. New material copyright © 1969 by Princeton University Press. Reprinted by permission of Princeton University Press and Routledge. *The Tibetan Book of the Great Liberation* (part of the General Introduction), translated by R. F. C. Hull, *The Bollingen Series* xx, *Volume 2: Experimental Researches.* Copyright © 1973 by Princeton University Press and Routledge.

KENNELLY, BRENDAN. "Good Souls to Survive" from *Good Souls to Survive* by Allen Figgis. Reprinted from *Irish Poets, 1924-1974*, edited by David Marcus. Copyright © 1975 by Pan Books Ltd.

KING, MARTIN LUTHER, JR. *Strength to Love.* Copyright © 1963 by Martin Luther King, Jr. Copyright renewed © 1991 by Coretta Scott King. *Stride Toward Freedom.* Copyright © 1958 by Martin Luther King, Jr. Copyright renewed © 1986 by Coretta Scott King. Reprinted by arrangement with The Heirs to the Estate of Martin Luther King, Jr., c/o Joan Daves Agency as agent for the proprietor.

KOESTLER, ARTHUR. *Arrow in the Blue.* Copyright © 1969 by Arthur Koestler. Reprinted by kind permission of Peters, Fraser & Dunlop Ltd.

KOWALSKI, GARY A. *The Souls of Animals.* Copyright © 1991 by Gary A. Kowalski. Reprinted by permission of Stillpoint Publishing.

KRISHNA, GOPI. *The Awakening of Kundalini: The Way to Self-Knowledge.* Copyright © 1975, 1984 by Gopi Krishna. Reprinted by kind permission of the Kundalini Research & Publication Trust. *Kundalini: The Evolutionary Energy in Man.* Copyright © 1967. Reprinted by kind permission of Shambhala Publications, Inc., P.O. Box 308, Boston, MA 02117.

MORGAN, ROBIN. "Another Parable," Part IV, Metaphysical Feminism from *Going Too Far: The Personal Chronicles of a Feminist*. Copyright © 1968, 1970, 1973, 1975, 1977 by Robin Morgan. Reprinted by permission of Random House, Inc., and Edite Kroll Literary Agency.

MOTHER TERESA OF CALCUTTA. *A Gift for God*, compiled and introduced by Malcolm Muggeridge. Copyright © 1975 by Mother Teresa Missionaries of Charity (Published by Collins Publishers).

MOTHER, THE. *Life Divine: The Mother's Talks, Words of the Mother, Part Two*. Reprinted by kind permission of Sri Aurobindo Ashram Trust.

MUGGERIDGE, MALCOLM. *Conversion: A Spiritual Journey*. Copyright © 1988 by Malcolm Muggeridge. Reprinted by permission of David Higham Associates, London. *Chronicles of Wasted Time*. Copyright © 1972 by Malcolm Muggeridge. Reprinted by permission of HarperCollins Publishers, Inc., and David Higham Associates, London.

MUKTANANDA, SWAMI. *Play of Consciousness* (pages 5, 214, 215, 216, 239, 249, 259). Copyright © 1971, 1972, 1978 SYDA Foundation. Copyright © 1990, fifth printing by SYDA Foundation South Fallsburg, New York, USA. All rights reserved. No part of this material may be reproduced without prior written permission. Printed by permission.

MURPHY, MICHAEL. *Golf in the Kingdom*. Copyright © 1972 by Michael Murphy. Reprinted by permission of Viking Penguin, a division of Penguin Books USA, Inc.

MURRAY, PAUL. "Introit" from *Ritual Poems* (Published by New Writers' Press, Dublin). Reprinted from *Irish Poets, 1924-1974*, edited by David Marcus. Copyright © 1975 by Pan Books Ltd.

O'CONNOR, FLANNERY. *The Habit of Being*, edited by Sally Fitzgerald. Copyright © 1979 by Regina O'Connor. Reprinted by permission of Farrar, Straus & Giroux, Inc.

PECK, M. SCOTT. *People of the Lie*. Copyright © 1983 by M. Scott Peck, M.D. Reprinted by permission of Simon & Schuster, Inc., and Rider, an imprint of Random House UK Ltd.

PIERCY, MARGE. "The Window of the Woman Burning" (Originally appeared in *Sunbury* #3, 1975). Copyright 1975, 1978 by Marge Piercy and Middlemarsh Inc. Reprinted by permission of the Wallace Literary Agency Inc.

PITTER, RUTH. "The Eternal Image." Copyright © the Estate of Ruth Pitter. Reprinted by kind permission of M. W. S. Pitter and the Estate of Ruth Pitter.

PLASKOW, JUDITH. "The Coming of Lilith." Copyright © 1972 by Judith Plaskow. Reprinted by kind permission of the author.

WHYTE, DAVID. *Where Many Rivers Meet.* Copyright © 1990 by David Whyte. Reprinted by kind permission of Many Rivers Company, P.O. Box 868, Langley, WA 360-221-1324.

WILBER, KEN. *Grace and Grit: Spirituality and Healing in the Life and Death of Treya Killam Wilber.* Copyright © 1991 by Ken Wilber. Reprinted by permission of Shambhala Publications, Inc., P.O. Box 308, Boston, MA 02117.

WILSON, COLIN. *The Essential Colin Wilson.* Copyright © 1985 by Colin Wilson. Reprinted by permission of Chambers Harrap Publishers Ltd., and David Bolt Associates. *The Outsider.* Copyright © 1956 by Colin Wilson. Reprinted by permission of Houghton Mifflin Co., and Victor Gollancz Ltd. All rights reserved.

WOLF, FRED ALAN. *Parallel Universes.* Copyright © 1988 by Fred Alan Wolf. Reprinted by kind permission of Fred Alan Wolf and Random House UK Ltd.

WOODMAN, MARION. *Addiction to Perfection: The Still Unravished Bride.* Copyright © 1982 by Marion Woodman. *Conscious Femininity.* Copyright © 1993 by Marion Woodman and Daryl Sharp. *The Pregnant Virgin.* Copyright © 1985 by Marion Woodman. Reprinted by kind permission of Inner City Books, Box 1271, Station "Q", Toronto, Ontario M4T 2P4.

YOGANANDA, PARAMAHANSA. *Autobiography of a Yogi.* Copyright © 1946 by Paramahansa Yogananda. Copyright renewed. Copyright 12th edition 1981 by Self-Realization Fellowship. Reprinted by kind permission of Self-Realization Fellowship.

ZUKAV, GARY. *The Seat of the Soul.* Copyright © 1990 by Gary Zukav. Reprinted by permission of Simon & Schuster, Inc., and Rider Books, an imprint of Random House UK Ltd.